Microprocessors and Microsystems, Volume 10

ScienceDirect

microprocessors and microsystems

vol 10 no 1 january/february 1986

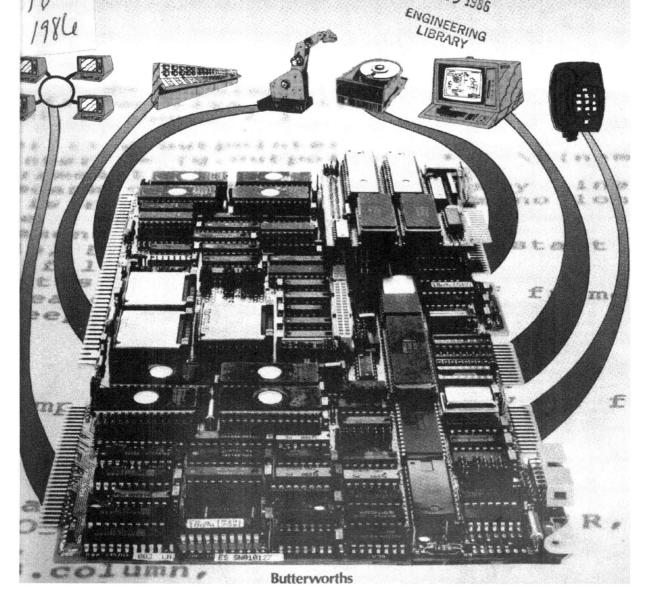

Butterworths

editorial advisory board

Microprocessors and Microsystems is an international journal published in February, March, April, May, June, August, September, October, November, December. *Editorial Offices:* Butterworth Scientific Ltd, PO Box 63, Westbury House, Bury Street, Guildford, Surrey GU2 5BH, UK. Tel: (0483) 31261. Telegrams and telex: 859556 SCITEC G. *Publishing Director:* John Owens. *Production:* Tony Lewis

Microprocessors and Microsystems is published by Butterworth Scientific Ltd. *Registered Office:* Butterworth Scientific Ltd, 88 Kingsway, London WC2 6AB, UK

Subscription enquiries and orders: Quadrant Subscription Services Ltd, Oakfield House, Perrymount Road, Haywards Heath, West Sussex RH16 3DH, UK. Tel: (0444) 459188

Annual subscription (10 issues): £89.00 Overseas rate (£22.00 for private individuals);

$160.00 US rate ($40.00 for private individuals)
UK subscription rates available on request.

Prices include packing and delivery by sea mail. Airmail prices available on request. Copies of this journal sent to subscribers in Bangladesh, India, Pakistan, Sri Lanka, Canada and the USA are air-speeded for quicker delivery.

Back issues: Prior to current volume available from Wm Dawson & Sons Ltd, Cannon House, Folkestone, Kent CT19 5EE, UK. Tel: (0303) 57421

US mailing agents: Expediters of the Printed Word Ltd, 515 Madison Avenue, Suite 1217, New York, NY 10022, USA. Second class postage paid at New York, NY. US Postmaster: Send address corrections to *Microprocessors and Microsystems*, c/o Expediters of the Printed Word Ltd, address as above.

Reprints: Minimum order 100, available from the publisher.

ISSN 0141 9331
MCRPD 10 (1) 1-56 (1986)

© Butterworth & Co (Publishers) Ltd 1986

Typeset by Tech-Set, Gateshead, Tyne & Wear, and printed by Dotesios (Printers) Ltd, Greenland Mills, Bradford on Avon, Wilts, UK.

microprocessors and microsystems

vol 10 no 1
january/february 1986

Editor Steve Hitchcock

Assistant Editor Andrew Taylor

Publisher Amanda Harper

notes for authors

Microprocessors and Microsystems

The Journal welcomes all articles on semi-conductor chip and PCB design, the application of microprocessors to industry, business and schools and on the development of microprocessor software. Articles can come from both academic and industrial research and should be 3000–5000 words in length. In addition to main articles, we welcome shorter case studies, design notes and teach-ins.

All submitted articles are refereed by two independent reviewers to ensure both accuracy and relevance, though it is the authors' sole responsibility that statements used are accurate. The author is also responsible for obtaining permission to quote material and to republish tables and illustrations.

Copyright

Before publication, authors are requested to assign copyright to Butterworth & Co (Publishers) Ltd. This allows the company to sanction reprints of the whole or part of the volume and authorize photocopies. The authors, however, still retain their traditional right to reuse or to veto third-party publication.

Preparation of scripts

As you can see from the Journal, every article published is stylized by us to keep consistency throughout each volume. We follow the Oxford English Dictionary. It would be helpful if you could follow the Journal style. The most important thing, though, is that you write (or rather type) in clear and concise English. Contributions should be typed double-spaced on one side of the paper. We would also appreciate it if you number each page and leave wide margins so we can prepare the article for the typesetters. Three copies of the article are preferred and should be sent to the editor.

Units

You should use, as far as possible, SI units. In circumstances where this is not possible, please provide a conversion factor at the first mention of the unit.

Illustrations

Line drawings

We have our own professional studio to ensure that line drawings are consistent with house style. We would prefer, however, to receive unlettered drawings (black ink on tracing paper) so we can put on the lettering ourselves. Drawings, if possible, should be of size consistent with the Journal, i.e. either 169 mm or 356 mm width. Single drawings should not extend over one page (500 mm) in height.

Computer printouts

Illustrations showing line printer listings, plotter output, etc should preferably be on unlined paper. Printouts will be reduced by us to the relevant size. Do not mark them as they will be used to make photographic copies for the typesetters. Only include sufficient lines for the reader to interpret the format and nature of the printout. Overlong printouts only cause confusion. Fuller explanation should appear in the caption and the text.

Photographs

Black and white glossy photographs (including Polaroid prints of VDU screens) should, where possible, be supplied unmounted. They should be labelled clearly on the back with a soft pencil. Photocopies of the photographs should be provided for the referees.

References

Our Journal style is to indicate the use of a reference in the text with a superscript as each one arises and give the full reference with the same number at the end. If a reference is cited more than once, the same number should be used each time. With a bibliography, the references are given in alphabetic order (dependent on the first author's surname). It would be helpful if you could follow this style. References take the following form:

(to journals)

1 Buckroyd, A 'Production testing of microprocessor-based equipment' *Microprocessors and Microsystems* Vol 5 No 7 (September 1981) pp 299–303

(to books)

2 Gallacher, J 'Testing and maintenance' in Hanna, F K (ed.) *Advanced techniques for microprocessor systems* Peter Peregrinus, Stevenage, UK (1980)

Proofs

Correspondence and proofs for corrections will be sent to the first named author, unless otherwise indicated. Authors will receive a copy of the galley proofs and copies of redrawn or relettered illustrations. It is important that these proofs should be checked and returned promptly.

Reprints

The first named author will receive 25 reprints of the technical article free of charge. Further copies, a minimum of 100, can be ordered at any time from the Reprints Department, Butterworth Scientific Ltd, Westbury House, PO Box 63, Bury Street, Guildford, Surrey GU2 5BH, UK.

Design and evaluation of a dual-microcomputer shared memory system with a shared I/O bus

V Lakshmi Narasimhan*, J K Ramachandra** and D K Anvekar***
describe a system which uses two microcomputers with a shared RAM and
I/O bus. Benchmarks indicate significant performance gains over a single-
processor unit

*The design, implementation and evaluation are described
of a dual-microcomputer system based on the concept of
shared memory. Shared memory is useful for passing large
blocks of data and it also provides a means to hold and
work with shared data. In addition to the shared memory, a
separate bus between the I/O ports of the microcomputers is provided. This bus is utilized for interprocessor
synchronization. Software routines helpful in applying the
dual-microcomputer system to realistic problems are
presented. Performance evaluation of the system is carried
out using benchmarks.*

microsystems   shared memory   I/O communication

Uninterrupted processing support at low cost, great
potential for system expansion and enhanced speed of
operation are the major factors which drive the current
trend towards multiprocessor systems. The first step
towards such systems is to work out a method for load
sharing and/or resource sharing. While the actual operating
system is unique for a multiprocessor system, plenty of
techniques are available for realizing the system[1, 2].
Various methods of operation and development using
different communication protocols may be applied,
depending on the needs of a given application[3].

One such organization for a multiprocessing scheme is
the incorporation of a shared memory in its architecture.
Arden[4] proposed a tightly coupled system with shared
memory for concurrent processing. A subset of this, a
dual-processor shared memory system, has been developed using Motorola 6809 microprocessors by Hoffner

and Smith[5], who also established a communication
protocol for the shared memory.

The present paper begins with the design of a parallel
bus for direct I/O communication between two processors, realized through a programmable I/O interface.
Implementation of the shared memory is achieved by
appropriately mapping the memory of the two processors.
This is done by buffering the address and data lines
accordingly; hardware details are provided. Software
development for this dual-processor system is illustrated
with some benchmark problems. Some typical performance factors, as presented by Firestone[6], are analysed
for the system. Some possible enhancements and
applications of the system are indicated.

DESIGN AND IMPLEMENTATION

Shared I/O bus for direct communication

Direct communication between the processors can be
established by either a serial link or a parallel bus. Parallel
communication is much faster than serial communication;
hence large blocks of data can be channelled through at
a faster rate. Parallel communication also aids system
modularity and gives potential for expansion. A serious
limitation of this scheme is that it employs more hardware
and so its reliability is poor unless special care is taken.
Also, parallel communication demands more complex
synchronization procedures, and the cost of implementing
this protocol is high[7]. However, applications of the shared
memory scheme demand a high rate of data transmission
and so a parallel link was developed.

Figure 1 shows a parallel bus established using the 8255
programmable peripheral interface chip, which is compa-

*University of Queensland, Brisbane 4067, Australia
**Indian Telephone Industries, Bangalore, India
***Indian Institute of Science, Bangalore, India

0141–9331/86/10003–08 $03.00 © 1986 Butterworth & Co. (Publishers) Ltd

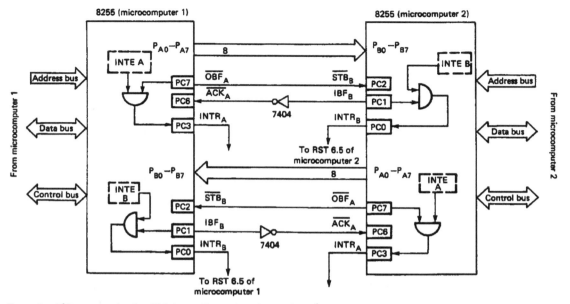

Figure 1. *I/O communication. This is used for process interaction. The OBF signal of one 8255 is used to strobe the second 8255 and the data is then transferred. When the data is fully passed on, the second IBF signal is activated, acknowledging receipt to the first. Thus handshaking is established. This data is passed on to the processor by interrupting it.*

tible with a variety of microprocessors. The 8255 has three modes of operation and its three available ports are individually programmable. In the present implementation port A is used as an output port and port B as an input. Port C is used for system synchronization and control. The 8255 is used in mode 1 configuration, ie strobed I/O mode. Strobing is done by connecting $\overline{OBF_A}$ (PC7) to the $\overline{STB_B}$ (PC2) of the second 8255. Thus, whenever data is loaded into the 8255, the output buffer becomes full $(\overline{OBF_A})$ and this strobes the second processor through $\overline{STB_B}$. The data can now be passed on to the second processor; when this process is complete the input buffer of the second processor becomes full and is indicated by IBF_B. This is indicated to the first processor by the connection of IBF_B and $\overline{ACK_A}$ through an inverter[8]. Figure 2 shows the timing diagram of the scheme.

Thus a handshaking protocol is constructed for I/O communication. The 8255 interrupts the processor whenever IBF_B becomes full and INTE B is enabled. Data can therefore be passed on to the other processor at any time. The INTE (interrupt enable) flipflops can be set or reset by controlling the pins in port C. So, if need be, I/O communication can be partially or totally inhibited. Also, since I/O communication is in general much slower than shared memory communication, it is preferable to assign it a low priority. However, if utilization of I/O communication demands alteration of priority, this can be achieved through software.

Indirect communication

There are three schemes to establish indirect communication through shared memory. The shared memory itself can be organized in two logical ways. In the present work, a time shared or common bus shared memory design of

the mailbox type was taken up. The reason for this choice of configuration was its simplicity of design and development. The cost of building the system is low and the system has a good expansion potential. A limitation of the system, however, is that the overall transfer rate is low compared to that of other configurations (ie multiple-bus shared memory system and multiport–multibus shared memory system). This limitation is due to the finite bandwidth and limited speed of the single common path[7].

The general configuration of the shared memory system is given in Figure 3. The main features in the development of a shared memory, memory mapping and devising a mechanism to resolve or prevent bus contention, are discussed below.

Memory mapping

In order that the shared memory be directly addressable by both processors, a 'proper slot' in the memory map of each processor has to be found dependent on the shared memory size required. The start and end addresses of the

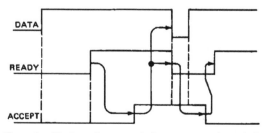

Figure 2. *Timing diagram of the request-acknowledge scheme (handshake protocol)*

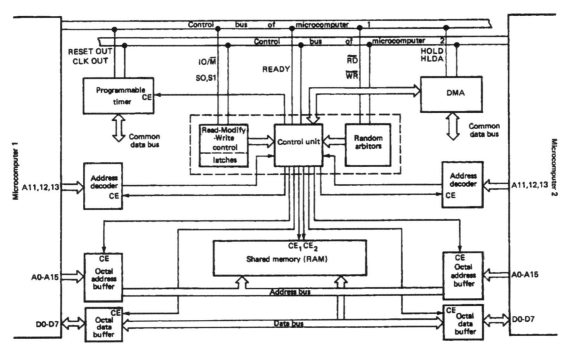

Figure 3. Organization of the shared memory system. The shared memory is useful for passing large blocks of data. It also provides a means to hold shared data and work with it.

shared memory may be the same for both processors, but in a general case they are different. The address lines for decoding and addressing the shared memory should be chosen so that they do not affect possible future developments for each individual processor.

Tristate bidirectional octal buffers are used to buffer the address and data lines before they are connected to the shared memory. Read and Write operations can be done by a judicious combination of signals from the microprocessors. The following control signals can be used: IO/$\overline{\text{M}}$, $\overline{\text{RD}}$, $\overline{\text{WR}}$, S0 and S1. (These signals refer to Intel's 8085 microprocessors[8]. IO/$\overline{\text{M}}$ specifies I/O operation or memory operation; $\overline{\text{RD}}$ and $\overline{\text{WR}}$ are signals indicating Read and Write operations. S0 and S1 can be used in conjunction with other signals to find the status of the bus.)

The appropriate logic is derived to enable and disable the various buffers and decoders, and this forms the central control unit as shown in Figure 3.

Bus contention

The main difficulty in this kind of system is resolving bus contention, ie preventing simultaneous memory access. Bus contention can be resolved by assigning priorities to the processors. There are various schemes of priority generation possible, but since this is not a complex system a random scheme can be used to resolve the conflict (Figure 4). Assignment is performed according to the inherent variations in circuit conditions at that particular time; it is determined mostly by the temperature and tolerance factors of the various components used in

the implementation[9]. The input control signals to the arbitor are $\overline{\text{RD}}$ and $\overline{\text{WR}}$. The central control unit appropriately produces wait states in case of bus contention, and encoding/decoding is done accordingly.

It is worth noting that hardware debugging in a multiprocessor environment is difficult, so the interconnections should be made systematically. Also, before implementation the compatibility of the various processors and components should be checked with their corresponding timing diagrams.

The expansion potential for the system is quite high — microcomputer peripherals and related chips can be attached. A display unit, CRT and teletype were attached to the present system. A direct memory access (DMA) path can also be built between the shared memory and

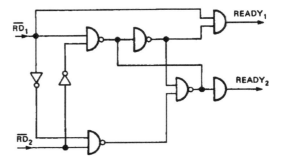

Figure 4. Example of a random arbiter. The circuit uses discrete components with different tolerance values to achieve 'random arbitration'

the processors for high-speed data transfer. The processors' HOLD and HLDA signals are used for this. The operation should again be made indivisible and the necessary decoding done by the central control unit.

SOFTWARE DEVELOPMENT

Problem decomposition and process interaction are the main features of the software development for multiprocessor systems[7, 10]. While decomposition depends mainly on the nature and complexity of the problem, process interaction mostly consists of exchange of data, addresses and control signals. In a shared memory system, process interaction can be accomplished by the common memory and also through the I/O channel. The nature of the process interactions and synchronizations plays a vital role in the swiftness of an algorithm.

Process synchronization

The major bottleneck in a direct shared memory scheme is due to the integrity of the shared data. This can be circumvented by synchronizing the accesses to the shared data. 'Semaphore' is one efficient method of doing this[11]. Semaphore provides a means to suspend the execution of a process until certain conditions are satisfied. Synchronization can be achieved if all processors perform semaphore operations in conjunction with shared memory accessing.

A crude form of this concept, called the Read-Modify-Write (RMW) operation, is implemented in the present system by maintaining a lock on that block of segment being used at the time in the shared memory. Locks are realized through a set of latches which can be individually controlled through software. So if one processor wants to perform an RMW operation it loads the corresponding segment lock. (The segment is determined by the address of the location in the shared memory that a processor wants to access.)

When one processor is performing an RMW operation, however, the other processor will be made to wait if it wants to access the same segment in shared memory. This is achieved by pulling down the other processor's READY line, thus preventing simultaneous use of the RMW operation. Operations on individual locks are made indivisible by the hardware.

Benchmark problems

The performance of the system can be evaluated by executing some benchmark problems on it. It can thus be shown that I/O communication is much slower than shared memory communication. In this case a 'producer-consumer algorithm'[5] was employed wherein, when one processor is transmitting or producing data, the other is receiving or consuming data. Signalling is also done by sending or receiving tokens to indicate that the data paths are cleared; these signals can be effectively used for various other purposes. The algorithm, which is the same for both processors, is given in Appendices 1 and 2 as a sequence of steps that can be translated into any computer language.

Matrix operation

At the heart of any problem in a multiprocessing operation is decomposition and interaction in the problem. Consider the matrix operation

$$E = A * B + C * D$$

where A, B, C, D and E are matrices. All data is assumed to be stored in the shared memory. Decomposition of E is accomplished as follows.

The first processor is made to perform the operation A * B, while the second processor computes C * D[12]. Then the first processor adds the corresponding elements in the odd rows and the second processor adds the respective elements in the even rows. Thus the algorithm employs both processors to work on the problem concurrently.

Process interaction is done by sending or receiving a token through the I/O communication bus, thus interrupting the processors and communicating the message. This sort of interaction should be carried out at different processing levels to complete the problem. The steps given in Appendix 3 epitomize the type of algorithm needed.

Search operation

In this dual-processor system linear search is done in shared memory by making one processor search from the top to the middle of the data segment and the other search from the bottom to the middle. With a little more modification in the nature of decomposition, a hash-search algorithm was tried[13]. Interaction in this case is done through the I/O channel.

Sort operation

A modified form of two-way merge-sort algorithm[14] was tried. The data block is divided into two segments. On the first pass the sorting is done in a mutually exclusive fashion. Merging of the two individually sorted blocks is done in the second pass. Here the process interaction is done through both the shared memory and the I/O communication link.

PERFORMANCE EVALUATION

The performance of the system can be summed up by looking at some performance factors, in this case throughput, cost-to-speed ratio and reliability.

Throughput is inversely related to the execution time for a problem. It has been shown analytically[6] that the throughput of a dual-processor system is higher than that of a single processing unit. Here it is demonstrated experimentally, by comparing the times taken to execute the above matrix-operation problem for matrices of different orders. The execution time for the program was found using an Intel 8253 timer; the execution time was read 'on the fly' when the program ended, this step being incorporated in the software. The complexity of the problem was increased by increasing the matrix order, and a plot of execution time versus relative complexity is shown in Figure 5.

When problem complexity was low, both single-processor and dual-processor systems were of similar efficiency. As the order of complexity was increased,

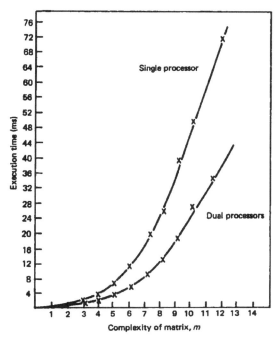

Figure 5. Execution time versus matrix complexity for single- and dual-processor systems. Matrix order is (m, m)

however, the dual-processor system gave better performance than the single processor.

The cost-to-speed ratio of the dual-processor system is lower than that of the single-processor system, mainly because the cost of the additional hardware needed for the dual system is small.

Enhanced reliability is achieved through one processor taking over the tasks of the 'diseased' processor in the event of failure. Protection of data in shared memory is also possible. Special hardware and software schemes have been developed to check and monitor failures.

CONCLUSION

From the above discussion it can be inferred that the performance of the dual-processor unit is better than that of a single-processor system. The dual-microcomputer system was designed to be upgradable to a fully fledged distributed system. Intel 8085 microprocessors were used in the implementation of the system, which can also be tailored to the needs of process control applications as well as for radar applications, robotic arm control, missile guidance systems etc. Process queueing, time-out mechanisms and deadlock prevention schemes could be worked out to improve the performance of the system, and an assembler may be tried to ease operation and debugging.

Indeed, adding a cache memory to the processors could be quite rewarding, but the main problem that might limit the system's expansion capability and performance would be enforcement of cache coherence. A mechanism must be devised to prevent the existence of replicate blocks of data on the different private caches.

The algorithms so employed should efficiently use both the global and private caches[15, 16]. A Markov model for multiple-bus multiprocessor systems has been given by Marsan[17]. A similar proposal can be made for the system described here, and this can be used to interpret the exact system performance.

ACKNOWLEDGEMENTS

The authors wish to thank Mr Rajan of the Indian Institute of Science ECE Department for help in the implementation of the hardware.

REFERENCES

1 **Enslow, P H** *Multiprocessors and parallel processing* John Wiley, New York, USA (1974)
2 **Enslow, P H** 'Multiprocessor organisation' *ACM Comput. Surv.* Vol 9 (March 1977) pp 47–71
3 **Davis, D W and Barbera, D L A** *Communication networks for computers* John Wiley, New York, USA (1973)
4 **Arden, B W and Ginoskar, R** 'MP/C: a multiprocessor/computer architecture' *IEEE Trans. Comput.* Vol C-31 (May 1982) pp 455–473
5 **Hoffner, Y and Smith, M F** 'Communication between two microprocessors through a common memory' *Microprocessors Microsyst.* Vol 6 No 6 (July/August 1982) pp 303–308
6 **Firestone, R M** 'An analytic model for parallel computation' *Proc. National Computer Conf., Dallas, TX, USA* Vol 46 (1977) pp 469–474
7 **Weitzman, C** *Distributed micro/mini computer systems* Prentice-Hall, Englewood Cliffs, NJ, USA
8 *Component data catalog* Intel, USA (1981)
9 **Muhlemank** 'Arbitors, priority, access conflicts and the glitch problem' *Proc. Euromicro Symp. Microprocessors and their Applications* (August 1979)
10 **Swan, R J, Fuller, S H and Sieworek, D P** 'Cm* — a modular multimicroprocessor' *Proc. National Computer Conf., Dallas, TX, USA* Vol 46 (1977) pp 637–644
11 **Dijakstra, E J** *Co-operating sequential processes* Mathematics Dept, Technological University, Eindhoven, The Netherlands (1965)
12 **Ahai Mov** 'An 8 × 8 multiplier and 8-bit microprocessor perform 16 × 16 bit multiplication' *EDN* (5 November 1979) pp 147
13 **Knuth, D E** *The art of computer programming. Vol 3: Fundamental algorithms* Addison-Wesley, Wokingham, UK (1968)
14 **Bitton, D, Dewitt, D J, Hsiao, D K and Jaishankar, M** 'A taxonomy of parallel sorting' *Comput. Surv.* Vol 16 No 3 pp 287–318
15 **Dubois, M and Briggs, R A** 'Effects of cache coherency in multiprocessors' *IEEE Trans. Comput.* Vol C-31 No 11 (November 1982)
16 **Dubois, M and Briggs, R A** 'Performance of a cache based multiprocessor' *Proc. ACM Conf. Measurement and Moulding Computers* Vol C-36 (February 1977)
17 **Marsan, M A and Gerla, M** 'Markov models for a multiple bus multiprocessor system' *IEEE Trans. Comput.* Vol C-31 No 3 (March 1982) pp 239–248

APPENDIX 1: PROGRAM FOR I/O COMMUNICATION

The processors check the presence of the transmission token before sending a data item. This token is used to initiate reception in the other processor and subsequently the address and the data are passed on. Upon completion, the second processor acknowledges the receipt of the data. Handshaking is thus completed.

PROGRAM: PRODUCER-CONSUMER — BUFFER CELL COMMUNICATION

```
                                    common for both processors
BEGIN
  REPEAT
    IF trans__flag = buff__empty        interrupt and check for transmission upon handshaking with the other
                                        processor
    THEN
      BEGIN
        INIT__trans                     initiate transmission
        WHILE token = true DO           while token for transmission is present
        BEGIN
          SEND__location                send start location
          SEND__data__item              send the data
          UPDATE__location              update the location
          CHECK__token                  check the token for transmission for exhausted output
        END;                            if false, end transmission
      END;
    ELSE
      IF recv__flag = buff__full THEN   interrupt and check for reception upon handshaking with the other
                                        processor
      BEGIN
        INIT__recv                      initiate reception
        WHILE token = true DO           while token for reception is present
        BEGIN
          RECV__location                receive start location
          RECV__data__item              receive the data
          UPDATE__location              update the location
          CHECK__token                  check the token for reception for exhausted input
        END;
      END;
    UNTIL switch__off                   till switch is off
    INTIMATE__failure                   intimate failure if one processor fails to function
END.
```

APPENDIX 2: PROGRAM FOR SHARED MEMORY COMMUNICATION

PROGRAM: SHARED__MEMORY__DIRECT__COMMUNICATION

```
5: BEGIN
    REPEAT
      IF read = true                    check permission for reading operation
      THEN
      BEGIN
        INIT__readop                    set up READ mode
        INIT__dma                       initiate DMA for reading
      END;
      WHILE location < = max__index DO   check location less than maximum
      BEGIN
        RECV__location                  identify location
        RECV__data__item                read data
        UPDATE__location                update the location
        WHILE rmw = true DO             check for Read-Modify-Write
        BEGIN
          SEMHO__RMW                     if yes, do semaphore for Read-Modify-Write operation
        END;
        CHECK__token                    check the read token
        IF token = false THEN GOTO 30    if read token is absent then goto write mode initiation
      END;
      ELSE
```

```
30:    BEGIN
           IF WRITE = true THEN              check permission for write operation
           BEGIN
              INIT__writeop                  set up WRITE mode
              INIT__dma                      initiate DMA for writing
           END;
           WHILE location < = max__index DO  check location less than maximum
           BEGIN
              SEND__location                 send location
              SEND__data__item               write data
              UPDATE__location               update location
              CHECK__token                   check write token
              IF token = false THEN GOTO 5   if write token is absent then goto read initiation
           END;
         END;
       UNTIL switch__off                     until switch is off
       INTIMATE__failure                     intimate failure if one processor fails to function
     END.
```

APPENDIX 3:   PROGRAM FOR MATRIX OPERATION

```
PROGRAM: DUAL__MATOP: E = A*B + C*D
                             all data in shared memory
BEGIN
   INIT__pointers            initialize data pointers for the matrix operation
   SEND ready__token         send ready intimation to the other processor
   MATMUL__multiply          do matrix multiplication — a subroutine
   CONVEY__mess__over        indicate when operation is over
   SEND token := true        send token appropriately
   WHILE recv__token = false DO
   BEGIN
     DO__otherop             until interrupt comes do other operations, if any
   END;
   IF interrupt = true THEN   when interrupt comes,
   IF recv__token = true THEN check for receive token
   BEGIN
     ADD__cor__elms          if yes, add the corresponding elements — a subroutine
     CONVEY__mess__over      convey message and operation over to operator
   END;
   ELSE
     DO__otherop             if no receive token is present, continue doing other operations, if any
END.
```

APPENDIX 4:   PROGRAM FOR LINEAR SEARCH

```
PROGRAM: LINEAR__SEARCH
                                      all data in shared memory
   BEGIN
     INIT__pointers                   initialize data pointers for search operation
     max__index := max__index/2       maximum index equals half the number of data
     WHILE location < = (top + max__index) DO  first processor searches from top to middle
     BEGIN
       IF data = token THEN
       BEGIN
         SEND__found__token           if searching is successful
         CONVEY__mess__over           then intimate other processor
         GOTO 10                      end search operation
       END;
       IF interrupt = true THEN GOTO 10   if the other processor is successful then this processor is inter-
                                          rupted and intimated
     END;
     CONVEY__search__fail             intimate search failure
10: END.
```

V Lakshmi Narasimhan was born in 1960 at Madras, India. He took bachelor's degrees in physics at the University of Madras and in electronics engineering at the Indian Institute of Science, Bangalore, India. He obtained his master's degree from the Madras Institute of Technology, and is currently working for a PhD at the University of Queensland, Brisbane, Australia. Research interests are in the fields of parallel processing and data-driven and demand-driven multiprocessing systems.

J K Ramachandra was born in 1959 in Karnataka, India. He took bachelor's degrees in physics at the Mysore University, Karnataka, and in electronics engineering at the Indian Institute of Science, Bangalore. Currently he is working as assistant executive engineer at Indian Telephone Industries, Bangalore. His fields of interest are parallel processing and signal processing.

D K Anvekar was born in Karnataka, India. He obtained his bachelor's degree in electronics engineering from the Bangalore University, India, and his master's degree from the School of Automation at the Indian Institute of Science, Bangalore, where he is currently working for a PhD in multiprocessing systems. Other fields of interest include robotics, missile guidance systems and philosophy.

Realtime implementation of the Viterbi decoding algorithm on a high-performance microprocessor

Microprocessor implementation of the Viterbi algorithm may unlock the potential of this powerful decoding tool. **S M Said and K R Dimond** present a software implementation on the MC68000 for realtime decoding

The complexity of the digital circuitry of the Viterbi decoder has prevented the algorithm from being fully exploited. One solution is to use a microprocessor to combat the complexity of the system. This paper presents a software implementation of the Viterbi algorithm on a high-performance microprocessor, for realtime decoding. The method implemented is based on forming a set of tables and using the internal structure of the processor for table manipulation rather than calculations. The paper gives a practical solution to the problem of memory management. The algorithm is reviewed mainly to define the necessary computational stages, with a detailed description of the software implementation of each stage. Also included is a comparison of the performance of the chosen processor with that of other processors, the results obtained showing a substantial improvement in performance over that of other microprocessor implementations published in the literature. This implementation would be suitable for low- and medium-speed data modems.

microprocessors   convolution   Viterbi decoding algorithm

In recent years, convolutional coding with Viterbi decoding has become one of the most widely used forward-error-correction techniques[1,2]. The large number of potential applications of the Viterbi algorithm provide sufficient motivation for a thorough investigation of possible means of implementing it using present state technology. But the complexity of the decoder hardware has always been a problem, preventing the algorithm from being fully exploited. This complexity arises from the fact that both the memory storage and the number of computations required to perform the algorithm increase

The Electronics Laboratories, University of Kent, Canterbury, Kent CT2 7NT, UK

exponentially with the constraint length of the code[3,4]. A straightforward implementation of the Viterbi algorithm is relatively costly. With the recent advance in LSI microprocessor technology, however, the circuit complexity and cost can be considerably reduced.

Memory management is the primary task of the designer of a Viterbi decoder, but much of the published literature treats the details of the memory management sketchily. Forney[2] suggests analogy with the fast Fourier transform, and implies that memory management can be used for the path metric calculation. These ideas have been developed in a practical form by Rader[5] and have provided the basis for some of the work presented in this paper.

The Viterbi decoding algorithm has been described by a large number of authors, but they have been concerned mostly with performance. Very few publications[6,7] have described practical implementation on microprocessor systems. This paper presents a software implementation of the Viterbi algorithm on the MC68000 microprocessor, providing a practical solution to the problem of memory management. In this, as in any other application, an understanding of the algorithm as well as the hardware capability is essential to achieve optimum performance. An overall view of the algorithm is given, mainly to define the necessary computation stages. The software considerations at each stage of computation are discussed in detail. The decoder speed, storage requirements and a comparison with the performance of other processors are also considered.

VITERBI DECODING ALGORITHM FOR CONVOLUTIONAL CODES

Two types of code are in common use today: (n, k) block codes and (n, k, K) convolutional codes. Both codes map a k-symbol input sequence into an n-symbol output sequence. The main difference between the encoders for these two codes is the presence or absence of memory. Conceptually, the block code encoder is a *memoryless* device, this term indicating that each n-symbol block depends only on a specific k-symbol and no other. The convolutional encoder, on the other hand, is a device with memory, where the output is determined by the current input and a span of the $(K-1)$ preceding inputs. The memory span parameter K is referred to as the 'constraint length' of the code.

Among the different techniques used to alleviate the effect of random errors in data communication systems, one of the most powerful is convolutional encoding combined with the optimal trellis search of the Viterbi decoding algorithm. To understand the Viterbi decoding algorithm, it is more convenient to expand the state diagram of the decoder in time. The resulting structure is called a trellis diagram, as shown in Figure 1. Each node corresponds to a distinct state at a given time, while every branch represents a transition to some new state at the next time instant. Consequently, to every possible input sequence there is a unique path through the trellis.

The basic theory behind the Viterbi decoding algorithm is explained in detail in many text books[3, 4]. The Viterbi algorithm[1] is based on finding a path through the trellis which matches the received sequence as closely as possible. The Hamming distance between the trellis branches and the received sub-block can be used as a metric, and the branch which minimizes this metric is selected. With this convention, a small branch metric represents a highly probable event, while larger metrics represent a less likely one. Therefore the Viterbi algorithm is optimum in the sense that it always finds the maximum likelihood path through the trellis. The algorithm is performed in four stages

Stage 1: branch metric computation. This is the basic computation element of the algorithm. With every received sub-block, a new set of metric values, with respect to all the trellis branches, have to be calculated.

Stage 2: path metric updating. The branch metrics are added to the previously stored path metrics. Then, for each node a comparison is made among all the merging paths, and the smallest path metric is selected and stored as the new path metric.

Stage 3: information sequence updating. Once the paths are chosen for all the nodes, the history of each path (information sequence) is updated and stored.

Stage 4: decoder output. The previous steps are repeated from the time $t=j$ to $t=j+L$, where j is an integer and L is the search length. At $t=j+L$, the survivor with the best metric is selected, and the oldest k bits on this path are chosen as the decoded bits.

After the first decoding, additional decoding decisions

are made in the same way for each new received block processed. Hence, the decoding decisions always lag the progress of the decoder.

SOFTWARE IMPLEMENTATION

In this implementation the main objective is to improve the decoder performance, ie its speed and accuracy. To achieve this, the program was written in machine code and optimized by using the powerful addressing modes of the processor.

The trellis structure allows an efficient implementation based on a table-driven program, where the internal registers of the processor are used as table pointers. Using the information provided about the encoder structure, the program calculates the number of branches N_B, the number of states N_S and the number of merging branches to each state N_M where

$$N_B = 2^K, \quad N_S = 2^{(K-k)} \quad \text{and} \quad N_M = 2^k \qquad (1)$$

The program uses the RAM workspace to form seven tables used during the trellis computation and assigns an address register as a pointer to each table, as in Figure 3. Three tables, Morder, Distan and Bitout, are required to generate the trellis. These tables exhibit dynamic properties, where the main program calculates their contents when the code is initially constructed. The other four tables Oldmetric, Oldsurviv, Newmetric and Newsurviv are formed during the trellis execution.

Branch metric calculation

Two methods are used to obtain the branch metric value, the conventional method and the table look-up method[3]. The first method is rather slow, since for each received sub-block $n2^K$ computations would be required to calculate its branch metrics. The second method is faster, but due to the table length, 2^{nk}, its speed depends on the method of accessing the table values. Normally, an entry table having the 2^n addresses of the submetric tables is used to access the look-up table.

The method implemented simplifies the calculations as follows:

(a) The trellis states are reordered and divided into groups, as in Figure 2, where the states within one group have branches merging from the same old states. The number of groups N_G is given by

$$N_G = 2^{K-2k} \qquad (2)$$

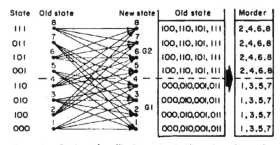

Figure 2. Basic subtrellis for a (n, 2, 5) code, where the states are reordered and divided into two groups

Figure 1. Trellis diagram for a (3, 1, 3) convolutional code, where each branch is labelled with its metric value

(b) The program calculates a merging order table (Morder) which contains the order of the old states S merging to the new state

$$S = i + (j - 1) N_G \quad \text{where } i = 1, 2, \ldots, N_G; \; j = 1, 2, \ldots, N_M \tag{3}$$

(c) Then it constructs a distance table (Distan) of length 2^{nK}. This table is divided into 2^n submetric tables where

- Each submetric table contains the Hamming distance between a certain input and all the trellis branches N_B. The order within the submetric tables depends on the value of n; for example, for $n = 4$ there are 16 submetric tables ordered as $n = 0000, 0001, \ldots, 1111$.
- The elements within each submetric table are re-ordered to match the trellis transition branches. In other words, all the branches merging to one state are successive within the submetric table. The branch number B is calculated as

$$B = i + (j - 1) N_S \quad \text{where } i = 1, 2, \ldots, N_S; \; j = 1, 2, \ldots, N_M \tag{4}$$

With this arrangement, the mechanism of accessing the look-up table becomes much simpler, as there is no need for the entry table. An internal address register is used as a distance pointer, and is always initialized to the beginning of the Distan table. When a new data sub-block n_1 is received, the pointer has to be displaced by $n_1 2^K$ in order to point at the appropriate submetric table. This is effectively equal to shifting n_1 to the left K times. Thus, within one processor shift instruction, the index value is calculated and added to the table start address to reposition the pointer, as shown in Figure 3.

Path metric updating

Three steps are necessary to perform the path metric updating:

(a) Addition of each branch metric to its old-state metric to form the path metric.
(b) Comparison between all branches merging at each state, to select the one with the smallest path metric. The others are discarded, since their likelihood can never exceed that of the survivor.
(c) When the proper branch is chosen, its path metric is stored as the new-state metric.

Since these steps have to be repeated with each state, tables are used to optimize the execution time of this stage as follows:

1 When a sub-block is received, the distance pointer is repositioned to the start of the appropriate submetric table as explained above. The submetric table elements were ordered as in Equation (4). Thus, the different branch metric values are obtained by successive reading of the table elements. The 'address register indirect with post-increment' (ARIP) addressing mode is used to move the distance pointer along the submetric table, as shown in Figure 3.

2 The old-state metric table (Oldmetric) is used in conjunction with the Morder table to obtain the old state corresponding to each branch. The Morder elements were calculated as in Equation (3) and used, as an index value in the Oldmetric table, to obtain the old-state metric. The Morder table pointer is moved using the ARIP addressing mode. With one ADD instruction to the processor, using the 'address register indirect with index' (ARII) address mode, the old-state metric is obtained and added to the branch metric to form the new path metric.

3 The previous steps are repeated 2^k times with each node, where each calculated value is compared with the previous value to choose the smallest. Since it takes longer to execute data operations within memory than with internal registers, the entire comparison for each node is performed using only the internal registers.

4 The new path metric values selected in step 3 are stored in the new-state metric table, Newmetric. The ARIP address mode is used to move the table pointer as data is stored, as shown in Figure 3.

Information sequence updating

Each node must be capable of storing the history of the surviving path along with its metric. Since the storage requirements increase exponentially with K, as in Equation (1), it is not practical to use K greater than 8. The tables and pointers used in this stage were as follows.

1 The main program forms the bit output table, Bitout, before executing the trellis. This table contains the information bits corresponding to each state, ordered according to the trellis diagram.

2 The selected paths determine the survivors to be updated from the old survivor table, Oldsurviv. Therefore the Morder values for the selected paths (in the previous stage) are used (after adjustment) as an index value into the Oldsurviv table pointer to obtain the required old survivors. This adjustment is needed since the Oldsurviv elements are long words. The ARIP addressing mode is used while accessing the Bitout table and storing the updated information sequences in the new survivor table Newsurviv, as shown in Figure 3.

Decoder output

The previous computational stages are repeated for a search length L before a decision can be made on the first received information block. The choice of L involves a trade-off between two conflicting factors. From the viewpoint of accuracy, it is desirable to have L as large as possible. The difficulty with large L, however, is the

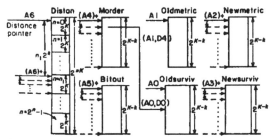

Figure 3. Basic construction of tables

decoding delay and the storage needed for the survivor's history (kL bit for each path). A compromise must be made.

In this implementation the survivor length (kL) is fixed to 32 bit and the main program determines the value of L according to the code used. This arrangement has two advantages

- It allows a long search length before a decision is made.
- The survivor's history can be manipulated easily by the processor as long words.

This stage is implemented as follows:

1 The program compares the number of input information blocks with the search length. If the search length is not reached (the first kL received bits), the program copies both the Newmetric and Newsurviv tables into the Oldmetric and Oldsurviv tables respectively, and repeats the first three computational stages with a new input information block.

2 When the search length is reached, the Newmetric elements are compared to select the smallest. The oldest k bit of the survivor corresponding to the selected new metric is the decoder output.

SIMULATION SYSTEM

A single 68000 microprocessor system was used to simulate a random data generator, the encoder, the transmission channel and the decoder, as in Figure 4a. The system hardware consists of a 68000 CPU board with a VIA (6522) as a timer (to measure the decoding speed) and a memory board[8]. The software implemented can be used in two modes

- Off-line mode: to allow the choice of different codes, and to analyse their performance and speed, as in Figure 3.
- On-line mode: where the encoder or the decoder can be connected to other hardware for realtime applications, as in Appendix 1.

Encoder All the necessary information about the code structure and the encoder connection matrix are provided by the user interactively. The implemented encoder model is a single binary shift register, with its data input obtained from a pseudorandom generator.

Transmission channel A software pseudo-noise generator[9] was used to simulate digital noise on the binary symmetric channel (BSC). The channel probability of error is chosen by the user during the measurements.

Measurements To obtain good statistical measurements the number of samples per measurement should be relatively high. In this implementation, the measurements are based on 100 kbyte sample. Figure 4a shows the measuring points, where the number of information bits, transmitted bits, channel errors and receiver errors are measured.

SYSTEM PERFORMANCE

Table 1 shows the decoding speed as a function of k and K for different codes implemented on a 68000 processor. Since the number of trellis branches is an exponential function of K, the speed decreases as K increases. The number of states and the number of groups are an inverse function of k, however, so as k increases the number of loop iterations within the software decreases, and the speed increases. The algorithm is implemented in such a way that the decoding speed is independent of the channel error rate.

A comparison with the performance of other processors is shown in Table 2. The work space required as a function of n and K is shown in Figure 5. Figure 6 shows the decoder performance for different convolutional codes.

Table 1. Speed of trellis decoder (bit s^{-1}) implemented on the MC68000L8 microprocessor

K	$n = 8$			
	$k = 1$, $L = 32$	$k = 2$, $L = 16$	$k = 3$, $L = 10$	$k = 4$, $L = 8$
2	61390	–	–	–
3	36312	–	–	–
4	20269	27061	–	–
5	10944	14814	–	–
6	5791	8055	9615	–
7	3034	4338	5177	–
8	1578	2253	2812	2987

Table 2. Speed of trellis decoder (bit s^{-1}) implemented on different microprocessors

K	MC68000L8	Z80*	MC6800*	8080*
2	61390	6793	6250	5764
3	36312	3709	3185	3082
4	20269	1944	1608	1596
5	10944	996	808	813
6	5791	504	405	410
7	3034	254	203	206

*From Reference 7 ($n = 2$, $k = 1$, $L = 32$)

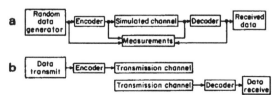

Figure 4. Simulation system implemented on the MC68000 processor: a, off-line mode; b, on-line mode

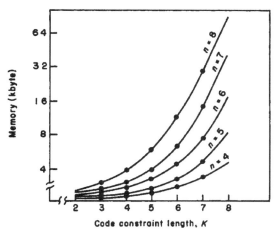

Figure 5. Work space against code constraint length K

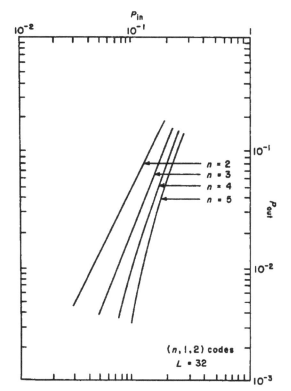

Figure 6. Decoder performance for different convolutional codes

rather than calculations in order to minimize execution time. The main software ideas and their implementation have been explained. A complete listing of the package is available from the authors.

In this implementation, the decoding speed is a function of k, K and independent of n (where $n < 16$). Therefore convolutional codes with higher values of n and k can be used to improve the decoding accuracy without affecting the decoding speed. The performance results obtained indicate that this implementation would be suitable for low- and medium-speed data modems.

For realtime applications, the decoding speed can be further increased by using a faster version of the same processor (eg by up to 40% with the MC68000L12). Also, in a system dedicated to this application, the maximum theory requirement would be 64 kbyte. Therefore if the memory is mapped from address zero upwards (ie $0000–$FFFF), the assembler will optimize the machine code by using a special addressing mode (absolute short)[10]. This would produce an 11% improvement in the decoding speed.

ACKNOWLEDGEMENT

Dr Said would like to acknowledge the Egyptian Government for their financial support. The authors would like to acknowledge the useful discussions with Professor P G Farrell, University of Manchester, UK.

REFERENCES

1 **Viterbi, A J** 'Convolutional codes and their performance in communication systems' *IEEE Trans.* Vol COM-19 (Oct 1971) pp 751–772

2 **Forney, G D Jr** 'The Viterbi algorithm' *Proc. IEEE* Vol 61 (March 1973) pp 268–278

3 **Clarck, G C and Bibb Cain, J** *Error-correction coding for digital communications* Plenum, New York, USA (1981)

4 **Viterbi, A J and Omura, J K** *Principles of digital communication and coding* McGraw-Hill (1979)

5 **Rader, C M** 'Memory management in a Viterbi decoder' *IEEE Trans.* Vol COM-29 (Sept 1981) pp 1399–1401

6 **Conan, J and Oliver, R** 'Hardware and software implementation of the Viterbi decoding algorithm for convolutional code' *Int. Symp. Mini and Microcomputers and their Applications, Toronto, Canada* (Nov 1979) pp 190–195

7 **Rashvand, H F** 'Implementation of microprocessor in trellis decoding of convolutional codes' *IEE Electron. Lett.* Vol 18 (Feb 1982) pp 121–123

8 **Said, S M and Dimond, K R** 'Design considerations for a hardware-refreshed memory card for the MC68000' *Microprocessors Microsyst.* Vol 8 No 8 (Oct 1984) pp 413–416

9 **Hurd, W J** 'Efficient generation of statistically good pseudo-noise by linear interconnected shift registers' *IEEE Trans.* Vol C-23 (Feb 1974) pp 146–152

10 *MC68000 user manual* Motorola, USA (1982)

CONCLUSION

This paper demonstrates an efficient implementation of the Viterbi algorithm on the MC68000 microprocessor. The method described is based on table manipulation

APPENDIX 1: ABSTRACT FROM SOFTWARE DESCRIBING TABLE MANIPULATION

```
1               MOVE       RXDATA, D1      *   D1 = received data sub-block
2               MOVE.B     K, D2           *   K = code constraint length
3               ASL        D2, D1          *   D1 = distance pointer displacement
4               ADDA       D1, A6          *   Reposition distance pointer
5       PASS1:  MOVE       NS, D3          *   NS = number of merging states
6               MOVE.B     #255, D7        *   Large initial comparison value
7       PASS2:  MOVE.B     (A6)+, D6       *   D6 = branch metric value
8               MOVE.B     (A4)+, D4       *   D4 = Oldmetric index value
9               ADD.B      0(A1, D4), D6   *   Path metric = old state + branch metric
10              CMP.B      D6, D7          *   Compare with previous value
11              BLS.S      PASS3           *   Branch if less than?
12              MOVE.B     D6, D7          *   Copy the path metric
13              MOVE       D4, D0          *   Copy the index value
14      PASS3:  SUBQ.B     #1, D3          *   Decrement merging counter
15              BNE.S      PASS2           *   Do another merging branch?
16              MOVE.B     D7, (A2)+       *   Store new state metric
17              ASL        #2, D0          *   Adjust index for long word table
18              MOVE.L     0(A0, D0), D3   *   Copy old survivor history
19              MOVE.B     (A5)+, D6       *   D6 = output bit
20              MOVE.B     k, D7           *   k = number of input bits
21              ASL.L      D7, D3          *   Prepare survivor for updating
22              ADD.B      D6, D3          *   Update survivor history
23              MOVE.L     D3, (A3)+       *   Store new survivor value
24              SUBQ.B     #1, D2          *   Decrement number of states
25              BNE.S      PASS1           *   Any more states?
```

S M Said was born in El-Fayom, Egypt, in 1949. He received his BSc in electrical engineering from the Military Technical College of Cairo, Egypt, in 1971. Between 1971 and 1976 he was involved in several communications projects for the Egyptian Army. Then from 1977 to 1981 he was a lecturer at the Military College. Since 1982 he has been working at the University of Kent at Canterbury, UK, and was awarded his PhD in 1985. His main interests lie in the application of microprocessors in digital communication.

Keith Dimond graduated in electrical engineering from the University of Manchester Institute of Science and Technology, UK, where he also undertook research. He was then a scientific officer at Government Communications Headquarters, Cheltenham, UK. Dimond joined the Electronics Laboratory at the University of Kent in October 1971. He became senior lecturer there in 1981. His interests are in CAD tools for digital and system design.

Emerging local area network technologies

Nigel Linge reviews current baseband local area network technologies, discussing the network topology and data transmission protocols of those technologies identified as potential market leaders

Many establishments now support a vast range of computer systems. A growing need has emerged to develop computer networks to achieve the interconnection of such systems for file transfer, electronic mail and similar purposes. This paper examines those baseband local area network technologies which are beginning to emerge as potential market leaders. In particular, the network topology, data transmission protocols, LSI network controllers and activities of world standards bodies are discussed.

microsystems   LANs   topology   protocols

The development of the microprocessor and the resulting computer revolution has led to a situation in which many offices and industries now support a large range of distributed computer systems. The concept of the electronic office, coupled with a desire to interconnect these systems for purposes such as central database access, file distribution facilities, electronic mail services and industrial plant monitoring[1-3], provided the incentive for the development of computer networks[4-12]. Computer networks are destined to play an important role within the sphere of information technology and, as a result, the computer network market continues to expand.

Networks in general can be classified with regard to four important design considerations. First, the distinction is made regarding the actual physical distance over which the network operates. A wide area network (WAN) spans tens to hundreds of miles; British Telecom's Packet Switchstream, which serves many of the principal cities in the UK as well as providing international communications, is a typical WAN. A local area network (LAN), on the other hand, is limited in size to approximately 2.5 km and is typically confined to a single building. Provision may be incorporated, however, for multiple LAN or LAN-to-WAN interconnections.

Second, networks are characterized depending on the way in which they use the available network bandwidth. A baseband network provides a single communications channel operating over the entire bandwidth. A broadband network divides the bandwidth logically into smaller frequency ranges and thus supports multiple independent communications channels.

Third, networks vary depending on the way in which the computer systems that are actively attached to the

network, the network nodes, are physically interconnected, ie the network topology. The set of rules (protocols) adopted by the network to govern reliable data transmission precisely forms a fourth method of classification.

This paper is intended to provide a general introduction to those baseband local area network technologies which are now beginning to emerge as potential market leaders. In particular, the network topology, data transmission protocols, the effects of proposed LSI network controllers and the activities of various international standards bodies will be discussed.

LAN TECHNOLOGIES

Those LAN technologies which are now being standardized and are therefore destined to become the market leaders can be characterized into two broad types depending on the network topology adopted. Bus topology networks employ a single transmission medium suitably terminated at the two open ends to prevent data reflections. Ring topology networks, on the other hand, support a closed loop transmission medium. Each of these two LAN types is considered in detail below.

Bus topology networks

Two separate LAN technologies have been defined using a bus topology. The first, CSMA/CD, originally known as Ethernet, implements a 'random access' algorithm for transmitting data over the network whereby each network node must compete for access to the bus on an equal priority basis. Techniques for overcoming bus contention and forcing transmission rescheduling are required.

The second technology, token bus, introduces a deterministic access algorithm whereby each network node is allocated access to the network bus in a negotiated sequential order.

CSMA/CD (Ethernet)

The Ethernet local area network (Figure 1), was developed at the Xerox Palo Alto research centre during 1972[13-17]. The design was originally formalized in the Ethernet Specification, a joint venture by Xerox, Intel and Digital Equipment Corporation. More recently the IEEE under subcommittee 802.3[18] has produced an equivalent specification which has been accepted as the international standard for this LAN technology.

Department of Electronic and Electrical Engineering, University of Salford, Salford M5 4WT, UK

0141-9331/86/10017–08 $03.00 © 1986 Butterworth & Co. (Publishers) Ltd

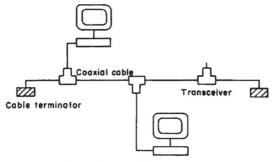

Figure 1. Ethernet bus topology

The network is configured either as a single coaxial cable segment, with a maximum permitted length of 500 m, or a series of such segments interconnected by repeaters such that no more than four repeaters exist between any given two nodes. The network nodes are attached to the bus by means of special transceivers which perform all the electrical signalling requirements.

Data to be transmitted over the LAN is first assembled into defined data packet structures (Figure 2). The absence of a master network synchronization clock forces each data packet to commence with a 7 byte preamble sequence of alternate ones and zeros followed by a 1 byte start of frame delimiter (10101011). The first 12 byte of the frame itself contains a 6 byte destination and 6 byte source address field. The addresses are followed by a 2 byte field which specifies the number of valid data bytes contained within the data field. The data field must contain a minimum of 46 byte and must not exceed 1500 byte. An optional pad field is included to overcome situations where a node wishes to transmit less data than the minimum limit. The packet is terminated with a 4 byte cyclic redundancy check sequence which operates over the entire data packet except for the initial preamble sequence.

Data packets are transmitted over the network using a special network protocol known as 'carrier sense multiple access with collision detection' (CSMA/CD). Under the conditions of CSMA/CD, a node with a correctly formatted data packet awaiting transmission must first establish whether the network bus is free, ie ensure that no other node is currently transmitting data. If data is detected on the bus (carrier sense), then a carrier sense signal is produced and the node delays transmission until the carrier sense signal has reset (a node is said to defer transmission). The node must wait for a predefined time, 9.6 μs (minimum packet spacing), before commencing its

transmission; this allows the network controllers time to recover from handling previous data packets.

Once a transmission commences, it takes a finite time for the data to propagate along the entire network. As a result, a second node could begin transmission not yet having sensed the carrier already on the bus. When this happens the two sets of data are said to collide and are in effect destroyed. As soon as a collision is detected, the transmitting nodes initiate a network jam routine which ensures that the collision occurs over the entire network length and hence every network node can detect its presence. Following the jam signal, all the transmitting nodes cease transmission and wait for a random period of time, the back-off period, before attempting a retransmission.

The worst-case time for detecting a collision is the sum of the time taken for data to propagate along the entire network, plus the time taken for the jam signal to travel all the way back, ie the round-trip delay. Clearly, the minimum data packet size must exceed this limit and is defined to be 64 byte (excluding the preamble sequence) in length. Similarly, no collisions can occur after the round-trip delay has expired and under these circumstances, the single transmitting node is said to have acquired the network. To prevent a single node from monopolizing this situation and taking sole control of the network, a maximum permitted data packet length of 1518 byte (excluding the preamble sequence) is defined.

Token bus

Under the conditions of the CSMA/CD network protocol, all nodes compete for access to the shared bus which can, under situations of excessive demand, produce significant increases in bus access time, severely reducing the effective point-to-point data rate. The token bus technique is a technology designed to maintain the network's bus topology, but to solve the contention problem by guaranteeing access to the bus within a maximum specified time. The technique is currently being formalized by the IEEE under subcommittee 802.4[19].

The token bus network protocol allows only one node access to the communications bus at any one time. This is achieved by the transmission of a special data packet, known as the network token, from node to node. Only that node to which the token is addressed is allowed to transmit data. Figure 3 illustrates the data/token format defined in the IEEE 802.4 specification. Each node continuously 'listens' to the network until it receives a data packet addressed to it. If the frame control byte indicates

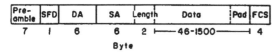

Figure 2. IEEE 802.3 Ethernet data packet format. SFD = start of frame delimiter; DA = destination address; SA = source address; FCS = frame check sequence

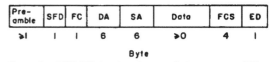

Figure 3. IEEE 802.3 token bus packet structures. SFD = start of frame delimiter; FC = frame control; DA = destination address; SA = source address; FCS = frame control sequence; ED = end of frame delimiter

that the packet is the token, then that node can take control of the network and transmit a variable length data packet.

Following either data transmission or the decision that the node has no data to transmit, the network token is retransmitted, addressed to the next node in the token passing sequence. Hence, each node must maintain a record of the node addresses either side of it in the token passing sequence, which tends to imply that the token bus technique is essentially a closed user system. It is the responsibility of the node currently in possession of the network token, however, to periodically permit the addition of new nodes by the transmission of a special 'solicit-successor' frame. This frame invites nodes, with an address between those specified within the frame, to demand entry onto the network. Nodes must respond to such a request within a specified time known as the response window. Deletion of a node is somewhat simpler in that when the node receives the token it transmits a 'set-successor' frame to the node from which it received the token. That node then issues the token to its new successor as specified within the 'set successor' frame.

After retransmission of the token, a node expects to detect data on the network, either a token or data frame, within a defined maximum time known as the 'slot time'. If no such data transmission is detected, then the node enters a fault recovery procedure whereby, as an initial step, the token is reissued. A second response failure results in the node assuming that its successor has gone inactive and so transmits a 'who-follows (successor)' frame. Hence, the node attempts to transmit the token to the next node beyond its normal successor. If this attempt also fails, then the node transmits a 'solicit-successor' frame specifying the entire network address range, hence inviting all nodes to respond. Finally, if a response has still not been received then the node assumes that a network failure has occurred and so resorts to 'listening' to the bus.

Under light network loads the CSMA/CD data transmission technique exhibits a reduced delay compared with the token bus, but under heavy network loads the token bus method provides overall a reduced network access time.

Ring topology networks

A ring topology network comprises a closed loop transmission medium which exhibits a known propagation delay. In addition, extra delays are introduced deliberately such that the whole ring can be considered as a data storage medium of fixed size. Two LAN technologies are defined using this topology: Cambridge Ring logically formats the ring storage capacity into a series of small data units known as slots, hence the adoption of the term 'slotted ring', token ring uses the topology in a way similar to token bus but the ring topology introduces advantages such that the effective data rate can be increased beyond that experienced with the bus equivalent network.

Cambridge Ring

The Cambridge Ring local area network was designed within the computer laboratory of the University of Cambridge[20, 21]. It is configured as a closed loop of cable, access to which is gained via any one of a series of network repeaters (Figure 4).

Each repeater, in addition to providing all the electrical data, encoding/decoding functions, introduces a propagation delay equal to approximately three data bits. A special unit known as the network monitor is then assigned the task of formatting the storage capacity logically into as many 40-bit minipackets as possible (Figure 5). The monitor together with the repeaters then establishes and maintains the cyclic motion of the minipackets at a ring data rate of 10 Mbit s^{-1}.

All nodes constantly examine the structure of the passing minipackets. The leader bit is designed purely to aid synchronization and is always set to logic 1. The full/empty flag indicates whether a particular minipacket contains valid information, ie whether it is available for use. If the minipacket is detected as empty and the node wishes to transmit data, then it sets the flag to full. The monitor pass bit is used by the network monitor and is always set by the transmitting node. As the minipacket circles the ring, the monitor resets the monitor pass bit. Any minipackets detected as being full, yet having the monitor pass bit cleared, will be marked empty automatically, hence preventing full minipackets from continually circulating the ring. The destination and source address fields convey the receiving and transmitting node addresses respectively. The data field contains the true data content of the minipacket. The type bits are under the control of higher level protocols and distinguish between communication request messages and normal

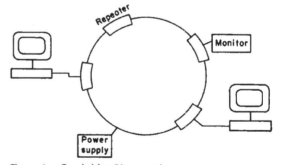

Figure 4.   Cambridge Ring topology

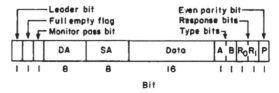

Figure 5.   Cambridge Ring CR82 minipacket format. DA = destination address; SA = source address

data transfers. Finally, the response bits are set to 1 and the parity bit adjusted accordingly.

If a full minipacket is detected, the node examines the destination address and compares it with its own network address. A negative comparison results in the node ignoring the remainder of the minipacket. If the comparison is true, the source address field is examined and compared with the node's internal source select register. The source select register contains the address of the node or nodes from which data will be accepted. If the register is set to zero, no minipackets will be accepted; if it is set to 255, all minipackets will be accepted. If the source select register contains a value in the range 1 to 254, only those minipackets addressed as having originated from that particular node will be accepted. Hence, the restrictions on the contents of the source select register limit a single Cambridge Ring to supporting a maximum of 254 independent nodes.

The contents of the source select register thus govern whether that particular node will copy the minipacket data field. Whatever the outcome, the node will always adjust the response bits. As each minipacket completes one revolution of the ring, it will naturally arrive back at the node from where it was originally transmitted. At that point, the response bits are analysed to determine whether the minipacket was successfully received. In all, the response bits can relay one of four possible states, as illustrated in Table 1.

Protocols for use over Cambridge Ring networks have now been formally detailed by the Joint Network Team in its CR82 specifications[22, 23].

Token ring

Initial research into the token ring network configuration was performed by the IBM research group in Zurich, Switzerland, along with contributions from IBM at Research Triangle Park, NC, USA[24]. In addition, specifications for the token ring technique are now under consideration by IEEE subcommittee 802.5[25].

With a token bus network, the token must be logically retransmitted to each active node, otherwise the token would be lost as it propagated to the ends of the network. The continuity of a ring system enables a single token to continually circle the ring, hence simplifying the token passing algorithm. The major difficulty associated with token ring networks is ensuring that the token field cannot possibly occur within a data packet; the token and data packet formats detailed in the IEEE 802.5 specification[25] are illustrated in Figure 6.

A node waiting to transmit data examines the network until a free network token is detected. The token bit contained within the access control field is then changed to indicate that the token has been accepted. Having obtained the token, a node is permitted to transmit data frames until either the transmission is complete or its token holding time (10 ms) expires. All data frames transmitted contain, as they complete their revolution, a frame status field which is adjusted by the destination node to indicate whether it successfully received the data. In addition, the end of frame delimiter contains an error bit which can be set by any node to indicate that a frame error has been detected.

The token ring technique can also establish a data prioritization scheme. The access control field of the token contains a 3-bit priority and a 3-bit reservation variable. Each node assigns a priority to its own data frame awaiting transmission. A node with priority exceeding that of the current busy token can reserve the next free token to the required priority level by adjusting the reservation variable accordingly. When the transmitting node finishes, it reissues the token at the new priority level. Network nodes with lower priority data are not allowed control of the token and so the token passes straight to the requesting node or to an intermediate node with an equal or higher priority data frame to transmit.

It is then the responsibility of the node which requested the higher priority to reissue the token at its previous lower value. To overcome situations where the token becomes permanently set to the highest priority level, each node maintains a record of the priority of the previous free token and can detect such situations, being able to reduce the priority accordingly.

Table 1. Cambridge Ring — minipacket response bit usage

Response bits		Interpretation
R0	R1	
1	1	The destination node is physically absent from the ring
1	0	Not selected — the destination node's source select register is set to a different address
0	1	Accepted — the destination node has received the minipacket and successfully copied the data content
0	0	Busy — the destination node has its source select register set correctly but is still busy processing the previously received minipacket

Token format

Data frame format

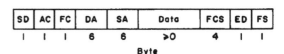

Figure 6.   IEEE 802.5 token ring packet structures. SD = start of frame delimiter; AC = address control; FC = frame control; DA = destination access; SA = source address; FCS = frame check sequence; ED = end of frame delimiter; FS = frame status

NETWORK PROTOCOLS

The network topology and data transmission technique adopted form only part of the overall networking task. In addition, special rules, or protocols, must be developed and implemented so as to define precisely the way in which the various computer systems actually communicate over the underlying network[26, 27].Typically, network protocols as a whole are subdivided into a number of discrete tasks or layers[28]. The lower-level layers perform only the most basic of functions achieving the transmission of individual data bits. Subsequently higher layers build on the functions provided by the lower layer, thus enabling data bits to be logically formatted into bit sequences and then into messages until, eventually, quite complex tasks such as reliable file transfer are being performed. Standards bodies throughout the world are now actively involved in the telecommunications and data networks area[29].

In particular, the International Standards Organisation (ISO) has, under technical committee (TC) 97, sub-committee (SC) 16, produced its own seven-layer reference model for network protocols (Figure 7)[30, 31].

Communication between network nodes commences at a particular protocol level in the transmitting node. Control is then successively passed down through each layer until the information reaches the transmission medium from where it travels to each node along the network. The information will arrive at the intended destination node and begin to 'climb' its way up through the layers until it reaches the layer equivalent to that from which it originated. As a result, information appears to simply pass from layer to corresponding layer, thus forming what is often termed a virtual link or peer-to-peer protocol.

The lower three layers, termed the subnet, are concerned with data transfer between adjacent network nodes and comprise the physical, data link and network layers. The physical layer is concerned with the actual electrical contact to the network and the transmission of data bits. The data link layer then enhances the unreliable physical layer to provide an efficient means of transferring data blocks. Finally, the network layer is concerned with issues of data routing and addressing.

The remaining four layers perform end-to-end functions, that is the higher levels (those above the subnet) will only be active within the transmitting and receiving nodes. Data will be rejected by the subnet structure of any intermediate network node (Figure 8). The transport layer performs an end-to-end set of functions similar to those provided by the network layer. The session layer sets up and maintains specific periods of communication, sessions, between communicating nodes and provides the 'dialogue' of the session, involving such functions as resynchronization following the 'lock up' of a communication through loss of data or reply information. The presentation layer is concerned with such issues as data formatting, encryption and file translation functions. Finally, the application layer represents the task which is actually being performed, ie access to databases, file transfer, remote terminal access etc.

The IEEE subcommittee 802 is now also actively involved in local area network technology[32, 33]. Its work is centred around producing definitions for the lower two layers of the ISO reference model to be installed onto CSMA/CD (802.3), token bus (802.4) and token ring (802.5) local area networks. The committee has identified that the data link layer can be subdivided into those functions which are independent of the underlying network, referred to as the logical link control layer (LLC)[34], and those functions which are network dependent, the media access control layer (MAC) (Figure 9).

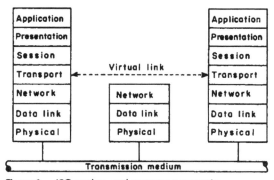

Figure 8. ISO end-to-end prototype operation

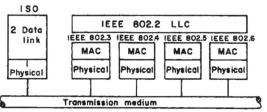

Figure 9. IEEE subcommittee 802 protocol standards. LLC = logical link control driver; MAC = media access control layer

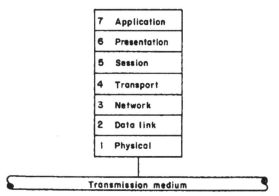

Figure 7. ISO seven-layer OSI reference model

Data is then transmitted as LLC and MAC frames. Typical MAC frames would be the 'who follows' or 'set-successor' frames of the token bus, whilst an LLC frame conveys information from the higher layers which could include normal data frames, connection requests etc.

In Europe, the International Telegraph and Telephone Consultative Committee (CCITT), which is part of the International Telecommunications Union, is also very active in the network field. The CCITT produces the V and X series protocols of which V24 (equivalent to RS232C) and X25 are probably the most commonly known. In particular, their recommendation X25 is seen as a realization of the lower three layers of the ISO reference model and is now adopted in many wide area networks including British Telecom's PSS[35-37].

The European Computer Manufacturers' Association (ECMA) is also active. Although their documents take the form of proposals and not standards, they represent a major influence. Documents produced to date follow the lines of the IEEE recommendations in that CSMA/CD, token ring and token bus LANs are preferred[38-43]. In addition, proposals for the transport and session layer protocols have been produced in accordance with the ISO seven-layer model[44, 45].

Before the ISO reference model had been formalized, a series of protocols was developed within the UK designed to work directly over level 3 of X25. Commonly known as the Rainbow Books, these protocols provided an interface to X25 (yellow book)[46] onto which various specialized protocols could be installed: file transfer facilities (blue book)[47], remote job entry and manipulation (red book)[48], electronic mail (grey book)[49], and terminal access (green book)[50]. The history of these protocols is such that they do not comply to the ISO standards and are therefore unlikely to receive worldwide attention although they are heavily used within the UK academic community.

LSI LOCAL NETWORK CONTROLLERS

Probably the most significant factor yet to be analysed in the development of LAN technologies is the effect of LSI network controllers. Within the last year major manufacturers have announced the availability of these components in production quantities.

Essentially, the majority of commercial products comprise two discrete integrated circuits. In general, one device performs data bit encoding/decoding, whilst the other implements the protocol for transmission and reception of data frames and provides an interface to a suitable host microprocessor. Hence, the controllers achieve a partial hardware realization of the physical and data link layers of the ISO seven-layer reference model.

The exception is the Texas Instruments controller, produced for the IBM token ring, which comprises five integrated circuits: a host microprocessor interface, communications processor, protocol handler, ring controller and ring transceiver. Table 2 lists known manufacturers of LSI controllers.

THE FUTURE

This paper has presented a review of the current local area network market. The various technologies currently being studied and standardized have been described and the many data communications protocol standards have been introduced.

The future of this market is difficult to predict, but a number of important factors can be outlined as significant controlling issues. Local area networks will inevitably become commonplace within the industrial and office

Table 2. LSI IC local area network controllers

Manufacturer	Device description	Network
Intel	82586 data link controller	Ethernet
	82501 Manchester encoder–decoder	Ethernet
AMD	Am7990 data link controller	Ethernet
	Am7991 Manchester encoder–decoder	Ethernet
	Am7995 cable transceiver	Ethernet
Rockwell	R68802 data link controller	Ethernet
Fujitsu	MB8795 data link controller	Ethernet
	MB502A Manchester encoder–decoder	Ethernet
National Semiconductor	DP8390 data link controller	Ethernet
	DP8391 Manchester encoder–decoder	Ethernet
	DP8392 cable transceiver	Ethernet
Mostek	MK68590 data link controller	Ethernet
	MK3891 Manchester encoder–decoder	Ethernet
Seeq	8003 data link controller	Ethernet
	8002 Manchester encoder–decoder	Ethernet
Swindon Silicon Systems	Cambridge Ring repeater and Type 1 interface chip set — under development	
Western Digital	WD2840 local network controller	Token passing
Standard Microsystems Corporation	COM9026 local network controller	Token passing
	COM9032 transceiver	Token passing
Texas Instruments	TMS380 set	Token Ring (IBM)

environments. Demands from industry indicate the necessity for deterministic data rates, eliminating technologies such as CSMA/CD. Office requirements are less stringent, however, and as such CSMA/CD, which has already achieved an early and important foothold in the form of Ethernet, will survive.

Industry will therefore have to decide between token ring and token bus. Already a major step has been made by General Motors, which has proposed its Manufacturing Automation Protocol (GM-MAP) in accordance with IEEE 802.4 token bus specifications. Higher-layer protocols within GM-MAP have adopted the ISO standards.

Another major factor to be considered is the recent announcement of the IBM Token Ring, currently operating at 4 Mbit s^{-1} but with a predicted data rate of 16 Mbit s^{-1}. Clearly, IBM has sufficient influence and customer base to be able to enter the office and possibly the industrial marketplaces.

Finally, the only true UK technology, Cambridge Ring, would appear to have an unfortunate future. Its late arrival on the international standards scene plus the lack of international manufacturing support could lead to the demise of the standard.

The only conclusion that can be made now is that the arrival of LSI controllers and the ensuing price reduction will, in the next few years, ensure that LANs become commonplace in many areas of the electronics industry.

REFERENCES

1 **Hanlon, P D** 'Use of local area networks within manufacturing systems' *Microprocessors Microsyst.* Vol 6 No 8 (Oct 1982) pp 425–429

2 **Weston, R H** 'The use of a commercial local area network in distributed machine and process control systems' *Electronics & Power* Vol 29 (May 1983) pp 401–404

3 **Nauman, J D** 'Managing computer networks in the steel industry' *Iron and Steelmaker* Vol 10 (June 1983) pp 17–23

4 **Clark, D D** 'An introduction to local area networks' *Proc. IEEE* Vol 66 No 11 (Nov 1978) pp 1497–1516

5 **Hutchison, D** 'Local area networks: a tutorial' *Software Microsyst.* Vol 2 No 4 (Aug 1983) pp 87–95

6 **Frisch, I T** 'The evolution of local area networks' *J. Telecomm. Networks* Vol 2 No 1 (1983) pp 7–23

7 **ICL** *The Principles of Data Communications — Communications Networks* Heinemann, in conjunction with ICL

8 **ICL** *The Principles of Data Communications — Structure in Data Communications* Heinemann, in conjunction with ICL (1983)

9 **ICL** *The Principles of Data Communications — Techniques in Data Communications* Heinemann, in conjunction with ICL

10 **Stallings, W** *Local Networks — An Introduction* Macmillan (1984)

11 **Green, P E Jr** (Ed) *Computer Network Architectures and Protocols* Plenum

12 **Davies, D W** *Computer Networks and their Protocols* John Wiley

13 **Shoch, J F** 'Evolution of the Ethernet local computer network' *Computer* (Aug 1982) pp 10–27

14 **Crane, E** 'Ethernet designers guide' *Microprocessors Microsyst.* Vol 6 No 8 (Oct 1982) pp 405–412

15 **Metcalfe, R M** 'Ethernet: distributed packet switching for local computer networks' *Commun. ACM* Vol 19 No 7 (July 1976) pp 395–404

16 **Posa, J G** 'Will Ethernet win computer-link race?' *High Technology* (April 1983) pp 12–15

17 **Hughes, H D** 'Simulation model of an Ethernet' *Computer Perf.* Vol 3 No 4 (Dec 1982) pp 210–217

18 'CSMA/CD access method and physical layer specifications' *IEEE Standard 802.3* (July 1984)

19 'Token passing bus access method and physical layer specifications; Draft D' *IEEE Standard 802.4* (Dec 1982)

20 **Wilkes, M V** 'The Cambridge digital communication ring' *Proc. LACN Symp.* (May 1979) pp 47–61

21 **Saltzer, J H** 'Why a ring?' *Computer Networks* Vol 7 (1983) pp 223–231

22 *Cambridge Ring 82 Interface Specifications* SERC and the Joint Network Team (Sept 1982)

23 *Cambridge Ring 82 Protocol Specifications* The Joint Network Team (Nov 1982)

24 **Dixon, R C** 'A token-ring network for local data communications' *IBM Syst. J.* Vol 22 Nos 1 and 2 (1983) pp 47 and 62

25 'Token ring access method and physical layer specifications; Working draft' *IEEE Standard 802.5* (23 Sept 1983)

26 **Pouzin, L** 'A tutorial on protocols' *Proc. IEEE* Vol 66 (Nov 1978) pp 1346–1370

27 **Sproull, R F** 'High level protocols' *Proc. IEEE* Vol 66 (Nov 1978) pp 1371–1386

28 **Witt, M** 'An introduction to layered protocols' *Byte* (Sept 1983) pp 385–398

29 **Kearsey, B N** 'International standardisation in telecommunications and information processing' *Electronics & Power* Vol 31 No 9 (Sept 1985) pp 643–651

30 **Zimmermann, H** 'OSI Reference Model — the OSI model of architecture for open systems interconnection' *IEEE Trans. Commun.* Vol COM-28 No 4 (April 1980) pp 425–432

31 *Open Systems Interconnection — Basic Reference Model* ITSU 1024

32 **Myers, W** 'Toward a local network standard' *IEEE Micro* (Aug 1982) pp 28–45

33 **Graube, M** 'Local area nets: a pair of standards' *IEEE Spectrum* (June 1982) pp 60–64

34 'Logical link control; Draft D' *IEEE Standard 802.2* (November 1982, revised March 1983, July 1983)

35 *X25 packet level protocol for data terminal equipment* ITSU 1010 Issue 3

36 *Description of the 1984 X25 LAPB-compatible DTE data link procedures* ITSU 1026 Issue 2

37 *OSI network protocol — X21 version* ITSU 1022

38 'Local area network layers 1 to 4: architecture and protocols' *ECMA-TR14* (Sept 1982)

39 'Local area networks: CSMA/CD baseband, coaxial cable system' *ECMA-80* (March 1984)
40 'Local area networks: CSMA/CD baseband, physical layer' (March 1984)
41 'Local area networks: CSMA/CD baseband, link layer' *ECMA-82* (March 1984)
42 'Local area networks: Token Ring technique' *ECMA-89* (March 1985)
43 'Local area networks: Token Bus technique' *ECMA-90* (Sept 1983)
44 'Transport protocol' *ECMA-72* (March 1985)
45 'Session protocol' *ECMA-75* (Jan 1982)
46 *A Network Independent Transport Service (Yellow Book)* Study Group Three of the Post Office PSS User Forum (Feb 1980)
47 *A Network Independent File Transfer Protocol (Blue Book)* High Level Protocol Group, revised by the Fife Transfer Protocol Implementors Group of the Data Communication Protocols Unit (Feb 1981)
48 *A Network Independent Job Transfer and Manipulation Protocol (Red Book)* JTP Working Party of the DCPU (Sept 1981)
49 **Bennett, C J** *JNT Mail Protocol (Grey Book)* University College London (Jan 1982)
50 *Character Terminal Protocols on PSS (Green Book)* Study Group 3 of the British Telecom PSS User Forum (Feb 1981)

Nigel Linge is a postgraduate in the Department of Electronic and Electrical Engineering at the University of Salford. He graduated from Salford in 1983 with an honours degree in electronics. He is now studying for a PhD in digital communications with special research interests in novel techniques for the interconnection of CSMA/CD local area networks.

Microprocessor-based delay generators

Saad Alshaban and Z Mansour have interfaced digital generators
to controlling micros

*Some digital techniques developed to generate time delays
are reviewed. These delay generators are interfaced to
microprocessors for control and storage of time delays.*

microsystems   delay generation   SEMs

Alshaban and Dinnis[1] developed a digital sampling
system for a scanning electron microscope (SEM) to
observe high-frequency signals. This system was based
mainly on digital principles of operation. The same
system was used to produce SEM colour stroboscopy for
imaging of timing in integrated circuits[2]. The digital delay
generator was controlled by microcomputer, to give
remote control of the sampling phase. Programmable
counters were used for delay generation.

Subsequent work, described here, has led to the
development of new models of delay generators which

Electrical Engineering Department, University of Technology,
Baghdad, Iraq

are easily interfaced to microprocessors such as the 8085.
This simplifies control circuitry and makes the system
portable and small in size.

System design

The system shown in Figure 1 was constructed to produce
digitally switched time delay. This delay generator is
implemented using a programmable counter in cascaded
form with eight delay tapings to count up or down the
pulses at the input. Time delay, which is selectable
between 0.1 μs and around 2 ms, can be adjusted and
programmed by the microprocessor, which is interfaced
to the delay generator through a decoder unit.

Previous work used complicated circuitry to interface
the digital sampling system, through the IEEE 488 general-
purpose interface bus (GPIB), to a microcomputer with
multiprogrammer kits. Machine code was used to control
time delay according to the flowchart shown in Figure 2.

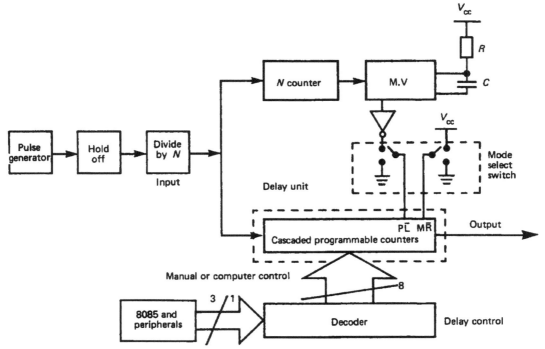

Figure 1.   Digital delay generator

0141-9331/86/10025–03 $03.00 © 1986 Butterworth & Co. (Publishers) Ltd

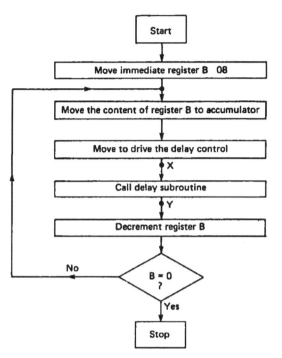

Figure 2. Time delay control by microcomputer

Saad Alshaban graduated from the University of Technology in Baghdad, Iraq, in 1973 with a BSc degree. From 1975 to 1977 he worked at Dundee University, UK, towards his MSc in amorphous semiconductor technology. From 1977 to 1980 he was an assistant lecturer at the University of Technology, Baghdad. He studied for a PhD in instrumentation in the Electrical Engineering Department of the University of Edinburgh, UK, from 1980 to 1983 before returning to the University of Technology.

Z Mansour obtained his BSc in electronics from the University of Salah Aldeen, Iraq, in 1982. Since 1984 he has been studying for an MSc in the electrical engineering department of the University of Technology, Baghdad, Iraq. His research interests include digital delay lines and digital filters.

Time delay storage for sampling input signals, or for when any time delay was in demand, was provided.

A further time-delay generator was designed using programmable shift registers in cascaded form, arranged as serial-in–parallel-out (Figure 3). Time delay can be programmed by microprocessor according to the flow-chart shown in Figure 4. Figure 5 gives a subroutine for

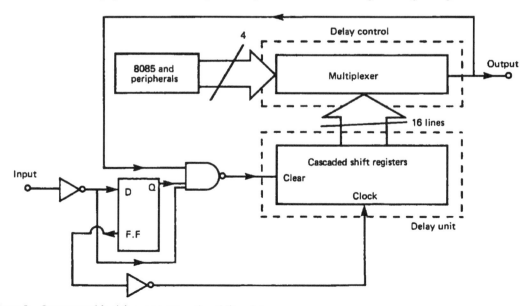

Figure 3. Programmable delay generator using shift registers

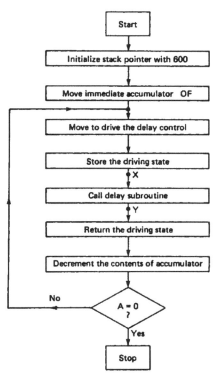

Figure 4. Time delay control for shift register system (Figure 3)

Figures 2 and 4. The problem of mismatching the input signal and the clock to the shift register, mentioned previously[1], has been solved in the present design by means of logic gates.

Conclusions

Previous work on delay circuitry required the construction of a series of costly circuits. The present microprocessor-based system simplifies the control setup and makes the system portable. This is useful for a variety of applications especially in digital filters, when different time delays are

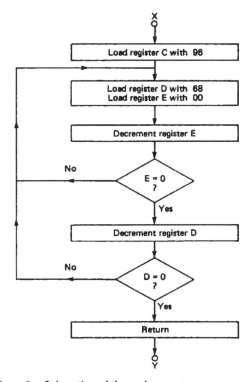

Figure 5. Subroutine of the main programs

required. It can also be used for correlation techniques, amongst other applications.

Comparison of the circuit designs for both delay generator models shows that the programmable counter is more stable and reliable than shift registers. Both may be interfaced to microprocessors for delay programming.

References

1 **Alshaban, S and Dinnis, A R** *J. Inst. Eng. (India)* Vol 65 (1984) pp 48–51
2 **Alshaban, S and Dinnis, A R** *Proc. Microcircuit Engineering Conf., Cambridge, UK* (1983) pp 510–516

design note

32008-based single-board microcomputer

Jacob Davidson describes a simple low-cost NS32008 evaluation board

A single-board microcomputer was built based on the NS32008 microprocessor. It was designed for evaluation of the processor's performance and ease of use, and illustrates some design ideas relevant to those evaluating 16/32-bit microprocessors in the 32000 series.

microprocessors   evaluation boards   NS32008

The advent of 16-bit and 32-bit microprocessors has led to the rapid replacement of their 8-bit counterparts in many applications. National Semiconductor's Series 32000 microprocessor family includes the NS32008, which has a 32-bit internal architecture, an 8-bit data bus and a 24-bit address bus, allowing for a total of 16 Mbyte of memory addressing. In this respect it compares favourably with Motorola's 68008 and Intel's 8088, both of which possess an 8-bit data bus and a 20-bit address bus. An application of the 32008 is in colour graphics terminal controllers, in which the amount of RAM associated with the graphics functions may exceed 1 Mbyte.

There are not many commercially available 32008-based microcomputers and potential users sometimes have trouble evaluating the performance and ease of use of this microprocessor. The design of the single-board microcomputer presented in this paper is intended for those considering the 32000 series for development of advanced microprocessor-based products.

NS32008 MICROPROCESSOR

The Series 32000 microprocessor family was designed around a 32-bit architecture with the goal of obtaining good performance, efficient management of large address space and facilities for high-level language program development. The main features of the 32008 are

- 32-bit internal architecture
- eight 32-bit general-purpose registers
- six 32-bit dedicated registers
- two 16-bit special registers
- one 4-bit configuration register
- 8-bit data bus
- 24-bit address bus creating a 16 Mbyte uniform addressing space

The configuration register is used to indicate the presence of different hardware units such as a floating point unit, an interrupt control unit or a custom slave processor. If the

University of Quebec at Montreal, Case postale 8888, Succursale 'A', Montreal PQ H3C 3P8, Canada

floating point bit is not set in the configuration register the respective instructions are trapped, allowing the implementation of floating point routines in software.

The instruction set is characterized by

- two address instructions
- addressing optimized for high-level language
- restricted instructions depending on the mode of operation (supervisor or user mode)
- instruction set expansion via traps or slave processors

The 32008 has two pins, INT and NMI, allowing for maskable or nonmaskable hardware interrupts. In addition, a set of internally generated traps is used for software interrupt service as a result of an exceptional condition or a specific trap instruction.

HARDWARE

The design goals were a simple low-cost 32008-based single-board microcomputer with two serial interfaces allowing crossassemblers and crosslinkers to be used on a host computer for software development.

The schematics in Figures 1 and 2 show the design of the board. This consists of 24 integrated circuits (ICs), the functions of which can be divided into timing, decoding, bus interface, communication interface and miscellaneous support. A list of components is given in Table 1.

Timing

The 32008 (labelled U1 in Figure 1) needs an NS32201 TCU (labelled U2) to provide timing signals. Clock signals ϕ_1 and ϕ_2 are received from the TCU which in turn is connected to a 4.9152 MHz crystal. The TCU also sends such signals as reset, address strobe, read, write and data bus enable.

Decoding

The memory map is shown in Table 2. Memory is divided into eight blocks of 8 kbyte each with the monitor residing at address 0. Decoding is done by two 74LS138 decoders (U17, U18) and a 74LS00 NAND gate (U20). At the output of the decoder there are eight memory select signals (CS0–CS7) and two select signals to enable the asynchronous interfaces at addresses C00000 and C00040.

0141–9331/86/10028–05 $03.00 © 1986 Butterworth & Co. (Publishers) Ltd

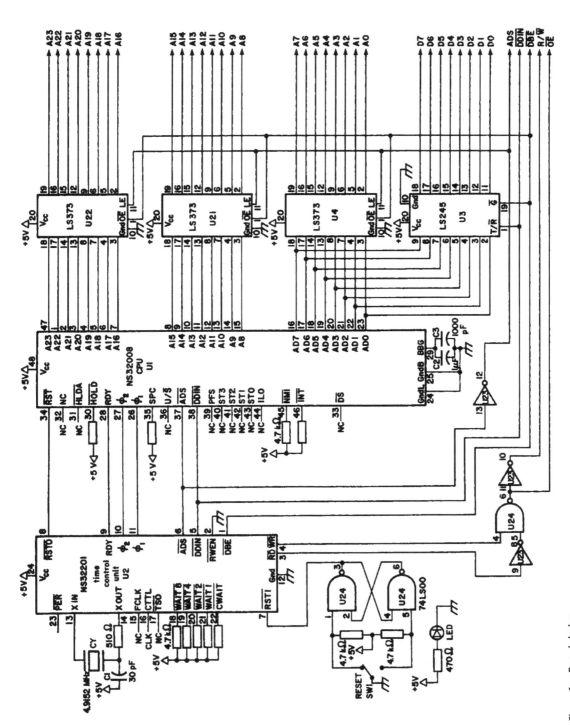

Figure 1. Board design

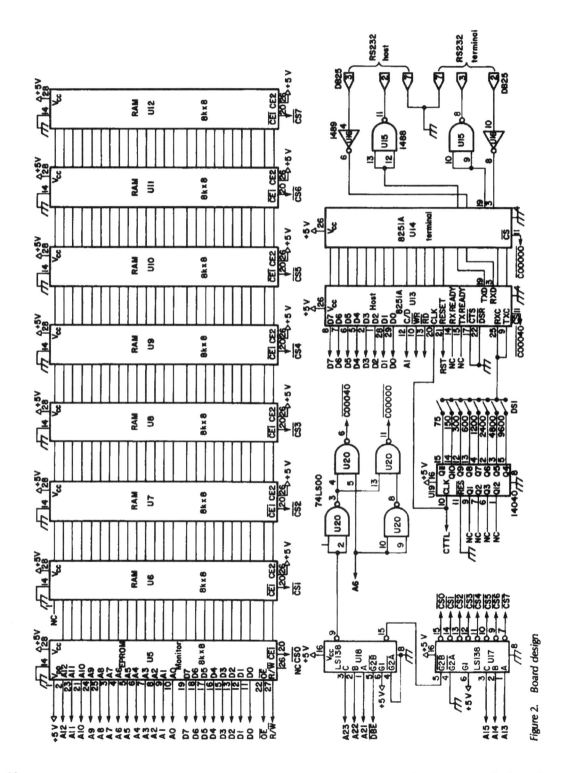

Figure 2. Board design

Table 1. Parts list

IC	Part number	Description
U1	NS32008-6	CPU
U2	NS32201-6	TCU
U3	74LS245	Data bus transceiver
U4	74LS373	Address bus latch buffer
U5	AM2764	EPROM (8 kbyte)
U6	HM6264	RAM (kbyte)
U7	HM6264	RAM (8 kbyte)
U8	HM6264	RAM (8 kbyte)
U9	HM6264	RAM (8 kbyte)
U10	HM6264	RAM (8 kbyte)
U11	HM6264	RAM (8 kbyte)
U12	HM6264	RAM (8 kbyte)
U13	I8251A	Host serial communication adapter
U14	I8251A	Terminal serial communication adapter
U15	1488	RS232 transmitter
U16	1489	RS232 receiver
U17	74LS138	Decoder 3/8
U18	74LS138	Decoder 3/8
U19	14040	12-stage counter (baud rate generator)
U20	74LS00	Quad two-input NAND gate
U21	74LS373	Address bus latch buffer
U22	74LS373	Address bus latch buffer
U23	74LS04	Hex inverter
U24	74LS00	Quad two-input NAND gate
CY	–	4.9152 MHz crystal
SW1	–	Push button reset switch
DS1	–	Eight-position DIP switch (baud rate switch)
–	–	Capacitors, resistors, connectors

Table 2. Memory map

Address	Device
$000000–$001FFF	(1) 8 kbyte EPROM (monitor)
$002000–$00FFFF	(7) 8 × 8 kbyte RAMs (56 kbyte memory)
$C00000–C000002	(1) Intel 8251A (terminal serial port)
$C00040–C000042	(1) Intel 8251A (host computer serial port)

Communication interface

The asynchronous communication interface consists of two Intel 8251A serial adapters (U13, U14). One is used to communicate with an alphanumeric terminal (address C00000) and the other with a host computer for program development (address C00040). A circuit 14040 (U19) is used as a baud rate generator deriving different baud rates from the frequency of 2.4576 MHz (half of the crystal frequency) by using the microprocessor signal CTTL. The DS1 dip switch is used for sending different baud rates to 8251A interfaces. The RS232C interface is obtained by using a 1489 RS232C receiver (U16) and a 1488 RS232C transmitter (U15). Both are transferring signals through two DB-25 connectors normally used for RS232 communication interfacing.

Bus interface

The address bus interface consists of three 74LS373 ICs (U4, U21, U22) and a 74LS245 transceiver (U3) is used for the data bus. All four circuits are enabled by the DBE (data bus enable) signal sent by the TCU. The U4 circuit is used to separate the 8-bit data bus from the lowest address byte (A0–A7).

MONITOR

The monitor program provides a set of program development services such as

- communication with a terminal and a host computer in transparent mode for program development via cross-support software
- debugging
- interrupt and trap handling
- object code downloading
- data manipulation
- program execution
- supervisor call routines

Monitor commands are received from the terminal as an ASCII string followed by a carriage return.

SOFTWARE

The NSX cross-support software package is provided by National Semiconductor for program development and debugging. The package runs on VAX/VMS systems and is composed of a crossassembler, a crosslinker, a cross PASCAL compiler (ANSI compatible), a librarian, an object code formatter and a symbolic debugger.

This software development package is intended to facilitate the development of software for Series 32000 based systems. The object code that is obtained (after the programs are edited and assembled on VAX computers) can be downloaded via the serial ports to the development board for execution and debugging.

A 'floating point support library' is also available. This provides floating point mathematical routines, which can be called from PASCAL or assembly language programs, and supports emulation of the NS32081 floating point unit.

design note

CONCLUSION

A simple low-cost single-board microcomputer based on the NS32008 8/32-bit microprocessor is described. This may be used as an evaluation board by microcomputer designers and engineers interested in Series 32000 microprocessors.

BIBLIOGRAPHY

Series 32000 data book National Semiconductor Corp, Santa Clara, CA, USA
NSW-ASSEMB-9VMR National Semiconductor Corp, Santa Clara, CA, USA
NSS-SYS32-3001 Pascal compiler National Semiconductor Corp, Santa Clara, CA, USA

Jacob Davidson is a professor of microelectronics at the University of Quebec in Montreal, Canada. He has participated in several computer process control projects in the Montreal area as chief engineer of the Computer Control and Automation Department at Tecsult International Inc, a consulting engineering company in Quebec, Canada. He obtained his PhD in electrical engineering from the Ecole Polytechnique, Montreal, Canada, in 1984. His current research interests include distributed computer control, microprocessor applications, robotics and digital communications.

applications

Example of the use of the BBC microcomputer for data collection

The BBC micro has been widely adopted in UK research laboratories. **P J Robertson and B Campbell** show how they use it to automate data acquisition in a photosynthesis experiment

An Acorn BBC model B microcomputer is applied to the collection and processing of data in a photosynthesis experiment. Interfacing to a pH meter and an oxygen meter are described in detail, as are necessary modifications to the BBC's reference circuitry. Data collection software is explained and a program listing given. Data processing software is covered briefly. All programming was done in BBC BASIC.

microsystems   BBC microcomputer   data acquisition

The Acorn BBC microcomputer has proved a valuable tool in the research laboratory, being an inexpensive microsystem offering a variety of interfaces. Use of the BBC micro for data collection has previously been described[1]. This paper describes a specific example where the collection and processing of data from an experiment can be handled by the BBC micro, resulting in greatly improved efficiency in using the experimental equipment.

There are three elements to the experimental apparatus, none very sophisticated in itself. Operational problems do arise, however, if data collection is to be done manually and simultaneously. Not only does the computer make the collection procedure easier but it makes feasible unattended data collection. In a situation where the time span of an experiment is measured in hours, this releases valuable time which the researcher can use elsewhere.

Experimental procedure

The research for which the system was designed is concerned with the effect of bicarbonate on the photosynthesis of macroalgae. An

Microcomputer Group, Computing Laboratory, University of St Andrews, Fife KY16 8XF, UK

experiment was designed to monitor the rate of photosynthesis (ie the rate at which oxygen is absorbed from the surrounding atmosphere and converted into carbon dioxide) in various species of plants as a function of ambient conditions, namely the pH of aqueous environment. (pH, which is the negative logarithm of the hydrogen ion concentration in a solution, is used as a measure of the acidity or alkalinity of the solution.)

The rate of oxygen uptake and the production of carbon dioxide are measured to allow calculation of the photosynthesis rate, which is compared for various pH settings. The pH is measured using a pH meter (model PHM 84 made by Radiometer of Copenhagen, Denmark) connected to a GK240 combined gas electrode in the solution. This produces an analogue output signal ranging between 0 and -7.5 V DC, ie 500 mV per unit of pH.

The oxygen is measured by a meter (Strathkelvin model 781) which is connected to an oxygen electrode (made by Instrumentation Laboratory). This combination produces another analogue signal in the range from 0 to $+1$ V DC. Finally, the carbon dioxide is measured by neutralizing the solution using an autoburette (Radiometer model ABU80).

The amount of solution which has been delivered by the burette is denoted as a TTL pulse on the output line for each 0.01 ml of neutralizing solution delivered. A microsystem which can cope with two analogue inputs and also provide a pulse counter is therefore required.

The BBC micro has four A/D converter channels available as well as a user port which is driven by a 6522 VIA (versatile interface adapter) chip. Among the facilities of the VIA device is the ability to count events. The chip has two 8-bit I/O ports each with handshaking ability and there are also two 16-bit programmable counters. One of the ports is usually reserved for the printer while the other provides the user port. Each of the bits of the user port can be individually programmed.

To use the port in a pulse counting mode, the maximum number of pulses which is expected is first loaded into the high-order counter register for timer 2. Subsequently, any negative-going edges which are input on pin 16 (ie the PB6 input) of the user port will cause the number in the counter register to be decreased by one. By examining this register (at hexadecimal address FE68 in the BBC memory map), the experimenter can calculate the number of pulses received.

The basic tools are therefore available within the BBC micro for the inputs supplied in this experiment. What remains is to check that the signals from the experimental apparatus are compatible with the required inputs for the ports on the BBC micro and to provide the software to run the data collection. A simplified diagram of the experimental layout is given in Figure 1.

0141-9331/86/10033-05 $03.00 © 1986 Butterworth & Co. (Publishers) Ltd

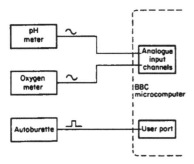

Figure 1. Schematic of experimental apparatus

Hardware

Neither of the analogue inputs was suitable for direct connection to the input of the BBC micro. Analogue signals normally require two elements of interfacing circuitry: one to adjust the voltage range to the required scale required by the A/D channels in the microcomputer, and the other to provide some protection from the voltage increasing sufficiently to damage the A/D circuitry.

To be effective, simple protection circuitry must often be designed to become active at a threshold which is within the normal working range of the equipment. Such circuitry has its price in loss of performance. Where this might be unacceptable and where the user is conscious of the need to take care to avoid excessive input levels, the circuitry can be simplified by the exclusion of protective components. This has the advantage of avoiding possible signal degradation (and possible added noise) within the normal working range. In cases where the user is likely to be less careful or is less sure about the nature of the input signals, limiting diodes can be added in the signal paths to clip signals at a safe level.

For this experiment, the user of the equipment opted to exclude protective components from the interface.

pH meter interface

In the case of the pH meter, which was connected to analogue channel

1 of the BBC micro, the normal absolute measurements of pH produce a negative DC voltage in the range from 0 to −7.5 V from the pH meter's recorder output. This corresponds to pH readings in the range from 0 to 14. As the BBC micro accepts inputs in the range from 0 to + 1.8 V, the signal requires both attenuation and inversion.

For this experimental set-up, the maximum pH encountered was to be 11. The design of the interface was therefore based on the requirement for a pH of 11, producing −5.5 V, to give a full-scale input to the BBC micro. Accordingly, an interface was provided in the form of an inverting DC amplifier with a gain of −0.3.

One channel of a single-rail quad operational amplifier (type LM324) proved suitable for this purpose, since a 5 V DC power supply was available from the BBC micro analogue port. Decoupling of the supply was performed adjacent to the LM324 itself. Due to the relatively slow sampling rate encountered in the experiment (sample intervals were of the order of tens of seconds), a certain amount of low-pass capacitive signal filtering was performed on this channel to improve the noise performance.

Oxygen meter interface

For the oxygen meter, which was connected to analogue channel 2, the output signal had a maximum value of about +1 V DC. Therefore amplification was required to bring this voltage up to a level suitable for the BBC micro analogue port. A noninverting amplifier with a gain of approximately +1.8 was provided using one of the remaining channels on the LM324.

It was noted that the video monitor (which tends to be used in close proximity to the microcomputer) was a potential source of extraneous noise, mainly from the line oscillator. Inductive pick-up hum from mains leads could also prove troublesome. Signal leads for this channel and the pH channel were therefore of the screened coaxial type. Care was also taken to avoid earth loops by avoiding multiple signal earthing.

The remaining two analogue channels on the BBC micro were unused for this experiment. The inputs to these channels were shorted to ground to prevent any noise signals present at these inputs coupling to the active channels.

Reference circuitry

Steps were taken to improve the performance of the 7002 A/D converter chip. The D7002C version of the chip fitted as standard to the BBC micro has a potential resolution of one part in 512, or approximately 0.2% based on a 9-bit conversion. A higher performance version of the chip, the D7002C-1, has a better resolution of 0.1%, ie 10-bit conversion accuracy. This corresponds to 1.8 mV referred to the full-scale input of 1.8 V. To achieve this level of performance the chip needs to be provided with a stable DC reference voltage, V_{ref}, having a peak-to-peak ripple voltage better than 1.8 mV.

In addition, for long-term measurements (eg a period of several days) the absolute value of V_{ref} must maintain long-term stability. The reference circuitry fitted to the standard BBC micro was inadequate for the demands of this experiment in both short- and long-term performance. Measurements of V_{ref} taken on a small sample of unmodified BBC model B microcomputers showed a peak-to-peak ripple of 50–60 mV superimposed on a DC level which drifted by 1–2% over a few hours.

Filtering of the ripple (as close to the chip as possible) and replacement of the three reference diodes (1N4148s) with two 1.2 V band gap devices (9491BJs) effected acceptable short- and long-term performance improvements. (The newer BBC model B+ has the 1 μF filter capacitor relocated closer to the chip to improve noise performance, but 1N4148s are still fitted.)

As the 7002 can accommodate a V_{ref} value up to 2.5 V, it is permissible to connect the new reference voltage directly to the V_{ref} input.

For this experiment, a potential divider was added to retain the original specification of 1.8 V. Due to the very small current drawn by the

V_{ref} input the divider does not degrade the DC performance of the reference, whereas it significantly improves the filtering of high-frequency 'mush'. A diagram of the interface circuitry and details of the modifications to the reference circuit appear in Figure 2.

Autoburette interface

The autoburette produced its output as a serial TTL pulse train and therefore required no electrical adjustment for connection to the TTL user port on the BBC micro. A simple connecting lead was the only interfacing hardware needed for this instrument.

Software

The software can be divided into two sections: a program to collect the data and a set of programs to do the necessary calculations on the results. This section concentrates on the former task since it is more concerned with the hardware described above.

Data collection

The collection program is written in BASIC. Because BBC BASIC is well equipped to sample data coming in at the A/D converter channels using the ADVAL function call, and because it is possible to address directly the memory locations relevant to the collection of data through the user port, there is no need to use 6502 assembly language for any of the program. Indeed, because the rate of change in this experiment was measured in seconds or even minutes, there were no pressing time constraints and the relatively slow BASIC functions were fast enough to cope with the experiment without any need to directly program the interface chips.

The initial section of the program asks the user for details of the experiment, viz the name of the file to be used for data collection, the experiment number, the date, what species is involved, the collection site, the temperature, the alkalinity, the lighting conditions and the salinity. Such information may be required when the final calculations on the data are carried out. A final entry is included for any comments that are to be added. The program then opens the output file and writes these items of information into it.

The user is then presented with a menu giving the various options for data collection. The first two options monitor drift in pH value of the solution; this may be done either alone or alongside monitoring of the oxygen uptake in the system. The other two options are to monitor the oxygen uptake at a static pH value either with or without carbon dioxide monitoring. The measurement of pH values and oxygen monitoring are carried out by sampling two of the A/D converter channels, while carbon dioxide measurement involves pulse counting using the port circuitry.

The next section of the program is common to all modes of collection and determines sampling details. The first question is to establish the sampling frequency required as the number of samples to be taken per hour. The next question asks whether or not sample monitoring is required.

In some of the experiments, the time intervals involved were large (eg several minutes between sampling) with reference to the computer's time scale. While the experiment itself may last much longer, perhaps four or five hours, a typical feature of this type of experiment is that most of the activity occurs early on with changes becoming slower later; a typical data curve is shown in Figure 3. Therefore a relatively rapid rate of sampling is required in the early stages of data collection compared to the later stages.

A simple form of data monitoring can be included to avoid large amounts of data being collected when there is little or no change in the experimental conditions, and to avoid the experimenter having to

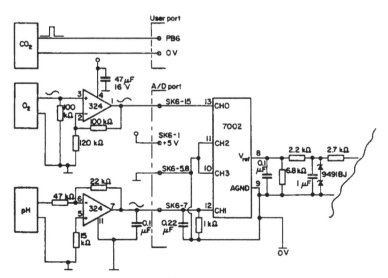

Figure 2. Circuit diagram of interfaces

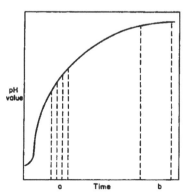

Figure 3. Typical graph of the change in conditions during an experiment. In section a, rapid sampling is needed while, in section b, only occasional samples are required.

occur oversee data collection to determine when the sampling rate should be reduced. It is possible to check whether or not the current reading on either or both of the A/D channels has changed significantly from the previous one collected. If this monitoring of the data is required, then a tolerance value is requested. This is the fraction of an accepted (stored) reading by which any subsequent reading must differ before that subsequent reading will be stored in the data file on disc (eg if a change of less than 0.5% is to be disregarded, the tolerance value would be 0.005).

The final query is the maximum length of time that the experiment should be allowed to run unattended. If this time is exceeded, the program closes down data collection automatically.

The program can proceed on either of two paths depending on whether or not the pH value is variable. In the first path, the change in pH against time is recorded and, if required, the oxygen content is also monitored.

In the second path, where the pH value is static, the user is first asked for the pH reading before sampling begins. During sampling the oxygen content is monitored and, if required, the counter readings from the autoburette are recorded. When the autoburette is being used, an initialization routine is required to set up the pulse counter while another function actually checks the count during the experiment. The value of the count can be recorded at regular intervals during the experiment by reading the memory address location corresponding to the appropriate register of the 6522 chip.

In all of the options, the experiment is finished when the specified time is overrun or the user presses the ESC key on the BBC micro keyboard. A common sequence is run to close the collection file and terminate the program. Should an

error occur for any reason during the running of the program, the program terminates by indicating what the error number is and in which line it occurred. (Fuller details of the error numbers are given in the BBC user guide[2].)

A listing of the data collection program is given in Appendix 1.

Data processing

To illustrate the steps expected in the data processing phase, one of the programs used for calculating results from collected information is outlined below.

The program consists of the experimental description and conditions recorded at the beginning of the file, followed by a series of data values with a corresponding series of time values. In the simplest case, the rate of change of the pH value of the solution is followed. From the initial information, the pH value can be converted to values for the total amount of inorganic carbon in the system, which is proportional to the rate of photosynthesis.

After some initial definitions, the program asks for the name of two files, the first being the file in which the data was collected and the other the file into which the results from this program are to be put. The program then reads in the experimental details from the first file, writes them to the output file and displays some of the information on the monitor screen. It then reads in the data points from the file, storing them in arrays, and the number of points collected is noted.

Next there is a call to a function to calculate the total carbon content. The program then asks for the chamber volume (ml) and the dry weight of the sample (g) before going on to calculate the experimental rate for the photosynthesis process.

A call is made to a procedure to calculate statistical means of the carbon, carbonate and bicarbonate

concentrations over each of the pH intervals. Another call is included to a procedure which presents some of the results graphically. The results of the calculations are stored in the output file.

As with the collection program, the program is written in BASIC; the code should trap any errors which arise and then print out the error number and the line in which one is found.

Conclusion

This experiment and the associated data processing contain no great practical difficulties either from the electronic or the programming point of view. However, on most popular computing systems, particularly in the low price range, the user would be faced with buying extra interfaces to accommodate the range of signals used here and also with the task of familiarization with the interfaces before being able to program them.

The attraction of the BBC microcomputer in this context is that the interfaces are already available on the system and the BBC BASIC language has the tools to enable the user to access them fairly readily. The interfaces are not flawless and, as has been indicated here, may need some adjustments to give an acceptable performance. Nevertheless, the relative simplicity of the interfacing process makes the BBC micro suitable for data collection applications such as the one described here.

References

1 Robertson, P J and Campbell, B 'The microcomputer as a data acquisition tool' Microprocessors Microsyst. Vol 8 No 3 (1984) pp 136–139

2 Coll, J The BBC microcomputer user guide BBC Publications, London, UK (1982) pp 474–482

Appendix 1: Listing of the data collection program

```
10 REM
20 REM
30 REM            Program to collect pH, oxygen
40 REM            and carbon dioxide readings
50 REM
                  Read experimental details
60 REM
70 MODE 7 CLOSE £0
80 PRINTTAB (6, 3),: INPUT "Which file for collection"; F$
90 PRINTTAB (10, 6),: PRINT "Experimental Details"
100 PRINTTAB (10, 8): INPUT"Experiment Number"; EXNO
110 PRINTTAB (10, 9): INPUT"Date              "; Day$
120 PRINTTAB (10, 10). INPUT"Species           "; SPEC
```

```
130  PRINTTAB (10, 11): INPUT "Collections site       "; SITES
140  PRINTTAB (10, 13):: PRINT"Conditions "
150  PRINT" "
160  PRINT" ": INPUT"Temperature                "; TEMP
170  INPUT"Alkalinity                    "; ALK
180  INPUT"Light                         "; LGHT
190  INPUT"Salinity                      ";SALT
200  PRINT" ": INPUT"Any comments        "; COMMS
210  REM                         Open file and write details
220  FILCH = OPENOUT (FS)
230  PRINT £FILCH, EXNO, DAYS, SPEC, SITES
240  PRINT £FILCH, TEMP, ALK, LGHT, SALT
250  PRINT £FILCH, COMMS
260  REM
270  REM                         Determine which option is required
280  REM
290  CLS: PRINTTAB (2, 3):: PRINT"Experiment Options"
300  PRINTTAB (8, 5): PRINT"1) pHDrift"
310  PRINTTAB (8, 7):: PRINT"2) pH Drift with Oxygen monitor"
320  PRINTTAB (8, 9):: PRINT"3) pH Stat and 02 monitor'
330  PRINTTAB (8, 11): PRINT"4) pH Stat. with CO2/02 monitor"
340  PRINT" "
350  INPUT"Choose which option is required", PICK
360  IF PICK < 1 OR PICK > 4 GOTO 340
370  IF PICK = 1 GOTO 430
380  IF PICK = 2 GOTO 430
390  IF PICK = 3 GOTO 790
400  IF PICK = 4 GOTO 790
410  REM
420  REM                         Collection variable pH
430  REM
440  CLS
450  PRINTTAB (6, 3):: PRINT "What is the sampling frequency "
460  INPUT "                        (per hour) "; FREQ
470  FREQ = 36 0000/FREQ
480  PRINTTAB (6, 6):: INPUT "Is sample monitoring required "; MONS
490  IF MONS < > "Y" AND MONS < > "N" GOTO 480
500  IF MONS = "Y" THEN INPUT"What tolerance (decimal fraction) "; TLANCE
510  PRINTTAB (6, 9):: PRINT"Maximum length of experiment ":
        INPUT"                (in hours) "; EOFEX
520  EOFEX = EOFEX*3600
530  IF PICK > 2 THEN GOTO 810
540  PRINTTAB (6, 13):: PRINT "Press any key to start sampling";: STS = GETS
550  PRINT " "
560  ON ERROR GOTO 1250
570  TIME = 0
580  PHLAST = 20
590  START = TIME
600  REPEAT UNTIL TIME = START + FREQ
610  TBASE = INT (TIME/100)
620  PH = ADVAL (1)/16
630  IF PICK = 2 THEN OXY = ADVAL (2)
640  IF PICK = 1 THEN PRINT TBASE, PH ELSE PRINT TBASE, PH, OXY
650  IF TBASE > EOFEX THEN GOTO 720
660  IF MONS ~ "N" GOTO 690
670  CHANGE = ABS (PH-PHLAST)/PHLAST
680  IF CHANGE < TLANCE GOTO 860
690  IF PICK = 1 THEN PRINT £FILCH, TBASE, PH ELSE PRINT £FILCH, TBASE, PH, OXY

700  PHLAST = PH
710  GOTO 590

720  PRINT " " : PRINT "Time completed"
730  CLOSEE0
740  GOTO 1310
750  REM
760  REM                                  Collection with static pH
770  REM
780  REM
790  CLS: PRINTTAB (6, 1):: INPUT " What is the pH value ";PH
800  GOTO 450
810  IF PICK = 4 THEN PROCsetup
820  PRINTTAB (6, 13):: PRINT "Press any key to start sampling";: STS = GETS
830  ON ERROR GOTO 1250
840  TIME = 0
850  OXLAST = 9999
860  START = TIME
870  REPEAT UNTIL TIME = START + FREQ
880  TBASE = INT (TIME/100)
890  OXY = ADVAL (2)/16
900  IF PICK = 4 THEN CO2 = FNPULSES
910  IF PICK = 3 THEN PRINT TBASE, OXY ELSE PRINT TBASE, OXY, CO2
920  IF TBASE > EOFEX THEN GOTO 990
930  IF MONS ~ "N" GOTO 960
940  CHANGE = ABS(OXY-OXLAST)/OXLAST
950  IF CHANGE < TLANCE GOTO 860
960  IF PICK = 3 THEN PRINT £FILCH, TBASE, OXY ELSE PRINT £FILCH, TBASE, OXY, CO2

970  OXLAST = OXY
980  GOTO 860
990  PRINT " ": PRINT "Time Completed"
1000 CLOSE £0
1010 GOTO 1310
1020 REM
1030 DEF PROCsetup
1040 REM
1050 REM                                  To set up pulse counter
1060 REM
1070 PULSES = 0
1080 ?&FE62 = 0
1090 ?&FE6B = 32
1100 ?&FE6D = &AO
1110 ?&FE6E = &AO
1120 ?&FE68 = &DO
1130 ?&FE69 = 09
1140 ENDPROC
1150 REM
1160 DEF FNPULSES
1170 REM
1180 REM                                  To read pulse count
1190 REM
1200 LOCAL TALLY, L%, H%
1210 L% = ?&FE68
1220 H% = ?&FE69
1230 TALLY = 2512 – (H%*256 + L%)
1240  = TALLY
1250 IF ERR < > 17 THEN GOTO 1280
1260 PRINT " ": PRINT "Escape pressed"
1270 GOTO 1290
1280 PRINT " ": PRINT "Error number "; ERR, "at line "; ERL
1290 CLOSEE0
1300 GOTO 1310
1310 END
```

Philip Robertson graduated from Edinburgh University, UK, in 1972 with a BSc in chemical physics. After studying for a PhD he began work as a computer programmer in 1975 at Edinburgh University. In 1977, he moved to the Computing Laboratory at the University of St Andrews, UK, as a computing advisor. Since 1980 he has been responsible for microcomputer support. Interests are primarily in microcomputer software, in particular applications software.

Bruce Campbell works in the Microcomputer Support Group in the Computing Laboratory at the University of St Andrews, UK. He has an electronics background and is concerned mainly with the hardware side of micro equipment and interfacing. He has an honours degree from the UK's Open University in electronics and has worked for Ferranti Ltd and the University of Dundee, UK.

book reviews

Major European suppliers lend weight to Unix standard

X/OPEN Group (Eds)

'X/OPEN portability guide' North-Holland, Amsterdam, The Netherlands (1985) DFI 275.00 pp xxviii + 702

A major problem in the development of the Unix market has been the large number of slightly different, and therefore incompatible, versions of Unix in existence. With the publication of the *System V interface definition* (SVID) in early 1985, AT&T took the first step towards the creation of a standard interface to the Unix operating system.

This idea of a standard Unix interface is important for the growth of the Unix market. It means that software written to conform to the standard is portable (at a source code level) to any Unix machine which itself conforms to the standard. So far the SVID has been widely endorsed by the major producers of Unix implementations (notably Microsoft, Digital Equipment and Unisoft). With the publication of the *X/OPEN portability guide*, the weight of major European suppliers of computer systems (ICL, Olivetti, Philips, Bull, Siemens and Nixdorf) has been added to the growing momentum behind the SVID.

The aim of the book is to define what it terms as a 'common applications environment', ie a standard interface to all the resources required from a Unix system by the applications writer. In the words of the preface, the book is designed 'to sit permanently on the desk, serving as a common reference point for anyone directly concerned with the practical side of software development'.

The overall structure of the guide is a collection of standards, each addressing a particular area of the common applications environment. The standards chosen are derived from standards already available and in use in the market. The majority of changes made to arrive at the X/OPEN versions are minor, and are for the most part concerned with clarity or correctness of the originals.

The guide is organized in an open-ended format and it is the intention to continue to add new standards and improve the existing ones. In this way, the guide will evolve with Unix rather than attempting to shape the growth of the operating system.

There is a section on future directions in the introduction which details the areas which the X/OPEN group intends to cover in future issues. These areas are mainly in the networking, graphics and internationalization areas.

The X/OPEN group has taken great pains to ensure that the guide is acceptable to its intended audience and, to this end, it has employed the services of three independent software houses to review the guide before publication. As a result of this, substantial changes were made before its publication. To roughly summarize the contents, the guide is divided into six parts.

- Common applications environment: a summary of the contents and intent of the guide giving an indication of the future directions in which the guide is intended to go
- X/OPEN system V specification: essentially a reprint of the AT&T *System V interface definition* with some slight modifications to improve the clarity and accuracy. Also, changes are made to reflect the expected future directions of the AT&T standard. Each section clearly states its relationship to the corresponding section in the SVID
- C language: a definition of the C language (taken from the *System V programming guide*) together with brief notes on portability of C programs
- X/OPEN ISAM definition: the definition of the indexed sequential file access method to be supported. This is a reproduction of a subset of the Relational Database Systems C-ISAM definition.
- X/OPEN COBOL definition: the standard used here is taken from the *Micro Focus* level II COBOL

language which is an implementation of the ANSI X3.23 1974 standard
- Source code transfer: a short section giving guidelines for the transfer of source code between different X/OPEN systems

The book itself comes in the form of an A5-sized boxed ring binder. It is well made and looks as if it would stand up to frequent use without falling to pieces — an important point if it is to live up to its aim of being a reference work. My one criticism of the packaging is that, due to the design of the metal bar which secures the pages, it is not always easy to keep the book open at any place other than the middle pages.

One criticism of the format is the omission of an index — each part has a contents listing at the start, but this is all that is provided. This is all very well for people familiar with Unix documentation, which has never been known for its 'user friendliness', but I think that if the book is to reach the widest possible audience, a comprehensive index is important.

I also feel that more room should have been devoted to the practical discussion of portability problems — after all, improving portability is the main aim of the guide. The section on C portability is good as far as it goes, but makes up an insignificant proportion of the guide.

A good idea would be for the guide to contain a register of portability problems. This may help to prevent the constant 'rediscovery of the wheel' which must surely go on as generation after generation of Unix programmers encounter and overcome the same old problems.

All in all, the *X/OPEN portability guide* is an important step in the direction of standardizing the Unix product. Although I would have liked more emphasis on the practical side of using the standard, I believe that its existence is a more significant fact than the precise nature of its contents. Provided its evolution is handled sensitively, there is no reason why the

Introducing the ever widening range of logic devices

Almaini, A E A

'Electronic logic systems' Prentice-Hall, Englewood Cliffs, NJ, USA (1985) £14.95 pp 452

Emphasizing the impact of VLSI integrated circuit developments on almost every aspect of human life, the book attempts to prepare the student for a comprehensive study of the principles and techniques of modern electronic systems. This is clearly a considerable task, even for a work of 450 pages.

The contents table occupies six densely packed pages of headings, such as topological principles, device descriptions and various families of digital circuits. These are interspersed with examples — some worked, others unanswered — and design data appendices.

Electronic logic systems is really two books. Part I is a text on logic devices and their circuit applications, with good illustrations of circuit schematics and clearly stated practical problems dealing with logic sequence generators, sequence controllers, a seven-segment display driver and a traffic light controller.

Explanations of some known logic families follow, starting with DTL and RTL functions. These obsolete families are perhaps given too much space, which might have been better used for more detailed examination of TTL and CMOS speed/power characteristics; brief mention is made of complementary high-performance MOS devices. An unusual convention is used for CMOS, HMOS, PMOS etc: these abbreviations are printed throughout the book as cMOS, hMOS, pMOS

X/OPEN portability guide
(continued)

X/OPEN portability guide should not earn its intended place on the desk of every serious Unix programmer.

Bill Bateson
Logica Software Products Ltd,
London, UK

---

etc, which the reader may find somewhat distracting.

Standard TTL device block diagrams are reproduced on several separate pages; the author might consider combining them in a comprehensive appendix, together with their truth tables, in a future edition.

Having indicated how logic functions may be implemented by the interconnection of standard commercially available gate packages, the author refers to a wide variety of circuits which can be constructed simply from multiplexers and demultiplexers. These are referred to as ULMs (universal logic modules), and more than a page would have been acceptable on this subject.

An important feature of the book is represented by semicustom and field programmable logic circuit diagrams, starting with the representation of ROMs and PROMs, as well as PLAs and FPLAs. This leads on to descriptions of gate arrays.

Reference to computer-aided design (CAD) tools is quite brief, although the reader is taken step by step through manual design and logic reduction procedures. As pointed out by Brothers[1], the heart of logic array design lies in CAD, with tools for the complete spectrum of schematic capture, simulation, test validation and generation.

On page 193 the reader is suddenly faced with a machine code program listing related to the traffic light example stated 30 pages earlier. An explanation of this program with illustrations and comments would be essential to make the listing useful; this material may have been lost during editing or production.

Chapter 4 contains a detailed compendium on the design of flip flops, shift registers and counters, including applications data; this should be useful to students and designers alike. Practical comments on race hazards are always useful and the author has attempted to deal with some of these in chapter 5, which also contains interesting primary and secondary plane methods for logic

design. Full bibliographical references could have been given here.

In part II of the book, the author discusses logic circuit optimization with respect to combinational and sequential logic, and gives examples of partitioning of synchronous and asynchronous circuits. This, of course, is the major area of current interest in VLSI design, where the pace of development is very rapid (represented for example by the special issue of *IEE Proceedings* on semicustom integrated circuits[2] and by the Fifth International Conference on Custom and Semicustom ICs[3]). The mainly manual methods described in this book, while of didactic value, should be related to the numerous automatic methods described in these references. Testability, for example, is an extremely important aspect of logic design, and more references to this would have been welcome.

One wonders, as always, whether computer program listings such as the minimization programs of appendices 7.3 and 7.4 will be of practical use — these occupy 28 pages.

Apart from the material on optimization which is contained in Part II, this work will form a useful introduction to the ever widening range of logic circuits and devices becoming available. The alphabetically organized bibliography of 118 items would be more helpful if references to particular items could be given in the text.

George Ettinger
Plessey, UK

References

1 **Brothers, J S** 'The megacell concept', *IEE Proc.* Vol 132 Parts E and I No 2 (March/April 1985) pp 91–98

2 **Bolton, M J P** 'Designing with programmable logic' *IEE Proc.* Vol 132 Parts E and I No 2 (March/April 1985) pp 73–85

3 *5th Int. Conf. Custom and Semicustom ICs,* London, UK November 1985

Programming text teaches fundamentals of MODULA-2

Ed Knepley and Robert Platt

'MODULA-2 programming' Reston Publishing, Reston, VA, USA (1985) £12.95 pp x + 390

The authors of this book believe that MODULA-2 will sweep the programming community in the 1980s, and their enthusiasm shows in their approach. This reviewer also believes that MODULA-2 will be a major programming language in the 1980s, particularly for industrial systems.

Who is the book aimed at? In one place the authors state that it is written for experienced programmers, in another that it assumes that the reader has very little programming experience. In fact, the book is very suitable for the latter as it sets out the fundamentals of MODULA-2 in an admirably clear manner.

The book is divided into three parts. The first two chapters make up part one and give an overview of MODULA-2. Part two is made up of the next six chapters which cover the fundamentals of MODULA-2 and present material that makes up from 80% to 90% of the lines of code in a typical program. The final part of the book comprises chapters 9–12, and covers 'advanced topics' such as recursion, low-level facilities and a reasonably large modular program.

Concentration is on the language features being introduced and not on the use of complex algorithms. Examples build upon one another. Many of the examples include the I/O statements as well as the algorithmic statements. I/O is a feature that is almost universally overlooked in textbooks. However, MODULA-2 with its InOut library module does make handling of this topic easier than in other languages.

Part one overviews the elements of MODULA-2 adequately, emphasizing that separate compilation is not only a powerful feature but indeed the main reason for its existence.

Part two covers the fundamentals of MODULA-2 with admirable clarity in chapters 3–7. Discussed here are data elements, assignments and control, I/O basics, data structures, and records and dynamic structures. In this section there is little for the experienced PASCAL programmer except syntactical differences particularly in the handling of records and pointers. However, much of this material is, even for the experienced person, worth reading just for the clear explanations. A small omission in the discussion on enumeration types is to say that a limitation of PASCAL has been carried forward into MODULA-2, in that the writing of enumeration variables is not permitted. The program containing the fragment

```
Type Fruit  =  (Apples, oranges);
Var Myfruit : Fruit;
Begin
    Myfruit  := Apples;
    WriteString (Myfruit);
```

is refused because of type incompatibility in the last line. Quite rightly so, because the formal parameter of WriteString is String. The problem can be got over with the use of a CASE statement, but it would be nice to be able to do it directly.

On page 127 there are two small errors in the example of the use of set operators. (This is mentioned merely to show that the reviewer has really read the book!) On page 133 CompareStr should have been discussed a little more fully. In particular it should be clearer that if an integer 0 is returned then not only are the strings equal in length but also on a character-to-character basis, ie CAT = CAT.

In chapter 8 is the real meat of the matter. The problems of program size, visibility of variables and side effects are addressed. How procedures assist the concept of data abstraction in solving these problems is clearly discussed. The desirability of local variables is emphasized, as is the fact that local variables exist only when their surrounding procedure exists. This, in many cases, forces the use of global variables which are fair game throughout the program. Discussion then proceeds to how modules, which support the concept of information hiding, assist with this problem by preventing a programmer from even knowing the details of an imported module. The creation of library modules to support modular compilation by the development of definition and implementation modules is dealt with.

So far, so good — even very good. It is to part three, 'Advanced topics', that some criticism must be directed. The chapters on recursion and low-level facilities are satisfactory. However, the chapters on advanced I/O and the modular word processor program suffer from their strong dependence upon a particular implementation of MODULA-2. This brings out the main problem with MODULA-2 at present, that is the difference between library modules of different implementations.

Be that as it may, the implementation dependence of the word processor program in chapter 12 makes it not only difficult to try out but indeed to follow in detail. A better approach for a textbook such as this would have been for the authors to develop library modules to support the application, and show the definition and implementation modules for these library modules.

The book is clearly written, well produced and has a good index and a good set of syntax diagrams. There are questions set at the end of each chapter, but answers are not provided. This book is recommended to all who wish to get a good grasp of MODULA-2 programming.

Joe Gallacher
Microprocessor Systems
Engineering Ltd,
Aberfeldy, UK

16-bit µP bas FORTH as its machine code

A 16-bit microprocessor whose machine code is the high-level programming language FORTH has been developed by Novix of the USA in consultation with FORTH inventor, Charles Moore.

The NC4000 is a 4000-gate CMOS array with an architecture that Novix describes as similar to that of a reduced instruction set computer (RISC). It has a 16-bit bus, can address up to 4 Mbyte of memory and provides 21 bit of I/O directly.

The processor has been designed specifically as a 'FORTH engine', says Novix, by optimizing it for the subroutine calls that provide the driving force of the language. This hardware–software match allows considerably higher operating speed than would otherwise be possible. For example, claims Novix, the NC4000 runs FORTH code over 20 times faster than a MC68000 runs machine code.

Processing throughputs of 4–40 MIFOPS (million FORTH operations per second) may be attained on the processor, though a typical rate is 12 MIFOPS. Versions with operating frequencies of 8 MHz and 10 MHz will be produced, with cycle times of 125 ns.

According to Novix, each addition instruction takes one cycle, although up to five such instructions may take place on a single cycle by accessing parallel buses. 16-bit signed multiply, divide and square root operations are quoted as taking 4 µs each, while invoking a FORTH word — the equivalent of a subroutine call — takes a single cycle.

The first batch of NC4000s, in 120-lead pin grid arrays, was made by Mostek during 1985. Novix intends that Mostek (now under the control of Thomson) should continue to supply the chip, although AMD and Harris are lined up as second sources.

Novix has also made available a development system for the NC4000, known as Beta Board, to enable systems designers to familiarize themselves with the chip. This is made almost entirely from CMOS components and has a power consumption of 600 mA. (The NC4000's power requirement is 75 mA maximum.) The board includes an NC4000 CPU, 56 kbyte of static RAM, 8 kbyte stack area, 8 kbyte of ROM containing PolyFORTH, two serial ports and two expansion sockets giving access to all address, data and I/O lines.

The PolyFORTH ROM contains a PolyFORTH compiler, a keyboard interpreter, a runtime package, a multitasker, and a terminal and remote link disc driver. This software links via one of the serial ports to an IBM PC or Apricot microcomputer, which acts as a VDU and disc peripheral to the Beta Board. (*Novix, 10590 North Tantau Avenue, Cupertino, CA 95014, USA. Tel: (408) 253-6930. European distributor: Computer Solutions Ltd, 1 Gogmore Lane, Chertsey, Surrey KT16 9AP, UK. Tel: (09328) 65292*) ☐

Intel's first ASICs

Intel has made an initial step in the direction of application-specific integrated circuits (ASICs) with a family of erasable programmable logic devices (EPLDs) and related computer-aided engineering (CAE) tools.

The EPLD family consists of the 5C121, 5C090 and 5C060 which have usable gate counts of 1200, 900 and 600 respectively. Programmable registers, latches and clock controls are provided as well as a flexible I/O architecture. The EPLD chips are manufactured in CMOS.

The 5C121 gives a maximum total propagation delay of 50 ns, an operating frequency of 15 MHz and a typical standby power dissipation of 15 mW, says Intel. The maximum total propagation delays of the 5C090 and 5C060 are quoted as 40 ns and 35 ns respectively, with operating frequencies of 33 MHz and 22 MHz respectively and 10 µW typical standby power dissipation. The 5C121 and 5C090 are housed in 0.6 in (1.5 cm) ceramic DIPs while the 5C060 comes in a 0.3 in (0.76 cm) 24-lead windowed ceramic DIP.

The hardware and software tools needed to design, verify and program the EPLDs are contained in Intel's iPLDS, which is designed to interface directly with schematic capture packages such as FutureNet's Dash series or PC Caps from US-based Personal CAD systems. This allows a system designer to use an IBM PC or compatible machine as a CAE logic design system. (*Intel Corp, 3065 Bowers Avenue, Santa Clara, CA 95051, USA. Intel Corp (UK) Ltd, Pipers Way, Swindon, Wilts SN3 1RJ, UK. Tel: (0793) 696006*) ☐

Linear macrocell arrays

Analogue semicustom ICs designed to replace entire printed circuit boards have been developed by US-based Raytheon Semiconductor. The RLA120 linear macrocell array is fabricated using a proprietary dual-layer metal bipolar process.

The RLA120 is a 24-pad dual metal chip holding a variety of predesigned programmable analogue cells and components that can be inter-connected by a single (top) layer of metal. The bottom layer of metal is used to fabricate architectural and structural components.

Devices are customized with the top-layer metal mask at the factory to implement the user's functional circuit configuration. Macrocell gain blocks can be configured as any combination of 4558, 324 or 3403 type operational amplifiers or as 339 or 365 type voltage comparators and can be programmed for specific quiescent currents and AC operating conditions.

Features of the macrocells include: slew rates to 15 V µs^{-1}; unity gain bandwidth to 20 MHz; and supply voltage from 2 V to 30 V. Completed circuits can be manufactured in plastic or ceramic dual inline or leadless chip carrier packages ranging from 14 pins to 24 pins. (*Raytheon Co, Semiconductor Division, 350 Ellis Street, Mountain View, CA 94039, USA. Tel: (415) 968-9211. Raytheon Semiconductor, Ogilvie Road, High Wycombe, Bucks HP12 3DS, UK. Tel: (0494) 450327*) ☐

Dual-buffer ADCs convert in 5 μs

A/D converters (ADCs) with double buffered registering have been introduced by Ferranti of the UK. The ZN439 series comprises a range of monolithic ADCs compatible with 8-bit microprocessors, including a clock generator, a trimmable 2.5 V bandgap reference and double buffered latches with three state outputs.

A full successive approximation conversion takes 5 μs on the ZN439, says the manufacturer. The double buffering set-up, which Ferranti believes to be the first of its kind, means that data can only enter the output buffer when it is not being read, so that the accessing microprocessor will always be presented only with valid data. Interfacing flexibility is increased as the microprocessor can read data at any time regardless of the conversion status.

Use of the bandgap reference is pin optional, and it can also act as a system reference to reduce the system component count and enhance temperature tracking. A choice of linearity and operating temperature is available within the series.

ZN439 devices are TTL and CMOS compatible and come in 22-lead plastic or ceramic dual inline packages. (*Ferranti Electronics Ltd, Fields New Road, Chadderton, Oldham, Lancs OL9 8NP, UK. Tel: 061–624 0515*)   □

Asynchronous SRAM comhines CMOS and NMOS

Both NMOS and CMOS techniques are used in the manufacture of the MB81C79, a 72 kbit asynchronous static RAM from Fujitsu. NMOS transistors are used for the memory cells while CMOS is used for the peripheral circuitry; this allows the devices to combine a high level of integration with low power consumption, says the manufacturer.

The MB81C79 comes in two versions with quoted address access times of 45 ns and 55 ns. Maximum power consumption is 660 mW, says Fujitsu, and power dissipation in standby mode is 83 mW. The memory is organized as 8k × 9 bit and the organization includes the parity bit.

The chip measures 5.8 mm × 7.24 mm and is housed in a 28-pin dual inline package. Single power supply is +5 V and inputs and outputs are TTL compatible. (*Fujitsu Ltd, 6-1 Marunouchi 2-chome, Chiyoda-ku, Tokyo 100, Japan. UK distributor: Fujitsu Mikroelektronik, Hargrave House, Belmont Road, Maidenhead, Berks SL6 6NE, UK. Tel: (0628) 76100*)   □

Calibration standards for wafer contamination

Surface contamination standards for wafers have been produced by US company VLSI Standards. The standards, which come in the form of silicon wafers, enable the user to check the calibration of virtually any type of surface contamination monitor, says the manufacturer, with an accuracy directly traceable to the US National Bureau of Standards.

Two types of standard allow either relative or absolute calibration. The relative standard has a pattern of scattering sites etched in a thin oxide layer on the surface of a clean silicon wafer. The sites are divided into four quadrants, each of which simulates a different particle size for a range of calibration capabilities.

The contamination detector scans the standard wafer until it reaches the user defined particle size, when the corresponding quadrant of the pattern appears and the particle count increases by a total of 525.

The absolute standard consists of calibrated latex spheres deposited on a wafer surface; these standards are available for particle sizes from 0.25 μm to 1.0 μm. (*VLSI Standards Inc, 2660 Marine Way, Mountain View, CA 94043, USA. Tel: (415) 961-3721. UK distributor: Chell Instruments Ltd, Tudor House, Grammar School Road, North Walsham, Norfolk NR28 9JH, UK. Tel: (0692) 402488*) □

VLSI relative standard, showing the chequerboard pattern of scattering sites

CMOS logic circuits operate at ~ 125 MHz

Advanced sub 2 μm CMOS logic circuits claimed to exceed the performance of low-power Schottky as well as existing high-speed CMOS devices have been introduced by Fairchild of the FRG. Devices currently available in the FACT (Fairchild advanced CMOS technology) range include 54AC/74AC74 D-type positive edge triggered flip-flops, 54AC/74AC240 and 54ACT/74ACT244 octal buffer/line drivers with three-state outputs, and 54ACT/74ACT373 octal transparent latches with three-state outputs.

FACT devices draw 0.1 mW per gate at 1 MHz operating frequency — three orders of magnitude less than equivalent Schottky TTL devices — says Fairchild. Some of the 80 or so devices which will form the full FACT range will have TTL-type input thresholds that allow them to be used as direct replacements for standard and advanced Schottky components.

Switching speed is almost twice that achieved by standard high-speed CMOS processes, says the manufacturer. A 74AC74, for example, has a worst-case propogation delay of 1–10 ns; typical operating speed is 125 MHz.

The 54AC series devices are capable of driving 75 Ω transmission lines within an operating temperature range of 55–125°C, while the 74AC series drives 50 Ω lines between −40°C and +85°C.

FACT devices may be packaged as dual inline packages, small-outline integrated circuits, flatpacks, leadless chip carriers or plastic chip carriers. (*Fairchild Semiconductor GmbH, Am Burgfrieden 1, 8090 Wasserburg Am Inn (Munich), FRG. Tel: (08071) 104-232*)

□

VLSI design station has CAE and silicon compiler

The SiliconMaster design system, a VLSI custom design workstation that combines silicon compilation and computer-aided engineering (CAE) techniques to automate design, has been introduced by Daisy Systems. Combining Silicon Compilers's Genesil software package with Daisy's own Logician software, SiliconMaster performs all stages of IC design from schematic entry through simulation to finished layout.

The system can also be used as an aid to board design, generating behavioural models of ICs that can be used in the verification of entire circuit designs. In addition, simulation is provided through the system's logic simulation and timing analyser functions.

Users of SiliconMaster need create only a high-level functional description of their circuit, says Daisy. The system automatically generates timing and simulation models, and a finished layout suitable for manufacture by specified fabrication plants. Layout definition is guided throughout by design rules which, claims Daisy, ensure that designs are correct the first time.

SiliconMaster uses a dual-processor architecture — a Series 32000 CPU and an 80286 are included — to speed up concurrent execution of tasks. One processor handles interactive functions, while the other performs automatic computation-intensive tasks. The system runs under Daisy Dnix, a version of Unix 4.2 BSD.

Schematic entry and verification interfaces from the Logician are utilized, and Daisy's ChipMaster full-custom mask editor can be bought as an option. Hardware includes a 140 Mbyte hard disc and 19 in (48 cm) colour monitor. The SiliconMaster is compatible with Daisy's other CAE tools.

Chips may be designed that incorporate data paths, programmable logic arrays and random logic functions. (*Daisy Systems Corp, 700 Middlefield Road, PO Box 7006, Mountain View, CA 94039, USA. Tel: (415) 960-0123. Daisy Systems Corp, Berk House, Basing View, Basingstoke, Hants RG21 2HG, UK. Tel: (0256) 64061*) □

CMOS device combines HDLC and DMA control

Plessey of the UK has launched what it claims to be the world's first low-power CMOS direct memory access (DMA) and high-level data link controller (HDLC) device. The MV6001 EXP comprises an HDLC transmitter and receiver combined with a DMA controller to relieve the host processor of most of the transmission overheads.

To transmit or receive a block of data, says Plessey, the processor merely specifies the start address and length of the block of data in memory; the MV6001 EXP then handles the block transfer and formatting without further processor intervention.

The device operates at DMA rates up to 8 MHz with HDLC frame length programmable up to 2 kbyte, and automatically appends a frame check sequence. (*Plessey Semiconductors Ltd, Cheney Manor, Swindon, Wilts SN2 2QW, UK. Tel: (0793) 36251*) □

Name	Description	Manufacturer/designer	Distributor/contact
CPUs			
80186-12	12.5 MHz version of the 16-bit 80186 microprocessor manufactured in 1.5 μm 'HYMOS-III', claimed to give a 30% smaller die size. Gives 6 Mbyte s^{-1} bus transfer rate	Intel Corp, 3065 Bowers Avenue, Santa Clara, CA 95051, USA	Intel Corp (UK) Ltd, Pipers Way, Swindon, Wilts SN3 1RJ, UK. Tel: (0793) 696006
Microcontrollers			
MB88201 H, MB88202 H	Single-chip microcontrollers in CMOS. Execution time is 1.5 μs. Masked ROM is 512 × 8 bit and 1 k × 8 bit respectively; static RAM 16 × 4 bit and 32 × 4 bit. Has 12 I/O lines and a 4 MHz clock generator. Supplied in 16-pin plastic DIPs	Fujitsu Ltd, 6-1 Marunouchi 2-chome, Chiyoda-ku, Tokyo 100, Japan	Fujitsu Mikroelectronik, Hargrave House, Belmont Road, Maidenhead, Berks SL6 6NE, UK. Tel: (0628) 76100
Arithmetic logic units			
L4C381	16-bit CMOS ALU with flexible onchip registers. Has a lookahead carry generator, operand multiplexers, two input registers and an output register in 68-pin grid array and PLCC packages	Logic Devices Inc, 628 East Evelyn Avenue, Sunnyvale, CA 94086-6459, USA. Tel: (408) 720-8630	Manhattan Skyline Ltd, Bridge Road, Maidenhead, Berks SL6 8DB, UK. Tel: (0628) 75851
Communications chips			
82588	VLSI local area network controller designed to replace 'spaghetti junction' stopgap networks. May be used in the implementation of StarLAN and IBM's PC network. Housed in a 28-pin DIP	Intel Corp, 3065 Bowers Avenue, Santa Clara, CA 95051, USA	Rapid Recall Ltd, Rapid House, Denmark Street, High Wycombe, Bucks HP11 2ER, UK. Tel: (0494) 26271
MC145406	16-pin RS232C driver–receiver in CMOS. Contains three drivers and three receivers, and is claimed to use one tenth the power of an equivalent bipolar device. Can operate at from ±4.5 V to ±12 V supply levels	Motorola Inc, 3501 Ed Bluestein Blvd, Austin, TX 78721, USA	Motorola Semiconductor Products Sector, 88 Tanners Drive, Blakelands, Milton Keynes MK14 5BP, UK. Tel: (0908) 614614
MC145411	Bit rate generator similar to the MC14411 but in a 16-pin package. Using a 1.8432 MHz or 3.6864 MHz crystal or external clock, 19 output bit rates are available	Motorola Inc, 3501 Ed Bluestein Blvd, Austin, TX 78721, USA	Motorola Semiconductor Products Sector, 88 Tanners Drive, Blakelands, Milton Keynes MK14 5BP, UK. Tel: (0908) 614614
D/A converters			
DAC1201KP-V	12-bit D/A converter in a 28-pin plastic DIP. Maximum settling time is 1 μs and linearity ±0.75 LSB at 25 °C	Burr-Brown International Ltd, Cassiobury House, Station Road, Watford, Herts WD1 1EA, UK. Tel: (0923) 33837	

Name	Description	Manufacturer/designer	Distributor/contact
DAC1600KP, DAC1600JP	16-bit DACs in 24-pin moulded DIPs. Provide ±10 V bipolar output with 13-bit (model JP) and 14-bit (KP) monotonicity over the temperature range 0–70°C	Burr-Brown International Ltd, Cassiobury House, 11–19 Station Road, Watford, Herts WD1 1EA, UK. Tel: (0923) 33837	

PROMs

Name	Description	Manufacturer/designer	Distributor/contact
HN27C64FP	One-time-programmable 8k × 8 bit CMOS EPROM in a plastic flat pack for surface mounting. Claimed to be half the size of conventional EPROMs. Response time is 2 ns	Hitachi Ltd, New Marunouchi Building No 5, 1-chome Marunouchi, Chiyoda, Tokyo, Japan	Hitachi Electronics Components (UK) Ltd, Hitec House, 221–225 Station Road, Harrow, Middx HA1 2XL, UK. Tel: 01-861 1414
KM2816A	2k × 8 bit E²PROM in NMOS with access times down to 300 ns. Memory has quoted 10 year retention capability. Onboard address/data latches, autotimed byte write and power up/down write protection. Claimed to have same features and in-system alterability as equivalent static RAMs	Samsung Semiconductor and Telecommunications Ltd, Main Building, 250, 2/KA Taepyung-Row, Chung-ku, Seoul, Rep. of Korea	Kord Distribution Ltd, Watchmoor Road, Camberley, Surrey GU15 3AQ, UK. Tel: (0276) 685741
63S285, 63S485	Titanium-tungsten replacements for the 6336 and 53/6341 NiCr PROM devices, respectively. Organized as 256 × 8 bit (63S285) and 512 × 8 bit (63S485) with maximum access times of 45 ns	Monolithic Memories Inc, 2175 Mission College Blvd, Santa Clara, CA 95054-1592, USA. Tel: (408) 970-9700	Monolithic Memories Ltd, Monolithic House, 1 Queens Road, Farnborough, Hants GU14 6DJ, UK. Tel: (0252) 517431

FIFO devices

Name	Description	Manufacturer/designer	Distributor/contact
67417	64 × 8 bit or × 9 bit serializing/deserializing FIFO memory for applications in microcomputers, LANs, data communications and disc controllers. Has three operation modes: serial in to parallel out, parallel in to serial out, serial in to serial out. In first mode data rate is 28 MHz in and 10 MHz out	Monolithic Memories Inc. 2175 Mission College Blvd, Santa Clara, CA 95054-1592, USA. Tel: (408) 970-9700	Monolithic Memories Ltd, Monolithic House, 1 Queens Road, Farnborough, Hants GU14 6DJ, UK. Tel: (0252) 517431
674219	First-in–first-out RAM controller provides control addressing and arbitration to make static RAM arrays act like FIFO buffers. Allows buffer sizes ranging from 512 kword up to 64 kword. Maximum read/write rate is 6 MHz (12 MHz when only read or write)	Monolithic Memories Inc, 2175 Mission College Blvd, Santa Clara, CA 95054-1592, USA. Tel: (408) 970-9700	Monolithic Memories Ltd, Monolithic House, 1 Queens Road, Farnborough, Hants GU14 6 DJ, UK. Tel: (0252) 517431

RAMs

Name	Description	Manufacturer/designer	Distributor/contact
CDM6264-3	64 kbit (8192 × 8 bit) CMOS static RAM with a maximum address access time of 150 ns. Operating temperature range: 0–70°C. Packaging: 28-lead DIP	RCA Ltd, Lincoln Way, Windmill Road, Sunbury-on-Thames, Middx TW16 7HW, UK. Tel: (09327) 85511	
12GO14 NanoRAM	256 × 4 bit gallium arsenide static RAM with access and cycle times quoted as 3 ns. Packaged in a 40-pin LCC	GigaBit Logic, 1908 Oak Terrace Lane, Newbury Park, CA 91320, USA. Tel: (805) 499-0610	Pronto Electronic Systems Ltd, City Gate House, 399–425 Eastern Avenue, Gants Hill, Ilford, Essex IG2 6LR, UK. Tel: 01-554 6222

product review

Name	Description	Manufacturer/designer	Distributor/contact
HM2064	8192 × 8 bit CMOS static RAM in a plastic DIP. Designed for low-power applications	Harris Systems Ltd, Eskdale Road, Winnersh, Wokingham, Berks RG11 5TR, UK. Tel: (0734) 698787	RR Electronics Ltd, St Martins Way, Cambridge Road, Bedford, UK. Tel: (0234) 47211
KM41256, KM41257	256 kbit NMOS dynamic RAMs (262k × 1 bit) in 16-pin DIPs. Version 256 has page-mode access while version 257 has nibble mode allowing serial access to up to 4 bit of data	Samsung Semiconductor and Telecommunications Ltd, Main Building 250, 2/KA Taepyung-Row, Chung-ku, Seoul, Rep. of Korea	Kord Distribution Ltd, Watchmoor Road, Camberley, Surrey GU15 3AQ, UK. Tel: (0276) 685741
MBM 10484, MBM 100484	4k × 4 bit bipolar ECL RAMs designed for main memory, control and buffer storage. Die size is 6.4 mm × 4.4 mm. Address access time: 15 ns; operating temperature ranges: 0–75°C and 0–85°C. Produced in 28-pin ceramic DIPs	Fujitsu Ltd, 6-1 Marunouchi 2-chome, Chiyoda-ku, Tokyo 100, Japan	Fujitsu Mikroelektronik, Hargrave House, Belmont Road, Maidenhead, Berks SL6 6NE, UK. Tel: (0628) 76100
MCM6164	'HCMOS' 8k × 8 bit static RAM designed using 1.5 μm rules. Available with access times of 45 ns, 55 ns or 70 ns. Comes in a 28-pin DIP	Motorola Inc, 3501 Ed Bluestein Blvd, Austin, TX 78721, USA	Motorola Ltd, Fairfax House, 69 Buckingham Street, Aylesbury, Bucks HP20 2NF, UK. Tel: (0296) 35252
TMM2018D	2k × 8 bit NMOS static RAM in a 24-pin ceramic DIP. Access times from 35 ns to 55 ns. Applications include cache memory, microcode store, image processing buffer and realtime A/D store	Toshiba, 1-chome, Uchisaiwai-cho, Chiyoda-ku, Tokyo, Japan	Toshiba UK Ltd, Semiconductor Division, Toshiba House, Frimley Road, Camberley, Surrey, UK. Tel: (0276) 62222
TMM2063P	NMOS static RAM organized as 8k × 8 bit in a narrow-line 28-pin plastic DIP. Access times for devices in the range are 100 ns to 150 ns. Operating current is 80 mA. Designed for use as microcomputer peripheral memory	Toshiba, 1-chome, Uchisaiwai-cho, Chiyoda-ku, Tokyo, Japan	Toshiba UK Ltd, Semiconductor Division, Toshiba House, Frimley Road, Camberley, Surrey, UK. Tel: (0276) 62222
TMM2078D	NMOS static RAM organized as 4k × 4 bit in a 22-pin ceramic DIP. Maximum access times are from 35 ns to 55 ns. Operating current in standby mode is 20 mA. Designed for cache memory and high-speed storage applications	Toshiba, 1-chome, Uchisaiwai-cho, Chiyoda-ku, Tokyo, Japan	Toshiba UK Ltd, Semiconductor Division, Toshiba House, Frimley Road, Camberley, Surrey, UK. Tel: (0276) 62222
Memory boards			
'Non-volatile mass storage system'	Two-board bubble memory system for Z80- and 8085-based STDbus configurations. Comprises a PCB-1 controller module and up to 16 memory modules of 128 kbyte or 256 kbyte capacity	Bubbl-tec, PC/M Inc, 6800 Sierra Court, Dublin, CA 94568, USA. Tel: (415) 829-8700	Amplicon Electronics Ltd, Richmond Road, Brighton, East Sussex BN2 3RL, UK. Tel: (0273) 608331
SM-256	Nonvolatile memory board for STEbus with oncard battery back-up. Eight 28-pin sockets allow combinations of 8 kbyte or 32 kbyte EPROMs or static RAMs. Access times range from 50 μs to 250 μs in 50 μs increments	DSP Design, UK	Dean Microsystems Ltd, 7 Horseshoe Park, Pangbourne, Berks RG8 7JW, UK. Tel: (07357) 5155

Name	Description	Manufacturer/designer	Distributor/contact
SAM-HCRAM	Multibus-compatible dynamic RAM board. Capacity ranges from 256 kbyte to 4 Mbyte using socket mounted 64k or 256k chips. Supports 24-bit address range and 8- or 16-bit data transfer	SGS-ATES Componenti Elettronici SpA, Stradale Primosole 50, 95121 Catania, Sicily, Italy. Tel: (3995) 599 111	SGS Systems Division, Planar House, Walton Street, Aylesbury, UK. Tel: (0296) 5977

Programming modules

Name	Description	Manufacturer/designer	Distributor/contact
L-stack	Programming 'stack' for the Universe 1000 system reads and programs 20- and 24-pin PALs. The stack can be interfaced to design and test software	Elan Digital Systems Ltd, 16–20 Kelvin Way, Crawley, West Sussex RH10 2TS, UK. Tel: (0293) 510448	
Series 1000	Parallel programmers for NMOS or CMOS PROMS, EPROMs and microcontrollers in up-to-40-pin packages. Programs up to 30 devices in parallel. Available in duplicator, downloader and virtual memory programmer (using an IBM PC) configurations	Data I/O Europe, World Trade Center, Strawinskylaan 633, 1077 XX Amsterdam, The Netherlands. Tel: (020) 622866	

CPU modules

Name	Description	Manufacturer/designer	Distributor/contact
MPA-1000	Multibus-compatible 80286 board with 2 Mbyte of onboard zero-wait-state dynamic RAM, 256 kbyte of EPROM, write pipelining to the iLBX bus and Multibus, 15 maskable interrupts and flexible memory mapping. Options include an 80287 numeric coprocessor and an 82258 DMA controller	Metacomp Inc, 9466 Black Mountain Road, San Diego, CA 92126, USA. Tel: (619) 578-9840	Micro-Marketing (Electronics) Ltd, Unit 4, Soho Mills Industrial Estate, Woobum Green, High Wycombe, Bucks HP10 0PF. UK. Tel: (06285) 29222
SYN-MP08	68008-based processor module for the G64 bus supporting up to 128 kbit of ROM or ROM–RAM mix, two RS232 or RS422 serial ports and multifunctional parallel I/O. Memory is expandable to 1 Mbyte by addition of SYN-EDM256 memory expander modules, which hold 256 kbyte of dynamic RAM and sockets for 128 kbyte of EPROM	Syntel Microsystems, Queens Mill Road, Huddersfield HD1 3PG, UK. Tel: (0484) 35101/2	

I/O adaptors

Name	Description	Manufacturer/designer	Distributor/contact
LDM422	Bidirectional RS232-to-RS422 converter with a complete electrical isolation barrier and heavy-duty surge protectors. Includes six diagnostic LED indicators	Burr-Brown International Ltd, Cassiobury House, 11–19 Station Road, Watford, Herts WD1 1EA, UK. Tel: (0923) 33837	

SAM-HCRAM Multibus memory board (left), L-stack programmer for the Universe 1000 system (centre) and LDM422 RS232-to-RS422 converter (right)

Name	Description	Manufacturer/designer	Distributor/contact
I/O adaptors (continued)			
GPIB-PC3	IEEE-488 interface board for IBM PCs, based on NEC's 7210 GPIB controller chip	National Instruments, 12109 Technology Blvd, Austin, TX 78759, USA. Tel: (512) 250-9119	Amplicon Electronics Ltd, Richmond Road, Brighton, East Sussex BN2 3RL, UK. Tel: (0273) 608331
LSI-11/DEC Euro Q adaptor board	Adaptor card allowing standard LSI-11 Q-bus boards to be plugged directly into DEC's Euro Q bus	BICC-Vero Electronics Ltd, Unit 5, Industrial Estate, Flanders Road, Hedge End, Southampton SO3 3LG, UK. Tel: (04892) 5824	
MPA 2160	CPU board and MPX module combined to form a Multibus-compatible 16-channel serial I/O communications controller board. Channels are operated by eight Z8530 multiprotocol communications controllers and a custom 32-channel DMA controller. Baud rates higher than 64 kbaud can be supported	Metacomp Inc, 9466 Black Mountain Road, San Diego, CA 92126, USA. Tel: (619) 578-9840	Micro-Marketing (Electronics) Ltd, Unit 4, Soho Mills Industrial Estate, Woodburn Green, High Wycombe, Bucks HP10 0PF, UK. Tel: (06285) 29222
MPV910, MPV910-NS, MPV910-LV	Digital input boards with 32 optically isolated discrete inputs. Available for VME-based micros, they offer protection from input voltage transients and field input malfunctions. Isolation between signal inputs is 600 V DC	Burr-Brown International Ltd, Cassiobury House, 11–19 Station Road, Watford, Herts WD1 1EA, UK. Tel: (0923) 33837	
MPV930-48	VMEbus TTL I/O board with 48 channels (six 8-bit ports). Designed for multipoint control and monitoring applications	Burr-Brown International Ltd, Cassiobury House, 11–19 Station Road, Watford, Herts WD1 1EA, UK. Tel: (0923) 33837	
VSIO	VMEbus serial/parallel I/O board offers two serial lines which can be configured as RS232C, RS422, 20 mA current loop and 1.2288 Mbaud I/O ports. Z8530 serial interface device supports synchronous and asynchronous data transfers. Can generate interrupt vector addresses	PEP Electronik Systeme GmbH, Am Klosterwald 4, D-8950 Kaufbeuren, FRG	Micro-Marketing (Electronics) Ltd, Unit 4, Soho Mills Industrial Estate, Woodburn Green, High Wycombe, Bucks HP10 0PF, UK. Tel: (06285) 29222
MPV902	VMEbus-compatible relay output interface board provides up to 32 switched output channels, each handling up to 10 W	Burr-Brown International Ltd, Cassiobury House, 11–19 Station Road, Watford, Herts WD1 1EA, UK. Tel: (0923) 33837	

LSI-11/DEC Euro Q adaptor board (left), MPV902 relay output board for VMEbus (centre) and EQC-3UBP Eurocard backplane

Name	Description	Manufacturer/designer	Distributor/contact
Backplanes			
EQC-3UBP	Eurocard backplane for prototyping. Gives up to 21 card positions. Each connector position is tracked to an adjacent 64/96-pin pattern into which IDC terminals are assembled	Dage (GB) Ltd, Rabans Lane, Aylesbury, Bucks HP19 3RG, UK. Tel: (0296) 33200	
Industrial controllers			
Chum One	Z80-based industrial controller with analogue and digital inputs and outputs, EPROM programmer, RS232 interface and realtime clock. Uses BASIC or Z80 machine code subroutines	Warwick Design Group, 12 St Georges Road, Leamington Spa, Warwks CV32 5PP, UK. Tel: (0926) 36326	
Development systems			
MICE II Z8	Micro in-circuit emulator which uses the development part of the Z8612 to emulate Z8611, Z8613 and Z8681 processors. Includes 4 kbyte of onboard emulation memory	Microtek International Inc, 6 Industrial East Road Three, Science-based Industrial Park, Hsin-chi, Taiwan. Tel: (035) 772155	ARS Microsystems Ltd, Doman Road, Camberley, Surrey GU15 3DF, UK. Tel: (0276) 685005
PEM1	Portable microprocessor monitor for debugging, commissioning and adapting 8-bit systems. Integral key pad and display	Thorn EMI Instruments Ltd, Archcliffe Road, Dover, Kent CT17 9EN, UK. Tel: (0304) 202620	
Test equipment			
4883	GPIB (IEEE 488) state analyser and memory with listener, talker and controller capabilities. Includes a 256 × 12 bit memory, word recognizer and hexadecimal LED display	Wasec, PO Box 161, Wallington, Surrey SM6 8BA, UK. Tel: 01-668 5400	
PM 8850/70	Microcracker disassembler for logic state analysis in 80186-based systems. Dissassembles the complete instruction set and can handle the processor's prefetched instructions. Presents interrupt handling on screen	Pye Unicam Ltd, York Street, Cambridge CB1 2PX, UK. Tel: (0223) 358866	
Software			
GPIB	Utility program which brings IEEE 488 bus facilities to control G64-based industrial microcomputers. Supports SYN-1488 Eurocard module. Program is invoked from the OS-9 shell. Device driver is supplied	Syntel Microsystems, Queens Mill Road, Huddersfield HD1 3PG, UK. (0484) 35101	

Chum One industrial controller (left), MICE-II Z8 emulator (centre) and Wasec's 4883 GPIB state analyser

ASIC manufacture — from design to silicon in a £2½M box

An integrated system for the design and manufacture of custom ICs has been launched by Lasarray Corp, a Swiss-financed company based in the USA.

The Lasarray Processing Module has been designed to enable an OEM to see its application-specific integrated circuits (ASICs) through from concept and design to fully tested Mil Spec silicon, without recourse to any outside centre or chip fab. Internal control over the whole process gives advantages of increased manufacturing efficiency, better operating profits and, most significantly, complete design security, says the manufacturer.

The Lasarray system is contained in a

The Lasarray pattern generator; this is housed within the class 10 clean area of the 'processing box'

'processing box', 12.5 m long × 7 m wide × 3.6 m high, supplied with mains power, water, gas and vacuum. This 'box' actually comes as three modules which are bolted together — a class 1000 clean room, a central services module and a class 100/10 module. The system is based on a Digital Equipment VAX 11/750 minicomputer with 3 Mbyte of memory running under VMS, plus design terminals and other peripherals.

The chief component of the software is Lattice Logic's Chipsmith gate array compilation package, supporting design simulation, autolayout and test of ASICs. This runs alongside a number of other design and auxiliary programs. A minimum of six people are required to staff the processing box — two in the clean room, two in packaging and two or more in design.

The starting block for IC fabrication is a 4 in (10 cm) wafer metallized using a patented 'grid' mask. After this stage, there is no need for any further 'personalized' masks, thanks to a proprietary laser

pattern generating technique from which Lasarray takes its name; considerable time and cost savings result from nonreliance on custom masks, says Lasarray.

The pattern generator uses a computer-controlled blue laser beam of 2 µm diameter to eliminate unwanted connections from the grid pattern. The wafer is covered in photoresist and manoeuvred beneath the laser beam, which is turned on and off under computer control. Thus, those areas between the gates on the wafer's photoresist which represent undesired connections are exposed to the laser; the areas so treated are then etched away using standard etching methods.

Up to four designs of chip can be exposed to the laser on one wafer, so the batch size for any particular ASIC can be less than the number of chips per wafer. The process is particularly suitable for batch sizes between 20 and 10 000, says Lasarray.

The positions where the wafer should be exposed are determined using layout database information from the silicon compiler. The wafer is positioned in relation to the blue laser using a red laser beam — the guidance beam — which is focussed on the same spot as the blue beam. Because the guidance beam is red, it does not affect the photoresist. However, the wafer surface reflects the red laser with different intensities, and the data needed for positioning is derived from these intensity variations.

Processing of a 4 in wafer with 200–240 chips takes around two hours, says Lasarray. The result of this process is a semicustom gate array in 4 µm CMOS, which is then electrically tested and hermetically sealed in a ceramic dual inline package or leadless chip carrier.

The cost of a complete turnkey system is quoted as £2.5M by UK distributor Quick Turnaround Logic (QTL). (*Lasarray Corp, 191 Lunar Drive, Scots Valley, CA 95066, USA. Tel: (408) 438-5440. UK distributor: QTL Ltd, Unit 4, Heron Industrial Estate, Spencers Wood, Reading, Berks RG7 1PG, UK. Tel: (0734) 883350*) □

Addenda

Ettinger, G M and Tillier, M L 'Memory-based logic sequence generation' *Microprocessors and Microsystems* Vol 9 No 9 (November 1985) pp 446–451

Add to 'Acknowledgements' section (p 451): 'This work was carried out in the Advanced Engineering Laboratories of Plessey PMSL Division at Poole, UK, and thanks are due to Plessey UK Ltd.'

Gould uses AlGaAs in transistor range

High-electron-mobility transistors (HEMTs) with quoted maximum operating frequencies of 18 GHz have been announced by US-based Gould Electronics. Designated H503, the devices use a lattice structure of aluminium gallium arsenide (AlGaAs) and gallium arsenide (GaAs) to give a speed some three times faster than conventional GaAs devices and ten times faster than the same devices in silicon.

A molecular beam epitaxy process is used to produce the HEMTs. According to Gould, this results in a precise structure that confines electron flow to a single layer, providing significantly lower noise levels than conventional GaAs. The H503 is equal to normal GaAs field-effect transistors in terms of reliability, says Gould, and has comparable geometry (0.5 μm × 280 μm).

The H503 is designed to replace GaAs devices in very high frequency applications such as satellite, radar and electronic warfare systems, where low noise levels are required. (*Gould Inc, 10 Gould Center, Rolling Meadows, IL 60008, USA. Tel: (312) 640-4113*) □

FORTH 83 standardized

An 'official' version of the FORTH-83 programming language has been published by the FORTH Interest Group. The *FORTH 83 standard* is designed to allow for portability of FORTH-83 standard programs between FORTH-83 standard systems, and is the only publication endorsed by the Forth Standards Team, the organization responsible for its development.

Besides defining the terms and requirements of the new standard, the publication addresses: references, compliance and labelling; usage; error conditions; glossary notation; required word set; assembler extension word set; system extension word set; and controlled reference words. It is available, priced $15.00, from *FORTH Interest Group, PO Box 8231, San Jose, CA 95155, USA, Tel: (408) 277-0668* □

UKAEA fights radiation induced errors

Research aimed at stamping out 'soft errors' — single-event upsets caused by alpha particle emissions from natural uranium or thorium impurities present in VLSI circuit materials and packages — is to be undertaken by the UK Atomic Energy Authority's Harwell Research Laboratory.

The 'Soft Errors R&D Club', set up by the Microelectronics Materials Centre at Harwell, is intended to bring together UK semiconductor manufacturers, users, process and materials suppliers in a collaborative research programme. This will use and extend the fission track autoradiography (FTA) technique developed at Harwell which can detect the presence of uranium in concentrations as low as 2×10^{-3} ppm (parts per million); such concentrations are undetectable by any other method.

'Soft errors' occur when the electrical charge released by an alpha particle alters the contents of a memory cell, giving rise to computational errors. As the density of memory cells increases, devices become more susceptible to single-event errors. The advent of VLSI has thus increased the demand for methods of detecting, and eventually eliminating, trace radioactive impurities in semiconductors.

The FTA technique will be used to investigate the extent of such impurities in currently used source and packaging materials. The research programme will look at the effect of circuit processing operations (eg deposition, etching and bonding) in introducing and retaining impurities, and will look at alternative packaging techniques to minimize contamination.

The Soft Errors Club is open only to UK organizations and to companies which have a significant manufacturing presence in the UK. Participants will pay an annual membership fee of £11 000. For further details, contact: *Ian Buckley-Golder, Microelectronics Materials Centre, Harwell Laboratory, Didcot, Oxon OX11 0RA, UK. Tel: (0235) 24141 ext 4309* □

Series 32000 heads for military marketplace

National Semiconductor has announced a number of hardware and software developments to make its Series 32000 microprocessor family suitable for military applications. These include sampling of 32000 devices in CMOS, development of military specifications and a military screening programme.

Selective sampling has commenced of a 32CO1616/32-bit CPU and a 32C201 timing and control unit (TCU), both in CMOS. These devices are currently specified at 10 MHz, but 12 MHz and 15 MHz versions will be available at a later date, says National.

A contract to characterize and develop 38510 JAN slash sheets (military specifications) for the 32000 series has been awarded by the US Air Force to Boeing Aerospace. National has also instituted its own internal military screening programme, known as MSP, to allow customers to obtain screened versions of certain VLSI devices faster than the full military qualification procedure would allow. Components covered by MSP include the 32016 CPU, the 32201 TCU and the 32081 floating point unit; CMOS parts complying with Mil Spec 883C will also be available in due course.

Other military-related programmes include the development of radiation-hardened Series 32000 versions by Sandia National Laboratories of the USA (*Microprocessors and Microsystems* Vol 9 No 7, page 369) and the adaptation of the ADA programming language to the 32000 series by US firm Verdix (ibid Vol 9 No 10, page 526).

'These developments put the 32000 family ahead of competing products in the military market,' claimed National's Werner Trattnig, 'making it the only 32-bit microprocessor family to offer complete solutions for military and other high-reliability applications.' □

Fully financed European Silicon Structures announces partners and plans

European Silicon Structures (ES2), the new European venture which plans to capture the short-run full-custom IC market using silicon compilation techniques, has reached its target of $65M required to finance full operation (*Microprocessors and Microsystems* Vol 9 No 9, page 468). This announcement follows the conclusion of cooperation agreements with a number of European companies, who have promised a total investment of $25M in ES2.

The remaining $40M will be obtained from the financial sector and certain other industrial companies ($20M) and from bank and government loans ($20M), says the firm.

Industrial partners in the venture now include Brown Boveri (Switzerland), Olivetti (Italy), Philips Gloeilampen Fabrieken (The Netherlands), Saab Scania (Sweden) through its Combitech Group, Telefonica (Spain), Bull (France) and British Aerospace (UK). According to ES2, these companies intend to make a long-term strategic investment in the venture, with a view to obtaining the benefits of fast-turnaround custom silicon.

'The corporate backing received today comes from different European countries and from major electronic market segments,' said ES2's managing director, Jean-Luc Grand-Clement. 'This is a brand new approach for European companies to cooperate in the field of high technology.'

A takeover bid by ES2 for UK-based CAE firm Lattice Logic has fallen through after both firms decided that acquisition was 'not appropriate'. Lattice, which has been associated with ES2 since the venture was announced in September 1985, has nonetheless agreed to negotiate commercial contracts with ES2 concerning its silicon compilation software packages Chipsmith and Shapesmith.

One definite transfer from Lattice to ES2 is John Gray, who joins the

Grand-Clement: 'brand new approach'

startup as vice president (methods and tools). Gray is to remain as a nonexecutive director of Lattice Logic. Other recent recruits to ES2 are Bernard Pruniaux, previously manager of Eurotechnique's Center for Production and Research, who becomes vice president (production and technology); and Rod Attwooll, former chief executive of Systime, who becomes managing director of Northern European operations.

Manufacture of ES2's ICs is to be done in a wafer production plant using electron-beam direct write onto wafers. ES2 plans to locate major operations in France, the FRG and the UK, with design centres in most European countries.

The company also intends to sponsor independently owned 'systems in silicon' design centres as part of Europe's Eureka project, whence extra financial support is being sought. A marketing deal signed with US CAD vendor SDA Systems means that SDA's ASIC design tools will be used in ES2's own centres, and ES2 will also be marketing the tools throughout Europe. □

Intel consults customers over 32-bit iRMX

Mitsubishi and Seiko are among several firms in the communications, industrial automation and CAE fields cooperating in a multimillion dollar Intel project to develop a new iRMX realtime operating system with a 32-bit capability. The operating system is to be used in the design of single-board computers and will be geared towards the 80386 microprocessor and its Multibus II architecture.

'Intel's purpose in forming a team of investors for this project is three-fold,' explained the company's William Lattin,' — to involve major customers early in the design process, to ensure high quality and thorough evaluation of the product, and to provide adequate resources for a job of this magnitude.'

Participants in the design of the operating system are attending regular meetings with Intel engineers and managers. They will receive advance copies of the finished product, giving them an early start on developing application software. □

End of the road for Array Logic

Low-volume semicustom IC manufacturer Array Logic of the UK has called in a receiver to wind down the company. Subcontractor delays on bringing new plant on stream, together with the depressed world semiconductor market, are blamed for the closure.

Set up in 1984 with £4M backing, Array Logic employed 30 staff, many of them highly qualified semiconductor professionals.

The company's managing director, Bob Whelan, commented: 'We have demonstrated our production technology and we know the market exists, but the current severe discounting, even on small volumes previously unattractive to the semiconductor majors, means that our funding was not sufficient to see us through the extended start-up period.' □

European Unix firms join forces

AT&T subsidiary Bell Telephone Systems of Belgium has teamed up with three European Unix specialist software/consultancy firms to form an association dedicated to 'European cooperation in Unix systems excellence'. The other firms involved in the venture, known as Unno, are Associated Computer Experts (The Netherlands), Axis Digital (France) and The Instruction Set (UK).

Among the aims of Unno are: to propose a coherent range of Unix products and services to clients within Europe; to facilitate European distribution, and eventually internationalization, of products developed by members; to jointly evaluate non-European products and jointly negotiate with US partners; to harmonize members' marketing strategies; to support the X/Open computer manufacturer's group; and, in the future, to develop products jointly.

Unno intends to accept other Unix companies into membership on two conditions: only one member company is allowed from any country, and that companies will only be accepted after 'serious technical evaluation'. □

68000s second sourced

A second sourcing agreement for VLSI peripheral chips of the 68000 family has been signed between Hitachi and US-based Signetics. The deal allows Signetics to manufacture Hitachi's HD63484 CRT (cathode ray tube) controller while Hitachi gains the rights to produce the Signetics SNC68562 dual universal serial communications controller (DUSCC), and also to the SCN2641 asynchronous communications interface (ACI) chip.

HD68562 (DUSCC) and HD2641 (ACI) devices are due for sampling in the first quarter of 1986. Signetics plans production availability of its 63484 ACRTC in the same quarter. □

SGS telecommunicates with Toshiba . . .

SGS Semiconductor and Toshiba have agreed on a joint development programme in the telecommunications IC sector. The agreement will, in the first instance, give Toshiba the right to second source SGS's M5913, CMOS pulse-code-modulation (PCM) codec IC, M9910 NMOS modem and MO88 NMOS PCM switching matrix.

SGS is to supply Toshiba with masks and relevant technical information, after which the Japanese company says it will be able to quickly supply chips needed for its own PBXs and personal computers as well as for outside customers. A number of Toshiba's telecommunications products are currently under evalua-

tion by SGS with a view to further alternative source arrangements. All devices will be marketed separately by the two companies.

● SGS has expanded its long-term 'strategic partner' agreement with Zilog to cover new Z8 parts developed by SGS. These products, which are to be produced by both companies, include a CMOS Z8 microprocessor, an NMOS Z8 with 8 kbyte of ROM and expanded RAM, Z8 versions with 4 kbyte or 8 kbyte of EPROM, and an incircuit emulator chip designed to support the 8 kbyte ROM and EPROM devices. □

. . . and has (logic array) designs on Daisy

Cooperative work between SGS and Daisy Systems has resulted in full electrical design kits for two families of SGS's CMOS logic arrays running on Daisy workstations. The HSG 3000 and 5000 logic array families are now fully supported on Logician series workstations, says SGS.

The HSG 3000 family uses a single-layer metal interconnection and offers functional complexity up to 2550 blocks, while the 5000 series arrays use double-layer metallization and give up to 6000-gate complexities.

Logician workstations can be used by SGS's customers on their own premises to perform the complete design cycle, including schematic capture, logic simulation, fault analysis and design rule checking. A netlist interface is provided to transfer the

Daisy Logician supports full design of HSG 3000 and 5000 gate arrays

database to one of SGS's design systems, located at a design centre, for final layout, routing and test generation. □

Harris, Analogic link on data acquisition

Harris Semiconductor and US-based Analogic are to collaborate on new product development under an agreement which also covers second sourcing of some recent Harris products. Joint development of a self-contained data acquisition system (designated HY-9600 by Harris) is already underway, say the companies.

Analogic is to provide a second source for the HY-9574/9674 sampling A/D converters and HY-9590/9591 data acquisition front end devices; these are the first such devices in Harris's VIP (vertically integrated products) line. Harris has been supplying data acquisition products to Analogic for over ten years. □

VMEbus 'will benefit most from 32-bit boom'

The presently sluggish microprocessor board market in the USA is about to be stirred by the growing popularity of 32-bit boards, says market research company Frost & Sullivan. And VMEbus, being the early market leader among the buses so far developed for 32-bit applications, stands to benefit most over the next five years.

VMEbus product consumption is set to increase from $75M in 1984 to $950M by 1989, says Frost & Sullivan's report, a surge that will be largely due to new products being developed for the 32-bit micro market. By 1989, VMEbus is expected to account for 38% of the board market in the USA; the report compares this with VMEbus's 11.5% of the worldwide market in 1983.

During the five-year forecast period, the US market will be driven by the emergence of computer integrated manufacturing (CIM), a sector which is expected to treble in volume to $42 000M. CIM is expected to represent the largest end user sector throughout the study period.

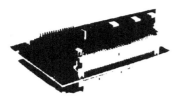

VMEbus: 32-bit market leader in the USA

In addition, says the report, over 600 VMEbus-compatible products will be available in the USA by 1989, from more than 120 vendors. These products will address such areas as computer-aided design and manufacturing, robotics, imaging, machine vision, medical scanning, seismology, infrared detection and weather analysis.

The report *The VMEbus-based product market in the US* is available, priced $1650, from *Frost & Sullivan Inc, 106 Fulton Street, New York, NY 10038, USA. Tel: (212) 233-1080.* ☐

Rapid growth is forecast for GaAs

Gallium arsenide (GaAs) consumption in Western Europe is set to increase from $378M in 1984 to $1150M by 1990, an annual growth rate of 20.5%, claims market research firm Frost & Sullivan. Breakthroughs in technology, particularly the development of the Czochralski method of crystal pulling, are pushing the worldwide market, including Europe, to new heights, says the company.

In 1984, GaAs products accounted for 8–9% of the total European semiconductor market. This figure will rise to 11% by 1990, says the report. While discrete components are expected to continue to dominate the GaAs market, with 1984 sales of $377.3M rising to $962.8M in 1990, integrated circuits are set for a faster rate of growth — from $714 000 in 1984 to $192.14M in 1990.

By country, the FRG has Europe's largest market — $88.6M in 1984 projected to rise to $289.2M by 1990. France comes in second with $83.96 (1984) rising to $255.56M (1990).

By end user, the military and aerospace sector now controls 55% of the market, though this will drop to 50% by 1990. Communications takes up another 37% of the 1984 market; this is expected to increase to 40% by 1990. The most important European activity for GaAs products is seen as being the development of ESPRIT (European strategic programme for research and development in information technology), a five-year programme aimed at making the EEC information technology industry competitive in world markets.

The report *The market for gallium arsenide semiconductors in Western Europe* is available, priced $2100, from *Frost & Sullivan Ltd, 104–112 Marylebone Lane, London W1M 5FU, UK. Tel: 01-486 2287* ☐

S/w firm seeks 'reverse engineering' ruling

Ruling on the principle of 'reverse engineering', whereby the performance and screen layout of a proprietary software package are reproduced by a different manufacturer using different source code, is being sought in a UK court of law.

UK software house Systems Union has issued a writ alleging that rival UK firm Simdell copied features of a Systems Union accountancy software package; the features in question include account types, analysis categories and column codes. Systems Union claims that, if its action reaches the High Court and is successful, it will establish that UK copyright law prevents the copying of features in a computer program — at present only source and object code appears to be covered.

Simdell denies the allegations contained in the writ, and is presently consulting legal advisors with a view to mounting a libel action against Systems Union.

According to Systems Union, this is the first case of its type to be initiated in the UK, although several similar cases are currently being heard in the USA. In the case of Whelan vs Jaslow, for example, a federal court has ruled that Jaslow copied Whelan's audiovisual display in breach of copyright; this case is subject to appeal. ☐

Date	Title	Contact	Place	Other details

1986

4–6 March	Semicon Europa	SEMI European Secretariat, CCL House, 59 Fleet Street, London EC4Y 1JU, UK	Zuspa Convention Centre, Zurich, Switzerland	European trade show and symposium. Includes technical sessions on wafer ecology, VLSI patterning and factory automation
4–6 March	DEXPO Europe 86	Expoconsul Europe Ltd, Axe & Bottle Court, 70 Newman Street, London SE1 1YT, UK	Olympia, London, UK	Exhibition and conference for the DEC and DEC-compatible industry
10–12 March	Computer Architecture and Operating Systems	Dr H P Louis, IBM Deutschland GmbH Laboratorium, Abt 3189, Schönaicher Strasse 220, 7030 Boblingen, FRG. Tel: (07031) 16-8796	University of Stuttgart, FRG	Ninth biannual conference, sponsored by the NTG, GI and IEEE
11–13 March	Electronic Production Efficiency Exposition 86 (EPEE)	Network Events Ltd, Printers Mews, Market Hill, Buckingham MK18 1JX, UK	Olympia, London, UK	Papers from users, developers, researchers and manufacturers who are involved with the technology and services surrounding the automated factory of the future
17–20 March	Hong Kong INFOTECH 86	Andry Montgomery Ltd, 11 Manchester Square, London W1M 5AB, UK	Hong Kong	Third international office communications, information and automation technology show
18–22 March	BIAS '86	BIAS Organizing Secretariat, Elettronica Oggi, Via Rosellini 12, Milan, Italy. Tel: (2) 688-09-51	Milan, Italy	20th international automation, instrumentation and microelectronics exhibition, with associated seminar on surface mounting technology to be held on 20 March
24–26 March	Speech Input/Output: Techniques and Applications	Conference Services, IEE, Savoy Place, London WC2R 0BL, UK	Institute of Education, London, UK	International conference on present research into speech-based input/output techniques, systems development, human factors in interface design and application to assist the physically or communication handicapped
2–4 April	Advances in Reliability Technology	Mrs R Campbell, NCSR, Wigshaw Lane, Culcheth, Warrington, Cheshire WA3 4NE, UK. Tel: (0725) 31244	University of Bradford, UK	Ninth symposium organized by the UK National Centre of Systems Reliability
7–11 April	MOS Integrated Circuit Design for Signal Processing and Data Conversion	Continuing Education Institute (Europe), Rörstorpsvägen 5, S-61200 Finspång, Sweden. Tel: (46 0122) 17570	Davos Congress Center, Switzerland	Course intended for engineers in the IC, aerospace, electronics or communications industries who are involved in use or design of integrated MOS signal or data processing circuits and systems
8–10 April	Unix Systems Exposition (Europe) '86	Network Events Ltd, Printers Mews, Market Hill, Buckingham MK18 1JX, UK	Palais des Congres, Paris, France	Second European Unix users' exhibition of software and hardware
15–17 April	The Computer as an Aid for those with Special Needs	The Conference Secretary, ACTIVE, Sheffield City Polytechnic, 37 Broomgrove Road, Sheffield S10 2BP, UK	Sheffield, UK	International conference for the computer community, educationalists and the disabled
15–17 April	5th Scottish Computer Show	Cahners Exhibitions Ltd, Chatsworth House, 59 London Road, Twickenham, Middx TW1 3SZ, UK. Tel: 01-891 5051	Scottish Exhibition and Conference Centre, Glasgow, UK	Trade exhibition
28–30 April	Expert Systems and their Applications	Jean-Claude Rault, Agence de l'Informatique, Tour Fiat — Cedex 16, 92084 Paris — La Défense, France. Tel: (331) 4796 4314	Palace of the Popes, Avignon, France	Sixth international workshop (conferences and exhibitions)

Date	Title	Contact	Place	Other details
13–15 May	Communications 86	Institution of Electrical Engineers, Savoy Place, London WC2R 0BL, UK. Tel: 01-240 1871	Metropole Hotel, Birmingham, UK	Eighth IEE conference and exhibition. Session headings include: the cellular scene; mobile radio update; office communications equipment; value added network services; satellite communications; recent developments in networks and services; ISDN becomes a reality.
13–15 May	Eurosoft/Nordcomp 86	Network Events Ltd, Printers Mews, Market Hill, Buckingham MK18 1JX, UK	Hamburg Exhibition Centre, FRG	European conference and exhibition on computer software and hardware
13–16 May	CommunicAsia 86	Andry Montgomery Ltd, 11 Manchester Square, London W1M 5AB, UK	Singapore	Fourth Asian international electronic communication show and conference
13–16 May	Hong Kong Elenex 86	Andry Montgomery Ltd, 11 Manchester Square, London W1M 5AB.	Hong Kong	Second Hong Kong international electrical and electronic engineering show
3–5 June	ComUnix '86	EMAP International Exhibitions Ltd, Abbot's Court, 34 Farringdon Road, London EC1R 3AU, UK. Tel: 01-608 1161	Tara Hotel, London, UK	Series of seminars concerning 'Unix solutions'. Sponsored by /usr/group/UK
3–6 June	International Conference on Consumer Electronics	ICCE, c/o TMA, 3553 North Milwaukee Avenue, Chicago, IL 60641, USA	Rosemont, IL, USA	Conference and exhibition on video and audio technology, home information systems, components, CADCAM and emerging technologies
10–12 June	Comdex International	The Interface Group Inc, 300 First Avenue, Needham, Massachusetts, USA	Nice, France	Display of software, small computer products, peripherals, accessories and other related items; miniconference on business, marketing and financial subjects of interest to computer industry marketers
10–12 June	Scottish Electronics Show	Network Events Ltd, Printers Mews, Market Hill, Buckingham MK18 1JX, UK	Anderson Centre, Glasgow, UK	Exhibition and conference covering equipment and services associated with the design, testing and manufacturing of electronic equipment and components
25–28 June	Communications: Message, Mind, & Machine	Canadian Association for Information Science, BC Research, 3650 Wesbrook Mall, Vancouver V6S 2L2, Canada	Canada	Conference and exhibition on information retrieval and systems design, artificial intelligence, expert systems, networking and distributed systems
2–4 July	International Workshop on Systolic Arrays	Will Moore, Systolic Array Workshop, Dept of Engineering Science, Oxford University, Oxford OX1 3PJ, UK	Oxford, UK	Papers on all aspects of systolic arrays and related SIMD architectures from abstract theory to practical applications and VLSI products
7–11 July	International Optical Computing Conference	Prof Joseph Shamir, Conference Chairman, 1986 IOCC, c/o Kopel Tours Ltd — Conventions, PO Box 4413, 61044 Tel Aviv, Israel	Jerusalem, Israel	Recent developments in optical computing including optical information processing, hybrid optical–digital processing systems, systolic array processors, integrated optical processing devices, electro-optic devices, optical interface techniques and application of optical bistability to computing
15–18 September	Euromicro 86	Mrs E C Snippe-Marlisa, TH Twente, PO Box 217, Dept INF, Room A306, 7500 AE Enschede, The Netherlands	Venice, Italy	Twelfth annual conference of micro-processing and microprogramming
15–20 September	Intercomm '86	Cahners Exhibitions Ltd, Chatsworth House, 59 London Road, Twickenham TW1 3SZ, UK	Beijing, China	International computer and communication congress/exposition for science and technology
29 September –3 October	ISATA 86	ISATA Secretariat, 62 High Street, Croydon CR0 1NA, UK	Ingolstadt, Austria	International symposium on automotive technology and automation

General Editor: Keith Baker (Plymouth Polytechnic, UK)

IMAGE AND VISION COMPUTING is the quarterly international and
interdisciplinary journal that provides communication between workers
in such diverse applications of computer imaging as astronomy, biomedicine,
robotics, remote sensing, broadcasting and video, metallurgy, seismology
and radar.

Topics covered include:

- mathematical foundations,
  including fast Fourier analysis
  and recursive filtering
- pattern recognition and artificial
  intelligence
- software techniques, including
  databases and data structures
- special-purpose hardware,
  including VLSI

- applications and case studies of
  image computing, including
  remote sensing robot vision,
  industrial quality control, video
  special effects and tomography
- experimental psychology
- image generation, including flight
  simulation and holography
- vision and perception theory

For further details and a sample copy please contact:

Mrs Sheila King
Butterworth Scientific
PO Box 63, Westbury House,
Bury Street, Guildford,
Surrey GU2 5BH, UK
Telephone: (0483) 31261
Telex: 859556 SCITEC G

microprocessors and microsystems

vol 10 no 2 march 1986

BACKPLANE BUS STANDARDS Special Issue

Butterworths

editorial advisory board

Microprocessors and Microsystems is an international journal published in February, March, April, May, June, August, September, October, November, December. *Editorial Offices:* Butterworth Scientific Ltd, PO Box 63, Westbury House, Bury Street, Guildford, Surrey GU2 5BH, UK. Tel: (0483) 31261. Telegrams and telex: 859556 SCITEC G. *Publishing Director:* John Owens. *Production:* Tony Lewis

Microprocessors and Microsystems is published by Butterworth Scientific Ltd. *Registered Office:* Butterworth Scientific Ltd, 88 Kingsway, London WC2 6AB, UK

Subscription enquiries and orders: Quadrant Subscription Services Ltd, Oakfield House, Perrymount Road, Haywards Heath, West Sussex RH16 3DH, UK. Tel: (0444) 459188

Annual subscription (10 issues): £89.00 Overseas rate (£22.00 for private individuals);

$160.00 US rate ($40.00 for private individuals)
UK subscription rates available on request.

Prices include packing and delivery by sea mail. Airmail prices available on request. Copies of this journal sent to subscribers in Bangladesh, India, Pakistan, Sri Lanka, Canada and the USA are air-speeded for quicker delivery.

Back issues: Prior to current volume available from Wm Dawson & Sons Ltd, Cannon House, Folkestone, Kent CT19 5EE, UK. Tel: (0303) 57421

US mailing agents: Expediters of the Printed Word Ltd, 515 Madison Avenue, Suite 1217, New York, NY 10022, USA. Second class postage paid at New York, NY. US Postmaster: Send address corrections to *Microprocessors and Microsystems,* c/o Expediters of the Printed Word Ltd, address as above.

Reprints: Minimum order 100, available from the publisher.

ISSN 0141 9331
MCRPD 10 (2) 57–136 1986)

© Butterworth & Co (Publishers) Ltd 1986

Typeset by Tech-Set, Gateshead, Tyne & Wear, and printed by Dotesios (Printers) Ltd, Greenland Mills, Bradford on Avon, Wilts, UK.

microprocessors and microsystems

vol 10 no 2
march 1986

Editor Steve Hitchcock

Assistant Editor Andrew Taylor

Publisher Amanda Harper

Special issue: Backplane bus standards

(continued)

microprocessors and microsystems

Special issue: Backplane bus standards
(continued)

Special issue:
Backplane Bus Standards

With the advance to ever more powerful microprocessors and modular, multiprocessor systems and the consequent need for communication links between components, backplane bus standards are growing in importance. For microsystem designers, a reliable bus standard simplifies design procedures, enabling them to concentrate on the functionality of individual components with the assurance that they will work together correctly at the hardware level.

Looking at the fast-changing field of backplane bus standards, this special issue is intended as an 'update' on today's major bus schemes, focussing particularly on recent developments, the present status and capabilities of these buses, and illustrating their application in advanced systems design. It is not intended to be a comprehensive guide to all bus standards, nor does it attempt to trace in detail past developments. As an indication of the rapid change that affects bus development an earlier 'backplane bus standards' issue of this journal (Vol 6 No 9, November 1982) covered, among others, Multibus I, Versabus and Eurobus, all now largely superseded by more recent bus designs.

Today, bus schemes proliferate — from 8- and 16- to 32-bit systems — both manufacturer-independent standards and manufacturers' de facto industry standards.

For advanced systems, manufacturer-independent standards such as the 32-bit buses Futurebus and Fastbus, discussed here by Roger Edwards and Dave Gustavson, have been developed by working parties sponsored by major institutions and thus benefit from the expertise and wide experience of the members of these groups; also, they do not tie the designer to any one manufacturer's products.

Futurebus has still to receive final approval as an official IEEE standard, but its advanced design features have ensured that already it finds applications. In this issue, Simon Peyton Jones highlights its use in a fifth-generation computer being developed at University College London, UK. Applications such as this push bus performance to its limits. It thus becomes necessary to consider the physical constraints of bus systems. Treatment of buses as transmission lines and the problems of driving buses are addressed by Rob Wilson, who presents some solutions, now implemented in silicon, for Futurebus.

Another manufacturer-independent bus, the 16-bit M3, was completed in 1982 under the auspices of the Computer Science Program of the Italian Research Council in response to the then inadequate capabilities of buses to fully support multiprocessor architectures. Dante Del Corso describes how the current status of the bus evolved and comments on its relation to other bus standards.

Manufacturer-developed 16- and 32-bit buses such as VME and Multibus II, on the other hand, have the advantage of wide product availability and support. Many companies promoting buses in fact see bus standards as a strong marketing and competitive tool, prompting market research company Frost & Sullivan to predict that no one standard will dominate the market this decade. And the potential worldwide market for buses is vast: F & S predicts that one of the leading buses, VMEbus, will reach a market value of $950 million by 1989 from today's level of $75 million, for example. Performance of the two most widely used manufacturer-supported buses can be compared in the papers by Steve Heath, who discusses some design applications of VMEbus, and Simon Muchmore, who describes the message passing facility of Multibus II.

More direct conclusions on the merits of all the 32-bit buses can be drawn from Paul Borrill's detailed comparisons of VME, Futurebus, Multibus II, Nubus and Fastbus.

We also cover some of the earliest buses to be developed — Q-bus, the STD bus and S100. These buses continue to survive, having been regularly upgraded to meet new system requirements whilst maintaining compatibility with existing products. Steve Dawes, Dave Batchelor and George W George illustrate how these buses have evolved to meet the needs of a changing marketplace.

It is clear that with so many bus schemes available, individual bias or preference for or against particular buses, for whatever reasons, is inevitable. To place this in perspective, Mike Rowe of the UK Independent Broadcasting Authority draws on his practical experience of bus systems to give an 'independent' user's view of backplane buses. The IBA maintains almost 1500 television and radio transmitters across the UK, and its equipment is required to be both reliable and maintainable. Mike's study of the bus-based microprocessor systems that best fit these requirements recommends combinations of three buses for optimum performance.

Acknowledgements

An expert editorial panel formed to coordinate this special issue provided many suggestions which have helped shape its content. We would like to acknowledge the valuable contributions of the members of this panel — Roger Edwards, Hugh Field-Richards, Bob Squirrell and Anthony Winter — and also Paul Borrill for his advice.

notes for authors

Microprocessors and Microsystems

The Journal welcomes all articles on semi-conductor chip and PCB design, the application of microprocessors to industry, business and schools and on the development of microprocessor software. Articles can come from both academic and industrial research and should be 3000–5000 words in length. In addition to main articles, we welcome shorter case studies, design notes and teach-ins.

All submitted articles are refereed by two independent reviewers to ensure both accuracy and relevance, though it is the authors' sole responsibility that statements used are accurate. The author is also responsible for obtaining permission to quote material and to republish tables and illustrations.

Copyright

Before publication, authors are requested to assign copyright to Butterworth & Co (Publishers) Ltd. This allows the company to sanction reprints of the whole or part of the volume and authorize photocopies. The authors, however, still retain their traditional right to reuse or to veto third-party publication.

Preparation of scripts

As you can see from the Journal, every article published is stylized by us to keep consistency throughout each volume. We follow the Oxford English Dictionary. It would be helpful if you could follow the Journal style. The most important thing, though, is that you write (or rather type) in clear and concise English. Contributions should be typed double-spaced on one side of the paper. We would also appreciate it if you number each page and leave wide margins so we can prepare the article for the typesetters. Three copies of the article are preferred and should be sent to the editor.

Units

You should use, as far as possible, SI units. In circumstances where this is not possible, please provide a conversion factor at the first mention of the unit.

Illustrations

Line drawings

We have our own professional studio to ensure that line drawings are consistent with house style. We would prefer, however, to receive unlettered drawings (black ink on tracing paper) so we can put on the lettering ourselves. Drawings, if possible, should be of size consistent with the Journal, i.e. either 169 mm or 356 mm width. Single drawings should not extend over one page (500 mm) in height.

Computer printouts

Illustrations showing line printer listings, plotter output, etc should preferably be on unlined paper. Printouts will be reduced by us to the relevant size. Do not mark them as they will be used to make photographic copies for the typesetters. Only include sufficient lines for the reader to interpret the format and nature of the printout. Overlong printouts only cause confusion. Fuller explanation should appear in the caption and the text.

Photographs

Black and white glossy photographs (including Polaroid prints of VDU screens) should, where possible, be supplied unmounted. They should be labelled clearly on the back with a soft pencil. Photocopies of the photographs should be provided for the referees.

References

Our Journal style is to indicate the use of a reference in the text with a superscript as each one arises and give the full reference with the same number at the end. If a reference is cited more than once, the same number should be used each time. With a bibliography, the references are given in alphabetic order (dependent on the first author's surname). It would be helpful if you could follow this style. References take the following form:

(to journals)

1   Buckroyd, A 'Production testing of microprocessor-based equipment' *Microprocessors and Microsystems* Vol 5 No 7 (September 1981) pp 299–303

(to books)

2   Gallacher, J 'Testing and maintenance' in Hanna, F K (ed.) *Advanced techniques for microprocessor systems* Peter Peregrinus, Stevenage, UK (1980)

Proofs

Correspondence and proofs for corrections will be sent to the first named author, unless otherwise indicated. Authors will receive a copy of the galley proofs and copies of redrawn or relettered illustrations. It is important that these proofs should be checked and returned promptly.

Reprints

The first named author will receive 25 reprints of the technical article free of charge. Further copies, a minimum of 100, can be ordered at any time from the Reprints Department, Butterworth Scientific Ltd, Westbury House, PO Box 63, Bury Street, Guildford, Surrey GU2 5BH, UK.

The physics of driving backplane buses

Treating backplane buses as transmission lines, **Rob Wilson** describes how solutions to bus loading problems have been implemented in silicon

Transmission line theory is surveyed briefly, showing the circumstances under which backplanes must be treated as transmission lines. The problems associated with practical design of transmission lines are covered with particular reference to crosstalk reduction and the capacitive loading problem. Solutions are presented which are implemented in silicon.

microsystems   transmission lines   backplane buses

A transmission line is a distributed network which can be represented by the circuit in Figure 1. This network has a characteristic impedance given by

$$Z_0 = \left(\frac{R + j\omega L}{G + j\omega C} \right)^{1/2}$$

At high frequencies, above 100 kHz, say, for practical lines, Z_0 can be considered as a constant which approximates to

$$Z_0 = (L/C)^{1/2}$$

The propagation delay t_p is also a constant

$$t_p = (LC)^{1/2} \text{ per unit length}$$

BACKPLANE BUSES AS TRANSMISSION LINES

A distributed network can be approximated to a lumped circuit only if the round-trip delay $2t_l$ is much less than the transition time t_t of signals on the network. Consider the example of a CCITT V24 data link covering a distance of 15 m. For twisted pair wiring the propagation delay of the network is approximately 5.9 ns m^{-1}, giving a round-trip delay of ~180 ns. The relevant V28 electrical specification limits the transition times of the signals to about 1 μs. So this link satisfies the condition $t_t \gg 2t_l$, and thus the lumped equivalent circuit is valid.

Now consider a backplane bus. For an unloaded bus the propagation delay will be typically 6.6 ns m^{-1}. So for a 0.6 m backplane the round-trip delay will be ~ 8 ns.

National Semiconductor (UK) Ltd, The Maple, Kembrey Park, Swindon, Wilts SN2 6UT, UK

Transition times for common logic types are about 5 ns. Thus this network cannot satisfy the condition for lumped circuit equivalence, and we must treat the backplane bus as a transmission line.

THE PRACTICAL BACKPLANE BUS

In the practical case of a backplane bus which has plug-in cards at regular intervals, the effect of capacitive loading of the transmission line is to reduce its impedance and to increase its propagation delay. In the case of a bus line having uniform capacitive loading C_x spaced at intervals l_x, the loaded impedance Z_L and propagation delay t_{pL} become

$$Z_L = Z_0/(1 + C_L/C)^{1/2}$$

where $C_L = C_x/l_x$, and

$$t_{pL} = t_p(1 + C_L/C)^{1/2}$$

For the backplane exampled quoted above the round-trip delay can be recalculated for a given capacitive loading. Using a figure of 15 pF per slot, with 65 slots m^{-1}

$$2t_l = 2 \times l \times t_l \times (1 + C_L/C)^{1/2}$$
$$(C_L = 15 \text{ pF} \times 65 \text{ slots m}^{-1})$$
$$= 2 \times 0.6 \times 6.6 \times (1 + 975/66)^{1/2}$$
$$= 31 \text{ ns}$$

which is now considerably greater than the transition time of the electrical signals on the bus.

The overall effect of this increase in propagation delay is to make the behaviour of the bus less like that of a lumped equivalent circuit, and more like that of a transmission line. The reduction of the bus impedance increases drive current requirements.

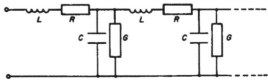

Figure 1. Equivalent circuit of a transmission line

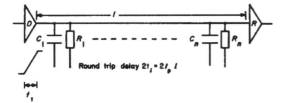

Figure 2. A distributed network

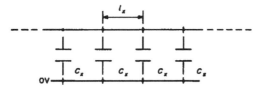

Figure 3. A uniformly loaded line

THE CROSSTALK PROBLEM

Attempts to drive backplanes hard in order to obtain high transmission rates have frequently resulted in short transition times, typified by peak slew rates up to 5 V ns^{-1}. In addition to the high supply current pulses required by these drivers, further problems are raised by the high frequency edges coupling to adjacent signal lines. The 'noise' so induced is commonly referred to as crosstalk.

Crosstalk, due to the distributed capacitive and inductive coupling between adjacent lines (C_c and L_c), has distinct features when measured at either end of a line. Amplitude of crosstalk is given by

$$V_{NE} = K_{NE} V_l \quad \text{for } t_t < 2t_l$$

where $K_{NE} = L (C_C Z + L_C/Z) 4t_l$ and V_l is the voltage swing on the driving line. Far-end crosstalk amplitude is

$$V_{FE} = K_{FE} L V_l / t_t$$

where $K_{FE} = (C_C Z - L_C/Z)/2$. From these expressions it can be noted that

- Crosstalk amplitude scales with driving amplitude.
- Crosstalk amplitude is proportional to slew rate V_l/t_t.
- Far-end crosstalk width is t_t.
- If $t_t < 2t_l$ then the near-end crosstalk amplitude as a fraction of V_l is a function of physical layout only.
- High values of t_t reduce the percentage of crosstalk relative to V_l.

From these observations we can deduce that

- Absolute noise levels do not matter; good noise performance is obtained by reducing the uncertainty region of the receiver threshold.
- Bus drive requirements can be reduced if signal amplitudes are reduced. By keeping the same transition times this reduction in V_l will also reduce crosstalk.
- A receiver which rejects pulses having widths less than t_t will eliminate far-end crosstalk.
- Careful layout is needed to reduce near-end crosstalk; increasing line spacing and introducing intermediate ground lines helps.
- Increasing the rise and fall times of the signals will reduce crosstalk.

A SOLUTION FOR CROSSTALK

Taking the above observations into account, the backplane can be driven with signals having a controlled transition time. If the receiver also has noise-rejecting properties in that it will reject pulses whose width is less than this transition time, then the far-end crosstalk problem will be eliminated.

National Semiconductor's DS3662 and DS3862 'trapezoidal' transceivers, intended for use with open-collector buses terminated in 120 Ω at each end, incorporate these facilities. Also, the receiver's threshold has a narrow uncertainty region of 400 mV, which is accurately centred in the middle of the 3.4 V bus swing. Figure 5 shows the driver circuit and its output waveform. It can be seen that the driver generates precise rising and falling edges, having a slew rate of 0.2 V ns^{-1}, giving a transition time of 15 ns which is independent of the driver's capacitive load. Even given this limit we can still drive the bus fast: the DS3662 can usefully transmit pulses with widths down to 20 ns.

The receiver uses a low-pass filter to reject pulses less than 20 ns in width, the width being measured at 2.5 V from either bus level. Figure 6 shows the receiver circuit and its behaviour with various input pulses.

In addition, the trapezoidal transceivers feature low bus loading (a maximum of 100 μA) under both power on and off conditions, and, importantly for backplane systems, 'glitch-free' power up and down protection.

THE BUS LOADING PROBLEM

As discussed above, the effects of loading the bus capacitively are to increase propagation delays and to reduce the bus impedance, thus increasing driver current requirements. If the bus is driven with insufficient current, then several round-trip delays will be incurred before the signal reaches an adequate level where a receiver can detect it. For example, consider a loaded bus having a net impedance of 10 Ω, a termination voltage of 3 V and a round-trip delay of 66 ns m^{-1}, as shown in Figure 7. A 300 mA driver will cause an immediate transition to 0 V, but a 50 mA driver will require between two and four round-trip delays to cross the normal TTL receiver threshold. This can cause multiple edge triggering on

Drive input

Driven line

Sense line

Near end crosstalk · · · For end crosstalk

Figure 4. Crosstalk

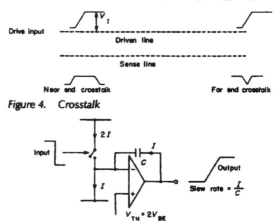

Figure 5. Trapezoidal driver and waveform

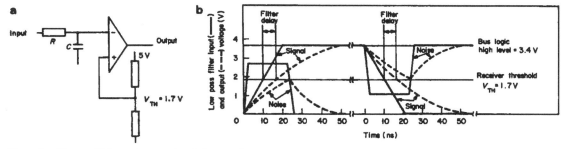

Figure 6. *Trapezoidal receiver: a, circuit; b, waveform*

clock and strobe signals, and limits the throughput of the bus. TTL devices suffer from this inadequate drive current, and thus a special driver is required.

However, if the drive current is simply increased, a larger output transistor is required for each driver on the bus. Unfortunately, the larger the transistor the higher its capacitance; adding to the bus capacitance and reducing the bus impedance even further requires even higher drive currents. Together with these problems, system power requirements are being increased adding to noise problems by increasing track voltage drops.

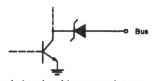

Figure 7. *Effect of insufficient drive current*

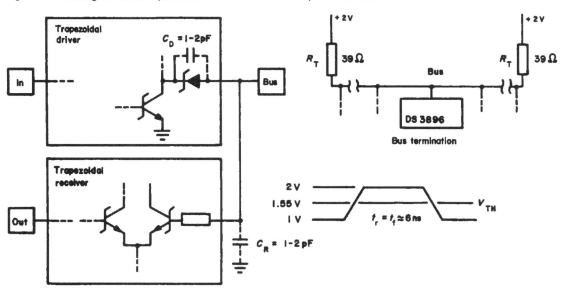

Figure 8. *Isolating the driver capacitance*

One way out of this situation is to tackle the problem via the driver capacitance. If each 'off' driver is isolated from the bus then the bus loading is reduced, bus impedance is increased and driver current requirements are reduced. A simple approach to this is to have a Schottky diode in series with the driver transistor's collector, as shown in Figure 8. If, when the transistor is off, the diode is reverse biased, a capacitance of only 1–2 pF will be presented to the bus.

One immediate objection could be raised here: the output low voltage of the driver will not meet traditional TTL levels. This is not a great problem. Crosstalk amplitude scales with signal amplitude, so the driver signal swing can be reduced as long as the receiver threshold is accurate.

FUTUREBUS TRAPEZOIDAL TRANSCEIVER

By coupling these features with the trapezoidal concept discussed above, National Semiconductor has produced the transceiver, the DS3896/7, which is recommended for use with the Futurebus backplane system. Shown in Figure 9, the transceiver is optimized for heavily loaded backplanes, and presents a capacitive load of less than 5 pF to the bus.

Figure 9. *The Futurebus transceiver*

The driver is intended for use with buses terminated at each end with 39 Ω to 2 V. The low termination value compared with conventional 120 Ω buses reduces reflections considerably. The signal swing is just 1 V, allowing the use of 50 mA drive, thus saving power. The transition times of the driver are approximately 6 ns, and the receiver rejects pulses of up to 12 ns width to virtually eliminate crosstalk. The device has 10 ns propagation delays which, coupled with low bus loading, increase bus throughput. Rates up to 50 Mbaud can be easily achieved.

For higher throughput the DS8393 quad Turbo Transceiver has been produced. Similar to the DS3896/7, this is designed for 20 Ω termination and has a 15 ns pair delay. The receiver has a built-in bandgap reference to provide an accurate threshold. Due to the higher speed, the controlled transition time facility has been excluded, so careful stripline design is needed to minimize noise. The transceiver can be used for Futurebus or, as with the DS3986/7, for custom backplane buses.

CONCLUSION

The difficult problems of backplane bus communications have been tackled. Implementing in silicon a three-pronged approach — reducing loading capacitance, reducing signal swing, and using trapezoidal driver waveforms together with a noise-rejecting receiver — provides designers with solutions that cut design time and simplify systems.

REFERENCES

1 **Balakrishnan, R V** 'Cut bus reflection, crosstalk with a trapezoidal transceiver' *EDN* (August 1983)
2 **Balakrishnan, R V** 'The proposed IEEE 896 Future-bus — a solution to the bus driving problem' *IEEE Micro* (August 1984) pp 23–27

Rob Wilson is National Semiconductor's European applications manager for advanced digital peripheral products. He joined the company in 1984, having previously worked as a design manager with Philips. A member of IEE, he holds a degree in engineering from Cambridge University, UK, and has written previously on telecommunications and computers.

Futurebus — the independent standard for 32-bit systems

Examining the likely trends in advanced microsystems, **Roger Edwards** explains how Futurebus fits into these systems, providing a manufacturer-independent, upgradable backplane bus standard that simplifies design procedures

Requirements for high-performance systems, many of which will use a multitasking, multiuser, multiprocessor architecture, are discussed. The performance of such systems is critically dependent on the backplane chosen and a properly designed backplane can very considerably simplify the designer's task. It is shown that the IEEE P896 (Futurebus) standard takes into consideration many of the problems likely to be encountered in a high-performance system and can offer economic solutions to most of them.

microsystems   backplane buses   Futurebus

Before defining the most suitable application areas for IEEE P896 (Futurebus) it would be sensible to hypothesize on the trends apparent in the development of microprocessor systems and to highlight some significant aspects of the bus specification.

The power of the 32-bit microprocessors and the availability of high-density, low-cost memory means that systems based on these devices will be able to perform tasks traditionally undertaken by the high-performance minicomputers and the smaller mainframe machines. These will typically be complex multitasking, multiuser, realtime transaction processing or control and monitoring applications. The comparatively low component costs of these computing and memory devices will enable a number of very high performance machines to be constructed for special applications.

These systems have a number of common features. As they become larger and more complex the effects of computer failure become more serious. Commercially this is just expensive. For an industrial control system, such as a nuclear power plant or defence system, however, human life can also be at risk. Failures do occur, but as hardware costs are falling in real terms it is expected that many new systems will be designed with some level of fault tolerance.

Also, because microprocessor and memory chips are relatively inexpensive, compared with the peripherals

Advantec Systems Ltd, Silhill House, 2235 Coventry Road, Sheldon, Birmingham B26 3NW, UK

and even the mechanical assemblies and power supplies, most high-performance systems will use a multiprocessor design. In most cases cards will be complete with processor, memory and other support chips. Consequently, the processors will, in general execute instructions from local memory rather than from global memory, implying that the bulk of traffic on the backplane bus will be block transfers of data, messages and programs between peripherals, global memory and processor subsystems.

Additionally, the major investment in a new computer system is no longer in the CPU and memory hardware; it is now in the operating system, other software and peripheral driver hardware. To keep his system at the forefront a manufacturer must therefore be able to redesign each individual part of the system — CPU, memory and peripherals — as new products are introduced. In particular, investment in a new machine can often be minimized by utilizing other standard products, perhaps from alternative specialist suppliers.

The very high performance machines will also require cache memory and perhaps special architectural features such as 'tagging'.

The above points have been carefully considered in the design of the P896 (Futurebus) backplane and it is therefore hoped that the bus will meet a wide cross-section of designers' requirements for 32-bit systems. It should be remembered of course that a bus structure does not do the designer's job for him/her; it enables effort to be concentrated on the functionality of each module with the assurance that all modules will work together correctly at the hardware level.

FAULT TOLERANT SYSTEMS

The level of fault tolerance varies widely from application to application. For example, a business system with 16 terminals handling primarily word processing and similar applications can afford a few hours down time each year, whereas a system controlling a nuclear power plant must operate *without* fail. There are three aspects to fault tolerance: fault detection, fault containment and fault recovery.

Fault detection is the most essential feature of any fault tolerant system since if a fault cannot be detected then no steps can be taken to correct it. Much of the fault detection system is up to the system designer; P896 helps by providing extensive checking and fault reporting mechanisms for both data transfers and arbitration. Data transfers are protected by priority bits for each byte of data, the control lines and, if used, the 'tag' bit. Furthermore, each data transfer is acknowledged separately by a set of status lines which define whether the transfer has been successful. Arbitration is protected by parity in the arbitration code and by a check to ensure that the winner of an arbitration does indeed have the same arbitration code as that placed on the bus by the arbitration process.

Futurebus helps to contain the fault because all bus facilities are fully distributed. There are no central clock or general service modules and consequently failure of no one module can disrupt the bus unless the failure is within the bus logic or drivers. The bus is completely contained on a single 96-way IEC 603-2 connector, which also assists with fault recovery as discussed below. The bus is also completely position independent, so reconfiguration to bypass a faulty module does not require physical alterations.

Fault recovery is helped by several facilities of the bus. As mentioned above, the bus is position independent and no central modules are required, so the faulty module can be removed by a software reconfiguration scheme. If the fault is within the bus logic an independent data path is required to isolate the faulty module. P896 makes provision for this as the bus is contained on one connector, but the preferred board height is triple Eurocard. Consequently, a very high security system could use three buses and implement a two-out-of-three majority voting system. Each implementation of the bus incorporates a serial bus which can be used for control messages to isolate a module.

Even if a system can recover from a single fault it is now running at a higher risk level and the faulty module will have to be replaced as soon as conveniently possible. P896 makes provision for the live insertion and extraction of modules covering both the physical live insertion of the module and the logical connection to the running system.

MULTIPROCESSOR DESIGNS

There are several reasons for expecting that the majority of new computer designs will be based on multiple processors. The devices are relatively inexpensive and modules can be easily constructed with a processor and a considerable amount of local memory and perhaps a number of special I/O controllers. This implies that many routine operating system commands can be offloaded to intelligent I/O modules with a correspondingly significant gain in performance. Furthermore, processor modules can now be optimized for particular tasks, eg scientific calculations are arithmetically intensive and warrant the use of relatively expensive arithmetic coprocessors, whereas a word processing application does not require extensive arithmetic but does require fast character manipulation. Also, to protect investment in software, a

general-purpose system could utilize processors from several different manufacturers.

The logical extension of this is to build a system around a pool of processors, each optimized for a specific range of tasks. These processors must all be able to communicate efficiently with each other and with global memory. The most common data transfers, however, will be large blocks of program code or data and a relatively few short control messages.

The backplane supporting such systems must therefore be manufacturer independent and must provide efficient arbitration mechanisms and fast block data transfer. In Futurebus the arbitration mechanism supports 31 devices in a priority system together with 31 devices operating a 'fair' algorithm. Devices may also dynamically change their priority as required, although of course the software must ensure that a consistent set of priority levels is maintained. This is helped by the 'geographical address' lines on the bus which can be used to give unique default values to the priority code. P896 also allows arbitration to take place concurrently with data transfer. This together with the efficient data transfer protocol and electrical specifications allows bus mastership to be changed after each data block with, in general, no time penalty.

The data transmission protocol has been optimized for the transmission of data in blocks, although the block length can be zero to 4 Gbyte. In practice, blocks will be kept short, say 256 byte, to ensure bus access within a given time period. The system designer has full control over this parameter. The data transmission protocol is asynchronous and uses a two-edged handshake. This enables data to be transferred on both the rising and falling edges of a strobe line and hence saves the time required to return the strobe signal to its released state. This enables data transfer rates of up to 117 Mbyte s^{-1} to be achieved, or realistically up to 60 Mbyte s^{-1} with currently available bus drivers and a 35 ns slave access time (Figure 1).

Another major problem with multiprocessor designs, or any other multiuser, multitasking system, is the protection of data. As P896 is a system bus it will in many cases be accessing memory shared by a local CPU, or in high security systems accessed by one or more other buses. Each of these cases can lead to data being changed during transmission unless suitable locking mechanisms are provided. In Futurebus, when a slave is accessed it may return a 'busy' status if the data is locked to another bus; the master can then take the appropriate recovery action which may simply be to try again. Futurebus can specifically request that data is locked until it is specifically released or bus mastership changes. Consequently, because it is the current master that determines when to release the bus, any number of read or write transfers may be made with the assurance that no other user can interfere. This is of particular importance when accessing system 'lock variables' or common cache memory.

Futurebus is the only bus that supports both broadcast and broadcall data transfers over the full 4 Gbyte address space, and also, as discussed below, fully supports both tagged architectures and various cache mechanisms.

TAGGED ARCHITECTURE

Many advanced computer architectures require that each word in memory is 'tagged'. The tag bit can be used for

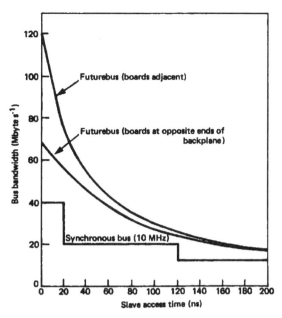

Figure 1. Comparison of bus bandwidth with slave access time. Note: the synchronous bus performance curve neglects clock latency problems for synchronization of board clock with bus clock

several purposes, but the most unusual is to distinguish between pointers (ie addresses) and other data. The LISP machine and Smalltalk, for example, require simple tagging of this kind. The tag bit is required with every word transferred between memory and processor, but if the tag is allocated to AD31 the data word is reduced to 31 bit which immediately becomes incompatible with the IEEE floating point arithmetic standard and creates problems. To overcome these problems, Futurebus transmits 34 bits; 32 bits are used as data and the remaining two bits are used as the tag and tag parity. It is up to the system designer how best to implement a system, and there is no *requirement* that a module makes use of the tag bit.

CACHE SUPPORT

Many machines have used a cache buffer memory between the system bus and local bus to improve performance. This is a relatively simple problem and does not fully utilize the advantages of cache memory, although it is one of the most effective ways of maintaining system performance in a multiprocessor system with shared access to a wide system address space. The major problem is to ensure that all data is coherent, and consequently most systems have used a cache memory only for instructions. Futurebus is the only standard bus to provide substantial support for cache memory and will fully support both a write-through and a write-back algorithm. This enables caches to be used effectively for both data and instructions and maintains full data coherence over the system. Write-through caches require only that the address cycle is broadcast. Write-back caches require, in addition, cache 'hit' indications from other masters on

read cycles. They also require cache invalidate indication and slave intervention. Furthermore, all masters must signal that they do or do not support the cache system so that they can coreside in the same system. Futurebus supports these mechanisms.

ELECTRICAL CHARACTERISTICS

To achieve maximum performance from a bus, which is always limited by transmission line theory, care has to be taken with the protocols used, the bus drivers and electrical characteristics of the backplane. A full-width fully loaded backplane behaves like a transmission line. To achieve the minimum response time a pulse injected at one end of the backplane must reach the other end with sufficient amplitude to be seen by the receivers before the first reflection occurs. Given enough time the amplitude of the pulse will of course be essentially the same at both ends of the backplane due to additive reflections. The amplitude of the original pulse, however, depends on two primary factors: the impedence of the backplane, and the amount of current that can be supplied by the drivers. The impedance of the backplane in turn depends on the connected capacitance. TTL drivers unfortunately have a relatively large capacitance and therefore a fully loaded backplane could have an impedance as low as 20–25 Ω. To achieve a sufficiently large signal at the far end of the backplane therefore requires, optimistically, at least 100 mA drivers. With their heavy power consumption these devices need large transistors to supply the current; the transistors in turn produce a higher output capacitance, reducing the bus impedance even further requiring even more powerful bus drivers.

To overcome this problem, P896 workers have designed a bus driver that tackles its primary cause. Futurebus drivers have a very low output capacitance which keeps the impedance of the fully loaded bus high and so requires a lower current to achieve a given signal amplitude. The drivers and receivers also have well defined and narrow thresholds which keep the voltage swings low, again minimizing the current requirements and also crosstalk between adjacent lines. Practical measurements have in fact shown that crosstalk is negligible with a properly designed backplane.

ADVANTAGES OF STANDARDIZATION

The advantages of using standards are particularly relevant for higher-performance systems. A high-performance system requires a correspondingly high-performance backplane bus and the design of such a critical component is a complex procedure involving trade-offs between many conflicting parameters. Any one manufacturer at a point in time has a preconceived idea as to the optimum balance of these parameters. Unfortunately for the designer, these parameters change with time and as new technologies become economically viable. Standards sponsored by the IEEE, rather than individual manufacturers' *de facto* standards, benefit from a wide range of expertise and are aimed at the widest possible market. The trade-off problems are exaggerated by this wide area of application and hence these standards generally take longer to develop, but the result is that the bus is truly manufacturer independent and, as far as is possible, technology independent.

This implies that the standard can support new devices and improvements in technology as these become available and still achieve a performance limited only by the new technology and by the laws of physics. Furthermore, this new technology can coexist and work alongside older devices. For example, a fast P896 master may currently work with a slow 100 ns access time slave and achieve a data transfer rate of 30 Mbyte s^{-1}. Alternatively the same master, at the next data transfer block, may work with a fast 10 ns access time slave and achieve a data transfer rate of 100 Mbyte s^{-1}. The performance increases smoothly between these two points.

In contrast, a manufacturer's 10 MHz synchronous bus would only achieve 13 Mbyte s^{-1} with the slow slave and would reach its maximum performance of 40 Mbyte s^{-1} with the fast slave.

This gradual increase in hardware performance means that a manufacturer can design a product with today's technology with the assurance that he/she can gradually upgrade the product as higher-performance devices become readily available. This maximizes product life and hence the return on the development costs.

Another important aspect of standards is that products will generally be available from more than one manufacturer. Consequently, a manufacturer can minimize its initial development costs by purchasing products from several sources and concentrating on particular market requirements. Once the product is in full production then bought-out cards can be replaced, if required, by cards optimized for the system. Conversely, the manufacturer can build a standard product and purchase cards outside for special purposes such as analogue and digital I/O.

CONCLUSIONS

It has been argued that there is a growing need for manufacturers and system integrators to build products based on manufacturer and technology independent standards. To a large extent the lower-performance systems are covered by STE (P1000). High-performance systems, however, present a whole new range of problems if they are to be able to keep up with advances in technology. Futurebus tackles seriously most of the problems that exist today and many that will become apparent over the lifetime of the standard. The solutions offered by the bus enable users to achieve a greater degree of manufacturer and technology independence and a markedly higher bus and overall system performance than is possible with other current or proposed bus standards.

Roger Edwards has over 20 years experience in the design of industrial computer systems. He obtained his Masters degree at Queen Mary College, London, UK, and then worked for the English Electric Company and later GEC, designing central processors and high-security computer and telemetry systems. He then spent five years with Leeds and Northrup Ltd before setting up his own consultancy, Advantec Systems Ltd. He is currently chairman of the IEE Computer Standards Working Party on Microprocessor Backplanes.

Using Futurebus in a fifth-generation computer

Simon Peyton Jones describes his design approach to a parallel fifth-generation computer, emphasizing its bus-based architecture

Despite the bandwidth limitations of a bus, a design is presented for a parallel computer (GRIP) based on Futurebus, which limits bus bandwidth requirements by using intelligent memories. Such a machine offers higher performance than a uniprocessor and lower cost than a more extensible multiprocessor, as well as serving as a vehicle for research into parallel architectures.

microsystems   fifth generation   graph reduction   Futurebus

In the future, computer programs will be executed by a large number of processors cooperating in a common task. The design and programming of such parallel machines is a major challenge, and is one of the principal objectives of the fifth-generation computer systems programmes which have sprung up in Japan, the USA and Europe.

The purpose of this paper is to present the architecture of a parallel fifth-generation computer called GRIP (graph reduction in parallel) based around a bus architecture. The main focus is on the hardware aspects of the design, and on the bus in particular, but the paper commences with a discussion of the challenges presented by a parallel architecture. This is followed by a brief overview of functional languages; this is the kind of language which GRIP is specifically designed to execute. Some of the options open to the designer of a parallel machine are discussed. Attention is then focussed onto GRIP and the bus chosen to implement it.

THE CHALLENGE OF PARALLELISM

Cooperation is expensive, yet it is the only way to get large tasks done quickly. This lesson is well illustrated by human organizations. Undoubtedly the most efficient way to get a task done is to assign a single individual to the task. There comes a time, however, when the sheer volume of work is more than a single individual can carry

out in the required period of time, so he/she employs assistants to help. Inevitably the assistants must be told what to do and how to do it, and a proportion of the time of all concerned is spent in internal communication rather than in doing profitable work.

As the company grows, the overheads of internal communication can become very burdensome. The amount of internally generated information grows with the company, but each individual's capacity to digest this information remains fixed. The solution is to partition the work of the company in such a way as to reduce the amount of interaction required between workers, so that they can spend more of their time on profitable work and less on internal communication. This may be easy if the company is engaged in a number of essentially independent activities, but it can be very difficult if the company's activities are highly interrelated.

A primary challenge facing computer architects is the effective exploitation of parallelism. Raw processing power is now cheap, through replication of silicon, but mechanisms for connecting processors together so that they cooperate to achieve a common goal is very difficult. Inextricably connected with this challenge is the challenge of programming a parallel machine, and of partitioning the program in a way that minimizes communication.

In specific application areas it may be fairly easy to partition the problem so as to minimize internal communication. For example, in a multiuser Unix machine it is easy to assign a processor to each process awaiting execution. Less trivially, vector processors such as the Cray-1, or array processors such as the ICL DAP, have an arrangement of processing elements specifically adapted for the efficient execution of vector or array structured problems.

Programming vector or array processors is, however, a highly skilled and somewhat arcane art. In order fully to exploit the parallelism of the machine the programmer needs an intimate understanding of its workings and of the workings of the compiler. The investment required to produce such programs is very large — several of them represent 10 man years of work or more — and small program modifications risk destroying their finely balanced optimizations. Furthermore, such programs are often extremely complex, not because the task is complex, but in order to exploit the architecture most effectively.

Department of Computer Science, University College London, Gower Street, London WC1E 6BT, UK

0141-9331/86/02069–08 $03.00 © 1986 Butterworth & Co. (Publishers) Ltd

An alternative approach is to have a number of processing elements connected together with some kind of network, each independently executing its own program: an MIMD (multiple instruction, multiple data) machine. Such a machine is relatively easy to build, but gives no clues about how best to program it. The problem of dividing the task up into concurrent subtasks, programming these subtasks in a sequential language and arranging the intertask communication is left entirely to the programmer. Even when the program is written it is hard to be sure that it is correct, and concurrency gives much scope for transient and irreproducible bugs which only occur under particular circumstances.

The challenge, then, is to produce a parallel programming system, including both architecture and a programming methodology, which

- is feasible to program; this is the overriding consideration
- is highly concurrent; this allows the developer to buy speed with raw processing power
- minimizes internal communication

FUNCTIONAL LANGUAGES AND GRAPH REDUCTION

Functional languages are fifth-generation programming languages which offer a powerful lever on programming parallel machines. The purpose of this section of the paper is to give a brief overview of where parallelism comes from, to set the rest of the paper in context. For full details of graph reduction, refer to Peyton Jones[1].

Programs written in a functional language can contain implicit parallelism. No new language constructs are required to write a parallel program, and the correctness of a program is no harder to establish than for a sequential functional program. This is in strong contrast with conventional procedural languages such as ADA, which require extra constructs to support parallelism, and where the parallelism has to be completely explicit.

To understand where the parallelism comes from, consider the following functional program

```
let f   x = (x + 1)* (x − 1)
in f   4
```

The 'let' defines a function f of a single argument x, which computes $(x + 1) * (x - 1)$. The program executes by evaluating 'f 4', ie the function f applied to 4. We can think of the program as its parse tree

where the @ stands for function application. Applying f to 4 produces the expression $(4 + 1) * (4 - 1)$, ie

We may now execute the addition and the subtraction simultaneously, giving

Finally the multiplication can be executed, to give the result

15

From this simple example it may be seen that

- Executing a functional program consists of evaluating an expression.
- A functional program has a natural representation as a tree or, more generally, a graph (in the sense of a network rather than a $y = mx + c$ graph).
- Evaluation proceeds by means of a sequence of simple steps, called reductions. Each reduction performs a local transformation of the graph (hence the term 'graph reduction').
- Reductions may safely take place simultaneously at different sites in the graph, since they cannot interfere with each other.
- All communication between processors performing concurrent reductions is implicit, mediated by the graph. No explicit communication between processors is required.
- Evaluation is complete when there are no further reducible expressions.

Graph reduction provides us with a simple and powerful execution model that can form the basis of a parallel implementation. The GRIP multiprocessor is designed to execute functional programs by performing graph reductions concurrently, exactly as described above. Despite the opportunities for parallelism offered by functional languages, only the ALICE project (at Imperial College, London, UK) has so far attempted a parallel implementation in hardware[2].

The smallest unit of concurrent computation is a single reduction, but this is a rather fine grain of parallelism, and there is a danger that the overheads of administering such small units will dominate the execution costs. To avoid this it is desirable (and possible) to choose certain reduction sequences to be the unit of concurrent computation, thus moving towards a coarser grain. The details of the generation, administration, execution and synchronization of concurrent computation are, however, beyond the scope of this paper. (The final chapter of Peyton Jones[1] could serve as a starting point for further reading.)

ARCHITECTURES FOR PARALLEL GRAPH REDUCTION

In this section we will discuss a range of possible architectures for a parallel graph reduction machine. This will set the scene for presentation of the GRIP architecture.

Almost any parallel reduction machine may be thought of as a variation of the scheme shown in Figure 1. The processing elements (PEs) are more or less conventional von Neumann processors, including some private memory.

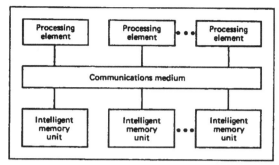

Figure 1. Physical structure of a parallel graph reduction machine

The intelligent memory units (IMUs) are the custodians of the graph, and may or may not also contain a processor.

This rather bland-looking diagram actually covers a huge spectrum of machine architectures. The two major axes along which variations are possible are: the intelligence of the IMUs; and the topology of the communications network.

Intelligence of the IMUs

The amount of intelligence contained in the IMUs has a radical effect on the architecture. The two extremes of the spectrum are as follows.

(1) The IMUs provide only the ability to perform read and write operations to the graph. All the intelligence required to perform reductions on the graph resides in the PEs. Such IMUs could be implemented with conventional memory boards, except that there would need to be some indivisible read–modify–write operation provided to assure mutual exclusion. This results in a classical tightly coupled system, where the graph is held in global memory and every access to the graph by a PE requires use of the communications medium.

(2) The IMUs each contain a sophisticated processor, sufficiently intelligent to perform graph reduction unaided. The PEs are now vestigial, since they have nothing left to do, and can be discarded altogether. This results in a collection of intelligent memories connected by a communications medium, which is a classical loosely coupled system (or distributed system). It is much cheaper for an IMU to access a graph node held in its own local memory than to use the communications medium to access remote nodes.

Between these two extremes there is a continuum of possible architectures. To move from one extreme to the other, imagine migrating functionality from the PEs into the IMUs. Moving along the spectrum, the IMUs become capable of more and more sophisticated functions. As will be seen later, GRIP occupies an intermediate point on the spectrum.

Communications medium

The purpose of the communications medium is to allow the PEs and IMUs to communicate with each other. A large amount of research has been done on optimal

network topologies for various sorts of computer architectures[3, 4], and this paper will do no more than lay out the major design issues, giving appropriate references. We will refer to a PE or an IMU as a box.

Before discussing possible network topologies, the characteristics sought after in the communications medium must first be established. Among these are

- cost — how much the network costs per box
- latency — how long it takes for a transaction to get from sender to recipient through the network
- bandwidth — how many transactions the network can handle simultaneously
- locality — whether or not it is essential that most transactions are local (ie between 'nearby' boxes)
- extensibility — whether the network can be expanded arbitrarily to accommodate more boxes

The sort of networks that are of interest break down into four main types, to be discussed according to the criteria given above.

Bus

A bus is the simplest form of interconnection; in a bus all the PEs and IMUs are connected to a common information highway (Figure 2a). Its cost is linear in the number of boxes, and its latency is roughly independent of the number of boxes. However, only one transaction can take place at a time over a bus, so its bandwidth is fixed and therefore places a fundamental limit on the extensibility of the bus communications medium. (The machine could, however, be extended by connecting together a number of independent buses through gateways, which would produce a hybrid of a bus system and a fully distributed system.) Locality is irrelevant since all boxes are equally accessible.

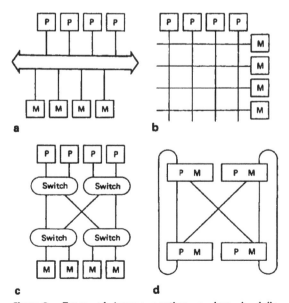

Figure 2. Types of interconnection: a, bus; b, fully connected network; c, partially connected network; d, fully distributed network

Fully connected networks

To avoid the bandwidth limitations of a bus, a crossbar switch (Figure 2b), in which simultaneous connections between any set of pairs of boxes are possible[5], may be considered.

For small numbers of boxes, this arrangement gives constant latency (although the latency becomes linear in the number of boxes for large systems, because the wire length becomes dominant), and no locality is required. Its bandwidth rises linearly with the number of boxes, but unfortunately the number of switch connections rises quadratically with the number of boxes, so its cost is prohibitive.

In theory crossbars are extensible, but their cost means that they are only practicable with rather small numbers of connections (eg 16×16[6,7]).

Partially connected networks

Limited-access partially connected networks are a compromise between buses and crossbars (Figure 2c). They have formed a particularly active focus of research work in recent years[3,5,8]. They are normally multistage networks (ie a message may go through a number of switching elements on its way to its destination) based on various permutation networks (banyan, perfect shuffle, shuffle exchange, omega networks etc).

They offer: a cost of $O(N\log N)$, where N is the number of boxes; a latency of $O(\log N)$; and a bandwidth of $O(N)$. This is a useful compromise between the extremes of buses and crossbars. It may not be possible to establish simultaneous paths between all pairs of boxes requesting one, so in general the latency is not bounded. The probability distribution of latency drops off very sharply, however, and the chances of long latency are very low. They can be reduced further by adding redundant paths; this also gives the possibility of fault tolerance. Again, no locality is required, and these networks are completely extensible in a modular way.

Networks of this sort are used in many machines, such as the NYU Ultracomputer[9], Cedar[10], TRAC[11], the BBN Butterfly[12] and ALICE[13].

Fully distributed networks

The last alternative seems more radical, though it relates closely to the previous one. A fully distributed network provides communications paths from each box to only a limited number of neighbouring boxes (Figure 2d). A box may communicate with a non-neighbouring box only through an appropriate neighbour. The work cited in the previous section is also applicable here, since we can obtain a distributed network from a multistage network by replacing the switching elements with IMUs (which must now also handle the forwarding of messages destined for other boxes).

Some boxes are therefore 'closer' than other boxes, so the latency will be nonuniform; to obtain good performance from such networks it is essential that most transactions take place between nearby boxes. The average latency is $O(N\log N)$, but the constant of proportionality is often considerably greater than for multistage network switching elements. Though the latency is nonuniform, the network can be made isotropic (or homogeneous) in the sense that the network looks the same when viewed from any box (the network has no edges).

The cost of such a distributed network is linear in the number of boxes, since each box normally has a fixed number of links to neighbours. The bandwidth also rises linearly. The networks are, of course, readily extensible.

Burton and Sleep have long advocated such networks as a basis for a reduction machine[14,15]. Recently a number of multiprocessors have become available — some commercially — based on cube-connected cycle networks, eg the CalTech Cosmic Cube[16] and the Intel Cube.

Summary

Table 1 summarizes our conclusions. It is easy to see the reason for the popularity of partially connected networks.

Locality

From Table 1 it is clear that if we could achieve locality then the way would be opened to cheap and extensible fully distributed communications networks. This is no mean feat, however.

The idea of locality is well established in conventional computer architecture. It is an observed property of most programs that they tend to reference data which has either been referenced in the recent past (temporal locality), or which is physically adjacent to recently referenced data (spatial locality)[17]. A conventional cache relies on locality of reference to hold the data in active use in fast memory close to the processor[18].

Functional programs are not so well behaved, since the physical adjacency of two cells bears no relation to their logical adjacency. Nevertheless, some sort of spatial locality is essential for a distributed loosely coupled network; otherwise the processors will spend all their time waiting to communicate rather than computing.

The analogy with a commercial company is again useful. The organization of the company is intended to enable workers to perform their tasks using mostly local communication — within an office, for example. An excessive proportion of nonlocal communication generally indicates an inefficiently organized company.

Locality is a heuristic property of programs, and the best we can hope to do is to develop effective heuristics. This is at present an area more of speculation than experiment, though some simulations have been performed[19,20].

The challenge of achieving locality in the execution of functional programs is at present an unsolved problem. Nevertheless, some researchers have chosen to confront the problem and build distributed machines requiring

Table 1. Comparison of interconnection networks

Type	Cost	Bandwidth	Latency	Locality essential?	Extensible?
Bus	N	1	1	No	No
Crossbar	N^2	N	N	No	Yes
Partially connected	$N\log N$	N	$\log N$	No	Yes
Distributed	N	N	$\log N$	Yes	Yes

locality[21, 22]. The ALICE project has chosen to use an extensible multistage partially connected network[13].

For the GRIP project we have chosen to avoid the problems of locality and the cost of a partially connected network by using a bus architecture. GRIP's architecture is discussed in more detail in the following section.

GRIP — A FUTUREBUS ARCHITECTURE

GRIP is intended to provide state-of-the-art performance at moderate cost by extracting maximum performance from a fast bus. This means that, within its performance range, GRIP should provide more power per unit cost than more extensible designs (such as ALICE). Our performance target for a fully populated GRIP is one million reductions per second.

We have chosen to implement the communications network using a fast bus, the IEEE P896 Futurebus. A bus offers a low-cost interconnection, but with the limitation that only one transaction can take place between a PE and an IMU at once, thus limiting concurrency. This places a fundamental limit on the parallelism achievable using GRIP, but it gives an extremely cost effective solution up to this limit.

The decision to use a bus was a hard one to take because of the inherent inextensibility of the design. However, the use of a bus allows us to address one research issue — parallel reduction — at a time, rather than to try to solve several difficult problems (locality, in particular) at once. By using a bus we therefore expect to produce a machine of higher performance than a uniprocessor, and lower cost than an extensible multiprocessor.

In the case of GRIP we anticipate being able to integrate up to 120 PEs or so, on 30 boards, before running out of bus bandwidth and physical space.

Intelligent memory units

GRIP's IMUs will consist of 1.25 Mbyte of RAM arranged in 40-bit words, with a fairly simple bit-slice microprogrammable processor on the front. Instead of supporting just read and write commands as normal memories do, the IMUs will support an instruction set of high-level operations, chosen to support parallel graph reduction. These operations are the unit of indivisibility supported by GRIP. (All concurrent machines must provide some indivisible operations to assure correct synchronization of parallel activities.) In addition the use of high-level operations reduces the bus bandwidth required to communicate with the IMUs.

The instruction set supported by the IMUs implements a view of memory as an unordered collection of cells. Each cell consists of a pair of 40-bit words, and is further structured as follows.

A cell contains two major fields, the head and tail. In addition, the tag field identifies the type of the cell, and the GC bits assist with garbage collection. The head and tail fields are structured as follows.

An atom:

| 0 | Data |

A pointer:

| 1 | Address of a cell |

Each can be an atomic data item (identified by a zero in the top bit) or a pointer to another cell (identified by a one). Later versions of the IMUs will support variable-length cells.

In addition to managing the cell storage, the IMUs will also be responsible for managing task queues and certain parts of the garbage collection activity. The design of the IMUs will be one of the major technical hardware challenges of the project.

Processing elements

The PEs are autonomous units responsible for performing reductions on the graph held in the IMUs. They will be of straightforward design, based around a microprocessor (eg Transputer, MC68020, NS32332), and will include their own private memory which is inaccessible to the rest of the system. The processor within a PE executes a program held in local memory.

A subsequent version of GRIP might replace a collection of microprocessor-based PEs with a single bit-slice PE, taking up the same board area, but whose architecture was more closely matched to the task of graph reduction. This is the approach taken by the SKIM uniprocessor[23].

Integrating PEs and IMUs

The conceptual architecture calls for distinct PEs and IMUs to plug into the common bus. In fact we propose to use a single board which contains some PEs and an IMU, interfaced to the bus with a common bus interface processor (BIP). The PE and IMU are still logically quite distinct and would operate concurrently on different internal buses. However, transactions which the PE addresses to the IMU that happens to be on its board will be 'short circuited' through, bypassing the BIP altogether.

Such an amalgamation gives an obvious advantage in that only one board and one BIP need be designed, making replication easier. However, it appears to suffer from the disadvantage that the ratio between PEs and IMUs cannot be changed to 'mix and match'.

. The argument to dispel this apparition is as follows. Standard Futurebus boards can be up to treble Eurocard size. This is far bigger than a PE would need — a PE consists only of a microprocessor, a couple of ROMs and some local RAM. It is also bigger than an IMU would need. A 40-chip memory array is the dominant space consumer, and this fits on less than a third of a treble Eurocard. In other words, we could fit several PEs and a respectable IMU on a single board. Other things being equal, this would be far preferable to having large amounts of empty and hence unproductive board area (on the PEs) plugged into the scarcest resource — the bus slots.

Many small IMUs are preferable to a few large ones, to gain maximum parallelism. Amalgamating an IMU with a

PE allows *n* IMUs in an *n*-slot bus, which is clearly the optimum situation. Amalgamation also allows maximization of the number of PEs, which is desirable because we want to have enough PEs to saturate the bus. PEs can always be depopulated to reduce bus loading (and cost). Looked at another way, putting a PE on the same board as an IMU allows up to 2*n* concurrent activities instead of only *n* (or more if there is more than one PE on a board).

As a corollary of amalgamation, it is now relatively easy to allow IMUs to become bus masters as well as slaves. This is useful for packet switching operations (discussed in the next subsection). Another spin off is that is should be possible to exploit to some degree the local access possible from a PE to its fellow IMU. No attempt would initially be made to exploit this locality.

In practice we hope to integrate four PEs and one IMU on each board.

Packet switching

Conventional microprocessor buses use circuit switching techniques. For instance, a memory read operation opens a circuit over the bus to memory that is held open during the entire read cycle, precluding any other unit from using the bus. During the memory access period the bus is inactive, and hence is used inefficiently.

Furthermore, at least some of the high-level memory operations supported by the IMUs will be considerably slower than even a memory read, worsening the inefficiency from circuit switching.

It is well known that packet switching can offer substantially better performance in cases where circuit switching makes inefficient use of the medium. In a packet switching regime a PE initiates a memory operation by writing a transaction request into a transaction buffer in the bus interface. The bus interface then acquires the bus (which might take some time), sends all pending transactions to the transaction buffers in the destination board(s) and relinquishes the bus. The request is then processed by the recipient IMU, which writes a reply transaction into its transaction buffer, whence it is returned to the initiating PE by the same mechanism.

This particular application of packet switching is sometimes known as split cycle bus operation. It makes more efficient use of the bus at the cost of increased overhead for each transaction, and increased latency. Because of these greater overheads we may want to circuit switch for some (fast) memory operations and packet switch for other (slow) ones.

Achieving an implementation of a packet switching protocol without imposing substantial latency on PE–IMU transactions is another of the major hardware challenges of the project.

IEEE P896 FUTUREBUS

Once the decision to use a bus was taken, we looked for a bus with the following characteristics

- high bandwidth, to alleviate the bottleneck as far as possible
- true multimaster capability, to reflect in the hardware the symmetry between the PEs; the arbitration time

should be very short, to allow rapid changes of bus mastership
- the ability to support high-level PE–IMU transactions, not simply read and write
- the ability to support packet switched as well as circuit switched protocols

We chose to use the IEEE P896 Futurebus to meet these objectives, for the following reasons.

- It is the fastest bus available to us. Special bus drivers and a novel backplane design ensure that no 'bus settling time' delays are required.
- It provides an ingenious fully distributed fair arbitration scheme with rapid settling time. Furthermore, arbitration can take place concurrently with data transfer, and so will often be complete by the time the bus is relinquished.
- Its protocols are powerful enough to support a mixture of packet and circuit switching. These protocols are tightly defined and debugged, thus saving the designers a lot of work.
- It can accommodate packet switched as well as circuit switched protocols. In addition, it offers broadcast and broadcall protocols, which turn out to be useful for system synchronization.
- It defines standard racks, backplanes and drivers. Due to careful design the drivers are relatively low powered, and eight of them are available in a single 0.3 in (7.6 mm) package; this gives a high packing density, and allows the drivers to be close to the connector pins.

Overview of Futurebus

This subsection comprises a brief overview of the Futurebus, seen from the standpoint of our machine. For more detail, a special issue of *IEEE Micro*[24] contains several articles about the bus design.

P896 is an asynchronous bus, using a 32-bit multiplexed address and data path. It incorporates a fair distributed bus arbiter for allocating bus access. When transferring multiple data items, it is capable of particularly fast operation by using a two-cycle handshake.

The P896 bus consists of: the address/data bus (34 bit wide); the command bus (5 bit wide, from master to slave); the status bus (3 bit wide, from slave to master); and the arbitration bus (11 bit wide — 7 bit device number, 3 bit + 1 bit control). We expect that a fully loaded bus will be capable of a transfer cycle time of 60–80 ns. Most transactions would transfer data as well as address, thus taking at least two cycles.

Synchronous *vs* asynchronous bus

Certain conventional wisdom has it that a synchronous bus is faster than an asynchronous one, since there are no timing interfaces. A timing interface manages the interaction between two systems running with different clocks, and is a great time waster, since the transmitting side of the interface has to wait for the receiving side's clock edge. Timing interfaces are also sources of latch metastability problems.

In practice, however, the fastest convenient clock speed for the bus is most unlikely to be the same as that for the processors, or the IMUs. This means that synchronous systems often have two timing interfaces. This makes an asynchronous system, which has only one timing interface, a faster bet if it is properly designed.

Asynchronous systems can also exploit actual-case gate and bus propagation times, rather than being tied to the worst case as synchronous systems are.

In order fully to exploit these speed advantages we plan to use an asynchronous finite state machine to control the transfer of data between transaction buffers across the bus.

Cache consistency protocols

Considerable effort has been expended in the Futurebus specification to develop protocols for maintaining multiple consistent caches in each processor, to avoid excessive bus use. These protocols rely on each cache manager 'snooping' on the bus to spot when a data item it holds has been altered by another processor.

Curiously, perhaps, we do not intend to use any of this work in GRIP. There are two reasons why it is not useful to us. First, it is closely tied to a simple read/write memory operation model, and would have difficulty in accommodating the more sophisticated instruction set supported by our IMUs.

Second, once a piece of graph is fully evaluated it can never alter. Hence it can be freely cached by any PE. Conversely, before it is fully evaluated only one PE should be given access to it, since otherwise several PEs would try to evaluate the same graph. Hence the situation in which several PEs might write to a location never arises.

CONCLUSIONS AND PROJECT STATUS

The use of a fast bus has enabled us to exploit a price/performance 'window' in parallel machine design. GRIP will be faster than a uniprocessor, and cheaper than a more extensible multiprocessor. More importantly, it will enable us to address many of the issues of parallel system design without requiring solution of all the problems at once.

The GRIP project is funded by the UK's Alvey directorate as a collaborative project between University College London (UCL), ICL, High Level Hardware Ltd and Research Software Ltd. Three full-time research assistants form the main team based at UCL, and work began in the late autumn of 1985.

We expect to have a working prototype after two years, and to spend the third year of the project tuning the design.

Simon Peyton Jones is a lecturer in computer science at University College London, UK. After graduating from Trinity College, Cambridge, UK, he worked in industrial computing for two years before taking up his present post. His main research interest is in functional programming languages and their implementation, and he is currently leading a team in an Alvey-funded project to design and build a high-performance parallel graph reduction machine called GRIP. He is writing a book[1] about the implementation of functional languages using graph reduction, due for publication in 1986.

REFERENCES

1 **Peyton Jones, S L** *The implementation of functional languages* Prentice Hall, Englewood Cliffs, NJ, USA (to be published)

2 **Darlington, J and Reeve, M** 'ALICE — a multiprocessor reduction machine for the parallel evaluation of applicative languages' *Proc. ACM Conf. Functional Programming Languages and Computer Architecture, NH, USA* (October 1981) pp 65–75

3 **Feng, T** 'A survey of interconnection networks' *IEEE Comput.* (December 1981) pp 12–27

4 **Thurber, K J and Masson, G M** *Distributed processor communication architecture* Gower, Farnborough, UK (1979)

5 **Broomell, G and Heath, J R** 'Classification categories and historical development of circuit switching topologies' *ACM Comput. Surv.* Vol 15 No 2 (June 1983) pp 95–134

6 **Wulf, W and Bell, C** 'C.mmmp — multi-miniprocessor' *AFIPS Proc. (FJCC)* Vol 41 No 2 (1972) pp 765–777

7 **Farmwald, P M** 'The S-1 Mark IIa supercomputer' in **Kowalik** (Ed.) *High speed computations* Springer Verlag, Berlin, FRG (1984)

8 **Siegel, H J** 'Interconnection networks for SIMD machines' *IEEE Comput.* (June 1979) pp 57–65

9 **Gottlieb, A et al** 'The NYU Ultracomputer — designing a MIMD shared memory parallel computer' *IEEE Trans. Comput.* Vol 32 No 2 (February 1983) pp 175–189

10 **Gajski, D et al** 'Cedar' *Proc. Compcon* (1984) pp 306–309

11 **Brown, J C** 'TRAC — an environment for parallel computing' *Proc. Compcon* (1984) pp 294–298

12 **Butterfly parallel processor overview** Bolt Beranek Newman (BBN) Laboratories, USA (June 1985)

13 **Cripps, M D and Field, A J** *An asynchronous structure-independent switching system with system-level fault tolerance* Dept of Computer Science, Imperial College, London, UK (1983)

14 **Burton, F W and Sleep, R** 'The zero assignment parallel processor (ZAPP) project' *Proc. Symp. Functional Languages and Computer Architecture, Goteborg, Sweden* (June 1981)

15 **Burton, F W and Sleep, R** 'Executing functional programs on a virtual tree of processors' *Proc. ACM Symp. Functional Languages and Computer Architecture, Portsmouth, UK* (October 1981)

16 **Seitz, C L** 'The cosmic cube' *CACM* Vol 28 No 1 (January 1985) pp 22–33

17 **Denning, P J** 'On modelling program behaviour' *Proc. Spring Joint Computer Conf. 40* AFIPS Press, USA (1972) pp 937–944

18 **Smith, A J** 'Cache memories' *ACM Comput. Surv.* Vol 14 No 3 (September 1982) pp 473–530

19 **Keller, R M and Lin, F C H** 'Simulated performance of a reduction based multiprocessor' *IEEE Comput.* Vol 17 No 7 (July 1984) pp 70–82

20 **Hudak, P and Goldberg, B** 'Distributed execution of functional programs using serial combinators' *IEEE Trans. Comput.* (September 1985)

21 **Hudak, P** *Functional programming on multiprocessor architectures — a survey of research in progress* Dept of Computer Science, Yale University, Newhaven, CT, USA (November 1985)

22 **Keller, R M** 'Rediflow architecture prospectus' *TR UUCS-85-105* Dept of Computer Science, University of Utah, USA (August 1985)

23 **Clarke, T J W, Gladstone, P J S, Maclean, C D and Norman A C** 'SKIM — the S K I reduction machine' *Proc. ACM Lisp Conf., Stanford, CA, USA* (1980)

24 Special issue on bus standards *IEEE Micro* Vol 4 No 4 (August 1984)

Introduction to the Fastbus

Conceived in the late 1970s as a standard data acquisition system for physics experiments, Fastbus is now in full commercial production. **David Gustavson** presents the original design goals of the bus and its subsequent implementation

Fastbus is a modular data bus system for data acquisition and data processing. It is a multiprocessor system with multiple bus segments which operate independently but link together for passing data. It operates asynchronously to accommodate very high and very low speed devices over long or short paths, using handshake protocols for reliability. It can also operate synchronously with pipelined handshakes for transfer of data blocks at maximum speed. The paper summarizes the goals, history and motivation for the Fastbus. The structure of the Fastbus system is described in general and some details of its operation are introduced.

microsystems   backplane bus standards   Fastbus

In 1975, several physicists active in high-energy elementary particle physics asked the US NIM (nuclear instrumentation modules) committee to consider development of a standard data acquisition system which would meet the needs of future physics experiments and which would also be of general utility. The NIM committee established a study group to examine the needs and determine objectives to be met by such a system. In 1977, a committee was formed to begin the design of a system which would meet these goals. The design and prototyping efforts were supported by the US Department of Energy.

The design committee essentially completed its work in 1983, publishing the Fastbus specification as Department of Energy report *DOE/ER-0189*. Fastbus became ANSI–IEEE standard 960 in 1984[1]. At the time of writing, Fastbus has reached routine commercial production; catalogues of off-the-shelf Fastbus equipment are available from several vendors. Committee work continues, now mainly focussed on standards for software supporting Fastbus.

The goals of the Fastbus design were

● highest possible speed, to handle the high data rates

Stanford University Linear Accelerator Center, PO Box 4349, Stanford, CA 94305, USA

encountered in complex particle detectors and to reduce the temptation to design custom systems for each application

● lowest possible cost, because huge volumes of electronics are required in modern experimental physics and any unnecessary cost is multiplied by a large factor

● modular construction, so that useful standard building blocks can be developed which can then be connected in various ways to meet the needs of various projects

● general utility, so that commercial use outside the physics community will raise vendor volume and lower user costs; and no special physics features which interfere with general-purpose use in other markets

● complete system design, including: power distribution and heat removal adequate for large high-speed systems; diagnostic facilities to speed discovery location and correction of faults; operating and maintenance aids such as rear access for cabling, machine readable module identifiers, standardized control and status registers

● multiple-processor organization, so that many low-cost computing elements can be brought to bear on parts of the data acquisition and analysis problem

● segmented organization, so that the multiple processors will not be overly limited by the bus bandwidth; segments of the bus should operate independently, joining together automatically as needed for passing data

● asynchronous operation, so that slow and fast modules can be mixed in the system, and so that the system speed can increase easily as technology advances

● synchronous operation, so that data transfer can occur at the full bandwidth capability of the transfer medium when ultimate performance is needed

● uniform protocols, so that no protocol translation is needed as data flows from segment to segment (Fastbus uses cable segments to join segment interconnect modules residing on backplane segments. CAMAC — IEEE 583, Fastbus's predecessor — used a branch-highway cable connecting crate controllers. The branch cable used a different protocol to that of the crate backplane.)

0141-9331/86/02077-09 $03.00 © 1986 Butterworth & Co. (Publishers) Ltd

- uniform addressing, so that each device can have as much address space as it needs, with no dedicated positions on backplanes: devices have an address which is unique in a connected system and which is independent of device position within a segment; all positions are equal in capability
- position-dependent addressing; this is needed, at least during system initialization, for addressing a module to tell it its assigned position-independent address
- sparse data scanning capability, because the relevant data is usually a tiny fraction of the data available (Most elements of a large detector are not hit by any particles at all in a typical event.)

These goals, though partially conflicting, have been met to a remarkable degree by the Fastbus design.

HARDWARE AND ORGANIZATION OF THE FASTBUS SYSTEM

The essential part of the Fastbus design is the bus protocol. Various electrical and mechanical implementations are possible which use this protocol and hence are easy to interface to one another, but only one electrical implementation and one module design have been chosen for standardization. However, module dimensions are specified so that the same module can be used in an air cooled or in a conduction cooled (water cooled) crate.

The most common implementation consists of a crate which fits in a standard 19 in (48 cm) rack, with a multilayer backplane at the rear and card guides at the top and bottom as shown in Figures 1 and 2. Cooling air flows vertically from bottom to top through the crate, driven by separate fan units which may serve several stacked crates. Water cooled rechillers can be mounted between crates as necessary. The design capacity of 2000 W per crate seems easily accommodated, and with care 3000 W is possible.

A crate holds 26 modules (Figures 3 and 4) which consist of circuit boards of approximately 366.7 mm (14.437 in) high by 400.0 mm (15.748 in) long, with optional front panels about 16 mm (0.63 in) wide. The rear edge of the boards has two box connectors which mate with square pins that protrude from the backplane. The main bus connector has two rows of 65 positions on 2.54 mm (0.1 in) centres. An optional auxiliary connector

has up to three rows of 65 positions, and connects to long 'nonbussed' pins which pass through the backplane so that user cabling can be attached to the backplane rather than to the module. Small card guides are optionally provided on the rear of the crate to aid connector alignment and cable retention.

The main connector supplies power and ground as well as signals, with one ground to every four signals. Power is distributed by heavy layers of copper in the backplane, providing for 300 A at +5 V and −5.2 V, 200 A

Figure 2. Fastbus crate and modules

Figure 3. SLAC snoop module

Figure 4. SLAC Mark II/SLC drift chamber postamplifier module

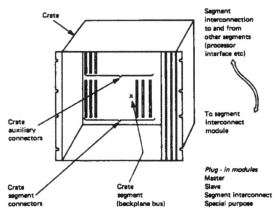

Figure 1. Basic Fastbus elements

Crate

Crate auxiliary connectors

Crate segment connectors

Crate segment (backplane bus)

Segment interconnection to and from other segments (processor interface etc)

To segment interconnect module

Plug - in modules
Master
Slave
Segment interconnect
Special purpose

at −2 V, 50 A at +15 V and −15 V, and 100 A at +28 V. A quiet analogue ground line is also provided. Power supplies are separate from crates, connected by remote sensing cables. Typically they will be mounted in the rear of the rack. The ±15 V and ±28 V supplies are optional.

Bus terminators and a small amount of logic associated with bus arbitration, broadcast timing and geographical addressing reside on small boards mated to extended main connector pins on the back of the backplane in the end positions. All bus signals are emitter coupled logic (ECL 10k) levels.

SEGMENTATION

The backplane bus in a single crate is a single segment, ie corresponding pins in all backplane connectors are directly connected by printed circuit traces, which means that the bus can be driven by only one device at a time. Thus, although multiple processors may be plugged into the crate and share the single backplane bus, they must take turns using it. An arbitration mechanism determines which processor can access the bus. Contention for the use of the bus may reduce the throughput of the system by causing processors to wait.

Distributing the processors among several crates reduces the contention problem if the data they need for operation is similarly distributed, but occasionally they will need access to shared data. In a Fastbus system, there may be many segments that operate independently most of the time, but which are temporarily linked together by segment interconnect modules when necessary for intersegment data transfers.

The cables which interconnect backplane segments are segments themselves, and may contain devices other then segment interconnect modules. Devices on cable segments obey the Fastbus protocols, but must provide their own power because power is not included in the cables. The term 'device' will often be used instead of 'module' to emphasize the logical similarity of devices, whether they fit in crates and attach to backplanes, or have arbitrary shapes and locations and attach to cable segments.

To transfer data, a device must first gain the right to use its bus segment via the arbitration mechanism, then assert onto the bus lines the address of the device with which it wants to communicate. After communication is established, the address is removed and the bus lines are used for transferring data either to (reading) or from (writing) the originating device.

Segment interconnect modules monitor activity on the two segments they connect, awaiting the appearance of any address in a set of addresses which they have been programmed to recognize. They respond to such an address by requesting use of their other segment and asserting the given address on that segment when they gain control. The two segments remain locked together until the operation is complete. An arbitrary number of segments can be linked successively as needed for a given operation. The programmed address contains all the information needed to direct the appropriate segment interconnects to respond and form the correct connection.

To use the address to provide the routing information in a practical way, the total address space available to the system is divided among the segments in such a way that the most significant bits of the address are sufficient to specify which segment is addressed. Every device on a given segment then has the same value for the high-order part of its address, and that value can be thought of as the segment number. The less significant bits serve to specify which device on the given segment is addressed, while the least significant bits specify the part or function within the device which is addressed.

The segment interconnect modules can thus be implemented simply by using the high-order address bits to address an internal memory which contains a 1 in the locations corresponding to addresses which are to be recognized and passed, and a 0 in the other locations. When the system is initialized, these memories are loaded with the patterns needed to route all operations correctly. The internal memories are called 'route tables', though actual connection routes are only determined by combination of all the route table memories in the system.

With this scheme there are no restrictions on the kinds of interconnection which may be made between segments. Segments may be connected in a tree structure with a big computer at the trunk and data acquisition devices at the leaves, for example. If heavy traffic between two widely separated segments causes excessive interference with the intermediate segments, a cable segment can be added which bypasses the intermediate segments. No device address changes are required for this change, and once the route tables in the segment interconnects are reinitialized to make use of the new route, the interfering traffic will disappear from the formerly intermediate segments. Tree, star and ring structures can all be accommodated. Figure 5 shows an example of a simple tree connection.

However, some rules must be obeyed when setting up the route table information for the segment interconnects. For example, only one interconnect module may respond to any given address on a segment, since there must be only one path used for a given operation. A procedure has been developed for creating the routing information

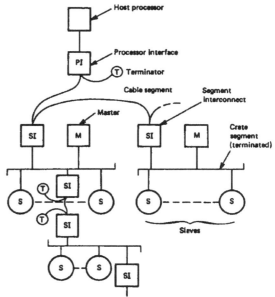

Figure 5.   Example of Fastbus system topology

automatically, which makes it easy to reconfigure the system as needs change. Dedicated systems which do not change may avoid the need for route table initialization by storing the necessary route information in permanent ROMs.

PROTOCOL

The Fastbus uses the same 32-bit parallel bus (AD) for addressing and for data transfer, by time multiplexing. It may seem strange to multiplex address and data in a system which strives for ultimate speed, but it turns out that the speed penalty is not nearly as great as is usually supposed, because the data cannot be used until address recognition is complete. The reduction in the number of bus lines, connections and transceivers results in significant economic and reliability advantages for multiplexing. To achieve maximum speed for data transfer, block transfer modes have been developed in which a single address word is followed by many data words, making the time penalty for multiplexing address and data insignificant.

To initiate a transfer, a master device asserts the slave's address on the 32 AD lines followed by the address strobe (AS), as shown in Figure 6. (A master is a device which initiates an operation by arbitrating to acquire control of the bus and then asserting an address. A slave is a device which responds to the address on the bus. A device may be able to act either as a master or as a slave at different times.) The address assertion sets up the path between master and slave, through segment interconnect modules if necessary. When the slave recognizes its own address, it responds with the address acknowledge signal AK.

AS and AK remain asserted until completion of the transfer, and serve to lock other users off the bus and cause them to ignore all bus activity. In fact, once the connection is established and the AS–AK lock is complete, the two devices could do almost anything with most other lines on the bus and no other devices would be disturbed. To facilitate the construction of compatible devices, however, standard protocols for most useful transfers have been specified.

When the master sees the AK response, it knows that the address information is no longer needed and removes it from the bus. It now asserts data and the data strobe DS, in case of a Write operation, waiting for the acknowledging DK from the slave before removing the data. For a Read operation, DS is asserted along with the read line RD as shown in Figure 6. The slave responds with data and DK. The transfer ends when the master sees DK and records the data on the AD lines, removes its signals including DS and AS, and the slave, seeing AS removed, removes its

signals including AK. The connection between master and slave always has full handshaking at the beginning and end of a transfer.

The transfer of single data words requires two strobe edges, the assertion of DS and then its removal. In effect, the first edge controls the assertion of data and the second edge controls its removal. This restores the bus to an undriven condition after each cycle, so that the direction of flow can be reversed between two cycles, as shown in Figure 7. Block transfers sacrifice the possibility of quick reversal and double the transfer rate by using both strobe edges to transfer data, as shown in Figure 8, without restoring the bus to its undriven condition until the very end of the block. Note that this is still a full handshake, so that the transfer cannot proceed without the agreement of both parties.

However, it is also possible to perform a block transfer with pipelined handshake, between devices which can handle the same data rates. In the case of a write, the master simply asserts data words and DS transitions at whatever rate is appropriate, without waiting for the DK responses. In effect, DS becomes a clock which the slave uses to find the data words in a synchronous transmission. For a read, the master sends DS and the slave replies with data and DK; the master uses each DK transition to find the data words in the received stream of signals. Handshake protected transfers require each data word to be on the bus for at least two bus-propagation delays, while the data flows to its destination and the acknowledge flows back to the source. On long cable segments, this delay can be significant, limiting system throughput. When pipelined handshake is used, however, several data words can be flowing through the bus transmission lines at once. With pipelined handshake, data can be transmitted at the full bandwidth capacity of the medium.

In most cases, transfers will use handshake protection. The handshake permits either party to pause for a moment if necessary (perhaps for refreshing dynamic memory chips), and allows either party to terminate an operation early (eg if a buffer overflows) with both parties having full knowledge of how many words were successfully transmitted. Transfers with pipelined handshake require the master to know the capabilities of the slave and the bandwidth of the entire path in order to choose a workable DS clock rate. If the transfer does not push this

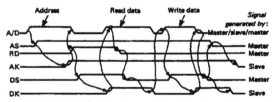

Figure 7. Address locked operation: Read–Modify–Write (as seen by master)

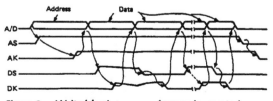

Figure 8. Write block transfer (as seen by master)

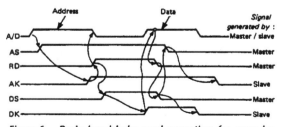

Figure 6. Basic handshake read operation (as seen by master)

rate near its limit, one could just as well have used full handshake protection and not had the worry.

The information that controls whether handshake or pipelined handshake is to be used and whether a block transfer (using both strobe edges) is to occur is encoded on two additional lines, the mode select (MS) lines. The MS code is also used with the address, to specify broadcast or normal addressing and to select normal data space or control register space access. Status information is supplied by the slave for each cycle, encoded on three SS lines, to inform the master of errors or unusual conditions. The MS lines act like extra AD lines which always carry address or data modifier information from master to slave, timed like address or write data. The SS lines always carry information from slave to master, timed like read data. Thus every cycle has timing compatible with both Write and Read, the only difference being the direction in which information is flowing on the AD lines.

ADDRESS-LOCKED AND ARBITRATION-LOCKED OPERATIONS

The transfers described above can be generalized to allow data flow to reverse direction without breaking the connection. For example, a read-modify-write operation as shown in Figure 7 asserts address, reads data, turns the AD lines around again by removing the RD signal, and writes the modified data back to the slave. Such a transfer is uninterruptable by any other processor, since it is locked the whole time by the AS–AK lock and no other device can use the bus. It thus forms the kind of indivisible operation needed in multiple-processor systems for coordinating use of shared resources.

This idea can be extended to even more complex operations, so long as master and slave agree on the meaning of each bus cycle. For example, the address which connects master and slave could be followed by a data word which the slave interprets as an internal address or special command, followed by another data word which the slave interprets as data. One of the MS codes is assigned the meaning 'internal address' to aid in this interpretation. Such a cycle is called a 'secondary address cycle' and is used frequently in the standard protocols, especially for accessing control and status registers.

Operations of this sort are referred to as address-locked operations. Note that the individual data words usually will not be sent as a block transfer, since the possibility of turning the bus around between words is being maintained, and the time needed for that is provided by the alternate edges of the data strobes. However, block transfers may be included within address-locked operations.

A still more general kind of transfer on the bus is called an arbitration-locked operation sequence. It consists of a series of (possibly complicated) address-locked operations, between which the master does not release the bus for arbitration, so no other master can get control. This can be very useful for synchronizing a set of slave devices which are shared by several processors so that a coherent set of operations can be performed without interference from other processors.

This mechanism even works if the slave devices are on various different segments, because the segment interconnect is designed to maintain any connection until the originating master gives up its bus, even if the current operation is not passing through that segment interconnect. This behaviour reduces system throughput, but is essential for solving the multiprocessor, multisegment resource management problem efficiently. Such behaviour can be avoided when it is not needed merely by allowing the master to release the bus after each access.

GEOGRAPHICAL ADDRESSING

In systems of any significant size, the amount of effort involved in correctly setting all module addresses by manual switches is unacceptably large. Furthermore, some means of automatically determining the locations of modules is needed, if only for use as a record or a check. When a system without switches is first turned on, the control registers which will contain the module address information are initialized randomly. Some other mechanism of addressing the modules is needed to load the device address register with the proper contents.

An addressing mechanism has been included in the Fastbus which allows a module to be accessed by its location in the system, or by its 'geographical' address rather than by its normal or 'logical address'. The geographical address of a location on a segment is the position or slot number of the location. The geographical address of a segment is given by the high-order bits assigned to addresses on that segment (as determined by segment interconnect route table entries). Thus the geographical address of a particular module in the system is given by the appropriate high-order bits specifying the segment, many intermediate zero bits, and five low-order bits specifying the position or slot number on the segment.

For economic reasons, addresses of this type are recognized by a geographic address controller packaged with the terminators at one end of the bus, which generates an EG (enable geographic) signal on the segment. Individual modules seeing EG compare the low-order address bits with the slot number as coded on five pins provided by the backplane and connector. It is permissible for modules to implement only this form of addressing, which makes them simple. Actually, the eight low-order address bits are used for geographic addressing, allowing for the combination of several physical crates into one logical crate, but only five bits are encoded in each backplane. On cable segments, no EG signal is provided and devices must decode the entire geographic address themselves. The cable 'geographic' address must be set by switches in the device.

The geographical addressing mechanism can be used to access the control and information registers in un-initialized devices so that an automatic procedure can be used to initialize them.

CONTROL AND STATUS REGISTER ADDRESSING

Certain registers and functions in devices need to be separated from the normal data registers in a way which provides some protection from accidental access and which does not interfere with the allocation of addresses to the normal data portions of the devices. For example, two memory devices should be able to have their addresses set so that the memories are adjacent in address space, allowing them to be used as one larger memory. However, they may contain control registers and status registers associated with logical address assignment, memory protection, or error detection and correction, and these registers must also be accessible in some way. Furthermore, it is desirable that devices have basic status and information registers in standard locations so that standard shared programs like the system initializer can find them easily.

The method chosen to accomplish this is a special case of the address-locked transfer. The device is selected by its address, with additional information on the MS lines to specify that this is really a control/status access. The first data word, called a 'secondary address' cycle and labelled by a special MS code, is the number of the internal control and status register (CSR), and the second is the data to be read or written. This three-cycle transfer provides a full 32-bit address for use within a device, providing sufficient address space to be allocated easily in standard ways. The more complex devices should include at least a ROM containing information about the device and its properties, which can be used by programs and people to make managing large systems easier. A large block of addresses within the device has been reserved for this purpose, and a file and directory structure has been defined. Standard locations have also been specified for all the usual control and status bits. One register is mandatory in all devices, containing a device identification code and several other useful bits.

With this scheme, the CSRs of any device in the system are easy to find. Either the device's geographical address or any logical address that it responds to may be used to establish contact, whereupon the desired register can be accessed via a secondary address cycle.

BROADCAST OPERATIONS

A broadcast operation is one in which a single master sends information to multiple slaves. Broadcasts can be used to synchronize devices or clear a bank of counters. Since more than one slave may be involved, no handshake between slave and master is possible. However, a system handshake has been devised which informs the master that its command has propagated to every segment to which it was addressed. The master asserts an address with a code on the MS lines indicating that a broadcast is to occur. The address may refer to a specific segment or may refer to all connected segments in a pattern controlled by the route tables in the segment interconnects, or it may specify all segments beyond a given segment in that predefined pattern.

The general address used for broadcasting has zero in its most significant bit positions, so that the route table entries corresponding to the zero address are used for routing broadcasts. For this entry, more than one segment interconnect may recognize the address and pass it on, since no handshakes are to be returned. The pattern formed by the pathways propagating from the broadcast master must form a simple tree with no cross connections, another rule to be applied by the initialization program.

When the broadcast address has propagated successfully throughout the system, the system handshake occurs and the master asserts the control register number to which it wishes to broadcast, following the protocol of the CSR addressing discussed above. When the system handshake is returned, the control data is asserted. Thus, any kind of standard control operation may be performed

simultaneously on a large set of devices by a broadcast. Broadcasts may also be made to ordinary data space, using a secondary-address data cycle to select the appropriate internal data location in the selected devices. (The address used for broadcast has no room for this information, and each device is at a different address anyway.) Data space broadcasts are rarely useful unless one of the selective broadcast modes is used, or the scope of the broadcast is limited to a part of the system containing many identical devices. Broadcast read (broadcall) is also permitted, but is only useful under special conditions because it results in the logical OR of the data provided by every selected device.

Broadcasts may take some time to start, since they must wait for completion of all conflicting use of the segments involved. Applications requiring very fast response to signals from a central controller may have to resort to direct cables, since there is no way to achieve fast response in a reliable way in a multiple-segment system. Once the system connection is complete, however, speed of execution of the data cycles is limited only by signal propagation delay, so a reasonably synchronous execution of the command is achieved. At least, one can be certain that all devices will see the command before any other bus operations occur.

SPARSE DATA SCANS AND THE T PIN

The Fastbus design includes a pin called the 'T' pin, which connects inside the backplane to the AD bus line corresponding to the module position number. Thus, a module in position 12 finds its T pin connected to AD12, for example. The T pin thus can be used for positional information.

The T pin was originally included in the Fastbus to provide a means for rapidly scanning sparse data in detector front-end modules. A controller on the backplane broadcasts a command to the front-end modules which causes them to assert their T pins if they contain data. The resulting pattern on the AD lines immediately shows the controller which modules need to be read out, thus avoiding the overhead of polling them one at a time. Other useful broadcast operations using the T pin have been defined, for discovering which crate positions are occupied or which devices are asserting the service request line. The T pin is simulated on cable segments.

INTERRUPTS ON THE FASTBUS

An interrupt is a request from some device to a processor for service or attention. Since interrupts may have to cross segment boundaries, and since they must carry information, they are handled by normal Fastbus operations. The interrupting device addresses an interrupt sensing control register in the processor, and writes its own address and possibly other information into the register. The processor then has all the information it needs to find the interrupting device and service it at later time.

In some systems, large numbers of simple devices may need to signal a request for service without having the capability of gaining bus mastership and performing an interrupt write. Within a single segment, such devices may assert a service request (SR) line. This can be monitored by a special interrupt service device which does have the circuitry to gain mastership and find the requester, whether by means of the T pin or by polling or some other means. The interrupt service device may then perform the necessary service itself, or it may send a normal interrupt message on behalf of the simple requester to some other processor. The SR lines may be passed through selected segment interconnect modules as well, allowing multiple-crate extensions of the simple SR system where appropriate.

ARBITRATION FOR BUS MASTERSHIP

Since several devices on a segment may wish to become master of the segment, some means is needed to prevent more than one device using the bus at any time. Ten lines on the bus are dedicated to the solution of this problem. Six of the lines are used to hold a 'priority' code that determines which competing device wins mastership, while the other four are used to synchronize the requests. The arbitration mechanism operates in parallel with use of the bus, so that little time need be wasted in switching from one master to another.

At a given time, each requester tries to assert its priority on the AL (arbitration level) lines. The lines perform a 'wire OR' function, so that any asserting requester overrides nonasserting requesters at each bit position. Each requester compares its level bit by bit with the level on the AL lines, from most to least significant. If it sees an AL line asserted which it did not assert, it removes its assertions of all less significant bits, because it knows that a higher priority requester is competing. After four bus propagation delays, only the highest arbitration level remains asserted and each requester knows whether it has won or lost.

Of the 64 possible levels, zero is not used because it is easily confused with an idle bus, 1–31 are available for use within the segment, and 32–63 are used as 'super' priorities which must be assigned uniquely throughout an entire connected system. The normal levels 1–31 must be assigned uniquely to devices within a given segment, but exist on every segment to be used over and over again. When a segment interconnect connects a master to another segment, the arbitration level used on the second segment will normally be the local level of the segment interconnect module rather than that of the originating master. However, if one of the super priorities was used by the master, the segment interconnect will propagate that level onto the second segment, which it is free to do since the super priorities are unique within the system. The super priorities can be useful in preventing undue delay for important broadcasts, and can help to expedite important messages which otherwise may suffer from fluctuating levels as they form paths through the system.

The current master determines when it will be finished with the bus, and releases the arbitration circuitry so that the next master can be selected before it finishes. It thus maintains ownership of the bus as long as it likes, which is the mechanism used to implement the arbitration-locked operations discussed above.

An 'assured access' protocol is also available, which provides a kind of round-robin access to the bus, avoiding 'bus hogging' by high priority devices. Assured access works by preventing a master from reapplying for mastership, once it has had it, until no other applicants remain. Most devices should use assured access in normal operation of a system, but the choice is up to the system configurer. Priority access can be mixed with assured access as appropriate — the priority devices simply apply for mastership and join the arbitration process whenever they wish.

The term 'priority' is somewhat misleading, because there is no mechanism to allow a high-priority device to preempt or force a lesser one off the bus. In a lightly loaded system, 'first come, first served' is the dominant mode of behaviour. The arbitration level only serves to break ties when simultaneous requests for use of the bus occur, or when requests become synchronized as a result of waiting for passing traffic. Thus arbitration priority should not be confused with the kind of priority which may apply to multitasking executive programs or computer interrupt systems which allow nesting.

DEADLOCK PREVENTION IN MULTIPROCESSOR SYSTEMS

Deadlock is a fundamental problem which must be solved in multiprocessor systems, caused by conflicting exclusive access requirements of processors for multiple resources. Fastbus provides some tools which help to solve this problem, eg address-locked operations allow reliable testing and setting of semaphores without interference by other processors. A 'user address register' allows administration of resource ownership in a distributed cooperative system without requiring a central software resource manager. Especially important in large systems, segment interconnects hold any paths which they establish until the master which originated the connection gives up the bus to another master. This allows one master to block access by any other to critical resources located on several other segments, to gather all the necessary resources and protect them before it begins taking any irreversible actions — if it cannot get access to all the required resources it releases the bus and tries again later.

When avoidance fails, Fastbus relies on a 'time out' to resolve deadlocks: a master that cannot gain access to resources gives up, waits for a random length of time and then tries again.

DIAGNOSTIC NETWORK

Diagnosing problems in a complex system with multiple bus segments requires powerful tools to set up tests and gather information from multiple sources; then to bring it together for analysis and display. Because the Fastbus interconnect system might be the point of failure, and because it is desirable to be able to collect information about the system without disturbing it, a secondary information path is needed.

Fastbus has allocated two lines in the backplane for use by a diagnostic serial network. The protocols have not yet been standardized, but the principles are clear. The network must be robust, easy to connect, available everywhere in the system, inexpensive and versatile. Two modules on the same backplane should be able to communicate just as well as modules that are widely separated. This can be achieved by using an Ethernet-like scheme, with every module transmitting on the TX serial line while listening to the RX serial line. The TX line is a normal wire-OR backplane signal line which is received by a network interface attached to the back of the backplane. (Eventually this should be part of the terminator/ancillary logic board.) The interface drives a network coaxial cable via isolating transformers, and also receives cable signals and drives the RX line with them. Thus the TX signal from any module on any backplane is visible at every module position in the system, on the RX line. The network cable must visit cable-segment devices individually as needed.

To make the cabling convenient, to reduce restrictions on cable flexibility, length and quality, and to reduce board space requirements in devices that wish to use the network, the data rate must be rather modest.

Work is underway at Stanford Linear Accelerator Center (SLAC), USA, on an implementation of the AppleTalk network, used primarily by the Apple Macintosh and LaserWriter, as a prototype diagnostic network. It operates at 230 400 bit s^{-1} and needs only half of a Zilog SCC 8530 communications chip in each device. Apple-Talk has about the right combination of attributes for this application.

The prototype implementation is being done in the SLAC Fastbus Snoop Module[2], a sort of specialized fast logic analyser which understands Fastbus protocols, can store a history of bus activity, set traps and triggers and act as a master to exercise remote parts of the system for test purposes.

CABLE SEGMENTS

The Fastbus cable segment contains all the protocol and data lines needed for full Fastbus operation. It does not carry power, daisy chains, T pins, geographical address encoding pins, serial network lines or free-use lines. The geographical address encoding must be provided by switches and the T pin connection must be simulated in the devices which attach to the cable segment. Otherwise, devices connected to cable segments act just like devices (modules) connected to backplane segments.

The wire-OR behaviour of certain Fastbus lines (especially the arbitration lines) is fundamental to the protocol. Wire-OR in the usual style (as used on the backplane segments) has certain unavoidable limitations[3] caused by the use of voltage-driver technology. On the backplane, circuit delays are used to overcome these problems, but on long cable segments this solution would cause unacceptable delays.

A new transceiver technology was therefore developed for use on Fastbus cable segments; this uses current drivers and voltage receivers to completely eliminate wire-OR problems. The signals from multiple drivers simply add, the laws of linear superposition applying, and the receivers are comparators which only need to discriminate between 0 and one or more logic levels. In addition, long cables are especially vulnerable to electrical noise, ground potential differences etc, so the cable segment uses differential signalling to cancel out these effects. The resulting system behaves in a nearly ideal way. Present implementations use hybrid technology for the transceivers, but monolithic technology is already capable of the required performance so fully integrated transceivers should eventually be available.

CONCLUSION

The Fastbus design has evolved over a seven-year period into a simple and cost-effective system that can solve a broad spectrum of problems. Its ability to cope with extremely fast as well as slow devices, its expandability, parallelism, modularity and multiprocessor support commend it for a wide range of applications.

Recent experience at CERN involving bids on large systems (private communication from Henk Verwij) reveals that Fastbus has begun to show its expected economic advantage. The cost of usable module area (after subtracting system interface overheads etc) for a complete system including power and cooling was found to be: SWFr 0.33 cm^{-2} for Fastbus, SWFr 0.55 cm^{-2} for CAMAC and SWFr 0.75 cm^{-2} for VME. VME is considered by many to be very inexpensive, so this result shows Fastbus in a good light. Further improvements are expected when Fastbus designs begin using LSI gate-array interface chips which are now available.

FURTHER READING

The status of the Fastbus is reported annually at the IEEE Nuclear Science Symposium. The symposium proceedings are published as the *IEEE Transactions on Nuclear Science*[4,5] each February. For current information, contact Louis Costrell, Chairman, US NIM Committee, National Bureau of Standards, Center for Radiation Research, Washington, DC 20234. Tel: (301) 921-2518.

Several useful articles discuss bus signal propagation[6], arbitration[7] and protocol[8], in particular for the IEEE P896 Futurebus, but that bus has some similarity to Fastbus and the physics problems are the same.

The Fastbus solution to the bus driving problem was the use of ECL 10k transceivers, which behave almost exactly like the new transceivers described by Balakrishnan[6] except that they operate at different voltage levels. Fastbus arbitration behaves just like the system described by Taub[7] except that the control mechanism is different. Signal diagrams for other buses are usually upside down compared to Fastbus, because ECL 10k signals perform the wire OR going positive while most other systems perform wire OR going negative (ie any transmitter being active pulls the signal low).

ACKNOWLEDGMENTS

This paper supersedes an earlier version published in 1980[9]. Several figures were taken from the Fastbus specification[1]. Helmut Walz and Louis Costrell were also helpful in providing figures. The author is grateful to Jerry Friedman and Ray Larsen for encouragement and support, and to Johannes Joemann and David Gelphman for their assistance with the AppleTalk project.

REFERENCES

1 'Fastbus modular high speed data acquisition and control system' *ANSI/IEEE Std 960* (1986)

2   Gustavson, D B and Walz, H V 'SLAC Fastbus Snoop Module — test results and support software' *IEEE Trans. Nucl. Sci.* (February 1986)

3   Gustavson, D B and Theus, J 'Wire-OR logic on transmission lines' *IEEE Micro* Vol 3 No 3 (June 1983) pp 51–55

4   Walz, H V and Barsotti, E J 'Fastbus review 1985' *IEEE Trans. Nucl. Sci.* (February 1986)

5   Verweij, H 'Fastbus in experiments in Europe' *IEEE Trans. Nucl. Sci* (February 1986)

6   Balakrishnan, R V 'The proposed IEEE 896 Futurebus — a solution to the bus driving problem' *IEEE Micro* Vol 4 No 4 (August 1984) pp 23–27

7   Taub, D M 'Arbitration and control acquisition in the proposed IEEE 896 Futurebus' *IEEE Micro* Vol 4 No 4 (August 1984) pp 28–41

8   Borrill, P and Theus, J 'An advanced communication protocol for the proposed IEEE 896 Futurebus' *IEEE Micro* Vol 4 No 4 (August 1984) pp 42–56

9   Gustavson, D B 'An introduction to the Fastbus' *Nucl. Phys.* A 335 (1980) pp 571–578

David B Gustavson has been a member of the Computation Research Group at the Stanford Linear Accelerator Center in Palo Alto, CA, USA, since 1977. He is currently working on a diagnostic system, human interface and local network for the Fastbus. He serves as chairman of the Fastbus Software Working Group and is a member of the hardware design team and of the executive committee. A member of the IEEE, IEEE Computer Society and ACM, Gustavson received a BS in physics and mathematics from the University of Nebraska, USA, in 1962, studied at the Georg August Universität in Göttingen, FRG, as a Fulbright Fellow in 1962–1963, and received a PhD in high-energy elementary particle physics from Stanford University in 1969.

Building up a system architecture using VMEbus

Steve Heath shows how the full potential of VMEbus can be realized in distributed processing and expanded 32-bit systems

VMEbus is designed for use in a wide range of systems, from the simple to the complex. The paper describes the design of VMEbus, its bus arbitration scheme, interrupts, and address and data widths. Some examples of VME systems are given, including simple systems, distributed processing systems, and systems upgraded to include 32-bit microprocessors.

microsystems   backplane buses   VMEbus

The VMEbus specification was announced in October 1981 by a manufacturers' group comprising Motorola, Mostek, Signetics and Thomson. The specification was based on Motorola's Versabus adapted for the Eurocard form factor which uses DIN 41612 connectors. Since its introduction, VMEbus has been accepted as an industry standard with over 200 manufacturers producing VMEbus products. It has an IEEE standardization number of P1014.

Applications of VMEbus range from the simple to the complex. Simple applications often treat VMEbus as a method of connecting a processor card, a memory card and some I/O, without considering the full potential that it offers. This paper describes the design concepts behind the bus and illustrates them with some examples.

VME BUS DESIGN

VMEbus is designed as a global parallel interconnect supporting 8-, 16- and 32-bit processors and data paths. Data transfers are based on a nonmultiplexed asynchronous protocol which allows transfers beween bus masters and slaves (eg processor and memory cards) to be performed at the highest speed that the slowest card will allow. This asynchronous communication allows speed upgrades to be performed without having to modify the entire system.

Multiprocessor support is essential for any bus to be accepted, and this is an integral part of the VMEbus specification. Such support requires a mechanism to prevent simultaneous bus access and to prioritize bus usage by multiple masters, a method of organizing and directing interrupt handling, system resource partitioning and, finally, a protocol to reconcile different processor data and address bus widths.

A description of the signal lines is given in Table 1.

Bus arbitration

Simultaneous bus access is prevented by the four-level bus arbitration scheme. This scheme also provides a method of prioritizing bus usage. For a master to use the bus it must request it by asserting one of the four bus request lines (BR0*–BR3*) and wait for the system bus arbiter to send the bus grant signal for that level. These signals are daisychained down the backplane using the BGIN* and BGOUT* signals (Figure 1). This means that for a particular arbitration level there is a hierarchy based on slot position.

In addition to this priority arbitration, single-level and round-robin schemes are supported. The bus arbiter located on the system controller in slot 1 can request a master to relinquish the bus after completion of its usage (release when done) or on the present bus cycle (release on request). The latter is very important for a realtime response. Bus arbitration is concurrent with data transfer to maximize throughput.

Interrupts

With a single-master system, all interrupts are handled by the master. However, with a multiple-master system, this

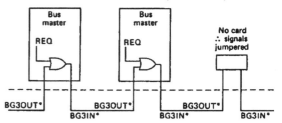

Figure 1.   Bus grant daisychaining

Semiconductor Products Sector, Motorola Ltd, Fairfax House, 69 Buckingham Street, Aylesbury, Bucks HP20 2NF, UK

0141–9331/86/02086–05 $03.00 © 1986 Butterworth & Co. (Publishers) Ltd

Table 1: VMEbus signals

Signal type	Lines	Description
Primary signals (P1 connector)		
Address bus	A01–A23	Primary address range (16 Mbyte)
Data bus	D00–D15	Primary data width (16 bit)
Address control	AS*	Address strobe
	AM0–AM5	Address modifiers
Data control	DS0*, DS1*	Data strobes
	WRITE*, DTACK*	Read/write, data transfer acknowledge
	LWORD*	Long word
Interrupts	IRQ1*–IRQ7*	Interrupt request (seven levels)
	IACK*, IACKIN*	Interrupt acknowledge (daisychain)
	IACKOUT*	
Bus arbitration	BR0*–BR3*	Bus request (four levels)
	BG01N*–BG3IN*	Bus grant (daisychain)
	BG0OUT*–BG3OUT*	
	BBSY*, BCLR*	Bus busy, bus clear
VMSbus	SERDAT	Serial data
	SERCLK	Serial clock
Error signals	SYSFAIL*	System failure
	BERR*	Bus error
	ACFAIL*	Power failure
Power	+5, +12, −12	Power includes standby for battery back-up
	+5 STDBY, GND	
Miscellaneous	SYSCLK	16 MHz system clock
	SYSRESET*	System reset
Expansion signals (P2 connector)†		
Extended address bus	A24–A31	Extended address range (4 Gbyte)
Extended data bus	D16–D31	Extended data width (32 bit)
Power	+5, GND	Additional power and ground lines
I/O	User I/O or VMXbus	64 pins in the two outside rows A and C available for I/O or VMXbus

†P2 can be used entirely as an I/O channel where an expanded bus is not required

is not acceptable and a more flexible arrangement is required. VMEbus provides a mechanism whereby interrupt handling can either be centralized on one master card or distributed throughout the system. Again, to optimize system performance the mechanism provides a priority scheme through daisychaining the interrupt acknowledge signals (IACKIN* and IACKOUT*).

An interrupt is started by asserting one of the interrupt request lines (IRQ1*–IRQ7*). The appropriate processor card's interrupt handler responds by requesting the bus, and then starts the acknowledge cycle. This asserts IACKIN* and places the interrupt level as a 3-bit code on the address bus. This tells the system which level the acknowledgement is for. The interrupter then places a vector number on the bus for the handler to use.

Each interrupt handler can respond to any level; this provides the method for distributed interrupt handling (Figure 2). The daisychaining then provides an additional priority scheme to the seven levels by adding slot priority within a level (Figure 3).

Address and data widths

VMEbus supports the use of any mix of 8-, 16- or 32-bit processors by using bus signals to indicate the data bus

size and addressing on a cycle-by-cycle basis. The two data strobes (DS0* and DS1*) indicate whether a word, an odd byte or an even byte is accessed. The two strobes are in fact a decoded address line A0. For 32-bit transfers the long word (LWORD*) signal is asserted. If a mismatch in size occurs then a bus error (BERR*) signal should be generated. Accessing a byte as a word is a typical example.

Different address widths are indicated by the use of address modifier codes to inform the system how many

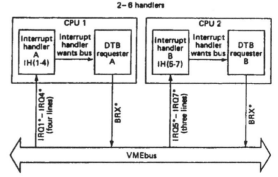

Figure 2. Distributed interrupt operation (2–6 handlers)

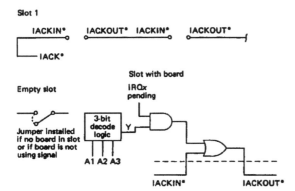

Figure 3. *IACKIN* and IACKOUT* control*

address bits are valid. Three sizes are supported: 16 bit, 24 bit and 32 bit, giving 64 kbyte, 16 Mbyte and 4 Gbyte addressing respectively. The address modifiers also indicate whether data/program, user/supervisor or some other user defined access is taking place. These modifiers allow hierarchical system partitioning, memory bank switching and similar schemes. Their use also provides fault tolerance in respect of failures of address generating components.

VME SYSTEMS

Simple systems

The simplest example of a VME system is based around an MVME110-1 CPU card, a RWIN1-1 disc controller and a MVME202 512 kbyte RAM card (Figure 4). This system has a simple architecture; it simply uses VMEbus as an interconnect between the various components. The CPU card provides its own system controller function and uses the VMEbus memory as its own private memory as it is the only bus master in the system. The disc controller is accessed via the I/O channel, an 8-bit local bus defined by Motorola which utilizes the user definable I/O pins on the P2 connector.

This system suffers from having no direct memory access (DMA) into the VMEbus RAM. This means that the onboard 68000 processor has a transfer overhead added to its software load and, during disc intensive activity, has a poor system response.

The SYS315 system (Figure 5), although it has a similar specification to the above system (ie CPU, RAM and disc controller), uses the VMEbus properly. The disc controller is intelligent and uses its onboard 68120 intelligent peripheral controller to load disc data directly into VMEbus memory. To do this, the controller acts as a bus master and competes with the CPU for bus access. The system uses the single-level (BR3*) arbiter provided by the CPU, and thus the CPU has priority due to its higher slot position.

All interrupts on the systems are dealt with entirely by the CPU card.

Although this type of system can be expanded by the addition of other cards, often with the cards acting as bus masters, there is little development of the architecture (Figure 6). Such expansions have a single interrupt handler

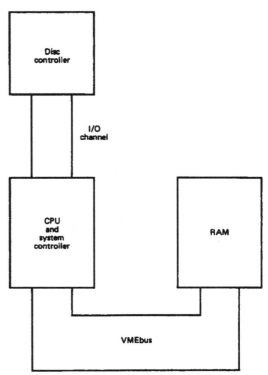

Figure 4. *Simple VME system with no VMEbus interrupts and a single bus master*

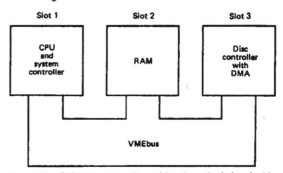

Figure 5. *SYS315 system. Bus arbitration: single level with slot priority (ie CPU has higher priority than disc controller). Interrupts: all handled by CPU (disc controller can interrupt CPU by VMEbus interrupt)*

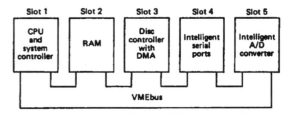

Figure 6. *Extended version of SYS315. Bus arbitration: single level with slot priority (slot 1 > slot 3 > slot 4 > slot 5). Interrupts: all handled by CPU; disc controller serial card and A/D converter interrupt CPU by VMEbus interrupts.*

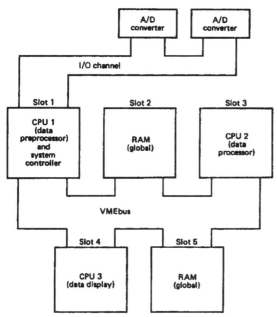

Figure 7. *Signal processing system. Bus arbitration: single level with slot priority (slot 1 > slot 3 > slot 4). Interrupts: CPU 1 handles level 2 VMEbus interrupts (from CPU 3); CPU 3 handles level 3 VMEbus interrupts (from CPU 1).*

and use simple arbitration. Each bus master is essentially independent and is controlled by the supervising CPU.

Distributed processing

The signal processor system shown in Figure 1 appears to be less complex than the previous example, but it uses more of the VMEbus potential. Data is collected from A/D converters on the I/O channel and is preprocessed by CPU 1. This card not only provides intelligence but acts as a gateway to the VMEbus, where the processed data is transferred to global memory. This memory is dual ported with CPU 2 which provides fast number crunching facilities for further data processing. The second-level data processing is initiated by CPU 1 changing a memory semaphore. When it is complete CPU 2 generates an interrupt on level 3 which is handled by CPU 3. This tells CPU 3 to fetch the data and send it to a graphics terminal for display. On completion of this task another interrupt is generated on level 2 which is handled by CPU 1, starting the process all over again.

This system uses distributed interrupt handling and either a single-level/slot-position or priority-level/slot-independence bus arbitration scheme could be used. The choice may depend on whether CPU 1 has system controller functions or not.

The system shown in Figure 8 takes the idea of distributed interrupt handling to an extreme. The system has seven CPU cards with three intelligent disc controllers and associated memory. One CPU runs Unix using one of the disc controllers while the others run realtime software, with two using the other disc controllers. The system has ten bus masters, all capable of generating interrupts. It is

impossible to allocate an individual interrupt level to each one and so some cards share an interrupt level. The priority of the cards sharing that level uses daisychaining and is thus determined by slot position.

With the four levels of arbitration available, more use is made of the daisychaining and card slot position, to determine the overall bus arbitration hierarchy.

With such a complex system running multiple software programs, there is always the danger of unwanted access to resources. Although such a situation can be prevented by having unique address ranges for the separate modules, this does rely on the software specification being well defined and adherend to. Future support and bug fixes may ignore these definitions.

The definitions can be easily implemented in VMEbus by the use of address modifiers to act as access descriptors. They operate in a similar way to a hardware memory management system. The modifiers are put on the bus, along with the address, and the slave must have a matching modifier code and address before it will respond. By using the user defined codes with 'don't care' bits, the system can be partitioned in a hierarchical scheme. This hardware partitioning exactly defines the

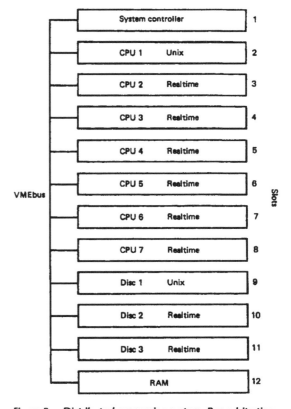

Figure 8. *Distributed processing system. Bus arbitration: four level with slot priority (level 3: CPU 2, disc 2; level 2: CPU 3, disc 3; level 1: CPU 4, CPU 5, CPU 6, CPU 7; level 0: CPU 1, disc 1). Interrupts: distributed (level 7 from disc 3 to CPU 3; level 6 from CPU 4 to CPU 3; level 5 from CPU 6, CPU 5 to CPU 3; level 4 from disc 2 to CPU 2; level 3 from CPU 6, CPU 5 to CPU 2; level 2 from CPU 7 to CPU 2; level 1 from disc 1 to CPU 1)*

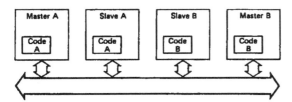

Figure 9. *System partitioning*

system access hierarchy irrespective of what software is running on it (Figure 9).

The use of address modifiers also increases fault tolerance with respect to address generation components.

Further expansion

The above system uses the VMEbus to provide a global parallel interconnect. However, today's technology, with the exception of the new generation of 32-bit processors, is not capable of transferring data down the bus as fast as the bus will allow. In such cases the solution is either to make the data transfers faster or to take them off the VMEbus. Using 32-bit processors will speed up data transfers, due to their wider data buses and faster clock rates. VMEbus traffic can be removed by increasing the integration on the individual cards or by using a local memory extension bus such as VMX or MVMX32.

Current trends in die integration, especially in memory, have allowed what was a three-card VME system two years ago to be integrated on a single card today. Realtime CPU cards, along with their associated memory and disc controllers, can be replaced with a single card using higher device integration. The Unix CPU card can be replaced by a card using a 68020 processor, with its 32-bit data path

and faster memory cycles. To reduce its use of the VMEbus, the 68020 accesses its memory resource via the MVMX32 local bus extension. This uses the user definable I/O pins on the P2 connector to provide the connections. To provide maximum flexibility the MVMX32 memory card is dual ported to the VMEbus.

CONCLUSIONS

The system examples discussed above show that VMEbus can be used to provide very simple or very complex architectures. The transition from the simple to the complex often requires only some thought and some minor hardware changes (usually done by jumpers). VMEbus's open architecture and the volume of product available for it offers the system builder solutions today with an open path to the future.

Steve Heath joined Mullard Semiconductors, now Signetics, in 1976 as a failure analysis technician. During this time he received an HNC in applied physics at Southampton Institute of Technology, UK. In 1980 he joined Thorn EMI Electronics as a senior reliability engineer to carry out design vetting for military and offshore electronic systems. He moved to Crellon Microsystems in 1982 as a field applications engineer supporting Motorola microsystems products, taking up a similar role with Motorola in 1984. He specializes in VME system integration.

Multibus II message passing

Simon Muchmore outlines the Multibus II message passing facility
which in multiprocessor systems frees the CPUs from waiting
for bus access

*The paper describes the system performance and cost
advantages of using the Multibus II message passing
facility for communication between modules in a
multiprocessor configuration. Classical multiprocessor
problems of interrupt resource and data sharing are
discussed and the solutions that message passing
offers the systems designer are presented.*

microsystems   message passing   interrupts   Multibus II

The demand for increased functionality and processing
power in microcomputer systems is growing faster than
single-processor solutions can satisfy. Multiprocessing
has proven to be a viable solution, largely because of
the advent of inexpensive memory and CPUs. To
improve performance and simplify the implementation
of multiprocessor systems, the Multibus II architecture
employs a mechanism called 'message passing'. This
paper discusses message passing and its benefits for
system design.

FUNCTIONAL PARTITIONING AND MICROPROCESSOR COMMUNICATIONS

There are two general types of multiprocessing: one
that employs transparent multiprocessing in a tightly
coupled system architecture, and one that uses a
heterogeneous mix of processors in a loosely coupled
architecture (Figure 1). A functionally partitioned
system is characterized by the use of a separate CPU
and memory on a board with an optimized local
environment. Other boards communicate via an
interface that is independent of the implementation of
the board. Future enhancements in the functional
module, therefore, can be easily integrated without
redesigning the entire system. Also, since I/O, CPU and
memory technology evolve at different rates, a
functionally partitioned system can be upgraded as
technology allows.

Key to the success of a functionally partitioned
system is the mechanism for communication between
the various functions. Multibus II was designed to

Intel Corporation (UK) Ltd, Pipers Way, Swindon, Wilts
SN3 1RJ, UK

resolve the problem of communication in multiprocessing systems by providing a unique message
passing approach to intermodule interrupts and data
movement. Further, the bus interface controller can be
implemented in a single coprocessor device that
augments the CPU.

VIRTUAL INTERRUPTS

In traditional systems, interrupts are propagated down
backplanes via discrete interrupt lines. To get *n*
processors to communicate with each other unam-
biguously, the bus needs $n(n - 1)$ interrupt lines. Since
existing buses usually provide up to eight interrupt
lines, designers have allowed multiple sources of
interrupts to be assigned to a line; the interrupted
processor may then poll all other processors to
determine the source of the signal.

In contrast, Multibus II uses message passing in a
virtual interrupt scheme to resolve this '$n \times n$ problem'
as well as to facilitate the more complex intertask
communication required for a multitasking operating
system. A virtual interrupt is a message that contains a

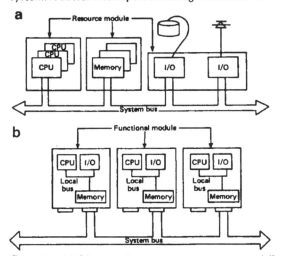

*Figure 1.   Multiprocessing systems: a, transparent (all
CPUs the same); b, heterogeneous mix of processors*

0141-9331/86/02091–03 $03.00 © 1986 Butterworth & Co. (Publishers) Ltd

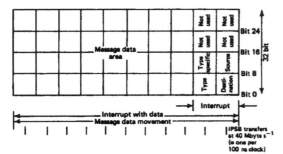

Figure 2. Message format: first two transfers form virtual interrupt

destination and a source address and 2 byte of qualifying information (Figure 2), and up to 28 byte of user data. The entire message is sent as one packet over the system bus at the maximum bus rate of 40 Mbyte s⁻¹. This method of interrupt with user data can be faster, when the software overhead is considered, than an interrupt mechanism constructed from discrete lines.

SHARING OF DATA AND VARIABLES

Traditionally, processors share data on a bus through a common block of memory. These data are either globally accessible by each sharing processor via the system bus or are resident in dual-port memory local to one or more of the processors. Several performance and cost trade-offs need to be evaluated for these different approaches.

It is necessary for one processor (in the dual-port case) and sometimes others (in the global case) to use the system bus to access the memory in question. When a processor uses the bus, it typically incurs an arbitration delay while waiting for the bus to become free and may also suffer the penalty of several wait states whilst actually performing the transfer, depending on how cleverly the memory system has been designed. In a dual-port approach, only one processor incurs this bus delay. However, the performance of the local processor is adversely affected by two factors. The first is the often complex dual-port control logic. The second is contention for its own local bus with the other processor, which is trying to access the same memory through the dual port via the system bus.

For systems where the data to be shared is small and accessed infrequently, the impact on performance may be small. As shared data requirements increase, however, the CPUs pay a noticeable penalty. At some point the system bus itself can also become a bottleneck. When systems software is required to coordinate and communicate the location of the shared memory, performance can degrade further. Finally, shared memory designs are complicated to debug and, most important of all, are difficult to extend beyond a pair of communicating CPUs.

MESSAGE PASSING

An ideal shared data system would have one CPU signal to another CPU that it has data to share, followed by the data becoming available to the second processor within its local memory. A good example of this requirement is that of a host CPU exchanging data with an intelligent disc controller where the CPU needs fast access on its local bus to the programs or data on disc. Getting this information to the CPU quickly is the key to high performance.

With Multibus II, the mechanism for moving data from one board to another is built into the bus interface hardware. The component which supports the requirements of message passing is referred to as the message passing coprocessor (MPC). MPC devices, one on each intelligent board, move the data from one board to the other. Figure 3 shows a typical message passing system with a host CPU and a disc controller using MPC devices to communicate. The following sequence of events occurs when the host requests a block of data from disc:

1. The host requests the data block from the controller using an interrupt message containing, in the user data field, the parameters needed to describe the file.
2. The disc controller responds to the host after retrieving the file and requests a memory buffer be made available.
3. The host signals that it has made a memory buffer available for use in its local memory.
4. The controller sends the data in 32 byte packets. Each packet is transmitted over the bus until all the data is at the host. Transfer is then complete.

Data is moved between the MPC devices at the maximum bus bandwidth of 40 Mbyte s⁻¹, or 100 ns per 32-bit packet. This rate is about five times as fast as the rate at which the fastest microprocessors can access real memory for sustained periods.

The MPC performs a speed matching function between the bus and the local microprocessor environment. Internal to the MPC are first-in–first-out memories which buffer the system bus from the local bus and provide the speed matching. Figure 4 shows the data flow in an MPC device. Data messages are broken into 32 byte packets because of the speed differences between the system bus and the burst data rates that can be supported on the board. The fastest microprocessor direct memory access (DMA) devices cannot keep pace with these data rates, and realtime performance is affected if the packets are too large. It is, therefore, advantageous to break a large data move-

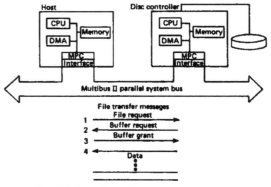

gure 3. File transfer using messages

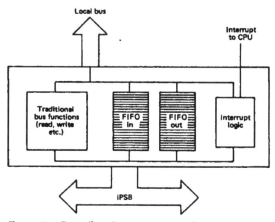

Local bus

Interrupt to CPU

Traditional bus functions (read, write etc.)

FIFO in

FIFO out

Interrupt logic

iPSB

Figure 4.   Data flow in message passing coprocessor

ment into smaller pieces and let the bus interface reconnect the pieces.

A 32 byte message packet takes 1 μs of bus time (a two-cycle header plus eight data cycles of 100 ns per cycle). This allows other boards to use the bus between the packets that make up a large data movement. In this way the system bus is not tied up for long periods of time when moving large chunks of data. For realtime applications the Multibus II protocol allows virtual interrupts to be sent without having to wait for a long data transfer to be completed.

PERFORMANCE

In the message passing example above (Figure 3), note that neither CPU needed to access the bus during the disc file request and transfer. The interrupt-like messages that request and set up the transfer as well as the transfer itself all occur through the MPC. When the MPC sends a message, the message is split into packets and moved at 40 Mbyte s^{-1} over the iPSB bus. Any bus overhead is thus paid only once per 32 byte data message.

In this way, the CPUs do not pay a penalty for arbitration or bus contention, nor do they incur any performance penalty associated with dual-port memory operation. The wait states that a CPU would traditionally incur are eliminated since the bus transfers are occurring at full bus bandwidth via the MPC and are independent of the CPU. If, in addition, the boards in our example each have their own local DMA device then the MPC may use a DMA channel to move data between itself and local memory, freeing the CPU to perform other tasks concurrently.

It is important to realize that the Multibus II architecture does not preclude the use of the more traditional dual-port or global memory techniques for data movement should the system designer wish to adopt those methods. Message passing is an incremental capability that enhances throughput by freeing the CPU to get on with processing.

SUMMARY

The design goals for message passing were to enhance performance and to make it easier to implement multiprocessor systems. Message passing solves the $n \times n$ interrupt problem, providing a high-performance solution to functionally partitioned systems that can be implemented in a single-chip solution.

Simon Muchmore is an applications engineer with Intel. He holds a degree in engineering from the University of Cambridge. His experience before joining Intel includes bit-slice microprocessor design and the system design of complex, realtime multiprocessor-based systems. Current research interests are in Multibus II interfacing and the problems of message communication between functionally distributed microprocessor systems.

Objective comparison of 32-bit buses

Paul L Borrill presents a comparison of five well known 32-bit buses — VME, Futurebus, Multibus II, Nubus and Fastbus

The major component of the paper is an extensive table giving an objective comparison of five 32-bit backplane bus standards: VMEbus, Futurebus, Multibus II, Nubus and Fastbus. Manufacturing support, performance, cost, complexity, maintenance, configurability, multiprocessor support, electrical and reliability issues, and protocol and physical features are considered. Because of the danger of reading too much into this table, and because of the potential for misunderstanding, many of the issues covered in the table are discussed and elaborated upon in the accompanying text.

**bus standards   VMEbus   Futurebus   Multibus II
Nubus   Fastbus**

The table presented in Appendix 1 compares various aspects of the 32-bit backplane bus standards VMEbus, Futurebus, Multibus II, Nubus and Fastbus. This table is believed to be entirely accurate; however, it is the nature of the backplane buses in question that their specifications, environment and commercial support change with time. Consequently, the table will be updated periodically, and the latest version should always be obtained when the most accurate and up-to-date comparisons are sought. The table presented here is version 3.0, dated 18 December 1985.

Throughout the table, 'Not supported' means that no direct provision has been made in the bus specification for the facility in question. This does not mean that the feature cannot be implemented by some non-standard means, or by future modification of the specification. However, since many of these features have significant architectural and protocol implications to the specification, the likelihood of being able to graft such features onto a specification adequately is remote.

SUPPORT

To avoid the numbers game which vendors tend to play when claiming multiple sources for compatible products, only the primary sponsor and supporters of each bus are given as an indication of the bus's genealogy.

Spectra-Tek (UK) Ltd, Swinton Grange, Malton, N. Yorks YO17 0QR, UK

PERFORMANCE

Bus bandwidth

The performance figures are, as far as possible, calculated values taking into account realistic assumptions applied consistently to each bus. Included in the calculations are: bus driver and receiver propagation delays; transmission line driving delays (the bus driving problem and signal propagation delays down the backplane); logic and backplane skews; set-up and hold times for latches; and slave access times. Since a synchronous bus must have a clock period slow enough to cope with a fully loaded system, the calculations for the asynchronous buses also assume a fully loaded system, even though this assumption may not always be valid: asynchronous buses may be faster with shorter backplanes or in a more lightly loaded typical system[1].

The performance figures for the Nubus and Multibus II are almost identical, because they both use a synchronous protocol clocked at 10 MHz. The performance in the single transfer mode for Multibus II and Nubus includes some concurrency, which is possible between the address decode, plus access time delays and the address and data multiplexing delays. The Nubus appears to have a faster arbitration time than Multibus II because its shorter backplane and fewer arbitration lines allow the logic to settle faster.

A simple calculation shows that the average distance between any two communicating boards on a backplane is one third of the backplane length, so this figure is used in the calculation of the backplane delays for the asynchronous protocols. Synchronous buses have a fixed clock period which must be long enough to cope with boards communicating from each extremity of the backplane; their performance is thus independent of which two boards happen to be communicating at any instant in time.

Identical fully loaded backplane delays were applied to the VMEbus, Futurebus and Fastbus, even though in the case of the Futurebus this would be an overestimation because Futurebus transceivers load the bus less. Fastbus and Futurebus use essentially the same protocol, and differences in bus bandwidth and arbitration performance are due primarily to the difference in technology currently available to implement the two (ie advanced Schottky TTL for the Futurebus — the same as for the VMEbus — and 10k ECL for Fastbus).

A noteworthy result is shown in the figures for single transfer mode, where all of the buses demonstrate very similar performances. This is primarily due to the fact that the VMEbus, which is nonmultiplexed, does not suffer the delays of multiplexing address and data on the same lines as do the other buses, and because there are transactional overheads in the protocol for the Futurebus and Fastbus besides the multiplexing: the Futurebus suffers delays to overcome the transmission line effect, called the wired-OR glitch[2], on the fully broadcast address transfers; and the Fastbus has a 40 ns clean-up delay at the end of each transaction (to solve effectively the same problem).

Address pipelining, which is possible only on the VMEbus because it is nonmultiplexed, is not taken into account in the calculations because of the complexity of the assumptions needed to justify the figures produced.

The burst transfer mode, which is the usual 'communications-oriented' assumption for transactions in a typical multiprocessor system, shows a wider difference in bus performance. Even in this case, however, performances start to equalize rapidly at the longer access times.

The lesson to be learnt from this is that a high-performance bus alone is not sufficient to guarantee a high-performance system. Some architectural means is necessary to fully utilize the bus's available bandwidth; for example, a method is needed to either reduce the amount of bus traffic each board generates, or to reduce the 'effective' bus access time. (This may be done by using blocks predominantly to communicate across the bus, and using static-column-address or nibble-mode-access RAMs on the memory boards.) Effective ways to reduce bus traffic are: cache memories between each processor and the bus; and local memories, either on each board or accessible through some kind of local extension bus. The former can be transparent to the programs; the latter is generally not transparent. Effective ways to force the system to pass blocks over the bus rather than single transfers are: cache memories; and restricting the system to a functionally distributed (message-passing) architecture. Cache memories and message passing are discussed below.

The highly artificial assumption of processor, memory and bus clock coherence is made in the figures for the performance of the synchronous buses. The clock latency problem would effectively add a half-cycle (50 ns) penalty to every transfer on Multibus II and Nubus, lowering their performance in many real implementations.

The clock latency problem can be viewed as follows. Because all bus-based multiprocessor systems would be limited by the bus being a bottleneck if the processors accessed all instructions and data directly through the bus, it is necessary to find ways to keep as much as possible of the instructions and data local to each processor, so that it can reduce its bus requirement. Therefore, for a large percentage of the time (say 90%), processors are executing and manipulating data locally, and only for a small percentage of the time (say 10%) do they need to use the bus. It therefore become pragmatic to optimize the processor to its local resources rather than to the bus, ie to choose a processor clock speed and memory access as the best economically available at the time. 12.5 MHz and 16.7 MHz processors are

typical currently, with 20 MHz and 25 MHz expected during the course of 1986.

This means that each local processor clock will be different and mutually asynchronous to the bus clock. Consequently, in the 10% of occasions on which the processor needs access to the bus, its interface must synchronize the two somehow to pass the data. This synchronization causes two problems: the delay needed to wait for the first valid bus clock edge, and the metastable state problems intrinsic to the synchronizer circuits.

On each transfer the processor makes through the bus, after the processor presents its request to the interface, the interface must wait for the first valid clock edge. The request may arrive just before a bus edge is due, so there would be no time to wait; or the request may arrive just after a bus clock edge has gone, so it must wait an entire cycle before another is due. On average, the delay will be half a clock cycle; this is the clock latency problem.

Multibus II recognises this problem by providing a method of buffering the timing of the processor from that of the bus, called message passing. Provided the implementor is prepared to accept the constraints of such an architecture, clock latency can be mostly overcome by this technique. Nubus also suffers from the clock latency problem but does not explicitly offer a facility such as message passing to help overcome it.

Asynchronous buses do not suffer the clock latency problem because the bus adopts the timing of the master. On the other hand, it is often claimed that synchronous buses are easier to design to, are more reliable and have less noise problems than asynchronous buses. This is a highly subjective argument which tends to generalize too much on categories of synchronous and asynchronous buses, without taking into account the details of how thoroughly the individual buses are designed.

Arbitration

The information needed to estimate the arbitration overhead, and the average bus acquisition latency, is given in algebraic form as well as in numbers, since it is very application specific. T_{arb} is the time for the arbitration system to resolve multiple requests, and is equivalent to the time it takes a master to acquire the bus when it is not in use, assuming it was previously not owned by that master. All the buses have an effective 'parking' mode, where there is essentially zero delay to acquire the bus if there is no change in mastership. This is called 'release on request' (ROR) in VMEbus terminology. 'Release when done' (RWD) is not normally useful except in master–slave-type multiprocessor architectures, to which the VMEbus is particularly well suited.

T_m is the time for mastership, ie the time any one master is allowed to keep the bus under normal circumstances. This is not always clearly specified for some of the buses, and others deliberately do not specify it, claiming it is the privilege and responsibility of the system implementor to set this number.

For the Nubus, T_m is built in to the protocol by the way it does the block transfer. For the VMEbus, T_m is arbitrarily chosen to ease implementation difficulties, and to solve the memory boundary problem for block transfers. For Multibus II, T_m is also an arbitrary limit, related to the maximum useful message size in the message-passing mode. For Futurebus and Fastbus, the system implementor is encouraged to program limits appropriate to his system; typically, 16 or 32 quadlets (128 byte or 256 byte) will be chosen as a maximum, and the boards will be programmed to split larger blocks into several smaller ones of this maximum size. However, it may make sense in some systems to set the maximum size at 1 kbyte (256 transfers) or more, to pass an entire page of virtual memory from the disc controller to the main memory, for example.

The time for a master to acquire each bus (T_{get}) is also given. This assumes 16-word limited blocks, 150 ns slave access times for the transactions, and 16 modules per system. The priority case, T_{get}(best), assumes there is only one high-priority master in the system. The fairness case, T_{get}(worst), assumes there are 16 modules all operating in fairness mode.

T_{get}(best) is the maximum time interval from when a high-priority module requests the bus in a heavily loaded system to when it obtains it. This may be of greatest importance in a system processing realtime data, or in one with a need to react to very fast events. Clearly, if the bus is in use then, even if an arbitration has taken place, the winner cannot assume control until the previous master has finished. There is, however, one more complication: a simple queueing model shows that, on average, there will be one board which is currently using the bus and one which has arbitrated, won, and is waiting to use the bus (the 'master elect'). Thus a new high-priority master requesting the bus must not only wait for the current master to finish, but also for the master elect to finish, even though the master elect may be of lower priority. This is reflected in the values for T_{get}(best) by the factor $2T_m$, ie the time for two masters to each use the bus for their maximum allotted time.

The only buses which do not show this $2T_m$ behaviour are the Futurebus and the Nubus. The Futurebus has an intrinsic facility called 'pre-emption' which allows a high-priority master to displace a lower-priority master elect before the bus is handed over. The Nubus does not have a priority mechanism for arbitration, so T_{get}(best) and T_{get}(worst) reflect the best- and worst-case access times, respectively, for the fairness algorithm. The VMEbus has a feature similar to Futurebus pre-emption, provided by the BCLR line, which could be used to inform the current master that a high-priority master is waiting to use the bus and may also be used to pre-empt the master elect. However, this is not fully specified in the specification, and so is not included in the comparison figures.

T_{get}(worst) is the maximum time from when a standard-priority module requests the bus in a heavily loaded system to when it obtains it. This figure reflects the fairness arbitration algorithm, which ensures all requestors get a turn. There is one further subtlety here, because the fairness scheme is not a true first-in–first-out algorithm, but merely an approximation to it. All masters have an assigned 'identity' in the fairness schemes of all these buses. Consider what happens when the fairness 'gate' is opened to let new requestors arbitrate for the bus. If all the modules but the one with the lowest identity make a request and the gate then closes for a period to service these requests, should the lowest-identity master then be ready to request immediately the gate closes, it may have to wait not only for the current queue to finish (a period of $(N-1)T_m$) but in the same queue a second time if all these masters (but the last) are ready to request the bus again when the fairness gate opens again (a further $(N-2)T_m$). The last master in the previous queue is assumed to have missed the second gate opening because it was still active. This accounts for the difference between the T_{get}(worst) and T_{get}(best) cases for the Nubus, which uses the fairness scheme exclusively.

COST AND COMPLEXITY

This section of the table was included as an indication of the relative cost effectiveness of each bus. All of the buses are expensive at the moment, but each proponent claims that its bus is less expensive than those of its competitors. Multibus II may appear expensive to implement at the moment, but this situation is likely to change: Intel claims that in the near future a crossover point will be reached where Multibus II becomes less costly than, say, VMEbus, because the interface will become more fully integrated, and the trend in the cost of silicon is always downwards. This view does tend to assume that semiconductor manufacturers supporting the VMEbus will not also attain a greater degree of integration, which is hardly likely. However, in the long term, the number of active signal lines is indicative of the ultimate cost effectiveness of the bus interface, since silicon cost is predominantly a result of interconnections.

As far as implementation cost is concerned, a more important question to ask of each bus is how much of the facilities provided must be implemented in order to use the bus, or to gain the principal advantages of the bus. For VMEbus, clearly, cost may be reduced by using implementations which are wholly 16 bit data and 24 bit address, although this does raise some compatibility issues with 32-bit systems.

The VMEbus also presents a somewhat simple appearance because of its traditional design, and its duplication of the familiar 68000 component-level signals. For the Futurebus and Nubus, it is always necessary to implement the full 32-bit-wide bus. This means that a minimum-cost implementation is less cost effective when using 16-bit processors only than in, say, VMEbus; however, it does overcome compatibility problems and eliminates some complexity for 32-bit processors due to hybrid arrangements. The cache facilities, message passing, broadcast facilities, and sophisticated control status register (CSR) functions can be eliminated or considerably reduced in cost-conscious implementations of the Futurebus. In particular, boards can be readily constructed using slower but more highly integrated parts such as programmable array logic (PAL) devices, and still ensure total compatibility because of the technology-independent asynchronous handshake, making a wide spectrum of costs and performances possibly.

For Multibus II, message passing is more or less essential to gain any real advantage of the bus over, say, Multibus I, because of the clock latency problem; and message passing is expensive in LSI, real estate and software redevelopment. However, Intel has an ingenious solution to this particular problem: the iSSB serial bus implements the same message-passing function as the parallel bus, so implementations which require low bandwidth and only one or two processors need use only the iSSB bus to be cost effective.

The philosophy of the Nubus is not to load down the user with unnecessary additional features. Nubus therefore has a refreshing sparcity of mechanism, which allows it to be considerably cheaper than, say, Multibus II by virtue of the more sophisticated features being unavailable. The Fastbus tends to be used in very high-performance systems, such as where large numbers of data acquisition subsystems are connected in a tree structured network, an application which is typical of the requirements of the nuclear physics community.

MULTIPROCESSOR SUPPORT

Cache

Cache memory requirements for a bus are often very widely misunderstood. All buses can implement some kind of cache system. The basic categories are instruction caches and data caches. With care, any bus can implement an instruction cache since the instructions are unlikely to be modified. Data or combined instruction-and-data caches, whilst considerably more useful than pure instruction caches, are more difficult. If a system programmer can define at least which data are 'private' and which data are 'shared' then he/she can, with help from a memory management unit, cause the cache system to treat all shared data as noncacheable. Whilst this is a low-performance, messy and nontransparent method, all buses can implement caches in this way.

Higher-performance systems, which are required to be transparent and/or to cache shared data, must have some basic facilities built into the bus in order to maintain consistency[3]. There are two basic consistency schemes possible: write through, where all write data is written through the cache to the main memory via the bus; and write back, where written data is simply stored in the cache until it is flushed at a later time. With the write-through scheme the transaction is visible on the bus and, provided the bus supports a fully handshaken broadcast mechanism, at least for the address, then other masters which have a stale copy of this data can invalidate it (or copy the updated data off the bus as it becomes available).

With the highest-performance write-back system, additional information must be stored along with each piece of data to define the ownership of the data. If the data is marked 'shared', then the scheme reverts to write through; if it is marked 'exclusive', then the write transaction need not appear on the bus. Data becomes shared or exclusive depending upon the status lines on the bus when the data is first read, or it may become invalidated whenever another processor is seen writing the same location over the bus. If a piece of data exists in a cache and is marked as exclusive, and if another board wishes to read the location in main memory that data belongs in, then the cache must intervene in the read cycle to inhibit the stale data from the main memory and provide the master with most recent data from within itself.

Only the Futurebus and the Fastbus support an adequate broadcast mechanism to fully support the write-through scheme, and only the Futurebus has the necessary bus status and protocol intervention facilities to support the high-performance write-back scheme[4].

ACKNOWLEDGEMENTS

The author would like to thank Steve Cooper, Shlomo Pri-Tal, George White and Dave Gustavson for their extensive comments on the first draft of the comparison table (Appendix 1).

REFERENCES

1   **Balakrishnan, R V** 'The proposed IEEE 896 Futurebus — a solution to the bus driving problem' *IEEE Micro* Vol 4 No 4 (August 1984) pp 23–27

2   **Gustavson, D B and Theus, J** 'Wire-OR logic on transmission lines' *IEEE Micro* Vol 3 No 3 (June 1983) pp 51–55

3   **Katz, R et al** 'Implementing a cache consistency protocol' *Proc. 12th Annual Computer Architecture Conf.* IEEE Computer Society Press pp 276–283

4   **Sweazey, P** 'The Futurebus cacheing system' *Proc. Midcon, Chicago, USA, September 1985* Electronic Conventions Inc, 8110 Airport Boulevard, Los Angeles, CA 90080, USA

5   **Borrill, P L and Theus, J** 'An advanced communications protocol for the proposed IEEE 896 Futurebus' *IEEE Micro* Vol 4 No 4 (August 1984) pp 42–56

6   **Siskind, E** in *IEEE Trans. Nucl. Sci.* (February 1985)

APPENDIX 1: COMPARISON OF 32-BIT BUSES

Aspect	VMEbus	Futurebus	Multibus II	Nubus	Fastbus
Support					
Standardization	IEEE P1014	IEEE P896.1	IEEE Pxxx	IEEE Pyyy	ANSI/IEEE 960
Status	Draft 1.2, IEC 821 draft	Draft 7.2, due for release early 1986	Intel Rev. C	Draft 1.0	Approved standard IEC45 (Sec. 243)
Primary sponsor	Motorola	IEEE P896 W.G.	Intel	Texas Instruments	US NIM committee
Primary supporters	Signetics, Mostek	Specification not yet released for commercial use	–	Lisp Machines Inc	Kinetic Systems, LeCroy Research, Dr B Struck
Present silicon support	Motorola, Signetics	National Semiconductor	Toshiba	None	Maruei Shoji Co, several gate arrays
Expected silicon support	–	Ferranti, Monolithic Memories, Signetics, Texas Instruments	Intel	Texas Instruments	Valtronic Inc, Integrated Networks, Phillips (Zurich)
Performance	Continuously variable	Continuously variable	Quantized – 100 ns wait states	Quantized – 100 ns wait states	Continuously variable
Bus bandwidth					
Sponsor claim	20–57 Mbyte s^{-1}	117.6 Mbyte s^{-1} (boards adjacent)	40 Mbyte s^{-1} (assumes 10 MHz clock)	37.5 Mbyte s^{-1} (16 cycle block)	160 Mbyte s^{-1}
Source	Motorola	*IEEE Micro*[5]	Intel	Texas Instruments	*IEEE Trans. Nucl. Sci.*[6]
Single transfer mode (average backplane delay = one third of backplane length)					
T_{acc} = 0 ns	25.0 Mbyte s^{-1}	37.0 Mbyte s^{-1}	20.0 Mbyte s^{-1}	20.0 Mbyte s^{-1}	37.0 Mbyte s^{-1}
T_{acc} = 50 ns	19.0 Mbyte s^{-1}	25.3 Mbyte s^{-1}	13.3 Mbyte s^{-1}	13.3 Mbyte s^{-1}	25.3 Mbyte s^{-1}
T_{acc} = 100 ns	15.4 Mbyte s^{-1}	19.2 Mbyte s^{-1}	13.3 Mbyte s^{-1}	13.3 Mbyte s^{-1}	19.2 Mbyte s^{-1}
T_{acc} = 150 ns	12.9 Mbyte s^{-1}	15.5 Mbyte s^{-1}	10.0 Mbyte s^{-1}	10.0 Mbyte s^{-1}	15.5 Mbyte s^{-1}
Burst transfer mode (handshaken, infinite length block, average backplane delay = one third of backplane length)					
T_{acc} = 0 ns	27.9 Mbyte s^{-1}	95.2 Mbyte s^{-1}	40.0 Mbyte s^{-1}	40.0 Mbyte s^{-1}	173.9 Mbyte s^{-1}
T_{acc} = 50 ns	20.7 Mbyte s^{-1}	43.5 Mbyte s^{-1}	20.0 Mbyte s^{-1}	20.0 Mbyte s^{-1}	54.8 Mbyte s^{-1}
T_{acc} = 100 ns	16.5 Mbyte s^{-1}	28.2 Mbyte s^{-1}	20.0 Mbyte s^{-1}	20.0 Mbyte s^{-1}	32.5 Mbyte s^{-1}
T_{acc} = 150 ns	13.6 Mbyte s^{-1}	20.8 Mbyte s^{-1}	13.3 Mbyte s^{-1}	13.3 Mbyte s^{-1}	23.1 Mbyte s^{-1}
Pipelined mode (nonhandshaken, infinite length block)	Not specified	Not specified	Not applicable	Not applicable	Unlimited
Ultimate future performance	~ 35 Mbyte s^{-1}	~ 280 Mbyte s^{-1}	40 Mbyte s^{-1*}	40 Mbyte s^{-1*}	~ 500 Mbyte s^{-1}
Message passing mode	Not defined	To be specified in P896.2	30 Mbyte s^{-1}	Not defined	Not defined
Fundamental limitations	Transition times, bus driving problem, logic delays, skew, backplane propagation delay, timing constraints built into the specification	Logic delays, skew, backplane propagation delay	100 ns between signal sampling; *ignores clock latency	100 ns between signal sampling; *ignores clock latency	Logic delays, skew, segment propagation delay
Arbitration					
Algorithms	RWD, ROR	Fair, priority	Fair, priority	Fair	Fair, priority
T_{arb}(typical)	200–400 ns	250 ns	300 ns*	200 ns*	150 ns
T_{arb}(best)	150 ns	150 ns	300 ns*	200 ns*	90 ns
T_m	$256T_t$	Unconstrained	$32T_t$	$16T_t$	Unconstrained
T_{get}(priority)	$T_{arb} + 2T_m$	$T_{arb} + T_m$	$T_{arb} + 2T_m$	$T_{arb} + (N-1) + 2T_m$	$T_{arb} + 2T_m$
T_{get}(fairness)	$T_{arb} + T_m[2(N-2) + 1]$	$T_{arb} + T_m[2(N-2) + 1]$	$T_{arb} + T_m[2(N-2) + 1]$	$T_{arb} + T_m[2(N-2) + 1]$	$T_{arb} + T_m[2(N-2) + 1]$
Comparison with T_{arb}(typical), and T_m limited to 16 transfers, in block transfer mode (150 ns access time)					
T_{get}(best)	9.8 µs	3.3 µs	9.9 µs	139.4 µs	5.8 µs
T_{get}(worst)	136.9 µs	89.5 µs	139.5 µs	139.4 µs	80.5 µs
Cost and complexity					
Address spaces	64	1	4	1	2
Connectors	2	1	1	1	1
Pins	128	96	96	96	130
Number of active signal lines	107	67	67	46	60
Interrupt lines	7	0	0	0	1
Power rails	+5 V, +5 V SBY, +12 V, −12 V	+5 V only	+5 V, +5 V battery, +12 V, −12 V	+5 V, −5.2 V, +12 V, −12 V	+28 V, +15 V, −15 V, +5 V, −5.2 V, −2.0 V
Electrical and reliability issues					
Bus interface	TTL mixture (48 mA and 64 mA); tristate and open collector	BTL (50 mA backplane transceiver logic), solves the bus driving problem	TTL mixture (48 mA and 64 mA); tristate and open collector	TTL mixture (48 mA and 64 mA); tristate and open collector	ECL 10k (nearly solves the bus driving problem)

Aspect	VMEbus	Futurebus	Multibus II	Nubus	Fastbus
Parity	None	Optional	Mandatory	Optional	Optional
Inhibit control	None	Via CSR space	None	Enable line	Enable line
Parallel bus	None	1 bit byte^{-1}	1 bit byte^{-1}	1 bit for A and D lines	1 bit for all
Control lines	None	1 bit	2 bit	None	None
Tag	None	1 bit	Not applicable	Not applicable	Not applicable
Arbitration	None	1 bit	None	None	None
Maintenance and configurability					
Live insertion	Not available	Fully supported	Not available	Not available	Partially supported (halt line)
Extender card	Not allowed for	Fully supported	Not allowed for	Not allowed for	Partially supported
Geographical addressing	None	5-bit slot ID	LACHn pin (T-pin technique with power-up initialization)	4-bit slot ID	5-bit ID
Autoconfiguration	Not supported	Fully supported at any time, including live insertion	Fully supported at power-up time only	Fully supported	Fully supported
Multiprocessor support					
Virtual interrupts	Not specified	Supported; further specified in P896.2	Supported	Supported; further specified in separate document	Supported
Arbitration	4-level daisychain	Fully distributed, asynchronous	Distributed, synchronous central clock	Distributed, synchronous central clock	Distributed, central timing element
Deterministic acquisition	Supported; four-deep round-robin system	Fully supported (fairness)	Fully supported (fairness)	Fully supported (fairness, 16 levels)	Fully supported (assured access mode, fairness)
Priority acquisition	Supported, four levels only except in round robin	Fully supported; 32 levels	Fully supported; 32 levels possible	Not supported	Fully supported; 32 levels
Message passing	Not supported	Format defined; fully specified in P896.2	Fully supported	Not supported	Not directly supported
Cache					
Write through	Limited capability	Fully supported	Limited capability	Limited capability	Limited capability
Writeback	Not supported	Fully supported	Not supported	Not supported	Not supported
Tagged architectures	Not directly supported; possible implementation with address modifiers	Fully supports tag bit with parity protection	Not directly supported	Not directly supported	Not directly supported
Protocol features					
Bus protocol	Asynchronous	Asynchronous; technology independent	Synchronous; 10 MHz clock	Synchronous; 10 MHz clock	Asynchronous with optional synchronous suboperations
Data path	Nonmultiplexed	Multiplexed	Multiplexed	Multiplexed	Multiplexed
Primary	16 bit	32 bit	32 bit	32 bit	32 bit only
Secondary	32, 24, 16 and 8 bit	32, 24, 16 and 8 bit	32, 24, 16 and 8 bit	32, 16 and 8 bit	Not supported
Justification	16 bit justified	Nonjustified	16 bit justified	Nonjustified	Nonjustified
Nonaligned 32/16-bit operations	Rev. C only	Fully supported	Fully supported	Not supported	Not supported
Byte orientation	Big end	Not constrained	Little end	Little end	Not applicable
Address spaces					
Primary	2^{24} byte	2^{32} byte	2^{32} byte	2^{32} byte	2^{32} quadlets
Secondary	2^{32} byte	Expandable	None	None	Expandable
Interconnect	In I/O space	In CSR space*	2^{14} byte	In CSR space*	In CSR space
I/O space	2^{16} byte	In CSR space*	2^{16} byte	In CSR space*	In CSR space
Broadcast (writes to multiple slaves)	Not supported	Broadcast on any write transaction	Message space only; not supported in memory or I/O space	Not supported	Broadcast on any write transaction; module subset and system subset selection facilities
Broadcall (reads from multiple slaves)	Not supported	Broadcall on any read transaction	Not supported	Not supported	Sparse data scan through T-pin
Bus repeater					
Circuit switched	Not supported	Bus repeater deadlock prevention	Bus repeater deadlock prevention	Bus repeater deadlock prevention	Fully supported
Packet switched	Not specified	Extension beyond the backplane is considered as a store and forward (packet switched) operation (896.2)	Fully specified message passing mechanism can be used for 256 nodes	Not specified	Supported, but packet-switched operations are not specified in ANSI/IEEE 960

*Control status register (CSR) space is located within main memory space in these buses

Aspect	VMEbus	Futurebus	Multibus II	Nubus	Fastbus
Provision for future expansions	One reserved line; spare address modifier states	Extended command mode built in to protocol to ensure compatibility	Two reserved lines; one reserved state on SC lines	No comment	Five reserved lines; protocols designed to permit expansion by additional levels of multiplexing
Locking					
Arbitration lock	Use BBSY* line and release when done	Release when done	Release when done when lock line is active	Continues request; relies on pure fairness mechanism	Release when done
Address lock	All transfers must be assumed locked	Fully supported (lock line)	Fully supported (lock line)	Not supported	Not supported
Single transaction lock	By AS* asserted through transaction	Fully supported (lock line)	Fully supported (lock line)	Not supported	By AS/AK lock
Multiple transaction lock	Not supported	Fully supported (unlocks on change of mastership)	Not supported	Not supported	Not supported
Bus diagnostic features					
Debugging	None	Fully handshaken broadcast mode; full extender board capability	None	None	Time-outs can be disabled; wait line can single step transactions
Monitor/snoop	None	Fully asynchronous connection phase to allow inspection of address transfer; slave intervention capability	Clocked for easy logic analyser inspection	Clocked for easy logic analyser inspection	Wait line to slow handshake for inspection
Bus utilities available to the user	Spare address modifier codes; 64 pins free on P2 connector	None: all user defined facilities are delegated to auxilliary connectors to ensure maximum interoperability of all boards	Extra power buses (+12 V, −12 V, +5 V battery)	Extra power buses (+12 V, −12 V, −5.2 V)	Extra power buses (+12 V, −12 V, −5.2 V); daisychain to right; daisychain to left; eight terminated lines; two unterminated lines; four unbussed pins
Physical features					
Board size					
Primary	233.35 mm × 160 mm	366.7 mm × 280 mm	233.35 mm × 220 mm	366.7 mm × 280 mm	366.7 mm × 400 mm
Secondary	100 mm × 160 mm	233.35mm × 280 mm	100 mm × 220 mm	None	None
Board area					
Primary	373 cm²	1027 cm²	513 cm²	1027 cm²	1467 cm²
Secondary	160 cm²	653 cm²	220 cm²	None	None
Connectors					
Dedicated (type)	2 (IEC 603-2)	1 (IEC 603-2)	1 (IEC 603-2)	1 (IEC 603-2)	(Multisourced: AMP 2-532956, or DuPont 66527-565 or SAE RTP 2525-1303)
Number of pins	2 × 96	96	96	96	130
Undedicated (type)	0 (64 pins spare) (IEC 603-2)	2 (IEC 603-2)	1 (IEC 603-2)	2 (IEC 603-2)	(Multisourced eg AMP 2-532981-1)
Number of pins	64 spare on second connectors	2 × 96	96	96	195 max.
Number of modules					
Logical modules	Not logically constrained	32 per backplane; 65536 message nodes	32 per backplane; 256 message nodes	16 per backplane	26 per backplane segment, 16777216 × 255 in fully connected system
Dedicated physical slots	1	0	1	0	0
Nondedicated physical slots	20	21 (48 cm rack)	19	16	26 (48 cm rack)

Paul Borrill has been technical manager at Spectra-Tek (UK) Ltd since autumn 1985, prior to which he was a research fellow at the University College London, UK, Mullard Space Science Laboratory. Before university he spent several years in the UK merchant navy as a radio and electronics officer. Graduating with an honours degree in physics from the University of Manchester, UK, in 1977, he has since been studying for a PhD in the field of space research applications of microprocessors (computer bus structures and fault-tolerant multiprocessor systems). He has acted as a consultant on computer system design, microprocessor system architecture and semiconductor device design for a number of European and US companies. He is also a member of the IEEE microprocessor standards committee, the IEE working party on standards and its subgroup on backplane buses, and the chairman of the IEEE P896 committee.

Experiences in designing the M3 backplane bus standard

M3 was developed at short notice to be a state-of-the-art multi-processor system bus for 16-bit micros. **Dante Del Corso** describes the design process

The M3 backplane bus was designed at the beginning of the 1980s with the goal of providing the backbone for development of a new family of multiprocessor systems. Being used by companies which are interested in the system market rather than in selling just boards, M3 did not receive widespread publicity. It did, however, apply some design solutions later incorporated in other better known buses. The paper focusses on the bus design process, and presents the environment and constraints of M3, its key features, current status and position with respect to other standards.

microsystems   backplane bus standards   M3 bus

The board designer's job is made much easier by following a well defined standard for the interconnection structure. Computer-aided design (CAD) tools presently available allow production of complete and reliable units in a short time if specifications are complete and correct. The main problem is now the writing of the specifications; that is, as far as this paper is concerned, the process of designing and specifying the communication structure — a backplane bus in most cases.

The 'design experience' described here refers to the process of bus design, not to module design. This paper describes how a backplane bus was defined, and the reasons behind some of the technical decisions which were made. The following sections present the goals of the M3 (modular multi micro) bus, the design trade-offs the 'design history' and the project environment — this last factor can contribute to the success of a design even more than purely technical aspects.

DESIGN PROCESS

Environment and history

Toward the end of the 1970s, new multiprocessor projects based on the then latest generation of 16-bit microprocessors were starting up. The status of backplane

Dipartimento di Elettronica, Politecnico di Torino, C. Duca degli Abruzzi 24, 10129 Torino, Italy

bus standards at that time was not adequate to fully support these architectures; the best available was Multibus I, and new standards like VME and P896 had still to come. In 1979 a large coordinated research effort on computer science was started in Italy (the Computer Science Program of the National Research Council). Some parts of it dealt with modular multiprocessor architectures, covering the various aspects from hardware to system and applications software, and it was therefore decided to follow a single standard for the new hardware expressly designed for these machines.

Since available bus standards were not satisfactory, the new M3 standard was defined[1] and used to build systems. The work started in October 1979; at the end of 1980 an experimental multiprocessor with three Z8001s was running[2]. The M3 specifications were refined and finally frozen in 1982[3]. Since then, M3 work has concentrated on documentation, industrial board design, application of new micros, and on further tests of some special functions of the protocol.

M3 is now used by both large and small companies involved in the industrial automation and control field. These companies are system builders, that is they usually sell complete machines and not boards, so a board market has not developed and the use of M3 is confined to the companies and research laboratories participating in the project. However, the results of this work are available to everybody interested in the use or design of M3 systems.

The design of M3 was carried out by a small group of people, as a joint effort between universities and industrial research laboratories. A key element for the success of the work was this cooperation, which put together experience from industry, research laboratories and international standardization committees (especially IEEE P896).

Goals

A condensed formulation of the M3 design goals would be

'Definition of a processor-independent system bus for high-performance multiprocessor machines based on 16-bit microprocessors'

In 1980, the main effort in this direction was the Futurebus (IEEE P896). Waiting for the final P896 specification was not feasible, because working systems had to be available within one year. However, the Futurebus project included ideas which were gaining a wide consensus of approval, eg board size and connector, A/D multiplexing, an asynchronous protocol, the 'event' concept and the serial bus. Some of these concepts were incorporated in M3, which therefore has many common features with the P896 specification as developed in 1980–81. Since then, P896 has evolved into a high-performance 32-bit bus, while M3 has been put to work with 16-bit machines.

A more extensive list of goals for M3 is

- to use standard board sizes and put all signals on a single indirect standard connector
- to support modular and easily reconfigurable systems, suitable for high-reliability applications
- to put emphasis on multiprocessor requirements — fast and flexible arbitration, bus lock primitives and special provisions for interprocessor communications
- to use the same specification for all buses available on a board connector (global, local or private)
- to define a protocol with handshake at the transaction level, being careful to minimize the complexity of interfacing with existing micros
- to provide hardware support to detect bus errors
- to define an extended set of bus operations, eg multiple interrupt structures, block transfers, indivisible operations and supervision capability
- to include an auxiliary serial bus for communications among intelligent units and as an emergency channel in case of failure of the parallel bus
- to obtain a good price/performance ratio

Some of the above listed goals were easily mapped into design constraints; others led to experiments before freezing the final design decisions. More details on the process of trading off desired features with acceptable complexity and cost are given below.

Mapping constraints into design decisions

The technical design decisions of M3 are presented here using a bottom-up approach (from physical to higher layers). The actual temporal sequence was not so straightforward; in many cases the choices at different levels interact, and loops were frequent in the design process.

One of the easy decisions was to use double Eurocard boards. This size was selected because it allows two connectors (ie two independent buses) and because it provides enough area to host the two bus interfaces and the core logic (memory, processor etc). Smaller boards cause unnecessary partitioning of functions (eg one board for the processor, another for the memory); larger ones may require multiple buffering and cause mechanical problems.

It was also decided to put all bus signals on a 64-pin DIN connector, both to limit the complexity of the board layout and to allow the use of standard flat cables for very short bus segments. The 64-pin limit put a severe challenge to the designer: pins became the most precious resource, and multiplexing became absolutely essential. Practical experience showed later that flat cables are not usable at run time because the propagation environment is too badly defined. Therefore a full 96-pin connector is now specified; the central row is used only for additional grounds, for a few infrequently used signals, and for 32-bit expansion. Flat cables are used only for connection to static test equipment.

After this step, the basic structure of typical M3 multiprocessor systems was defined. As shown in Figure 1, an M3 rack has two backplanes: a continuous one for the global bus, and a segmented one for local or private buses. Since all the buses accessible on board connectors follow the same M3 specification and the global bus is 'folded' on a segment of the other level, the same units can go on the global or local/private levels.

At the electrical level, the key decision is the electrical technology of the bus. The design group chose to use TTL devices, even at the expense of speed. Some experiments were carried out to select the best backplane configuration and a good compromise for terminations. Current M3 systems use 48 mA drivers on four- or six-layer backplanes with 200 Ω terminations.

Some discussions arose on the transfer protocol organization: should the main information path (address and data) be multiplexed or not? Most existing buses were fully parallel, and some people in the design group were concerned about performance and complexity penalties of multiplexing. However, most 16-bit microprocessors are already multiplexed, and a properly designed slave needs in any case a layer of bus buffers. Speed and chip count are therefore not very different for the two choices. The final decision was to multiplex, the other main arguments in favour of this being the 64 pin limit and power saving.

It is worth noting that, in the first implementations, both true and inverted address and data lines were used. An inverting buffer is, in principle, faster than a noninverting buffer, but the final choice was for a true bus because of the lack of inverting latches.

Having decided in favour of multiplexing, M3 exploited this technique to the full. As shown in Figure 2, arbitration, addressing, data, interrupts and event vectors are multiplexed and pipelined on the same lines (INF 0–29). A bus signal (ADDREN*) indicates the use of INF lines (selection phase or data transfer phase). Within each phase the other signals control the action sequences for addressing, arbitration, data transfer and interrupt requests.

The number of INF lines (a total of 30) emerged as a compromise between the address and status bits required by 16-bit microprocessors (24 bit + 6 bit) and the pin count limit.

TECHNICAL FEATURES

Arbitration

The selection of the arbitration protocol considered factors like speed, number of masters, variable priority and

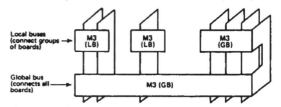

Figure 1. Physical structure of an M3 system

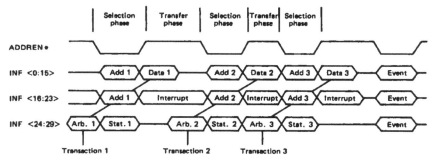

Figure 2. Multiplexing and pipelining of information. The figure shows three data transfers and one event cycle

visibility of current master. The final choice was a distributed arbiter with coded priority[4]. Arbitration priorities are carried by a subset of INF lines during the transfer phase. There were initially seven priority bits (on INF 24–29), but this number was later reduced to four to lower the arbitration delay and because, to limit bus loading, more than 16 masters cannot be fitted onto the same backplane.

The arbiter is the only bus unit which relies on a central timing signal (4 MHz clock) — experiments with distributed self synchronization were not satisfactory, and it seemed impossible to define a fully asynchronous reliable protocol (as in the current version of P896).

To get fair priority, a module which already has access to the bus cannot make another arbitration cycle as long as other requests are pending. A BUSREQ* signal has been defined for this purpose alone.

Addressing and data transfer protocol

The basic addressing cycle in the M3 bus is synchronous, and all the timing is guaranteed by the master. The slaves must be fast enough to catch the address information, but this is easy to accomplish because they have in any case a latch to store the multiplexed address.

The addressing phase uses a static qualifier (ADDREN*) and a strobe (CYCLE*). There is redundancy, but this makes the interface circuits of slave boards simpler.

The signals used in M3 bus for the data transfer are a WRITE* line and a pair of byte strobes, LODAVAL* and HIDAVAL*. Even though the first processor put to work on M3 was the Zilog Z8000, the two-strobe approach was selected rather than the byte/word technique in order to simplify interfacing with the MC68000 family. The penalty is a slower cycle for ECC memories in byte write operations; the error correcting circuitry must wait for the data strobes to compute the code.

The data transfer protocol uses a pair of handshake signals to allow broadcast or broadcall, as shown in Figure 3. This was another hard decision; the broadcast is necessary, but should all operations provide the time-consuming three-wire handshake? One possibility is to specify the type of operation at compile time by extracting it from system memory allocation tables. But if we allow the configuration to change at run time, the master cannot know if a transfer is single or multiple partner, so it was decided to use the three-wire handshake for all operations.

Block transfers were included in M3, even though no existing processor performs this operation directly. It emerged from some experimental implementations of the block protocol that this feature is useful only if directly supported by the processor on one side and by a direct memory access (DMA) controller on the other.

The only viable way to protect information within the 64 pin constraint is parity. Parity is expensive in terms of time and board area, so it was decided to keep it as an optional feature. Boards with or without parity can be mixed; those which generate parity activate a parity enable signal (PAREN*), thus enabling the parity checkers on the modules which receive the information.

Interrupt and interprocessor communication

Since M3 has to be used both at local level (for a single processor) and as a global bus (multiprocessor), two types of interrupt-like communication must be supported: interrupt requests from peripherals and 'events' from processors. Interrupt requests are activated by the peripherals requiring service by lowering one of the INF < 16:23 > lines in the data transfer phase. The complete interrupt structure, shown in Figure 4, is quite similar to the Multibus I or VME approach.

Events, if needed, use a special cycle which allows the transfer of a 30-bit vector from a commander to units provided with a special processor control register. This operation is controlled by a strobe (PROCINT*) allocated at first on external rows. The first implementations showed that this signal was very seldom used, because interprocessor communications were carried out by means of write cycles on shared memory areas. (This operation generates a normal interrupt towards the processor which

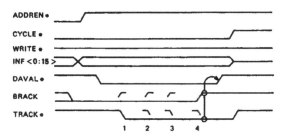

Figure 3. Broadcast data write cycle

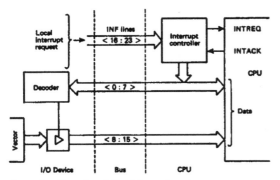

Figure 4. Transfer of the interrupt vector

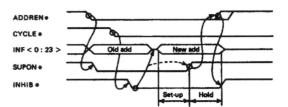

Figure 5. Address replacement with a supervisor

hosts the memory.) PROCINT* was left in the specification, but moved to the central row to make room for a more useful PWDOWN* signal.

Supervisor protocol

The M3 parallel bus protocol exploits a distributed control technique[5] to allow special operations performed by modules called supervisors. A supervisor can slow the operations and replace the information (address and data) both in the selection and in the transfer phases. Supervisors use only two dedicated lines on the bus backplane: SUPON* and INHIB*.

SUPON* always acts as a not-valid command. For instance, when SUPON* is active in the address phase, the slaves do not accept the address. INHIB* disables the bus drivers of the current commander. Figure 5 shows a cycle with address replacement: the supervisor inhibits the slaves from accepting the address by activating SUPON* at the beginning of the cycle, reads the address issued by the current commander and validated by the falling edge of CYCLE*, then disables the master address buffers using the INHIB* line, issues the new address, and signals that the address is valid by deactivating the SUPON* line.

These and other information transfer primitives can be used as debug aids, or to get memory protection,

distributed memory management, cache management, and error detection and recovery[6]. The supervisor approach was debated in the P896 committee, and a similar set of functions has been kept for distributed cache management.

Serial bus

A serial bus connects all boards plugged into an M3 system. This uses two lines, with a modified I^2C (inter integrated circuit) protocol[7]. A device which performs most of the functions assigned to the M3 serial bus is the Philips–Signetics MAB8400 microprocessor. An experimental chip for the modified I^2C protocol was designed and built within a multiproject chip[8].

Up to now, the serial bus has been used only for experimental implementations. The key point is, however, the availability of two backplane lines as an independent communication structure. If an IEEE standard for serial backplanes is defined, M3 will adopt it.

Timing and pinout

The final M3 protocol emerged as a trade-off between the synchronous and asynchronous approaches; the timing constraints were defined from measurements of propagation and settling time. A summary of timing specifications is given in Figure 6.

The complete pinout of the M3 bus is shown in Table 1. It was defined with the intention of being 'almost' compatible with P896, draft 4.1.

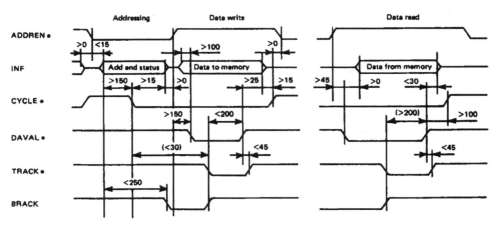

Figure 6. Timing specifications for M3 operations (not complete)

Table 1.   M3 bus pinout

	A	B	C
1	GND	GND	GND
2	+5	+5	+5
3	INF 0	res	INF 1
4	INF 2	res	INF 3
5	INF 4	res	INF 5
6	INF 6	res	INF 7
7	INF 8	res	INF 9
8	INF10	res	INF11
9	INF12	res	INF13
10	INF14	res	INF15
11	INF16	res	INF17
12	INF18	res	INF19
13	INF20	res	INF21
14	INF22	res	INF23
15	INF24	res	INF25
16	INF26	res	INF27
17	INF28	res	INF29
18	PAREN*	res	DAER*
19	WRITE*	GND	CYCLE*
20	LODAVAL*	GND	HIDAVAL*
21	ADDREN*	GND	TRACK*
22	PAR 0	res	BRACK
23	PAR 1	res	PAR 3
24	PAR 2	res	SERCK*
25	SUPON*	res	INHIB*
26	BREQ*	GND	BBSY*
27	PWFAIL*	GND	SERDAT*
28	NMI*	GND	RESET*
29	PROCDW*	res	−15
30	+15	PROCINT*	SCK
31	+5	+5	+5 backup
32	GND	GND	GND

DEVELOPMENT PROCESS AND CURRENT STATUS

Documentation and education

The best standard is completely useless if not fully and clearly documented. Care has been taken from the beginning to produce, maintain and propagate complete design documentation for M3.

Designing and putting into practice complex multiprocessor systems is not only a matter of backplane organization. In order to give as much information as possible to the user, the following support has been provided.

- preparation (and maintenance) of a technical document which includes not only the bus specification, but also general aspects of multiprocessor architectures, bus protocols and bus interface design; the latest document for M3 addresses all these subjects
- publication of a user bulletin, which presents bus design problems and examples of interfacing in a didactic way, and discusses in detail the particular features of M3

- organization of seminars and workshops on the hardware and system aspects of multiprocessors

The most complete document on M3 is that by Civera et al[3], which can be requested directly from the author of this paper. A shortened version can be found in Civera et al[9].

Systems and boards

According to different system requirements, families of boards with and without parity have been developed. The former are optimized for high reliability, and provide hardware support to recover safely from error conditions, at the expense of less dense integration (more boards for the same functions).

Most M3 processor boards are designed for multiprocessor architectures, that is they include a dual-port memory and two bus interfaces (global and local). The list of processors in use includes the Zilog Z8000 family, Intel's iAPX 286, and the Digital Equipment J11. Prototype boards with the Motorola 68000 and National Semiconductor 32016 have been built, mainly to verify the interface complexity. These designs showed that a complete M3 interface requires, besides bus transceivers, only a few programmable array logic devices. Because of this, no custom IC for the interface has been developed.

Slave boards include ECC memories and various types of I/O controllers (disc, local area network, intelligent general purpose etc).

Comparison with other standards

Since a bus specification originates from trade-offs between a number of constraints, only specific features, eg speed, width or cost, or technical problems, eg arbitration or handshake, can be compared. From this point of view, a comparison between M3 and other buses which address the same class of systems is shown in Table 2.

Table 2 does not answer the key question 'Which bus is best?' (From which point of view?) Neither will it tell a designer which bus to pick. (For which application?) The choice must be made for each specific case, and depends on technical and nontechnical factors related both to the standard itself (eg board availability, second sourcing, certification) and to the user's experience or attitude. (Proprietary design may be a means of discouraging competitors.) Many companies which have started to use M3 are continuing to use it for some applications, and consider other choices when needed. Some are joining the M3 group while others are considering different standards; design expertise gained during work with M3 can enable them to switch without problems.

Review of M3 after five years

There is now enough experience on M3 systems for M3's design choices to be revised and its constraints to be reconsidered.

The weakest point of M3 is speed: a transaction cannot be completed in less than 450 ns (150 ns per data item in

Table 2. Comparison of M3 with other bus standards

Feature	Multibus I	VME	M3	Multibus II (iPSB)	IEEE P896
Address/data					
(One connector)	20/16	24/16	24/16 (32/32)	32/32	32/32
(Two connectors)	–	32/32	–	–	–
Organization	Parallel	Parallel	Multiplexed	Multiplexed	Multiplexed
Timing	Asynchronous two-wire	Asynchronous two-wire	Synch./asynch. three-wire	Synchronous with wait	Asynchronous three-wire
Arbitration	Daisychain	4 daisychain	Distributed self selection 4 lines	Distributed self selection 5 lines	Distributed self selection 7 lines
Interrupts	8 lines	Daisychain	8 lines	Message passing	Message passing
Error detection	–	–	Parity	Parity	Parity
Serial bus	No	Yes	Yes	Yes	Yes
Centralized unit	Optional for arbitration	Needed for arbitration	Needed for clock	Needed	–

block operations). This limit is caused by the three-wire handshake, and by the possible existence of supervisors. After some experience on M3, the usefulness of the supervisor approach seems questionable. To provide for a full-function supervisor in the protocol costs time, and up to now it has been used only in laboratory experiments. Supervisor-like units with reduced functionality have been used as debug aids, indicating that a minimum of 'extended' functions (eg the three-wire handshake) must be kept in the protocol. These functions should be defined in such a way as to have a minimum performance penalty, and then only when required.

The handshake protocol is not technology independent because there is a constraint on the activation delay of BRACK. A true full handshake would have required a three-wire protocol also in the address phase, as in P896, but this again increases delays.

The pin allocation could have been better designed. (In fact, P896 improved upon it a few months later!) In M3 the grouping of bits is not optimized for 8-bit transceivers, and more grounds should be interleaved. (They were later allocated to the central row.)

Today it is quite easy to design complex semicustom ICs. This makes it possible to define a more complex protocol to gain speed (eg as in P896 block operations).

CONCLUSIONS

The M3 project put into practice many innovations in the area of tightly coupled multiprocessors and bus design. The results were new hardware and a fallout of design experience in a number of industries and universities. While for industrial applications M3 relies on defined design rules, it is still a test vehicle for research on communication structures and evaluation of multi-processor architectures[10, 11].

The tight project deadline played a key role in the fulfillment of the design goals, forcing the design group to take decisions optimized for existing machines. However, in the five following years the communication primitives supported by integrated CPUs did not show any real advances. The constraint of having to design an advanced

bus for today rather than a more advanced one for tomorrow resulted in a protocol which requires simple interfaces towards CPUs and memories, thus making more space available for the core functions on the boards.

The design time constraint also resulted in an important nontechnical decision — probably the most important decision taken overall — to start experiments (build prototypes) very early, and to freeze the specification just after operational verification, without looking for further improvements. An essential role in achieving results quickly can be played by people from industry, provided that their companies are really interested in the project.

REFERENCES

1 **Del Corso, D and Duchi, G** 'M3BUS: system specification for high performance multiprocessor machines' Proc. BIAS 81, Milan, Italy (October 1981) pp 329–342

2 **Conte, G et al** TOMP80 — a multiprocessor prototype' Proc. Euromicro 81, Paris, France (September 1981) pp 401–410

3 **Civera, P et al** 'Multiprocessors: M3BUS systems and TOMP architectures' CNR PFI-MUMICRO report (September 1983)

4 **Taub, D M** 'Contention resolving circuits for computer interrupt systems' Proc. IEE (September 1976) pp 845–850

5 **Del Corso, D** 'A test technique for microprocessor-based machines' Alta Frequenza (February 1979) pp 63–67

6 **Del Corso, D and Maddaleno, F** 'Extension of bus protocols: a technique for modular upgrade of processing systems' Proc. Euromicro 82, Haifa, Israel (September 1982) pp 169–179

7 **Moelands, A P M** 'Serial I/O with the MAB8400 series microcomputers' Philips Electron. Components Appl. Vol 3 No 1 (November 1980)

8 **Reyneri, L et al** 'An integrated controller for modified inter integrated circuit protocol' Microproc. Microprog. (submitted for publication)

9 **Civera, P et al** 'Some examples of multiprocessor buses' in Multiprocessor systems for realtime applications Kluwer, Dordrecht, The Netherlands (1985) pp 165–223

10 **Pasero**, E 'Multiprocessor benchmarks' in *Multi-microprocessor systems for real-time applications* Kluwer, Dordrecht, The Netherlands (1985) pp 279–299

11 **Danese**, G *et al* 'A new retry algorithm implemented on the standard microprocessor M3 bus' *FTCS-86* (submitted for presentation)

ACKNOWLEDGEMENTS

All work on M3 systems was sponsored by the Computer Science Program of the National Research Council (CNR), Italy, as part of the projects MUMICRO and MODIAC. The first experiments were carried out at the Dipartimento di Elettronica of the Politecnico di Torino. The companies mainly involved in the design and test process were Ansaldo/Esacontrol (Genova) and Prima Progetti (Torino).

M3 is a trademark of the CNR. Those who received official credit for its development are M Belluca, D Del Corso, G Duchi, G Girardi, G Neri, E Pasero and A Serra.

Dante Del Corso received a Dr. Ing. degree in electronics from the Politecnico di Torino, Italy, in 1970, after which he became a researcher at the Department of Electronics at the same Politecnico. He was involved there in the development of the M3 backplane bus standard. In 1982 he was made associate professor of electronics. During 1984 he took sabbatical leave at the Laboratoire de Microinformatique of EPFL, Switzerland. His current research interests are computer communication structures (especially buses), protocol design and verification techniques, multiprocessor architectures and VLSI design techniques. He is a member of IEEE (CS), Euromicro and AEI.

Why the Q-bus lives on

Digital Equipment's Q-bus has been in use for over 12 years, and has been continually adapted to take account of advancing technology.
Steve Dawes explains how it has been possible to 'teach an old bus new tricks'

The paper describes how the Q-bus has evolved in the 12 years since its original specification. Use of 'spare lines', the addition of parity memory and methods of increasing direct memory access (DMA) bandwidth are covered. Accessing of the I/O page is discussed. Changes to the Q-bus interrupts are reviewed and the Micro PDP-11/83's private memory interconnect (PMI) scheme for speeding memory access is described.

microsystems   backplane buses   Q-bus

The Q-bus was designed by Digital Equipment Corp. (DEC) over twelve years ago. Since 1974 it has been used with at least twelve new processors and countless Q-bus interface and memory boards have been designed. In that time the bus has almost doubled its effective bandwidth, and has increased its address space by 64 times. This paper examines how that growth has been possible whilst maintaining backward compatibility with older designs. The techniques discussed here could also be applied to preserve the usefulness of other buses.

Much of the information has been obtained by experience alone, although some basic reference sources are quoted. The reader is assumed to have a passing knowledge of Q-bus, or a more detailed knowledge of the Unibus.

The Q-bus is a multiplexed bus; it was conceived by DEC as a low-cost implementation of the company's Unibus. Originally Q-bus consisted of

- sixteen multiplexed address and data lines (BDAL ⟨15:00⟩)
- six data transfer control lines (BBS7, BDIN, BDOUT, BRPLY, BSYNC, BWTBT)
- six system control lines (BHALT, BREF, BEVNT, BINIT, BDCOK, BPOK)
- seven interrupt and direct memory access (DMA) control lines (BIAKI, BIAKO, BDMGI, BDMGO, BIRQ4, BDMR, BSACK)
- nine spare lines

Although the Q-bus is defined by its active lines, DEC included nine spare lines for future use. Furthermore, many of the control lines are only defined at certain times,

so that spare capacity is available by using the same lines at different times within the cycle.

When the Q-bus was originally designed, it was for just one processor, core memory planes, RAM memory with external refresh, and very few interface cards. Gradually the Q-bus has had to increase in power to match the power of the boards plugged into it. It has done so by using some of its spare capacity. In addition to the originally defined lines, the bus definition now includes

- two multiplexed address/parity lines (BDAL ⟨17:16⟩)
- four extended address lines (BDAL ⟨21:18⟩)
- three additional interrupt request lines (BIRQ5, BIRQ6, BIRQ7)

The following power, ground and spare lines are also defined

- eight ground lines
- three +5 V supply lines
- two +12 V and two −12 V supply lines
- three battery backup supply lines
- two spare lines to prevent damage if modules are inserted incorrectly
- four maintenance spaces for test purposes
- four unassigned spares, used mainly by processors

The other method of increasing performance in a system is to implement the bus scheme as closely as possible to the official definition. The actual bus timing relationships for Q-bus have been published[1], but it is interesting to note that much of the bus's backward compatibility has come from designing interfaces to the official definition of the bus rather than to the performance of each newly available processor.

For example, consider the implementation of control signals shown in Table 1. The LSI-11/23 read cycles were $(190 − 130) + (285 − 196) + (720 − 220) = 649$ ns shorter than on the previous processor, the LSI-11/2. They could, in theory, be up to 146 ns shorter and still be within the original design specification and hence work with all existing boards in the range.

ACCESSING THE I/O PAGE

DEC learnt an important lesson from its experiences with Unibus. The Unibus was limited in its growth potential because all of the I/O page devices decoded a normal

Rapid Systems Ltd, Denmark Street, High Wycombe, Bucks HP11 2ER, UK

0141–9331/86/02108–07 $03.00 © 1986 Butterworth & Co. (Publishers) Ltd

Table 1. Implementation times of Q-bus control signals

	Q-bus specification	KD11-F (LSI-11/2)	KDF11-A (LSI-11/23)
BSYNC L — BDIN L	100 ns minimum	190 ns	130 ns
BSYNC L — BDOUT L	200 ns minimum	285 ns	260 ns
Address set-up time	150 ns minimum	285 ns	196 ns
Address hold time	100 ns minimum	100 ns	100 ns
Reply to DIN/DOUT	150 ns minimum	720 ns minimum	220 ns minimum
inactive time		1120 ns maximum	285 ns maximum

address pattern. All PDP-11s, however, have the I/O page in the top 4k words of address space, which means that the effective address changes according to the size of the total address space. The address space of a PDP-11 is either 16 bit, 18 bit or 22 bit according to its mode, but the Unibus was limited to 18-bit addressing because every I/O device decoded its 18-bit address from the bus.

The designers of the Q-bus made provision for growth by getting the bus master (usually the processor) to generate a new signal, BBS7. The signal originally stood for 'bus bank 7 select', a hangover from the days of banked memory. BBS7 is interpreted by all I/O devices as meaning: 'All address bits above 12 are asserted.' Use of BBS7 simplifies the design of the interface cards, but also means that the address range could be arbitrarily changed from 16 bit to 18 bit and finally to 22 bit without affecting the design of the interface cards.

There appears to have been an internal fight inside DEC over this issue, with a Unibus-style faction opposed to the BBS7 faction. The conflict was resolved by the company's introduction of the LSI-11/23 in 1978.

PARITY MEMORY ON THE Q-BUS

Another innovation which was added to the Q-bus after its original design was parity — not parity protection of the data over the bus, but the detection of parity errors within memory modules. What was required was a method to detect the parity errors when the data was being read from memory.

Of course, it is possible for the memory subsystem not to respond when it detects a parity error, and so to trap the processor. However, it was considered preferable to generate a special interrupt for this case.

The upper multiplexed lines BDAL 16 and BDAL 17 are not defined during either read or write data cycles, and it was proposed that these lines be used. The new processors (at the time) would monitor BDAL 16 and BDAL 17, and if both were asserted during a read then a parity error would be detected by the memory board. This would produce a trap through vector 114[1].

Similarly, if the parity detection logic was to be tested, then some method of introducing parity errors was required. BDAL 16 is used to indicate to the memory to 'write wrong parity'. This condition can then be detected by subsequent memory reads.

More recent memory subsystems have their own parity logic which captures the address of the offending location, but they still use the BDAL 16 and 17 technique for notifying the processor of an error.

INCREASING DMA BANDWIDTH

One of the primary parameters of any bus system is the rate at which data can be transported from a DMA device to memory — the DMA bandwidth. This was recognized to be one of the limiting factors behind the original Q-bus design. This section describes how the bandwidth was almost doubled using a technique known as block-mode DMA.

What is block-mode DMA?

Block-mode DMA is a method of data transfer which increases throughput due to the reduced handshaking necessary over the Q-bus. It was realized that most of the DMA transactions were to sequential locations in memory, not to random addresses. Therefore, if the memory was made intelligent enough it could increment the address, rather than needing to send the address with every word of data transferred. In order to implement block-mode DMA both the master and slave devices must understand the block-mode protocol. If either device does not have block-mode capability the transfers proceed via standard DATI (data word input) or DATO (data word output) cycles.

Conventional DMA on the Q-bus

Under conventional DMA operations, after a DMA device has become bus master it begins the data transfers. This is accomplished by gating an address onto the bus followed by data being transferred to or from the memory device. If more than one transfer is performed by the temporary bus master the address portion of the cycle must be repeated for each data transfer. Since the Q-bus is a multiplexed bus, the address transfers take a significant period of time.

Block-mode DMA on the Q-bus

Under block-mode DMA operations, an address cycle is followed by multiple word transfers to sequential addresses. Data throughput is therefore increased, due to the elimination of the address portion of each transfer after the initial transfer.

It is the ingenious use of the control signals which is of interest here. This method of DMA transfer has been implemented in a manner which is backward compatible with older devices and does not use any additional control signals. The philosophies behind the various DMA techniques[2] are introduced below.

Single-cycle mode

Single-cycle-mode DMA on the Q-bus requires that the DMA device gains control of the bus through an arbitration cycle. During the arbitration cycle the DMA device becomes bus master by first asserting a DMA request (BDMR). When the arbiter acknowledges this request it issues a DMA grant (BDMGO). In the event that there is more than one DMA device in the backplane the grant signal is daisychained from device to device. Eventually the device that issued the DMA request will latch the grant signal and take control of the bus, and proceed with the DMA transfer.

On becoming bus master the device asserts BSACK and is allowed to do one word transfer to or from memory, during which time the CPU is idle. Certain processors, such as the KDJ11-B series (used in the PDP-11/73 plus and PDP-11/83), have a cache memory with dual tag store which allows them to process data while DMA transfers are occurring. Regardless of which processor type is used, only one transfer is allowed in single-cycle mode. If the device must perform additional transfers, it must go through the bus arbitrator cycle again (Figure 1).

In single-cycle mode, the theoretical transfer rate across the Q-bus is 1.66 Mbyte s^{-1} (833k word s^{-1}). A device such as the DRV11-B or the newer 22-bit-compatible DRV11-WA can transfer data at a rate of 250k word s^{-1} while in single-cycle mode.

Burst mode

It soon became obvious that there would be occasions where the single-cycle transfer rate would not be sufficient. In special cases a DMA device, once granted bus mastership, may hold on to it for as long as it wishes. This technique is called burst mode.

Burst-mode DMA can be performed by devices such as the DRV11-B. Once the DMA controller has become bus master (through the arbitration routine described above for single-cycle mode) and has asserted BSACK, the DMA transfers can begin. Each data word that is transferred is accompanied by an address that the data word is targeted for. In burst mode, loading an octal value into the 16-bit word count register (WCR) allows for that number of words (64 kbyte maximum) to be transferred under one arbitration (Figure 2). This differs from single-cycle mode, where the WCR can be loaded with the same value but each single word transfer requires a new arbitration cycle (ie in order to transfer 64 kbyte of data it would require 65 536 arbitration cycles).

The theoretical transfer rate across the Q-bus in burst mode remains at 1.66 Mbyte s^{-1}, although a device such as the DRV11-WA operating in burst mode can transfer data at a rate twice that of a DRV11-WA operating in single-cycle mode, at 500k word s^{-1}. In burst mode the DMA bus master maintains control of the bus until it has transferred all of the required data. Burst mode has the advantage of moving large blocks of memory across the bus with no delay, but it has the disadvantage that no other device (including the CPU) has access to the bus during that time; this can have a severe impact on system performance.

DMA compromise

Since single-cycle mode requires a rearbitration for every data transfer, and burst mode can adversely affect system performance in some cases, DEC made some compromises with certain DMA controllers. Most DEC devices will perform limited burst-mode operation. These controllers (eg the RXV21 and RLV12) are allowed up to four words of data transfer per arbitration cycle (Figure 3). Each word being transferred is preceded on the bus by an address that the data word is targeted for. This allows data to move across the bus with a minimum of rearbitration. However, when a group of four transfers is finished, the DMA devices must again go through the arbitration cycle in order to allow other devices the opportunity to use the bus. If no other bus requests are pending at a higher priority, then bus mastership will be returned to the device for the next set of data transfers. The bus request priority is determined solely by the physical distance from the bus arbiter (the processor) as the grant signals are chained down the bus.

Block mode

Block-mode DMA may be implemented on devices designed for use with memories that support this type of transfer, giving increased throughput. Block-mode DMA devices only operate in block mode when required to do so; they may operate like single-cycle-mode devices if they are only doing a single word transfer, and they will always look like single-cycle-mode devices when used with non-block-mode memory.

Once a block-mode device has arbitrated for the bus, the starting memory address is asserted, followed by data for that address, then by data for consecutive addresses (Figure 4). By eliminating the assertion of the address for each data word, the transfer rate is almost doubled. The DMA device should monitor the BDMR line; if the line is not asserted after the seventh transfer then the device can continue. This allows a maximum of 16 data transfers for one arbitration cycle. If the BDMR line is not monitored by the DMA device then a maximum data transfer of eight words is allowed after completing one bus arbitration

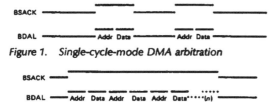

Figure 1.   Single-cycle-mode DMA arbitration

Figure 2.   Burst-mode DMA arbitration

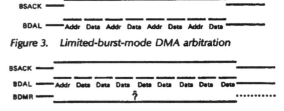

Figure 3.   Limited-burst-mode DMA arbitration

Figure 4.   Block-mode arbitration

cycle. Block-mode DMA transactions can be described either as DATBI (block mode data in) or DATBO (block mode data out).

Block-mode devices such as the DEQNA, the RQDX1 and the MSV11-P memories can transfer data across the bus at rates that approach twice that of DMA devices in burst mode. The actual rate is dependent upon the device itself.

Control implementation

Special attention should be paid to the use of BREF and BBS7 signals when performing a DATBO cycle. The original definitions of these signals were for external memory refresh and I/O page selection respectively. However, the definition of these signals referred only to particular combinations of control lines; there was no definition for them at other times. Block-mode DMA has now used this previously 'inactive' time to implement the new protocol.

MORE FLEXIBLE INTERRUPTS

Interrupts are generated on the Q-bus by devices that wish to gain the attention of the processor for service. When the Q-bus was originally defined there were very few devices available and a very simple scheme was implemented. However, as systems became more complex a method was required which ensured that all of the old devices still operated, but which gave the processor (and hence the operating system) much finer control over the permitted interrupts. The final design provides for a two-dimensional four-level automatic priority interrupt scheme.

Interrupt overview

The processor has three bits in the processor status word (PSW) which encode to form the priority level (0–7). Each interrupt class has a priority level associated with it. If a device with an interrupt priority higher than the current processor running priority asserts BIRQn, then the processor will honour the interrupt at the end of the current instruction.

The bus arbiter will then assert BIAKO. This signal is daisychained down the bus, passing through every card (entering as BIAKI and leaving as BIAKO). When the device has received the interrupt acknowledge, it does not pass the acknowledge signal any further; it places a vector onto the bus and asserts BRPLY.

The processor receives the vector and uses it to find the service routine. The device clears down the signals on the bus[3].

Single priority interrupts

When the LSI-11 was first introduced, there was only one interrupt request line — BIRQ4. The interrupts were therefore either effectively ON or OFF as determined by the processor priority being less than four, or greater than or equal to four, respectively. Some element of priority for the various interrupt sources could be given by the

physical distance from the processor. Those devices nearest the processor would always get their interrupts granted, even if another device further down the bus was also requesting interrupt service.

Multiple priority interrupts

By the time the LSI-11/23 was introduced, it had become obvious that multiple-priority interrupt request lines would be required. The bus architects had forseen this and had reserved some of the 'spare' lines for the extra three request lines. However, since most of the DEC devices were designed to the original scheme, a single interrupt acknowledge line still had to be used. The solution was for the interrupting device to assert more than one line, as described below.

BIRQ4 is asserted by all devices, for backward compatibility with earlier LSI-11 processors. The interrupt level required is also asserted. A special case exists for level 7 devices, which must also assert BIRQ6; this is done to simplify the monitoring and arbitration by level 4 and 5 devices.

In the full implementation, any interrupting device can be placed anywhere in a system backplane. To ensure that the single interrupt grant is picked up by the highest-priority interrupting device, every device must monitor the interrupt request lines to determine whether there is a higher-priority interrupt pending (Table 2).

Unfortunately, none of the DEC devices have ever monitored the interrupt request lines (although some devices have made provision for a DC103 chip by mounting the DC003 in a socket and feeding the extra request lines to the socket). Fortunately, a compromise system can be built where the devices are inserted in the backplane in priority order, thus preventing an interrupt grant being 'stolen' by a low-priority device, and without the need for the devices to monitor the other request lines.

MicroVAX II interrupt latency improvement

The newer block-mode DMA devices have the ability to hold the Q-bus for quite a long time, increasing interrupt (and DMA) latency. The block-mode DMA specification includes a feature to reduce DMA latency, which can also be used to reduce interrupt latency.

Any block-mode DMA device can transfer up to 16 words at a time. However, it must monitor the Q-bus signal BDMR (DMA request) after seven words have been transferred. If it sees that another device is requesting access to the bus it must close down the transfer after only eight words and rearbitrate for the bus. This gives other devices a chance to access the bus.

Table 2.   Four-level interrupt control lines

Module interrupt level	Asserts	Monitors
Level 4	BIRQ4	BIRQ5, BIRQ6
Level 5	BIRQ5, BIRQ4	BIRQ6
Level 6	BIRQ6, BIRQ4	BIRQ7
Level 7	BIRQ7, BIRQ6, BIRQ4	–

The MicroVAX II also uses this trick to reduce interrupt latency. If it detects an interrupt request (IRQ, BEVNT or power fail) and a block-mode DMA is in progress, it raises the BDMR line to get the current bus master to relinquish the bus as soon as possible. This effectively halves the worst-case interrupt latency time.

FASTER ACCESS TO MEMORY

The most critical function of a bus system is to transport data between the processor and main memory. As the speed of processors and memories began to rise, it became obvious that some new technique would be required to increase the bandwidth still further.

Various techniques involving direct memory connection (ie not via the bus) have been used in the case of the MicroVAX II processor. While these techniques solved the problem of speed, they did not use the bus and are hence outside the scope of this discussion. Note that the MicroVAX memory is not on the Q-bus (Figure 5), and can only be accessed via the Q-bus scatter gather map or Q-bus mapping registers (a technique which is very similar to the Unibus mapping on the PDP-11/70).

Various other techniques involving cache memory have also been used on the J-11 based processors (ie the PDP-11/73, PDP-11/73 plus and PDP-11/83). While they decreased the net access time to memory, however, they did not alter the actual transfer time from CPU to memory.

The foundation for the solution was laid some time ago, when the backplanes for the newer generation of systems, the MicroPDP-11s, were designed. Provision was made then for extra interboard connections using a scheme called CD interconnect (Figure 6). The four contact fingers of a quad module are designated A, B, C and D. The Q-bus is normally only accessed on fingers A and B. In these backplanes, the first three or four slots are wired with Q-bus on A and B, but the top side of C and D connects to the bottom side of the next slot position. By connecting top and bottom contacts together on a board, a 'short haul' bus can be built.

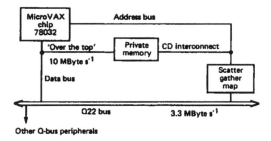

Figure 5. MicroVAX II private memory interconnect

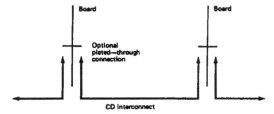

Figure 6. CD interconnect

Each CD interconnect connects all the pins on one side of a board to the pins on the opposite side of the next board in the backplane. If a board connects the pins on one side to those on the other side, then the bus is extended to the next slot. This pseudobus, designated private memory interconnect (PMI), is described below for the MicroPDP-11/83 system. The description is not intended to be a design guide for PMI, since no devices other than the CPU and memory will make use of it.

PMI general description

A MicroPDP-11/83 system consists of the KDJ11-B CPU and one or more MSV11-J memories in a Q-bus backplane (Figure 7). The slots used for the CPU and memory use the CD interconnect. In a MicroPDP-11/83 configuration, the first one or two slots in a BA23 backplane (an eight-slot backplane with the first three slots Q/CD) are reserved for MSV11-J memory. The CPU is put in the third slot.

Putting the CPU after the memory ends the PMI because the PMI signals from the CD side of the CPU board are only on the component side of the CPU board. 'Private memory interconnect' is the addition of 14 unique signals to the Q-bus. These new signals use the CD part of the backplane in a KDJ11-B Q-bus system for communications between the KDJ11-B CPU and one or two MSV11-J memories. Only the CPU and memory may communicate over this bus (hence the description 'private'). The Q-bus address and data lines are used for passing addresses and data between the CPU and memory. All other Q-bus transactions proceed as before.

It is important to appreciate that only the extra control signals pass over the CD interconnect; the actual data transfer takes place over the Q-bus as before. In practice the PMI protocols take advantage of the predictability of accessing memory: there are considerably less handshakes involved in a data transfer since both the processor and the memory 'know' what is involved. Furthermore, the MSV11-J memory is implemented in such a manner that not only is error correcting code used but two words are delivered in quick succession over the 16-bit Q-bus, a technique referred to by DEC as double pumping.

The PDP-11/84 Unibus system uses the KTJ11-B Unibus adaptor, KDJ11-B CPU, and one or two MSV11-J memories. No Q-bus devices may be configured with the PDP-11/84 system. Five of the PMI signals are used only with Unibus systems and will not be discussed further. All communications between Unibus devices and the KTJ11-B occur according to the Unibus protocol. The KTJ11-B provides the interface between PMI and Unibus protocols.

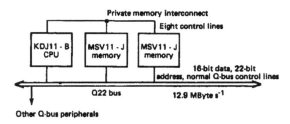

Figure 7. PDP-11/83 private memory interconnect

(Note that the specification for the private memory bus provides for only three slots, a maximum of 10 cm of wire.)

To understand PMI it is necessary to describe some of the bus cycles used by PMI and compare them with ordinary Q-bus cycles. There are four PMI cycles used in the MicroPDP-11/83 system: DATI (data word input); DATIP (data word input with pause); DATO (data word output); and DATOB (data byte output).

Control implementation

As with block-mode DMA, PMI has been implemented in a fashion which preserves backward compatibility for the other bus users. Most of the extra control signals, however, are provided on the CD side of the boards. One control line has been used from the normal Q-bus.

Q-bus signals such as TWTBT[4] are used differently during a PMI cycle than during a normal Q-bus transaction (Table 3); TWTBT is not normally used during a DATI cycle, for example.

It becomes evident that there is an essential difference between normal Q-bus transactions and PMI transactions. Q-bus transactions are all based on handshaking. During a DATI Q-bus transaction, the memory responds with BRPLY after BDIN from the processor; there must be these signals between the devices to indicate that the transaction has taken place. During a PMI DATI transaction, a strobe signal from the memory passes between the memory and CPU; the only further communication between memory and CPU is the actual data transfer. Only upon the transmission of the second possible data word is parity information sent along with the second data word. No other memory-CPU signalling occurs.

Timing comparisons

At this point it is interesting to make some timing comparisons between Q-bus and PMI DATI transactions. Considering a Q-bus DATI transaction, the cycle time (timing from BSYNCH to TRPLY, ignoring addressing time) is 510 ns for MSV11-M. The MSV11-M was chosen because its cycle time does not include the ECC overhead of the MSV11-J. Add to this a 320 ns access time and the total time to transfer one word from memory to CPU is 830 ns. Now, if two words are to be transferred in this manner, 300 ns must be added due to the delay between RRPLY and TSYNCH, so that other Q-bus devices can access the bus. This results in a 1130 ns total delay for a two-word transfer using MSV11-M parity memory.

The MSV11-J memory access time (time from RPBCYC to PRDSTB) is 417 ns. The CPU receives the second data word 58 ns later, at the trailing edge of PRDSTB. This means that PMI is approximately 2.5 times faster than Q-bus on two-word reads from memory to CPU. (This also accounts for the time the ECC requires to do its modified

Table 3. Private memory bus cycle types

BWTBT L	PBYT L	Description
H	H	DATI or DATBI cycle
H	L	DATIP cycle
L	H	DATO cycle
L	L	DATOB cycle

Steve Dawes leads a team of DEC support engineers at Rapid Systems, a division of Rapid Recall Ltd based at High Wycombe, UK. After studying physics and mathematics at Cambridge University, UK, he turned to engineering and finally to systems programming. His first experience of the DEC PDP-11 minicomputer was in 1976, when he designed and implemented a compiler and multiuser operating system; subsequently he spent two years working with PDP-11 and VAX minicomputers on an English language query program suite for the Total database. Currently his work involves presales consultancy and postsales support for Q-bus systems based on PDP-11s and MicroVAXs.

Hamming code versus the MSV11-M parity check.) For each 18 bit of MSV11-J memory there is 6 bit used for ECC. This accounts for the space needed on the MSV11-J for 2 Mbyte of memory, where 4 Mbyte is possible on the same board area in the MSV11-Q.

CONCLUSIONS

The Q-bus has survived by not only evolving, but also maintaining backward compatibility. The strict use of a bus specification, and the strict adherence of designers to that specification, has enabled designers to take full advantage of improvements as they are made.

The improvements fall into three main classes. First, as each new processor is developed the implementation of the bus has been brought closer to the formal definition. This improvement can almost always be made to any asynchronous bus, and is especially useful if the bus is multiplexed.

Second, several of the edge connectors which were 'reserved for future use' have been used. There is obviously a limit to the amount of expansion which is possible by this means. Any bus designer could make provision within his/her specification for spare signal lines.

Third, various control signals have been used at different times and in different ways to provide new types of bus cycle. This technique is only possible if the bus was originally defined sufficiently accurately to ensure that no existing design would be confused by the new protocols.

There have been many other minor modifications to the Q-bus specification during its lifetime, but the highlights have been presented here. If the Q-bus can still be useful after 12 years, then perhaps we should all look in more detail at the spare capacity of other existing bus architectures rather than spending our time defining new ones.

REFERENCES

1   *Microcomputers and memories handbook* (EB-20912-20) Digital Equipment, Maynard, MA, USA (1983) pp 210–213

2   *Microcomputers and memories handbook (EB-20912-20)* Digital Equipment, Maynard MA, USA (1983) pp 219–262

3   *Microcomputers and memories handbook (EB-20912-20)* Digital Equipment, Maynard, MA, USA (1983) pp 196–200, 236

4   *Microcomputers and memories handbook (EB-20912-20)* Digital Equipment, Maynard, MA, USA (1983) pp 224–225, 239

5   *PDP-11 architecture handbook (EB-23657)* Digital Equipment, Maynard, MA, USA (1982) Chapters 9 and 10, Appendix E

6   *Micro PDP-11 handbook (EB-24944-18)* Digital Equipment, Maynard, MA, USA (1983) Appendix E

7   *MicroVAX I technical description (EK-KD32A-TD)* Digital Equipment, Maynard, MA, USA (1984) Chapter 9 and Appendix 1

8   *PDP-11/70 processor handbook* Digital Equipment, Maynard, MA, USA (1975)

9   **Kent, P** *Micronotes* Digital Equipment, Maynard, MA, USA (1985)

Advances in STD system capability

Designed as an 8-bit industrial control system, the STD bus might seem outmoded by today's standards. But **David Batchelor** argues that STD is evolving to address 16-bit technology and a wider variety of applications

The paper is concerned with the work of the STD Manufacturers Group in defining and maintaining standards. Attention is given to the 8088 standard and to the CMOS STD bus. The impact of these advances on STD architectures is discussed along with the arbitration methods for multimaster CPU implementation. These concepts are expanded to include hybrid industrial systems comprising an IBM PC alongside STD.

microsystems   backplane buses   STD

When it was introduced in 1978, the STD bus was conceived as a universal 8-bit microprocessor bus standard. The idea was to provide a low-cost system to be used in the industrial control environment as a replacement for discrete logic implementations; the basic STD system architecture is shown in Figure 1.

The STD bus has, however, found wider application than was originally intended in areas far removed from industrial control, such as office systems and ticket dispensing machines. Ironically, STD has become a victim of this diversification: while manufacturers promoted the bus as an 8-bit fully defined system, consumers were using the product in applications where the greater power of 16-bit and quasi-16-bit processors could clearly be used to advantage. It is no surprise that exponents of other bus structures exploited this apparent flaw in the STD marketing strategy.

STD vendors have been slow to respond to the challenge to their bus, but the designers have been quietly keeping pace with advancing technology.

Perhaps the poor market image of STD bus is due to its wide range of manufacturers. The bus standards were not developed by a major silicon producer and are still not copyrighted, making STD one of the most successful nonproprietary bus structures in the world. Controlling and monitoring the STD bus standards is the responsibility of the STD Manufacturers Group (STDMG) which now has over 88 member companies[1]. The STDMG is a voluntary organization that maintains close technical contact and

exists to maintain and enhance the STD standard. The group has issued a document, *STD specification and practice*[2], which resolves many issues such as priority

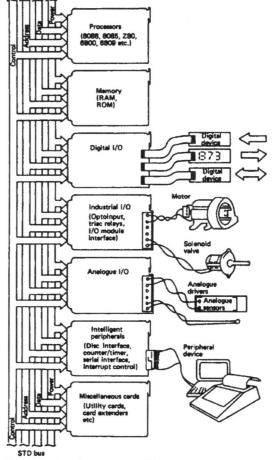

Figure 1.   STD bus system architecture

Technitron Ltd, Doman Road, Camberley, Surrey GU15 3DH, UK

0141-9331/86/02115-05 $03.00 © 1986 Butterworth & Co. (Publishers) Ltd

interrupt, bus priority keying, backplane practice and memory expansion. Of particular interest at present is the work of the STDMG in the area of 16-bit processors.

STD BUS STANDARDS

The latest proposed STD bus connector pin assignment is shown in Table 1. It can be seen that this assignment makes provision for up to 24-bit memory addressing and full 16-bit data words using a multiplexing technique. The address bus extension is achieved by multiplexing lines A16–23 onto eight data bus lines, while the data bus extension is implemented by multiplexing D8–D15 onto their corresponding address bus signals.

Since the STD bus accommodates many processors and yet remains a synchronous system, it is necessary to define certain pins for specific processors. Table 2 shows how this is done.

The pins are carefully selected when new CPU chips are added to the STD specification to ensure existing I/O

Table 2. Pin definitions for different microprocessors

Processor	MCSYNC	STATUS 1	STATUS 0	MEMEX	A0
8085	ALE	S1	S0	–	
Z80	(RD + WR + INTAK)	M1	–	–	
NSC800	ALE	S1	S0	–	
8088	ALE	DT/R	SS0	–	
8086*	ALE	DT/R	SS0	BHE	A0
6800	Q1	UMA	R/W	–	
6809E	EOUT (Q2)	LIC	R/W	–	
6502	Q2	SYNC	R/W	–	
68000*	AS	M1		LDS	UDS

*Proposals being reviewed by STDMG

and memory cards remain compatible. In the cases of the 68000 and the 8086, new word-wide memory cards have still to be developed to accommodate 16-bit data transfers. Once the concept of special memory cards for 16-bit applications is accepted it becomes possible to introduce memory cards which allow the processors to run without wait states. This provides a bus transfer rate of

Table 1. Proposed STD bus pin connector assignment, with address lines A8–A15 multiplexed to incorporate 16-bit processors

		Component side					Circuit side		
	Pin	Signal name	Signal flow	Description		Pin	Signal name	Signal flow	Description
Logic power bus	1	V$_{cc}$	In	Logic power (+5 V DC)		2	V$_{cc}$	In	Logic power (+5 V DC)
	3	GND	In	Logic ground		4	GND	In	Logic ground
	5	VBB#1/VBAT	In	Logic bias #1/Battery power		6	VBB#2/DCPD*	In	Logic bias #2/Power down
Data bus	7	D3/A19	In/Out	Data bus/address extend		8	D7/A23	In/Out	Data bus/address extend
	9	D2/A18	In/Out			10	D6/A22	In/Out	
	11	D1/A17	In/Out			12	D5/A21	In/Out	
	13	D0/A16	In/Out			14	D4/A20	In/Out	
Address bus	15	A7	Out	Address bus		16	A15/D15	Out	Address bus/Data bus extend
	17	A6	Out			18	A14/D14	Out	
	19	A5	Out			20	A13/D13	Out	
	21	A4	Out			22	A12/D12	Out	
	23	A3	Out			24	A11/D11	Out	
	25	A2	Out			26	A10/D10	Out	
	27	A1	Out			28	A9/D9	Out	
	29	A0	Out			30	A8/D8	Out	
Control bus	31	WR*	Out	Write to memory or I/O		32	RD*	Out	Read memory or I/O
	33	IORQ*	Out	I/O address select		34	MEMRQ*	Out	Memory address select
	35	IOEXP	In/Out	I/O expansion		36	MEMEX	In/Out	Memory expansion
	37	REFRESH*	Out	Refresh timing		38	MCSYNC*	Out	CPU machine cycle synchronize
	39	STATUS 1*	Out	CPU status		40	STATUS 0*	Out	CPU status
	41	BUSAK*	Out	Bus acknowledge		42	BUSRQ*	In	Bus request
	43	INTAK*	Out	Interrupt acknowledge		44	INTRQ*	In	Interrupt request
	45	WAITRQ*	In	Wait request		46	NMIRQ*	In	Nonmaskable interrupt
	47	SYSRESET*	Out	System reset		48	PBRESET*	In	Pushbutton reset
	49	CLOCK*	Out	Clock from processor		50	CNTRL*	In	AUX timing
	51	PCO	Out	Priority chain out		52	PCI	In	Priority chain in
Auxiliary Power bus	53	AUX GND	In	AUX ground		54	AUX GND	In	AUX ground
	55	AUX + V	In	AUX positive (+12 V DC)		56	AUX -V	In	AUX negative (−12 V DC)

*Low-level active indicator

8 MHz; using the most recent design of four-layer motherboard, this can be achieved without loss of system integrity. While the 8086 and 68000 (true 16-bit) implementations are, at the time of writing, pending STDMG approval, the 8088 is fully approved and the subject of many product innovations. The 8088 simply restricts the above to 20-bit memory addressing and 10-bit I/O addressing with the data highway at 8 bit.

The demultiplexing of the address/data bus is achieved by using the rising edge of the signal MCSYNC to latch the upper address lines, while the data word demultiplexing combines MEMEX and A0. For example, the scheme currently being assessed for the 8086 is shown in Table 3.

8088 MULTIMASTER ARBITRATION INTERFACE

To optimize the performance of systems using 16-bit processors, it is necessary to provide a scheme of bus arbitration that permits multiple CPUs to be active and share global resources. The arbitration interface on the STD bus permits up to 16 CPUs to exist on the bus simultaneously and involves five of the standard control lines. BUSRQ and BUSAK are used by the arbitration logic to indicate when a processor requests the bus and when the bus is in use. The priority chain signals PC1 and PC0 are used to prevent bus contention arising from simultaneous access. The final signal is the CNTRL line, which is used to synchronize all the CPU interfaces. Figure 2 shows a typical multimaster CPU block diagram.

The arbitration logic can be configured to operate in one of four modes, as described below.

Hardware lock

In this configuration the CPU sets an output port lock signal which, when sensed by the bus arbiters, keeps BUSAK asserted, thus preventing other processors from accessing the bus. Current implementations allow this to be deselected by on-card jumpers.

Software lock

This operates in a similar manner to the hardware lock but is initiated by executing an instruction with a 'lock' prefix. BUSAK is released when the processor has completed execution of the locked instruction.

Equal access

This mode allows all processors to share the bus with equal priority. Any arbiter can initiate a BUSRQ provided

Table 3. Implementation under assessment for the 8086

MEMEX	A0	Characteristic
0	0	Whole word transfer
0	1	Upper byte transfer
1	0	Lower byte transfer
1	1	No transfer

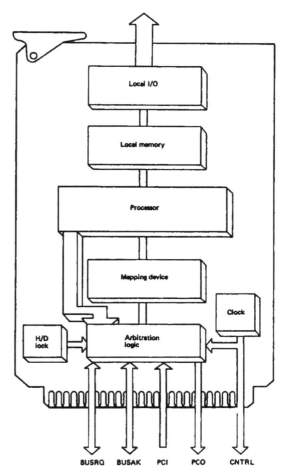

Figure 2. Typical multimaster processor card

that the signal is not already asserted by another processor. When BUSRQ is asserted the processor currently using the bus must release it at the end of its current machine cycle. The requesting processor then acquires the bus as shown in Figure 3. If there is no pending BUSRQ, arbitration does not occur and the bus remains a resource of the present processor.

DMA lock

This mode permits external devices to access the global bus resources under direct memory access (DMA). The

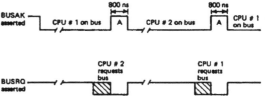

Figure 3. Multimaster CPU timing

highest card on the priority chain must be configured for DMA lock. This special configuration disables all arbiters on the chain when DMA occurs. The BUSRQ and BUSAK signals are then returned to their normal operating modes to accommodate the DMA transfer.

Implementation

Practical implementations of this arbitration strategy also combine a timer function with the bus arbitration facility so that more complex bus access schemes can be implemented. For example, using the timer to time out the hardware lock makes it possible to achieve a rotating master priority scheme; alternatively, by gating timer signals with the bus accesses it is possible to achieve time multiplexed arbitration. The slight redefinition of the BUSAK and BUSRQ signals does not undermine the bus standard since these signals are only used by DMA controllers and processor cards. The arbitration scheme accommodates the DMA controller, and it would never be required to use monomaster CPUs and multimaster CPUs together on the same bus.

CMOS STD BUS

One recent advance in STD bus is the trend towards fully CMOS versions of standard cards; in fact many manufacturers now design the CMOS card and retrofit standard MOS components. The standard STD bus temperature range is from 0°C to 60°C, but the CMOS bus that was approved by STDMG in 1985 has an extended temperature range from −40°C to +85°C. STD is one of the few buses actively supporting CMOS in this manner.

There are, at present, five members of the STDMG who actively manufacture a CMOS product line; this allows designers of systems for harsh environments to use STD bus as a standard component. Applications in which it is advantageous to use CMOS include: battery-backed or battery-operated systems; systems placed in industrial environments that are subject to electrical noise; and systems placed remotely (eg underground in direct heat or in subzero temperatures).

In the past, speed, price and availability have hindered the use of CMOS technology. The 74HC-type logic family and CMOS processor, memory and peripheral chips now provide CMOS advantages at essentially the same speed as NMOS parts. Although prices of CMOS parts remain slightly higher, some of the costs are offset by the lower price of packaging and reduced power consumption. CMOS processors currently supported by STD include the 80C85, the Z80C, the NSC800 and the 80C88.

LINKING STD TO THE IBM PC

Another area of system enhancement stems from the impact which the IBM PC has made on the industrial environment. Although it was not designed for industrial situations, the PC is becoming more prevalent day by day. The internal bus of the PC is very similar to the STD bus, and once 8088 CPUs became common it was inevitable that PC-STD link packages would emerge. (In fact an STD system has now been manufactured which

includes ROM-based MS-DOS 3.1; this system provides direct access to the largest pool of software tools and applications software available today.)

There are presently two connection methods to link STD bus to the PC: an I/O-only link (tight coupling) or a distributed processing system (loose coupling); these are shown in Figure 4.

In Figure 4a, STD and the PC are linked to form a distributed system able to communicate over RS232 or RS422 serial lines. This is a typical configuration of applications that require a combination of rugged monitoring or control with the data processing and display facilities of the PC. It has the advantage that several STD bus systems can be interconnected, providing complex local control functions under the control of a central computer.

The STD system is totally self contained and runs independently of the PC. The two systems communicate via a bidirectional 'mail box' which is port addressable and allows PC-STD data transfers under polled, interrupt or DMA control.

Figure 4b shows an STD system, with no processor, configured in a remote rack sited up to 45 m from the host. This system remains at all times under the direct control of the PC and simply permits the use of STD industrial I/O cards to be linked to the range of MS/PC-DOS software available for the PC. This approach provides the host with access to all STD memory and I/O facilities and permits the handling of STD interrupts.

Both systems are interconnected via a flat ribbon cable. Direct connection is used for short links while an optically isolated version can be used over large distances.

CONCLUSIONS

The STDMG has continually approved updates to the STD bus to allow the system to keep up with technology. The bus is now capable of handling 16-bit processors with

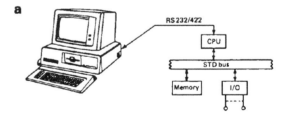

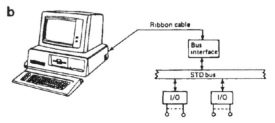

Figure 4. Hybrid IBM PC-STD systems: a, distributed system; b, remote I/O system

transfer rates of 8 MHz whilst keeping its original objectives of small card size and simple interfacing. The multimaster CPU concept further extends the STD bus to give solutions to yet more complex system problems. CMOS STD is actively supported by many vendors, and this will undoubtedly add to its popularity.

That STD is controlled by a committee should be seen as an advantage. All manufacturers have an opportunity to influence the direction of the technical advances made by the STD bus. The result is a product that does not aim specifically at using the latest silicon — nor does it exclude this — but rather at providing solutions to real industrial problems.

REFERENCES

1 *STD Manufacturers Group register STDMG (1984)* (available from Technitron Ltd, Camberley, UK)
2 *STD specification and practice STDMG (1984)* (available from Technitron Ltd, Camberley, UK)

David Batchelor graduated in electrical engineering from Brunel University, UK, where he specialized in computers and digital systems. On completion of a UK Ministry of Defence student training programme, he joined the Engineering Department of Technitron Ltd and became involved in the development and commissioning of several realtime industrial systems; these were based on a variety of bus structures and processors. After two years away from Technitron, during which time he was employed by Solartron as product specialist for digital instruments, he returned to take over the company's Microprocessor Division. In this capacity he is responsible for the company's marketing strategy and product direction in the areas of microprocessor buses and support instruments.

S100 in commercial applications

S100 bus, which can be found in systems in research laboratories, machine rooms, offices and banks, survives because of its performance/price characteristic, says **George W George**

IEEE 696/S100 is a well established industry standard bus. The large variety of proprietary S100 cards available allows the designer to tailor hardware to particular system requirements, with the advantage of reduced design cycle time and consequently lower product cost. This paper discusses the development of the bus and highlights aspects which give the bus its flexibility for systems design. The commercial advantages of S100 continue to be exploited by OEMs and some examples of applications are presented.

microsystems   multiprocessors   S100

Simplicity is the key theme in applications design. It is the essential element required to ensure cost-effective manufacture, test and maintenance of a product, and reflects directly on the marketability of a product. Universal acceptance of this principle maintains the popularity of modular systems design based on a standard backplane.

In the past it was system complexity that demanded the disciplines of modular design. Paths which carried data and other signals from module to module within a large system were a means to an end when it was physically impossible to condense the whole system onto a single board. The concept of one function per board had its benefits, not least in the areas of testing and maintenance.

In microprocessor system design the use of a backplane bus in early systems to carry signals from one functional board to another did not constitute a radical design decision; it would have been a departure from convention not to have included a backplane within a design. The important step, however, was the recognition of the benefits of an industrial standard backplane. Pro-Log opened the field in 1973 with the STD bus, which was announced in the hope that manufacturers with applications expertise would design the many different functional cards required to closely tailor hardware for specific system designs. The original STD specification had many inherent disadvan-

tages, not the least of which was the mixing of I/O and processor signals on the same restricted bus — the bus was based on a 56-pin edge connector card. Some years later Pro-Log, jointly with Mostek and IEEE P846 working party, redefined the bus. In the mean time a new bus had arrived.

In *Popular Electronics* (Jan. 1975) MITS introduced an 8-bit computer kit based on the Intel 8080 microprocessor. The computer, named the Altair, was designed around a backplane with 100-pin edge connector sockets. Selection of these sockets was apparently due to their availability as surplus stock from a supplier. The Altair became popular as a hobby computer, encouraging many companies to begin manufacturing Altair bus-compatible boards. The ready availability of a growing range of functional boards made system design simple. The Altair bus was therefore incorporated into other microcomputer systems, causing a further growth of the available range of bus-compatible boards. Cromemco adopted the name 'standard 100 bus', or S100, to give a common name to what many manufacturers were claiming was their own bus.

In 1983 a working party set up by the IEEE forced a redesign and enhancements to the S100 bus definition to include multiprocessor and full 16-bit capability. The resulting specification was formalized in the standard IEEE 696. S100's continuing popularity with systems designers and end users ensures that it is well supported by manufacturers worldwide.

Since the early 1970s a variety of bus specifications have emerged. A favoured few have earned popular success by their suitability for particular applications. VME, for example, is suited to high-level scientific applications and applications dominated by the Motorola 68000 family, while Multibus has found application with high-end industrial systems and multiuser single-processor systems. S100 spans a diversity of systems, ranging from small industrial control applications to multiuser electronic office systems running proprietary database and word processing software, autodial and telephone answering control systems and fully interactive information display systems. The bus can be found in systems in

High Technology Electronics Ltd, 303–305 Portswood Road, Southampton SO2 1LD, UK

0141-9331/86/02120–05 $03.00 © 1986 Butterworth & Co. (Publishers) Ltd

betting shops and banks, in machine shops and research laboratories (Figure 1).

BUS SUMMARY

IEEE 696/S100 consists of a set of signal and control lines used to carry information among interconnecting devices. The bus standard, formalized in 1983, specifies clearly the design limitations which must be applied to any S100 compatible board. The specification in its basic form defines a 127 mm × 254 mm PCB. A double height board is allowed within the standard though this is rarely used — the basic board is considered adequate for many applications.

The bus itself, and the interface between each card and the bus, must adhere to the bus loading and termination impedances specified. Many of the early problems of compatibility between different manufacturers' boards were related to bus loading effects giving signal reflections and crosstalk. More particularly, signal timings, now strictly defined in the standard, were at one time variable between manufacturers, making it difficult to mix boards from different origins in the same system.

The bus is subdivided into eight sets of signal lines and one set of power lines, as shown in Table 1. The full signal allocation list is given in Garetz[1].

The functional cards in an S100 system are generally termed the bus 'master' or bus 'slave'. The bus master is normally a device capable of initiating any bus cycle: memory read/write, port addressing etc. A slave is not capable of initiating a bus cycle, but merely responds to it. One of the most popular uses for S100 systems is to exploit its multiprocessor capabilities. In this type of system individual users can obtain exclusive use of peripheral facilities even with other users on the system. Each additional processor card must take control of the bus for a number of bus cycles each time a disc access is required, for example. Thus each

Table 1. Signal and power lines of the S100 bus

Data bus	DO 0–7, DI 0–7	16 lines
Address bus	A 0–23	24 lines
Status bus	s XXX	8 lines
Control output bus	p XXX	5 lines
Control input bus	RDY, NMI etc	6 lines
Temporary master	TMA 0–3	
access control bus	+ transfer signals	8 lines
Vectored interrupt bus	VI 0–7	8 lines
Utility bus	Reset etc	16 lines
Power bus	0, +8, +16, −16	9 lines

additional processor card has the capability of becoming a temporary bus master.

The data bus can be configured into two unidirectional 8-bit buses for byte operations, or a single bidirectional bus for 16-bit word operations. There is an interesting problem regarding 16-bit word transfers in a system capable of supporting a variety of processors simultaneously: should the least significant byte be transferred on the DI bus or the DO bus? Processors of the Intel family store 16-bit words with the least significant byte first, whereas the 6800, 9900 and Z8000 store the most significant byte first. The problem is solved by determining where each byte is to be written, assigning the even byte, that going to a location with A0 = 0, to the DO bus and the odd byte to the DI bus. Switching from two unidirectional 8-bit buses to the composite 16-bit bidirectional data bus is made using the sixteen request control line (sXTRQ*) and sixteen acknowledge (SIXTN*).

The extended 24-bit address bus has 16 Mbyte of contiguous memory address space available. Functional slaves having onboard memory, video cards, for example, can be installed within a contiguous memory system such that the card memory overlays the system memory. In this application the slave asserts the PHANTOM* signal, which disables the coincident

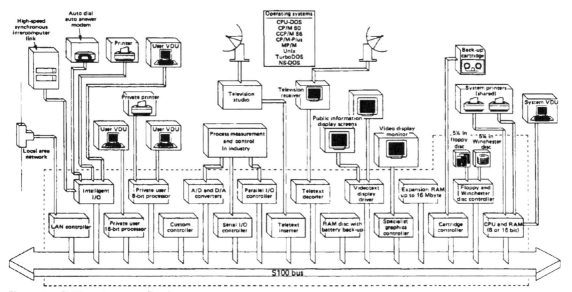

Figure 1. S100 systems applications

portion of system memory, whenever its memory is accessed.

S100 is a synchronous bus with a maximum specified switching rate of 6 MHz, below the practical limit of well designed S100 systems utilizing selected processors and reliable bus interface techniques. Table 2 shows examples of the data transfer rates for some off-the-shelf processor cards that can be used in 3,10 or 20 slot systems. Figure 2 shows the layout of the HTE 68000 processor card.

Power is distributed to all cards on the bus as unregulated voltages, requiring the installation of regulators on each card. Although this uses board space for heat sinks, it ensures power supply isolation between boards. Some manufacturers offer systems fitted with 5 V switch mode supplies, removing the regulators from the individual cards. This contravenes the standard but allows smaller, lighter and more power-efficient units to be constructed.

MULTIPROCESSOR OPERATION

A multiprocessor system can be implemented in one of two ways. The simplest is to employ a master processor with a series of slave processors operating under a suitable network operating system such as DPC/OS or TurboDOS. Within such a system the slave processors exist on the I/O bus and request disc and peripheral access through the bus master. This requires that the master processor polls the slaves, or responds to interrupts from the slaves, transferring data through

Table 2. S100 bus transfer rates

Card*	Processor	Clock frequency (MHz)	Data transfer rate (byte μs^{-1})
EPIC	Z80B	6	2
SB-186	80186	8	4
68K	68000	10	4

*Cards available from High Technology Electronics

the bus as parallel I/O or memory accesses. The simplicity of this type of system, and its expansion capabilities beyond the 16 true temporary masters catered for in the IEEE 696 specification, makes this a popular implementation. The alternative is to implement a true multimaster system which has benefits of speed over the master/slave processor systems and, in addition, allows processors and operating systems to be mixed simultaneously on the bus.

Arbitration

For a temporary master to make use of the bus, control must be transferred from the permanent master to the temporary master and from one temporary master to another in such a way as to avoid the generation of spurious signals, which may cause false bus cycles, on the control output lines. At an intermediate stage both the permanent master and the temporary master drive

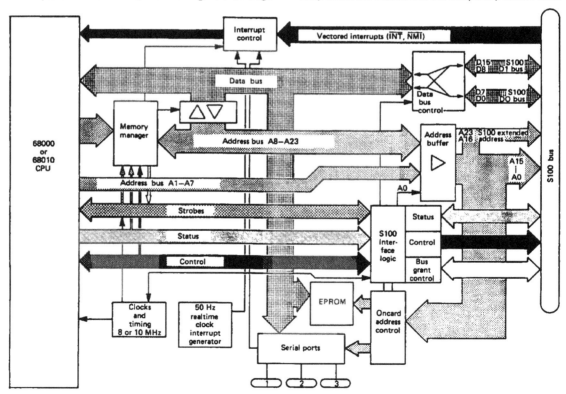

Figure 2. Block diagram of the HTE 68 K processor card

the control output lines simultaneously, and a similar situation exists when control is passed back. The actual transfer protocol follows well defined steps

Idle	The temporary master either does not require access to the bus, or it is waiting for the bus to become free.
Arbitration	The bus is available, signified by HOLD* and pHLDA being false. The temporary master is now in a position to contest bus access against other temporary masters in the system.
Mine	The bus has been granted to the temporary master. Hold request is asserted, and the transfer of bus control from the permanent to the temporary master begins at the rising edge of hold acknowledge. If more than one temporary master is simultaneously requesting the bus the lower-priority requestor returns to the Idle state.
Transfer State 1	The bus transfer control circuit on the permanent master asserts the signals

Disable address lines	ADSB*
Disable status signals	SDSB*
Disable data lines	DODSB*

Simultaneously these signals enable the control output drivers of the temporary master. Transfer becomes complete by the assertion of the CDSB* signal by the bus transfer control circuit.

The temporary master now has complete control of the bus. All other temporary masters are in the Idle state, either not interested or waiting for HOLD* and pHLDA to return to their normal state at which time the device with the next highest priority may contend for the bus.

Return of control to the permanent master takes the system through Transfer State II, the reverse of Transfer State I, prior to the temporary master reassuming the Idle state.

UTILITIES

S100 supports both 8- and 16-bit processors, simultaneously if necessary. Almost every type of 8- and 16-bit processor from the 8080 to the iAPX 286 is supported on the bus. To emphasize its manufacturer independence, most of the Motorola range is supported, as is the National Semiconductor range including the NS32016 processor.

Over 100 manufacturers actively ensure that new devices are designed onto the S100 bus shortly after release since there is a ready market for such cards. Systems can be constructed from an efficient three-slot unit to a powerful 22 slots.

The maximum clock speed specified for the bus is 6 MHz. The stability of the bus in its standard form, however, allows it to perform with clock rates up to 10 MHz, and some manufacturers supply cards up to

12 MHz, although these speeds are incompatible with the standard and will only work reliably in small systems, eg 2–3 cards. For applications such as image analysis the data acquisition rate is particularly critical. Proprietary S100 boards are available for activities such as video frame grabbing, digital image editing and video graphics mixing. Since processing is normally localized for these applications, bus bandwidth is not a problem. Being CPU/coprocessor bound rather than bus bound, S100 easily accommodates these 32/16-bit processor applications.

The ability of the S100 bus to support large amounts of main memory is one of its most important facilities. The bus is large enough to hold the boards required physically for large RAM. Advanced processors are available that can handle megabyte address spaces and operating systems, and languages are available that make use of the address space. As an example, CompuPro's CPU board based on the NS16032 includes the NS16082 memory management unit (MMU) to implement demand-paged memory managment. In a multiuser environment, each user has access to 16 Mbyte virtual address space. When running under a multiuser operating system such as TurboDOS, the full allocation of up to 16 slave processors per master can be installed on the system.

The ability to span processor generations offers advantages for the user; the new Z80H/80286 combination CPU from CompuPro enables 8-bit Z80 software to be run up to six times faster while anticipating developments in operating systems (eg Concurrent DOS/286). Multiprocessor systems extend the scope of S100. There are a number of these systems on the market — North Star Dimension, Comart, HMS, Armstrong etc. Some have taken the IBM PC pathway, using 80186 slaves, while others use the 68000–Unix combination (Figure 3). There is no reason why the two processors cannot be mixed on the same bus[2].

SOFTWARE SUPPORT

S100 accommodates most popular operating systems, from single-user 8-bit to multiuser, multitasking 16-bit systems. If, however, this element of flexibility is not sufficient for the systems integrator, many manufacturers supply dual-processor units (DPUs) which enhance the range of operating systems portable on a single board. Cromemco's DPU, for example, includes a 68000 for access to newer software and operating

Figure 3. HTE Spirit ST3 three-slot 68000 system configured for Unix

systems, plus a Z80A for compatibility with a large existing base of 8-bit software. In operation, the DPU switches back and forth between 8- and 16-bit data path widths according to the type of memory or I/O being accessed. Furthermore, the full 16 Mbyte address space of the S100 is supported directly by the 68000 and, through a paging scheme, by the Z80A. Another example is Macrotech's MI-286 CPU board featuring both the 286 and the Z80B processors.

To take advantage of the large base of DEC software, manufacturers are introducing board-level products based on the J-11 and T-11 microprocessors. Abacus Technology Systems, for example, offers the PC11, an S100 card based on the T-11. Similar in performance to the PDP-11/03, the RT-11 operating system is included in the package.

Unix is gaining popularity through two distinctive groups of users. The undoubted power of Unix as a software development tool, with its ability to allow the user to connect programs and to create his own environment through the shell, is ensuring an enthusiastic following in academic and R & D circles. In the less exotic commercial world, acceptance is a little slower, although the market potential is much greater. The distinction between the two groups is blurred, however; the former group is to some extent developing utilities for the latter.

In its various guises Unix is now ported to many S100 products. UnixQuix markets a range of Unix systems based on HTE 68000 cards. Its smallest unit, and probably the smallest Unix system available, is a three-slot motherboard unit 6.4 cm high. This system, containing the processor card, a 1 Mbyte DRAM card and a disc controller card with a 20 Mbyte hard disc, supports up to three users simultaneously, bringing an efficient Unix system to the small business user.

VIRTUAL DISC ON S100

Increased performance of disc and tape subsystems both in single-user microcomputers and multiuser computer systems has been the focus of efforts of many manufacturers, primarily because it remains one area where system access times can still be improved dramatically.

New add-in memory boards from Macrotech, for example, are intended to boost main memory to 1 Mbyte, taking up only one slot in the S100 bus. The boards come with 'Macrocache', a software package on a 13.3 cm floppy disc that can provide both RAM disc emulation (virtual disc) and full cache memory capability. Through the Macrocache virtual disc, a user specified portion of the memory board can be addressed as if it were a disc drive, enabling the add-on memory to simulate a second or a third disc drive via software. Virtual disc can speed up program execution significantly, especially where disc accesses are frequent. Microcache software employs dynamic memory allocation in both virtual disc and cache memory modes. For example, the cache may act as an expanding and contracting buffer that responds automatically to changing virtual disc requirements. As virtual disc storage area increases, cache buffer size decreases proportionally, providing flexibility for programs with memory blocks of frequently varying sizes.

CONCLUSION

S100 is a defined bus standard and suitability for a particular task can be easily determined by applying this standard. For example, an 8-bit system using the maximum specified clock speed of 6 MHz in a master/multiple-slave processor configuration, using synchronized parallel I/O data transfer between master and slave processor, transfers 1 byte in 23 bus clock cycles. This gives a data transfer rate of 261 kbyte s^{-1}. If each of 16 users requests a file of 56 kbyte simultaneously, the final user in the queue will be serviced within 4 s (no account has been taken of disc access and directory search time). Such a speed of response proves adequate in most applications requiring configurations of this type. It is true to say that some high-performance bus systems can offer a great bus bandwidth; what favours S100 is its price/performance characteristics.

REFERENCES

1 **Garetz, M** 'P696/S100 — a bus which supports a wide range of 8- and 16-bit processors' *Microprocessors Microsyst.* Vol 6 No 9 (1982) pp 466–470
2 **Moody, G** 'Many hands make light work' *Pract. Comput.* Vol 8 No 11 (Nov. 1985) pp 115–117
3 **Libes, S and Garetz, M** *Interfacing to S100/IEEE 696 microcomputers* Osborne/McGraw Hill
4 **Kalish, R and Plomgren, D** 'Consider using the S100 bus to host your 16-bit microprocessor' *EDN* (9 Aug. 1984)

FURTHER INFORMATION

Armstrong Micro Electronics Ltd, Castle Hill, Dudley, West Midlands DY1 4QQ, UK
Comart Computers Ltd, Little End Road, Eaton Socon, St Neots, Huntingdon, Cambs PE19 3JG, UK
Compupro, Oakland Airport, CA 94614, USA
Cromemco Inc, Box 7400, 280 Bernardo Avenue, Mountain View, CA 94039, USA
HM Systems, Minstrel House, 220 The Vale, London NW11 8HZ, UK
Macrotech International Corp, 9551 Irondale Avenue, Chatsworth, CA 91311, USA
North Star Dimensions, Kilbarry Park, Cork, Ireland
UniQuix Ltd, 109 Connaught Avenue, Frinton, Essex CO13 9PS, UK

George W George graduated from the University of Reading, UK, in 1973. After working in the transport industry as a manager for some years he joined the UK Royal Navy in a technical training role. He then became a senior software engineer for a company manufacturing intelligent display systems. He is now the systems manager at High Technology Electronics Ltd, which manufactures S100 and other bus-based systems.

An independent user's view of backplane bus standards

Choice of a bus standard for a piece of equipment should involve a variety of factors. **Mike Rowe** elucidates the decision-making process

The general characteristics of the UK Independent Broadcasting Authority are examined in respect of its transmitter site construction and maintenance activities, and these are related to particular requirements in respect of processor-based equipment. Past experience with bus-based systems is discussed, with particular reference to Multibus I. The requirements derived from this experience are discussed and currently available bus systems are considered with a view to recommendations for use on future projects. Bus system interoperability, and upgrade paths especially, are considered. The paper recommends that the best apparent couplings are between STE (P1000), VME (P1014) and Futurebus (P896).

**microsystems   backplane buses   Multibus I   STEbus
VMEbus   Futurebus**

The UK Independent Broadcasting Authority (IBA) has a variety of technical responsibilities, as well as many of a nontechnical nature, given to it by Government. The IBA's principal area of involvement with bus standards is the requirement that it should 'own, operate and maintain' broadcast transmitters for Independent television (ITV) and independent local radio (ILR). There are, at present, about 1460 such transmitters spread over some 760 sites throughout the UK. In order to maintain and control this system, the IBA has some 26 mobile maintenance bases and four regional operations centres, as well as an engineering headquarters near Winchester, UK.

Not all transmitting sites have remote control and interrogation equipment, only those which are particularly important by virtue of population served, proportion of coverage in an ITV region, importance within a network or difficulty of access. Thus the control system has a relatively small number of controlled sites in terms of its large geographical coverage. The sites tend to be on the highest piece of lowest conductivity rock in the area, quite often with difficult access. They are

Independent Broadcasting Authority, Crawley Court, Winchester, Hants SO21 2QA, UK

provided with an aerial and support structure up to 416 m above ground level; this tends to attract lightning. The electrical noise level can also be high, particularly if there is a close or cosited medium wave transmitter.

The teams which service these sites are expected to be capable of maintaining virtually all technical equipment on site, with some specialist exceptions. There tends to be a lower degree of familiarity with digital equipment, however, not only because of its greater inherent reliability, but also because equipment directly in the programme path (which is entirely analogue) normally takes priority. No matter how thorough a team's training, if equipment does not break down with sufficient frequency, the team will never become truly familiar with it! In order to adequately cover this problem — as well as that of the increasing cost of specialized test and repair equipment — certain team bases now specialize in the repair of particular classes of equipment. There is also a central repair service to provide further back-up.

It should be noted that the in-service life of equipment is long by industrial standards. For example, equipment now being replaced under the ITV1 replacement project will have been in service for about 18 years.

The functional specification of equipment is written in consultation with operations and maintenance staff, both at headquarters and regionally. Procurement is by invited competitive tender, although the range of potential suppliers is rather small for some classes of equipment. The IBA will normally only develop and/or design equipment itself where no adequate commercial equipment is available, in view of both cost and manpower considerations. Maintenance and modifications or extensions are normally carried out using internal resources.

EQUIPMENT SPECIFICATION AND CHOICE CONSIDERATIONS

From the above it will be clear that all equipment purchased by the IBA should have certain general characteristics, certainly in areas that are subject to modification. These are as follows

- design and construction such that maintenance, modification and extension are as easy as possible over an extended period
- compliance with the maximum number of relevant standards in order to ease the burden of specification as much as possible, and to assist in obtaining and assessing technically equivalent competitive tenders

In the particular context of microprocessor-based equipment — whether it be a unit having its own separate identity or part of a larger piece of equipment within which it performs some control function — these general requirements strongly suggest the use of some standard means of linking together the boards making up the system. The system will be functionally decomposed into boards in a logical manner, each board carrying one or more subsets of functions depending on system size, system complexity and what it is possible to fit on a board of a given size at the time of design. Thus the bus system is formed. Such a system must, of course, be specified for whatever type of use it is intended; each specification is divided into two main areas: mechanical and electrical.

The mechanical specification covers such variables as board size, board type, number of connectors and means of extraction. The electrical specification covers: connector pin allocations for both power and signals; signal levels, rise times and relative timing; addressing capability; data width; multiplexing of data and addresses; synchronous or asynchronous operation; multiprocessor capability; geographical addressing; processor priority and processor family dependence etc. These variables are far from independent and affect each other in a complex manner.

There is another nontechnical variable: whether a particular combination of variables actually possesses a definitive specification, either proprietary or in the public domain.

Taking into account all these variables, it is hardly surprising that there is a very wide choice of available bus systems, a choice which has appeared to increase almost weekly over the last few years and which presents a very confusing picture to anyone who actually has to make it. All proponents of bus systems claim that theirs is the finest in its class — a claim which is not dissimilar to that made by the proponents of any type of microprocessor.

In reality, if certain specific uses which heavily capitalize on the use of certain features peculiar to a processor or bus are excluded, there is technically very little to choose between rival systems in any particular class for the great majority of uses. In fact there are large areas of overlap between different classes of bus. It is uncommon and, indeed, bad practice for a system to be stretched to its limits at the time of initial design, even if it gets there in the course of meeting the specification requirements!

As will be appreciated, the factors affecting the choice of a bus system are complex and certainly not limited to hardware considerations. Although the effect of software choice and availability is not considered in this paper, the systems are utterly dependent upon it. Limitations in this area may well cause one bus system to be preferred to another despite technical advantages. For instance, a realtime executive that is only available to run particular proprietary boards may have the effect either of locking a user into a particular board set, or of stopping use of that executive in the first place.

The penalties attached to an inappropriate (or unlucky) choice of a bus standard can be severe, particularly if the required capability has been substantially underestimated or if it ceases to be available. Thus, any microprocessor system embodying a bus should be the object of a specific choice, made in the full knowledge of the possible consequences, rather than as the result of current whim and fashion.

Processor systems in particular are notorious for initial underestimation of software requirements. It is generally much safer and less expensive in the long term (and sometimes in the short term as well) to choose a system with greater capabilities than initially appear necessary. A restricted range of boards, limited memory or processing capacity and uncertain future availability all impose penalties at different stages in a system's life.

PREVIOUS EXPERIENCE WITH BUS-BASED SYSTEMS

The IBA's first experience in the specification, supply and use of bus-based systems on a large scale occurred as a result of the Fourth Channel construction programme. Under this programme, four different pieces of equipment were supplied by four different manufacturers in which a bus-based microprocessor system was present. In three of these, the bus system was only 'incidentally' present in that it was there as part of a piece of equipment rather than as a microprocessor system in its own right; all three were proprietary, limited to use with the supplier's equipment; one is now obsolete. The fourth case involved a controller intended to coordinate the operations of station equipment and to provide telemetry functions; this was overtly a microprocessor system.

Prior to the issue of the specification for this last unit, it was established that the long-term interests of the IBA would best be met if the processor and associated boards used were to conform to a well established and widely used bus specification, having multiple sources of supply. The main reasons for this were

- continued supply of functionally compatible boards would be assured for maintenance and extension purposes over an extended period
- smaller likelihood of 'bugs'
- easy design of boards for 'special' functions
- competitive tenders would be easier to obtain and assess, a wide variety of boards being available from a variety of technically and financially sound manufacturers
- increased probability of directly compatible software

In practice, it appeared that there were only three systems that met these requirements at the time: Intel's Multibus I; Digital Equipment's LSI-11 bus; and STD bus. The other available bus systems either had unacceptable technical deficiencies or restricted sourcing. Many of the systems which were investigated at the time have now disappeared from the market. STD bus, though technically sound and widely available, could only use a single processor, and so had to be discounted. Out of five tenders for the piece of equipment in question, three offered Multibus I based systems; one of these was the successful tender.

The equipment which was supplied has proved flexible and reliable. If so required, it would be readily extendable as compatible boards are freely available from many sources. Thus it has fulfilled its requirements so far.

FUTURE DEVELOPMENT

To have an unnecessarily large variety of microprocessor systems in service makes problems in many areas. Maintenance and support become more difficult and uncertain, particularly when it is desired to modify or extend systems over an extended period of time. The design life of a board may be short. The board may have to pass through a number of revisions; some of these will be due to the superseding of complex-function integrated circuits, which will make maintenance of earlier boards difficult if not impossible. It thus becomes essential in the bus used that functional replacement of obsolete boards is most likely to be possible.

A greater degree of common ground between systems would make it more economically viable to build standard test jigs and to hold improved stocks of spares. It would also reduce staff training requirements and make system fault diagnosis easier.

For any standard requirement to be effectively imposed upon a supplier, it must be very carefully chosen with an eye to both technical requirements and acceptability. Apart from overcoming the 'not invented here' syndrome, any system — especially if manufactured by a commercial rival — would have to show benefits such as reduced development effort, ready availability and reduced cost.

The boards should also fit into their chosen racking standard with the minimum of problems. The use of a well regarded bus standard with a choice of processor to conform with internal preferences is also desirable.

To conform to these requirements, the bus standard should be one whose use is freely available (ie a nonproprietary bus) and it should have clearly defined and straightforward interfacing requirements to ease the design of any special boards necessary.

The majority of the available bus systems have been evolved independently and spontaneously by manufacturers or even hobbyists; many were incompletely specified. As a consequence, even where formal standards have been written, these are a mass of compromises to ensure, as far as possible, that earlier boards continue to work with later ones and to meet the demands of competing manufacturers.

In recent years, there has been a concerted effort to produce nonproprietary standards by international committees in advance of hardware production; these efforts have been made under the aegis of the US Institute of Electrical and Electronic Engineers (IEEE), but with support from the UK Department of Trade and Industry and with a disproportionally large UK presence. These standards should be particularly well examined.

To benefit fully from the use of a bus system or complementary bus systems, the use of the chosen bus should be made a requirement of the specification. It should not appear as a real restriction as the buy/design-or-purchase decision is entirely in the supplier's hands and subject to the same economic and other considerations as any other choice.

CONSIDERATION OF MULTIBUS I FOR FUTURE PROJECTS

As Intel's Multibus I has already been used by the IBA in one major application and is being used in several minor ones, it must be seriously considered for future projects. It does, however, have a number of disadvantages which would prejudice its use in a number of situations. These are

- large board size; this makes the boards expensive in terms of front panel space as convection cooling is required to increase system reliability
- nonmodular boards; this makes them difficult to mount in conjunction with any other boards
- high unit cost for limited function requirements, due to the large size of the board; the cost of a small increase in functions can be particularly expensive if it pushes the functions just over a board size boundary
- low reliability of the direct edge connector
- dated design: Intel has announced that it intends to end new design production in 1988 although several new suppliers have entered the market in the UK recently

GENERAL CONSIDERATION OF BUS SYSTEMS FOR FUTURE PROJECTS

The bus systems presently available or shortly to become available fall into two broad categories: those that are Eurocard based and 'the rest'. There seems to be no good reason to consider any other non-Eurocard system apart from Multibus I: no two systems appear to have anything in common apart from a leaning towards odd sized boards and 0.156 in (4 mm) pitch direct edge connectors. The low cost and ready availability of Eurocard mounting hardware and compatible units such as power supplies give advantages of cost and convenience to Eurocards, as well as the reliability of the DIN connector; this is a considerable advantage because, as a general rule, the cost of housing and powering a set of processor boards is between 30% and 50% of the overall hardware cost of that unit.

Within the Eurocard-based systems two levels of capability may be clearly distinguished, although with considerable overlaps. These levels are also reflected in the basic cost at each level.

Low-level buses

The lower level uses an 8-bit data bus, with an address range varying from 64 kbyte to several megabytes. This

Table 1. Comparison of buses under consideration

Bus	Number of manufacturers	Processors currently available on bus
STE (P1000)	> 8	8085, 80188, Z80A, NSC800, 64180, 65186, 6809, 68008
Eurobus (IIOC)	> 4	8085, 8088, Z80A, 6800, 6802, 6809, 68008
G64	> 6	8085, 8088, Z80, 6800, 6802, 6809, 68008
MMD	2	8085, 8088
SMP	1	8080, 8031, 8085, 8088, 80188

level may be viewed as being particularly suitable for I/O intensive applications, although the use of 16- or 32-bit internal processors makes a lot of power available.

The power may be further enhanced on some bus systems by the use of multiple processors. There tends to be a concentration on serial or parallel I/O board types. Considering the variety of boards, number of manufacturers and range of processors offered, it seems particularly worthwhile to consider the 8-bit bus systems shown in Table 1.

Technically, there is not a great deal to choose between these bus systems, although STE is the only one capable of supporting multiple processors on the bus. All appear to be well supported and technically sound. The STEbus appears to be gaining ground, but has not yet attracted a major manufacturer. It has, however, the widest range of manufacturers and processor families and a comprehensive internationally agreed specification. The other buses are well established, but have a smaller range of manufacturers and processors.

High-level buses

At the higher capability level, choice is more restricted. In terms of Eurocard bus systems currently available in Europe with a wide variety of boards, the choice lies between AMSbus (Siemens), VMEbus (P1014) and Multibus II (Intel).

The Futurebus (P896) specification is now near final ratification and working devices are available for the bus drivers. There has been an enormous volume of work put into Futurebus by many individuals on behalf of many organizations, both large and small; the bus should therefore be considered for any project requiring considerable processing power, for which hardware is not required within the next year or so. Apart from its power in terms of speed and processor capability, Futurebus offers ease of maintenance and reliability through an extensive range of fallback operation modes in the event of a bus fault. There is

also the potential to insert live and dynamically reconfigure, at the expense of a considerable increase in system software complexity.

INTERWORKING OF BUS SYSTEMS

An area which is of vital importance is the capability to upgrade a system. This has been discussed above in terms of adding or changing processor boards on the same bus standard, but there are limits on the extent to which this can be done particularly if the existing system is running near the limit of its bus data capacity.

If a lower-capacity system can be run as a peripheral of a more powerful system then it is possible to minimize disruption while preserving much of the earlier investment. This may also be a desirable initial design strategy, as 8-bit bus boards tend to be significantly cheaper than those having a greater data width. The arrangement is especially beneficial for I/O intensive applications keeping I/O transactions off the main data bus as well as providing some system fault isolation and potential I/O redundancy.

For such a scheme to be entirely satisfactory, rather than just a convenient 'bodge', demands that the component systems should have some fundamental areas of compatibility, ie some common exchange protocol and power supply requirements (apart from mechanical standards). If the systems use a common board size, it is doubly desirable that power supply pinning on the connectors should be compatible. Sooner or later, someone is likely to plug the wrong board into a slot; even if the board cannot function, no damage should be caused.

This kind of system interworking may be achieved by the use of bus adaptors which are now available to link STE to VME[1], Eurobus to VME, G64 to VME and SMP to AMS. It appears highly probable that adaptors will become available to link AMS to Multibus II, STE to Futurebus and VME to Futurebus. This gives a number of clear upgrade or expansion paths.

The adaptors may appear in several forms, principally either as dual-port memory or as a bus protocol converter.

CONCLUSIONS

At the end of the day, choices or firm recommendations have to be made. The recommendations will reflect a mixture of technical evaluation, commercial considerations, engineering judgement and balancing of rival claims, together with a dash of personal prejudice.

My recommendation is that, for the purposes of the IBA, the most promising couplings are those between STE, VME and Futurebus. There is, of course, an element of arbitrariness about this recommendation, and other organizations may weigh the various considerations differently according to their situations. But one question all must ask is: 'What is the real cost of the bus system or systems?' It may be higher than is initially envisaged. The buyer must be prepared to insist upon, and even (perhaps apparently) to pay more for, the system that suits his/her application best, rather than that which would benefit an intending supplier the most.

ACKNOWLEDGEMENTS

The author would like to thank the director of engineering of the IBA for permission to publish this paper, which is based upon an internal technical report. Thanks are also due to colleagues, both within and without the IBA, who have assisted in forming my ideas and prejudices and to those bus system suppliers who have provided helpful seminars and much documentation. The views expressed in this paper do not represent the official view of the IBA.

REFERENCES

1 **Elsmore, T** 'STE bus as an I/O bus in VME bus systems' (1986) (submitted for publication)

Mike Rowe undertook a student apprenticeship at the Westinghouse Brake and Signal Co. Ltd, at Chippenham, UK, after which he continued with the company as an engineer on telemetry and automation systems. He then moved to Redifon Air Trainers at Aylesbury, UK, working principally on the design of hardware and software for aircraft simulators. He is currently a senior telemetry engineer in the Station Design and Construction Department of the IBA, where he has been for the last 15 years. His principal technical interests have always been in realtime digital systems, with a particular emphasis on interfacing requirements, system reliability, EMI control and, more recently, bus-based systems, in which he provides internal consultancy.

IEE P896 Futurebus Colloquium

31 January 1986, London, UK

Futurebus is intended to be the ultimate backplane bus. Setting the tone of this colloquium, Paul Borrill, Chairman of the P896 Futurebus Committee, predicted that it would be the long-term, technology-independent bus standard that will outperform all other buses for as long as systems design is bus based. But P896 is not yet an official IEEE standard and it does not currently have the widespread support of the major semiconductor companies, some of which have created *de facto* industry standards of other 32-bit buses.

Many of the features of the P896 Futurebus specification do bear favourable comparison with other 32-bit buses, as evidenced by Borrill's detailed table of comparisons discussed at the meeting and published on page 94 of this issue. It is the fastest bus, with the widest bandwidth (apart from the specialized Fastbus); it is asynchronous, multiplexed and has multimaster capability; it fully supports tagged architectures and is eventually to be upgraded to support caching and to offer a live insertion facility.

Manufacturing support

Features such as these were cited by two speakers currently developing fifth-generation computers as why they had chosen to base their systems on Futurebus. Simon Peyton Jones of University College London is developing GRIP, a parallel graph reduction machine (page 69 of this issue), and Simon Wiseman of RSRE is working on a 'capability' computer, where capabilities are unforgeable addresses for objects and are used as the basis of a secure communications processor.

For industry in general, however, the lack of dedicated parts for Futurebus and the lack of major manufacturing support will restrict its widespread use, a point emphasized by Paul Dixon of Ferranti Computer Systems. The success of the bus depends on persuading the major semiconductor companies to make the parts, he said. To achieve this a new design based on a common specification is required for the internal hardware of the bus, in order to present a unified approach to manufacturers.

Such an approach will be enhanced by official IEEE standardization of Futurebus. Progress in this direction was reported by Hugh Field-Richards, editor of the draft specification, who said that work on the specification was now winding down. A draft document P896.1 has been produced and members of the P896 Working Party have been balloted on its contents. An agreed specification resulting from the ballot is expected to be published in April; thereafter final ratification will come through the IEEE. P896 members are hopeful that Futurebus could become an official standard by November. Two facilities still being developed for the bus, message/event passing and cache control, are being considered in a separate document, P896.2, which could be incorporated in the main specification within a year, said Field-Richards.

Synchronization and locking

Moving on to technical features of the bus, Mike Griffiths of RMCS described synchronization and locking on Futurebus. In multiprocessor systems, the processors will clearly need to access, via the bus, a set of shared variables in memory. In certain cases, where variables need to be altered by an indivisible sequence of operations to maintain internal consistency, a particular software process, called the critical section of the program, will require exclusive access to the shared store. Futurebus accommodates such a process, explained Griffiths, by providing a three-tier lock mechanism: at the lowest level, read-modify-write to a single address is protected by the AS/AK lock; read-modify-write to more than one address is protected by not allowing a bus master to be pre-empted; at the highest level an 'advisory lock' between bus tenures is provided by allocating space in control and status registers.

To reduce loss of bandwidth through wait states and lock test processes, a further facility of the bus is its 'half-duplex' memory. This is a local read, global write mechanism whereby a processor is able to test a local copy of the lock flag without using the bus.

Fault tolerance and acquisition control

For fault-tolerance purposes, a feature of Futurebus is that all locks are cleared automatically whenever bus mastership is changed or reset. The bus is designed to support fault-tolerant architectures in general, Roger Edwards pointed out, to detect, report, contain and recover bus errors. Fault detection is achieved in three ways: software errors are detected because the bus is asynchronous; illegal transfers are detected by status codes; and byte parity protects data transfers. Being a fully distributed system without any central services module, the bus can also contain, isolate and recover faults. The basic triple Eurocard format holds up to three buses, and a fault on one bus cannot be propagated to another.

Developments to the bus control acquisition scheme were reported by Matthew Taub (IBM). Deficiencies had been identified in the 1983 draft scheme. In the control transfer sequence of the original scheme a situation could arise whereby a 'priority' class module — one that can compete for bus access at any time regardless of previous bus use — when in urgent need of the bus would be unable to gain access to it. In the redrafted scheme this problem is solved, Taub said, by a pre-emption mechanism which allows the priority module to effectively abort the current bus transfer as if it had detected an arbitration error.

Caching

Transaction facilities necessary to accommodate high-speed cache memory — broadcast and broadcall modes and burst-mode transfers, for example — are included on Futurebus. Current work at Tektronix in Wilsonville, OR, USA, is aimed at implementing caches on the bus and was described by Paul Sweazey. Sweazey briefly outlined cache operation and discussed cache models designed to ensure coherency, in particular the MOESI state model which applies to Futurebus. MOESI assigns five characteristics — modified, owned, exclusive, shared and invalid — that define cache data, and it is the key to maintaining cache coherency, said Sweazey. When fully developed,

Futurebus will be the only 32-bit bus to fully support cache architectures.

Full cache implementation on Futurebus will take another year or so to develop and could be the 'icing on the cake'. The success of the bus, however, may depend on developments in the more immediate future. Next month will see publication of the draft document by the P896 Committee; this will offer the first chance to gauge the reaction of the manufacturers needed to support Futurebus products. Prospects for its success in the competitive industrial markets could become evident very quickly.

Steve Hitchcock

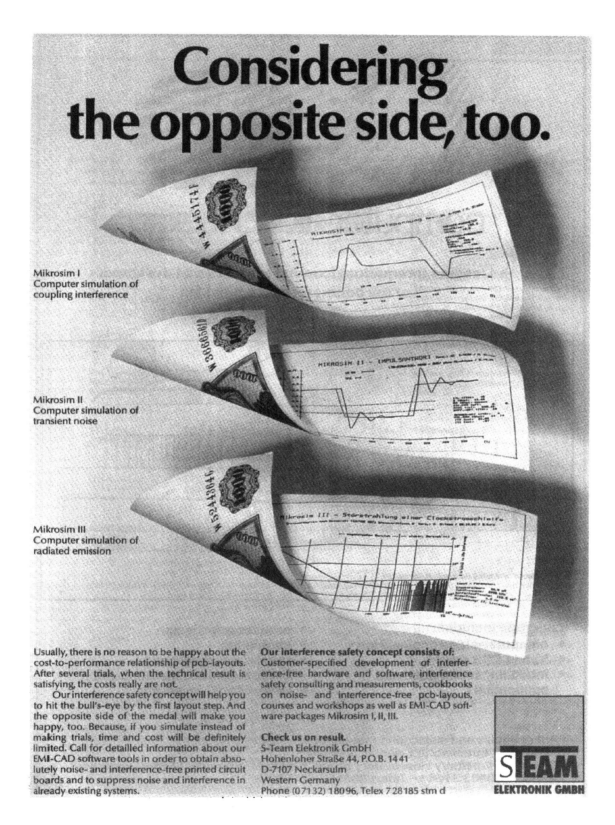

Considering the opposite side, too.

Mikrosim I
Computer simulation of coupling interference

Mikrosim II
Computer simulation of transient noise

Mikrosim III
Computer simulation of radiated emission

Usually, there is no reason to be happy about the cost-to-performance relationship of pcb-layouts. After several trials, when the technical result is satisfying, the costs really are not.

Our interference safety concept will help you to hit the bull's-eye by the first layout step. And the opposite side of the medal will make you happy, too. Because, if you simulate instead of making trials, time and cost will be definitely limited. Call for detailed information about our EMI-CAD software tools in order to obtain absolutely noise- and interference-free printed circuit boards and to suppress noise and interference in already existing systems.

Our interference safety concept consists of:
Customer-specified development of interference-free hardware and software, interference safety consulting and measurements, cookbooks on noise- and interference-free pcb-layouts, courses and workshops as well as EMI-CAD software packages Mikrosim I, II, III.

Check us on result.
S-Team Elektronik GmbH
Hohenloher Straße 44, P.O.B. 14 41
D-7107 Neckarsulm
Western Germany
Phone (0 71 32) 1 80 96, Telex 7 28 185 stm d

sTEAM
ELEKTRONIK GMBH

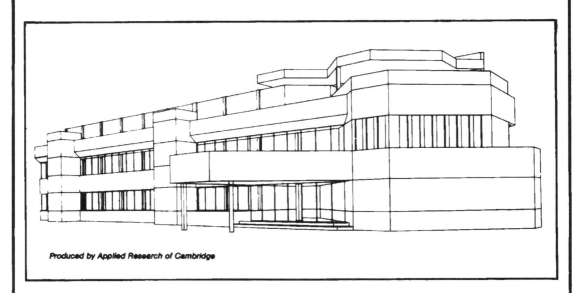

Date	Title	Contact	Place	Other details

1986

Date	Title	Contact	Place	Other details
2-4 April	Advances in Reliability Technology	Mrs R Campbell, NCSR, Wigshaw Lane, Culcheth, Warrington, Cheshire WA3 4NE, UK. Tel: (0725) 31244	University of Bradford, UK	Ninth symposium organized by the UK National Centre of Systems Reliability
7-10 April	IEEE Computer Society 2nd International Conference on ADA Applications and Environments	David Fisher, Incremental System Corp, 319 South Craig Street, Pittsburgh, PA 15213, USA. Tel: (412) 621-8888	Konover Hotel, Miami, FL, USA	Sponsored jointly by the IEEE and TC-Comp Lang
7-11 April	MOS Integrated Circuit Design for Signal Processing and Data Conversion	Continuing Education Institute (Europe), Rörstorpsvägen 5, S-61200 Finspång, Sweden. Tel: (46 0122) 17570	Davos Congress Center, Switzerland	Course intended for engineers in the IC, aerospace, electronics or communications industries who are involved in use or design of integrated MOS signal or data processing circuits and systems
8-10 April	Unix Systems Exposition (Europe) '86	Network Events Ltd, Printers Mews, Market Hill, Buckingham MK18 1JX, UK	Palais des Congres, Paris, France	Second European Unix users' exhibition of software and hardware
15-17 April	The Computer as an Aid for those with Special Needs	The Conference Secretary, ACTIVE, Sheffield City Polytechnic, 37 Broomgrove Road, Sheffield S10 2BP, UK	Sheffield, UK	International conference for the computer community, educationalists and the disabled
15-17 April	5th Scottish Computer Show	Cahners Exhibitions Ltd, Chatsworth House, 59 London Road, Twickenham, Middx TW1 3SZ, UK. Tel: 01-891 5051	Scottish Exhibition and Conference Centre, Glasgow, UK	Trade exhibition
21-24 April	EUUG Spring Conference and Exhibition	European Unix User Group, Owles Hall, Buntingford, Herts SG9 9PL, UK. Tel: (0763) 73039	Florence, Italy	Three-day technical programme (22-24 April), plus an industrial programme and a series of advanced tutorials, on aspects of Unix systems
28-30 April	Expert Systems and their Applications	Jean-Claude Rault, Agence de l'Informatique, Tour Fiat — Cedex 16, 92084 Paris — La Défense, France. Tel: (331) 4796 4314	Palace of the Popes, Avignon, France	Sixth international workshop (conferences and exhibitions)
13-15 May	Communications 86	Institution of Electrical Engineers, Savoy Place, London WC2R 0BL, UK. Tel: 01-240 1871	Metropole Hotel, Birmingham, UK	Eighth IEE conference and exhibition. Session headings include: the cellular scene; mobile radio update; office communications equipment; value added network services; satellite communications; recent developments in networks and services; ISDN becomes a reality.
13-15 May	Eurosoft/Nordcomp 86	Network Events Ltd, Printers Mews, Market Hill, Buckingham MK18 1JX, UK	Hamburg Exhibition Centre, FRG	European conference and exhibition on computer software and hardware
13-16 May	CommunicAsia 86	Andry Montgomery Ltd, 11 Manchester Square, London W1M 5AB, UK	Singapore	Fourth Asian international electronic communication show and conference
13-16 May	Hong Kong Elenex 86	Andry Montgomery Ltd, 11 Manchester Square, London W1M 5AB.	Hong Kong	Second Hong Kong international electrical and electronic engineering show
19-23 May	International Conference on Distributed Computing Systems	Dr Ming T Liu, Ohio State University, 2036 Neil Avenue, Columbus, OH 43210, USA. Tel: (614) 422-1837	Hyatt Regency, Cambridge, MA, USA	Sponsored by the IEEE Computer Society and the ACM

calendar

Date	Title	Contact	Place	Other details
26–30 May	3rd Software Engineering Conference	Jean Pierre Finance, AFCET Informatique 156, Blvd Pereire 75017, Paris, France	Versailles, France	Sponsored by AFCET and the IEEE Computer Society
3–5 June	13th Annual International Conference on Computer Architecture	Dr Hideo Aiso, Dept of Electrical Engineering, Keio University, 3-14-1 Hiyoshi, Kohohu-ku, Yokohoma 223, Japan	Tokyo, Japan	Sponsored by IPSJ (Japan), the ACM, the IEEE Computer Society and TC–CA
3–5 June	ComUnix '86	EMAP International Exhibitions Ltd, Abbot's Court, 34 Farringdon Road, London EC1R 3AU, UK. Tel: 01-608 1161	Tara Hotel, London, UK	Series of seminars concerning 'Unix solutions'. Sponsored by /usr/group/UK
3–6 June	International Conference on Consumer Electronics	ICCE, c/o TMA, 3553 North Milwaukee Avenue, Chicago, IL 60641, USA	Rosemont, IL, USA	Conference and exhibition on video and audio technology, home information systems, components, CADCAM and emerging technologies
10–12 June	Comdex International	The Interface Group Inc, 300 First Avenue, Needham, Massachusetts, USA	Nice, France	Display of software, small computer products, peripherals, accessories and other related items; miniconference on business, marketing and financial subjects of interest to computer industry marketers
10–12 June	Scottish Electronics Show	Network Events Ltd, Printers Mews, Market Hill, Buckingham MK18 1JX, UK	Anderson Centre, Glasgow, UK	Exhibition and conference covering equipment and services associated with the design, testing and manufacturing of electronic equipment and components
11–13 June	Microelectronics Packaging	Center for Professional Advancement, Palestrinastraat 1, 1071 LC Amsterdam, The Netherlands. Tel: (020) 623050	Caransa Crest Hotel, Amsterdam, The Netherlands	Intensive course covering: packaging chips and subcircuits; microjoining and bonding; encapsulation of microelectronics; materials, techniques and equipment for moulding and casting; microelectronics reliability; and thermal management
16–19 June 1986	National Computer Conference	AFIPS, 1899 Preston White Drive, Reston, VA 22091, USA. Tel: (703) 620–8900	Las Vegas, NV, USA	Conference sponsored by the American Federation of Information Processing Societies
25–28 June	Communications: Message, Mind, & Machine	Canadian Association for Information Science, BC Research, 3650 Wesbrook Mall, Vancouver V6S 2L2, Canada	Canada	Conference and exhibition on information retrieval and systems design, artificial intelligence, expert systems, networking and distributed systems
2–4 July	International Workshop on Systolic Arrays	Will Moore, Systolic Array Workshop, Dept of Engineering Science, Oxford University, Oxford OX1 3PJ, UK	Oxford, UK	Papers on all aspects of systolic arrays and related SIMD architectures from abstract theory to practical applications and VLSI products
7–11 July	International Optical Computing Conference	Prof Joseph Shamir, Conference Chairman, 1986 IOCC, c/o Kopel Tours Ltd — Conventions, PO Box 4413, 61044 Tel Aviv, Israel	Jerusalem, Israel	Recent developments in optical computing including optical information processing, hybrid optical–digital processing systems, systolic array processors, integrated optical processing devices, electro-optic devices, optical interface techniques and application of optical bistability to computing
15–18 September	Euromicro 86	Mrs E C Snippe-Marlisa, TH Twente, PO Box 217, Dept INF, Room A306, 7500 AE Enschede, The Netherlands	Venice, Italy	Twelfth annual conference of micro-processing and microprogramming
15–20 September	Intercomm '86	Cahners Exhibitions Ltd, Chatsworth House, 59 London Road, Twickenham TW1 3SZ, UK	Beijing, China	International computer and communication congress/exposition for science and technology

Argus M700.
The military computer
for tomorrow's systems.

Some computers come and go.

Not Argus M700. Ferranti is committed to the continuing enhancement and support of this proven range.

As new generations of hardware and software come along we'll be making them compatible with the M700 you have now. And we shall be continuing to give you full service and product support.

Recently the M700/40 joined the range, the first M700 to be implemented purely in LSI form, giving more power and versatility.

And don't forget the Argus M700s are rugged, reliable machines designed for real time applications in all spheres of defence – land, sea and air.

Start using the Argus M700 range and look forward to a growing family of computer capability.

Contact:
Cwmbran (06333) 71111 Bracknell (0344) 483232
Oldham (061) 624 0281

Ferranti Computer Systems Limited,
Product Sales,
Ty Coch Way, Cwmbran, Gwent NP44 7XX
Telex: 497636 FERCWM G

FERRANTI
Computer Systems

microprocessors and microsystems

vol 10 no 3 april 1986

Butterworths

editorial advisory board

Microprocessors and Microsystems is an international journal published in February, March, April, May, June, August, September, October, November, December. *Editorial Offices:* Butterworth Scientific Ltd, PO Box 63, Westbury House, Bury Street, Guildford, Surrey GU2 5BH, UK. Tel: (0483) 31261. Telegrams and telex: 859556 SCITEC G. *Publishing Director:* John Owens. *Production:* Tony Lewis

Microprocessors and Microsystems is published by Butterworth Scientific Ltd. *Registered Office:* Butterworth Scientific Ltd, 88 Kingsway, London WC2 6AB, UK

Subscription enquiries and orders: Quadrant Subscription Services Ltd, Oakfield House, Perrymount Road, Haywards Heath, West Sussex RH16 3DH, UK. Tel: (0444) 459188

Annual subscription (10 issues): £89.00 Overseas rate (£22.00 for private individuals);

$160.00 US rate ($40.00 for private individuals)
UK subscription rates available on request.

Prices include packing and delivery by sea mail. Airmail prices available on request. Copies of this journal sent to subscribers in Bangladesh, India, Pakistan, Sri Lanka, Canada and the USA are air-speeded for quicker delivery.

Back issues: Prior to current volume available from Wm Dawson & Sons Ltd, Cannon House, Folkestone, Kent CT19 5EE, UK. Tel: (0303) 57421

US mailing agents: Mercury Airfreight International Ltd Inc., 10B Englehard Avenue, Avenel, NJ 07001, USA. Second class postage paid at Rahway, NJ. US Postmaster: Send address corrections to *Microprocessors and Microsystems* c/o Mercury Airfreight International Ltd Inc., address as above.

Reprints: Minimum order 100, available from the publisher.

Copyright: Readers who require copies of papers published in this journal may either purchase reprints or obtain permission to copy from the publisher at the following address: Butterworth Scientific Ltd, PO Box 63, Westbury House, Bury Street, Guildford, Surrey GU2 5BH, UK. For readers in the USA, permission to copy is given on the condition that the copier pay the stated per copy fee through the Copyright Clearance Center Inc., 26 Congress Street, Salem, MA 01979, USA, Tel: (617) 744-3350, for copying beyond that permitted by Sections 107 and 108 of the US Copyright Law. Fees appear in the code at the foot of the first page of major papers.

ISSN 0141 9331
MCRPD 10 (3) 137–192 1986

© Butterworth & Co (Publishers) Ltd 1986

Typeset by Tech-Set, Gateshead, Tyne & Wear, and printed by Dotesios (Printers) Ltd, Greenland Mills, Bradford on Avon, Wilts, UK.

microprocessors and microsystems

vol 10 no 3
april 1986

Editor Steve Hitchcock

Assistant Editor Andrew Taylor

Production Tony Lewis

Publisher Amanda Harper

THE UNIVERSITY
OF MICHIGAN

JUL 07 1986

ENGINEERING
LIBRARY

notes for authors

Microprocessors and Microsystems

The Journal welcomes all articles on semiconductor chip and PCB design, the application of microprocessors to industry, business and schools and on the development of microprocessor software. Articles can come from both academic and industrial research and should be 3000–5000 words in length. In addition to main articles, we welcome shorter case studies, design notes and teach-ins.

All submitted articles are refereed by two independent reviewers to ensure both accuracy and relevance, though it is the authors' sole responsibility that statements used are accurate. The author is also responsible for obtaining permission to quote material and to republish tables and illustrations.

Copyright

Before publication, authors are requested to assign copyright to Butterworth & Co (Publishers) Ltd. This allows the company to sanction reprints of the whole or part of the volume and authorize photocopies. The authors, however, still retain their traditional right to reuse or to veto third-party publication.

Preparation of scripts

As you can see from the Journal, every article published is stylized by us to keep consistency throughout each volume. We follow the Oxford English Dictionary. It would be helpful if you could follow the Journal style. The most important thing, though, is that you write (or rather type) in clear and concise English. Contributions should be typed double-spaced on one side of the paper. We would also appreciate it if you number each page and leave wide margins so we can prepare the article for the typesetters. Three copies of the article are preferred and should be sent to the editor.

Units

You should use, as far as possible, SI units. In circumstances where this is not possible, please provide a conversion factor at the first mention of the unit.

Illustrations

Line drawings

We have our own professional studio to ensure that line drawings are consistent with house style. We would prefer, however, to receive unlettered drawings (black ink on tracing paper) so we can put on the lettering ourselves. Drawings, if possible, should be of size consistent with the Journal, i.e. either 169 mm or 356 mm width. Single drawings should not extend over one page (500 mm) in height.

Computer printouts

Illustrations showing line printer listings, plotter output, etc should preferably be on unlined paper. Printouts will be reduced by us to the relevant size. Do not mark them as they will be used to make photographic copies for the typesetters. Only include sufficient lines for the reader to interpret the format and nature of the printout. Overlong printouts only cause confusion. Fuller explanation should appear in the caption and the text.

Photographs

Black and white glossy photographs (including Polaroid prints of VDU screens) should, where possible, be supplied unmounted. They should be labelled clearly on the back with a soft pencil. Photocopies of the photographs should be provided for the referees.

References

Our Journal style is to indicate the use of a reference in the text with a superscript as each one arises and give the full reference with the same number at the end. If a reference is cited more than once, the same number should be used each time. With a bibliography, the references are given in alphabetic order (dependent on the first author's surname). It would be helpful if you could follow this style. References take the following form:

(to journals)

1 Buckroyd, A 'Production testing of microprocessor-based equipment' *Microprocessors and Microsystems* Vol 5 No 7 (September 1981) pp 299–303

(to books)

2 Gallacher, J 'Testing and maintenance' in Hanna, F K (ed.) *Advanced techniques for microprocessor systems* Peter Peregrinus, Stevenage, UK (1980)

Proofs

Correspondence and proofs for corrections will be sent to the first named author, unless otherwise indicated. Authors will receive a copy of the galley proofs and copies of redrawn or relettered illustrations. It is important that these proofs should be checked and returned promptly.

Reprints

The first named author will receive 25 reprints of the technical article free of charge. Further copies, a minimum of 100, can be ordered at any time from the Reprints Department, Butterworth Scientific Ltd, Westbury House, PO Box 63, Bury Street, Guildford, Surrey GU2 5BH, UK.

Design for testability and built-in self-test for VLSI circuits

Built-in self-test is gaining favour in the search for new methods of testing VLSI circuits. **Hideo Fujiwara** reviews self-test approaches, highlighting microprocessor-based implementations

The special characteristics of VLSI and VHSI (very high-speed integrated) circuits — their high speed of operation and their poor accessibility to external probing — have aggravated the problems of test-pattern generation and testing. As circuit technologies advance to higher speeds and larger scales of integration, new approaches will be required to test the high speed and very dense circuits which may contain both multiple 'stuck' type and non 'stuck' type faults. Hence, it might be necessary to consider testing approaches in a new light. This paper surveys built-in self-test approaches, which seem to be preferred over external testing and have a good potential for future testing requirements. Built-in self-test schemes implemented in microprocessor-based systems are highlighted.

microprocessors   self test   random logic

With the growth in the complexity of VLSI circuits, testing has become more difficult and more expensive. The only way to test circuits cost effectively is not simply to use computer-aided design tools, but also to make use of testable structures in the design process — design for testability. Testability can be defined as the ease of testing, or as the ability to test easily or cost effectively[1]. Testability should be adopted as one of the circuit design parameters. This is supported by the fact that the cost of hardware is decreasing steadily relative to the cost of testing.

Approaches to testing can be divided into two categories: external testing and built-in self-testing. In external testing the test equipment is external to the unit (chip, board or system) under test; ie test patterns are applied by the external tester and the responses are then evaluated. In built-in self-testing the test equipment is built into the unit under test, and the unit tests itself by

Department of Electronics and Communication, Meiji University, 1-1-1 Higashi-Mita, Tama-Ku, Kawasaki 214, Japan

applying test patterns and by evaluating output responses internally without the use of external test equipment.

Many of the popular design-for-testability approaches have been concerned with external testing, for example scan design techniques[2-6] such as scan path[3] and level-sensitive scan design (LSSD)[4], and universally testable design for programmable logic arrays (PLAs)[7-13]. Although these design-for-testability techniques based on external testing have succeeded in reducing the difficulty of testing, some drawbacks still remain: it is necessary to store huge amounts of test patterns and the responses to them; test-pattern generation is still troublesome for scan design approaches because special test-pattern generation software is required; and testing is slow because patterns have to be shifted through the scan path.

In this paper, first those design-for-testability techniques based on external testing are described, and then various built-in self-test techniques for random logic are surveyed.

DESIGN FOR TESTABILITY

Approaches to design for testability can be categorized as *ad hoc* or structured. Examples of the *ad hoc* methods are the techniques of dividing a circuit and enhancing its controllability and/or observability. Figure 1 shows two examples of logical partitioning using extra degating logic. By dividing the circuit into small sections, it can be tested more easily. This approach is based on the 'divide and conquer' approach. The bus-structured architecture shown in Figure 2 is another example of partitioning. The buses make it easier to test the microcomputer by applying test patterns separately to each module.

The controllability and observability of a circuit can be enhanced by adding test points. Figure 3 shows an example of enhancing the 0-controllability by adding an AND gate. Figure 4 shows how a JK flip-flop can be made directly resettable.

These *ad hoc* techniques are heuristic rather than systematic. They are intended to make a given design

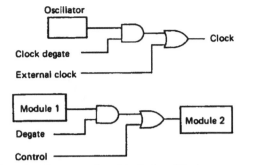

Figure 1. Two examples of logical partitioning

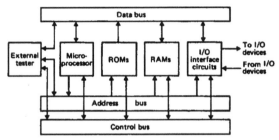

Figure 2. Bus-structured microcomputer

more testable in a simple and inexpensive way. Structured techniques on the other hand are aimed at solving the general problem of testing with a design methodology that uses a set of design rules to achieve good testability. Two examples of the structured approach are described below: scan design for sequential circuits and universally testable design for PLAs.

Scan design

In general, the problem of generating tests for sequential circuits is so difficult that it may not be solved in reasonable computing time if high fault coverage is required. Several structured design approaches have been reported to give the ability to control and observe the internal states of a circuit[2-6].

Figure 5 shows a scan design proposed by Williams and Angel[2]. A double-throw switch is inserted at each input of every flip-flop in the circuit and in one of the primary outputs of each flip-flop. It has two modes of operation: a normal-function mode and a shift-register mode. These modes are switched by mode control p. In the shift-register mode, all the flip-flops are connected in a chain. By switching to the shift-register mode it is possible to control and observe easily the internal state or content of the flip-flops, ie all flip-flops can behave as primary inputs/outputs. Hence, the test generation problems for sequential circuits can be reduced to that of combinational circuits.

The procedure for testing such circuits is:

(1) Switch to the shift-register mode and check the shift-register operation by feeding an alternating sequence of 1s and 0s.
(2) Set the initial state into the shift register.

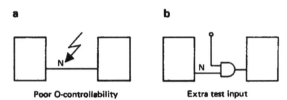

Figure 3. Test point for enhancing testability: a, original circuit; b, with additional control gate

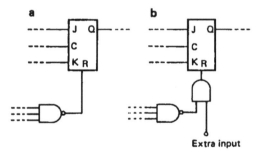

Figure 4. Test point for direct resetting: a, original circuit; b, with additional control gate

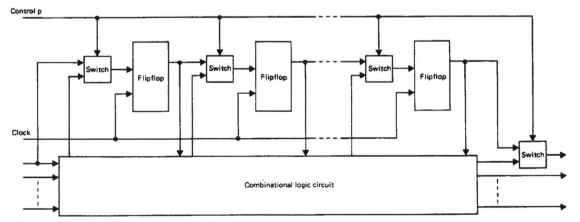

Figure 5. Shift register modification

(3) Return to the normal mode and apply the input test pattern.
(4) Switch to the shift-register mode and shift out the final state while setting the starting state for the next test. Return to step 3.

Many variations of the scan design approach have been proposed: scan path[3], level-sensitive scan design (LSSD)[4], scan/set logic[5] and random-access scan[6]. Figure 6 shows the shift register latch (SRL) used as the basic memory element in LSSD. The polarity-hold SRL consists of two latches, L_1 and L_2, which have the scan input I, data input D, system clock C, and two shift-control inputs A and B. Figure 7 shows a general structure for double-latch LSSD using SRLs, in which all feedback inputs into the combinational circuit N are taken from the L_2 latch. All storage elements are implemented as a set of master-slave latches L_1 and L_2. In the normal-function mode, each of the master–slave latches is clocked by two non-overlapping clocks C_1 and C_2, where C_2 is equivalent to B. In the shift-register mode, the SRLs are chained to form a shift register under the control of clocks A and B.

Universal testing

Optimal design to minimize the cost of test-pattern generation can be accomplished by a technique called universal testing or function-independent testing. Universal testing is performed with a test set that is independent of the function realized by the circuit under test. A PLA, which is conceptually a two-level AND-OR circuit, is attractive in VLSI because of its memory-like array structure and has become a popular and effective tool for implementing logic functions. The first universally testable PLA designs were proposed independently by Fujiwara et al[7-8] and Hong and Ostapko[9]. Since then, much work has been done on the design of easily testable PLAs[10-13].

The PLA design of Fujiwara[13] can achieve high fault coverage with low overhead. A PLA consists of three main sections: the decoder, the AND array and the OR array, as shown in Figure 8. To design an easily testable PLA, a given PLA is augmented by adding extra logic as shown in Figure 9. This can be obtained by adding a shift register, two

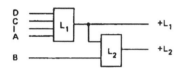

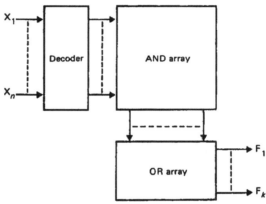

Figure 8. General structure of a PLA

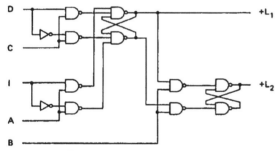

Figure 6. Polarity-hold shift register latch

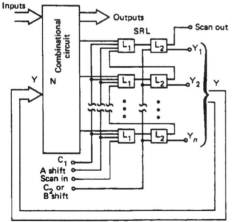

Figure 7. General structure for double-latch level-sensitive scan design (LSSD)

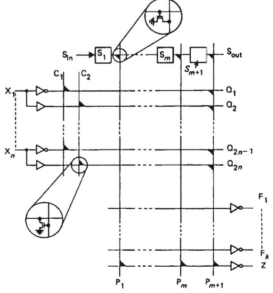

Figure 9. Augmented PLA

columns between the decoder and the AND array, and one column and one row to the AND and OR arrays, respectively. Note that NOR-NOR logic in NMOS technology is assumed.

A shift register is added to select a column (product line) and in the AND array. Each column P_i is AND gated by the complement of each variable S_i of the shift register:

$$P_i = p_i \bar{S_i} \qquad \text{for } i = 1, 2, \ldots m$$

where p_i is a product term generated by the ith column of the original AND array. Two extra control lines C_1 and C_2 are added to disable all $\bar{X_i}$ and X_i respectively

$$Q_{2i-1} = \bar{X_i} C_1$$
$$Q_{2i} = X_i \bar{C_2} \qquad \text{for } i = 1, 2, \ldots n$$

where X_i is the ith input line and Q_j is the jth row of the AND array. An extra product line P_{m+1} has devices on all crosspoints in the AND array, ie

$$P_{m+1} = \bar{Q_1} \bar{Q_2} \ldots \bar{Q_{2n}} \bar{S}_{m+1}$$

where Q_i is the ith row of the AND array. An extra output line Z also has devices on all product lines, ie

$$Z = P_1 + P_2 + \ldots + P_m + P_{m+1}$$

The universal test set for the augmented PLA is given in Table 1. The test set detects all multiple faults such as any combination of the following types of faults which can occur simultaneously:

(1) 'Stuck-at' faults in the augmented PLA, ie stuck-at-0 and stuck-at-1 faults on lines, X_i, C_i, Q_i, P_i, F_i, Z and S_i.
(2) Crosspoint faults (missing or extra device fault at crosspoints) in the control array, the AND array and the OR array.
(3) Adjacent line bridging faults in the control array, the AND array and the OR array, ie bridging faults between C_1 and C_2, Q_i and Q_{i+1}, P_i and P_{i+1}, F_i and F_{i+1}, and F_k and Z.

BUILT-IN SELF-TESTING

Scan design approaches have succeeded in enhancing high testability by reducing the difficulty of testing sequential logic. This type of testing still has some drawbacks, however, in respect of cost/performance

- Storage is required for a large amount of test patterns and the response to them.
- Test pattern generation is still troublesome since special test generation software is required for scan design.

Table 1. Universal test set

	$X_1 \ldots X_i \ldots X_n$	C_1	C_2	$S_1 \ldots S_j \ldots S_m S_{m+1}$
I^1	$0 \ldots\ldots 0$	1	0	$1 \ldots\ldots 1$
I_j^2	$0 \ldots\ldots 0$	1	0	$1 \ldots 0 \ldots 1$
($j = 1, \ldots, m+1$)				
I_{m+1}^3	$1 \ldots\ldots 1$	0	1	$1 \ldots\ldots 10$
I_{ij}^5	$1 \ldots 0 \ldots 1$	0	1	$1 \ldots 0 \ldots 1$
($i = 1, \ldots, n$; $j = 1, \ldots, m+1$)				
I_{ij}^7	$0 \ldots 1 \ldots 0$	1	0	$1 \ldots 0 \ldots 1$
($i = 1, \ldots, n$; $j = 1, \ldots, m+1$)				

- Testing is slow due to the shifting of patterns through the scan path.
- Automatic test equipment (ATE) is becoming expensive as circuit performance and complexity increases.

As circuit technologies advance to higher speeds and larger scales of integration, new approaches will be needed to test, at high logic speeds, large complex circuits that may contain both multiple 'stuck' type and non 'stuck' type faults. The built-in self-testing approaches that are surveyed in this paper appear to be a solution to this problem.

Signature analysis

In built-in self-testing, linear feedback shift registers (LFSRs) are used as both a pseudorandom pattern generator and a data compressor. Two types of serial LFSRs are shown in Figure 10; Figure 11 shows two types of

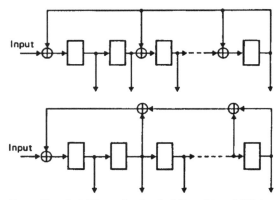

Figure 10. Serial linear feedback shift registers (LFSRs)

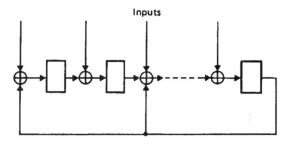

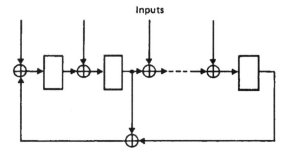

Figure 11. Parallel linear feedback shift registers (LFSRs)

parallel LFSRs. Data compression using LFSRs is based on cyclic redundancy check (CRC) codes, which are widely used in systems where data are transmitted or received. Fundamental results on CRC codes can be found in algebraic coding theory[14].

When an LFSR is used as a data compressor it is called a signature register or a signature analyser. After data compression the final contents of, or the remainder in, the LFSR are called a signature. By analysing the signature, one can determine whether or not the circuit under test is faulty. Some faults are not detected, however, when erroneous sequences caused by the faults are compressed to the same signature as a correct sequence. Analytical results on the probability of failing to detect an error by LFSRs have been reported[15-19].

Frohwerk[15] and Smith[16] showed that for a k-bit response sequence, if all possible error patterns are equally likely, then the probability p of failing to detect an error by a serial LFSR of length r (Figure 10) is

$$P = \frac{2^{k-r} - 1}{2^k - 1}$$

For long response sequences, the probability of not detecting an error approaches $1/2^r$, and hence the error coverage approaches $1 - 1/2^r$. For a 16-bit LFSR, this gives

rise to a probability of 99.998% that an error, if present, can be detected, although these measures are of questionable validity because of unrealistic fault or error assumptions.

The same result holds for parallel LFSRs[17]: let the response sequence consist of L vectors of m bits each. If all possible error sequences are equally likely, then the probability P of failing to detect an error in the response sequence by an r-bit parallel LFSR is

$$P = \frac{2^{mL-r} - 1}{2^{mL} - 1}$$

Carter[19] showed that if the order of the L test patterns is chosen randomly, then the probability of failing to detect an error in the response sequence by an r-bit parallel LFSR is less than $4/L$, where $r > \log_2(L - 1)$. This result holds for a set of randomly generated or algorithmically generated test patterns.

Built-in logic block observer

Using LFSRs, Koenemann et al[20] proposed a built-in self-test approach called the built-in logic block observer (BILBO). Figure 12 shows the logic diagram of an 8-bit BILBO. By controlling inputs B_1 and B_2, the BILBO register

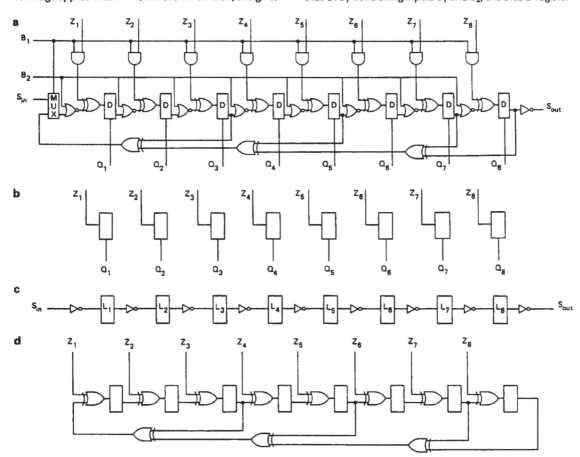

Figure 12. BILBO registers: a, logic diagram of BILBO; b, normal mode ($B_1 = 1$, $B_2 = 1$); c, shift-register mode ($B_1 = 0$, $B_2 = 0$); d, parallel-input LSFR mode ($B_1 = 1$, $B_2 = 0$)

can realize four modes. Figure 12b–d shows the normal mode ($B_1 = B_2 = 1$), the shift-register mode ($B_1 = B_2 = 0$) and the LFSR mode ($B_1 = 1$, $B_2 = 0$). The fourth mode ($B_1 = 0$, $B_2 = 1$) is used for resetting the contents of the register.

Figure 13 illustrates an application of BILBOs to modular bus-oriented systems. Each module has two BILBOs; one is used as a pseudorandom test-pattern generator, the other as a parallel signature analyser to compress the test responses into a signature. The shift-register mode is used to initialize the BILBOs and to observe the resulting signatures. Each module can therefore be tested automatically, separately from the rest of the system, by means of the BILBOs.

Self-testing with scan design

Another approach to built-in self-test has been proposed[23] in which the scan design concept and LFSRs are combined[21-24] (Figure 14). All primary inputs and primary outputs are buffered by additional shift register latches (SRLs) that act as 'see through' latches in normal-function mode. These SRLs form a shift-register string for parallel and serial pattern loading and unloading. The first group of SRLs form a pseudorandom pattern generator and the last group of SRLs form a signature analyser. Self-testing proceeds as follows:

(1) Initialize all SRLs to 0, but initialize the pseudorandom pattern-generator latches to 1 to provide a determination point for the self-test. After all latches have been initialized, apply the first test pattern to the combinational logic.
(2) Shift out all interior and output latches to compress the responses into a signature by means of the signature analyser (the last group of the SRLs). While the contents of latches are shifted, pseudorandom patterns are shifted from the pattern generator (the first group of the SRLs) into the interior latches.
(4) Repeat steps 2 and 3 until the test is complete.
(5) Compare the final signature compressed in the signature analyser with the expected signature.

There is also another built-in self-test approach, called self-verification[25], which merges off-line and on-line testing techniques. In this approach, on-line fault detection circuits such as parity checkers and self-checking comparators are used instead of signature registers. These on-line fault detection circuits detect errors caused by test patterns produced from off-line test-pattern generators.

BUILT-IN SELF-TEST FOR MICROPROCESSORS

Built-in self-testable architectures for microcomputers have been reported in which parallel/serial signature analysis techniques are implemented as on-chip testing aids.

Fasang[26] reported a microprocessor-based system in which a built-in self-test technique called 'Microbit' was implemented. Figure 15 is a block diagram of Microbit I. The system is typically bus oriented and composed of the following major blocks: a microprocessor (8085), clock and reset circuits, ROM, RAM, parallel I/O ports, a serial I/O port and an external system bus arbitrator. In addition to these standard blocks, Microbit has two BILBOs: a pseudorandom pattern generator (PRPG) and a parallel signature analyser (PSA). The PRPG generates a repetitive sequence of 255 pseudorandom patterns which are used for testing RAM and the Multibus adaptor.

In the Microbit system, basic functional or operational testing is performed. The 8085 microprocessor runs a test program. The most fundamental test, called the kernel

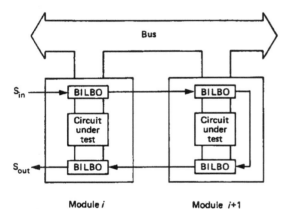

Figure 13. Modular bus-oriented design with BILBOs

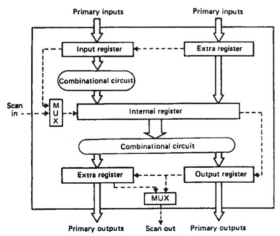

Figure 14. Built-in self-test with scan design

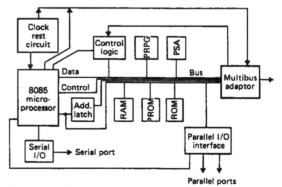

Figure 15. Block of diagram of Microbit I

test, checks the processor with respect to only a few instructions, as well as the address, data and control buses. The remaining instructions of the processor are then executed and compared with the expected results. The BILBOs (PRPG and PSA) are not used in this process but are used for testing RAM, ROM, the Multibus adaptor, and themselves. In the ROM test, the contents of the ROM are read out, one byte at a time, and compressed by the PSA. The final contents of the PSA are compared with the expected signature by the 8085. In the RAM test, the first 256 byte of RAM are filled with 256 patterns from the PRPG, the next 256 byte with the 256 patterns from PRPG+1, etc. When all RAM is filled, the contents are transferred to the PSA, one byte at a time, and compressed into a signature. The signature is then transferred to the 8085 and compared with the expected signature stored in PROM. In this way Microbit implements a microprocessor-based system with a built-in self-test function.

Thatte et al[27] proposed an architecture for on-chip built-in testable VLSI processors. The methodology proposed is based on a bit-sliced, bus-oriented architecture which is amenable to on-chip built-in implementation using BILBOs. Figure 16 shows the general configuration of the processor. In general, a typical single-chip VLSI processor has three main sections: a data path, control and an on-chip memory. The data-path section stores, manipulates and transfers data. It is usually composed of registers, arithmetic logic units (ALUs) and data buses. The control section, which decodes machine instructions and generates control signals for the data-path section and other logic, is composed of a control ROM, PLA and decoders. Other on-chip memory, such as program ROM for storing machine-level programs and data RAM for storing data, is contained in the on-chip memory section.

The testable processor proposed has two monitors, a control monitor and a data monitor. Both are the same and have four modes of operation: normal, signature-analysis, scan (shift) and rotate modes. Except for in the rotate mode, the monitors work in the same way as a BILBO. The control monitor can be configured as a parallel signature analyser to monitor the control signals of the data-path section. The control ROM is tested by reading out the entire contents of the ROM and compressing the control signals into a signature. In a similar way, the data monitor is configured as a parallel signature analyser to monitor and compress the output data produced by the data-path section. Each functional test pattern for the data-path section consists of control signals and data operands: data operands can be generated by the use of simple hardware such as counters and shifters; control signals can be generated by a microprogram stored in an additional ROM or by a machine code program. The on-chip program ROM is tested by reading out the contents of the ROM and compressing the ROM outputs into a signature by means of the data monitor. For data RAM testing, test patterns stored in the on-chip program ROM are applied to the RAM and the outputs compared with the expected values by means of a comparator.

Built-in self-test approaches using LFSRs have also been implemented on commercial MOS micro-computers, the MC6804P2[28] and the MC68020[29]. Figure 17 is a block diagram of the MC6804P2, which is designed for 4-bit and low-end 8-bit applications: its ALU and buses are all 1 bit wide. Due to its serial architecture, a 16-bit serial signature analyser, an LFSR, is used to compress test responses from each module such as the ALU, RAM, ROM, timer, ports etc.

In the MC68020 32-bit microprocessor, a combination of structural and functional testing is used. To produce structural tests of the control section, the processor is partitioned by a bus-oriented structure with the addition of some microcode and multiplexers to enable the PLAs, ROMs and the cache to be separated from the rest of the circuitry. A built-in self-test approach using a signature register, an LFSR, is partly adopted for testing the on-chip PLAs. Each PLA under test can be separated from the rest of the circuit by test microcode. Two types of test sets are applied to the PLAs: a deterministic (algorithmically generated) test set and an exhaustive test set from an on-chip register. The output response from each of the PLAs is compressed via a 16-bit signature register, and the signature is read out to compare with the expected signature.

A built-in self-test design for modular structured microprocessors in which the testing hardware, composed of LFSRs, is centralized and shared among modules was reported by Yamaguchi et al[30]. The basic configuration is illustrated in Figure 18. The hardware necessary for self-testing is not distributed but centralized, ie the test-pattern generator and signature register are not built into each individual module, but self-test resources are centralized

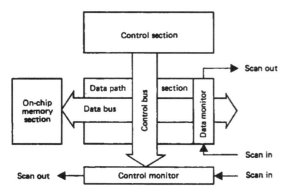

Figure 16. A configuration of built-in testable VLSI processors

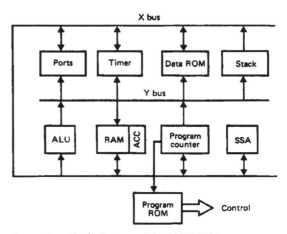

Figure 17. Block diagram of the MC6804P2

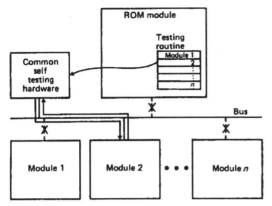

Figure 18. *Basic configuration of self-testing for modular structured microprocessors*

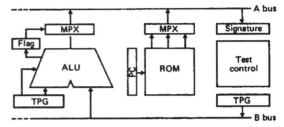

Figure 19. *Module examples and self-testing hardware*

and shared with all modules to obtain a self-test scheme with low area overhead. Each module is composed of either combinational circuits of memory elements without feedback loops, and is tested by test patterns from the common self-test hardware and/or from its own additional test-pattern generator. The response of each module is transferred to the signature register of the common self-test hardware and is compared with the expected signature. These self-testing processes are controlled by a microprogram using a special microinstruction which is provided only for self-testing the modules. This micro-instruction selects the module to be tested, forms the data path between the selected module and the common self-testing hardware, specifies the number of test patterns to be applied, and performs self-testing of the module. This design achieves a high fault coverage (90% of single stuck-at faults) with low area overhead (7%) when applied to a VLSI hard disc controller.

BUILT-IN SELF-TEST FOR PROGRAMMABLE LOGIC ARRAYS

As universal testing or function-independent testing needs no test-pattern generation, it seems to be an optimum design for testability when external testing is considered. Due to the regularity of universal test patterns, universal testing is also suited to built-in self testing and has been used in much of the research work done on built-in self-test PLAs[31-36]. The approach of Treuer et al[36] is based on the universally testable PLA design described above[13] and has produced built-in self-testable PLAs in which high fault coverage is achieved with low area overhead — all single and almost all multiple stuck-at, crosspoint and bridging faults are detected with an area overhead of about 15% for large PLAs.

CONCLUSIONS

Various approaches to design for testability and built-in self-testing have been surveyed in this paper, focussing particularly on the latter. Many techniques have been proposed, some of which are already in practical use but

most of which need further research. Built-in self-testing is seen as a potential solution to VLSI testing problems and the advancement of future test technology could very much depend upon the progress of current research on built-in self-testing. Although today's built-in self-test technologies offer many advantages, further research efforts are necessary to find

- effective built-in self-test schemes to achieve high fault coverage with low area overhead
- effective means for determining the test lengths needed to get the expected fault coverage in a pseudorandom testing environment
- cost-effective means for evaluating fault coverage.

REFERENCES

1 **Fujiwara, H** *Logic testing and design for testability* MIT Press (1985)
2 **Williams, M J Y and Angell, J B** 'Enhancing testability of large scale integrated circuits via test points and additional logic' *IEEE Trans. Comput.* Vol C-22 No 1 (Jan 1973) pp 46–60
3 **Funatsu, S, Wakatsuki, N and Arima, T** 'Test generation systems in Japan' *Proc. 12th Design Automation Symp.* Vol 6 (1975) pp 114–122
4 **Eichelberger, E B and Williams, T W** 'A logic design structure for LSI testability' *Proc. 14th Design Automation Conf.* (1977) pp 462–468
5 **Stewart, J H** 'Future testing of large LSI circuit cards' *Proc. 1977 Semiconductor Test Symp.* (1977) pp 6–17
6 **Ando, H** 'Testing VLSI with random access scan' *Proc. Compcon* (1980) pp 50–52
7 **Fujiwara, H, Kinoshita, K and Ozaki, H** 'Universal test sets for programmable logic arrays' *Proc. 10th Int. Conf. Fault-Tolerant Comput.* (1980) pp 137–142
8 **Fujiwara, H and Kinoshita, K** 'A design of programmable logic arrays with universal tests' *IEEE Trans. Comput.* Vol C-30 No 11 (Nov. 1981) pp 823–838
9 **Hong, S J and Ostapko, D L** 'FITPLA: A programmable logic array for function independent testing' *Proc. 10th Int. Conf. Fault-Tolerant Comput.* (1980) pp 131–136
10 **Saluja K K, Kinoshita, K and Fujiwara, H** 'An easily testable design of programmable logic arrays for multiple faults' *IEEE Trans. Comput.* Vol C-32 No 11 (Nov. 1983) pp 1038–1046
11 **Ramanatha, K S and Biswas, N N** 'A design for testability of undetectable crosspoint faults in programmable logic arrays' *IEEE Trans. Comput.* Vol C-32 No 6 (June 1983) pp 551–557
12 **Khakbaz, J** 'A testable PLA design with low overhead and high fault coverage' *IEEE Trans. Comput.* Vol C-33 No 8 (Aug. 1984) pp 743–745

13 **Fujiwara, H** 'A new PLA design for universal testability' *IEEE Trans. Comput.* Vol C-33 No 8 (Aug. 1984) pp 745–750

14 **Peterson, W W and Weldon, E J** *Error-correcting codes* MIT Press (1972)

15 **Frohwerk, R A** 'Signature analysis: a new digital field service method' *Hewlett-Packard J.* (May 1977) pp 2–8

16 **Smith, J E** 'Measures of the effectiveness of fault signature analysis' *IEEE Trans. Comput.* Vol C-29 No 6 (June 1980) pp 510–514

17 **Bhavsar, D K and Heckelman, R W** 'Self-testing by polynomial division' *Proc. 1981 IEEE Test Conf.* (1981) pp 208–216

18 **Sridhar, T, Ho, D S, Powell, T J and Thatte, S M** 'Analysis and simulation of parallel signature analysis' *Proc. 1982 IEEE Test Conf.* (1982) pp 656–661

19 **Carter, J L** 'The theory of signature testing for VLSI' *Proc. 14th ACM Symp. Theory of Computing* (1982) pp 66–76

20 **Koenemann, B, Mucha, J and Zwiehoff, G** 'Built-in logic block observation techniques' *Proc. 1979 IEEE Test Conf.* (1979) pp 37–41

21 **Segers, M T M** 'A self-test method for digital circuits' *Proc. 1981 IEEE Test Conf.* (1981) pp 79–85

22 **Bardell, P H and McAnney, W H** 'Self-testing of multichip logic modules' *Proc. 1982 IEEE Test Conf.* (1982) pp 200–204

23 **Komonytsky, D** 'LSI self-test using level sensitive scan design and signature analysis' *Proc. 1982 IEEE Test Conf.* (1982) pp 414–424

24 **Eichelberger, E B and Lindbloom, E** 'Random-pattern coverage enhancement and diagnosis for LSSD logic self-test' *IBM J. Res. Develop.* Vol 27 No 3 (1983) pp 265–272

25 **Sedmak, R M** 'Design for self-verification: an approach for dealing with testability problems in VLSI-based designs' *Proc. 1979 IEEE Test Conf.* (1979) pp 112–120

26 **Fasang, P P** 'A fault detection and isolation technique for microprocessors' *Proc. 1982 IEEE Test Conf.* (1982) pp 214–219

27 **Thatte, S M, Ho, D S, Yuan, H T and Powell, T J** 'An architecture for testable VLSI processors' *Proc. 1982 IEEE Test Conf.* (1982) pp 484–492

28 **Kuban J and Bruce, B** 'The MC6804P2 built-in self-test' *Proc. 1983 Int. Test Conf.* (1983) pp 295–300

29 **Kuban, J and Salick, J** 'Testability features of the MC68020' *Proc. 1984 Int. Test Conf.* (1984) pp 821–826

30 **Yamaguchi, N, Funabashi, T, Iwasaki, K, Shimura, T, Hagiwara, Y and Minorikawa, K** 'A self-testing method for modular structured logic VLSIs' *Proc. Int. Conf. CAD* (1984) pp 99–101

31 **Daehn, W and Mucha, J** 'A hardware approach to self-testing of large programmable logic arrays' *IEEE Trans. Comput.* Vol C-30 No 11 (Nov. 1981) pp 829–833

32 **Grassl, G and Pfleiderer, H J** 'A self-testing PLA' *Proc. 1982 IEEE Int. Solid-state Circuits Conf.* (1982) pp 60–61

33 **Hassan, S Z and McCluskey, E J** 'Testing PLAs using multiple parallel signature analysers' *Proc. 13th Int. Symp. Fault-Tolerant Comput.* (1983) pp 422–425

34 **Yajima, S and Aramaki, T** 'Autonomously testable programmable logic arrays' *Proc. 11th Int. Symp. Fault-Tolerant Comput.* (1981) pp 41–43

35 **Hua, K A, Jou, J Y and Abraham, J A** 'Built-in tests for VLSI finite-state machines' *Proc. 14th Int. Symp. Fault-Tolerant Comput.* (1984) pp 430–435

36 **Treuer, R, Fujiwara, H and Agarwal, V K** 'Implementing a built-in self-test PLA design' *IEEE Design and Test of Computers* Vol 2 No 2 (April 1985) pp 37–48

37 **Williams, T W and Parker, K P** 'Design for testability — a survey' *IEEE Trans. Comput.* Vol C-31 No 1 (January 1982) pp 2–15

38 **McCluskey, E J** 'Built-in self-test techniques' *IEEE Design and Test of Computers* Vol 2 No 2 (April 1985) pp 21–28

39 **McCluskey, E J** 'Built-in self-test structures' *IEEE Design and Test of Computers* Vol 2 No 2 (April 1985) pp 29–36

Hideo Fujiwara is an associate professor in the Department of Electronics and Communication at Meiji University, Japan. Prior to this he was in the Department of Electronic Engineering at Osaka University, Japan. Fujiwara received the BE, ME and PhD degrees in electronic engineering from Osaka University in 1969, 1971 and 1974, respectively. His research interests include switching theory, design for testability, test pattern generation, fault simulation, built-in self-test and fault-tolerant computing. He is a senior member of the IEEE, also a member of IECE of Japan and the Information Processing Society of Japan.

Minimal M68000 system controllers for fast-acting multi-input multi-output processes

Realtime aircraft tracking system controllers have, in the past, typically included 8-bit processors. **A Bradshaw, P Konnanov and M A Woodhead** describe how a 16-bit micro can improve control simulation performance

The paper describes a high-performance microprocessor system for use in realtime multivariable control applications. The system concept and hardware is discussed and an example of its use, in the simulated control of a combat aircraft undergoing enhanced manoeuvres, is given.

microsystems   68000   flight control simulation

The effective use of fast-acting microprocessor-based controllers in realtime tracking systems has been demonstrated for enhanced manoeuvre flight control of an experimental combat aircraft[1, 2]. Controllers of this type have incorporated 8-bit CPUs such as the Motorola 6800 and the Rockwell 6502[3] along with 12-bit data acquisition circuitry and hardware arithmetic logic units (ALUs) for efficient arithmetic manipulation.

With the advent of increasingly sophisticated control strategies has come the demand for further improvements in processing capacity and speed. This paper presents a 68000-based system designed to meet the requirements of high-order control algorithms, and results demonstrating the system's use in realtime flight control simulation of the YF-16 aircraft undergoing enhanced pitch pointing and vertical translation manoeuvres.

SYSTEM OVERVIEW

The controller is designed for high-speed processing of analogue data, and consists of a microprocessor module

based on the 68000 CPU, a data acquisition unit for data handling and processing between the system and external equipment, and a variable hardware interrupt unit for accurate cycle timing. Figure 1 shows a simplified configuration of the main system components.

The microprocessor circuitry is focussed on the Apollo 68000 standalone computer module. This module provides the user with a means of interfacing the CPU efficiently to peripheral devices through an 8255 parallel peripheral interface (PPI), an 8250 asynchronous communications element (ACE) for serial data, or directly via the bus, depending on the data format required. The module was chosen mainly for the speed of the CPU (10 MHz), for the 68000 instruction set which permits efficient onchip arithmetic processing, and for the 16-bit data bus which minimizes operation data transfers.

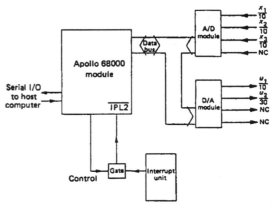

Figure 1.   Controller configuration

Department of Aeronautical and Mechanical Engineering, University of Salford, Salford M5 4WT, UK

The data acquisition system consists of a high-level A/D module and an analogue-output D/A module is configured within the memory map of the computer unit. The modules were purpose designed for compatibility with the CPU specification and require a minimum of software control.

The basis of the hardware interrupt unit is a divider-chain configuration applied to the 10 MHz clock signal. Various frequencies are manually selectable. The resulting signal is optionally admitted to the CPU interrupt pin IPL2 via the user software to avoid system corruption during monitor operations, where interrupt priority is not under user control.

Apollo 68000 module

The Apollo 68000 single-board computer incorporates a 68000 CPU. This processor runs at 10 MHz and has 17 internal 32-bit registers and a 24-bit program counter. The board is supplied with a comprehensive monitor on EPROM which provides full debug facilities, single step and trace, downline loading and a programming handler. Also on the board is 4 kbyte of fast static RAM (expandable to 16k of EPROM (expandable to 32k), some of which is used for the monitor; a 24-line parallel interface; and an RS232 interface with a wide range of transmission rates.

Although programming the module is possible by means of the monitor program and a standard terminal, the most efficient method is via a host computer. The Epson QX-10, an 8-bit Z80 CP/M machine with a disc-based 68000 crossassembler, has been used successfully in this role. When the user's program is inserted and assembled on the host system, the object code is transferred to the module via the serial interface. Figure 2 shows the memory map of the system. The monitor requires the RAM area from 400000H to 4003FFH; consequently, user object files may be inserted at any location beyond 400400H.

D/A conversion module

The conventional method of obtaining multichannel D/A action is to use one D/A converter chip along with multiplexing and sample-and-hold (SH) circuitry. With the present system, one converter per channel is employed to attain maximum performance, thus eliminating the relatively lengthy SH acquisition time. Although the associated analogue circuitry has to be duplicated for each channel and the chip count is generally higher, the technique is justified by the speed of data throughput compared to that of conventional methods.

Each D/A channel is based around a 12-bit monolithic, multiplying D/A converter, the RS7544, incorporating a six-word deep, 12-bit wide, first-in first-out (FIFO) stack register which acts as a buffer store for digital information.

When wired in a simple configuration, operation requires only two controls, a chip enable line from the decoding circuitry and the CPU RD/WR line.

As the write-to-data hold time is 270 ns minimum, latches are required when interfacing the 68000. Two octal edge-triggered flipflops, the outputs of which are constantly enabled by hardwiring, are incorporated for this purpose. New data is clocked in, upon every CPU

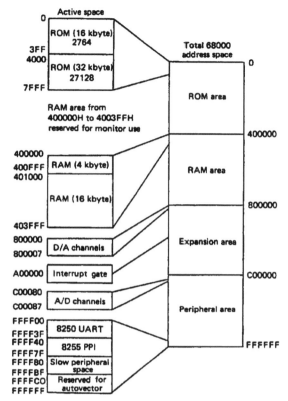

Figure 2. System memory map

operation accessing the D/A module, via the external select line EXSEL.

With memory-mapped interfacing, D/A operations consist of simply writing data to the memory location assigned to the particular channel. The module is fast enough to be implemented at full CPU speed, allowing successive operations to be carried out immediately, without the use of wait states.

Analogue operational amplifier circuitry is required to transform the converter outputs into bipolar form. Trimmers are provided so that each channel may be set up to give a voltage output of 10 V for a digital input value of 07FFH, −10 V for an input of 0800H and 0 V for an input of 0H. Operation is therefore simple as the magnitude and polarity of the voltage output correspond to those of the digital input.

A/D conversion module

A/D conversion is a notoriously time-consuming operation. Standard multichannel systems are generally arranged in multiplexed sequential configurations. When several channel conversions are required, the total conversion time consists of the sum of the conversion and software initialization times of each channel. To increase efficiency, the method employed in the present system is to invoke conversion of all channels simultaneously. The total conversion time merely consists of the execution time of one memory operation plus the length of the longest conversion cycle. With this technique, any number of channels may be converted with no increase in either initialization or total conversion time.

As with the D/A module, one converter per channel is used. Each channel, apart from the decoding circuitry, consists almost entirely of the converter chip RS574. This chip is a complete 12-bit successive-approximation A/D converter with three-state output buffer circuitry for direct interfacing to the microprocessor bus. Chip operations are simple via the general control lines: chip enable (CE), chip select ($\overline{\text{CS}}$) and Read/$\overline{\text{Convert}}$. Decoding is arranged such that memory read operations will access any desired converter whereas a write operation to any of the chips will initiate conversion on all of them.

As the average length of conversion is 25 μs — a relatively short period — the situation is simplified by halting CPU operations during acquisition time; for this purpose, use has been made of the RS574 status flags, which are normally held low. Status flags become high while conversions are taking place.

A simple logical arrangement monitors the status flags from each channel. When any one or all of these becomes active (high), the 68000 bus request (BR) line is brought low, inhibiting further CPU operations. This situation continues until all status flags have returned to the low state, indicating that all channel conversions are complete. With this configuration the data read instructions may follow the conversion write command immediately in the software, greatly simplifying user operational considerations.

A similar bipolar conversion format is employed to that of the D/A module. A 10 V input produces a digital output value of 07FFH; 0 V gives a value of 0H; and −10 V produces 0800H. Two trimmer potentiometers per channel are provided to adjust zero and range characteristics.

Interrupt hardware

The interrupt arrangement was designed for flexibility and simplicity. A frequency divider chain provides a range of interrupt signals derived, ultimately, from the 10 MHz clock signal. Selection is by means of hard wiring or, optionally, switching.

For correct interrupt operation, the CPU requires a trigger pulse width of at least 44 clock periods. Suitable logic circuitry is included to ensure that the selected signal satisfies this requirement.

The nature of the Apollo system is such that all interrupt levels are enabled following monitor subroutines. Additional circuitry was thus necessary to allow regulation of the flow of interrupt pulses to the CPU. A tristate switch, gated by the action of a bistable flipflop, is used for this purpose. The bistable flipflop is toggled from two sources. The system reset gates the throughput of interrupt signals OFF whilst a decoded CPU operation gates interrupts ON. Thus, once the interrupt signal is enabled under software control, it can only be disabled by a system reset. This form of signal control is adequate for present purposes. The interrupt signal destination is CPU pin IPL2.

Mapping and decoding

The data acquisition modules are configured in a memory-mapped arrangement with the CPU, not only for the sake of efficiency but also in order to leave the PPI 24-line port free for EPROM programmer expansion if required.

The Apollo 68000 system provides a 4 Mbyte expansion area which requires the return of DTACK and a peripheral area, part of which is reserved for PPI and ACE mapping, along with autovector and 32-word slow peripheral space. The D/A module is implemented at full speed within the general expansion space from 800000H onwards; the data-valid requirements are within the 100 ns clock period of the CPU. The A/D module, however, requires longer pulse times and is thus configured within the slow peripheral area from FFFF80H onwards. Due to simple address decoding, the Apollo 68000 active address space is mapped into the 16 Mbyte total address space many times. This allows the D/A module to be addressed from C00080H, greatly simplifying the decoding of both D/A and A/D modules.

Interrupt signal switching is mapped within the expansion space at memory location A00000H. This is a convenient location, outside the range of the module decoder. The decoder signal activates a bistable switch enabling the flow of interrupt pulses to the CPU.

MICROPROCESSOR CONTROL APPLICATION

In the example below, the system is used in realtime control simulation. In the study, the controller is required to effect fuselage pitch pointing and vertical translation manoeuvres for an analogue computer representation of a YF-16 aircraft. The control loop is arranged as in Figure 3.

The results of Bradshaw and Porter[4, 5] indicate that tight noninteracting control of multi-input multi-output processes is, in general, achievable by fast sampling error-activated controllers. It has been shown[6, 7], however, that in many situations a time delay of several sampling periods may occur in the control implementation. For this reason, the original control methodology[2] has been modified to accommodate multiple period delays.

Discrete-time tracking systems with finite time delay compensation

The controller design procedure used here is described in the open-half interval $0 < t < +\infty$ by state, output and measurement equations of the forms, respectively

$$\begin{bmatrix} \dot{x}_1(t) \\ \dot{x}_2(t) \end{bmatrix} = \begin{bmatrix} A_{11}, A_{12} \\ A_{21}, A_{22} \end{bmatrix} \begin{bmatrix} x_1(t) \\ x_2(t) \end{bmatrix} + \begin{bmatrix} 0 \\ B_2 \end{bmatrix} u(t) \qquad (1)$$

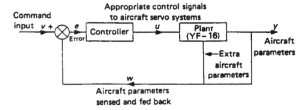

Figure 3. System configured within the control loop

$$y(t) = [C_1, C_2] \begin{bmatrix} x_1(t) \\ x_2(t) \end{bmatrix} \qquad (2)$$

$$w(t) = [F_1, F_2] \begin{bmatrix} x_1(t) \\ x_2(t) \end{bmatrix} \qquad (3)$$

together with fast sampling error-actuated digital controllers governed on the discrete-time set $T_T = \{0, T, 2T, \ldots\}$ by control law equations of the form

$$s(kT) = f[K_o e(kT) + K_1 z(kT)] \qquad (4)$$

and computational time-delay compensation equations of the form

$$r(kT) = s(kT) - \sum_{i=1}^{m} \gamma_i r[(k-i)T] \qquad (5)$$

where

$$e(kT) = v(kT) - w(kT) \qquad (6)$$

and

$$z(kT) = z(o) + T \sum_{j=0}^{j=k-1} e(jT) \qquad (7)$$

In equations (1)–(7):

$x_1(t) \in R^{n-l}$;

$x_2(t) \in R^l$;

$u(t) \in R^l$;

$y(t) \in R^l$;

$w(t) \in R^l$;

$A_{11} \in R^{(n-l)(n-l)}$;

$A_{12} \in R^{(n-l)l}$;

$A_{21} \in R^{l(n-l)}$;

$A_{22} \in R^{ll}$;

$C_1 \in R^{l(n-l)}$;

$C_2 \in R^{ll}$;

$F_1 \in R^{l(n-l)}$;

$F_2 \in R^{ll}$;

rank $C_2 B_2 < l$;

rank $F_2 B_2 = l$;

$r(kT) \in R^l$;

$s(kT) \in R^l$;

$v(kT) \in R^l$;

$e(kT) \in R^l$;

$z(kT) \in R^l$;

$K_o \in R^{ll}$;

$K_1 \in R^{ll}$;

and $f = 1/T$ is the sampling frequency; $\gamma_i (i = 1, 2, \ldots, m) \in R$ are the delay compensation parameters. Since the computational time delay is m sampling periods, the digital controller is required to generate the control input vector

$$u(t) = r[(k-m)T] \qquad t \in [kT, (k+1)T] \qquad kT \in T_T \quad (8)$$

to cause the output vector $y(t)$ to track any constant command input vector $v(t)$ on T_T in the sense that

$$\lim_{k \to \infty} \{v(kT) - y(kT)\} = 0 \qquad (9)$$

as a consequence of the fact that the error vector $e(t) = v(t) - w(t)$ assumes the steady-state value

$$\lim_{k \to \infty} e(kT) = \lim_{k \to \infty} \{v(kT) - w(kT)\} = 0 \qquad (10)$$

for arbitrary initial conditions. In the case where

$$[F_1, F_2] = [C_1 + MA_{11}, C_2 + MA_{12}] \qquad (11)$$

it is evident from Equations (2), (3) and (11) that the vector

$$w(t) - y(t) = [MA_{11}, MA_{12}] \begin{bmatrix} x_1(t) \\ x_2(t) \end{bmatrix} \qquad (12)$$

of extra measurements, such that $v(kT)$ and $y(kT)$ satisfy the tracking condition (Equation (9)) for any $M \in R^{l(n-l)}$ if $e(kT)$ satisfies the steady-state condition (Equation (10)), since Equation (1) clearly implies that

$$\lim_{t \to \infty} [A_{11}, A_{12}] \begin{bmatrix} x_1(t) \\ x_2(t) \end{bmatrix} = 0 \qquad (13)$$

in any steady state. However, the condition that rank $F_2 B_2 = l$ requires that C_2 and A_{12} are such that M can be chosen so that

$$\text{rank } F_2 = \text{rank } (C_2 + MA_{12}) = l \qquad (14)$$

It can be shown that stability is assured by requiring that

$$F_2 B_2 K_o = \text{diag} (\sigma_1, \sigma_2, \ldots, \sigma_l) \qquad (15)$$

where $(1 - \sigma_j) \in R \cap D^- (j = 1, 2, \ldots, l)$. If, in addition, M is chosen such that both 'slow' and 'fast' transfer function matrices are diagonal, then increasingly non-interacting tracking will occur as $f \to \infty$.

Aircraft simulation

The linearized longitudinal dynamics of the YF-16 aircraft flying at a Mach number of 0.8 at sea level are governed by the state equation

$$\begin{bmatrix} \dot{x}_1(t) \\ \dot{x}_2(t) \\ \dot{x}_3(t) \end{bmatrix} = \begin{bmatrix} 0, & 1 & , & 0 \\ 0, & -2.068, & 10.029 \\ 0, & 0.985, & -2.155 \end{bmatrix} \begin{bmatrix} x_1(t) \\ x_2(t) \\ x_3(t) \end{bmatrix}$$

$$+ \begin{bmatrix} 0 & , & 0 \\ -35.44 & , & -5.124 \\ -0.238 & , & -0.308 \end{bmatrix} \begin{bmatrix} u_1(t) \\ u_2(t) \end{bmatrix} \qquad (16)$$

where $x_1(t)$ is the change in pitch angle; $x_2(t)$ is the rate of change of pitch angle; $x_3(t)$ is the change in angle of attack; $u_1(t)$ is the elevator deflection; and $u_2(t)$ is the flaperon deflection. In the realtime simulation studies described in this paper, Equation (16) was represented as shown in Figure 4 by a suitably programmed EAL Pace 48 analogue computer.

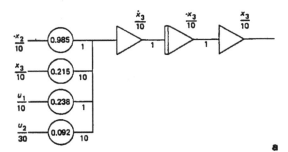

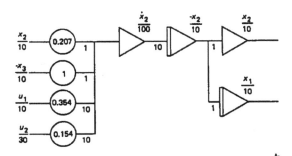

Figure 4. Analogue computer flow diagrams: a, for incidence angle, b, for pitch rate and pitch angle

Vertical translation manoeuvre

The vertical translation manoeuvre requires the aircraft to track a command on the angle of attack whilst suppressing any variation in pitch angle. The corresponding output equation is therefore

$$\begin{bmatrix} y_1(t) \\ y_2(t) \end{bmatrix} = \begin{bmatrix} 1,0,0 \\ 0,0,1 \end{bmatrix} \begin{bmatrix} x_1(t) \\ x_2(t) \\ x_3(t) \end{bmatrix} \tag{17}$$

Hence, in the case

$$\{\sigma_1,\sigma_2\} = \{0.4,0.4\};$$

$$\gamma_i = 1/6 (i = 1,\ldots,5);$$

$$K_0^{-1}K_1 = \text{diag}\{\rho_1,\rho_2\} = \text{diag}\{2.5,2.5\};$$

$$M = \begin{bmatrix} 0.25 \\ 0 \end{bmatrix} \tag{18}$$

it follows from Equations (3), (5), (8) and (15) that the corresponding transducers and fast sampling error-actuated digital controllers with finite time-delay compensation are governed on T and T_T by the respective measurement and control law equations

$$\begin{bmatrix} w_1(t) \\ w_2(t) \end{bmatrix} = \begin{bmatrix} 1,0.25,0 \\ 0,0 \quad,1 \end{bmatrix} \begin{bmatrix} x_1(t) \\ x_2(t) \\ x_3(t) \end{bmatrix} \tag{19}$$

and

$$\begin{bmatrix} r_1(kT) \\ r_2(kT) \end{bmatrix} = f \left\{ \begin{bmatrix} -0.051, & 0.211 \\ 0.039, & -1.462 \end{bmatrix} \begin{bmatrix} e_1(kT) \\ e_2(kT) \end{bmatrix} \right.$$

$$+ \begin{bmatrix} -0.127, & 0.528 \\ 0.098, & -3.655 \end{bmatrix} \begin{bmatrix} z_1(kT) \\ z_2(kT) \end{bmatrix} \right\}$$

$$-\frac{1}{6} \sum_{i=1}^{5} \begin{bmatrix} u_1\{(k-i)T\} \\ u_2\{(k-i)T\} \end{bmatrix} \tag{20}$$

As the asymptotic transfer function assumes diagonal form, the direct digital flight-mode control system for the vertical translation manoeuvre of the aircraft, with a time delay of five sampling periods in the implementation of the control action, will exhibit increasingly noninteracting tracking behaviour as $f \to \infty$ when the piecewise-constant control input vector is generated by the fast sampling digital controller governed on T_T by Equation (20).

Fuselage pitch pointing manoeuvre

The fuselage pitch pointing manoeuvre requires the aircraft to track a command on the pitch angle whilst suppressing any variation in flight path angle. The corresponding output equation is therefore

$$\begin{bmatrix} y_1(t) \\ y_2(t) \end{bmatrix} = \begin{bmatrix} 1,0, & 0 \\ 1,0, & -1 \end{bmatrix} \begin{bmatrix} x_1(t) \\ x_2(t) \\ x_3(t) \end{bmatrix} \tag{21}$$

Hence, in the case $\{\sigma_1,\sigma_2\} = \{0.4, 0.4\}$, $\gamma_i = 1/6 (i = 1,\ldots,5)$, $K_0^{-1}K_1 = \text{diag}\{2.5,2.5\}$, and

$$M = \begin{bmatrix} 1.25 \\ 0 \end{bmatrix} \tag{22}$$

it follows from equations (3), (5), (8) and (15) that the corresponding transducers and fast sampling error-actuated digital controllers with finite time-delay compensation are governed on T and T_T by the respective measurement and control law equations

$$\begin{bmatrix} w_1(t) \\ w_2(t) \end{bmatrix} = \begin{bmatrix} 1,0.25, & 0 \\ 1,0 \quad, & -1 \end{bmatrix} \begin{bmatrix} x_1(t) \\ x_2(t) \\ x_3(t) \end{bmatrix} \tag{23}$$

and

$$\begin{bmatrix} r_1(kT) \\ r_2(kT) \end{bmatrix} = f \left\{ \begin{bmatrix} -0.051, & -0.211 \\ 0.039, & 1.462 \end{bmatrix} \begin{bmatrix} e_1(kT) \\ e_2(kT) \end{bmatrix} \right.$$

$$+ \begin{bmatrix} -0.127, & -0.528 \\ 0.098, & 3.655 \end{bmatrix} \begin{bmatrix} z_1(kT) \\ z_2(kT) \end{bmatrix} \right\}$$

$$-\frac{1}{6} \sum_{i=1}^{5} \begin{bmatrix} u_1\{(k-i)T\} \\ u_2\{(k-i)T\} \end{bmatrix} \tag{24}$$

The asymptotic transfer function assumes diagonal form, so the direct flight-mode control system for the fuselage pitch pointing manoeuvre of the aircraft, with a time delay of five sampling periods for control action implementation, will exhibit increasingly noninteracting tracking behaviour

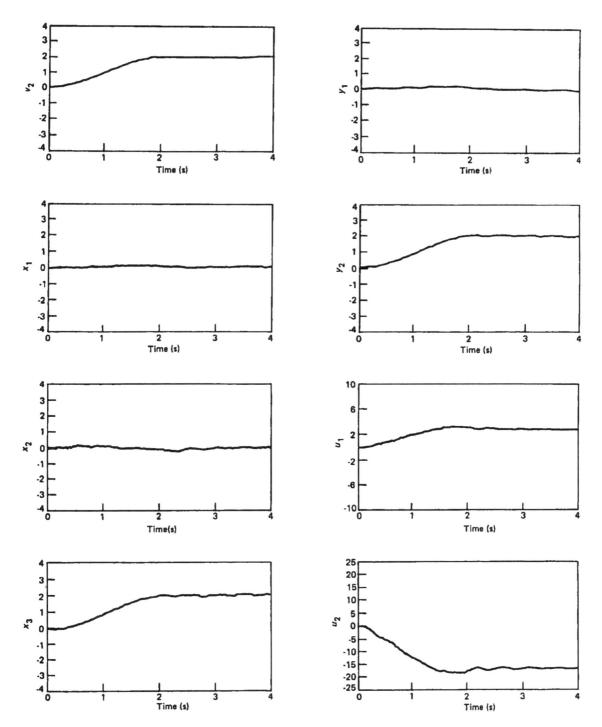

Figure 5. Simulated vertical translation manoeuvre (time delay = 0.1 s)

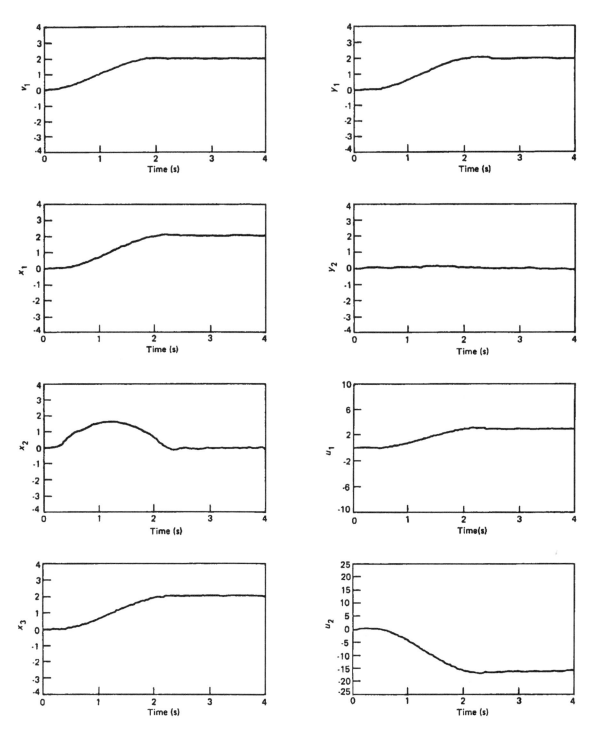

Figure 6. *Simulated fuselage pitch pointing manoeuvre (time delay =0.1 s)*

as $f \to \infty$ when the piecewise-constant control input vector is generated by the fast sampling digital controller governed on T_T by Equation (24).

SIMULATION RESULTS

The simulated behaviour of the YF-16 aircraft is shown for vertical translation mode (Figure 5) and fuselage pitch pointing mode (Figure 6) when controlled in accordance with Equations (20) and (24); the command input vectors are 'ramped up' in 2 s to the steady-state values $[v_1(t), v_2(t)]^T = [0,2]^T$ deg (Figure 5) and $[v_1(t), v_2(t)]^T = [2, 0]$ deg (Figure 6). In all cases a sampling period of 0.02 s is used and it is evident that highly accurate noninteracting behaviour is achieved despite the control action time delay of five sampling periods. It is also apparent from Figures 5 and 6 that both vertical translation and fuselage pitch pointing manoeuvres are effected without the use of excessive transient control surface deflections.

CONCLUSIONS

A minimal 68000-based controller for advanced control of multi-input multi-output processes has been presented. The controller was relatively inexpensive to construct, is flexible and simple to effect, and offers a much greater algorithm-to-sample rate ratio than was possible with any of its 8-bit predecessors.

The results of the YF-16 simulation example show that tight noninteracting control is maintained even when the applied control is delayed by 0.1 s. Thus both the adequacy of the theory and the ability of the controller to implement the theory in real time are demonstrated.

REFERENCES

1   **Porter, B and Bradshaw, A** 'Design of direct digital flight-mode control systems for high-performance aircraft' *PROC. IEEE National Aerospace and Electronics Conf.* Dayton, USA (May 1981)
2   **Porter, B, Bradshaw, A, Garis, A and Woodhead, M A** 'Microprocessor implementation of fast sampling direct digital flight-mode controllers' *AGARD-CP-321 Conf. Advances in Guidance and Control Systems,* Lisbon, Portugal (October 1982)
3   **Beurms, W, van den Abeele, M, Boullart, L, de Keyser, R and d'Hulser, F** 'Use of a low-cost microcomputer to control SISO processes' *Journal A* Vol 22 No 2 (1981) pp 63–71
4   **Bradshaw, A and Porter, B** 'Singular perturbation methods in the design of tracking systems incorporating fast-sampling error-actuated controllers' *Int. J. Systems Sci.* Vol 12 (1981) pp 1181–1191
5   **Bradshaw, A and Porter, B** 'Singular perturbation methods in the design of tracking systems incorporating inner-loop compensators and fast-sampling error-actuated controllers' *Int. J. Systems Sci.* Vol 12 (1981) pp 1207–1220
6   **Butler, G F, Corbin, M J, Mepham, S, Stewart, J F and Larson, R R** 'NASA/RAE collaboration on non-linear control using the F-8C digital fly-by-wire aircraft' *AGARD-CP-321 Conf. Advances in Guidance and Control Systems,* Lisbon, Portugal (October 1982)
7   **McRuer, D** 'Progress and pitfalls in advanced flight control systems' *AGARD-CP-321 Conf. Advances in Guidance and Control Systems,* Lisbon, Portugal (October 1982)

Alan Bradshaw has been for 15 years with the Department of Aeronautical and Mechanical Engineering at the University of Salford, UK, as a lecturer and senior lecturer. Research interests have included multivariable control system theory with particular emphasis on the design of active flight control systems. Before this he was head of engineering analysis with Mirrlees Blackstone Ltd, responsible for the introduction and development of computer-aided design methods. He is an active industrial consultant on the dynamics and control of vehicles and machinery.

Peter Konnanov is a research assistant in the Department of Aeronautical and Mechanical Engineering at the University of Salford, UK. He graduated from Salford in 1980 with a degree in electronics. He then went on to research the use of microprocessor technology in the investigation of drug effects upon human performance, for which he was awarded a PhD in 1985. In his present post he designs microprocessor systems for use in realtime control simulation studies.

Mike Woodhead was employed as a graduate aeronautical engineer involved with flight simulation and aerodynamic analysis for Hawker Siddeley Aviation. Research into optimal model control theory was followed by a lectureship in the Department of Aeronautical and Mechanical Engineering at the University of Salford, UK. His main interests relate to aircraft design, flight dynamics and aircraft handling qualities and the synthesis of fast-acting integrated flight control systems. He is a Chartered Engineer and a Member of the Royal Aeronautical Society and the American Institute of Aeronautics and Astronautics.

Message-passing primitives for multimicroprocessor systems

Single-processor kernels in multiprocessor systems must be enhanced to cope with the kernel primitives now available. **K W Ng** presents a model implementation for communication and synchronization primitives based on message passing

Concurrent and distributed processing systems based on multiple microprocessors are both feasible and desirable. Processes residing on different processors execute in parallel while processes allocated on the same processor execute in a multiprogramming environment. These processes normally have to communicate and synchronize in order to achieve a common goal. Communication and synchronization are usually achieved by calling primitives supplied by a kernel. The paper describes a model of implementation for message-passing primitives which must be added to a single-processor kernel for communication and synchronization purposes in multi-microprocessor systems.

microsystems   multiprocess structuring   message passing

A software design methodology for single-processor systems that is gaining popularity and becoming a *de facto* standard is the multiprocess structuring approach[1]. The multiprocess structuring approach divides the job to be handled by the software into a number of tasks; these tasks then become communicating sequential processes that can be executed concurrently. Software processes and the means of interprocess communication are implemented by a kernel that forms the interface between the processor and processes that operate concurrently. The multiprocess structuring approach is powerful in structuring and organizing software and has therefore been in use for some time, with *ad hoc* implementations of the kernel functions. Nowadays, versions of realtime multitasking kernels or executives suitable for ROM storage are available for a wide range of 8- and 16-bit microprocessors (eg ZRTS for the Z8000, RMX86 for the 8086, RMS68K for the 68000). These

Department of Electrical and Computer Engineering, University of Wollongong, Wollongong, NSW 2500, Australia

kernels provide primitives to perform the following functions[2]

- process dispatching
- I/O support
- job management
- interprocess communication and synchronization
- exception handling
- other runtime services

Recent advances in hardware technology have made it feasible to construct a general-purpose system out of many independent microprocessors with common and/ or distributed storage. The multiprocess structuring approach is still applicable and even essential here, but the single-processor kernel must be suitably enhanced to cope with the new environment. In particular, the communication and synchronization primitives must be able to deal with distributed storage. Therefore communication and synchronization mechanisms based on the monitor[3] and the guarded command[4] must be supplemented by a set of message-passing primitives[4, 5]. The following sections describe an implementation model for these message-passing primitives which could be added to the single-processor kernels to allow them to function in a multimicroprocessor environment.

MESSAGE PASSING

The monitor construct enables two or more processes to exchange information provided that they can access some shared memory. However, processors in a distributed system may not share memory, so the most common form of interprocess communication in a distributed software system is by means of message-type protocols. Processes send and receive messages instead of reading and writing shared variables. The message-passing mechanism provides a means for process communication because a process, upon receiving a message, obtains

0141-9331/86/03156–05 $03.00 © 1986 Butterworth & Co. (Publishers) Ltd

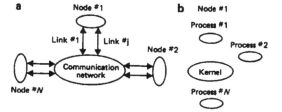

*Figure 1.   General model of multimicroprocessor systems:
a, overall organization; b, node structure*

values from some sender process. Synchronization is achieved because a message can be received only after it has been sent, which constrains the order in which these two events can occur.

A general model of multimicroprocessor systems is shown in Figure 1. The overall organization is depicted in Figure 1a, where the processes and processors are grouped together into nodes connected through a communication network. Each node has a number of communication links into the network. The assumption here is that those processes that are closely coupled logically or have to be close together physically are put into the same node; otherwise, they could be put into different nodes. The kernel within each node as depicted in Figure 1b is responsible for providing dispatching, I/O support etc and message-passing primitives.

General principles of concurrent programming and implementations of monitors, guarded commands and kernels can be found in Ben-Ari[4], Hemenway[6], Hoare[7] and Holt[8]. Higher-level message-passing constructs are discussed by Andrews[5]. This paper concentrates on the basic message-passing primitives; thus, processes within the same node can communicate and synchronize using the monitor construct or message passing, whereas processes residing in different nodes must use the message-passing construct. The underlying machine model is supported by several high-level concurrent and distributed programming languages such as CSP[9], OCCAM[10], ADA[11], SR[12] and GDPL[13]. These languages have built-in message passing and handling facilities.

The message-passing mechanism supported by the kernel is based on the concept of mailboxes[4, 5]. Each process in the system can own zero or more mailboxes. If a process has N mailboxes, each one must assume a unique mailbox number within the range from 1 to N. A process can send a message to another process by placing the message into one of the other processes' mailboxes. On the other hand, a process can receive a message by retrieving it from one of its own mailboxes.

Each node and process in the system must have a network number and a process number respectively. These numbers must be positive whole numbers greater than zero, and processes residing in the same node must have different process numbers. The network number and process number together uniquely identify a process in the system.

DATA STRUCTURES

A kernel employs a number of different data structures in order to perform its functions. The most important one is the process descriptor, which contains all the necessary

information about the corresponding process and resides on various queues managed by the kernel. This section contains descriptions of additional data structures required to deal with the message-passing mechanism; these must be suitably modified to adapt to relevant data structures in an existing kernel and environment.

Message slot

A message is contained in a message slot (Figure 2) which contains all the attributes of the message. 'Mailbox #' is the number of the mailbox where the message is to be placed. The 'wait for reply' flag indicates whether the sender process would wait for a reply from the destination process.

Mailbox

Each mailbox is implemented as a queue chaining a list of message slots. When a message slot arrives at a mailbox, it is placed at the tail of the queue. A process always gets the first slot out when it tries to receive a message from a particular mailbox. The message slots within a mailbox are chained using the 'pointer to next message' field.

Message frame

If a process wishes to send or receive messages during execution, it must contain a message frame (Figure 3). Two pointers pointing to the first and the last message slot on a mailbox queue are stored in the message frame.

Sender's network #
Sender's process #
Receiver's network #
Receiver's process #
Mailbox #
Pointer to next message
Pointer to message
Wait for reply flag

Figure 2.   Message slot

Pointer to process descriptor (owner)
Expected network #
Expected process #
Address of receiving location
Pointer to process descriptor (reply)
Number of mailboxes
Mailbox #1 queue head
Mailbox #2 queue tail
Mailbox #N queue head
Mailbox #N queue tail

Figure 3.   Message frame

Link_array

Link_array is an external array containing the network numbers of those nodes connected to the local node via the communication links. Each link in the node is numbered ascendingly from one. Therefore Link_array[n] contains the network number of the node connected to the local node via link n. This array is used to initialize the protocol table within the kernel.

Protocol_table

The kernel maintains a protocol table (Figure 4) which contains the information of each link connected to the node. An entry in the table describes the information of a link. The table is initialized before the user processes are allowed to execute. 'Flag' denotes whether there is any process being responsible for controlling the outstream of the particular link. Initially it is set to zero, but when a process claims to be the master of the link it is set to one. If the Flag field is set, the field Message_frame_address points to the message frame of the master process for the link. The Network_number field is loaded from the externally initialized array Link_array.

Frame table

The kernel maintains an internal frame table (Figure 5) containing the addresses of the message frames of all the processes. Frame_table[i] contains the address of the message frame for process i. The table is initialized before the processes start execution, and the maximum number of entries in the table depends on the maximum number of processes. Flag indicates whether the entry has been initialized, and the field Message_frame_ptr is a pointer pointing to the message frame of the process.

MESSAGE-PASSING PRIMITIVES

This section provides a detailed description of the five basic message-passing primitives: Init_message; Message_sender; Send_message; Receive_message; and Available_message.

	Flag	NETWORK_NUMBER	MESSAGE_FRAME_ADDRESS
1			
2			
N			

Figure 4. Protocol table

	Flag	MESSAGE_FRAME_PTR
1		
2		
N		

Figure 5. Frame table

Init_message

```
Init_message( PROCESS_NO    :positive_integer
     var WHICH_MESSAGE_FRAME : MESSAGE_FRAME
     NO_OF_MAILBOX        :positive_integer )
```

The above notation is used throughout this section and its meaning is explained in Appendix 1. The message frame of the process is initialized by clearing all fields except the Number_of_mailbox field, which is set to the value of No_of_mailbox. Process_no is used to identify the desired entry in the frame table where the address of the message frame is stored.

Message_sender

```
Message_sender( LINK_NO    :positive_integer
     var  WHICH_MESSAGE_FRAME : MESSAGE_FRAME
     NO_OF_MAILBOX : positive_integer )
```

To ensure the compactness of the kernel, remote message passing is assumed to be performed by the application system. Two processes are required for each link connected to a node. One process is responsible for receiving a message from the kernel and controlling the operation of message sending over the communication link. The other reassembles the data coming from the communication link into a complete message and then sends the message to the proper process. These two processes can be combined into a single process performing two functions, but they are usually separated for flexible operation.

The application system should also design a proper message protocol and a strategy for routing, error control and retransmission according to the particular requirements of the application. The process controlling the Out_stream of a link must use this primitive to identify itself to the kernel. When this primitive is invoked, the message frame of the process is initialized as usual. Then the address of the message frame is stored into the protocol table using Link_no as the index.

Send_message

```
Send_message( var WHICH_MESSAGE_FRAME : MESSAGE_FRAME
     MESSAGE_INFORMATION : MESSAGE_SLOT
     WAIT_FLAG        :unsigned_integer )
```

A process sends a message to another process by this routine. The message slot Message_information is examined to determine whether the message is to be sent to a remote node. If so, the protocol table is searched to see which link the message is to be sent over and to find out the message frame of the process controlling that link. Then the message is appended to the message frame of the master process.

However, if the message is to be sent to a process in the local node, the table Frame_table is searched to find out the message frame for the destination process. If the message is a reply and the destination process is waiting for the reply, the destination process is simply woken up. If the message is not a reply and the destination is not waiting for a message then the message is stored in a proper mailbox. If the receiver process is waiting for a message, the attributes of the message are compared to that required by the receiver. If the attributes match, the receiver process is woken up and the message slot is placed in a specified location; otherwise the message slot is inserted into the mailbox queue.

If the sender process wishes to wait for a reply (blocking send), it is pre-empted, its process descriptor is inserted into the message frame and a process on the ready queue is then dispatched. For systems that must meet realtime response constraints, an extra parameter indicating the maximum period of time for which the process is prepared to wait can be included.

Receive__message

```
Receive__message( var ITS__MESSAGE__FRAME : MESSAGE__FRAME
                MESSAGE__TYPE        : positive__integer
                LOCATION__PTR        : address
                EXPECTED__NETWORK     : positive__integer
                EXPECTED__PROCESS     : positive__integer )
```

In using the Receive__message primitive, the process has to supply the identification of the expected message slot, ie the network number, the process number and the mailbox number. However, it is not necessary to supply all this information. A process can receive a message slot under any of the following conditions

- expected network number, process number of the sender and mailbox number specified; the process needs to receive a message of a specified type and from a particular sender
- expected network number and process number of the sender specified; the message can be any type, provided it comes from the required source
- expected network number of the sender specified; the message can be of any type, provided it comes from a process in a specified node
- expected mailbox number specified; the message must be of a particular type but can come from any source
- expected network number of the sender and mailbox number specified; the message must belong to the required type and come from a process in the specified node
- all fields left unspecified; the source and the type of the message are immaterial to the process

When a process hopes to accept a message via the Receive__message primitive, the mailbox queue is searched .ᵓ see whether a candidate message satisfying the requirements of the process is available. If there is such a message, the message slot is removed from the mailbox queue and inserted into the place specified by the process and control is returned to the process. If there is no message satisfying all the requirements, the process is suspended until the expected message arrives. The process descriptor and the attributes of the expected message are stored in the process's message frame. If the process does not care about the network number, the process number of the sender or the mailbox type, the corresponding fields in the message frame are filled with zeros. If the process wishes to accept any message, the mailboxes are searched in ascending order of mailbox number.

The strategy applied to a message when the source and destination processes reside on the same node is different from that used if they reside on different nodes. If the source and destination processes are in the same node, the kernel controls the complete routing of the message. Otherwise, the message will be attached to the mailbox of the process controlling the particular link through which the message is to be sent.

Available__message

```
Available__message( WHICH__MESSAGE__FRAME : MESSAGE__FRAME
                  WHICH__MAILBOX : positive__integer )
                  : boolean
```

This primitive is provided to make the message-passing system complete; it enables a process to test whether there is any message in a particular mailbox. The head field of the queue of the mailbox specified is examined to see whether there is any message slot, then a boolean result is returned.

Examples

Two examples are given here to illustrate the direct support given by the message-passing primitives to concurrent or distributed programming languages.

The first example is a group of processes that function as coroutines through the simulation of the resume statement. The simulation is accomplished through the message-passing mechanism. Assume that process P is one of the processes which function as coroutines and it wants to resume another process Q at some place. After the resume message is accepted by Q, control is transferred from P to Q. P must wait until another process resumes it. The program, written in GDPL[13], is as follows

```
message resume__slot = int;
node coroutines;              {Assume that this node contains all the
                               processes that function as coroutines}
   begin
   process P;
var resume: resume__slot;
begin
      messin (resume);
      skip;
      messout Q(resume);
      messin (resume);
      skip;
   end P;
   process Q;
var resume: resume__slot;
begin
      messin (resume);
      skip;
      messout R (resume);
      messin (resume);
      skip;
   end Q;
   | . . . |
   end coroutines;
```

The first statement specifies that a message type of integer will be used in the program. A translator can create a message frame and a mailbox (for the resume message) for each process; the 'messin' and 'messout' statements can be translated into calls to the kernel primitives Receive__message and Send__message respectively.

The second example is a program to input a single value via an input channel and then output the fourth power of the value via an output channel. It is assumed that two squaring processes will be used with a communication channel between them. The program written in OCCAM[10] is as follows

```
PROC square (CHAN input, output) =
   WHILE TRUE
      VAR x:
      SEQ
         input ?x
         output !x*x:
CHAN comms:
PAR
   square (chan 1, comms)
   square (comms, chan2)
```

Again, the message-passing statements (shown in italics) can be translated into calls to kernel primitives; the only difference is the use of synchronous message passing in OCCAM. Therefore, after each Receive_message call, the translator has to insert a Send_message call to send a message back to the sending process.

CONCLUSIONS

A model of implementation for communication and synchronization primitives based on message passing has been presented. A single-processor kernel, when augmented with these primitives, will be able to support concurrent and distributed processing. The primitives have been successfully implemented on a system consisting of a number of Z8000-based microcomputers in support of application programs written in the GDPL language. The kernel is written in the PLZ/ASM low-level system language from the PLZ family[14] and has a code size of less than 3 kbyte. The application programs are modules belonging to an ongoing project on distributed operating systems.

Experiments are under way using different topologies and network protocols[15] with the same kernel primitives; these are a direct result of the separation of basic mechanism from policy in the design of the kernel. The link table and protocol table deal with the topology of the communication network whereas the Message_sender process deals with the network protocol. The message-passing primitives are suitable for systems with static processes. For systems with dynamic processes, additional primitives for dealing with the dynamic creation and retrieval of data structures or memory must be added.

REFERENCES

1 **Cheriton, D R** *The Thoth system: multi-process structuring and portability* Elsevier, Amsterdam, The Netherlands (1982)
2 **Lorin, H and Deitel, H M** *Operating systems* Addison-Wesley, Wokingham, UK (1983)
3 **Hoare, C A R** 'Monitors: an operating system structuring concept' *Commun. ACM* Vol 17 (1974) pp 549–557
4 **Ben-Ari, M** *Principles of concurrent programming* Prentice-Hall, Englewood Cliffs, NJ, USA (1982)
5 **Andrews, G R and Schneider, F B** 'Concepts and notations for concurrent programming' *ACM Comput. Surv.* Vol 15 No 1 (1983) pp 1–44
6 **Hemenway, L** 'Virtual-kernel design makes multi-processing go' *EDN* (1 September 1982) pp 215–220
7 **Hoare, C A R** *Communicating sequential processes* Prentice-Hall, Englewood Cliffs, NJ, USA (1985)
8 **Holt, R C** *Concurrent Euclid, the Unix system, and Tunis* Addison-Wesley, Wokingham, UK (1983)
9 **Hoare, C A R** 'Communicating sequential processes' *Commun. ACM* Vol 2 (1978) pp 666–677
10 **Inmos Ltd** *OCCAM programming manual* Prentice-Hall, Englewood Cliffs, NJ, USA (1984)
11 'ANSI/MIL-STD1815A' *ADA reference manual*
12 **Andrews, G R** 'The distributed programming language SR — mechanisms, design and implementation' *Software Practice and Experience* Vol 12 (1982) pp 719–753
13 **Ng, K W and Li, W K** 'GDPL — a generalized distributed programming language' *Proc. 4th Int. Conf. Distributed Computing Systems* (May 1984) pp 69–78
14 **Snook, T et al** *Report on the programming language PLZ/SYS* Springer-Verlag, Berlin, FRG (1978)
15 **Tanenbaum, A** *Computer networks* Prentice-Hall, Englewood Cliffs, NJ, USA (1981)

APPENDIX 1: CALLING CONVENTION FOR PRIMITIVES

Using the Init_message primitives as an example

```
Init_message( PROCESS_NO       : positive_integer
       var     WHICH_MESSAGE_FRAME : MESSAGE_FRAME
               NO_OF_MAILBOX : positive_integer )
```

The notation means that this primitive requires three parameters, Process_no, Which_message_frame and No_of_mailbox. They should be supplied to the kernel by pushing them into the stack before calling the primitive. If the type of the parameter is a scalar and the parameter is passed by value, the value of the parameter is pushed into the stack. Scalar types include integer, byte, word, positive_integer, unsigned_integer and boolean. However, if the parameter is a structure, an array or a scalar which is passed by reference (there is a 'var' preceding the formal parameter), the address of the actual parameter should be pushed into the stack. The parameters should be pushed into the stack according to their order in the declaration.

The Init_message primitive should be invoked using a calling sequence written in PLZ/ASM as follows

```
PUSH   @SP,PROCESS_NO
PUSH   @SP,#WHICH_MESSAGE_FRAME
PUSH   @SP,NO_OF_MAILBOX
CALL   Init_message
LDA    SP,6(SP)
```

The first instruction pushes the Process_no into the stack since it is a scalar and is passed by value. The second instruction pushes the address of the message frame into the stack since it is a structure. The third instruction pushes the value of No_of_mailbox into the stack since it is a scalar and is passed by value. The primitive is then called. The last instruction pops out all the parameters.

Kam Wing Ng obtained his PhD in electronics engineering at the University of Bradford, UK, in 1977. He then returned to Hong Kong and worked as a microprocessor engineer for Conic Investment Ltd, before joining the Department of Computer Science of the Chinese University of Hong Kong as a lecturer in August 1978. He has been teaching courses on digital systems, programming languages and systems programming since then. He is now with the Department of Electrical and Computer Engineering at the University of Wollongong in Australia. His main interests are new-generation computing and logic programming.

Simple IC tester using a database technique

An automatic IC tester has been developed to perform static testing of SSI and MSI circuits using a database technique. **Ala A Wahab, R Nagarajan and Dakhil H Jerew** show how to construct from the database some test data sets for specific ICs

A simple and efficient tester based on an Intel 8085 microcomputer system has been proposed for static testing of SSI and MSI circuits[1]. The tester uses a database technique to provide input data to the IC under test; the response of the IC to the data can then be compared with the 'correct' response as stored in memory. The test database is designed such that an operator need make only a few simple circuit connections. This paper details some test data sets suitable for testing some particular ICs. Pin 'stuck at' faults and short circuits can be detected.

microsystems   static testing   databases   digital ICs

In a digital system, faults are generally classified into two types[2]: logical faults and parametric faults. Any input or output can be 'stuck at' 0 or 'stuck at' 1. For example, a stuck-at-1 fault in x_1 on a two input AND gate, with x_1 and x_2 as inputs, causes the output to be x_2 instead of $x_1.x_2$. This is a logical fault. Other faults such as short circuits and open circuits can also be modelled as logical faults. Logical faults usually occur during manufacture of the system or can be introduced into the system during servicing. They may also be caused if the system is subjected to high currents or high voltage.

Parametric faults alter the magnitude of a circuit parameter causing a change in operational characteristics such as voltage level, current level or speed of response. They cannot be treated as logical faults and usually occur due to long storage or ageing, or due to environmental factors such as changes in temperature and humidity, or leakage from sealed elements.

For reliable system operation it is essential that these two types of faults are detected and, if possible, recovered. Three types of testing procedure are available for detecting these faults in digital systems[1]:

● DC testing (static or functional)
● AC testing (dynamic or parametric)
● clock rate testing

Department of Electrical Engineering, University of Basrah, Basrah, Iraq

In DC testing, preprogrammed input data are fed into the system and the system response is measured. The measured output data are then compared with the known correct or ideal output data. Based on this comparison the system can be judged to be working correctly or not.

AC testing is concerned with parametric faults. It verifies the time-related behaviour of the system and involves measuring the actual voltage and current levels at various points in the system. AC testing is usually performed manually.

Clock rate testing is similar to DC testing but the test input data are applied at a frequency nearer to that specified for the operation of the system under test. It is usually performed on systems where it is impractical to detect parametric faults. This test is essentially performed on dynamic devices whose stored memory, eg RAM, is continually refreshed during operation.

DC testing of digital ICs, particularly small-scale integration (SSI) and many medium-scale integration (MSI) chips, is considered to be important and is performed more frequently than other tests. Equipment capable of performing at least the test is considered essential for manufacturers and systems designers. This paper discusses a DC tester controlled by an Intel 8085 microprocessor. Hardware and software to interface this microcomputer development board with the IC under test, referred to below as the test IC, were described in an earlier paper[1] and are reviewed here. The paper then concentrates on the design and selection of specific test data sets for various test ICs.

INTERFACE HARDWARE

The microcomputer development system employed in this work is the MP-85/EV based on the Intel 8085 microprocessor[3]. The system has a keyboard, an LED display, 1k ROM containing the system software and 1k of user RAM. The proposed interface circuit, which connects the development board to the test IC, is controlled by three addressable Intel 8255A programmable peripheral interfaces (PPIs) and a set of tristate buffers. The tristate

0141-9331/86/03161-08 $03.00 © 1986 Butterworth & Co. (Publishers) Ltd

buffers are connected to all pins of the socket in which the test IC is placed. Each pin of the socket is provided with a pull-up resistor to accommodate testing of ICs with open collector outputs. Data flow between the socket and the microcomputer is controlled by the test software.

Figure 1 shows the interface arrangement for testing an IC having 24 pins or less. The PPIs are operated under program control in mode 0 (ie their output data are latched) basic I/O[4]. Their inherent data latching property is exploited in PPI1 and PPI2[5]. The PPIs route the required input test data from the tester to the test IC through the first group of tristate buffers (74126), which have individual control lines[6]. The control words (each of 1 byte) are designed such that when they are applied to the control pins of the tristate buffers, the input pins of the test IC are connected to the respective PPI ports and the output pins are kept in a high impedance state. This enables the operator to connect the suppy voltage V_{cc} and ground from an external source. (Connections of V_{cc} and ground on the test IC could be made in software but in this case the maximum power required by the test IC

could not be transferred via the pull-up resistors. In addition, perfect earthing of the ground pin of the test IC is not possible in software.) The input data and the response of the test IC are sampled by PPI3. The sample control words to the second group of tristate buffers (74241) are generated through one of the ports of PPI3. These buffer chips have a provision to make common control lines[6].

DATABASE MANAGEMENT

Testing ICs requires many different sets of stored data, collectively known as the testing database. Each data set pertains to one type of IC, and is identified by the first 2 byte which are arranged such that they indicate the type number of the IC. The complete database can be either loaded into RAM from a peripheral device prior to testing the IC, or can be stored in ROM.

The database developed during this work is suitable for SSI and MSI circuits. It is designed so that the operator

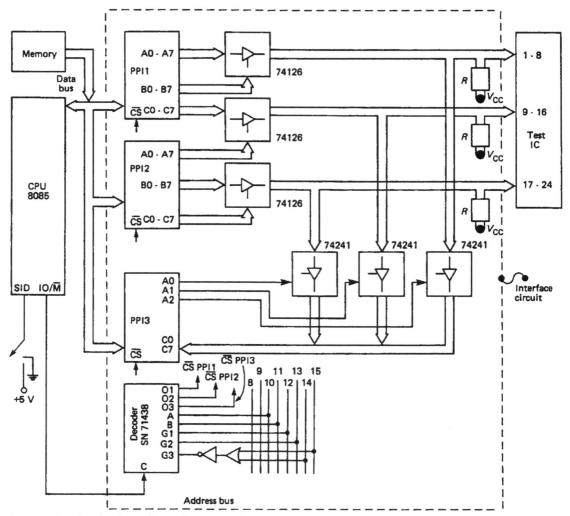

Figure 1. Interface hardware (R = pull-up resistor)

does not need an *a priori* knowledge of the function and pin details of the test IC, nor does he need a data sheet. The database technique requires only minimum interaction between the operator and the test equipment; the operator simply inserts the test IC into its proper socket and connects V_{cc} and ground pins to $+5$ V and 0 V respectively.

The data sets developed in this work consist of scalar, vector and matrix data words arranged as shown below. The number of bytes required for, and the presentation (hex or decimal) of, each data set is also indicated. A whole data set is represented by

$$(C_1, C_2, N, P, V, G, [D_p], [T_{np}])$$

where C_1, C_2 are the type number of the test IC (2 byte, decimal); N is the number of tests required to completely test the IC (1 byte, hex); P is a predefined number which depends on the total number of pins on the IC socket (1 byte, hex); V is the pin number of the socket connected to V_{cc} (1 byte, decimal); G is the pin number of the socket connected to ground (1 byte, decimal); $[D_p]$ is a vector data word defining the I/O pins of the test IC (P byte, hex, $p = 1,2,\ldots,P$); and $[T_{np}]$ is a matrix data word which contains the input-correct output data patterns of the test IC (PN byte, hex, $p = 1,2,\ldots,P; n = 1,2,\ldots,N$).

P indicates the size of the socket (in terms of pin numbers) in which the test IC is placed: $P = 01$ for an 8-pin socket; $P = 02$ for 16 pins; $P = 03$ for 24 pins etc. P is also useful in deciding the number of control words sent to the 74126 tristate buffers and the number of sample control words sent to the 74241 tristate buffers.

These data contain all the allowable input sets including 'don't care' conditions, and are arranged such that even short circuits, between input pins, between output pins or between input and output pins, can be detected. This type of fault cannot be detected by the IC tester developed in earlier work[7].

The fact that each data set contains $(P + PN + 6)$ byte is employed in searching for that set which is particular to any given test. Note that for ICs having a type number of five digits, the first four digits (from the right) are taken as the type number of the IC. Design details of data sets for some specific SSI and MSI chips are explained below.

SOFTWARE OPERATION

Software for the microcomputer tester was developed from the flow chart shown in Figure 2. The first test phase identifies the required data set from the database. The microcomputer displays the pin numbers of the socket to which V_{cc} and ground are to be connected. The operator connects V_{cc} and ground to the respective socket pins. The software then sends the vector data $[D_p]$ from the database to the control pins of the 74126 tristate buffers, enabling the input pins of the test IC to be connected to the respective output ports of PPI1 and PPI2. The output pins of the test IC are isolated from PPI1 and PPI2 by the tristate buffers. Thus all the pins of the test IC are identified.

When designing a data set for a test, the V_{cc} and ground pins are considered as 'output' pins since they are also isolated from the output ports of PPI1 and PPI2. The pin identification vector $[D_p]$ in the data set is decided accordingly.

During the second test phase many test data files are output and latched at the input pins of the test IC. After a

software delay introduced to stabilize the input and output pins of the test IC, the complete input-measured output of the test IC is transferred to the CPU (Figure 3). This data transfer is performed byte by byte via the 74241 tristate buffers. Control for this set of tristate buffer is generated in software and is latched at the respective pins via port A of PPI 3. The input-measured output of the test IC is now compared with the input-correct output data held in the database. The result of the comparison is indicated on the LED display unit; if the test IC fails this is displayed and a buzzer sounds.

Since there are insufficient ports available on the MP-85/EV development system, an additional PPI is connected. An address decoder (SN74LS138) is used to select this extra PPI, as shown in Figure 4. The decoder inputs are connected to the address bus, and through its truth table (Table 1) the decoder selects the PPI as shown in Table 2[6].

The complete machine language program for the tester is listed in Figure 5.

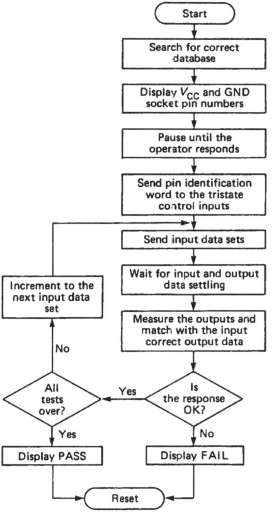

Figure 2.   Software for the digital IC tester

Table 1. Truth table of the SN74LS138 address decoder

Inputs						Outputs							
$\overline{G1}$	$\overline{G2}$	$\overline{G3}$	A	B	C	CS0	CS1	CS2	CS3	CS4	CS5	CS6	CS7
0	0	1	0	0	0	0	1	1	1	1	1	1	1
0	0	1	1	0	0	1	0	1	1	1	1	1	1
0	0	1	0	1	0	1	1	0	1	1	1	1	1
0	0	1	1	1	0	1	1	1	0	1	1	1	1
0	0	1	0	0	1	1	1	1	1	0	1	1	1
0	0	1	1	0	1	1	1	1	1	1	0	1	1
0	0	1	0	1	1	1	1	1	1	1	1	0	1
0	0	1	1	1	1	1	1	1	1	1	1	1	0

Table 2. PPI selection by the address decoder

	Address bus word								Selected output pins
	A15	A14	A13	A12	A11	A10	A9	A8	
	A7	A6	A5	A4	A3	A2	A1	A0	
Decoder input	G3	G3	$\overline{G2}$	$\overline{G1}$	B	A			
Hex word 03	0	0	0	0	0	0	1	1	CS4
07	0	0	0	0	0	1	1	1	CS5
0B	0	0	0	0	1	0	1	1	CS6
0F	0	0	0	0	1	1	1	1	CS7

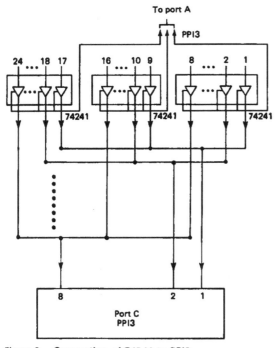

Figure 3. Connection of 74241 to PPI3

DATABASE DESIGN

The important components in the data set of any IC are the vector data $[D_p]$ and the matrix data $[T_{np}].[D_p]$ are used to identify the functions of the various pins of the test IC such as input, output, V_{cc} and ground, and pins with no connection. It is these data which free the operator from needing to know pin details of the test IC. The matrix data $[T_{np}]$ include many sets of input-correct response data for the test IC. These data files have to be selected carefully and arranged so that faults of the test IC, such as stuck at 0, stuck at 1 and short circuits between pins, are detected. This section describes the design and selection of data for various test ICs.

Data sets for SSI chips

This section presents a number of design examples of data sets for various SSI chips. In each case the definition

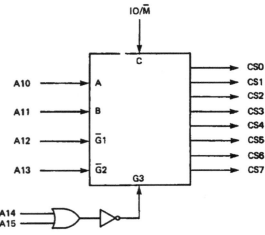

Figure 4. Decoder connection for selecting PPIs

M400, 4FF
```
0400   21  FE  06  46  23  4E  21  00  05  7B  BE  23  C2  14  04  79
0410   BE  CA  26  04  23  7E  23  5E  23  3C  16  00  19  3D  C2  1C
0420   04  23  23  C3  09  04  23  5E  23  56  23  0E  05  CD  AD  04
0430   23  CD  AD  04  2B  20  17  D2  2B  04  23  23  43  4A  7E  D3
0440   00  0D  23  7E  D3  06  0D  CA  4E  04  23  AE  D3  01  3E  80
0450   D3  0B  3E  00  D3  0A  23  4A  7E  D3  08  0D  23  7E  D3  04
0460   0D  CA  68  04  23  7E  D3  09  1E  FF  1D  C2  6A  04  4A  7A
0470   FE  02  C2  7A  04  1E  02  C3  7C  04  1E  04  7B  D3  0A  17
0480   5F  DB  05  BE  C2  A2  04  2B  C2  7C  04  05  CA  97  04  5A
0490   16  00  19  53  C3  52  04  3E  00  D3  01  21  F8  04  CD  DA
04A0   04  76  3E  20  D3  01  21  FC  04  CD  DA  04  76  3E  F0  A6
04B0   0F  0F  0F  0F  CD  BE  04  3E  0F  A6  CD  BE  04  C9  22  05
04C0   07  21  E0  02  06  00  B8  CA  CF  04  23  04  C3  C6  04  7E
04D0   D3  00  79  D3  01  0D  2A  05  07  C9  0E  05  7E  D3  00  79
04E0   D3  01  23  0D  FE  02  C2  DE  04  2B  2B  2B  20  17  04  04
04F0   DA  04  C9  FF  FF  FF  FF  FF  C5  88  92  92  8E  88  F9  C7 ...
```

Figure 5.   IC tester software (machine code program)

vector data $[D_p]$ and the matrix data $[T_{np}]$ are defined in the tables shown. Test patterns are chosen such that even short circuits, between input pins, output pins, or between input and output pins, can be detected.

7400 quad two-input NAND gate

Table 3 defines $[D_p]$ and $[T_{np}]$ for this test IC, which has four identical gates as shown in Figure 6[6]. $[T_{np}]$ are derived so that all possible input combinations are applied to each gate in the test IC. As the gates are independent of each other, all the gates can be tested simultaneously.

The number of the tests required for a test IC is equal to 2^r, where r is the number of inputs in a gate. For the 7400, $r = 2$, so four tests are required. It has been found that four tests are enough to detect a malfunction in the test IC, but short circuits cannot be detected with just these four tests.

For example, referring to Table 3, the binary sequences for pins 2 and 12 are identical and hence a possible short between the two input pins cannot be detected. Similarly for pins 5 and 15. To detect these faults an additional test is required, bringing up to 5 the total number of tests necessary. Hence N in the data set is 05.

The 7400 has 14 pins and thus should be placed in a 16-pin socket. P in the data set becomes 02. Pins 8 and 9 of the socket are not connected although they are considered as input pins for the pin definition vector $[D_p]$.

From Table 3, the data set for the 7400 is:

(74, 00, 05, 02, 16, 07, 9B, 6D, AB, 9B, B5, E3, A6, BD, 9C, D7, 9D, BD)

7415 triple three-input AND gate

The 7415 is an open collector type. Table 4 shows the data set designed for this chip. It is clear from the table that eight tests are required for complete testing. The possibility of short circuits between pins is also detected by these eight tests, so there is no need for additional tests.

The complete data set for the 7415 is:

(74, 15, 08, 02, 16, 07, $[D_p]$, $[T_{np}]$)

Table 3. $[D_p]$ and $[T_{np}]$ for the 7400

	Socket pin number										Socket pin number						
	16	15	14	13	12	11	10	9			8	7	6	5	4	3	2	1
Pin identification	V_{cc}	1	1	0	1	1	0	NC			NC	GND	0	1	1	0	1	1
D_2 = 6D	0	1	1	0	1	1	0	1	D_1 = 9B		1	0	0	1	1	0	1	1
T_{12} = 9B	1	0	0	1	1	0	1	1	T_{11} = AB		1	0	1	0	1	0	1	1
T_{22} = E3	1	1	1	0	0	0	1	1	T_{21} = B5		1	0	1	1	0	1	0	1
T_{32} = BD	1	0	1	1	1	1	0	1	T_{31} = A6		1	0	1	0	0	1	1	0
T_{42} = D7	1	1	0	1	0	1	1	1	T_{41} = 9C		1	0	0	1	1	1	0	0
T_{52} = BD	1	0	1	1	1	1	0	1	T_{51} = 9D		1	0	0	1	1	1	0	1

V_{cc} is supply voltage; GND is ground; NC is no pin connection

Table 4. $[D_p]$ and $[T_{np}]$ for the 7415

	Socket pin number										Socket pin number						
	16	15	14	13	12	11	10	9			8	7	6	5	4	3	2	1
Pin identification	V_{cc}	I13	O1	I33	I32	I31	O3	NC			NC	GND	O2	I23	I22	I21	I12	I11
D_2 = 5D	0	1	0	1	1	1	0	1	D_1 = 9F		1	0	0	1	1	1	1	1
T_{12} = 91	1	0	0	1	0	0	0	1	T_{11} = 84		1	0	0	0	0	1	0	0
T_{22} = 95	1	0	0	1	0	1	0	1	T_{21} = 89		1	0	0	0	1	0	0	1
T_{32} = 99	1	0	0	1	1	0	0	1	T_{31} = 8E		1	0	0	0	1	1	1	0
T_{42} = 9F	1	0	0	1	1	1	1	1	T_{41} = 93		1	0	0	1	0	0	1	1
T_{52} = CD	1	1	0	0	1	1	0	1	T_{51} = 94		1	0	0	1	0	1	0	0
T_{62} = C5	1	1	0	0	0	1	0	1	T_{61} = 99		1	0	0	1	1	0	0	1
T_{72} = C9	1	1	0	0	1	0	0	1	T_{71} = BE		1	0	1	1	1	1	1	0
T_{82} = E1	1	1	1	0	0	0	0	1	T_{81} = 83		1	0	0	0	0	0	1	1

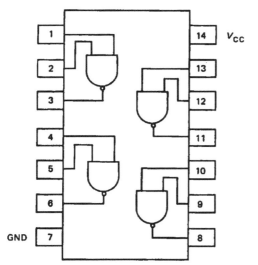

Figure 6. Pin configuration of the 7400

where

$[D_p] = [95\ 5D]$

and

$$[T_{np}]^T = \begin{bmatrix} 84 & 89 & 8E & 93 & 94 & 99 & BE & 83 \\ 91 & 95 & 99 & 9F & CD & C5 & C9 & E1 \end{bmatrix}$$

where the superscript T represents the transpose of the matrix.

Data sets for MSI chips

This section describes the design of data sets for some MSI chips, illustrating methods of clock generation, such as flipflops and counters, required for some ICs. Note that the 'don't care' condition at any inputs is taken into account in deciding the total number of test patterns required. For ICs with two identical flipflops, the input files in the data sets are staggered so that any possible short circuit between pins is detected.

7442 BCD-to-decimal decoder

The 7442 is a multipurpose decoder designed to accept four binary-coded decimal (BCD) inputs and provide ten mutually exclusive decimal outputs[6]. $[T_{np}]$ for the decoder consists of 16 sets which include all the possible combinations of the inputs. $[D_p]$ and $[T_{np}]$ are defined in Table 5.

The complete data set for the 7442 is:

$(74, 42, 10, 02, 16, 08, [D_p], [T_{np}])$

where

$[D_p] = [00\ 78]$

and

$$[T_{np}]^T = \begin{bmatrix} 7E & 7D & 7B & 77 & 6F & 5F & 3F & 7F & 7F & 7F & 7F & 7F & 7F & 7F & 7F & 7F \\ 87 & C7 & A7 & E7 & 97 & D7 & B7 & F6 & 8D & CB & AF & EF & 9F & DF & BF & FF \end{bmatrix}$$

7473 dual JK master-slave flipflop

In the 7473, JK information is loaded into the master flipflop while the clock is 'high' and is transferred to the slave on the high-to-low transition[6]. Thus it is a negative edge-triggered flipflop. The clock is generated through the data set itself, as shown in Table 6.

$[T_{np}]$ includes all allowable input combinations, including the 'don't care' conditions. As this is a dual-type chip, there is the possibility of short circuits between pins of different flipflops. The input data in the data set are staggered so that such faults, if any, are detected. The complete data set for the 7473 is:

$(74, 73, 0F, 02, 04, 13, [D_p], [T_{np}])$

where

$[D_p] = [F7\ 89]$

and

$$[T_{np}] = \begin{bmatrix} 98 & 89 & 9C & CD & D8 & C9 & DC & AD & BE & EF & FA & AB & BA & AB & BA \\ 43 & 4B & 4B & 43 & C3 & CB & CB & CB & 4D & 43 & C3 & C5 & 25 & 25 & 23 \end{bmatrix}$$

Table 5. $[D_p]$ and $[T_{np}]$ for the 7442

	Socket pin number									Socket pin number							
	16	15	14	13	12	11	10	9		8	7	6	5	4	3	2	1
Pin identification	V_{cc}	A0	A1	A2	A3	$\overline{9}$	$\overline{8}$	$\overline{7}$		GND	$\overline{6}$	$\overline{5}$	$\overline{4}$	$\overline{3}$	$\overline{2}$	$\overline{1}$	$\overline{0}$
$D_2 = 78$	0	1	1	1	1	0	0	0	$D_1 = 00$	0	0	0	0	0	0	0	0
$T_{12} = 87$	1	0	0	0	0	1	1	1	$T_{11} = 7E$	0	1	1	1	1	1	1	0
$T_{22} = C7$	1	1	0	0	0	1	1	1	$T_{21} = 7D$	0	1	1	1	1	1	0	1
$T_{32} = A7$	1	0	1	0	0	1	1	1	$T_{31} = 7B$	0	1	1	1	1	0	1	1
$T_{42} = E7$	1	1	1	0	0	1	1	1	$T_{41} = 77$	0	1	1	1	0	1	1	1
$T_{52} = 97$	1	0	0	1	0	1	1	1	$T_{51} = 6F$	0	1	1	0	1	1	1	1
$T_{62} = D7$	1	1	0	1	0	1	1	1	$T_{61} = 5F$	0	1	0	1	1	1	1	1
$T_{72} = B7$	1	0	1	1	0	1	1	1	$T_{71} = 3F$	0	0	1	1	1	1	1	1
$T_{82} = F6$	1	1	1	1	0	1	1	0	$T_{81} = 7F$	0	1	1	1	1	1	1	1
$T_{92} = 8D$	1	0	0	0	1	1	0	1	$T_{91} = 7F$	0	1	1	1	1	1	1	1
$T_{A2} = CB$	1	1	0	0	1	0	1	1	$T_{A1} = 7F$	0	1	1	1	1	1	1	1
$T_{B2} = AF$	1	0	1	0	1	1	1	1	$T_{B1} = 7F$	0	1	1	1	1	1	1	1
$T_{C2} = EF$	1	1	1	0	1	1	1	1	$T_{C1} = 7F$	0	1	1	1	1	1	1	1
$T_{D2} = 9F$	1	0	0	1	1	1	1	1	$T_{D1} = 7F$	0	1	1	1	1	1	1	1
$T_{E2} = DF$	1	1	0	1	1	1	1	1	$T_{E1} = 7F$	0	1	1	1	1	1	1	1
$T_{F2} = BF$	1	0	1	1	1	1	1	1	$T_{F1} = 7F$	0	1	1	1	1	1	1	1
$T_{102} = FF$	1	1	1	1	1	1	1	1	$T_{101} = 7F$	0	1	1	1	1	1	1	1

7493 four-bit binary ripple counter

This counter is divided into two sections (Figure 7): the first is for division by 2 and the second for division by 8. Both the sections are triggered by the high-to-low transitions of the clock input.

$[T_{np}]$ have the following features

- a test to reset all outputs
- consideration that the data are transferred on the high-to-low transition of the clock input

- consideration that the counting mode consists of three possible combinations
- two different inputs applied: the first for the divide-by-2 section, the second for the divide-by-8 section

The complete data for the vector $[D_p]$ and the matrix $[T_{np}]$ are shown in Table 7, giving the data set for the 7493 in the form

$$(74, 93, 12, 02, 05, 12, [D_p], [T_{np}])$$

Table 6. $[D_p]$ and $[T_{np}]$ for the 7473

	Socket pin number									Socket pin number							
	16	15	14	13	12	11	10	9		8	7	6	5	4	3	2	1
Pin identification	J1	$\overline{Q1}$	Q1	GND	K2	Q2	$\overline{Q2}$	NC		NC	J2	RD2	CP2	V_{cc}	K1	$\overline{RD1}$	$\overline{CP2}$
$D_2 = 89$	1	0	0	0	1	0	0	1	$D_1 = F7$	1	1	1	1	0	1	1	1
$T_{12} = 43$	0	1	0	0	0	0	1	1	$T_{11} = 98$	1	0	0	1	1	0	0	0
$T_{22} = 4B$	0	1	0	0	1	0	1	1	$T_{21} = 89$	1	0	0	0	1	0	0	1
$T_{32} = 4B$	0	1	0	0	1	0	1	1	$T_{31} = 9C$	1	0	0	1	1	1	0	0
$T_{42} = 43$	0	1	0	0	0	0	1	1	$T_{41} = CD$	1	1	0	0	1	1	0	1
$T_{52} = C3$	1	1	0	0	0	0	1	1	$T_{51} = D8$	1	1	0	1	1	0	0	0
$T_{62} = CB$	1	1	0	0	1	0	1	1	$T_{61} = C9$	1	1	0	0	1	0	0	1
$T_{72} = CB$	1	1	0	0	1	0	1	1	$T_{71} = DC$	1	1	0	1	1	1	0	0
$T_{82} = CB$	1	1	0	0	1	0	1	1	$T_{81} = AD$	1	0	1	0	1	1	0	1
$T_{92} = 4B$	0	1	0	0	1	0	1	1	$T_{91} = BE$	1	0	1	1	1	1	1	0
$T_{A2} = 43$	0	1	0	0	0	0	1	1	$T_{A1} = EF$	1	1	1	0	1	1	1	1
$T_{B2} = C3$	1	1	0	0	0	0	1	1	$T_{B1} = FA$	1	1	1	1	1	0	1	0
$T_{C2} = C5$	1	1	0	0	0	1	0	1	$T_{C1} = AB$	1	0	1	0	1	0	1	1
$T_{D2} = 25$	0	0	1	0	0	1	0	1	$T_{D1} = BA$	1	0	1	1	1	0	1	0
$T_{E2} = 25$	0	0	1	0	0	1	0	1	$T_{E1} = AB$	1	0	1	0	1	0	1	1
$T_{F2} = 23$	0	0	1	0	0	0	1	1	$T_{F1} = 8A$	1	0	0	0	1	0	1	0

Table 7. $[D_p]$ and $[T_{np}]$ for the 7493

	Socket pin number									Socket pin number							
	16	15	14	13	12	11	10	9		8	7	6	5	4	3	2	1
Pin identification	$\overline{CP0}$	NC	Q0	Q3	GND	Q1	Q2	NC		NC	NC	NC	V_{cc}	NC	MR2	MR1	$\overline{CP1}$
$D_2 = C1$	1	1	0	0	0	0	0	1	$D_1 = EF$	1	1	1	0	1	1	1	1
$T_{12} = C1$	1	1	0	0	0	0	0	1	$T_{11} = FF$	1	1	1	1	1	1	1	1
$T_{22} = 41$	0	1	0	0	0	0	0	1	$T_{21} = FE$	1	1	1	1	1	1	1	0
$T_{32} = C1$	1	1	0	0	0	0	0	1	$T_{31} = FD$	1	1	1	1	1	1	0	1
$T_{42} = 65$	0	1	1	0	0	1	0	1	$T_{41} = FC$	1	1	1	1	1	1	0	0
$T_{52} = E5$	1	1	1	0	0	1	0	1	$T_{51} = FD$	1	1	1	1	1	1	0	1
$T_{62} = 43$	0	1	0	0	0	0	1	1	$T_{61} = FC$	1	1	1	1	1	1	0	0
$T_{72} = C3$	1	1	0	0	0	0	1	1	$T_{71} = FB$	1	1	1	1	1	0	1	1
$T_{82} = 67$	0	1	1	0	0	1	1	1	$T_{81} = FA$	1	1	1	1	1	0	1	0
$T_{92} = E7$	1	1	1	0	0	1	1	1	$T_{91} = FB$	1	1	1	1	1	0	1	1
$T_{A2} = 51$	0	1	0	1	0	0	0	1	$T_{A1} = FA$	1	1	1	1	1	0	1	0
$T_{D2} = D1$	1	1	0	1	0	0	0	1	$T_{B1} = F9$	1	1	1	1	1	0	0	1
$T_{C2} = 75$	0	1	1	1	0	1	0	1	$T_{C1} = F8$	1	1	1	1	1	0	0	0
$T_{D2} = F5$	1	1	1	1	0	1	0	1	$T_{D1} = F9$	1	1	1	1	1	0	0	1
$T_{E2} = 53$	0	1	0	1	0	0	1	1	$T_{E1} = F8$	1	1	1	1	1	0	0	0
$T_{F2} = D3$	1	1	0	1	0	0	1	1	$T_{F1} = F9$	1	1	1	1	1	0	0	1
$T_{102} = 77$	0	1	1	1	0	1	1	1	$T_{101} = F8$	1	1	1	1	1	0	0	0
$T_{112} = F7$	1	1	1	1	0	1	1	1	$T_{111} = F9$	1	1	1	1	1	0	0	1
$T_{122} = E1$	1	1	1	0	0	0	0	1	$T_{121} = F8$	1	1	1	1	1	0	0	0

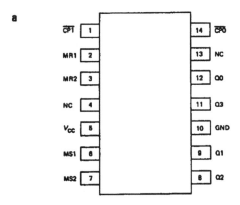

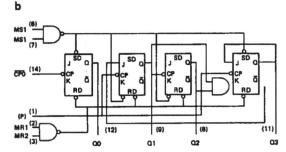

Figure 7.   7490: a, pin configuration; b, logic diagram

where

$$[D_p] = [EF\ C1]$$

and

$$[T_{np}]^T = \begin{bmatrix} FF & FE & FD & FC & FB & FC & FB & FA & FB & FA & F9 & FB & F9 & FB & F9 & FB & F9 & F8 \\ C1 & 41 & C1 & 65 & E5 & 43 & C3 & 67 & E7 & 51 & D1 & 75 & F5 & 53 & D3 & 77 & F7 & E1 \end{bmatrix}$$

CONCLUSION

An Intel 8085-based microcomputer development board has been used for testing static faults in both SSI and MSI digital ICs. Faults such as IC malfunction, short circuits between pins, stuck at 0 and stuck at 1 can be detected by the scheme developed.

Data sets have been designed for particular SSI and MSI chips. These sets consist of details regarding input and output pins of the given IC, also files of carefully selected input-correct output data for the test IC. These data include all allowable input sets including those terms specified incompletely (don't care). It is noted that all data sets are stored in the development microcomputer, and that the format suggested in this work will enable data sets for other test ICs to occupy a smaller memory space.

REFERENCES

1   **Wahab, A A, Nagarajan, R and Jerew, D H** 'Database management in a microcomputer-controlled IC tester' *Microprocessors Microsyst.* Vol 8 No 9 (Nov. 1984) pp 488–491

2   **Breuer, M A and Friedman, A D** *Diagnosis and reliable design of digital systems* Computer Science Press, Woodland Hills, USA (1976)

3   *Operator manual: MP-85/EV microcomputer basic board and expansion board* Electronic Veneta, Italy (1980)

4   *The 8080/8085 microprocessor book* John Wiley (1980)

5   **Goldsbrough, P** *The bugbook IV, microcomputer interfacing using the 8255 PPI chip with experiments* Blacksburg Group, USA (1979)

6   **KawaKami, P and McCarthy, R (eds)** *Logic-TTL Signetics technical handbook* Mullard, USA (1978)

7   **West, G L, Troy, H T and Nelson, V P** A microcomputer-controlled testing system for digital integrated circuits *IEEE Trans. Ind. Electron. Control Instrum.* Vol IECI-27 No 4 (Nov. 1980) pp 279–283

Ala A Wahab received the degrees of BSc in electrical engineering and MSc from Basrah University, Iraq, in 1980 and 1982 respectively. He joined Basrah Technical Institute as a lecturer in 1983.

R Nagarajan received a BE in electrical engineering from Madras University, India, an MTech from IIT, Kanpur, India, and a PhD from Madras University in 1961, 1969 and 1977 respectively. He worked at PSG College of Technology, Coimbatore, India, from 1961 to 1966 and from 1970 to 1979 in various teaching positions. He joined the University of Basrah, Iraq, in 1979 and is currently assistant professor in the Control and Computer Section of the Department of Electrical Engineering. His teaching and research interests are adaptive control, and microcomputers applied to adaptive control implementation.

Dakhil H Jerew obtained a BSc in electrical engineering from London University, UK, in 1966 and an MSc in system engineering and a PhD from Brunel University, UK, in 1967 and 1972 respectively. He was assistant lecturer at Southall College of Technology, UK, for one year and later worked with the English Electric Co. in the UK as an assistant engineer. He joined Basrah University, Iraq, in 1968 as assistant lecturer and became the president of the University in 1985.

Logical operations on flag bits X5 and CY, definition of D3 and an undocumented feature of instruction DADrp in the 8085

It is well known that, in the 8085 microprocessor, arithmetic and logical operations are carried out by the ALU and that flag bits are affected by the results of operations. We have observed previously[1] that the X5 flag bit, defined by Dehnhardt and Sorensen[2], can be used in comparing signed arithmetic data, and that it can be modified by the joint effect of results of ALU operations and their corresponding two operands[1]. The X5 flag bit, together with the twos complement overflow (V) flag bit[2] and the D3 flag bit, are not defined in Intel's 8085 user manuals[3,4].

As an extension to our previous work[1] we have studied theoretically the various logical relations between flag bits X5 and CY for n-bit operand lengths. Experimental verification of our studies has been obtained using 8-bit and 16-bit addition and subtraction operations. Definition of the D3 flag bit and the proper documentation of flag bits for the DADrp instruction are reported here on the basis of experimental results.

Logical relations are derived, assuming that there is a set of full adder (FA) units present to perform the addition and subtraction operations. Figure 1 shows the most significant FA unit, where inputs A_{n-1} and B_{n-1} are the most significant bits of operands A and B respectively; C_{n-2} is the carry bit from the next most significant FA unit; results R_{n-1} and C_{n-1} are the sign (S) and carry (CY) flag bits respectively. For an addition operation, we have

$$R_{n-1} = A_{n-1} \oplus B_{n-1} \oplus C_{n-2} \qquad (1)$$

$$CY = A_{n-1}.B_{n-1} + (A_{n-1} \oplus B_{n-1}).C_{n-2} \qquad (2)$$

$$X5 = A_{n-1}.B_{n-1} + A_{n-1}.R_{n-1} + B_{n-1}.R_{n-1} \qquad (3)$$

Equations (1)–(3) yield

$$X5 \, \Delta \, CY = A_{n-1} \, \Delta \, B_{n-1}$$

$$\overline{X5} \, \Delta \, \overline{CY} = \overline{A}_{n-1} \, \Delta \, \overline{B}_{n-1} \qquad (4)$$

where Δ is a logic operator (OR, AND or XOR). From equations (4), various other logical relations may be derived, for example

$$(\overline{X5} + CY).(X5 + \overline{CY}) = \overline{A_{n-1} \oplus B_{n-1}} \qquad (5)$$

For subtraction and comparison operations, we have (considering B as the second operand)

$$X5 \, \Delta \, Br = A_{n-1} \, \Delta \, \overline{B}_{n-1}$$

$$\overline{X5} \, \Delta \, \overline{Br} = \overline{A}_{n-1} \, \Delta \, B_{n-1} \qquad (6)$$

where Br is the borrow flag bit. Relations similar to Equation (5) may thus be realized.

To verify the above relations, we have used 8-bit operands: $A = FC_H$, $B = 08_H$ and the flag byte due to an

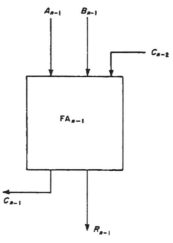

Figure 1. Most significant full adder unit

addition operation is 11_H. Then $A_{n-1} = A_7 = 1$; $B_{n-1} = B_7 = 0$; and $X5 = 0$, $CY = 1$. Thus

$$X5 \cdot CY = A_7 \cdot B_7 = 0$$
$$X5 + CY = A_7 + B_7 = 1$$
$$X5 \oplus CY = A_7 \oplus B_7 = 1$$

In a similar way, other relations can be verified for 8-bit and 16-bit operands. Note that the above relations were not borne out by experiment for 16-bit addition using the DADrp instruction, but that they are experimentally valid using 8 bit × 8 bit addition operations.

Table 1 gives our experimental results. These show that 16-bit addition using DADrp affects not only CY, as documented[3,4], but also the undocumented V flag bit. The undefined D3 flag bit is reset to zero when any instruction is executed. This instruction may or may not affect the other status code.

Equations (4)–(6) show that logical relations between X5 and CY (or Br) depend only upon the most significant bits of operands A and B. This means that, for a given pair of operands A and B, A_{n-1} and B_{n-1} are known. So if CY is to be affected by an addition or subtraction operation, as usually happens, then X5 should also be affected in such a way that both satisfy the above relations. We therefore suspect that X5 is affected by DADrp; we are not yet able to verify this experimentally, although we have verified it for 16-bit addition using 8 bit × 8 bit operations.

It may be that 16-bit addition using DADrp is not carried out by the ALU in the usual way, but by another means whereby the complete status of the operands and results is not registered, except for V and CY. On the other hand, since subtraction is performed by adding the twos complement of the second operand to the first one, it is surprising that the above relations are found to be true for 16-bit subtraction using the DSUB instruction.

Equations (4)–(6) may be applied in simultaneous transfer of logic control using hardware and software. As equations (6) may be derived from equations (4) by substituting Br for CY and $\overline{B}_{n-1}$ for B_{n-1}, let us use equations (6) to illustrate a

0141-9331/86/03169-02 $03.00 © 1986 Butterworth & Co. (Publishers) Ltd

research note

Table 1. Experimental results

	Addition		Subtraction		Result (hex)		Flag byte (hex)	
	First operand (hex)	Second operand (hex)	First operand (hex)	Second operand (hex)	Addition	Subtraction	Addition	Subtraction
8-bit operation	7F	7F	7F	7F	FE	00	92	54
	FC	08	FC	08	04	F4	11	B0
	04	F8	04	F8	FC	0C	A4	05
	81	81	81	81	02	00	23	54
16-bit operation	7FFF	7FFF	7FFF	7FFF	FFFE	0000	02	54
	8001	7FFF	8001	7FFF	0000	0002	01	26
	7FFF	8001	7FFF	8001	0000	FFFE	01	97
	8001	8001	8001	8001	0002	0000	03	54
8-bit × 8-bit operation	7FFF	7FFF			FFFE		96	
	8001	7FFF			0000		55	
	7FFF	8001			0000		55	
	8001	8001			0002		67	

logical transfer of control. It may be seen from Table 1 that the logical relation $X5 \cdot Br = 1$ implies a 'less than (signed)' condition and $X5 \cdot Br = 0$ implies a 'greater than (signed)' condition for two operands of opposite sign. So these two logical conditions may be checked using software.

On the other hand, using Equations (6), the same logical conditions may be realized by logic circuits interfaced to a microprocessor system, as A_{n-1} and B_{n-1} may be accessed to external circuitry while calling the operands A and B. This hardware logical output signal, corresponding to the above logic conditions, may be simultaneously used to trigger other logic circuits for any requirements

under microprocessor control. Moreover, when Equations (4)–(6) indicate complex logic conditions, and software realization becomes costly in terms of computation and memory requirements, time penalties can be minimized using hardware realization; then the hardware logical output is used for software control of transfers within the program.

As the V flag bit is affected by DADrp, it can be used for checking the overflow condition in 16-bit addition using the RSTV instruction. It has also been observed that X5 can be used instead of CY in binary comparison of operands using the JX5 and JNX5 instructions. X5 can also be used for comparing signed operands[1] where CY alone is not

applicable. For example, let the first operand be 04 (hex) and the second 08 (hex). When 04 and 08 are compared using the CMP instruction, CY will set to 1 and JC can be used for the proper jumping. It has been observed[1] that X5 is also set to 1 and JX5 can be used for the same process, ie CY can be replaced by X5. If a first operand −04 (signed decimal) and a second operand 08 (signed decimal) are compared using CMP, however, then CY will not set to 1 but X5 will set to 1; thus CY alone cannot check this condition, while X5 can.

P K Chakraborty
J C Biswas
Indian Institute of Technology,
Kharagpur 721302, India

REFERENCES

1   **Chakraborty, P K and Biswas, J C** 'Undocumented features of the X5 flag bit in the 8085 microprocessor' *Microprocessors Microsyst.* Vol 9 No 6 (July/August 1985) pp 296–299
2   **Dehnhardt, W and Sorensen, V** 'Unspecified 8085 op-codes enhance programming' *Electronics* Vol 52 (18 January 1979) pp 144–145
3   *MCS-85 user manual (preliminary)* Intel, Santa Clara, CA, USA (January 1978)
4   *MCS-80/85 family user manual* Intel, Santa Clara, CA, USA (October 1979)

Thesis gives first-hand insights into RISC design

Manolis G H Katevenis

'Reduced instruction set computer architectures for VLSI' MIT Press, Cambridge, MA, USA (1985) £33.50 pp 215

When I first picked up this book I was surprised to find that it was headed 'ACM Doctoral Dissertation Award 1984'. It is relatively unusual for a doctoral thesis to be read by more than its author, supervisor and examiner — most theses are far too specific to appeal to more than a handful of people. However, this thesis is more a review of a subject area than an in-depth investigation into an esoteric topic.

At the moment, the reduced instruction set computer (RISC) architecture is the star turn of the microprocessor world. Over the last few years microprocessor architectures have gradually become more and more complex as the area of silicon available to the designer has increased, while channel widths have decreased. This progress has given us powerful microprocessors with advanced instruction sets and a wealth of addressing modes. The RISC architecture, developed at Berkeley University in 1985, represents a movement away from today's complex architectures. The reason for this apparently retrograde step is that complex architectures carry out their sophisticated operations relatively slowly. RISC architectures, on the other hand, execute their primitive instructions so rapidly that they are frequently faster than their more complex brothers.

Before starting to read the book, I expected the impenetrably dense style of the typical thesis. This is not so. *Reduced instruction set computer architectures for VLSI* is as readable as any book written for a student audience and is well laid out and nicely typeset. It is not a facsimile of a thesis.

Like any other thesis, important statements are referenced and there is a seven-page bibliography at the end. Consequently, I regard this work as an excellent primer for any student or engineer moving into the field of microcomputer architecture or VLSI.

It is no good pulling a new architecture out of a hat and then proclaiming its advantages. The first part of this book analyses the nature of computer calculations in terms of the amount of CPU time required by various programs. It comes as no surprise that the majority of computer operations are not sophisticated arithmetic operations but are the rather mundane operations of copying data from one buffer to another or testing and branching. By optimizing the RISC architecture to execute these actions rapidly, it becomes possible to design a high-speed processor without a sophisticated set of arithmetic operations.

Chapter 3 describes the original Berkeley RISC I and II machines. Their design philosophy, instruction set and register set are included here. A section on pipelining shows how overlapping instruction fetch and execute cycles are implemented to increase the speed of RISC I. The chapter ends with an indication of RISC II's performance by comparing it with the 68000, the VAX's 11/780 and other processors. The RISC II requires 67% more instructions than the VAX but executes a set of benchmarks written in C in half the time taken by the VAX.

Later chapters deal with the microarchitecture of the RISC II, including both the structure of the chip in terms of its internal buses and registers and the timing of its micro-operations. Some details of the physical structure of the chip are also included. A short debugging and test section describes how the RISC II chip was debugged; we are given, for example, a list of the errors uncovered by the switch-level simulation.

The final chapters of the book leave the Berkeley RISC chips and look at some issues raised by RISC architectures. Topics vary from 'multiwindow register files *versus* cache memories' to 'support for fast instruction fetching and sequencing' and 'multiport memory organization'.

At the end of the book, Appendix A gives a detailed description of the RISC II architecture.

Because this is a doctoral thesis and is written by someone involved in the RISC project, it is authoritative and provides many first-hand insights into the design of RISC architectures. It is well written and I strongly recommend it to all final year students of computer architecture.

Alan Clements
Teesside Polytechnic,
Middlesbrough, UK

Unix introduction is informative and practical

R J Whiddet, R E Berry, G S Blair, P N Hurley, R J Nicol and S J Muir

'UNIX — a practical introduction for users' John Wiley, New York, USA (1985) £9.50 pp 195

Aimed at a very general readership, namely 'those who will be using Unix as a tool in their work', this book is a guide to the main facilities to be found in Unix. It does not (and is not intended to) provide an introduction to the C programming language; C is mentioned only in passing.

The seven chapters occupy 172 pages and cover the following subjects: introduction to Unix; files

(continues over page)

and the filestore; text preparation; software tools; pattern matching; document preparation; and the shell.

It is stated that 'No particular knowledge is assumed, but some familiarity with computers would be an advantage.' Whilst the book remains generally faithful to this statement, there are certainly areas which require a little more than 'some' familiarity with computers.

For example, chapter 2 fluctuates to an appreciable degree. On the one hand there are clear introductions to **inodes** and some commands such as **ln**, **mv** and **cp**. The reader then transits a section on directories which includes the somewhat bewildering sentence 'The "sub-directories" of a directory not only include those directories most directly contained in the directory but also all their subdirectories in a recursive manner, ie all their descendents in the family tree.' Finally the reader passes on to sections dealing with some of the system calls and devices. Whilst the summary at the end of the chapter readily admits that this section 'may be ignored by non-programmers', the warning is really a little late.

An initial concern upon receipt of the book was the fact that it had six authors. Would this mean fluctuating style and lack of continuity? The various and discrete subjects covered by each chapter meant that the latter of these concerns was not so important. However, the style of each chapter does fluctuate and I feel this to be important. Some subjects are easier to treat than others. The **vi** editor (which receives excellent treatment in chapter 3) is a much easier topic than the **awk** programming facility, but even taking the difficulty factor into account, the book would benefit from a more consistent presentation.

This fluctuation in style manifests itself in several areas. The following are some of the more noticeable varying aspects:

- clarity and presentation of the diagrams and figures
- frequency of use of examples to illustrate a point
- amount of intellectual effort required to follow the examples (some of the **egrep** and **awk** examples in chapter 5 are more difficult to follow than, say, the **shell** examples in chapter 7)
- the approach adopted in each chapter to explain a subject (chapter 4, for example, adopts a somewhat academic approach when discussing filters commencing with the 'single canonical form' of a Unix tool)
- frequency of small errors, eg incorrect spelling and missing words (chapters 3, 4, 5 and 6 are relatively free of such errors, but I noticed about 20 in the other three chapters)

The chapters do have a similarity in format, however, each having a useful introduction and summary.

There is a detailed description of the **nroff** text formatter in chapter 6, along with its related pre- and postprocessors. This section may be of limited interest to the commercial world where word processors which encompass a degree of formatting facilities are gaining ground.

There are some useful appendices in the book, including a command summary and quick reference sheets for the **vi** and **ex** text processors.

The book covers a wide range of general topics and many specific commands within each topic. Most of the topics are well illustrated with examples. Chapter 1 provides a very gentle introduction for the naive computer user. The book as a whole is very informative about Unix whatever your degree of experience with computers. The authors point out clearly that it is not a reference book; indicators to further reading on a topic are frequently given. Generally the book fulfils its intention of being 'useful and usable' and does take a 'practical bias throughout'.

Karl Farrell
Istel Ltd,
Redditch, UK

Digital test text caters for academia and researchers

Hideo Fujiwara

'Logic testing and design for testability'
MIT Press, Cambridge, MA, USA
(1985) £34.95 pp x + 284

For reasons that escape me, there is a shortage of books on digital testing. Nobody now denies that the subject is just as important as digital design and yet books on design must outnumber books on testing by at least 20 to one. A new book on testing is therefore an event which should be heralded with due ceremony, provided it contributes to the topic in an authoritative way. Professor Fujiwara's book does just that but in a limited way.

The book has been organized into two major sections: the first part on logic testing and the second part on design for testability. Both sections follow a classical sequence of topics. Part 1 introduces the testing requirement and comments briefly on types of failure mechanisms and their related fault effects. The core of Part 1 concentrates on test generation algorithms and fault simulation techniques, with detailed discussion of the Boolean difference, D-algorithm, PODEM and FAN algorithms, followed by the principles of parallel, deductive and concurrent fault simulation techniques. The presentation of these topics is mathematically based (where appropriate) but only lightly illustrated through very simple examples.

Part 2 starts with a discussion on what 'testability' means and how, in the end, it is related to cost. The author then pursues the ways in which the costs of test application and test generation can be reduced by such techniques as designing for minimum test sequences or partitioning. During the course of this discussion the author also introduces the topics of syndrome testability and Read–Muller canonical forms. Part 2 concludes with a chapter on scan design (with discussion of the LSSD, scan-set and random-access variants) and built-in test (use of linear-feedback-style registers and BILBO).

The book has clearly been written by an academic and is of most value to other academics. From a practitioners viewpoint, there is too much missing. For example, there is nothing on the use of fault collapsing or sampling techniques to reduce the fault-simulator target fault lists, and hence run time. The important subject of testing LSI and VLSI devices such as ROM, RAM and even microprocessors is also ignored. The RAPS variant of PODEM is not described; neither is the concept of the serial shadow shift register discussed despite the fact that this particular form of scan design is an important and powerful means of implementing scan through the use of standard off-the-shelf (merchant) devices.

I also found the book to be light on illustrative examples. Algorithms and procedures that are illustrated are done so with very simple examples. The reader wishing to extrapolate to larger and more realistic problems will have some difficulty. The real world differs quite considerably from the illustrative five-gate example!

For this reason, I hesitate to recommend the book for students, although as a course reference text the book is useful. I would be concerned, however, at the lack of commercial judgement on the topics. The Boolean difference technique is not used in industry other than by those engaged in 'semi-academic' research, whereas an algorithm such as PODEM is used extensively. Judgements of this sort are missing in the text.

Overall, I would say that the book is useful to those entering the subject at an academic research level. It is of limited value to students and even less so to engineers and their managers in industry. Nevertheless, Professor Fujiwara has produced a useful reference text and, for anybody who is seriously trying to progress the 'state of the art', I would recommend purchase.

R G Bennetts
GenRad DEG, Fareham, UK

Data comms for industry and management

Fred Halsall

'Introduction to data communi-
cations and computer networks'
Addison-Wesley, Wokingham, UK
(1985) £12.95 pp ix + 27

This book is well titled in that it deals exclusively with data communications between computers themselves and their peripheral data entry and data exit devices, as well as the various networking methods that are being evolved to allow satisfactory implementation of a data communication service.

The author claims that a primary aim has been to assemble much of the published information which is only available in standard documents into a form suitable for use by a student or practising engineer wishing to gain a general understanding of the subject. I believe he has succeeded in this objective.

The book is based upon a series of lectures given to electronics engineering and computer science students and no attempt is made to hide its origins. Each chapter commences with a list of points that are to be presented to the reader and concludes with a number of problems which the reader should be able to tackle successfully if he has absorbed the material thoroughly.

Chapters and subsections have been written as complete entities

(continues over page)

book reviews

Halsall (Continued)

and consequently there is considerable repetition of basic statements. This structure makes it irritating to read in lengthy sessions, but since the book is intended to be used as either a teaching aid or a reference book into which the engineer can dip at will to learn about a particular aspect, this is of little consequence.

The layout of the book will make it quite attractive to management as well as to students and designers. It is well illustrated and the diagrams and tables are well located in the text. It is only occasionally that the explanations become heavy going — this is almost inevitable where the subject matter is very complex.

After a brief description of distributed system architectures taking up some nine pages, the book expands into data transmission basics including control circuits, synchronization and error detection methods. The jargon of the subject is introduced and well explained and then subsequently used in context with a handy glossary at the end to jog the memory. The subjects of error control, flow control and link management are dealt with in some depth before the various types of electrical interface are described. The importance of modems and how they contribute in the communication function is given adequate attention.

Having covered the basic features of data transmission, networks are dealt with in a useful fashion. Both wide area and local area networks (LANs) are encompassed and the common as well as the distinguishing characteristics are highlighted. The subject of the ubiquitous ISO seven-layer model has a chapter dedicated to it and for the curious it is possible, for example, to get a sensible understanding of the purpose and behaviour of any particular layer without having to plough through a lot of introductory material.

The various topologies of LANs are described and the characteristics of the several access methods discussed. The depth is adequate for a general understanding of the subject and the diagrams are quite helpful as are the comments on performance

criteria. It is understandable that, with the speed at which developments are occuring in this area, applications of LANs in industry are not dealt with, nor is the MAP activity promoted by GM mentioned.

The book concludes with two appendices giving some insight into the mysteries of forward error control and data encryption.

In my view, this is a book to be recommended for technical libraries

in industry and managers' book cases alike. It is useful for anyone wishing to learn quickly what data communication is about generally, or alternatively to find out a bit more about some particular aspects. It is a bonus that the set problems even allow you to test for what you have learned!

Lionel Thompson
Hawker Siddeley Ltd,
Welwyn Garden City, UK

Interactive graphics guide based on IBM PC

Chan S Park

'Interactive microcomputer graphics'
Addison-Wesley, Wokingham, UK
(1985) £36.95 pp xviii + 458

This hardback text is intended for students and practitioners of computer graphics, and uses the IBM PC as a basis for much of the description and as a host for the software examples given, which are numerous. This choice should ensure that a large proportion of readers are able to experiment with the techniques described. The book is targetted as an introductory text to computer graphics, or to supplement more advanced programming and management science courses; the latter is covered by the fourth part of the text.

The hardware and graphics characteristics of the IBM PC are described in part one, at an easily assimilated level. The basic commands available on the PC are described and examples are given of their use. Exercises for the reader, and references, are given at the end of each chapter.

As might be expected, the text is liberally illustrated with clear figures and several full-colour graphics examples.

Part two covers basic mathematics behind 2D and 3D graphics, and hidden line and surface removal. Coordinate systems and 3D rotation are covered in an easy-to-read manner, as are the other topics.

Having covered some basic concepts in parts one and two, part three describes the design of a graphics package, again for the IBM

PC, although it could be ported to other systems without much difficulty. This package handles 2D and 3D plotting, rotation, scaling and translation, data manipulation and input from the keyboard. Complete program source listings in BASIC are provided and the reader is urged to extend the programs for their own applications.

Part four covers the application of graphics to a particular task, namely management decision making. While this may seem an odd subject for inclusion in a text on interactive microcomputer graphics, the author justifies it on the pretext that it provides a complete discrete example of a real application. I think he is justified in this, although the inclusion is clearly due to a personal interest in this topic.

Multiple regression analysis and economic risk simulation are covered, with software provided.

An appendix covers methods of plotting 3D histograms and stacked bar charts.

One useful feature in the book is a tear-out postcard, offering to dispatch an IBM-compatible floppy disc with all the software in the book for $49.95. There is also a card enabling the reader to take out a licensing agreement — it would be interesting to know what proportion of readers take this up.

At £36.95 the book is not cheap. However, its clear illustrations, easy reading style and the material covered make it a worthwhile acquisition for anyone interested in interactive graphics.

Ian Leslie
Logica, Swindon, UK

Understanding networking, without too much detail

Colin Pye

'Networking with microcomputers'
NCC Publications, Manchester, UK
(1985) £12.50 pp 196

Computer networks are now becoming an important area within the information technology industries; this is reflected in the large number of proprietary and 'standard' networks now being produced by manufacturers. To date, books on the subject have tended to concentrate on detailed descriptions of network technologies and protocols, ignoring such issues as comparison of networking techniques and installation practices.

Networking with microcomputers is a book with a different emphasis. It is deliberately aimed at the manager who is responsible for ensuring that the right network is purchased and installed correctly. Hence, technical issues are treated in a superficial manner, with concentration focussed instead on the advantages and disadvantages of various networking solutions.

To fulfill this aim the book is carefully structured. It begins by broadly characterizing networks into wide area, local area, and personal computer, illustrating the significant differences between all three. To ensure an appropriate choice of network it is essential to understand the requirements of the environment in which the inclusion of a network is planned.

The book presents an analysis of a number of typical applications, with major emphasis on electronic office systems. Having specified the environmental requirements it examines the specific micro-computer and associated network characteristics. This description is by far the most useful in the book, for it presents the complete range of questions which need to be answered before a network choice can be made. For instance, the internal hardware of the computers

governs the ease with which network interfaces can be attached and the computer operating system determines the ability of computers to communicate.

The author also explores those points which are often considered to be secondary, but which can significantly contribute to networking costs, ie staff training, after-sales support, cable installation and system commissioning.

Currently available network technologies are described in a general way in terms of the various transmission media, topologies and access protocols. A short description of the OSI seven-layered reference model is presented as an example of a major international standardization activity. The book concludes by taking a look towards the future with a short description of ISDN and the newly proposed S5/8 serial interface for microcomputers.

This 196-page book is on the whole well written and easy to follow with sufficient diagrams to assist understanding. One extremely useful feature is the inclusion, at well chosen intervals, of summary tables which review in a very convenient and concise way the major points of the preceding text. In particular, a five-page table reviewing over 60 manufacturers' proprietary networks is presented as an appendix. These

tables will undoubtedly prove useful when the book is used as a source of reference.

Throughout the book abbreviations prevail but in most cases the full form of the abbreviation is presented first. A glossary has been included for reference and, although useful, it could have been more suitably structured by presenting the abbreviation first rather than the expanded form. The book also cites a rather disappointing number (29) of references; however, this is probably a direct result of the overall emphasis of the book.

Priced at £12.50 the book falls in line with similar sized publications and proves to be an easily readable and undoubtedly useful checklist of the 'do's and 'do not's of specifying and installing a computer network. It should therefore satisfy the needs of the manager who wishes to obtain a working knowledge of systems without being swamped by the intricate technical detail normally associated with existing computer network publications. The book should also prove to be of interest to anyone who wishes to obtain a general understanding of the subject without exploring issues in too much depth.

Nigel Linge
University of Salford, UK

Unix catalogues

'Unix micros catalog, edition 2'
European Unix Systems User Group (EUUG), Buntingford, Herts, UK (1985) £7.50 pp 78

Catalogue of Unix microsystem hardware. Some 50 European and US system and peripheral manufacturers are listed in alphabetical order, with entries covering: system name(s); CPU and speed; system bus; memory availability; Unix version supported; porting company; controller vendors; peripheral vendors; basic

configuration; applications; remarks and distributors.

'Unix products for Europe'
Springer-Verlag, Heidelberg, FRG (1985) DM 98,– pp xii + 207

Catalogue composed by EUUG listing nearly 300 Unix products, including systems and other hardware, publications, consultancies, courses, services and software. Information is supplied covering: manufacturer name and address; installation date; source language; required hardware; availability; and price.

μp introduction gains strength by its completeness

J Ffynlo Craine and Graham R Martin

'Microcomputers in engineering and science' Addison-Wesley, Wokingham, UK (1985) £13.95 pp ix + 444

Among my many books on cooking I have one which describes meals made almost entirely from left-over scraps. *Microcomputers in engineering and science* rather reminds me of this cookbook because its ingredients include odds and ends from several different sources. I do not make this remark disparagingly: the authors have put together an introductory book on microprocessors for engineering students and have included a remarkably broad spectrum of topics ranging from an introduction to programming to local area networks and design for testability.

It is a brave author that brings out a new introductory text on microprocessors. Clearly, the books of the late 1970s cannot simply be rewritten and updated to include new technology. Each new book must have something different to say. The strength of this book is its completeness: unless the student is taking several in-depth courses on microprocessors, it should prove to be an ideal introduction to the broad range of topics associated with microcomputers in engineering. Equally, the book's weakness is that it does not deal with any one topic in depth, and would therefore be less useful to a student majoring in microprocessor technology.

Microcomputers in engineering and science is well written, clearly laid out and is as up to date as one could expect from a textbook. It begins with a brief introduction to number systems, basic gates and flipflops. I see little point in some of this as it does not lead to any discussion of the structure of the microprocessor itself. It seems that all introductory books on microprocessors begin in the same way and authors never stop to think.

The second chapter, 48 pages long, introduces algorithmic design and describes both BASIC and PASCAL. I am glad to see that the major examples are related to engineering. However, I do wonder if the depth of treatment is sufficient to save the student the cost of a book devoted entirely to PASCAL. Perhaps it would

have been better if the first chapter had been scrapped and the second expanded.

A chapter entitled 'Inside the microprocessor' deals with assembly language programming. This topic is treated adequately in the limited space available and I am glad to see that a discussion of high-level language constructs in assembly language is provided. Even better, the 6809 is chosen as the target processor.

The bulk of this book is devoted to interfacing. Following a chapter on conventional interfacing (parallel ports, handshaking, interrupts, DMA) there is a chapter on the electrical interface. It is at this point that the text departs from many others. Interfaces ranging from optoisolators to Schmitt triggers are described. Analogue interfaces are described in depth, although the sampling theorem and its consequences are neglected. The basic interfacing section ends with an introduction to sensors and transducers. Taken together, these chapters form the core of a course in microprocessor-based instrumentation and control.

A chapter is also included on computer communication. In keeping with the general nature of this book, topics range from the mundane serial interface to local area networks.

The final chapter, 'System design and development', provides an overview of the design process and the debugging of digital systems.

It is difficult to provide a definitive comment on this book, as a book dealing with so many topics could be considered as a 'Jack of all trades and a master of none' or as a workhorse covering an entire subject area. My feeling is that this is a valuable book to someone taking a first course in the engineering applications of micro-processors because it includes such a wide range of topics. At least the student gets the whole picture and not just one tiny part of it. No student could ever hope to encounter such a wealth of experience without reading half a dozen other books.

Alan Clements
Teesside Polytechnic,
Middlesbrough, UK

Microsystem design text is marred by dated reference sources

Michael F Hordeski

'Design of microprocessor sensor and control systems' Reston Publishing, Reston, VA, USA (1985) £37.40 pp xv + 376

Microprocessor system design and programming, and systems using sensors and control systems, are the subjects covered in this book. The concept of the book is good, but the detailed content does not match the stated objectives. The shortfall is in five major areas, as follows.

- There are so many typographical errors and minor errors of detail that they seriously distract from the flow of the text. These are particularly prevalent in the examples of program code.
- There are some errors in details of concept descriptions. There are inconsistencies in concept descriptions. There are many trivial points discussed at length. There are some important concepts mentioned but not explained.
- Some of the concepts and mathematical formulae are introduced in such a way that they could only be understood by those who already know the subject matter.
- The many photographs of equipment do not explain what the equipment does, how it is used, or how it functions. System block diagrams would have been better than the photographs of the equipment front panels.
- The contents are dated. This was a continual frustration when reading the text, and was only confirmed by looking at the bibliography. Many of the references are dated. For instance Norton's *Handbook of transducers for electronic measuring systems* (1969) is quoted. Norton's more recent replacement for this, *Sensor and analyser handbook* (1982), is not quoted.

There are parts of the book which might be a useful reference, probably best as an *aide memoire* for a person who already knows the topic well. A newcomer to the field should look elsewhere to get a more modern approach to the subject.

The discussions on programming are particularly dated. It is therefore not suitable for what I had hoped to use it as — a textbook for computer science students taking an option on sensor and control systems.

The best summary of the book might be provided by a bar chart showing the publication dates of references in the bibliography. This is shown in the following table.

Table: Dates of references quoted in the bibliography

Year	Number of references
1966	
1967	R
1968	RR
1969	RRR
1970	RRRRRRRR
1971	RRRRR
1972	RRRRRRRRRRRRRR
1973	RRRRRRRRRR
1974	RRRRRRRRRRRRRR
1975	RRRRRRRRRRRRRRRRRRR RRRRRRRRH
1976	RRRRRRRRRRRRRRHHHHH
1977	RRRRRRRRRRRRRRRHHH HHHHHH
1978	RRRRRRRRRRRRRRRRRRHHH
1979	RRRRRRRRRRRRRRRH
1980	RRRRRRRRR
1981	RR
1982	HHHH
1983	H
1984	
1985	

R = reference to other authors
H = reference to M F Hordeski

Don Fay
Queen's University of Belfast,
UK

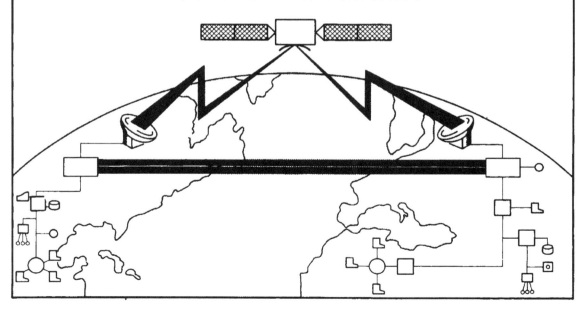

32-bit board-level micro features 'scoreboard' mechanism

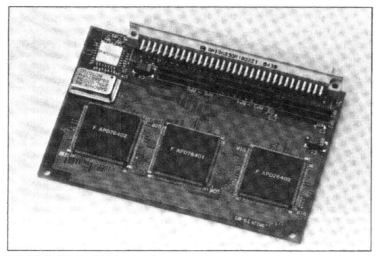

Fairchild's Clipper 32-bit module

Fairchild of the FRG is poised to enter the 32-bit marketplace with Clipper, a microprocessor module optimized for the Unix operating system. According to the manufacturer, instruction rates of over 5 MIPS (million instructions per second) can be achieved with the module.

Clipper has full 32-bit internal and external architecture and runs at 33 MHz. The module consists of three chips: a CPU with onchip floating point unit, and two 4 kbyte combination cache and memory management chips — one each for instructions and data. The instruction set has the basic elements of RISC (reduced instruction set computer) architecture, says Fairchild, coupled with a macroinstruction unit that provides high-level instructions and functions. Hard wired rather than microcoded instructions are used to achieve peak performance levels quoted as up to 33 MIPS.

The two cache chips are linked to the CPU via dual 32-bit buses. An additional synchronous multiplexed address/data bus — Clipper's system bus — allows the chip set to interface with main memory and with a range of industry standard peripheral chips. The bus structure permits byte, half word, word and quad word transfers.

'Unlike other microprocessors, Clipper has a load-store architecture with instruction prefetch overlapped with integer and floating point execution units,' explained Fairchild's Howard Sachs. 'The key to its performance is a 'scoreboard' mechanism used to simultaneously keep track of events taking place in all resources — until now, scoreboarding has only been used by supercomputer supplies such as Cray and Control Data.'

Clipper's CPU chip has four major functional blocks: an integer pipe with a three-port 32 × 32 register file,

serial 64-bit double bit shifter and 32-bit arithmetic logic unit; a 64-bit floating point unit with its own register file of eight 64-bit registers; prefetch logic to support an 8 byte instruction buffer; and a macro-instruction ROM used to execute sequences of standard machine instructions.

The basic instruction set is streamlined, says Fairchild, to both maximize performance and facilitate compilation into efficient code of high-level language programs such as those typically used with Unix (eg C, FORTRAN and PASCAL). Because the CPU's 101 basic instructions are hard wired instead of microcoded, time-consuming operations such as microcode ROM sequences are eliminated and most instructions execute in one 30 ns clock cycle, says the firm.

The two cache chips are identical, the instruction cache being distinguishable from the data cache only by the activation of an onboard program counter that allows prefetch activities into cache memory. The prefetch activity improves the instruction cache hit ratio to greater than 96%, says Fairchild. Cache access time is quoted as 90 ns average, 120 ns maximum. Clipper implements several cacheing schemes, including write-through, noncacheable and copyback, designed to enhance performance in the Unix–C environment.

The Clipper chips are fabricated in 2 μm CMOS and packaged in 132-pin ceramic leadless chip carriers. The module is a 3 in × 4.5 in (7.6 cm × 11.4 cm) printed circuit card which plugs into the user's system via a 96-pin connector. Initial software offerings for the product will include a port of Unix system V.2, FORTRAN, C and PASCAL compilers, and an assembler.

Clipper is due for sampling in mid 1986, with production volumes scheduled for fourth quarter 1986. *(Fairchild Semiconductor GmbH, Am Burgfrieden 1, 8090 Wasserburg Am Inn (Munich), FRG. Tel: (08071) 104-232)*

□

FOLLOWING UP SOMETHING YOU'VE JUST SEEN?

PLEASE MENTION

MICROPROCESSORS AND MICROSYSTEMS

Test system supports range of processors and buses

A performance test system for bus-structured boards — including those that use 32-bit microprocessors — has been launched by Zehntel Performance Systems of the UK. The system differs from most others in that it is oriented towards a bus rather than to a specific microprocessor, says Zehntel.

The Z3200 tester supports a range of microprocessors that currently includes the 6502, NSC800, Z80, 8086, 8088, 80186, 6800, 6808, 6809 and 68000. It is designed to support new microprocessors as they become available; pods for the 80286, 80386, 68020 and 32032 are in development, says the manufacturer. The system is also designed to test boards with multiple bus structures and/or multiple processors: up to eight emulators are available, of which two can be used simultaneously.

The Z3200 consists essentially of a 6809–68000-based host computer, together with four dedicated hardware units optimized for their respective applications. At the heart of the system is the performance test unit, which incorporates two emulation modules each designed for realtime emulation, at 25 MHz, of 32-bit buses and microprocessors.

The performance test unit uses Zehntel's bus timing emulation technique which was introduced in 1979 in the C2000 test system. This technique provides a high-level test language which can be used with all microprocessor and bus types, and single commands for testing CPUs, ROM, RAM etc.

The other three main hardware modules are: the 12 MHz functional test unit, which provides up to 512 I/O lines with selectable interfaces to

permit connection to various logic families; the measurement unit, which provides parallel measurement of signals and buses with flexible triggering and strobing facilities, and also observation of internal nodal activity via probe and clip units; and the analogue test unit, which provides stimulus and measurement of analogue signals with signal routing via an integral switch matrix.

Synchronization mechanisms employed within the system allow the four test units to operate simultaneously, giving true realtime testing across the unit under test, says Zehntel. Alternatively, the test units may be used 'stand alone'.

The Z3200 is being aimed chiefly at systems which use their manufacturers' own purpose-built backplane buses, and also at VME

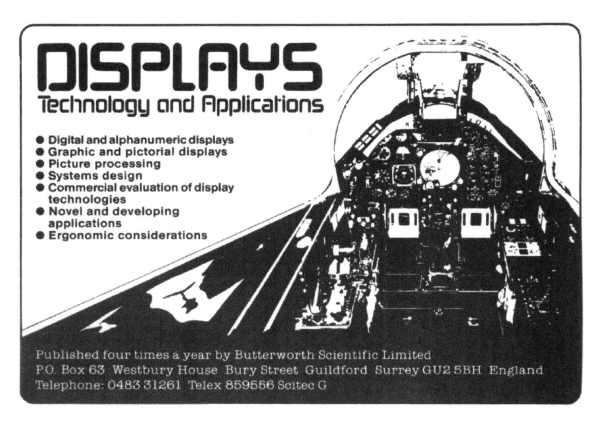

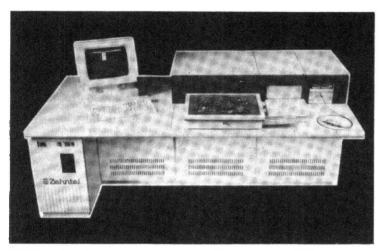

Z3200: designed to test new processors as they become available

and Multibus systems. However, facilities for new buses, as for new processors, are expected to be added as demand dictates. According to Zehntel's Malcolm Hay, structures such as the IEEE Futurebus 'could probably be covered' under the system.

The cost of a typical Z3200 system (in the UK) is quoted as around £175 000. (*Zehntel Performance Systems Ltd, Hanover Way, Windsor, Berks SL4 5NJ, UK. Tel: (0753) 858771. US contact: Zehntel Inc, 2625 Shadelands Drive, Walnut Creek, CA 94598, USA. Tel: (415) 932-6900*) □

Evaluation boards for Series 32000 and F9450

Evaluation and prototyping boards have been introduced by National Semiconductor for its Series 32000 microprocessor family and by Fairchild for its F9450 16-bit processor.

National's DB32000 board is designed for evaluation of the complete 32000 computing cluster. Its standard configuration comprises the NS32032 CPU, 32081 floating point unit, 32082 memory management unit, 32202 interrupt control unit and the 32201 timing and control unit. Onboard RAM of 256 kbyte (expandable to 1 Mbyte), up to 256 kbyte of EPROM, two serial ports and 24 programmable parallel I/O lines are also included.

A TDS monitor is provided in EPROM to edit, assemble and debug Series 32000 software, and 32016 or 32008 processors may be used instead of the 32032. The board can be used either standalone or in

host-associated mode. Cross software packages are available for a range of hosts, including the IBM PC, VAX/VMS and Unix machines.

The DB32000 is available in 6 MHz and 10 MHz versions.

Fairchild's SBC-50 board is described as the company's first evaluation and prototyping tool for designers of F9450-based systems. It incorporates 64k × 16 bit dual-port static RAM, two sockets for up to 16k × 16 bit of EPROM and two RS232C serial ports. The system bus is functionally compatible with the Multibus I standard, says Fairchild, while a further iSBX-compatible bus allows expansion of onboard I/O via plug-in cards.

Onboard firmware includes the Debug-50 monitor in EPROM, for user control and debugging of SBC-50 code. An optional peripheral module is available which contains the 9451 memory management unit and the

EPROMs aimed at PROM market

16 kbit CMOS 'reprogrammable PROMs' with access times down to 25 ns (maximum) have been introduced by Cypress Semiconductor of the USA. These devices are fabricated in the same floating-gate CMOS technology which Cypress uses for its existing EPROMs but, because of their improved speed of access and lower power consumption, are aimed at the bipolar PROM rather than the EPROM market.

The advantage of using 'rePROMs' instead of conventional bipolar PROMs is that the former do not have to be scrapped in the event of incorrect programming, says Cypress.

The devices are available in standard (CY7C291) and registered (CY7C245) versions, the latter of which has a clock-to-output time quoted as 12 ns. They are organized as 2k × 8 bit, and have power consumptions down to 60 mA. Byte-wide intelligent programming algorithms are supported, allowing typical programming times of 2.5 ms for a byte, says the manufacturer.

The parts are implemented using a differential EPROM memory cell and are delivered in an erased state; the erased condition can be checked via two 'blank-check' modes in which locations from 0 to 2047 are addressed and read. Encapsulation is in a slim bipolar-compatible dual inline package. (*Cypress Semiconductor Corp, 3910 North 1st Street, San Jose, CA 95154, USA. Tel: (408) 943-2600 UK distributor: Pronto Electronic Systems Ltd, City Gate House, 399–425 Eastern Avenue, Gants Hill, Ilford, Essex IG2 6LR, UK. Tel: 01-554 6222*) □

9452 block protect unit. (*National Semiconductor GmbH, Industriestrasse 10, D-8080 Furstenfeldbruck, FRG. Tel: (08141) 103376. Fairchild Semiconductor GmbH, Am Burgfrieden 1, 8090 Wasserburg Am Inn, Munich, FRG. Tel: (08071) 104232*) □

products in brief

Name	Description	Manufacturer/designer	Distributor/contact
CPUs			
Z84C00 families	2 μm (from Toshiba) and 3 μm (from SGS) CMOS versions of the Z80 CPU and associated peripheral devices. Clock rates of 2.5 MHz, 4 MHz and 6 MHz are available	SGS-ATES Compenenti Elettronici Spa, Stradale Primsole 50, 95121 Catania Sicily, Italy. Tel: (3995) 599 111 Toshiba, 1-chome, Uchisaiwai-cho, Chiyoda-ku, Tokyo, Japan	SGS Systems Division, Planar House, Walton Street, Aylesbury, Bucks, UK. Tel: (0296) 5977 Toshiba UK Ltd, Toshiba House, Frimley Road, Camberley, Surrey, UK. Tel: (0276) 62222
Digital signal processors			
'VME digital signal processing card'	VMEbus-compatible module based on Texas Instruments's TMS32020 VLSI digital signal processor. Double-Eurocard format	Racal Microelectronic Systems Ltd, Worton Grange, Worton Drive, Reading, Berks, UK	Racal Central Publicity & Information Services, 21 Market Place, Wokingham, Berks RG11 1AJ, UK. Tel: (0734) 782158
D/A converters			
DAC70BH, DAC72BH	16-bit DACs providing 14-bit monotonicity over the temperature range from −25°C to 85°C; maximum nonlinearity of ±0.003% at 25°C. Upgraded versions of the DAC70 and DAC72 in 24-pin DIPs	Burr-Brown International Ltd, Cassiobury House, 11–19 Station Road, Watford, Herts WD1 1EA, UK. Tel: (0923) 33837	
DT216	Dual 16-bit voltage-output DAC module containing two DACs which can be changed independently (200 kHz aggregate throughput) and are addressed sequentially. Includes proprietary deglitching circuit. Comes in an insulated and shielded steel case (117 mm × 76 mm × 9.5 mm)	Data Translation Inc., 100 Locke Drive, Marlboro, MA 01752, USA	Data Translation Ltd, The Business Centre, Molly Millar's Lane, Wokingham, Berks RG11 2QZ, UK. Tel: (0734) 793838
Gate arrays			
AV family	1.8 μm CMOS gate arrays with typical propagation delay per gate quoted as 1.4 ns, typical access time as 26 ns. Basic AV series devices have from 2640 to 8000 gates and up to 160 signal pins. The AVM series integrates a gate array (2375, 1000, or 4000 gates) and a RAM block on a single chip. AVB series devices (300–2052 gates) have 10 mA output drive capability and are designed with input pull-up/pull-down resistor options, a CMOS-level input buffer and a Schmitt trigger input	Fujitsu Ltd, 6-1 Marunouchi 2-chome, Chiyoda-ku, Tokyo 100, Japan	Fujitsu Mikroelektronik, Hargrave House, Belmont Road, Maidenhead, Berks SL6 6NE, UK. Tel: (0628) 76100
ROMs			
CDM5364, CDM5365	64 kbit (8192 × 8 bit) mask-programmable CMOS ROMs with maximum address times of 250 ns, in 24-pin (5364) and 28-pin (5365) plastic DIPs (−40°C to 85°C) or side-brazed ceramic packages (−55°C to 125°C)	RCA, Camden, NJ 08101, USA	RCA Ltd, Lincoln Way, Windmill Road, Sunbury-on-Thames, Middx TW16 7HW, UK. Tel: (09327) 85511

Name	Description	Manufacturer/designer	Distributor/contact
EPROMs			
EDH5832	256 kbit (32k × 8 bit) E²PROM in 28-pin module. Single byte write time is 5 ms (typical) and 10 ms (maximum)	Electronic Designs Inc, Hopkinton Industrial Park, 35 South Street, Hopkinton, MA 01748, USA. Tel: (617) 435-9077	Electronic Designs Europe, Shelley House, The Avenue, Lightwater, Surrey GU18 5RF, UK. Tel: (0276) 72637
M28C256	256 kbit (32 k × 8 bit) CMOS E²PROM in 28-pin ceramic DIP or LCC. Byte write time is quoted as 2.5 ms; maximum data read time is 250 ns	Seeq Technology Inc, 1849 Fortune Drive, San Jose, CA 95131, USA. Tel: (408) 942-2313	Seeq International Ltd, Dammas House, Dammas Lane, Old Town, Swindon, Wilts SN1 3EF, UK. Tel: (0793) 694999
P27256	One-time-programmable 256 kbit EPROM in a windowless plastic DIP. Programmed in as little as 4 s with Intel's Quick-Pulse Programming algorithm implemented on Intel programmers or on Data I/O gang programmers	Intel Corp, 3065 Bowers Avenue, Santa Clara, CA 95051, USA	Intel Corp (UK) Ltd, Pipers Way, Swindon, Wilts SN3 1RJ, UK. Tel: (0793) 696006
RAMs			
CY7C167	16 kbit (16 384 × 1 bit) static RAMs in CMOS, with access times of 25 ns, 35 ns and 45 ns and active power consumption of 550 mW (commercial versions) and 605 mW (military versions). Packaged in 20-pin DIPs or 20-contact LCCs	Cypress Semiconductor Corp, 3910 North 1st Street, San Jose, CA 95134, USA. Tel: (408) 943-2600	Pronto Electronic Systems Ltd, City Gate House, 399–425 Eastern Avenue, Gants Hill, Ilford, Essex IG2 6LR, UK. Tel: 01-554 6222
M5M4256J	256 kbit (256k × 1 bit) dynamic RAM in a J-leaded chip carrier. Access times down to 120 ns; power consumption 260 mW (typical)	Mitsubishi Electric Corp, 2–3 Marunouchi 2-chome, Chiyoda-ku, Tokyo 100, Japan	Mitsubishi Electric (UK) Ltd, Hertford Place, Denham Way, Maple Cross, Rickmansworth, Herts WD3 2BJ, UK. Tel: (0923) 770000
M5M5165FP	8 k × 8 bit static RAM with resistive-load NMOS memory cells and CMOS peripherals, in a 28-pin flat pack. Access times down to 70 ns; power consumption 50 mA when active	Mitsubishi Electric Corp, 2–3 Marunouchi 2-chome, Chiyoda-ku, Tokyo 100, Japan	Mitsubishi Electric (UK) Ltd, Hertford Place, Denham Way, Maple Cross, Rickmansworth, Herts WD3 2BJ, UK. Tel: (0923) 770000

 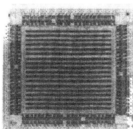  

From left: Racal VME DSP card incorporating the TMS32020 digital signal processor; Fujitsu's C2000 gate array from the AVB series; Electronic Designs' 28-pin EPROM; and Mitsubishi M5M4256J and M5M5165FP memories

products in brief

Name	Description	Manufacturer/designer	Distributor/contact
RAMs (continued)			
Am2130	Dual-port static RAM, organized as 1k × 8 bit, allowing independent read or write access to any of the 8192 memory locations. Access times quoted as 70 ns, 100 ns or 120 ns. Comes in a 48-pin plastic DIP	Advanced Micro Devices Inc, 901 Thompson Place, Sunnyvale, CA 94086, USA	Advanced Micro Devices (UK) Ltd, AMD House, Goldsworth Road, Woking, Surrey GU21 1JT, UK. Tel: (04862) 22121
Am99C88, Am99CL88	8k × 8 bit CMOS static RAMs with access times down to 70 ns over both military (−55°C to 125°C) and commercial temperature ranges. CL88 is a low-power version (commercial temperatures only) drawing 220 mW when active. C88 draws 330 mW when active	Advanced Micro Devices Inc, 901 Thompson Place, Sunnyvale, CA 94086, USA	Advanced Micro Devices (UK) Ltd, AMD House, Goldsworth Road, Woking, Surrey GU21 1JT, UK. Tel: (04862) 22121
HM3-6116-5	16 kbit (2k × 8 bit) CMOS static RAM with access time quoted as 120 ns, maximum power consumption as 440 mW. Housed in a 24-pin plastic or ceramic DIP	Harris Systems Ltd, Eskdale Road, Winnersh, Wokingham, Berks RG11 5TR, UK. Tel: (0734) 698787	RR Electronics Ltd, St Martins Way, Cambridge Road, Bedford, MK42 0LF, UK. Tel: (0234) 47211
Single-board computers			
Microbox III	Single-Eurocard colour graphics computer based on Motorola's 68000 CPU and RMS (Raster management system) graphics chip set. Includes 512 kbyte of RAM and up to 192 kbyte of EPROM, and gives three modes of video generation: bit plane graphics, list-mode graphics and true objects	Micro Concepts, 2 St Stephens Road, Cheltenham, Glos GL51 5AA, UK. Tel: (0242) 510525	
Processor boards			
CPU-2RT	Double-Eurocard VMEbus module incorporating a 12.5 MHz 68000 CPU, realtime clock, up to 512 kbyte of dual-port RAM and up to 128 kbyte of EPROM. Can be used as a Unix subsystem	Electronic Modular Systems GmbH, Robert-Koch-Strasse 1–3, D-6078 Neu-Isenburg, FRG. Tel: (06102) 3117	MCP Electronics Ltd, 26–32 Rosemont Road, Alperton, Wembley, Middx HA0 4QY, UK. Tel: 01-902 6146
SX180 series	STEbus CPU boards and accessories based on the HD64180 processor, on single Eurocards. Provides an extended Z80 instruction set, 8k or 32k SRAM, EPROM and 256k DRAM sockets, two RS232 serial channels, and full use of on-chip DMA handler and interrupt channels via ATNRQ* lines. 3 MHz and 6 MHz versions are available	DSP Design, LNTN Building, 100 St Pancras Way, London NW1 9ES, UK	Dean Microsystems Ltd, 7 Horseshoe Park, Pangbourne, Berks RG8 7JW, UK. Tel: (07357) 5155
SYN-VM020	VME processor module combining a 68020 CPU (and 68881 coprocessor) with a G-64 interface on the P2 connector. Features 1 Mbyte of onboard (32-bit-wide) memory, realtime calendar–clock, status indicators and two RS232/422 serial ports. Runs under OS9/68000	Syntel Microsystems, Victoria Works, Queen's Mill Road, Huddersfield HD1 3PG, UK. Tel: (0484) 535101	

Name	Description	Manufacturer/designer	Distributor/contact
GESMPU-18	80286-based CPU card (8 MHz) giving up to 16 Mbyte of directly addressable memory, on a single-height Eurocard. Compatible with the G-64/G-96 bus. Optional 80287 processor extension.	Gespac Inc, 100 West Hoover Avenue, Suite 11, Mesa, AZ 85202, USA. Tel: (602) 962-5559	Gespac SA, 3 ch. des Aulx, CH-1228 Plan-les-Ouates, Geneva, Switzerland. Tel: (41-22) 71 34 00
KPI	IBM PC compatible board with Z80B processor and 256 kbyte of RAM is designed to provide realtime emulation of 8- and 16-bit microsystems and logic analysis on the PC	Kontron Electronics Ltd, Blackmoor Lane, Croxley Centre, Watford, Herts WD1 8XQ, UK. Tel: (0923) 45991	
MVME372	Network interface board compatible with VMEbus and the MAP 2.1 (manufacturing automation protocol) protocol standard. Includes a 68020 CPU, 68824 token bus controller and 640 kbyte RAM array	Motorola Inc, 3501 Ed Bluestein Blvd, Austin, TX 78721, USA	Motorola Ltd, Fairfax House, 69 Buckingham Street, Aylesbury, Bucks HP20 2NF, UK. Tel: (0296) 35252

I/O boards

Name	Description	Manufacturer/designer	Distributor/contact
GESMFI-1	Universal interface module implemented on a single-height Eurocard compatible with the G-64/G-96 bus. Includes two serial RS232C ports, two 8-bit parallel ports, a triple programmable timer and a CMOS clock-calendar unit	Gespac Inc, 100 West Hoover Avenue, Suite 11, Mesa, AZ 85202, USA. Tel: (602) 962-5559	Gespac SA, 3 ch. des Aulx, CH-1228 Plan-les-Ouates, Geneva, Switzerland. Tel: (41-22) 71 34 00
PC-I/O series	Range of input and output modules for interfacing microcomputers to an array of analogue and digital events. Interfaces to host computer via RS232, RS422 or IEEE 488 links, with communication controlled by an 8088-based CPU module. Range of ROM-based software functions, and RAM expandable to 32 kbit, on board	Analogic Corp, Audubon Road, Wakefield, MA 01880, USA	Analogic Ltd, 68 High Street, Weybridge, Surrey KT13 8BN, UK. Tel: (0932) 56011
PME S10-3	VMEbus terminal interface handler for Unix-based systems. Operates as an eight-channel intelligent I/O board with data rates up to 9600 baud on each channel. Includes 16 kbyte of dual-port DRAM and eight asynchronous RS232C ports	Plessey Microsystems Ltd, Water Lane, Towcester, Northants NN12 7JN, UK. Tel: (0327) 50312	

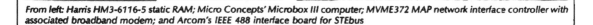

From left: Harris HM3-6116-5 static RAM; Micro Concepts' Microbox III computer; MVME372 MAP network interface controller with associated broadband modem; and Arcom's IEEE 488 interface board for STEbus

products in brief

Name	Description	Manufacturer/designer	Distributor/contact
I/O boards (continued)			
SIEEE	IEEE 488 interface board for STEbus systems, based around the 7210 intelligent GPIB controller. Functions include source and acceptor handshaking; talker/extended talker and listener/extended listener; service request; remote local, remote or local parallel poll; device clear and trigger	Arcom Control Systems Ltd, Unit 8, Clifton Road, Cambridge CB1 4WH, UK. Tel: (0223) 242224	
Syscon	STEbus system controller with bus timeout, watchdog timer and power fail monitor functions; onboard system clock and reset options. Can be configured to refuse access to a particular master. Includes a Centronics parallel interface and an LCD controller	Arcom Control Systems Ltd, Unit 8, Clifton Road, Cambridge CB1 4BW, UK. Tel: (0223) 242224	
Memory boards			
PT-VME 201	VMEbus memory module of 256 kbyte, 512 kbyte, 1 Mbyte or 2 Mbyte capacity with write and read times of 180 ns and 280 ns respectively. Double-height Eurocard format	Performance Technologies Inc, 300 Main Street, East Rochester, NY 14445, USA	Dean Microsystems Ltd, 7 Horseshoe Park, Pangbourne, Berks RG8 7JW, UK. Tel: (07357) 5155
VMI-1	Bubble memory board of 256 kbyte capacity, expandable up to 32 Mbyte using VX series expansion modules. Memory access time quoted as 82 ns (maximum) and effective transfer rate as 125 kbit s^{-1}	Bubbl-tec, PC/M Inc, 6800 Sierra Court, Dublin, CA 94568, USA. Tel: (415) 829-8700	Amplicon Electronics Ltd, Richmond Road, Brighton, E Sussex BN2 3RL, UK. Tel: (0273) 608331
Backplanes			
Pressfit	DEC-compatible backplane system designed for use in robotics and industrial control systems	EMS Inc, 4546 Beltway Drive, Dallas, TX 75244, USA. Tel: (214) 392-3473	EMS UK Ltd, Bray House, Martin Road, Cordwallis Industrial Estate, Maidenhead, Berks SL6 7DE, UK. Tel: (0628) 76062
PROM programmers			
Z-2000B	Universal PROM, EPROM and E^{2}PROM programmer with self test and self diagnostics, for use with some 700 fuse-link bipolar memories as well as PALs, FPLAs and Intel microcomputers. System comprises a Z-1000B programmer with 64 kbyte of CMOS, SRAM, a DMA controller, disc controller and IEEE 488 components, with integral 8 in floppy disc drives set up for CP/M operation	Sunrise Electronics Inc, 524 South Vermont Avenue, Glendora, CA 91740, USA. Tel: (213) 914-1926	Petratec, Unit 1, Glanty House, The Causeway, Egham, Surrey, UK. Tel: (0784) 36254
Development systems			
303A-009 version V02, 303A-006 version V02	CMOS program/test adaptors which enable Data I/O's 29B/LogicPak programmable logic development system to program a total of 58 new logic devices	Data I/O Corp, 10525 Willows Road NE, PO Box 97046, Redmond, WA 98073-9746, USA. Tel: (206) 881-6444	Microsystem Services, PO Box 37, Lincoln Road, Cressex Industrial Estate, High Wycombe, Bucks HP12 3XJ, UK. Tel: (0494) 41661

Name	Description	Manufacturer/designer	Distributor/contact
EtherTarget	Cross software development system with in-circuit emulation and networking capabilities. Comprises an EtherSeries CPU with 2 Mbyte of RAM, 45 Mbyte Winchester disc, cartridge tape streamer and appropriate crosscompiler and in-circuit emulator for the 68000/68010, Z80B, 8085, 8086, 8048, 6809 or 6502. Runs under Uniplus+ system V	Logic Replacement Technology Ltd, 7 Arkwright Road, Reading, Berks RG2 0LU, UK. Tel: (0734) 751087	
KPDS	Development system for 8- and 16-bit microprocessors which can be integrated into a Unix network and may be used for VT100 terminal emulation. Used with the KSA slave logic analyser, it allows simultaneous logic analysis and microprocessor emulation	Kontron Electronics Ltd, Blackmoor Lane, Croxley Centre, Watford, Herts WD1 8XQ, UK. Tel: (0923) 45991	

Test equipment

Name	Description	Manufacturer/designer	Distributor/contact
K115	Logic analyser designed for design, debugging and test of 8-, 16- and 32-bit micros. Provides 32 or 64 channels at 20 MHz and a maximum clock speed of 200 MHz on up to eight channels. Pushbutton state/timing facility on main channels	Gould Electronics, 1870 Lundy Avenue, San Jose, CA 95131, USA. Tel: (408) 263-7155	Gould Electronics Ltd, Roebuck Road, Hainault, Ilford, Essex IG6 3UE, UK. Tel: 01-500 1000
REL-4100A	Wafer probing system for wafers of diameter up to 6 in (15.2 cm), with 10 s scanning capability, zero backlash on movement and 1 μm resolution. Options include digital position readouts and a programmable 166-location memory	Alessi Inc, 16871 Noyes Avenue, Irvine, CA 92714, USA. Tel: (714) 863-0430	Dage (GB) Ltd, Intersem Division, Rabans Lane, Aylesbury, Bucks HP19 3RG, UK. Tel: (0296) 33200

Software

Name	Description	Manufacturer/designer	Distributor/contact
Log/IC	Software design package for logic devices, including PALs, IFLs; PROMs, gate arrays and microprogrammable logic. Combines optimization methods, error checking and automatic vector generation. Runs on IBM PCs, VAX, Prime, Apollo and Siemens machines	Elan Digital Systems Ltd, 16–20 Kelvin Way, Crawley, W Sussex RH10 2TS, UK. Tel: (0293) 510448	

From left: Analogic I/O modules for PCs; Syscon STE system controller; EMS Pressfit backplane system; and Gould's K115 logic analyser

IBM microsystem uses RISC processor and Unix V

An in-house designed 32-bit microprocessor with RISC (reduced instruction set computer) architecture, and a new proprietary operating system based on Unix system V, are features of IBM's recently announced 'personal CADCAM workstations', the 6150/6151 (PC RT) range.

According to IBM press officer Mike Levy, the company has been working on RISC architectures at its Vermont, USA, facility since the mid 1970s. Apart from a RISC component in the IBM 3090, however, this is the first time that such IBM-designed processors have been used in commercial machines: the PC microcomputer range has always been based on Intel CPUs. While refusing to speculate on future use of IBM proprietary chips in specific product ranges, Levy commented that he 'could not believe that the expense of developing the RT's microprocessor could be justified by just one product'.

The RT CPU , known as ROMP (IBM research/OPD microprocessor), is fabricated using a 2 µm NMOS process. Its 7.65 mm × 7.65 mm package contains some 45 000 devices on a 36 mm ceramic substrate.

IBM 6150 (PC RT) workstation in use with a 5080 graphics system

The workstations are assembled at IBM's Austin, USA, plant. An anomaly has arisen over the naming of the machines: their micro-based nature led to them being released as the PC RT range in the USA. As the machines require different software to the existing PC range (unless an optional PC AT coprocessor card is used), however, they are being marketed in Europe as the 6151 model 10 (desktop) and 6150 models 20 and 25 (floor-standing) systems.

The operating system AIX (advanced interactive executive) has been developed by IBM to support the 6150/6151 processors. It is based on Unix system V but, according to Levy, some 50% of the code has been developed by IBM. Additional functions to standard system V include installation aids, multiple-user interfaces, virtual memory support and selected Berkeley 4.2 functions.

IBM states its target markets for the 6150/6151 to be technical and commercial professionals, scientists and engineers in industry, academia and government. 'You might say it's everything to everyone,' proclaimed Levy, 'but we tend to point it at the engineering workstation market.' The system has been designed as a multiuser system for up to eight users on local and remote terminals.

The systems incorporate 1–4 Mbyte of main memory, two or more disc/diskette drives and a 16-bit PC AT I/O bus. A 32-bit data bus is dedicated to data transfers between microprocessor, virtual memory management unit and optional floating point accelerator card. IBM's UK prices for the workstation start at around £10 000; the AIX operating system costs £2627. □

Quick-turnaround ASICs — Thomson–Marconi venture challenges ES2

Following the lead taken by European Silicon Structures (ES2, see *Microprocessors and Microsystems* Vol 9 No 9 p 468, Vol 10 No 1 p 52), GEC of the UK (through its Marconi Electronics subsidiary) and Thomson of France have announced their intention to collaborate on the design and manufacture of quick-turnaround application-specific integrated circuits (ASICs).

In its initial stages, the Thomson–Marconi project will involve research work aimed at improving circuit design software, developing a sophisticated expandable cell library and implementing a 1.25 µm CMOS process using electron beam lithography. Within five years, the two companies hope to able to produce prototype cell arrays to their customers' specification inside two weeks.

Marconi's David Westgarth explained that the company had been in a natural position to launch such a venture for some time due to its already heavy commitment to short-run ASICs for 'idiosyncratic' defence applications throughout Europe, and Westgarth expects Thomson to follow suit with its own facilities. The aim of the project was to make the provision of ASICs 'comparable in cost and time to that for printed circuit boards'.

The project has been submitted for partial funding to the administration of Eureka, the programme designed to foster cooperation on high technology between the European nations.

● ES2 announced the opening of its first design centres, at Munich, FRG, and Paris, in January of this year. A third centre at Bracknell, near London, UK, is due to open shortly. The company's first custom chips are scheduled to be delivered from a pilot plant at Exel, CA, USA, around the middle of 1986. □

interface

Semicon. top ten

The depressed semiconductor market has had a marked impact on major suppliers, according to Dataquest's 1985 survey, with the top 13 companies all recording lower dollar sales than during 1984. The total world market registered a decline of 16.4%, with bipolar and MOS segments declining by 21.4% and 22.6% respectively. Linear and discrete/opto markets fared rather better, declining by only 3.7% and 6.8% respectively, so suppliers with presence in these areas were generally better off than their IC-only competitors.

NEC has taken over the position, held for many years by Texas Instruments, of overall largest semiconductor supplier with a dollar sales decline of only 11.9% (from $2251M to $1984M); TI fell to third place with a market decline of 28.8% ($2480M to $1766M). Motorola, with a 20.3% drop from $2320M to $1766M, remained in second place. The top ten suppliers for 1985 (with position in parentheses and market change in brackets) were

1 (3) NEC [−11.9%]
2 (2) Motorola [−20.3%]
3 (1) Texas Instruments [−28.8%]
4 (4) Hitachi [−18.6%]
5 (5) Toshiba [−6.5%]
6 (6) Philips/Signetics [−19.4%]
7 (9) Fujitsu [−14.3%]
8 (8) Intel [−15.1%]
9 (7) National [− 25.6%]
10 (12) Matsushita [−2.4%]

Dataquest's figures for the US market show a decline of some 28%, while preliminary results for the European market show an essentially zero change from 1984, with Philips/Signetics, Texas Instruments and Motorola the top three European suppliers.

Meanwhile, the market research department of Hitachi has predicted a semiconductor boom in 1988, with the North European market crossing the $2000M threshold for the first time ever. Much of this growth is expected in the MOS segment, particularly in CMOS and related technologies. □

in brief

Supercomputer project

A joint UK–French supercomputer project based on transputers has been awarded funding under the European Community's Esprit programme. The project aims eventually to produce a modular parallel processing computer capable of 500 MFLOPS (million floating point operations per second), which should cost only 10% of what it now costs to build a machine of equivalent power. Participants in the project are Telmat, Apsis, Laboratoire de Genie Informatique and the University of Grenoble (France), and the Royal Signals and Radar Establishment, Southampton University, Inmos and Thorn EMI (UK). It is intended to construct the computer from nodes, each typically comprising 16 floating point transputers, connected by a programmable switching network.

RCA–GE merger

RCA and General Electric Co of the USA have announced a $6000M merger agreement. The move has been approved by the boards of both companies, but is subject to the approval of shareholders and US government agencies such as the Federal Communication Commission.

Lattice in the USA

Lattice Logic of the UK has set up a wholly owned subsidiary, Lattice Logic USA, with offices in Santa Clara, CA. The company is about to sign OEM deals with several major companies in the USA, according to the new company's executive vice-president, Mike Jenkins, formerly president of US IC design consultancies Applied Silicon Technology and Independent Resource Corp.

Fujitsu design centre

Fujitsu has appointed Wolfson Electronics of the UK to act as an approved design house for its custom and semicustom VLSI gate arrays. Fujitsu's 1.8 μm 'extended building block array' standard cells are covered by the agreement. Formerly a research institute with Edinburgh University, UK, Wolfson set up as an independent company at the beginning of 1985.

UK micro drop-outs

Some 30% of existing UK microcomputer hardware suppliers withdrew from the market in the year up to January 1986, according to a National Computer Centre survey of the UK micro market. Of 583 suppliers identified in January 1985, only 409 were known to be still manufacturing or importing, the remainder having merged, been taken over, returned to previous businesses or closed down. However, the overall number of suppliers was swelled over the year by 241 newcomers. Only 35% of hardware items sold in the UK are now of UK manufacture, said the survey.

letter to the editor

Systems Union *versus* Simdell

Sir,

You have recently published an item concerning this matter (*Microprocessors and Microsystems* Vol 10 No 1 p 54) and I considered that I should appraise you of the present situation.

Simdell is set to embark upon what could be a two-year legal tussle to clear its name of allegations that Simdell's Libra Accounts software package infringes Systems Union Copyright in Sun Account. While the law states that someone is innocent until proven guilty, this accusation has the opposite effect. We are, therefore, forced into a position of denying something of which we should never have been accused. Some relevant facts:

- The first alleged similarity identified in the writ issued by Systems Union states 'Four types of accounts are defined: debtor, creditor, profit and loss and balance sheet.' One is led to wonder how an accounting system can be designed without such fundamental definitions and just who has copyright in them.
- The reason why software packages are copied is to save development time and cost, and also bring a competitive product quickly to the marketplace. Our Libra Accounts Software took two man years to develop and cost in excess of £50 000.
- Systems Union has said that Libra Accounts has been developed by 'reverse engineering', where the performance and screen design of programs are reproduced using different source code. Not only is the functionality of Libra Accounts totally different, but input screen designs contain no similarity whatsoever.
- Software package developers agree that the development of any new software package is based upon the previous experience of its authors, coupled with ideas and concepts gained from researching other comparable products. The existence of similarities, which can be found in most equivalent packages, cannot form the basis of copyright infrigement. If this were the case, not only could the software industry be plunged into confusion, but package development would stagnate.

As a member of the Computing Services Association, my company supports the work of FAST and the legitimate fight against piracy and infringement of copyright. We are just as strongly opposed to wrongful accusations, including those made by Systems Union.

Yours faithfully,

J Peter Westwood
Managing Director, Simdell Ltd

Date	Title	Contact	Place	Other details
1986				
12–15 May	CICC '86	Roberta Kaspar, 20 Ledgewood Drive, Rochester, NY 14615, USA. Tel: (716) 865-7164	Rochester, USA	IEEE custom integrated circuits conference, with technical and tutorial sessions covering CAD tools macro-based designs, full custom ICs, fabrication technology, custom applications, digital signal processing, test, reliability, packaging and custom GaAs
13–15 May	Communications 86	Institution of Electrical Engineers, Savoy Place, London WC2R 0BL, UK. Tel: 01-240 1871	Metropole Hotel, Birmingham, UK	Eighth IEE conference and exhibition. Session headings include: the cellular scene; mobile radio update; office communications equipment; value added network services; satellite communications; recent developments in networks and services; ISDN becomes a reality.
13–15 May	Eurosoft/Nordcomp 86	Network Events Ltd, Printers Mews, Market Hill, Buckingham MK18 1JX, UK	Hamburg Exhibition Centre, FRG	European conference and exhibition on computer software and hardware
13–16 May	CommunicAsia 86	Andry Montgomery Ltd, 11 Manchester Square, London W1M 5AB, UK	Singapore	Fourth Asian international electronic communication show and conference
13–16 May	Hong Kong Elenex 86	Andry Montgomery Ltd, 11 Manchester Square, London W1M 5AB.	Hong Kong	Second Hong Kong international electrical and electronic engineering show
19–23 May	International Conference on Distributed Computing Systems	Dr Ming T Liu, Ohio State University, 2036 Neil Avenue, Columbus, OH 43210, USA. Tel: (614) 422-1837	Hyatt Regency, Cambridge, MA, USA	Sponsored by the IEEE Computer Society and the ACM
20–22 May	StanCon '86	StanCon '86, 1730 Massachusetts Avenue, NW Washington, DC 20036-1903, USA. Tel: (202) 371-0101	Ramada Renaissance Hotel, San Francisco, CA, USA	IEEE Computer Society computer standards conference
26–30 May	3rd Software Engineering Conference	Jean Pierre Finance, AFCET Informatique 156, Blvd Pereire 75017, Paris, France	Versailles, France	Sponsored by AFCET and the IEEE Computer Society
28–30 May	IMC 86	Secretariat of IMC 86, c/o Japan Convention Services Inc., Nippon Press Center Building 2-2-1, Uchisaiwai-cho Chiyoda-ku, Tokyo 100, Japan. Tel: (03) 508-1213	International Conference Center, Kobe, Japan	Fourth international microelectronics conference
2–5 June	ISCA '86	Secretariat ISCA '86, Business Center for Academic Societies Japan, Conference Department, Yamazaki Building 4F, 40-14 Hongo 2-chome, Bunkyo-ku, Tokyo 113, Japan	Sunshine Prince Hotel, Tokyo, Japan	13th international symposium on computer architecture, sponsored by IEEE Computer Society, ACM and the Information Processing Society of Japan
3–5 June	13th Annual International Conference on Computer Architecture	Dr Hideo Aiso, Dept of Electrical Engineering, Keio University, 3-14-1 Hiyoshi, Kohohu-ku, Yokohoma 223, Japan	Tokyo, Japan	Sponsored by IPSJ (Japan), the ACM, the IEEE Computer Society and TC-CA
3–5 June	ComUnix '86	EMAP International Exhibitions Ltd, Abbot's Court, 34 Farringdon Road, London EC1R 3AU, UK. Tel: 01-608 1161	Tara Hotel, London, UK	Series of seminars concerning 'Unix solutions'. Sponsored by /usr/group/UK

calendar

Date	Title	Contact	Place	Other details
3–6 June	International Conference on Consumer Electronics	ICCE, c/o TMA, 3553 North Milwaukee Avenue, Chicago, IL 60641, USA	Rosemont, IL, USA	Conference and exhibition on video and audio technology, home information systems, components, CADCAM and emerging technologies
10–12 June	Comdex International	The Interface Group Inc, 300 First Avenue, Needham, Massachusetts, USA	Nice, France	Display of software, small computer products, peripherals, accessories and other related items; miniconference on business, marketing and financial subjects of interest to computer industry marketers
10–12 June	Scottish Electronics Show	Network Events Ltd, Printers Mews, Market Hill, Buckingham MK18 1JX, UK	Anderson Centre, Glasgow, UK	Exhibition and conference covering equipment and services associated with the design, testing and manufacturing of electronic equipment and components
11–13 June	Microelectronics Packaging	Center for Professional Advancement, Palestrinastraat 1, 1071 LC Amsterdam, The Netherlands. Tel: (020) 623050	Caransa Crest Hotel, Amsterdam, The Netherlands	Intensive course covering: packaging chips and subcircuits; microjoining and bonding; encapsulation of microelectronics; materials, techniques and equipment for moulding and casting; microelectronics reliability; and thermal management
16–19 June	National Computer Conference	AFIPS, 1899 Preston White Drive, Reston, VA 22091, USA. Tel: (703) 620–8900	Las Vegas, NV, USA	Conference sponsored by the American Federation of Information Processing Societies
25–28 June	Communications: Message, Mind, & Machine	Canadian Association for Information Science, BC Research, 3650 Wesbrook Mall, Vancouver V6S 2L2, Canada	Canada	Conference and exhibition on information retrieval and systems design, artificial intelligence, expert systems, networking and distributed systems
2–4 July	International Workshop on Systolic Arrays	Will Moore, Systolic Array Workshop, Dept of Engineering Science, Oxford University, Oxford OX1 3PJ, UK	Oxford, UK	Papers on all aspects of systolic arrays and related SIMD architectures from abstract theory to practical applications and VLSI products
7–11 July	International Optical Computing Conference	Prof Joseph Shamir, Conference Chairman, 1986 IOCC, c/o Kopel Tours Ltd — Conventions, PO Box 4413, 61044 Tel Aviv, Israel	Jerusalem, Israel	Recent developments in optical computing including optical information processing, hybrid optical–digital processing systems, systolic array processors, integrated optical processing devices, electro-optic devices, optical interface techniques and application of optical bistability to computing
21–23 July	Simulation of Semiconductor Devices and Processes	Dr K Board, Department of Electrical and Electronic Engineering, University College of Swansea, Singleton Park, Swansea SA2 8PP, UK	University College of Swansea, UK	Second international conference on semiconductor device and process simulation
21–24 July	CAD/CAM in Electronics	Center for Professional Advancement, Palestrinastraat 1, 1071 LC Amsterdam, The Netherlands	Crest Hotel, Amsterdam, The Netherlands	Course covering computer-aided design, manufacturing and testing in electronics. Includes circuit analysis for integrated and analogue circuits, logic simulation for digital circuits and systems, PCB design and manufacture, VLSI, automatic testing, system implementation and electronics engineering workstations
28–30 July	SCSC '86	Society for Computer Simulation (SCS), PO Box 17900, San Diego, CA 92117, USA. Tel: (619) 277-3888	Reno, NV, USA	SCS conference covering artificial intelligence, simulation in medicine, physics, chemistry, engineering, ecology, government and defence, data communications systems, simulation credibility and validation etc

Date	Title	Contact	Place	Other details
8–11 September	ESSDERC '86	Clive Jones, Institute of Physics, 47 Belgrave Square, London SW1X 8QX, UK. Tel: 01-235 6111	University of Cambridge, UK	16th European solid-state device research conference organized by the Institute of Physics and cosponsored by IEE, IEEE, IERE and the European Physical Society. Coverage includes CMOS, silicon bipolar device modelling, process modelling, thin oxide metallization, defects, submicron lithography, solid-state sensors
8–11 September	International Test Conference (ITC 1986)	ITC, Millbrook Plaza, Suite 104D, PO Box 264, Mount Freedom, NJ 07970, USA. Tel: (201) 895-5260	Sheraton Hotel, Washington, DC, USA	Tutorials, workshops and user group meetings on IC testing. Sponsored by the IEEE Computer Society
9–13 September	Fabritec 86	Secretariat Fabritec 86, c/o Swiss Industries Fair, Postfach, CH-4021 Basel, Switzerland. Tel: (061) 26 20 20	Swiss Industries Fair, Basel, Switzerland	Second international trade fair for fabrication installations in electronics
15–18 September	Euromicro 86	Mrs E C Snippe-Marlisa, TH Twente, PO Box 217, Dept INF, Room A306, 7500 AE Enschede, The Netherlands	Venice, Italy	Twelfth annual conference of micro-processing and microprogramming
15–20 September	Intercomm '86	Cahners Exhibitions Ltd, Chatsworth House, 59 London Road, Twickenham TW1 3SZ, UK	Beijing, China	International computer and communication congress/exposition for science and technology
23–24 September	Customized ICs	Professor R W Hartenstein, Universität Kaiserlautern, Bau 12/4, Postfach 3049, D-6750 Kaiserlautern, FRG	Kaiserlautern, FRG	European conference on customer-vendor interfaces in microelectronics, sponsored by the Commission of the European Communities
23–25 September	Microsoftware 1986	Dr R A Adey, Computational Mechanics Institute, Suite 6200, 400 West Cummings Park, Woburn, MA 01801, USA. Tel: (617) 933-7374	Boston, USA	International conference on microsoftware in engineering, covering codes developed for personal computers, workstations and expert systems
30 September –2 October	ATE '86	Network Events Ltd, Printers Mews, Market Hill, Buckingham MK18 1JX, UK	Palais des Congres, Paris, France	Fifth automatic testing and test instrumentation exhibition and conference
6–10 October	ISATA 86	ISATA, 42 Lloyd Park Avenue, Croydon, Surrey CR0 5SB, UK. Tel: 01-686 7026	Flims, Switzerland	15th international symposium on automotive technology and automation, covering manufacturing information systems, factory networks (MAP), realtime operating systems, man–machine communications, artificial intelligence, expert systems, CADCAM etc
15–17 October	19th Annual Workshop on Microprogramming	Stanley Habib, City College of New York, Computer Science Department, New York City, NY 10031, USA. Tel: (212) 690-6631/2	Graduate Center, City University of New York, USA	Workshop on microarchitecture design, firmware engineering, compaction and optimization, specification languages, graphics hosts, microprogramming languages, RISC/CISC machines and microprogrammed VLSI. Sponsored by ACM Sigmicro and the IEEE Technical Committee on Microprogramming

IMAGE AND VISION COMPUTING

General Editor: Keith Baker (Plymouth Polytechnic, UK)

IMAGE AND VISION COMPUTING is the quarterly international and interdisciplinary journal that provides communication between workers in such diverse applications of computer imaging as astronomy, biomedicine, robotics, remote sensing, broadcasting and video, metallurgy, seismology and radar.

Topics covered include:

- mathematical foundations, including fast Fourier analysis and recursive filtering
- pattern recognition and artificial intelligence
- software techniques, including databases and data structures
- special-purpose hardware, including VLSI

- applications and case studies of image computing, including remote sensing robot vision, industrial quality control, video special effects and tomography
- experimental psychology
- image generation, including flight simulation and holography
- vision and perception theory

For further details and a sample copy please contact:

Geraldine Hills
Butterworth Scientific
PO Box 63, Westbury House,
Bury Street, Guildford,
Surrey GU2 5BH, UK
Telephone: (0483) 31261
Telex: 859556 SCITEC G

microprocessors and microsystems

vol 10 no 4 may 1986

Butterworths

editorial advisory board

Microprocessors and Microsystems is an international journal published in February, March, April, May, June, August, September, October, November, December. *Editorial Offices*: Butterworth Scientific Ltd, PO Box 63, Westbury House, Bury Street, Guildford, Surrey GU2 5BH, UK. Tel: (0483) 31261. Telegrams and telex: 859556 SCITEC G. *Publishing Director*: John Owens. *Production*: Tony Lewis

Microprocessors and Microsystems is published by Butterworth Scientific Ltd. *Registered Office*: Butterworth Scientific Ltd, 88 Kingsway, London WC2 6AB, UK

Subscription enquiries and orders: Quadrant Subscription Services Ltd, Oakfield House, Perrymount Road, Haywards Heath, West Sussex RH16 3DH, UK. Tel: (0444) 459188

Annual subscription (10 issues): £89.00 Overseas rate (£22.00 for private individuals); $160.00 US rate ($40.00 for private individuals)
UK subscription rates available on request.

Prices include packing and delivery by sea mail. Airmail prices available on request. Copies of this journal sent to subscribers in Bangladesh, India, Pakistan, Sri Lanka, Canada and the USA are air-speeded for quicker delivery.

Back issues: Prior to current volume available from Wm Dawson & Sons Ltd, Cannon House, Folkestone, Kent CT19 5EE, UK. Tel: (0303) 57421

US mailing agents: Mercury Airfreight International Ltd Inc., 10B Englehard Avenue, Avenel, NJ 07001, USA. Second class postage paid at Rahway, NJ. US Postmaster: Send address corrections to *Microprocessors and Microsystems* c/o Mercury Airfreight International Ltd Inc., address as above.

Reprints: Minimum order 100, available from the publisher.

Copyright: Readers who require copies of papers published in this journal may either purchase reprints or obtain permission to copy from the publisher at the following address: Butterworth Scientific Ltd, PO Box 63, Westbury House, Bury Street, Guildford, Surrey GU2 5BH, UK. For readers in the USA, permission to copy is given on the condition that the copier pay the stated per copy fee through the Copyright Clearance Center Inc., 26 Congress Street, Salem, MA 01979, USA, Tel: (617) 744-3350, for copying beyond that permitted by Sections 107 and 108 of the US Copyright Law. Fees appear in the code at the foot of the first page of major papers.

ISSN 0141 9331
MCRPD 10 (4) 193-248 1986)

© Butterworth & Co (Publishers) Ltd 1986

Butterworths
Leading the Campaign against Copyright Erosion

Typese... ...ne & Wear, and ... ...nters) Ltd, Greenl... ...von, Wilts, UK.

microprocessors and microsystems

vol 10 no 4
may 1986

Editor Steve Hitchcock

Assistant Editor Andrew Taylor

Publisher Amanda Harper

notes for authors

Microprocessors and Microsystems

The Journal welcomes all articles on semiconductor chip and PCB design, the application of microprocessors to industry, business and schools and on the development of microprocessor software. Articles can come from both academic and industrial research and should be 3000–5000 words in length. In addition to main articles, we welcome shorter case studies, design notes and teach-ins.

All submitted articles are refereed by two independent reviewers to ensure both accuracy and relevance, though it is the authors' sole responsibility that statements used are accurate. The author is also responsible for obtaining permission to quote material and to republish tables and illustrations.

Copyright

Before publication, authors are requested to assign copyright to Butterworth & Co (Publishers) Ltd. This allows the company to sanction reprints of the whole or part of the volume and authorize photocopies. The authors, however, still retain their traditional right to reuse or to veto third-party publication.

Preparation of scripts

As you can see from the Journal, every article published is stylized by us to keep consistency throughout each volume. We follow the Oxford English Dictionary. It would be helpful if you could follow the Journal style. The most important thing, though, is that you write (or rather type) in clear and concise English. Contributions should be typed double-spaced on one side of the paper. We would also appreciate it if you number each page and leave wide margins so we can prepare the article for the typesetters. Three copies of the article are preferred and should be sent to the editor.

Units

You should use, as far as possible, SI units. In circumstances where this is not possible, please provide a conversion factor at the first mention of the unit.

Illustrations

Line drawings

We have our own professional studio to ensure that line drawings are consistent with house style. We would prefer, however, to receive unlettered drawings (black ink on tracing paper) so we can put on the lettering ourselves. Drawings, if possible, should be of size consistent with the Journal, i.e. either 169 mm or 356 mm width. Single drawings should not extend over one page (500 mm) in height.

Computer printouts

Illustrations showing line printer listings, plotter output, etc should preferably be on unlined paper. Printouts will be reduced by us to the relevant size. Do not mark them as they will be used to make photographic copies for the typesetters. Only include sufficient lines for the reader to interpret the format and nature of the printout. Overlong printouts only cause confusion. Fuller explanation should appear in the caption and the text.

Photographs

Black and white glossy photographs (including Polaroid prints of VDU screens) should, where possible, be supplied unmounted. They should be labelled clearly on the back with a soft pencil. Photocopies of the photographs should be provided for the referees.

References

Our Journal style is to indicate the use of a reference in the text with a superscript as each one arises and give the full reference with the same number at the end. If a reference is cited more than once, the same number should be used each time. With a bibliography, the references are given in alphabetic order (dependent on the first author's surname). It would be helpful if you could follow this style. References take the following form:

(to journals)

1 **Buckroyd, A** 'Production testing of microprocessor-based equipment' *Microprocessors and Microsystems* Vol 5 No 7 (September 1981) pp 299–303

(to books)

2 **Gallacher, J** 'Testing and maintenance' in **Hanna, F K (ed.)** *Advanced techniques for microprocessor systems* Peter Peregrinus, Stevenage, UK (1980)

Proofs

Correspondence and proofs for corrections will be sent to the first named author, unless otherwise indicated. Authors will receive a copy of the galley proofs and copies of redrawn or relettered illustrations. It is important that these proofs should be checked and returned promptly.

Reprints

The first named author will receive 25 reprints of the technical article free of charge. Further copies, a minimum of 100, can be ordered at any time from the Reprints Department, Butterworth Scientific Ltd, Westbury House, PO Box 63, Bury Street, Guildford, Surrey GU2 5BH, UK.

Graphbug — a microprocessor software debugging tool

Software tools for program design work could make better use of the facilities of modern VDUs. Adopting this approach **A C Davies and A S Goussous** have designed a debugging tool with an improved graphics-based user interface

Principles of traditional debugging tools have been analysed to identify ways of improving the user interface. In this paper a software tool for assembly-language programming which provides an improved user interface by making use of the facilities of modern visual display units is described. The tool, Graphbug, is designed for the Z80 microprocessor and runs under the CDOS operating system. Internal operation of Graphbug is illustrated.

microprocessors   program monitoring   debugging

It is normal practice during the development of assembly-language programs for microprocessors to use a debugging tool, such as Digital Research's DDT[1], to monitor program execution. Such tools typically provide a user interface suitable for slow teletypewriter output, although this output is now usually displayed in a much speeded-up form on a visual display unit (VDU). No use is made of any of the features of modern VDUs, such as selective screen updating, cursor addressing, reverse video and graphics, which enable a quite different style of user interface to be developed[2,3]. These features are commonly used in business computing software for desk-top microcomputers, but rarely in software tools for scientific or engineering program design work.

This paper describes a debugging tool that provides a much better user interface, giving an improved environment for monitoring program execution, both for program development and as a teaching aid[4]. The tool is designed for the Z80 microprocessor (with minor modifications it could be used for the 8085). It runs under the Cromemco CDOS operating system and in its present form requires a Lear Siegler ADM5 or compatible terminal modified by the inclusion of a Tektronix 4010-compatible graphics board. However, it has been designed in such a way that it

Centre for Information Engineering, The City University, Northampton Square, London EC1V 0HB, UK

could be modified easily to run under the Digital Research CP/M operating system, and with any terminal which supports line-drawing graphics. CDOS is very similar to CP/M, so the modifications required are slight. A simplified version using only character graphics is possible and can, for example, be used with an unmodified ADM5 terminal, but many of the features of the tool cannot then be supported. Although the basic principles could be used for any other microprocessor, major modifications would be needed for use with an operating system which was not similar to CP/M.

Purists may argue that debugging tools should not be used; programs should be created correct and, in the event of erroneous execution, a high-level language version of the program should be re-assessed and revised rather than tinkering around with the program at the hexadecimal level. In reality, however, a substantial amount of microprocessor software is still developed in assembly language, and debugging tools offer considerable help. Additionally, for those who need to understand the details of processor operation at the machine-code level, they provide a good educational aid.

PRINCIPLES OF MAN–MACHINE INTERFACE DESIGN

Software tools originally conceived for use with tele-typewriters are constrained by the slow output response of such devices, typically only 10 characters s^{-1}. This is so slow that brief (and hence uninformative) computer messages in response to user actions are appropriate. Detailed explanatory messages and helpful menus of commands take too long to print and their benefits are outweighed by the slowing down of the man–machine interaction and the mechanical noise generated.

Fast silent VDUs operating at 960 characters s^{-1} or more are typical today, and yet there has been no widespread change in the format of the computer output. Many program development environments do not even provide the screen editors extensively used in word processing. In some respects, the tendency to scroll the VDU output upwards puts users in a worse environment than using a slow teletypewriter: the lines of text may move upwards so quickly that they cannot read them, and they have no means of scrolling in reverse to review past output (with a teletypewriter, they could go back over the mounting rolls of paper that had accumulated on the floor).

A fast VDU enables users to be prompted with a list of all command options available at each step (instead of inherently meaningless single-character prompts), and since the computer can monitor the speed of users' responses it is a simple matter to provide additional 'help' information automatically for a slow user and suppress information for a fast (and, presumably, expert) user. The need to keep a 'user guide' alongside the terminal can be virtually eliminated.

A VDU that supports rapid screen clearing and updating and fast cursor control will permit the design of a screen format which does not scroll upwards and which displays various categories of information in predetermined areas of the screen. For example, the top lines of the screen might be reserved for a brief menu of available commands that is continually updated as the options change; the left side of the screen might be used to record relevant aspects of the dialogue between user and computer; and the right side might be used to display information generated by the software tool being used (eg in the case of a debugging tool this might be a display of CPU registers or contents of a memory region).

The cursor prompt can be maintained in a specific screen location so that the user always knows where to expect it. Since individual characters or groups of characters can be erased quickly, redundant or unnecessary information can be removed and the display updated rapidly.

Techniques such as those described in the three preceding paragraphs are now commonplace in software for business applications and personal computers, but are rarely encountered in software development environments.

FEATURES OF TRADITIONAL DEBUGGING TOOLS

A typical debugging tool, of which the Digital Research DDT and Cromemco Debug[5] are good examples, provides the user with the means of executing a program under test in a controlled way. For example, the user can normally

- initiate execution of the program from any desired instruction, having initialized CPU register and memory locations if required
- interrupt program execution at any desired instruction by prior insertion of a breakpoint
- single-step the program one instruction at a time with the opportunity to display or change registers and memory between each step.

The more sophisticated tools (including Debug) allow the simultaneous insertion of multiple breakpoints and can associate a count N with each breakpoint so that it is acted upon only on the Nth pass through the breakpoint location — this is of considerable assistance in monitoring

the behaviour of iterative loops. Often a disassembler is incorporated in the tool so that instructions may be displayed to the user as mnemonics rather than hexadecimal numbers, and this then makes it relatively easy also for instructions to be entered in mnemonic form, providing a line-by-line assembler facility.

Figure 1 shows a typical register display resulting from the single-step execution of part of the following Z80 program segment (which outputs seven stored ASCII characters from a port)

```
        ORG   103H      ; program start address
CHARS   EQU   7         ; number of characters to
                        ; output
START   LD    HL, LIST  ; point to start of character
                        ; list
        LD    B, CHARS  ; initialize invariant
LOOP    LD    A, (HL)   ; loop invariant is number of
        OUT   18H, A    ; characters left to output
        INC   HL        ; and equals contents of B.
        DJNZ  LOOP      ; on exit, no more to output
        JP    0         ; exit to operating system
                        ; restart
LIST    DEFB  'ABCDEFG'
        END   START     ; start is label of first executable
                        ; statement
```

Although the display appears to be giving the user a direct view of the internal registers of the CPU, the actual operation makes use of a 'register save' area of user memory; following execution of each instruction an interrupt routine is entered which copies the contents of each register from the CPU to predetermined locations in the 'save' area, so forming an image of the state of the processor at the end of the instruction. From the 'save' area, this image is used to provide the data for the register display. When the user gives the command to execute the next instruction, the whole of the image is copied back into the CPU, ending with the contents of the program counter, so that execution continues from the break. In this way the user is given the illusion of being able to change directly the contents of registers within the CPU, whereas really the contents of memory locations are changing in the 'save' area.

FACILITIES OF GRAPHBUG

The graphics-based debugging tool, called Graphbug, is loaded from disc by the command

GRAPHBUG < filename >

where < filename > is optional; if present it denotes the name of an executable binary file which is to be executed under the control of Graphbug.

The VDU screen then displays the main Z80 registers and a menu of commands, as shown in Figure 2. The present version does not incorporate a disassembler, so that the 'next instruction' (defined as the instruction starting at the current contents of the program counter) is displayed in hexadecimal format. By selecting various alternatives from the menu the user is presented with alternative displays as shown by the typical examples in Figures 3 and 4. The same program segment as used above was loaded into memory for these figures. The display layouts were designed with the objective of eliminating unnecessary information where possible, so

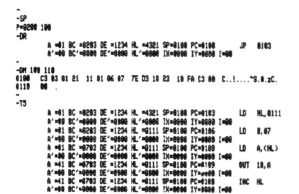

Figure 1.   Register display from Cromemco Debug

that the user's attention can be directed to the aspects of concern.

Notice that it is possible to show not only the contents of HL, but also (Figure 3) the contents of the memory location HL is pointing to and also of several adjacent locations. Figure 4 shows the display following insertion of a breakpoint at 10BH to operate on the fourth pass around the loop and additional breakpoints at 106H and 10EH. The display is updated as the breakpoints are encountered. (Static photographs do not, of course, give a realistic impression of using this debugging tool, since dynamic aspects — screen updating, user interaction, etc — are the most important feature.)

The version illustrated requires a graphics VDU to draw the rectangular register outlines, to provide the necessary resolution to place the text in the required positions, and to permit more information to be displayed using a smaller character size. A VDU having a conventional 80

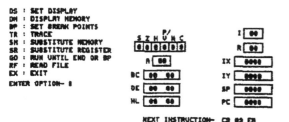

Figure 2.   Initial display on loading Graphbug

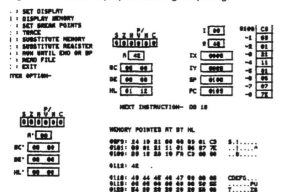

Figure 3.   Full display including display of stack

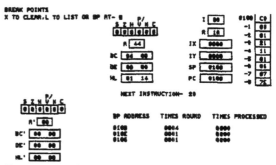

Figure 4.   Breakpoint insertion and display

column, 24 line display can be used, however, to give a primitive pictorial display provided the VDU can support cursor addressing and rapid screen clearing. Without these features the screen-update time would be much too long for practical use.

Figure 5 shows an example from a simpler debug tool, developed to run on any ADM3 or ADM5 terminal. Several enhancements are needed (for example, displaying the flag register in hexadecimal form is rather useless!), but further development has not so far been carried out because completion of Graphbug in the time available was considered more worthwhile. Graphbug occupies about 10 kbyte in memory, which is similar to other debug tools, but an increase would be inevitable if a full disassembler and line-by-line assembler were to be incorporated.

ESSENTIALS OF THE OPERATING SYSTEM INTERFACE

To understand the internal operation of Graphbug, the way that it interacts with the operating system must first be understood. The outline which follows is based on CDOS, but CP/M and several other disc operating systems for the Z80 differ in only minor aspects[6,7].

The first 256 byte of memory (0 to 0FFH) form the 'system parameter area', and a large block of some 10 kbyte from 0FFFFH downwards contains the remainder of the operating system, consisting of the I/O system (IOS), disc operating system (DOS) and console processor

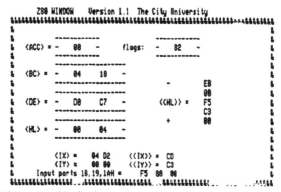

Figure 5.   Display from 'character-graphics' version

(CONPROC). The exact size of memory area required depends upon the version number of the operating system. The lowest address is referred to by the mnemonic label OSSTART (Figure 6a). In CP/M literature, these are known as the basic I/O system (BIOS), basic disc operating system (BDOS) and console command processor (CCP). The user memory is thus from 100H to OSSTART-1. This is also known as the 'transient program area'.

When a command is given to execute a program stored on disc (which will have a file-name with extension COM to denote a binary, executable program), the object code is copied from disc to user area and an absolute jump to the program start address is written to locations 100H, 101H and 102H. The operating system then initiates execution by loading 100H into the program counter. Typically, such programs are arranged to occupy memory from 103H upwards, but even then 103H may not be the start address since the object code may begin with data tables, so that the absolute jump to the actual start address is still required.

Relocation of systems programs

Certain systems programs (for example BASIC interpreters, or debug tools) need to be able to load in other programs for subsequent execution, and therefore need to be able to clear the bottom end of user memory (from 103H) to create the maximum amount of space for these programs. They achieve this by relocating themselves to the top of user memory as shown in Figures 6b and c. Assuming the system program occupies SIZE bytes, the process is

1) system program loaded from disc into 103H to PROGTOP (where PROGTOP = 103H + SIZE)
2) location of OSSTART determined, available at memory locations 6 and 7
3) program copied from [103H . . . PROGTOP] to [(OSSTART − SIZE − 1) . . . (OSSTART − 1)] (recalculating all absolute addresses in the program).

After relocation the system program commences its normal mode of execution, typically either by displaying a prompt to the user or by loading from disc into user memory any files which were given as operands in the command line which initiated operation of the system program. For example, if the system program were a BASIC interpreter, the prompt might be '>'; if the name of an existing BASIC program had been given as an operand in the command line, this program would be loaded into the bottom of the user area, ready to be RUN or LISTed. In the case of a debugging program, which for the purposes of this example will be assumed to have the filename BUG.COM, being used to debug an assembled linked program stored on disc under the name PUT.COM (PUT chosen as a mnemonic for 'program under test'), the command line would be

    BUG PUT

which would cause the operating system and the debugging program to manage the following actions in the sequence

1) BUG.COM copied from disc to 103H upwards (as Figure 6b)
2) BUG.COM relocated to top of user RAM (as Figure 6c)
3) PUT.COM copied from disc to 103H upwards (overwriting initial location of BUG.COM)
4) 'register save' area in RAM set up for initial execution of PUT (all images of CPU registers cleared except that the program counter is set to 100H ready for the user to initiate execution of PUT). The stack pointer may also be set to 100H to provide an initial small stack area in case the designer of PUT has failed to include stack pointer initialization
5) prompt displayed for user.

Execution of PUT could then be initiated by user command, either in single-step or continuous mode, possibly after setting some breakpoints and initializing various registers and memory locations.

The actual operations which follow the user command to execute would be: copy current values of registers (as stored in 'register save' area) into CPU, the last action being to copy 100H into the program counter. The result of this would be a jump to the start address of the user program (typically, but not essentially, 103H) which would then run until an interrupt (or system reset) occurred. The interrupt might be caused by encountering a breakpoint, or when in single-step mode it might occur after completion of each instruction. The interrupt initiates the copying of register values from CPU to the 'register save' area, and then prompts the user to display and/or modify these values, enter new breakpoints etc, before execution is resumed.

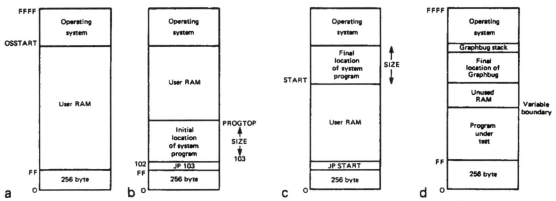

Figure 6. a Memory map of operating system, b system program (such as Graphbug) before relocation, c system program after relocation, d after relocation of Graphbug and loading of program under test

INTERNAL OPERATION OF GRAPHBUG

This section describes general aspects of the structure and operation of Graphbug, with details of those aspects which seem either least obvious or most interesting. Graphbug is built from a number of separate modules which can be described independently. The most important aspect to understand is the breakpoint processor, since this is involved in both the breakpoint and single-step actions.

Breakpoint processor

After calling Graphbug, if a filename (for a program to be debugged) is given in the command line then Graphbug loads this program into the user memory area and inserts a jump instruction to the breakpoint-processing routine in locations 30H, 31H, 32H. This ensures that whenever an RST6 instruction is encountered, control passes to the breakpoint processor. Implementing breakpoints involves inserting RST6 (single byte) instructions in the program. Although it would be possible to insert these RST6 instructions in the program as part of the breakpoint setting process, this would have the disadvantages that if the user were to then list the program, he/she would see the RST6 instructions instead of the original program instructions. Therefore, actual insertion of RST6 instructions is delayed until the GO processor is invoked (see below).

The breakpoint status is stored in a table BPTABLE, which takes the form of eight records, each record having three fields: breakpoint address; number of passes before break; number of times already encountered. BPTABLE and a memory location, BPCOUNT, used to keep a record of the number of breakpoints entered, are initialized to zero on entry to Graphbug and when breakpoints are cleared by the user.

The first two fields of BPTABLE are entered by the user, who can thus set up to eight breakpoints, each with an optional associated count. The third field is incremented every time the corresponding breakpoint is encountered, and execution is stopped and the program status displayed when the second and third fields become equal for any breakpoint. When the user requests execution of the program, the first byte of the instruction at the address is saved in an eight-location table BYTETAB, and replaced by an RST6 instruction. An RST6 instruction may be present in the program under test either because a breakpoint has been inserted or because single-step (trace) operation has been selected. These two alternatives are distinguished by a flag TRTEST.

On encountering an RST6 instruction, the jump instruction at locations 30H–32H transfers control to module BPROCESS, which operates as follows: the contents of all registers are transferred to the 'register save' area. The program counter (PC) is saved by a POP instruction, since execution of the RST6 puts < PC > on the stack

if < TRTEST > = 1 then single-step process,
else true-breakpoint process

Single-step process

Replace RST6 by original instruction. If previous instruction was transfer of control type (eg JR, JP, CALL, or RET) replace second RST6 also.

True-breakpoint process

Locate breakpoint in BPTABLE (by searching field 1). Increment field 3.

if field 2 > field 3 then return to GO
else replace RST6 instruction(s)
by original byte(s) and return to
user

endif

GO processor

A program can be run within Graphbug using the GO option. With the facility of setting breakpoints the progress of the program can be monitored at any suitable point.

As explained above, the GO processor inserts RST6 instructions in the program, where breakpoints have been set. Before inserting the RST6 instructions the GO processor checks if the execution start address (the contents of the user's program counter) is a breakpoint. This situation normally occurs when execution of the program is restarted after encountering a breakpoint.

The following mechanism was developed to ensure that execution of the start instruction is carried out correctly

- A copy of the instruction at the start address is put in memory at a location called SUBCALL followed by a RET instruction (note that if the instruction is a jump-relative, an equivalent absolute jump is put at SUBCALL)
- The user's stack pointer is restored
- The address of the instruction following the start instruction is pushed onto the stack
- The rest of the user's registers are restored
- A jump to location SUBCALL is executed. This has the effect of executing the instruction at SUBCALL then returning to the user's program via the return address on the stack.

Stack display

Graphbug displays the contents of the top eight locations of the user's stack plus the location currently pointed at by the stack pointer. The stack is displayed in nine boxes stacked vertically. The top box is labelled with the address contained in the stack pointer. The other eight boxes are labelled $-1, -2, -3, -4, -5, -6, -7, -8$, with -8 being the bottom box in the display (see Figure 3).The stack display is updated every time a breakpoint is encountered (including every instruction in single-step mode) or when the contents of the stack pointer are changed explicitly using the modify register option.

Next-instruction display

Even in machine-code format, displaying the next instruction following a breakpoint or when in single-step mode presents a problem because Z80 instructions may be from 1 byte to 4 byte long. The instruction length must be determined from a knowledge of the first and, in some cases, the second byte. The Z80 instruction set is unfortunately unsystematic in structure and there is no simple way to determine the instruction length. It is possible, however, to reduce the alternatives to a small number of categories, and a subroutine, LEN, of 188 byte was written, requiring associated tables of 257 byte. IY is use as a pointer to the start address of the instruction and the number of bytes N is returned in A.

The algorithm used is given below. The ith byte of the instruction pointed to by IY is denoted by b_i (eg the instruction is $b_1 b_2 \ldots b_N$, with $1 <= N <= 4$) (where $<=$ denotes 'less than or equal to').

```
if (80 <= b₁ <= C1) or (3F < b₁ < 7F) then N:= 1
    elseif (b₁ = CB) then N:= 2
    elseif (b₁ = DD or FD) then DDCHECK (N)
    elseif (b₁ = ED) then EDCHECK (N)
    else SEARCHTAB (N)
endif
```

DDCHECK (N):

```
if (b₂ = (CB or 21 or 22 or 2A or 36) ) then N:= 4
    else SEARCHTABDD (FOUND)
        if (FOUND) then N:= 2
                    else N:= 3
        endif
endif
```

EDCHECK (N):

```
SEARCHTABED (FOUND)
if (FOUND) then N:= 2
            else N:= 4
endif
```

SEARCHTAB (N):

```
Search LENTAB for b₁
N:= < ADDR + 1 >
```

where ADDR is the location containing b_1. Three tables are required:

TABDD contains all second bytes for 2-byte instructions starting with DD or FD
(11 entries: 09, 19, 23, 29, 2B, 39, E1, E3, E5, E9, F9)

TABED contains all second bytes for 4-byte instructions starting with ED
(6 entries: 43, 4B, 53, 5B, 73, 7B)

LENTAB contains the first byte of all instructions not included elsewhere, together with the length of each instruction (120 entries of 2 byte each)

It was realized subsequently that the subroutine LEN could have been improved by shortening LENTAB to contain only 2 byte and 3 byte instructions. Anything not found in LENTAB would then be a 1 byte instruction, requiring a change in SEARCHTAB (N) to include:

```
if (found at ADDR) then N:= < ADDR > + 1
                    else N:= 1
endif
```

This would reduce LENTAB from 240 byte to 100 byte.

For the Z80, there are no unused op. codes. In the case of processors with undefined or illegal op. codes, it would of course be necessary to add a method of indicating their occurrence.

Relocation

As described above, Graphbug needs to relocate itself into the top end of user memory after it has been loaded. Although more recent microprocessors (eg 6809) have been designed to operate with position-independent code so that programs can be located anywhere in memory without change, this is not the case for the Z80.

To move a program from one region to another, all the locations which contain absolute addresses (eg operands of CALL and JP instructions, absolute loads, etc) need to be changed to correspond to the new region, with the exception of references to fixed addresses (such as calls to routines provided by the operating system)[8]. Two alternative approaches are possible.

Suppose that the program has been assembled into the range 103H to TOP, and that relocation to a start address of (103H + N) is required. One possible method is to scan through the assembled program to find all op. codes corresponding to CALL or JP instructions or absolute LOADs, and for each one found to check if the next two bytes (the operand) form an address in the range 103H to TOP. If so, N is added to the address. Addresses outside the range are assumed to be system calls not requiring alteration. Apart from a need to have a stored table of all the op. codes which have absolute-address operands, this method has a further disadvantage that any stored-data regions within the program (for example, ASCII text strings) could be corrupted if they contained bytes equal in numerical value to certain op. codes, since there would be no way to distinguish data and instructions.

An alternative method, using a 'bit-map', is preferable and is used by Graphbug. The bit-map is an array having 1 bit corresponding to each byte in the program to be relocated; a set bit '1' indicates that the byte is an absolute address which needs modifying; a reset bit '0' indicates a byte for which no change is needed during relocation.

To construct the bit-map, the program is assembled twice, with two different origins. The two assembled programs differ only in those bytes which change during relocation. The two origin addresses are arbitrary except that the procedure is substantially simpler if the least significant byte is chosen to be zero for both. Only the most significant bytes then differ, and relocation by any integer multiple of 256 byte is still possible. A byte-by-byte comparison of the two assembled programs enables the bit-map to be easily constructed; subsequently, during runtime of a selfrelocating program (such as Graphbug), the bit corresponding to each byte in the program is checked and, if set, the required offset is added prior to copying it at its new location.

The bit-map is one-eighth of the size of the program to be relocated. Additionally, space is needed for the instructions of the relocating procedure, but storage space is not a serious problem.

MODIFICATIONS FOR CP/M AND OTHER DEVELOPMENTS

The CDOS operating system is very similar to CP/M, and most function calls have direct equivalents. Two CDOS function calls used by Graphbug, however, do not have direct CP/M equivalents.

- CDOS call 80H, which reads a character from the console keyboard without echo, can be replaced by a similar CP/M call 6.
- CDOS call 86H, which formats a file name string into a file control block (FCB) has no CP/M equivalent, but a Z80 subroutine to emulate it has been written,

must be completed within a given time, it ignores interrupts. Should the computer decide to respond to the interrupt, it must carry out the following sequence of actions.

(1) Complete its current instruction. All instructions are indivisible, which means they must be executed to completion. A more sophisticated architecture might allow the temporary suspension of an instruction.

(2) The contents of the program counter must be saved in a safe place, so that the program can continue from the point at which it was interrupted after the interrupt has been serviced. The program counter is invariably saved on the stack so that interrupts can, themselves, be interrupted without losing their return addresses.

(3) The state of the processor is saved on the stack. Clearly, it would be unwise to allow the interrupt service routine to modify, say, the value of the carry flag, so that an interrupt occurring before a BCC instruction would affect the operation of the BCC after the interrupt had been serviced. In general, the servicing of an interrupt should have no effect whatsoever on the execution of the interrupted program. (This statement is qualified below in dealing with software interrupts, which are a special type of synchronous event.)

(4) A jump is then made to the location of the interrupt handling routine, which is executed like any other program. After this routine has been executed, a return from interrupt is made, the program counter restored, and the system status word returned to its pre-interrupt value.

Before examining the way in which the 68000 deals with interrupts, it is worthwhile considering some of the key concepts emerging from any discussion of interrupts.

Nonmaskable interrupts

An interrupt request is so called because it is a request, and therefore carries the implication that it may be denied or deferred. Whenever an interrupt request is deferred, it is said to be masked. Sometimes it is necessary for the computer to respond to an interrupt no matter what it is doing. Most microprocessors have a special interrupt request input called a 'nonmaskable interrupt input' (NMI). Such an interrupt cannot be deferred and must always be serviced.

Nonmaskable interrupts are normally reserved for events such as loss of power. In this case, a low voltage detector generates a nonmaskable interrupt as soon as the power begins to decay. This forces the processor to deal with the interrupt and perform an orderly shutdown of the system before the power drops below a critical level and the computer fails completely. The 68000 has a single (level 7) nonmaskable interrupt request.

Prioritized interrupts

In an environment where more than one device is able to issue an interrupt request, it is necessary to provide a

mechanism to distinguish between an important interrupt and a less important one. For example, if a disc drive controller generates an interrupt because it has some data ready to be read by the processor, the interrupt must be serviced before the data is lost and replaced by new data from the disc drive. On the other hand, an interrupt generated by a keyboard interface probably has from 250 ms to several seconds before it must be serviced. Therefore an interrupt from a keyboard can be deferred if interrupts from devices requiring urgent attention are pending.

For the above reasons, microprocessors are often provided with prioritized interrupts. Each interrupt has a predefined priority, and a new interrupt with a priority lower than or equal to the current one cannot interrupt the processor until the current interrupt has been dealt with. Equally, an interrupt with a higher priority can interrupt the current interrupt. The 68000 provides seven levels of interrupt priority.

Vectored interrupts

A vectored interrupt is one in which the device requesting the interrupt automatically identifies itself to the processor. Some 8-bit microprocessors lack a vectored interrupt facility and have only a single interrupt request input (IRQ*). When IRQ* is asserted, the processor recognizes an interrupt but not its source. This means that the processor must examine, in turn, each of the peripherals that may have initiated the interrupt. To do this, the interrupt handling routine interrogates a status bit associated with each of the peripherals.

More sophisticated processors have an interrupt acknowledge output line, IACK, which is connected to all peripherals. Whenever the CPU has accepted an interrupt and is about to service it, the CPU asserts its interrupt acknowledge output. An interrupt acknowledge from the CPU informs the peripheral that its interrupt is about to be serviced. The peripheral then generates an 'identification number' which it puts on the data bus, allowing the processor to calculate the address of the interrupt handling routine appropriate to the peripheral. This is called a vectored interrupt. The 68000 provides the designer with both vectored and nonvectored interrupt facilities.

PRIVILEGED STATES AND THE 68000

Having introduced the interrupt the next step is to look at how the 68000 handles exceptions, which are a more general form of interrupt.

The 68000 is an unusual processor because it always operates in one of two states: either supervisor state or user state. User and supervisor states are only relevant to multitasking systems in which several user tasks are run under control of the operating system. By executing the operating system in the supervisor mode and the user tasks in the user mode, it becomes relatively easy to prevent one user task from accessing the memory space of another task or of the operating system.

The supervisor state is the higher state of privilege and is in force whenever the S bit of the status register is true. All the 68000's instructions can be executed while the processor is in this state. The user state is the lower state of privilege, and certain instructions cannot be executed in this state. Each of the two states has its own stack pointer, so that the 68000 has two A7 registers. The user-mode A7 is called the user stack pointer (USP) and the supervisor-mode A7 is called the supervisor stack pointer (SSP). Note that the SSP cannot be accessed from the user state, whereas the USP can be accessed in the supervisor state by means of the instructions MOVE USP,An and MOVE An,USP. Figure 1 shows the register arrangements of the 68000. The program counter, status register, data registers and address registers A0–A6 are common to both operating modes. Only A7 is duplicated.

All exception processing is carried out in the supervisor state, because an exception forces a change from user to supervisor state. Indeed, the only way of entering the supervisor state is by means of an exception. Figure 1 shows how a transition is made between the 68000's two states. Note that an exception causes the S bit in the 68000's status register to be set and the supervisor stack pointer to be selected at the start of the exception, with the result that the return address is saved on the supervisor stack and not on the user stack. The 68000 puts out a function code on its three function code pins, FC0–FC2, which informs any external memory management unit whether the CPU is accessing user or supervisory memory space. This enables the memory management unit to

protect the supervisor's memory space from any illegal access by user programs.

The change from supervisor to user state is made by clearing the S bit of the status register. This change is carried out by the operating system when it wishes to run a user program. Four instructions are available for this operation: RTE; MOVE.W < ea >, SR; ANDI.W #$XXXX, SR; and EORI.W #$XXXX, SR. The #$XXXX represents a 16-bit literal value in hexadecimal form. The RTE (return from exception) instruction terminates an exception handling routine and restores the value of the program counter and the old status register stored on the stack before the current exception was processed. Consequently, if the 68000 were in the user state before the current exception forced it into the supervisor state, an RTE would restore the processor to its old (ie user) state.

In the user state, the programmer must not attempt to execute certain instructions. For example, the STOP and RESET instructions are not available to the programmer, because the RESET instruction forces the RESET* output of the 68000 low and resets any peripherals connected to this pin. Some of these peripherals may be in use by another program. The whole philosophy behind user and supervisor states is to prevent this type of thing from happening. Similarly, a STOP instruction has the effect of halting the processor until certain conditions are met, and is not allowed in the user state because a user program should not be allowed to bring the entire system to a standstill.

Any instructions affecting the S bit in the upper byte of the status register (ie RTE; MOVE.W < ea>,SR; ANDI.W #$XXXX,SR; ORI.W #$XXXX,SR; EORI.W #$XXXX,SR) are also not permitted in the user mode. Note that no instruction that performs useful computation is barred from the user mode. Only certain system operations are privileged.

Suppose a programmer tries to set the S bit by executing an ORI.W #$2000,SR; obviously, there is nothing to stop him/her from writing the instruction and running the program containing it. When the program is run, the illegal operation violates the user privilege by trying to enter the supervisor mode and forces an exception to be generated. This causes a change of state from user to supervisor, ie the 'punishment' for trying to enter the supervisor state is to be forced into it.

In fact, the effect of attempting to execute an ORI.W #$2000,SR is to raise a software exception called a privilege violation, forcing a jump to a specific routine dealing with this type of exception. (The way in which exception states are entered and processed is dealt with below.) Once the exception handling routine dealing with the privilege violation has been entered, the user no longer controls the processor. The operating system has now taken over and it is highly probable that the exception handling routine will deal with the privilege violation by terminating the user's program.

EXCEPTION TYPES

There are a number of different exception types supported by the 68000, some of which are associated with external

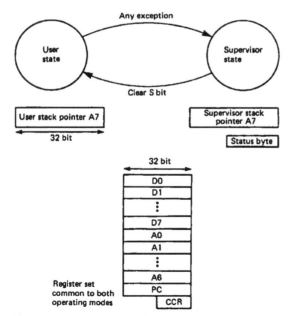

Figure 1. State diagram of user and supervisor state transitions

hardware events such as interrupts, and some of which are associated with internally generated events such as privilege violations. Below is a list of the exception types currently implemented. The way in which these exceptions are implemented is described later.

Reset

An externally generated reset is caused by bringing the RESET* and HALT* pins low for 10 clock pulses (or 100 ms on power up), and is used to place the 68000 in a known state at start up or following a totally irrecoverable system collapse. The reset is a unique exception, because there is no 'return from exception' following a reset.

Bus error

A bus error is an externally generated exception, initiated by hardware driving the 68000's BERR* pin active low. It is a 'catch-all' exception, because the systems designer may use it in many different ways, and it is provided to enable the processor to deal with hardware faults in the system. A typical use of the BERR* input is to indicate either a faulty memory access or an access to a nonexistent memory.

Interrupt

The 68000 has three interrupt request inputs, IPL0–IPL2, which are encoded and indicate one of seven levels of interrupt. To obtain maximum benefit from the interrupt request inputs, it is necessary to apply an eight-line to three-line priority encoder to convert one of seven interrupt request inputs from peripherals into a 3-bit code. The eighth code represents no interrupt request.

Address error

An address error exception occurs when the processor attempts to read a 16-bit word or a 32-bit longword at an odd address. Attempting to read a word at an odd address would require two accesses to memory — one to access the odd byte of an operand and the other to access the even byte at the next address. Address error exceptions are generated when the programmer makes a mistake. Consider the following fragment of code

```
MOVE.L #$7000,A0   (Load A0 with $00 7000)
MOVE.B (A0)+,D0    (Load D0 with the byte pointed at by A0, and
                    increment A0 by 1)
MOVE.W (A0)+,D0    (Load D0 with the word pointed at by A0, and
                    increment A0 by 2)
```

The third instruction results in an address error because the previous operation, MOVE.B (A0)+ D0, causes the value in A0 to be incremented from $7000 to $7001. Therefore when the processor attempts to execute MOVE.W (A0)+, D0 it finds it is trying to access a word at an odd address. In many ways, an address error is closer to

an exception generated by an event originating in the hardware than to one originating in the software. The bus cycle that leads to the address error is aborted, as the processor cannot complete the operation.

Illegal instruction

In 8-bit microprocessors, it was an intriguing diversion to find out what effect 'unimplemented' op. codes had on the processor. For example, if the value $A5 did not correspond to a valid op. code, an enthusiast would try and execute it and then see what happened. This was possible because the control unit (ie the instruction interpreter) of most 8-bit microprocessors was implemented by random logic.

To reduce the number of gates in the control unit of the CPU, some manufacturers have not attempted to deal with illegal op. codes; after all, these are not supposed to be executed. In keeping with the 68000's approach to programming, an exception is generated whenever an operation code is read that does correspond to the bit pattern of the first word of one of the 68000's legal instructions.

Divide by zero

If a number is divided by zero, the result is meaningless and often indicates that something has gone seriously wrong with the program attempting to carry out the division. For this reason, the designers of the 68000 decided to make any attempt to divide a number by zero an exception generating event. Good programs never try to divide a number by zero, so the divide-by-zero exception should not arise; it is intended merely as a failsafe device, to avoid the meaningless result that would occur if a number was divided by zero.

CHK instruction

The 'check register against bounds' instruction (CHK) has the assembly language form CHK < ea >,Dn, and has the effect of comparing the content of the specified data register with the operand at the effective address. If the lower-order word in the register, Dn, is negative, or is greater than the upper bound at the effective address, an exception is generated. For example, when the instruction CHK D1,D0 is executed, an exception is generated if

$$[D0(0: 15)] < 0$$

or

$$[D0(0: 15)] > [D1(0:15)]$$

The CHK instruction works only with 16-bit words, and therefore cannot be used with an address register as an effective address. The CHK exception has been included to help compiler writers for languages such as PASCAL which have facilities for the automatic checking of array indexes against their bounds.

TRAPV instruction

When the 'trap on overflow' instruction (TRAPV) is executed, an exception occurs if the overflow bit, V, of the condition code register is set. Note that an exception caused by dividing a number by zero occurs automatically, while TRAPV is an instruction equivalent to:
IF V = 1 THEN exception ELSE continue.

Privilege violation

If the processor is in the user state (ie the S bit of the status register is clear) and it attempts to execute a privileged instruction, a privilege violation exception occurs. Apart from any instruction that attempts to modify the state of the S bit, the following three instructions cannot be executed in the user state: STOP; RESET; MOVE < ea >,SR.

Trace

A popular method of debugging a program is to operate in a trace mode, in which the contents of all registers are printed out after each instruction has been executed. The 68000 has an inbuilt trace facility. If the T bit of the status register is set, a trace exception is generated after each instruction has been executed. The exception handling routine called by the trace exception can be constructed to offer programmers any facilities they need.

Line 1010 emulator

Operation codes whose four most significant bits (bits 12–15) are 1010 or 1111 are unimplemented in the 68000, and therefore represent illegal instructions. However, the 68000 generates a special exception for op. codes whose most significant nibble is 1010 (also called line ten). The purpose of this exception is to emulate instructions on future versions of the 68000. Suppose a version of the 68000 is designed which includes floating point operations as well as the normal 68000 instruction set. Clearly, it is impossible to run code intended for the floating point processor on a normal 68000. But by using 1010 as the four most significant bits of each of the new floating point instructions, an exception is generated each time the 68000 encounters one, and the line 1010 exception can emulate its more sophisticated counterpart.

Line 1111 emulator

The line 1111 (or line F) emulator behaves in almost exactly the same way as the line 1010 emulator, except that it has a different exception handling routine.

Uninitialized interrupt vector

The 68000 supports vectored interrupts, so that an

interrupting device can identify itself and allow the 68000 to execute the appropriate interrupt handling routine without having to poll each device in turn. Before a device can identify itself, it must first be correctly configured by the programmer. If a 68000 series device is unconfigured and yet generates an interrupt, the 68000 responds by raising an 'uninitiated interrupt vector' exception. 68000 series peripherals are designed to supply the initialized interrupt vector number ($0F) during an IACK cycle, if they have not been initialized by software.

Spurious interrupt

If the 68000 receives an interrupt request and sends an interrupt acknowledge, but no device responds, the CPU generates a spurious interrupt exception. To implement the spurious interrupt exception, external hardware is required to assert BERR* following the nonappearance of either DTACK* or VPA* a reasonable time after an interrupt acknowledge has been detected.

TRAP (software interrupt)

The 68000 provides sixteen instructions of the form TRAP #1, where $I = 0, 1, \ldots, 15$. When this instruction is executed an exception is generated and one of sixteen exception handling routines called. Thus TRAP #0 causes TRAP exception handling routine 0 to be called, and so on.

The TRAP instruction is very useful. Suppose a program is written which is to run all 68000 systems. The greatest problem comes in dealing with input or output transactions. One 68000 system may deal with input in a very different way to every other 68000 system. However, if everybody agrees that, say TRAP #0 means input a byte and TRAP #1 means output a byte, then the software becomes truly portable. All that remains to be done is for an exception handler to be written for each 68000 system to actually implement the input or output as necessary.

EXCEPTION VECTORS

Having described the various types of exception supported by the 68000, the next step is to explain how the processor is able to determine the location of the corresponding exception handling routine. Every exception has a vector associated with it, and that vector is the 32-bit absolute address of the appropriate exception handling routine. All exception vectors are stored in a table of 512 words, extending from address $00 0000 to $00 03FF. A list of all the exception vectors is given in Table 1, and Figure 2 shows the physical location of the 512 vectors in memory. The left-hand column of Table 1 gives the vector number of each entry in the table. The vector number is a value which, when multiplied by four, gives the address, or offset, of an exception vector. For example, the vector number corresponding to a privilege violation is 8, and the

Table 1.   Exception vectors and the 68000

Vector number	Vector (hex)	Address space	Exception type
0	000	SP	Reset — initial supervisor stack pointer
1	004	SP	Reset — initial program counter value
2	008	SD	Bus error
3	00C	SD	Address error
4	010	SD	Illegal instruction
5	014	SD	Divide by zero
6	018	SD	CHK instruction
7	01C	SD	TRAPV instruction
8	020	SD	Privilege violation
9	024	SD	Trace
10	028	SD	Line 1010 emulator
11	02C	SD	Line 1111 emulator
12	030	SD	(Unassigned — reserved)
13	034	SD	(Unassigned — reserved)
14	038	SD	(Unassigned — reserved)
15	03C	SD	Uninitialized interrupt vector
16	040	SD	(Unassigned — reserved)
:	:	:	:
23	05C	SD	(Unassigned — reserved)
24	060	SD	Spurious interrupt
25	064	SD	Level 1 interrupt autovector
26	068	SD	Level 2 interrupt autovector
27	06C	SD	Level 3 interrupt autovector
28	070	SD	Level 4 interrupt autovector
29	074	SD	Level 5 interrupt autovector
30	078	SD	Level 6 interrupt autovector
31	07C	SD	Level 7 interrupt autovector
32	080	SD	TRAP #0 vector
33	084	SD	TRAP #1 vector
:	:	:	:
47	0BC	SD	TRAP #15 vector
48	0C0	SD	(Unassigned — reserved)
:	:	:	:
63	0FC	SD	(Unassigned — reserved)
64	100	SD	User interrupt vector
:	:	:	:
255	3FC	SD	User interrupt vector

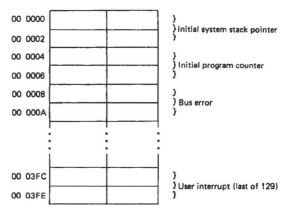

Figure 2.   Memory map of the 68000 vector table

because, until a stack is defined, the 68000 cannot deal with any other type of exception. Once the stack pointer has been set up, the reset exception vector is loaded into the program counter and processing continues normally. The reset exception vector is, of course, the initial (or 'cold start') entry point into the operating system.

There is yet another difference between the reset vector and all other exception vectors. The reset exception vector and the intial value of the supervisor stack pointer both lie in the supervisor program space, denoted by SP in Table 1. All other exception vectors lie in supervisor data space.

USING THE EXCEPTION TABLE

In any 68000 system, an exception vector table must be maintained in memory. Although the complete table is 512 words (1024 byte) long, it is not necessary to fill it entirely with exception vectors. For example, if the system does not implement vectored interrupts, the memory space from $00 0100 to $00 03FF does not need to be populated with user interrupt vectors. It is a good idea to reserve the memory space $00 0000 to $00 03FF for the exception vector table unless forced to do otherwise, even if the whole of the table is not being used. All unused vectors can be preset to the spurious exception handling routine vector. This approach is in line with the philosophy of always providing a recovery mechanism for events which could possibly happen, and which would cause the system to crash if not adequately catered for.

The 8-bit microprocessor also has its own vector table; these contain relatively few vectors corresponding to the limited exception handling facilities of most 8-bit devices. The table is invariably maintained in the same ROM that holds the processor's operating system or monitor. An advantage of putting exception vectors in ROM is that the table is always there immediately after power up, but a disadvantage is its inflexibility. Once a table is in ROM, the vectors cannot be modified to suit changing conditions. In practice, whenever a vector has to

appropriate exception vector is to be found at memory location 8 × 4 = 32 = $20. Therefore, whenever a privilege violation occurs, the CPU reads the longword at location $20 and loads it into its program counter.

Although there are normally two words of memory space devoted to each 32-bit exception vector, as stated above, the reset exception (vector number 0) is a special case. The 32-bit longword at address $00 0000 is not the address of the reset handling routine, but the initial value of the supervisor stack pointer. The actual reset exception vector is at address $00 0004. Thus the reset exception takes four words of memory instead of the usual two.

The first operation performed by the 68000 following a reset is to load the system stack pointer. This is important

be variable, 8-bit processors use a vector pointing to another table in read/write memory containing the actual exception handling vector.

As the 68000 is so much more sophisticated than 8-bit devices and a dynamic or flexible response is sometimes required for the treatment of exception handling routines, the exception vector table is frequently held in read/write memory rather than in ROM. The operating system, held either in ROM or loaded from disc, sets up the exception vector table early in the initialization process following a reset.

A problem here is the reset vector. The two things that *must* be in ROM are the reset vector and the system monitor or bootstrap loader. Clearly, when the system is powered up and the RESET* input asserted, the reset exception vector and supervisor stack pointer, loaded from $00 0004 and $00 0000 respectively, must be in ROM. At first sight, it might be thought that it is necessary to place the whole exception vector table in ROM, as it is not possible to get a four-word ROM just for the reset vector, and a (512 − 4)-word read/write memory for the rest of the table. Hardware designers have solved the problem by locating the exception vector table in read/write memory and overlaying this with ROM whenever an access in the range $00 0000 to $00 0007 is made.

Consider a situation in which 4 kbyte of memory in the range $00 0000–$00 0FFF are provided by read/write memory. As explained later, the region of RAM at $00 0000–$00 0007 cannot be accessed by the processor. Read/write memory extending from $00 0008 to $00 03FF holds the exception vector table, which is loaded with vectors as dictated by the operating system. The remaining read/write memory from $00 0400 to $00 0FFF, is not restricted in use, and is freely available to the user or the operating system.

The 4 kbyte of memory space from $00 1000 to $00 1FFF is populated by ROM. The first 8 byte of this ROM, from $00 1000 to $00 1007, contains the reset vectors. It is necessary to arrange the hardware of the 68000 system so that a read access to the reset vectors automatically fetches them from the ROM rather than the read/write memory. One way of achieving this is demonstrated by the circuit in Figure 3. The read/write memory and ROM elements are supplied by conventional 2k × 8 bit chips, and their circuitry is entirely straightforward. Read/write memory is selected when CSRAM* is active low, and ROM when CSROM* is active low. Whenever an access is made to the region $00 0000–$00 0007, the output of IC6 (RVEC*) goes active low. The effect of this is to deselect the read/write memory and to select the ROM containing the reset vectors.

EXCEPTION PROCESSING

The 68000 responds to an exception in four identifiable phases.

In phase one, the processor makes a temporary internal copy of the status register and modifies the current status register ready for exception processing. This involves setting the S bit and clearing the T bit (ie

trace bit). The S bit is set because all exception processing takes place in the supervisor mode. The T bit is cleared because it is undesirable to have the processor in the trace mode during exception processing. (The trace mode forces an exception after the execution of each instruction. If the T bit were set, an instruction would trigger a trace exception which would, in turn, cause a trace exception after the first instruction of the trace handling routine had been executed. In this way an infinite series of exceptions would be generated.) Two specific types of exception have a further effect on the contents of the status word. After a reset, the interrupt mask bits are automatically set to indicate an interrupt priority of level 7. An interrupt causes the interrupt priority to be set to the same value as the interrupt currently being processed.

In phase two, the vector number corresponding to the exception being processed is determined. Apart from interrupts, the vector number is generated internally by the 68000 according to the exception type. If the exception is an interrupt, the interrupting device places the vector number on data lines D00–D07 of the processor data bus during the interrupt acknowledge cycle, signified by a function code (FC2, FC1, FC0) of 1, 1, 1. Once the processor has determined the vector number, it multiplies it by four to extract the location of the exception processing routine within the exception vector table.

In phase three, the current 'CPU context' is saved on the system stack. The CPU context is all the information required by the CPU to return to normal processing after an exception. Phase three of the exception processing is complicated by the fact that the 68000 divides exceptions into two categories, and saves different amounts of information according to the nature of the exception. The information saved by the 68000 is called the 'most volatile portion of the current processor context', and is saved in a data structure called the exception stack frame.

Figure 4 shows the structure of the exception stack frame. Note that exceptions are classified into three groups. The information saved during group 1 or group 2 exceptions is only the program counter (two words) and the status register, temporarily saved during phase one. This is the minimum of information required by the processor to restore itself to the state it was in prior to the exception.

The three groups of exception are categorized in Table 2. A group 0 exception originates from hardware errors (the address error has all the characteristics of a bus error but is generated internally by the 68000) and often indicates that something has gone seriously wrong with the system. For this reason the information saved in the stack frame corresponding to a group 0 exception is more detailed than that for groups 1 and 2. Figure 4b shows the stack frame of group 0 exceptions.

The additional information saved in the stack frame by a group 0 exception is a copy of the first word of the instruction being processed at the time of the exception and the 32-bit address that was being accessed by the aborted memory access cycle. The third new item saved is a 5-bit value giving the function code which was displayed on FC2, FC1 and FC0 when the exception

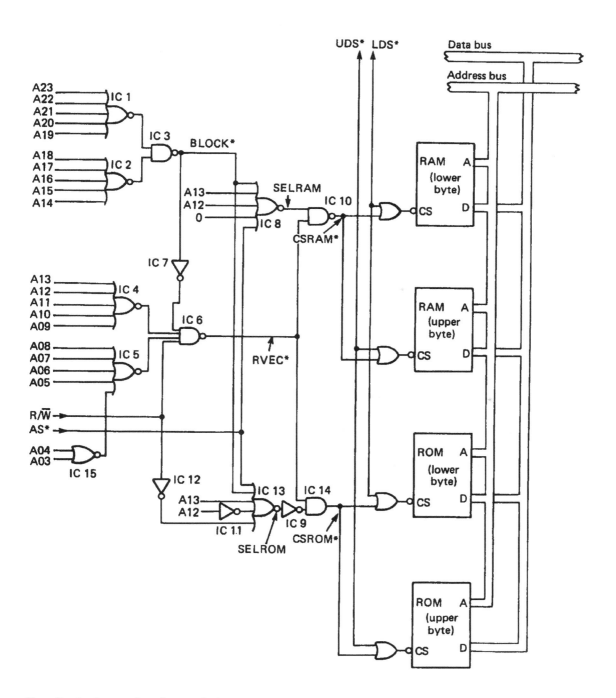

Figure 3.   Implementation of an overlaid reset vector

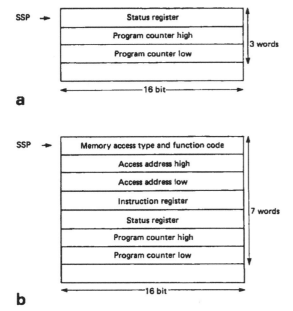

SSP →

Status register
Program counter high
Program counter low

3 words

←——— 16 bit ———→

a

SSP →

Memory access type and function code
Access address high
Access address low
Instruction register
Status register
Program counter high
Program counter low

7 words

←——— 16 bit ———→

b

Figure 4. Stack frames: a, for group 1 and group 2 exceptions; b, for group 0 exceptions

occurred, together with an indication of whether the processor was executing a read or a write cycle, and whether is was processing an instruction or not. This is diagnostic information which may be used by the operating system when dealing with the cause of the exception.

The fourth and final phase of the exception processing sequence consists of a single operation — the loading of the program counter with the 32-bit address pointed at by the exception vector. Once this has been done, the processor continues executing instructions normally.

When an exception handling routine has been run to completion, the instruction 'return from exception' (RTE) is executed to restore the processor to the state it was in prior to the exception. RTE is a privileged instruction and has the effect of restoring the status register and program counter from the values saved on the system stack. The contents of the program counter and status register, just

Table 2. Exception grouping according to type and priority

Group	Exception type	Time at which processing begins
0	Reset Bus error Address error	Exception processing begins within two clock cycles
1	Trace Interrupt Illegal op. code Privilege	Exception processing begins before the next instruction
2	TRAP TRAPV CHK Divide by zero	Exception processing is by normal instruction execution

prior to the execution of the RTE, are lost. RTE cannot be used after a group 0 exception to execute a return.

The second part of this paper, to be published in *Microprocessors Microsyst.* Vol 10 No 5 (June 1986), looks at the way in which interrupt handling is actually implemented in the 68000.

Alan Clements obtained an honours degree in electronics at the University of Sussex, UK, in 1971 and a doctorate from Loughborough University, UK, in 1976. During the two years he spent at Loughborough University as a research fellow, he studied the application of microprocessor technology to adaptive equalizers for distorted digital signals. In 1977 he joined the Department of Computer Science at Teesside Polytechnic, UK. In the last few years, he has devoted much of his spare time to writing. His first book, Microprocessor systems design and construction, *was published in 1982 and this was followed by* Principles of computer hardware *in 1985.*

Transputer communication link

Point-to-point communication links are better able to support the high level of integration offered in transputer systems than are conventional backplane buses. **Richard Taylor** explains the operation of these links

The transputer communication link is a new standard for system interconnection. It uses the capabilities of VLSI to offer simple, easy-to-use and cheap interconnection for computer systems. This paper describes the transputer's communications link and the considerations which have influenced its design. The advantages of the link are shown in a conventional application. The link adaptor, which interfaces a communications link to the outside world, is introduced. Inmos makes two types of link adaptor. Each is described with example applications.

microsystems   transputers   communication links

The idea of a backplane bus as an open standard for system interconnection is more than 15 years old. In that time enormous advances have been made in silicon fabrication — the standard RAM has grown from 256 bit to 256 kbit for example. However, although there are now a great variety of backplane bus standards, they have not made the same progress in offering increased capabilities and performance. Moreover, because buses are parallel they have not been able to use the higher levels of integration offered in silicon.

The transputer communication link is a new standard for system interconnection. It uses the capabilities of VLSI to offer simple, easy-to-use and cheap interconnection for computer systems. The link is a fundamental component of, and was developed as part of, the transputer architecture[1, 2]. The transputer is a single VLSI device with memory, processor and communications links for direct connection to other transputers. It is a programmable component which enables systems to be constructed from a collection of transputers that operate concurrently and communicate through links (Figure 1).

HARDWARE ISSUES

In a system constructed from integrated circuits (ICs) much of the physical bulk arises from connections between devices. The size of the package for an IC device is determined more by the number of connection pins than by the size of the device itself. In addition, the connections between devices on a printed circuit board consume a considerable amount of space. The speed of communication between electronic devices is optimized by the use of one-directional signal wires, each connecting only two devices. If many devices are connected by a shared bus, the electrical problems of driving the bus require that the speed of signal propagation is reduced. Additional control logic and wiring is required to control bus sharing.

To provide maximum speed with minimal wiring, the transputer uses point-to-point serial communication links. Communication is synchronized to prevent loss of data and simplify programming, particularly when devices of different speeds communicate. To provide synchronization, each communication link requires an acknowledge signal be sent in the opposite direction to data. The advantages of synchronized communication almost certainly justify this cost. A transputer link therefore consists of two signal wires to provide one communication channel in each direction. Each signal wire

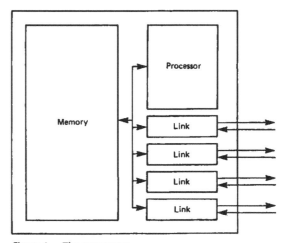

Figure 1.   The transputer

Inmos Ltd, Whitefriars, Lewins Mead, Bristol BS1 2NP, UK.

0141–9331/86/04211–05 $03.00 © 1986 Butterworth & Co. (Publishers) Ltd

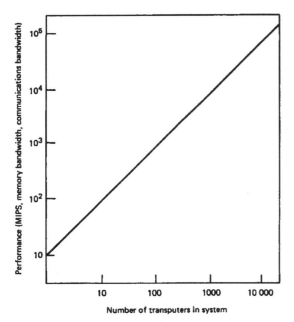

Figure 2. *Transputer system performance*

uses a simple protocol to multiplex the data on one channel and the synchronizing acknowledge signals on the other.

Transputers communicate only through links, allowing the memory to be dedicated entirely for use by the processor. Integration of the processor and memory in the same device results in a considerable performance gain as memory access does not require communication outside the device. The choice of point-to-point communication links means that a system can be constructed from an arbitrary number of transputers. As the number of transputers in a system increases, the total processing power, memory bandwidth and communication bandwidth of the system grows proportionally (Figure 2).

SOFTWARE ISSUES

OCCAM is a programming language designed in conjunction with the transputer[3, 4]. The hardware is designed to allow systems to be constructed from many transputers; the main design objective of OCCAM therefore is to provide a language for programming a network of transputers. Another important design objective is that the same concurrent programming techniques can be used for programming both a single computer and a network of transputers.

OCCAM enables a system to be described as a collection of concurrent processes which communicate with each other and with peripheral devices through named channels. An OCCAM program is built from three primitive processes, which are

$v := e$	assign expression e to variable v
$c \, ! \, e$	output expression e on channel c
$c \, ? \, v$	input a value from channel c to variable v

The primitive processes are combined by constructors to form constructs. There are three main constructors, which differ in the way in which their component processes are executed

SEQ	execute component processes one after another
PAR	execute component processes together
ALT	execute the first ready component process

IF and WHILE constructs are also provided. A construct is itself a process and may be used as a component of another construct.

The components of a parallel construct are concurrent processes which may only communicate via channels. A channel provides a communication path between two concurrent processes. Communication is synchronized and takes place when both the inputting and outputting processes are ready. The data to be output is then copied from the outputting process to the inputting process, and both processes continue.

As an OCCAM channel is point-to-point, synchronized and unbuffered it can be implemented without needing a message queue, a process queue or a message buffer. Data is copied from the outputting process to the inputting process when this is necessary for communication between transputers. Microcode is used to make copying fast within a transputer.

In many respects, OCCAM is the assembly language for a network of transputers. There is a one-to-one relationship between concurrent processes and transputers, and between OCCAM channels and transputer links.

IMPLEMENTATION

A link between two transputers provides a pair of OCCAM channels, one in each direction, and is implemented by connecting a link interface on one transputer to a link interface on another using two one-directional signal lines (Figure 3). Each signal line carries data and control information.

Communication through a link involves a simple protocol (Figure 4) which provides the synchronized communication of OCCAM. The use of a protocol providing for the transmission of an arbitrary sequence of bytes allows transputers of different wordlength to be connected. Each message is transmitted as a sequence of single byte communications, requiring only the presence of a single byte buffer in the receiving transputer to ensure that no information is lost. Each byte is transmitted as a start bit followed by a '1' bit, the eight data bits and a stop bit. After transmitting a data byte, the sender waits until an acknowledge is received, consisting of a start bit followed

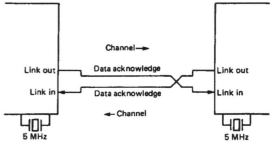

Figure 3. *Transputer links*

Data packet

Acknowledge packet

Figure 4.   Link protocol

by a '0' bit. The acknowledge signifies both that a process was able to receive the acknowledged byte, and that the receiving link is able to receive another byte. The sending link reschedules the sending process only after the acknowledge for the final byte of the message has been received. Data bytes for one channel and acknowledges for the other channel are multiplexed on each signal line.

The transputer external clock is nominally 5 MHz. For compatibility, all future transputers will use this same frequency. This clock is used to generate two internal clocks, one for the links and the other for the processor. The external clocks at either end of a link must be the same to within strict frequency tolerances, but there are no other constraints, so separate clocks can be used if required.

Data is transmitted at a universal data rate that is double the clock frequency. Data can also be transmitted at a faster rate which is related to the processor clock. While data is transmitted synchronously to its clock, reception is asynchronous. Advantages of the clocking scheme are

- a transputer has a relatively slow external clock which is independent of the processor performance
- the asynchronous link protocol removes the need to generate and distribute high frequency deskewed clocks
- circuit design is simplified; the only requirement for reliable link operation is that the input clock frequencies of interconnected devices are within 400 ppm of one another.

Example

Design of the links is best motivated by a simple example. This example is a common configuration of microprocessor components which go to make up a workstation or high performance personal computer. Figure 5 shows three transputer components, a disc controller, a graphics controller and a 32-bit transputer connected by standard communications links. The 32-bit processor runs applications programs; the other two transputer components are dedicated to controlling their respective peripherals.

In a conventional system a common bus would be used for system interconnection. It would also be used by the applications processor for accessing memory. In a transputer-based system each processor has its own local memory, and links are used for system interconnection.

Using links to connect the system has a number of design and performance advantages

- Using just two line connections simplifies board layout. A link consumes less area than a traditional bus.
- System bottlenecks are removed by having many parallel paths through which data is routed. For instance, the disc controller can transfer pictures to the graphics controller without affecting the applications processor.
- Systems can be built easily with transputers of different word length. In this example, a 32-bit transputer is connected to 16-bit device controllers.

A further advantage of the link is that it is programmed in a high level language. The workstation is described and programmed in OCCAM at all levels from the overall structure down to the details of the device drivers. Concurrency corresponds to the implementation which is functionally distributed over the three transputers. Communication over channels corresponds to connections by links. Because the connections to peripherals are channels, device drivers can be written in OCCAM.

Apart from the link interfaces, a transputer has a separate external memory interface. The 32-bit transputer has a 32-bit multiplexed path for data and addresses and generates all the timing strobes necessary to access static or dynamic RAM. Thus the memory interface needs a minimum of external 'glue' components. Separation of the interfaces is beneficial because

- each interface is optimized for its purpose; the memory interface is dedicated to accessing memory while peripherals and other transputers are connected to links
- each interface has a high bandwidth; for example, a link interface, whose design is not constrained by existing standards, has a throughput of 10 Mbit s^{-1} through two pins
- a dedicated interface can be designed so that it needs few external components and is easy to use.

THE LINK ADAPTOR

The link adaptor is a simple peripheral chip which turns an Inmos serial communication link into a parallel link, ie it is a serial-to-parallel and parallel-to-serial converter. The serial side is a standard Inmos communication link which uses three pins: data in, data out and clock. Inmos makes two versions of the link adaptor which have different parallel sides. These are the C001, which has separate parallel input and output ports, and C002, which has a bidirectional port.

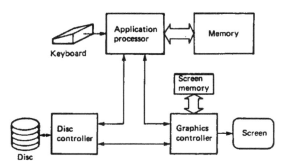

Figure 5.   Application example

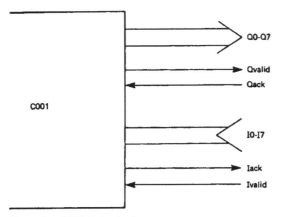

Figure 6. C001 link adaptor

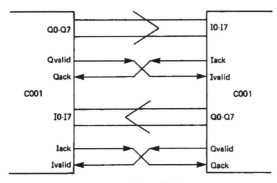

Figure 7. Two connected C001 link adaptors

C001 link adaptor

The C001 converts between an Inmos serial link and two fully handshaken byte-wide interfaces (Figure 6). One interface is for data coming from the serial link and one for data going to the serial link. Transfers may proceed in both directions at the same time.

IValid and IAck provide a simple two-wire handshake. Data is presented to the link adaptor on I0–I7, and IValid is taken high to commence the handshake. The adaptor transmits the data to the serial link, and acknowledges receipt of the data on IAck when it has received the acknowledge signal from the serial link and all the data bits have been transmitted. IValid is then taken low, and the link adaptor completes the handshake by taking IAck low.

The link adaptor receives data from the serial link, presents it on Q0–Q7, and takes QValid high to commence the handshake. Receipt of the data is acknowledged on QAck, and the link adaptor then transmits an acknowledgement on the serial link. The link adaptor takes QValid low and the handshake is completed by taking QAck low.

The simplest use of the C001 is connection to simple I/O devices such as switches and LEDs, or for controlling hardware via counters and latches. Two link adaptors, directly connected via their byte-wide interfaces and inserted into an Inmos serial link (Figure 7), will correctly maintain the handshaken link protocol. Uses for this

include communication between transputers running at different clock frequencies and monitoring activity on the link.

C002 link adaptor

The C002 link adaptor (Figure 8) provides an interface between an Inmos serial link and a bidirectional bus, via an 8-bit interface. It has status/control and data registers for both input and output accessed via the byte-wide interface. The C002 enables transputers to communicate with conventional peripheral controllers and microprocessor systems.

The C002 is controlled at the parallel interface by read/write status/control registers, and by read/write data registers. Two interrupt lines are provided: one indicates that the link adaptor is ready to output a byte to the link, and the other indicates that it is holding a byte that it has read from the link.

The 8-bit data path can connect directly in small systems, but in larger systems a bus transceiver must be included to drive the bus load. The only external circuitry required in a small system is to generate the control lines for chip select, read/write and reset (Figure 9). The device can be polled by the microprocessor, in which case no further hardware is required. An alternative solution is to connect the input-interrupt and output-interrupt lines of the C002 to either the interrupt system of the micro or to a DMA controller. Transfer is then handled by the operating system kernel or by hardware, and is transparent to the user program.

Link adaptors do not need to be used in conjunction with transputers. An interesting application is to use two

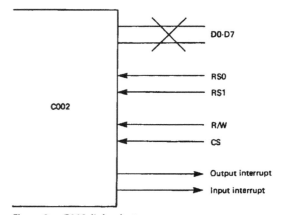

Figure 8. C002 link adaptor

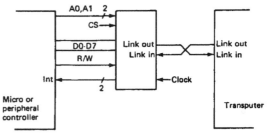

Figure 9. C002 connection

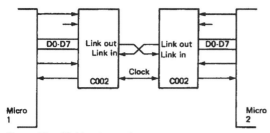

Figure 10. Linking two micros

link adaptors connected via their links to provide a high-speed connection between two traditional microprocessor or standard buses (Figure 10).

REFERENCES

1   **Barron, I M et al** 'The Transputer' *Electronics* Vol 17 (Nov. 1983) pp 109–115

2   *Transputer reference manual* Inmos Ltd (1985)
3   *Inmos: OCCAM programming manual* Prentice-Hall (1984)
4   **May, M D and Taylor, R J B** 'OCCAM — an overview' *Microprocessors Microsyst.* Vol 8 No 2 (March 1984) pp 73–79

Richard Taylor took a first degree in computer science from Manchester University, UK. He worked on protection in operating systems at Cambridge University, UK, and on distributed systems at Warwick University, UK, before joining Inmos in 1979. Since then he has worked on OCCAM and the transputer and their applications.

Microcomputer for the dynamics laboratory

James Martin and Jaeho Kim explain the design of a microcomputer
optimized for control tasks in dynamics experiments

*A microcomputer developed for use in a dynamics
laboratory of a mechanical engineering department is
discussed. The microcomputer is based on the Motorola
6802 microprocessor and includes an EPROM burning
circuit for flexibility. Special mathematical routines have
been developed for the computer. These routines are
designed for use with 4-digit floating-point numbers to gain
speed with minimal sacrifice of accuracy. The special
routines include a data approximation and smoothing
routine for signal processing, and routines to compute
frequently used mathematical functions. The routines are
written in 6802 assembly language and are stored in
2 kbyte of external EPROM. An application of the microcomputer used as a component in a speed controller is
also discussed.*

microsystems   laboratory instrumentation   control

In laboratory R&D experiments a computer is often
desirable to improve the speed and accuracy of measurements. At the New Jersey Institute of Technology a
situation arose where a low-cost computer with moderate
processing speed was needed for the dynamics laboratory.
Since dedicated personal computers or minicomputers
for realtime control are expensive, it was decided to build
a microcomputer to provide the required capabilities.
Development of the microcomputer would also provide
experience that would be invaluable in teaching
mechanical engineers how to exploit microprocessor-
based instruments in mechanical engineering work.
Figure 1 shows a block diagram of the microcomputer
developed.

REQUIREMENTS OF THE MICROCOMPUTER

For the dynamics laboratory the microcomputer needed
to

- be portable
- be readily modifiable to read and display the outputs
  of various sensors and devices used in the laboratory
- have an analogue output
- have a data processing capability with minimum
  sacrifice of speed
- be able to process floating-point numbers: 4-digit
  floating-point numbers were used for the first application of the present 6802-based unit
- receive input from a keyboard or terminal.

HARDWARE DETAILS

CPU control

Control is provided by a 4 MHz clock and reset circuits,
CPU address outputs and read/write (R/W) lines.
Implementation of each control is by the techniques
presented in Reference 1.

RAM

A 128 byte RAM on the CPU is supplemented by 1 kbyte
of external RAM. The RAM on the CPU is currently the
only RAM storage used by the main system monitor
program, data processing routines and control program
developed for the initial system application.

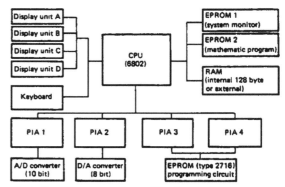

Figure 1.   Microcomputer architecture

Mechanical Engineering Department, New Jersey Institute of Technology,
200 Central Avenue, Newark, NJ 07102, USA

0141–9331/86/04216–06 $03.00 © 1986 Butterworth & Co. (Publishers) Ltd

Display system

The display system employs 14 TIL 308s and consists of four separate units. Two of these each have four 308s to give a 4-digit display. The two other units each have three 308s. The four units are accessible at one of eight addresses A200-A207, decoded by a 74138.

Keyboard

A standard ASCII keyboard with parallel data output is employed as the main input device. The keyboard is accessable at address A000 through a 74241 data buffer. An 'enable' signal for the data buffer is generated using the address lines, a 7442 decoder and a 7427 NOR gate. The keyboard is full ASCII, but only alphanumeric keys are recognized by the system monitor program. The keys 'A', 'B', 'C', 'D', 'E' and 'F' are used for hexadecimal character input. When used, other alphabetic keys are encoded by the monitor program as command keys.

A/D converter

An Analog Devices A/D converter AD571JD, a 10-bit converter with 25 μs conversion time, is interfaced by one of four 6821 peripheral interface adapters (PIAs). The converter is wired for bipolar operation. Data ports DB0–DB7 of the converter are connected to PA0–PA7 of PIA 1; DB8 and DB9 are connected to PB0 and PB1 of PIA 1, accessible at addresses A100-A103. PIA 1 controls the operation of the converter through its CA1 and CA2 control lines. CA2 is configured as an output by the PIA 1 initializing program. By writing 0 at CRA-3 of the control register A of PIA 1, CA2 is made to drive the conversion start input of the converter low, starting A/D conversion. On completion, the converter sends a 'data ready' signal to PIA 1 by driving CA1 low through the converter's Data Ready output.

D/A converter

An Analog Devices AD558, an 8-bit D/A converter, is interfaced by a second 6821 (PIA 2). The data bus DB0–DB7, is connected to PB0–PB7 of PIA 2. The operation of the converter is controlled by the CB2 output of PIA 2. The output of the D/A converter is wired for 0–10 V operation.

Other outputs

Port A of PIA 2 operates remote on-off switches which are used to configure a Wheatstone bridge, one of the units in a speed controller for dynamic strain sensing. The initial application of the microcomputer was as a component of the speed controller.

An EPROM (2716) burning circuit was provided by using two other 6821s (PIA 3 and PIA 4). This circuit is intended for expansion, alteration and generation of monitor programs for this and other 6800-based controllers.

Hardware operating characteristics

When operating at the minimum clock frequency the microcomputer described can receive, process and display data in 45 ms and can sample (at the A/D converter) and convert 10-bit data to floating point form in 100 μs. The basic system, when used with a faster microprocessor, eg 68B00, 68B02 or 68B08, and compatible supporting chips can perform the display operation in half this time.

The microcomputer can also compare received data with theoretical results calculated from approximation and ramp (linear interpolation) routines. The level of sophistication in developing theoretical results for comparison with received data is limited but significant.

SOFTWARE

System software is set in 4 kbyte of ROM in two 2716 EPROMs: one EPROM contains the unit monitor program; the other contains the maths library (a series of programs which execute all calculations). This arrangement was dictated by the sizes of the monitor program, of the maths library and of the 2716 chip — the monitor program and maths library combined were too large for a single 2716 but could be readily contained in the two.

Since the monitor program provides the computer essentials and the maths library provides the computer personality, to provide for a flexible computer personality it was decided to store the library on a separate chip.

The monitor program and maths library begin at addresses F800 and F000, respectively. Using this arrangement, address lines 14 and 15 are used to decode either the monitor programs or the library routines; addresses above F800 and F000 are used to identify monitor subprograms or library subroutines.

For the initial application of the microcomputer all necessary code was generated by the onboard firmware. As the authors' command of the potential applications for the controller and the available resources for controller development has grown, the need to make provisions for configuring the controller to accept code generated by a host computer has become clear, and modifications directed to this end are now in progress.

Monitor program

The monitor contains

- an initialization procedure
- keyboard decoding programs for interpreting
  - ○ numercal information as hexadecimal instructions
  - ○ input from the keyboard, in the form of a single stroke of a letter-labelled key, as a command instruction
- a display control program
- A/D and D/A servicing programs
- a remote on-off switching program
- other routines for program development and EPROM programming.

Maths library

Routines of the maths library handle all arithmetic

operations in floating-point form. All numbers are handled in 3 byte form (2 byte for the mantissa and 1 byte for the exponent) giving 0.003% accuracy. This Arrangement has been made to suit the available A/D converters and to provide the desired 4-digit decimal accuracy. If an integer result is necessary, a routine from the library converts the floating-point source to a fixed-point form.

Approximations used by the computer in control functions are calculated by one of the maths library routines (using an optimal polynomial evaluation routine[2]). Data smoothing and error compensation calculations are also performed by routines from the maths library. These routines are described in Figures 2 and 3.

PERFORMANCE EVALUATION THROUGH SIMULATION

A dynamic strain measuring experiment was introduced in the dynamics laboratory of NJIT in 1975. In this experiment strain at a point in an eccentrically loaded rotating beam (Figure 4) is sensed, amplified and displayed. Since the centre of mass of the end masses and the centre line of

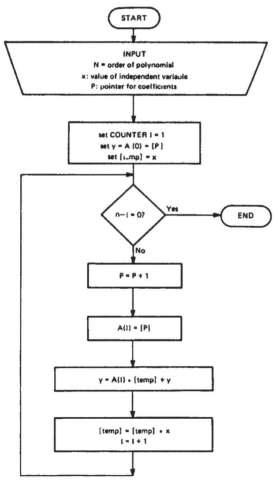

Figure 2. POLY flowchart (*polynomial calculation:* $y = A(O) + \ldots A(n) * x^{**} (n - 1)$)

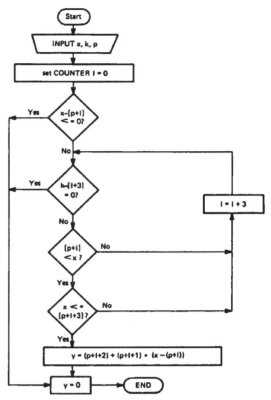

Figure 3. RAMP flowchart (*piecewise linear compensation* $\sum_{i=0}^{k} A(i) + B(i) * [x - C(i) * (U(C(i)) - U(C(i + 1)))]$, *where x is an independent variable, k is number of intervals, p is pointer for coefficients*

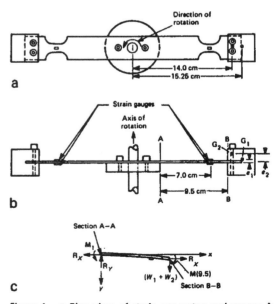

Figure 4. **a** *Plan view of strain generator and sensor,* **b** *cross-section of strain generator and sensor,* **c** *free body diagram of strain sensor*

the supporting beam are not colinear, the sensed strain can be uniaxial or combined strain[3]. The strain sensing and amplifying circuit is shown in Figure 5. With the shunt switches open the sensed strain is uniaxial; with the shunt switches closed the strain is combined flexural and uniaxial strain.

The dynamic strain measuring unit was chosen to be the first application of the microcomputer controller, in a speed control experiment. In this application the controller reads the current combined strain, computes the current frequency of applied strain in revolutions per minute (rpm) from the combined strain, compares the current rpm with the rpm supplied from the keyboard and outputs, via the D/A converter, a signal that increases or decreases, as appropriate, the current rpm. This process repeats until the rpm computed from the combined strain is within 20 rpm of the value supplied from the keyboard.

Simulation results

A routine was written to simulate the system performance of the dynamic strain measuring unit and controller. The output of this routine is shown in Figure 6b. The strain variations that develop during the change in rpm rate are shown in Figure 6a. Figure 6c shows the result of a least-squares determination of the relation between rpm and combined (ie total or ce) strain, a relation that is used in the simulation program. Figure 7 is a flow chart of the simulation program. The output from the simulation program shows that the controller will accept analogue signals in the range −5 V to +5 V, compute selected performance characteristics and output appropriate adjustments of the controlled parameters. Coefficients in the approximating polynomials and ramp functions, used for interpolating in error compensating procedures, are used to select performance characteristics calculated by the maths library routines.

SUMMARY

A low-cost 6802-based microcomputer employing simple hardware has been developed for use as a component in a number of dynamics laboratory controllers and measuring instruments. The software of the microcomputer maths library, especially the polynomial evaluation and ramp or interpolation routines, is effective in generating some functions and in data smoothing, and enables use of the computer in situations where more expensive computers

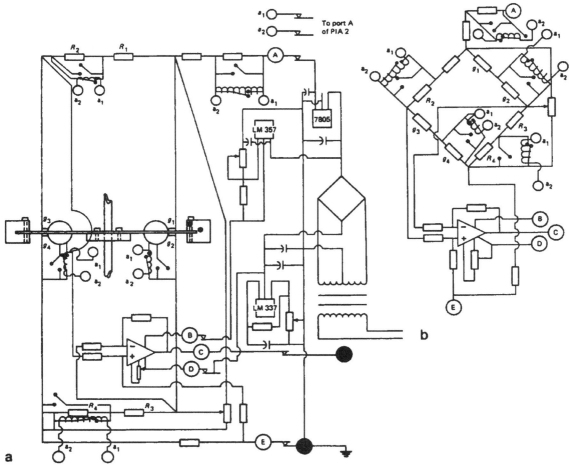

a
b

Figure 5. **a** *Strain generator, sensor and amplifier with power supply,* **b** *circuit of strain sensor and amplifier*

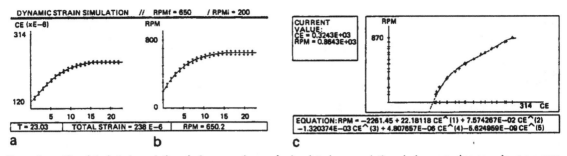

Figure 6. **a** *Simulated strain variation during rpm change,* **b** *simulated rpm variation during rpm change,* **c** *least squares approximation of ce, rpm relation*

are routinely employed.

The maths library, stored in 2 kbyte of ROM with addresses F000–F7FF, can be accessed as subroutines from any 6800, 6802 or 6808-based system permitting extensive use of the software.

REFERENCES

1   *The complete microcomputer data library* Motorola Technical Information Center, Motorola Semiconductor Production Inc, Phoenix, AZ, USA (1978)

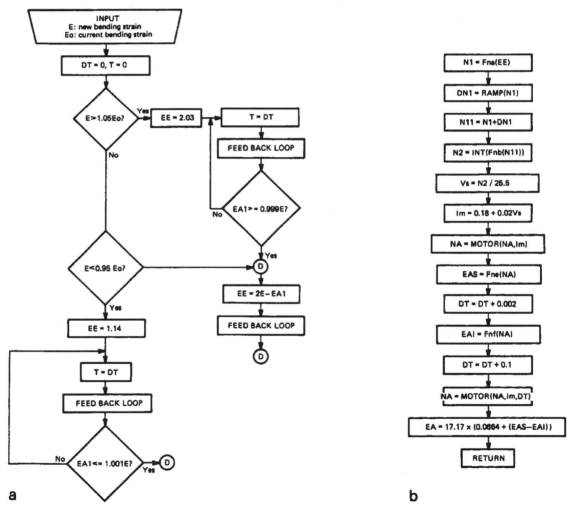

Figure 7. **a** *Flow chart of main simulation program,* **b** *flow chart of subroutine for simulation program*

2 Carnahan, B and Wilkes, J O *Digital computing and numerical methods* John Wiley, NY, USA (1973) p 291

3 Mott, R L *Machine elements in mechanical design* E. Merrill Publishers, Columbus, OH, USA (1985) p 66

James L Martin joined the mechanical engineering faculty of Newark College of Engineering in 1965. He has lectured courses primarily in mechanisms, machine design and solid mechanics, and has done research in motion measurements and human blood flow. In the last seven years his activities with respect to motion measurement have involved increasing study and application of ICs and microcomputers.

Jaeho Kim holds a BSME from Hanyang University, Korea, and an MSME from the New Jersey Institute of Technology. At present he is a doctoral student at NJIT. In Korea he was involved in a jet engine overhaul and manufacturing project. His interests are microprocessor application and manufacturing, CAD/CAM, and optimization of numerical methods for microsystems. Currently he is developing an IBM PC based CAM program using graphics for laser-based contour cutting tools.

Flexible interface based on the peripheral interface structure

Instead of interfacing a microcomputer at the processor bus level, a PIA port can be used as the basis of a flexible interface structure. **Malcolm Taylor** shows how

A technique whereby a single port of a peripheral interface adaptor (PIA) is used as the basis of a flexible interface structure is described. In this way, all peripheral interfacing may be accomplished through the single PIA port. The technique finds application in the connection of interface units to desk-top microcomputers where it may not be appropriate to interface at the processor bus level. Interface modules designed in this way will be compatible with any microcomputer offering a single PIA port.

microsystems   interfacing   peripheral interface adaptor

Development of interface modules can be accomplished at either the microcomputer bus level[1] or at the equipment level, utilizing standards such as the S100 bus and IEEE 488 respectively. The peripheral interface adaptor (PIA) or programmable peripheral interface (PPI) may also be applied as the standard interface at the equipment level. PIAs and PPIs offer two or three 8-bit bidirectional data ports and associated control signals depending on the particular manufacturer, eg MOS 6520[2] or Intel 8255[3]. For the MOS 6520 PIA, two 8-bit ports, A and B, are available. Port A has bidirectional data lines described as PA0–7 and two control lines CA1 and CA2. Port B is described in a similar way.

The basic application of PIA ports is for the connection of byte-oriented action/status devices, such as printers. More flexible structures, facilitating the connection of many interface modules to a single PIA port, can be developed with the addition of a small amount of external logic.

BCD INTERFACE UNIT

To consider the flexibility of applying a single PIA port to interface design, a binary coded decimal (BCD) interface will be considered as an example.

Simple output unit

Consider the requirement to connect 16 BCD output registers via a single PIA port. Figure 1 illustrates how this may be accomplished. The 8-bit data port is partitioned

Department of Computer Science, University of Liverpool, PO Box 147, Liverpool, L69 3BX, UK

into two output blocks, PA0–3 and PA4–7, to provide data (D0–3) and address (A0–3) highways respectively. Data is loaded into a particular 4-bit register by routing the strobe pulse generated on the CA2 control line through a 1-of-16 line decoder to the clock terminal (CLK) of the addressed register. The reset (RES) signal clears the register array on system power up.

Simple input unit

Figure 2 illustrates the method required to connect 16 BCD inputs. In this case the 8-bit data port is partitioned into an input section, PA0–3, and an output section, PA4–7, to provide the data and address highways respectively. Four 16-line input multiplexers are required to select a particular BCD character on the input data highway. This is effected when an enabling pulse is generated on the CA2 control line.

General input/output unit

In a realistic system it may be necessary to have a mix of several input and output modules. A simple solution

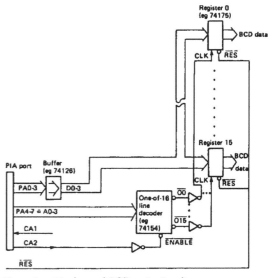

Figure 1.   16 channel BCD output unit

0141–9331/86/04222–04 $03.00 © 1986 Butterworth & Co. (Publishers) Ltd

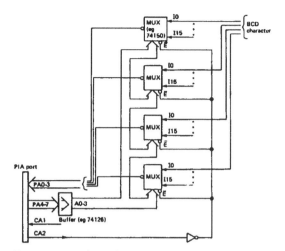

Figure 2.   16 channel BCD input unit

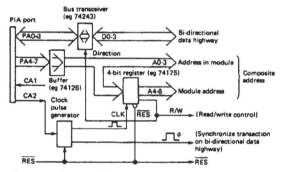

Figure 3.   System block diagram of general unit

would be to connect each individual unit to its own PIA port. A more flexible solution is illustrated in Figure 3 and connects up to eight input and eight output modules to a single PIA port.

The 8-bit data port is again partitioned into two equal sections: PA0–3 acts as a bidirectional highway (D0–3), and PA4–7 acts as a multiplexed address highway (A0–3). A 4-bit register is attached to the address highway; three bits provide the module address (A4–6) and the fourth bit acts as a read/write (R/W) control line to define the direction of the transaction on the data highway (logic 0 specifying output from the PIA port) and switch the bus transceiver accordingly. A composite 7-bit address is then defined by A0–3 and A4–6.

Pulses generated on the CA2 control line drive a clock pulse generator which produces the register strobe pulse and the data highway transaction synchronizing pulse φ. Figure 4a defines the state diagram of this logic. In state S0, CA2 is routed to C; in state S1, CA2 is routed to φ. The corresponding logic diagram is shown in Figure 4b.

The system timing diagrams for this arrangement are illustrated in Figure 5. The sequence of operations is first to load the module address and state of the R/W line into the 4-bit register with CA2 pulse 0, and then effect the data highway transaction with CA2 pulse 1. The relative operations and their timing are defined by assembler code running on the microcomputer to which the PIA port is attached.

The simple input and output modules described previously require some minor modifications to be compatible with this more flexible bus arrangement. In the case of the output module (Figure 1) the 1-of-16 line decoder would be enabled by Aw.R̄/W̄, where Aw is the module or base address derived from A4–6. In a similar way, the input unit (Figure 2) would require the 16-line input multiplexers to be enabled by Aw.R/W. φ. The outputs of the multiplexers would also require isolating

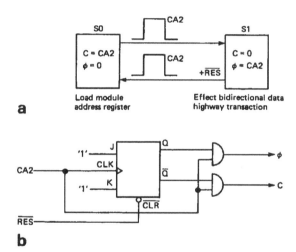

a

b

Figure 4.   a State diagram of clock pulse generation logic for the general unit, b clock pulse generation logic diagram

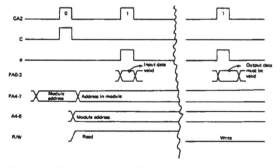

Figure 5.   System timing diagrams for read and write operations in the general unit

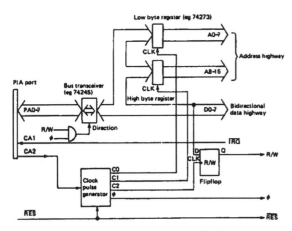

Figure 6. System block diagram of flexible interface structure

by tristate drivers since the data highway is bidirectional, and they would also be enabled by Aw.R/W. φ.

FLEXIBLE INTERFACE STRUCTURE

The basis of the structure is a 16-bit address highway, an 8-bit bidirectional data highway and two control signals: R/W and φ. Figure 6 illustrates the system block diagram that achieves this. The 8-bit data port provides the basis of the bidirectional data highway (D0–7). Two 8-bit registers are also attached to this highway to latch the multiplexed low and high order address bytes. The outputs of the two registers then form the address highway (A0–A15). A R/W flip-flop, also loaded from the data highway, defines the direction of the transaction on the data highway when φ is high.

A clock pulse generator provides the necessary clock pulses to load the two registers (C0 and C1), load the R/W flip-flop (C2) and effect the transaction on the data highway (φ). Figure 7 gives the state diagram of this logic. A 2-bit counter and a 2-to-4 line decoder form the basis of the generator.

The bus transceiver is normally set in its output mode (data from the PIA port to the data highway) and is only able to respond to the state of the R/W line (logic 0 defining a write transaction) when φ is active.

Figure 8 illustrates the system timing diagrams for the read and write transactions. The sequence of operations is

- load the low byte of the address with CA2 pulse 0
- load the high byte of the address with CA2 pulse 1
- load the R/W flip-flop with CA2 pulse 2
- effect the data highway read or write transaction with CA2 pulse 3

The structure of the software driving routine on the microcomputer to effect a write transaction is as follows (port A is already set to the output mode)

- load low byte of address: write low address byte to port A
  set CA2 high
  set CA2 low
- load high byte of address: write high address byte to port A
  set CA2 high
  set CA2 low
- load R/W flip-flop: write logic 0 to PA0
  set CA2 high
  set CA2 low
- write data byte to addressed location: write data byte to port A

  set CA2 high
  set CA2 low

The read transaction is similar in that the first two operations are concerned with the loading of the 2 byte address. The final two operations are

- load R/W flip-flop: write logic 1 to PA0
  set CA2 high
  set CA2 low
- read data byte from addressed location: set port A to input mode

  set CA2 high
  read data byte from port A
  set CA2 low
  set port A to output mode

In the case of the MOS 6520 PIA, the CA1 control line may be configured into an input mode such that on placing the line low a corresponding pin on the processor bus side of the PIA is also placed low to assert an interrupt request to the processor. This interrupt request is also maskable, under software control, within the PIA. It is therefore possible to provide a maskable interrupt request facility

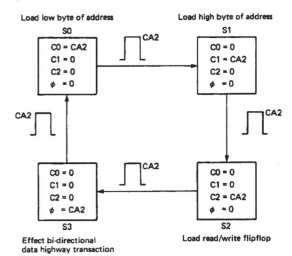

Figure 7. State diagram of clock pulse generation logic for the flexible interface

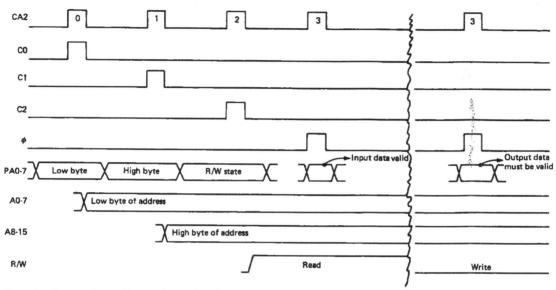

Figure 8.   System timing diagram for read and write operations in the flexible interface

(IRQ) by way of the CA1 control line. If more than one interrupt source is to be connected then an interrupt sorting module[1] will be required to generate the single interrupt IRQ. In this case it is necessary first to identify the source of the interrupting device by reading the status (address) contained in the sorting module and then use this information to activate the corresponding service routine.

The interface structure derived is similar to that available at the processor bus level, although the speed of transactions is reduced due to the multiplexed nature of the bidirectional data highway. Interface modules may be readily designed to conform to this interface specification.

CONCLUSION

A technique has been described whereby a single PIA port is used as the basis of a flexible interface structure. The technique may be applied in the connection of interface modules to desk-top microcomputers where a PIA port is the only available interfacing facility because it is not appropriate to interface at the processor bus level. Interface modules designed in this way are compatible with any microcomputer offering a single PIA port.

REFERENCES

1   **Zissos, D** *System design with microprocessors* Academic Press, New York, USA (1978)
2   *MCS 6500 microcomputer family hardware manual* MOS Technology (1976)
3   *Intel component data catalog* Intel Corp (1984)

Malcolm Taylor is a lecturer in the Department of Computer Science at Liverpool University, UK. He was previously employed as a hardware specialist (1976–1978) and then as a lecturer (1978–1982), both in the Computer Laboratory at Liverpool University. His research interests include microprocessor applications, medical computing and hardware design techniques. He holds a BSc in electrical engineering from Salford University, UK, as well as an MSc and PhD in digital electronics from Manchester University, UK.

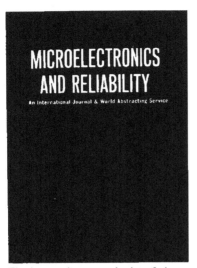

Pulse operating system textbook casts doubts on ADA

D Keeffe, G M Tomlinson, I C Wand
and A J Wand

'PULSE: an ADA-based distributed operating system' Academic Press, Orlando, FL, USA (1985) £15.50 pp xiii + 244

I have approached the review of this book unashamedly from the ADA point of view. My own interest is in the language, rather than in distributed operating systems, and I was encouraged that the authors had set themselves, as one of their goals, the assessment of the influence ADA has had on their design of Pulse. It is good that the first round of standard ADA textbooks is now being supplemented with books of a more specialist nature, such as this one.

ADA has now moved on from its initial definition phase. Validated compilers for the language do exist. Much of the embedded systems industry, particularly in the defence sector where ADA will be a prerequisite, is now taking the decision to use ADA for its systems. The industry is evaluating both ADA and ADA compilers and deciding how to map their applications onto the language.

Since this book represents an early case study of the use of ADA for a real system, I was interested in finding out the authors' views on whether the language features had helped them in the design and structuring of their operating system and, secondly, whether the tasking features of the language were found to be adequate and sufficiently efficient for programming a realtime system. ADA tasking in particular is now becoming a controversy, especially in applications of a time critical nature such as avionics where a very fast response to external stimuli and fast context switching are required.

The authors of this book criticize the ADA tasking model in several respects, eg the constant growth in program size when tasks are created dynamically, and the difficult compiler optimizations that are required (and not yet achieved by

any available compiler) to spot the conditions under which expensive task context switching can be removed.

In many ways, ADA has become part of the problem, rather than the solution to the perceived crisis in the software industry. The production of fast, good-code-quality compilers, rather than the solution of embedded systems problems, is still engaging the brains of most ADA experts. There is a strong temptation in the industry to get around the problems imposed by ADA by finding solutions outside the language, which is precisely what the DoD wanted to avoid through the compiler validation service.

The authors used the ADA compiler produced at York, which is only for a subset of the language. Generics, derived types and private types were unavailable to the team, which severely restricted their evaluation of the use of ADA. The authors make the interesting comment that they underestimated, as did most other compiler groups, the amount of effort that would be required to produce a compiler. They observe that the code quality generated by the York compiler is poor and that sophisticated optimization techniques such as Habermann–Nassi are required if task communication is to be made efficient.

The book itself presents the results of a five-year research programme into distributed systems. An operating system called Pulse, which is like Unix but is distributed across a network of personal computers, is discussed. The design and implementation of the distributed file system, combining the individual machines' disc storage into a single hierarchical file store, is described. The design and implementation of the kernel is presented as are its facilities for running user programs. These facilities are made available to the user program through a set of ADA system packages.

The authors state in the preface that the book assumes the reader has some familiarity with the ADA

language, and this is certainly true; any reader with less than a sound knowledge of the language would soon lose the thread of the argument. Statements are frequently made which would make no sense to a novice, and yet which serve no purpose to the specialist. For example

> 'Tasks are explicitly declared objects and can be created by the use of task access types and the "new" operation, or by declaration on task or scope entry.'

The book is well argued, weighing up the alternatives confronting the designers at each decision point. However, there are several minor annoying characteristics in the argument.

The argument is often presented superficially. The authors frequently justify their argument by recourse to a long list of references, without running through, even briefly, the arguments presented in those references. Thus the justification for structuring the operating system as a set of separate but cooperating ADA programs is made in one paragraph. If, as the authors state, the main problem is to do with the use of shared variables between tasks on processors without shared memory, then why use shared variables?

Obviously, a mechanism has to be provided for allowing separate user programs to communicate with each other, and the description in chapter 2 of 'medium' tasks acting as buffers between the user program and the kernel is interesting; but it is less obvious that each of the kernels residing on each of the machines could not have been developed as a single program spanning the entire network. This topic is of particular interest to the ADA community where distributed targets are being increasingly used for embedded systems. I would have liked to have been presented with a more reasoned justification for the authors'

(continues over page)

book reviews

Broad treatment of micro-based measurement and control

George C Barney

'Intelligent instrumentation' Prentice-Hall, Englewood Cliffs, NJ, USA (1985) £12.95 pp 532

Intelligent instrumentation deals with microprocessor applications in measurement and control. It deals with them in four main parts, and has a fifth part dealing with case studies. The four main parts cover measurements, digital computation, interfacing and software.

In just over 500 pages every aspect of these subjects is touched on: from expansion thermometers to chemical analysis in the measurement field; from number systems to computer performance measurements in digital computation; from D/A conversion to local area networks via standard interface systems such as IEEE 488 and CAMAC in the interfacing field; and from assembly language to the design of realtime operating systems in software. As the author states the very broad nature of topic requires a very broad treatment.

It is intended that this broad approach be supported by selected references given in the bibliography at the end of each chapter. Some of the references are familiar, but I did not see two of my favourite instrument books, Spink's *Flow meter engineering* and Considine's *Process instruments*.

The book is intended for the use of students taking undergraduate courses in measurements, control, digital electronics, computer science and instrumentation; for postgraduate courses which provide conversion from a scientific discipline to an applied technology (eg from mathematician to control engineer); and for applications engineers entering the intelligent instrumentation field for the first time. However, the book is really a student textbook. This view is reinforced by the exercises, which have a distinctly undergraduate flavour about them (including some of the form 'Go to the library and select any six books on instrumentation/transducers . . .'

In view of the avowed philosophy of this book, ie a broad approach supported by references, it is difficult to fault it on the grounds that a particular aspect has not been treated in sufficient depth. However, the subject of the book, microprocessor applications in measurement and control, requires that aspects apposite to this subject are more fully treated than those that are not. In the section on temperature measurement, for instance, microcomputer cold junction compensation and linearization of thermocouple measurements deserve a fuller treatment. Also three-wire, as against four-wire, connection of resistance thermometers merits consideration as it is common practice in industry.

Suffixes have been omitted from one part of the book, and the definition of terms from one of the equations (5.11). This is not too important as the meaning is still clear. Part 2 (digital computation), which includes chapters 9–12, covers the elements of the structure of the digital computer and its I/O interface. The important question of interrupts *versus* polling is dealt with. Chapter 12 touches on computer power and performance — difficult subjects to deal with so briefly. The discussion on benchmarks brings out the point that benchmark programs and their results require careful interpretation; an example given in the book shows three tests on the 'same' machine yielding different results because of differences in peripheral configuration, operating system, compilers and runtime systems. The benchmark must be relevant to the application and results must be related to the computer, operating system and compiler combination.

In the chapter on analogue signal processing the dual-ramp A/D converter is a notable omission as it is much used in industrial systems because of its good CMR.

Part 4 deals with software and covers realtime languages, programming realtime systems and realtime operating systems. A useful discussion on the user and language requirements for a realtime language is followed by a review of some realtime languages. However, section 18.6.6(a) on separate compilation fails to state that separate or modular compilation is a requirement of modern industrial microcomputer systems programming.

MODULA-2, an omission from the review list, overcomes the objections raised to separate compilation. With

---

Keeffe *et al.*
(continued)

choice than just a set of references to the literature.

The authors also make some most esoteric statements, such as

'ADA is similar to DP in that it presents an asymmetric naming scheme.'

This reviewer has never heard of DP. Sorry.

One final negative criticism is to a statement encountered on page 1 of the book:

'Unix has recently emerged as a *de facto* industrial standard operating system.'

This simply is not true. Most of industry, and particularly that connected with ADA, uses other operating systems. Such a statement coming on page 1 can prejudice a reader for the remainder of the book.

However, these last criticisms I have of the book are minor. The book is an interesting case study of ADA, and can be recommended to the small circle of specialists in the area of distributed operating systems development. The conclusions reached on ADA add to a continuously growing view of its inadequacy in the tasking model, and are disturbing for the language.

Moss Mossakowski
Systems Designers,
Camberley, UK

VLSI design course provides timely telecomms tutorial

Y Tsividis and P Antognetti (Eds)

'Design of MOS VLSI for telecommunications applications' Prentice-Hall, Englewood Cliffs, NJ, USA (1985) £37.40 pp xiv + 620

An advanced course in the design of MOS VLSI for telecommunications, held in June 1984 at L'Aquila, Italy, provided the origin of this book, which is a timely addition to the growing literature of VLSI design methods covering a field that has not received the attention that it deserves.

The book is aimed at the advanced reader with a knowledge of telecommunication systems. Although MOS technology is introduced in the first part, readers with MOS design experience will find the book much easier to use than will the novice. The book will also be found useful by many who have interests other than in telecommunications systems.

The material is divided into three parts. After a brief but clear introduction to MOS technology, the main circuit building blocks are discussed in some detail with particular emphasis on analogue design methods. This part comprises about two thirds of the book. In the final part some representative applications of the techniques that have been covered in the second part are described. This partitioning is particularly appropriate, and allows readers with different preferences to approach the book in their own way.

The content of part 2 is worth reviewing in some detail. As noted above, it concentrates on analogue and switched capacitor design methods which obviously represent the prejudices of the editors and authors. Only one chapter (36 out of the 370 pages in part 2) is devoted to digital design (in contrast to part 3, the applications section, where a much more balanced view of the digital/analogue debate is presented). In his 36 pages the author, Walter Ulbrich of Siemens, covers a large amount of ground within a review format, but there would have been plenty of scope for the editors to expand this section at the expense of some of the repetition in the other chapters.

This complaint aside, the quality of the remaining chapters is high; the main criticism is again levelled at the editors, who have not exercised sufficient control over the content. For example, although the chapter on micropower techniques is very interesting, most of the material is of limited relevance to the basic theme of MOS VLSI for telecommunications. Similarly, it is doubtful whether it is necessary to have two chapters on op. amps (one on CMOS, one on NMOS) bearing in mind the dominance of CMOS technology.

I found the chapters on CMOS operational amplifiers, by Bedrich Hosticka, and continuous-time filters, by Yannis Tsividis, particularly well though out. In addition, Paul Gray *et al* have put together the sort of high-quality expositions on A/D conversion and switched capacitor filters that we have come to expect from them. Part 2 therefore provides a good grounding in analogue IC design techniques which is relevant to many system disciplines — not just telecoms.

Part 3 is something of a miscellany, as you might expect for an applications section. The authors have generally resisted the temptation to describe just their own chip sets and have tried to present a general picture of the state of VLSI for telecoms. However, they have described several practical integrated systems, ranging from analogue modems to digital TV. Lothar Lerach from Siemens gives a good overview of the current developments in telecoms and Russel Apfel from AMD does something to redress the balance against digital implementations in his chapter on digital signal processing modems.

In summary, this book provides a good grounding in analogue design techniques for telecoms (and other) applications. It does, however, underrates the value of digital methods in an increasingly digital telecommunications network. The book merits a place on the bookshelves of any IC design group just starting with analogue IC design or systems groups that wish to keep abreast of developments in analogue IC design. One final criticism directed at the publishers of this book: how can they justify the very high cost (£37.50) of a book which has been prepared from camera ready copy (of occasionally dubious quality) on which they have performed minimal additional work?

P A Ivey
British Telecom,
Martlesham Heath, UK

Barney
(continued)

regard to the review of realtime languages, BASIC and FORTRAN could well have been omitted and C and MODULA-2 added.

Chapter 20 deals with realtime operating systems — adequately for the level of the book.

Part 5 consists of 15 case studies. These draw attention to application fields but do not take the reader much further. In the main they consist of short descriptions of background, requirements, proposed solution, implementation and commentary. The reader is obviously expected to get the details from the reference. In 11 of the 15 cases the reference is a PhD thesis or an MSc dissertation. These may or may not be available to the general reader.

The book has a glossary, a reasonable index, tutorials and revision sections. It would appear to be an undergraduate student textbook; its use to applications engineers could only be as a first-level reference book.

Joe Gallacher
Microprocessor Systems
Engineering Ltd,
Aberfeldy, UK

book reviews

Variety of papers introduces specialized computers

L Snyder, L H Jamieson, D B Gannon and H J Siegel (Eds)

'Algorithmically specialized parallel computers' Academic Press, Orlando, FL, USA (1985) £24.00 pp xiii + 252

Based on a workshop of the same title held in 1982 at Purdue University, USA, this book is a collection of papers which describe work on various aspects of parallel computers that are specialized towards executing particular algorithms. Although part of a 'rapid manuscript' series, work described by the papers is quite old, but none the less interesting. The papers are arranged into four sections concerning the use of VLSI, innovative parallel architectures, speech and image processing, and numerical computations.

The book is best suited to people with an academic interest in special-purpose parallel computers or computer architecture in general. A knowledge of mathematics is not essential as only a few papers go into the mathematical detail of the algorithms involved. I found the book a 'good read' because of the way it introduces a wide range of architectures and techniques.

The editors have tried to link the subject areas by providing them with short introductions. Most of these amount to little more than the abstracts of the following papers, however, though at least this helps you find your way around. The book has been reproduced directly from the authors' manuscripts, so the papers are in a variety of styles. The text and diagrams are quite clear, although in one paper two pages are transposed!

The subject matter tackled by the book is really 'specialized computers', though it quickly becomes clear that in practice this also means parallel computers: hence the title. Many of the papers are concerned with architectures that give efficient parallel implementations of particular algorithms, such as sorting chips. Some papers take this a stage further and propose special-purpose architectures which have some generality, such as the 'programmable systolic chip'.

Most of the papers are quite readable, though one or two suffer from bad English which makes them hard to follow. Some are of a practical nature, showing how a special-purpose computer can be built and used effectively. One such that is particularly interesting is Batcher's description of the 'massively parallel processor', an SIMD (single instruction multiple data) stream system for satellite image processing.

Other papers are of a theoretical nature, exploring algorithm complexity or new ways of implementing algorithms. Bronson and Jamieson's paper, for example, describes a system for exploring algorithms for continuous speech understanding. This comprises a pipeline of computers of various architectures, including SIMD machines, each specially tailored for its task.

Three short papers which end the book are of a philosophical nature, under the heading 'Does general purpose mean good for nothing?' These represent a summary of a panel discussion held at the workshop and offer definitions of the terms 'special purpose' and 'general purpose', suggesting how things should progress in the future.

Overall the book covers a wide range of topics, from layout techniques for VLSI devices, through raster graphics generators and processors for special numerical computations, to image processing architectures and speech recognition and understanding machines. I found it a good introduction to the topic and there are plenty of references to follow up the bits that really interest you.

Simon Wiseman
Royal Signals and Radar Establishment, Malvern, UK

Control text is pitched at undergraduate level

S A Money

'Microprocessors in instrumentation and control' Collins, Glasgow, UK (1985) £20.00 pp viii + 246

Microprocessors in instrumentation and control covers a wide range of topics, from basic number sequences through the components of data acquisition and control systems to simple examples of software requirements. The components include microcomputer architecture, parallel and serial I/O, A/D and D/A converters and interrupts all applied to realtime systems. An interlude on control theory is included.

The book is well written and understandable, but a large part of it is not about microprocessors but about systems aspects in instrumentation and control. There are no examples of specific or control systems although there are generally a good many illustrations of technique given in the text. Occasionally the book drifts down to transistor circuitry, which is not relevant today.

The level of the book is below degree level, being particularly perhaps to appropriate to technician-level courses, trainee engineers, sixth formers with interests in micro-computing and to early years of some undergraduate courses. This comment is not intended to be derogatory, but merely to recommend its use to these groups of readers.

It is a pity that the title is almost the same as that for R J Bibbero's book!

George Barney
University of Manchester Regional Computer Centre, UK

Microsystems text makes good sense for engineers

John Ferguson

*'Microprocessor systems engineering'
Addison-Wesley, Wokingham, UK
(1985) £12.95 pp xi + 303*

Reviewing a book is like detective work. Just as the detective must go back in time from the scene of the crime, the reviewer works backwards from his or her only evidence — the book itself. Ferguson leaves so many clues that it is not difficult to determine the probable origin of this book. Books may be written specifically as books; or they may be commissioned; or they may arise out of a set of lecture notes. All the evidence points to lecture notes as the precursor of *Microprocessor systems engineering*.

Microprocessor systems engineering is, ostensibly, an introductory course which begins with 'bits, bytes and hex' and ends with the rudiments of system servicing. *En route* the reader meets the 6502, the Z80, the 8088/8086 and the 68000 which, according to the blurb on the back of the book, are covered in detail. There is, of course, no way in which these topics can be covered in any reasonable depth in approximately 300 pages. The 68000, for example, gets 12 pages; I wish I could describe the 68000 in 12 pages!

Ferguson's book is not appropriate as an introductory text. For example, the 6502 has a three-page introduction followed by several assembly language programs which make use of indexed addressing and indirect addressing. The average student could not even begin to follow this text.

The book would seem, in fact, to have been written for readers who have had some experience with digital technology and who are being retrained to work with microprocessors. When viewed in this light, it makes good sense.

The early part of the book provides an overview of some of the popular microprocessors. Assembly language programs for the 6502 and the Z80 are introduced with virtually no explanation. The average student would have great difficulty in following this text; on the other hand, an engineer would find the introduction useful because it compares different microprocessors without spending page after page on elementary material.

The second part of *Microprocessor systems engineering* introduces 'software production' starting with assembly language programming. The author assumes that the reader understands assembly language concepts, and concentrates on showing the reader some examples of actual programs.

The next section is devoted to 'testing and debugging', both of which are topics of particular relevance to the engineer. In keeping with the rest of the text, the author provides a readable introduction to these topics. Having dealt with system design, 'interfaces and peripherals' are introduced; I would have placed this chapter earlier in the book. The usual interfaces are described in varying degrees of detail together with an extensive introduction to the IEEE 488 bus. A short section on local area networks briefly introduces network topologies and then describes how a particular version of Ethernet is programmed at the system level.

A short final chapter looks at the important subject of 'system servicing'. Given the limited space devoted to this topic, all the author can do is list the various servicing tools. However, the signature analyser, which is mainly used in production line testing, is given a reasonably detailed treatment.

Microprocessor systems engineering will be of interest to the engineer with a limited background in digital technology who is faced with the design or servicing of digital equipment. It is reasonably well written and its illustrations are rather better than average. However, Ferguson's treatment of his material is not consistent in the sense that equal weighting is not given to equal topics. For example, the relatively unimportant topic of signature analysis dominates the chapter on servicing. This is not always a bad thing: the occasional in-depth treatment of a specific topic in an introductory text is often better than a totally bland coverage of everything. Equally, I am left with the feeling that this is a collection of lecture notes written by Ferguson which has been turned into a book.

*Alan Clements
Teesside Polytechnic,
Middlesbrough, UK*

Practical guide to BBC Micro interfacing

Roger Morgan, Winston McClean and Joan Rosell

'Interfacing your BBC Micro-computer' Prentice-Hall, Englewood Cliffs, NJ, USA (1985) £8.95 pp ix + 179

At last here is a book that can be fully recommended as much to the home computer user as to the student for whom it has been produced.

Interfacing your BBC Micro-computer does not set out to teach all about electronics and electrical engineering, but assumes some knowledge of these. In my opinion this is a thoroughly reasonable approach in a book of this size, accompanied as it is by a recommendation on page one to work through an introductory text first if the reader has no previous experience of electronics. It also assumes a working knowledge of the BBC model B, using BASIC.

However, there is a very practical approach to all aspects of interfacing.

(continues over page)

book reviews

Morgan *et al*
(continued)

This starts with how the computer stores numbers and covers conversion between binary and hexadecimal numbers. The versatile interface adaptors (VIAs) are described, including their location in the computer and how they can be programmed to send or receive on each connection.

Enough details are given about how to construct an interface box, with switches for inputs and lamps for output, but a supplier has also been arranged for complete working boxes. There is an adequate refresher course on the electronics needed to couple lamps, relays, 12 V motors and stepper motors. In each case these are accompanied by BASIC programs for their use. Throughout the book, each chapter ends with a few problems on developing programs to extend the work covered. Programs

are provided in the answer section at the end of the book.

Analogue and digital I/O lines and transducers, burglar alarms etc are covered in good practical detail. The measurement of voltage, temperature and light are followed by the control of simple devices like an oven made from a metal waste paper basket heated by two lamps; this starts with 'bang bang' control followed by the introduction of proportional, integral and then differential control.

In many cases the computer draws graphs of how the system settles down to the desired value. Algorithms are discussed to provide near optimum response. Where mains supplies are involved a warning of the danger is given and the use of optical isolators and solid-state relays advocated.

The use of the interrupt flag and peripheral control registers are explained, as are the use of the internal timers. Making a morse code generator, driving seven segment

displays, making and using a light pen, adding external A/D and D/A converters and programming so that second processors can be used over the tube are all illustrated.

A closing chapter gives very clear guidance on the use of assembly code, again using it for practical purposes such as high-speed sampling of input waveforms and the display of the result.

An appendix lists the components used in the various projects, four suppliers and their catalogue numbers for the components. Oddly, one of these is given as Radio Shack, Tandy Corp, at its US address, with little indication that Tandy shops are all over the UK or that they have a postal service.

There is a reasonable index with many page numbers quoted against most entries. The book is good value for money.

W H P Leslie
East Kilbride, UK

VLSI chips and network kit put Motorola on the MAP

Motorola is claiming to have taken a lead in 'the race to provide components for MAP-compatible equipment' by introducing its MC68824 token bus controller (TBC), the first VLSI component to be made commercially available for the MAP (Manufacturing Automation Protocol) networking standard. MAP, which is based on the ISO/OSI seven-layer model, is a standard for connecting manufacturing systems, CAE work-stations and offices in a factory-wide communications system.

The 68824 implements the IEEE 802.4 media access control sublayer of the ISO data link layer, and is designed to relieve the host processor of frame formatting and token management functions. Features of the chip include four-channel direct memory access with bus master capability, a 32-bit address range and a 40 byte first-in-

MAP network developer's kit: VMEbus interface boards, software, broadband network hardware, cables

first-out memory. Serial data rates of 1, 5 and 10 Mbyte s^{-1} are supported, says Motorola.

A 68020-based VME module incorporating the 68824, the MVME372 MAP interface controller, is due from the company in mid 1986.

Further Motorola support for MAP comes in the form of 'MAP network developer's kits', providing all the elements (apart from host computer) required to implement a 10 Mbyte s^{-1} two- or four-node network — VME-compatible network interface boards, Unix V software and broadband network hardware, including cabling.

The MVME370kit-1 is a two-node MAP development kit with two interface board sets, one head-end remodulator plus cables and terminators. Network management and demonstration software are also provided. MVME370kit-2 is identical except that it provides four sets of network interface modules instead of two. (*Motorola Inc. 3501 Ed Bluestein Blvd, Austin, TX 78721, USA. Motorola Ltd, 88 Tanners Drive, Blakelands, Milton Keynes MK14 5BP, UK. Tel: (0908) 614614*) □

product news

'Structured cells'

'Structured Cell technology' is the epithet given by US-based LSI Logic to the process it uses for its LSC20 family of logic arrays, standard cells, memories and 'megacells'. Implemented in 2 μm dual-layer CMOS, the 'structured cells' are based on predefined, precharacterized cells with designs built up from base silicon using a custom diffusion process.

LSC20 offers up to 14k random gates, up to 32 kbit of metal-configurable static RAM, up to 128 kbit of metal-configurable ROM plus VLSI 'megacell' building blocks. Design elements include LSI Logic's LST20 standard cell family, LL7000 logic array series, LL8000 series of high-drive I/O pads and buffers, and single-port and multiport RAMs, ROMs and megacells. Typical applications for the LSC20 family would include electronic data processing, telecommunications and digital signal processing (DSP), says the manufacturer.

Scan testing has been built into all LSC20 memories and megacells. The family is supported by the LSI Logic Design System simulation, verification, text extraction and layout tools, and is TTL compatible. (*LSI Logic Corp, 1551 McCarthy Blvd, Milpitas, CA 95035, USA. Tel: (408) 263-9494. LSI Logic Ltd, Grenville Place, The Ring, Bracknell, Berks RG12 1BP, UK. Tel: (0344) 426544*)

● LSI Logic has added five new device configurations to its LSA2000 series of CMOS structured arrays. The additions are: a combination of eight 2901 bit-slice micro ALUs with a 64k ROM and 3500-gate logic array, allowing design of a 32-bit CPU (LSA2006); a DSP device containing two 16 × 16 multiplier-accumulators and a 5000-gate logic array (LSA2008); a 5000-gate logic array with 11.5 kbit of RAM (LSA2009); a general-purpose combination of 2 kbit RAM, 64k ROM and 3200 gates of logic array (LSA2011); and a device containing four 2901 ALUs, a 16 × 16 multiplier-accumulator and a 5000-gate logic array for DSP and CPU applications (LSA2011). □

CMOS computers from Mitsubishi . . .

Mitsubishi has brought onto the market its first in-house designed CPU chips, the 740 Series of 8-bit single-chip microcomputers in 2 μm CMOS. The family's 16 members are all upward code compatible, though of different architecture to, the 6502 microprocessor, says the manufacturer.

The microcomputers are designed around application-specific functional blocks, including UARTs, A/D and D/A converters, LCD and vacuum fluorescent drivers, stepper motor control and I/O ports. It is in the last of these, according to Mitsubishi, that the devices score over conventional microcontrollers — the market at which they are aimed. While microcontrollers tend to lack I/O space, the 740 devices are configured with up to 56 parallel I/O lines.

On-chip memory sizes range from 96 byte to 256 byte of RAM and from 3 kbyte to 8 kbyte of ROM, and all devices can be programmed to make use of external memory (up to 128 kbyte). Current consumption of the devices is quoted as 3–6 mA in active mode and 10 μA on standby. Operating speeds up to 8 MHz are now available, with 12 MHz versions due out in mid 1986. Operating temperature range is from −40°C to +85°C.

Other features of the devices include 69 machine code instructions (6502 compatible), 19 addressing modes and development support including crossassembler, dynamic debugging software and piggyback EPROM evaluation chips. An in-circuit emulator is also available, running on an IBM PC or compatibles.

The 740 Series originated in a family of 4-bit computers designed for use by Mitsubishi in its own equipment, mostly in consumer electronics. The devices were first introduced commercially as discrete components in Japan two years ago, whence they spread to the USA and now to Europe. 16-bit versions are currently in development, says the company.

Standard packaging is a 52-pin or 64-pin 'shrink-DIP', with surface mounting versions planned for later. A one-time-programmable EPROM version is scheduled for late 1986, although some devices already have piggyback EPROM for development purposes. (*Mitsubishi Electric Corp, 2-3 Marunouchi 2-chome, Chiyoda-ku, Tokyo 100, Japan. Mitsubishi Electric (UK) Ltd, Hertford Place, Denham Way, Maple Cross, Rickmansworth, Herts WD3 2BJ, UK. Tel: (0923) 770000*) □

One of Mitsubishi's 740 Series microcomputers installed in a video recorder

product news

... and from Hitachi

Hitachi has produced a CMOS microcomputer which it claims to be the first 8-bit single-chip ZTAT (zero turnaround time) computer with an on-chip A/D converter. The HD63705Z has 68 parallel I/O ports, a serial communications interface, eight channel × 8 bit A/D converter and a slave processor mode allowing its use as an intelligent peripheral.

On-chip memory consists of 8 kbyte of EPROM and 384 byte of RAM. The chip has five 16-bit timers and a software programmable pulse-width-modulation timer. Packaging is in a flat pack either with a window for EPROM programming or as a windowless one-time-programmable version. (*Hitachi Ltd, New Marunouchi Building No 5, 1-chome Marunouchi, Tokyo, Japan. Hitachi Electronic Components (UK) Ltd, Hitec House, 221–225 Station Road, Harrow, Middx HA1 2XL, UK. Tel: 01-861 1414*) □

VME–STE net cards

Networking cards for use in VME–STE multicomputing systems have been made by GMT Electronics of the UK. The 'VME Networking Card' which has been designed for compatibility with GMT's STE System 1000 network controller, allows data communication over a shared medium with up to 254 nodes connected in a logical ring.

Based on the WD2840 LSI communications chip, the VME cards use Manchester encoding and decoding and have an RS422 interface providing a minimum two-wire connection. The Manchester signals are alternatively available for use with custom designed interfaces.

Access to the STE controller's 16 on-chip registers is via a selectable-address I/O interface; the VME card decodes the short I/O address range with selectable privilege. On-card dual-port static RAM provides for message passing between the VME card and the controller. The

11-bit memory driver

Recent moves to 1 Mbit dynamic RAMs have prompted Advanced Micro Devices (AMD) to introduce an 11-bit-wide dynamic memory drivers designed to increase efficiency beyond that offered by 8-bit and 9-bit devices.

The increased drive capacity of the Am2976's 11 drivers will enable designers to reduce substantially the system part count and hence system costs, according to the manufacturer. It also allows all memory array RAS and CAS lines to be driven by one chip, minimizing skew times between devices.

The Am2976 can drive up to 88 dynamic RAMs with densities up to 1 Mbit, says AMD, typically for applications in mainframes and superminicomputers.

Packaging options for the Am2976 include 0.3 in (7.6 mm) plastic and ceramic DIPs PLCCs and LCCs. (*Advanced Micro Devices Inc, 901 Thompson Place, Sunnyvale, CA 94086, USA. Advanced Micro Devices (UK) Ltd, AMD House, Goldsworth Road, Woking, Surrey GU21 1JT, UK. Tel: (04862) 22121*) □

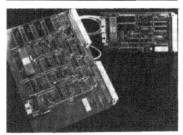

GMT's VME Network Card (foreground) links to the STE System 1000 network controller

contiguous block resides on a jumper-selectable address boundary; the VME card decodes the standard address range with selectable privilege and data type.

The STE controller interrupt can be connected to the system bus and obeys the relevant protocol on both the VME and STE cards (vectored and nonvectored respectively). (*GMT Electronic Systems Ltd, Woodlands Road, Epsom, Surrey KT18 7HN, UK. Tel: (03727) 42333*) □

Microprogram sequencers

Microprogram sequencers in 'CEMOS II' have been added to IDT's Microslice range

12-bit and 16-bit CMOS microprogram sequencers with 16 control functions have been introduced by US-based Integrated Device Technology (IDT) as part of its Microslice microprocessor range.

The IDT39C10B and IDT49C410 have 12-bit and 16-bit loop control counters, respectively, and provide control of up to 4k and 64k words of microprogram memory. Addresses are selected from one of four sources: the microprogram address register, external direct input, internal register–counter or a 33-deep LIFO (last-in-first-out) stack. The LIFO provides for subroutine return linkage and looping capabilities for highly nested microcode applications, says IDT.

The devices have been designed for speed, drive and instruction compatibility with the 2910A bipolar sequencer, but for lower power consumption. Packaging is in 44-pin LCCs or 40-pin DIPs (39C10B) and 48-pin LCCs, DIPs or 'shrink-DIPs' (49C410). (*Integrated Device Technology Inc, 3236 Scott Blvd, PO Box 58015, Santa Clara, CA 95052-8015, USA. Tel: (408) 727-6116. Integrated Device Technology (Europe) Ltd, 5 Bridge Street, Leatherhead, Surrey KT22 8BL, UK. Tel: (0372) 377375*) □

products in brief

Name	Description	Manufacturer/designer	Distributor/contact
RAMs *(continued)*			
HM51256P, HM51256LP	256 kbit CMOS dynamic RAMs with battery back-up capability. Page-mode access times quoted as 55 ns, 65 ns or 80 ns and normal-mode times as 100 ns, 120 ns or 150 ns. Low-power (LP) version consumes 60 mA, 50 mA or 40 mA (maximum) in active mode, 300 μA (average) in standby mode, and has to refresh every 32 ms	Hitachi Ltd, New Marunouchi Building No 5, 1-chome Marunouchi, Chiyoda, Tokyo, Japan	Hitachi Electronic Components (UK) Ltd, Hitec House, 221–225 Station Road, Harrow, Middx HA1 2XL, UK. Tel: 01-861 1414
MN411000, MN411001	1 Mbit dynamic RAMs using 1.2 μm NMOS technology. MN411000 provides page-mode access while MN411001 is designed for nibble mode. Maximum access times are given as 100 ns and 120 ns respectively (row access), 50 ns and 60 ns respectively (column access); cycle times as 190 ns and 220 ns respectively. Current dissipation from a 5 V supply is 4.5 mA (standby) and 95 mA (active)	Matsushita Electronics Corp, Nagaokakyo, Kyoto 617, Japan. Tel: (07592) 1-8151	Panasonic Industrial UK Ltd, 280–290 Bath Road, Slough, Berks SL1 6JG, UK. Tel: (0753) 73181
TC5564PL	64 kbit (8192 × 8 bit) static RAM in CMOS, pin compatible with 64 kbit EPROMs. Maximum operating current is 5 mA at 5 MHz cycle frequency; standby current is typically 0.01 μA. Battery back-up and operation are possible. Operating temperature range: −30°C to +85°C	Toshiba, 1-chome Uchisaiwai-cho, Chiyoda-ku, Tokyo, Japan	Toshiba UK Ltd, Semiconductor Division, Toshiba House, Frimley Road, Camberley, Surrey, UK. Tel: (0276) 62222
First-in–first-out (FIFO) memories			
67411A, 67412A	'Fall-through' FIFOs organized as 64 × 4 bit and 64 × 5 bit respectively. Has a 35 MHz shift-in-shift-out rate, and is pin compatible with the F3341 FIFO	Monolithic Memories Inc, 2175 Mission College Blvd, Santa Clara, CA 95154-1592, USA. Tel: (408) 970-9700	Microlog Ltd, The Cornerstone, The Broadway, Woking, Surrey GU21 5EZ, UK. Tel: (04862) 29551
Register files			
Am29334	32-bit dual-access four-port register file with access time quoted as 24 ns, designed to support system cycle times of 80 ns. Organized as 64 × 18 bit, with horizontal and vertical cascading capability allowing for expansion	Advanced Micro Devices Inc, 901 Thompson Place, Sunnyvale, CA 94086, USA	Advanced Micro Devices (UK) Ltd, AMD House, Goldsworth Road, Woking, Surrey GU21 1JT, UK. Tel: (04862) 22121
Interface modules			
EF68230	Parallel interface and timer 8 bit or 16 bit wide, operable in either unidirectional or bidirectional mode. Timer contains a 24-bit-wide counter and a 5-bit prescaler. Ports allow for five vectored or autovectored interrupts Compatible with the EF68000 bus	Thomson–CSF, 5–7 rue de Milan, 75009 Paris, France. Tel: (1) 280-6711	Hawke Components Distribution, Amotex House, 45 Hanworth Road, Sunbury-on-Thames, Middx TW16 5DA, UK. Tel: 01-979 7799

Name	Description	Manufacturer/designer	Distributor/contact
'IEEE-488 interface for MicroVAX II'	IEEE-488 (GPIB) support kit for Digital Equipment's MicroVAX II computer, comprising an interface board, connecting cable, operator's manual and software. Provides data transfer speeds up to 330 kbyte s^{-1} between the IEEE-488 bus and Q-bus, and implements all IEEE-488 functions. Software provides FORTRAN and MACRO high- and low-level function calls	National Instruments, 12109 Technology Blvd, Austin, TX 78759, USA. Tel: (512) 250-9119	Amplicon Electronics Ltd, Richmond Road, Brighton, East Sussex BN2 3RL, UK. Tel: (0273) 608331
Inlab/Thinklab	Interface systems for IBM, Apricot, Victor/Sirius, Apple, Commodore, Acorn BBC and other microcomputers, selectable from some 40 modules. Three additions to the range of modules available are: a 4.5-digit A/D converter with eight differential amplifiers and multiplexer; a 12-bit A/D converter with 25 μs conversion time and sample-and-hold amplifier; and an eight-digit universal counter-timer with a crystal controlled programmable oscillator	3D Digital Design and Development Ltd, 18–19 Warren Street, London W1P 5DB, UK. Tel: 01-387 7388	

Processor boards

Name	Description	Manufacturer/designer	Distributor/contact
CPU3183	8085-based STD bus CPU card allowing for 64 kbyte of onboard memory: two JEDEC-type sockets accept up to 32 kbyte EPROM chips while two further sockets take 8 kbyte CMOS RAM chips (the contents of which are protected by a rechargeable Ni–Cd battery). Can be used as processor card for the Apoloco Flexy S industrial microcomputer	Apoloco Ltd, 90 King Street, Newcastle, Staffs ST5 1JB, UK. Tel: (0782) 620519	
PMM 86C	Range of computer modules architecturally identical to the PMM 86 families, but incorporating ceramic packaged CMOS components. Elements of the modules include microprocessor, dual-port memory, 1553B interface and system bus monitor. Temperature range is from −40°C to 85°C	Plessey Microsystems Ltd, Towcester, Northants NN12 7JN, UK. Tel: (0327) 50312	

 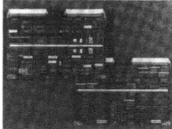 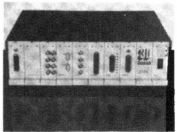

Apoloco 3183 CPU board (left); Plessey PMM 86C computer modules (centre); and 3D Thinklab microcomputer interface systems (right)

Name	Description	Manufacturer/designer	Distributor/contact
MLD 32008	STEbus board includes a 32008 CPU (6MHz, 8 MHz and 10 MHz options), 32081 floating point coprocessor, 32201 timing control unit and 32202 interrupt control unit. Memory capacity is up to 40 kbyte of SRAM, EPROM and/or ROM. Software support includes monitor, TDS and 32000 assembler	MLD, London, UK	Dean Microsystems Ltd, 7 Horseshoe Park, Pangbourne, Berks RG8 7JW, UK. Tel: (07357) 5155
MLD 64180	STEbus controller board based on Hitachi's 64180 CMOS Z80-based CPU (4 MHz and 6 MHz options). Features two serial channels, two DMA channels, counter-timers and a 512 kbyte main memory address range. Provides for two ROMs (8 kbyte or 16 kbyte each) and four RAMs (8 kbyte each)	MLD, London, UK	Dean Microsystems Ltd, 7 Horseshoe Park, Pangbourne, Berks RG8 7JW, UK. Tel: (07357) 5155
PT-VME 103	VME/VMX 68010 processor module with two sockets for up to 128 kbyte of ROM, PROM or EPROM, and two sockets for a further 32 kbyte of RAM or 128 kbyte of ROM. Also includes a 68901-based async./sync. RS232C serial port, dual general-purpose timers and provision for a 68881 floating point coprocessor. Packaging: 160 mm dual-height Eurocard with front panel controls including Reset/Abort switch, Run, Halt and Fault LEDs	Performance Technologies Inc, 300 Main Street, East Rochester, NY 14445, USA	Dean Microsystems Ltd, 7 Horseshoe Park, Pangbourne, Berks RG8 7JW, UK. Tel: (07357) 5155
Single-board computers			
SBC 01	68000-based VMEbus SBC, running at 8 MHz. Includes 128 kbyte of DRAM and four 28-pin sockets for up to 256k of additional ROM, PROM, EPROM or SRAM; two RS232 serial ports; parallel I/O; and a realtime clock	MicroSys GmbH, Amzinger Strasse, 800 Munich, FRG. Tel: (089) 638-0132	Dage (GB) Ltd, Eurosem Division, Rabans Lane, Aylesbury, Bucks HP19 3RG, UK. Tel: (0296) 33200

Name	Description	Manufacturer/designer	Distributor/contact
Test equipment			
K450	Logic analyser with 5 ns resolution on up to 24 channels and 10 ns resolution on up to 48 channels. Designed for concurrent analysis of multiprocessor systems — both CMOS and TTL devices can be debugged simultaneously. By connecting two instruments together (96 channels, 10 ns resolution), wide bus systems and 32-bit microprocessors can be debugged. Features 16 independent levels of trace control (maximum 20 ns between levels)	Gould Electronics, 1870 Lundy Avenue, San Jose, CA 95131, USA. Tel: (408) 263-7155	Gould Electronics Ltd, Roebuck Road, Hainault, Ilford, Essex IG6 3UE, UK. Tel: 01-500 1000
Development systems			
AT51	IBM PC based development system for Intel's 8051 series of single-chip microcontrollers, providing software development, in-circuit emulation and PROM programming. Optional file transfer package available to exchange data between the AT51 and Intel systems	Ashling Microsystems Ltd, Enterprise House, Plassey Technological Park, Limerick, Ireland. Tel: (061) 338177	Instrumatic UK Ltd, First Avenue, Globe Park, Marlow, Bucks SL7 1YA, UK. Tel: (06284) 4426
LANalyzer EX5000E	IBM PC compatible package for developing, debugging and characterizing local area networks, monitoring traffic and measuring performance. Designed for Ethernet versions 1.0 and 2.0 and IEEE 802.3 compatible networks. Comprises the EXOS 225 controller board plus system software on floppy disc	Excelan, Weir Bank, Bray-on-Thames, Maidenhead, Berks SL6 2ED, UK. Tel: (0628) 34281	
MICE 8/16/32	Family of in-circuit emulators based on a 32-bit bus, embodying the features of the MICE 2+ together with serial and parallel ports, five breakpoints, filtered trace with date stamping and 256 kbyte of emulation memory with operation up to 14 MHz. MICE 8 (for the Z80) and MICE 32 (for the 68020) are now available, with MICE 16 (for the 8086 or 68000 families) to follow in third quarter 1986	Microtek International Inc, 6 Industrial East Road Three, Science-based Industrial Park, Hsin-chi, Taiwan. Tel: (035) 772155	ARS Microsystems Ltd, Doman Road, Camberley, Surrey GU15 3DF, UK. Tel: (0276) 685005

From left: MLD 32008 CPU board; MicroSys SBC 01 single-board computer; Gould K450 logic analyser; and Ashling AT51 microcontroller development system

products in brief

Name	Description	Manufacturer/designer	Distributor/contact
Development systems (continued)			
MicroForce 1A	VMEbus-based microcomputer running Unix system V, designed for use in software development, as a decentralized workstation or for other system V applications. Includes a 68010 CPU with 68451 memory management unit and 68450 DMA controller, four serial I/O channels, 128 kbyte static RAM, 2 Mbyte system memory, 1 Mbyte Winchester disc and C and FORTRAN 77 compilers	Force Computers GmbH, Daimlerstrasse 9, D-8012 Ottobrunn — Munich, FRG. Tel: (089) 609-2033	
MicroPSE	'Microprocessor programming support environment' comprising emulators for the Z80, 8086 and MC68000; a CORAL crosscompiler, assembler and linker for the M68000 series; and assembler-linkers for the Z80 and MC14500. Hosted on a MicroVAX running under VMS, it is capable of concurrent simulation of the same or different microprocessors	Marconi Defence Systems Ltd, The Grove, Warren Lane, Stanmore, Middx HA7 4LY, UK. Tel: 01-954 2311	
Multi-V Systems	Software development systems, hosted on VAX family computers, for the 68020 and 80286 microprocessors. Language support is via CLANDS II (C language development system), including a C compiler, C language directed editor, 32-bit macroassembler, relocating linker, an integration control system and a C debugging system. Hardware–software integration support includes emulators for the 68020 and 80286	Tektronix Inc, PO Box 500, Beaverton, OR 97077, USA	Tektronix UK Ltd, Fourth Avenue, Globe Park, Marlow, Bucks SL7 1YD, UK. Tel: (06284) 6000
Software			
CGEN	BASIC-to-DOS conversion package now available for use with the DOS operating system (original version runs under Unix)	MS Associates Ltd, St Marks House, 1 Station Road, Bourne End, Bucks SL8 5QF, UK. Tel: (06285) 24999	
Express BASIC	Version of the BASIC language developed for use with the Chameleon Controller single-board computer. Employs a form of tokenized code claimed to make it faster than other interpreted languages. Features include: eight interrupt sources; fully 'ROMable' code; integrated disc filing system; autostart facility; interactive program error checking; and compatibility with Tiny BASIC as used on the Essex Tiny BASIC computer	Essex Electronics Centre, University of Essex, Colchester, Essex CO4 3SQ, UK. Tel: (0206) 865089	RCS Microsystems Ltd, 141 Uxbridge Road, Hampton Hill, Middx TW12 1BL, UK. Tel: 01-979 2204
pSOS-68K	Realtime pSOS operating system kernel for the 68020 microprocessor	Unit-C Ltd, Dominion Way, West Broadwater, Worthing, W Sussex BN14 8NT, UK. Tel: (0903) 205233	

'The worst is over,' say semiconductor manufacturers

Semiconductor companies are optimistic about business prospects despite continuing announcements of large operating losses into 1986. Presenting National Semiconductor's sales figures for the quarter to 9 March, president Charles Sporck pointed out that the semiconductor division had 'experienced increased booking for the second consecutive quarter as business conditions in the semiconductor industry continued to improve'.

Motorola has announced higher sales and earnings for the first quarter of 1986 compared with the same period in 1985. The company's Semiconductor Products Sector is shown to have returned to moderate profit levels after two consecutive quarters of substantial losses. Robert W Galvin, chairman and chief executive, said that the company was pleased with the increase in orders

for the semiconductor business and that this is contributing to the company's confidence in moderate, continuing growth.

Big losses at Intel during 1985 have caused the company to lay off about 700 employees, mainly in the USA. Gordon Moore, company chairman, conceded that the climb back to profitability was a long one, but said: 'We believe we've seen the worst of this cycle; prices are firming in some areas and demand for certain products is increasing.'

National most recently reported sales totalling $328.9M in the quarter to March 1986, producing a net loss of $32M. This compares with net earnings of $1.5M in the corresponding period in 1985. Sales quoted overall for the first three quarters of the fiscal year 1986 are $1.1 billion, giving a net loss of $120.3M. This again compares

unfavourably with the previous year, when a net gain was reported.

First quarter sales reported by Motorola, covering all its major operations, are $1.34 billion, up from 1985's $1.32 billion. This gave net earnings of $45M, an increase of $4M on last year.

Intel's reported results for 1985 showed a net income of $2M, but this is down from $198M made in 1984. Revenues were $1.4 billion, down from $1.6 billion one year earlier.

In contrast to the giants, US start-up CMOS manufacturer Cypress Semiconductor has announced a profit in its seventh trading quarter, leading the company to claim that it is the fastest-growing semiconductor company in the world. Specializing in 1.2 µm CMOS products — RAMs, PROMs, PALs and bit-slice microprocessors — the company says it has achieved annual sales of $20M. ☐

VSB supersedes VMX in bus market

Four major companies — Motorola, Philips, Plessey and Thomson — have announced support for VSB, the intended new standard 32-bit VME subsystem bus to supersede the existing expansion buses, VMX and MVMX-32. The companies say that the new bus will be better able to meet the requirements of the developing VME market, a lucrative market which it is estimated will be worth $1.2 billion by 1990.

VSB is to become an official bus standard and is in the final stages of standardization with the International Electrotechnical Committee (IEC), a recognized standards body. Copies of the specification will be available from the VMEbus International Trade Association (VITA).

Some features of the VMX series of buses have been incorporated in the new bus, although VSB and VMX products are not compatible. VSB is designed to be used in multimaster applications to expand the local resources of main system processors. The bus offers 32-bit parallel address and data paths, and has asynchronous transfer protocols. Cache-based architectures will be supported.

Motorola has already announced its introduction of VSB-compatible board-level products, including processor boards, RAM, intelligent mass storage and graphics controllers. Initial shipments will begin in the second half of 1986.

Although concentrating on VSB, Motorola says this does not preclude support of VMX if there is demand for it. The company says, however, that its future developments centre on 32-bit and highly integrated 16-bit systems, which are not suitable for VMX. (*VITA, 5726 E. Leith Lane, Scottsdale, AZ 85254, USA. Tel: (602) 951-8866*) □

AMD and Sony seek 'next generation of ICs'

In a bid to break into consumer markets, US chip manufacturer Advanced Micro Devices has joined forces with the Japanese electronics giant Sony Corporation 'to cooperatively develop, produce and market the next generation of ICs'. The agreement, formalized in a letter of intent signed in February by both companies, envisages each company having access to the other's designs.

Commenting on the agreement, AMD president W J Sanders III hoped that it would 'maximize AMD's return on investment in process technology development by extending participation in VLSI products into the consumer markets'. AMD claims to have spent more than $180M on IC research and development in 1985.

Sony's president Norio Ogha hoped that the agreement would be 'an example for future co-operation between Japanese and US firms'.

Together, the two companies achieved worldwide sales of $7.6 billion in 1985 and employ 59000 people. □

109 join RACE to digital telecomms

Thirty one projects, involving 109 European organizations, have been approved as part of the RACE (research in advanced communications for Europe) Definition Phase, the first part of a 10-year programme to establish a pan-European advanced wideband telecommunications network. The programme was first announced in September 1985.

Advanced semiconductors, control software and optoelectronics have been identified as the main research areas in the programme, which aims to replace today's analogue telephone systems with digital integrated networks capable of handling voice, text, graphics and video signals.

Results of the 18-month definition phase are expected to fall into two categories: specification of networks by the telecommunications administrations; and development by manufacturers of sophisticated terminal equipment. Other groups taking part in the programme include university researchers and broadcasters.

RACE is coordinated by the Information Technologies and Telecommunications Task Force, set up in 1983 by the Commission of the European Communities. This is the second project launched by the Task Force, following the setting up of ESPRIT.

Further decisions on the development of RACE will be made by ministers who will consider results of the definition phase at the end of 1986. (*Commission of the European Communities, Rue de la Loi 200, B-1049 Brussels, Belgium. Tel: 235 11 11*) □

FOLLOWING UP SOMETHING YOU'VE JUST SEEN?

PLEASE MENTION

MICROPROCESSORS AND MICROSYSTEMS

'Silicon micro-system' research commences

UK collaborative research on 'silicon microsystems' is to be one of the first projects to be set up under a new scheme announced by the British Government's Department of Trade and Industry. Under the scheme, the National Electronics Research Initiatives, industrial collaborators are encouraged to locate precompetitive work on a single site, so overcoming some of the geographical inefficiencies apparent in some group research programmes.

Work on silicon microsystems concerns the development of silicon motherboards, or superhybrids. Using silicon as a substrate allows fine interconnections between mounted chips, thus increasing the density of components possible on a board. The programme will investigate electrical, mechanical, optical and thermal properties of these superhybrids, as well as studying design methodologies, methods of attachment and sealing, and packaging techniques.

Initial partners in the work are RSRE, which will act as the central base for the project, also British Aerospace, British Telecom, GEC, Lucas, Mars Electronics, Smiths, Plessey and Thorn-EMI. Money is being made available from Government to meet the cost of support staff, services, new plant and equipment at the central location, although participants will bear the costs of their researchers' salaries and related costs.

The only other project so far involved in the scheme concerns pattern recognition approaches for machine intelligence. Potential initiatives in advanced semiconductors and molecular electronics are being considered. Companies interested in participating should contact: *B R Arthur, Electronics Applications Division, Department of Trade and Industry, 29 Bressenden Place, London SW1E 5DT, UK. Tel: 01-213 4780* □

BA supports ADA

ADA software and support is provided for military computer hardware built by British Aerospace Naval Weapons Division following the company's agreement with ADA support house High Integrity Systems of the UK. BA's MC5-80 computer modules are based on Intel designs, and incorporate the 8086 and 80286 processors. HIS, which is Intel's recommended ADA support house in Europe, is providing a package encompassing its Multibox-286 ADA development workstation, US company SofTech's ADA Language System, and training and consultancy services.

Intel innovation award

Intel has been awarded the Corporate Innovation Recognition of the IEEE, the first time this distinction has been granted. Also selected to receive this first award was the electric utilities company, Southern California Edison Company of Rosemead, CA, USA. Established in 1985, the award is to recognize innovative development and realization of products or services in fields of interest to the IEEE. Intel was cited for 'its pioneering efforts in the development of the microprocessor and associated technologies which have transformed the electronics industry'. The company introduced the world's first microprocessor in 1971.

Xerox copies National ICs

To assist its development of VLSI systems based on application specific integrated circuits (ASICs), Xerox Corporation has signed a long-term agreement with National Semiconductor, for the supply of 2 µm CMOS semicustom ICs. National will also supply advice on design, tooling and packaging, as well as CAD/CAM software for Xerox's proprietary-design workstations. Under the agreement the two companies hope to codevelop new cells and functional blocks. Semicustom ICs supplied to Xerox will be manufactured at National's new $100M facility at the US company's site in Arlington, TX, which has just begun production. At present, gate arrays are the primary product at Arlington, but standard cells and cell-based custom circuits will follow within a few months, the company says.

Raytheon CMOS source

Military supplier Raytheon Semiconductor is the latest company to second-source LSI Logic's LL 7000 family of 2 µm CMOS logic arrays. Toshiba and Gold Star already have second-sourcing arrangements for the devices. The arrays, which range up to 10k gates, were announced just over a year ago and are described by Raytheon as having reached 'production maturity'. For Raytheon, the arrays provide an immediate production source of CMOS devices to complement its bipolar products. Intended markets for the arrays are the US and European military, for small volume applications.

VME dept for BICC-Vero

BICC-Vero has confirmed its commitment to VMEbus, establishing a new division devoted to systems based on the bus. Located at the company's Southampton, UK, plant, the new 'microsystems' division will offer boards and software, as well as its existing range of bus accessories such as backplanes, prototyping boards and extender cards.

Pronto takes G64/G96

Pronto Electronic Systems has signed a franchise agreement with Gespac to market the Swiss company's G64/G96 Eurocards in the UK. The G64/96 bus is the only 16-bit bus dedicated to the single-height Eurocard format, says Pronto, and it supports 8, 16 and 32-bit processors. Products based on the bus are aimed at 'mid-range' industrial automation applications.

calendar

Date	Title	Contact	Place	Other details
1986				
2–5 June	ISCA '86	Secretariat ISCA '86, Business Center for Academic Societies Japan, Conference Department, Yamazaki Building 4F, 40-14 Hongo 2-chome, Bunkyo-ku, Tokyo 113, Japan	Sunshine Prince Hotel, Tokyo, Japan	13th international symposium on computer architecture, sponsored by IEEE Computer Society, ACM and the Information Processing Society of Japan
3–5 June	13th Annual International Conference on Computer Architecture	Dr Hideo Aiso, Dept of Electrical Engineering, Keio University, 3-14-1 Hiyoshi, Kohohu-ku, Yokohoma 223, Japan	Tokyo, Japan	Sponsored by IPSJ (Japan), the ACM, the IEEE Computer Society and TC–CA
3–5 June	ComUnix '86	EMAP International Exhibitions Ltd, Abbot's Court, 34 Farringdon Road, London EC1R 3AU, UK. Tel: 01-608 1161	Tara Hotel, London, UK	Series of seminars concerning 'Unix solutions'. Sponsored by /usr/group/UK
3–6 June	International Conference on Consumer Electronics	ICCE, c/o TMA, 3553 North Milwaukee Avenue, Chicago, IL 60641, USA	Rosemont, IL, USA	Conference and exhibition on video and audio technology, home information systems, components, CADCAM and emerging technologies
10–12 June	Comdex International	The Interface Group Inc, 300 First Avenue, Needham, Massachusetts, USA	Nice, France	Display of software, small computer products, peripherals, accessories and other related items; miniconference on business, marketing and financial subjects of interest to computer industry marketers
10–12 June	Scottish Electronics Show	Network Events Ltd, Printers Mews, Market Hill, Buckingham MK18 1JX, UK	Anderson Centre, Glasgow, UK	Exhibition and conference covering equipment and services associated with the design, testing and manufacturing of electronic equipment and components
11–13 June	Microelectronics Packaging	Center for Professional Advancement, Palestrinastraat 1, 1071 LC Amsterdam, The Netherlands. Tel: (020) 623050	Caransa Crest Hotel, Amsterdam, The Netherlands	Intensive course covering: packaging chips and subcircuits; microjoining and bonding; encapsulation of microelectronics; materials, techniques and equipment for moulding and casting; microelectronics reliability; and thermal management
16–19 June	National Computer Conference	AFIPS, 1899 Preston White Drive, Reston, VA 22091, USA. Tel: (703) 620–8900	Las Vegas, NV, USA	Conference sponsored by the American Federation of Information Processing Societies
25–28 June	Communications: Message, Mind, & Machine	Canadian Association for Information Science, BC Research, 3650 Wesbrook Mall, Vancouver V6S 2L2, Canada	Canada	Conference and exhibition on information retrieval and systems design, artificial intelligence, expert systems, networking and distributed systems
1–3 July	16th Fault Tolerant Computing Symposium	Professor H Kopetz, Institut fur Praktische Informatik, Technische Universitat Wien, Gubhausstrasse 30/180, A-1040 Wien, Austria. Tel: (222) 56-01	Vienna, Austria	Organized by the IEEE Computer Society and the Austrian Computer Society
2–4 July	International Workshop on Systolic Arrays	Will Moore, Systolic Array Workshop, Dept of Engineering Science, Oxford University, Oxford OX1 3PJ, UK	Oxford, UK	Papers on all aspects of systolic arrays and related SIMD architectures from abstract theory to practical applications and VLSI products
7–11 July	International Optical Computing Conference	Prof Joseph Shamir, Conference Chairman, 1986 IOCC, c/o Kopel Tours Ltd — Conventions, PO Box 4413, 61044 Tel Aviv, Israel	Jerusalem, Israel	Recent developments in optical computing including optical information processing, hybrid optical–digital processing systems, systolic array processors, integrated optical processing devices, electro-optic devices, optical interface techniques and application of optical bistability to computing

Date	Title	Contact	Place	Other details
14–16 July	Computer Networks for Realtime Applications	Cindy Barnes, Frost & Sullivan Ltd, 104–112 Marylebone Lane, London W1M 5FU, UK. Tel: 01-935 4433	Portman Hotel, London, UK	Seminar covering communications and organizational networks, mission-oriented networks, issues related to distributed databases, and analytical tools relating to network design
14–18 July	Modern Digital Signal Processing	Cindy Barnes, Frost & Sullivan Ltd, 104–112 Marylebone Lane, London W1M 5FU, UK. Tel: 01-935 4433	Cumberland Hotel, London, UK	Tutorial seminar on DSP problem analysis and solution
21–23 July	Simulation of Semiconductor Devices and Processes	Dr K Board, Department of Electrical and Electronic Engineering, University College of Swansea, Singleton Park, Swansea SA2 8PP, UK	University College of Swansea, UK	Second international conference on semiconductor device and process simulation
21–24 July	CAD/CAM in Electronics	Center for Professional Advancement, Palestrinastraat 1, 1071 LC Amsterdam, The Netherlands	Crest Hotel, Amsterdam, The Netherlands	Course covering computer-aided design, manufacturing and testing in electronics. Includes circuit analysis for integrated and analogue circuits, logic simulation for digital circuits and systems, PCB design and manufacture, VLSI, automatic testing, system implementation and electronic engineering workstations
21–26 July	Third International Conference on Logic Programming	Doug DeGroot, IBM Research, PO Box 218, Yorktown Heights, NY 10598, USA	Imperial College, London, UK	Sponsored by the IEEE Computer Society
28–30 July	SCSC '86	Society for Computer Simulation (SCS), PO Box 17900, San Diego, CA 92117, USA. Tel: (619) 277-3888	Reno, NV, USA	SCS conference covering artificial intelligence, simulation in medicine, physics, chemistry, engineering, ecology, government and defence, data communications systems, simulation credibility and validation etc
8–11 September	ESSDERC '86	Clive Jones, Institute of Physics, 47 Belgrave Square, London SW1X 8QX, UK. Tel: 01-235 6111	University of Cambridge, UK	16th European solid-state device research conference organized by the Institute of Physics and cosponsored by IEE, IEEE, IERE and the European Physical Society. Coverage includes CMOS, silicon bipolar device modelling, process modelling, thin oxide metallization, defects, submicron lithography, solid-state sensors
8–11 September	International Test Conference (ITC 1986)	ITC, Millbrook Plaza, Suite 104D, PO Box 264, Mount Freedom, NJ 07970, USA. Tel: (201) 895-5260	Sheraton Hotel, Washington, DC, USA	Tutorials, workshops and user group meetings on IC testing. Sponsored by the IEEE Computer Society
9–13 September	Fabritec 86	Secretariat Fabritec 86, c/o Swiss Industries Fair, Postfach, CH-4021 Basel, Switzerland. Tel: (061) 26 20 20	Swiss Industries Fair, Basel, Switzerland	Second international trade fair for fabrication installations in electronics
15–18 September	Euromicro 86	Mrs E C Snippe-Marlisa, TH Twente, PO Box 217, Dept INF, Room A306, 7500 AE Enschede, The Netherlands	Venice, Italy	Twelfth annual conference of micro-processing and microprogramming
15–20 September	Intercomm '86	Cahners Exhibitions Ltd, Chatsworth House, 59 London Road, Twickenham TW1 3SZ, UK	Beijing, China	International computer and communication congress/exposition for science and technology

calendar

Date	Title	Contact	Place	Other details
23–24 September	Customized ICs	Professor R W Hartenstein, Universität Kaiserlautern, Bau 12/4, Postfach 3049, D-6750 Kaiserlautern, FRG	Kaiserlautern, FRG	European conference on customer–vendor interfaces in microelectronics, sponsored by the Commission of the European Communities
23–25 September	Microsoftware 1986	Dr R A Adey, Computational Mechanics Institute, Suite 6200, 400 West Cummings Park, Woburn, MA 01801, USA. Tel: (617) 933-7374	Boston, USA	International conference on microsoftware in engineering, covering codes developed for personal computers, workstations and expert systems
30 September –2 October	ATE '86	Network Events Ltd, Printers Mews, Market Hill, Buckingham MK18 1JX, UK	Palais des Congres, Paris, France	Fifth automatic testing and test instrumentation exhibition and conference
6–10 October	ISATA 86	ISATA, 42 Lloyd Park Avenue, Croydon, Surrey CR0 5SB, UK. Tel: 01-686 7026	Flims, Switzerland	15th international symposium on automotive technology and automation, covering manufacturing information systems, factory networks (MAP), realtime operating systems, man–machine communications, artificial intelligence, expert systems, CADCAM etc
15–17 October	19th Annual Workshop on Microprogramming	Stanley Habib, City College of New York, Computer Science Department, New York City, NY 10031, USA. Tel: (212) 690-6631/2	Graduate Center City University of New York, USA	Workshop on microarchitecture design, firmware engineering, compaction and optmization, specification languages, graphics hosts, microprogramming languages, RISC/CISC machines and microprogrammed VLSI. Sponsored by ACM Sigmicro and the IEEE Technical Committee on Microprogramming
28–30 October	Test + Transducer '86	Norma Thewlis, Trident International Exhibitions Ltd, 21 Plymouth Road, Tavistock, Devon PL19 8AU, UK. Tel: (0822) 4671	Wembley Conference Centre, London, UK	Exhibition and conference covering materials testing, solid-state transducers, optical sensors for robots, automotive sensors, data acquisition and microprocessors, test in hazardous environments etc
2–6 November	FJCC 86	Stanley Winkler, FJCC 86, 1730 Massachusetts Avenue, NW Washington, DC 20036-1903, USA	Dallas, USA	IEEE/ACM joint computer conference and exhibition, covering database management systems, artificial intelligence, software engineering, operating systems, VLSI, graphics, electronic education, languages, parallel computing and networks
11–14 November	Compec '86	Reed Exhibitions, Surrey House, 1 Throwley Way, Sutton, Surrey SM1 4QQ, UK. Tel: 01-643 8040	Olympia, London, UK	Exhibition of computers, peripherals and systems for professional and business users
17–18 November	Computer Networking Symposium	IEEE Computer Society Administrative Office, 1730 Massachusetts Avenue, NW Washington, DC 20036-1903, USA	Washington, DC, USA	IEEE symposium covering long-haul networks, local area networks PBX systems, satellite systems, video systems, protocols, teleconferencing, standards design, network testing, network procurement and internetworking
17–21 November	AutomAsia 86	Andry Montgomery Ltd, 11 Manchester Square, London W1M 5AB, UK. Tel: 01-486 1951	Singapore	Third South East Asian conference and show on automated manufacturing technology and robotics
21–22 November	8th Annual FORTH convention	FORTH Interest Group, PO Box 8231, San Jose, CA 95155, USA. Tel: (408) 277-0668	Doubletree Hotel, Santa Clara, USA	US FORTH convention including exhibition, vendor booths, hands-on tutorials, lectures and user group meetings

BASIC Mechanical Vibrations

A J PRETLOVE

The subject of vibration is of great importance to the mechanical engineer as it influences wear, metal fatigue, noise and physical comfort of machine operators and transport passengers. It is also of growing importance in civil engineering, for instance in bridges and prestressed concrete structures. This book introduces the subject both in theory and practice, and will be useful to degree and diploma students as well as to engineers who need a quick refresher course on vibrations backed with some useful BASIC programs.

Contents: Preface • The BASIC computer language • Simple systems with no damping • Two degree of freedom systems • Systems with several degrees of freedom • Bending vibrations • Further reading • Index

| May 1985 | 216 × 138 mm | 0 408 01554 3 | Softcover | 128 pages | £8.95 |

BASIC Theory of Structures

K R F ANDREWS
MSc(Eng), CEng, MICE

Taking the standard Theory of Structures syllabus which is essential to the study of civil and mechanical engineering, this book introduces the reader to computer methods for the solution of a wide range of typical problems. In doing so it enhances the reader's appreciation of the principles of the subject and engenders a fluency in the appropriate computational techniques.

With its introduction to the analysis of trusses and influence line diagrams, this book will be useful to the degree or diploma student in his first year as well as to the engineer for the solution of straightforward structural problems. This book complements *BASIC Stress Analysis* by M J Iremonger.

Contents: Introduction to BASIC • Numerical analysis • Force analysis of trusses • Displacement analysis of trusses • Beam theory • Influence line diagrams • Programs • Worked examples • Index

| September 1985 | 216 × 138 mm | 0 408 01357 5 | Softcover | 176 pages | £8.95 |

BASIC Stress Analysis

M J IREMONGER
BSc(Eng), PhD, ACGI, CEng, MIMechE
Professor, Head of Department of Materials, Royal Military College of Science, Shrivenham, Wiltshire

"This is a competitively priced text and one of an excellent series which introduces programming to engineering students in their own environment."
International Journal for Numerical Methods in Fluids

Contents: Introduction to BASIC • Introduction to stress analysis • Direct stress and strain • Shear and torsion • Bending • Complex stress and strain • Failure • Axisymmetric systems • Index

| 1982 | 216 × 138 mm | 0 408 01113 0 | Softcover | 176 pages | £8.95 |

For details of other Butterworth Scientific titles, please contact the appropriate office.
Orders should be sent to the appropriate office listed below.
The UK headquarters serves all UK and overseas markets except where there is a local Butterworths office

United Kingdom
Butterworths, Borough Green
Sevenoaks, Kent TN15 8PH
England

Australia & Papua New Guinea
Butterworths Pty Ltd, PO Box 345
North Ryde, New South Wales 2113
Australia

Customers in Asia may order through:
Butterworth & Co (Asia) Pty Ltd
PO Box 770, Crawford Post Office
Singapore 9119, Republic of Singapore

New Zealand
Butterworths of New Zealand Ltd
33-35 Cumberland Place
Wellington 1, New Zealand

South Africa
Butterworth & Co (South Africa)
(Pty) Ltd Box No 792
Durban 4000, South Africa

USA & Canada
Butterworth Publishers
80 Montvale Avenue
Stoneham, MA 02180 USA

SPECIAL ISSUE: MARCH 1986

microprocessors and microsystems

The authoritative international journal on microsystem technology and applications for designers

BACKPLANE BUS STANDARDS

With the development of ever more powerful microprocessors and modular multiprocessor systems, and the consequent need for effective communication links between components, backplane bus standards are becoming increasingly important. For microsystems designers a reliable bus standard simplifies design procedures, enabling them to concentrate on the functionality of individual components with the assurance that they will work together at the hardware level.

Today, bus schemes proliferate; from 8-bit and 16-bit to 32-bit systems, and from manufacturer-independent standards to manufacturers' *de facto* industry standards. The March 1986 issue of *Microprocessors and Microsystems* is devoted to the fast-changing field of backplane bus standards, and is a wide-ranging update of today's major bus schemes. It focuses particularly on recent developments and present status and capabilities and illustrates applications in advanced systems design.

Contents

Special issue orders, bulk orders, requests for subscription details and/or sample copies of the journal should be addressed to:

Geraldine Hills, *Microprocessors and Microsystems*, Butterworth Scientific Limited, PO Box 63, Westbury House, Bury Street, Guildford, Surrey GU2 5BH, UK. Telephone 0483 31261. Telex 859556

microprocessors and microsystems

vol 10 no 5 june 1986

Butterworths

editorial advisory board

Microprocessors and Microsystems is an international journal published in February, March, April, May, June, August, September, October, November, December. *Editorial Offices:* Butterworth Scientific Ltd, PO Box 63, Westbury House, Bury Street, Guildford, Surrey GU2 5BH, UK. Tel: (0483) 31261. Telegrams and telex: 859556 SCITEC G. *Publishing Director:* John Owens. *Production:* Tony Lewis

Microprocessors and Microsystems is published by Butterworth Scientific Ltd. *Registered Office:* Butterworth Scientific Ltd, 88 Kingsway, London WC2 6AB, UK

Subscription enquiries and orders: Quadrant Subscription Services Ltd, Oakfield House, Perrymount Road, Haywards Heath, West Sussex RH16 3DH, UK. Tel: (0444) 459188

Annual subscription (10 issues): £89.00 Overseas rate (£22.00 for private individuals); $160.00 US rate ($40.00 for private individuals)
UK subscription rates available on request.

Prices include packing and delivery by sea mail. Airmail prices available on request. Copies of this journal sent to subscribers in Bangladesh, India, Pakistan, Sri Lanka, Canada and the USA are air-speeded for quicker delivery.

Back issues: Prior to current volume available from Wm Dawson & Sons Ltd, Cannon House, Folkestone, Kent CT19 5EE, UK. Tel: (0303) 57421

US mailing agents: Mercury Airfreight International Ltd Inc., 10B Englehard Avenue, Avenel, NJ 07001, USA. Second class postage paid at Rahway, NJ. US Postmaster: Send address corrections to *Microprocessors and Microsystems* c/o Mercury Airfreight International Ltd Inc., address as above.

Reprints: Minimum order 100, available from the publisher.

Copyright: Readers who require copies of papers published in this journal may either purchase reprints or obtain permission to copy from the publisher at the following address: Butterworth Scientific Ltd, PO Box 63, Westbury House, Bury Street, Guildford, Surrey GU2 5BH, UK. For readers in the USA, permission to copy is given on the condition that the copier pay the stated per copy fee through the Copyright Clearance Center Inc., 26 Congress Street, Salem, MA 01979, USA, Tel: (617) 744-3350, for copying beyond that permitted by Sections 107 and 108 of the US Copyright Law. Fees appear in the code at the foot of the first page of major papers.

ISSN 0141 9331
MCRPD 10 (5) 249–304 1986

© Butterworth & Co (Publishers) Ltd 1986

Butterworths
Leading the Campaign
against
Copyright Erosion

Typeset by Tech-Set, Gateshead, Tyne & Wear, and printed by Dotesios (Printers) Ltd, Greenland Mills, Bradford on Avon, Wilts, UK.

microprocessors and microsystems

vol 10 no 5
june 1986

Editor Steve Hitchcock

Assistant Editor Andrew Taylor

Publisher Amanda Harper

notes for authors

Microprocessors and Microsystems

The Journal welcomes all articles on semi-conductor chip and PCB design, the application of microprocessors to industry, business and schools and on the development of microprocessor software. Articles can come from both academic and industrial research and should be 3000–5000 words in length. In addition to main articles, we welcome shorter case studies, design notes and teach-ins.

All submitted articles are refereed by two independent reviewers to ensure both accuracy and relevance, though it is the authors' sole responsibility that statements used are accurate. The author is also responsible for obtaining permission to quote material and to republish tables and illustrations.

Copyright

Before publication, authors are requested to assign copyright to Butterworth & Co (Publishers) Ltd. This allows the company to sanction reprints of the whole or part of the volume and authorize photocopies. The authors, however, still retain their traditional right to reuse or to veto third-party publication.

Preparation of scripts

As you can see from the Journal, every article published is stylized by us to keep consistency throughout each volume. We follow the Oxford English Dictionary. It would be helpful if you could follow the Journal style. The most important thing, though, is that you write (or rather type) in clear and concise English. Contributions should be typed double-spaced on one side of the paper. We would also appreciate it if you number each page and leave wide margins so we can prepare the article for the typesetters. Three copies of the article are preferred and should be sent to the editor.

Units

You should use, as far as possible, SI units. In circumstances where this is not possible, please provide a conversion factor at the first mention of the unit.

Illustrations

Line drawings

We have our own professional studio to ensure that line drawings are consistent with house style. We would prefer, however, to receive unlettered drawings (black ink on tracing paper) so we can put on the lettering ourselves. Drawings, if possible, should be of size consistent with the Journal, i.e. either 169 mm or 356 mm width. Single drawings should not extend over one page (500 mm) in height.

Computer printouts

Illustrations showing line printer listings, plotter output, etc should preferably be on unlined paper. Printouts will be reduced by us to the relevant size. Do not mark them as they will be used to make photographic copies for the typesetters. Only include sufficient lines for the reader to interpret the format and nature of the printout. Overlong printouts only cause confusion. Fuller explanation should appear in the caption and the text.

Photographs

Black and white glossy photographs (including Polaroid prints of VDU screens) should, where possible, be supplied unmounted. They should be labelled clearly on the back with a soft pencil. Photocopies of the photographs should be provided for the referees.

References

Our Journal style is to indicate the use of a reference in the text with a superscript as each one arises and give the full reference with the same number at the end. If a reference is cited more than once, the same number should be used each time. With a bibliography, the references are given in alphabetic order (dependent on the first author's surname). It would be helpful if you could follow this style. References take the following form:

(to journals)

1 **Buckroyd, A** 'Production testing of microprocessor-based equipment' *Microprocessors and Microsystems* Vol 5 No 7 (September 1981) pp 299–303

(to books)

2 **Gallacher, J** 'Testing and maintenance' in **Hanna, F K (ed.)** *Advanced techniques for microprocessor systems* Peter Peregrinus, Stevenage, UK (1980)

Proofs

Correspondence and proofs for corrections will be sent to the first named author, unless otherwise indicated. Authors will receive a copy of the galley proofs and copies of redrawn or relettered illustrations. It is important that these proofs should be checked and returned promptly.

Reprints

The first named author will receive 25 reprints of the technical article free of charge. Further copies, a minimum of 100, can be ordered at any time from the Reprints Department, Butterworth Scientific Ltd, Westbury House, PO Box 63, Bury Street, Guildford, Surrey GU2 5BH, UK.

Hardware system for realtime signal processing software development

Signal processing devices are now available at comparatively low cost, but they are complex and require specific development tools. **John Dunlop and Manal Al-Kindi** show how they have adapted a development system for the TMS32010 processor

A solution to the development of hardware for realtime signal processing applications using an existing Unix-based microprocessor development system is described. The system used is based upon a single special purpose digital signal processor controlled by a general purpose microprocessor. The modularity of the approach allows the possibility of control of several signal processing modules performing concurrent tasks. A particularly attractive feature of this development system is that it may be extended at low cost to accommodate new processors as they become available from manufacturers.

microprocessors   signal processing   software development

Until relatively recent times the application of sophisticated signal processing algorithms has been restricted to expensive mini or mainframe computers usually operating in nonrealtime environments. This situation has changed dramatically with the introduction by several manufacturers of fast, special purpose signal processing devices at comparatively low cost. Such devices are complex and require specific development tools for the design process. The system described in this paper is based on a multiuser microprocessor development system[1] which can be adapted cheaply to cater for a wide range of general purpose and special purpose microprocessor devices.

The main feature of the special purpose microprocessors is a high-speed parallel multiplier, as the limiting factor in most signal processing applications is the time required to perform multiplications. Another common feature of these devices is the use of a Harvard architecture[2] which allows the separation of data memory (containing signal processing coefficients) and program memory. This means that data may be manipulated whilst the next instruction is being fetched and decoded from the program memory. The TMS32010, on which the current system is based, can perform a 16×16 bit multiplication in 200 ns, for example.

The architecture of the TMS32010 is described fully in Reference 2, but its salient features are

- the majority of instructions, including 16×16 bit multiplication, are single cycle, having an execution time of 200 ns
- the device has a 16-bit data bus and instruction word
- the device has a 144×16 bit onchip data RAM and (on some versions) a 1536×16 bit onchip program ROM; on the versions with no onchip ROM, 4k words of external memory may be addressed externally
- the device has eight input and eight output channels which are addressed by the three least significant bits of the address bus
- a 16×16 bit multiplication and accumulate, which is the basis of virtually all signal processing algorithms, is executed in 400 ns.

These hardware features are specially designed for signal processing applications, and the accompanying instruction set is optimized from this point of view also. However, the instruction set does not have a software interrupt which is a common feature of general purpose microprocessors. The ability to interrupt a processor under software control is an essential requirement during the debugging phase of any software development and the implementation of such an interrupt, with this device, is described in detail below.

SYSTEM OVERVIEW

The design methodology adopted is one of using an existing multiuser microprocessor development system to support software and hardware design based on

Department of Electronic and Electrical Engineering, University of Strathclyde, Glasgow G1 1XW, UK

special purpose digital signal processing chips. The existing system consists of a large minicomputer running the Unix operating system and is equipped with a crossassembler for each processor supported. The cross-assemblers are all written to a common template using a standard Unix utility (Yacc)[3].

The detail of the multiuser system is described elsewhere[1], but essentially it consists of a number of target systems designed to accommodate a range of 8-bit general purpose microprocessors. Each target system is connected to the host by means of a 9.6 kbaud serial link. Object code is generated on the host machine and downloaded to the target system for local execution. The target systems are able to function independently of the host machine and all the normal development aids, such as single stepping of programs for debugging etc, are catered for.

In this paper we describe the essential problems involved in adapting the system to perform similar functions with special purpose signal processing chips, with particular reference being made to the TMS32010. This assumes the installation of a Yacc generated cross-assembler for the TMS32010 processor.

The data transfer between host, target system and VDU is normally handled by whichever processor happens to be resident in the target system using standard ACIAs operating at a clock frequency of 1 MHz. It became clear at an early stage in the design process that using the TMS32010 for normal serial data transfer and local software debugging is not an attractive proposition. The reasons for this are summarized below:

(a) Interfacing the TMS32010 with serial devices operating at a clock frequency of 1 MHz is not advised as this is below the minimum frequency of operation recommended by the manufacturer. The minimum frequency is actually one third of the maximum speed of 5 MHz.

(b) There is a limit to the 'off-chip' addressable memory of 4k (16 bit) words which should be devoted to as little communications overheads as possible.

(c) The processor lacks a general purpose instruction set (eg a software interrupt) which makes it difficult to incorporate functions essential for software development such as starting user program execution at a specific address, inserting breakpoints, single stepping through a user program, and examining the processor's internal registers.

(d) The TMS32010 has a specialized control bus which is not easily interfaced with the bus architecture of the target systems, the latter being designed for general purpose processors.

It was decided, because of these difficulties, to control the operation of the TMS32010 by means of an MC6809 8-bit general purpose processor. The 6809 handles communication with the host, loads the debug software for the TMS32010 and controls program execution. An additional advantage of using the 6809 as the master processor is that it is possible to supervise the operation of a number of TMS32010 cards, which allows the possibility of a multitasking environment.

HARDWARE FEATURES

A schematic of the MC6809/TMS32010 system is shown in Figure 1. This consists of two Eurocards plugged into the target system backplane. The 6809 card has onboard 4k of EPROM, containing the system monitor, and 4k of static RAM, which is the standard configuration for the multiuser development system. The 6809 processor has access, via the backplane, to RAM (8k × 8 bit and 4k × 1 bit) on the TMS32010 card. The 8k × 8 bit RAM is actually reconfigured to 4k × 16 bit when the TMS32010 is active. The 6809 also has access to serial I/O, via the backplane, for communication with the host and local VDU (this is not shown in Figure 1). On resetting the 6809, the TMS32010 is held in its 'reset' state by a toggle flip-flop. Under these circumstances all TMS32010 output lines, except the address lines, are in a high impedance state. The bus available (BA) and bus status (BS) outputs of

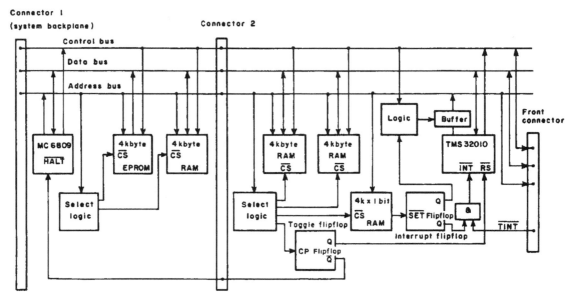

Figure 1. Schematic of the 6809/TMS32010 system

the 6809 are used to disable the buffer between the TMS32010 and the system address bus, thus isolating the TMS32010. The 6809 then has access to all memory on the TMS32010 card. Essentially, object code from the host is transferred to the 'dual port' RAM on the TMS32010 card under control of the 6809 and then execution is transferred to the special purpose processor.

The dual port RAM is the program memory for the TMS32010. This is arranged as two blocks of 4k × 8 bit bytes (using four IMS1420 devices) which are loaded separately by the 6809 and are then reconfigured to (4k × 16 bit) when the TMS32010 commences program execution at the full clock speed of 5 MHz. The reconfiguration is achieved by hardware using bilateral switches (CD4016). The TMS32010 card also contains a (4k × 1 bit) RAM which serves as the breakpoint RAM. This RAM is loaded with a 0 by the 6809 at whichever address it is required to generate a software interrupt for the TMS32010. When the TMS32010 output address matches the address at which a 0 has been stored this produces an active signal on the $\overline{INT}$ input of the processor, thus simulating a software interrupt.

The special purpose card is designed such that the TMS32010 will either be executing a program contained in the dual port RAM or be held in the reset state. In the latter case the internal registers of the TMS32010 are destroyed and so it is necessary to ensure that the contents of these registers are transferred to external RAM before the reset state is entered. The toggle flip-flop is used for transferring control between the 6809 and TMS32010 in such a way that the 6809 processor will be held in a 'halt' whilst the TMS32010 is executing a user program. When the HALT pin of the 6809 is held low its address and data buses assume a high impedance state.

PRINCIPLES OF OPERATION

When the TMS32010 is released from its reset state, program execution is vectored via locations > 000, > 001 (> is the manufacturer's symbol for a hexadecimal number). Hence, prior to releasing the TMS32010 from this state the 6809 must load this location with the start address of the debug program execution. (When executed by the TMS32010 the debug software loads the processor registers and the contents of the stack from RAM; the stack contains the start address of the user program.) A flow chart describing the sequence of operations is shown in Figure 2, and the TMS32010 memory map is shown in Figure 3. The 6809 commences by loading the dual port RAM according to Figure 3. In addition to the user program object code the RAM must be loaded with various vectors, initial contents of the TMS32010 internal registers and data memory and the resident debug software. The single bit RAM is then loaded with 0s at the desired breakpoint addresses.

The TMS32010 memory map is configured in such a way that the last 256 locations are reserved as follows

- from > F00 to > F8F accommodate the contents of the internal data memory and registers of the TMS32010 (the last 12 locations in page 2 of the data memory are allocated to store the register contents)
- from > F90 to > FE8 are allocated to the resident debug software; amongst other functions this software transfers the contents of registers and data memory

from RAM before program execution, and in the reverse direction when a simulated software interrupt occurs.

HARDWARE DETAILS

A schematic of the TMS32010 card is shown in Figure 4. At system power up the reset line $\overline{NRST}$ goes low, resetting a flip-flop whose Q output is connected to the $\overline{RS}$ pin of the TMS32010 and whose $\overline{Q}$ output is connected to the HALT pin of the 6809. Under these circumstances the 6809 is active and operates under the control of the monitor

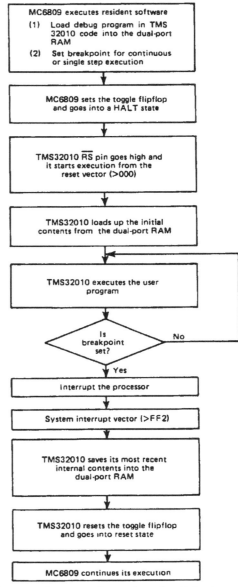

Figure 2. Sequence of operation of 6809/TMS32010 target system

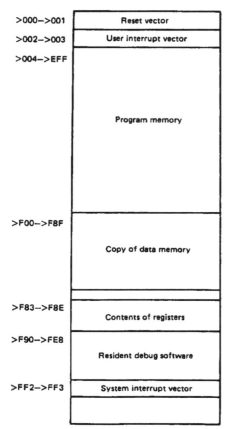

>000->001	Reset vector
>002->003	User interrupt vector
>004->EFF	Program memory
>F00->F8F	Copy of data memory
>F83->F8E	Contents of registers
>F90->FE8	Resident debug software
>FF2->FF3	System interrupt vector

Figure 3. *TMS32010 program memory map*

program present in the 4k EPROM on the 6809 card. The 6809 is able to toggle this flip-flop by placing $93XX, which is decoded as PAG93, on its address bus ($ is the Motorola standard symbol for hexadecimal). This signal toggles the flip-flop, thus placing a high level on the $\overline{RS}$ pin of the TMS32010, when the BS and BA outputs of the 6809 indicate that it is in the 'halt' state.

When the TMS32010 is active, control may be transferred back to the 6809 by once again toggling the flip-flop. This is done at the end of an interrupt sequence initiated by a 0 appearing on the data output of the 4k × 1 bit breakpoint RAM. The simulated 'software interrupt' causes the TMS32010 to enter its interrupt routine vectored via locations > FF2, > FF3. This routine transfers the internal registers of the processor to locations > F83 to > F8E and the data memory to locations > F00 to > F82 and outputs > 007 on the TMS32010 address bus. This address is decoded as $\overline{RST}$ and toggles the flip-flop which forces the TMS32010 to its reset state and allows the 6809 to regain control of the buses. The 6809 is then able to access the contents of the dual port RAM and, in particular, to display the stored contents of all the internal registers of the TMS32010.

A breakpoint is set by the 6809 by writing a logic 0 to the desired breakpoint address(es) in a HM6147-45 high-speed RAM. When the address bus of the TMS32010 matches a breakpoint address a low level will appear at the DOUT pin of the breakpoint RAM. This pulse will set the

interrupt flip-flop (Figure 4) which then interrupts the processor by means of its Q output. Clearly it is desirable to preserve the normal hardware interrupt features of the TMS32010 in addition to allowing simulated software interrupts. This has been made possible by using the Q output of the interrupt flip-flop to indicate when the interrupt is a simulated software interrupt.

The normal interrupt response of the TMS32010 is to vector via locations > 002, > 003. For a simulated software interrupt the vector address is effectively changed to > FF2, > FF3. This is achieved by disabling the eight most significant bits of the TMS32010 address buffer by the Q output of the interrupt flip-flop when the address > 002 appears on the TMS32010 output pins. This is achieved using address decoding, as shown in Figure 4. When this buffer is disabled the outputs go high by means of pull-up resistors. Hence when the interrupt vector addresses > 002 or > 003 appear on the address pins of the processor, the address actually on the bus is > FF2 or > FF3.

The toggle flip-flop is reset by placing the address > 007 on the TMS32010 bus. This is actually achieved using an Out 7 instruction or a table write (TBLW) to location > 007. Since address > 007 is decoded to produce the $\overline{RST}$ pulse for the toggle flip-flop, a TBLW to location > 007 or an Out 7 instruction should not appear in a user program.

A/D INTERFACE

The processor card is interfaced via a 40-way connector to a high-speed A/D and D/A converter card. Input and output of data is accomplished by In and Out instructions via the data ports of the TMS32010 (except port 7).

PROGRAM DEVELOPMENT EXAMPLE

This section describes the realization of a fast Fourier transform (FFT) algorithm for processing real analogue data, based upon the hardware described above. The FFT is a widely used technique[4] for evaluating the discrete Fourier transform of a sampled signal. A general block diagram of the FFT processor is shown in Figure 5. The analogue interface board contains a 12-bit A/D converter type ADC80-12 and a 12-bit D/A converter type AD565AJD. The applied analogue signal is sampled under processor control and the samples are stored in specific locations of the data memory. When sufficient data is available the processor then commences the arithmetic-intensive algorithm for evaluating the discrete Fourier transform of the stored samples.

The transform algorithm is based upon a 32-point radix 2 decimation in time algorithm. The basic unit of this algorithm, commonly referred to as a 'butterfly', accepts two complex numbers as input and produces two complex numbers as output. A 32-point transform is optimum for the TMS32010 as all 32 complex coefficients may be held in the data memory at the same time (provision is also required for intermediate storage of 16 variables). If more than 32 data points are considered, ie 64, 128 etc, coefficients must be transferred from the external memory which will slow the execution time of the algorithm considerably. A general flow chart of the FFT algorithm is shown in Figure 6.

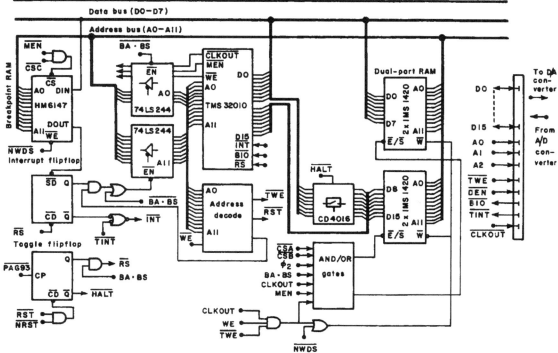

Control bus [$\overline{PAG\,93}$, $\overline{NRST}$, $\overline{NWDS}$, $\overline{HALT}$, BA, BS, $\overline{CSA}$, $\overline{CSB}$, $\overline{CSC}$, ϕ_2 (MC 6809 system clock)]

Figure 4. Schematic of the TMS32010 card

The constants referred to in block 1 are pointers for the input data locations and initialization values for the analogue interface board. Blocks 2 and 3 are self explanatory. When the 32 real data samples are available a window function is implemented (Hanning) by weighting the samples appropriately. In block 4 a bit reversal re-ordering routine is performed on the input data. This scrambling of data is necessary to carry out data point computations in place and hence minimize storage requirements. This routine has been timed using a synchronized counter and has an execution time of 200 µs. Block 5 is the FFT algorithm which is based on the signal flow graph of Figure 7.

The algorithm is split up into the computation of a number of arrays with complex coefficients. If the number of data points is $N = 2^{**}NP$ then NP is the number of arrays to be computed and the number of butterflies required is $N/2$. (When the data is real, the real part of the spectrum has even symmetry about (sampling frequency) /2 and the imaginary part of the spectrum has odd symmetry about the same frequency). The weighting

factors $W' = \cos (2\pi n/N) + j \sin (2\pi n/N)$ are constants and are stored in data memory as two 16-bit quantities. The coefficients are stored in the data memory as a 15-bit binary representation of the decimal fraction; in the case

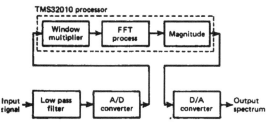

Figure 5. TMS32010 based FFT processor

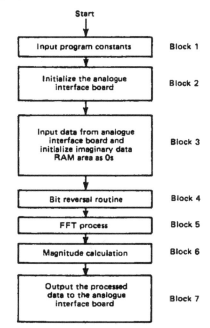

Figure 6. Flow chart for the FFT algorithm

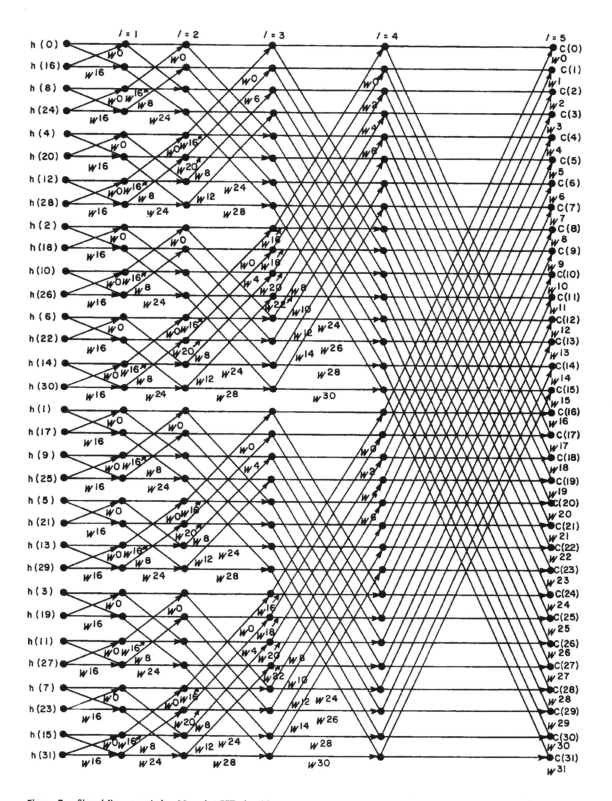

Figure 7. Signal flow graph for 32-point FFT algorithm

of the FFT algorithm all coefficients will be within the range -1 to $+1$. If the input signal is also in the range -1 to $+1$ this means that the result of a computation at any point in the algorithm will be the sum of two multiplications. Each multiplication will have a maximum value of 1 (since all coefficients and data samples have a maximum value of unity), and thus the sum of two multiplications will have a maximum value of 2. Overflow is avoided in this algorithm by truncating the result of each multiplication to 15 bits and dividing by 2, prior to forming the sum. The overall effect of this division is to scale the output of the transform by $1/N$. The modulus of each component is calculated in block 6 and the data scaled pending transfer to the D/A converter for display. The execution time of block 5 is 1.25 ms.

It is worth mentioning here that the FFT algorithm was specifically designed to minimize the number of multiplications because this was the slowest arithmetic operation in many digital computers. The TMS32010 is equipped with a high-speed multiplier which completes a 16 bit $\times$ 16 bit multiplication in one machine cycle (200 ns). This is exactly the time required for a 16-bit addition. This means that there is no advantage in reducing the number of multiplications at the expense of more additions. Hence, in the case of the TMS32010 and other like processors it is important to reduce the overall number of arithmetic operations rather than the number of multiplications, to achieve the fastest computation times.

CONCLUSIONS

This paper has described a flexible and low incremental cost method of supporting development of hardware and software for the latest special purpose microprocessor chips now appearing on the market. The methodology adopted is to use a general purpose microprocessor to control a special purpose device and handle normal serial data communications. Apart from the attractiveness of employing existing standard cards, this approach also allows a single processor to sequence a number of special purpose cards performing concurrent tasks. Such techniques will be a valuable intermediate method of introducing realtime signal processing to signal bandwidths beyond the capability of a single processor.

REFERENCES

1 **Dunlop, J** 'Multiuser microprocessor development system for undergraduate training' *Proc IEE* Vol 131, Part A No 3 (1984) pp 170–173

2 *TMS32010 user's guide*, Texas Instruments, USA (1983) Chapter 2

3 **Dunlop, J and Lorimer, A G** 'A development system for special purpose signal processing applications' *Signal Proc.* Vol 9, No 3 (1985) pp 207–213

4 **Brigham, O** *The fast Fourier transform* Prentice Hall, Englewood Cliffs, NJ, USA (1974)

John Dunlop graduated in electrical engineering from University College Swansea, UK, in 1966 and was awarded a PhD by the University of Wales, UK, in 1970. He joined the lecturing staff at the University of Strathclyde, UK, in 1969 and is currently a senior lecturer in the Department of Electronic and Electrical Engineering. His research interests include local area communications networks, mobile communications, bandwidth compression, distributed processor systems and underwater communications. Dr Dunlop is an author of undergraduate and postgraduate texts in telecommunications engineering and signal processing. He is also a consultant in the application of microprocessors to medical and industrial instrumentation systems.

Manal J Al-Kindi received the degree of BSc in electrical engineering from the University of Technology, Baghdad, Iraq, in 1978. He was subsequently employed as a demonstrator at the University until 1984. Mr Al-Kindi is currently at the Department of Electronic and Electrical Engineering, University of Strathclyde, Glasgow, UK, working on a postgraduate programme within the Communications Group. His research interests include realtime digital signal processing, adaptive systems and multiprocessor systems.

Exception handling in the 68000, Part 2

In the second of two tutorial papers, **Alan Clements** examines in detail the implementation of hardware and software initiated exceptions on the 68000, with particular emphasis on interrupts

The paper discusses the implementation by the 68000 microprocessor of hardware and software initiated exceptions. The three categories of hardware exception — resets, bus errors and interrupts — are covered first, with detailed discussion of how vectored and autovectored interrupts are processed. The software initiated exceptions discussed are illegal operation codes, traces, emulator-mode exceptions and traps. An example of the use of a trap handler is given.

microprocessors   exceptions   interrupts   68000

Part 1 of this paper[1] introduced the concept of the exception, a mechanism employed by computers to deal with certain events. These events cannot easily be handled by normal 'inline' programming techniques and require the processor to temporarily interrupt its normal processing. Part 2 of the paper examines how the 68000 implements asynchronous exceptions, and introduces the software exception.

HARDWARE INITIATED EXCEPTIONS

Three types of exception are initiated by events taking place outside the 68000 and are communicated to the CPU via its input pins; they are the reset, the bus error and the interrupt. Each of these three exceptions has a direct effect on the hardware design of a 68000-based micro-computer. This section examines each of these systems in more detail, beginning with a look at the control of the RESET* pin.

Reset

It was stated in Part 1 of the paper[1] that the exception vector table is frequently located in read/write memory, and that the circuit shown in Figure 3 of Part 1 can be used to overlay the first 8 byte of the read/write memory with ROM containing the reset vectors. The only other circuitry associated with the 68000's reset mechanism is that connected to the RESET* pin itself.

The designers of the 68000 have made RESET* a bidirectional I/O, which complicates the design of the reset circuitry. In normal operation the RESET* pin is an

Department of Computer Science, Teesside Polytechnic, Middlesbrough, Cleveland TS1 3BA, UK

input. Almost all microprocessor systems connect every device that can be reset to the RESET* pin. This means that all devices are reset along with the 68000 at power up or following a manual reset. The 68000 is also capable of executing a software reset instruction which forces its RESET* pin active low, resetting all devices connected to it. This facility was provided to permit a system reset under software control that does not affect the processor itself. Consequently the RESET* pin of the 68000 cannot be driven by gates with active pull-up circuits. RESET* must be driven by open-collector or open-drain outputs.

Another aspect to note about hardware initiated resets is that both RESET* and HALT* must be asserted simultaneously. Like RESET*, the HALT* pin is bidirectional and must also be driven by an open-collector or open-drain output. If RESET* and HALT* are asserted together following a system crash, they must be held low for at least 10 clock cycles to ensure satisfactory operation. However, at power up they must be held low for at least 100 ms after the V_{cc} supply to the 68000 has become established.

A possible arrangement of a reset circuit for the 68000 is given in Figure 5. IC1, a 555 timer, generates an active-high pulse at its output terminal shortly after the initial application of power. The timer is configured to operate in an astable mode, generating a single pulse whenever it is triggered. The time constant of the output pulse (ie the duration of the reset pulse) is determined by resistor R_2 and capacitor C_2. R_1 and C_1 trigger the circuit on the application of power. The output is buffered and inverted by IC2a to become the system active-low power-on-reset pulse (POR*), which can be used by the rest of the system as appropriate. A pair of crosscoupled NAND gates provides a manual reset facility.

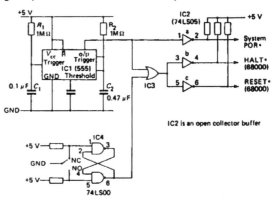

Figure 5.   *Control of RESET* in a 68000-based system*

0141–9331/86/05258–10 $03.00 © 1986 Butterworth & Co. (Publishers) Ltd

Bus error

A bus error is an exception raised in response to a failure by the system to complete a bus cycle. As there are many possible failure modes, the details of each depending on the type of hardware used to implement the system, the detection of a bus error is left to the systems designer rather than to the 68000 itself. All the 68000 provides is an active-low input, BERR*, which generates a bus error exception when asserted.

Figure 6 gives the timing requirements that the BERR* input must satisfy. To be recognized during the current bus cycle, BERR* must fulfil one of two conditions: it must either be asserted at least time t_{ASI} (the asynchronous input set-up time) before the falling edge of state S4; or it must be asserted at least time t_{BELDAL} (BERR* low to DTACK* low) before the falling edge of DTACK*. It is necessary to maintain BERR* active low until time t_{SHBEH} (AS* high to BERR* high) after the address and data strobes have become inactive. The minimum value of t_{SHBEH} is zero, implying that BERR* may be negated concurrently with AS* or LDS*/UDS*. It is important to realize that, if BERR* meets the timing requirement t_{ASI}, it will be processed in the current bus cycle irrespective of the state of DTACK*.

There are a number of reasons why BERR* may be asserted in a system. Typical applications of BERR* are as follows.

● Illegal memory access. If the processor tries to access memory at an address not populated by memory, BERR* may be asserted. BERR* may also be asserted if an attempt is made to write to a read-only memory address. The decision as to whether to assert BERR* in these cases is a design decision. (All 8-bit microprocessors are quite happy to access nonexistent memory or to write to ROM!) The philosophy of 68000 systems design is to trap events which may lead to unforeseen circumstances. If the processor tries to write to ROM, the operating system can intervene because of the exception raised by BERR*.

● Faulty memory access. If error-detecting memory is employed, a read access to a memory location at which an error is detected can be used to assert BERR*. In this way the processor will never try to process data that is in error due to a fault in the memory.

● Failure to assert valid peripheral address (VPA*). If the processor accesses a synchronous bus device and VPA* is not asserted after some time-out period, BERR* must be asserted to stop the system hanging up and waiting for VPA* forever.

● Memory privilege violation. When the 68000 is used in a system with some form of memory management, BERR* may be asserted to indicate that the current memory access is violating a privilege. This may be an access by one user to another user's program. In a system with virtual memory, it may result from a page fault, indicating that the data being accessed is not currently in read/write memory.

Bus error sequence

When BERR* is asserted by external logic and satisfies its set-up timing requirements, the processor negates AS* in state S6. As long as BERR* remains asserted the data and address buses are both floated. When the external logic negates BERR*, the processor begins a normal exception processing sequence for a Group 0 exception. Figure 4b (Part 1 of the paper[1]) shows that additional information is pushed onto the system stack to facilitate recovery from the bus error. Once all phases of the exception processing sequence have been completed, the 68000 begins to deal with the problem of the error in the BERR* exception handling routine. It must be emphasized that the treatment of the hardware problem which led to the bus error takes place at a software level within the operating system. For example, if a user program generates a bus error, the exception processing routine may abort the user's program and provide him/her with diagnostic information to help deal with the problem. The information stored on the stack by a bus error exception (or an address error) is to be regarded as diagnostic information only and should not be used to institute a return from exception. In other words, the 68000 does not support a return from a Group 0 exception (although the 68010 does).

Rerunning the bus cycle

It is possible to deal with a bus error in a way which does not involve an exception. If, during a memory access, the external hardware detects a memory error and asserts both BERR* and HALT* simultaneously, the processor attempts to rerun the current bus cycle.

Figure 7 illustrates a rerun cycle. A bus fault is detected in the read cycle and both BERR* and HALT* are asserted simultaneously. As long as the HALT* signal remains asserted, the address and data buses are floated and no external activity takes place. When HALT* is negated by the external logic, the processor will rerun the previous bus cycle using the same address, the same function codes, the same data (for a write operation) and the same

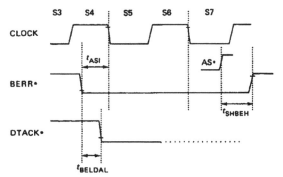

Figure 6. Bus error input (BERR*) timing diagram: t_{ASI} = 20 ns (min.); t_{BELDAL} = 20 ns (min.); t_{SHBEH} = 0 ns (min.)

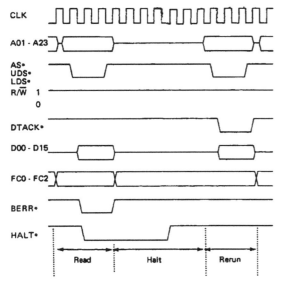

CLK

A01 - A23

AS•
UDS•
LDS•
R/W̄   1
        0

DTACK•

D00 - D15

FC0 - FC2

BERR•

HALT•

Read | Halt | Rerun

Figure 7.   Rerunning the bus cycle

control signals. For correct operation, the BERR* signal must be negated at least one clock cycle before HALT* is negated.

A possible implementation of bus error control in a sophisticated 68000-based system might detect a bus error and assert BERR* and HALT* simultaneously. The rising edge of AS* can be used to release BERR* and HALT* at least one clock cycle later. This guarantees a rerun of the bus cycle. Of course, if the error is a 'hard' error (ie is persistent), rerunning the bus cycle will achieve little and external logic will once again detect the error. A reasonable strategy would be to permit, say, three reruns and assert BERR* alone on the next cycle, forcing a conventional bus error exception.

Interrupt

As discussed in Part 1[1], an interrupt is a request for service generated by some external peripheral, which the 68000 implements within the framework of its overall exception handling procedures. The 68000 offers two schemes for dealing with interrupts. One is intended for peripherals specifically designed for 16-bit processors, while the other is more suited to earlier 8-bit (6800 series) peripherals.

An external device signals its need for attention by placing a 3-bit code on the 68000's interrupt request inputs (IPL0*, IPL1* and IPL2*). The code corresponds to the priority of the interrupt and is numbered from 0 to 7. A level 7 code indicates the highest priority, level 1 the lowest priority and level 0 the default state of no interrupt request. While it would be possible to design peripherals with three interrupt request output lines on which they put a 3-bit interrupt priority code, it is easier to have a

single interrupt request output and to design external hardware to convert its priority into a 3-bit code suitable for the 68000.

Figure 8 shows a typical scheme for handling interrupt requests in a 68000 system. A 74LS148 eight-line to three-line priority encoder is all that is needed to translate one of the seven levels of interrupt request into a 3-bit code. Table 3 gives the truth table for this device. Input EI* is an active-low enable input, used in conjunction with outputs GS and EO to expand the 74LS148 in systems with more then seven levels of priority.

As the enable input and expanding outputs are not needed in this application of the 74LS148, Table 3 has been redrawn in Table 4 with inputs 1-7 renamed IRQ1*–IRQ7*, respectively, and outputs A0–A2 renamed IPL0*–IPL2*. It must be appreciated that all inputs and all outputs are active low, so that an output value 0, 0, 0 denotes an interrupt request of level 7, while an output 1, 1, 1 denotes a level 0 interrupt request (ie no interrupt).

Inspecting Table 4 reveals that a logical zero on interrupt request input i forces interrupt request inputs 1 to $i - 1$ into 'don't care' states (ie if interrupt IRQi* is asserted, the state of interrupt request inputs IRQ1* to

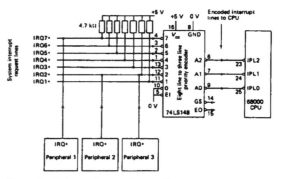

Figure 8.   Interrupt request encoding

Table 3.   Truth table for the 74LS148 eight-line to three-line priority encoder

Inputs									Outputs				
EI*	0	1	2	3	4	5	6	7	A2	A1	A0	GS	EO
1	X	X	X	X	X	X	X	X	1	1	1	1	1
0	1	1	1	1	1	1	1	1	1	1	1	1	0
0	X	X	X	X	X	X	X	0	0	0	0	0	1
0	X	X	X	X	X	X	0	1	0	0	1	0	1
0	X	X	X	X	X	0	1	1	0	1	0	0	1
0	X	X	X	X	0	1	1	1	0	1	1	0	1
0	X	X	X	0	1	1	1	1	1	0	0	0	1
0	X	X	0	1	1	1	1	1	1	0	1	0	1
0	X	0	1	1	1	1	1	1	1	1	0	0	1
0	0	1	1	1	1	1	1	1	1	1	1	0	1

0 = low-level signal (< VIL); 1 = high-level signal (> VIH);
X = 'don't care'

Table 4.   Truth table for a 74LS148 configured as in Figure 8

Inputs								Outputs		
Level	IRQ1*	IRQ2*	IRQ3*	IRQ4*	IRQ5*	IRQ6*	IRQ7*	IPL2*	IPL1*	IPL0*
7	X	X	X	X	X	X	0	0	0	0
6	X	X	X	X	X	0	1	0	0	1
5	X	X	X	X	0	1	1	0	1	0
4	X	X	X	0	1	1	1	0	1	1
3	X	X	0	1	1	1	1	1	0	0
2	X	0	1	1	1	1	1	1	0	1
1	0	1	1	1	1	1	1	1	1	0
0	1	1	1	1	1	1	1	1	1	1

0 = low-level signal (< VIL); 1 = high-level signal (> VIH); X = 'don't care'

IRQ[i − 1]* has no effect on the output code IPL0*-IPL2*). It is this property that the microprocessor systems designer relies on. Devices with high-priority interrupts are connected to the higher-order inputs. Should two or more levels of interrupt occur simultaneously, only the higher value is reflected in the output code to the 68000's IPL pins.

Figure 8 demonstrates that the 74LS148 does not restrict the system to only seven devices capable of generating interrupt requests. More than one device can be wired to a given level of interrupt request as illustrated by peripherals 2 and 3. If peripheral 2 or 3 (or both) asserts its interrupt request output (IRQ*), a level 2 interrupt is signalled to the 68000, provided that levels 3-7 are all inactive. The mechanism used to distinguish between an interrupt from peripheral 2 and one from peripheral 3 is called 'daisychaining' and enables several devices to share the same level of interrupt priority while permitting only one of them to respond to an IACK cycle. Daisychaining is implemented by feeding the IACK* response from the CPU into the first peripheral in the daisychain. When an IACK cycle is executed, the first peripheral receives the IACK* signal from the CPU. If this peripheral generated the interrupt, it responds to the IACK*. If it did not generate the interrupt, it passes the IACK* signal onto the next peripheral in the chain. Note that, in this arrangement, each peripheral requires an IACK_IN* pin and an IACK_OUT* pin.

Processing the interrupt

All interrupts to the 68000 are latched internally and made pending. Group 0 exceptions (reset, bus error, address error) take precedence over an interrupt in Group 1. Therefore, if a Group 0 exception occurs, it is serviced before the interrupt. A trace exception in Group 1 takes precedence over the interrupt, so that if an interrupt request occurs during the execution of an instruction while the T bit is asserted, the trace exception has priority and is serviced first. Assuming that none of the above exceptions have been raised, the 68000 compares the level of the interrupt request with the value recorded in the interrupt mask bits of the processor status word.

If the priority of the pending interrupt is lower than or equal to the current processor priority denoted by the interrupt mask, the interrupt request remains pending and the next instruction in sequence is executed. Interrupt level 7 is treated slightly differently, as it is always processed regardless of the value of the interrupt mask bits (ie a level 7 interrupt always interrupts a level 7 interrupt if one is currently being processed). Any other level of interrupt can be interrupted only by a higher level of priority. Note that a level 7 interrupt is edge sensitive and is interrupted only by a high-to-low transition on IRQ7*.

Once the processor has made a decision to process an interrupt, it begins an exception processing sequence as described earlier. The only deviation from the normal sequence of events dictated by a Group 1 or Group 2 exception is that the interrupt mask bits of the processor status word are updated before exception processing continues. The level of the interrupt request being serviced is copied into the current processor status. This means that the interrupt cannot be interrupted unless the new interrupt has a higher priority.

Example. Suppose that the current (ie pre-interrupt) interrupt mask is level 3. If a level 5 interrupt occurs, it is processed and the interrupt mask is set to level 5. If, during the processing of this interrupt, a level 4 interrupt is requested, it is made pending even though it has a higher priority than the original interrupt mask. When the level 5 interrupt has been processed, a return from exception is made and the former processor status word is restored. As the old interrupt mask was level 3, the pending interrupt of level 4 is then serviced.

Unlike other exceptions, an interrupt may obtain its vector number externally from the device that made the interrupt request. As stated above, there are two ways of identifying the source of the interrupt, one vectored and one autovectored.

Vectored interrupt

After the processor has completed the last instruction before recognizing the interrupt and stacked the low-order word of the program counter, it executes an interrupt acknowledge cycle (IACK cycle). During an IACK cycle, the 68000 obtains the vector number from the interrupting device, with which it will later determine the appropriate exception vector.

Figure 9 shows the sequence of events taking place during an IACK cycle; it can be seen that an IACK cycle is just a modified read cycle. Because the 68000 puts out the special function code 1, 1, 1 on FC2, FC1 and FC0 during an IACK cycle, the interrupting device is able to detect the IACK cycle. At the same time, the level of the interrupt is put out on address lines A01–A03. The IACK cycle should not decode memory addresses A04–A23 and memory components should be disabled when FC2-FC0 = 1, 1, 1. The device that generated the interrupt at the specified

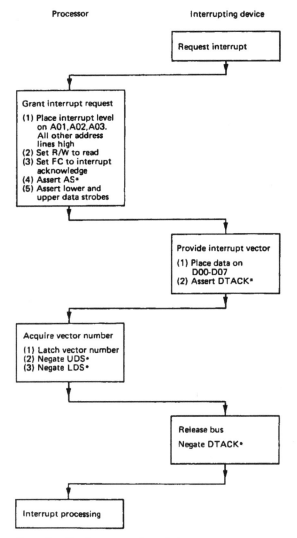

Figure 9. The interrupt acknowledge sequence

level then provides a vector number on D00–D07 and asserts DTACK*, as in any normal read cycle. The remainder of the IACK cycle is identical to a read cycle. Figure 10 gives the timing diagram of an IACK cycle. Note that the IACK cycle falls between the stacking of the low-order word of the program counter and the stacking of the high-order word.

After the peripheral has provided a vector number on D00–D07, the processor multiplies it by four to obtain the address of the entry point to the exception processing routine from the exception vector table. Although a device can provide an 8-bit vector number giving 256 possible values, there is space reserved in the exception vector table for only 192 unique vectors. This is more than adequate for the vast majority of applications. (However, a peripheral can put out vector numbers 0–63, as there is nothing to stop these numbers being programmed into the peripheral and the processor does not guard against this situation. In other words, if a programmer programs a peripheral to respond to an IACK cycle with, say, a vector number 5, then an interrupt from this device would cause an exception corresponding to vector number 5 — the value also appropriate to a divide-by-zero exception. While at times this might be useful, it seems an oversight to allow interrupt vector numbers to overlap with other types of exceptions.)

A possible arrangement of hardware needed to implement a vectored interrupt scheme is given in Figure 11. A peripheral asserts its interrupt request output, IRQ5*, which is encoded by IC3 to provide the 68000 with a level 5 interrupt request. When the processor acknowledges this request, it places 1, 1, 1 on the function code output, which is decoded by the three-line to eight-line decoder IC1. The interrupt acknowledge output (IACK*) from IC1 enables a second three-line to eight-line decoder, IC2, which decodes address lines A01–A03 into seven levels of interrupt acknowledge. In this case, IACK5* from IC2 is fed back to the peripheral, which then responds by placing its vector number onto the low-order byte of the system data bus. If the peripheral has not been programmed to supply an interrupt vector number it should place $0F on the data bus, corresponding to an uninitialized interrupt vector exception.

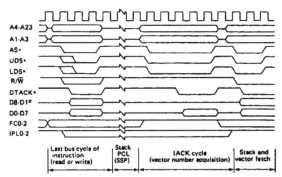

Figure 10. Interrupt acknowledge and the IACK cycle

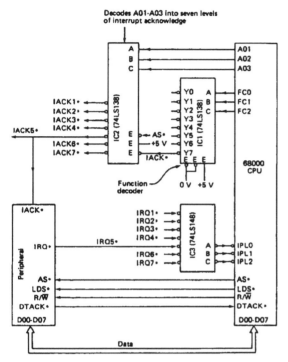

Figure 11. *Implementing the vectored interrupt*

Autovectored interrupt

As set out above, a device which generates an interrupt request must be capable of identifying itself when the 68000 carries out an interrupt acknowledge sequence. This presents no problem for modern 68000-based peripherals such as the 68230 parallel interface-timer.

Unfortunately, older peripherals originally designed for 8-bit processors do not have interrupt acknowledge facilities and are unable to respond with the appropriate vector number on D00–D07 during an IACK cycle. The systems designer could overcome this problem by designing a subsystem which supplied the appropriate vector as if it came from the interrupting peripheral. Such an approach is valid but a little messy: a single-chip peripheral would need several components just to provide a vector number in an IACK cycle.

An alternative scheme is available for peripherals that cannot provide their own vector numbers. An IACK cycle, like any other memory access, is allowed to continue to state S5 by the assertion of DTACK*. If, however, DTACK* is not asserted but VPA* is asserted, the 68000 carries out an autovectored interrupt.

Valid peripheral address, VPA*, belongs to the 68000's synchronous data bus control group of signals. When asserted, VPA* informs the 68000 that the present memory access cycle is to be synchronous and to 'look like' a 6800 series memory access cycle. If the current bus

cycle is an IACK cycle, the 68000 executes a 'spurious read cycle', ie an IACK cycle is executed but the interrupting device does not place a vector number on D00–D07. Nor does the 68000 read the contents of the data bus; instead, it generates the appropriate vector number internally.

The 68000 reserves vector numbers 25–31 (decimal) for its autovector operation (see Table 1). Each of these autovectors is associated with an interrupt on IRQ1*–IRQ7*. For example, if IRQ2* is asserted followed by VPA* during the IACK cycle, vector number 26 is generated by the 68000 and the interrupt handling routine address read from memory location $000068.

Should several interrupt requesters assert the same interrupt request line, the 68000 will not be able to distinguish between them. The appropriate interrupt handling routine must poll each of the possible devices in turn (ie the status register of each peripheral must be read to determine the source of the interrupt).

The timing diagram of an autovector sequence is given in Figure 12 and is almost identical to the vectored IACK sequence of Figure 10, except that VPA* is asserted shortly after the interrupter has detected an IACK cycle from FC0–FC2. Because VPA* has been asserted, wait states are introduced into the current read cycle in order to synchronize the cycle with VMA*. Note that this is a dummy read cycle as nothing is read. (The autovector is generated internally and no device places data on D00–D07 during the cycle.)

The hardware necessary to implement an autovectored interrupt is minimal. Figure 13 shows a possible arrangement involving a typical 6800 series peripheral which requests an interrupt in the normal way by asserting its IRQ* output. This is prioritized by IC3 and an acknowledge signal is generated by ICs 1 and 2.

The interrupting device cannot, of course, respond to an IACK* signal. Instead, the appropriate interrupt acknowledge signal from the 68000 is combined with the

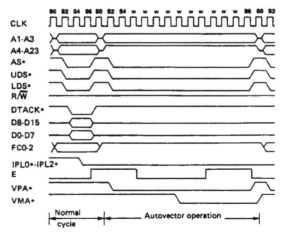

Figure 12. *Timing diagram of an autovectored interrupt*

teach-in

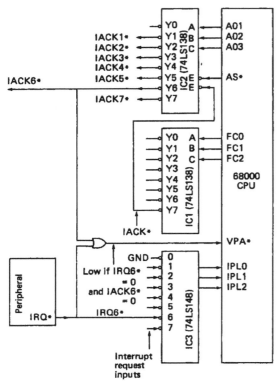

Figure 13. Hardware needed to implement an autovectored interrupt

interrupt request output from the peripheral in an OR gate. Only when the peripheral has asserted its IRQ* and the correct level of IACK* has been generated does the output of the OR gate go low to assert VPA* and force an autovectored interrupt.

SOFTWARE INITIATED EXCEPTIONS

A software initiated exception is one that occurs as the result of an attempt to execute certain types of instruction (not the address error which is classified as a hardware initiated interrupt). Software initiated interrupts fall into two categories: those executed deliberately by the programmer and those representing a 'cry for help'.

The 'help' group comprises the illegal op. code, privilege violation, TRAPV and divide-by-zero exceptions. These are all exceptions that are normally generated by something going wrong; therefore the operating system needs to intervene and sort things out. The nature of this intervention is very much dependent on the structure of the operating system. Often, in a multiprogramming environment, the individual task creating the exception will be aborted, leaving all other tasks unaffected.

Software exceptions initiated by the programmer are the trace, the trap and the emulator. The trace exception mode is in force whenever the T bit of the status word is set. After each instruction has been executed, a trace exception is automatically generated if the T bit is set. This is done to allow the user to monitor the execution of a program.

Illegal op. code exceptions

Consider the illegal op. code exception. This is raised when the 68000 attempts to execute an op. code that does not form part of the 68000's instruction set. The only way that this can happen is when something has gone seriously wrong — an op. code has been corrupted in memory or a jump has been made to a region containing nonvalid 68000 code. The latter event frequently results from wrongly computed GOTOs. Clearly, once such an event has occurred, it is futile to continue trying to execute further instructions as they have no real meaning. By generating an illegal op. code exception, the operating system can inform users of the problem and invite them to do something about it.

Trace exceptions

The simplest trace facility would allow the user to dump the contents of all registers on the CRT terminal after the execution of each instruction. Unfortunately, this leads to the production of vast amounts of utterly useless information. For example, if the 68000 were executing an operation to clear an array by executing a CLR.L (A4)+ instruction 64k times, the human operator would not wish to see the contents of all registers displayed after the execution of each CLR.

A better approach is to display only the information needed. Before the trace mode is invoked, the user informs the operating system of the conditions under which the results of a trace exception are to be displayed. Some of the events which can be used to trigger the display of registers during a trace exception are

- execution of a predefined number of instructions (eg contents of registers may be displayed after, say, 50 instructions have been executed)
- execution of an instruction at a given address (equivalent to a break point)
- execution of an instruction falling within a given range of addresses, or the access of an operand falling within the same range
- as last event, but with the contents of the register displayed only when an address generated by the 68000 falls outside the predetermined range
- execution of a particular instruction (eg contents of the registers may be displayed following the execution of a TAS instruction)
- any memory access which modifies the contents of a memory location (ie any write access)

It is possible to combine several of the above conditions to create a composite event. For example, the contents of registers may be displayed whenever the 68000 executes write accesses to the region of memory space between $3A 0000–$3A 00FF.

Emulator-mode exceptions

Emulator-mode exceptions provide the systems designer with tools to develop software for new hardware before that hardware has been fully realized. Suppose a company is working on a coprocessor to generate the sine of a 16-bit fractional operand. For commercial reasons, it may be necessary to develop software for this hardware long before the coprocessor is in actual production.

By inserting an emulator op. code (ie an exception call) at the point in a program at which the sine is to be calculated by the hardware, the software can be tested as if the coprocessor were actually present. When the emulator op. code is encountered, a jump is made to the appropriate emulator handling routine. In this routine, the sine is calculated by conventional techniques.

Trap exception

The trap is the most useful software user initiated exception available to the programmer. Indeed, it is one of the more powerful functions provided by the 68000. There are no significant differences between traps and emulator exceptions; they differ only in their applications. There are sixteen traps, TRAP #0–TRAP #15, which are associated with exception vector numbers 32–47 (decimal) respectively.

Just as emulator exceptions are used to provide functions in software that will later be implemented in hardware, trap exceptions create new operations or 'extra codes' not provided directly by the 68000 itself. However, the purpose of the trap is to separate the details of certain 'housekeeping' functions from the user- or applications-level program.

Consider I/O transactions. These involve real hardware devices and the precise nature of an input operation on system A may be very different from that on system B, even though both systems put the input to the same use. System A may operate a 6850 ACIA in an interrupt-driven mode to obtain data, while system B may use in Intel 8055 parallel port in a polled mode to carry out the same function. Clearly, the device drivers (ie the software which controls the ports) in these systems differ greatly in their structures.

Applications programmers do not wish to consider the fine details of I/O transactions when writing their programs. One solution is to use a jump table and to thread all I/O through this table. Table 5 illustrates this approach. It can be seen that the applications programmer deals with all device-dependent transactions by indirect jumps through a jump table. For example, all console input at the applications level is carried out by BSR GETCHAR. At the address GETCHAR in the jump table,

the programmer inserts a link (JSR INPUT) to the actual routine used in his/her own system.

This is a perfectly acceptable approach to the problem of device dependency. Unfortunately, it suffers from the limitation that the applications program must be tailored to fit on to the target system. This is done by tagging on the jump table. An alternative approach, requiring no modification whatsoever to the applications software, is provided by the trap exception. This leads to truly system-independent software.

When a trap is encountered, the appropriate vector number is generated and the exception vector table interrogated to obtain the address of the trap handling routine. Note that the exception vector table fulfils the same role as the jump table (Table 5). The difference is that the jump table forms part of the applications program while the exception vector table is part of the 68000's operating system.

An example of a trap handler is found on the Motorola educational single board (ECB) computer. This is known as the 'TRAP #14 handler' and provides the user with a method of accessing functions within the ECB's monitor software without the user having to know their addresses.

The versatility of a trap exception can be increased by passing parameters from the user program to the trap handler. The TRAP #14 handler of Tutor (the monitor on the Motorola ECB) provides for up to 255 different functions to be associated with TRAP #14. Before the trap is invoked, the programmer must load the required function code into the least significant byte of D7. For example, to transmit a single ASCII character to port 1, the following calling sequence is used.

```
OUTCH  EQU       248        (Equate the function
                             code to name of
                             activity)
       MOVE.B  #OUTCH, D7   (Load function code
                             in D7)
       TRAP    #14          (Invoke TRAP #14
                             handler)
```

Table 6 gives a list of the functions provided by the TRAP #14 exception handler of the Tutor monitor on the ECB.

Table 5. The jump table

	ORG	$001000	Jump table
GETCHAR	JMP	INPUT	
OUTCHAR	JMP	OUTPUT	INPUT, OUTPUT
GETSECTOR	JMP	DISK_IN	DISK_IN, DISK_OUT
PUTSECTOR	JMP	DISK_OUT	Provided by user

BSR	GETCHAR	input a char

BSR	PUTSECTOR	write sector

Application program (address of subroutines not system dependent)

teach-in

Table 6. Functions provided by the TRAP #14 handler on the EBC

Function value	Function name	Function description
255	—	Reserved functions — end of table indicator
254	—	Reserved function — used to link tables
253	LINKIT	Append user table to TRAP14 table
252	FIXDAOD	Append string to buffer
251	FIXBUF	Initialize A5 and A6 to BUFFER
250	FIXDATA	Initialize A6 to BUFFER and append string to BUFFER
249	FIXDCRLF	Move CR, LF string to buffer
248	OUTCH	Output single character to port 1
247	INCHE	Input single character from port 1
246	—	Reserved function
245	—	Reserved function
244	CHRPRNT	Output single character to port 3
243	OUTPUT	Output string to port 1
242	OUTPUT21	Output string to port 2
241	PORTIN1	Input string from port 1
240	PORTIN20	Input string from port 2
239	TAPEOUT	Output string to port 4
238	TAPEIN	Input string from port 4
237	PRCRLF	Output string to port 3
236	HEX2DEC	Convert hex values to ASCII-encoded decimal
235	GETHEX	Convert ASCII character to hex
234	PUTHEX	Convert one hex digit to ASCII
233	PNT2HX	Convert two hex digits to ASCII
232	PNT4HX	Convert four hex digits to ASCII
231	PNT6HX	Convert six hex digits to ASCII
230	PNT8HX	Convert eight hex digits to ASCII
299	START	Restart Tutor; perform initialization
228	TUTOR	Go to Tutor; print prompt
227	OUT1CR	Output string plus CR, LF to port 1
226	GETNUMA	Convert ASCII encoded hex to hex
225	GETNUMD	Convert ASCII encoded decimal to hex
224	PORTIN1N	Input string from Port 1; no automatic line feed
223–128	—	Reserved
127–0	—	User-defined functions

Alan Clements obtained an honours degree in electronics at the University of Sussex, UK, in 1971 and a doctorate from Loughborough University, UK, in 1976. During the two years he spent at Loughborough University as a research fellow, he studied the application of microprocessor technology to adaptive equalizers for distorted digital signals. In 1977 he joined the Department of Computer Science at Teesside Polytechnic, UK. In the last few years, he has devoted much of his spare time to writing. His first book, Microprocessor systems design and construction, *was published in 1982 and this was followed by* Principles of computer hardware *in 1985.*

CONCLUSIONS

These two papers have looked at the way in which the 68000 implements exception handling.

Over the past few years, microprocessors have become faster and are able to access much larger memory spaces than those available to earlier 8-bit machines. However, the improvements in the exception handling mechanisms of today's microprocessors are as significant as advances in microprocessor performance (ie throughput). Exception handling carried out within the framework of the 68000's user/supervisor operating modes brings new security mechanisms to microcomputers. Modern multiuser, multitasking systems require more than mere performance. They must have mechanisms which protect one task from illegal access by another task. Equally, they require mechanisms which protect the system from a wide range of 'abuses'.

The 68000 provides all these facilities. The operating system interface is furnished by the trap; protection from some forms of abuse is provided by invalid instruction exceptions, uninitialized interrupt exceptions etc. Hardware exceptions (eg bus error) protect the system from faulty hardware.

266

microprocessors and microsystems

REFERENCE

1 **Clements, A** 'Exception handling in the 68000, Part 1' *Microprocessors Microsyst.* Vol 10 No 4 (May 1986) pp 202–210

BIBLIOGRAPHY

Bacon, J *The Motorola MC68000* Prentice-Hall, Englewood Cliffs, NJ, USA (1986)

Eccles, W J *Microprocessor systems — a 16-bit approach* Addison-Wesley, Wokingham, UK (1985)

Jaulent, P *The 68000 hardware and software* Macmillan, London, UK (1985)

Triebel, W A and Singh, A *The 68000 microprocessor — architecture, software and interfacing techniques* Prentice-Hall, Englewood Cliffs, NJ, USA (1986)

The VMEbus specification manual Printek, Benton Harbour, MI, USA (1985)

MC68000 educational computer board user's manual (MEXKECB/D2) Motorola, Austin, TX, USA (1982)

The MC68000 data manual Motorola, Austin, TX, USA (1983)

Interactive development environment for single-board computers

Andrew Haley, Howerd Oakford and Chris Stephens explain how a personal computer can be used as an *in situ* development tool for polyFORTH-based target hardware

An effective development environment has been designed for single-board microprocessor products, providing many of the advantages of conventional development systems but without the high cost of special purpose development hardware, such as in-circuit emulation. The use of a low-cost personal computer combined with the polyFORTH programming language running on the single-board computer solves the problems of cheap access to mass storage and the wish to interact with the hardware during development.

microprocessors   *in situ* **development**   **polyFORTH**

This paper is concerned with a development environment for single-board computers which uses the polyFORTH programming language. PolyFORTH is a professional multi-tasking version of the high level programming language FORTH, which has been employed for many years in control and instrumentation applications. FORTH's strength is that it allows applications to be developed and tested interactively without imposing intolerable speed overheads. Interaction has been found to be particularly useful in those fields where a significant part of the application involves complex I/O handling and control.

The polyFORTH package provides more than 400 primitive operators (words) for data and I/O manipulation, any one of which may be executed by typing its name at the terminal. The programmer constructs new words by entering a sequence of existing words; once defined, the new word may be executed by typing its name. The process of defining a word is simple

: NEW A B C D ;

The FORTH word ':' defines a word called NEW, whose action is made up of the sequence of primitives A then B then C then D. At the end of the definition (;) control will

be returned to the keyboard, or, if NEW was itself called from within another higher level word, control returns to that word.

The process of developing a program consists of building increasingly application-specific words and tools, culminating in one word which performs the entire application. Alternatively, where an operator is in control, a wide range of options can be selected via the keyboard. Where appropriate, the operator can simply define his own sequences.

The time taken to compile a word such as NEW is less than the time to output a carriage return to the VDU; the word is then available immediately for execution. If there is any doubt about the correctness of the definition it is necessary only to enter each individual part in sequence to check its detailed actions. To test a hypothesis, it is not necessary to write a program, as any group of primitives or modules can be tested by using the keyboard interpreter. This is one of the benefits of polyFORTH when debugging complex hardware/software combinations.

Additional facilities provided within the language include conditional and looping structures, as well as the ability to define variables, constants and sophisticated data structures. As well as being able to produce high level definitions, polyFORTH systems also allow words to be defined by sequences of assembler mnemonics. These execute at full machine code speed and allow access to all of the machine's features. The assembler, compiler and editor are bound together by the keyboard interpreter (which is responsible for taking in words from the terminal). Disc editing commands are provided, which allow programs to be held on mass storage to provide a powerful development environment. Moving between I/O testing, program editing, compiling and testing is rapid because all these units are resident in memory, usually in less than 8k of RAM. Typically, a 10 s delay occurs between identifying a correction and testing it. This high speed turnaround allows FORTH programmers to achieve rapid development times and flexibility to modify or enhance products.

Computer Solutions Ltd, 1 Gogmore Lane, Chertsey, Surrey KT16 9AP, UK

The advantages of this interaction are best realized if the system being used for development is the same as the one on which the application will finally run. Once the program has been tested thoroughly, it will normally be necessary to generate a ROM-based or embedded product, at which time the development terminal, discs and much of the software overhead associated with development may be removed. The utility that does this is known as the 'target compiler', which is capable of stripping out unwanted code (such as editor and compiler), leaving an overhead of less than 600 byte and allowing simple, but non-trivial, programs to run in under 2k of ROM.

CROSS TARGET COMPILERS

PolyFORTH is available in compatible 16-bit configurations for a large number of processors: 8086, 8085, 6809, 1802 PDP-11, 6301, 6803, 6502. With minor modifications to suit individual machines (eg high/low byte swapping), all the target compilers for these machines are the same, making it relatively simple to use a development system for micro A to produce code that will run on micro B. This is sometimes known as 'host/target compilation'. With the wide availability of low-cost personal computers there is a large financial incentive to use these machines as development systems, even if their CPU is not going to be used in the application. (In this paper the abbreviation PC is used to refer to any low-cost computer having disc storage.) Typical examples available are the IBM PC, its clones, CP/M and MS-DOS machines as well as the BBC microcomputer.

When one is familiar with using FORTH to interact with the hardware during development, however, the process of cross target compiling a complex realtime application into a dedicated board can mean slow turnaround and isolation from the hardware.

It is worth identifying which capabilities inherent in FORTH are lost if cross compilation is used

● It is not possible to test the machine code parts of any application without transferring to the target board.
● It is not possible to check the speed of critical words without transferring to the target board.
● It is not possible to check interrupt handling. Hence, it is not possible to fully test multitasking areas.
● It is not possible to access the I/O on the application. Hence, it is not possible to test the performance of interfaces, actuators, transducers etc.

The last point is particularly important. It should be stressed that these are not faults in FORTH; no other cross target compiler system provides these facilities. Rather, they are advantages of FORTH which are lost because of the remoteness of the target environment from the development environment.

The first, and most straightforward, way to improve the development process is to use a ROM emulator that can be loaded from the development system. This cuts out the ROM burning step as well as the mechanical removal and replacement of chips. Whilst this improves the turnaround time, it still means that, for a complex realtime task with significant I/O and multitasking, the chances of a significant program change solving the problem under consideration are small; a number of iterations are still needed.

IN SITU DEVELOPMENT

In situ development is a technique designed to overcome the problems of developing code for single-board computers (SBCs) which cannot be made part of a conventional development system. Clearly, if the application SBC uses a popular bus system such as Multibus or VME, then the most advantageous way to develop software for that board is to add disc drivers and any other cards required, so that the development is done on that card. If the card is bought in for a specific application, however, then the costs of the disc interface and the chassis may represent a high overhead for a single job. If the board is to be manufactured specially for a product, the overhead would be intolerable.

The idea of *in situ* development is to provide a development system that will run on the target hardware, that will require the minimum of hardware construction and offers the maximum ability to re-use equipment. The arrangement necessary for *in situ* development is shown in Figure 1.

The majority of intermediate sized projects that we have encountered with high I/O content and multitasking have not had a disc but have had in excess of 8k ROM, at least 4k RAM and a serial I/O device. This configuration is sufficient for polyFORTH, which packs the normal editor, assembler, compiler, interpreter, nucleus words and I/O drivers into 7k and requires 2k of RAM for disc buffers. A typical arrangement with a polyFORTH target board is shown in Figure 2.

An analysis of the requirements of the disc controller and interface shows that it must be compatible with other media and that its transfer rate, although the higher the better, does not need to be very fast. During development, the interface is typically transferring only one or two 1k blocks for each cycle of program development (human response time/boredom tolerance ~ 4 s). This means that, with suitable software, the disc controller and

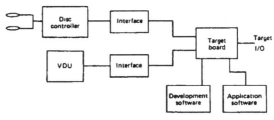

Figure 1.   Arrangement for in situ development of target hardware

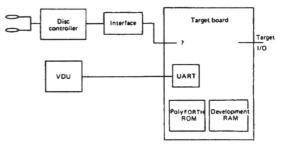

Figure 2.   Arrangement for in situ development of polyFORTH-based target board

VDU could share an RS232 serial interface. This suggests the use of a low-cost PC as a display–floppy combination communicating with the target via a serial link (Figure 3).

A suitable program, written in FORTH and residing on the host, can now take input from the host's keyboard and pass it to the target. In the target, normal FORTH keyboard interpretation takes place and terminal output goes back up the serial line to the host where it is routed to the screen. Should a command to load a program be entered at the host end, it is transmitted to the target as a character string, interpreted by the target FORTH system and the disc driver in the target called. This disc driver calls the serial driver to pass a control character requesting a source disc block from the host. The host program does not display this control character, but instead transmits the required block back to the target. Compilation of the source and its execution then takes place on the target system. By this technique, the target board becomes a full development system capable of providing the programmer with normal program compilation facilities, as well as rapid interactive access to FORTH words and hence to timings and I/O control. The breakdown of responsibilities between the processors is shown diagrammatically in Figure 4.

In this configuration, there is no reason why the host and target should be the same CPU. If the development RAM can be large (eg 32k) then, once the application has been tested on the target board, that system would be quite capable of target compiling to ROM. With the RS232 link, however, this would be slow and would not provide the means to initially generate the target polyFORTH ROM. If a cross target compiler on the host is used, it can both generate the target FORTH system, and later allow compilation of tested code to replace the polyFORTH ROM with the application ROM.

If the target hardware does not have enough ROM and RAM space or serial I/O to allow even the basic 8k system then, to provide any necessary extra development hardware, it is usually easy to build a board which piggybacks onto the target system via the CPU socket.

Protocol

The link protocol between the host and target is simple, as the target is always the master and controls the link operation. The only handshake used is at the end of a block transfer when the host responds with ACK if no disc failure has occurred or NAK if a disc fault was present. Only three control codes are emitted by the target; these are shown in Table 1.

Host end

Two tasks exist in the host: one to service the display and keyboard — this is the normal keyboard task called OPERATOR; the second is the normal serial I/O device task, TYPIST. Communications are via two byte variables, 'IN and 'OUT.

TYPIST task

The TYPIST task runs a program COMMS which cycles testing two things.

1 If a character has been received by the UART (?KEY is non-zero), then either a disc Read/Write is performed or it is sent to 'IN as soon as that variable is empty. This test ensures that the target does not exceed the speed at which a potentially slow operating system can output to the display.

Table 1. Control codes emitted by the target

Code	Action	Description
0	NULL	No special action — used to allow null characters
1	READ	Target read followed by an ASCII five-character disc block number, 1k data from the disc and an ACK/NAK are transmitted by the host
2	WRITE	Target write followed by an ASCII five-character disc block number and 1k of data. An ACK/NAK is transmitted by the host once it has placed the data on the disc

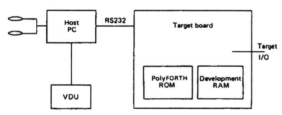

Figure 3. Host PC linked to the target board

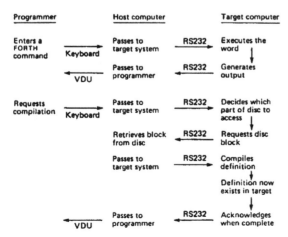

Figure 4. Schematic of programmer–host computer-target computer interaction

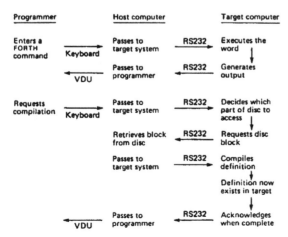

Figure 5. Interaction of host-end tasks, TYPIST and OPERATOR

2   If the variable 'OUT holds a character, it is removed and output to the target without any tests, thus ensuring that the system cannot lock, even if the target is in an infinite loop.

```
: COMMS
    BEGIN PAUSE ?KEY
```
cycle, looking at the keyboard for an input
```
        IF DUP 3 <
```
if a key has been hit, checks to see if it is one of the control codes
```
        IF ACTION ELSE >OPERATOR THEN
```
if so, performs the desired action, otherwise sends it to the operator task
```
    THEN
        'OUT C@ ?DUP
```
has a character come in from the operator?
```
        IF EMIT 0 'OUT C! THEN
```
if so, output it and clear the character to show it has been processed
```
    AGAIN ;
```

The word PAUSE is used to force a task switch. C@ and C! are character memory read and write operators. The constituent words are then

```
:  >OPERATOR ( n)
```
(n) indicates that it expects to find one argument in the stack
```
        BEGIN PAUSE 'IN C@ 0= UNTIL
```
cycles, looking at 'IN until it is empty
```
        'IN C! ;
```
once 'IN is empty it puts the character it was passed into 'IN

ACTION executes one of the following words depending on the value

```
: READ ASK BLOCK
```
gets in the number of the block to be read by the target (ASK) then gets the block from disc (BLOCK)
```
        1024 >TYPE FLUSH
```
outputs it to the target and clears own buffers
```
        .ACK ;
```
send ACK/NAK depending on the disc status
```
: WRITE ASK
```
gets in the number of the block to be written by target
```
        PAD 1024 STRAIGHT
```
sends the 1024 byte from the target using the word STRAIGHT that performs no CR or DEL character processing
```
        BUFFER PAD SWAP 1024 MOVE
```
copies the data from PAD into the allocated disc buffer
```
        UPDATE FLUSH .ACK ;
```
copies the buffer to the disc and transmits ACK/NAK to the target

OPERATOR task

The OPERATOR task runs SERVICE, which outputs the contents of 'IN to the screen and inputs from the keyboard, if there is a character there, then to 'OUT unless it is an 'escape' character in which case control is returned to the host's keyboard interpreter.

```
: SERVICE
    BEGIN
        BEGIN 'IN C@ 0 'IN C! PAUSE ?DUP
```
examines the input character buffer and clears it
```
        WHILE EMIT REPEAT
```
while it continues to have something in it, then display it to the operator
```
        ?TER
```
if there was nothing in it then there is time to look at the terminal
```
        IF DUP 27 =
```
if there was anything, was it an escape character?
```
            IF DROP EXIT THEN
```
if it was then throw away the character and return to the interpreter
```
            'OUT C!
```
if not an ESC then put it in the output buffer
```
        THEN
    AGAIN ;
```
continue cycling doing this return

The package also allows the host or PC to be used as a terminal that has numerous applications in other areas.

Target end

In the target hardware it is necessary to produce the standard polyFORTH primitive BLOCK, which is the normal disc handling word. This word is usually defined in high level and the only ports that will need to be written for this configuration are the 'pseudo disc' read and write primitives TREAD and TWRITE.

```
: TREAD (n a)
```
the comment indicates two arguments on the stack, n the block number and a the buffer's address
```
        01 EMIT SWAP .VAL
```
output the code for read then output the block number required
```
        1024 STRAIGHT
```
read in the ACK/NAK character and put in into the target disc status flag
```
        !ACK ;
```
read in the ACK/NAK character and put it into the target disc status flag
```
: TWRITE (n a)
        02 EMIT SWAP .VAL
        1024 TYPE !ACK ;
```

To enable the user to distinguish between the two systems, the usual lower-case 'ok' prompt is changed to upper case on the target.

The production of a target polyFORTH ROM is perhaps the most complex part of setting up an *in situ* development system. The standard polyFORTH source provides initialization code and drivers for the 'normal' UART for the particular CPU. If that is the chip set to be used, it is simply a case of setting up ROM, RAM and I/O addresses and replacing the disc drivers with the versions described above. If a 'foreign' or new UART or interrupt structure is to be used, then the first step is to cross target compile on the host a target ROM that will communicate normally with a VDU. Once this is running, the serial link drivers may be installed and tested.

SPEED CONSEQUENCES

Four possible factors limit the speed of the system:-

- Output of the characters to the screen by the OPERATOR task; this is a problem with MS-DOS systems which have slow character handlers.
- It is assumed that keyboard speed will limit the rate at which values will be input to the host.
- Input speed for disc blocks to the target may be limited by slow CPUs if polled I/O is used (eg 1802).
- Input speed to the host from the target may be limited if an operating system is being used.

The use of hardware or XON/XOFF character handshakes would significantly limit systems that could be linked and complicate writing their drivers, and so was rejected.

In the worst case (MS-DOS host, 1802 target), all communications can take place without faults at 2400 baud. This speed is workable but the programmer tends to use the host for editing and adopts a testing strategy that minimizes the number of full system loads required. This is considered good FORTH practice, and so is no hardship.

The experienced polyFORTH programmer is encouraged to modify the code to best suit particular hardware. The most useful enhancement to the system is interrupt-driven queued input from the target to COMMS. This queue needs to be 2 kbyte deep, then the system can easily handle 19200 baud links to the target. At this speed, interaction with the system is not perceptibly different to a normal development system; editing takes place on the target without switching backwards and forwards to the host.

CONCLUSIONS

A package that would both generalize and simplify the procedure of linking a target single-board computer with a personal computer, to provide a robust development system, has been designed. The package described, which uses the polyFORTH language, can be used by the novice FORTH programmer but does not jeopardize the expert's ability to optimize the configuration where that is possible. This new technique enables a range of applications, that would not otherwise do so, to use polyFORTH.

BIBLIOGRAPHY

Moore, C H 'FORTH: a new way to program a computer' *Astronomy and Astrophysics Suppl.* Vol 15 (1974) p 497
Rather, E D and Moore, C H 'The FORTH approach to operating systems' *ACM Proc.* (1976)
Harris, K 'FORTH extensibility or how to write a compiler in 25 words or less' *Byte* (August 1980)
Brodie, L *Starting FORTH* Prentice-Hall, NJ, USA
Brodie, L *Thinking FORTH* Prentice-Hall, NJ, USA
Winfield, A *The complete FORTH* Sigma Technical Press

After receiving an honours degree and diploma in applied physics from the University of Hull, UK, in 1967, Chris Stephens carried out research for 12 years at Imperial College, London, UK, in the automation of astronomical instrumentation. During this time he worked on a number of international telescope projects including the Anglo-Australian Telescope, the UK Infrared Telescope, the Canada-France-Hawaii Telescope and the Northern Hemisphere Observatory. In 1979 he set up Computer Solutions Ltd to market and use the polyFORTH language in industrial applications. His technical interests are centred around the optimization of hardware/software resources and man-machine interfacing.

Howerd Oakford is a polyFORTH consultant specializing in efficient programming environments. Having received an honours degree in physics from Oxford University, UK, in 1976, he spent 18 months servicing, and later designing, hardware for the Computer Electronics CR 6000 range computers, drifting into software 'by necessity'. He then joined the team working on the Sinar Agritec 'Moisture Computer', an agricultural grain analyser programmed in FORTH, which won the British Microprocessor Award in 1980. As a consultant since 1981, he has worked in the UK for Computer Solutions, and in Alabama, USA, for six months with a team from Forth Inc. on the King Khaled International Airport project.

Andrew Haley studied at Leicester Polytechnic, UK. Subsequently, he worked as an electrical design engineer and is now a software engineer for Computer Solutions, where one of his projects has been implementing a version of polyFORTH to run under the MS-DOS operating system. His main technical interests are programming languages and techniques for improving program quality.

Microcomputer processing of 10 MHz acoustic signals

Processing signals at megaHertz frequencies usually requires the power of a minicomputer, but **W H Chen and I S Chang** have used a microcomputer, interfaced to high-speed RAM and control circuitry, to process 10 MHz acoustic signals

A microcomputer has been developed to process signals with frequencies up to 10 MHz. The system uses a 30 MHz A/D converter and a high-speed RAM interface. Distorted 10 MHz ultrasonic echoes have been processed using the microcomputer system, demonstrating the feasibility of using a microcomputer system to process realtime VHF signals.

microsystems   signal processing   acoustic waves

Signal processing using computers is important in many system applications that involve the radar, sonar, medical imaging and ultrasonic nondestructive testing (NDT). In these applications the frequency of signals to be processed is usually in the range of a few megaHertz, so a high-speed computer, at least a minicomputer, is needed to sample and handle such high-frequency signals. Some waveform analysers which are available can process signals of 100 MHz or even higher. Both systems, however, are expensive and involve complicated operations.

In this paper, the development of a microcomputer in conjunction with hardware electronics and software programs capable of processing signals or waveforms with carrier frequencies in the VHF range or of accepting signals with pulse widths in the 100 ns range is described. The system consists of an Apple II microcomputer, a high-speed buffer RAM interface and control circuits. System design, the control circuit and timing sequences will be described. Results demonstrating the feasibility of using a low-cost microcomputer to process high-frequency signals or waveforms are presented from an application of processing 10 MHz overlapped ultrasonic echoes using the Weiner filtering technique.

SYSTEM DESIGN

The Apple II microcomputer is the main control unit of the system. A hardware interface has been designed and implemented which can sample 10 MHz input signals and feed into a 1 MHz machine cycle microcomputer. A block diagram of the system is shown in Figure 1.

The microcomputer sends out a 10 MHz control signal to the control network via the I/O interface. The 10 MHz clock signal is transmitted by the control network simultaneously to the A/D converter and the high-speed buffer RAM. Input sampled signals are sequentially written, read and stored in the microcomputer via the control network.

Figure 2 shows the system control circuitry. The complete system has two different clock signals: one is the 1 MHz machine cycle of the computer, and the other is the 10 MHz write/read converting clock. The operating period is therefore confined to 100 ns. The high-speed RAM used is a Fairchild 93415A which has a read time of 25 ns and write time of 20–25 ns. The transmission path of the signal is designed to be as short as possible to eliminate unnecessary delays. A small CR value is preferable to reduce the circuit time constant. The power supplies are connected in parallel to reduce propagation delays due to large resistance. The time delay between transistor gates was calculated carefully.

At high-frequency operation, the large transient current variations at S and $\bar{S}$ may affect the stability of the source voltage. This current variation effect is reduced by connecting a 0.1 μF ceramic capacitor to each V_{cc} of the transistors. Molybdenum capacitors (47 μF) are added to eight other transistors to filter the low-frequency noise of the power supply. Figure 3a shows the noise generated by the transient current variation with no capacitor connected to the transistors. Figure 3b reveals that the noise is substantially reduced by connecting the appropriate

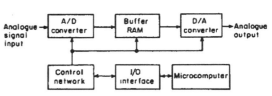

Figure 1.   System block diagram

Department of Applied Physics, Chung Cheng Institute of Science and Technology, Tahsi, Taoyuan, Taiwan 335

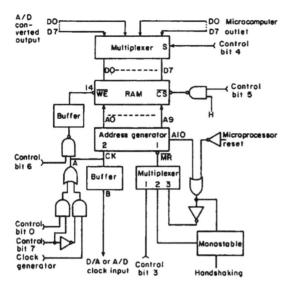

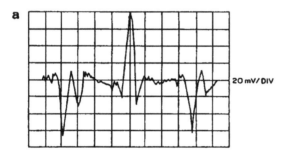

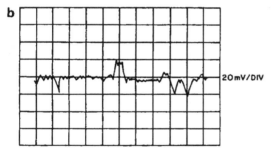

Figure 2. System control circuitry

Figure 3. **a** Noise generated by the transient current variation with no capacitor connected to the transistors; **b** noise is substantially reduced by connecting the appropriate capacitors to the transistors

capacitors. The A/D converter used is a TRW TDC1007PCB which has a conversion time of 30 megasamples s^{-1} and can handle 10 MHz analogue signals. Input impedance is 75 Ω. The converting input voltage of -0.5 V to 0.5 V is fed into the Nth pin of the converter to control the converting clock.

Each input analogue signal is sampled 1024 times, requiring eight 1k × 1 bit RAM as the buffer memory. The RAM has 25 ns read time, 20–25 ns write time, and a 15 ns

safety time interval; thus only 40 ns is needed to write in or read out the data. The 11 address selection pins are connected in parallel. The address generator consists of three 4-bit binary counters. As shown in Figure 4, the first pulse of the clock triggers the generator which counts from 1 to 1023; at the end of the count, Q_2 of the third counter transmits a high-level voltage through the control circuit to reset the generator as shown in Figure 2, then the count begins again, ie the addresses are generated by counting from 1 to 1023 to 0, making 1024 counts in total.

In Figure 2, control bit 7 is used to select the control bit. The address generator clock is controlled by bit 0, and the clock count is transmitted by the pulse generator when bit 0 is low. Bit 6 controls write or read operations as shown when high and low respectively. The buffer is used to enhance driving capability. Memory is enabled only when control bit 5 is high.

Data may be sent to the buffer memory system from the microcomputer or from the A/D converter, which is controlled by bit 4. Bit 3 is used to select the reset address. The reset address signal can be delayed to allow the microcomputer to alter the parameters of the control bit. The system can also be used in a nondelay mode so that read/write operations can be continued; this is controlled by bit 3.

TIME SEQUENCE ANALYSIS

As can be seen from Figure 2, the key clocking sequence begins with the signal arriving at point A which initiates counting. Signals at each 74LS244 buffer gate (point B) are delayed for 18 ns, and are then fed into the A/D or D/A converters. It takes 50 ns to convert an analogue signal into 8-bit data, which then appears, via a multiplexer, at outputs D0–D7 of the A/D converter (Figure 5f). Decoding of the address generator takes 37 ns. RAM port $\overline{WE}$ delays the clock signal by 40.5 ns (Figure 5c). Figure 5e shows that the address is locked 37 ns after the clock signal arrives at point A. The write signal has a pulse width of 50 ns, which is larger than the safety write period. Figure 5f shows that converted data are locked in 25 ns after the end of WR. The system can therefore be operated for frequencies below 10 MHz.

CONTROL CIRCUIT

The control circuit, as shown in Figure 6, has two 6522 interface ICs with a minor modification to control the storage, read and write operations. Three 74LS05 inverters

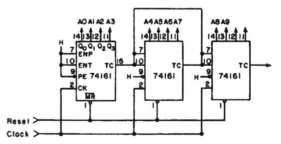

Figure 4. Address generator, consisting of three 4-bit binary counters

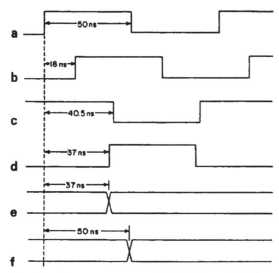

Figure 5. Time sequences: **a** clock signal at point A (see Figure 2); **b** clock signal at the A/D input; **c** phase delay of the clock signal at RAM port $\overline{WE}$; **d** decoding time of the address generator; **e** time taken for RAM to lock the address; **f** data transmission time from the A/D converter to the RAM input

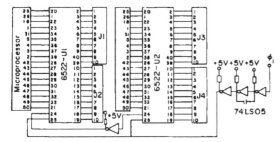

Figure 6. Control interface circuitry

are used to synchronize the signal phases between the microcomputer and the interface cards.

J1 is the input port connected to the output of high-speed RAM. J2 is the output port connected to the input of a multiplexer. J4 controls the 8-bit data from D0 to D7 and is connected to control bits 0–7. Table 1 indicates the application of each control bit. As can be seen, the data can be read into the high-speed buffer RAM from the A/D converter output when J4 sends a control signal byte 011100XX. Another control signal byte 101XX0X0 transfers

data from RAM to the microcomputer and changes bit 0, which controls the clock pulse. Byte signal 1110X0X0 controls data transfer from the microcomputer to RAM. Byte 001X11XX transfers the data from the RAM to the D/A converter output.

Assembly language is used by the computer to perform the signal processing effectively, such as the Weiner filtering, fast Fourier transform (FFT) etc. The circuit diagram for the high-speed RAM write/read system is shown in Figure 7.

APPLICATION

Ultrasonic nondestructive testing (NDT) of materials is one of the important applications of high-frequency acoustic waves. Due to the finite bandwidth of the transducers used, the impulse response of the transducer is usually far from a bipolar or a tripolar waveform. Return echoes from two adjacent defects in the material may overlap because of the broad impulse response of the transducer used in the pulse–echo NDT system. The overlapped waveform is one kind of amplitude-distorted waveform that can be decomposed using the Weiner filtering technique. This has been demonstrated by using a surface acoustic wave (SAW) filter[1] or by a software method[2]. Using the software method to perform Weiner filtering to decompose the overlapped echoes has great flexibility and could be important in NDT applications. In this approach, however, at least a minicomputer would be needed to perform the software Weiner filtering because the frequencies used in ultrasonic NDT are usually in the range of a few megaHertz, and only a mainframe computer or a minicomputer could sample signals at such high frequencies. This may inherently limit the scope of the ultrasonic NDT applications owing to the high cost and the size of the computer used.

We used the microcomputer signal processing system to perform Weiner filtering of acoustic echoes up to 10 MHz. In practice, the amplitude-distorted or overlapped echoes are fed into the microcomputer through the A/D converter and the high-speed RAM. The FFT and Weiner filtering are performed in the microcomputer in the frequency domain. The time required to FFT the data, to process the data in the frequency domain and to inverse FFT the resultant output spectrum is typically of the order or a few microseconds, which is comparable to the time taken by a computer system interfaced to a commercial digitizer.

To demonstrate the usefulness of the system, an ultrasonic transducer was used to transmit a pulse approximately 100 ns wide and detect the reflected echoes from two holes drilled in an aluminium block approximately 1 mm apart. The reflected echoes over-

Table 1. State control table

Bit	7	6	5	4	3	2	1	0
High	Clock input from bit 0	Write	CS enable	Data input from A/D	Reset	Analogue output enable	No effect	Pulse generation
Low	Clock input from counter	Read	CS disable	Data input from microcomputer	Delay reset	Analogue output disable	No effect	

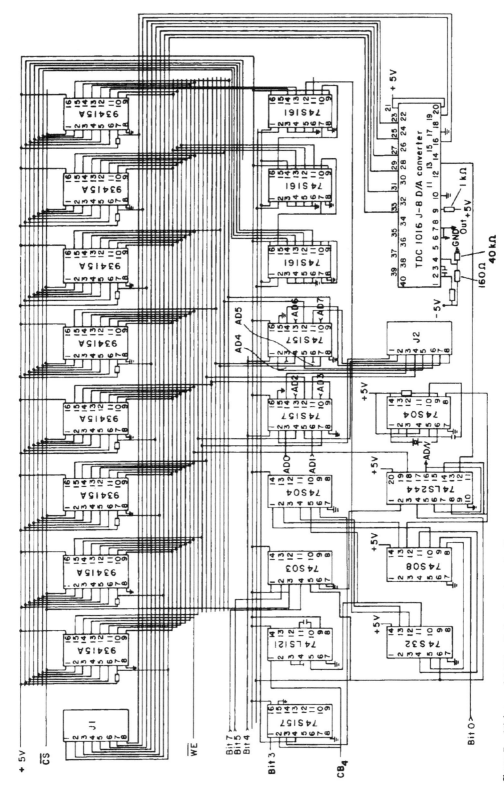

Figure 7. High-speed RAM write/read system circuitry

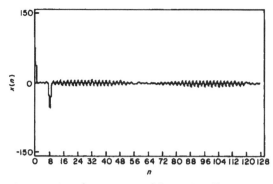

Figure 8. Impulse response of the Weiner filter

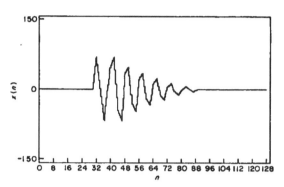

Figure 9. Overlapped echoes from n = 31 and n = 40

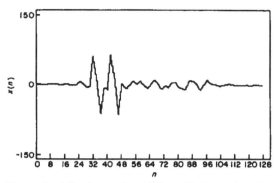

Figure 10. Waveform after Weiner filtering using the microcomputer signal processing system. The waveform represents two separated echoes reflected from two defects located inside a material

REFERENCES

1 **White, R M et al** 'Surface acoustic wave Weiner filter' Proc. IEEE Ultrasonics Symp. (1976)
2 **Murakami, Y and Kino, G S** 'Application of Weiner filtering to nondestructive evaluation' Appl. Phys. Lett. Vol 33 (1978) pp 685–687

Wen-Hsien Chen was born in Taiwan, Republic of China, in 1946. He received a PhD in electrical engineering from Stanford University, USA, in 1979. He is currently a professor in the applied physics department of Chung Cheng Institute of Technology, Taiwan, and is a programme manager of the National Science Council of the Republic of China. He is also a consultant for Chung Shan Institute of Science and Technology, Taiwan. His present research interests include sensing and signal processing for optical and acoustic devices, optical phase conjugation, and acoustics and nondestructive testing. Professor Chen has served as a committee member for various associations in Taiwan. He is a member of IEEE.

lap due to the bandwidth limitations of the transducer and electronics used. The impulse response function of the Weiner filter was obtained by normalizing the impulse response function of the transducer to an assigned ideal delta-function impulse response in the frequency domain. Figure 8 shows the impulse response of the filter. Figure 9 is the echo signal after the inverse FFT, representing the overlapped waveform of the echoes from the two adjacent holes. Weiner filtering was performed in the frequency domain using the computer. The output waveform, after the operation of Weiner filtering, is shown in Figure 10. It is evident that the two echoes are separated.

This result demonstrates the feasibility of using a microcomputer to process very high frequency signals and therefore avoiding the need to use an expensive minicomputer.

6800 coprocessor for a 6502 bus

The 6800 is a popular model for teaching microprocessors. **B T G Tan and L C Sia** have
designed a board that interfaces this processor to the popular Apple II computer for
practical teaching exercises

*The 6800 is favoured as a teaching model in many
educational establishments. Often, these establishments
will have Apple II microcomputers installed, and these
systems could be useful for teaching the 6800 architecture
in practice if a suitable interface board was available. This
paper describes the construction of a 6800 board designed
for this purpose which interfaces the Apple's 6502
processor. A test program has been run on the board to
assure its operation.*

microprocessors   interfacing   6800   Apple II

The 8-bit 6502 microprocessor has been one of the most
widely used microprocessors, particularly in small
personal computers. One of the most popular personal
computers using the 6502 is the Apple II computer and its
derivatives. The Apple II motherboard incorporates an
eight-slot I/O bus which greatly facilitates I/O interfacing.
The I/O bus is allocated a 4k space in the 6502's 64k
memory map, and each slot has a portion of this 4k space
allocated to it and decoded on the motherboard. Though
the slots are primarily meant for I/O, the I/O bus actually
includes the complete 6502 bus including the entire 16-
bit address bus.

Several interface boards have been designed for the
6502 which make use of the accessibility of the 6502 bus
on the I/O slots to provide coprocessors for the 6502. The
most popular coprocessor used in this way is the Z80,
which enables the widely used CP/M operating system to
be run on the Apple II[1]. Other processors which have
been interfaced to the bus include the 6809, and 16-bit
processors with 8-bit data buses such as the 8088 and
68008.

The 6502 is itself a derivative of the Motorola 6800,
both processors having similar bus structures. The 6800 is
still widely used in dedicated applications, especially in its
single-chip microcomputer version, the 6801. Its elegant
architecture and well structured instruction set have
favoured it as a microprocessor teaching model, and it is
still widely used as such in microprocessor courses and
textbooks[2]. The availability of a 6800 board for the Apple
II would be useful for teaching 6800 architecture and
machine code, in situations where an Apple II was already
at hand; however, such a 6800 board is at present not
available commercially. This paper describes the design
and construction of such a 6800 board for the Apple II
which was intended to fulfil these aims.

Department of Physics, National University of Singapore, Kent Ridge,
Singapore 0511

The 6800 board was designed initially to take over the
Apple II bus automatically from the Apple's 6502 when
power was switched on. The design of the board was
subsequently improved to include a 'softswitch' which
enables the 6502 to transfer control of the bus to the 6800
under 6502 software control. This is accomplished by
incorporating an onboard control register which resides
within the device address space allocated to the slot into
which the board is plugged. In addition, the board
includes a 2k 2716 EPROM which may contain a monitor
program for the 6800.

6800 BOARD DESIGN

The circuit design of the 6800 board is shown in Figure 1.
There are a total of 12 ICs on the board, including the
6800 and the 2716 EPROM. The external connections are
all made to the Apple II bus, the lines of which are
identified by a designation and number[3]. The data bus
lines from the 6800 are connected to the Apple II data bus
via a 74LS245 8-bit bidirectional tristate buffer. Similarly,
the 6800's address bus and R/$\overline{W}$ line are connected to the
equivalent Apple II bus lines via three 74LS367 hex
unidirectional tristate buffers. These four buffers can be
enabled by the 6800's VMA line via an inverter. The
direction of data flow through the 74LS245 buffer when it
is enabled is determined by the R/$\overline{W}$ line and hence by
whether a read or write operation is taking place with
respect to the 6800.

The 2716 EPROM was included on the board to
provide a means of carrying a dedicated 6800 program,
such as a simple monitor program. The address range for
the 2716 was allocated to the range $F800 to $FFFF so that
it would include the 6800's interrupt vectors which are
from $FFF8 to $FFFF. The chip enable ($\overline{CE}$) and output
enable ($\overline{OE}$) lines of the 2716 are pulled low, thus enabling
the chip, when the address lines A11 to A15 from the 6800
and the VMA line go low. This ensures that the 2716
responds to the address range $F800 to $FFFF only when
the 6800 is generating a valid memory address.

The 6800 is activated by a 74LS259 memory register
chip. This chip has one input line and eight output lines
each of which is enabled by a 3-bit binary address. The
three address lines are connected to A0, A1 and A2 of the
Apple II address bus. The 74LS259's enable ($\overline{E}$) line is
connected to the device select ($\overline{DS}$) line of the Apple II
bus. This effectively places the 74LS259 in the address
range $C080 + $n0 to $C087 + $n0 where n is the slot
number (n = 0–7), ie within the space in the Apple II
memory map reserved for the slot I/O. The input line is

0141-9331/86/05278-04 $03.00 © 1986 Butterworth & Co. (Publishers) Ltd

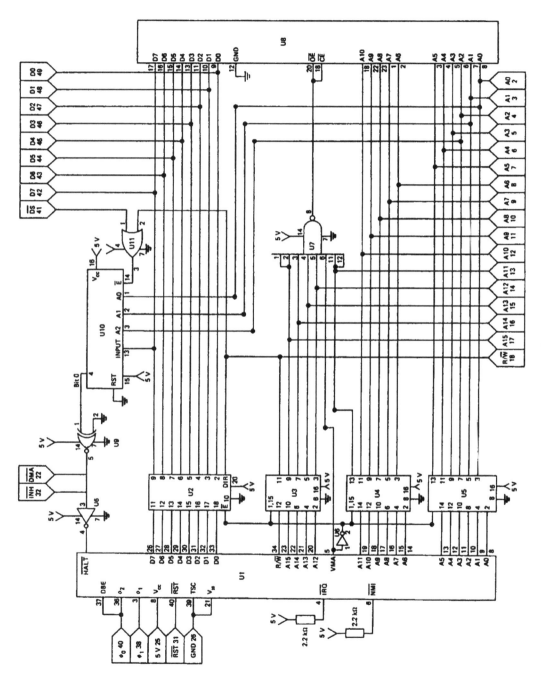

Figure 1. Circuit diagram for the 6800 board. U1 = 6800 microprocessor; U2 = 74LS245; U3, U4, U5 = 74LS367; U6 = 74LS04; U7 = 74LS30; U8 = 2716; U9 = 74LS266; U10 = 74LS259; U12 = 74LS232. Decoupling capacitors (1 μF) at U1, U2, U3, U4, U5 and U7.

connected to the D7 line of the data bus, and the reset line to the reset ($\overline{RST}$) of the Apple II bus. Thus when the Apple II is powered up, all the eight output lines of the 74LS259 are reset to '0'. If data is now placed on the data bus to make D7 carry a '1', then any one of the above eight addresses would enable the corresponding output line to go to a '1'. The device select line is ORed with the R/$\overline{W}$ line to ensure that data from D7 will be input to the 74LS259 only during a write cycle, otherwise spurious data might be input.

Only one of the output lines of the 74LS259, ie that corresponding to I/O address $C080 + $n0 is actually used. This output line is connected to the $\overline{DMA}$ and $\overline{INH}$ lines of the Apple II bus, and to the $\overline{HALT}$ line of the 6800 via an inverter. An open-collector NOR gate was used to buffer the 74LS259 output line from the $\overline{DMA}$ and $\overline{INH}$ lines, as the latter are pulled high by resistors to the 5 V power line.

At the moment of powering up the Apple II, all the output lines of the 74LS259 are reset to 0. Thus the $\overline{DMA}$ and $\overline{INH}$ lines are held high and the $\overline{HALT}$ line is pulled low. In this state the 6800 is halted and isolated from the Apple II bus. By addressing the 74LS259 appropriately and putting a 1 on the D7 line of the data bus, the output line of the 74LS259 can be set to 1. This will then pull the $\overline{DMA}$ and $\overline{INH}$ lines low; the $\overline{INH}$ will then isolate the Apple II's ROMs on the motherboard from the bus and the $\overline{DMA}$ line will halt the Apple II's 6502 and isolate it from the bus as well. The $\overline{HALT}$ line is then pulled low, thus activating the 6800 and connecting it to the bus. The converse operation, that of deactivating the 6800 and activating the 6502, can be performed by the 6800 by addressing the 74LS259 and setting D7 to 0.

TESTING

A test program was written and programmed into the 2716 onboard EPROM (Appendix 1). The EPROM occupies the addresses $F800 to $FFFF. The program first sets the Apple II screen to the text mode and clears the screen. It then puts a blinking cursor at the top of the blank screen and waits for the input of four hex characters from the Apple II keyboard. When these four characters are received, they are used as pointers to a particular address in the memory map. The contents of this address will then be retrieved and displayed in hex characters on the screen. In this way, the program enables the contents of any memory location to be displayed.

This simple program worked successfully as intended, showing that the 6800 was truly in control of the Apple II bus and memory map. The EPROM could easily be made to carry a complete monitor program which would enable the contents of memory locations to be changed as well as displayed, and machine language programs to be run. This would enable the board to be used to teach 6800 machine language programming using the Apple II. It would also be possible to write a disc booting routine which would boot up one of the standard 6800 operating systems such as FLEX, which is already available for commercial 6809 coprocessor boards.

It is hoped that this simple 6800 coprocessor board design will be of use to those who may wish to run 6800 machine language programs on the Apple II bus or any other microcomputer using a 6502-based bus.

REFERENCES

1   *Microsoft Softcard (Z80 card) reference manual*
2   **Levanthal, L A** *Introduction to microprocessors: software, hardware, programming* Prentice-Hall Englewood Cliffs, NJ, USA (1978)
3   *Apple II reference manual*

APPENDIX 1: LISTING OF TEST PROGRAM

F800					ORG		$F800	
F800	B6	C0	51		LDA	A	$C051	set screen mode to text
F803	B6	C0	51		LDA	A	$C051	clear keyboard strobe
F806	CE	04	00		LDX		#$0400	first location of screen
F809	86	A0			LDA	A	#$A0	ASCII code for blank
F80B	A7	00		LOOP	STA	A	$0, X	clear the screen location
F80D	08				INX			
F80E	8C	07	F8		CPX		#$07F8	last location?
F811	26	F8			BNE		LOOP	no, do again
F813	CE	03	01		LDX		#$0301	
F816	86	60		START	LDA	A	#$60	ASCII code for blinking cursor
F818	A7	FF			STA	A	$FF, X	at top line of the screen
F81A	F6	C0	10	KEY	LDA	B	$C010	read keyboard register
F81D	2A	FB			BPL		KEY	no key depressed, do again
F81F	E7	FF			STA	B	$FF, X	got key, display it at cursor position
F821	B6	C0	10		LDA	A	$C010	clear keyboard strobe
F824	C1	C0			CMP	B	#$C0	greater than 9?
F826	2B	02			BMI		PLUS	no

F828	CB	09			ADD	B	#$09	yes, add offset
F82A	C4	0F		PLUS	AND	B	#$0F	masking to get actual key value
F82C	E7	00			STA	B	$0, X	and store it
F82E	08				INX			next address byte
F82F	8C	03	05		CPX		#$0305	four bytes?
F832	26	E2			BNE		START	no, do again
F834	86	BA			LDA	A	#$BA	ASCII code for colon
F836	B7	04	04		STA	A	#$0404	display it
F839	86	04			LDA	A	#$04	
F83B	78	03	01	AGN	ASL		$0301	
F83E	78	03	03		ASL		$0303	
F841	4A				DEC	A		
F842	26	F7			BNE		AGN	shift values
F844	B6	03	01		LDA	A	$0301	
F847	BA	03	02		ORA	A	$0302	
F84A	B7	03	01		STA	A	$0301	
F84D	B6	03	03		LDA	A	$0303	
F850	BA	03	04		ORA	A	$0304	
F853	B7	03	02		STA	A	$0302	address bytes stored in 0301 and 0302
F856	FE	03	01		LDX		$0301	
F859	A6	00			LDA	A	$0, X	data byte stored in accumulator
F85B	36				PSH	A		
F85C	84	F0			AND	A	#$F0	get most significant bit first
F85E	44				LSR	A		
F85F	44				LSR	A		
F860	44				LSR	A		
F861	44				LSR	A		
F862	81	0A			CMP	A	#$0A	greater than 9?
F864	2B	02			BMI		ADD2	no
F866	8B	07			ADD	A	#$07	yes and offset
F868	8B	B0		ADD2	ADD	A	#$B0	add offset
F86A	B7	04	05		STA	A	$0405	display it
F86D	32				PUL	A		
F86E	84	0F			AND	A	#$0F	get least significant bit
F870	81	0A			CMP	A	#$0A	greater than 9?
F872	2B	02			BMI		ADD3	no
F874	8B	07			ADD	A	#$07	yes, add offset
F876	8B	B0		ADD3	ADD	A	#$B0	add offset
F878	B7	04	06		STA	A	$0406	display it
F87B	01			STOP	NOP			
F87C	20	FD			BRA		STOP	
					END			

Bernard Tan graduated in 1965 with an honours degree in physics from the University of Singapore, and in 1968 with a DPhil from Oxford University, UK. He is a chartered engineer and a member of the IEE and the IERE. Since 1968 he has taught at the National University of Singapore where he is now an associate professor in physics. His research interests include microwave properties of semiconductors, computer-assisted acoustical analysis and synthesis, and microprocessor applications.

L C Sia obtained an honours degree in physics from the National University of Singapore in 1984. He is now teaching physics at St. Andrew's Junior College, Singapore. He is also doing part-time research in high energy physics for an MSc at the National University of Singapore.

book reviews

Interfacing text tackles area frequently passed over

Chris Georgopoulos

'Interfacing fundamentals in micro-processor-controlled systems' Kluwer, Dordrecht, The Netherlands (1985) £24.95 pp xix + 364

One of the potentially most difficult and error prone areas in the implementation of designs where microprocessors are to be used in conjunction with other equipment is in the interfacing, where two discrete units have to be harnessed together. It is an area which is sometimes skipped over in texts on microprocessors, and frequently treated even more shortly in manufacturers' literature for scientific equipment. This book tackles the problem of interfacing by first looking at the microprocessor itself, then considering how it relates to

peripheral devices, including memory access, and then moving into interfacing with other computers and equipment. The second half of the book considers several application areas ranging from the diffuse topic of communications to specialized automotive electronics.

The book is part of a series on microprocessor-based systems engineering and is derived from the author's lecture course. It assumes some background knowledge of electronics although not necessarily of microprocessors and is intended to be used by both students and practising engineers.

Each chapter includes at the end a set of questions and problems on the text as well as a set of references.

In the first chapter, the author takes time to indicate the importance of interfacing and points out that, to be successful, it is necessary to have

an understanding of both the microprocessor and the 'outside world' to which it is to be interfaced. It is this guideline which determines the development of the book.

The book is certainly packed with information, to the extent that some of the diagrams seem cluttered. The author succeeds in providing a comprehensive coverage of the subject and has coped reasonably well with the perennial problem of this type of book — to keep up to date. He acknowledges the growing impact of CMOS circuitry and includes a table of 32-bit processors. The transitions from the description of the microprocessor to its interfacing with peripherals, and also from the general description of interfacing to specific examples, are unobtrusively made. This gives the feel of a single text which is an improvement on some books based

on lecture courses where the separate sections are thrown together. The common interface standards — IEEE488, SCSI, VME and many others — are described in various sections of the text; this is quite impressive in the range of applications which are considered.

The presentation of the book is not as good as it might be. It has obviously been prepared as camera-ready copy on some computer system. There are sections where the printer has had trouble following a straight line and the text has more than the usual number of spelling and typographical errors.

The range of example application areas for the microprocessor underline its ubiquity in modern technology; for example there are applications in the home, in the factory, in the car and in the office. The final chapter is a useful look at the impact of VLSI on the topics which have just been described and it emphasizes that, great though the changes of the last decade have been, we are not yet at the end of the road.

In summary, this is a book which provides a useful addition to the library of those working in this area. The information has been thoroughly researched and is clearly written. It is not unreasonably priced for the information which it contains and it is as up to date as is possible.

Philip Robertson
University of St Andrews
Computing Laboratory, UK

Human approach to systems design

Andrew Monk (Ed.)

'Fundamentals of human–computer interaction' Academic Press, New York, USA (1984) £22.50 pp xvii + 293

A bad computer system is one that is difficult for users to operate: the disharmony between user and system will eventually lead to general rejection of such a system. Why has this happened? It is because the system designer has failed to adapt the system to the abilities of the users. It is therefore imperative that user-system harmony is of the highest priority in system design, and this is what *Fundamentals of human-computer interaction* sets out to encourage.

The book consists of three major parts. In part 1, the nature of the human being is examined in order to expose its limitations in using its natural senses to extract information. Detailed explanations are given on the capacities of the eyes and the brain as mechanisms for input to the human information processing system, and at attempt is made to explain how the human brain processes information. The aim of this part of the book is to provide some information on the nature of the computer user.

The second part of the book focusses attention on how to collect and evaluate data on the behavioural pattern of man. Both qualitative and quantitative methods are covered to some extent. The concluding section of this part described an experiment on evaluating speech synthesizers as output devices.

The final part of the book attempts to give some guidelines on how to apply the knowledge of the user in designing truly user-oriented computer systems. The specific emphasis is on user-computer dialogue through sight and voice.

One defect of the book is the lack of proper demarcation between fundamentals and applications of some principles. For example, while human sight is introduced well in part 1 before many applications are touched on in parts 2 and 3, this is not the case with human speech. The reader suddenly encounters synthesizers in chapter 7 without previous basic understanding of how the human being speaks. Although a brief introduction to speech articulation is given in chapter 12, this is too late to be of any use to the inexperienced reader.

In addition, the human hearing system as well as the vocal system should have been treated in detail in part 1; visual perception is very well treated.

The book concludes with many useful references. The main strength of the book, which far outweighs its shortcomings, is that it consists of current material from many reputable authors. In addition, the book covers a wide range of topics.

In computer systems development, once things go wrong at the design stage there will never be user-system harmony; this book helps towards avoiding this. Therefore first and foremost I would like to recommend the book for all those connected with designing computer systems. In addition, because the language used in the book is clear, it should be readable for both teachers and students of computer science as well as systems managers.

O R Omotayo
University of Ibadan,
Nigeria

Books received

Pelloso, Pierre *'Practical digital electronics'* John Wiley, Chichester, UK (1986) £12.95 pp viii + 219

Originally published in 1983 in French, this textbook is intended to educate first-degree students and teachers in the design and realization of digital circuits and subsystems using SSI, MSI and LSI components. The six chapters cover: basic functions; technology of integrated circuits; combinational systems; sequential systems; arithmetic systems; and digital systems. Particular attention is given to correct interfacing (especially using buses) and avoiding timing problems by the correct use of signals. An index is provided.

Digital brings 32-bit 'Backplane Interconnect' to VAX systems

The 32-bit successor to the Q-bus and Unibus backplane buses, the VAX Backplane Interconnect (VAXBI), has been introduced by Digital Equipment. The company's primary purpose for the bus is to act as an interconnection for VAX clusters and future generation VAX systems. In a system configuration the bus can be used as a combined memory and I/O channel for single processors, as simply a memory bus in multiprocessing systems, or as a dedicated I/O bus on some single-board computers.

Operation of the bus is synchronous, at a rate of 5 MHz, with address, arbitration and data transmission time-multiplexed over the 32 lines. Physical address space is 1 Gbyte. Data transmission, although at fixed lengths of 4, 8 and 16 byte, within these lengths can be from 1 to 16 byte in any transaction. Maximum data transfer rate quoted by DEC is 13.3 Mbyte s^{-1} for 16-byte transfers; for a single 32-bit word the transfer rate is said to be 6.6 Mbyte s^{-1}.

Arbitration on the bus is distributed rather than controlled by a central, dedicated arbiter. Arbitration algorithms are handled by the interface chips at each bus node on a dual 'round-robin' basis. According to DEC, because the maximum block-mode transfer is 16 byte, no node can monopolize the bus. The bus provides connection for up to 16 nodes, each of which can be a mix of processors, memories and adaptors.

The interface on each node between the bus and the user interface logic is a single chip, the BIIC, which implements the bus protocol. It also performs self test before system operation begins to verify the bus control logic and the accessibility of bus registers. In addition, each node checks its own logic and the result of the BIIC's self test.

The standard VAXBI hardware module is a 20.32×23.32 cm multilayered printed wiring board which is 0.236 cm thick, divided into bus-defined and user-defined areas. The latter has approximately 90% of the available surface space, says DEC. (*Digital Equipment Co. Ltd, PO Box 110, Reading RG2 0TR, UK. Tel: (0734) 856117*) □

Bipolar logic arrays — 'speed with low power'

High-speed bipolar logic arrays, the DS series of uncommitted logic arrays (ULAs), have been announced by Ferranti. In sticking with bipolar the company emphasizes the speed advantages of the technology, but also claims to have dramatically reduced power requirements, the conventional drawback with bipolar devices, by using a design that it says is unique to bipolar.

'Differential logic' is based on steering current through a logic tree by means of differential pairs of transistors stacked across the supply rail. A differential pair of transistors has a linear and sharp characteristic, enabling gates to operate with logic swings of 100 mV, says Ferranti. Discrimination between logic levels is claimed to be no worse than with single-ended circuits that have logic swings of typically 400 mV, giving a power saving for differential pairs of 4:1 with no compromise in speed, the company says.

Overall system speed of the DS series of arrays is rated at 100 MHz for gate complexities from 500 to 10k gates. Clock-to-input delay is 1.5 ns at a 250 MHz toggle rate. Power dissipation at this frequency is 750 µW with a 5 V supply, or 300 µW

Connection patterns of a 2600-gate DS series bipolar array

with a 2 V supply.

Ferranti is keen to point out that gate delay and flip-flop speed are virtually independent of fan-out and supply voltage. For clock and reset lines where high fan-outs are typical, the DS clock drivers are claimed to handle fan-outs up to 100 without loss of performance.

The arrays are fabricated in an advanced bipolar technology using double layer metal and with a 1.5 µm feature size.

CAE software is available and covers design, simulation and, using silicon compilation techniques, autolayout and verification of application-specific IC (ASIC) solutions. The complete range of functions can only be run on a VAX computer. Other CAE workstations — Daisy, Mentor or Valid — handle just the design and simulation functions. (*Ferranti Electronics Ltd, Fields New Road, Chadderton, Oldham, Lancashire OL9 8NP, UK. Tel: 061-624 0515*)

● UK availability of bipolar logic arrays, the Q3500 series, has been announced by AMCC. The arrays have mixed ECL/TTL-mode I/O. Typical gate delays are claimed to be up to 0.7 ns, achieving a maximum operating frequency of 300 MHz. Power consumption quoted is 1 mW per gate. Arrays are available with 1300, 2400 and 3500 equivalent gates. An array can be supplied with 1600 gates and 1280 bit of configurable static RAM on the chip. A software design kit supports the arrays for semicustom applications and runs on most popular CAE workstations. (*Applied Micro Circuits Corp, Slington House, Rankine Road, Basingstoke RG24 0PH, UK. Tel: (0256) 460219*) □

Frame grabber speeds PC AT imaging

Frame grabber and auxiliary processor boards from Data Translation speed image processing on the IBM PC AT

Image processing using the IBM PC AT computer can be performed 250 times faster than is possible with the AT alone using a frame grabber combined with an auxiliary frame processor announced by Data Translation. The company claims that its DT2851 grabber and DT2858 auxiliary boards perform a three-by-three convolution on a typical 512 × 512 × 16-bit image frame in 0.85 s. Image processing algorithms are implemented on the boards using the DT-IRIS software package.

The frame grabber is designed around CMOS gate arrays developed by Data Translation, but it derives its speed of operation from the memory architecture used. This architecture has two 256 kbyte memory buffers onboard, which provide storage for two image frames. This double buffered architecture allows parallel processing of multiple images.

The auxiliary processor has a 16-bit pipelined architecture for arithmetic-intensive operations. The principal elements on the board are a RAM conversion table and a 16-bit ALU. Both boards are connected together and to the AT via external I/O ports kept separate from the PC bus so that their operations are not slowed by the PC.

Applications targetted for the processor are in machine and robot vision, medical imaging and scientific research. (*Data Translation Ltd, The Business Centre, Molly Millar's Lane, Wokingham, Berks RG11 2QZ, UK. Tel: (0734) 793838)* □

32-bit Z80 000 set for production

Zilog has marked its entry into the 32-bit field with the Z80 000 CPU. This 10 MHz processor in NMOS is suited for large system tasks or, configured under software control to use 16-bit logical addresses, it can be used for high-speed controller applications. Three major markets targetted for the processor are military and defence applications, graphics processing and signal processing. As it uses the Z-bus, the chip is compatible with the existing range of Z8000 peripheral chips.

The Z80 000 has 256 byte onchip cache and memory management unit (MMU). Via a six-stage instruction pipeline, the chip executes instructions at a rate of up to one instruction per processor cycle, it is claimed.

The MMU translates the most recently used logical addresses generated by the CPU into the physical addresses used by the memory system. Each address is checked to determine its permissibility. The MMU can also be used to implement a virtual memory.

Packaged in an 84-pin grid array, the processor is to be produced at Zilog's Nampa, ID, USA, facility. Production quantities of the processor will be available in the third quarter of 1986. (*Zilog (UK) Ltd, Zilog House, Moorbridge Road, Maidenhead, Berks SL6 8PL, UK. Tel: (0628) 39200* □

32 × 32 MAC is rated at 80 ns

A 32 × 32-bit fixed point multiplier-accumulator (MAC) launched by LSI Logic is, the company claims, the first and the fastest such MAC available. Manufactured in 1.5 μm HCMOS, the L64032 computer-compiled IC is specified to operate at 80 ns in versions designed for commercial applications, or at 100 ns in versions for military conditions. Double precision 64 × 64-bit multiplication can be achieved in four clock cycles, the company says.

Available off the shelf, the MAC is primarily intended for digital signal processing applications, but can also be used in graphics and image processing. The device can be used as a megacell in LSI Logic's application specific ICs (ASICs) or as a standalone customized circuit.

The MAC is designed with scan testability of all internal registers within the device. This facility allows the user to monitor internal states by activating a single test pin.

Supplied in a 132-pin ceramic PGA package, the MAC is now available in production quantities. (*LSI Logic Ltd, Grenville Place, The Ring, Bracknell, Berks RG12 1BP, UK. Tel: (0344) 426544)* □

Multitasking op. system

A microprocessor-based multitasking operating system, MTOS-UX, that allows tasks and related support structures to be created dynamically while an application is running, has been launched by IPI Europe. The system interfaces via a serial link to Unix System V, which can be used as a software development environment. In this way, the company says, the integrity of this realtime system is maintained rather than grafting development tools onto the realtime kernel itself.

The first version of UX runs on the 68000. A version for the Intel processor family is due for release.

UX is the latest in the series of MTOS operating systems dating back to 1976 which operate on the 6800, 8080/8085 and 8086/8088 processors, and on the 68000 but without the dynamic object creation and Unix interfacing facilities. IPI claims that these operating systems are the only systems available with built-in support for tightly coupled multiprocessors. Similar realtime systems require extra software development to serve multiple processors. (*IPI Europe Ltd, Science Park, University of Warwick, Coventry CV4 7EZ, UK. Tel: (0203) 417091)* □

MicroVAX II gains board-level array processor

Board-level array processors have been produced for Digital Equipment's MicroVAX II microsystems. US firm Sky Computers has ported its Warrior array processor, capable of accelerating both 32-bit and 64-bit floating point operations, onto the DEC machines to give what Sky claims as a 100-fold performance increase in some number-crunching applications.

'This is the first time a board-level array processor has been integrated into any VAX product,' announced John Cavill of UK distributor Data Translation; he also claimed that the result was 'the most aggressive price: performance product in the industry'.

The basic Warrior configuration costs just over £16 000 (UK price) and includes a 15 MFLOPS (million floating point operations per second) array processor with 64 kbyte of cache memory, 2 Mbyte of data memory and over 100 routines callable from VAX/VMS applications. This set-up uses three quad boards on the MicroVAX backplanes: two for the basic array processor and one for the dual-ported 2 Mbyte memory board. Cache memory is expandable to 256 kbyte and data memory to 10 Mbyte.

Software support for the MicroVAX version of Warrior is provided by enhancing the capabilities of the VAX/VMX high-level languages through a subroutine library. The Warrior is also available with VMEbus and Versabus interfaces. (*Sky Computers Inc, Foot of John Street, Lowell, MA 01852, USA. Tel: (617) 454-6200. Data Translation Ltd, The Business Centre, Molly Millar's Lane, Wokingham, Berks RG11 2QZ, UK. Tel: (0734) 793838*) □

Surface-mount PLD programmer

As surface mount devices (SMDs) find increasing popularity, programming devices for these components are now emerging in the market. From Stag Electronic Designs is the ZL30A logic programmer for a range of programmable logic devices (PLDs), which the company claims is the first dedicated programmer to cater for the latest packaging styles, including surface mount. Built-in ZIF sockets are provided for 20, 24 and 28-pin devices, but for SMDs an optional adaptor module is available.

Functions provided with the programmer include: load and program operations; empty, verify and vector testing; input and output of data; and an editing facility. The programmer can be used as a standalone unit, in conjunction with a host computer via an RS232C link.

SMD programmers that do not require socket adaptors or caps have been introduced by Data I/O. The Series 1000 EPROM gang programmers have pop-in, pop-out socket rails for SMDs, so reducing handling time the company claims. Sockets are 15-to-a-rail and can set up in a single or double rail configuration. At any one time the programmers can handle up to 30 EPROMs in PLCC packages. (*Stag Electronic Designs Ltd, Stag House, Tewin Court, Welwyn Garden City, Herts AL7 1AU, UK. Tel: (0707) 332148. Data I/O Europe, World Trade Center, Strawinskylaan 633, 1077 XX Amsterdam, The Netherlands. Tel: (020) 622866*) □

Mbit CMOS EPROM

Am27C1024, a 1 Mbit EPROM fabricated in 1.5 μm CMOS

Claimed to be a world first, a 1 Mbit CMOS EPROM has been introduced by Advanced Micro Devices. Organized as 64k × 16 bit, the Am27C1024 has a quoted access time of 200 ns.

With a 16-bit-wide architecture, the EPROM can be interfaced directly to 16- and 32-bit systems. Typical applications could be in systems requiring high density storage to save board space, or in portable systems with low power consumption requirements. In active mode, power consumption is rated at 250 mW. This is reduced to 5 mW in standby more or, by deselecting the chip-enable input, power dissipation can be brought down to 1 mW.

Constructed in a 40-pin side-brazed package, the device will be available in production quantities in the third quarter of 1986. (*Advanced Micro Devices (UK) Ltd, AMD House, Goldsworth Road, Woking, Surrey GU21 1JT, UK. Tel: (04862) 22121*) □

'Final' NMOS EPROM

Two 512 kbit EPROMs with access times of 250 ns and 300 ns have been launched by Hitachi. Designated HN27512G, the devices are the last EPROMs Hitachi intends to make using NMOS technology: all future EPROMs will be CMOS, says the company, starting with a high-integration 1 Mbit chip.

The HN27512G devices use a programming voltage of +12.5 V, and may be programmed using a 'High Performance Programming Algorithm' designed to increase programming speed without voltage stress or deterioration of data reliability. Standby current is quoted as 40 mA (maximum). The chips require no clock, says Hitachi, and their inputs and outputs are TTL compatible in both Read and Program modes.

The EPROMs are supplied in 28-pin DIL packages. (*Hitachi Ltd, New Marunouchi Building No 5, 1-chome Marunouchi, Chiyoda, Tokyo, Japan. Hitachi Electronic Components (UK) Ltd, 21 Upton Road, Watford, Herts WD1 7TB, UK. Tel: (0923) 46488*) □

products in brief

Name	Description	Manufacturer/designer	Distributor/contact
Microcontrollers			
Microgem	Programmable controller designed to replace (economically) as few as six relay circuits. Measuring 250 mm × 75 mm × 116 mm, it has 32 software counters, 32 counters, four sequencers, 80 internal flags, 12 input circuits and eight output circuits. A hand-held programmer and battery support RAM and EPROM options are available	GEC Industrial Controls Ltd, Kidsgrove, Stoke-on-Trent, Staffs ST7 1TW, UK. Tel: (07816) 3511	
MTE100	Range of small programmable controllers based on four modules: processor (with memory capacity of 1000 instructions), I/O, input expansion and analogue input. Systems can be configured to a maximum of 32 inputs and 32 outputs in increments of eight inputs and eight outputs. Programming can be carried out with a dedicated hand-held LCD programmer or an IBM-compatible personal computer	MTE Ltd, Leigh-on-Sea, Essex SS9 5LS, UK. Tel: (0702) 527111	
Bit-slice microprocessors			
CY7C901-23	CMOS version of the 2901 4-bit slice microprocessor. Claimed to be 25% faster than the NMOS version. Power consumption is 70 mA	Cypress Semiconductor Corp, 3910 North 1st Street, San Jose, CA 95134, USA. Tel: (408) 943-2600	Advanced Technology Devices, Pronto Electronic Systems Ltd, City Gate House, 399–425 Eastern Avenue, Gants Hill, Ilford, Essex IG2 6LR, UK. Tel: 01-554 6222
Communications chips			
Am7996	Single chip transceiver with collision detection for IEEE 802.3 Ethernet and Cheapernet networking applications. Supports signal recognition up to 1000 m without repeaters over Ethernet, up to 305 m over Cheapernet	Advanced Micro Devices Inc, 901 Thompson Place, Sunnyvale, CA 94086, USA	Kudos Electronics Ltd, Handpost Corner, Finchampstead Road, Wokingham, Berks RG11 3LP, UK. Tel: (0734) 794515
53C80	CMOS version of the 5380 small computer system interface (SCSI) chip which when introduced was claimed to be the first chip capable of driving the SCSI bus directly without requiring external logic. The CMOS version has had four ground lines added to reduce ground plane noise and to increase the switching speed of output buffers	NCR Corp, Micro Electronics Mianisburg, 8181 Byers Road, Mianisburg, OH 45342, USA. Tel: (513) 866 7471	Manhattan Skyline Ltd, Bridge Road, Maidenhead, Berks SL6 8DB, UK. Tel: (0628) 75851
Programmable arrays			
SPL series	CMOS PLDs based on EPROM technology for the development of custom circuits. Can be implemented using a logic programmer. The product range comprises 20-pin latch and register devices	Sprague World Trade Corp, 18 Avenue Louis Casai, 1209 Geneva, Switzerland. Tel: (98) 4071	ITT Multicomponents, The Mill House, Barry Avenue, Windsor, Berks SL4 1QS, UK. Tel: (0753) 840201

products in brief

Name	Description	Manufacturer/designer	Distributor/contact
Programmable arrays (continued)			
HG28	Two ranges, E and A, of gate arrays with 0.8 ns gate delays and power dissipation of 0.22 mW per gate at 10 MHz. The E range has up to 1k gates and an output drive of 24 mA; the A range has up to 2.5k gates and output drive of 8 mA. Suitable applications are graphics, dynamic DRAM control and hard disc drives	Hitachi Ltd, New Marunouchi Building No 5, 1-chome, Marunouchi, Chiyoda, Tokyo, Japan	Hitachi Electronics Components (UK) Ltd, 21 Upton Road, Watford, Herts WD1 7TB, UK. Tel: (0923) 46488
A/D converters			
AD7578	12-bit A/D converter with 100 µs conversion time. Unadjusted error is ± 1 least significant bit. Power dissipation is 150 mW. Supplied in a 24-pin 'skinny' DIP	Analog Devices Ltd, Central Avenue, East Molesey, Surrey KT8 0SN, UK. Tel: 01-941 0466	BA Electronics Ltd, Hitchin Road, Arlesey, Beds SG15 6SG, UK. Tel: (0462) 834744
MC145040/ 145041	8-bit CMOS A/D converters with serial interface ports. Maximum nonlinearity is ± 0.5 least significant bit. Version 40 uses an external clock, version 41 has an internal clock and an end-of-conversion signal	Motorola GmbH, Arabella strasse 17, 8000 München 81, FRG. Tel: (089) 92720	ITT Multicomponents, The Mill House, Barry Avenue, Windsor, Berks SL4 1QS, UK. Tel: (0753) 840141

Name	Description	Manufacturer/designer	Distributor/contact
D/A converters			
PM-7524	8-bit CMOS buffered converter. Supply voltage is 5 V or 15 V. Linearity is ± 11/8 least significant bit. Supplied in a 16-pin ceramic DIL package	Precision Monolithic Inc, 1500 Space Park Drive, Santa Clara, CA 95052-8020, USA. Tel: (408) 727-9222	Hi-Tek Electronics, Ditton Walk, Cambridge CB5 8QD, UK. Tel: (0223) 213333
PM-7528	A dual 8-bit converter which is CMOS and TTL compatible. Comes in a 20-pin DIL package. Designed for battery-operated equipment, operation is from a 5–15 V single power supply, and power dissipation is 20 mW. Relative accuracy is ± 1/2 least significant bit	Precision Monolithics Inc, 1500 Space Park Drive, Santa Clara, CA 95052-8020, USA. Tel: (408) 727-9222	Hi-Tek Electronics, Ditton Walk, Cambridge CB5 8QD, UK. Tel: (0223) 213333
Single-board computers			
PG8000	68008-based, VME-compatible single-board computer running at 8 MHz. Hardware timing is via a 16-bit timer that can activate interrupts. Two 28-pin sockets are left free for memory devices. Two RS232C serial ports are provided, or the board can be used in a standalone configuration	Philips Bv, Eindhoven, The Netherlands. Tel: (40) 756785	Unit-C, Dominion Way, West Broadwater, Worthing, West Sussex BN14 8NT, UK. Tel: (0903) 205233

products in brief

Name	Description	Manufacturer/designer	Distributor/contact
Single-board computers (continued)			
PMM 68K-2	68000 or 68010-based Multibus compatible single-board computer with dual cache to minimize wait states. The 8 kbyte dual cache consists of two memory sections each with a 2k word capacity. Board operating speed is 12.5 MHz. Onboard is a 19.2 kbit s^{-1} universal asynchronous receiver transmitter (UART) to communicate with a terminal console. Eight Multibus interrupt lines are provided with levels defined by PALs	Plessey Microsystems Ltd, Water Lane, Towcester, Northants NN12 7JN, UK. Tel: (0327) 50312	
Processor boards			
ET-68020	25 MHz version of this VMEbus processor board. Earlier versions ran at 12 or 16 MHz. Speed is achieved by using asynchronous RAM access, says the manufacturer	Integrated Micro Products Ltd, No. 1 Industrial Estate, Medomsley Road, Consett, Co. Durham DH8 6TJ, UK. Tel: (0207) 503481	
Model 300	4 MHz Z80A board with 1 Mbyte RAM onboard (with an associated power supply unit); also 64 kbyte EPROM and 12 kbyte static RAM. The board has six serial I/O ports	Rotec International, 15 Osyth Close, Brackmills Industrial Estate, Northampton NN4 0DY, UK. Tel: (0604) 63611	
7865/6	Two 8088-based boards for the STDbus. Both boards have an optional 8087 maths coprocessor and sockets for up to 128k of ROM and 64k RAM. The 7865 board has a dual serial communications controller providing RS232 and RS422 channels, and is suited for industrial applications. The 7866 board has two Intel SBX connectors for customized I/O (eg A/D, D/A, IEEE 488 etc)	Pro-Log Corp, 2411 Garden Road, Monterey, CA 93940, USA. Tel: (408) 372-4593	Technitron, Doman Road, Camberley, Surrey GU15 3DH, UK. Tel: (0276) 26517
Bus boards			
Bus-Tech	Series of VMEbus-based boards. So far 14 boards are available, covering processors, memory disc controllers, I/O and graphics	High Technology Electronics, 303–305 Portswood Road, Southampton SO2 1LD, UK. Tel: (0703) 581555	

GP Industiral Electronics PAL programmer (left), HTE Bus-Tech VME boards (centre) and Data I/O model 201 EPROM programmer (right)

Name	Description	Manufacturer/designer	Distributor/contact
Development systems			
miniForce 2P21	A 32-bit VMEbus development system with a 68020 running under PDOS, a realtime multiuser, multitasking operating system. Within the system are: a 68884 floating point coprocessor, 512 kbyte zero wait state static RAM and Winchester and floppy disc storage. The housing chassis has nine slots for VMEbus motherboards, with six slots available for user applications	Force Computers GmbH, Daimlerstrasse 9, D-8012 Ottobrunn/München, FRG. Tel: (089) 6092033	
Pascal-2	Cross development system that enables application software, including realtime programs to be developed on VAX machines for MC68000-based hardware. Consists of a cross-compiler, a cross-linker/assembler that runs on VAX/VMS and a VersaDOS support library	Oregon Software, OR, USA. Tel: (503) 245-2202	Unit-C Ltd, Dominion Way, West Broadwater, Worthing, West Sussex BN14 8NT, UK. Tel: (0903) 205233
Uniware common tool set	A modular tool set for the development of assembly language microprocessor software. Contains a macro preprocessor, a link editor, an archiver and various formatters and downloaders. Target processors supported include 8051, 8086/8088, Z80, 6800, 68000 and HD64180	Software Development Systems, IL, USA. Tel: (312) 971-8170	Unit-C, Dominion Way, West Broadwater, Worthing, West Sussex BN14 8NT, UK. Tel: (0903) 205233
Compilers			
BSO/C	c compilers for the Motorola 68000/010/020 and Intel 8086/186/286 processors, with full Ultrix support on the VAX and MicroVAX II computers. Versions are also available for Unix 4.2, VMS and MicroVMS	BSO Inc, 128 Technology Center, Waltham, MA 02254-9164, USA. Tel: (617) 894-7800	BSO UK, 16 Fernhill Road, Farnborough, Hants GU14 9RX, UK. Tel: (0252) 510014
Programmers			
Model 201	Single socket EPROM programmer aimed at entry-level users. Programs MOS and CMOS EPROMs and E^{2}PROMs. Based on the company's existing eight-socket model 280 set programmer	Data I/O Corp, 10525 Willows Road NE, PO Box 97046, Redmond, WA 98073-9746, USA. Tel: (206) 881-6444	Data I/O Europe, World Trade Center, Strawinskylaan 633, 1077 XX Amsterdam, The Netherlands Tel: (020) 622866
PAL programmer	'Intelligent' system for programming 20 and 24 series PALs. Comprises an EPROM programmer, a universal programming module and a PAL programming adaptor. The system accepts fuse plots generated and downloaded in the Jedec format, and can be used with most logic compiler software	GP Industrial Electronics Ltd, Unit E, Huxley Close, Newnham Industrial Estate, Plymouth PL7 4JN, UK. Tel: (0752) 342961	
Promac 16-III	Gang and set programmer for MOS devices. Can program up to 16 devices at a time. Includes a 1 Mbyte RAM buffer. The programmer has edit facilities and remote control via an RS232C interface	Japan Macnics Corp, 516 Imaiminami-cho, Nakahara-ku, Kawasaki City, Kanagawa-ken 211, Japan. Tel: 044 (711) 0330	Technitron, Doman Road, Camberley, Surrey GU15 3DH, UK. Tel: (0276) 26517

products in brief

Name	Description	Manufacturer/designer	Distributor/contact
S125GD/L/GL	Standalone family of multiprogrammers which can program PROMs, EPROMs, E^{2}PROMs, single chip microprocessors and logic arrays. 16 devices can be programmed simultaneously	Bytek Inc, PO Box 15555, Minneapolis, MN 55415, USA	Trident Microsystems Ltd, Trident House, 53 Ormside Way, Redhill, Surrey RH1 2LS, UK. Tel: (0737) 65900
Z-400	Programmer designed for NMOS and CMOS EPROMs and bipolar PROMs. Does not require pinout adaptors for different devices. Has 64k × 8 bit RAM and two serial I/O ports with data buffering	Sunrise Electronics Inc, 524 South Vermont Avenue, Glendora, CA 91740, USA. Tel: (213) 914-1926	Petratec Ltd, Glanty House, The Causeway, Egham, Surrey, UK. Tel: (0784) 36254

Memory boards

Name	Description	Manufacturer/designer	Distributor/contact
DPR cards	Dual-ported RAM cards that allow Z80A processors to communicate via common RAM in control and logging applications. The cards are compatible with Kemitron's industrial and scientific computer range. Using the cards a master microprocessor can communicate with up to four slave processors. Each slave holds a 16 kbyte block of RAM which handles data at up to 80 kbyte s^{-1}	Kemitron Ltd, Hawarden Industrial Park, Manor Lane, Deeside, Clwyd CH5 3PP, UK. Tel: (0244) 536123	
MII-1	512 kbyte bubble memory on a Multibus II module with an onboard intelligent controller. The controller communicates with host processors via unsolicited messages and message queues in shared memory. Full message passing is supported. Has a built-in self-test facility. Can be expanded to 32 Mbyte	Bubbl-tec, PC/M Inc, 6800 Sierra Court, Dublin, CA 94568, USA. Tel: (415) 829-8700	Amplicon Electronics Ltd, Richmond Road, Brighton, East Sussex BN2 3RL, UK. Tel: (0273) 608331
PSB-1	128 kbyte bubble memory for Z80 or 8085-based systems running on STDbus. Finds applications in process control and in communications equipment. Data transfer rate is 68 kbit s^{-1} with a maximum access time of 82 ms. An intelligent controller is provided onboard and self-test diagnostics are included	Bubbl-tec, PC/M Inc, 6800 Sierra Court, Dublin, CA 94568, USA. Tel: (415) 829-8700	Amplicon Electronics Ltd, Richmond Road, Brighton, East Sussex BN2 3RL, UK. Tel: (0273) 608331
SDRAM	Dynamic RAM board on a single Eurocard for STEbus systems. Four possible memory sizes are offered: 64, 128, 256 or 512 kbyte. Read/write access times are claimed to be 240 ns	Arcom Control Systems Ltd, Unit 8, Clifton Road, Cambridge CB1 4WH, UK. Tel: (0233) 242224	
SVME 328	2 Mbyte dynamic RAM board on a double Eurocard for the VMEbus. With 8-, 16- or 32-bit data, and 24- or 32-bit address. The memory array is partitioned into two banks of 1 Mbyte; each bank is subdivided into four blocks of nine 256k × 1 bit devices, the ninth device providing parity if required	DY-4, 888 Lady Ellen Place, Ottawa, Ontario, Canada. Tel: (613) 728-3711	Dage (GB) Ltd, Eurosem Division, Rabans Lane, Aylesbury, Bucks HP19 3RG, UK. Tel: (0296) 33200

Name	Description	Manufacturer/designer	Distributor/contact
EPROMs			
MBM27C1000/ 1024/1028	Series of 1 Mbit CMOS EPROMs with access times from 150 ns to 250 ns. 1000 version is a 32-pin package organized as 131k × 8 bit; 1024 is 65k × 16 bit in a 40-pin DIP; 1028 is either 65k × 16 bit or 131k × 8 bit, available in both a 28-pin DIP or a 32-pin LCC	Fujitsu Ltd, 6–1 Marunouchi 2-chome, Chiyoda-ku, Tokyo 100, Japan	Fujitsu Mikroelektronik, Hargrave House, Belmont Road, Maidenhead, Berks SL6 6NE, UK. Tel: (0628) 76100
RAMs			
Am90C255/ 256/257	256kbit CMOS dynamic RAMs organized as 256k × 1 bit. Access times are 100 ns. With a maximum standby current of 100 mA, these RAMs are suited for battery back-up applications. The three versions offer nibble, enhanced page and static column modes of address, respectively. Production quantities are available in 16-pin plastic and ceramic DIPs, or in PLCCs	Advanced Micro Devices Inc, 901 Thompson Place, Sunnyvale, CA 94086, USA	Advanced Micro Devices (UK) Ltd, AMD House, Goldsworth Road, Woking, Surrey GU21 1JT, UK. Tel: (04862) 22121
EDH84H64C	256 kbit RAM supplied in DIL package. Organized as 64k × 4 bit for video and computer graphics applications. Versions with access times of 45, 55 or 70 ns are available. Power consumption is 1.5 W maximum	Electronic Designs Inc, Hopkinton Industrial Park, 35 South Street, Hopkinton, MA 01748, USA. Tel: (617) 435-9077	Electronic Designs Europe, Shelley House, The Avenue, Lightwater, Surrey GU18 5RF, UK. Tel: (0276) 72637
M5M5187P/ 5188P	64k CMOS static RAMs organized as 64k × 1 bit and 16k × 4 bit respectively. With an onchip power down facility which is claimed to reduce typical operating power from 200 mW to 5 µW. Versions are available with access times of 45 or 55 ns. Supplied in 22-pin plastic DIL package. The 5188 has common I/O lines, the 5187 has separate terminations	Mitsubishi Electric Corp, 2-3 Marunouchi 2-chome, Chiyoda-ku, Tokyo 100, Japan	Mitsubishi Electric (UK) Ltd, Hertford Place, Denham Way, Maple Cross, Rickmansworth, Herts WD3 2BJ, UK. Tel: (0923) 770000

From left: Electronic Designs 84H64C static RAM; Arcom SDRAM STEbus memory board; Fujitsu MBM27C1028 1 Mbit EPROM; and DY-4 SVME 328 dynamic RAM board

products in brief

Name	Description	Manufacturer/designer	Distributor/contact
RAMs (continued)			
F100415/ F10415	High-speed ECL static RAMs organized as 1k × 1 bit with maximum access times said to be 10 ns. Designed for high-speed scratchpad, control and buffer-storage applications. Available in 16-pin DIL packages and 16-pin quad-sided flatpacks	Fairchild Semiconductor GmbH, AM Burgfrieden 1, 8090 Wasserburg Am Inn, FRG. Tel: (08071) 104232	
TC514256P-10/ J-10	1 Mbit CMOS dynamic RAMs organized as 256k × 4 bit. Cycle time is 55 ns. Standby current is 1 mA. Available in a 20-pin plastic DIP (P version) or a 20-pin plastic SOJ (J version)	Toshiba, 1-chome, Uchisaiwai-cho, Chiyoda-ku, Tokyo, Japan	Toshiba (UK) Ltd, Semiconductor Division, Toshiba House, Frimley Road, Camberley, Surrey, UK. Tel: (0276) 62222
TMM 2089C	8k × 9 bit NMOS static RAM designed for high-speed applications, particularly cache memory and high-speed storage. Maximum access time is claimed to be 35 ns. Operating current is 120 mA, but is 10 mA on automatic standby mode. Available in a 28-pin ceramic DIP	Toshiba, 1-chome, Uchisaiwai-cho, Chiyoda-ku, Tokyo, Japan	Toshiba (UK) Ltd, Semiconductor Division, Toshiba House, Frimley Road, Camberley, Surrey, UK. Tel: (0276) 62222
TMM 41256T	256 kbit dynamic RAM in a surface mount package — an 18-pin 'J' leaded package measuring 13.51 × 8.31 × 3.51 mm. Organized as 256k × 1 bit. Operating power is 275 mW, or 28 mW on standby	Toshiba, 1-chome, Uchisaiwai-cho, Chiyoda-ku, Tokyo, Japan	Toshiba (UK) Ltd, Semiconductor Division, Toshiba House, Frimley Road, Camberley, Surrey, UK. Tel: (0276) 62222
Bubble memory			
'Profile' bubble memory	4 Mbit bubble memory chip for video and graphics storage. The chip can store 2 h of video time. Average access times for the 'profile' bubbles is 485 ns. Chip size is 15 × 15 mm	Hitachi Ltd, New Marunouchi Building No 5, 1-chome, Marunouchi, Chiyoda, Tokyo, Japan	Hitachi Electronic Components (UK) Ltd, 21 Upton Road, Watford, Herts WD1 7TB, UK. Tel: (0923) 46488
Software			
BWS BASIC	Multitasking Z80-based BASIC interpreter that allows the creation and execution, in real time, of BASIC programs controlling up to 16 tasks. Located on a 7806 CPU card, the ROM-based interpreter handles standard BASIC commands, with some additions: WHENP and WHENT check I/O port and timing port and timing prior to executing a task; the AUTO command allows automatic task execution on power up or reset. Timing routines are not required. The module can be connected to a host computer and programs executed on the target system or downloaded to a PROM programmer	Pro-Log Corp, 2411 Garden Road, Monterey, CA 93940, USA. Tel: (408) 372-4593	Technitron, Doman Road, Camberley, Surrey GU15 3DH, UK. Tel: (0276) 26517
bMasm; bMd	Microcode assembler and debugger (respectively) written in C, designed for use on any microcode programmable bit-slice system	benchMark Technologies Ltd, benchMark House, 2 Lower Teddington Road, Hampton Wick, Kingston-upon-Thames, Surrey KT1 4ER, UK. Tel: 01-943 4393	

Microprocessors assure constant measures in pubs and clubs

Microprocessors are being used to increase the speed and accuracy of drinks dispensing in UK clubs and public houses. Developed by UK firm Anglo Services at a cost of some £¼M, the Z80A-based Optronic drinks dispenser is now undergoing field trials with several major brewery groups.

The Optronic is designed to replace the familiar mechanical 'optic' dispenser for

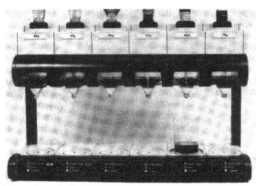

Micro-based dispenser: quicker and more accurate spirit measures

wines and spirits. Dispense is controlled by two sets of sensors: a sensor pad beneath the dispenser causes a measure of liquid to be released whenever a glass is placed on it; and a level sensor, which is situated within a 'dispensing chamber' beneath the inverted bottle, assures that a constant volume of liquid is dispensed. The sensors are linked to a Z80A system, which records the number of drinks dispensed as well as providing more detailed information.

Advantages claimed for this method of electronic dispense include speed (up to eight times that of mechanical dispense); improved accuracy of the measure dispensed; no possibility of bar staff manipulating the size of the measure; and more convenient stock control. An on-screen 'cocktail menu' display is available as an option.

The microprocessor system comprises a Z80A running at 4MHz with 8 kbit of EPROM and 2 kbit of battery-backed RAM; 96 I/O lines and an RS232/422 serial interface are included on board. The processor scans all input buttons and sensors — level sensors, dispense sensors which monitor the status of the bottle (full/empty etc), and enable (pressure pad) sensors. It monitors and controls actuator timings, warns of possible errors, and can also communicate with other equipment such as a master computer or a till.

The basic eight-bottle Optronic dispenser will sell for £795 in the UK, and Anglo Services envisages potential sales of around £20M by 1988 in this country alone. ☐

Action puts PC bus into industrial control

The IBM PC bus has been put into a modular, industrial computer for the first time in the A-PAC BC-12, according to Action Instruments Europe who developed the system. The computer is used in industry

A-PAC BC-12 industrial computer extends the IBM PC bus to the factory floor

'Supermicro' assists acoustics research

Acoustic intensity measurement of building insulation characteristics is being assisted by a super-microcomputer in a research project currently underway at Liverpool Polytechnic, UK.

The Masscomp MC5500 was chosen for its high-speed data acquisition capability which, says Deryk McNeill of the research group, is essential in acoustic research. A vital component in this respect is the computer's 1M sample per second A/D converter combined with a sample-and-hold unit enabling simultaneous sampling of 64 channels. In the acoustics research at Liverpool, signals are sampled at rates of up to 50 kHz per channel, typically over of the order of five channels.

Acoustic intensity rather than acoustic pressure is now the standard parameter for the characterization of acoustic fields, and the current project is intended to consolidate and refine application of these techniques to the measurement of building characteristics, says McNeill.

The MC5500 is a 68000-based virtual memory Unix computer and was introduced by Masscomp in 1984. Industrial and scientific R&D are its primary target markets. ☐

typically for factory automation and process control.

In contrast to what AIE calls the PC's 'hard-to-get-to' motherboard installation, the BC-12's 8088 CPU is installed on a plug-in card which fits into any of the eight PC bus slots. This modular configuration is also applied to other major components — communications, memory, I/O etc — of the system. Other manufacturers' IBM-compatible cards can also be accepted.

To protect the cards against rough handling and harsh operating environments, each card is enclosed within a metal case. Using nonvolatile bubble memory modules, providing up to 2 Mbyte of storage, eliminates the need for cooling fans or filters and reduces susceptibility of the system to high temperature and shock. ☐

Hand-held computer 'gives desk-top power'

UK computer software company Psion claims to have built the data processing capability and programming facilities of a desk-top office microcomputer into a hand-held computer measuring 142 × 78 × 29 mm and weighing 250 g. Called the Organiser II, the new computer is a redesigned version of an earlier model introduced in 1984. The circuitry of the earlier model has been condensed into a single custom IC, and the computer is provided with a built-in operating system and programming language.

The processor used is a Hitachi CMOS 6303X running at 10 MHz, with up to 32 kbit of ROM and up to 32 kbit of RAM available internally. Onboard memory can be expanded to 304 kbit. An RS232 interface enables the computer to be connected to printers and other computers. Dual solid-state drives comparable to disc drives port to the back of the computer and accept program packs.

Built into ROM is the computer's operating system and its structured programming language, OPL. OPL has 112 commands and functions. Psion says the language incorporates functions of C, PASCAL and ARCHIVE whilst remaining similar to BASIC. It can deal with integers, floating point arithmetic, string handling and database fields. Accuracy is to 12 significant figures for scientific and accounting requirements. OPL allows programmers to access directly routines in ROM, giving the benefits of using machine code. Programs can be written using the built-in multiline editor and are compiled using the TRANslate command before saving in object or source code. For professional purposes, a development system can be supplied to run on the IBM PC range. □

Secret software scans the streets

Secret microprocessor software is at the heart of an in-car navigation device developed by Plessey. Called Pace (Plessey adaptive compass equipment), the device is said to solve a problem that motor manufacturers worldwide have been trying to solve — that of developing an in-car route-finding system capable of navigation through complex street patterns.

For the car driver, the device displays directions on a small panel on the instrument facia. All the driver needs to know initially is the grid reference of the car's starting point, and the destination. Once this data is entered, the computer works out precise directions.

Currently, demonstration examples of the compass device are being shown to car manufacturers. Plessey is hoping that the compass will be fitted in new cars during the manufacturing process. It is expected that the system hardware will be specified more clearly when customers' requirements have been determined.

Plessey says its scientists have taken seven years to develop the software, now a closely guarded secret, that is capable of correcting instantly the frequent false indications that can affect compass readings. Such indications can be caused, for instance, by changes in the earth's magnetic field or by the proximity of large metallic objects. Inbuilt accuracy of Pace is 1% of distance travelled, it is claimed. The microprocessor-controlled compass continually monitors the vehicle's speed and direction and updates its location.

A map of the UK has been digitized, says Plessey, and can be incorporated into the system software. It is also planned to provide maps for other areas of the world. An ordnance survey map can be digitized in 26 min, it is claimed.

The device could also be used to deter car thieves, suggests the manufacturer, as it could be linked to a radio receiver/transmitter which would broadcast the vehicle's grid location. Military application in combat aircraft is another possible use of the compass to be explored. □

Pilots' computer vision includes Z80

An STEbus based 'intelligent' data logger is being used in trials on a system for helicopter flight control that could enable helicopters to fly regardless of poor visibility conditions. The so called 'visually coupled' system that is being evaluated on a Westland Mk.5 Lynx helicopter at RAF Farnborough, UK, will also allow the pilot to hand over tasks such as target tracking to the co-pilot.

The visually coupled system consists of a sensor platform at the nose of the aircraft carrying the camera — several camera types can be used — and a miniature helmet-mounted CRT display that gives the pilot a realtime picture of what he would see with proper visibility. The sensor is driven by signals from a head position tracker and, via a closed loop system, is claimed to operate rapidly enough to match the pilot's head movements under normal flying conditions.

Processor boards forming the data logger are supplied by Arcom Control Systems of the UK, and consist of the CPUA Z80 CPU board with an onboard floppy disc controller, the SCRAM realtime clock board, an 8-bit A/D converter, a 40-line parallel I/O board and a video display board. A new board, the Disync synchronizer, overlays signals on the video display.

Helmet installation of visual tracking and display system that could enable 24 hour helicopter flying regardless of visibility

Normal video mixing techniques were not possible, says Arcom, but the new board is claimed to lock the overlay signals frame-by-frame.

Software that controls the feeding of information to the computer board is being written by flight systems personnel at Farnborough and is developed on a ground rig similar to the airborne computer system being used. □

8085A controls jet fuel system tests

Testing procedures used during the manufacture of fuel systems and control equipment for aircraft jet engines at Lucas Aerospace in Birmingham, UK, are being carried out with a microprocessor-based controller. The controller recently supplied by UK company Negretti Automation is its MPC84 system, originally introduced in 1984.

Based on the Intel 8085A processor, the system also has 3k of PROM firmware, 16k of E^{2}PROM for user applications and 16k of CMOS static RAM. Designed for process control and monitoring of continuous or batch processes, the system has 32 analogue input and 16 analogue output channels that can handle signals up to 20 mA; 64 I/O lines are available for digital signals.

Typically, input signals may be from strain gauge applications or thermocouples, for example, where data rates are not expected to be high. The update time of the system is 100–250 ns. Using Negretti-developed SENZTROL software, which the company likens to BASIC, the system is claimed to control eight proportional integral derivative (PID) loops and can run 16 sequence programs simultaneously. □

FPS 'supercomputer' uses 16k transputers

Transputers have been implemented in a new series of 'massively parallel' supercomputers introduced by US company Floating Point Systems which, the company says, are more powerful than any machine currently available. Peak operating speed quoted for the largest computer in the T-series, the T/4000, is 262 GFLOPS (billion floating point operations per second).

'Nodes' within the computer consist of a transputer with 16 multiplexed links, a vector processor and extra memory to supplement the transputer's insufficient onchip memory. Each node is said to act as a complete scientific computer in its own right. Peak arithmetic speed of a single node is quoted to be 16 MFLOPS. Each node has 1 Mbyte of high-speed memory and can access directly up to 1 Gbyte of disc storage. The number of nodes contained within the different computers in the new series ranges from eight in the smallest model, the T/10, which has a peak speed of 128 MFLOPS. The largest model has 16 384 nodes.

Conventionally, the architecture of supercomputers has been based on parallel arithmetic units with individual adder, multiplier and integer address functions.

Software is based on the transputer's OCCAM programming language. Although the library of software routines is currently small, a compiler, operating system and maths library are available with first orders of the system.

Despite using a radically different architecture in this new series of supercomputers, FPS intends to market the systems to the traditional scientific and engineering users of supercomputers in academia and in industry. □

SPECIAL ISSUE: MARCH 1986

microprocessors and microsystems

The authoritative international journal on microsystem technology and applications for designers

BACKPLANE BUS STANDARDS

With the development of ever more powerful microprocessors and modular multiprocessor systems, and the consequent need for effective communication links between components, backplane bus standards are becoming increasingly important. For microsystems designers a reliable bus standard simplifies design procedures, enabling them to concentrate on the functionality of individual components with the assurance that they will work together at the hardware level.

Today, bus schemes proliferate; from 8-bit and 16-bit to 32-bit systems, and from manufacturer-independent standards to manufacturers' *de facto* industry standards. The March 1986 issue of *Microprocessors and Microsystems* is devoted to the fast-changing field of backplane bus standards, and is a wide-ranging update of today's major bus schemes. It focuses particularly on recent developments and present status and capabilities and illustrates applications in advanced systems design.

Contents
Price: £10 UK, £11 OS, $20 USA

Special issue orders, bulk orders, requests for subscription details and/or sample copies of the journal should be addressed to:

Geraldine Hills, *Microprocessors and Microsystems*, Butterworth Scientific Limited, PO Box 63, Westbury House, Bury Street, Guildford, Surrey GU2 5BH, UK. Telephone 0483 31261. Telex 859556

Manufacturing Automation Protocol — ten firms join to support, interoperahility is evaluated

Ten European companies have joined forces to begin work on a project aimed at encouraging wider acceptance and use of industrial network communications standards based on the International Standards Organization's model for Open Systems Interconnection (OSI). Called 'Communications network for manufacturing applications' (CNMA), the project will be partly funded by the Commission of the European Communities under the Esprit programme.

General Motors' Manufacturing Automation Protocol (MAP) initiative and the related Technical and Office Protocol (TOP) programme from Boeing are two well known schemes that according to British Aerospace, one of the companies involved in CNMA, have done much to further OSI. Despite the success of these schemes, the target of open, multivendor systems has yet to be realised, says BA, so CNMA is intended to lend further weight to the momentum established by MAP and to overcome its limitations.

Limitations of MAP highlighted by the project group include its inadequate take up among European equipment vendors. The group also

points out the currently limited progress in implementing the upper layer services of the ISO model in the MAP specifications. Implementations of the MAP automation protocols are few and far between, they say. While attempting to maintain compatibility with MAP, CNMA will concentrate on the development of the relevant automation protocols and is supporting the IEEE 802.3 baseband Ethernet local area network (LAN). This approach is beginning to be adopted for MAP, it is said, although strictly MAP is limited to the IEEE 802.4 token broadband LAN.

Aimed particularly at European vendors of factory automation equipment, CNMA intends to encourage the development and marketing of products conforming to the emerging standards through a programme of work to select, implement and demonstrate profiles of existing and emerging standards. This programme will assisted by the publication of implementation guides and the development of conformance testing tools and procedures. A publicity and technical awareness campaign will also be coordinated.

The companies taking part in the project are: British Aerospace, acting as the prime contractor, and GEC (UK); Bull, Peugeot and TITN/CGE (France); BMW, Nixdorf and Siemens (FRG); and Aeritalia and Olivetti (Italy). Work on the project began at the beginning of this year and will continue into 1988.

● MAP network interoperability has been evaluated by two US companies who claim to have successfully integrated different equipment under the same network protocols. Data was exchanged between Allen-Bradley's VistaMAP 802.4 10 Mbyte s^{-1} modem and a 10 Mbyte s^{-1} token net head-end remodulator from Concord Data Systems. The tests performed are described as preliminary and did not determine the error rate of the system nor the extent to which the equipment used conformed to the IEEE 802.4 specification.

● Intel has joined the recently formed corporation for Open Systems, the first OEM supplier to do so. Open Systems is a nonprofit organization of computer makers formed to facilitate communications standards based on OSI. ☐

Four software houses sign up to develop compilers for the 80386

Intel has signed agreements with four US software houses to develop compilers for the 80386 microprocessor. Silicon Valley Software, Green Hills Software, Language Processors and Ryan-McFarland are all due to have 80386 compilers, running under Unix system V/386, available by October this year.

Silicon Valley Software is working on packages with both global and local optimizations which will support simultaneous symbolic debugging of FORTRAN, PASCAL and C code segments. Green Hills's compilers will perform special

optimization functions such as register colouring, strength reduction and loop invariant removal, and will translate FORTRAN, PASCAL and C programs. The Language Processors compilers, with user selectable optimization levels, a source-level debugger and support for polyglot programming, will be available for four GSA-certified languages: FORTRAN, COBOL, PASCAL and BASIC.

As well as 80386 code, these three companies' compilers will be designed to generate code for the 80387 numeric coprocessor and Weitek's 1167 floating point chip set

when operating with the 80386.

Ryan-McFarland intends to produce a FORTRAN-77 compiler based on its GSA-certified RM/FORTRAN language which implements the ANSI X3.9-1978 standard. The package will perform local and global optimizations and supply code for the 80387 when it is used with the 80386. An RM/COBOL-SX (ANSI X3.23-1974) compiler is also being developed. Both compilers will support a number of IBM and Digital (DEC) mainframe extensions as well as symbolic debugging. ☐

Project will study transputer systems

A novel high-speed computer based on Inmos transputers is the key goal of a new development project, named 'Parsifal'. Supported to the tune of nearly £2M by the UK's Alvey directorate and coordinated by Logica, the project will involve the participation of three other UK companies — FEGS, GEC Research and Inmos — as well as the Universities of Cambridge and Manchester and the Polytechnic of Central London (all UK).

The basic computer, 'T-rack', will consist of 64 transputers, each with 1 Mbyte of memory. The transputers will be connected through a switching matrix to allow the effect of different configurations to be examined; it will be possible to switch several racks together to provide more powerful machines.

The Parsifal project is also aiming to develop software tools to enable users to maximize the performance of transputer-based programs. T-rack and its software systems will allow measurement of program performance, emulation of topologies not directly achievable on the T-rack, and simulation of systems running on very large transputer networks. This last facility provides the name of the complete system — PSF (parallel simulation facility) — as well as the 'Parsifal' project name.

The results of performance analysis and simulation experiments will be presented on colour monitors via the 'graphical representation of activity interconnections and loadings' (GRAIL) being produced by GEC and the Polytechnic of Central London (PCL); GRAIL is intended to show up 'hot and cold spots' in the activity of a program. PCL is also working on the Transim simulation package for large transputer systems.

The PSF hardware and switch control software is to be designed at Manchester University, and will be made available to researchers via Janet, the UK's Joint Academic Network. Inmos will work on improved multitransputer loading and debugging systems, while Logica will be responsible for converting the

IBM PC-AT is used for 'almost realtime' speech recognition

A microcomputer-based speech recognition system has been demonstrated by staff from IBM's Thomas J Watson Research Centre in the USA. The system, which is still in the experimental stage, is based on a modified PC-AT, and can transcribe dictated sentences with more than 95% accuracy within 2 s, claims IBM.

At the heart of the system are two subsystems, each of which incorporates a digital signal processor (DSP) chip and associated circuitry mounted on three boards, controlled by the PC-AT's processor. The DSP chip, which has some 6000 gates and is capable of 30M operations per second, was developed at IBM's laboratories in Switzerland and France and has previously been used in the company's modems.

The first subsystem is designed to encode the speaker's words, while the second matches them with those in the system's 5000-word vocabulary using a custom-designed memory management unit. These two subsystems have allowed IBM to condense the speech recognition power of a mainframe computer and three auxiliary processors, which represented the company's previous efforts in the field, into desktop form.

Before use, the PC-AT must first be taught the characteristics of the user's voice; each user must read a short standard document into the system. Dictation can then commence, with short pauses between words, and the speech can be transcribed as printed copy or displayed for editing, by voice or keyboard.

Speech is recognized using a statistical method whereby a limited number of building blocks are used to compose words. As sounds are

Transputer Development System to run under Unix.

In addition to the trial programs which will be run by all the participants in Parsifal, large-scale demonstration programs will be written at Cambridge University and its neighbouring company, FEGS Ltd. □

IBM's PC-AT based speech recognition system can display dictated sentences on screen 'almost as fast as the words are spoken'.

detected, the system chooses 'candidate' words using a statistical model which IBM has drawn from an analysis of 25M words of office correspondence. As speech continues, new candidates are chosen and the initial candidates are re-evaluated in the context of their successors; thus the system can (usually) distinguish between phonetically similar words such as 'to', 'too' and 'two'.

IBM is currently testing the system in office environments to gauge its adaptability to different speakers and ambient noise levels, and to assess user reaction to the technology. Further work will concentrate on expanding the vocabulary, improving tolerance to noise, and increasing speed to eliminate the need for the speaker to pause between words. □

4 Mbit DRAMs and 'virtual' SRAMs

Researchers at Toshiba are claiming two breakthroughs in RAM technology: the development of a 4 Mbit dynamic RAM, and the world's first 1 Mbit 'virtually' static RAM, dubbed 'VSRAM'.

The 4 Mbit dynamic RAM, which is fabricated in submicron CMOS, is due for commercial sampling in 2–3 years. Access times of 80 ns (static column) and 40 ns (fast page) are quoted by Toshiba, with power dissipation given as 300 mW (operating) and 2.5 mW (standby). Two architectures have been developed: 4M × 1 bit and 1M × 4 bit.

The VSRAM chips are so named because, although they are made from dynamic RAM cells (one transistor, one capacitor) rather than static RAM cells (4–6 transistors), they do not require the refresh circuits normally associated with dynamic RAMs. Instead, refreshing is performed automatically by specially developed function circuits such as refresh counter, arbiter and buffer register.

The refresh operation takes place in parallel with either address decoding or output driving, when word lines and bit lines are not occupied by normal access operation. The refresh timer determines when a refresh operation is needed and intermittently generates a refresh request signal. If the memory cell array is occupied with a normal access, the refresh waits until the cell data is transferred to a buffer register, which drives the output circuit; similarly a normal access must wait until the end of a refresh. An arbiter selects between normal and refresh modes.

VSRAMs are fabricated in 1 μm CMOS and give address access times of 62 ns, says Toshiba. Current requirement is 21 mA (operating) and 30 μA (standby), and the chips are organized as 128k × 8 bit. Packaging is presently a 5.99 mm × 13.8 mm 32-pin DIP.

The first VSRAM samples will be available in about a year's time, says Toshiba.   □

Network conformance testing

The Commission of the European Communities has taken steps towards establishing conformance testing services for networked systems. Contracts have been signed with a number of test centres in Europe to develop facilities and 'cooperative procedures' to check conformance of information technology (IT) equipment to international standards, such as those of the ISO and IEC, and the CCITT technical recommendations. Equipment passing the tests will be capable of interchanging data throughout the European community, says the Commission, and would benefit from current proposals for mutual recognition on type approval for IT and telecommunications systems. The conformance testing project will initially be 50% financed by the European Commission (to the tune of just under 10M European Currency Units), but the centres will eventually be expected to continue the work on a commercial basis.

Tandem–Triplex MAP link

The UK arm of US-based Tandem Computers has announced a 'strategic alliance' with Triplex, a manufacturer of programmable logic controllers (PLCs). In exchange for the investment of an undisclosed sum by Tandem in Triplex, Tandem will market Triplex's PLCs in conjunction with its own NonStop system to offer what it describes as 'comprehensive fault-tolerant solutions for computer integrated manufacturing'. The main communications link between the two companies' components will be Tandem's implementation of the Manufacturing Automation Protocol (MAP).

Sperry joins X/Open

Sperry has joined the X/Open group of computer manufacturers, set up to work towards a 'common applications environment' for Unix applications, based on AT&T's system V interface definition. Other members of the group are Bull, DEC, Ericsson, ICL, Nixdorf, Olivetti, Philips and Siemens. 'Sperry's membership of X/Open reflects our commitment to open systems and standards,' commented the company's European marketing director Mats Bosrup.

GKS-PHIGS compatibility sought

A project is being undertaken in the FRG to implement a combined version of the GKS-3D and PHIGS computer graphics standards. The present lack of compatibility between the two standards is not a technical requirement of the systems, says Professor J Encarnacao, who is directing the project at the TH Darmstadt Department of Interactive Computer Graphics, but it nevertheless endangers manufacturers' investments in GKS- or PHIGS-compatible graphics equipment. Therefore a 'PHI-GKS conception' is being sought by a consortium of FRG-based and other researchers; it is hoped that this will be available for evaluation by late autumn 1986.

GE produces Quik-Chip

General Electric (GE) of the USA is to market and produce the Laserpath Quik-Chip family of prototype laser-programmable gate arrays. Laserpath's aim with the Quik-Chip range is to supply 'one-day gate arrays' for design verification, system development, prototypes, beta sites and test marketing from its Sunnyvale, CA, USA, plant. GE intends to produce production volumes of the chips from its existing semiconductor facility in North Carolina. 'GE's manufacturing and marketing strengths complement our Quik-Chip instant prototype capability' commented Laserpath's Michael Watts, 'and ultimately we will achieve one-day fab turnaround.'

Telecomms logic agreement

Cypress Semiconductor and Weitek of the USA are to jointly design a series of VLSI logic circuits for the telecommunications market. Major design work will be carried out by Weitek and the chips will be manufactured using Cypress's 1.2 μm CMOS process.

calendar

Date	Title	Contact	Place	Other details
1986				
1–3 July	16th Fault Tolerant Computing Symposium	Professor H Kopetz, Institut fur Praktische Informatik, Technische Universitat Wien, Gubhausstrasse 30/180, A-1040 Wien, Austria. Tel: (222) 56-01	Vienna, Austria	Organized by the IEEE Computer Society and the Austrian Computer Society
2–4 July	International Workshop on Systolic Arrays	Will Moore, Systolic Array Workshop, Dept of Engineering Science, Oxford University, Oxford OX1 3PJ, UK	Oxford, UK	Papers on all aspects of systolic arrays and related SIMD architectures from abstract theory to practical applications and VLSI products
7–11 July	International Optical Computing Conference	Prof Joseph Shamir, Conference Chairman, 1986 IOCC, c/o Kopel Tours Ltd — Conventions, PO Box 4413, 61044 Tel Aviv, Israel	Jerusalem, Israel	Recent developments in optical computing including optical information processing, hybrid optical–digital processing systems, systolic array processors, integrated optical processing devices, electro-optic devices, optical interface techniques and application of optical bistability to computing
14–16 July	Computer Networks for Realtime Applications	Cindy Barnes, Frost & Sullivan Ltd, 104–112 Marylebone Lane, London W1M 5FU, UK. Tel: 01-935 4433	Portman Hotel, London, UK	Seminar covering communications and organizational networks, mission-oriented networks, issues related to distributed databases, and analytical tools relating to network design
14–18 July	Modern Digital Signal Processing	Cindy Barnes, Frost & Sullivan Ltd, 104–112 Marylebone Lane, London W1M 5FU, UK. Tel: 01-935 4433	Cumberland Hotel, London, UK	Tutorial seminar on DSP problem analysis and solution
21–23 July	Simulation of Semiconductor Devices and Processes	Dr K Board, Department of Electrical and Electronic Engineering, University College of Swansea, Singleton Park, Swansea SA2 8PP, UK	University College of Swansea, UK	Second international conference on semiconductor device and process simulation
21–24 July	CAD/CAM in Electronics	Center for Professional Advancement, Palestrinastraat 1, 1071 LC Amsterdam, The Netherlands	Crest Hotel, Amsterdam, The Netherlands	Course covering computer-aided design, manufacturing and testing in electronics. Includes circuit analysis for integrated and analogue circuits, logic simulation for digital circuis and systems, PCB design and manufacture, VLSI, automatic testing, system implementation and electronic engineering workstations
21–26 July	Third International Conference on Logic Programming	Doug DeGroot, IBM Research, PO Box 218, Yorktown Heights, NY 10598, USA	Imperial College, London, UK	Sponsored by the IEEE Computer Society
28–30 July	SCSC '86	Society for Computer Simulation (SCS), PO Box 17900, San Diego, CA 92117, USA. Tel: (619) 277-3888	Reno, NV, USA	SCS conference covering artificial intelligence, simulation in medicine, physics, chemistry, engineering, ecology, government and defence, data communications systems, simulation credibility and validation etc
12–22 August	International Conference on Parallel Processing	Tse-Yun Feng, Department of Electrical Engineering, EE East Building, Pennsylvania State University, University Park, PA 16802, USA. Tel: (814) 863-1469	Pheasant Run Resort, St Charles, IL, USA	Sponsored by the IEEE Computer Society

Date	Title	Contact	Place	Other details
18–20 August	5th Annual Microelectronic Interconnection Conference	Bert Letrondo, Sundstrand Data Control, Overlake Industrial Park M/S 29, Redmond, WA 98052, USA. Tel: (206) 885-8183		Sponsored by the International Society for Hybrid Electronics (Northwest Chapter)
7–12 September	Industrial Digital Control Systems	Institution of Electrical Engineers, Savoy Place, London WC2R 0BL, UK. Tel: 01-240 1871	Somerville College, Oxford, UK	IEE 'vacation school' covering digital signals in simple control systems, microprocessor control systems, adaptive and selftuning control, computer-aided control systems design, problems of commissioning computer control systems etc .
8–11 September	ESSDERC '86	Clive Jones, Institute of Physics, 47 Belgrave Square, London SW1X 8QX, UK. Tel: 01-235 6111	University of Cambridge, UK	16th European solid-state device research conference organized by the Institute of Physics and cosponsored by IEE, IEEE, IERE and the European Physical Society. Coverage includes CMOS, silicon bipolar device modelling, process modelling, thin oxide metallization, defects, submicron lithography, solid-state sensors
8–11 September	International Test Conference (ITC 1986)	ITC, Millbrook Plaza, Suite 104D, PO Box 264, Mount Freedom, NJ 07970, USA. Tel: (201) 895-5260	Sheraton Hotel, Washington, DC, USA	Tutorials, workshops and user group meetings on IC testing. Sponsored by the IEEE Computer Society
9–13 September	Fabritec 86	Secretariat Fabritec 86, c/o Swiss Industries Fair, Postfach, CH-4021 Basel, Switzerland. Tel: (061) 26 20 20	Swiss Industries Fair, Basel, Switzerland	Second international trade fair for fabrication installations in electronics
14–19 September	Semi-custom IC design VLSI	Institution of Electrical Engineers, Savoy Place, London WC2R 0BL, UK. Tel: 01-240 1871	University of York, UK	Fifth IEE 'vacation school' to introduce the various types of semicustom ICs that are available and instruct in logic design, system architecture and partitioning, use of CAD tools, hardware description languages and testing
15–18 September	Euromicro 86	Mrs E C Snippe-Marlisa, TH Twente, PO Box 217, Dept INF, Room A306, 7500 AE Enschede, The Netherlands	Venice, Italy	Twelfth annual conference of microprocessing and microprogramming
15–20 September	Intercomm '86	Cahners Exhibitions Ltd, Chatsworth House, 59 London Road, Twickenham TW1 3SZ, UK	Beijing, China	International computer and communication congress/exposition for science and technology
21–26 September	Software Engineering for Microprocessor Systems	Institution of Electrical Engineers, Savoy Place, London WC2R 0BL, UK. Tel: 01-240 1871	City University, London, UK	Fourth IEE 'vacation school' on software engineering for those with an electronics/hardware or assembly language background
23–24 September	Customized ICs	Professor R W Hartenstein, Universität Kaiserlautern, Bau 12/4, Postfach 3049, D-6750 Kaiserlautern, FRG	Kaiserlautern, FRG	European conference on customer-vendor interfaces in microelectronics, sponsored by the Commission of the European Communities
23–25 September	Microsoftware 1986	Dr R A Adey, Computational Mechanics Institute, Suite 6200, 400 West Cummings Park, Woburn, MA 01801, USA. Tel: (617) 933-7374	Boston, USA	International conference on microsoftware in engineering, covering codes developed for personal computers, workstations and expert systems

calendar

Date	Title	Contact	Place	Other details
23–26 September	HCI '86	Conference Department, British Computer Society, 13 Mansfield Street, London W1M 0BP, UK. Tel: 01-637 0471	University of York, UK	International conference on human–computer interaction. Includes: practical experience of user-centred design; user interface evaluation; user modelling; task analysis; interface tools and techniques; systems for the handicapped
30 September –2 October	ATE '86	Network Events Ltd, Printers Mews, Market Hill, Buckingham MK18 1JX, UK	Palais des Congres, Paris, France	Fifth automatic testing and test instrumentation exhibition and conference
5–10 October	ICCD '86	ICCD '86, 1730 Massachusetts Avenue, NW Washington, 20036-1903, USA. Tel: (202) 371-0101	Ryetown Hilton, New York, USA	International conference on computer design, sponsored by the IEEE Computer Society
6–10 October	ISATA 86	ISATA, 42 Lloyd Park Avenue, Croydon, Surrey CR0 5SB, UK. Tel: 01-686 7026	Flims, Switzerland	15th international symposium on automotive technology and automation, covering manufacturing information systems, factory networks (MAP), realtime operating systems, man–machine communications, artificial intelligence, expert systems, CADCAM etc
6–11 October	Interkama 86	Nowea Dusseldorfer Messegesellschaft mbH, Postfach 32 02 03, Stockumer Kirchstrasse, D-4000 Dusseldorf 30, FRG. Tel: (0211) 4560-01	Dusseldorf, FRG	Tenth international congress (8–10 October) and exhibition for instrumentation and automation
15–17 October	19th Annual Workshop on Microprogramming	Stanley Habib, City College of New York, Computer Science Department, New York City, NY 10031, USA. Tel: (212) 690-6631/2	Graduate Center City University of New York, USA	Workshop on microarchitecture design, firmware engineering, compaction and optmization, specification languages, graphics hosts, microprogramming languages, RISC/CISC machines and microprogrammed VLSI. Sponsored by ACM Sigmicro and the IEEE Technical Committee on Microprogramming
28–30 October	Test + Transducer '86	Norma Thewlis, Trident International Exhibitions Ltd, 21 Plymouth Road, Tavistock, Devon PL19 8AU, UK. Tel: (0822) 4671	Wembley Conference Centre, London, UK	Exhibition and conference covering materials testing, solid-state transducers, optical sensors for robots, automotive sensors, data acquisition and microprocessors, test in hazardous environments etc
2–6 November	FJCC 86	Stanley Winkler, FJCC 86, 1730 Massachusetts Avenue, NW Washington, DC 20036-1903, USA	Dallas, USA	IEEE/ACM joint computer conference and exhibition, covering database management systems, artificial intelligence, software engineering, operating systems, VLSI, graphics, electronic education, languages, parallel computing and networks
11–14 November	Compec '86	Reed Exhibitions, Surrey House, 1 Throwley Way, Sutton, Surrey SM1 4QQ, UK. Tel: 01-643 8040	Olympia, London, UK	Exhibition of computers, peripherals and systems for professional and business users
17–18 November	Computer Networking Symposium	IEEE Computer Society Administrative Office, 1730 Massachusetts Avenue, NW Washington, DC 20036-1903, USA	Washington, DC, USA	IEEE symposium covering long-haul networks, local area networks PBX systems, satellite systems, video systems, protocols, teleconferencing, standards design, network testing, network procurement and internetworking

EUROMICRO 86
15 - 18 SEPTEMBER

The 12th Euromicro symposium on Microprocessing and Microprogramming

will be held in

VENICE

Keynote addresses:

SURENUM - a MIMD Multimicroprocessor for Large Scale Scientific Computing
Comparing Causes for System Failure
Semiconductor Industry in Europe vs. Japan & the United states

Programme highlights:

- Software Engineering Tools
- Software Eng. Environments
- Development Tools
- Embedded Systems
- Industrial Automation
- Microprocessor Applications
     in Artificial Intelligence

- Multimicroprocessors
- Distributed Systems
- Specialised Architectures
- Local Area Networks
- Silicon Compilation
- High Level Systems
- Hardware Description Languages

- VLSI : Hardware and Software
- Test Generation
- Fault Tolerance
- Systems Performance
- Data Store Organisation
- Simulation

and the European Finals of the Robot Ping-Pong competition

For further information write to:
EUROMICRO, T.H. Twente, P.O. Box 217, 7500 AE ENSCHEDE, The Netherlands

microprocessors and microsystems

vol 10 no 6 july/august 1986

Butterworths

editorial advisory board

Microprocessors and Microsystems is an international journal published in February, March, April, May, June, August, September, October, November, December. *Editorial Offices:* Butterworth Scientific Ltd, PO Box 63, Westbury House, Bury Street, Guildford, Surrey GU2 5BH, UK. Tel: (0483) 31261. Telegrams and telex: 859556 SCITEC G. *Publishing Director:* John Owens. *Production:* Tony Lewis

Microprocessors and Microsystems is published by Butterworth Scientific Ltd. *Registered Office:* Butterworth Scientific Ltd, 88 Kingsway, London WC2 6AB, UK

Subscription enquiries and orders: Quadrant Subscription Services Ltd, Oakfield House, Perrymount Road, Haywards Heath, West Sussex RH16 3DH, UK. Tel: (0444) 459188

Annual subscription (10 issues): £89.00 Overseas rate (£22.00 for private individuals); $160.00 US rate ($40.00 for private individuals)
UK subscription rates available on request.

Prices include packing and delivery by sea mail. Airmail prices available on request. Copies of this journal sent to subscribers in Bangladesh, India, Pakistan, Sri Lanka, Canada and the USA are air-speeded for quicker delivery.

Back issues: Prior to current volume available from Wm Dawson & Sons Ltd, Cannon House, Folkestone, Kent CT19 5EE, UK. Tel: (0303) 57421

US mailing agents: Mercury Airfreight International Ltd Inc., 10B Englehard Avenue, Avenel, NJ 07001, USA. Second class postage paid at Rahway, NJ. US Postmaster: Send address corrections to *Microprocessors and Microsystems* c/o Mercury Airfreight International Ltd Inc., address as above.

Reprints: Minimum order 100, available from the publisher.

Copyright: Readers who require copies of papers published in this journal may either purchase reprints or obtain permission to copy from the publisher at the following address: Butterworth Scientific Ltd, PO Box 63, Westbury

*Butterworths
Leading the Campaign
against
Copyright Erosion*

Typeset by Tech-Set, Gateshead, Tyne & Wear, and printed by Dotesios (Printers) Ltd, Greenland Mills, Bradford on Avon, Wilts, UK.

microprocessors and microsystems

vol 10 no 6
july/august 1986

Editor Steve Hitchcock

Assistant Editor Andrew Taylor

Publisher Amanda Harper

notes for authors

Microprocessors and Microsystems

The journal welcomes original papers from both academic and industrial contributors on the research, design, development, evaluation and application of all microprocessor-based systems and on the development and use of microsystem software. Papers should illustrate practical experience and show the applicability of the work described. Typically, full-length papers are approximately 5000–7000 words long plus illustrations. In addition to full-length papers, the journal welcomes shorter design notes, tutorial papers and case studies of up to 3000 words.

REFEREEING

All submitted articles are refereed by two independent reviewers to ensure both accuracy and relevance, though it is the authors' sole responsibility that statements used are accurate. The author is also responsible for obtaining permission to quote material and to republish tables and illustrations.

PREPARATION OF SCRIPTS

Three copies of the manuscript, typed *double spaced* on one side of A4 paper should be sent to:

● The Editor, Microprocessors and Microsystems, PO Box 63, Westbury House, Bury Street, Guildford, Surrey GU2 5BH, United Kingdom.

Each page of the manuscript should be numbered. Wide margins should be left so that the paper can be prepared for the typesetters. Please remove tables and figures from the main body of the script and attach them at the end of the paper. Each table or figure should be reproduced on a single sheet. Please list figure captions on a separate sheet and attach this sheet at the end of the paper.

English is the sole language used by the journal, and we follow the Oxford English Dictionary. All papers should be written in English. To maintain consistency throughout each volume, every paper published is stylized by the journal's editorial staff.

Biographical notes

It is the journal's practice to include biographical notes on the authors of published papers. Biographical notes can be up to 100 words, briefly describing career details and current research interests, and should be accompanied by a black-and-white portrait photograph. To speed processing of the paper it is helpful if biographical notes can be attached to the submitted manuscript.

UNITS

SI units should be used. In circumstances where this is not possible, please provide a conversion factor at the first mention of the unit.

ILLUSTRATIONS

Line drawings

We use our own professional studio to ensure that line drawings are consistent with house style. We would prefer, however, to receive one set of unlettered drawings (black ink on tracing paper) so we can put on the lettering ourselves. Drawings, if possible, should be of a size consistent with the journal, i.e. either 169 mm or 366 mm wide. Single drawings should not extend over one page (500 mm) in height.

Computer printouts

Illustrations showing line printer listings, plotter output, etc should preferably be on unlined paper. Printouts will be reduced by us to the relevant size. Do not mark them as they will be used to make photographic copies for the typesetters. Only include sufficient lines for the reader to interpret the format and nature of the printout. Overlong printouts can cause confusion. Fuller explanation of the printout should appear in the caption and the text.

Photographs

Black-and-white glossy photographs (including Polaroid prints of VDU screens) should be supplied unmounted. They should be labelled clearly on the back with a soft pencil. Photocopies of the photographs should be provided for the referees.

REFERENCES

The journal style is to indicate the use of a reference in the text with a superscript as each one arises and give the full reference with the same number at the end of the paper. If a reference is cited more than once, the same number should be used each time. With a bibliography, the references are given in alphabetical order (dependent on the first author's surname). It would be helpful if you could follow this style. References take the following form:

(To journals)

1 **Buckroyd, A** 'Production testing of microprocessor-based equipment' *Microprocessors and Microsystems* Vol 5 No 7 (September 1981) pp 299–303

(To books)

2 **Gallacher, J** 'Testing and maintenance' in **Hanna, F K (ed.)** *Advanced techniques for microprocesor systems* Peter Peregrinus, Stevenage, UK (1980)

PROOFS

Correspondence and proofs for corrections will be sent to the first named author, unless otherwise indicated. Authors will receive a copy of the galley proofs and copies of redrawn or relettered illustrations. It is important that these proofs should be checked and returned *promptly*.

COPYRIGHT

Before publication, authors are requested to assign copyright to Butterworth & Co (Publishers) Ltd. This allows the company to sanction reprints of the whole or part of the volume and authorize photocopies. The authors, however, still retain their traditional right to reuse or to veto third-party publication.

OFFPRINTS AND REPRINTS

The first named author will receive 25 offprints of the paper free of charge as well as a complimentary copy of the journal. Further reprint copies, a minimum of 100, can be ordered at any time from the Reprints Department, Butterworth Scientific Ltd, Westbury House, PO Box 63, Bury Street, Guildford, Surrey GU2 5BH, UK.

Evolution and use of the VME subsystem bus — VSB

VSB is soon to be ratified officially as the single standard VME subsystem bus. **John Alexander** assesses the role of the VME subsystem bus and highlights the characteristics of VSB

To overcome the bandwidth limitations of a system bus in multiprocessor implementations each processor can be allocated a 'subsystem bus' over which it can access its own private resources. Since 1983 buses such as VMX and MVMX32 have been widely used as VME subsystem buses. They have been defined through a number of revisions but never standardized. Now the International Electrotechnical Committee intends to standardize on a single VME subsystem bus, called VSB. This paper discusses the need for a subsystem bus and shows how features of VMX and MVMX32 have been incorporated in the specification for VSB. The role of subsystem buses in VME-based data acquisition systems used in particle physics experiments is illustrated.

microsystems   backplane buses   VME   VSB

A special working group of International Electrotechnical Committee (IEC) committee SC47B is currently working on the definition of a VME 'subsystem bus', designated VSB. It is hoped that this work will be completed in time for acceptance by the IEC in September 1986. This paper examines the history of the VSB and its precursors, the VMX and MVMX32 buses, and also discusses the need for a subsystem bus and some of the uses to which it can be put.

HISTORY OF VME SUBSYSTEM BUSES

Table 1 shows the publication dates of the various revisions of the VME, VMX and MVMX32 buses. This shows that the need for a subsystem bus was not apparently perceived until some 3 years after the VME bus was first defined. Thus the subsystem bus has had to fit on only half the number of bus lines used by VME, which has led inevitably to multiplexed use of some lines (unlike VME). This has also led to a proliferation of secondary buses to meet differing requirements, a situation the IEC are hoping to rectify by the definition of a single standard, VSB.

Daresbury Laboratory, Warrington WA4 4AD, UK

NEED FOR A SUBSYSTEM BUS

VMEbus provides a defined mechanical and electrical environment for the implementation of data processing systems. Being an 'open' specification it enables a system builder to choose from a wide range of cards, from many different manufacturers, with which to assemble a system. This has the benefits of such an approach: not being tied to one manufacturer's product line, competitive pricing, and the availability of a wide range of functional modules.

VMEbus has an arbitration mechanism that enables several bus masters to use it in a time sharing mode. This permits, for example, an 'intelligent' I/O board to transfer data between a memory card and a mass storage device while a general-purpose processor, which may have directed the I/O card to implement the transfer, still has access to the bus to carry on with its processing tasks. This is the familiar configuration of many minicomputers — a central CPU with several I/O processors or direct memory access (DMA) channels.

With the availability of cheap and powerful microprocessors, however, many computer systems are now becoming more complex. In particular, processing tasks which once time shared a central CPU can be distributed among many processors, either on the basis of one or more tasks permanently allocated to each processor (eg the control of a particular section of machinery), or by a distributed operating system which allocates tasks to processors as they become available. Advantages of such an approach are increased data throughput and increased reliability: if one processor fails the rest of the system can continue to operate, and in the case of a distributed system no functionality is lost, only a decrease in throughput is experienced.

Such a multiprocessor system can be built in VME. However, it immediately becomes apparent that if all the processors use the VMEbus to access their I/O devices and memory, as well as for communicating with each other, the bandwidth of the bus becomes a limiting factor. One solution is to build each processor card with sufficient memory and I/O resources for its own use, leaving the VMEbus for interprocessor communication and access to shared resources. This has two major

Table 1. Publication dates for VME and subsystem buses

	VME	VMX	MVMX32	VSB
1980	Revision A			
1981				
1982	Revision B (August)			
1983		Revision A (October)		
1984		Revision B (December)	MVMX32 (April)	
1985	Revision C (February)		Revision φ (August)	
1986				VSB (September?)

drawbacks: the size of a VME card is often insufficient for the required private resources, and the system loses the concept of modularity at this 'private resource' level. Another solution is to provide a private 'subsystem bus' for each processor over which it can access its private resources without burdening the system bus, while retaining its ability to access the system bus. Figure 1 illustrates the concept.

FEATURES REQUIRED IN A SUBSYSTEM BUS

The desirable features of a subsystem bus are similar to those of a system bus: it should be a standard, it should provide high transfer speeds (ideally a processor should be able to access resources over the subsystem bus as fast as resources on its own card), and it should be simple to interface to for reasons of price and board area occupied by the interface logic. In addition it should be mechanically compatible with the system bus, and have multimaster capability so that I/O processors or DMA devices can access the memory of the main processor. An interrupt capability is desirable, but this need not be complex since in most cases there will be a single 'controlling' processor for the bus which will handle all interrupts.

In any multiprocessor system it is necessary to have a 'booking' mechanism to control accesses to common resources if these cannot handle concurrent accesses from several processors. This is often achieved by a 'test and set' operation on a 'booking flag', and is usually implemented as a read–modify–write operation on a

memory location. Additionally for multiported devices, such as a memory card accessible from both the system and subsystem buses, a mechanism is required which gives a processor indivisible access to the device over one port while locking out accesses from other ports.

VME SUBSYSTEM BUSES

All the VME subsystem buses defined to date achieve mechanical compatibility with the VMEbus by utilizing the pins of the outer two rows of connector J2/P2, which in the VME specification are designated as 'User Defined'. Thus a standard (double height) card has access to both VME and the subsystem bus. The subsystem bus is implemented as a ribbon cable or a flexible printed circuit card with connectors which can be pushed onto the protruding pins of the connectors mounted on the J2 backplane. Thus the user can configure a VME crate to contain as many subsystem buses as he/she needs, each consisting of between two and six card positions (six being the maximum number of cards permitted by the specifications published to date).

As noted above the restriction of the subsystem bus to 64 pins means that it cannot retain the parallel 32 address lines and 32 data lines of the VMEbus. Obviously a compromise is necessary, and as is often the case in such situations this has led to more than one solution becoming available.

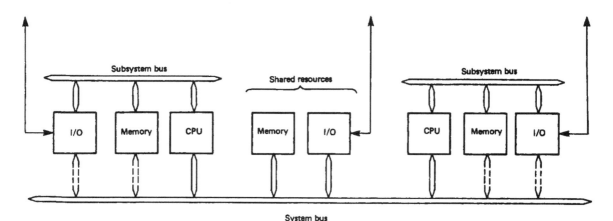

Figure 1.   Example of two processors, each with a subsystem bus, sharing a system bus

The first subsystem bus to be defined was the VMX (VME memory extension) bus. The name implies that the primary purpose of this bus was simply to enable larger 'private' memories to be attached to processor cards, but an arbitration mechanism to permit a primary and a secondary master to share the bus is included (this is increased to five secondary masters in revision B of the specification). The bus provides 24-bit addressing capability by multiplexing the address onto 12 lines while providing, in parallel, 32 data lines. This seems a reasonable restriction on address space when viewed as providing 16 Mbyte of 'local' addresses in addition to the capabilities of the VMEbus. The need to multiplex, however, compromises on transfer speed and ease of interfacing. VMX revision B supersedes revision A and, while providing virtually the same facilities, is incompatible with it, largely due to the inversion of one signal (without changing its use) and the specification of higher current bus drivers. The Lock signal of revision A, which provides for indivisible access to multiported devices, is also replaced by an interrupt line, yet spare 'Reserved' lines exist.

Soon after the publication of the VMX revision A specification, Motorola defined its own (proprietary) memory extension bus for use with the 68020 microprocessor — the MVMX32 bus. This closely resembles the 68020's own bus: it has 32 multiplexed address/data lines, and control signals very similar to those of the 68020. VMX uses control signals resembling those of the 68000, as does VME. This raises an interesting question: why not have several alternative subsystem bus standards, each optimized for a particular microprocessor? The main argument against this is of course that it would entail different versions of memory and peripheral cards to do the same job for different microprocessors. Arguments for it, however, are that something very akin to the microprocessor's own bus can be used as the subsystem bus, thus simplifying interface logic requirements, increasing throughput (particularly if multiplexing can be avoided) and allowing support chips designed for the microprocessor to be easily integrated into subsystem cards. This approach appears to be behind the design of MVMX32. Further, at the Geneva-based European Centre for Nuclear Research (CERN) a 'VMC' subsystem bus has been defined which is essentially the 68000's bus. VMC provides 24-bit address and 16-bit data in parallel[1].

Between them the MVMX32 and VMC buses would appear to make VMX redundant. VMX is certainly not optimized for any particular microprocessor. But, it being the only public standard for a VME subsystem bus published to date, there is already an established market of boards designed to both revision levels. This was also the situation when, in 1985, it was proposed that the IEC should adopt a subsystem bus standard to go with the IEC 821 (VME) standard on which it was then working. It was suggested that both VMX revision B and MVMX32 should be adopted, but the IEC rejected this in favour of a single standard, and set up a subcommittee to define one which would incorporate all the best features of the two buses, and which was designated VSB.

CHARACTERISTICS OF VSB

The majority of the VSB specification now appears to be established, leaving a few minor points and some editorial changes to be finalized. Functionally it is very similar to

the MVMX32 bus, with several enhancements. The only discernible influence from the VMX specification is in the electrical characteristics of the signal lines. Table 2 summarizes the signals and their usage. Features of the VSB are as follows.

Features derived from MVMX32

- 32 multiplexed address/data lines
- Dynamic bus sizing. A master specifies, for each bus cycle, whether it is attempting to transfer 1, 2, 3 or 4 byte of data, and the responding slave indicates whether it is an 8, 16 or 32-bit port. If the slave indicates that it can only handle a portion of the data transfer requested by the master, it is up to the master to initiate further bus cycle(s) to transfer the remainder, if it so wishes.
- Block transfers: Multiple data transfer subcycles can accompany a single address subcycle, to increase data throughput on the bus. The VSB specification adds a mechanism whereby the responding slave can signal to the master when to terminate a block transfer.
- An arbtration mechanism similar to the 'single level' arbitration mechanism of VME, with the same choice of 'release on request' or 'release when done' requester algorithms. The VSB specification adds a parallel arbitration mechanism as an alternative. (The two mechanisms cannot coexist on a single VSB backplane.) The parallel mechanism has the advantage that the priority of a board need not be position dependent, and can be altered dynamically, but has the disadvantage that it cannot operate in parallel with data transfers, as can the alternative mechanism, and may therefore reduce the data throughput obtainable on the bus.
- A Lock signal is provided, whereby a master can inform a multiported slave to lock out accesses from other ports during an indivisible operation.
- A single interrupt line is provided. The VSB specification adds a mechanism to select, in a single bus operation, the highest priority board requesting an interrupt, and for this board to return an interrupt vector to the 'interrupt handling' master. This selection mechanism is essentially the same as the parallel arbitration mechanism, so the interrupters' priorities need not be position dependent and can be dynamically altered.
- A cache signal is provided so that slaves can indicate whether the data being transferred can be cached (eg memory data can usually be cached, whereas the contents of a status register or I/O port cannot).

Additional features

- Broadcast and broadcall facilities. Data can be transferred to several VSB boards simultaneously, with the cycle timing being automatically adjusted to suit the slowest board involved. To achieve this all participating boards may prolong the address subcycle by holding the Address Control line low, and the data subcycle by holding the Wait line low. A master must not end a subcycle until the appropriate line is released, thereby ensuring that all participating slaves have had time to process the address or data on the bus. It must also wait for appropriate Acknowledge timing signals from the (single) slave directly addressed by the operation before it can determine that the subcycle has been successful.
- Each board position is provided with a unique 3-bit Geographical Address code hard wired on the backplane.

Table 2. VSB signals and their usage

No. of lines	Name	Description	Used during
32	ADi	Address/data lines	
2	SPACEi	Address-space selection	Address transfer
2	SIZEi	Specify 1, 2, 3 or 4 byte transfer	Address transfer
1	WR*	Write direction control	Address transfer
1	LOCK*	Controls indivisible access	Address transfer
1	PAS*	Physical address strobe	Address transfer
1	CACHE*	Indicates cacheable data	Address acknowledge
1	AC	Address control (for address broadcast control)	Address acknowledge
2	ASACKi*	Address strobe acknowledge (and port width indication)	Address acknowledge
1	DS*	Data strobe	Data transfer
1	WAIT*	Data broadcast/broadcall control	Data acknowledge
	(AC)	(Block transfer termination)	Data acknowledge
1	ACK*	Data strobe acknowledge	Data acknowledge
1	ERR*	Error (alternative to ACK*)	Data acknowledge
1	IRQ*	Interrupt request	
1	BREQ*	Bus request	Arbitration
1	BUSY*	Bus busy	Arbitration
1	BGIN*	Bus grant in (daisy chain)	Arbitration
1	BGOUT*	Bus grant out (daisy chain)	Arbitration
3	GAi	Geographical address	
9	GND	Signal ground	

* indicates low-active or low-true signals

i (eg ADi) indicates signals are numbered from 0 (indicating least significance within a field) upwards

The board places this in the least significant half of a 6-bit priority code used during parallel arbitrations or interrupt source selections. The most significant half of the code is user supplied. Thus each board is ensured a unique priority code without the need for onboard patching, while at the same time users can alter the relative priority of boards to suit their systems.

It can be seen that the VSB provides a comprehensive set of features, including some of a more recent concept than those provided by VME, within a relatively low pin count. It could even be considered as an alternative to VME (within the restriction of six board positions), and the specification allows for this by defining those pins of the connector's centre row not used for power or ground as 'User Defined'.

OTHER USES FOR A SUBSYSTEM BUS

A system and subsystem bus pair can be viewed simply as two standard buses for which dual-ported memory and processor cards are commercially available. This viewpoint has been exploited at CERN and other European experimental physics laboratories to construct data acquisition systems based on the VME and VMX buses.

Experiments carried out on the Super Proton Synchrotron at CERN (a proton/antiproton accelerator achieving particle energies of 300 GeV) can involve huge composite detectors, several metres in length and diameter, having many thousands of parallel data outputs. As these can be activated every few microseconds, a very high rate of data reduction to look for 'meaningful' events must be achieved. This is usually done by 2, 3 or 4 levels of event filtering, executing progressively more comprehensive event analysis, to reduce the 'interesting event' rate by factors of 10 to 100 at each level. Microprocessors are widely used for such event analysis, and to control the flow of data through the various levels of filtering. As the 68000 and, more recently, 68020 microprocessors are used in many of these experiments the VMEbus is also becoming widely used as it enables the use of commercially produced processor, memory and I/O cards.

Systems as large as these naturally require many tens of VME crates interconnected by high-speed parallel data paths, in many cases simply to produce an effective 'VME crate' with 100 slots or more. In the absence of any published specification from the VME manufacturers to meet this need, various different systems have been built[2-6]. Two of these make use of the VMX revision A and MVMX32 buses 'stretched' between crates[2, 3]: in the former case this is done by simply exceeding the VMX length specification to connect two adjacent crates; in the latter by the use of a 'daughter card' connected to the rear of the J2 connector to produce a differentially driven version of the bus.

Another and very important reason for using a VMX-style bus to interconnect units in different crates is to achieve the required data throughput rates. To do this data and control paths are kept separate, and data flow is constrained to be largely unidirectional, ie the data is not transferred across the same bus twice. An example of this is illustrated in Figure 2[2]. The figure shows part of the data acquisition system, which is dedicated to an identifiable subsection of the experimental apparatus. Other crate pairs handle other subsections. The detector bus drivers read the detector modules, via the detector buses, in response to commands from the readout supervisor, and put the data into the dual-port memories. The CPUs are used to examine a subset of the data and, together with the readout supervisor, perform one level of event filtering. If the event is to be accepted for further processing the data from all the dual-port memories are read, via the event data bus and crate linker, by the event builder; this can be done concurrently with reading in data from the next event. The event builder has access to all the event data buses in the system via a high-speed parallel bus connected to the crate linkers, and can thus assemble the complete set of data from a single experimental event.

CONCLUSIONS

The history of VME subsystem buses to date has been far from ideal, with several alternatives being defined. It is to be hoped that the emergence of VSB will rectify the situation, but this is not a foregone conclusion. There are two main obstacles to its adoption: market inertia — units using VMX (both versions) and MVMX32 are already in the field and working — and the complexity of VSB — unless dedicated chips to drive the bus become available at an early stage, simply fitting a VSB and a VME interface on the same card will be a major achievement. However, there does already appear to be considerable commercial interest in VSB, with Motorola, Plessey, Philips and Thompson having announced that they intend to support it.

As the current situation has followed from the fact that VME was originally specified without a subsystem bus, it is interesting to speculate what would happen if the VME/VSB pair were to be specified today. In view of the trend towards systems of semi-independent computing nucleii intercommunicating via a system bus, it might well be that the bandwidth requirement of the subsystem bus would be considered greater than that of the system bus, leading to the subsystem bus being allocated the greater portion of available connections to allow non-multiplexed operation. Even if this were not the case, at least the basic protocols of the two buses would surely be harmonized, making the designer's job easier and allowing a single interface chip set to service both.

Finally a word about intercrate buses. It has been mentioned that many European physics laboratories have found VME to be a cost effective way of implementing data acquisition and accelerator control systems, but that they frequently use many times the number of cards that can fit in a single VME crate. This has already led to several fast, parallel intercrate link systems being defined — a situation analogous to the current situation with subsystem buses. As a result of this and other factors, the ESONE committee (a collaborative organization that exists to standardize electronic equipment practice among European laboratories) has set up a working group to recommend standard practices for the use of VME in the laboratory

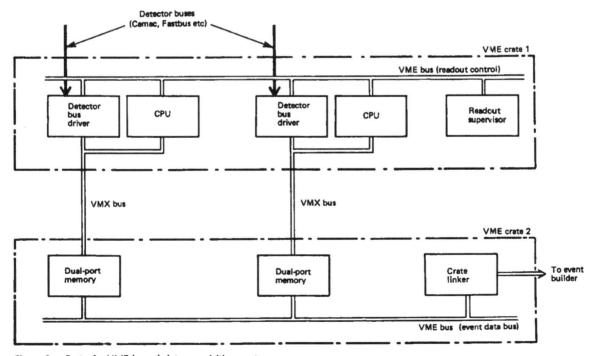

Figure 2. Part of a VME-based data acquisition system

environment, to include the use of multicrate systems. The group is of course in contact with the IEC and other bodies to prevent duplication of effort, but so far no other work is being done in this area.

REFERENCES

1   *VMCbus specification manual* LEP/SPS Controls Group, CERN, 1211 Geneva 23, Switzerland
2   **Cittolin, S** 'The UA1 data readout system' *VMEbus in Physics Conf., Cern, Switzerland* (October 1985)
3   **Brisson, J C et al** 'The OPAL VMEbus-based data collection system' *VMEbus in Physics Conf., CERN Switzerland* (October 1985)
4   **Pietarin, E** 'VMEbus crate interconnect' *VMEbus in Physics Conf., CERN, Switzerland* (October 1985)
5   **Bovier, J and Worm, F** 'Vertical bus for multi-crate VME systems' *VMEbus in Physics Conf., CERN, Switzerland* (October 1985)
6   **Alterber, J et al** 'A VME multiprocessor architecture for the LEP/SPS controls system' *VMEbus in Physics Conf., CERN, Switzerland* (October 1985)

John Alexander obtained an honours degree in physics and electronic engineering at Manchester University, UK. He then worked in the Post Office (now British Telecom) research department for three years on high-speed digital transmission systems. Ten years ago he moved to his current job at Daresbury Laboratory, one of the Science and Engineering Research Council's research establishments. Here he has been involved in the definition and design of computer-based data acquisition systems and computer communication systems. He recently designed a VME interface to an IBM (mainframe) computer, which is in use as part of a system transferring experimental data directly to the laboratory's central computer over Ethernet. He is currently investigating the application of the VMEbus to data acquisition systems.

Teaching computer-aided engineering on the BBC microcomputer

It no longer takes a mainframe to introduce students to CAE: **G D Alford** shows how his teaching department has adapted the BBC microcomputer for the purpose

Teaching computer-aided engineering (CAE) to students has in the past been based almost exclusively on mainframe computers supporting a number of terminals. Some of this work can now be performed on microcomputers, as their relatively simple I/O facilities enable them to be used for data acquisition and interactive machine control applications. The paper describes the development of general-purpose hardware and software designed to adapt the Acorn BBC microcomputer for demonstrating CAE applications in a teaching environment. Student experiences with the system are discussed.

microsystems   CAE   teaching   BBC microcomputer

Courses in computer-aided engineering (CAE) taught within the Department of Mechanical Engineering at Teesside Polytechnic, UK, cover general topics such as mechanical design and production as well as more specialized topics such as finite element analysis, thermofluid mechanics and dynamics. Computing power available for this work is based on three Prime 750/9750 machines supporting 200 terminals. A computer-aided design (CAD) unit, consisting of 16 Apollo computers, is networked and linked to the Prime system.

Now, however, the trend is for a proportion of the work to be carried out on microcomputers, the relatively simple I/O facilities on such systems facilitating their use for data acquisition and machine control applications. The Prime system is still necessary for the main number-crunching tasks such as finite element packages and storage of large databases. Interfaces between microcomputers and the Prime system have been developed to allow progress towards integration similar to that found in flexible manufacturing systems (FMSs) and computer integrated manufacturing (CIM) systems in industry.

CHOICE OF MICROCOMPUTER

Early work with microcomputers was based on the CBM

Department of Mechanical Engineering and Metallurgy, Teesside Polytechnic, Middlesbrough, Cleveland TS1 3BA, UK

Pet but more recently tutors have been looking for a more advanced machine to suit their teaching and researching needs. The actual choice of machine was based on four criteria:

- unit cost
- computing power
- versatility
- user friendliness

With a limited budget in a difficult financial climate, it was considered preferable to choose more machines of low cost than fewer at high cost; this was necessary for class teaching. Although not the cheapest computer, the BBC machine had established a reputation for reliability and good value for money.

In terms of computing power, the Department was interested primarily in data acquisition, graphics and machine control applications for which memory was not crucial. A standard BASIC language with extensions to facilitate these applications was required. The fast extended BASIC of the BBC machine, together with its assembler and choice of sideways ROMs, were considered valuable for such applications.

The different applications envisaged also demanded versatility. The BBC possesses a good range of standard I/O channels, serial/parallel and digital/analogue, together with provision for add-on units such as second processors (through the Tube), user expansion (through the 1 MHz bus) and speech synthesis. The Econet system also appeared to be a useful facility to economize on peripheral devices.

In a teaching environment, the system must also be user friendly. Acorn's BBC machine offered several advantages in this respect, such as the use of long variable names and structured BASIC-based procedures. Most UK schools have standardized on the BBC microcomputer, so that new students would be familiar with its use. Generally the range and standard of software for the machine is good.

Having decided on the BBC as its main teaching computer the Department now has 16 machines.

GENERAL-PURPOSE HARDWARE

Apart from the usual disc drives, printers and plotters, the Department has developed its own range of interfaces for general-purpose data acquisition and machine control applications (Table 1). These units have been designed on a modular basis to allow a variety of uses. A simple student-proof plug-in system has been adopted and found to be user friendly, quick to use and versatile in application.

The digital I/O units provide two 8-bit ports and are of two types: one works directly from the printer and user ports, and the other from the 1 MHz bus using an additional I/O chip. Both types employ Darlington driver chips to provide limited DC amplification of output signals from each port bit. LED arrays provide visualization of I/O signals and DIL switches can be used to simulate digital inputs. Students are introduced to basic digital I/O programming with these units alone.

Reed-relay boxes are employed for interfacing with AC/DC circuits. Typical applications are controlling solenoid valves and multiplexing input channels. Programs to control simple cylinder sequencing circuits are developed using these interfaces.

Stepping motors can be driven through various interfaces. Chips are available to drive small motors using two bits of a port, one pulsing for each step and the other setting the direction of rotation. For larger motors, more powerful amplification is required; boxes have been developed to drive the four coils of such motors directly from four bits.

Programs to drive such motors form the next stage of output programming.

A variety of chips is available for A/D and D/A conversion; however, these do not teach the student the fundamental principles involved. To satisfy this need, large scale resistance ladder networks with buffered inputs and output to an operational amplifier have been designed. These can be driven from a computer port to demonstrate the D/A conversion directly, using the operational amplifier as a simple buffer. Alternatively, using the operational amplifier as a comparator with a set analogue input, the conversion process can be examined on the same unit using a simple count-up procedure and more efficient progressive weighting technique. These units together with the BBC's A/D converters are then used to interface with transducers to measure strain, pressure, temperature etc.

Analogue control of heating, lighting, valve position and motor speed can be provided through an analogue power amplifier. This plugs directly into the D/A converter unit described above. The student can now combine the processes of analogue output and input to design software for controlling heating or cooling of a model factory, for example.

Digital H-type amplifiers are also provided for more effective motor speed control using pulse-width modulation. Software to drive this involves fairly complex machine code programming by the student at a later stage of his/her development

The above interfaces were produced within the Department, but other general-purpose devices have

Table 1. General-purpose interfaces and drive units

| | Purpose | Contents | External connectors | |
			Inputs	Outputs
A	I/O interface	Darlington arrays, DIL switch inputs, LED outputs	26- and 20-way IDC for printer and user port	2 × 25 way D sockets, sources and sinks
B	Two additional ports and I/O interface	As above, plus I/O chip	34-way IDC or 1 MHz bus	As above
C	AC/DC interface	Reed relays (eight)	25 W D plug for A or B	2 × 8-way sockets (0–24 V AC/DC, 500 mA)
D	Stepping motor driver	Power amplifiers (eight)	25 W D plug for A or B	2 × 5-way DIN sockets (25 V DC, 5 A)
F	Large A/D or D/A converter	Resistance ladder, operational amplifier, switch and trimmers	25 W D plug for A or B	3-way DIN socket, analogue I/O
G	Proportional motor driver	Operational and power amps	3-way DIN plug for F	5-way DIN socket (−15 V to +15 V DC, 5 A)
H	Pulse-width modulation driver	Operational and H-type power amplifiers	25 W D plug for A or B	5-way DIN socket (−15 V to +15 V DC, 3 A)

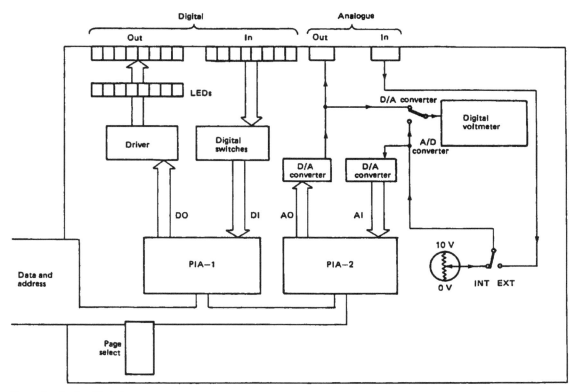

Figure 1. Junior Rexagan

been bought commercially. The Junior Rexagan* (Figure 1) is one useful and versatile I/O device, providing four 8-bit ports from the 1 MHz bus. The first of these is dedicated for digital output, the second for digital input, the third for analogue input and the fourth for analogue output. A/D and D/A converter chips are built into the unit. Junior Rexagan is used for basic I/O teaching using its menu-based software but, using the reed-relay boxes mentioned above, can allow multichannel analogue input measurements, typically a feature of several student projects.

The Cubex unit† also offers a way of expanding the BBC system through the 1 MHz bus. The memory map may be extended by up to 1 Mbyte: additional processors, memory, A/D serial or parallel I/O and prototype boards can be incorporated in this space to suit a specific application.

CAE APPLICATIONS

A range of software has been developed for the BBC microcomputer in areas of CAE. Some of this software has to be treated as a 'black box', but the author has developed programs to demonstrate the essential features of the application and also allow students to develop and improve the software themselves: such software could be

*Labcon Ltd, South Parade, Croft-on-Tees, Darlington DL2 2SR, UK

†Control Universal Ltd, Andersons Court, Newnham Road, Cambridge CB3 9EZ, UK

dubbed a 'glass case' allowing the inner workings of the program to be seen and understood. Such an approach is essential if the student is to play a significant part in developing software in the future.

Some particular applications are considered below.

Research and development

In industry this particular heading might in many cases involve data acquisition or data logging and processing. With four built-in analogue channels the BBC enables a straightforward demonstration of these principles. Further programmed multiplexing of the channels using reed relays (Figure 2) offers the student a simple way of using these principles in more detailed project and research work. In this work presentation of results is important: the

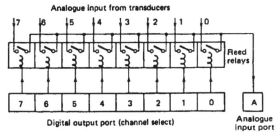

Figure 2. Multiplexing A/D converter with reed relays

word processor and spreadsheet ROMs can be employed usefully.

Computer-aided design

Facilities used for teaching the use of commercial CAD systems on the Apollo system include two-dimensional (2D) drafting using Diad, 3D modelling using Romulus, and other skills in this area using other packages. However, teaching at this level uses the computer and software as a 'black box'.

A simple program was written for the BBC computer to introduce the essential principles of drafting with a simple menu. This has been described in detail in a previous paper[1] and only a brief outline is given here. Input control boxes were produced to use the four analogue input channels for menu selection and graphics cursor motion (Figure 3). A simple digitizer was constructed from two linked arms; this also uses two of the analogue channels for point coordinate definition. The menu for the simple drafting program consists of

CLEAR	(clear the whole screen)
LINTY	(select line type — full or broken)
SLINE	(draw straight line through two defined points)
CURVE	(draw circular arc through three defined points)
CIRCL	(draw circle with given centre and radius)
CENTR	(draw centre cross in previous circle)
HEXGN	(draw circumscribed hexagon around circle)
DIMLIN	(draw dimensioned line between two points)
TITLE	(add text to specified position on drawing)
PRINT	(dump screen contents to a printer)

This program is relatively short — about 100 lines of multi-statement BASIC. The procedural structure makes the working of the program easy to follow, so that students can develop it to include additional features as assignment exercises. For example, in its basic form the program has no data structure for storage of points, lines etc, apart from the screen memory, making selected editing of the drawing impossible; neither has it any scaling built in, all dimensions being in screen coordinates. Successful assignments have been set for students to include these facilities; thus they learn how more complex drafting packages are put together — the 'glass case' idea. Incorporation of a graphics tablet for creative menu use, as found in larger drafting systems, is another suitable exercise for the student. Other specific commercial drafting programs are under evaluation by the Department, including Denford's Easicad and Bitstick II.

Some students have basic difficulties in 3D visualization. Before they can progress to 3D modelling some fundamental training is essential in this area. The author has produced a program for 3D coordinate transformation allowing rotation of solid objects about any axis.

Design of mechanisms is another area of CAD in which complex packages are available. 'Link' is a program developed for the BBC computer to demonstrate some fundamental principles of mechanism design. The program is based on a four-bar chain and allows several variations on this original theme: Figure 4 shows a summary of the main variables involved in the theory of this type of linkage. Using different menu options, input of the link dimensions can either be made numerically or digitized using the analogue ports. The linkage is then drawn on the screen and can be rotated in either direction; the relative velocity and acceleration of the driven link is continuously displayed during this process. One option allows the inflexion circle to be drawn and the path of any point attached to the coupler link to be plotted. Another option allows the linkage to be synthesized by defining a given I/O set of angles. A list option produces a hard copy of the link geometry, the full set of joint angles and details of the inflexion circle and coupler point selected. A screen dump gives a hard copy of the screen contents.

Finite elements

Many thousands of man years have been spent in the development of finite element (FE) packages for mainframe systems. Such general-purpose programs demand large slices of memory for element libraries, databases for

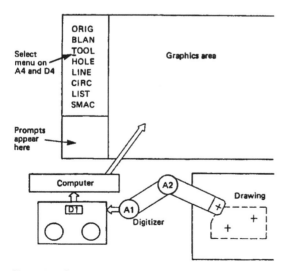

Figure 3. CAD hardware

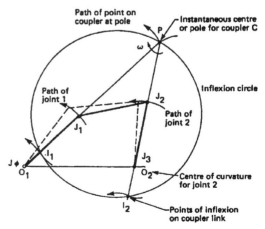

Figure 4. Four-bar chain variables

model coordinates and element topologies, and stiffness arrays for the solution of displacements etc. In mainstream work in this area the BBC computer, with its 8-bit architecture and small memory, cannot compete. However, in teaching and in low-cost industrial applications, FE programs with a limited choice of elements and size of mesh have already been developed[2, 3]. Such programs employ the graphics ability of the computer to provide user friendly facilities for data checking and display of the results using displaced-shape and stress-contour plots. The special techniques developed for full-size packages to use memory and time efficiently can be employed on the BBC machine. The total process may be broken down into a series of phases, such as

- geometry input
- automatic mesh generation
- mesh drawing check
- application of loading and restraints
- restraints drawing check
- solution for displacements
- displaced shape drawing
- solution for stresses
- stress contour drawings

To save memory, these phases can be CHAINed together consecutively, saving and reloading data as necessary. Memory can also be saved in this application by using byte vectors to hold nodal coordinates and element topology as an integer between 0 and 255 inclusive. Alternatively these items can be combined into a single integer array as in Table 2. A project is currently underway to use these ideas in an integrated program for the BBC computer.

The system will normally allow both manual and automatic mesh generation. A method of automatic mesh generation suitable for the BBC computer was developed, which involves generating two lines of nodes with variable spacing, each consisting of several straight lines and/or circular arcs as in the drafting program. Points defining these lines may be digitized from a prepared drawing or drawn directly on the screen using the analogue boxes described above. The number of elements between the lines is then specified and the mesh of elements is filled in automatically on the screen. Figure 5a shows the process of mesh generation for a well known component. It should be noted that it is not necessary for the number of nodes to be the same along each original line: the program automatically fills the main block as a quadrilateral, but additional nodes on one side are dealt with in a triangular block (Figure 5b).

Programs for graphical numerical control (GNC)

GNC is one package used on the Apollo for general-purpose teaching on numerical control. It calculates and

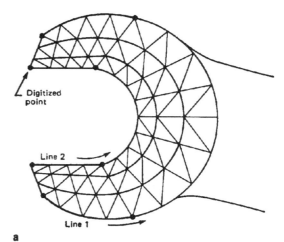

a

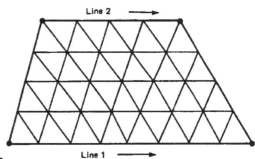

b

Figure 5. Finite element mesh generation: a, line/circle fill; b, unequal triangle fill

displays tool path motion from a definition of the solid surface profile. A similar program, Orion, is used in the Department for part programming on a Denform Easiturn lathe and Bridgeport miller, both controlled by a North East Electronics PNC2C system.

A simple program to demonstrate these principles has been developed for the BBC computer. Full details of the program have been published[1], but an outline is given here. A drawing of the required component is digitized into the computer using the following menu:

ORIG   (defines home position for tool changing)
BLAN   (defines four corners of the blank)
TOOL   (changes tool and defines diameter)
HOLE   (drills a hole at a defined position)
LINE   (mills a straight line through point specified)
CIRC   (mills a circular arc through points specified)
LIST   (lists the part program produced)
SMAC   (simulates the total machining process)

Table 2. Single integer array of nodal coordinates and element topology

XYZ%(N%)	Nodal coordinates			TPL%(E%)	Element topology				
	X	Y	Z		N1	N2	N3	ET	MT
	(10 bit each)							Element type (2 bit)	Material type (3 bit)
						Nodes (9 bit each)			

The points digitized under the LINE or CIRC options are on the required profile; the program calculates the required tool centre coordinates to produce this profile. The SMAC option first draws the blank as a white block on the screen, tool changes are requested, holes are drilled and lines and curves are milled in the order in which they were programmed. The cut surfaces then appear in the background colour. (Figure 6 illustrates the progression of the process from the digitized points in numerical order to the simulated machining output.) Again this program is used for 'glass case' teaching. One suitable project is to develop the LIST option: the format is changed to produce output on tape or through the RS432 interface to suit a specific machine tool.

Other programs are available to use the computer to prepare part programs off line for Denford's Orac, Triac and Easiturn machines. These also allow the machining process to be simulated before cutting metal: editing facilities are included to rectify any errors. The final programs are then transferred to the machine control system to actually cut the parts.

Robotics

The Department is well equipped with industrial robots. The Unimate Puma 600 is a versatile machine allowing programming in a variety of methods (lead-by-the-hand, teach-base driving, different coordinate systems, numerical control, VAL high-level language). VAL (Vic's assembly language), incorporated in Unimation's operating system, is based on BASIC and offers the engineer a user friendly and versatile method of programming the robot. The original VAL system is virtually invisible to the user. Because of this the interfacing of other user systems such as vision, though not impossible, is not straightforward. The new VAL II system aims to make interfacing with other systems easier; this is essential for adaptive control and flexible manufacturing system (FMS) applications.

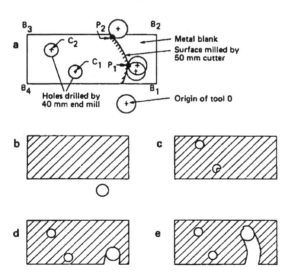

Figure 6. Stages in CNC simulation: a, example program; b, blank with tool at origin; c, two holes nearly completed; d, straight line completed; e, circular arc nearing completion

To enable students to understand the basic processes involved in robotics control and coordinate transformation, various 'glass case' control programs have been designed using the BBC computer, some as student projects. The simplest of these is an x–y plotter driven by two stepping motors. Figure 7 shows the general layout of the slides with a moving bed and head unit, which has replaceable actuators. The plotter features

- four colour pens with solenoid control
- rotating pen to simulate a milling cutter
- electromagnet to simulate a robotic warehouse
- electoprobe to simulate a testing machine
- optical sensor to digitize a drawing automatically

The part of the program to control operations is of course different for each head, but the x–y positional program controlling the operation of the stepping motors is similar. The plotter and miller modes have special routines to produce linear and curved increments. The standard interfaces described above are sufficient to drive the motors and solenoids involved.

A robotic container crane model (Figure 8) is a development along similar lines to the plotter. It has three-axis control: the rail traverse is powered by a servomotor as it moves the whole mass of the structure; the other two axes are controlled by stepping motors. A solenoid is used to pick and place model containers in a predefined pattern.

Selective-compliance-assembly robot arms (SCARA) are particularly suited to rapid assembly tasks. A small SCARA robot has been designed and built as another project. The general arrangement of this machine is shown in Figure 9. It has two servomotors controlling

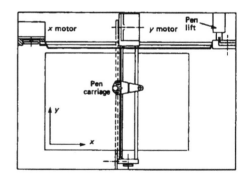

Figure 7. x–y plotter

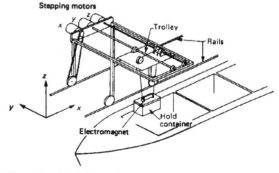

Figure 8. Model container crane

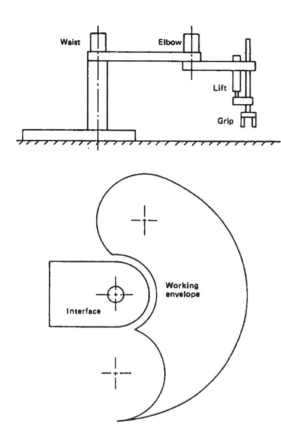

Figure 9. SCARA robot

rotation of the main vertical axes and two single-acting air cylinders for vertical motion and gripper actuation. Plastic potentiometers are used as encoders for the servos; these are interfaced directly to the analogue ports of the BBC. Other motor bits are taken from the user port through appropriate interfaces.

The three projects have proved to be particularly successful as design-and-make exercises for the practical engineering applications component of our BEng course. The students have worked in small groups and motivation has been excellent as they have developed the systems bit by bit.

Production of a Turtle robot has been the subject of another student project. The usual plotting mode of this machine is shown in Figure 10a. The device is driven by two stepping motors with wheels sized and spaced to allow 1 mm linear motion and 1° of turn per step. A central pen is lifted by a solenoid. Software has been designed to allow basic procedures to be combined and developed to a high level, as follows:

0 — PROCPENO (U%)   [pen operation (U% = 0/1 down/up)]
1 — PROCLINE (L%)   [move on straight line, length L% mm]
2 — PROCTURN (A%)   [turn through angle A% degrees (steps)]
3 — PROCIRCA (A%, R%)   [move in circular arc through angle A% with radius R%]

4 — PROCGRID (NX%, NY%, SX%, SY%, PO%)   [create rectangular grid with NX%, NY% spaces of size SX%, SY% with pen options P% = 0 (pen up), 1 (plot node points), 2 (draw axes), 3 (draw frame), 4 (draw grid)]
5 — PROCDIGI (SC%)   [create points with digitizer scaled by SC%]
6 — PROCMOTO (N%)   [move to point number N%]
7 — PROCJOIN (P$)   [join up to 26 different points created in arrays X%(0), Y%(0), . . ., Y%(25) referred to by letters A . . . Z in string]
8 — PROCHARD (C$, D%)   [draw character defined by C$ at size D%]
9 — PROCWORD (W$, S%)   [print word defined by W$ at size S%]

The basic program contains these procedures, those with higher numbers using those of lower orders. For example, a circle is drawn by a series of straight lines and turns. The grid can be used to draw graphs or create a frame for characters as shown in Figure 10b; the character 'A' is then simply created in the procedure PROCHARD by

```
DEF PROCHARD (C$, S%)
SG% = S%/4: PROCGRID (5, 4, SG%, SG%, 0)
IF C$ = "A" PROJOIN ("AOU"): PROCJOIN ("HR")
IF C$ = "etc
.
.
.
ENDPROC
```

The procedure PROCWORD consists of

```
DEF PROCWORD (W$, S%)
L% = LEN (W$): FOR N% = 1 To L%
C$ = LEFT$ (W$, 1): W$ = RIGHT$ (W$, L%-N%)
PROCHARD (C$, S%): NEXT N%
ENDPROC
```

A dummy procedure PROCDRAW initial consists of

```
2000 DEF PROCDRAW
4000 ENDPROC
```

and can be entered using a menu option in the program. The user may enter any sequence of the above procedures into this space, eg to print the word 'CAD' at a height of 100 mm would simply involve entering a new line:

```
2010 PROCWORD ("CAD", 100)
```

Other procedures may be edited to suit the user. PROCHARD above contains the standard upper case alphanumeric set only, but it can be expanded to draw special symbols. To produce a diode symbol, for example, the extra statement

```
IF C$ = "DIODE" PROCJOIN ("CHJRBH"):
    PROCJOIN ("PT"): PROCJOIN ("RW")
```

should be added. The robot can thus be used as a quite powerful plotter suited to any size of paper, or even for large-scale lofting. It is capable of storing a set of special symbols for circuit layouts etc.

The Turtle robot can also be converted to model a quite different application, an automatic guided vehicle (AGV) as used in FMS to transfer parts and products between manufacturing cells and warehouse. For this, the

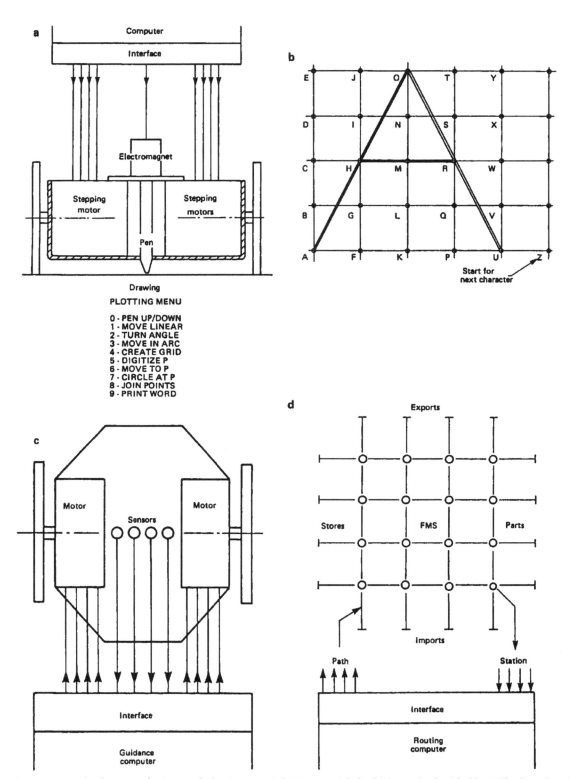

Figure 10. Turtle plotter: a, plotting mode; b, character definition; c, guided vehicle mode; d, grid of line LEDs for guided vehicle mode

pen is replaced by a set of four phototransistors which are used for line following (Figure 10c).

A full-size AGV would normally follow the field from a live wire set in the factory floor; but this is invisible to the observer. To show the route visibly for teaching purposes, a grid of line LEDs was constructed on a base board as shown in Figure 10d. At the grid intersections are 16 stations, each containing a photodiode to report back the robot's position to the routing computer through a suitable decoder. From each station, the robot can be guided through the network by lighting the path in the N, S, E or W directions using four outputs from the routing computer (which contains user friendly software to define the route as a string of characters). Appropriate algorithms in the guidance computer correct any errors to keep the vehicle on course.

The Mitsubishi RM101 robot is driven by six stepping motors to control waist, shoulder, elbow, and wrist rotation and gripper actuation. It contains a microcomputer in its base to recognize primitive commands sent from a host computer. Some of these commands are

N	[move to nest or home position]
Iw, s, e, h, t, g	[move waist motors etc the steps specified by w, s etc]
Pn, w, s, e, h, t, g	[define a position number *n* as being w etc steps from home]
Mn	[move to position number *n*]
Ss	[set speed to s(0–4)]
C	[close gripper fully]

A student project has developed a user friendly menu-based operating program on a BBC host computer to enable this robot to be taught positions in the following ways:

- from a 'teachbox' or numerically
- using relative or absolute dimensions
- in joint angles, global or tool displacement

These positions can be saved and reloaded, run through and edited as required. Once a set of positions is produced, another program can be CHAINed to add control and move through these positions in any sequence. Basic procedures have been written to

- define I/O channels to interface with other machines
- set outputs and read inputs
- activate the gripper
- set speed and cause delays
- move to home position
- move to any position taught
- move through a sequence of positions

Any program can be built up from these procedures using all the BBC BASIC functions by editing statements into a dummy PROCRUN procedure[4] in a similar way to the PROCDRAW procedure on the Turtle. The programs have proved to be very useful in robotic teaching, allowing students to learn at their own pace from simple beginnings, but capable of stretching them at a later stage into quite complex tasks.

All the facilities of an industrial robot can be taught on a small scale, and the programs are simple enough for students to comprehend their structure in terms of kinematics, coordinate transformation, I/O interfacing, sequencing, looping etc. This fundamental idea of splitting the positional teaching and control phases with a menu-based program can, of course, be applied to any

robot, and it is currently being used to convert other machines in the Teesside Polytechnic Robotics Laboratory to a unified teaching approach.

Figure 11 shows the port allocations used on a Genesis P101 robot. This machine has hydraulic actuators and coils wrapped around the cylinders allowing the piston rod to produce a linear variable displacement transformer (LVDT) position measurement system. It was built up as a kit as a student project, but this resulted in an electronic circuit which did not work! Parts of the system were salvaged and converted for use with the menu-based approach. Internal control details of the program are very different from the stepping motor system on the RM101, but the menu options appear similar to the student user.

A salvaging operation is also being applied to a Pendar Placemate 5 robot. This machine has pneumatic rotary actuators, brakes and incremental position encoders on the main axes. A control system is currently being developed for this robot as a student project. The position encoders have been linked to 12-bit counters to allow absolute positions to be fed to the computer. Control problems are to be expected with this combination of hardware; hence the control of a single joint is currently being studied using the simple port connections shown in Figure 12a. An elementary control program for this single joint is as follows:

```
10    DRC=&FD22 : DRD=&FD23
20    PTC=&FD20 : PTD=&FD21         [define the ports]
30    ?DRC=&F0 : ?DRD=&00
40    ?PTC=&A0 : K=INKEY(1000)      [move to zero stop]
50    ?PTC=&10 : ?PTC=&00           [reset counters]
60    INPUT "TYPE IN POSITION",     [define required position]
      RPOS%
70    APOS%=256*(?PTC AND ?0F)      [read actual position]
      +?PTD
80    ERR%= RPOS%-APOS%             [calculate position error]
90    IF ERR% > 0 ?PTC=&C0:GOTO 70
100   IF ERR% < 0 ?PTC=&A0:GOTO 70  [set outputs accordingly]
110   ?PTC=&00 : GOTO 60            [until position reached]
120   END
```

In practice this is likely to cause the motion to hunt wildly and require refinements to measure velocity on the encoder and cut off the supply before the required position is reached. No speed control is possible with this machine, and the approach involved is necessarily empirical. Once this process has been proved for a single joint a system for running all joints together must be derived. Figure 12b shows one method of interfacing all joints to the computer; latches are used to multiplex the I/O lines, operating one joint at a time.

Computer-aided manufacturing (CAM)

A well designed database is the heart of many modern manufacturing systems. Database management systems have been devised to set up data in an efficient manner; such systems are beyond the needs of a department in an educational establishment and considerable time is needed to learn the correct use of the process. In a syllabus under pressure on time for new applications, it is difficult to justify spending time on teaching the use of databases. It would seem more sensible to teach the

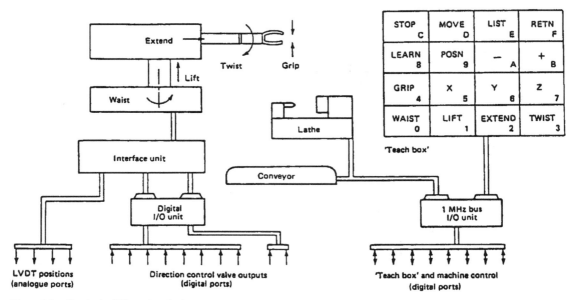

Figure 11. Control of Genesis robot

fundamental theory and structure involved in such systems with practical experience on a simple system. Suitable programs are now available on the BBC computer as sideways ROM (eg Starbase, Masterfile).

A similar program was previously developed by the author which allows load/save of file on disc, specification

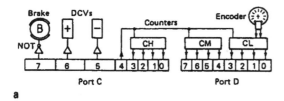

a

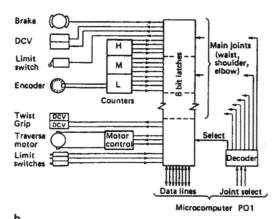

b

Figure 12. Placemate robot: a, single joint control; b, multiple joint control

of print format, printing of selected fields, selection of specific records and addition/deletion/altering of fields/records. A typical student project using this program entails the creation of an efficient database for storage of details on suppliers and parts. This might take the form of: names and addresses of parts suppliers; specification of these parts; supplier–part relationships (price and delivery); and cross references between these data files. Armed with these insights, the student will quickly learn the specific methods involved in a full database management system when placed in the industrial environment.

Databases can also help the student to gain quick access to information on literature surveys, material or fluid properties, design data on bearings, springs, gears, belts, fastenings, motors, valves etc. Some of these groups might be of a suitable size to mount on disc-based BBC computers but it might be more sensible to use the Prime mainframes for larger files. Project work is currently in progress to improve facilities for students in this direction.

The introduction of BEng courses has encouraged educational establishments into more practical aspects of engineering including estimation of the costs of producing components. A project is underway to produce a computer program to perform this task for standard components. This may be done using a database involving costs of materials, labour, tools, forming, machining, bought-out parts, fabrication and assembly[5]. The costs of different methods of producing components and assemblies can be compared in this way; in particular, the variation of cost with batch size is facilitated by this approach, enabling a direct comparison of manual, flexible manufacturing and hard automation methods of production.

Several textbooks on manufacturing systems (eg Ramalingham[6]) contain programs for critical path analysis, PERT, machine scheduling, stock control, decision tree analysis, job assignment, allocation of resources etc, with listings in FORTRAN. These have been developed and converted to BBC BASIC for use in teaching.

Study of FMSs by students is normally confined to visiting lectures from involved industrialists together with a limited number of films and videos on the subject. One method used in industry to study the scheduling and bottlenecks arising in the layout and operation of such systems is the simulation program. Several commercial packages are available for this purpose, eg Seewhy and Siman. The author has designed a program for the BBC computer which illustrates and quantifies the variables involved in the operation of an FMS. The screen display in Figure 13 represents a plan view of the system, which includes

- machining centres
- two fabrication/assembly robots
- automatic guided vehicles
- an automatic warehouse
- a production schedule

Commercial programs of this type can involve a large slice of memory. On the BBC computer memory is at a premium and, because of this, special features have been incorporated in the program. Mode 7 has been employed instead of the graphics modes; in practice this is not felt to be a limitation as, instead of graphics symbols for machines and AGVs, more meaningful numerical groups are moved over the screen. The total process is limited to the use of eight different tools, materials, parts and assemblies; although this is an obvious oversimplification for an industrial situation, as an educational aid the data preparation required to run the program is not too complex.

In a similar way, data to define the routing of the part through the machines and the part program associated with those machines has also been simplified to allow the eight parts or assemblies to be transferred to up to four different machines. Each part program can involve up to four operations with different tools and cutting times. Details of machine routing and part programs are held in memory as byte vectors. A master production schedule is held as a string array of 32 words, each of three characters, the first defining the part letter (A–H) or assembly (I–P) and the other two the number of parts or assemblies required (00–99). The leading 10 items of this schedule are displayed on the screen.

As the program is run the first item on the schedule is examined. Stock is reduced and the materials and tools required are placed on a pallet which is routed to the first machine by prefixing the schedule item by a machine letter code (A–J). To give sufficient speed of operation, a machine code program has been written to transfer the job along conveyors or on AGVs. When the job reaches the machine it is taken into that machine's queue where it again appears in three-character form as in the schedule. The machine takes the first item from this queue and simulates the machining operation by a count-down process with the following order of change displayed for each machine:

(1) machining time using a particular tool
(2) tool number according to the part program
(3) number off for job in queue as each part is completed

When work on the job is completed on one machine, it is tagged with a prefix code for the next machine and sent there by conveyor as before. When all machining is completed on the job, a tag of 'S' for stock is added. The conveyor returns the finished job back to the warehouse. On arrival there the stock of that part or assembly is increased accordingly; the kit of tools originally despatched to produce the part is also returned to replenish the tool stock.

Default data to run a simulation exercise is contained within the program. The student is encouraged to study the effect of using this data, observe operational bottlenecks and slack times, and modify the data to improve the process. The program itself is not capable of rescheduling automatically, but it can be used to test schedules from other programs in a graphical way similar to the approach used on other more complex and expensive commercial packages.

CONCLUSIONS

This paper has given an account of the wide range of activities for which the author has employed the BBC microcomputer in the field of CAE. Others at Teesside Polytechnic have used this computer for different applications, eg robot vision, CNC programming and address labels.

Since embarking on these activities, a considerable variety of commercial hardware and software has become available for the BBC computer. As mentioned above, various general-purpose interfaces can now be obtained; a number of 2D drafting and simple FEM programs have been developed; CNC programs are available for particular CNC machines; several robots are now controlled by the BBC computer; integrated packages incorporating word processor, spreadsheet and database components can be obtained.

The computer is still being developed in the Master series with specific versions giving increased speed, wider scientific facilities, greater memory capacity etc. The range of software available makes it unnecessary to develop one's own programs; the total cost of doing so (including programmer time) would not be competitive. However, new applications, for which software is not available, are continually being presented for student projects and staff research. Future work might include speech analysis and synthesis for robot control, use as a controller in an FMS cell, and graphics simulation of robot–machine interaction.

The complexity of modern machines and processes can lead to them being accepted as 'black boxes'. However, the engineer must be encouraged to continue

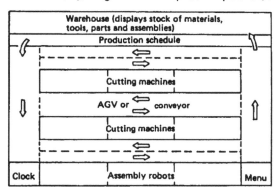

Figure 13.   Screen layout for FMS simulation

perpetually to ask the question 'How does it work?' To attempt to encourage this, the complex systems must be broken down into some basic building blocks, simplified as necessary so that they may be viewed as 'glass cases'. The author has attempted to show how this can be achieved in several engineering applications. The BBC microcomputer has shown itself to be a reliable, versatile and user friendly machine for this introductory task, encouraging students to progress to more complex computer systems.

REFERENCES

1   Alford, G D 'CAD/CAM programs for a microcomputer' *4th Polytechnic Symposium on Manufacturing Engineering, Birmingham Polytechnic, UK* (May 1984)
2   Ross, C T F 'Microcomputer applications to field problems' in Schrefler, B A, Lewis, R W and Odorizzi, S A (Eds) *Engineering software for microcomputers* Pineridge (1984)
3   Hodge, M H 'FE analysis on microcomputers' NAFEMS (1986)
4   Alford, G D and Chadwick, H G 'A high-level robot language' *CAE Conf., University of Warwick, UK* (December 1984)
5   Henry, T A 'A costing system suitable for use in the teaching of design' *I. Mech. E. Proc.* Vol 189 (1975)
6   Ramalingham, P 'Systems analysis for managerial decisions' Wiley, Chichester, UK (1976)

G D Alford graduated from Loughborough College, UK, with a BSc and a DLC in aeronautical engineering. He lectured in aerodynamics, the mechanics of flight and fluid mechanics at Hull College of Technology, UK, from 1965 to 1970, and then moved to Teesside Polytechnic, UK, where he was involved in setting up and developing new laboratories in microprocessor applications and robotics. Currently he is involved in teaching computer-aided engineering, finite element methods, robotics and digital systems. His research interests include hardware and software development for machine control applications.

Data acquisition and control system for laboratory experiments

M Chmielowski has designed a low-cost analogue interface system to link laboratory apparatus to a personal computer

The design and implementation of a multichannel 12-bit data acquisition and control system for laboratory use is described. The system is provided with software capable of recording experimental data directly as a function of experimental parameters. Control logic, data acquisition, high- and low-speed D/A conversion and system software are discussed. The properties of the system were tested during spectroscopic measurements on metal–insulator–semiconductor (MIS) transistors in the far infrared region of the spectrum.

microsystems   data acquisition   control

The improved capability of low-price personal computers (PCs) has led to an increase of interest in the use of these devices in laboratory control. The bidirectional high-performance analogue interface between the experimental apparatus and the microcomputer is of great importance if a PC is to be used as a laboratory tool. An efficient software system, capable of realtime acquisition of analogue input data and control of experimental parameters, is also necessary. If the interface system is to be combined with a low-cost PC in small laboratories or in schools, it is crucial that it is inexpensive.

DESIGN REQUIREMENTS

A specification relating to the user's needs must be established before a laboratory control system is designed. It is usual in laboratory practice to measure physical quantities as a function of some experimental parameters. Here the assumption is that the experimental apparatus transforms the values of these physical quantities to analogue voltages within a standard range, and that at least some of the experimental parameters can be controlled more or less precisely using analogue electrical signals.

Institute of Physics, Polish Academy of Sciences, St. 32/46 Lotnikow, Warsaw 02-668, Poland

The recording of physical quantities is simple if only one parameter is changed steadily while the others are kept constant. Unfortunately, some experimental parameters may be very difficult to control precisely, and it may be impossible to avoid their fluctuations; pressure and temperature at extreme values and the power of far infrared lasers are examples of such parameters. It may also be impossible to keep these parameters constant, so that more than one parameter will vary in some experiments.

One of the possibilities for recording data in such situations is to measure the values of the physical quantities and the experimental parameters together and then record all the data as a function of time. This method requires a multichannel data acquisition system with a sufficient number of input channels to measure all the physical quantities and parameters. A short throughput time is necessary since an information stream must be produced for each of the inputs.

Recording the data as time functions, i.e. with a constant sampling rate, has two main disadvantages:

- Additional memory is required to store the parameter values as time functions.
- If the parameters vary slowly but in an inconsistent way, the method described leads to the recording of useless, identical data.

In some experimental situations it is better to measure physical quantities alongside parameters, and to use system software which allows storage of the physical quantity values in computer memory as a function of the experimental parameters. This method overcomes the difficulties involved when the time dependence of the physical quantities is to be transformed into parameter dependence. It also avoids multiple recording of identical data because new values of physical quantities are stored only when the parameter value changes noticeably (regardless of sampling rate). Thus the effective rate of data storage follows the rate of change of the parameter.

This method limits the throughput rate, however, as the processor needs some time for realtime analysis of all data arriving from the A/D converter prior to storing it in computer memory. This method can be applied only if the changes in parameter values are so slow that the physical quantity values follow them without significant delay.

As mentioned above, it is usually desirable to keep all but one experimental parameter constant during the course of an experiment. The choice of values for the constant parameters and the correction of any deviation from these values requires some analogue outputs in our system. In properly designed experimental apparatus the parameters should need correction so rarely that slow, inexpensive, low-resolution D/A converters can usually be used for the purpose. However, one or two high-speed analogue outputs may be useful to control a parameter which is changed during the course of an experiment or for testing the experimental apparatus.

HARDWARE

This paper describes the design of a multichannel data acquisition system combined with a multichannel D/A conversion system. The analogue interface has been designed to collect the values of physical quantities and to measure the experimental parameters on 16 input channels with 12-bit resolution, within programmed voltage ranges. The analogue outputs were designed to control up to 10 experimental parameters with 12-bit or 6-bit resolution. The maximum sampling frequency was 50 kHz per analogue input channel and the output voltage setting times were 1 μs and 1 ms for the high- and low-speed output channels respectively. The total cost of the interface system is less than that of a low-price personal computer.

The functional elements of the analogue interface system are shown in Figure 1. The unit consists of

- control logic and computer bus buffer
- data acquisition board
- high-speed D/A converter board
- low-speed D/A converter board
- power supplies

Control logic

The control logic provides address decoding, interrupt control and timing control between the unit and the microprocessor system. The circuit shown in Figure 2 was designed for connecting to the 6502-based Apple IIe personal computer.

The information transfer between the microprocessor data bus (buffered lines D0–D7) and the data registers or output buffers of the analogue interface system is controlled by the use of 10 signals (CS1–CS10). Each of these signals is activated by the control logic during the read or write operation by use of the corresponding address. The 12- bit data are transferred using two 8-bit words and the right-justified format. The eight least significant bits (LSBs) reside in the first byte while the upper four most significant bits (MSBs) occupy the lower half of the second byte.

The interrupt request (IRQ) signal is generated when the A/D conversion is completed (the EOC signal goes active) and it is cancelled by reading of the A/D converter outputs.

After setting the power on, or after resetting the microprocessor, the control logic inactivates the AOE signal which switches off the outputs of the D/A

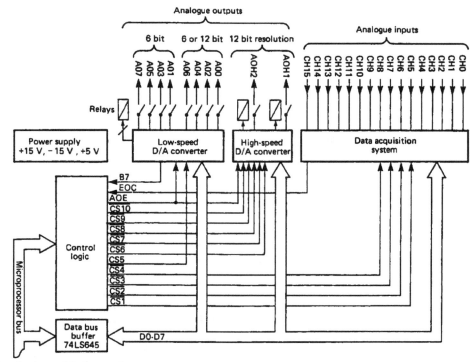

Figure 1. Analogue interface system

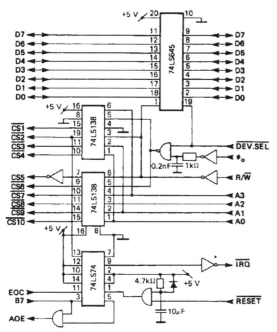

Figure 2. Control logic and data bus buffer (*indicates the open collector output)

converters to avoid generating spurious output voltages. The analogue outputs can be switched on under software control by changing bit 7 from 0 to 1 (signal B7) in the register situated on the low-speed D/A converter board.

Data acquisition system

To reduce the number of integrated circuits and to simplify the system, the Datel Intersil HDAS-16MC hybrid 12-bit data acquisition system[1] was used. This hybrid circuit includes a 16-channel multiplexer, the channel address register, the resistor gain programmable instrumentation amplifier, the sample-and-hold circuit and the A/D converter with three-state outputs. The input voltage range can be selected by the value of the R_{GAIN} resistor from 10 mV to 10 V. However, selection of a voltage range below 100 mV decreases the effective resolution of the system.

The conversion time is 9 μs. The minimum acquisition time is also 9 μs but it can be increased by the use of an R_{DELAY} resistor to increase system accuracy.

The HDAS-16 input channels are protected at up to 20 V beyond supply voltage; overvoltage protection can be increased by adding input series resistors (R_{PROT}), but these resistors increase the multiplexer setting time and a longer acquisition time must be used.

Figure 3 shows the data acquisition system with sixteen input channels (CH0-CH15) protected up to 120 V. The input voltage range can be selected by the relays, as can unipolar or bipolar conversion mode (relay 5). There are four possible input voltages: 10 V (acquisition time 9 μs) switched by relay 1; 5 V (acquisition time 16 μs) switched by relay 2; 2 V (acquisition time 16 μs) switched by relay 3; and 1 V (acquisition time 16 μs) switched by relay 4. The relays have been used because they separate the

analogue signals from the control logic better than the much faster MOS switches. The positions of the relays are controlled by the outputs of the eight-line D flipflop (74LS574). Loading of data to this register from the data bus (lines D0–D8) is controlled by the CS4 signal. The switching time of the relays is about 10 ms, and the program-controlled delay is inserted after each change of the input voltage range.

The falling edge of the $\overline{CS3}$ signal loads the multiplexer channel address register from the data bus, initiates the acquisition and (after a delay) the conversion of the analogue signal. The end of conversion is signalled by the rising edge of the EOC signal. The 12-bit output data can then be read out. The active CS1 signal causes transfer of the lower eight bits and the active CS2 signal transfers the upper four bits.

High-speed D/A converters

Two high-speed analogue outputs (AOH1 and AOH2) are driven by two 12-bit Analog Devices AD567KD D/A converters[2] with setting times of about 1 μs (Figure 4). The AD567 bus interface logic is double buffered to avoid generation of spurious analogue voltages during data transfer. The 12-bit data are subsequently loaded from the data bus to the first-rank latches of all AD567s without affecting the output voltages. Signals CS9 and CS10 load the lower 8 bit and the upper 4 bit of data, respectively, to the latches of the first converter. Signals CS7 and CS8 do the same for the second converter. The dummy write operation with active CS6 signal strobes the second-rank registers of both AD567s, upon which both analogue outputs (AOH1 and AOH2) are updated simultaneously.

Low-speed D/A converter

All eight low-speed analogue outputs (AO0–AO7) are driven by a single Fairchild μA9706DC multichannel D/A converter[3] (Figure 5). Each channel gives 6-bit resolution with a setting time of about 1 ms. Two channels can be summed to increase the resolution up to 12 bit (outputs AO0, AO2, AO4 and AO6).

The data for the μA9706 are transmitted in sequence under software control. Suitable bytes are subsequently loaded from the data bus to the eight-line D flipflop (74LS574) on every rising edge of the CS5 signal. Three outputs of this register are used to generate data and timing signals for the converter. Bits 1, 3 and 5 correspond to the W/$\overline{R}$ signal of the converter, to the DATA CLOCK signal and to the DATA INPUT signal respectively. The DATA INPUT signal is used to transfer the data controlling the output voltages. The control data for each channel (the 6-bit channel data followed by the 3-bit channel address) are transferred in sequence (LSB first) to the converter on the high-to-low transition of the DATA CLOCK signal.

The four D flipflop outputs which correspond to bits 0, 2, 4 and 6 are used to control relays which switch to 6- or 12-bit resolution of conversion on the AO0, AO2, AO4 and AO6 analogue output channels, respectively.

SYSTEM SOFTWARE

The system software allows storage in computer memory of the raw values of physical quantities as functions of the

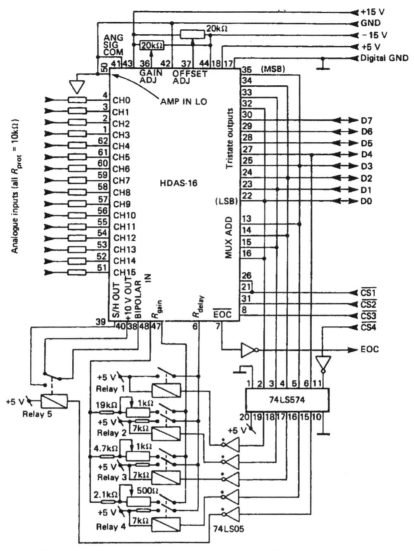

Figure 3. Data acquisition unit (*indicates the open collector output)

experimental parameters, and controls the experimental apparatus using the analogue output channels. In outline, the method of operation is as follows.

For each physical quantity (i.e. for the information stream corresponding to that quantity) which we want to record as a function of a selected subset of the experimental parameters, the array of 2 byte words is defined before the start of the experiment. The number of dimensions of each of the identical arrays is equal to the number of selected experimental parameters that vary during the course of the experiment.

If, for example, we want to record three different physical quantities as functions of two experimental parameters, the data memory must be arranged as shown in Figure 6a. The values of each physical quantity are recorded in a separate array (arrays 1, 2 and 3). These arrays are two dimensional because, in this example, the

data are recorded as a function of two experimental parameters. The value of the first parameter indicates the array row and the value of the second one indicates the array column. Each parameter is measured with 12-bit resolution, although a smaller number of bits is usually used for array indexing because of memory size limitations. In the example shown in Figure 6a, only the five most significant bits of the first parameter and eight bits of the second one are taken into account. Thus the first parameter can take 32 and the second parameter 256 different values. Each dimension of the data arrays is of equivalent size to the number of different values that the index corresponding to the dimension can take: the arrays in the present example are 32 × 256.

All experimental parameters (not only those which are used as array indexes) and physical quantities are measured in sequence during the experiment. The

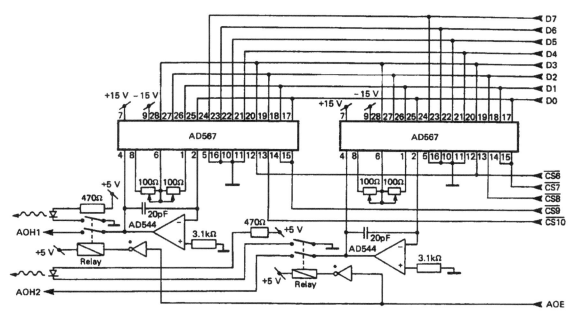

Figure 4.   High-speed D/A converters (*indicates the open collector output)

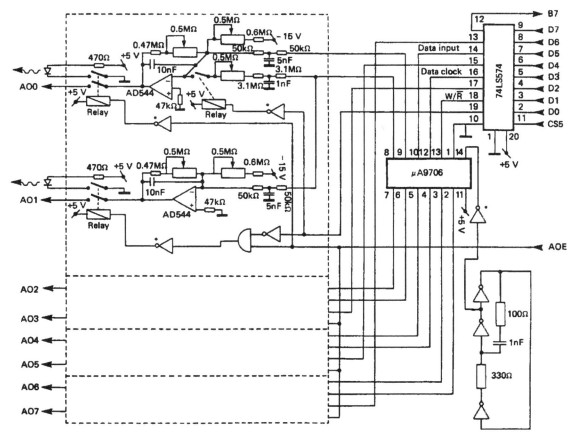

Figure 5.   Low-speed D/A converter (*indicates the open collector output)

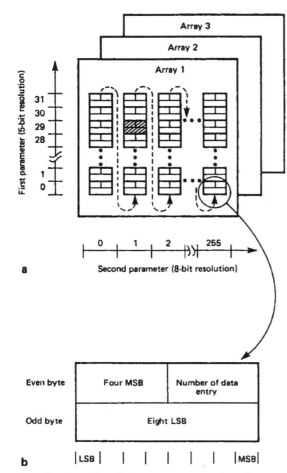

 with labels: Array 3, Array 2, Array 1, First parameter (5-bit resolution) 31 30 29 28 1 0, Second parameter (8-bit resolution) 0 1 2 255, **a**

Even byte | Four MSB | Number of data entry

Odd byte | Eight LSB

b | LSB | | | | | | MSB |

Figure 6. Example of data memory configuration: a, arrays for recording the experimental results; b, array word (broken line shows the computer memory address in increasing order)

current values of the previously selected parameters are used as indexes to indicate a certain site, the same for each array. At this site the current values of the measured physical quantities are stored in the appropriate arrays (12 bits in a 2 byte word — see Figure 6b). The sequence of measurements is then repeated.

Suppose, in the example shown in Figure 6a, that the value of the first parameter is 29 and that of the second is 1. Then the actual data will be stored in a 2 byte word corresponding to these index values, i.e. 29th row and 1st column (the shaded box in Figure 6a). If the values of the parameters have changed at the time of the next measurement sequence, the new data will be stored in the word corresponding to the new values. In this way the data will be recorded directly as a function of the experimental parameters.

The same combination of index values may occur many times during the experiment because of the repeated measurements. In such a situation the array word pointed by the recurring index combination contains the average of all data corresponding to that word. The number of data acquisitions (up to 15) used to calculate

the average value is stored in the remaining four most significant bits of the even byte in every word of the arrays (Figure 6b). Averaging many measurements increases data accuracy but decreases the throughput rate. So, when high data acquisition speed is necessary, the averaging is switched off and only the latest data value is stored.

For each experimental parameter (not only for those parameters which are used as array indexes) a range is defined inside which that parameter value ought to be kept during the experiment. When some of the experimental parameters are outside the defined ranges the program controlling D/A converters is activated. This program simulates the proportional integral derivative (PID) type controller and changes the analogue outputs (controlling the experimental apparatus) in such a way that the parameter values return to the defined ranges. The limits of the required parameter range can be changed during the experiment as defined time functions. Thus the program simulating the PID regulator can also be used to change the parameter values with time in a predetermined way.

The system software consists of three main parts. The first part allows the operator to define all options and program parameters used by the second part of the program before starting the measurements. The second part of the program controls the realtime operations of the analogue interface, performs online data analysis, stores data in the computer memory, displays actual information and controls the analogue outputs. The third part is used, after all data have been collected, for standard offline data analysis, and allows the operator to store data on floppy disc or to plot them on an x,y recorder.

The first and third parts of the software were written in Apple BASIC, while the second part was written in assembly language to increase the data acquisition speed.

APPLICATION EXAMPLE

The analogue interface system described above was used with an Apple IIe personal computer to control the far infrared magnetospectroscopic measurements of the inversion n channel in HgCdTe and HgMnTe metal-insulator–semiconductor field-effect transistors (MISFETs)[4].

The optical and electrical properties of bulk HgMnTe are a complicated function of both magnetic field and temperature. To extract the properties related to the inversion channel it is necessary to measure several physical quantities simultaneously, viz:

- reflected and transmitted far infrared radiation
- source-drain conductivity and Hall voltage
- capacitance between gate and bulk contacts

Recording of these physical quantities as a function only of the two physically interesting experimental parameters — magnetic field and MISFET temperature — is impractical because the output power of the far infrared laser changes randomly during the experiment. It is therefore necessary to relate the measured experimental results to the current laser power, which is taken as an additional parameter.

The multichannel analogue interface system presented in this paper made it possible to record and correlate all the important physical quantities (up to five information streams) as functions of two or three variable experimental paramters. The data collected during the experiments were used to investigate surface cyclotron resonance of the inversion carriers, channel conductivity, quantum Hall effects, and the surface states at the insulator–semiconductor interface.

ACKNOWLEDGEMENTS

The author acknowledges Professor F. Koch for his interest and financial support. Thanks are also due to Mr P Sobkowicz and Mr P Kruk for their helpful remarks.

REFERENCES

1   *Data conversion components* Datel Intersil, USA (1983/1984)
2   *Data acquisition databook, Vol 1: Integrated circuits* Analog Devices, USA (1982)
3   *Linear integrated circuits* Fairchild, USA (1984)
4   **Chmielowski, M, Dietl, T, Koch, F, Sobkowicz, P and Kossut, J** 'Far-infrared spectroscopy of the space–charge layers in p-HgMnTe' *Acta Physica Polonica* Vol A69 (1986) p 929

Marek Chmielowski graduated with an MSc in physics from the Warsaw University, Poland, in 1980. Since then he has been studying for a doctorate at the Institute of Physics of the Polish Academy of Sciences, Warsaw, researching into magnetospectroscopic and magnetotransport properties of the space–charge layers in narrow-gap semi-magnetic semiconductors. From 1983 to 1984 he undertook postgraduate training at the Institute of Physics, Technical University of Munchen, FRG, where the first version of the analogue interface system described in this paper was constructed. Research interests include the surface properties of semiconductors containing magnetic atoms, using conversion electron Mossbauer spectroscopy, far infrared spectroscopy and electron quantum transport in two-dimensional charge layers; and the practical application of microprocessors to control physical and biophysical experiments.

Pingpong-playing robot controlled by a microcomputer

Will robots one day be capable of playing table tennis against human opponents?
John Knight and David Lowery describe a first step in this direction — the winner of
last year's European robot pingpong competition

In 1983, a competition was announced to build a micro-processor-based robot to play pingpong. The paper describes one of the systems built in response to the article, 'Robot Charlie', which is the current European robot pingpong champion after winning the finals of the competition in September 1985. System details and associated software are outlined, and a discussion of the robot's vision system and mechanics are given.

microsystems   robot pingpong   tracking

The rules for a competition to design and build a microprocessor-controlled robot to play pingpong (table tennis) were sketched out by John Billingsley in an article published in September 1983. A fully dimensioned drawing of the proposed table was given, and this is shown in Figure 1. Within the constraints laid down, we felt that it would require only limited resources to compete, and a start was made in May 1984.

It was seen from the outset that the vision system presented the biggest challenge, and a start was made by studying the flight of the ball. A video camera was set up with a side view of a table approximating to the one shown in Figure 1. A grid with 10 cm squares was placed immediately behind it and a game was simulated by two human players.

The video tape was examined to find sequences showing the extremes of speed, height and angle that could be expected in the course of a game. These parameters were plotted and their maximum and minimum values were measured. This data was used in the construction of the vision system,

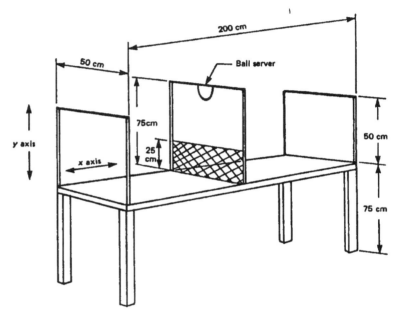

Figure 1.   Robot pingpong table specifications

and was again useful later when developing the mathematical model of the flight of the ball, needed for the prediction routine.

Vision system

The rules of the competition specified that the ball would always be served from the same position, and with this in mind two approaches presented themselves: to build a camera with a narrow but mobile field of vision and physically track the ball's movement in the playing area; or to give the camera a broader field of vision covering the whole playing area,

thereby avoiding the mechanical difficulties of tracking a ball through a bounce.

After building a succession of different cameras designed along these lines, it was decided to opt for a hybrid machine which combined the two approaches. In this design, the angle of view on the horizontal axis was reduced and the camera was given the facility to physically track the ball across the table. The larger angle of view on the vertical axis was retained.

A further refinement was to give the camera a crude peripheral vision on the horizontal axis, to come into use if the ball was lost from the central field of vision.

Camera construction

The final version of the camera used a mechanical scanning system, with two lenses mounted on a drum which revolves at about 1700 rpm (revolutions per minute). As the camera must move to track the ball, it was decided to integrate the camera with the robot.

The essential components of the robot are shown in Figure 2. The bat assembly is mounted on a vertical slider to enable upward and downward movement; this slider together with the camera are in turn mounted on a horizontal slider. This arrangement allows the camera to track the ball and in doing so automatically aligns the bat with the ball on the vertical axis.

The basic layout of the camera is shown in Figure 3. Light from the ball is focussed onto the photodiodes by two lenses mounted on the edge of the drum. Four photodiodes form a horizontal array looking forward directly at the ball; a fifth looks upwards through the top mirror and a sixth looks down through the bottom mirror.

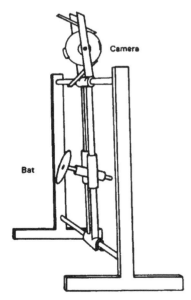

Figure 2. Design of the pingpong robot

Tracking the ball

The forward-looking array consists of four large-area PIN photodiodes mounted behind a slit mask as shown in Figure 4. The image for a ball 1 m from the camera is also outlined to show the effect of the astigmatic lenses. As the distorted image moves over the slit mask a steep-sided pulse is produced which can easily be detected.

With the ball directly in front of the camera, half of the image falls on each of the central pair of photodiodes. If the image moves to one side then their output becomes unequal, resulting in an error signal which is used to control the horizontal servo motor. This motor realigns the camera with the ball and the resulting feedback loop keeps the camera locked onto the ball. The outer two photodiodes supply the peripheral vision; their signals are used if that of the central pair falls below a preset level. If the signal from all four diodes is too feeble then the camera is centralized. The analogue and logic circuitry used to realize this scheme is described below.

The top and bottom diodes are part of a separate system which determines the height of the ball and its distance from the home end of the table.

When a pulse is received from the top photodiode it indicates that the reflected image of the ball, the lens and the diode are aligned. The drum position is then recorded and taken to be a bearing on the ball. When a pulse is recorded from the bottom photodiode the same logic applies and it provides a second bearing, but from a displaced viewpoint.

These bearings are the main input to the computer and enable the software to calculate the eventual interception point for the ball and bat.

Software

The software is involved not only in predicting and controlling the height of the bat but also, at an earlier stage, in collecting data from the camera's sensors and recording the bearings.

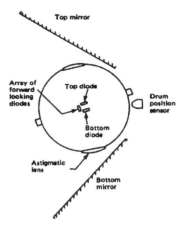

Figure 3. Camera layout

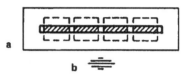

Figure 4. Forward-looking photodiode array: a, layout; b, image of ball 1 m from the camera

Once two consecutive pairs of bearings have been collected, the prediction routine is entered.

To simplify calculations the ball's movement is considered to have two components, a vertical and a horizontal velocity. The horizontal velocity is taken to be constant, and the vertical velocity is taken to be that of a body in free fall. These assumptions introduce errors, but the prediction calculation and the adjustment of the bat height are repeated every time a new set of bearings is received (every 18 ms). This enables the bat to home in on the interception point as the ball gets closer.

The bearings provided by the camera are used as pointers to look up the position of the ball as (x,y) coordinates in a table. This table is stored as a two-dimensional array and occupies 6k of computer memory. Only the current and previous coordinates are used to make the prediction. Should the camera fail to produce an acceptable set of bearings then the previous prediction stands. Figure 5 shows the flow diagram of the program.

The time interval between readings is essentially constant at 18 ms; by subtracting x_2 from x_1 (where x_2 is the current horizontal coordinate and x_1 is the previous horizontal coordinate) the speed of the ball is obtained. If the result is negative then the ball is moving away from the camera and the prediction routine is aborted. The 'time to arrival' for the ball at the home end of the table is given by $x_2/(x_1 - x_2)$ in 18 ms time units. Now only a prediction of the ball's height at the arrival time is required to position the bat at the interception point.

The central element of the final part of the program is the time–distance table. This holds the time taken for a ball to drop a given distance and provides a time value for a range of distances from 0 to 255 cm. The time–distance table provides a model of the ball's motion, with the pointer representing the ball's present position and the base representing the ball at the top of its bounce.

Thus, to position the pointer, the distance between the ball's present position and the top of bounce must be calculated. This is done by calculating the ball's vertical velocity using y_1 and y_2, and then using this value as a pointer in the Base table containing the distance a ball must drop to obtain a given velocity. This provides the offset for the pointer in the time–distance table. The model is now complete and can be used to predict the height of the ball for the previously calculated time to arrival.

Predicting the ball's height

To use the model to predict the ball's movement the pointer is stepped through the table. The sign of $(y_1 - y_2)$ gives the ball's direction, and hence the direction to step the pointer (increment it if the ball is falling or decrement it if the ball is rising). Once the pointer has been stepped to the new position, the value read from the table is the time taken for the ball to move 1 cm, given its present velocity. A tally of these time values is kept as the pointer is stepped through the

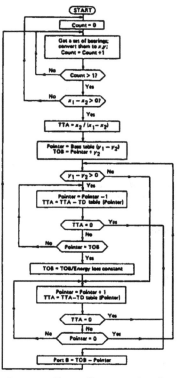

Figure 5. Flow diagram of robot software

table and, when it is equal to the time to arrival, the end point is reached and the pointer can be used to calculate a height for the bat.

Two conditions can interrupt this process. If the pointer is being decremented and reaches zero, then the ball has reached the top of its bounce, and the pointer is incremented to model the ball falling. If the pointer is being incremented and reaches the 'top of bounce' value, then the ball is about to bounce and the pointer should be decremented to model the ball rising. But, before this can happen, the 'top of bounce' value must be reduced to allow for the loss of momentum in the bounce; this is done by simply dividing the pointer by a constant.

The bat's height is obtained by subtracting the pointer from the current 'top of bounce' height to give a height for the bat above the table surface (in-cm).

This completes one cycle of the

main program, which on average takes 4.4 ms leaving 13.6 ms free before testing of the photodiodes is required. This time is used to display the ball's position on a VDU.

Microcomputer and interface circuitry

The analogue and digital circuitry used to interface the sensors and drive the motors is outlined here at function block level. The computer used was a Dragon 32 microcomputer, with a 6809 CPU running at 0.9 MHz. The computer was modified to include a 6522 versatile interface adaptor; it is this unit that provides the two ports used by the system.

The interface circuitry is shown in Figure 6. The inputs from the four forward-looking diodes are AC amplified and passed to the rate detectors. These filter out all 'non-ball-like' pulses by passing only positive-going signals whose rate of change exceeds a preset level. The digital output from these units goes through 'one shots' to expand their pulse widths from (typically) 100 µs to 20 ms, so that successive pulses produce a continuous signal. The logic circuitry uses these signals to decide which of the four voltages is to be applied to the servo motor. In the normal 'locked on' condition the error signal is selected, but otherwise the state of the outer two diodes determines the selection.

The error signal is derived from the central pair of diodes. Each output feeds a type of sample-and-hold circuit which maintains on its output a voltage proportional to the peak-to-peak voltage of the input pulse. The difference in these signals is then nonlinearly amplified to complete the processing of the error signal.

This nonlinear stage is used to part compensate for the variation in light levels received by the sensor as the ball travels the length of the table. A typical variation of 25 to 1 produces a similar variation in the error signal, which this stage helps to reduce. In moderation this effect is useful as it reduces the servo response time as the ball nears the bat.

The signals from the top and bot-

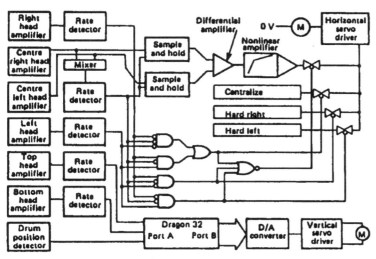

Figure 6. Microcomputer interface circuitry

ing and hitting a pingpong ball served towards it. Since then, various modifications have been made to the system with a view towards this year's competition. It is hoped to improve the software model of the ball's trajectory to allow for air resistance and spin, and further work has been done on the horizontal-error signal processing hardware.

If these and other modifications are successful we have high hopes for this year's competition, and we look forward to the day when a pingpong-playing robot is capable of taking on a human opponent.

The authors are pictured here with part of their winning pingpong robot, 'Charlie'. When the work described in this paper was carried out, John Knight (right) was a computer technician at Highbury Technical College, UK; he has since moved to Portsmouth Polytechnic in the same capacity. Dave Lowery (left) is currently working as a lorry driver.

tom diodes go through AC amplifiers and rate detectors. Their outputs are fed directly to the computer on two lines of the input port. A third line receives the signal from a slotted opto switch used to sense the position of the camera drum. Having digested the input provided at port A, the computer presents an 8-bit byte at port B. This, via a D/A converter, controls the bat's height.

The computer has one further function: to release the bat when the ball breaks one of six infrared beams which cross the area immediately in front of the bat. The signals from the six infrared sensors are NANDed and fed to one of the four handshake control lines provided by the 6522. This

input generates an interrupt whose service routine simply introduces a delay before releasing the bat. The purpose of the delay is to moderate the force of the return stroke by preventing the bat from reaching full speed when it makes contact with the ball. The duration of the delay is derived from the horizontal velocity of the ball, a value provided by the main program.

Conclusions

At the 1985 competition, 'Robat Charlie' was found to be capable on most occasions of successfully track-

Assembler–monitor package to teach assembly language

Assembly language can be difficult to teach and study. **Ivan Tomek and Peter Steele** describe a collection of assembler tutorial programs which run on CP/M and MS-DOS systems

The paper describes a software package designed to make the study of assembly language programming easier. The package, called AMS, consists of a set of programs that have been implemented for CP/M and MS-DOS systems. The main parts of each package are a text editor, a code generator, and a simulator. The simulator, which is the essential component of the package, simultaneously displays the source code being executed, memory and register contents, and timing information. In its single-step mode the simulator highlights the currently executing instruction both in source form and in hexadecimal code, and updates the screen after each individual instruction. AMS is related to debugging tools; therefore a comparison between AMS and two recently announced MS-DOS debuggers is given.

microprocessors   assembly language   simulator

Assembly language programming can be one of the more difficult programming courses to study. The main reasons for this are

- the relative difficulty of implementing I/O with limited previous knowledge of assembly language, and the lack of feedback from the computer without I/O
- the subtle effect of machine instructions on an array of registers, status flags and memory, all dynamically changing their values without the student getting a chance to observe them

Different instructors use different strategies to deal with the problems. Some solutions are: developing special-purpose I/O macros; starting the course with subroutines and operating system I/O calls[1]; and using the system debugger to visualize CPU operation[2]. All these approaches are useful and can even be combined. In the authors' opinion, however, none of them achieves their ultimate goal — to let the student see what is happening when an assembly language program executes, and correlate this with the source program. A tutorial package that achieves this goal has been designed and implemented on CP/M- and MS-DOS-based computers. The package is called AMS (assembly language programming made simple). The basic idea of AMS resembles the principle of PMS (PASCAL made simple), developed for the student of PASCAL[3, 4].

Components of AMS

AMS is a combination of a text editor, a code generator and a special-purpose simulator. An assembler and a set of I/O macros are also included in the package.

The editor is screen oriented and allows the user to create assembly language programs. The code generator is essentially an assembler. It converts the source code into code executable by the simulator, generating extra information and extra code to allow the simulator to execute the program and perform the specialized functions described below. The simulator uses the binary code generated by the

code generator and executes user programs, continuously displaying and updating the following information:

- the contents of 256 byte of memory (in hexadecimal)
- the contents of registers (in hexadecimal and, in the CP/M version, in binary)
- a section of the source program currently under execution
- timing information (CPU cycles spent executing the program)
- a menu of commands

Some examples of program displays are given in Appendix 1.

In normal use the simulator loads an object code file requested by the user and displays its first source instructions, and the initial contents of memory (instruction and data codes) and registers. The user then prompts the simulator to execute the program step by step. (Continuous execution is also available.) At each step the simulator highlights the next source instruction and the code of the corresponding machine instruction in memory. If the instruction operates on memory, the simulator highlights the data code. The source code is automatically scrolled so that the user can always see a few instructions surrounding the current one in context.

The simulator executes binary code and the execution of instructions is thus not simulated. To run, for example, the Z80 version of AMS the user must have a CP/M-based computer.

The assembler is a macroassembler generating ordinary executable code. Its purpose is to complete the package so that no further software is required for the course. It is also required for the use of the macros provided in the package.

The macros (at present developed only for the CP/M version) are mainly

School of Computer Science, Acadia University, Wolfville, Nova Scotia, Canada B0P 1X0

0141-9331/86/06336–04 $03.00 © 1986 Butterworth & Co. (Publishers) Ltd

I/O macros that perform more complicated functions such as string and numerical I/O in various formats. Their purpose is to give the student a set of tools to allow him/her to write interesting programs without the need to spend time developing the necessary I/O subroutines or macros. Note that, although the AMS tools make it possible for the student to avoid writing I/O code, they do not isolate him/her from I/O operations: they teach low-level I/O by operating system calls. The simulator provides a specialized display when an operating system function is called.

Teaching assembly language with AMS

The authors cannot report any scientifically conducted experiment to prove the value of AMS. However, the package, and a text written for it[5], have been used in an assembly language course during September 1985, and have received favourable comments from students.

AMS can be used as a demonstration tool in lectures (with classroom TV monitors or a projector) or as a student aid for individual study. Students can use the simulator to learn the basic operation of the CPU and the operating system as well as for the debugging of small assignments. Use of the simulator as an auxiliary tool is recommended; students should use an assembler for larger assignments.

Comparison of AMS with related programs

Although the authors are not aware of any other programs designed specifically for the teaching of assembly language programming, there is a category of programs somewhat related to AMS — debugging tools. We will now compare AMS with debuggers in general, and with two recent advanced MS-DOS debuggers in particular.

The main function of debuggers is, of course, to help an advanced software designer in the development of programs at machine level. A typical debugger such as the MS-DOS Debug provides functions to load

object files and execute them from a specific address, step-by-step execution, setting of breakpoints, and display and modification of memory and register contents. Other instructions provided by some debuggers are memory searches and comparisons and primitive single-instruction assembly. Debuggers are normally written in assembly language to minimize memory requirements and interference with the debugged program.

The difference between AMS and debuggers is in their purpose — AMS is a tutorial package, debuggers are development tools — hence the differences between their features. Since AMS was not intended to replace a debugger it does not provide some debugging functions such as memory search and comparison and the setting of breakpoints. It does not allow the patching of instruction codes in the simulation mode. AMS is written in PASCAL and partially interprets code execution.

Most of the differences between AMS and a debugger are due to the primary goal of AMS — to allow the simultaneous viewing of the source code as written by the user (including labels, constant definitions and named operands) and machine-level operations of the CPU. This feature is not available in debuggers, which at best disassemble object code without providing any symbolic information other than op. code mnemonics. This may cause problems since mechanical disassembly can lead to some bizarre and misleading results when code inserted into a program is 'disassembled' into instructions, possibly invalidating the rest of the disassembly. The lack of the feature in debuggers is understandable since the intended user of a professional debugger is an expert assembly language programmer. This consideration applies also to another AMS function not present in debuggers — display of the description of operating system call functions, when encountered in the program. The display of machine cycle count provided in AMS would seem useful even for debuggers, but is not provided in those with which the authors are familiar.

For the purposes of comparison, two advanced MS-DOS debuggers[6] are described briefly below. These

are AFD (advanced full screen debugger) by IBM and PDF (professional debug facility) by Puttkamer Software and Microcomputertechnic of the FRG.

Unlike traditional debuggers but in keeping with the general trend in recent software, both PDF and AFD are screen oriented. This means that they provide a display of memory and registers somewhat similar to AMS (rather than the traditional command-driven line-by-line display) and that some of their functions, such as changing of memory and register values, are cursor driven. In addition to the standard debugging functions listed above they provide the following extra features:

- use of two displays, one for the execution of the program being debugged and one for the debugger display
- user control over screen definition with an option to set up several coexisting definitions for use with different areas of the program
- special display and operating modes for operation with disc files
- additional (simulated) registers for use with search and compare functions as well as for the definition of breakpoints
- conditional breakpoints with complex conditions including execution counts
- several kinds of trace functions both at instruction and subroutine call level
- a hardware card for the activation of nonmaskable interrupts.

Advanced debuggers such as AFD and PDF are much better suited for teaching than traditional debuggers, but they still lack some features of AMS that the authors consider useful for the typical student of assembly language programming. A combination of AMS and either AFD or PDF (which cost $110 and $150 respectively) may be used by those who wish to learn assembly language programming from the start and pursue it in a serious manner.

Conclusions

The response of students to AMS has indicated that its use can help to speed up assembly language tutorial courses and provide students with a deeper insight. AMS does not rely on any special terminal characteristics and runs on any CP/M or MS-DOS computer with the standard amount of memory.

In addition to its instructional use, AMS can be used as a debugging tool for small programs. AMS is to be marketed commercially in due course.

References

1 **Hutty, R** *Programming in Z80 assembly language* Macmillan, London, UK (1984)
2 **Singh, A and Triebel, W A** *IBM PC/ 8088 assembly language programming* Prentice-Hall, Englewood Cliffs, NJ, USA (1985)
3 **Tomek, I, Muldner, T and Khan, S** 'A program to make learning Pascal easier' *Computers and Education* Vol 9 No 4 (1985) pp 205–211
4 **Tomek, I and Muldner T** *A Pascal primer with PMS* McGraw-Hill, New York, USA (1985)
5 **Steele, P and Tomek, I** *Z80 assembly language programming with AMS* Computer Science Press (in press)
6 **Carden, J C** 'Professional debug facility and advanced fullscreen debug' *Byte* Vol 11 No 4 (April 1986) pp 249–255

Ivan Tomek is a professor of computer science at Acadia University, Canada. His main professional interests are VSLI design and developing tools for teaching computer science. He has developed a number of tutorial computer programs including Josef (a PASCAL-like programming language), Hard (a hierarchical hardware simulation package) and PMS ('visual PASCAL').

Peter W Steele received a BSc in computer science from Acadia University in 1980. He then undertook graduate studies at the University of Western Ontario, Canada, and was awarded an MSc in computer science by Acadia University in 1982. Since then he has been lecturing at Acadia University and developing software for MicroNova.

Appendix 1: Display of three consecutive steps in the execution of a program as produced on screen by the AMS simulator (MS-DOS version). Op. codes are shown in brackets; accessed data is marked by asterisks

```
                                                          | File: TEST2.888
                                                          | Time: 202
----------------------------------------------------------|-----------------------
0100  48*49* FF  C7  C7  00  00  C7  C3  00  01  E4  03  F6  C0  04 |  JZ LUPE
0110  74  F9 <8A 01>80  F8  FF  74  06  E6  02  47  E9  EC  FF  CD>>>  MOV AL, [BX + DI]
0120  20  00  00  00  00  00  00  00  00  00  00  00  00  00  00  00 |  CMP AL, 0FFH
0130  00  00  00  00  00  00  00  00  00  00  00  00  00  00  00  00 |  JZ DONE
0140  00  00  00  00  00  00  00  00  00  00  00  00  00  00  00  00 |  OUT 2,AL
0150  00  00  00  00  00  00  00  00  00  00  00  00  00  00  00  00 |
0160  00  00  00  00  00  00  00  00  00  00  00  00  00  00  00  00 |
0170  00  00  00  00  00  00  00  00  00  00  00  00  00  00  00  00 |  — —SINGLE STEP MENU— —
0180  00  00  00  00  00  00  00  00  00  00  00  00  00  00  00  00 |     M — Main Menu
0190  00  00  00  00  00  00  00  00  00  00  00  00  00  00  00  00 |     S — Single Step
01A0  00  00  00  00  00  00  00  00  00  00  00  00  00  00  00  00 |     Q — Quit/Restart
01B0  00  00  00  00  00  00  00  00  00  00  00  00  00  00  00  00 |     X — Exit
01C0  00  00  00  00  00  00  00  00  00  00  00  00  00  00  00  00 |
01D0  00  00  00  00  00  00  00  00  00  00  00  00  00  00  00  00 |
01E0  00  00  00  00  00  00  00  00  00  00  00  00  00  00  00  00 |
----------------------------------------------------------|
      :  :  :  :  :  :  :  :  :  :  :  :  :  :  :  :  | > Memory Access
----------------------------------------------------------|
AX-0004   BX-0100   CX-0000   DX-0000   SP-0032   SI-0000 |
CS-0000   DS-0000   ES-0000   SS-04FF   BP-0032   DI-0001 |
FLAGS- ... oditsz.a.p.c                 IP-0112           |
```

File: TEST2.888
Time: 207

```
0100   48  49  FF  C7  C7  00  00  C7  C3  00  01  E4  03  F6  C0  04      JZ LUPE
0110   74  F9  8A  01<80  F8  FF>74  06  E6  02  47  E9  EC  FF  CD        MOV AL, [BX + DI]
0120   20  00  00  00  00  00  00  00  00  00  00  00  00  00  00  00  > > >  CMP AL, 0FFH
0130   00  00  00  00  00  00  00  00  00  00  00  00  00  00  00  00      JZ DONE
0140   00  00  00  00  00  00  00  00  00  00  00  00  00  00  00  00      OUT 2,AL
0150   00  00  00  00  00  00  00  00  00  00  00  00  00  00  00  00
0160   00  00  00  00  00  00  00  00  00  00  00  00  00  00  00  00
0170   00  00  00  00  00  00  00  00  00  00  00  00  00  00  00  00      — —SINGLE STEP MENU— —
0180   00  00  00  00  00  00  00  00  00  00  00  00  00  00  00  00          M — Main Menu
0190   00  00  00  00  00  00  00  00  00  00  00  00  00  00  00  00          S — Single Step
01A0   00  00  00  00  00  00  00  00  00  00  00  00  00  00  00  00          Q — Quit/Restart
01B0   00  00  00  00  00  00  00  00  00  00  00  00  00  00  00  00          X — Exit
01C0   00  00  00  00  00  00  00  00  00  00  00  00  00  00  00  00
01D0   00  00  00  00  00  00  00  00  00  00  00  00  00  00  00  00
01E0   00  00  00  00  00  00  00  00  00  00  00  00  00  00  00  00
```

```
AX-0049    BX-0100    CX-0000    DX-0000    SP-0032    SI-0000
CS-0000    DS-0000    ES-0000    SS-04FF    BP-0032    DI-0001
FLAGS- . . . oditsz.A.p.C                   IP-0114
```

File: TEST2.888
Time: 211

```
0100   48  49  FF  C7  C7  00  00  C7  C3  00  01  E4  03  F6  C0  04      JZ LUPE
0110   74  F9  8A  01  80  F8  FF<74  06>E6  02  47  E9  EC  FF  CD        MOV AL, [BX + DI]
0120   20  00  00  00  00  00  00  00  00  00  00  00  00  00  00  00      CMP AL, 0FFH
0130   00  00  00  00  00  00  00  00  00  00  00  00  00  00  00  00  > > >  JZ DONE
0140   00  00  00  00  00  00  00  00  00  00  00  00  00  00  00  00      OUT 2,AL
0150   00  00  00  00  00  00  00  00  00  00  00  00  00  00  00  00
0160   00  00  00  00  00  00  00  00  00  00  00  00  00  00  00  00
0170   00  00  00  00  00  00  00  00  00  00  00  00  00  00  00  00      — —SINGLE STEP MENU— —
0180   00  00  00  00  00  00  00  00  00  00  00  00  00  00  00  00          M — Main Menu
0190   00  00  00  00  00  00  00  00  00  00  00  00  00  00  00  00          S — Single Step
01A0   00  00  00  00  00  00  00  00  00  00  00  00  00  00  00  00          Q — Quit/Restart
01B0   00  00  00  00  00  00  00  00  00  00  00  00  00  00  00  00          X — Exit
01C0   00  00  00  00  00  00  00  00  00  00  00  00  00  00  00  00
01D0   00  00  00  00  00  00  00  00  00  00  00  00  00  00  00  00
01E0   00  00  00  00  00  00  00  00  00  00  00  00  00  00  00  00
```

```
AX-0049    BX-0100    CX-0000    DX-0000    SP-0032    SI-0000
CS-0000    DS-0000    ES-0000    SS-04FF    BP-0032    DI-0001
FLAGS- . . . oditsz.A.p.C                   IP-0117
```

R&D reports

'R & D reports' surveys the recent scientific and technical literature, highlighting papers on all matters affecting the research, development and application of microprocessor-based systems.

Applications

Betts, W R
'Multiplexing for the automotive industry' *GEC Rev.* Vol 2 No 1 (1986) pp 32–36

Modern automobiles are, says the author, a complex amalgam of dissimilar technologies. This, together with the range of models available in the market, creates problems for suppliers and manufacturers of vehicle electrical systems. The paper describes the implementation of the microprocessor-based Salplex Series 4000 automotive multiplexing system which it is claimed fulfils the requirements of being cheap, reliable, safe, and easy to install, maintain, test and repair.

El-Dhaher, A H G, Hassan, T S and Safar, J A
'Microprocessor-based system for measurement of conductivity in amorphous semiconductors' *J. Microcomput. Appl.* Vol 9 No 2 (April 1986) pp 83–94

Hobson, L, Webb, D W and Christopher, R
'Microprocessor control of a transistorized induction-heating power supply' *Int. J. Electronics* Vol 59 No 6 (December 1985) pp 735–745

Kadhim, M A H, Sadiq-Hussain, S B and Danial, K
'A new approach for the measurement of AC arc parameters using microprocessors' *J. Microcomput. Appl.* Vol 9 No 2 (April 1986) pp 95–104

Kakatsios, B, Petrou, L and Kleftouris, D
'A microprocessor-based high availability irrigation control system' *J. Microcomput. Appl.* Vol 9 No 1 (January 1986) pp 27–38

Smith, M F
'A taxonomic classification of dedicated microprocessor applications' *J. Microcomput. Appl.* Vol 9 No 1 (January 1986) pp 63–81

Taxonomically derived characteristics of dedicated microprocessor applications may be of value in producing more efficient designs. Principles and uses of taxonomic classification are discussed and illustrated by mapping a population of devices produced by the author into the classification scheme.

Buses

Harold, P
'Low-cost buses add industrial I/O to VME, Multibus II' *EDN* Vol 31 No 9 (1 May 1986) pp 175–196

Wallace, C and Koch, D
'TTL-compatible multiport bus' *Computer Syst. Sci. Eng.* Vol 1 No 1 (October 1985) pp 47–52

An experimental multiprocessor system with sixteen 32-bit processors sharing sixteen memory modules has been developed. It is estimated that peak traffic rates in the system will be of the order of 30 data transfers μs^{-1}, requiring a 32-port bus with a cycle time not exceeding 33 ns. A nonstandard TTL-compatible bus with built-in tolerances on these requirements is described.

Communications

Burd, N C
'A communication protocol for single chip processors' *J. Microcomput. Appl.* Vol 9 No 2 (April 1986) pp 105–111

Whilst standards for communication systems such as local area networks are in an advanced stage of their evolution, similar standards for smaller processors do not exist. The paper describes an implementation of a communication protocol using single-chip microprocessors as slave devices in a master/slave system with a serial bus architecture.

Sánchez, M, Méndez, J A, Núñez, A
'A microprocessor-based concentrator/distributor system' *Mundo Electronico* No 161 (April 1986) pp 79–82 (in Spanish)

A system that is intended to serve as an alternative to computer terminal multilinks is described. The system is built around an 8085A with an RS232C interface.

Hardware

Aguiló, J, Deschamps, J P, Schutz, E and Valderrama, E
'The future of full custom integrated circuits' *Mundo Electronico* No 163 (June 1986) pp 91–98 (in Spanish)
Compares three types of custom ICs: gate arrays, standard cells and full custom circuits. Systems consisting of standard components are compared with equivalent systems of specific components.

Balde, J W
'Status and prospects of surface mount technology' *Solid State Tech.* Vol 29 No 6 (June 1986) pp 99–103

Bridge, A
'DSP chips multiply fast' *Systems Int.* (June 1986) pp 37–38
Dedicated digital signal processor (DSP) chips are being accepted enthusiastically by designers and the market for these products is booming. Single-chip DSPs are analysed in the article and potential applications surveyed.

Cushman, R H
'Support chips mature to upstage the host microprocessor' *EDN* Vol 31 No 6 (20 March 1986) pp 116–167

The microprocessor is no longer the sole, central system chip but just another component, according to EDN's chip directory for 1986. New trends to be identified in the support chip area are that manufacturers are increasingly supplying their chips in standard silicon form or as CAD megacells; also ISDN chip sets are nearly complete and are waiting for final standards.

Smith, D
'Programmable logic devices' *EDN* Vol 31 No 10 (15 May 1986) pp 94–109

In the past two years the operating speeds of bipolar PLDs have doubled and CMOS PLDs have emerged offering four times more circuitry per chip than older bipolar versions. This 'special report' surveys developments and products.

Multiprocessor systems

Corsini, P, Prete, C A and Simoncini, L
'MuTEAM: an experience in the design of robust multimicroprocessor systems' *Computer Syst. Sci. Eng.* Vol 1 No 1 (October 1985) pp 23–35

MuTEAM is an experimental multi-processor prototype supporting concurrent programming and decentralized non-hierarchical policies for both resource management and fault treatment. Experimentation is aimed at the interrelationship between these issues and their influence on the applications supported by the system.

Spyropoulos, C D and Evans, D J
'Performance analysis of priority-driven algorithm for multiprocessor model with independent memories: mean flow time criterion' *Computer Syst. Sci. Eng* Vol 1 No 1 (October 1985) pp 36–46

Networks

Bowen, J
'Design of a simple Cambridge Ring interface adapter' *Computer Syst. Sci. Eng.* Vol 1 No 2 (January 1986) pp 93–98

The Cambridge Ring, while accepted in the academic community, is not so widely used in industry due to the lack of commercially available interfaces, says Bowen. The interface described in this paper is between a type 1 Cambridge Ring node and the Motorola 68230 parallel interface/timer chip.

Brookes, G R, Manson, G A and Thompson, J A
'Lattice and ring array topologies using transputers' *Computer Comm.* Vol 9 No 3 (June 1986) pp 121–125

Development of a parallel processor architecture using transputers is described for the example of a desk-top parallel processing computer. For such a workstation a general array is required and two alternative processor topologies — lattice and ring arrays — are compared. The ring array is found to offer significant advantages.

Chen, T N
'Ring network reliability and a fault-tolerant Cambridge Ring architecture' *JIERE* Vol 56 No 5 (May 1986) pp 179–183

Ring networks have inherent reliability problems — a single node failure can bring down the network. Duplicate rings could avoid such a failure but are expensive. An alternative, the Centre-Switching Ring-Star, is proposed which is designed to bypass faulty nodes. The system is designed specifically for the Cambridge Ring network.

Dunlop, J and Rashid, M A
'Improving the delay characteristics of standard Ethernet for speech trans-mission' *JIERE* Vol 56 No 5 (May 1986) pp 184–186

Delay in the transmission of speech packets on Ethernet is caused by collisions with other packets. Performance can be improved by truncating the standard binary exponential back-off generated by nodes experiencing a collision, which, as shown in the paper, can be implemented in special-purpose VLSI devices.

Mataix, J and de la Puente, J A
'Local area computer networks for industrial process control' *Mundo Electronico* No 163 (June 1986) pp 57–63 (in Spanish)

Reviews current local area networks from the viewpoint of the design of distributed control systems. Emphasis is on token bus networks.

Suda, T and Yemini, Y
'Architectures for integrated service networks' *Computer Comm.* Vol 9 No 1 (February 1986) pp 3–8

Teo, E H and Georganas, N D
'Design and validation of a transport protocol for local area networks' *Computer Comm.* Vol 9 No 3 (June 1986) pp 115–120

Parallel processing

Salzwedel, M and Baisch, F
'Parallel processing suits real-time applications' *EDN* Vol 31 No 6 (20 March 1986) pp 213–220

A parallel processing computer has been developed by the Aerospace Medicine Institute of the West German Space Agency for realtime data acquisition, analysis and control applications. Called Spacemed, the system processes electrocardiogram and impedance-cardiogram waveforms from astronauts during space shuttle missions, at rates from ×1 to ×10 realtime, and at sampling rates from 1 kHz to 10 kHz. The development of the system is explained.

R & D reports

Power sources

Javier, M and Fanjul, A
'High volumetric efficiency capacitors in microprocessor-based systems' *Mundo Electronico* No 159 (February 1986) pp 69–73 (in Spanish)

Electric double layer capacitors are beginning to replace batteries and accumulators as standby power sources for volatile memories in microprocessor systems. The paper reveals the main characteristics and the advantages and disadvantages of these high-efficiency capacitors which are claimed to have 10 to 50 times greater capacity per unit volume than conventional aluminium electrolytic capacitors.

Semiconductors

Rust, R D and Doane, D A
'Growing interdependence within the microelectronics industry: an overview perspective' *Solid State Tech.* Vol 29 No 6 (June 1986) pp 125–128

The three 'sister' industries, say the authors — integrated circuit, printed circuit and hybrid circuit manufacturing — are moving from a historical position of independence towards greater interdependence. The article defines the primary 'forces of change' within these industries and describes their effects.

Software

Jones, D-W
'Learning ADA on a micro' *Dr. Dobb's J. Software Tools* Vol 11 No 2 (February 1986) pp 42–58

Validated ADA compilers are expensive but, says the author, there is an affordable ADA subset that runs on CP/M-80 systems that is complete enough to provide useful experience. Examples of the US Defense Department's 'favourite' language presented in this article were written and tested by the author on a 62K CP/M system using what is now the Supersoft A compiler.

Testing

Boswell, C, Saluja, K K, and Kinoshita, K
'Design of programmable logic arrays for parallel testing' *Computer Syst. Sci. Eng.* Vol 1 No 1 (October 1985) pp 5–16

VLSI

Bartlett, C J
'Advanced packaging for VLSI' *Solid State Tech.* Vol 29 No 6 (June 1986) pp 119–123

Dimond, K R and Bagherli, J
'Custom VLSI circuits for man-machine interaction: an automatic design method' *JIERE* Vol 56 No 2 (February 1986) pp 79–85

As single ICs become more powerful and complex some of the processing capability of the chips must be used to make digital systems more 'user-friendly' for non-computer specialists, the authors say. It is proposed that the only solution is to have an automatic system capable of designing ICs for processing man–machine interaction, and the paper describes a method of realizing such a design system.

Liao, Y-Z, Chen, N-P and Gau, T
'Symbolic layout software accelerates IC design' *Electron. Des.* Vol 35 No 13 (12 June 1986) pp 89–96

Spaanenburg, L
'Efficient silicon compilation of digital control specifications' *JIERE* Vol 56 No 4 (April 1986) pp 142–146

Efficiency of IC design in terms of signal throughput and area utilization is often sacrificed for execution speed of CAD aids such as silicon compilers. But the most important requirement should be to create a design technology rather than just CAD software, says Spaanenburg, who introduces the concepts of hierarchy and regularity which he says will shorten design time.

Books received

These books have been received recently by the Editorial Office. They may be reviewed in a later issue.

Banks, S P
'Control systems engineering' Prentice-Hall (1986) £29.95 pp 624

Cooling, J E
'Real-time interfacing: engineering aspects of microprocessor peripheral systems' Van Nostrand Reinhold (1986) £19.95 pp 236

Furht, B and Parikh, H
'Microprocessor interfacing and communication using the Intel SDK-85' Reston (1986) £31.00 pp 510

Gorsline, G W
'Computer organization: hardware/software (2nd edition)' Prentice-Hall (1986) £43.80 pp 638

Hörbst, E (Ed.)
'VLSI 85: VLSI design of digital systems' North-Holland (1986) $53.50 Dfl 155 pp 443

Proceedings of the conference on Very Large Scale Integration held in Tokyo, Japan, in August 1985, organized by the International Federation for Information Processing.

Jermann, W H
'Programming 16-bit machines: the PDP-11, 8086 and M68000' Prentice-Hall (1986) £39.95 pp 447

Kelly, M G and Spies, N
'FORTH: a text and reference' Prentice-Hall (1986) £19.10 pp 500

Kowalik, J S (Ed.)
'Parallel MIMD computation: HEP supercomputer and its application' MIT Press (1985) £37.75 pp 425

Contains fifteen contributions that discuss multiprocessor architectures, concurrent programming and parallel algorithms in relation to the HEP supercomputer, a general-purpose MIMD computer.

Toy, W and Zee, B
'Computer hardware/software architecture' Prentice-Hall (1986) £41.70 pp 464

Introduction to 68000 is 'excellent' for teaching

Jean Bacon

'The Motorola MC68000: an intro-duction to processor, memory and interfacing' Prentice-Hall, Englewood Cliffs, NJ, USA (1986) £14.95 pp 319

Based largely on foundation courses in computer systems organization at Hatfield Polytechnic, UK, this book uses the 68000 chip to explain the fundamentals of microprocessor systems software. It is aimed at students and serious microprocessor users, and assumes no previous experience of machine-level design or programming.

As with any introductory text, the maximum benefit will be gained only if the reader has the opportunity of hands-on experience using the example programs, of which this text has many. A small 68000 development system available from Motorola, Tutor, is used throughout the book to show how theory can be put into practice.

The author covers most of her aims well. There is a straightforward introduction to describe the path that will be taken, then the book is split into two parts. The first introduces how a microprocessor works, and how it interprets instructions to run programs. Simple machine code programs are developed so that examples may be run on the development system. A description of assembly-level programming in a host-target development environment is given.

This part of the text is very well presented. In particular, the use of stacks to implement block structured programming is described in detail, and should present no problem for inexperienced readers.

The second part of the book deals with the connection of the 68000 chip to the outside world via serial I/O, interrupts and exceptions. There are several long examples, including a fully interrupt driven I/O program.

By the end of the book, the reader should be able to see how a 68000 chip operates at the heart of an operating system, handling a multiprocessing or even a multiuser environment. The book's appendices describe several of the peripherals which can be attached; these appear to be copies from the 68000 literature, and seem to be for interest only as, apart from a description of the PIA, they are not referenced in the text.

I liked the clear style, although it is very slow at times. The example programs are well commented and easy to understand; it should not be difficult to get them up and running on the Tutor system, or any similar development board. There are no suggested programming exercises, which is a little unusual since writing your own programs is a better way to learn than typing in someone else's.

Although aimed primarily at students as a foundation course, the book is meant to be used by people to 'upgrade' from 8-bit micros. The pace is certainly too slow for those with even a minimal knowledge of microprocessor programming and, although some chapters can be missed out, a more concise approach would be better suited to these readers.

For a book of this cost, it would be nice if it could be used as a reference book when the user becomes more experienced. Finding details on individual instruction codes is tiresome, involving a lot of hunting through the pages. There is a summary of instructions, but this may be rather terse for the novice user. Readers would probably need to purchase a reference manual once they had covered this book, which seems rather a waste.

One minor point which applies to this and a number of computing texts is that although the main text is well printed, all of the examples are in a low quality typeface which is not as easy to read and spoils the otherwise high quality of the printing. However, the book is well bound in an attractive cover which should shrug off the occasional coffee spill and last well.

The book is certainly to be recommended to those who have had no previous experience of programming microprocessors. It is an excellent teaching book, and probably covers a single term's course for a computer science student or a longer course for students in less closely related disciplines. However, I feel that most readers will put it back on the shelf fairly quickly once they have mastered the basics of the chip, and will be looking around for a text which is more usable in the long term.

Roderick Manzie
Trading Technology Ltd,
London, UK

German–English microelectronics dictionary

Y H Attiyate and R Swan

'Dictionary of microelectronics and microcomputer technology' VDI Verlag, Dusseldorf, FRG (1986) DM78,- pp 470

On first use this dictionary gives the impression of a small, handy reference book with very clear typing; but on account of its low volume there is a tendency to doubt that it could possibly contain all technical terms on the subject. After going through just a few such terms, however, readers will realize that by confining themselves strictly to the field of microelectronics and microcomputer technology the authors have in fact succeeded in covering almost all the terms presently in use.

Working with this book, the reader soon comes to appreciate the short explanations given in addition to the literal meaning, that are so very much to the point. They are longer for more complicated terms and are given for both the book's languages: once for the German keyword and again for

(continues over page)

Welcome addition to the growing 8085A library

Barry B Brey

The 8085A microprocessor: software, programming and architecture' Prentice-Hall, Englewood Cliffs, NJ, USA (1986) $29.95 pp 354

Intel's 8085A is the longest surviving member of a growing family of 8-bit microprocessors based on the same architecture as that of the 8080. Its popularity has not diminished since its introduction some ten years ago; throughout the world, it has been found to be an ideal vehicle for educational and training courses introducing students to the concepts of microprocessing. It is not surprising, therefore, to find that new titles such as this one by Barry Brey are still being produced, even when everybody in the profession is talking about 32-bit micros. It is certainly worth having a closer look inside to find out what this book has to offer us.

The book is written as a text for students of engineering, computing and other scientific disciplines who are attending courses on microprocessing. To this end, every chapter starts with clear-cut objectives setting out the purpose of topics under discussion and ends with a summary of the main points, a glossary of the new terms introduced and some further exercises to strengthen the material studied in the chapter. The topics discussed are illustrated with appropriate diagrams and exemplified by software listings wherever possible. I was pleasantly surprised by the depth of the treatment of topics which were often neglected by earlier books on the subject.

One of the difficult tasks for course organizers is to decide where and how to start the teaching of microprocessing — logic gates, architecture of devices, system hardware or software?

The neophytes are anxious to see something happening in front of their eyes rather than exposing themselves to endless talk on internal architecture, data paths, timing diagrams, abstract machines and hypothetical instruction sets. To this effect, Brey is very honest in his title as regards the content of the book. After a bird's eye view of microprocessors in general, he concentrates only on the 8085A and its associated

---

Attiyate and Swan
(continued)

the English one. Modern computer-aided printing technology made this possible and it is by no means a waste of space, saving the user a lot of turning over and over the leaves.

The dictionary was evidently written by skilled technicians. It is aimed at technicians, particularly those with good general control of English (or German) as a foreign language, who want to familiarize themselves with the subject or who just want the exact translation of one special word.

This book will be particularly helpful for translators: usually they know something about the subject, but rather often they are at a loss when it comes to subtle distinctions. The explanations readily available in both languages give the exact meaning of the word and the context so that they need not fall back upon numerous reference books in order to verify their own translations.

The typeface, size and hard cover of the book are further assets and it is not a great problem that the brackets that are meant to separate the explanations from the actual translation are not always there.

However, I do find fault with the fact that the keyword is sometimes at the bottom of one page and the translation at the top of the next. This is certainly a consequence of computer typesetting and very difficult if not impossible to avoid, but it must be mentioned as a drawback if we point out all the merits of the book.

One of these merits — and a very important one too — is that the authors have included in their dictionary the numerous abbreviations that are so often to blame when beginners have difficulty understanding articles or papers or even handling instructions. Many of these abbreviations are explained briefly, and the explanations can also be found in full under the keyword. So, for instance, it says under IEC bus that this standard interface is also given under IEEE-488, GPIB or HPIB bus. Only someone who has had to identify what the letters 'GPIB' mean can really appreciate this feature.

The decision which abbreviations to include and which to omit may well have been a difficult one to take, since it happens that some terms out of a specific group are given whereas others of equal importance in the context are missing. So, for instance, the term DTR (data terminal ready) is given, whereas TXD (transmit data), RXD (receive data) and RTS (request to send) are not although they are on 'the same level'.

Considering the abundance of expressions and terms, it really has to be tolerated if minor mistakes have escaped the authors', or editors', attention: kilobyte (kB) is not the abbreviation for 1000 bytes but for 1024 bytes (2 to the power of 10); LED (light emitting diode) must not be applied for infrared radiation — it would have to be IRED (infrared emitting diode), which is described correctly under this keyword.

I would not want to fail to mention as an important asset: that numerous terms and expressions that have come up only very recently are considered in this book. Microelectronics and microcomputer technology are developing very rapidly and a dictionary that manages to keep pace is of the greatest value.

To conclude, I would like to say that to buy this book is certainly a good investment for all those who are not always sure what means what in microelectronics and microcomputer technology.

Norbert Nessler
Universität Innsbruck,
Austria

programming and software development. He has left the hardware components and system architecture to the last chapter, where he prepares students for more advanced courses in those areas. Given a low-cost board-level teaching aid and following the book chapter by chapter, students are not likely to be disappointed.

The first three chapters of the book are devoted to understanding microprocessors, the software development process and the internal architecture of the 8085A from the programmer's point of view. The introduction to modern programming approaches and the steps in designing the software are also outlined. Here I agree with the author that the correct approach to practical software design is a combination of top-down, modular, structured programming, an approach which is emphasized subsequently.

Once this basic ground is prepared, the next three chapters are devoted to understanding all the basic instructions in three broad categories — data transfer, arithmetic/

logic and program control — with numerous worked examples. The use of assembler and pseudo-operations is covered in a following chapter while most subsequent chapters develop commonly used software building blocks in data manipulation and conversion, fixed- and floating-point arithmetic, look-up tables and sorting algorithms.

The penultimate chapter is entirely devoted to diagnostic software. I would like this chapter to be further expanded to include some introduction to operating systems and software debugging techniques for runtime errors.

The last chapter on system architecture is followed by six appendices. The first three cover the usual instruction set summary, data sheets and ASCII code. One of the interesting aspects of the 8085A processor, and of great research interest even to this date, is the discovery of ten undocumented instructions and three unspecified bits in the flag register; these are listed in another appendix. Nobody yet knows why Intel keeps the

undocumented features a secret. The last appendix contains answers to all the even numbered questions of the exercises in the book (but the odd numbered questions are to be answered by the students).

The book is attractively bound in a hard cover. The layout of chapters and illustrations reflects the traditional Prentice-Hall image and the text is very readable throughout. It can be recommended as a second semester undergraduate course, the students having been exposed to TTL logic in the first semester (in order to comprehend the logical instructions of chapter 5).

It is also suitable for specialized short courses on microprocessing. The experienced engineer and programmer will find it useful too as a handy source of over 170 program examples. The book lives up to expectations and is a welcome addition to the growing library on the subject.

D M Vaidya
Westfield College,
London, UK

Alley, Charles L and Atwood, Kenneth W

'Microelectronics' Prentice-Hall (Reston), Englewood Cliffs, NJ, USA (1986) £40.60 pp xi + 542

Intended as a basic introduction to electronic devices and their application to various circuits and systems, the book comprises chapters on semiconductors, diodes, junction transistors, transistor characteristics and models, transistor amplifier configurations and amplifier design, field-effect transistors (FETs), FET amplifiers, direct coupled amplifiers, multistage amplifiers, negative feedback, linear integrated circuits, active filters, power amplifiers, power supplies and oscillator circuits. □

Brindley, Keith

'Radio and electronics engineer's pocket book, 16th edition' Newnes, Twickenham, UK (1986) £5.50 pp 170

This is a pocket-sized compendium of facts, figures and formulae written with the radio/electronics designer, student and service engineer in mind. Shows a distinct UK bias, e.g. in its coverage of the BBC (British Broadcasting Corporation) radio services. Includes listings and pin-out diagrams of TTL and CMOS components, and a 'semiconductor glossary'. □

Motorola

'M68000 8-/16-/32-bit microprocessors — programmer's reference manual, fifth edition' Prentice-Hall, Englewood Cliffs, NJ, USA (1986) £16.50 pp xii + 218

The new edition of Motorola's manual is extended from the 68000, 68008 and 68010 to cover the 68012 extended virtual memory processor (but not, despite the title, the 68020). Four main sections cover: architectural description; data organization and addressing capabilities; instruction

set summary; and exception processing. Appendices on condition code computation, instruction set details, instruction format, instruction execution times for each of the four processors and 68010/012 loop-mode operation are included. □

Sinclair, Ian R

'Practical electronics handbook (revised edition)' Newnes, Twickenham, UK (1986) £5.95 pp 199

Standard circuits, rules of thumb and design data for engineers, students and electronics hobbyists are presented in five chapters: passive components; active discrete components; discrete component circuits; linear ICs; and digital ICs. Functions of typical circuits are described, and a table of standard metric wires and a short bibliography are provided. The handbook, first published in 1980, has been revised to give more details on computers and microprocessors. □

Microcontroller family is based on common 16-bit CPU

A family of 16-bit 'high-performance micro-controllers' (HPCs) that are configurable to the requirements of specific applications has been inaugurated. The devices are based on a modular internal architecture, says manufacturer National Semiconductor: each member of the HPC range has the same core processor chip, but with a different combination of memory, onboard peripherals and I/O.

The core processor is a 16-bit CPU rated at 16 MHz, and has six working registers, a microinstruction ROM, a clock generator, a serial I/O bus, four 16-bit timer-counters, three capture registers, control logic and watchdog and reset circuitry. It also includes National's Microwire/Plus interface.

Internal data paths and arithmetic logic unit are 16 bit wide, and direct internal or external addressing through 64 kbyte of memory space allows

The HPC's emulator, Mole, includes built-in modem interface and PROM programmer

interfacing to external memory, peripherals or hosts.

The first member of the family to be released is the HPC16040, which includes 4 kbyte of ROM, 256 byte of RAM, 52 general-purpose I/O lines, four extra 16-bit timers and an onchip UART, as well as the core processor; this device is designed for 'applications

requiring efficient data communications', says National. Other combinations of ROM and RAM, I/O options and peripheral functions — e.g. UARTs, pulse-width timers, A/D converters, CRT controllers, local area network controllers and a 480-gate array — are scheduled for introduction later this year and beyond.

The HPC instruction set features a variety of single-byte multifunction instructions and nine addressing modes. All memory, I/O options, onboard peripherals and registers are memory mapped into the controller's address space, says National, allowing flexibility in the control of data.

Development support for HPCs includes the Mole (microcontroller online emulator) two-board set, which can be used standalone or in conjunction with a host system. In addition to emulating the HPC chip, Mole has a built-in modem interface and an onboard PROM programmer. (*National Semiconductor Corp., 2900 Semiconductor Drive, PO Box 58090, Santa Clara, CA 95052–578090, USA. Tel: (408) 733-2600. National Semiconductor, Industriestrasse 10, D-8080 Fürstenfeldbruck, FRG. Tel: (08141) 103486)* □

Filtering repeater extends LANs

Signals on Ethernet LANs can be transmitted beyond the nominal 2.5 km limit with EFE, a protocol independent filtering repeater from Logic Replacement Technology. The filter facility built into the repeater enables multiple, locally sited Ethernets to be logically linked together and to carry packet transmissions simultaneously, thereby increasing the usable bandwidth of the network. Individual segments of the network are fully secured against data packet intrusions from other segments, says LRT.

The repeater comprises two VMEbus-based Ethernet controller cards and a 68010 processor. Filtering and queueing mechanisms are built

Evaluation kits have been made available for the Astron IC cards made by Astar of Japan. The kit, designated AEK 001, allows the designer to develop interface techniques between his/her hardware and the IC card, says UK distributor Cumana. It includes 38 pin connectors — four with right-angle pins and four with straight pins — ten 16 kbyte Astron cards, six 32 kbyte cards and a programming adaptor to fit standard EPROM blowers. The Astron IC card is available with four memory types: ROM, one-shot PROM, E^2PROM and CMOS RAM. (Astar International Co. Ltd, 2/14/10 Denpa Building, Soto Handa, Chiyoda-ku, Tokyo 101, Japan. Cumana Ltd, The Pines Trading Estate, Broad Street, Guildford, Surrey GU3 3BH, UK. Tel: (0483) 503121)

into software. A system management function enables access permissions to be established and statistical information on the performance of the logical link to be displayed.

Protocol independence of the repeater allows data access and routing to be controlled by the absolute Ethernet addresses of the communicating workstations. Operation of the repeater is thus effectively transparent to users, enabling them to use the same commands between networks as for the local system. (*Logic Replacement Technology Ltd, 7 Arkwright Road, Reading, Berks RG2 0LU, UK. Tel: (0734) 751087*)

□

32-bit barrel shifter

A 32-bit CMOS barrel shifter and normalizer designed to replace external logic circuits in floating-point normalization, word pack/unpack and field extraction applications is being manufactured by US firm Logic Devices.

Designated the LSH32, the chip can eliminate the space and power needs of 32 SSI funnel shifter and multiplexer devices in designs using a single-clock 32-bit barrel shift, says the manufacturer. A power requirement of 60 mW is quoted for the LSH32, which is also claimed to give an order of magnitude speed increase in conventional 1 bit per cycle instructions.

The LSH32 has 32 data inputs which may be configured for any shift operation (fill or wrap mode). Operations are performed with a propagation delay of 42 ns (commercial versions) or 50 ns (military versions), says Logic Devices. Output from the device is multiplexed into 16-bit segments, and several devices can be cascaded for long word normalization. The device features an integral priority encoder with independent outputs for block floating-point operations.

Packaging of the LSH32 is in a ceramic 68-pin grid array or a plastic leaded chip carrier. (*Logic Devices

IBM PC develops for over 40 micros

An IBM-PC-based single-user development system which deals with over 40 different target microprocessors has been developed by Philips. The PMDS3 consists of a PC AT running Xenix, a hardware emulation subsystem called PIDS (Philips integration and debug station) and development software.

Separation of dedicated and universal hardware in the system allows realtime transparent emulation at clock rates of up to 10 MHz (16 MHz for the 68000 and 68010) with or without emulation memory. Universal hardware — up to two universal debug units, memory and trace facilities — is housed in the PC extension box. These components operate independently of the target processor, which is placed in a separate 'microprocessor adaptor box'. Emulation memories from 16 kbit static to 1 Mbit dynamic are available for testing software before the hardware is ready.

Speed of operation is a major feature of the PMDS3, says Philips. Tight coupling of the PIDS to the PC AT by an extension of the PC's own bus, via a parallel connection, results in speeds of about ten times those of PC-based emulators which use an RS232C serial link. Another feature is the ability to debug a program in the same high-level language as it was written in; PASCAL and C debugging are available currently, says Philips, with development work on PL/M in progress.

Cross software available for the PMDS3 includes cross compilers for 'virtually any' combination of target processors and the high-level languages C, PASCAL and PL/M as well as assembler. (*Philips Test and Measurement Instruments, Pye Unicam Ltd, York Street, Cambridge CB1 2PX, UK. Tel: (0223) 358866*) □

Inc., 628 East Evelyn Avenue, Sunnyvale, CA 94086-6459, USA. Tel: (408) 720-8630. UK distributor: Manhattan Skyline Ltd, Manhattan House, Bridge Road, Maidenhead, Berks SL6 8DB, UK. Tel: (0628) 75851)* □

product news

Graphics coprocessor 'has capabilities of a dedicated 32-bit engineering subsystem'

Graphics functions equivalent to those provided by dedicated 32-bit subsystems in engineering workstations can now be implemented in personal computers (PCs) with a single-chip graphics coprocessor introduced by Intel. Complex graphics routines can be performed on PCs using software, but Intel claims that for certain functions, such as line drawings, its 82786 graphics coprocessor operates up to 100 times faster than software methods.

Offloading pixel-intensive graphics operations from the CPU to the coprocessor speeds the throughput of a PC. 'The graphics coprocessor will do for graphics what numerical coprocessors did for floating-point arithmetic,' says Dave House, vice-president of Intel's Microcomputer Group. The coprocessor, which has a 16-bit architecture, can be interface to any 8-, 16-or 32-bit microprocessor, the company says.

The chip is intended for use particularly in office workstations and PCs, where it is predicted that graphics applications will gain a greater share of the office software market currently dominated by spreadsheet, database and word processing packages.

According to Intel, the coprocessor requires little support logic and integrates more functions on chip than similar coprocessors. On chip are two processors — one for graphics processing operations and the other for display — that operate concurrently, a bus interface unit and a dynamic RAM controller. The chip has access to 4 Mbyte of memory divided between external system memory and 82786-supported graphics memory.

This volume of memory is necessary to support bit maps, which is how the coprocessor handles graphics and text. Bit maps are rectangular drawing areas comprising a number of pixels which serve as the canvas for graphics operations, such as line drawing, colour filling or polygon creation.

A unique facility of the coprocessor, says Intel, is the ability to perform instantaneous windowing.

As graphics for each application can be drawn into separate regions of memory, each can be displayed instantly by relaying the data to the screen. The on-chip graphics processor can manipulate individual bit maps independently of the display and, using an internal shift register, the display processor can assemble several windows on the screen from different bit maps in memory. The host CPU is required simply to point to instruction lists in memory rather than create lists. In this way a multitasking PC fitted with the coprocessor can alter the screen display instantly for scrolling, panning and new windows without having to continually redraw the contents from memory.

The display supported by the coprocessor has 640 × 480 × 8 pixel resolution with standard dynamic RAMs, providing up to 256 colours simultaneously. Performance can be improved with video dynamic RAMs. The chip can create eight horizontal windows and an unlimited number of vertical windows.

Industry graphics standards such as the Computer Graphics Interface (CGI) and applications standards such as CGA are supported on the chip, which has an instruction set that closely follows these ANSI standards. This has been done to give users access to existing applications software based on the standards, and provides compatibility with software produced by many of the major vendors. Of these vendors, Ashton-Tate, Digital Research, Lotus and Microsoft, among others, are said to have committed support to the 82786 and are currently sampling the chip to work on applications software, board products and development tools.

Sample quantities of the coprocessor are also available generally, and volume production is scheduled to begin by the end of 1986. (*Intel Corp., 3065 Bowers Avenue, Santa Clara, CA 95051, USA. Intel Corp. (UK) Ltd, Pipers Way, Swindon SN3 1RJ, UK. Tel: (0793) 696020*)

□

E²PROM cells

'Supercells' which allow nonvolatile memory arrays to be easily added to integrated circuits have been made by NCR. Introduced as part of NCR's standard cell library, the product is a CMOS E²PROM device which can be added to a standard cell with just a single additional mask step, bringing remote programmability to application-specific integrated circuits (ASICs).

Implementation and features of the modular E²PROM supercell are identical to those of standard E²PROM devices, says the manufacturer; the supercell consists of a programming voltage generator and control block and a modular E²PROM array block.

Rather than fabricating the E²PROM capacitor between two layers of polysilicon, using perhaps three or more masking steps, NCR fabricates it using a single additional layer of silicon, reducing manufacturing costs and also reducing programming voltage to 15 V.

The device features include a direct write operation, fully synchronous static operation and a three-line control architecture (write enable, chip select and output enable).

The E²PROM supercell is 'essentially the same' as NCR's ROM, RAM and other supercells, says the firm, and is supported on engineering workstations compatible with the NCR computer-aided design system. (*NCR, 11010 Torreyana Road, San Diego, CA 92121, USA. Tel: (408) 452-1020. NCR Ltd, 206 Marylebone Road, London NW1 6LY, UK. Tel: 01–725 8248*)

□

Errata

Microprocessors Microsyst. Vol 10 No 4 (May 1986) p 242, under 'Software — CGEN': 'BASIC-to-DOS conversion package' should read 'BASIC-to-C conversion package'.

STEbus development system marks BT's micros dehut

An STEbus development system and a set of related board-level products have been launched by British Telecom (BT). The Martello development system, which represents the UK telecommunications company's first venture into commercial computing systems, is described by BT as the first 'completely manufacturer independent' system of its type, due to its use of the industry standard STEbus structure.

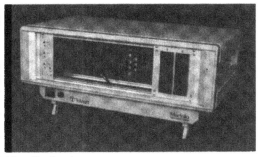
Martello development system

The Martello system comprises a software development environment called Martello FORTH, configured in ROM and floppy disc. Hardware consists of two board-level products: a customer-specified CPU module, which may be the Martello 8085 CPU board; and the Martello disc controller installed in a disc subsystem which provides two 1 Mbyte 3.5 in floppy disc drives.

The complete system is housed in a custom designed BICC-Vero Diplomat enclosure and includes a 19 in (48 cm) KM6 3U height card frame and a 10-slot STEbus backplane.

The 8085 CPU card features 4 byte wide memory sites which may be configured for up to 32 kbyte of ROM, static RAM and pseudostatic RAM. It contains a UART, an RS232C interface, two 8-bit parallel I/O ports, five counter-timers, eight-level priority interrupt controller and high-level monitor. All peripheral devices are addressed in isolated I/O with the 8085 allowing access to 256 I/O addresses.

A flexible address decoding mechanism is employed. When used as part of an STE system, the card acts as a master with or without onboard arbitration, depending on the position of the link. It also provides SYSSCLK, TFRERR (bus time out) and SYSRST system functions.

The floppy disc controller acts as a slave and is addressed in the I/O space on any 08H boundary between 0H and FFFH. A WD 1772 controller is used, which allows all normal disc operations, says BT. Link fields are provided, so that the DATRQ and INTEQ signals from the controller chip can be allocated to ATNRQ0* or ATNRQ1*.

The Martello development system and its associated boards are being distributed worldwide by Dean Microsystems. (*British Telecom Research Laboratories, Martlesham Heath, Ipswich IP5 7RE, UK. Tel: (0473) 642933. Dean Microsystems Ltd, 7 Horseshoe Park, Pangbourne, Berks RG8 7JW, UK. Tel: (07357) 5155*) □

CMOS cell library is jointly launched

A family of CMOS standard cell functions known as SystemCell has been jointly developed and introduced by Texas Instruments (TI) and Philips–Signetics.

The initial release of the SystemCell library contains nearly 300 cell types including SSI, MSI and I/O integrated functions. The common library includes all the cell functions currently available from TI and Philips–Signetics, says the latter's UK subsidiary Mullard, plus a number of new cell types. The chips are fabricated in 2 μm double-layer metal CMOS with an effective gate length of 1.6 μm.

SystemCell libraries can be installed on the customers' own engineering workstations, or the chips can be designed at any of 25 centres worldwide. The two companies intend to continue their joint development programme with the release of new and more complex functions for the SystemCell library. (*Texas Instruments Inc., PO Box 1444, Houston, TX 77001, USA. Philips Electrologica BV, PO Box 245, Oude Apeldoornseweg 41, Apeldoorn, The Netherlands. Mullard Ltd, Mullard House, Torrington Place, London WC1E 7HD, UK. Tel: 01-580 6633*) □

Compact disc ROM gains SCSI interface

Philips has introduced a small computer systems interface (SCSI) that enables its compact disc (CD) ROM to be interfaced to micros other than the IBM PC. Until now only users of PCs and Q-bus compatibles have been able to use the CD drive through a controller installed inside the PC. The SCSI controller is integrated into the drive itself.

By providing double buffering on the controller, the SCSI is claimed to give a faster stream of data than was previously possible. A drive fitted with the SCSI — such a drive is called the CM-110 — has a block transfer rate of 500 kbyte s^{-1}. Track-to-track positioning time is less than 1 ms, says the manufacturer, and built-in error correction assures a bit-error rate of the order of 1 in 10^{15}.

CD ROMs, which each have a capacity of 600 Mbyte, are already having an impact in electronic publishing, database storage and software distribution, says Philips. The company hopes that the SCSI drive will open the way for OEMs and systems integrators to address the non-IBM-PC market with optical discs. (*Philips, PO Box 523, 5600 AM Eindhoven, The Netherlands. Tel: (040) 757061*) □

products in brief

Name	Description	Manufacturer/designer	Distributor/contact
A/D converters			
AD7572	12-bit CMOS ADC with 'guaranteed' 5 µs conversion time. Power consumption is 215 mW, data address time 70 ns (max.) and bus relinquish time 40 ns (max.). Packaging: 24-pin DIP or 28-pin LCC	Analog Devices Ltd, Central Avenue, East Molesey, Surrey KT8 0SN, UK. Tel: 01-941 0466	Pronto Electronic Systems Ltd, City Gate House, 399–425 Eastern Avenue, Gants Hill, Ilford, Essex IG2 6LR, UK. Tel: 01-554 6222
MC6108	8-bit A/D converter with conversion time down to 1.8 µs, allowing direct connection to a microprocessor bus. Power supply requirement is +5 V and − 5.2 V and dissipation is 415 mW (max.). Includes 2.5 V internal reference. Packaging: 28-pin plastic DIP, pin compatible with the Am6108	Motorola Inc., 3501 Ed Bluestein Blvd, Austin, TX 78721, USA	Motorola Ltd, 88 Tanners Drive, Blakelands, Milton Keynes MK14 5BP, UK. Tel: (0908) 614614
D/A converters			
HS9378	16-bit DAC with dual storage registers, internal reference and an output amplifier, designed for use with 8-bit or 16-bit microprocessors	Hybrid Systems Corp., 22 Linnell Circle, Billerica, MA 01821, USA: Tel: (617) 667-8700	Hybrid Systems UK Ltd, 333 London Road, Camberley, Surrey GU15 3HQ, UK. Tel: (0276) 28128
Development systems			
HP64000	Revised version of the 64000 logic development system, described as giving advantages of cost and flexibility. The new system is designed to integrate with other workstation-based CAE/CAD solutions; network to certain microcomputers; provide in-circuit emulators, languages and analysis tools for 8-, 16- and 32-bit microprocessors; and integrate with all HP software engineering tools	Hewlett-Packard Ltd, Miller House, The Ring, Bracknell, Berks RG12 1XN, UK. Tel: (0344) 424898	Literature Section, Hewlett-Packard Ltd, Eskdale Road, Winnersh Triangle, Wokingham, Berks RG11 5DZ, UK. Tel: (0734) 696622
Digital signal processors			
ADSP-2100	Single-chip 16-bit DSP with a 24-bit address bus. Processor cycle time is quoted as 125 ns; all instructions are executed in a single cycle	Analog Devices, Central Avenue, East Molesey, Surrey KT8 0SN, UK. Tel: 01-941 0466	
PCB5010, PCB5011	CMOS single-chip DSPs, the first members of Mullard's SP50 family, featuring two 16-bit data buses, a two-operand multiply/accumulate unit and a two-operand ALU. 5010 has on-chip ROM and RAM; 5011 uses on-chip ROM and external memory	Mullard Ltd, Mullard House, Torrington Place, London WC1E 7HD, UK. Tel: 01-580 6633	

Section headings in this issue's 'Products in brief' are

A/D converters	**EPROMs**	**Microprocessors**	**Programmable arrays**
D/A converters	**Language software**	**Microprogram sequencers**	**PROMs**
Development systems	**Microcomputers**	**Operating systems**	**Programming modules**
Digital signal processors	**Microcontrollers**	**Processor boards**	**RAMs**

Name	Description	Manufacturer/designer	Distributor/contact
TMS320C25	Pin-compatible CMOS version of the TMS32020, giving faster instruction cycle time and additional hardware and software features. Instructions and data words are 16 bit and the ALU and accumulator are 32 bit. 16 input and 16 output channels are included. Internal clock rate is 32 MHz or 40 MHz. Packaging: 68-pin plastic LCC	Texas Instruments Inc., PO Box 1444, Houston, TX 77001, USA	Texas Instruments Ltd, Manton Lane, Bedford MK41 7PA, UK. Tel: (0234) 63211
Wordslice family: ADSP-1401; -1410; -1101; -1110A; -3210; and -3220	1.5 µm CMOS DSP range comprising (respectively): a program sequencer; address generator; integer ALU; single-port multiplier/accumulator; floating-point multiplier; and floating-point ALU	Analog Devices, Central Avenue, East Molesey, Surrey KT8 0SN, UK. Tel: 01-941 1066	

EPROMs

Name	Description	Manufacturer/designer	Distributor/contact
2864A	64 kbit E^{2}PROM with a read access time of 200 ns. Has a page-mode write capability, which allows programming of up to 16 byte in a single write cycle without external hardware. Pin 1 is unconnected to provide an upgrade capability for higher-density devices. Supplied in a standard 28-pin ceramic DIP. Military versions will be added to the range in the near future	Intel Corp, 3065 Bowers Avenue, Santa Clara, CA 95051, USA.	Intel Corp (UK) Ltd, Pipers Way, Swindon, Wilts SN3 1RJ, UK. Tel: (0793) 696006
M5L 27512K	64k × 8 bit EPROM with access times down to 200 ns. Power consumption is 100 mA (max.) when active and 40 mA (max.) on standby. Programming voltage is 12.5 V. Packaging: 28-pin DIP	Mitsubishi Electric Corp., 6–3 Marunouchi, 2-chome Chiyoda-ku, Tokyo 100, Japan	Mitsubishi Electric (UK) Ltd, Hertford Place, Denham Way, Maple Cross, Rickmansworth, Herts WD3 2BJ, UK. Tel: (0923) 770000
M9306	16 × 16 bit E^{2}PROM with a clock frequency of 500 kHz. Operating current is 1.5 mA and minimum erase/write pulse width is 5 ms	SGS-ATES Componenti Elett-ronici SpA, Stradale Primosole 50, 95121 Catania, Sicily, Italy. Tel: (3995) 599 111	SGS Systems Division, Planar House, Walton Street, Aylesbury, Bucks, UK. Tel: (0296) 5977
TMM27512D	65k × 8 bit NMOS EPROM with access time of 200 ns. Programming voltage is 12 V; supply requirement is 5 V ± 5% or ± 10%. Packaging: 28-pin ceramic DIP, pin compatible with i27512 devices	Toshiba, 1-chome Uchisaiwai-cho, Chiyoda-ku, Tokyo, Japan	Toshiba UK Ltd, Toshiba House, Frimley Road, Camberley, Surrey, UK. Tel: (0276) 62222

Language software

Name	Description	Manufacturer/designer	Distributor/contact
Assembler II for 68020	68020 assembler running on VAX and MicroVAX systems. All executable instructions and addressing modes are identical to Motorola's assembly syntax, and the assembler supports all data storage directives including real number constants and 32-bit expressions	BSO Inc., 128 Technology Center, Waltham, MA 02254-9164, USA. Tel: (617) 894-7800	BSO UK, 16 Fernhill Road, Farnborough, Hants GU14 9RX, UK. Tel: (0252) 510014

products in brief

Name	Description	Manufacturer/designer	Distributor/contact
Optim-2	c compiler optimizer, designed to reduce the size and increase the speed of programs written in c. Principal areas of optimization are: removal of loop invariant computations from loops; elimination of common subexpressions; register allocation; elimination of copies; elimination of redundant stores and fetches; simplification of loop expressions; and machine-specific optimizations	Root Computers Ltd, Saunderson House, Hayne Street, London EC1A 9HH, UK. Tel: 01-726 6501	
PL/M-51	PL/M compiler for the 8051 micro-computer running on VAX and MicroVAX systems under VMS or Ultrix. Speed on these systems is around 5000 lines of PL/M code per minute; the compiler can also run more slowly on Philips development systems	Philips Electrologica Bv, PO Box 245, Oude Apeldoornseweg 41, Apeldoorn, The Netherlands	Philips Test & Measurement Instruments, Pye Unicam Ltd, York Street, Cambridge CB1 2PX, UK. Tel: (0223) 358866
Whitesmiths c version 3.0	Revised version 3.0 c compiler for the 8086, 80186 and 80286. Enhancements include the ability to read high-level source code, assembler source code and generated codes on the same listing, and source-level interactive debugging with breakpoints and variable display	Whitesmiths Inc., 97 Lowell Road, Concorde, MA 01742, USA. Tel: (617) 369-8499	Real Time Systems Ltd, PO Box 70, Viking House, Nelson Street, Douglas, Isle of Man, UK. Tel: (0624) 26021

Microcomputers

Name	Description	Manufacturer/designer	Distributor/contact
HVME-SB286	VMEbus single-board computer featuring the 80286 CPU running at 8 MHz (part of the Bus-Tech range). Includes 1 Mbyte of dual-ported DRAM, optional 80287 numeric coprocessor, built-in bus arbiter and interrupt, and two serial and two parallel I/O ports. 80286/287 line assembler–disassembler is provided	High Technology Electronics Ltd, 303–305 Portswood Road, Southampton SO2 1LD, UK. Tel: (0703) 581555	
ICM-3232	Second member of the ICM (integrated computer module) product range (see *Microprocessors Microsyst.* Vol 9 No 8, page 415), based on a 32032 CPU with 2 Mbyte of memory and a separate I/O processor. Basic module is a single Euro-card, expandable by RAM cards (up to 14 Mbyte). The Sigma H124N 'tower' enclosure is available to house either the 3232 or the previously launched 3216 ICM	National Semiconductor Corp., 2900 Semiconductor Drive, PO Box 58090, Santa Clara, CA 95052-578090, USA. Tel: (408) 733-2600	National Semiconductor, Industriestrasse 10, D-8080 Fürstenfeldbruck, FRG. Tel: (08141) 103486
SVME 109	68000-based VME-compatible single-board computer designed as an intelligent communications processor. Has four serial I/O channels, 128 kbyte or 512 kbyte of dynamic RAM, an interrupt handler and system controller functions. I/O is based on two 68564 controllers with programmable data rates up to 19.2 kbit s^{-1} (asynchronous) and 500 kbit s^{-1} (synchronous)	DY-4, 888 Lady Ellen Place, Ottawa, Ontario, Canada. Tel: (613) 728 3711	Dage (GB) Ltd, Eurosem Division, Rabans Lane, Aylesbury, Bucks HP19 3RG, UK. Tel: (0296) 33200

Name	Description	Manufacturer/designer	Distributor/contact
Systems 121, 1131	VMEbus systems designed for OEMs and software developers, based on the 68010 (121) or the 68020 (1131), which run under the system V/68 operating system. Systems include Winchester and floppy disc storage, user DRAM, system controller, RS232 ports and expansion slots for up to five (121) or up to six (1131) VMEbus modules	Motorola Inc., 3501 Ed Bluestein Blvd, Austin, TX 78721, USA	Motorola Ltd, 88 Tanners Drive, Blakelands, Milton Keynes MK14 5BP, UK. Tel: (0908) 614614
VMElab	Workstation designed for high-level teaching environments, based on the PG2010 VMEbus single-board computer with an 8 MHz 68000 CPU and 20 kbyte of SRAM. Includes five-slot backplane and rack, power supply, pSOS operating system and pROBE debugger	Unit-C Ltd, Dominion Way, West Broadwater, Worthing, Sussex BN14 8NT, UK. Tel: (0903) 205233	

Microcontrollers

WD33C92, WD33C93	CMOS interface controller for the SCSI bus, implementing arbitration, disconnect, reconnect, parity and synchronized data transfers. Features an 8-bit data bus, multifunction commands and synchronous data transfer at up to 4 Mbyte s^{-1}. WD33C93 includes additional 48 mA drivers	Western Digital Corp., 2445 McCabe Way, Irvine, CA 92714, USA	Pronto Electronic Systems Ltd, City Gate House, 399-425 Eastern Avenue, Gants Hill, Ilford, Essex IG2 6LR, UK. Tel: 01-554 6222

Microprocessors

Am29C01; Am29C101	CMOS plug-in replacement for the Am2901 4-bit bipolar microprocessor slice (29C01); and 16-bit CMOS microprocessor slice combining the functions of four 2901 4-bit slice microprocessors and a 2902 carry look-ahead device onto a single chip (29C101)	Advanced Micro Devices Inc., 901 Thompson Place, Sunnyvale, CA 94086, USA	Advanced Micro Devices (UK) Ltd, AMD House, Goldsworth Road, Woking, Surrey GU21 1JT, UK. Tel: (04862) 22121
MC68020	20 MHz version of Motorola's 32-bit CPU now available in sample quantities. Full production is scheduled for third quarter 1986	Motorola Inc., 3501 Ed Bluestein Blvd, Austin, TX 78721, USA	Motorola Ltd, 88 Tanners Drive, Blakelands, Milton Keynes MK14 5BP, UK. Tel: (0908) 614614

From left: the Unit-C VMElab educational workstation; the Am29C101 16-bit microprocessor slice from AMD; and HTE's SB286 VMEbus processor board

products in brief

Name	Description	Manufacturer/designer	Distributor/contact
Microprogram sequencers			
Am29331	16-bit microprogram sequencer combining 16 address bits, realtime interrupt facilities, two branch or input address ports and a 33-level deep stack. System cycle time is quoted as 80 ns when used with other members of the Am29300 bipolar microprocessor family	Advanced Micro Devices Inc., 901 Thompson Place, Sunnyvale, CA 94086, USA	Advanced Micro Devices (UK) Ltd, AMD House, Goldsworth Road, Woking, Surrey GU21 1JT, UK. Tel: (04862) 22121
Operating systems			
STD-DOS prototyping and OEM systems	Two products for integrating ROM-based MS-DOS 3.1 into a solid-state disc system for the STD bus. Development, testing and debugging are carried out on an IBM PC or compatible. Prototyping system includes an 8088 CPU card, memory cards, cage and card extender; OEM system provides just cards and software	Pro-Log Corp., 2411 Garden Road, Monterey, CA 93940, USA. Tel: (408) 372-4593	Technitron, Doman Road, Camberley, Surrey GU15 3DH, UK. Tel: (0276) 26517
Processor boards			
GesMPU-4A	G64-bus Eurocard with an 8 MHz 68000 CPU, being promoted as being low in price. Includes paging lines to allow up to 512 kbyte memory addressing. Contains a programmable RS232 serial port, three 16-bit timers and sockets for up to 16 kbyte of SRAM and 128-kbyte of EPROM. Runs under OS-9 and CP/M-68K	Gespac Inc., 100 West Hoover Avenue, Suite 11, Mesa, AZ 85202, USA. Tel: (602) 962-5559	Pronto Electronic Systems Ltd, City Gate House, 399-425 Eastern Avenue, Gants Hill, Ilford, Essex IG2 6LR, UK. Tel: 01-554 6222
PME 68-15	VMEbus CPU board with a cache algorithm to minimize wait states of the 68000 or 68010 processors. Memory management unit implements Sun-type architecture, giving a 50 ns propagation delay for address translation. Board includes console port and realtime clock, and was designed to run under Unix	Plessey Microsystems Ltd, Water Lane, Towcester, Northants NN12 7JN, UK. Tel: (0327) 50312	Dean Microsystems Ltd, 7 Horseshoe Park, Pangbourne, Berks RG8 7JW, UK. Tel: (07357) 5155

 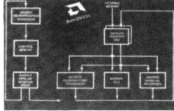 

From left: Plessey's PM 68-15 VMEbus 68000/010 board; the Am29331 16-bit microprogram sequencer, part of AMD's 29300 32-bit MPU family; and the Arcom SC88T STE board with 80188 processor

Name	Description	Manufacturer/designer	Distributor/contact
SC88T	8 MHz 80188-based STEbus board with 16 kbyte SRAM, 128 kbit EPROM sockets and two RS232C channels with handshaking. An EPROM monitor is available for evaluation, and applications can be developed in c using either an 80188-based STE system (DOS, MS-DOS or CP/M Plus) or an IBM PC	Arcom Control Systems Ltd, Unit 8, Clifton Road, Cambridge CB1 4WH, UK. Tel: (0223) 242224	
TP20	Three-board sets in VMEbus or Multibus I formats. Each set comprises: a 68020 CPU card (12.5 or 16 MHz) with 2 Mbyte of memory and Motorola's PMMU memory management unit; a 4 Mbyte memory card; and a 16-user 68010 intelligent I/O card. Runs under Virtual Unix V.2	Tadpole Technology plc, 151 Cambridge Science Park, Milton Road, Cambridge CB4 4GG, UK. Tel: (0223) 861112	

Programmable arrays

Name	Description	Manufacturer/designer	Distributor/contact
SCL family	Standard cell family comprising a library of fixed-height cells and functional blocks in 2 µm CMOS. The fixed-height cells include some 150 SSI and MSI logic functions and CMOS- and TTL-compatible I/O functions encompassing the macro library of the SCX gate array family. The functional blocks available are dual-port RAMs, the 16450 UART and high-current output drivers	National Semiconductor Corp., 2900 Semiconductor Drive, PO Box 58090, Santa Clara, CA 95052-578090, USA. Tel: (408) 733-2600	National Semiconductor, Industriestrasse 10, D-8080 Furstenfeldbruck, FRG. Tel: (08141) 103486
XC2064	General-purpose CMOS ICs consisting of an 8 × 8 array of logic cells with a string of 58 I/O cells around them. Configuration circuitry allows complete reconfiguration within the user's system. Logic cell storage elements can be programmed as either a transparent latch or an edge-triggered flipflop. Another feature is controllable I/O architecture. The XACT logic array development system is available, running on an IBM PC XT	Xilinx, 2069 East Hamilton Avenue, San Jose, CA 95125, USA	Ambar Cascom Ltd, Rabans Close, Aylesbury, Bucks HP19 3RS, UK. Tel: (0296) 34141

PROMs

Name	Description	Manufacturer/designer	Distributor/contact
CY7C281/2	1k × 8 bit CMOS PROMs with 30 ns access time and quoted 100% programming yield. V_{cc} tolerance specified as 10%. Packaging: 24-pin DIPs (normal temp.) and LCCs (military temp. range)	Cypress Semiconductor Corp., 3910 North 1st Street, San Jose, CA 95134, USA. Tel: (408) 943-2600	Advanced Technology Devices, 466-478 Cranbrook Road, Gants Hill, Ilford, Essex IG2 6LE, UK. Tel: 01-554 5700
DM87SR183	8 kbit (1k × 8 bit) registered PROM with asynchronous initialize. Set-up time is 40 ns maximum. Clock-to-output time is 25 ns maximum. Fabricated in Schottky process with titanium-tungsten fuses.	National Semiconductor, Industriestrasse 10, D-8080 Fürstenfeldbruck, FRG. Tel: (08141) 103376	

products in brief

Name	Description	Manufacturer/designer	Distributor/contact
MB7111/2L	Bipolar, low-power 256 kbit Schottky PROM, suitable for applications in car electronic ignition circuits says the manufacturer. Power supply current is 40 mA max from a 5 V source. Organized as 32k × 8 bit, the PROM has an address access time of 50 ns maximum	Fujitsu Ltd, 6–1 Marunouchi 2-chome, Chiyoda-ku, Tokyo 100, Japan	Fujitsu Mikroelektronik, Hargrave House, Belmont Road, Maidenhead, Berks SL6 6NE, UK. Tel: (0628) 76100

Programming modules

P-Stack	PROM and EPROM programming stack for the Universe 1000 programming system, allowing a selection of pin configurations and eliminating all external cabling	Elan Digital Systems Ltd, 16–20 Kelvin Way, Crawley, West Sussex RH10 2TS, UK. Tel: (0293) 510448	
Z-3000	Gang programmer for EPROMs, E²PROMs and microcomputers from Intel and Motorola. Programming boards contain thirty-two 24- or 23-pin programming sockets. A 'quick change' programming facility permits sockets of one board to be unloaded and reloaded while another board is programming. Through these facilities, the board is claimed to be up to four times faster than similar programmers	Sunrise Electronics Inc, 524 South Vermont Avenue, Glendora, CA 91740, USA. Tel: (213) 914-1926	Petratec Ltd, Glanty House, The Causeway, Egham, Surrey, UK. Tel: (0784) 36254

RAMs

IMS 2800 family	256 kbit CMOS dynamic RAMs with access times down to 60 ns	Inmos International plc, Whitefriars, Lewins Mead, Bristol BS1 2NP, UK. Tel: (0272) 290861	
STC 2018	2048 × 8 bit static RAM in NMOS, with access times of 35 ns, 45 ns, 55 ns or 70 ns. Typical power dissipation is 350 mW (active) and 40 mW (standby). Packaging: 24-pin slim, plastic or ceramic DIP; 32-bit ceramic LCC	STC Semiconductors, Maidstone Road, Foots Cray, Sidcup, Kent CA14 5HT, UK. Tel: 01–300 3333	Norbain Technology Ltd, Norbain House, Boulton Road, Reading, Berks RG2 0LT, UK. Tel: (0734) 866766

Sunrise Electronics Z-3000 gang programmer (left); and the P-stack fitted to Elan's Universe 1000 programmer (right)

'Flood' of 32-bit boards is expected

Board-level computers represent a market which is alive and growing, though at a slower rate than had once been envisaged. This is the conclusion of a Dataquest TCSIS report, *Board computers.*

The board computer is playing an increasingly important role in technical applications — particularly industrial and laboratory automation and realtime and medical applications — by replacing older minicomputers, says Dataquest. In this respect the market has been helped by US radio-frequency emission legislation, which has restricted the sale of many 'traditional' minicomputers.

The worldwide board computer industry grew (in terms of factory revenues) by 11% from 1984 to 1985, says Dataquest, reaching a total value of $574M. This growth rate is significantly lower than the computer industry's 'normal' growth rate of 20–25%; board-level growth has been slowed by a reduction in prices by many vendors in response to increased competition.

A breakdown of the 1985 bus market, again in terms of factory revenues, shows Intel's Multibus structures to be leading the field with 39% of the market. The Digital Equipment (DEC) Q-bus remains in second place with 37%, while Motorola's VMEbus has gained ground significantly from its 1984 position to reach a third placed 11%.

Dataquest expects 1986 to see a peak in the revenues of the 8-bit board market segment, as 16-bit products take over as the mainstream of the market. A flood of 32-bit products, based particularly on the 68020 and 80386, is also forecast — an annual growth rate of over 120% is predicted up to 1990.

This growth rate is based on a 1985 unit shipment volume of only around 1000 32-bit boards, leaving the competing 32-bit bus architectures Multibus II and VMEbus almost completely devoid of CPU board shipments last year. The survey expects both of these buses to survive their initial struggle, however.

Little improvement is forecast for the fortunes of the other high-speed 32-bit buses such as Nubus, Futurebus and Fastbus. These still lack significant vendor support, says Dataquest, and will continue to do so as the industry concentrates on relatively low-speed applications. DEC's Q-bus replacement, the 32-bit VAX backplane interconnect (VAXBI), is unlikely to make any impact on the industry until 1987; the bus is currently available only on expensive ($130k or more) computer systems, and its structure is being kept a secret by the manufacturer.

The report forecasts a total worldwide shipment for board computers of 1.2M units in 1986, rising to 2.5M by 1990. An applications breakdown (in terms of factory revenues) for 1990 shows the market divided into 35% industrial automation, 20% realtime data acquisition and control, 16% communications, 9% laboratory automation, 8% medical applications and 12% others. (*Dataquest Inc., 1290 Ridder Park Drive, San Jose, CA 95131-2398, USA. Tel: (408) 971-9000*)   □

European research networks link up

A West European consortium of national research networks, to be known as RARE (*Réseaux Associés pour la Recherche Européene*), has been set up in The Netherlands. This will represent organizations such as the Dutch research network Surfnet, the UK's Janet (joint academic network) and DFN (*Deutsche Forschungsnetz*) in the FRG.

The objective of RARE is to establish 'a European infrastructure for the benefit of communication between scientists and research workers within Europe, as well as between Europe and other parts of the world'. This infrastructure is intended to give access to all the important computer centres in Europe and to support international scientific databases.

The ongoing activities of RARE, organized through technical working groups, are stated as: identification of protocols and selection of implementation options; selection of data transmission facilities; directory services, and information services.

The organization has declared its support for the principles of OSI (open systems interconnection), but also intends to collaborate with the European Commission and other bodies in the establishment of functional standards to achieve harmonization and internetworking of networks. It is already helping to develop the specification of the Cosine (cooperation for open systems interconnection networking in Europe) project.

The address of RARE for correspondence is: *RARE Secretariat, c/o JMA, de Boelelaan 873, 1082 RW Amsterdam, The Netherlands. Tel: (31) 20 462243.*   □

Semiconductor growth

Annual European semiconductor sales of nearly $13 000M — up from a 1985 level of $4900M, using a constant dollar rate — are predicted in a recent Frost & Sullivan report, *Semiconductor market in Europe.* The 1985 markets for semiconductors in integrated circuits ($3500M) and in discrete devices ($1400M) are expected to grow at the rates of 20% a year and 9.7% a year respectively up to 1991.

The highest rate of growth will be in security applications with an annual increase of 25%, according to the report. Another rapid growth area will be automotive applications, e.g. in electronic ignition, antiskid braking and display systems; this market is set to grow by 23% a year.

On a country-by-country basis, the report expects the FRG to have 'by far the best' growth prospects. The FRG already represents more than a quarter of the European market in both ICs and discrete devices — some DM 2400M and DM 913M respectively in 1985. Of European suppliers, Philips leads Texas Instruments in terms of sales, with Motorola and Siemens in third and fourth places; together these four companies account for more than half the European market. (*Frost & Sullivan Ltd, 104–112 Marylebone Lane, London W1M 5FU, UK. Tel: 01-935 3190*)   □

___

Burroughs and Sperry merge

Following several failed attempts and improved offers, Burroughs has persuaded Sperry to accept an acquisition proposal under which the former buys 31M of the latter's shares for $76.50 each. The two companies will now be merged, resulting in the second largest computer company in the world in terms of revenue — smaller than IBM but ahead of Digital Equipment (DEC). But the independence of Sperry and Burroughs products will be maintained 'in perpetuity', says Michael Blumenthal, chairman of the new joint corporation.

Unix penetrates UK

The Unix operating system has already achieved 'a significant market presence' in the UK and is likely to represent over 25% of the UK market within five years, says a report carried out by Alliance Marketing on behalf of UK firm SyFA Data Systems. A sur-vey of 4000 organizations within the UK, which yielded an 18% reply rate, showed Concurrent DOS to have the second highest growth rate, with PC-DOS, MS-DOS and CP/M on the decline.

Exhibiting the fifth generation

Fifth-generation computers will be among the topics covered at the 1988 British Electronics Week. The organizers of the show, Evan Steadman, recognize that it will be some time before commercial fifth-generation products will be available in quantity and variety, but nonetheless hopes to have a 'beneficial, though not large-scale' presentation ready by April 1988, the time of the show.

TI supports IBM Token Ring

Texas Instruments is to move to volume production of boards for IBM's Token Ring local area network based on the TMS380 chip set. The boards, which include a 380 chip set and necessary logic devices, will enable 8- and 16-bit communication with IBM-compatible PCs and peripherals, says the manufacturer. An IBM-compatible software interface, Net-Bios, is also being produced; the IBM standard hardware and software is part of a portfolio of products aimed at covering the whole of the token ring market, says TI.

Intel-INI MAP link

Intel has gained exclusive marketing rights for a MAP (manufacturing automation protocol) compatible token bus controller, broadband modems and Multibus I boards from US firm Industrial Networking Inc. (INI). The two companies have also initiated a joint development program for token bus devices. Full conformance testing and validation to ensure interoperability with other vendors' products will be implemented, says Intel.

Date	Title	Contact	Place	Other details

1986

7–12 September	Industrial Digital Control Systems	Institution of Electrical Engineers, Savoy Place, London WC2R 0BL, UK. Tel: 01-240 1871	Somerville College, Oxford, UK	IEE 'vacation school' covering digital signals in simple control systems, microprocessor control systems, adaptive and selftuning control, computer-aided control systems design, problems of commissioning computer control systems etc
8–11 September	ESSDERC '86	Clive Jones, Institute of Physics, 47 Belgrave Square, London SW1X 8QX, UK. Tel: 01-235 6111	University of Cambridge, UK	16th European solid-state device research conference organized by the Institute of Physics and cosponsored by IEE, IEEE, IERE and the European Physical Society. Coverage includes CMOS, silicon bipolar device modelling, process modelling, thin oxide metallization, defects, submicron lithography, solid-state sensors
8–11 September	International Test Conference (ITC 1986)	ITC, Millbrook Plaza, Suite 104D, PO Box 264, Mount Freedom, NJ 07970, USA. Tel: (201) 895-5260	Sheraton Hotel, Washington, DC, USA	Tutorials, workshops and user group meetings on IC testing. Sponsored by the IEEE Computer Society
9–13 September	Fabritec 86	Secretariat Fabritec 86, c/o Swiss Industries Fair, Postfach, CH-4021 Basel, Switzerland. Tel: (061) 26 20 20	Swiss Industries Fair, Basel, Switzerland	Second international trade fair for fabrication installations in electronics
10–12 September	Software Engineering 86	British Computer Society, 13 Mansfield Street, London W1M 0BP, UK. Tel: 01-637 0471	University of Southampton, UK	Cosponsored by the BCS and IEE
14–19 September	Semi-custom IC design and VLSI	Institution of Electrical Engineers, Savoy Place, London WC2R 0BL, UK. Tel: 01-240 1871	University of York, UK	Fifth IEE 'vacation school' to introduce the various types of semicustom ICs that are available and instruct in logic design, system architecture and partitioning, use of CAD tools, hardware description languages and testing
15–18 September	Euromicro 86	Mrs E C Snippe-Marlisa, TH Twente, PO Box 217, Dept INF, Room A306, 7500 AE Enschede, The Netherlands	Venice, Italy	Twelfth annual conference of micro-processing and microprogramming
15–20 September	Intercomm '86	Cahners Exhibitions Ltd, Chatsworth House, 59 London Road, Twickenham TW1 3SZ, UK	Beijing, China	International computer and communication congress/exposition for science and technology
21–26 September	Software Engineering for Microprocessor Systems	Institution of Electrical Engineers, Savoy Place, London WC2R 0BL, UK. Tel: 01-240 1871	City University, London, UK	Fourth IEE 'vacation school' on software engineering for those with an electronics/hardware or assembly language background
22–25 September	EUUG Fall '86 Conference	European Unix Systems User Group, Owles Hall, Buntingford, Herts SG9 9PL, UK. Tel: (0763) 73039	Manchester, UK	Technical workshop on distributed Unix systems
23–24 September	Customized ICs	Professor R W Hartenstein, Universität Kaiserlautern, Bau 12/4, Postfach 3049, D-6750 Kaiserlautern, FRG	Kaiserlautern, FRG	European conference on customer-vendor interfaces in microelectronics, sponsored by the Commission of the European Communities

calendar

Date	Title	Contact	Place	Other details
23–25 September	Microsoftware 1986	Dr R A Adey, Computational Mechanics Institute, Suite 6200, 400 West Cummings Park, Wobum, MA 01801, USA. Tel: (617) 933-7374	Boston, USA	International conference on microsoftware in engineering, covering codes developed for personal computers, workstations and expert systems
23–26 September	HCI '86	Conference Department, British Computer Society, 13 Mansfield Street, London W1M 0BP, UK. Tel: 01-637 0471	University of York, UK	International conference on human–computer interaction. Includes: practical experience of user-centred design; user interface evaluation; user modelling; task analysis; interface tools and techniques; systems for the handicapped
30 September –2 October	ATE '86	Network Events Ltd, Printers Mews, Market Hill, Buckingham MK18 1JX, UK	Palais des Congres, Paris, France	Fifth automatic testing and test instrumentation exhibition and conference
6–8 October	11th Conference on Local Computer Networks	Bob Lutnicki, Computer Network Technology, 9440 Science Center Drive, New Hope, MN 55428, USA	Minneapolis, MN, USA	Topics will include software protocols, network management, gateways and interfaces
6–9 October	ICCD 86	M R Wayne, IBM East Fishkill Facility, Department 156, Building 503–92A, Route 52, Hopewell Junction, NY 12533, USA	New York, USA	IEEE international conference on computer design, this year concentrating on VLSI in computers and processors. Interactions between system design, logic circuit design, memory design architecture, software, CAD, testing, physical design and VLSI technology will be emphasized
6–10 October	ISATA 86	ISATA, 42 Lloyd Park Avenue, Croydon, Surrey CR0 5SB, UK. Tel: 01-686 7026	Flims, Switzerland	15th international symposium on automotive technology and automation, covering manufacturing information systems, factory networks (MAP), realtime operating systems, man–machine communications, artificial intelligence, expert systems, CADCAM etc
6–11 October	Interkama 86	Nowea Dusseldorfer Messegesellschaft mbH, Postfach 32 02 03, Stockumer Kirchstrasse, D-4000 Dusseldorf 30, FRG. Tel: (0211) 4560-01	Dusseldorf, FRG	Tenth international congress (8–10 October) and exhibition for instrumentation and automation
8–10 October	FOC/LAN 86	Information Gatekeepers Inc., 214 Harvard Avenue, Boston, MA 02134, USA. Tel: (617) 232-3111	Orange Country Civic Center, Orlando, FL, USA	Tenth annual international fibre optic communications and local area networks exposition
15–17 October	19th Annual Workshop on Microprogramming	Stanley Habib, City College of New York, Computer Science Department, New York City, NY 10031, USA. Tel: (212) 690-6631/2	Graduate Center City University of New York, USA	Workshop on microarchitecture design, firmware engineering, compaction and optmization, specification languages, graphics hosts, microprogramming languages, RISC/CISC machines and microprogrammed VLSI. Sponsored by ACM Sigmicro and the IEEE Technical Committee on Microprogramming
27–30 October	International Conference on Computer Languages	Joseph Urban, Center for Advanced Computer Studies, University of Southwestern Louisiana, PO Box 44330, Lafayette, LA, USA. Tel: (318) 231-6304	Konover, Hotel, Miami Beach, FL, USA	Sponsored by the IEEE Computer Society

Date	Title	Contact	Place	Other details
28–30 October	Test + Transducer '86	Norma Thewlis, Trident International Exhibitions Ltd, 21 Plymouth Road, Tavistock, Devon PL19 8AU, UK. Tel: (0822) 4671	Wembley Conference Centre, London, UK	Exhibition and conference covering materials testing, solid-state transducers, optical sensors for robots, automotive sensors, data acquisition and microprocessors, test in hazardous environments etc
28–29 October	Secure Communication Systems	Institution of Electrical Engineers, Savoy Place, London WC2R 0BL, UK. Tel: 01-240 1871	London, UK	Second international conference covering commercial and military system design, authentication and security in data networks, video, audio and speech encryption, impact of VLSI on security etc.
2–6 November	FJCC 86	Stanley Winkler, FJCC 86, 1730 Massachusetts Avenue, NW Washington, DC 20036-1903, USA	Dallas, USA	IEEE/ACM joint computer conference and exhibition, covering database management systems, artificial intelligence, software engineering, operating systems, VLSI, graphics, electronic education, languages, parallel computing and networks
5–7 November	ISDN Europe 86	IGI Europe Inc., c/o AKM, PO Box 6, CH-4005 Basel, Switzerland. Tel: (061) 25-51-11	World Trade and Convention Center, Basel, Switzerland	Conference covering ISDN terminal equipment, access, protocols and standards, services, implementations, internetworking, PBXs and LANs, field trials plus broadband ISDN and future directions
11–14 November	Compec '86	Reed Exhibitions, Surrey House, 1 Throwley Way, Sutton, Surrey SM1 4QQ, UK. Tel: 01-643 8040	Olympia, London, UK	Exhibition of computers, peripherals and systems for professional and business users
17 November	Electronic Interference: Practical Design and Construction Techniques	Institution of Electrical and Electronics Incorporated Engineers, Savoy Hill House, Savoy Hill, London WC2R 0BS, UK. Tel: 01-836 3357	London, UK	Symposium covering: good engineering design; circuit layout and internal wiring; power supply design and layout; system installation and environmental considerations; test and diagnostic techniques; etc.
17–18 November	Computer Networking Symposium	IEEE Computer Society Administrative Office, 1730 Massachusetts Avenue, NW Washington, DC 20036-1903, USA	Washington, DC, USA	IEEE symposium covering long-haul networks, local area networks PBX systems, satellite systems, video systems, protocols, teleconferencing, standards design, network testing, network procurement and internetworking
17–21 November	AutomAsia 86	Andry Montgomery Ltd, 11 Manchester Square, London W1M 5AB, UK. Tel: 01-486 1951	Singapore	Third South East Asian conference and show on automated manufacturing technology and robotics
18–20 November	International Open Systems Conference	Online International, 989 Avenue of the Americas, New York, NY 10018, USA. Tel: (212) 279-8890	Moscone Center, San Francisco, USA	Conference geared towards assessing the possibilities of OSI systems using MAP and TOP as case studies
21–22 November	8th Annual FORTH Convention	FORTH Interest Group, PO Box 8231, San Jose, CA 95155, USA. Tel: (408) 277-0668	Doubletree Hotel, Santa Clara, USA	US FORTH convention including exhibition, vendor booths, hands-on tutorials, lectures and user group meetings
25–26 November	MIL-STD-1553B: Applications, Developments and Components	Laura Christie, ERA Technology Ltd, Cleeve Road, Leatherhead, Surrey KT22 7SA, UK. Tel: (0372) 374151	Regent Crest Hotel, London, UK	Seminar concerning applications of the US 'aircraft internal time division command/response multiplex data bus'

microprocessors and microsystems

vol 10 no 7 september 1986

Butterworths

Microprocessors and Microsystems is an international journal published in February, March, April, May, June, August, September, October, November, December. *Editorial Offices:* Butterworth Scientific Ltd, PO Box 63, Westbury House, Bury Street, Guildford, Surrey GU2 5BH, UK. Tel: (0483) 31261. Telegrams and telex: 859556 SCITEC G. *Publishing Director:* John Owens. Production: Nick Wilson

Microprocessors and Microsystems is published by Butterworth Scientific Ltd. *Registered Office:* Butterworth Scientific Ltd, 88 Kingsway, London WC2 6AB, UK

Subscription enquiries and orders, UK and overseas: Quadrant Subscription Services Ltd, Oakfield House, Perrymount Road, Haywards Heath, West Sussex RH16 3DH, UK. Tel: (0444) 459188; *North America:* Butterworth Publishers, 80 Montvale Avenue, Stoneham, MA 02180, USA

Annual subscription (10 issues): £98.00 overseas rate (£24.00 for private individuals); $176.00 US rate ($43.00 for private individuals)
UK subscription rates available on request.

Prices include packing and delivery by sea mail. Airmail prices available on request. Copies of this journal sent to subscribers in Bangladesh, India, Pakistan, Sri Lanka, Canada and the USA are air-speeded for quicker delivery.

Back issues: Prior to current volume available from Wm Dawson & Sons Ltd, Cannon House, Folkestone, Kent CT19 5EE, UK. Tel: (0303) 57421

US mailing agents: Mercury Airfreight International Ltd Inc., 10B Englehard Avenue, Avenel, NJ 07001, USA. Second class postage paid at Rahway, NJ. US Postmaster: Send address corrections to *Microprocessors and Microsystems* c/o Mercury Airfreight International Ltd Inc., address as above.

Reprints: Minimum order 100, available from the publisher.

ISSN 0141 9331
MCRPD 10 (7) 361–416 (1986)

© Butterworth & Co (Publishers) Ltd 1986

Butterworths
Leading the Campaign
against
Copyright Erosion

Typeset by Tech-Set, Gateshead, Tyne & Wear, and printed by Dotesios (Printers) Ltd, Greenland Mills, Bradford on Avon, Wilts, UK.

microprocessors and microsystems

vol 10 no 7
september 1986

Editor Steve Hitchcock

Assistant Editor Andrew Taylor

Publisher Amanda Harper

Microprocessors and Microsystems

The journal welcomes original papers from both academic and industrial contributors on the research, design, development, evaluation and application of all microprocessor-based systems and on the development and use of microsystem software. Papers should illustrate practical experience and show the applicability of the work described. Typically, full-length papers are approximately 5000–7000 words long plus illustrations. In addition to full-length papers, the journal welcomes shorter design notes, tutorial papers and case studies of up to 3000 words.

REFEREEING

All submitted articles are refereed by two independent reviewers to ensure both accuracy and relevance, though it is the authors' sole responsibility that statements used are accurate. The author is also responsible for obtaining permission to quote material and to republish tables and illustrations.

PREPARATION OF SCRIPTS

Three copies of the manuscript, typed *double spaced* on one side of A4 paper should be sent to:

● The Editor, Microprocessors and Microsystems, PO Box 63, Westbury House, Bury Street, Guildford, Surrey GU2 5BH, United Kingdom.

Each page of the manuscript should be numbered. Wide margins should be left so that the paper can be prepared for the typesetters. Please remove tables and figures from the main body of the script and attach them at the end of the paper. Each table or figure should be reproduced on a single sheet. Please list figure captions on a separate sheet and attach this sheet at the end of the paper.

English is the sole language used by the journal, and we follow the Oxford English Dictionary. All papers should be written in English. To maintain consistency throughout each volume, every paper published is stylized by the journal's editorial staff.

Biographical notes

It is the journal's practice to include biographical notes on the authors of published papers. Biographical notes can be up to 100 words, briefly describing career details and current research interests, and should be accompanied by a black-and-white portrait photograph. To speed processing of the paper it is helpful if biographical notes can be attached to the submitted manuscript.

UNITS

SI units should be used. In circumstances where this is not possible, please provide a conversion factor at the first mention of the unit.

ILLUSTRATIONS

Line drawings

We use our own professional studio to ensure that line drawings are consistent with house style. We would prefer, however, to receive one set of unlettered drawings (black ink on tracing paper) so we can put on the lettering ourselves. Drawings, if possible, should be of a size consistent with the journal, i.e. either 169 mm or 366 mm wide. Single drawings should not extend over one page (500 mm) in height.

Computer printouts

Illustrations showing line printer listings, plotter output, etc should preferably be on unlined paper. Printouts will be reduced by us to the relevant size. Do not mark them as they will be used to make photographic copies for the typesetters. Only include sufficient lines for the reader to interpret the format and nature of the printout. Overlong printouts can cause confusion. Fuller explanation of the printout should appear in the caption and the text.

Photographs

Black-and-white glossy photographs (including Polaroid prints of VDU screens) should be supplied unmounted. They should be labelled clearly on the back with a soft pencil. Photocopies of the photographs should be provided for the referees.

REFERENCES

The journal style is to indicate the use of a reference in the text with a superscript as each one arises and give the full reference with the same number at the end of the paper. If a reference is cited more than once, the same number should be used each time. With a bibliography, the references are given in alphabetical order (dependent on the first author's surname). It would be helpful if you could follow this style. References take the following form:

(To journals)

1 **Buckroyd, A** 'Production testing of microprocessor-based equipment' *Microprocessors and Microsystems* Vol 5 No 7 (September 1981) pp 299–303

(To books)

2 **Gallacher, J** 'Testing and maintenance' in **Hanna, F K (ed.)** *Advanced techniques for microprocesor systems* Peter Peregrinus, Stevenage, UK (1980)

PROOFS

Correspondence and proofs for corrections will be sent to the first named author, unless otherwise indicated. Authors will receive a copy of the galley proofs and copies of redrawn or relettered illustrations. It is important that these proofs should be checked and returned *promptly*.

COPYRIGHT

Before publication, authors are requested to assign copyright to Butterworth & Co (Publishers) Ltd. This allows the company to sanction reprints of the whole or part of the volume and authorize photocopies. The authors, however, still retain their traditional right to reuse or to veto third-party publication.

OFFPRINTS AND REPRINTS

The first named author will receive 25 offprints of the paper free of charge as well as a complimentary copy of the journal. Further reprint copies, a minimum of 100, can be ordered at any time from the Reprints Department, Butterworth Scientific Ltd, Westbury House, PO Box 63, Bury Street, Guildford, Surrey GU2 5BH, UK.

Industrial computer networks and the role of MAP, Part 1

The MAP initiative has been widely welcomed, but to many it remains shrouded in mystery. **Richard H Weston, Chris M Sumpter and Jack D Gascoigne** explain the reasoning behind MAP and its derivation from the ISO/OSI reference model

The first of two review papers introduces the ISO/OSI reference model and explains how and why the manufacturing automation protocol (MAP) was derived from it. The seven layers of the ISO/OSI model are described, and entities, primitives and peer processes are defined. Some commonly used implementations of the model are discussed. The paper then goes on to discuss the MAP initiative in relation to ISO/OSI.

microsystems   MAP   ISO/OSI reference model   CIM

During the last three decades increased levels of automation have been established within UK manufacturing industry, resulting in improved production efficiency. This increased efficiency can be identified with reduced product cost and improved product quality, thereby generally improving the profitability and market position of the company concerned. Automation has usually been identified with mass production or high production levels, where machines are dedicated to the manufacture of a single product, but with the availability of relatively low-cost computational power comes the opportunity to automate flexibly many processes involved in batch manufacturing.

The need for flexible automation is promoted by worldwide market pressures for product variety, which implies the need to manufacture products in smaller batches. Thus product lead times must be reduced both for new products (i.e. shorter product design cycles are required) and for existing products where it is necessary to respond rapidly to customer orders. If conventional automation is used, so that inflexible manufacturing methods are employed, the direct result is often significant work in progress to reduce the effect of long delays involved in product change; this results in high capital investment in stock and thus increased product cost.

To reduce work in progress and lead times implies not only the need for flexible production machines, but also

Department of Engineering Production, Loughborough University of Technology, Leics LE11 3TU, UK

for efficient management/organizational and design systems. Computer-based production analysis, planning and control systems as well as CADCAM systems are now becoming commonplace in manufacturing[1, 2]. Computer-based automated machinery is also commonplace; examples include machines controlled by PLCs (programmable logic controllers), computer-controlled processes, NC (numerically controlled) machines, robots and automatic guided vehicles (AGVs), which provide flexibility on the shop floor[3, 4, 5]. As yet, however, fully integrated manufacturing systems where management, design and production functions operate collectively and automatically are not common.

Another major factor influencing the trend towards computer integrated manufacture (CIM) is the need to improve product quality. In the manufacture of automobiles, for example, improved quality and improved inspection techniques can have significant financial benefit with respect to reducing the cost of warranty periods on cars supplied to the consumer. In particular, improved testing of components, boards and systems can lead to increased productivity and profitability in the manufacture of electronic products.

CIM systems of the future will also require another form of flexibility, namely the property of reconfigurability. Product life cycles have reduced dramatically in recent years, largely as the direct result of high technology allowing product innovations to be introduced which can allow a company to achieve a significant market lead. Thus there is the need for reconfigurable plant, organization and design systems.

The need for integrated manufacturing systems imposes new problems of information transmission, processing and storage. Central to the issues involved is the need for efficient information flow between the computer-based equipment operating at each level within manufacturing systems. This equipment, however, is inevitably supplied by a multitude of vendors (for example, there are some 200 manufacturers of industrial robots alone, each basing its robot controller on its own choice of computer hardware) who will generally specify their own communication protocols by which information can be transmitted to and from the equipment. (A protocol implies a set of rules or conventions. Communication protocols generally define both the hardware and software requirements to be observed when transmitting or receiving information.) Most vendors adopt quasistandard communication protocols (e.g. RS232, RS422, IEEE488, DDCMP), but in practice vendor-specific software-based protocols will necessarily be involved as the commonly used communication standards do not fully define the way in which information should be transferred.

Communication with equipment of this type can be considered to be 'closed' in the sense that equipment from two different vendors can only communicate if conversion between the two vendor specified protocols is accomplished by some specially engineered method. It has been reported from a number of sources that the cost of engineering solutions to the problems of intercomputer communication can be greater than 50% of the total cost of installing plant automation schemes. Furthermore the same solutions are derived many times over by different system builders and the user is left with very little support for his/her purchased equipment in the face of obsolescence or, possibly more importantly, if his/her automation scheme needs to be enhanced at some future date. What is required to overcome these problems is for an 'open' communication standard to be adopted by all vendors which fully defines all types of information transfer between the elements of manufacturing systems. In such an arrangement a vendor would be responsible for providing a standard interface to his/her equipment, thereby offering 'plug compatibility' with equipment from other vendors supporting that standard.

Although open communication standards suitable for use in manufacturing systems are not yet a reality, two major landmarks have been reached. First, the business world of computing and the associated requirements of information technology have led to the International Standards Organization's definition of a framework within which modern computer networks should be designed. This framework is referred to as the International Standards Organization/Open Systems Interconnection (ISO/OSI) model[6] and outlines the interface architecture which should be used between computers communicating via a network or networks. Secondly, the General Motors MAP (manufacturing automation protocol) initiative[7] has encouraged equipment vendors and users to seek an agreed implementation of the ISO/OSI model which will lead to first-generation products demonstrating a level of open system interconnection capability in the near future.

This first part of a two-part paper concentrates on a description of the ISO/OSI model framework and the role of MAP. The second part of the paper will consider the availability of future MAP-based products and outline the possible impact that such products will have on the design of manufacturing systems.

PURPOSE OF THE ISO/OSI REFERENCE MODEL

Considerable interest has been generated worldwide in emerging computer network standards. In the manufacturing sector most multinational companies have now formed a team of personnel whose brief is to study, and often contribute to, developments in such standards and associated products. However, much confusion still exists about the purpose and technical details of the ISO/OSI

model for open systems interconnection and indeed the emergence of MAP.

It should be understood that the ISO/OSI model can be more clearly described as the ISO/OSI reference model. This reference model was developed to provide an architecture, or framework, for the orderly development of standard protocols, thus allowing computer systems to interconnect and communicate regardless of their manufacturer, make, age or level of complexity. The ISO/OSI model, being an abstract model, provides a conceptual and functional framework to allow groups of experts working internationally to develop the standards for open systems interconnection. It purposely does not specify how the protocols are to be implemented in a particular computer system. The only users for which the reference model is intended are designers of protocol standards. The model provides a common basis for ISO and other standards organizations to coordinate their standards development, placing existing standards in perspective and identifying areas where new standards need to be developed or improved.

Thus, the ISO/OSI reference model is sufficiently abstract that it neither describes nor limits the technology to be used in implementing open systems.

Layers of the reference model

The ISO/OSI reference model uses the technique of layering to divide the interconnection problem into manageable subproblems[6]. The layers form a hierarchy, each layer defining a subset of functions necessary for open systems interconnection.

Seven layers were considered to be sufficient to divide the problem into structurally similar but logically distinct functions. Figure 1 illustrates the layered structure; the lower-layer functions are the more basic and are prerequisites for the higher-layer functions. In the ISO/OSI reference model this is expressed by saying that each layer (layer N) uses the services of the adjacent lower layer (layer $N - 1$) while providing its services to the next higher layer (layer $N + 1$).

Commercial users of equipment incorporating ISO standards, and managers responsible for computer operations in organizations, will want to know the kind of problems they address without having a detailed knowledge of the actual protocols involved. Similarly, systems and applications programmers employed by commercial users will only require a knowledge of the facilities provided and how to access them. In contrast to this, a detailed knowledge of protocols used will be required by equipment manufacturers or persons connected with the standards oganizations.

This paper is directed towards the commercial user and as such will not provide a detailed description of the ISO/OSI reference model or the various implementations of that model. However, it will outline the function of each layer in the ISO/OSI reference model so that the relative merits of commercially available implementations can be assessed separately by the user.

Physical layer

The physical layer provides the mechanical, electrical, functional and procedural characteristics to access the physical medium[8]. Thus for a particular reference model

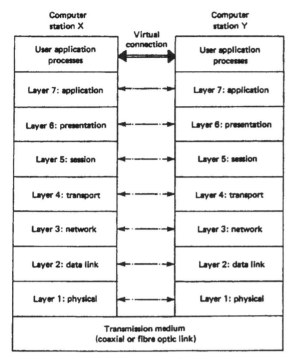

Figure 1. ISO/OSI reference model

The diagram shows two columns for Computer station X and Computer station Y connected by a Virtual connection, with the following layers:

Computer station X	Computer station Y	Description
User application processes	User application processes	User applications software — not part of the ISO/OSI model
Layer 7: application	Layer 7: application	Provides network services to the application processes
Layer 6: presentation	Layer 6: presentation	Formats the data to/from the network into a standard format
Layer 5: session	Layer 5: session	Synchronization and data management; name/address translation; access security
Layer 4: transport	Layer 4: transport	Provides transport data transfer between end systems
Layer 3: network	Layer 3: network	Accomplishes message routing to/from stations on other networks
Layer 2: data link	Layer 2: data link	Accomplishes message routing, error detection; retries between stations on local networks
Layer 1: physical	Layer 1: physical	Encodes/decodes messages and transfers data to/from the transmission medium

Transmission medium (coaxial or fibre optic link)

implementation the physical layer characterizes the type of plug(s) and socket(s) used, their pin configuration, the required electrical signal levels and timing arrangements, the type of modulation technique (baseband or broadband) etc., these being closely related to the chosen transmission medium which commonly in manufacturing environments will be coaxial or fibre optic cable.

Data link layer

The data link layer provides the functional and procedural means to transfer data between network entities (these concepts are described below) and to detect and possibly correct errors which may occur in the physical layer. The functions provided by protocols in this layer typically include facilities for synchronization, error control and flow control.

The responsibility of this layer lies in accomplishing the transfer of frames of data to an address on the same network, supplied as an interface parameter by the network layer. This address may not necessarily be the final destination but one of many intermediate stations (depending on the network topology). To achieve this goal, the data link layer organizes, for a given network station, media access to a single local area network (LAN) resolving contention, detecting noise, selecting frames addressed to the station, delimiting data frames and accomplishing network retries when needed.

Network layer

The network layer provides a network independent (i.e. independent from the actual data transfer technology as well as relaying and routing considerations) service for the

higher levels of the ISO/OSI model. Thus the next layer (the transport layer) will not require a knowledge of whether optical fibres, packet switching, a wide area network (WAN) or a LAN are being used.

Some of the main functions performed by the network layer are to route and relay information between stations, which may be located physically on different networks, to direct the message (contained in network packets) to its intended destination. This is achieved by using globally unique station addresses which are passed as parameters from the transport layer. However, the route which the message takes is determined by the network layer. The address information of intermediate stations (required by the data link services) is obtained either locally from resident 'look-up' tables or remotely from a network 'router' station. Error notification, but not necessarily correction, is also performed.

Transport layer

The transport layer accomplishes the transparent transfer of data over an established link providing an end-to-end service with high data integrity, this being achieved by using acknowledgement-based protocols involving transmission, retries and error recovery. It also provides a multiplexing and mapping facility allowing numerous different ports (or sockets) in a station to communicate separately via the shared network access. Data flow control, required to ensure that local and remote message buffers are not overrun, is also included.

Inherent in this layer is a data streaming facility (i.e. the breaking up of an arbitrarily large continuous block of data into smaller, discrete, manageable packets) making the problem of transferring large files transparent to the higher layers. This layer also provides the association of a logical channel (i.e. connection number) used by the higher layers and the physical addresses required by the lower layers.

Session layer

The session layer provides the mechanisms for organizing and structuring the interactions between two entities. In this way it provides grounds for an orderly dialogue between the entities, allowing two-way simultaneous operation, the establishment of major and minor synchronization points (such as the start of transfers or job execution) and the definition of special tokens for structuring the exchange. This layer can provide the association between logical names and logical channels, i.e. names that can relate directly to the application entity, and the connection number used by the transport services.

Presentation layer

The presentation layer frees the application processes from concern with differences in data presentation, e.g. syntax. Thus the presentation layer interprets data following agreed rules of encoding and decoding. For example, NC data is usually transferred to machine tool controllers in one of two internationally agreed formats (ISO or EIA messaging formats)[9], while robots often use vendor-specific codes. The presentation layer could define a set of rules so that each end entity understands the context and content of a message.

Application layer

The application layer does not provide services to any other layer of the ISO/OSI reference model. The primary concern of the application layer is with the semantics of the application. All application processes reside in the application layer. However, only those aspects of the application processes concerned with interprocess communication over networks are within the scope of the ISO/OSI reference model. (Application processes are user programs which may be operating concurrently to achieve user-defined objectives. They need have no knowledge of where the communicating processes reside, i.e. in the same or a different computer station.)

The application layer processes concerned with inter-process communication will perform management functions, establishing a link in terms of the application, independent of the physical location or interconnections. The fact that the two communicating application processes may reside in the same computer or on different computers or even on different LANs can be made transparent at this level.

Entities, primitives and peer processes

The functions of each layer are said to be carried out by one or more entities in the layer. The entities are abstract and should not be confused with a program or software module. In an actual system the entities correspond to one or more software modules or hardware elements. Generally, though, an entity is an abstraction of 'whatever it is to carry out a given function'.

The entities in each layer communicate or interact with each other and with entities in adjacent layers. The interactions between adjacent layers are carried out using primitives, these being the sole means by which adjacent layer entities in the same system can interact and exchange parameters (see Figure 2).

This technique for describing the functions of a layer is similar to techniques in structured programming where only the functions performed by a module are known to the user. The internal functions of the module are not known. In the ISO/OSI reference model each layer performs a specific function and the interaction between layers is characterized by well defined primitives (which relate to parameter transfer between layer entities).

Communication between two systems can be viewed as communicating between corresponding layer entities in each system. The interactions between entities in the separate systems are referred to as peer protocols. Peer protocols exist at all layers of the ISO/OSI reference model, i.e. between entities at the physical layer, data link layer etc. (see Figures 1 and 2).

Thus the ISO/OSI reference model provides a design framework for systems interconnection. It does not, however, specify the detailed functioning of each layer nor the details of the peer protocols. It is the work of standards bodies to develop and specify alternative protocols. The use of such protocols is common in our normal lives, e.g. the special conventions and procedures followed in the exchange of information between taxi drivers, aircraft pilots etc. and their respective control personnel. This paper now considers the characteristics of a few real, commonly used, open computer networks.

Commonly used implementations

It must not be thought that two systems, each of which can rightly claim to conform to the ISO/OSI seven-layer reference model, will be able to communicate with each other directly. To accomplish direct compatibility there must be an agreed implementation specifying each of the seven layers. This is the prime aim of MAP and this initiative is discussed below. This subsection briefly considers common practices in computer communications. The reader should note that the MAP initiative set out to select, where possible, appropriate and already widely used individual layer implementations of the ISO/OSI reference model.

Since the ISO/OSI reference model came into existence, many standards bodies have been busy preparing speci-

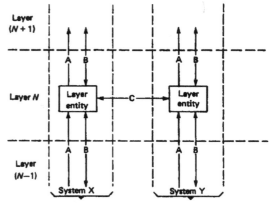

Figure 2. Concept of a layer entity. A = layer services; B = primitives or parameters; C = peer protocols

fications consistent with the model for the various layers. In the LAN area possibly the most notable of these has been IEEE project 802. This project was initiated in the early 1980s[10] for the development of a local network standard and by 1982 had separate subcommittees investigating three key areas[11]: a high-level interface; datalink and machine access; and the physical layer.

Project 802 has achieved considerable success particularly with respect to layers 1 and 2, with a number of the now familiar 802.x series of working party specifications becoming full ISO standards and with others at the draft international standard stage. Figure 3 summarizes the area of consideration of the various 802.x working parties and it can be seen that several implementations of layers 1 and 2 have evolved in an attempt to optimize performance in differing application scenarios.

A closer look at individual layer specifications reveals that, within a particular specification, a choice exists as to the class of service provided by that layer in any one implementation of that specification (e.g. datalink class 1, transport class 4). The wider implications of this will be discussed in Part 2 of this paper, particularly considering layer services with respect to a reduced network architecture.

As much of the activity has centred on the lowest layers of the reference model we will consider classes of such systems with the major classification being made with respect to network topology (see Figure 4).

Direct point-to-point data link[8]

This is still the most commonly found method of linking individual system elements together within manufacturing systems. Examples are particularly common with CADCAM and FMS systems[12, 13]. Systems of this type are acceptable when the complexity is low and only a few computer stations are involved preferably with a natural supervisor-slave hierarchy. However, the use of such a network topology can soon lead to disorder as new system elements are added. As stated earlier flexibility, in the sense that the system can expand easily, is an increasingly common requirement of modern manufacturing systems. However, with a 'star' topology of this type, every new link requires another computer port at each end and software modifications to cope with the load. Other major disadvantages of this approach are that the system is susceptible to failure of the central computer (or

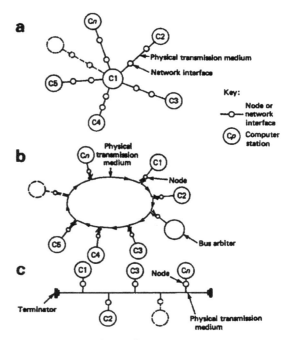

Figure 4. Network topology: a, star network; b, ring network; c, bus network

supervisor), that communication between slaves requires relay system elements and hence will be slow, and that cable runs will be long and hence cabling costs may be unacceptably high.

Ring networks

System extension is greatly simplified if all the computer stations are linked via a computer port (or node) to a continuous ring (see Figure 4). Here each system element need make only one connection into the network irrespective of the number of nodes (or computers) linked to the ring[8].

With such a ring network, provision must be made to regulate data traffic on the ring, this function being performed by entities operating in layers 1 and 2 of the interface architecture at each node or computer station. The most common method used to regulate traffic, with ring networks, is to pass a logical token round the ring. Only the node having the possession of the token is allowed to initiate message transfer.

Each message must contain the address(es) of the intended recipient(s). All nodes listen to transmitted messages on the ring and pass them on to the next node; the only nodes to take notice of the message are those recognizing their addresses. The transmitting node waits to receive its own message after it has circulated around the ring then it removes the message from the ring and passes on the token to the next node. This method of allocating bus access guarantees that a time allocation is allowed for each node (i.e. the ability to transmit is said to be 'deterministic'). The major problem with this approach is that a 'control node' (or 'bus arbiter') is required to monitor activity on the ring to see if the message passes twice or to detect other fault conditions which indicate

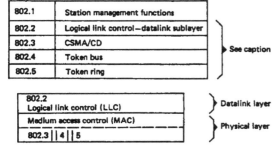

802.1	Station management functions	
802.2	Logical link control—datalink sublayer	
802.3	CSMA/CD	See caption
802.4	Token bus	
802.5	Token ring	

802.2 Logical link control (LLC)	Datalink layer
Medium access control (MAC)	Physical layer
802.3 | | 4 | | 5	

Figure 3. IEEE 802 subcommittees. Particular implementations of the specifications are referenced by a subcommittee section number extension, e.g. IEEE 802.4.4 refers to a token bus physical layer using broadband duobinary amplitude modulated phase shift keying (AM-PSK) modulation

that a node is faulty. The need for a control node can pose reliability problems, as can the fact that a break in the ring will stop all communications.

Token ring network systems have been used in office environments, and many proprietary products implementing layers 1 and 2 of the ISO/OSI reference model, as defined by the IEEE 802 project specifications, have been available for a number of years.

Bus networks

With a bus network each node is identified by an address and connected to a common cable as illustrated by Figure 4. Each node can broadcast a message along the bus but only the nodes addressed by the broadcast message will take part in the data transfer. There are two major classes of mechanism used to gain access to the bus; these are described below.

Contention systems. These are systems in which each node listens to the messages on the bus; if it detects that there is no bus traffic it attempts to transmit a message. If two or more nodes attempt to transmit at the same time a collision will occur and such an event will be detected by each node; the nodes then 'back off' for a random time period before trying again. Obviously it is impossible to predict the maximum time taken for a node to transmit a high-priority message. Hence the contention systems can be considered to be probabilistic.

However, contention systems do not require a master controller, with each node being equal. In this respect they can be considered to be more reliable in the event of a station failure.

It has been found that contention systems cope very well with loads of up to 50% of the theoretical capacity and with a bus loading of this magnitude provide a very efficient mechanism for high-speed bus access[14]. However, with loads exceeding 80% of capacity the performance falls off dramatically: as a node fails in a contention situation it is even less likely to succeed next time it tries. It is interesting to note that the results of performance testing carried out in relation to the MAP project[15] indicate that high bus loading has a more dramatic effect on performance than was suggested by Bux[14].

Contention bus network systems are also very common in office environments, with many proprietary products being available implementing layers 1 and 2 of the ISO/OSI reference model as defined by the IEEE 802.3 specification. Ethernet is such a network implementation which is based on a CSMA/CD (carrier sense multiple access/collision detect) technique for overcoming bus contention, and there are many Ethernet systems employed worldwide with a variety of network services available to the user. Generally, however, contention systems are not considered to be suitable for realtime control, where it must be possible to predict what the worst-case response will be.

Token passing. A way of avoiding bus contention and granting access to the bus in realtime control situations is to have a logical token which, in similar fashion to a token ring system, passes from one node to another. In such a scheme only the node having possession of the token can transmit and when it is finished it must pass the token to another node.

In a token bus system the token is passed to a node having a specified address rather than to the next node physically on a ring (as with the token ring). If no use is made of the token it can be passed to lower-priority nodes. Thus, not only is it possible to determine the worst-case response time, it is also possible to assign a priority to individual nodes. The performance of a token bus system has been shown to fall almost uniformly over a wide range of bus loadings and to be better than an equivalent contention bus system under heavy loads[15]. One disadvantage of the token bus, when compared with a token ring, is that the minimum response time will generally be longer.

A range of proprietary token passing bus network products are now becoming available, such as Proway, which implements the IEEE 802.4 specification at layers 1 and 2 of the ISO/OSI reference model. The widespread use of these products will become inevitable as the IEEE 802.4 specification provides

- desirable characteristics for manufacturing environments, particularly in accomplishing information transfer to and from shop-floor production equipment; this encouraged the MAP initiative to recommend the use of token passing bus systems
- a system which is currently within the IBM recommended strategic solution for communications in industrial environments, although IBM is also committed to using token ring technologies in office environments; clearly the influence that IBM has is extremely important

Modulation techniques

Of major importance in choosing a network system is the type and total amount of information it must transfer[8]. In this respect it is necessary to consider two available options which have found widespread use in manufacturing industry, namely baseband and broadband network systems. These two types of transmission system are briefly described below; in the context of the ISO/OSI reference model they are alternative technologies which can be used to form part of layer 1 (i.e. layer 1 network entities) and provide the physical link or transmission medium.

Baseband network systems. Here some form of time division multiplexing is used for the transmission of digital data between computers. Thus each node can use the full capacity (or bandwidth) of the cable on a time sharing basis. In a modem baseband computer network the bandwidth of the cable will extend between DC and tens of megaHertz; this upper frequency limit is able to cope with the maximum digital switching speeds involved in the serial transmission of bits on the cable (i.e. 10 Mbit s^{-1}).

In baseband systems relatively low-cost cabling is required, as the bandwidth requirement is fairly easily achieved. Similarly, relatively low-cost and simple interface electronics is required to accomplish baseband transmission in every node.

The reader should be aware that two major forms of baseband network system are commonly used. In one form the physical medium transmits digital data by sequentially switching between two voltage levels to form the bits which encode the data. In the second form the two states of each bit correspond to two different carrier frequencies so that bits encoding the digital data are transmitted on the physical medium by sequentially switching between these two frequencies. Ethernet LANs use the former type of transmission mechanism while the second mechanism is referred to as carrier band transmission to distinguish it from the amplitude switching baseband technique. Carrier band transmission is proposed for use in the realtime segments of MAP networks as discussed below and in Part 2 of the paper.

Broadband network systems. Here a mixture of frequency division and time division multiplexing techniques are used to carry signals covering a frequency spectrum of up to 100 MHz. Because of their large bandwidth, broadband systems can concurrently transmit digital-data video signals and speech which in some manufacturing environments will offer significant benefit. To facilitate concurrent transmission frequency division multiplexing is used. Thus a single cable can support several simultaneous, but separate, communications, each communication channel having its own bandwidth and carrier frequency; for example Ethernet, token passing and closed-circuit TV networks might share a common cable. Using such a scheme it is possible to allocate a channel for the transmission of digital data with the channel shared on a time division basis between nodes as for a baseband network system.

The major advantage of broadband systems, from the manufacturing point of view, is that a cable can be laid down, without knowledge of the future traffic, knowing that whatever the future needs might be there should be sufficient bandwidth to accomplish data transfer. However, the cost and complexity of the interface electronics and the cost of cabling (either coaxial or fibre optic) will be higher than that for baseband systems.

THE MAP INITIATIVE

The General Motors (GM) MAP initiative promises to be a major step towards providing true open systems interconnection, or 'plug compatibility', between computer-based automation equipment and systems. MAP provides a framework of rules for information exchange within manufacturing plants, and is gaining significant support worldwide. Although it is primarily user driven, most of the leading vendors of computer systems are committed to providing MAP interfaces to their equipment.

The basic ideas behind MAP were formulated by GM and, mainly during 1984, interest spread rapidly to many of the leading computer users and suppliers in the USA. In March 1985, GM brought a powerful team over to Europe which led ultimately to the formulation of the European MAP Users Group (EMUG), the secretariat of which is now based at Cranfield Institute of Technology, UK. The MAP specification is constantly being enhanced under the direction of a GM MAP task force, but version 2.1[7] has been partially frozen as a specification to which the vendors of computer systems can work in providing commercially available products. A variety of version 2.1 products are promised by late 1986 and some of these products will be considered in Part 2 of this paper.

Again it should be emphasized that the MAP initiative is not attempting to define an independent set of standards. The whole concept is based on the framework of the ISO/OSI reference model and where possible seeks

Table 1. MAP 2.1 specification (April 1985)

Layer 7 (Application)	ISO — case subset
	ISO — file transfer subset
	MAP messaging (MMFS)
	MAP directory services
	MAP network management
Layer 6 (Presentation)	Null/MAP transfer
Layer 5 (Session)	ISO session kernel
Layer 4 (Transport)	ISO transport class 4
Layer 3 (Network)	ISO CLNS inactive and subset
Layer 2 (Data link)	IEEE 802.2 type 1
Layer 1 (Physical)	IEEE 802.4 token bus on
Physical transmission medium	Broadband backbone or baseband realtime segments

to select a set of pre-existing standards, most of which are internationally accepted, corresponding to each layer within the model. MAP version 2.1 has selected pre-existing, widely used protocols for layers 1–5 of the reference model (see Table 1). Layer 6 is essentially null although MAP-defined messaging structures accomplish transfer between layers 5 and 7. File and message representation schemes are also defined by MAP as part of the layer 7 specifications. It is primarily at layer 7 where the MAP initiative has sought to define internationally acceptable standards for which previously available vendor protocols were not considered to be generally suitable in manufacturing automation. Thus layer 7 of MAP version 2.1 provides a range of network management, file transfer, interconnection, directory and application interface facilities. Part 2 provides a more detailed description of MAP version 2.1; the implications of the choices made in protocol selection will be considered with respect to manufacturing applications.

The proposed MAP backbone network will be based on the use of a broadband transmission system which will facilitate communication between local factory sites and between major computers within a site. It is envisaged that, for the realtime control of machines, the response time which could be guaranteed on the Backbone network might not be acceptable in a situation where many computer stations are connected to the network, and that the cost of the interface electronics might be prohibitive. Thus, within the MAP initiative a carrier band implementation is proposed for realtime control which will be used to interconnect factory floor terminals and machine controllers. The proposed bandwidth of the carrier band system will be 12 MHz and each segment will have its own token, guaranteeing a maximum response time of not more than 25 ms.

The backbone and realtime segments of the network will operate using the same set of rules and be linked via 'bridge units'. The bridge units will be necessary to match the essential differences in implementation of the ISO/OSI layers 1–2 on broadband and baseband systems.

MAP AND MANUFACTURING

The need for the MAP initiative has thus grown from the emergence, from many sources, of computer-based equipment performing managerial, design and production functions. To increase the flexibility, and hence the efficiency, of future manufacturing systems it will be necessary to achieve an integrated functioning of the whole; hence the need for efficient and reliable communication between plant computers. When MAP version 2.1 products become generally available they will provide plug compatibility or a network architecture between the elements of manufacturing systems and this will represent a major step forward in the evolution of computer integrated manufacturing systems.

Many unanswered questions remain, however, and many questions have not yet been asked. These will inevitably lead to enhanced versions of the MAP specification being adopted in future product generations. The MAP initiative is committed to minimizing upgrade requirements, and it is hoped that each new MAP release will include information specifying methods which will enable new implementations to recognize and communicate with lower-version systems, the base version being 2.1.

Part 2 of this paper, to be published in a future edition of *Microprocessors and Microsystems*, will consider some of the problems which remain with regard to achieving a consistent 'application architecture' which is suitable for the range of manufacturing environments encountered. It will also outline some of the problem areas which have not yet been considered within the MAP initiative.

REFERENCES

1 **Ranky, P** *Computer integrated manufacture* Prentice-Hall, Englewood Cliffs, NJ, USA (1986)
2 **Groover, M P and Zimmers, W** *CAD/CAM* Prentice-Hall Englewood Cliffs, NJ, USA (1984)
3 **Heginbotham, W B** (Ed.) *Programmable assembly* IFS, Bedford, UK (1984)
4 **Husband, T** (Ed.) *Proc. 2nd Int. Conf. Robots in the Automotive Industry* IFS, Bedford, UK (May 1985)
5 **Batchelor, B G, Hill, D A and Hodgson, D C** *Automated visual inspection* IFS, Bedford, UK (1985)
6 **Zimmerman, H** 'OSI reference model — the OSI model of archictecture for open system interconnection' *IEEE Trans. Commun.* Vol 28 (April 1980) pp 425–432
7 **General Motors** *MAP specification — version 2.1* Obtainable from EMUG Secretariat, Cranfield Institute of Technology, Bedford, UK (March 1985)
8 **Mayne, A J** *Linked local area networks* October Press, Fareham, UK (1982)
9 **Bachelor, A T** 'EIA and ISO numerical control standards for automated manufacturing systems' in **Gardner, L B** (Ed.) *Automated manufacturing, ASTM Special Technical Pub.* 862 ASTM, 1916 Race Street, Philadelphia, PA, USA (April 1985) pp 21–30
10 **Clancy, G J Jr** 'A status report on the IEEE project 802 local network standard' *Local Network* No 81 (1981) pp 263–295
11 **Sze, D T W** 'IEEE LAN project 802 — current status' *Local Network* No 82 (1982) pp 109–120
12 **Popplewell, F and Schmoll, P** 'The road to FMS' *Proc. 1st Int. Conf. FMS* (October 1983) pp 501–513
13 **Hatvany, J** (Ed.) *World survey of CAM* Butterworths, Guildford, UK (1983)
14 **Bux, W** 'Local area subnetworks — a performance comparison' *IBM Technical Report* (February 1981)
15 **Allen Bradley Inc.** *CSMA/CD and token bus performance testing* Ship Star Associates, 36 Woodhill Drive, Newark, DE 19711, USA (1985)

Richard Weston was employed until 12 years ago in the UK Scientific Civil Service, involved in the design of HF, VHF and digital communication systems. Since then he has been project manager for government and industry sponsored research work at Loughborough University, UK, on the design of distributed process and machine controls. Much of this work has centred on the design of robotic systems, e.g. evolving new controller and manipulator forms for robots, the most recent studies centring on the use of MAP interfaces in flexible assembly systems. He is a retained consultant in flexible manufacturing for Haiste Automation and Baker Perkins.

Chris Sumpter has worked in an industrial consultancy whose typical projects would involve the design of fixtures and machine tooling for clients (including Rolls Royce and British Rail), and for a period of several years as an equipment design engineer for a major lamp manufacturer; this involved the design and integration of conventional hard automation into both pilot and mainstream production. During the last three years as a research associate at Loughborough University he has been conducting research into data/information transfer, using a LAN (MAP of late) between elements of a flexible assembly system, with particular interest in flexible cell supervision techniques.

Jack Gascoigne spent two years researching the design of computer-controlled pneumatic servos for modular robots. This involved the design of realtime control algorithms to accomplish motion control and the design of novel hardware for position and velocity measurement. During the last four years as a research associate at Loughborough University he has worked in the design of intelligent interfaces for robots and machines. Here, computer hardware and software have been produced to facilitate the remote programming and control of industrial robots performing assembly and inspection functions.

'Transparent' interfacing of speech recognizers to microcomputers

For applications such as speech input for the disabled, it is desirable that standard software packages can be used with speech recognizer–microcomputer systems. **H H Dabbagh, R I Damper and D P Guy*** detail their work towards this goal using 'transparent' interfacing

'Transparent' interfacing allows nonstandard input devices such as speech recognizers to emulate the de facto standard input device, the keyboard, enabling standard commercial software to accept input from speech recognizers, touch sensitive devices, bar code readers etc. without modification. The paper describes experiences with the transparent interfacing of a number of different speech recognizers to microcomputers in order to study the issues involved. Two such systems are described: an Interstate VRM recognizer interfaced to an Acorn BBC model B microcomputer to allow computer access for the physically disabled; and an Interstate VRT300 device interfaced to a Cromemco Z-2D computer to investigate the potential of speech recognition to assist in the preparation of television subtitles. The extent to which the manufacturer of the speech recognizer had provided for transparent interfacing was found to have a profound impact. A number of human factors were also revealed as salient. The authors conclude that transparent interfacing, vital if the potential of new input technologies is to be realized, demands considerable forethought. Manufacturers of novel input devices and of microcomputers should make their products as flexible as possible in terms of I/O capability.

microsystems   speech recognizers   interfacing

In spite of the emergence of novel I/O techniques, e.g. speech, the conventional keyboard remains the standard computer input device. Hence, the vast majority of software is written to accept such input. The system designer seeking to exploit speech recognition capabilities is therefore faced with the need to make input from nonstandard devices, e.g. speech recognizers, emulate keyboard entry if modifications to existing and readily available applications software (word processors, spreadsheets etc.) are to be avoided. This is referred to as transparent interfacing, because the computer is unable to distinguish between keyboard input and input from the nonstandard device. We believe transparency in man–machine interaction to be an important yet underrated subject.

Although the topic is really much wider, transparent input has received most attention in the context of disabled persons unable to use standard keyboard input. Indeed, a sizeable part of the work described in this paper focusses on this user group. The problems of achieving transparent operation are most keenly felt when interfacing to microcomputers of limited processing power such as those typically used in systems for the disabled.

This paper considers the possible ways of realizing transparency in general, before describing two implementations featuring speech input. One system used the Interstate VRM speech recognizer whereas the other used the VRT300 device from the same company. The VRM was interfaced to the Acorn BBC model B microcomputer: the application of interest was computer access by speech for the physically disabled[1]. The BBC computer was chosen because it is both typical of current machines and popular. In the course of other work on speech data entry in television subtitling[2] the VRT300 was interfaced to a Cromemco Z-2D microcomputer. The important technical issues which emerged as a result of the work are then discussed. A number of human factors were revealed as salient and are dealt with subsequently.

In what follows, the term 'host' is used to refer to the computer running standard applications software. The reader is warned that this terminology may differ from that

Man–Machine Systems Laboratory, Department of Electronics and Information Engineering, University of Southampton, Southampton SO9 5NH. UK
*Royal Naval Staff College, Greenwich, London SW10 9NN, UK
This paper is based on a presentation at the IEE conference 'Speech I/O: techniques and applications' held in London, UK (March 1986)

0141-9331/86/07371-06 $03.00 © 1986 Butterworth & Co. (Publishers) Ltd

of other workers who use the term to refer to the computer controlling the speech recognizer.

APPROACHES TO TRANSPARENT INTERFACING

Vanderheiden[3] identified three degrees of transparency in the context of computer access for the disabled using nonstandard input devices. The categorization is equally valid and useful in other application areas.

'Complete (or full) transparency' avoids modification to the host software and, as a consequence, allows any standard software to be run. This is not the case for the other two schemes to be discussed. However, complete transparency does involve at least some additional interfacing hardware, which usually takes the form of a module placed between the computer and the keyboard. This module accepts input from the nonstandard device and converts it to a form comprehensible to the computer. A good example of a fully transparent implementation is the so-called 'MOD keyboard' described by Nelson et al.[4]

By contrast, 'semitransparent' interfacing requires no additional hardware but is less flexible in terms of the software which can be run. The basic principle is that of indirection: the operating system is modified slightly so that its vectors point to specially written software servicing the nonstandard input device rather than to the normal keyboard servicing routines. This special software is placed in infrequently used portions of memory to minimize interference as much as possible. The major disadvantage of this technique is that avoidance of memory clashes between the commercial software and the interfacing software cannot be guaranteed.

The third approach to transparency involves multitasking, i.e. the ability of the computer to run several programs seemingly at once by transferring resources rapidly back and forth between them. The simplest such implementation would be a dual tasking system in which one of the programs is the specially written interfacing software and the other could be any desired commercial program, together with the scheduler for the dual tasking. As far as systems for the disabled are concerned, they are typically based on inexpensive home computers of a type which simply do not have the power or facilities to make dual tasking worth considering. Although our subtitling work used a relatively powerful machine, at the time this had only a single-user operating system (CDOS). This made the multitasking approach unattractive.

Our choice is therefore essentially between the completely transparent and semitransparent approaches. In the main, we have employed the former, essentially because it is the most flexible and has proved the simplest to implement.

INTERFACING USING TWO COMPUTERS

Hardware

During work on the development of a speech-controlled word processor for disabled users[5] it was necessary to interface an Interstate VRM recognizer to a BBC microcomputer. The VRM is a speaker-dependent isolated word recognizer with a 100-word capability[6]. Communication with a controlling computer is either serial or parallel.

When a spoken command is recognized, the VRM sends information on the recognized word (template number, difference between winner and runner-up scores etc.) bracketed by framing characters. The BBC microcomputer's I/O capabilities[7] include a serial RS423 line, a parallel interface intended for printer communication (the 'printer port') and a similar port specifically provided for the user's own purpose (the 'user port'). Both the printer and user ports are taken from a common 6522 versatile interface adaptor (VIA) chip.

Although the information sent by the VRM is coded in ASCII at the symbol level, for transparent operation the symbol strings must first be converted into a form meaningful to the BBC microcomputer. For complete transparency, the conversion must be effected external to the host. This is conveniently done using an additional BBC microcomputer. Thus, two computers are used, one to run the target software (the host machine), and the other (the interface processor) to control the speech recognizer, decode its responses and pass this information to the host. Although this appears an expensive solution, it is a very powerful approach. There is, of course, no reason why the second microcomputer should not ultimately be replaced by a dedicated microprocessor board once system design is completed, and should this prove cheaper.

There are, however, only two I/O facilities on the BBC computer capable of accepting user-generated input without modifications to the operating system — the keyboard port and the RS423 interface. Hence, for complete transparency, one of these must be used for communication from the interface processor to the host. There is no difficulty in getting the keyboard interface to accept input since this is its designed function. In addition, the serial RS423 line can be made to accept ASCII characters transparently by use of a single operating system command[7, 8], .∗FX2,1. This command directs the operating system to treat the RS423 buffer as if it were the keyboard buffer.

However, there is a very significant problem with keyboard emulation by routing input via serial lines. Although this would work for all keyboard selections which place ASCII codes in the keyboard buffer, not all selections operate in this fashion; examples which do not do this include ⟨break⟩, ⟨caps_lock⟩, ⟨shift_lock⟩ and the function keys. Clearly, the most direct way to access these selections is via the keyboard connector. Thus, use of the RS423 line can only offer semitransparency whereas input via the keyboard connector can be fully transparent. The latter approach, which is advocated as a general strategy by Massena[9] and which we adopted, is facilitated by the recent availability of products for the BBC microcomputer like Keymaster[10] and the keyboard adaptor unit for CID (computer interface for the disabled) marketed by Elfin Systems. Somewhat arbitrarily, we chose to use Keymaster rather than the CID adaptor unit.

Keymaster allows serial ASCII input to be converted to the appropriate parallel format required by the BBC computer's keyboard interface. It was designed to give disabled people transparent access to the BBC microcomputer using a much reduced set of switches, e.g. just a single switch. It is, however, useful for interfacing other nonstandard input devices such as speech recognizers. The Keymaster fits between the keyboard and the main computer circuit board and accepts input from both the keyboard and the nonstandard input device (in this case, the interface processor), routing it to the keyboard connector. The host's keyboard remains fully functional.

Note that the Keymaster requires serial input from the interface processor and the BBC processor has only one serial line. Thus, communication between the interface processor and the VRM must be parallel. This parallel communication turned out not to be entirely straightforward. The VRM has two unidirectional 8-bit buses, one acting as input and the other as output, rather than a single bidirectional port. Hence the interface processor requires two parallel ports, so both the user port and printer port are needed. The printer port is buffered so that it can only act as output from the BBC computer. However, the user port only allows handshaking when it is used as output[11]. Thus, there is a problem in using one or other of the two ports for communication in the VRM-to-BBC direction. Our solution was to remove the buffering from the printer port so that it could be used for input. The 74LS244 buffer and line driver package is simply removed and replaced with a dual in-line socket adaptor with appropriate short circuit connections between pins.

A block diagram of the complete two-computer system is shown in Figure 1. We consider the Keymaster, the interface processor and the speech recognizer together to constitute the 'keyboard emulator'.

Software

The functions of the interface processor are essentially to control the VRM and process its responses, but it was also considered sensible to use this processor to handle those parts of the user dialogue which are speech specific (see below). Control of the VRM will involve switching between training and recognize modes, setting rejection thresholds, template transfer between disc and VRM etc. Processing of the VRM's response to an utterance is simply a matter of translating the ASCII string into a form understandable by the Keymaster (see below). Appropriate software must be provided for all these functions.

The Keymaster allows the depression of any key to be simulated using a proprietary three-character code, which is converted into the correct electrical signals to be fed to the keyboard connector. In addition, the coding is sufficiently flexible to allow continuous key depression to be emulated. For key selections which place characters in the keyboard buffer there is the option of sending the selections to the Keymaster as ASCII coded data rather than using the three-character coding.

The translation from VRM response to Keymaster input is conveniently done by table look-up using a translation

table which resides in the memory of the interface processor. The fact that provision has not been made for this translation process in the recognizer itself is the reason the second computer is needed. The translation software is written in BASIC and occupies approximately 2 kbyte of memory. (Of course, the VRM control and dialogue control software is appreciably more substantial.)

INTERFACING USING A SINGLE COMPUTER

The recognizer used in the work described above, the Interstate VRM, was first introduced in 1979 and is now obsolete (but still widely used). Subsequent work on speech input in television subtitling has used the more up-to-date VRT300 recognizer[12] in conjunction with a Cromemco Z-2D host computer. Transparency was an important issue because the speech input facility was to be added to existing, commercially successful subtitling software called Newfor[13]. Clearly, we wished to avoid any modifications to Newfor.

Enhancements by the manufacturer to the newer recognizer have made it possible to achieve transparency without use of a second computer. The main reason for this greater ease of interfacing is that many speech-specific functions have been made board resident. In particular, an onboard editor allows the user to pre-enter the ASCII string which is to be output on recognition of any particular command. Thus, the translation process referred to above is effectively incorporated within the recognizer rather than requiring external processing.

The VRT300 recognizer is installed in a C. Itoh CIT101 (DEC VT100 equivalent) video terminal, which acts primarily as the computer monitor, and is interfaced to both the terminal and the Cromemco computer by two serial RS232C lines (Figure 2). All communication between the terminal and the computer takes place through the recognizer. The VRT300 has two modes of operation: 'terminal' and 'maintenance' modes. In terminal mode, speech input can be accepted. Keyboard input is merely passed via the VRT300 to the computer, except for a special command to change modes. Additionally, the VRT300 can be controlled by commands from the computer. In maintenance mode, data transfer between the terminal and the computer is blocked. The recognizer is controlled by the CIT101 keyboard.

Note that, in a single-computer arrangement, the computer must at different times operate both as controller for the recognizer and as host for the target software. This contrasts with the two-computer arrange-

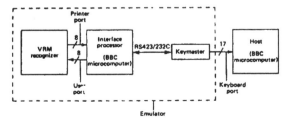

Figure 1. Transparent interfacing scheme using a VRM speech recognizer and two BBC microcomputers (interface processor plus host)

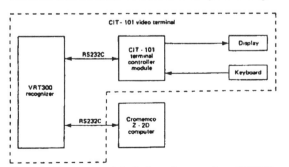

Figure 2 Transparent interfacing scheme using a VRT300 recognizer and a single Cromemco microcomputer

ment, where different machines (interface processor and host) play these separate roles at the same time. When the single computer is controlling the recognizer, operation cannot (by definition) be transparent, but this is unimportant since running of the target software will be suspended.

Although the VRT300 is a more modern device, its I/O capabilities are more restricted than those of the VRM. They consist of two serial RS232C lines only for communication with terminal and computer respectively (Figure 2); there are no parallel ports. This is reasonable, since the VRT300 is specifically intended for installation in a DEC VT100 equivalent terminal. Thus, flexible in' facing facilities are not required. For system designers wi .ing to interface to other machines, Interstate have made available a 'standalone' version of the VRT300, called SYS300[14]. Thus, as an alternative to the two-computer system described above, SYS300 could be used to realize a transparent single-computer system for the disabled based on the BBC model B. Unfortunately, the restricted and inflexible I/O provision of the VRT300 — two serial lines only — has been retained. Further, the SYS300 has the same operational modes (terminal and maintenance) as the VRT300 and this predetermines which serial line must be used in any given circumstance. Thus the two lines are not freely available as alternatives to the system designer. Problems could therefore be expected with the SYS300 and, indeed, an instance is given in the work of Stephens[15]. He describes a single-computer system, using this recognizer in conjunction with the BBC computer, which necessitated additional hardware for transparent operation. This degree of difficulty in interfacing is bound to limit the appeal and applicability of speech input whatever its other attractions.

HUMAN FACTORS

In any computer-based task, the user requires feedback at two essentially different levels. At the higher level, feedback on the progress of the task itself is needed, and this is conventionally achieved using a visual monitor. At a lower level, however, the user must be able to check the integrity of the input actions. With conventional keyboard input, no special provision is normally necessary as the device itself gives inherent proprioceptive, tactile or acoustic feedback. In the case of speech input, this sort of feedback is absent unless provided by the system designer. Since users typically have low confidence in speech input as a result of high error rates, good feedback to facilitate error correction assumes particular importance. The combination of transparent operation and speech input makes it especially difficult to achieve this.

If the two levels of feedback referred to above are to be provided, two separate displays are necessary. With the two-computer system, there is no problem: the displays are conveniently derived from the separate computers. Thus, the monitor of the host (the central display) provides the higher-level feedback on the task itself, whereas the interface processor monitor (the local display) can be used to give the lower-level feedback on the recognizer's responses. Note that, for fully transparent operation, the central display cannot be used to provide the lower-level feedback since this would require modification to the host software e.g. by provision of 'windows'. Use of two displays, however, leads to a problem of division of attention, with the user unsure

where to look in certain circumstances. Appropriate placement of the displays can minimize some of the effects of this problem. In our system, a small black-and-white monitor is used for the local display and this is placed immediately adjacent to the larger colour monitor serving as the central display.

In most circumstances, the two monitors will display essentially the same information but in somewhat different form. That is, the local monitor displays a record of spoken commands whereas the central monitor reflects the effects of the commands transmitted to the host. In a few cases, however, there is no such observable effect. For instance, dialogue control commands which change the active vocabulary are unobservable: no data is transmitted to the host in this case. Normally, however, it will be quite sufficient for the user's attention to be focussed on the central monitor. In the case of an unobservable effect, however, attention should be diverted to the local display. The designer can assist the user by indicating when this is necessary. We do this by giving an audible signal.

Thus far, we have not considered the way that the interface processor transmits its output to the host computer. This is an important issue since, for instance, a misrecognized command might lead to a file being erroneously deleted unless some opportunity exists for error correction before transmission. The transparent switch input system of Nelson et al.[4] deals with this problem by providing 'deferred' modes of operation in addition to the immediate transmission mode. In immediate mode, any errors in selection must be corrected on the host; in deferred modes, corrections can be made before verification is given to allow transmission to the host. In our experience, routine use of such a deferred mode is to be discouraged since it leads to frequent switching of attention between the displays. Therefore, immediate transmission is normally used with deferred mode reserved for the commands with unobservable effects. Typically, the situation is that a multicommand string is built and verified before transmission. The individual commands have unobservable effects but the transmitted string does not.

Turning to the single-computer system, although this is apparently a more compact and economic realization, there are some associated drawbacks. First, only one monitor is available for provision of feedback. This creates a problem in that the lower level of feedback referred to above cannot be given. Suppose a dialogue control command is mistaken for another command with an unobservable effect. The user has no way of telling that a misrecognition has occurred resulting in breakdown in the dialogue. Only when a subsequent incorrect observable effect is seen can the user detect this. If several such errors were to occur in succession, it could conceivably be impossible for the user to determine what had gone wrong. This type of problem was minimal in our speech input subtitling work since, for other reasons, syntactic division of the vocabulary was avoided[2] and most commands had observable effects. The second difficulty relates to the restricted nature of the recognizer's processing capabilities compared to those of a general-purpose microcomputer (used as an interface processor). For instance, dynamic structuring of the vocabulary by software running on the interface processor was readily implemented in our two-computer system. Such structuring was found useful in certain circumstances, e.g. deactivating misrecognized selections when error correction is invoked prevents the same misrecognition from recurring. In contrast, use of a single-computer system forces us to rely on the recognizer's onboard editor for the provision of such facilities, and this editor cannot be accessed dynamically. As a consequence, the two-computer approach gives the system designer much greater freedom to provide additional facilities as deemed useful.

The next issue which must be considered is the design of the dialogue itself — in particular, the choice of command names. The dialogue must be as natural as possible, to promote acceptability and speed up transactions by avoiding syntactic violations and out-of-vocabulary utterances. Thus, the words chosen must be easy to say, come readily to mind, conform with prompting and feedback messages and be consistent in meaning with the responses they elicit. However, the words also need to be phonetically distinctive if good recognition accuracy is to be achieved, and this requirement sometimes conflicts with the others. As an example, we have used the so-called 'pilot's alphabet' (Alpha, Bravo, Charlie, ...) in place of conventional letter names in word processing applications. Although this violates some of the above criteria, some such substitution is necessary if adequate accuracy is to be attained.

An obvious way to design the dialogue would be to have a one-to-one correspondence between every key of the keyboard being emulated and a command name. In this case, the command name may or may not be meaningful in the context of a given task. For example, to delete a line of text on a particular word processor may require a CTRL-Y command: the corresponding spoken command might be either control__y or delete__line. The former is not really meaningful but has the advantage of being task independent. Thus the recognizer vocabulary can be independent of the applications software being run. By contrast, delete__line (and its associated string) only has meaning in the context of the particular word processor. Thus a different vocabulary and translation table would, in general, need to be loaded for any given task.

It is also possible to have a one-to-many correspondence between spoken commands and the transmitted command string length. For instance, saving a file may require the two-command string CTRL-K, S to be entered. Rather than forcing the user to speak two separate commands, the single command save__file could be automatically expanded by the interface processor, reducing time and effort on the part of the user. Clearly this string expansion technique is inherently task specific.

Word processing is one particular task where transparent string expansion is very attractive. As an alternative to entering words character by character using the pilot's alphabet, we can use a small number of whole words as selections. Thus, 'the' can be entered as a single spoken selection which the system expands to the character string ⟨t⟩⟨h⟩⟨e⟩ ⟩. The potential to exploit this whole word technique is limited by the poor recognition accuracy associated with a large, syntactically undivided vocabulary. It is a simple matter, however, to replace common words such as 'the', 'of' or 'people' with abbreviated codes ('short forms'), viz, 't', 'o' and 'p' respectively. We have implemented a semitransparent short-form expansion system[16] based on the BBC computer. The short-form dictionary and expansion software reside in sideways RAM[17]. Using indirection techniques, this software is executed in place of the normal keyboard servicing routines.

CONCLUSIONS

Transparency is an important issue when nonstandard input devices, such as speech recognizers, are used for computer access. With current recognizers and micro-computers, the realization of transparent operation may not be straightforward. From the system designer's point of view, recognizers should be provided with a reasonable choice of I/O facilities. Further, speech-specific functions should be handled by the recognizer itself; this is especially important during normal speech input operation. In other words, the opportunities that modern micro-electronics offers to make recognizers more intelligent should be exploited. Similarly, microcomputer manufacturers should make their products as flexible as possible in accepting different, even multiple, input devices. For example, making keyboards pluggable and using standard communications protocols between keyboard and CPU, providing a reasonable variety of I/O facilities and including operating system calls to reroute input to the keyboard buffer would all ease the difficulties of achieving transparency. Although this would arguably add to the computer's cost, overall system costs would almost certainly be reduced. Interestingly, Vanderheiden[18] has recently reviewed a number of developments in the field of microcomputers which are heading precisely in the directions suggested above.

Both recognizers used in the work described in this paper were from the same manufacturer (Interstate) and are now relatively old. Experience with recognizers from other manufacturers (Votan V5000, Marconi SR128) has revealed that Interstate's products are not atypical in terms of interfacing provision. As a general point, it appears that manufacturers of speech recognizers need to consider the requirements of transparent interfacing more seriously than hitherto. There are some indications that more recent — although admittedly more costly — products (e.g. Marconi's Macrospeak) will go some way toward alleviating some of the problems considered in this paper. We hope to have the opportunity to report on work with such devices in the future.

ACKNOWLEDGEMENTS

The work was supported financially by the UK Department of Health and Social Security, Oracle Teletext Ltd and the Ministry of Education, Government of Kuwait. The generosity of these bodies is gratefully acknowledged. We are indebted to Dr R M Stephens for suggesting the use of the Clwyd Technics Keymaster to realize transparency in interfacing to the BBC computer.

REFERENCES

1 **Damper, R I** 'Voice-input aids for the physically disabled' *Int. J. Man–Machine Studies* Vol 21 (1984) pp 541–553

2 **Damper, R I, Lambourne, A D and Guy, D P**
   'Speech input as an adjunct to keyboard entry in
   television subtitling' in **Shackel, B** (Ed.) *Human-
   computer interaction — Interact '84* Elsevier,
   Amsterdam, The Netherlands (1985) pp 203–208

3 **Vanderheiden, G C** 'Computers can play a dual
   role for disabled individuals' *Byte* Vol 7 (September
   1982) pp 136–162

4 **Nelson, P J, Korba, L, Park, G and Crabtree, D**
   'The MOD keyboard' *IEEE Micro* (August 1983)
   pp 7–17

5 **Dabbagh, H H and Damper, R I** 'Text composition
   by voice: design issues and implementations'
   Augmentative and Alternative Communication Vol
   1 (1985) pp 84–93

6 *Voice recognition module (VRM) reference manual,
   revision 3* Interstate Electronics Corp., Anaheim,
   CA, USA (April 1981)

7 **Coll, J** *The BBC microcomputer user guide* British
   Broadcasting Corporation, London, UK (May 1984)

8 **Bray, A C, Dickenson, A C and Holmes, M A** *The
   advanced user guide for the BBC microcomputer*
   Cambridge Microcomputer Centre, Cambridge,
   UK (August 1983)

9 **Massena, R** 'Speech recognition and bar code
   keyboards — input peripherals' *Proc. Speech Tech.
   '85, New York, USA* (April 1985)

10 *The Newtech Keymaster: preliminary user guide for
   dual switch control of the scanning keyboard*
   Clwyd Technics Ltd, Rhydymwyn, Clwyd, UK
   (1984)

11 **Osborne, A and Kane, G** *4 and 8-bit microprocessor
   handbook* Osborne/McGraw-Hill, Berkeley, CA
   (1981)

12 *Voice recognition terminal model VRT300 operation
   and maintenance manual, revision 2* Interstate Electronics Corp., Anaheim, CA, USA (February 1983)

13 **Lambourne, A D** 'NEWFOR — an advanced subtitle
   preparation system' *IBA Tech. Rev.* Vol 20 (1983)
   pp 69–74

14 *Voice recognition system model SYS300 operation
   and maintenance manual, revision 1* Interstate
   Electronics Corp., Anaheim, CA, USA (July 1983)

15 **Stephens, R M** 'Voice recognition for the BBC
   microcomputer: an aid for handicapped children'
   *IEE Conf. Publ. 238, Speech Input/Output: Techniques
   and Applications, London, UK* (March 1986)
   pp 230–233

16 **Damper, R I, Smith, J W and Dabbagh, H H**
   'Shortforms: abbreviated natural language for
   computer text entry' *IEEE Trans. Systems, Man,
   Cybernetics* (to be submitted)

17 **Smith, B** *The BBC Micro ROM book: sideways
   ROMs and RAMs* Collins, London, UK (1985)

18 **Vanderheiden, G C** 'Alternate access to all standard
   computers for disabled and non-disabled users'
   *Proc. Rehabilitation Engineering Society of North
   America Conf., Memphis, TN, USA* (June 1985)
   pp 279–281

*Hani Dabbagh received his
BSc in electronic engineering
from the University of Birmingham, UK, in 1981. After a
year at Hewlett-Packard in
Geneva, Switzerland, working
on database applications, he
joined the Department of
Electronics and Information
Engineering at Southampton
University, UK, as a research
student. He received his
PhD in 1986 for his thesis entitled 'A voice operated
word processor: an aid for the disabled'. Dr Dabbagh's
research interests are in the applications of speech
technology, and particularly the man–machine
interaction aspects.*

*Bob Damper holds an MSc in
Physics (1973) and a PhD in
Electrical Engineering (1979),
both from the University of
London, UK. He is a lecturer
in electronics at the University
of Southampton, UK, and is
also active as a consultant.
He has wide research interests
including microprocessor-
based aids for the disabled,
speech I/O, computational
linguistics and VLSI testing. He is a Chartered Engineer
and Chartered Physicist, a Member of the Institution of
Electrical Engineers and the Institute of Physics, and a
Fellow of the Institute of Acoustics. Dr Damper serves
on the IEE's Computing and Control Divisional Board,
is chairman of the IEE's Professional Group C5 (man–
machine interaction) and is a member of the Institute
of Acoustic's Speech Technology Assessment Group.*

*David Guy joined the Royal
Navy in 1973 as an engineering
student. He graduated from
Bristol University, UK, in 1976
with a BSc in electrical
engineering. From 1982 to
1983 he was on leave at the
University of Southampton,
UK, where he received the
degree of MSc in electronics.
While at Southampton, he
conducted research into the
application of speech recognition technology to
television subtitling. Lt Cmdr Guy is now an engineering
officer in the Royal Navy and is currently at the Royal
Naval Staff College, Greenwich, UK.*

Handprinted text reader that learns by experience

Handwritten text presents problems for machine readers due to the infinite variety of character shapes possible. **R Malyan and S Sunthankar** explain how a microcomputer-based 'intelligent' system can be taught to recognize the handwriting of different users

A microcomputer-based handprinted text reader whose reading performance it is intended will improve with experience is currently being developed. This paper explains the principles behind the 'intelligent' machine reading system which when fully developed will be capable of reading unconstrained handwriting styles. Text is analysed syntactically, enabling the optical text reader to offer tolerance to the variability of character shapes in the handprinted text. Some preliminary results are presented to illustrate the performance of the present system which is based on the BBC microcomputer. When fully implemented the system will be capable of continually improving its performance by retaining the vocabulary of the text being read and also by memorizing all the variable shapes characters take when written by the user over a period of time. The motivation for the research is the development of a low-cost effective reading aid for the blind.

microsystems   machine reading   handprinted text

Machine simulation of human reading can be broadly classified as being of one of three types: fixed-font, multi-font and handprinted. Machine printed fixed and multi-font character reading is easily achievable, but the problem with handwritten characters is their infinite variation in shape. Even human beings make approximately 4% errors[1-3] when reading isolated characters. The variability of character shapes is caused by many factors[1,4] which include psychological, environmental and purpose-related factors.

Two approaches that have been adopted for minimizing the effects of variability are: character readers that require the writers to be trained to a constrained handprinting style; and character readers which are trained to recognize unconstrained handprinted characters. Constrained character readers[1,5] are now being developed and manufactured to recognize character sets developed by

Faculty of Engineering, Kingston Polytechnic, Penrhyn Road, Kingston upon Thames, Surrey KT1 2EE, UK

national standards organizations, e.g. the US National Standards Institute X3.45-1974 standard developed by the OCR Committee for alphanumeric character shapes for handprint. The more natural approach must be the category of character readers which are trained to recognize a person's style of writing.

The basic structure of the proposed reader is shown in Figure 1. The system implemented currently uses the BBC microcomputer to control an optical scanning read head. The microcomputer then processes and recognizes the digital character images. No provision is made in the present system to build in the 'learning' features, the character classifier and corrective feedback loop and the contextual postprocessor, which update the character and word knowledge bases. These will be incorporated after further development. Below, this paper explains the principles behind the operation of the proposed system generally, and presents some preliminary results to illustrate the performance of the system as it is currently implemented.

BASIC STRUCTURE OF THE SYSTEM

The character recognition system shown in Figure 1 receives character images which are preprocessed in terms of transforming a spatially analogue signal into a spatially quantized binary signal. The resulting binary image is applied to a primitive detector which extracts topological features[4] present in the character image. The system functions in two modes: training and reading.

In the training mode, the system is taught to recognize the writer's handprinted characters. This is achieved by presenting a predetermined string of training characters which constitutes samples of all character images the character recognition system will be expected to read. Topological features extracted from each sample of character image are then forwarded to an inference machine[6] as a syntactic string[6-8]. The inference machine generates a character dictionary[9] for use by the character classifier to parse[6] unknown syntactic strings for character recognition.

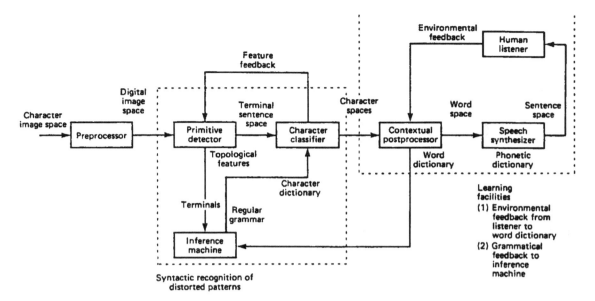

Figure 1. Basic structure of the reader

When in the reading mode, each character image applied to the primitive detector causes the generation of syntactic strings which describe the topological structures of the image character. The character classifier parses the syntactic strings and groups them into sets of alphabetical characters or unknown characters.

Contextual information, shown conceptually in Figure 2, can be modelled in a hierarchical form. At the lowest level information is extracted from the topological features and is used to describe the character images. This enables the character to be classified by considering the structural characteristics of the image character and not just by comparison of isolated measurements made on the image. This is known as the decision theoretic[6] (discriminant approach to pattern recognition).

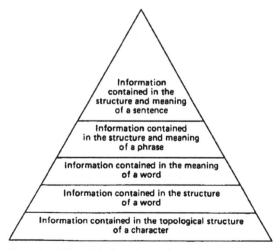

Figure 2. Hierarchical structure of context

The next contextual hierarchical layer takes advantage of redundancy in the spelling of words. The contextual postprocessor can be considered to receive corrupted text from the character classifier which is correctly spaced into words and develops a small, fast dictionary representative of the vocabulary used in text currently being read. The dictionary is used only for word identity, and does not provide any semantic information. All words are grouped according to length and the dictionary is structured for speed of operation in performing word comparisons. The contextual postprocessor works on the principle that if the incoming word matches an entity in the dictionary then it is assumed that no errors have occurred in the character recognition for that word. If the incoming word fails to match with any entity in the dictionary and differs by only one character from a single entity, then the incoming word is assumed to be in error and the offending character substituted. If the incoming word differs by one character from more than one dictionary entity then the entity from the highest occurrence in the text is chosen as the intended word and this is passed on to the speech synthesizer. If the incoming word differs by more than one character from all entities in the dictionary then it is considered to be a new word with no errors.

Word outputs from the contextual postprocessor are fed to the unlimited vocabulary speech synthesizer which builds up a phonetic dictionary of the words contained in the text. The actual speech is uttered in sentences. This enables the person listening to the text to provide additional error correction by making use of the higher layers of contextual information contained in the meaning of words, phrases and sentences. For words which are synthesized incorrectly, the listener stops the reading and makes any corrections necessary to the dynamic dictionary. This forms a correction feedback loop from the environment to the handprinted character reader, enabling it to learn as it reads.

FEATURE DETECTION

To represent handprinted characters adequately in digital form, at least 500 bit of memory is required[1]. Characters are hand printed onto orthogonally lined paper. The boxes produced by this quadruled paper are used as character delimiters. The character images are spatially quantized into 24 × 24 binary images.

There are numerous types of features[10] that can be employed for handprinted character recognition. The requirements for a suitable set of features are that they should provide the maximum amount of data reduction, tempered with the need to be sufficiently discriminatory for handprinted character classification. The features selected should also be easy to detect without the need for large amounts of processing.

The topological features chosen are detected and encoded into hexadecimal character strings which structurally describe the character images. The features are detected from the character images after thay are centralized and normalized onto a 3 × 3 rectangular grid. Figure 3 shows how the 12 grid lines are numbered arbitrarily. The square grid is centralized and normalized to the size of the spatially quantized character image in a manner shown in Figure 4.

Topological features are generated by noting which of the 12 grid lines are crossed by the character image. Figure 5 demonstrates how the topological features for 'B' are generated. The topological features are represented by a 12-bit code with digits 1 to 12 representing the 12 grid lines. If a grid line is crossed the binary character corresponding to the rectangular grid line is set to a binary 1; if the grid line is not crossed then a binary 0 is generated. The 12-bit code describes the structural characteristics of the character image when referenced to the 3 × 3 rectangular grid. The 12-bit code is represented as a three-digit hexadecimal code.

The criteria used for determining when a character image has crossed a rectangular grid line is illustrated in Figure 6. The vertical lines 1, 2, 5, 6, 10 and 12 are deemed to have been crossed if a single picture element, a pixel, on one side of a line has an adjacent pixel or diagonal pixel on the other side of the grid line. The same criteria is used for determining when one of the horizontal lines 3, 4, 7, 8, 9 or 11 has been crossed.

The square grid has been found to offer a large tolerance to the variability in character shape but is also effective in discriminating character types. Table 1 shows the hexadecimal coded strings of characters generated by an example of a set of upper and lower case handprinted characters.

When the single global 3 × 3 grid is unable to discriminate between character images as indicated by the asterisk in the four rows for characters 'D', 'O', 'a' and 'o' in Table 1, a second, more sensitive level of local

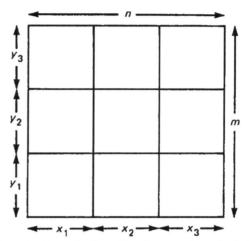

Figure 4. Normalization of 3 × 3 rectangular grid. n is the quantized width of the character image, m is the quantized height of the character image. When n is divisible by 3 then $x_1 = x_2 = x_3 = n/3$; when m is divisible by 3 then $y_1 = y_2 = y_3 = m/3$; when n is odd and not divisible by 3 then $x_1 = x_3 = (n - 1)/3$ and $x_2 = (n + 2)/3$; when n is even and not divisible by 3 then $x_1 = x_3 = (n + 1)/3$ and $x_2 = (n - 2)/3$; when m is odd and not divisible by 3 then $y_1 = y_3 = (m - 1)/3$ and $y_2 = (m + 2)/3$; when m is even and not divisible by 3 then $y_1 = y_3 = (m + 1)/3$ and $y_2 = (m - 2)/3$

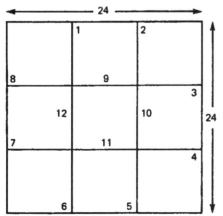

Figure 3. 3 × 3 square grid used for topological feature detection

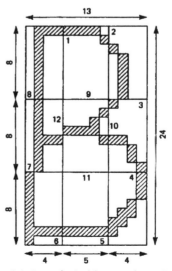

Figure 5. Global topological features for a 'B'

topological features is employed. This is achieved by superimposing local 3 × 3 square grids onto each of the nine areas formed from the original global sized 3 × 3 grid. The position and number of the local 3 × 3 square grids are shown in Figure 7.

Using the sample set of characters in Table 1 it was found that only local grid area 1 was required to provide the additional discrimination necessary to classify correctly the four character images with the same global features. Figure 8 illustrates how the local features in area 1 were detected, enabling discrimination between 'D' and 'O'. The result of this second level of topological feature detectors is shown in Table 2.

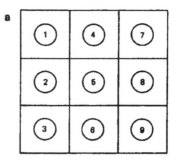

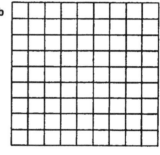

Figure 7. Local features generated by 3 × 3 square grids superimposed on the global feature grid

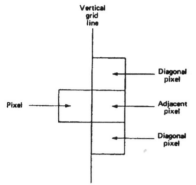

Figure 6. Criteria used for line crossings. 1, 2, 5, 6, 10, 12 are vertical lines; 3, 4, 7, 8, 9, 11 are horizontal lines

Table 1a. Global topological character dictionary for capital letters

	Topological feature lines												Topological syntactic strings
	1	2	3	4	5	6	7	8	9	10	11	12	
A	1	1	1	1	0	0	1	1	0	1	0	1	F35
B	1	1	1	1	1	1	1	1	0	1	0	1	FF5
C	1	1	0	0	1	1	1	1	0	0	0	0	CF0
D	1	1	1	1	1	1	1	1	0	0	0	0	FF0*
E	1	1	0	0	1	1	1	1	0	1	0	1	CF5
F	1	1	0	0	0	0	1	1	0	1	0	1	C35
G	1	1	0	1	1	1	1	1	0	1	0	0	DF4
H	0	0	1	1	0	0	1	1	0	1	0	1	335
I	1	1	0	0	1	1	0	0	1	0	1	0	CCA
J	1	1	0	0	0	1	1	1	1	0	1	0	C7A
K	0	1	0	0	1	0	1	1	1	0	1	1	8BB
L	0	0	0	0	1	1	1	1	0	0	0	0	0F0
M	1	1	1	1	0	0	1	1	1	0	0	0	F38
N	1	0	1	1	1	0	1	1	1	0	1	0	BBA
O	1	1	1	1	1	1	1	1	0	0	0	0	FF0*
P	1	1	1	0	0	0	1	1	0	0	0	0	E30
Q	1	1	1	1	1	1	1	1	0	0	1	0	FF2
R	1	1	1	1	0	0	1	1	0	1	0	1	F35
S	1	1	0	1	1	1	0	1	0	1	0	1	DD5
T	1	1	0	0	0	0	0	0	1	0	1	0	C0A
U	0	0	1	1	1	1	1	1	1	0	0	0	3F0
V	0	0	1	1	1	1	1	1	0	1	1	1	217
W	0	0	1	1	1	1	1	1	1	0	1	0	3FA
X	1	1	0	1	0	0	0	0	1	1	0	0	D0C
Y	1	1	1	0	0	0	0	0	1	0	1	0	E0A
Z	1	1	0	0	1	1	0	0	1	0	0	0	CC8

Table 1b. Global topological character dictionary for lower case letters

	Topological feature lines												Topological syntactic strings
	1	2	3	4	5	6	7	8	9	10	11	12	
a	1	1	1	1	1	1	1	1	0	0	0	0	FF0*
b	0	0	0	1	1	1	1	1	0	1	0	1	1F5
c	1	1	0	0	1	1	1	1	0	0	0	0	CF0
d	0	0	1	1	1	1	1	0	0	1	0	1	3E5
e	1	1	1	0	1	1	1	1	1	1	0	1	EFD
f	1	1	0	0	0	0	1	1	0	1	0	1	C35
g	1	1	1	1	1	1	0	1	0	1	0	1	FD5
h	0	0	0	1	0	0	1	1	0	1	0	1	135
i	0	0	0	0	0	0	0	0	1	0	1	0	00A
j	0	0	1	1	1	0	0	0	0	0	0	0	3C0
k	0	1	0	0	1	0	1	1	1	0	1	1	8BB
l	0	0	0	0	1	1	1	1	0	0	0	0	0F0
m	1	1	1	1	0	0	1	1	1	0	1	0	F3A
n	1	1	1	1	0	0	1	1	0	0	0	0	F30
o	1	1	1	1	1	1	1	1	0	0	0	0	FF0*
p	1	1	1	0	0	0	1	1	0	1	0	1	E35
q	1	1	1	1	0	0	0	1	0	1	0	1	F15
r	1	1	0	0	0	0	1	1	0	0	0	0	C30
s	1	1	0	1	1	1	0	1	0	1	0	1	DD5
t	0	0	0	0	1	1	1	1	0	1	0	1	0F5
u	0	0	1	1	1	1	1	1	0	0	0	0	3F0
v	0	0	1	0	0	0	0	1	0	1	1	1	217
w	0	0	1	1	1	1	1	1	1	0	1	0	3FA
x	0	1	0	0	1	0	1	1	1	0	1	1	4BA
y	0	0	1	1	1	1	0	1	0	1	0	0	3D4
z	1	0	0	1	1	0	0	0	1	1	1	0	98E

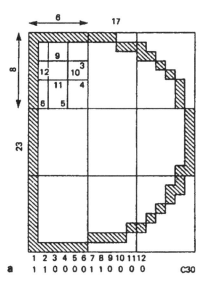

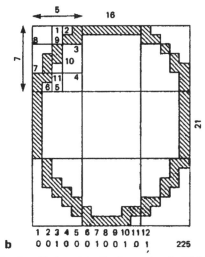

```
          6        17
1 2 3 4 5 6 7 8 9 10 11 12
a  1 1 0 0 0 0 1 1 0 0 0 0        C30
```

```
          5        16
1 2 3 4 5 6 7 8 9 10 11 12
b  0 0 1 0 0 0 1 0 0 1 0 1        225
```

Figure 8. Local feature detection in area 1: a, for 'D'; b, for 'O'

Table 2. Topological syntactic strings generated by local 3 × 3 square grid in global area 1 described by global topological syntactic string FFO

	Local topological feature lines												Topological syntactic strings
	1	2	3	4	5	6	7	8	9	10	11	12	
D	1	1	0	0	0	0	1	1	0	0	0	0	C30
O	0	0	1	0	0	0	1	0	0	1	0	1	225
a	0	0	1	0	0	0	1	0	0	1	0	1	222
0	0	0	1	0	0	1	0	0	0	1	1	0	246

CHARACTER RECOGNITION

Syntactic character recognition[11] is a method of pattern recognition achieved by considering the topological strings describing the image character to sentences of an artificial language. The artificial language acts as a pattern description language[6-8] consisting of an alphabet or vocabulary and a set of syntactic rules. The vocabulary consists of the hexadecimal characters, known as primitives, used to describe the topological features of the image pattern and the syntax which is determined by the grammatical rules governing the allowed sequence of primitives.

A regular or finite–state grammar[6] can be specified from two viewpoints, generation and recognition of syntactic strings. The recognition viewpoint is expressed in terms of the sets of syntactic strings that are accepted by the finite-state recognition device. A finite-state automaton A is defined by a quintuple

$$A = (\Sigma, Q, \delta, q_0, F)$$

where Σ is a finite set of input symbols, Q is a finite set of states, δ is a mapping $Q \times \Sigma$ into Q (next space functions), $q_0 \in Q$ the initial state, and $F \in Q$ the set of final states.

The parsing of the syntactic strings is performed by a character dictionary implemented in two levels. The first level of recognition consists of the global automata shown in Figure 9 and is defined by

$$A_G = (\Sigma_G, Q_G, \delta_G, q_G, F_G)$$

where $\Sigma_G = \{0, 1, 2, 3, 4, 5, 6, 7, 8, 9, A, B, C, D, E, F\}$

$Q_G = \{$S0, A, B, C, D, E, F, G, H, I, J, K, L, M, N, P, Q, R, S, T, U, V, W, X, Y, Z, *, SPACE, NEW$\}$

$F_G = \{$A, B, C, D, E, F, G, H, I, J, K, L, M, N, P, Q, R, S, T, U, V, W, X, Y, Z, *, SPACE NEW$\}$

$q_G = $ S0

δ_G:

S0 — F35A	S0 — E30P	S0 — FD5G
S0 — FF5B	S0 — FF2Q	S0 — 135H
S0 — CF0C	S0 — F35R	S0 — 00AI
S0 — FF0*	S0 — DDSS	S0 — 3C0J
S0 — CF5E	S0 — C0AT	S0 — F3AM
S0 — C35F	S0 — 3F0U	S0 — F30N
S0 — D4FG	S0 — 217V	S0 — E35P
S0 — 335H	S0 — 3FAW	S0 — F15Q
S0 — CCAI	S0 — D0CX	S0 — C30R
S0 — C7AJ	S0 — E0AY	S0 — 0F5T
S0 — 8BBK	S0 — CC8Z	S0 — 4BAX
S0 — 0F0L	S0 — 1F5B	S0 — 3D4Y
S0 — F38M	S0 — 3E5D	S0 — 98EZ
S0 — BBAN	S0 — EFDE	S0 — 000SPACE

New state functions were obtained from the topological character dictionary shown in Table 1.

The final-level global automata comprise a look-up table with 4096 entries. If the syntactic string of terminals is disjoint from other classifications then its entry in the address specified by the string has a binary 1 followed by the 7-bit ASCII code for the classified character. If the syntactic string of terminals is not disjoint from other classifications then the entry will be a binary 0 followed by a 7-bit code of a root symbol required by the second level of classification. The third possibility is that the address specified by the string has not previously been classified as being a grammar associated with a character, in which case the binary 1 is followed by the 'null' ASCII code to represent a new syntactic string for learning.

The second level of recognition is entered only if the syntactic strings of terminals describing the global features

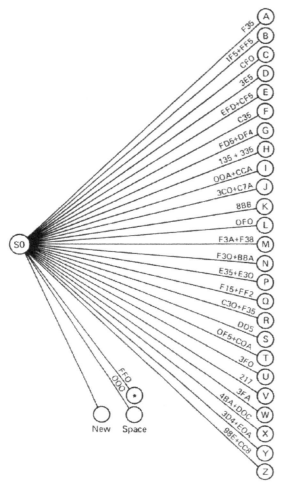

Figure 9. State transition diagram for identifying characters using global features

in the first level of recognition are not disjoint from other classifications. The second level makes use of the local primitives associated with the nine local areas shown in Figure 7. The character classifier instructs the primitive detector to extract the local primitives in area 1 which are then forwarded to the classifier as a syntactic string for second-level parsing. If area 1 does not generate a disjoint syntactic string then the primitive areas are sequenced through until a unique classification occurs.

An example of local-level primitive strings of a nondisjoint global string is shown in Table 2. Second-level parsing is not implemented as look-up tables as it is possible that a further nine blocks of 4096 entries would be required. To reduce the memory requirements, finite-state machines with internal states are used to recognize the local syntactic strings. The single root transition diagram required by the finite-state machine to recognize the local syntactic strings of Table 2 is shown in Figure 10. The local automata required for Figure 10 are defined by

$$A_{L1} = (\Sigma_{L1}, Q_{L1}, \delta_{L1}, q_{L1}, F_{L1})$$

where

$$\Sigma_{L1} = \{0, 2, 3, 4, 5, 6, C\}$$

$$Q_{L1} = \{SL1, S1, S2, S3, S4, S5, A, D, O, NEW\}$$

$$F_{L1} = \{A, D, O, NEW\}$$

$$q_{L1} = S_{L1}$$

$$\delta_{L1}: \quad
\begin{array}{ll}
SL1 - CS1 & S1 - 3S2 \\
SL1 - 2S3 & S1 - 3\ NEW \\
SL1 - (C + 2)\ NEW & S2 - OD \\
S3 - 2S4 & S2 - ONEW \\
S3 - 4S5 & S4 - 5\ O \\
S3 - (2 + 4)\ NEW & S4 - 2A \\
S5 - 6\ O & S4 - (5 + 2)\ NEW \\
 & S5 - 6\ NEW
\end{array}$$

The NEW state is used for the occasion when the syntactic string is a new experience to the automaton in which case the 'null' ASCII is passed to the contextual postprocessor for 'learning'.

CONTEXTUAL POSTPROCESSOR

Research has shown that people experience an error rate of approximately 4% when reading handprinted characters in isolation. It is therefore unrealistic to expect a machine to have a superior performance. The error rate experienced by people when reading text as opposed to isolated characters is drastically reduced. The improved reading performance is achieved by making use of the large amount of redundancy inherent in English text for error correction.

The contextual postprocessor (CPP) makes use of a word dictionary[12-16] which receives ASCII characters blocked into words from the character classifier. The ASCII words are separated from each other by space codes, one space code for word separation and two space codes for sentence separation. The CPP is structured as a dynamic dictionary, all the word entries in the dictionary reflecting the vocabulary of the text currently being read. Words in the dictionary are ordered into lists of words of the same length. The purpose of the dictionary is to perform error correction on the received words by means of word recognition. Higher levels of context shown in Figure 2, such as analysis and meaning of words, are not

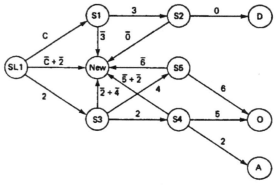

Figure 10. State transition diagram required for recognizing undecided characters using local primitives from area 1

included in the dictionary. This aspect of context is processed by the listener who in turn updates the dictionary by means of the correction feedback loop shown in Figure 1.

The dynamic dictionary is initialized to contain a small core of words which are normally part of most English text. This dictionary is built gradually up in the manner described above. In the early part of the text there will inevitably be a large number of apparent errors which are not errors, also a large number of words which differ by more than one character, so causing the system to spell the word to the listener. As the text is being read, the dictionary is built up dynamically, reflecting the vocabulary of the text in a similar manner to the way the contents of a cache memory reflect the currently used data or instructions in a computer system. The more experience the system has of a text, therefore, the more the dynamic cache dictionary will reflect the vocabulary of the person writing the text, hence providing a more effective mechanism for error correction.

UNLIMITED VOCABULARY SPEECH SYNTHESIS

Speech synthesis can be broadly grouped into two categories. The first category makes use of recording human utterances and applying various coding schemes to reduce the amount of data required for storage of speech. This category normally provides speech of good quality but of finite vocabulary as it is impractical to encode every word which a text reader is likely to read.

The second category synthesizes utterances by modelling the human vocal tract electronically to produce the basic sounds of a language, called phonemes. These phonemes can then be concatenated to synthesize any human utterance. This technique is employed for text-to-speech systems and has the advantage of having an unlimited vocabulary, but it suffers the disadvantage of sounding very machine-like.

The unlimited vocabulary speech synthesizer builds up a phonetic dictionary in a similar manner to that employed by the dynamic cache word dictionary of the contextual postprocessor. Words of text are applied to the synthesizer which translates them into their respective phonemes. The synthesizer translates all the words in a sentence before starting to utter the complete sentence.

TRAINING AND LEARNING

The optical text reader is operated in two modes, training and reading. In the training mode the text reader is taught to recognize a finite set of topological shapes. This is achieved by the text reader scanning an example of every handprinted character shape, known as the 'training set', it will be expected to read. The training set of handprinted characters is entered in a predetermined order and a complete set of global and local primitives determined and then stored. The inference machine generates the character dictionary which consists of look-up tables, for parsing the global syntactic strings of primitives, and finite-state tables needed for parsing the local syntactic strings of primitives required for the parsing of global syntactic strings which are nondisjoint. The character

dictionary is used by the character classifier for character recognition in the reading mode.

The novel feature of this optical text reader is that it improves its reading skills with experience. This ability to learn is facilitated by two feedback loops. In the reading mode, speech is synthesized into sentences. This enables the listener to capitalize on the use of context up to sentence level, shown in Figure 2. This high level of context is the source of the environmental feedback to the contextual postprocessor. The feedback is entered into the system via an alphabetic keyboard. The sentence which has just been synthesized is held in temporary storage in three different forms: in the primitive detector as digital images, in the contextual postprocessor as a sentence of ASCII words, and finally in the speech synthesizer as a sentence of phonetic words.

The environmental feedback corrects any misspelt words in the sentence stored in the contextual post-processor. The corrected ASCII encoded words are then forwarded to the speech synthesizer to correct the phonetic words. The corrected characters are also fed back via the grammatical feedback loop to the inference machine, as shown in Figure 1. This causes the inference machine to re-enter its training mode to learn the character images that were previously undefined and also to reclassify the character images which were incorrectly classified. During this learning phase the corrected ASCII encoded words are entered into the dynamic cache dictionary and the corrected phonetic words are entered into the phonetic dictionary.

IMPLEMENTATION AND PRELIMINARY RESULTS

A handprinted optical character reader has been developed based on the BBC microcomputer (Figure 11). The microcomputer controls a read head consisting of a photodiode array which produces a binary character image of 24 × 24 pixels. The character images are smoothed and skeletonized before applied to the feature detector. The feature detector generates syntactic strings which describe only the global topological features.

Figure 11. Handprinted optical character reader

The syntactic strings which describe global features are used to generate the character knowledge base during the training mode by applying the predefined character string

'THE QUICK BROWN FOX JUMPED OVER THE LAZY DOGS BACK‖the quick brown fox jumped over the lazy dogs back‖'

The position of each character in the string shown in Table 3 determines the character set to which its global syntactic string belongs. Character spaces are ignored and sentences are delimited by black squares. The training set produced the character knowledge base depicted in Figure 9. The character knowledge base produced by the training set is then used for character classification in the reading mode by generating ASCII codes representing the character images. Character images which do not produce disjoint sets of global syntactic strings, i.e. those which have a one-to-many mapping, output ASCII characters separated by the ASCII '/' character. At this stage of its development the computer does not have provision for error correction or further learning by feedback from the user and is therefore not capable of having its character knowledge base enhanced after training.

The handprinted characters are written inside square boxes whose sizes match the 24 pixel dimensions of the photodiode array. The boxes are used to enable the writer to maintain the correct index of each character with respect to the top left-hand corner of the page and also to encourage the writer to use the full resolution of 576 pixels for each character image.

Table 4 conveys the average dimensions of the character images used in training sets. The table shows that the upper-case characters utilized more of the area in

Table 3. Position of characters in the training set

Character	Position in training string
A	31, 39, 72, 80
B	9, 38, 50, 79
C	7, 40, 48, 81
D	22, 34, 63, 75
E	3, 21, 25, 29, 44, 62, 66, 70
F	14, 55
G	36, 77
H	2, 28, 43, 69
I	6, 47
J	17, 58
K	8, 41, 49, 82
L	30, 71
M	19, 60
N	13, 54
O	11, 15, 23, 35, 52, 56, 64, 76
P	20, 61
Q	4, 45
R	10, 26, 51, 67
S	37, 78
T	1, 27, 42, 68
U	5, 18, 46, 59
V	24, 65
W	12, 53
X	16, 57
Y	33, 74
Z	32, 73

Table 4a. Average size and resolution for upper-case characters in the training set

Character	Average size	Average resolution (pixels)
A	24 × 16	384
B	24 × 13	312
C	23 × 17	391
D	23 × 17	391
E	23 × 17	391
F	22 × 15	330
G	24 × 17	408
H	23 × 13	299
I	22 × 11	242
J	23 × 16	368
K	24 × 13	312
L	21 × 15	315
M	23 × 14	322
N	23 × 15	345
O	21 × 16	336
P	24 × 14	336
Q	22 × 17	374
R	24 × 14	336
S	22 × 16	352
T	20 × 18	360
U	21 × 13	273
V	22 × 14	308
W	22 × 18	396
X	22 × 16	352
Y	24 × 17	408
Z	21 × 19	399

Table 4b. Average size and resolution for lower-case characters in the training set

Character	Average size	Average resolution (pixels)
a	19 × 16	304
b	24 × 11	264
c	20 × 17	340
d	21 × 11	231
e	20 × 18	360
f	23 × 15	345
g	21 × 12	252
h	23 × 12	276
i	22 × 2	44
j	19 × 9	171
k	21 × 12	252
l	21 × 8	168
m	17 × 16	272
n	19 × 14	266
o	19 × 16	304
p	22 × 11	242
q	21 × 16	336
r	18 × 11	198
s	20 × 14	280
t	23 × 11	253
u	17 × 15	255
v	20 × 15	300
w	19 × 19	361
x	21 × 15	315
y	20 × 11	220
z	20 × 13	260

the boxes than the lower-case characters. The average number of pixels for upper-case characters was 348 compared with an average of 264 pixels for lower-case characters. Although the lower-case characters had 24% lower resolution than the upper-case characters, the syntactic strings describing the lower-case characters were more discriminant than for the upper-case characters. The syntactic strings were unable to discriminate between 'a' and 'o' for lower-case, whereas for upper-case characters 'A' and 'R' were indistinguishable, as were 'D' and 'O'. The problem would be rectified by classifying the characters by their local features described by the more detailed local syntactic strings.

CONCLUSION

Preliminary investigations have shown that the character classifier used for discriminating global syntactic strings would be able to discriminate between approximately 90% of both upper- and lower-case handprinted characters. This would be greatly enhanced by using a multistage classifier, contextual postprocessor and corrective feedback to update the character and word knowledge bases.

When the scheme is realized, the training mode will need to be entered only once for each writer to generate the character dictionary for that writer. After reading text from one writer, the contents of the character, word and phonetic dictionaries will be loaded into a backing memory to make space for another writer. With these capabilities it would then be possible to either train the text reader to a new writer or to read text from a known writer. When it is required to read text from a known writer whose handprinting has already been learnt and experienced, the character, word and phonetic dictionaries for the writer will need to be loaded from backing memory. The text reader is thus able to capitalize on its previous experience of the writer.

REFERENCES

1 **Suen, C Y, Berthod, M and Mori, S** 'Automatic recognition of handprinted characters — the state of the art' *Proc. IEEE* Vol 68 No 4 (April 1980) pp 469–483
2 **Reisser, U and Weene, P** 'A note on human recognition of hand-printed characters' *Information and Control* Vol 3 (1960) pp 191–196
3 **Suen, C Y and Shillman, R J** 'Low error rate optical character recognition of unconstrained handprinted letters based on a model of human perception' *IEEE Trans. Systems, Man and Cybernetics* (June 1977)
4 **Tou, J T and Gonzalez, R C** 'Automatic recognition of handwritten characters via feature extraction and multi-level decision' *Int. J. Comput. Information Sci.* Vol 1 (1972) pp 491–495
5 **Tersoff, A I** 'Man-machine considerations in automatic handprint recognitions' *IEEE Trans. Systems, Man and Cybernetics* Vol SMC-8 No 4 (April 1978) pp 279–282
6 **Fu, K S** *Syntactic pattern recognition and applications* Prentice-Hall, Englewood Cliffs, NJ, USA (1982)
7 **Narasimhan, R** 'Syntax-directed interpretation of classes of pictures' *Comm. ACM* Vol 9 No 3 (March 1966) pp 166–173
8 **Aleksander, I** *Advanced digital information systems* Prentice-Hall, Englewood Cliffs, NJ, USA (1985)
9 **Yamamoto, K and Mori, S** 'Recognition of handprinted characters by an outermost point method' *Pattern Recognition* Vol 12 (1980) pp 229–236
10 **Ullmann, J R** *Pattern recognition techniques* Butterworths, Guildford, UK (1973)
11 **Shridhar, M and Badreldin, A** 'A high-accuracy syntactic recognition algorithm for handwritten numerals' *IEEE Trans. Systems, Man and Cybernetics* Vol SMC-15 No 1 (Jan./Feb. 1985) pp 152–158
12 **Duda, R O and Hart, P E** 'Experiments in the recognition of handprinted text, part 2: context analysis' *Proc. Fall Joint Comput. Conf.* (1968) pp 1143–1149
13 **Burr, D J** 'Designing a handwriting reader' *IEEE Trans. Pattern Anal. Machine Intell.* Vol PAMI-5 No 5 (Sept. 1983) pp 554–559
14 **Hanson, A R, Riseman, E M and Fisher, E** 'Context in word recognition' *Pattern Recognition* Vol 8 (1976) pp 35–45
15 **Shinghal, R and Toussaint, G T** 'A bottom-up and top-down approach to using context in text recognition' *Int. J. Man-Machine Studies* (1979) pp 201–212
16 **Hall, J J, Srihari, S N and Choudhari, R** 'An integrated algorithm for text recognition: comparison with a cascaded algorithm' *IEEE Trans. Pattern Anal. Machine Intell.* Vol PAMI-5 No 4 (July 1983) pp 384–395

Ron Malyan served an apprenticeship in electronics whilst serving in the UK Royal Navy for 12 years. He obtained a degree in technology from the Open University, UK, and a Masters degree in electronics from UMIST, UK. After leaving the Services he spent a further 12 years in the computer industry. He is currently researching pattern recognition and artificial intelligence techniques in character recognition.

Sunny Sunthankar is a senior lecturer in computer engineering and data communications at Kingston Polytechnic, UK. He graduated from London University, UK, with a degree in electrical engineering in 1958, with an MPhil from Reading University, UK and in 1971 with a PhD (CNAA) in 1974. His research interests are pattern recognition, prosthetic limbs and robot vision.

design note

New design for an 82720-based colour graphics generator

Conventional high-resolution graphics generators do not take full advantage of the speed of modern dynamic RAMs. **P Prabhakar Rao and S Srinivasan*** describe a design approach which overcomes this failing, as well as reducing chip count and board space requirement

A low-cost Multibus-compatible graphics generator has been designed for a resolution of 512 × 512 pixels with a 3-bit colour code per pixel. The heart of the system is an 82720 graphics display controller (GDC). Usual designs of colour graphics generators use three different memory planes, each containing information corresponding to one of the three primary colours of the cathode ray tube (CRT). However, this approach requires a large PCB area and a large number of memories and transceivers. Further, the design does not use the full speed of present-day dynamic RAMs, as the three planes are read in parallel during display. In the scheme presented in this paper, the memory is partitioned into segments, three of which store graphics information corresponding to three colours. The three segments are read sequentially within each GDC read cycle, using the full speed of the dynamic RAMs. Moreover, memory segmentation reduces the chip count and PCB area considerably. The system can produce a character display of 40 rows with 64 characters in each row, and can magnify any part of the display by a factor of up to 16.

microsystems   graphics controllers   display memory

The making of colour graphics generators that are high in resolution but low in cost is the key to producing engineering workstations and equipment for the automated office. With the introduction of dedicated LSI peripheral integrated circuits such as Intel's 82720 graphics display controller (GDC) and the Thomson–Efcis EF9367 graphics display processor (GDP), it has become possible to produce a high-performance graphics generator at low cost. These chips have not only reduced the burden on the CPU as far as display memory management, figure drawing and raster timings are concerned, but have also minimized the design complexity of graphics systems. The GDC can be used in low-end or high-end engineering displays; but research has shown that, for office automation products, a 512 × 512 pixel display is quite acceptable, and that colour is often a requirement. As an example of the types of display that can be built for office products

Department of Electrical Engineering, Indian Institute of Technology, Madras 600036, India
*Department of Electronics and Electrical Engineering, California Polytechnic State University, San Luis Obispo, CA 93407, USA

using the 82720 GDC, we consider the design of a 512 × 512 three-colour plane graphics display on a single Multibus-compatible board; this is capable of producing eight colours from a palette of 64.

The 82720 has certain features[1] which give flexibility to the design of graphics systems. These include variable resolution, figure drawing commands, support for colour displays, compatibility with most microprocessors, high-level commands for offloading host processors and support for mixed-mode displays of graphics and characters. Because of its powerful commands and memory management abilities, the 82720 is used most widely in low-cost graphics generators.

Some recent designs[1,2] with the 82720 have used the standard technique of three separate memory planes, one for each colour, as shown for example in Figure 1. The GDC's internal architecture is such that it prefetches 16 pixels of data from each colour plane in each display read cycle and stores them in the corresponding latches to convert them into video information in the next cycle. The parallel reading of colour memory planes in the above scheme, as can be seen in Figure 2, makes it necessary to use separate memory banks for each colour

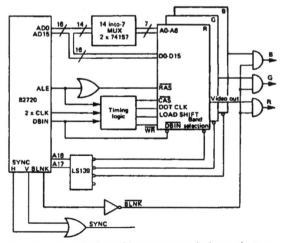

Figure 1.   Standard graphics generator design technique using three memory banks

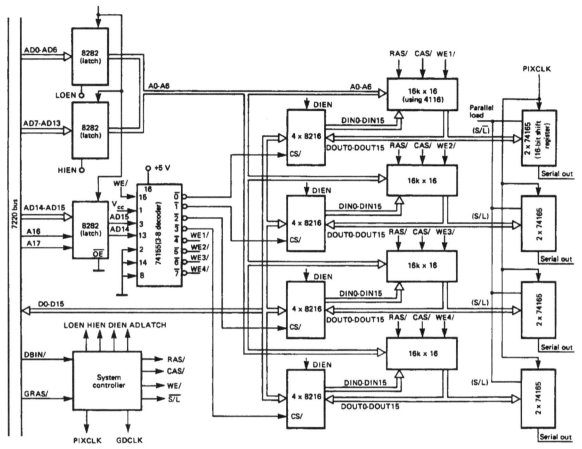

Figure 2.   Display memory and its interfacing to the GDC

plane. This increases the chip count and board area considerably. Further, the full memory speed is never used in such designs.

NEW DESIGN TECHNIQUE

With high-density high-speed RAMs now available at low cost, it is desirable to use only one set of sixteen 64k × 1 bit RAM chips for all the colour memory planes. Since the memory requirement for each colour plane is 16k × 16 bit word length the total memory can be divided into four segments, with address lines A14 and A15 forming the segment address for representing the colour planes. Each read cycle of the GDC is modified into three read cycles by means of external hardware. In each of these cycles one colour segment is read sequentially and stored in the corresponding 16-bit latch. At the end of each GDC display read or read–modify–write cycle, the data is transferred to a 16-bit shift register. Thus, by converting

parallel reading of three colour planes into a sequential read operation, a drastic reduction in the number of memory chips and associated buffers is achieved. In mixed-mode operation, with a 2.5 MHz GDC clock and a 10 MHz pixel clock, the GDC takes 1.6 µs for each display read operation as it has to display 16 pixels during that time. In the case of read–modify–write operation, only about 700 ns out of the 1.6 µs is available for the sequential reading of the three memory planes, as shown in Figure 3. This gives an access time of more than 200 ns for reading each segment in a 3-bit colour graphics system. Since present-day RAMs require only about 100 ns access time, six to eight sequential read operations can be performed in each GDC read cycle, making it possible to increase greatly the number of colour planes.

As well as the reduction in chip count and PCB area, the new technique has the following advantages:

● The system controller is designed around a ROM to obtain precise timings.

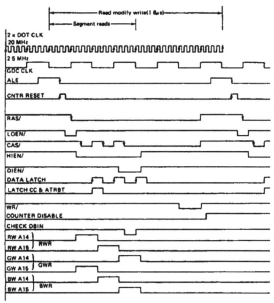

Figure 3. Control signals and their timings

- Extra segments available in display RAM can be used for generation of characters.
- The design can be extended to high-resolution displays.

HARDWARE IMPLEMENTATION

The block schematic of the Multibus-compatible graphics generator is shown in Figure 4. Three segments of display memory are used for red, green and blue planes and the fourth segment is used for storing character code and attributes. The fourth segment of memory is selected by the GDC whenever it is in character mode. In all, the GDC can store four screens of character information in this segment of memory. Each screen comprises 40 rows with 64 characters per row.

The schematic of the system controller is shown in Figure 5. This controller receives ALE, DBIN/, A14, A15, A16, A17, HSYNC, VSYNC and blanking signals from the GDC and generates the control signals required for performing the sequential read of the display memory. A 20 MHz master clock is used to drive the system controller, from which a 2.5 MHz GDC clock and 10 MHz basic dot clock are derived. On receiving an ALE from the GDC, the system controller generates a counter reset pulse which, when applied to the 5-bit sequence counter, enables counting to start from zero.

The 5-bit output of the sequence counter forms the address for PROMs I and II (74S188s). While PROM I outputs eight control signals, PROM II outputs only two. The remaining outputs are used for generating three different sequences of A14 and A15. The A14 and A15 address lines form the segment selection lines for the display memory. It is necessary to read all three colour segments during each display read cycle. This is performed by reading one segment after another in succession. The

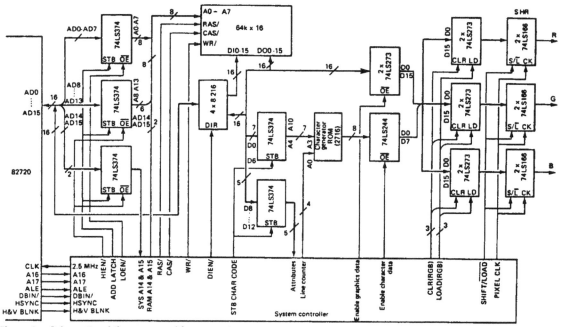

Figure 4. Schematic of the new graphics generator

INPUTS

OUTPUTS

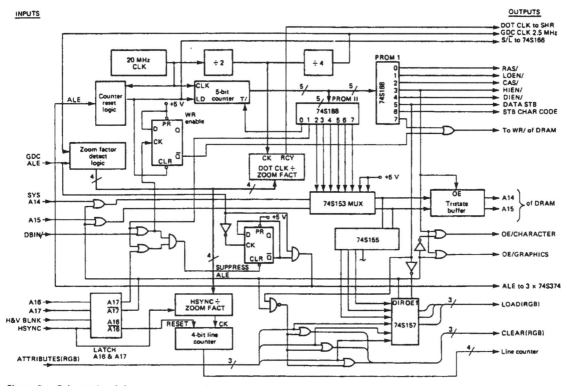

Figure 5. Schematic of the system controller

sequence in which the segments are read does not matter for a display read cycle. However, for a read–modify–write cycle, the last address read should correspond to the A14 and A15 address generated by the GDC so that the following write cycle is performed in the correct location. To satisfy this requirement three different sequences of segment addresses are programmed into PROM II. The GDC-generated A14 and A15 address selects the appropriate sequence. The segment coding and sequence selection are shown in Tables 1 and 2.

The sequence counter is disabled when the counter reaches 26 (decimal). This is done by the LSB (least significant bit) output of PROM II. The termination of counting ensures that the counter does not overrun during the zoomed display mode. The counter is once again enabled when it is reset by the following ALE.

For character-mode display the system controller has a 4-bit line counter, the output of which forms the lower significant four address bits (A0–A3) of character generator ROM. A zoom factor determining logic is also provided to automatically sense and correct the dot clock rate and line counter depending on the zoom factor set. The zoom factor determining logic counts the number of GDC clocks between two ALEs at the commencement of every new field and holds the zoom factor value until the next field commences.

In the character mode of display, data from the character generator ROM is loaded into the RGB data latches in parallel. The three colour attributes in the

Table 1. Segment coding

Segment	Code	
	A15	A14
Red	0	0
Green	0	1
Blue	1	0
Character	1	1

Table 2. Read sequence selection

GDC address		Segment I read	II read	III read and write
A15	A14			
0	0	Red	Green	Blue	Red
0	1	Green	Blue	Red	Green
1	0	Blue	Red	Green	Blue

design note

character data control the loading and clearing of the RGB data latches.

The program table for generating the waveforms shown in Figure 3 is given in Tables 3 and 4. This ROM-based implementation simplifies the circuit design and reduces the chip count.

CONCLUSION

A new design technique has been presented which considerably reduces the chip count of 82720-GDC-based graphics generators. The advantage of such a graphics subsystem is that it can be interfaced to any Multibus-compatible system to give a graphics option. It can also be configured as a dedicated low-cost graphics terminal with an 8-bit microprocessor. In addition to the composite colour video signal, the subsystem is designed to give a modulated RF output for use with commercially available TV receivers. The system controller, which is actually responsible for converting the parallel read operation of the GDC into a sequential one, can be suitably modified to read up to seven or eight memory segments; this is more than adequate for any engineering application. Thus the design technique allows designers of graphics subsystems to make good use of the new generation of high-speed high-density RAMs.

REFERENCES

1 **Olson, M and May, B** 'Graphics chip makes low-cost, high-resolution color displays possible' *Intel microsystem component handbook* Vol 2 (1984) pp 8-99 to 8-105
2 **Manohar, S et al.** 'Design of a Multibus-compatible graphics subsystem' *Microprocessors Microsyst.* Vol 8 No 6 (July/August 1984) pp 284–289
3 *Data sheets on the 82720 graphics display controller* Intel, Santa Clara, CA, USA (1984)

Table 3.   Program table for PROM I (74S188)

Address	Bit 7 (WR/)	Bit 6 (CCL)	Bit 5 (DATL)	Bit 4 (DIEN/)	Bit 3 (HIEN/)	Bit 2 (CAS/)	Bit 1 (LOEN/)	Bit 0 (RAS/)
00	1	0	0	1	1	1	0	1
01	1	0	0	1	1	1	0	0
02	1	0	0	1	0	1	1	0
03	1	0	0	1	0	0	1	0
04	1	0	0	1	0	0	1	0
05	1	1	1	1	0	1	1	0
06	1	1	1	1	0	1	1	0
07	1	0	0	1	0	0	1	0
08	1	0	0	1	0	0	1	0
09	1	0	1	1	0	1	1	0
0A	1	0	1	0	0	1	1	0
0B	1	0	0	0	0	0	1	0
0C	1	0	0	0	0	0	1	0
0D	1	0	1	0	0	0	1	0
0E	1	0	1	1	1	0	1	0
0F	1	0	0	1	1	0	1	0
10	1	0	0	1	1	0	1	0
11	1	0	0	1	1	0	1	0
12	1	0	0	1	1	0	1	0
13	1	0	0	1	1	0	1	0
14	1	0	0	1	1	0	1	0
15	0	0	0	1	1	0	1	0
16	0	0	0	1	1	0	1	0
17	0	0	0	1	1	0	1	0
18	0	0	0	1	1	0	1	0
19	1	0	0	1	1	1	1	1
1A	1	0	0	1	1	1	1	1
1B	1	0	0	1	1	1	1	1
1C	1	0	0	1	1	1	1	1
1D	1	0	0	1	1	1	1	1
1E	1	0	0	1	1	1	1	1
1F	1	0	0	1	1	1	1	1

Table 4. Program table for PROM II (74S188)

Address	Bit 7 (SEQ 1 A15)	Bit 6 (SEQ 1 A14)	Bit 5 (SEQ 2 A15)	Bit 4 (SEQ 2 A14)	Bit 3 (SEQ 3 A15)	Bit 2 (SEQ 3 A14)	Bit 1 (STB DBIN/)	Bit 0 (DIS CTR)
00	0	0	0	0	0	0	1	0
01	0	0	0	0	0	0	1	0
02	0	0	1	0	0	1	1	0
03	0	0	1	0	0	1	1	0
04	0	0	1	0	0	1	1	0
05	0	0	1	0	0	1	1	0
06	0	1	0	0	1	0	1	0
07	0	1	0	0	1	0	1	0
08	0	1	0	0	1	0	1	0
09	0	1	0	0	1	0	1	0
0A	1	0	0	1	0	0	1	0
0B	1	0	0	1	0	0	0	0
0C	1	0	0	1	0	0	0	0
0D	1	0	0	1	0	0	0	0
0E	0	0	0	0	0	0	1	0
0F	0	0	0	0	0	0	1	0
10	0	0	0	0	0	0	1	0
11	0	0	0	0	0	0	1	0
12	0	0	0	0	0	0	1	0
13	0	0	0	0	0	0	1	0
14	0	0	0	0	0	0	1	0
15	0	0	0	0	0	0	1	0
16	0	0	0	0	0	0	1	0
17	0	0	0	0	0	0	1	0
18	0	0	0	0	0	0	1	0
19	0	0	0	0	0	0	1	0
1A	0	0	0	0	0	0	1	1
1B	0	0	0	0	0	0	1	1
1C	0	0	0	0	0	0	1	1
1D	0	0	0	0	0	0	1	1
1E	0	0	0	0	0	0	1	1
1F	0	0	0	0	0	0	1	1

P Prabhakar Rao is a technical officer in the Department of Electrical Engineering at the Indian Institute of Technology, Madras, where he is involved in the development and maintenance of microprocessor-based systems. He received his bachelor's degree in electronics from Anna University, Madras. Currently he is working for an MS in electrical engineering. His fields of interest are three-dimensional television, computer-aided design and graphics systems.

S Srinivasan was educated at the University of Madras and at the Indian Institute of Technology, Madras. Until recently he served on the faculty of the Indian Institute of Technology. He is currently teaching at the California Polytechnic State University at San Luis Obispo, USA. During 1977–78, he visited the FRG as a DAAD Fellow. During 1983–85, he was a visiting professor at the University of California at Davis, USA. His current research interests are in the fields of digital image processing and microprocessor applications. He is a Fellow of the Institution of Electronics and Telecommunication Engineers (India).

Development equipment with switched memory decoding

Microprocessor development systems can be expensive and their use consequently favours complex systems. For low-cost microprocessors that perform control tasks, **G D Bergman** proposes a simpler development system with switched memory decoding

A simple microprocessor development system is described in which memory address assignment and decoding allow the system to be switched directly from a state where it is under the control of a monitor program to a state where it is under the control of an applications program. Using this system immediate change can be made between a state in which programs can be developed, tested and modified, and a state where the applications program can be test run, demonstrated, critically assessed and, finally, run as a prototype unit with the target equipment. This ability can greatly streamline the implementation of microprocessor enhanced equipment for a number of industrial control applications. An example of the switched address technique as applied to an MC6800 system is given.

microprocessors   development systems   6800 switched memory decoding

An increasing number of microprocessor applications are being identified, particularly in conjunction with industrial equipment, in which the microprocessor performs a relatively simple control function which has previously been effected by other means. In addition to the control function, advantage is taken of the data handling ability of the microprocessor to implement quite complicated features which enhance the behaviour of the equipment to which it is attached. For example, a keyboard and display can be used to prompt an equipment operator to enter a necessary selection and quite elaborate displays can be provided which clearly indicate the state of equipment. Some specific applications that have been considered are in the control of mode selection, safety interlocks, start-up and shut-down in jig cutting and ultraviolet drying equipment, and in the control of ingredient selection, metering and sequence timing in ingredient mixing equipment.

The development of 'microprocessor enhanced' equipment of this type generally has some special requirements. First, as the microprocessor provides a control function that is already being achieved satisfactorily by other means, the budget that can be justified for its development is usually quite small. Secondly, a large number of variations of data entry and information display are available. There is a strong incentive to make rapidly

Department of Electronic and Electrical Engineering, King's College London, Strand, London WC2R 2LS, UK

available hardware which can be run on the equipment to enable a choice to be made from the various possibilities on the basis of operator experience. In this context it is frequently desirable to make functional changes on site without the time penalty of returning to a development laboratory.

The strategy and tools for microprocessor system development have become widely accepted over the past few years[1]. In general these are admirably suited to the tasks that need to be performed. For the development of 'microprocessor enhanced' equipment as described above, however, they are often not ideal. There are two reasons for this.

- Available microprocessor development systems can cater for the development of systems of varying degrees of complexity, but since they are generally designed to cover the whole spectrum of applications, from the simple to the very complex, from the point of view of cost relative to complexity their use tends to favour the more complex systems. Most microprocessor enhanced equipment is at the lower end of the complexity spectrum. For example, systems of this type could typically involve the use of an 8-bit microprocessor, a small number of I/O ports and a control program which can be stored in less than 2 kbyte of memory. Such microprocessor enhanced equipment consequently has a relative development cost disadvantage on the grounds of its low complexity.
- The transfer of a microprocessor unit from a development system to a reasonable, well engineered prototype that can be run on the target equipment is usually not trivial, and it is preferred not to use a full microprocessor development system on site.

In this paper a simple microprocessor system is described which overcomes these two disadvantages. It is designed with memory address assignment and decoding which allows the system to be switched directly between a state where it is under the control of a monitor program and a state where it is under the control of an applications program[2]. Using this sytem, immediate change can be made between a state in which programs can be developed, tested and modified and a state where the applications program can be test run, demonstrated, critically assessed and finally run as a prototype unit with the target equipment.

In addition, irrespective of the state into which the system has been switched, the applications program can access procedures in the monitor program and *vice versa* without any need to make address changes. This is particularly important for applications program testing. It also allows monitor programs to be used which have been tailored to contain a large number of necessary procedures for a certain type of application. The applications program can be written to call freely upon these procedures in a prototype system.

These abilities can greatly streamline the implementation of microprocessor enhanced equipment of the type described and often overcome the development cost barrier which frequently inhibits the implementation of some attractive microprocessor systems.

SYSTEM ORGANIZATION

The basic idea of the system described can be applied readily to the majority of 8-bit microprocessors available. A block diagram which shows the organization of the system for an 8-bit microprocessor is given in Figure 1. The microprocessor is linked to a number of support elements via an address, data and control bus in the normal way. The support elements required are for the input and output of data: RAM, to implement a stack and intermediate value storage; a nonvolatile RAM which stores the applications program; and some form of ROM in which a monitor program is stored. Intermediate values and data on the stack do not need to be retained when the equipment is switched off and so can be stored in volatile RAM. The applications program, which is initially written in the development laboratory and is later modified on site, must be retained when the equipment is switched off and so is stored in nonvolatile RAM. The monitor program is predetermined for a particular type of system and is stored permanently in ROM.

The provision for input and output of data depends on the specific application or class of applications for which the system is intended; it also depends on the I/O requirements of the monitor program that is to be used for program development. For many systems some form of keyboard input and alphanumeric display output is desirable. Frequently this part of the I/O unit can be chosen so that it can be shared by the applications and the monitor program.

The volatile RAM for stack and intermediate value storage has no special requirements. In simple systems the RAM included in some microprocessors will be sufficient for these functions.

The nonvolatile RAM can be implemented in a number of ways, but a battery-backed CMOS RAM is usually the least expensive choice. The applications program is stored in the nonvolatile RAM during program development, debugging and testing. It remains in the nonvolatile RAM for prototype running. A switch that can set the nonvolatile memory into a read only mode should be provided to protect the program from accidental overwriting during prototype tests.

The monitor program stored in ROM can be fairly simple for systems of low complexity. Typically, a program

that allows memory examination and change via a keyboard and alphanumeric display and that allows program running with selected break points is suitable. The monitor ROM will also contain procedures which are required particularly by the class of application being considered and these procedures can be called by the application program when required.

The final element shown in Figure 1 is the switched address decoding. The design of this circuit decides the allocation of addresses in the memory or I/O map for the various units on the data bus. For noncomplex systems by no means all of the memory map will be used and some redundant addressing of units can be tolerated to simplify the decoding circuit. The decoding unit is designed so that, irrespective of what other range of addresses the nonvolatile RAM and the monitor ROM can be accessed at, there is a range of addresses for each of these elements at which they can always be accessed. Linkage between program segments in these two elements is thus not changed by other changes in the address decoding.

For the majority of 8-bit microprocessors there are a number of fixed special addresses in the memory map, generally either at the highest or lowest addresses, which exercise vital control over program execution. These are the addresses which the processor accesses to determine its operation on switch-on, restart, after an interrupt, etc.

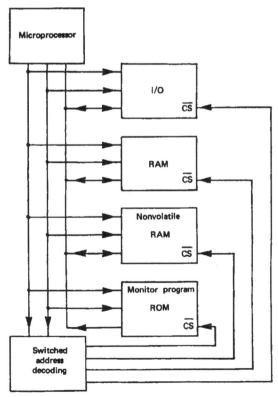

Figure 1. System organization

The memory unit which is accessed at these address locations exercises a master control over the operation of the system. When a program is being developed using a monitor program the monitor should respond to these addresses. When an applications program is being run in a prototype, it is the applications program which should respond to these addresses.

The function of the switched decoding unit is to allow the decoding to be switched so that during program development under the control of the monitor, the special addresses are accessed in the range of addresses allocated to the monitor program ROM. When the prototype is to be run, the decoding is switched so that the special addresses are accessed in the range of addresses allocated to the nonvolatile RAM containing the applications program. In this way a switched address decoding scheme allows rapid transfer from a program development mode to a prototype running mode, and back again.

MC6800-BASED DEVELOPMENT SYSTEM

An example of the switched address technique is considered as applied to a simple development system based on the MC6800 microprocessor. The MC6800 has 16 address lines (A0–A15) which can access 64k memory address locations. If the address decoding is arranged so that the monitor program is selected when address lines A12 and A14 are at a logical 1 and A15 is at zero (i.e. $A12.A14.\overline{A15}$), then the monitor program will be accessed in the two bands of 4k address locations which lie between hexadecimal address locations 5000 and 5FFF and 7000 and 7FFF shown in the memory map for the system given in Figure 2. Similarly, if the applications program is selected by $A12.A14.\overline{A15}$ then the applications program will be accessed in the two bands of 4k address locations which lie between hexadecimal address locations 1000 and 1FFF and 3000 and 3FFF shown in Figure 2. The MC6800 has special address locations for restart and interrupts located at the high address range of the memory map. A program selected by A12.A15 will be accessed by the four bands of 4k address locations which lie between hexadecimal addresses 9000 and 9FFF, B000 and BFFF, D000 and DFFF and F000 FFFF shown in Figure 2. A program selected by A12.A15 would consequently be selected by the highest addresses, would have control of the restart and interrupt behaviour and would be in control of the system.

In a development system with switched address decoding based on the MC6800 this is used to select which program, the monitor or the applications program, is in control of the system. When the monitor is in control, it is selected by the address lines

$$A12.A14.\overline{A15} + A12.A15$$

and the applications program is selected by

$$A12.\overline{A14}.\overline{A15}$$

When the applications program is in control it is selected by address lines

$$A12.\overline{A14}.\overline{A15} + A12.A15$$

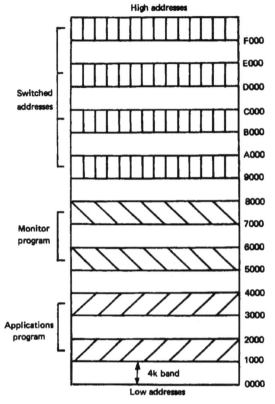

Figure 2. MC6800 system memory map

and the monitor is selected by

$$A12.A14.\overline{A15}$$

A change-over switch can be used to select between these two decoding modes.

A circuit which implements this switched decoding scheme for an MC6800 system is shown in Figure 3. It uses 12 standard NAND gates, two resistors and a single-pole change-over switch. The input signals to this circuit are the three lines from the microprocessor address bus A12, A14 and A15 and two signals from the microprocessor control bus, E (enable) and VMA (valid memory address). The two outputs from this circuit provide enable signals ($\overline{CS}$) for the monitor ROM and the nonvolatile RAM.

With the change-over switch in the position shown in Figure 3, the monitor program will be accessed when the following logical expression is true

$$VMA.E.(A12.A14.\overline{A15} + A12.A15)$$

and the applications program will be accessed when the following logical expression is true

$$VMA.E.A12.\overline{A14}.\overline{A15}$$

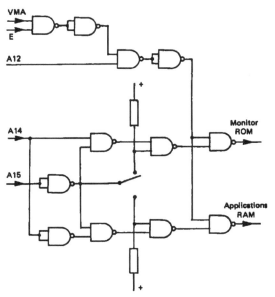

Figure 3.   Switched decoding circuit

restart and interrupt vectors at high-value addresses. For the Intel 8085 or the Z80 microprocessors the controlling addresses are located at low-value addresses. For a comparable system using these microprocessors the switchable block of memory would be located between hexadecimal addresses 0000 and 0FFF which would contain these addresses. The rest of the system would remain substantially the same as for the MC6800.

CONCLUSIONS

A simple microprocessor development system has been designed in which, by means of a single change-over switch, the memory address decoding can be changed. This allows for rapid changes to be made between a program development phase and a prototype testing phase in a microprocessor system development, which can greatly decrease the overall development time and cost. The decoding scheme can be designed so that irrespective of the switch position the system monitor and the applications program can always be acccessed at fixed address locations. This allows the applications program to use procedures in the monitor program without any need for address changes.

With the change-over switch in the position shown in Figure 3, the monitor program will be accessed by the highest value addresses and will be in control of the system. If the change-over switch is set to the other position, the monitor program will be accessed when

$$VMA . E . A12 . A14 . \overline{A15}$$

is true and the applications program when

$$VMA . E . (A12 . \overline{A14} . \overline{A15} + A12 . A15)$$

is true. With the switch in this position the applications program will be in control of the system.

The decoding circuit shown in Figure 3 only provides enable signals for the monitor ROM and the applications program RAM. Similar decoding circuits could be used to provide enable signals for the I/O units and RAM. These would, of course, be fixed decoding circuits and the decoding for these units would be designed so that they would be accessed at address locations which are not allocated to the applications program or the monitor.

One of the features of the address decoding scheme described is that although, depending upon the switch setting, either the applications program or the monitor program is accessed at address locations defined by A12.A15, the applications program is always accessible at locations defined by A12.$\overline{A14}$.$\overline{A15}$ and the monitor at locations defined by A12.A14.$\overline{A15}$. This means that applications can use useful routines in the monitor program as they can always be accessed at certain fixed address locations irrespective of the setting of the change-over switch.

The system described above is for an MC6800 type microprocessor which has the special addresses for the

REFERENCES

1   **Tseng, V** *Microprocessor development and development systems* Granada (1982)
2   *British patent application No 8606469*

G D Bergman obtained a PhD in 1955 at King's College London for research in hybrid computers. He was then engaged in guided missile simulation for the Fairey Aviation Company. From 1957 to 1968 he worked for the semiconductor division of GEC on power semiconductor applications and design. He was then appointed chief research engineer at Ultra Electronics where he was chiefly concerned with the introduction of programmable computer control of gas turbine engines. In 1974 he was appointed lecturer in electronics at King's College London. Dr Bergman's research interest is in microprocessor application to industrial control and instrumentation. He is a member of Bermount Technology Associates, where he is involved with the Microprocessor Applications Project, and he acts as a microprocessor consultant to Dowty Electronics Ltd.

'R & D reports' surveys the recent scientific and technical literature, highlighting papers on all matters affecting the research, development and application of microprocessor-based systems.

Applications

Kingswood, N, Dagless, E L, Belchamber, R M, Betteridge, D, Lilley, T and Roberts, J D M
'Image reconstruction using the transputer' *IEE Proc. E* Vol 133 No 3 (May 1986) pp 139-144

Shows how parallelism may be used to improve the performance of image reconstruction algorithms for computer tomography.

See, P S and Boyle, J T
'A 6502-based matrix handling package for finite element analysis on a microcomputer' *Microsoftware for Engineers* Vol 2 No 2 (April 1986) pp 82-95

Computer security

Lautzenheiser, D P
'Semicustom IC offers new possibilities for software protection' *EDN* Vol 31 No 12 (12 June 1986) pp 177-182

The development of 'trapdoor' algorithms and random-keyed schemes, which can be implemented in hardware or software, has improved the security of data encryption. Now a semicustom logic device, called a logic cell array, can integrate these security schemes into system hardware, safeguarding not just data and instruction words, but also the decryption routines themselves, says the author.

Control

Moreno, L, Serra, I, Luque E and Bosch, J
'An extension on sub-optimal control strategy for microprocessor implementation' *Microcomput. Appl.* Vol 5 No 2 (1986) pp 49-54

Witting, P A
'Controller realization via VLSI signal processors' *Microcomput. Appl.* Vol 5 No 1 (1986) pp 28-31

Reports the application of the British Telecom FAD signal processor as a controller. The author shows that the device is suitable for the implementation of adaptive controllers and for model-reference schemes.

Fault tolerance

Antola, A, Erényi, I and Scarabottolo, N
'Transient fault management in systems based on the AMD 2900 microprocessors' *Microproc. Microprog.* Vol 17 No 4 (April 1986) pp 205-217

Graphics

Ohr, S
'How silicon ICs are reshaping the graphics picture' *Electronic Des.* Vol 34 No 15 (26 June 1986) pp 72-80

Hardware

Birenbaum, R I and King, D R
'VME imaging boards target machine vision' *Digital Des.* Vol 16 No 8 (May 1986) pp 28-32

Machine vision is being propelled into prominence within computer-integrated manufacturing. VMEbus has proved apt for the machine vision industry, say the authors: it supports 32-bit microprocessors and is designed to serve in tough environments. VMEbus also has a user-defined section of the backplane available for high-speed communication paths, which is essential for machine vision and image processing. The authors, from Imaging Technology, a company that develops VME imaging boards, discuss the design and operation of some of these boards.

Lea, R M
'SCAPE: a single-chip array processing element for signal and image processing' *IEE Proc. E* Vol 33 No 3 (May 1986) pp 145-151

Mennie, D
'Hybrid circuits: meeting tough challenges in tough environments' *Electronic Des.* Vol 36 No 14 (19 June 1986) pp 64-76

Proctor, J J
'Micropower ICs conserve power in linear systems' *Electronic Des.* Vol 36 No 14 (19 June 1986) pp 129-134

Linear ICs have always consumed more power than their CMOS digital equivalents, but according to Proctor low-power linear ICs are changing this. These low power devices, called 'micropower ICs', dissipate less than 1 mW under quiescent conditions, and in some cases can operate with voltages of 2 V, he says.

Segal, M
'Hardware sorting chip steps up software pace' *Electronic Des.* Vol 34 No 15 (26 June 1986) pp 85-91.

Advanced Micro Devices has developed a hardware sorting device based on a new architecture, an articulated first-in, first-out register, to reduce software processing bottlenecks. The device manipulates data files up to 500 times faster than software routines, says Segal.

IC design

Darby, B J and Orton, D W R
'Structured approaches to design' *IEE Proc. E* Vol 133 No 3 (May 1986) pp 123-126

Current techniques in system design do not often result in regular global architectures. This disorder makes it necessary to provide and support a structured design process which leads a designer through the design stages and minimizes the complexity of each design task. The design tools available and the use of pre-existing cell libraries to reduce design time and to give efficient implementations are discussed.

Fox, J
'Cell-based design: a review' *IEE Proc. E* Vol 133 No 3 (May 1986) pp 117-122

R&D reports

Memory

Bagnall, P and Furnweger, C
'Hierarchical memory features multi-level access paths' *Digital Des.* Vol 16 No 8 (May 1986) pp 67–70

MOS memories have polarized towards the slow DRAM or the expensive SRAM. A hierarchical RAM (HRAM) from Visic, claim the authors, offers performance at reasonable cost by using a new three-level hierarchy in the memory organization, which gives three levels of access time. Features of the memory are presented.

Cantrell, T
'Static RAM uses smarts to control dual-port access' *Electronic Des.* Vol 34 No 15 (26 June 1986) pp 115–120

Smart dual-port RAMs merge standard memory features with intelligence to cater for arbitration disputes in multi-processor systems. An example of a smart dual-port RAM from Hitachi is described.

Microprogramming

Davidson, S
'Progress in high-level micro-programming' *IEEE Software* Vol 3 No 4 (July 1986) pp 18–26

Meuller, R A and Duda, M R
'Formal methods of microcode verification and synthesis' *IEEE Software* Vol 3 No 4 (July 1986) pp 38–48

Vegdahl, S R
'Microcode optimization: examples and approaches' *IEEE Software* Vol 3 No 4 (July 1986) pp 59–68

Winner, R I and Carter, E M
'Automated vertical migration to dynamic microcode: an overview and example' *IEEE Software* Vol 3 No 4 (July 1986) pp 6–16

These four papers appear in a special issue on 'Firmware engineering: the interaction of microprogramming and software technology'. Davidson examines several approaches to high-level microprogramming. A high-level microprogramming language would decouple algorithm design from microcoding, he says, but although higher level languages are an active field of microprogramming research, a widely accepted language has not yet emerged. Microcode has traditionally been written in assembly language, but optimizing compilers can reduce the workload on firmware engineers. These compilers do not produce code as efficient as that produced by a good microprogrammer, however. Vegdahl examines compilers for micro-machine target architectures.

Multiprocessors

Axelrod, T S
'Effects of synchronization barriers on multiprocessor performance' *Parallel Comput.* Vol 3 No 2 (May 1986) pp 129–140

While most theoretical analyses predict that speed increases monotonically with the number of processors, actual experience with large numbers of processors shows that a speed maximum occurs at a 'discouragingly' small number of processors. The reason for this discrepancy, says Axelrod, is almost always due to the synchronization requirements of the algorithms used and on the method of implementing synchronization on the hardware. A form of synchronization, the barrier, and its effect on multiprocessor performance are discussed.

Chao, Y
'Multiple-microprocessor/microcomputer performance: what to acquire and how to evaluate: a status report' *Microproc. Microprog.* Vol 17 No 5 (May 1986) pp 267–276

Velardi, P and Forcina, A
'Reliability analysis of multipath interconnection networks' *Microproc. Microprog.* Vol 17 No 5 (May 1986) pp 255–265

Multistage interconnection networks (MINs) are employed for switching systems and multiprocessor computers. The paper presents the architecture of a particular multipath MIN and compares its reliability performance with two multipath networks described in the literature.

Networks

Nagasawa, M, Hiramatsu, Y and Takami, K
'Packet switching network access protocols for multi-media packet communications' *JIERE* Vol 56 No 6/7 (June/July 1986) pp 243–247

Integration of data, voice and video communications based on packet switching principles is, say the authors, becoming promising from the economic and user interface standpoints. Up to now, voice and video have been carried out on circuit switched networks. On the other hand, data communications use packet switched and circuit switched networks. The paper proposes a multi-media packet protocol for packetized data, voice and video communications.

Realtime systems

Annunziata, M, Cima, G, Mantica, P and Sechi, G R
'A Daisy architecture for the multiprocessor real time data acquisition system of the Thor Tokamak experiment' *Microproc. Microprog.* Vol 17 No 5 (May 1986) pp 285–296

The Thor machine is a Tokamak type device for toroidal plasma magnetic confinement, and is used in thermo-nuclear fusion research. The hardware system built for the Thor Tokamak experiment consists of several micro-computers controlled by a central minicomputer. Solutions adopted for data acquisition, storing, processing and displaying and for error handling are described.

Halang, W A
'On methods for direct memory access, without cycle stealing' *Microproc. Microprog.* Vol 17 No 5 (May 1986) pp 277–283

R&D reports

If a computer system contains peripheral devices that perform direct memory access (DMA) by 'stealing' memory cycles from the CPU, it becomes difficult to specify task run times accurately. This is a drawback for realtime environments, where it is necessary to determine run times in advance to guarantee short reaction times. The author describes some DMA methods which do not use cycle stealing and which overcome the problem.

Software

Anderson, B R
'MODULA-2: a 68000 cross assembler Parts 1 and 2' *Dr Dobbs J. Software Tools* Vol 11 No 4 (April 1986) p 52 and Vol 11 No 5 (May 1986) p 44

Djavaheri, M and Osborne, S
'MODULA-2: an alternative to C for system programming' *J. Pascal, Ada, Modula-2* Vol 5 No 3 (May/June 1986) pp 47–52

A number of MODULA-2 implementations now exist for Unix systems. The paper contrasts MODULA-2 with PASCAL and C, and discusses its implementation for the MC68000/Unix environment.

El-Dessouki, O, Huen, W and Evens, M
'Optimal partitioning of sequential jobs on a network computer' *J. VLSI Comput. Syst.* Vol 1 No 4 pp 377–397

Partitioning is one of the central problems of software design for distributed systems. The partitioning problem is to find suitable algorithms for dividing software to achieve load balancing, faster execution and smaller communication overhead. The paper considers partitioning sequential jobs to run on a network of processors.

Marshall, J L and Goldstein, R D
'Software engineering in MODULA-2: implementing the GPIB (IEEE 488) in a laboratory' *J. Pascal, Ada, Modula-2* Vol 5 No 3 (May/June 1986) pp 28–46

Oldfield, J V
'Logic programs and an experimental architecture for their execution' *IEE Proc. E* Vol 133 No 3 (May 1986) pp 163–167

Only recently have languages for logic and functional programming become prominent, says Oldfield. Although these programs are presently executed on conventional 'Von Neumann' computers, the way in which they are executed is unusual, providing scope for new hardware architectures. The paper illustrates the distinctive features of logic programming and shows how execution can be speeded up by using concurrency at differing levels of implementation.

Sonnenschein, M
'An extension of the language C for concurrent programming' *Parallel Comput.* Vol 3 No 1 (March 1986) pp 59–71

Wegmann, A
'Object-orientated programming using MODULA-2' *J. Pascal, Ada, Modula-2* Vol 5 No 3 (May/June 1986) pp 5–17

Object-oriented languages were developed as a new approach to programming. Rather than splitting a program into data and procedures, the program is divided into objects and messages. The objects are the components of the system and the messages define the interaction between the objects. The paper shows how the object-oriented concepts can be used in MODULA-2.

VLSI

Lea, R M
'VLSI and WSI associative string processors for structured data processing' *IEE Proc. E* Vol 133 No 3 (May 1986) pp 153–162

Sayers, I L, Kinniment, D J and Chester, E G
'Design of a reliable and self-testing VLSI datapath using residue coding techniques' *IEE Proc. E* Vol 133 No 3 (May 1986) pp 169–179

Books received

These books have been received recently by the Editorial Office. They may be reviewed in later issues.

Ammeraal, L
'Programming principles in computer graphics' John Wiley (1986) £11.50, pp 176

AT&T
'The Unix system user's handbook' Prentice-Hall (1986) £14.74, pp 98
'The Unix system user's manual' Prentice-Hall (1986) £32.05, pp 646

Bose, S J
'Digital systems: from gates to microprocessors' John Wiley (1986) £12.95, pp 424

Carr, J J
'Single-board computer applications' Tab Books (1986) $16.95, pp 271
Hobbyists' source book that shows how to interface 6502 or Z80-based micros, or commercial micros, to I/O devices, keyboards, displays and communications systems.

Hammond, J L and O'Reilly, P J P
'Performance analysis of local computer networks' Addison-Wesley (1986) £21.95, pp 426

Jenkins, R A
'Supercomputers of today and tomorrow; the parallel processing revolution' Tab Books (1986) $16.95, pp 222

According to the publishers, this is 'a view of future technology from the birth of modern computer science to the development of today's most advanced fifth generation computers'. The book is a journalist's account of the current 'technological breakthroughs' in computing — with sections on parallelism, artificial intelligence, expert systems and computer vision — and the expected impact of these developments in science and industry.

Miczo, A
'Digital logic testing and simulation' Harper and Row (1986) £24.95, pp 428

vol 10 no 7 september 1986 399

product news

Single-chip digital signal processors announced by Plessey and Motorola

Plessey and Motorola have both announced their entry into the digital signal processing (DSP) market, the debut of each company being marked by a CMOS single-chip digital signal processor.

Plessey's device, the PDSP16112, is a 16 × 12 bit complex number multiplier in 2 μm CMOS. Designed using Plessey's Megacell semicustom technique, the chip operates at 10 MHz and replaces four multipliers and two adders, says the manufacturer.

The device has a fully pipelined architecture and is designed to yield one 16 × 12 bit complex multiply every 100 ns. The multiplier pipeline comprises a three-row, six-column array of full adders so that the four real or imaginary parts of the products are combined in two pipeline 16-bit adders.

Input data format is twos complement. The PDSP16112 comes in a 120-pin grid array and is TTL compatible. (*Plessey Semiconductors Ltd, Cheney Manor, Swindon, Wilts, UK. Tel: (0793) 36251*)

Motorola's product, the DSP56000, is not due for sampling until first-quarter 1987, but 'design-in' software is already available in the form of a simulator and assembler package, says the manufacturer.

The DSP56000 is described as a fourth-generation, 10.25 MIPS (million instructions per second) user programmable DSP device in 1.5 μm technology. It is designed to maximize throughput in data intensive applications without sacrificing dynamic range or resorting to straight line code, says Motorola.

A multiply–accumulate operation with convergent rounding and two independent data moves can be performed in less than 100 ns, claims Motorola, allowing optimization of throughput. Four 24-bit data buses give a 144 dB external dynamic range, while an internal dynamic range of 335 dB is provided by a 56-bit ALU and accumulators.

The device can be programmed in assembly language without reference to its architecture or block diagram: as for familiar microprocessors, just the memory map and programmer's model will suffice, according to Motorola. An orthogonal instruction set with 62 instruction types makes the DSP56000 pipeline virtually invisible, making the device suitable for high-level language compilers.

Internal memory is addressed over three unidirectional 16-bit buses, while external memory spaces are addressed via a single unidirectional address bus plus memory space select lines. Four memory spaces — X data, Y data, program data and peripherals — can be addressed, and up to 192k of memory can be addressed externally over a 24-bit expansion data bus.

DSP56000 on-chip peripherals include a serial communications (RS232C-type) interface, a full duplex synchronous serial interface and a host/DMA interface. The host interface is an 8-bit parallel port which allows communication with a host microprocessor or DMA controller.

The DSP56000 is an 88-pin device in surface mount or pin grid array packages. (*Motorola Inc., 3501 Ed Bluestein Blvd, Austin, TX 78721, USA. Motorola Semiconductor Products Sector, 88 Tanners Drive, Blakelands, Milton Keynes MK14 5BP, UK. Tel: (0908) 614614*) □

Following up something you've just seen?

Please mention *Microprocessors and Microsystems*

Encoder–CPU chip protects software

Special microprocessors designed to protect software against unauthorized copying have been produced by Swiss firm SPL.

The chips are hybrid microprocessor-encoder devices, plug compatible with standard CPUs, which encrypt programs using randomly generated encryption algorithms so that only equipment using the same type of SPL processor and the same algorithmic 'key' can load and run the program. 'Protective standard microprocessors', as the devices are known, are currently available for the 8085A and Z80, with 8086 versions to follow.

Traditional software protection methods have prevented copying of discs, or have stored programs in coded form and decoded them during loading to the system. Such methods remain susceptible to manipulation into unprotected form by the experienced 'hacker', however. The SPL approach allows the protective process to be integrated into the program execution by means of a processor retrofit, after which the program can be used as normal.

Software is encoded by an encryption circuit, with an internal EPROM programmer, built into the standard microprocessor casing. The SPL processors use standard source code, and only those parts of the program which contain operation code are encrypted — operands, constants and variables which are eventually incorporated into the software remain in unencrypted form.

The manufacturer envisages applications for 'protective standard microprocessors' in individualizing OEM products, preventing unauthorized modification of software by users, control of licensees and distribution control of software updates. (*SPL Software Protect Ltd, Geissacher 6, 8126 Zumikon, Switzerland. Tel: (01) 918-15-00. UK distributor: Altek Microcomponents Ltd, 22 Market Place, Wokingham, Berks RG11 1AP, UK. Tel: (0734) 791579*) □

Unix V.3 has networking facilities

Unix system V release 3.0, which incorporates the networking facility 'Streams' and other multiuser features, has been launched by AT&T. The new release allows a 'transparent interface' for sharing files, applications software and devices without regard to the underlying protocols or network hardware requirements, says the company.

Among the features of system V release 3.0 is RFS (remote file sharing), which uses the underlying network to share files and peripherals. Thus different users can access information files of different computers as if on a local area network. RFS allows existing applications to be installed and executed in the RFS environment without any changes, says AT&T.

The Streams mechanism provides protocol and media independence for the system. A change in transmission medium or protocol can be accommodated by substituting Streams modules without modifying the applications software. Protocol software can also be developed in modules, and software for network services acquires portability through the isolation of hardware dependencies in various modules. Development is simplified, says AT&T, because Streams modules can be combined to perform more sophisticated network services and to use the same modules over different media and in different architectures.

The TLI (transport level interface) and TPI (transport provider interface) features of release 3.0 allow the user to run applications independent of the underlying network; for example, users running RFS over a Starlan network can substitute another type of network without losing the applications. TLI specifies user-level functions providing access to standard protocol services defined in the ISO transport service interface; TPI specifies the capabilities required of a Streams-based transport provider, and also the interface required for consistency with the TLI library.

The Unix 'uucp' commands have been modified to use the TLI library,

making the uucp family network independent and usable on all transport providers. This eliminates the need for different file transfer commands for different networks.

A further facility, 'shared libraries', means that functions are stored only once on disc and once in memory and are shared by all files or processes using them. This feature saves disc and memory space and eases incorporation of corrections or enhancement of shared library functions.

Unix system V release 3.0 is available as source code for porting onto a variety of processors. It is also available in binary form on AT&T's 3B2 computers, and will eventually become the standard operating system for all the company's products. (AT&T Unix Europe Ltd, International House, Ealing Broadway, London W5 5DB, UK. Tel: 01-567 7711)

● National Semiconductor has already ported system V release 3.0 onto its Series 32000 processor family, and this is now available for the 32016, 32032 and 32332. (National Semiconductor, Industriestrasse 10, D-8080 Furstenfeldbruck, FRG. Tel: (08141) 103376) □

'PDP-11 on VMEbus' boards and systems

A VME module with onboard Digital Equipment (DEC) J-11 microprocessor is part of a range of VMEbus board- and system-level products being manufactured by Yugoslavian-based company Iskra Delta Computers (IDC) at its Austrian production plant.

The 'VMEx module' series includes a choice of three CPU boards. The VMEx J-11 is a 15 MHz single-board computer which is claimed to be completely software compatible with DEC's entire range of PDP-11 minicomputers. PDP-11 and floating-point instruction sets are supported, says IDC.

The other two CPU boards are the VMEx 286, an 80286/287 board

Trident series microsystem

running at 16 MHz, and the VMEx 681, with a 10 MHz 68010 CPU, a 68451 virtual memory management unit and a 32081 floating-point unit. A variety of other features are to be found on the different CPU boards, but each includes 512 kbyte or more of dynamic RAM, two EPROM sockets, a realtime clock, RS232 ports, interrupt handling and bus arbitration.

IDC'S VMEx module range also includes a memory board (512 kbyte or 2 Mbyte); a hard disc controller; a graphics and text card; and a Z80-based intelligent communications controller for six serial channels and one local area network. A 48 cm nine-slot industrial rack designed for the VMEx boards includes a hard disc drive (up to 80 Mbyte), a 5¼ in floppy disc drive and a 100–240 V AC power supply.

While the boards are being marketed as separate components, they also form the basis of the Trident range of microsystems, which are aimed at OEMs and business users. These can be configured with a combination of VMEx modules, which can be readily substituted by the user at a later data. Operating systems available are Xenix, MS-DOS, Unix, RSX-11, IRMX, CP/M 86, OS-9 and Delta M. (*ID Computers, Sales and Support Center, Karl-Benz-Strasse 35, D-6000 Frankfurt-Main 61, FRG, Tel: (069) 7139-76. UK distributor: MCP Electronics Ltd, 26–32 Rosemont Road, Alperton, Wembley, Middx HA0 4QY, UK. Tel: 01-902 6146*) □

products in brief

Name	Description	Manufacturer/designer	Distributor/contact
Development systems			
HMA and SBE families	Crossassembler packages (HMA), interface software and serial RS232 linked in-circuit emulators (SBE) for 8-bit microprocessors including the 6502, 6809 and Z80 families. Development software may be hosted on MS-DOS, CP/M-80 or CP/M-86 systems, but is particularly intended for IBM PCs. Each crossassembler package consists of a relocatable macroassembler, linker, library manager and crossreference generator	Huntsville Microsystems Inc., PO Box 12415, 4040 South Memorial Parkway, Huntsville, AL 35802, USA. Tel: (205) 881-6005	Chiptech Ltd, Alban Park, Hatfield Road, St Albans, Herts AL4 0JJ, UK. Tel: (0727) 40476
EPROMs			
DQ28C256	256 kbit (32k × 8 bit) E^2PROM in 1.25 μm CMOS, with on-chip timer, automatic erase before write, page and byte write modes and 'write cycle complete' indication. Access times down to 250 ns are quoted, while operating current is 60 mA operating and 100 μA on standby from a 5 V power supply. Packaging: 28-pin ceramic DIPs and LCCs	Seeq Technology Inc., 1849 Fortune Drive, San Jose, CA 95131, USA. Tel: (408) 942-2313	Seeq International Ltd, Dammas House, Dammas Lane, Old Town, Swindon, Wilts SN1 3EF, UK. Tel: (0793) 694999
First-in-first-out (FIFO) memories			
CY7C401, 420, 403 and 404; CY3341	CMOS dual-port FIFOs with 25 MHz operating frequency and power consumption less than 75 mA. Capacities are 64 × 4 bit (401, 403 and 3341) and 64 × 5 bit (402 and 404). 403 and 404 feature an output enable. 3341 is a replacement for the PMOS 1 MHz part of the same name	Cypress Semiconductor Corp., 3910 North 1st Street, San Jose, CA 95134, USA. Tel: (408) 943-2600	Advanced Technology Devices, 466–478 Cranbrook Road, Gants Hill, Ilford, Essex IG2 6LE, UK. Tel: 01-554 5700
MV66401, 66402, 66403, 66404 and 66030	CMOS FIFOs designed to operate at 25 MHz while dissipating 200 mW. 66401 is a 64 × 4 bit device, 66402 is 64 × 5 bit, 66403 is 64 × 4 bit with output enable, 64404 is 64 × 5 bit with output enable and 66030 is 64 × 9 bit with output enable. The devices are low-power Schottky TTL compatible and feature last word retention	Plessey Semiconductors Ltd, Cheney Manor, Swindon, Wilts, UK. Tel: (0793) 36251	

Section headings used in this issue's 'Products in brief' are

Development systems	**Networking products**	**Programming modules**
EPROMs	**Operating systems**	**RAMs**
First-in-first-out (FIFO) memories	**Peripheral controllers**	**RAM controllers**
Graphics boards	**Processor boards**	**Shift registers**
I/O boards	**Programmable arrays**	**Software**
Memory boards	**PROMs**	**Test equipment**

Name	Description	Manufacturer/designer	Distributor/contact
Graphics boards			
DBSGP series	STEbus graphics boards based on Hitachi's 63484 ATETC graphics processor and the Inmos G170 D/A converter and colour palette, giving programmable resolution of up to 1024 × 1024 in four colours or 800 × 640 in 16 colours. Windowing with up to four partitions, horizontal and vertical scrolling and zooming, drawing commands and two cursors are provided	Data Beta Ltd, 8 Alben Drive, Binfield, Berks, UK	Dean Microsystems Ltd, 7 Horseshoe Park, Pangbourne, Berks RG8 7JW, UK. Tel: (07357) 5155
ULUT1/68K	VMEbus graphics extension board with a hardware universal look-up table. Converts up to 8 bit of video input with any programmable combination of 256 colours from a palette of 256k colours. A pixel mask register is provided, and pixel dot clock rates of up to 55 MHz are supported in the video channel. All output signals to the CRT comply with specification RS170	Eltec Elektronik GmbH, PO Box 65, Galileo Galilei Strasse 11, D-6500 Mainz 42, FRG. Tel: (061) 31-50031	Hawke Systems, Amotex House, 45 Hanworth Road, Sunbury-on-Thames, Middx TW16 5DA, UK. Tel: (0932) 785577
I/O boards			
CDI-488	STEbus interface board to the IEEE-488 (GPIB) bus, programmable as a talker, listener or controller, based on the TMS 9914 GPIB adaptor IC. May be either polled or interrupt driven. Includes software readable GPIB address switches and eight GPIB status indicators	Computer Dynamics Inc., 105 South Main Street, Greer, SC 29651, USA. Tel: (803) 877-7471	Amplicon Electronics Ltd, Richmond Road, Brighton, East Sussex BN2 3RL, UK. Tel: (0273) 608331
DPR-002	Two-board STEbus expander providing up to 32 kbyte of transparent dual-ported RAM, to enable large blocks of data to be passed between STE processor systems up to 2 m apart. Each system has common access to the onboard memory, with the ability to alter any location at will. Local uncontested accesses take about 200 ns, remote uncontested accesses are selectable between 350 ns and 550 ns, while contested access times are typically up to 2 μs	Scazon Systems, 23 Agard Street, Derby DE1 1DZ, UK	Dean Microsystems Ltd, 7 Horseshoe Park, Pangbourne, Berks RG8 7JW, UK. Tel: (07357) 5155

Scazon's DPR-002 STEbus expander (left), the Huntsville SBE-8031 in-circuit emulator for the 8031 micro family (centre) and a Data Beta DBSGP series graphics board (right)

products in brief

Name	Description	Manufacturer/designer	Distributor/contact
I/O boards (continued)			
SCSI-A	SCSI interface board for STEbus, to control up to eight devices. Control facilities are provided by an NCR5380	Arcom Control Systems Ltd, Unit 8, Clifton Road, Cambridge CB1 4WH, UK. Tel: (0223) 242224	
Memory boards			
VMH-1 Bubbl-Board	Bubble memory 'mass storage' for VMEbus systems. 512 kbyte of storage is provided on a dual-width module; 128 kbyte of this is located on a removable cartridge which can be plugged in through a front panel. In addition to a bubble memory device, each cartridge has an integrated sense amplifier, the whole device being contained in a shielded metal package about 7.5 cm square. A controller on the main storage system handles device formatting, control and interfacing to VMEbus	Bubbl-Tec, PC/M Inc., 6800 Sierra Court, Dublin, CA 94568, USA. Tel: (415) 829-8700	Amplicon Electronics Ltd, Richmond Road, Brighton, East Sussex BN2 3RL, UK. Tel: (0273) 608331
Networking products			
EtherTerm	68000-based Ethernet windowing terminal with integrated TCP/IP networking protocol, capable of opening multiple shells on single or multiple host computers. Opened shells can be monitored on up to four windows using on-screen icons and mouse commands; each window emulates DEC VT100 terminal functionality. Designed as a low-cost alternative to the usual terminal-connector Ethernet arrangement	Logic Replacement Technology Ltd, 7 Arkwright Road, Reading, Berks RG2 0LU, UK. Tel: (0734) 751087	
SICC-X.25	Double-height card for linking VMEbus systems to X.25 networks, featuring an X.21 bis interface, support of Q, M and D bits and permanent and switched virtual connections for incoming and outgoing calls. Provides 63 channels, 12 of which can be active at the same time. Transmission rate is up to 19.2 kbaud	Stollmann GmbH, Computer und Kommunikations Technik, Max Drauer Allee 81, D-2000 Hamburg 50, FRG. Tel: (040) 38-9003	Unit-C Ltd, Dominion Way, West Broadwater, Worthing, West Sussex BN14 8NT, UK. Tel: (0903) 205233
Operating systems			
Dayval CP/M+	Implementation of CP/M+ for the Hitachi 64180 when used on STEbus in the DSP Designs SX180 series or Arcom SFDC boards. Installation of the operating system allowing for system variables, such as processor speed, disc controller chip etc, is simplified using a flexible boot EPROM. The operating system is available on disc with boot EPROM or in the Step series of STE development systems	Dayval Designs Ltd, UK	Dean Microsystems Ltd, 7 Horseshoe Park, Pangbourne, Berks RG8 7JW, UK. Tel: (07357) 5155

Name	Description	Manufacturer/designer	Distributor/contact
Peripheral controllers			
SVME-716	Nine-track tape controller based on the 68000 and VMEbus, supporting drives with a standard Pertec/Kennedy/Cipher interface. Uses command control blocks to perform tape and memory transactions, supports contiguous block or scatter/gather modes and features a 68450 DMA controller. Automatic retry is provided	DY-4 Systems Inc., 888 Lady Ellen Place, Ottawa, Ontario, Canada K1Z 5M1. Tel: (613) 728 2711	Dage (GB) Ltd, Rabans Lane, Aylesbury, Bucks HP19 3RG, UK. Tel: (0296) 33200
Processor boards			
ARC 50	Single-Eurocard controller based on Intel's 8052AH-basic microcontroller chip, a mask programmed 8052 with a built-in 8k BASIC interpreter. Board also includes a battery-backed realtime clock, 16k RAM, two EPROM sockets and a high-voltage regulator for onboard programming, two RS232 lines, 16 parallel I/O lines and six interrupt/counter–timer lines to the CPU	Arcom Control Systems Ltd, Unit 8, Clifton Road, Cambridge CB1 4WH, UK. Tel: (0223) 242224	
CPU1100 series	Family of STEbus boards designed to provide multitasking and multiuser features for the STEbus, running under OS-9 level 2 but also capable of running level 1. Four types of board are available: a CPU board with 8-bit 2 MHz 68B09E processor, onboard proprietary MMU which expands the processor's 16-bit address space to 21 bit, 1 Mbyte of memory and 4 kbyte of I/O on the STEbus; an 8085-based intelligent floppy disc controller; a 68B09E-based serial I/O board with four RS232 ports and a Centronics interface; and a memory board with 250 kbyte of static RAM	Datapulse Ltd, Quebec Road, Henley-on-Thames RG9 1HA, UK	Dean Microsystems Ltd, 7 Horseshoe Park, Pangbourne, Berks RG8 7JW, UK. Tel: (07357) 5155

From left: DY-4 Systems SVME-716 tape controller; the Datapulse CPU1100 STEbus processor board; Arcom's ARC 50 single-board controller; and the same company's SCSI interface board for STEbus

products in brief

Name	Description	Manufacturer/designer	Distributor/contact
Processor boards (continued)			
DBC 286	80286-based Multibus single-board computer in 6 MHz and 8 MHz versions, software compatible with Intel's 286/10 SBC. Includes up to 3.5 Mbyte of dual-port dynamic RAM, three I/O ports, four PROM sockets, a programmable timer and (optionally) an 80287 coprocessor	Microbar Inc., 1120 San Antonio Road, Palo Alto, CA 92303, UK. Tel: (415) 964-2862	Data Design Techniques Ltd, 68–70 Tewin Road, Welwyn Garden City, Herts AL7 1BD, UK. Tel: (07073) 34774
MT68020	68020-based single-board computer for Multibus II. Includes 2 Mbyte of RAM expandable to 12 Mbyte, and an optional 68851 allows 4 Gbyte of logical addressing and supports page, segment/page or segment-only memory management. 12.5 MHz and 16.67 MHz clock rates are available	Microbar Inc., 1120 San Antonio Road, Palo Alto, CA 92303, USA. Tel: (415) 964-2862	Data Design Techniques Ltd, 68–70 Tewin Road, Welwyn Garden City, Herts AL7 1BD, UK. Tel: (07073) 34774
Programmable arrays			
ACE 30T00	Faster version of the type 3000 logic array from Mullard's 'advanced customized ECL' (ACE) family manufactured by a 2 µm 'Subilo-N' process. Contains 1450 gates, 36 major cells and 1280 bit of RAM and gives 250 ps equivalent gate delay, RAM access time of 4 ns and flipflop toggle frequency of 600 MHz	Mullard Ltd, Mullard House, Torrington Place, London WC1E 7HD, UK. Tel: 01-580 6633	
FGE0050	ECL 100-gate array giving clock rates up to 600 MHz and typical propagation delays of 225 ps. Contains 12 external cells, four internal cells, two bias driver cells and 21 I/O cells and shares a common macro library with other FGE series devices. Packaging: 24-pin flat pack or ceramic DIP; commercial and military versions are available	Fairchild Semiconductor GmbH, Am Burgfrieden 1, 8090 Wasserburg Am Inn, Munich, FRG. Tel: (08071) 104-232	Fairchild Semiconductor Ltd, 230 High Street, Potters Bar, Herts, UK. Tel: (0707) 51111
PROMs			
CY7C235	1k × 8 bit registered PROM made using a CMOS EPROM process, with an access time for clock transition of 15 ns and a 30 ns address set-up time. Current consumption is 90 mA, and a 1025-bit user programmable initialization word is provided	Cypress Semiconductor Corp., 3910 North 1st Street, San Jose, CA 95134, USA. Tel: (408) 943-2600	Advanced Technology Devices, 466-478 Cranbrook Road, Gants Hill, Ilford, Essex IG2 6LE, UK. Tel: 01-554 5700
Programming modules			
E9B	Eight gang editing copier for EPROMs and E²PROMs. Can be remotely controlled via an RS232 port using Elan's EasyCom driver or an IBM PC, and can be used for set programming different data by blocks into the eight sites. Intel's 1 Mbit 27010 is supported	Elan Digital Systems Ltd, 16–20 Kelvin Way, Crawley, West Sussex RH10 2TS, UK. Tel: (0293) 510448	

Name	Description	Manufacturer/designer	Distributor/contact
RAMs			
EDH8832HC, EDH8832CL	256 kbit (32k × 8 bit) static RAM modules comprising four 16k × 4 bit chips (HC version) or four 8k × 8 bit CMOS chips (CL version) mounted on JEDEC-compatible DIPs. Modules also hold decoupling capacitors and control logic. Access times are down to 45 ns (HC commercial version), 55 ns (HC military version) and 150 ns (CL version)	Electronic Designs Inc., Hopkinton Industrial Park, 35 South Street, Hopkinton, MA 01748, USA. Tel: (617) 435-0977	Electronic Designs Europe, Shelley House, The Avenue, Lightwater, Surrey GU18 5RF, UK. Tel: (0276) 72637
GR281, GR881 and GR3281	Static RAM and lithium cell hybrids with capacities of 2k × 8 bit (281), 8k × 8 bit (881) and 32k × 8 bit (3281). Pinout is JEDEC standard and compatibility with standard static RAMs is claimed. Access times (T cycle) are 150 ns (881 and 3281) and 200 ns (281). Current power requirements are 4 mA (deselected) and 30 mA (selected)	Greenwich Instruments Ltd, The Crescent, Main Road, Sidcup, Kent DA14 6NW, UK. Tel: 01-302 4931	
M5M 4256P	256k × 1 bit dynamic RAMs with access times down to 100 ns and power consumption of 300 mW. Operating modes supported are: RMW; RAS-only or CAS-before-RAS refresh; and early write for common I/O. 256 refresh cycles are needed every 4 ns. Packaging: 16-pin plastic DIP, LCC or zigzag inline package	Mitsubishi Electric Corp., 6–3 Marunouchi, 2-chome Chiyoda-Ku, Tokyo 100, Japan	Mitsubishi Electric (UK) Ltd, Hertford Place, Denham Way, Maple Cross, Rickmansworth, Herts WD3 2BJ, UK. Tel: (0923) 770000
MB84256	Combined CMOS–NMOS static RAM (32k × 8 bit) on a 6.0 mm × 9.7 mm chip. Power consumption is 5.5 mW or 1.65 mW; access time 100 ns or 150 ns. May be used as nonvolatile memory with battery back-up. Packaging: 28-pin DIP or flat pack; 32-pad LCC	Fujitsu Ltd, 6–1 Marunouchi, 2-chome Chiyoda-ku, Tokyo 100, Japan	Fujitsu Mikroelektronic, Hargrave House, Belmont Road, Maidenhead, Berks SL6 6NE, UK. Tel: (0628) 76100
RAM controllers			
74LS764	Dynamic RAM controller allowing two microprocessors, microcontrollers etc to share the same block of up to 1 Mbyte of memory. Provides arbitration and controls RAS, CAS, REFRESH and WRITE ENABLE. Clock frequency is 30 MHz. Packaging: 40-pin plastic DIP or 44-pin plastic LCC	Mullard Ltd, Mullard House, Torrington Place, London WC1E 7HD, UK. Tel: 01-580 6633	
Shift registers			
Am29524	8 bit wide, 14 word deep micro-programmed shift register with random-access data read, direct I/O pass-through and zero-byte output features. A 24 mA current output drive allows the data port to be connected directly to the system bus. Cycle time is quoted as 21 ns	Advanced Micro Devices Inc., 901 Thompson Place, Sunnyvale, CA 94086, USA	Advanced Micro Devices (UK) Ltd, AMD House, Goldsworth Road, Woking, Surrey GU21 1JT, UK. Tel: (04862) 22121

products in brief

Name	Description	Manufacturer/designer	Distributor/contact
Software			
Clipper Cross Support Package	Software development and simulation tools for Fairchild's Clipper 32-bit microprocessor module. Consists of Unix system V development tools; an optimized c compiler, assembler, linker and debugger; and a simulation environment including software simulator, timing analyzer and instruction profiler. Runs on VAX and MicroVAX II systems	Fairchild Semiconductor GmbH, Am Burgfrieden 1, 8090 Wasserburg Am Inn, Munich, FRG. Tel: (08071) 104-232	Fairchild Semiconductor Ltd, 230 High Street, Potters Bar, Herts, UK. Tel: (0707) 51111
LPA PROLOG Professional	Implementation of PROLOG, including compiler and interpreter, for IBM PCs and some other MS-DOS machines. Written in 8086 assembler, the package includes extended support for windows, files and floating-point arithmetic. Development environment supports Edinburgh and standard PROLOG dialects	Logic Programming Associates Ltd, Studio 4, Royal Victoria Patriotic Building, Trinity Road, London SW18 3SX, UK. Tel: 01-871 2016	
Physical Tool Kit	Package for designing RCA's PA50000 series CMOS gate arrays designed to be used with Daisy's MegaGatemaster workstation in conjunction with the PA50000 Electrica Kit	RCA, Camden, NJ 08101, USA	RCA Ltd, Lincoln Way, Windmill Road, Sunbury-on-Thames, Middx TW16 7HW, UK. Tel: (09327) 85511

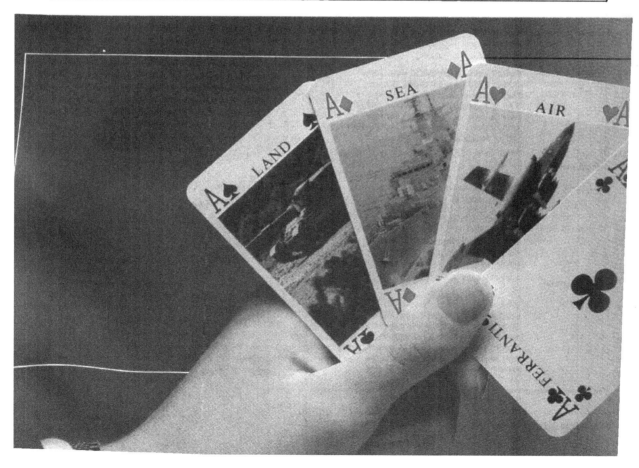

Name	Description	Manufacturer/designer	Distributor/contact
S400 IBM PC	Suite of utilities for hardware and software development for the HMCS400 series of microcomputers, running on the IBM PC. Comprises four main parts: a crossassembler with relocatable code and macro facilities; a linker; emulator interface software; and a PROM programmer interface	Hitachi Ltd, New Marunouchi Building No 5, 1-chome Marunouchi, Chiyoda, Tokyo, Japan	Hitachi Electronic Components (UK) Ltd, 21 Upton Road, Watford, Herts WD1 7TB, UK. Tel: (0923) 46488
X68000	Crossassembler for the 68000, 68008 and 68010 microprocessors, a member of Real Time System's XA8 series. Available for VMS or Unix running on a VAX machine, Idris or Unix on a PDP-11 or 68000-based machine and PC-DOS or MS-DOS on the IBM PC or compatibles	Real Time Systems Ltd, PO Box 70, Viking House, Nelson Street, Douglas, Isle of Man, UK. Tel: (0624) 26021	
Test equipment			
TSI-8150	Reconfigurable IEEE-488 controlled target device interface for automatic test equipment, consisting primarily of a main chassis and a device-under-test adaptor. Can handle signal switching from low-level DC to 18 GHz AC	Tektronix Inc., PO Box 500, Beaverton, OR 97077, USA	Tektronix UK Ltd, Fourth Avenue, Globe Park, Marlow, Bucks SL7 1YD, UK. Tel: (06284) 6000

UK government sponsors MAP awareness schemes

Three government-sponsored bodies are promoting initiatives aimed at providing UK industry with a 'technical forum' on multivendor computer communications, in particular the Manufacturing Automation Protocol (MAP) and technical office protocol (TOP) schemes, and their role in advanced manufacturing technology (AMT) generally.

As part of its advanced manufacturing awareness programme, the UK Department of Trade and Industry (DTI) is underwriting a £5.5M MAP demonstration to be held on 1–5 December 1986 at the National Exhibition Centre in Birmingham. The DTI has also begun moves towards setting up a MAP test and conformance centre, awarding a contract for joint work between the UK National Computer Centre and University of Leeds Industrial Services Ltd to define the requirements for establishing such a centre.

In addition, the British Standards Institution (BSI) has announced that it has consolidated all its AMT activities into a single coherent programme under a new standards committee to be known as AMT/–.

The trend in industrial automation is to link 'islands of technology' such as machine tools, robots or engineering workstations on the shop floor, providing fully integrated systems under computer control. The MAP/TOP schemes are intended to enable effective communication between these 'islands'. For example US car manufacturer General Motors (GM), which launched MAP, estimates that it uses 40 000 intelligent shop floor devices in its 'islands', and forecasts that this figure will rise to 200 000 by the end of the decade. Furthermore, GM claims that 85% of the devices installed today are 'incompatible', i.e. they share no common communication standard. MAP was introduced as the company's solution to this problem.

Over 50 competing companies are to collaborate in the 'live' MAP network demonstration, including IBM, ICL, DEC, British Telecom, Intel, Motorola and manufacturing

Butcher: 'Vital tool in achieving competitiveness'

companies such as British Aerospace, Jaguar Cars, Lucas and Unilever. Announcing the demonstration, the UK government's industry under secretary John Butcher said that the project is 'an example of UK initiative which is setting the pace for the rest of the world'. Alarm has been expressed by some sources, however, that the UK is lagging in converting to computer integrated manufacturing. GM is reported to be using the technology already in three US bus and truck plants, and by 1988 it will build its first cars using MAP as the sole communication specification. GM claims that all its plants will be MAP compatible within five years.

Butcher went on to say that the demonstration was important to alert UK manufacturers to the emergence of multivendor computer communications; to encourage vendors of AMT equipment to recognize the importance of MAP and TOP in opening up their products to wider markets; and to establish a pool of expertise in the UK in planning, implementation and conformance testing for the emerging communications systems.

Directing his comments at company managers, Butcher remarked that: 'It is open to any company to compete on a world scale. I believe that this communications technology provides management with a vital tool in achieving competitiveness.'

MAP is one example of many unconnected worldwide initiatives providing individual standards which are slowly converging to provide a unified framework for the development of advanced manufacturing technology. Initial graphics exchange specification (IGES) for CADCAM data exchange is another example. Recognizing this, BSI has formed the AMT/– committee to provide industry with information and guidance on the current status of all emerging AMT standards.

The scope of AMT/– includes: numerically controlled machine tools, robotics, control languages for manufacturing equipment, CADCAM data exchange, reference models for AMT, mechanical and electrical standards for AMT equipment, interdevice communication, process control and coordinate measuring. Each area will be served by a specialist technical committee. Through the pooled expertise on the committee, BSI hopes to be able to influence the development of international standards through its membership of the International Standards Organization (ISO) and other world standards bodies.

According to BSI, what is emerging are loose, de facto industry standards that are 'snapshots' of a fast moving technology. Due to the ponderous procedures for obtaining formal approval of ISO drafts for publication as standards, the BSI says it will make 'relatively stable' approved drafts available as 'drafts for development' (DDs) even though these may change prior to the publication of the standard. A list of DDs and British Standards for OSI, local area networks and computer graphics is available from British Standards Institution, 2 Park Street, London W1A 2BS, UK. Tel: 01-629 9000.

● A multivendor factory communications and MAP demonstration will be featured at the 1986 International Symposium on Automotive Technology and Automation (ISATA), the organizers have announced. The symposium, which is being held on 6–10 October at Flims in Switzerland, will focus on computer integrated manufacturing. □

Design centre boom

Regional VLSI design centres will be used by over 60% of systems designers to develop application-specific integrated circuits (ASICs) by the year 1990, says market research firm ETP. In the report *Customizing VLSI integrated circuits update — a user's guide to the IC design centre,* the firm predicts that design centre sales will represent 75% of a $7200M ASIC market by the end of the decade.

'The worldwide electronics industry is undergoing an unprecedented shift, with the future emphasis on service, design assistance and support,' asserts report author Osvaldo Viva. 'At the centre of this shift is the emergence of the VLSI design centre.

There is still a shortage of IC design expertise in the OEM area, however. The report estimates that there are between 3000 and 4000 expert IC designers worldwide, and that nearly 65% of them are employed by semiconductor manufacturers. While this population has not changed appreciably over the last decade, and is expected to remain unchanged into the next, the number of system designers has tripled in the same period and will double again by 1990.

The ratio of IC designers to systems designers has thus steadily dropped, says ETP, creating an unparalleled demand for IC design expertise which has led to the emergence of the VLSI design centre. (*Electronic Trend Publications, Nordre Ringvej 201, 2600 Glostrup-Copenhagen, Denmark. Tel: (452) 63-20-44*) □

$2M implanter sold

Applied Materials in the UK has shipped its first Precision Implant 9000 automated ion implant system (see *Microprocessors Microsyst.* Vol 9 No 9 (November 1985), page 470). The system, which normally sells for around $2M, was bought by Siemens for its Perlach Centre in Munich, FRG. It will be used primarily for a pilot line of 4 Mbit CMOS devices, and also in the production of 1 Mbit CMOS chips. □

Standard is introduced for CD ROM

The two companies that pioneered compact disc (CD) technology, Philips and Sony, have published specifications to enable applications to access data from a CD ROM system independently of the hardware and operating system being used. The final specification is expected by the end of 1986.

By avoiding confusion caused by noncompatible systems, the companies hope to spur the rapidly growing market for CD ROM. A recent report *CD-ROM markets* from US market research company IRD estimates that shipments of CD ROM players will be worth over $1000M early in the 1990s, the main application being business databases.

The CD ROM specifications will define a logical format standard for what is called the 'CD interactive media system' (CD-I). By harmonizing the file system of CD ROM and CD-I, CD ROM discs will be playable on any CD-I player conforming to the specifications. Features specified include how various types of data stored on CD are identified, how data are encoded and how tracks, files and records are laid out on the disc.

Prior to the CD-I specifications a CD ROM drive could act as a computer peripheral and information stored on CD ROM disc could be retrieved with a personal computer via floppy disc. CD-I players, however, are standalone units with their own intelligence, eliminating the need for floppy disc support.

The CD digital audio system, the precursor to CD ROM, was jointly developed by Philips and Sony in 1980, Agreements for CD ROM applications were reached between the two companies in 1983, and in 1985 they announced the physical format specification for CD ROM, which laid the groundwork for storing character and graphic information. (*International Resource Development, 6 Prowitt Street, Norwalk, CT 06855, USA. Tel: (203) 866-7800*) □

AI researchers have missed the point, says critic

Fifth-generation researchers have missed the basic point of Artificial Intelligence (AI) by trying to surmount mathematical obstacles that are irrelevant to their goals, according to Paul Bassett, vice president of research with Canadian software firm Netron.

Speaking at the Digital Equipment user show DECUS at Dallas, USA, Bassett accused researchers, especially in Japan, of being 'hung up on formal logic and failing to see that AI is all about ambiguity and inconsistency — the bread and butter of natural intelligence'. He quotes the reported abandonment of Delta, the Japanese parallel inference engine, as evidence of the country's faltering fifth-generation programme, and contested that this apparent failure made it more important than ever that models for inconsistency be applied to achieve the programme's aims.

'The world of AI will be revolutionized when "piecewise consistent systems" can be reconciled with the deterministic, consistent behaviour of the computer. Until sufficient models for inconsistency are utilized, inference machines such as those under development by the Japanese will be limited to complete information domain (CID) situations, such as payroll systems, in which all the information necessary to solve a problem is available,' Bassett said.

The difficulty, according to Bassett, is that most real-world problems occur in partial information domain (PID) situations, in which the data and/or algorithms necessary to solve problems are either complete or inconsistent, or both. 'Just as one rationalizes when personally held beliefs or principles conflict with one another, a computer can be made to cope when its individually consistent (piecewise consistent) models of reality are collectively inconsistent.' □

Translation system uses Esperanto

Buro voor Systeemontwikkeling (BSO) of the Netherlands is using the 'international language' Esperanto to implement a distributed system for translating between two European languages.

The aim of the DLT (distributed language translation) project, which is sponsored to the tune of £3M by the European Economic Commission, is to produce machine translation systems which translate first from the source language into Esperanto, and then into the target language. Esperanto was picked as an intermediary language because it was conceived and drawn up to be logical and consistent.

As the DLT systems are to be distributed, the final versions will be able to translate the source language into Esperanto at a teletext or word processor unit and send the Esperanto version by telephone to another computer station for translation to the target language. An English-to-German prototype is currently in development and BSO has been encouraged by the results of the feasibility study.

Among the problems which remain to be solved is maximization of text comprehension by the computer station, to keep interrogation time of the inputter to a minimum. This may entail incorporation of artificial intelligence. □

Voice processing markets forecast

Voice processing markets will leap from a value of $25M last year to $601M (in constant dollar terms) by 1994, predicts market research company Frost & Sullivan.

Voice processing owes its basic viability to the plummeting cost of computer power, but there are in fact five separate technologies involved: voice recognition, voice synthesis, voice compression, speaker verification and speech understanding. Each of these is advancing at its own pace, says the report *European market for voice processing*. The report goes on to identify several areas as potentially major applications for voice processing:

- Voice messaging, being essentially a sophisticated answering machine networked to PABXs, is easily the largest application at present with some $20M revenues projected for this year. Such devices are already well established in the USA and are likely to become a standard feature on most new PABXs in the next decade. Thus the report predicts a $223M market by 1994.
- Voice I/O by telephone involves touch-tone input via a telephone with output of a synthesized and compressed voice. Europe's telephone networks are likely to encourage its spread to increase their own revenues, resulting in a

$67M equipment market by 1994.
- Voice-activated office devices are aimed ultimately towards the voice-driven typewriter — F&S expects commercial versions to see the light of day by 1990. This market is set to grow from $0.5M in 1985 to $55M by 1994.
- Industrial applications are expected to reach a 1994 market value of $50M.
- Consumer products currently account for a tiny share of the market and are unlikely to improve their position much, although the number of residential appliances will increase over the next five years.
- Military and aerospace markets provided $5M revenue in 1985 due to the high hardware cost involved and in spite of the fact that the technology found very limited application in cockpit controls and cartography. These markets are expected to reach a 1994 level of $63M.

Other applications include systems to aid the handicapped and speaker verification systems for security of databases and building entry. These markets will grow from $5M expected this year to $77M in 1994. (*Frost & Sullivan Ltd, 104–112 Marylebone Lane, London W1M 5FU, UK. Tel: 01-935 3190*) □

The UK National Computing Centre has started an information base on software engineering, and is helping to organize a training course for engineers in the same field. It also provided the validation for Systems Designers' ADA compiler for MIL-STD-1750A

Software engineering at NCC

A 'comprehensive information base' of software engineering tools and methods is being set up at the UK's National Computing Centre (NCC) in Manchester. The project will involve staff from two programmes currently financed by the UK Department of Trade and Industry: STARTS (software tools for application to realtime systems), which is also currently updating its guide for the development of complex software systems, and the Software Tools Demonstration Centre (STDC). Software engineering suppliers who wish to be included in the information base and/or the START Guide should contact *STDC, NCC Ltd, Oxford Road, Manchester M1 7ED, UK. Tel: 061-228 6333.*

● Also in the software engineering field, the NCC is collaborating with the Institute of Electrical Engineers (IEE) on a UK certification course for Chartered and Technician Engineers, to be introduced in October 1987. This action has been prompted by the concern in both organizations over 'the current shortage of high-quality engineers' in engineering, communications and control.

UK software skills shortage

The concerns of the IEE and NCC are borne out by the findings of a Policy Services Institute (PSI) survey on the use of microelectronics in UK factories. The survey of some 1200 companies, which was sponsored by the UK government, points to software problems and a lack of suitably trained staff as the major barriers to the adoption of microelectronics, although over half of the UK's factories now use micro components in their products or processes — a 2.5-fold increase on 1982 levels. Nearly half of the microelectronics users reported difficulties in obtaining programming staff, and more then half said that programming took longer than expected.

ISDN chip-set link

Semiconductor design and compatible manufacturing technologies for a range of ISDN products conceived by Canadian-based Northern Telecom (NT) are to be researched by Motorola under the terms of a recent agreement. NT is providing Motorola with network and system architectures, semiconductor device specifications and ISDN (integrated services digital network) evaluation results for a chip set that includes CCITT-defined S/T interface devices and U interface transceivers for ISDN terminal, network termination and line card applications. Motorola's role will be to develop a process suitable for low-

cost, high-volume manufacturing, as well as marketing and distribution of the resulting silicon. The agreement also calls for the adoption of a generic interchip digital link for use as high-speed I/O for the S/T and U interfaces and other ISDN devices.

Eureka accepts ES2

Quick-turnaround custom chip maker European Silicon Structures (ES2) was among the projects approved for financial support under the Eureka programme at a recent meeting of European ministers. ES2 has also given the first public demonstration of its Solo 2000 ASIC design system, based on SDA tools and running on a Sun 3 microcomputer. The demonstration showed the closed loop verification system comparing schematics with physical layout.

ADA validated for 1750A

What is claimed to be the first validated ADA crosscompiler for the MIL-STD-1750A microprocessor has been announced by UK-based firm Systems Designers. Defined in 1980 for US Air Force weapons systems, conformance to MIL-STD-1750A is now a requirement for 16-bit micros in a wide variety of avionics applications, with devices being manufactured by Fairchild, Ferranti, GEC and Sperry amongst others. The original language specified was JOVIAL J73, but this is now being superseded by ADA, says Systems Designers.

Zilog takes 64180

Hitachi's HD64180 8-bit CPU, which is software compatible with the Z80, is to be manufactured and marketed by Zilog. As part of the deal between the two companies, Zilog will also gain nonexclusive production rights to the HD4186 as well as future product extensions, and Hitachi will be providing a modified version of the 64180 specifically designed for total compatibility with Z80 peripherals. The 64180 will be marketed by Zilog as the Z64180.

Date	Title	Contact	Place	Other details

1986

21–26 September	Software Engineering for Microprocessor Systems	Institution of Electrical Engineers, Savoy Place, London WC2R 0BL, UK. Tel: 01-240 1871	City University, London, UK	Fourth IEE 'vacation school' on software engineering for those with an electronics/hardware or assembly language background
22–25 September	EUUG Fall '86 Conference	European Unix Systems User Group, Owles Hall, Buntingford, Herts SG9 9PL, UK. Tel: (0763) 73039	Manchester, UK	Technical workshop on distributed Unix systems
23–24 September	Customized ICs	Professor R W Hartenstein, Universität Kaiserlautern, Bau 12/4, Postfach 3049, D-6750 Kaiserlautern, FRG	Kaiserlautern, FRG	European conference on customer–vendor interfaces in microelectronics, sponsored by the Commission of the European Communities
23–25 September	Microsoftware 1986	Dr R A Adey, Computational Mechanics Institute, Suite 6200, 400 West Cummings Park, Woburn, MA 01801, USA. Tel: (617) 933-7374	Boston, USA	International conference on microsoftware in engineering, covering codes developed for personal computers, workstations and expert systems
23–26 September	HCI '86	Conference Department, British Computer Society, 13 Mansfield Street, London W1M 0BP, UK. Tel: 01-637 0471	University of York, UK	International conference on human–computer interaction. Includes: practical experience of user-centred design; user interface evaluation; user modelling; task analysis; interface tools and techniques; systems for the handicapped
30 September –2 October	ATE '86	Network Events Ltd, Printers Mews, Market Hill, Buckingham MK18 1JX, UK	Palais des Congres, Paris, France	Fifth automatic testing and test instrumentation exhibition and conference
6–8 October	3rd International Symposium on Molecular Electronic Devices	Forrest L Carter, Chemistry Division, Code 6170, Naval Research Laboratory, 4555 Overlook Avenue, SW Washington, DC 20375-5000, USA	Pentagon City, Arlington, VA, USA	Symposium emphasizing experimental progress in the synthesis of nanocomposite structures and the generation, transport and control of signals in such structures
6–8 October	11th Conference on Local Computer Networks	Bob Lutnicki, Computer Network Technology, 9440 Science Center Drive, New Hope, MN 55428, USA	Minneapolis, MN, USA	Topics will include software protocols, network management, gateways and interfaces
6–9 October	ICCD 86	M R Wayne, IBM East Fishkill Facility, Department 156, Building 503-92A, Route 52, Hopewell Junction, NY 12533, USA	New York, USA	IEEE international conference on computer design, this year concentrating on VLSI in computers and processors. Interactions between system design, logic circuit design, memory design architecture, software, CAD, testing, physical design and VLSI technology will be emphasized
6–10 October	ISATA 86	ISATA, 42 Lloyd Park Avenue, Croydon, Surrey CR0 5SB, UK. Tel: 01-686 7026	Flims, Switzerland	15th international symposium on automotive technology and automation, covering manufacturing information systems, factory networks (MAP), realtime operating systems, man–machine communications, artificial intelligence, expert systems, CADCAM etc

Date	Title	Contact	Place	Other details
6-11 October	Interkama 86	Nowea Dusseldorfer Messegesellschaft mbH, Postfach 32 02 03, Stockurner Kirchstrasse, D-4000 Dusseldorf 30, FRG. Tel: (0211) 4560-01	Dusseldorf, FRG	Tenth international congress (8-10 October) and exhibition for instrumentation and automation
8-9 October	NCC TOP seminar	National Computing Centre, Oxford Road, Manchester M1 7ED, UK. Tel: (061) 228-6333	Ladbroke Westmorland Hotel, London, UK	Seminar presenting the current state of work on the technical and office protocols (TOP) specification, including electronic mail, word processing, text interchange, file transfer, graphics, videotext, database etc.
8-10 October	FOC/LAN 86	Information Gatekeepers Inc., 214 Harvard Avenue, Boston, MA 02134, USA. Tel: (617) 232-3111	Orange Country Civic Center, Orlando, FL, USA	Tenth annual international fibre optic communications and local area networks exposition
15-17 October	19th Annual Workshop on Microprogramming	Stanley Habib, City College of New York, Computer Science Department, New York City, NY 10031, USA. Tel: (212) 690-6631/2	Graduate Center City University of New York, USA	Workshop on microarchitecture design, firmware engineering, compaction and optimization, specification languages, graphics hosts, microprogramming languages, RISC/CISC machines and microprogrammed VLSI. Sponsored by ACM Sigmicro and the IEEE Technical Committee on Microprogramming
19-26 October	Semiconductor Technology	International Information Service Ltd, Room 103, Wing On Plaza, Tsimshatsui East, Kowloon, Hong Kong	Xiangshan Hotel, Beijing, China	International conference on semiconductor and IC technology, organized by the Chinese Institute of Electronics and the University of California, USA
27-28 October	CCVLSI '86	CCVLSI '86, Dept of Electrical Engineering, McGill University, 3480 University Street, Montreal, Quebec, Canada H3H 2A7	Montreal, Canada	Canadian conference on VLSI
27-29 October	Interface International in Europe	World Trade Center, Strawinskylaan 1245, 1077 XX Amsterdam, The Netherlands	Parc des Expositions, Paris, France	Conference discussing and analysing communications technology issues such as ISDN, ISO and CCITT standards, future roles and policies of the PTTs, multinational networks, videotex, software, voice-data integration and communication satellites
27-30 October	International Conference on Computer Languages	Joseph Urban, Center for Advanced Computer Studies, University of Southwestern Louisiana, PO Box 44330, Lafayette, LA, USA. Tel: (318) 231-6304	Konover, Hotel, Miami Beach, FL, USA	Sponsored by the IEEE Computer Society
27-30 October	Systec 86	Münchener Messe und Ausstellungs GmbH, Messelgelände, Postfach 121009, D-800 München 12, FRG. Tel: (089) 5107-0	Munich Trade Fair Centre, FRG	First international trade fair for computer integration in logistics, development, design, manufacture and quality assurance
28-30 October	Test + Transducer '86	Norma Thewlis, Trident International Exhibitions Ltd, 21 Plymouth Road, Tavistock, Devon PL19 8AU, UK. Tel: (0822) 4671	Wembley Conference Centre, London, UK	Exhibition and conference covering materials testing, solid-state transducers, optical sensors for robots, automotive sensors, data acquisition and microprocessors, test in hazardous environments etc

calendar

Date	Title	Contact	Place	Other details
28–29 October	Secure Communication Systems	Institution of Electrical Engineers, Savoy Place, London WC2R 0BL, UK. Tel: 01-240 1871	London, UK	Second international conference covering commercial and military system design, authentication and security in data networks, video, audio and speech encryption, impact of VLSI on security etc.
2–6 November	FJCC 86	Stanley Winkler, FJCC 86, 1730 Massachusetts Avenue, NW Washington, DC 20036-1903, USA	Dallas, USA	IEEE/ACM joint computer conference and exhibition, covering database management systems, artificial intelligence, software engineering, operating systems, VLSI, graphics, electronic education, languages, parallel computing and networks
4–6 November	6th International Conference on Custom and Semicustom ICs	Prodex Ltd, 9 Emson Close, Saffron Walden, Essex, CB10 1HL, UK	Heathrow Penta Hotel, London, UK	
5–7 November	ISDN Europe 86	IGI Europe Inc., c/o AKM, PO Box 6, CH-4005 Basel, Switzerland. Tel: (061) 25-51-11	World Trade and Convention Center, Basel, Switzerland	Conference covering ISDN terminal equipment, access, protocols and standards, services, implementations, internetworking, PBXs and LANs, field trials plus broadband ISDN and future directions
11–14 November	Compec '86	Reed Exhibitions, Surrey House, 1 Throwley Way, Sutton, Surrey SM1 4QQ, UK. Tel: 01-643 8040	Olympia, London, UK	Exhibition of computers, peripherals and systems for professional and business users
11–14 November	Structured Design and Programming	ICS Publishing Co., 3 Swan Court, Leatherhead, Surrey KT22 8AD, UK. Tel: (0372) 379211	London, UK	Tutorial course on systematic techniques for structured design and coding in realtime engineering and scientific applications
17 November	Electronic Interference: Practical Design and Construction Techniques	Institution of Electrical and Electronics Incorporated Engineers, Savoy Hill House, Savoy Hill, London WC2R 0BS, UK. Tel: 01-836 3357	London, UK	Symposium covering: good engineering design; circuit layout and internal wiring; power supply design and layout; system installation and environmental considerations; test and diagnostic techniques; etc.
17–18 November	Computer Networking Symposium	IEEE Computer Society Administrative Office, 1730 Massachusetts Avenue, NW Washington, DC 20036-1903, USA	Washington, DC, USA	IEEE symposium covering long-haul networks, local area networks PBX systems, satellite systems, video systems, protocols, teleconferencing, standards design, network testing, network procurement and internetworking
17–21 November	AutomAsia 86	Andry Montgomery Ltd, 11 Manchester Square, London W1M 5AB, UK. Tel: 01-486 1951	Singapore	Third South East Asian conference and show on automated manufacturing technology and robotics
18–20 November	International Open Systems Conference	Online International, 989 Avenue of the Americas, New York, NY 10018, USA. Tel: (212) 279-8890	Moscone Center, San Francisco, USA	Conference geared towards assessing the possibilities of OSI systems using MAP and TOP as case studies
20–21 November	SMT '86	French Trade Exhibitions, French Chamber of Commerce House, 54 Conduit Street, London W1R 9SD, UK. Tel: 01-439 3964	Paris, France	Convention on surface-mount technology, organized in association with Pronic '86
21–22 November	8th Annual FORTH Convention	FORTH Interest Group, PO Box 8231, San Jose, CA 95155, USA. Tel: (408) 277-0668	Doubletree Hotel, Santa Clara, USA	US FORTH convention including exhibition, vendor booths, hands-on tutorials, lectures and user group meetings

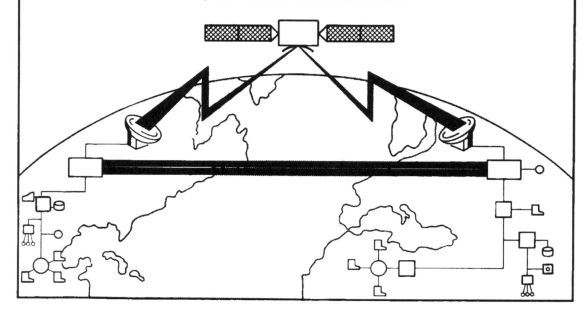

microprocessors and microsystems

vol 10 no 8 october 1986

Butterworths

editorial advisory board

Microprocessors and Microsystems is an inter-
national journal published in February, March,
April, May, June, August, September, October,
November, December. *Editorial Offices:*
Butterworth Scientific Ltd, PO Box 63, Westbury
House, Bury Street, Guildford, Surrey GU2 5BH,
UK. Tel: (0483) 31261. Telegrams and telex:
859556 SCITEC G. *Publishing Director:*
John Owens. *Production:* Nick Wilson

Microprocessors and Microsystems is published
by Butterworth Scientific Ltd. *Registered Office:*
Butterworth Scientific Ltd, 88 Kingsway,
London WC2 6AB, UK

*Subscription enquiries and orders, UK and
overseas:* Quadrant Subscription Services Ltd,
Oakfield House, Perrymount Road, Haywards
Heath, West Sussex RH16 3DH, UK. Tel: (0444)
459188; *North America:* Butterworth Publishers,
80 Montvale Avenue, Stoneham, MA 02180, USA

Annual subscription (10 issues): £98.00 overseas
rate (£24.00 for private individuals); $176.00 US
rate ($43.00 for private individuals)
UK subscription rates available on request.

Prices include packing and delivery by sea mail.
Airmail prices available on request. Copies of
this journal sent to subscribers in Bangladesh,
India, Pakistan, Sri Lanka, Canada and the USA
are air-speeded for quicker delivery.

Back issues: Prior to current volume available
from Wm Dawson & Sons Ltd, Cannon House,
Folkestone, Kent CT19 5EE, UK. Tel: (0303)
57421

US mailing agents: Mercury Airfreight International Ltd Inc., 10B Englehard Avenue,
Avenel, NJ 07001, USA. Second class postage
paid at Rahway, NJ. US Postmaster: Send
address corrections to *Microprocessors and
Microsystems* c/o Mercury Airfreight International Ltd Inc., address as above.

Reprints: Minimum order 100, available from
the publisher.

Copyright: Readers who require copies of
papers published in this journal may either
purchase reprints or obtain permission to copy
from the publisher at the following address:
Butterworth Scientific Ltd, PO Box 63, Westbury

ISSN 0141 9331
MCRPD 10 (8) 417-472 (1986)

© Butterworth & Co (Publishers) Ltd 1986

*Butterworths
Leading the Campaign
against
Copyright Erosion*

Typeset by Tech-Set, Gateshead, Tyne & Wear,
and printed by Doteslos (Printers) Ltd,
Green' ... ... yon, Wilts,
UK.

microprocessors and microsystems

vol 10 no 8
october 1986

Editor Steve Hitchcock

Assistant Editor Andrew Taylor

Publisher Amanda Harper

Industry demonstrates OSI

Eurosinet, a consortium of computer vendors set up to prove to customers that OSI (open systems interconnect) internetworking can work, has demonstrated a 'state-of-the-art' multivendor network in the UK. The network achieved data transfer between the hardware of Eurosinet members Cray, DEC, Hewlett-Packard, Honeywell, ICL, Intel and Tandem over a network supplied by British Telecom. While the consortium admits that such demonstrations will not in themselves result in the availability of OSI products, it is intended to indicate the internetworking capabilities that will soon be on offer.

Automated wafer fabrication: only 27.7% growth but Europe still an important market

ISDN architecture standard

Philips and Siemens have announced a 'standardized' modular architecture for the VLSI circuits needed to connect the voice, data and video communication services of telephone subscribers to an integrated services digital network (ISDN). The modularity of the so-called IOM (ISDN-oriented modular) architecture minimizes the number of different ICs required and reduces their individual complexity, says Philips.

Telecomms giants merge

The French state-owned electronics group CGE has been given government approval to take over the information technology interests of ITT of the USA, at a cost of $1800M. The deal will make CGE the second largest telecommunications company in the world after AT&T.

Automated wafer fabs in Europe

The European automated wafer fabrication market will grow from just $12.1M estimated for 1986 to a forecast $66.9M by 1993, roughly one tenth the size of the US market, says market research company Frost

& Sullivan. This represents a compound rate of increase (constant dollar terms) of 40.3% per year until 1990 followed by a flattening of the sales curve, giving an overall growth rate of only 27.7% up to 1993. But Europe's importance in the worldwide movement to wafer fab automation will be far greater than numbers suggest, says F&S, with cooperative research projects ensuring that the results of automation experiments become public more quickly than those in the USA, where individual corporations' investigations are constrained by antitrust laws. (*Frost & Sullivan Ltd, 104–112 Marylebone Lane, London W1M 5FU, UK. Tel: 01-935 3190*)

Silicon compiler workstation

CAE software developer Lattice Logic has launched its first workstation, to be known as the ASE (application-specific engine) silicon compiler workstation. The system is configured specifically for the design of ASICs and, priced at under £20 000, provides 'a breakthrough in price and performance for CAE workstations', says the manufacturer. Lattice Logic has reportedly already received orders for the system worth £0.5M from European Silicon Structures, with which it has an OEM agreement.

SMT to reach 50% of PCBs

Surface mounted technology (SMT) will be used in 50% of all printed circuit boards by 1990, market research firm ETP is predicting. According to the report *Surface mount technology*, advances in design, assembly and test equipment coupled with the availability of a complete range of SMT devices have already reduced board space requirements by up to 70% and costs by up to 50%. It is forecast that, by 1990, 41% of active and passive electronic components will be surface mounted. (*Electronic Trend Publications, Nordre Ringvej 201, 2600 Glostrup, Copenhagen, Denmark. Tel: (45) 2-63-20-44*)

Futurenet supports ASIC design

Support for the complete symbol library of Motorola's HCA6000 series of 2 µm and 3 µm macrocells has been incorporated into Futurenet's IBM PC based Dash workstations. Futurenet will be selling Motorola design kits which include the symbol library for development of semicustom ICs on Dash systems; the company will also be distributing simulation models for functional design verification. A further ASIC deal means that Gould's 3 µm standard cell library will be offered on the Dash-4 workstation. Design engineers will be able to complete logic definition (via Dash schematic entry), simulation and circuit timing on the Dash-4, says Futurenet.

ANSI '85 certified COBOL

Micro Focus has had its VS COBOL compiler certified to the ANSI '85 COBOL standard at intermediate level 'without errors' — the first time this has been achieved, says the company. This type of certification will be required for all US Federal COBOL procurements after October 1987. ANSI '74 functionality of the VS COBOL compiler is not affected by the ANSI '85 additions, says Micro Focus.

Simulation experiences in the development of software for digital signal processors

Software engineers tend to prefer in-circuit emulation to simulation for DSP software development, but **Jim Chance** considers simulation far superior. Here he explains why

The data streams which have to be handled by digital signal processors are quite different from the asynchronous events which are the normal input and output signals of general-purpose realtime systems. Simulation of the instruction sets of low-cost microprocessors on more powerful general-purpose computers is a well known technique. However, software engineers do not seem to like simulation when a hardware alternative is available. Considerable experience has been gathered with the author's digital signal processor (DSP) simulators for the TMS320 processor series. The aim of the paper is to demonstrate that, in DSP debugging situations, the simulator can be a superior alternative to in-circuit emulation. Enough experience has been acquired of TMS320 development in simulated environments for the author to be confident in recommending the method even in extremely hardware-oriented situations. Practical examples are used as illustrations.

digital signal processors   simulation   TMS320 series

'Digital signal processor' (DSP) is a term used to describe a generation of microprocessors, developed over the last four years, which are specialized for fast realtime arithmetic processing. Invariably the basic design includes a fast parallel multiplier executing in a single machine cycle. A Harvard-type architecture with a program memory space separate from data areas is often used, so that instruction fetches may be made concurrently with data processing. Usually many other internal processes are also highly parallel. To maximize processing speed, this parallelism is accompanied by a fast clock rate and programs are almost always written in assembly language.

The TMS32010[1] was one of the first DSP chips. With a 16-bit data bus and a 32-bit accumulator, specialized instructions directed to realtime filtering and similar operations such as multiply and accumulate are included. Address pointers can be manipulated and shift operations (for data scaling) can be accomplished concurrently with execution of an instruction, with zero time penalty.

Nevertheless, there are signs that applications outside the realtime signal processing area are becoming important for the digital signal processor. The TMS32010 has been followed by the TMS32020 and TMS320C25, with faster cycle times and more specialized instructions but with enough address space to be of great interest in many speed critical applications.

The method preferred by most practising engineers for testing and debugging small microprocessor-based systems is in-circuit emulation. The in-circuit emulator (ICE) allows full-speed operation of a microprocessor-based circuit while permitting the setting of 'break points' to stop program execution as desired. The great disadvantage of the ICE has always been its high cost, which has limited its use to high-volume production or research establishments. The obvious alternative method for program development in such systems is to simulate the chosen microprocessor on a larger computer. The advantages — low cost per workstation, at least in the context of a reasonable number of users, and a consistent user interface for several different target microprocessors — seem worthwhile. However, such simulation tools have never become popular as development aids.

It was against this background that simulation on a general-purpose computer was chosen[2] as the best method for setting up a development system for a digital signal processor. The TMS32010 was the chosen processor but the arguments apply equally to other signal processors.

SIMULATION OR IN-CIRCUIT EMULATION?

The argument for creating a simulated TMS32010 software development environment rests primarily on the reali-

Microprocessor Systems Laboratory, Gisbert Kapp Building, University of Birmingham, PO Box 363, Birmingham B15 2TT, UK

zation that, even with the benefit of an ICE, testing signal processing software would not be easy. The essence of most signal processing relies on the representation of analogue signals by sampling as frequently as possible. The problem of delivering data streams to a signal processing system makes an ICE difficult to use effectively. Normal analogue signal generators suffer from several disadvantages:

● It is not usually possible to freeze the output from a conventional analogue generator. This means that if a break point is reached while testing software, a discontinuity in the test signal will occur on restarting the processor.
● It is difficult to repeat a data stream exactly. Waveform phase may be difficult on different occasions and conversion to digital values by means of an A/D converter involves errors. (Even a single-bit conversion error may be important in a situation where, for example, an arithmetic overflow situation is being examined.)
● Where multiple data streams are being processed, the above problems are compounded because of the difficulty of synchronizing the generators with each other and with the ICE, often in a complex manner.

These problems can be overcome by the use of digital signal generators and custom built generator–ICE interfaces, but suitable devices are not yet readily available and constructing them is beyond the resources of most laboratories.

If the signal processing system produces output data streams, expensive storage and analysis equipment is necessary to evaluate them. A 'simple' logic analyser or spectrum analyser is often not capable of this. Synchronization with ICE operation is also desirable for output streams.

Such problems can only be solved in realtime hardware with extremely complex digital storage systems. However, when the microprocessor can be simulated on a general-purpose computer, input data streams can be held in the form of files on disc. The author's first signal processor simulator was directed at the Texas Instruments TMS32010.

TMS32010 SIMULATOR

This simulator was written by the author after the idea of designing a hardware debugging environment for the development of DSP devices had been rejected on the grounds of cost and complexity. The basic design has a program capable of simulating every instruction of the particular processor. (There are three simulators: for the TMS32010, TMS32020 and TMS320C25.)

The user first assembles the DSP source file using the author's assembler for the appropriate TMS320 series processor. The assembler produces TMS320 machine code which can be loaded by the simulator, and a file of symbols created by the user and their values. The simulator presents the user with a display of TMS320 registers and is able to display program and data memory. The simulator user can run the TMS320 program up to a 'break' address, single step through the program one instruction at a time and in general use the simulator in the same way as in-circuit emulator. Obviously, speeds are very much slower than the target device would achieve,

but the operator gets a machine cycle count. Real execution time does become more important when simulating a great many TMS320 machine cyles but local users commonly set a 'break' address after a run of more than 1 000 000 simulated cycles. The TMS32010 simulator is more fully described elsewhere[2]. The important conclusions reached during this and subsequent work are:

● Input and output data streams should be numbers suitable for arithmetic processing rather than a direct copy of input and output patterns appearing on the data bus; in the present case, this means ASCII strings representing decimal values between + 32767 and − 32768 rather than hexadecimal or binary representations as produced by most microprocessor simulators. This makes the input and output streams compatible with most arithmetic software packages such as fast Fourier transformers as well as giving the user the option to create and manipulate simple data streams with a text editor. Thus simpler generation and analysis of these streams either by standard packages or specially written software are achieved. The ability of the simulator to take data directly from and present data directly to other software is a major advantage in arithmetic work.
● The system must be able to include user-designed peripheral circuits. Many TMS32010 circuits require, for example, external RAM connected as an I/O device. Without the capability to simulate such peripherals, the simulation of a great deal of software becomes impossible.

Recent work on the TMS32010 simulator has been directed primarily towards making it available on operating systems other than Unix (MS-DOS in the first instance), improving the interface with the user and extending the range of processors simulated.

Simulator under MS-DOS

MS-DOS, unlike Unix, is an operating system capable of supporting only one task at a time. Therefore it is not possible to support user-defined TMS320 peripheral devices by executing their simulations as separate processes running concurrently with and communicating with the TMS320 simulator. The method adopted, therefore, has been to make the object code version of the TMS320 simulator available to the user, who can then link his/her own simulated peripherals to create a new simulator.

The primary way that this has been done is to use a C function called 'userio' which outputs to screen the TMS320 input and output operations. The user can replace this with a new version of 'userio' which manipulates input and output operations in such a way as to simulate the user's peripheral hardware. Figure 1 shows a 'userio' listing which simulates RAM external to a TMS32010[3]. Two variables are passed to the routine, one giving the port address and two flags representing the TMS32010 signals DEN and WE to distinguish 'in' from 'out', and the other sending or expecting to receive the I/O information (i.e. equivalent to the data bus). This has proved a satisfactory method for dealing with such situations in the absence of multitasking. However, some worthwhile advantages not possible when using a separate task to simulate the user peripheral have become evident.

```
userio(rwpad, dat) int *rwpad, *dat; {

£define ramsiz 4096
£define ramtop ramsiz — 1

    static int counter, ram[ramsiz], addr;

    switch (*rwpad){

        case 0 × 100: { /* write to counter*/
                    counter = *dat; return;
                    }
        case 0 × 101: { /*write to RAM*/
                    addr = counter++ & ramtop;
                    ram[addr] = *dat; return;
                    }
        case 0 × 81:  { /*read from RAM*/
                    addr = counter++ & ramtop;
                    *dat = ram[addr]; return;
                    }
        default:        return;
            }
}
```

Figure 1. C simulation of RAM external to a TMS32010[3]

All important TMS320 registers, and other important items such as the machine cycle count, are represented as global variables, i.e. variables accessible to any function in the simulator. These can be used for quite sophisticated debugging techniques. A typical example is the way that a complicated error situation can be trapped by examining the peripheral data with all the facilities available in a high-level language. The value of the TMS320 program counter, for example, can then be displayed to the user. Figure 2 lists such a program fragment (which is more fully described below).

A disadvantage arises when working under MS-DOS because there is no accepted resident C compiler; the writing of simulated peripherals is most easily done when using the compiler chosen for the TMS320 simulator.

User interface

The main improvement in the user's view of the simulator has been the provision of a user symbol table. This means that any symbols that the user has defined in the TMS320 assembler source code become accessible to the simulator user; this facility is common on modern ICE systems. For example, in response to the simulator prompt 'break at?' the user may respond 'labell', where 'labell' is a symbol in the user's TMS320 source code. The provision of a library of user peripherals is an appreciated convenience. A library of software signal generators, e.g. sine wave, noise, signal mixer, is also worthwhile.

```
extern int pc; /* TMS320 program counter */
...........................................
if(addr == *dat == 0) {
                printf("error trapped at %4x/n", pc);
}
...........................................
```

Figure 2. Example of error trapping instructions in a simulated peripheral

Extension to other target and host processors

Adaptation of the development software to MS-DOS systems has been mentioned. In fact the simulator and its associated assembler and other support packages have been ported to several 16- and 32-bit Unix machines without any changes in the C sources. The ability for the user to switch host machines easily has proved invaluable, for example to work initially with the speed of a 32-bit minicomputer and to move to a portable IBM PC compatible for field work.

The same principles have been used to create companion assemblers and simulators for the other members of the TMS320 family, the TMS320 and the TMS320C25. Users often wish to move a project onto a more powerful target processor. A consistent user interface for the debugging tools is helpful. Some tools such as simulated user peripherals, software signal generators and analysers need not be changed at all.

Users and projects

The rest of this paper uses results from TMS320-based projects to illustrate some of the techniques possible when debugging a digital signal processor with a simulator. Users have included, as well as the author, undergraduate and postgraduate students and experienced electronics engineers. Projects have ranged from small educational ones to major commercial prototypes.

RMS VOLTAGE MEASUREMENT

In 1975, Gilbert[4] described a 'novel technique for RMS–DC conversion based on the difference of squares'. Figure 3 shows the system, which is an analogue one. V_{in} is the AC input voltage and V_{out} the DC output voltage. The multiplier is arranged to compute $(V_{in} - V_{out}) (V_{in} + V_{out})$. The multiplier output $V_x = V_{in}^2 - V_{out}^2$ is applied to an integrator whose output is V_{out}. A unity gain inverter produces $-V_{out}$. In operation, the feedback loop reduces the multiplier output to a very low level. Taha and Abdul-Karim[5] described a version of this in hard-wired digital form; this maps acceptably onto the TMS320.

TMS320 RMS voltmeter simulation

Figure 4 shows a flowchart of the method used to simulate the RMS voltmeter. To test the system on the simulator, a file of input voltage samples has to be supplied. An

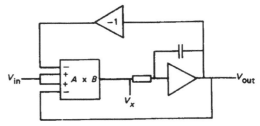

Figure 3. The Gilbert analogue method for RMS voltage measurement

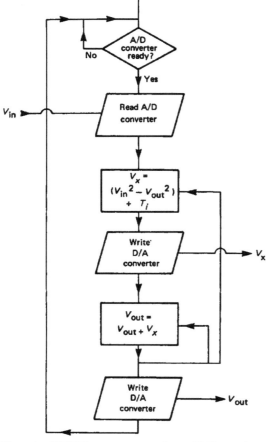

Figure 4. TMS320 program for RMS voltage measurement

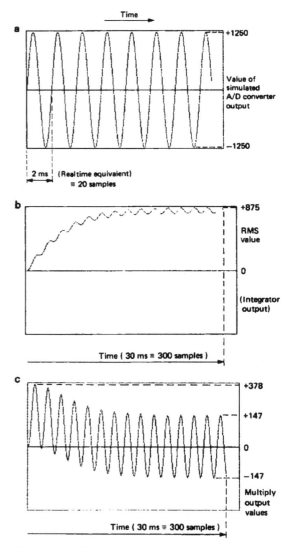

Figure 5. RMS program: a, simulator input file (V_{in}) at 500 Hz; b, simulator output file RMS value (V_{out}); c, simulator output file multiply output (V_x)

example of such a file (300 samples of a 500 Hz sine wave sampled at 10 kHz) was created by a standard software sine generator. The output samples (V_{out}) are saved on file. To clarify the method, a further output data stream is collected from the multiplier output V_x. Figure 5 shows screen dumps of the input file and the two output files generated by the simulator for a correctly working system, and Table 1 shows the listings for each. Note how V_x gradually reaches a mean value of approximately zero. The amount of ripple on the output is determined by the integrator time constant and is a compromise value determined by the time in which the system is expected to reach an accurate value of V_{out}. The value of T_i (Figure 4) effectively determines the integration time and is important. For the analogue case (Figure 3)

$$\frac{dV_x}{dt} = \frac{i}{C} = \frac{V_{out}}{CR}$$

where C and R are the integrator capacitor and resistor values and i is the current flowing through R.

In the digital case (Figure 4), when the sampling interval S is short, the equivalent equation is

$$\frac{V_x}{T_i S} = \frac{V_{out}}{CR}$$

Figure 6 shows output from these files, giving the value of V_{out} when T_i is set to 16 (instead of 32 768 × 16). In other words the programmer has computed

$$V_x = V_{in}^2 - V_{out}^2$$

to a 32-bit result from two 16-bit values of V_{in} and V_{out}. Instead of dividing the upper 16 bit of the result by 16 as intended, the whole 32-bit product has been divided by 16 and only the least significant 16 bit used.

This project demonstrates how simple it is with simulation not only to obtain graphical output equivalent to the oscilloscope in realtime working, but also to obtain streams of numbers in a form suitable for analysis. For example, errors in the RMS value can be computed directly and easily from the V_{out} output file. Another point

Table 1. Simulator input and output listings for the RMS voltage program

Number	V_{in} (Figure 5a)	V_{out} (Figure 5b)	V_x (Figure 5c)
000	0	0	0
001	195	0	9
002	386	2	36
003	567	7	78
004	734	15	131
005	883	27	190
006	1011	43	249
007	1113	62	301
008	1188	83	343
009	1234	106	370
010	1250	130	378
057	567	599	−10
058	386	596	−52
059	195	591	−78
060	0	586	−86
061	−195	581	−75
062	−386	578	−47
133	1113	871	120
134	1011	875	64
135	883	875	3
136	734	872	−56
137	567	865	−108
138	386	856	−147

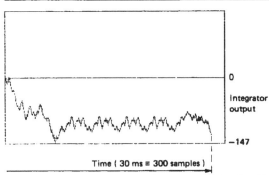

0

Integrator output

−147

Time (30 ms ≡ 300 samples)

Figure 6. RMS program: simulator output (V_{out}) with arithmetic overflow

to note is the ability to observe a transient condition extremely easily when using simulation. With real hardware, the V_{out} and V_x data streams would normally only be observed in the steady-state condition.

LIGHTNING INTERFERENCE ELIMINATION

This item has been included because it provides a good example of the difficulty of generating some types of input signal in order to test a DSP system. In a DSP system used for processing a radar signal to remove interference produced by lightning, it is of course necessary to create a reasonable representation of the signal to be processed in the laboratory. In this case, the various components of the signal are

● the Bragg return signal from the sea (a 1 Hz sine wave)

● the Doppler return from the target (a lower-amplitude sine wave, about 9 Hz)
● pulse repetition frequency (20 Hz)
● noise burst due to lightning of about 250 ms duration
● background noise

Figure 7 shows the hardware used to create this waveform for input to a TMS320-based system from the type of equipment available in a normal laboratory. The hardware is complicated, and the lightning pulse generator had to be specially constructed. For reasons of convenience, some degree of simulation is desirable even in hardware and, in fact, continuous rather than pulsed signals have been used with a frequency scaling factor of 10. A more important deficiency is that any particular waveform cannot be repeated. The two sine generators cannot be synchronized, noise sources add a further uncertainty and, most important of all, the emulated lightning pulse is impossible to control in relation to the other signals and to the oscilloscope used to record results.

In the simulation environment, standard or at least simple software sine and noise generators have been used to create input data files for testing the system. The lightning pulse can be inserted into the data file with a standard text editor. The ability to repeat a particular fault situation until the software error is found is invaluable. This type of input data, which is difficult to replicate except by recording, is not an uncommon situation in signal processing.

BURRUS-PARKS HARDWARE SIMULATION

The well known book by Burrus and Parks about fast Fourier transforms[3] uses a counter technique for addressing RAM external to the TMS320. As this RAM address cannot be supplied by the TMS320 address bus, it is normally latched in external hardware by a TMS320 output instruction. This makes RAM access slow as two operations

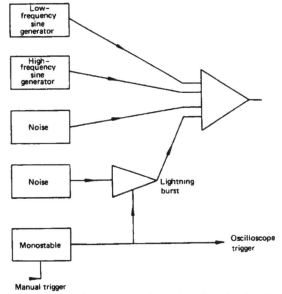

Figure 7. Hardware simulation of radar signal with lightning noise

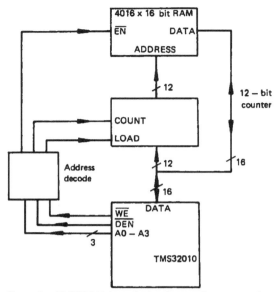

Figure 8. *TMS32010-based hardware for executing Burrus–Parks algorithms*

need to be carried out: to set the RAM address and then to read or write RAM data.

Burrus and Parks supply the RAM address from a binary counter (Figure 8) which is incremented every time a RAM data read or write is performed. A starting value can be written into this counter. The technique for using this hardware is to write a RAM address into the counter and then output data values which will be written into sequential RAM locations. It is clear that the presence of this hardware is essential to the execution of the algorithm to be tested.

Figure 1 shows a C source of the 'userio' routine which simulates hardware suitable for the Burrus–Parks and similar algorithms[1]. When this has been compiled, the object file is linked to the object file of the TMS320 simulator to create a new simulator. This can be used to test Burrus–Parks or other similar software. The C RAM simulation is quite short and simple. Note that in the newly created simulator, only input and output operations relating to RAM access are directed to the simulated RAM. Other I/O instructions can be linked to disc files to supply input values or store output values in the usual way.

Figure 2 shows the type of addition that can be made to simulated peripherals like that in Figure 1 to trap an error condition. In this case, a value of zero has unaccountably appeared in external RAM data at an address of zero. This was a real situation caused by an arithmetic rounding error. The error would be difficult to trap in hardware not only because the peripheral RAM is not in TMS320 address space but also because it only occurs after many accesses of address zero. The power of using a high-level language to create an error trap cannot be understated. Because it is simulated, the programmer can probe into any part of a peripheral device.

PWM HARDWARE SIMULATION

One of the most complex pieces of hardware designed by the author with the TMS320 has been used to generate

pulse width modulated (PWM) waveforms exemplified by Figure 9. The TMS320 has to perform an appreciable amount of arithmetic in solving the equations to determine the waveform characteristics. A full description of the equations to be solved is given by Taufiq et al.[6], but the basic equations are as follows.

For $NP_1 \leqslant 0.8$

$$\Delta_k = 0.4025 \sin\left[\frac{(k - 0.5)\, 59.184°}{m} + 60.408°\right]$$

$$\alpha_k = 60° \frac{(k + 1)}{(m + 1)} - \left[\frac{120°}{(m + 1)} \frac{\Delta_k\, NP_1}{0.8}\right] - \Delta D_k$$

where $\Delta D_k = 0$, and

For $NP_1 > 0.8$

$$\Delta D_k = \frac{(NP_1 - 0.8)^2}{0.09} \frac{13}{m}\left[\sin\frac{180°\, k}{(m + 5)}\right]$$

$$\text{for } k \text{ odd} \quad (1)$$

For $NP_1 \leqslant 0.8$

$$\Delta_k = 0.381 \sin\left[\frac{k}{(m - 1)}\left(58.558° - \frac{1.135° \times 11}{(m - 2)}\right)\right]$$

$$\alpha_k = \frac{60°\, k}{(m + 1)} + \left[\frac{120°}{(m + 1)} \Delta_k \frac{NP_1}{0.8}\right] - \Delta D_k$$

where $\Delta D_k = 0$, and

For $NP_1 > 0.8$

$$\Delta D_k = \frac{(NP_1 - 0.8)^2}{0.09} \frac{14}{m} \sin\left[\frac{180°\, (k - 1.5)}{m}\right]$$

$$\text{for } k \text{ even} \quad (2)$$

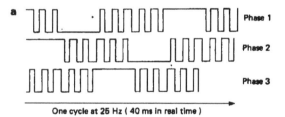

One cycle at 25 Hz (40 ms in real time)

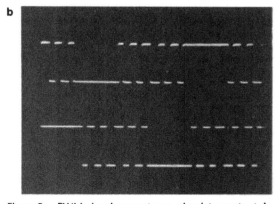

Figure 9. *PWM signal generator: a, simulator output; b, real hardware output*

These equations must be repeatedly solved in real time in response to two changing analogue input signals from which the values of NP_1 and m can be derived. k is the number of switching angles per quarter cycle and varies from 0 to m. Sine and cosine values are obtained quickly by table look-up. Multiplication and division are the main consumers of processing time. The purpose of the signal generator is to create a PWM waveform which gives the minimum harmonic content, for driving high-power induction motors. The output frequency range is up to 150 Hz.

It might be thought that the high speed of the TMS320 is not necessary for generating waveforms such as that shown in Figure 9 at such low frequencies. However, both analysis and experiment have shown that the 8086 and the Z8000, for example, are only barely able to compute these equations and update the peripheral hardware with a limited upper frequency range. On the other hand, use of the TMS32010 has given spare computing capacity which will be used in eliminating other system hardware.

A potential disadvantage of the TMS32010 and other DSP chips in this context is the lack of suitable counter-timer peripherals due to the fast cycle time. This has provided the impetus to use an unusual hardware method for waveform generation. The simulation of this hardware has been essential to the successful completion of the project and has in fact resulted in a lower chip count than in the conventional design.

The basic mechanism uses a RAM whose address is generated by a free running counter. The TMS320 is able to write data into RAM and read its contents at any RAM address. A bit pattern in RAM is used to generate the required pulse train by setting or resetting a latch. The operation of this hardware is rather complex not only because the waveform for three phases are generated, but also because RAM 'write switching angle' accesses are not made in the order in which they will be output by the hardware. Important design features are

- The integer arithmetic must be tested against high-level language floating-point algorithms which are known to be correct.
- The output waveforms are generated entirely by hardware, i.e. by the RAM which is being cycled through its addresses by a binary counter.
- The generated waveforms must be analysed for harmonics.

Testing of the TMS320 arithmetic can be done most easily and thoroughly by using the simulator to create data streams on file, as already demonstrated in the RMS voltage generator. In this project it was achieved as follows.

Input data samples from files fed the simulator to create an output file, in this case a file of waveform switching angles. Only the TMS320 software which computes the equations was executed at this stage. The output file was used as one input to a program written in BASIC on the IBM PC. The other inputs were the input data streams used in the TMS320 simulation.

The BASIC program computed the same algorithm as the TMS320 but in a high-level language and using floating-point arithmetic. A comparison was thus made between the TMS320 results and a correct data stream, the output being a list of errors for all the data samples. The advantage of this method of testing an algorithm is that is is so simple to perform when compared to, for

example, collecting real data that a large number of values can be computed. Confidence in the accuracy of the results is therefore much increased. If this testing were to be carried out using real hardware, TMS320 input and output data would have to be transferred from the collecting device (probably a logic analyser) to a general-purpose computer for analysis. In many laboratories this would have to be done by hand.

Waveform generation is a more complex problem as the waveform generator (RAM plus counter etc.) is a special-purpose hardware item. The software required to write the bit patterns into RAM is in fact more complicated and error prone and consumes more processor time than the algorithm calculation. The solution to the problem of creating a suitable debugging environment was to write a simulation of the waveform generation hardware. The external RAM is easily represented by an array of integers. The potential problem in this simulation is the representation of the counter, which is being incremented by hardware. The TMS320 reads the current counter value and waits in a polling loop until bit 11 of the counter toggles. Thus the processor does not in fact make use of all counter values. The values 0, 1, 2047, 2048, 2049 and 4095 are kept in an array in the simulated peripheral and returned in turn each time the TMS320 demands a counter value, cycling to 0 after 4095. This simple technique provides the necessary synchronization between TMS320 and peripheral simulations. Note that, although a pragmatic approach has given rise to this satisfactory solution, there are potential problems.

True synchronization with every TMS320 machine cycle is not possible when the simulated peripheral is only accessed by means of input or output instructions. In the above example, this means that an error condition, where the counter toggles bit 11 before the TMS320 reaches the polling loop, is not correctly simulated. Also, if bit 11 had been used to raise an interrupt on the TMS320, this would have been difficult to simulate. Although these problems have solutions, it is worth recording that they have not been demanded by simulator users so far, so perhaps they are of more theoretical than practical interest.

The simulated peripheral hardware needs to communicate not only with the simulated TMS320 but also with the user. Different C functions were linked to the simulated peripheral to produce

- a graphical display updated in each cycle of the generated waveform
- a file of numbers representing switching angles suitable for harmonic analysis

The latter is different from the values generated by the equation calculator as it includes errors due to the waveform generator hardware and its associated software. Figures 9a and 9b demonstrate a sample PWM waveform from the simulator and the real hardware respectively. This particular comparison was performed by reading input values used by the real hardware and putting them into the input files used by the simulator.

Note particularly that the graph of Figure 9a represents quite a different simulation environment to the graphs of Figures 5 and 6. The latter were simply plots of data files produced by a simulation run. Figure 9a, on the other hand, is an interactive display created while the programmer is actually using the simulator.

The problems of debugging this system in real time would have been considerable and it would certainly not have been attempted without the simulation capability. Producing correct pulse widths is the essence of the problem. The difficulty arises from the fact that the pulse width values do not exist directly outside the TMS320. They could only be measured digitally by directly timing the intervals with some special-purpose device. Neither is this information of much assistance in debugging. The time interval is made up from the difference between two external RAM addresses (low part of interval) and the number of times that the RAM address counter has been cycled (high part of interval). It is hoped that details of this PWM generation system will be published shortly. Up-to-date details are available from the author.

CONCLUSIONS

Software methods for executing signal processing algorithms create problems in the program debugging situation which are different from those in conventional microprocessor-based systems. These arise from the necessity to handle large streams of data rather than asynchronous events. Examples covering several different situations have been used as illustrations in the use of simulation of target system hardware. The advantages of simulation as a major preliminary step to the testing of hardware may be summarized as follows.

- Checking the correctness of arithmetic in a DSP system can be done most easily if the system produces lists of numbers in a computer file. The RMS voltage meter and PWM generator illustrate this point.
- Transient signals or others difficult to generate in the laboratory are prime candidates for digital processing. Simulation in software, as exemplified by the removal of the effects of a lightning strike from a radar signal, is simpler than simulation in hardware.
- Strangely, where a digital processing system includes an unusual piece of hardware, simulation of the hardware together with the DSP device is a superior method of program evaluation to testing in the hardware itself. The reason for this is that, if this hardware is outside the immediate processor environment, it is not supported by the usual ICE environment.

The projects described are only the 'tip of the iceberg' concerning simulation of the TMS320. Those of us who have access to TMS320 in-circuit emulation tend to relegate it to the job of hardware testing and expect our software to work the first time that it is put into real hardware; those who do not have such access create working DSP systems with a fast PROM emulator as practically the only hardware development tool. At least 14 projects local to the author are known to have used this system during the last year. This year the number will be about 25.

The suggestion is put forward that simulation is a superior alternative to in-circuit emulation in digital signal processing, in contrast to the position of using conventional processors for realtime computing. The use of simulation in application-specific integrated circuits is well known, and it is becoming an everyday technique for devices such as programmable logic arrays. The practical application of digital signal processors could well follow a similar pattern.

REFERENCES

1   *TMS32010 user's guide* Texas Instruments, Houston, TX, USA (1983)
2   **Chance, R J** 'TMS320 digital signal processor development system' *Microprocessors Microsyst.* Vol 9 No 2 (March 1985) pp 50–56
3   **Burrus, C S and Parks, T W** *DFT/FFT and convolution algorithms* John Wiley, New York, USA (1985)
4   **Gilbert, B** 'Novel technique for RMS–DC conversion based on the difference of squares' *Electron. Lett.* Vol 11 No 8 (17 April 1975) pp 181–182
5   **Taha, S M R and Abdul-Karim** 'Implicit digital RMS meter design' *IEEE Trans. Instrumentation and Measurement* Vol IM-33 No 4 (December 1984) pp 257–258
6   **Taufiq, J A, Mellitt, B and Goodman, C J** 'A novel algorithm for generating near optimal PWM waveforms for AC traction drives' *Proc. IEE* Vol 133 Part B No 2 (March 1986) pp 85–94

Jim Chance originally trained as a biochemist at Birmingham University, UK, but his working life has been spent mostly in the field of electronics. Having been involved with microprocessors since 1976 and mainframe computing since 1963, he joined the Microprocessor Systems Laboratory at Birmingham University in 1980. As a senior computer officer in the laboratory, he now works at the interface between electronic engineering and computing science. His day-to-day activities include the design of special-purpose microprocessor-based systems for research throughout the University and the mounting of specialized courses for postgraduate staff. Particular interests are single-chip microcomputers, microprocessor development tools and, over the last three years, digital signal processors.

Speech recognition system using Walsh analysis and dynamic programming

As an alternative to more expensive speech recognition techniques using FFTs or banks of analogue band pass filters, **Jon Tyler** has been working on a Z80-based system which uses Walsh–Hadamard transformation. Here he describes progress on the project

The paper describes the implementation of a demonstration speech recognition system which uses Walsh analysis and dynamic programming techniques to enable speaker-dependent discrete utterances to be recognized. The purpose of the implementation was to develop a low-cost system based on a readily available microprocessor to test the algorithms in terms of speed of operation. The system uses the Z80 microprocessor, and the software was developed under the CP/M operating system. The modular nature of the software and the fact that is was written almost entirely in PASCAL means that there is considerable scope for optimization. The aim of the current project is the specification of a system, based on the algorithms described here, which will operate in real time.

microsystems   speech recognition   Walsh transformation

Many algorithms for whole-word speech recognition have been reported[1-4]. These algorithms operate by comparing an unknown input utterance with a selection of master templates obtained previously. The master templates constitute the vocabulary of the speech recognition system. A distance score is obtained by comparison of the input with each of the master templates in turn, the word spoken being identified as the word whose distance score is lowest. The minimum distance criterion is quite successful for a limited vocabulary recognizer used under carefully controlled, low ambient noise conditions. Recognition scores in excess of 95% have been reported in such systems[3].

Most of the systems described make use of either a bank of parallel analogue band pass filters or fast Fourier transforms to obtain measurements of spectral power from the input signal. The current project is concerned with developing a system for low-cost realtime recognition,

and has therefore made use of Walsh–Hadamard transformation (WHT), a technique which has previously been applied successfully in speech processing and recognition[5-8].

Typical commercial implementations of speech recognition systems are designed to recognize whole words with brief pauses between the words (continuous speech) giving a 'realtime' response within, say, 500 ms of the end of a word[9-10]. Such systems are designed for office, military and industrial applications.

RECOGNITION ALGORITHM

A total sampling time greater than the maximum duration of the expected utterances is chosen. Sampling is carried out after a particular amplitude threshold has been passed, at a rate of 10k samples per second. These values are stored in memory and end point detection is carried out by detecting the last occurrence of a series of samples whose amplitudes exceed the selected threshold. The samples occurring before the end point are then transformed using WHT, and values of the power (compressed using a logarithmic function) for the sequence spectrum are accumulated into 16 equal time frames; this is known as linear time warping. Features are then extracted using the following rules.

If the values of power for n sequence spectra are

$$P_0, P_1 \ldots, P_{n-1}$$

then the corresponding feature vectors will be

$$F_0, F_1, \ldots, F_{n-2}$$

where

$$F_m = 1 \text{ if } P_{m+1} > P_m$$

$$F_m = 0 \text{ if } P_{m+1} < P_m \text{ or if } P_{m+1} = P_m = 0$$

$$F_m = F_{m-1} \text{ if } P_{m+1} = P_m \neq 0, m \neq 0$$

$$F_0 = 1 \text{ if } P_1 = P_0 \neq 0$$

School of Mathematical Sciences and Computer Studies, Robert Gordon's Institute of Technology, St Andrew Street, Aberdeen AB1 1HG, UK

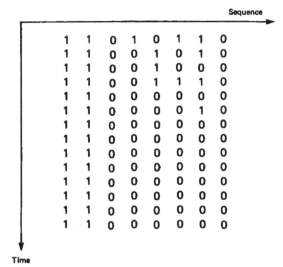

```
1 1 0 1 0 1 1 0
1 1 0 0 1 0 1 0
1 1 0 0 1 0 0 0
1 1 0 0 1 1 1 0
1 1 0 0 0 0 0 0
1 1 0 0 0 0 1 0
1 1 0 0 0 0 0 0
1 1 0 0 0 0 0 0
1 1 0 0 0 0 0 0
1 1 0 0 0 0 0 0
1 1 0 0 0 0 0 0
1 1 0 0 0 0 0 0
1 1 0 0 0 0 0 0
1 1 0 0 0 0 0 0
```
Sequence

Time

Figure 1.   Feature template for the word 'two'

The templates thus obtained contain only 1 or 0 values. In this context, the presence of a 1 in any position of the template is assumed to denote the existence of a feature. An example of a feature template is given in Figure 1.

Dynamic time warping

The unknown utterance template is compared with each of the master utterance templates in turn. This is carried out by modulo-two addition of each of the feature vectors from the unknown utterance template to each of the master template feature vectors. Thus, for $k (= n - 1)$ elements and t time frames, a similarities matrix is obtained which contains kt^2 binary values. The k values for each of the t^2 entries correspond to the number of differences during that time frame from master template time frames. The numbers of differences form a similarities matrix S which, for a perfect match, will have a diagonal of zeros.

A number of algorithms have been described for dynamic programming (DP) to obtain the optimal path through the similarities matrix; these have been shown to be applicable to isolated word recognition systems[3, 11]. Comparative studies have also been reported[12]. The method adopted here is the symmetric DP algorithm of Sakoe and Chiba[13] using a slope parameter of zero. For the input template u and the master template m, the distance $d(u, m)$ along the optimum warping path is found by dividing the final cumulative distance score by the normalization factor, i.e.

$$d(u, m) = g(t, t)/N$$

where $N = 2t$. The DP matrix g is constructed by evaluating the DP equation for all i and j.

$$g(i, j) = \min [g(i - 1, j) + s(i, j), g(i - 1, j - 1) + 2s(i, j), g(i, j - 1) + s(i, j)]$$

with initial conditions given by $g(1, 1) = 2s(1, 1)$.

SYSTEM IMPLEMENTATION

The system is made up of the data acquisition subsystem, comprising the analogue circuit given in Figure 2 and the

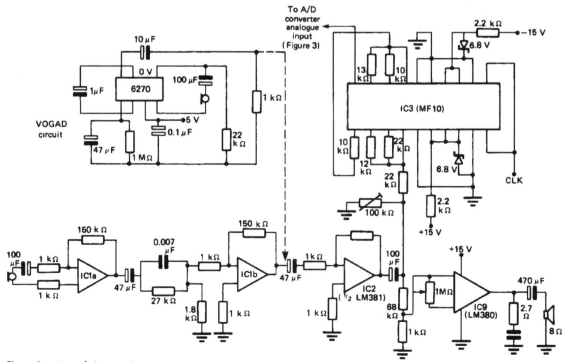

Figure 2.   Speech input subsystem

interface circuit of Figure 3, together with an assembly language program (Samp), two main PASCAL modules (Create and Speak) and seven PASCAL submodules. The operation of the system software is shown diagrammatically in Figure 4.

The software was implemented on an Ithaca Intersystems DPS-8 S100-based microcomputer, using PASCAL/ Z and Z80 assembly language under the CP/M operating system. The Z80 has the advantage over some other 8-bit microprocessors of being able to operate at a 4 MHz clock rate, allowing data to be acquired at a 10 kHz sampling rate. It is also available in CMOS form, allowing a battery or telephone line powered system to be implemented.

Speech input subsystem

Experiments were initially carried out using a voice-operated gain adjusting device (VOGAD) designed to accept signals from a low-output microphone and producing an essentially constant output signal of 90 mV for a 60 dB input range. In the configuration used, the attack time for the output to return to within 10% of its original value following a 20 dB increase in input signal was estimated to be 20 ms.

The results obtained with this configuration were disappointing, and further experimentation revealed that, although the optimum attack time of the VOGAD was of

the order of 20 ms, this incurred a decay time of 1 s to return to the previous level of gain following an equivalent fall in input amplitude. Thus the overall amplitude envelope was distorted for short utterances. A conventional linear amplifier was therefore used, as shown in Figure 2. This comprised a differential input stage (IC1a) followed by a pre-emphasis stage (IC1b), a preamplifier (IC2) and a fourth-order low pass Butterworth filter realized by a dual switched capacitor device (IC3). A monolithic power amplifier (IC9) and a loudspeaker were used for monitoring purposes.

The digital circuit components are shown in Figure 3. These perform decoding of the microprocessor input and output signals, generation of the A/D converter 'start conversion' signal and synchronization of these signals with the A/D converter clock waveform. The address, data and control lines correspond to IEEE-696 S100 standard signals.

IC4 is an 8-bit successive-approximation A/D converter with a minimum conversion time of 15 μs, implemented with a free running clock generated by IC5 (a 74123 dual monostable). IC6 consists of a dual D-type flipflop, of which the first stage is set by an incoming start signal from the computer. The 'start convert' signal to the A/D converter is formed by the inverted output of the second stage, ensuring synchronization with the next negative-going edge of the clock waveform. This ensures that half a clock period elapses between the end of the start convert

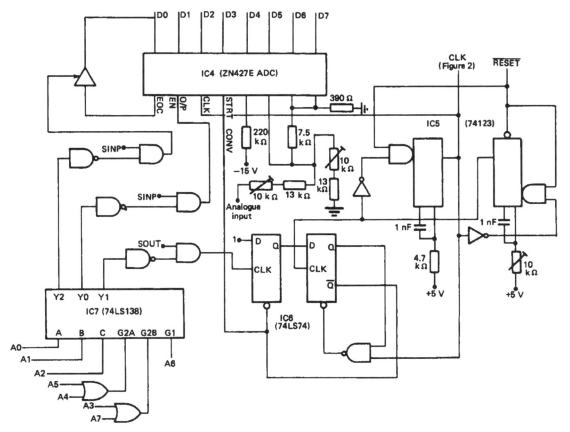

Figure 3.   Interface circuit

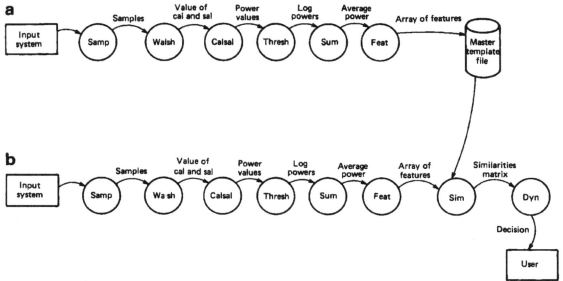

Figure 4. Overall system structure: a, Create; b, Speak

signal and the next negative-going edge of the clock waveform. The clock frequency was set to 480 kHz, giving an approximate conversion time of 18.75 μs.

Operation of recognition software

The system operates in one of two modes, as shown in Figure 4. Program Create performs the initial or 'training' mode, during which a set of master templates are constructed; these are required before any new user may use the system for recognition. Program Speak performs the recognition function using a previously constructed set of master templates.

In the initial mode (Create) a set of master templates is produced in response to the user saying each of the words of the vocabulary a given number of times. Experience has shown that optimum performance is attained with between three and ten repetitions of each word in the vocabulary. Averaging is then used to produce a composite template for each word. (An alternative to this would be to have multiple templates for each word.) In the present configuration, the master templates are stored on floppy disc, but in a practical system they would be stored in E²PROM or a low-power RAM device.

SAMPLING SOFTWARE

The program module Samp carries out speech sampling. The microprocessor system clock, which is controlled by a 4 MHz resonant-mode crystal, is used to control the speed of operation. It was discovered that 40 typical instructions could be executed in the time between the samples being read from the A/D converter, including 14 which were required to input and store the data.

The output of program module Samp consists of 10 240 8-bit speech samples. Walsh transformation (see for example Beauchamp[14]) is carried out on each block of 16 consecutive samples, using a 16-point transform, in program module Walsh. The output of this module

represents sets of eight 'cal' and eight 'sal' values (the equivalents of cosine and sine terms, respectively, in Fourier analysis), derived from the 16 input samples. There are thus 640 sets of 16 output values.

If $S_0, S_1, \ldots, S_{14}, S_{15}$ represent 16 successive samples, and

$$W(S_0, S_1, \ldots, S_{14}, S_{15}) = w_0, w_1, \ldots, w_{14}, w_{15}$$

where W represents discrete Walsh transformation, then

$$w_{cal(0)}, w_{cal(1)}, \ldots, w_{cal(6)}, w_{cal(7)} = w_0, w_2, \ldots, w_{12}, w_{14}$$

and

$$w_{sal(1)}, w_{sal(2)}, \ldots, w_{sal(7)}, w_{sal(8)} = w_1, w_3, \ldots, w_{13}, w_{15}$$

Each value is normalized by division by 16. Since Walsh transformation is phase sensitive, a power spectrum of 'sequences' is obtained by combining the squares of the 'cal' and 'sal' components. Program module Calsal accepts each set of sixteen cal–sal components, $w_{cal(0)}$–$w_{cal(7)}$ and $w_{sal(1)}$–$w_{sal(8)}$, and produces nine power spectral components, P_0–P_8, where

$$P_0 = w_0{}^2$$
$$P_1 = w_1{}^2 + w_2{}^2$$
$$P_2 = w_3{}^2 + w_4{}^2$$
$$P_3 = w_5{}^2 + w_6{}^2$$
$$P_4 = w_7{}^2 + w_8{}^2$$
$$P_5 = w_9{}^2 + w_{10}{}^2$$
$$P_6 = w_{11}{}^2 + w_{12}{}^2$$
$$P_7 = w_{13}{}^2 + w_{14}{}^2$$
$$P_8 = w_{15}{}^2$$

There are therefore a total of 640 sets of nine values of power (P). Calsal divides each input value by 8 prior to the squaring and adding operations, giving values in the range from 0 to $[\pm (128/8)^2 \pm (128/8)^2]$, i.e. 0 to 512.

Program module Thresh accepts the sets of nine power values and converts each value into a number in the range 0–3. This is an approximation to logarithmic compression. Inputs in the range 0–16 are output as 0, inputs in the range 17–45 become 1, inputs between 46 and 256 become 2, and values over 256 become 3. Program module Sum averages over 40 successive sets of nine values to give 16 sets of nine output values. Each value may therefore be in the range 0–120.

Program module Feat performs feature extraction by translating the nine input power spectral values into eight binary values as described above. An example of a feature template for the word 'two' is shown in Figure 1.

Program module Sim takes each set of eight binary values (a 'feature vector') output from module Feat and compares it with each feature vector from a master template. The master template would normally represent an average of several renderings of the same utterance, each produced by the same process as the test input. The comparison is performed by an exclusive OR on each pair of binary inputs in corresponding positions of the test input and the master vectors. This process is repeated for all test input vectors (a_1 to p_1); each test input is compared with each master vector (a_2 to p_2).

The number of bits which are set in each of the 8-bit elements of the resulting array are counted. This count represents a measure of the dissimilarity of the input test vector when compared with the vectors of the master template.

Program module Dyn accepts the 256-element similarities matrix and creates a dynamic programming array. The vertical axis, i.e. the first column of the matrix, is formed by accumulation of the values from the first column of the similarities matrix.

$$D_{0,0}, D_{1,0}, D_{2,0}, \ldots, D_{16,0} = 2S_{0,0}, 2S_{0,0} + 2S_{1,0},$$
$$2S_{0,0} + 2S_{1,0} + 2S_{2,0},$$
$$\ldots, 2S_{0,0} + \ldots + 2S_{16,0}$$

where D represents the dynamic programming array and S represents the similarities matrix.

The horizontal axis, i.e. the first row of the dynamic programming array, is produced in a similar way to the first column using the values from the first row of the similarities matrix. The remainder of the array is completed by traversal of each row from column 1 to column 15, taking as the value the minimum value found using the DP equation given above. A sample of the output from the dynamic programming procedure is shown in Appendix 2.

The decision as to which word has been spoken is based upon a comparison of the total distance score obtained from the dynamic programming array for each of the master templates. The values are sorted into ascending order, the lowest four results being presented to the user. In the case of two scores being identical, use could be made of the duration of the two master utterances in comparison with the duration of the test utterance to establish a further criterion for selection.

Sample runs of the Create and Speak programs are given in Appendices 3 and 4 respectively.

CONCLUSIONS

The system described gives recognition scores for digits from 0 to 9 of between 85% and 95%. Thus it has met its

objectives, and has demonstrated that the algorithms used are practical. The final stage of this project will be concerned with the translation of the time-critical PASCAL modules into functionally identical hardware modules to implement a system which will operate in real time. This will include investigation of the effects of variations in the parameters of the system, including the duration and number of time frames used, and the number of points used in the Walsh transform. The system will then be used for an investigation of algorithms for continuous speech recognition.

ACKNOWLEDGEMENTS

Thanks are due to Dr John Seymour at Thames Polytechnic, London, UK, for his valued advice and assistance in the preparation of this paper, and to Dr Peter Lee, of the South Bank Polytechnic, London, UK, for his work in speech recognition which laid the foundations for much of the work described here.

REFERENCES

1 **Davis, K H, Biddulph, R and Balashek, J** 'Automatic recognition of spoken digits' *J. Acoust. Soc. Amer.* Vol 24 (1952) pp 634–645

2 **Shearme, J N and Leach, P F** 'Some experiments with a simple word recognition system' *IEEE Trans. Audio Electroacoust.* Vol AU-16 (1968) pp 156–261

3 **White, G M and Neely, R B** 'Speech recognition experiments with linear prediction, bandpass filtering and dynamic programming' *IEEE Trans. Acoust., Speech, Signal Process.* Vol ASSP-24 (1976) pp 183–188

4 **Kuhn, M H and Tomachewski, H H** 'Improvements in isolated word recognition' *IEEE Trans. Acoust., Speech, Signal Process.* Vol ASSP-31 (1983) pp 157–167

5 **Gulamhusein, M N** 'Short-time Walsh analysis-synthesis with applications to digital speech processing' *PhD Thesis* Cambridge University, UK (1973)

6 **Edwardes, I M and Seymour, J** 'Discrete Walsh functions and speech recognition' *Proc. Theory Applications Walsh Functions* Hatfield Polytechnic, UK (1980)

7 **Abu El-Ata, M A** 'A speech recognition system using Walsh Hadamard analysis with a small computer' *PhD Thesis* Thames Polytechnic, London, UK (1980)

8 **Lee, P A** 'Speech recognition by microprocessor using Walsh analysis and dynamic programming' *PhD Thesis* Thames Polytechnic, London, UK (1984)

9 **Kurzweil, R** 'The technology of the Kurzweil voice writer' *Byte* (March 1986) pp 177–186

10 **Wilson, J** 'How to benefit from speech recognition — a designer's view' *Proc. Int. Conf. Speech Input/Output Techniques and Applications* London, UK (1986) pp 24–30

11 **Itakura, F** 'Minimum prediction residual principle applied to speech recognition' *IEEE Trans. Acoust., Speech, Signal Process.* Vol ASSP-23 (1975) pp 67–72

12 **Myers, C, Rabiner, L R and Rosenburg, A E** 'Performance tradeoffs in dynamic time warping algorithms for isolated word recognition' *IEEE Trans. Acoust., Speech, Signal Process.* Vol ASSP-28 (1980) pp 623–635

13 **Sakoe, H and Chiba, S** 'Dynamic programming algorithm for spoken word recognition' *IEEE Trans. Acoust., Speech, Signal Process.* Vol ASSP-26 (1978) pp 43–49

14 **Beauchamp, K G** 'Applications of Walsh and related functions' Academic Press, London, UK (1984)

Jon Tyler graduated from Leicester Polytechnic, UK, in 1976 with a degree in electronic engineering. Research into software for a hybrid computer, also at Leicester, led to an MPhil degree. From 1978 to 1983 he was a lecturer and subsequently a senior lecturer at Thames Poly-technic, London, UK. He is currently a senior lecturer in computer science at the Robert Gordons Institute of Technology in Aberdeen. Current research interests include novel computer architectures, particularly architectures for realtime speech recognition.

APPENDIX 1: SIMILARITIES MATRIX FOR THE WORD 'TWO'

```
3 2 5 2 2 3 3 3 3 3 1 3 3 3 3 2
0 1 2 1 1 2 2 2 2 2 2 2 2 2 2 1
1 2 1 2 2 1 1 1 1 3 1 1 1 1 1 2
1 2 3 0 0 3 3 3 3 3 1 3 3 3 3 0
2 1 2 3 3 0 0 0 0 0 2 0 0 0 0 3
1 0 3 2 2 1 1 1 1 1 1 1 1 1 1 2
2 1 2 3 3 0 0 0 0 0 2 0 0 0 0 3
2 1 2 3 3 0 0 0 0 0 2 0 0 0 0 3
2 1 2 3 3 0 0 0 0 0 2 0 0 0 0 3
2 1 2 3 3 0 0 0 0 0 2 0 0 0 0 3
2 1 2 3 3 0 0 0 0 0 2 0 0 0 0 3
2 1 2 3 3 0 0 0 0 0 2 0 0 0 0 3
2 1 2 3 3 0 0 0 0 0 2 0 0 0 0 3
2 1 2 3 3 0 0 0 0 0 2 0 0 0 0 3
2 1 2 3 3 0 0 0 0 0 2 0 0 0 0 3
2 1 2 3 3 0 0 0 0 0 2 0 0 0 0 3
```

APPENDIX 2: DYNAMIC PROGRAMMING FOR THE WORD 'TWO'

→ i

```
12 16 26 30 34 40 46 52 58 64 66 72 78 84 90 94
 6  7  9 10 11 13 15 17 19 21 23 25 27 29 31 32
 8  9  9 11 13 13 14 15 16 17 20 21 22 23 24 26
10 11 12  9  9 12 15 18 19 20 19 22 25 26 27 24
14 12 14 12 12  9  9  9  9  9 11 11 11 11 11 14
16 12 15 14 14 10 10 10 10 10 11 12 12 12 12 14
20 13 15 17 17 10 10 10 10 10 12 11 11 11 11 14
24 14 16 19 20 10 10 10 10 10 12 11 11 11 11 14
28 15 17 20 23 10 10 10 10 10 12 11 11 11 11 14
32 16 18 21 24 10 10 10 10 10 12 11 11 11 11 14
36 17 19 22 25 10 10 10 10 10 12 11 11 11 11 14
40 18 20 23 26 10 10 10 10 10 12 11 11 11 11 14
44 19 21 24 27 10 10 10 10 10 12 11 11 11 11 14
48 20 22 25 28 10 10 10 10 10 12 11 11 11 11 14
52 21 23 26 29 10 10 10 10 10 12 11 11 11 11 14
56 22 24 27 30 10 10 10 10 10 12 11 11 11 11 14
```

↓
j

APPENDIX 3: SAMPLE RUN OF 'CREATE' PROGRAM

Master template filename ?test
input data from microphone or disc (m or d) ?m
Number of words in master vocabulary ?1
Number of repetitions of each word ?1
start threshold ?20
end threshold ?20
Enter text for word no.   1:two
repetition no.   1
press return when ready to say two
sampling now
sampling completed
blocksize =   9
accept? (y or n) y
transforming now
forming power spectral values
taking log of power values
accumulating sums
forming features

accept ? (y or n)y

APPENDIX 4: EXAMPLE RUN OF 'SPEAK' PROGRAM

Master template filename ?digits.dat
test data from microphone or disc (m or d) ?m
print processes ? (y or n) :y
print data ? (y or n) :n
start threshold ? 20
end threshold ? 20
press return when ready to speak
sampling
sampling completed
blocksize = 9
transforming
forming spectral values of power
taking log of power values
accumulating values
forming features
form similarities matrix with word 1
perform dynamic programming
score for word one   is 68
form similarities matrix with word   2

```
perform dynamic programming                    score for word seven        is 106
score for word two          is 25               form similarities matrix with word   8
form similarities matrix with word  3          perform dynamic programming
perform dynamic programming                    score for word eight        is 60
score for word three        is 36               form similarities matrix with word   9
form similarities matrix with word  4          perform dynamic programming
perform dynamic programming                    score for word nine         is 38
score for word four         is 64               form similarities matrix with word   10
form similarities matrix with word  5          perform dynamic programming
perform dynamic programming                    score for word zero         is 55
score for word five         is 47               word five            score 47
form similarities matrix with word  6          word three           score 36
perform dynamic programming                    word nine            score 38
score for word six          is 69               word two             score 25
form similarities matrix with word  7
perform dynamic programming                    repeat ? (y or n)n
```

Crossassembler for the TMS32010 digital signal processor

The requirements of realtime signal processing often force software developers into assembler programming. **D R Campbell, C Canning and K Miller** have written a crossassembler for the TMS32010, running on Prime minicomputers

Software to support the development of TMS32010 assembler programs on a Prime computer system has been written using BASIC. The software consists of three main modules: a crossassembler, a format converter and a downloader. The software, which allows macro definition and the linking of previously written source code modules, has been tested and is now being used successfully.

digital signal processors   crossassemblers   TMS32010

Microprocessors specifically designed to perform common digital signal processing (DSP) operations efficiently are now available from several manufacturers. Applications of these devices are widespread, particularly in the telecommunications area. One such device is the Texas instruments (TI) TMS32010 processor.

The architecture of these devices and the requirements of realtime signal processing frequently force the use of assembly language programming on software developers. Software development for the TMS32010 is at present supported by crossassemblers running on Digital Equipment VAX minicomputers and TI minicomputers and microcomputers operating under MS-DOS, PC-DOS or CP/M. At the minicomputer level the choice of machines is limited, while at the microcomputer level the number of simultaneous users per system is restricted by the cost of networking hardware and software, and by multiuser software licensing.

To broaden the choice of host machines and provide a facility for a large number of users to develop TMS32010 software, cross support software has been written to run on the Paisley College computer system which is based on several Prime Series 50 minicomputers providing a time sharing and batch processing service. This software should be of interest to academic and industrial organizations that use the TMS32010 processor family.

The software described here was partitioned fairly naturally between crossassembly, format conversion and downloading. Processor simulation was not addressed in this project but it is intended to attempt this at a later date. A top-down, modular, structured design process[1] was adhered to and resulted in reasonably error free, easily debugged software. A prime requirement of the crossassembler, designated XAssem320, was that it should support modular programming for the target microprocessor.

The software is written in a subset of BASIC which, if used carefully, capitalizes on the following advantages.

● It is the most commonly available language on the vast array of large and small computers in use today and thus offers a large degree of portability.
● It features powerful string handling routines which are required for crossassembly processing.
● It is familiar to a large number of engineers and scientists from its previous widespread use as a teaching language.

DESCRIPTION OF XASSEM320

A comprehensive discussion of compiler design is given by Aho and Ullman[2]. A straightforward approach was taken for XAssem320 which translates TMS32010 assembly language source programs into TMS32010 hexadecimal machine code, in the process creating two files. The first is the 'output listing' file generated for documentation purposes, containing a formatted version of the source program including the translated hex machine code and program address of each source statement. The second is a 'hex' file that contains only the translated machine code which will ultimately be executed by the target TMS32010 microprocessor. XAssem320 prompts for input and allows

Department of Electrical and Electronic Engineering, Paisley College of Technology, High Street, Paisley PA1 2BE, UK

macro definition and the linking of previously written source code modules.

Macro facility

XAssem320 provides the user with the option of either defining a macro[2] in the source program, in which case the corresponding macro expansion is confined to that particular program, or predefining a macro in the 'macro library' file, in which case the macro can be expanded in any source program. A macro defined in a source program is given precedence over one with the same name existing in the macro library. Up to three parameters may be specified with each macro.

Labels are allowed within macro routines. When such a macro is expanded more than once in the same source program, each label and corresponding operand reference is renamed with a unique macro code. This avoids multiple definition of labels which would result in an assembly error. Thus it is possible to write complex macros employing branching within the macro. Macros cannot be nested.

Linking facility

Independently written source programs may be linked into a main source program using XAssem320 directives. If the origin address of each linked program is not defined and all program memory locations are referenced by labels, the linked source programs are completely relocatable. A control program may then be used to arrange the final position of each program in the microprocessor program memory. This allows program modules to be developed and evaluated independently before being merged with other programs.

'User friendly' facilities

User friendliness and convenience are enhanced by providing

- *Prompts.* The crossassembler prompts the user when it requires information. If the user returns an illegal reply to the prompt then this is indicated at the terminal and the user is requested to re-enter the information.
- *Help facility.* Whenever the user is prompted for an input and is uncertain of the required response, an explanatory response may be obtained by returning HELP to the prompt. On completion of the help routine, the user is given the option to either continue from where the help facility was invoked or to quit from XAssem320.
- *Error detection.* Error checks are made during the translation process which detect illegal use of machine instructions, assembler directives and operands. XAssem320 indicates source lines which are in error and the type of error detected on the 'output listing' file.
- *User-defined symbols.* The contents of the symbol table are written to the output listing to show each user-defined symbol with its value in the decimal and hexadecimal number system. This process is repeated for user-defined labels. The distinction between a symbol and a label is clarified below.

- *File management.* Before any translation process is attempted, XAssem320 performs a number of file management functions on the user file directory (UFD) which contains a list of the names and attributes of the files created by the user. This reduces the possibility of any files in the UFD being corrupted or deleted by the XAssem320 file processing. In doing this it also maintains a file name protocol. The 'source' file is required to have a '.SRC' extension and the two output files, 'output listing' and 'hex', are assigned the same name as the 'source' file but with the respective extensions '.LST' and '.HEX'.
- *Development option.* When the translation process is completed, a yes/no option is provided to allow the user to continue with the development process and run Format320. Format320 converts the contents of the 'hex' file into a format suitable for transmission along the RS232 data link from the host computer to the target TMS32010 system. If the above option is taken, a further yes/no option is available for the user to perform the data transfer by running Download320. Format320 and Download320 can also be entered independently of XAssem320.

OPERATION OF XASSEM320

The crossassembler is not a conventional two-pass assembler since it translates all source code during the first pass. Any forward reference labels that are encountered on the first pass will be translated to a numerical value of zero. Once the initial pass is completed and a complete 'label' table has been constructed, a 'pseudo' second pass is performed solely to replace each forward reference with the appropriate numerical address from the label table. This allows XAssem320 to process faster than some conventional two-pass assemblers, although no rigorous speed optimization exercise has yet been attempted.

Source format

A source statement for processing by XAssem320 is made up of five fields: ⟨LINE NO.⟩, ⟨LABEL⟩, ⟨MNEMONIC⟩, ⟨OPERAND(S)⟩ and ⟨COMMENT⟩. The line number field, if present is automatically removed before the source statement is translated. The label field holds a symbolic name that represents the numerical address of the machine instruction. The mnemonic field holds the TMS32010 machine instruction. The operand field holds the data to be operated on by the machine instruction; this data may be written in numerical form (decimal, binary, hex or octal) or may be represented by user-defined symbols. The comment field holds a statement (no longer than 20 characters) that is used to document the program, and it is ignored by XAssem320. Only the mnemonic field is mandatory; the rest are optional. The source program format accepted by XAssem320 is as follows:

- Statements are written in free format, i.e. there is no restriction on which column the statement fields start in. All fields are delimited by at least one space.
- Comments may exist independently of an instruction line if preceded by the '*' character and are limited to 120 characters.

- Standard TMS32010 mnemonics and operand formats are accepted. Operands to a maximum of three are delimited by a comma. The first six characters of symbols and labels must be unique. This restriction was imposed to maintain compatibility with TI's own crossassembler product. Addressing symbols (*, * +, and *–) may be represented by user-defined symbols. A number of assembler-defined symbols may be used. These are AR0 and AR1, which represent the two auxiliary registers, and PA0–PA7 which represent the eight I/O port addresses of the TMS32010.
- Among the directives provided are AORG, DATA, EQU, SET, LINK, END and macro commands. A macro definition command consists of the macro name preceded by '$$'. A macro expansion command consists of the macro name preceded by '$'. Mnemonic symbols are predefined by the XAssem320 program and cannot be altered by the user. Operand symbols and their numerical values are defined by the user. Label names are also defined by the user but the numerical value of the label is determined by XAssem320 during the translation process.

Translation process

The process of translating a source statement is essentially that of replacing each label, mnemonic and operand by a predefined numerical value and assembling the values into the correct machine code[3]. To do this, XAssem320 requires access to a number of look-up tables that store symbolic names and equivalent numerical values. Labels and symbols are local to the particular source program and are stored in the 'symbol', 'label' and 'forward reference' tables, which are temporary tables constructed during the translation process and later deleted. A pseudocode algorithm for the translation process is shown in Appendix 1.

Assemblers for most general-purpose microprocessors place symbols and labels in the same table so that both types of symbolic name may be used as operands by any of the microprocessor instructions. However, the TMS32010 employs a modified Harvard architecture in which program memory and data memory lie in two separate address spaces with machine instructions provided to operate on either program memory or data memory. It follows that, in the source program, labels are only used by program memory instructions and symbols are only used by data memory instructions.

To maintain this restriction in the development process, symbols and labels are stored in separate tables, with access to each table restricted to the appropriate instructions. Although this is true for most instructions, TI has provided a crossover path between program and data memory which is especially useful for reading tables of constant coefficients from nonvolatile program memory into volatile data memory, where they may be used in arithmetic operations. The associated table read (TBLR) and table write (TBLW) instructions require a program memory address to be placed in the accumulator prior to their execution. This is often achieved using the multiply immediate (MPYK) instruction with the immediate operand being the required program memory address, e.g. the start of a data block. Thus a label may exist as a data item in program memory and an item in data memory may be used to reference an address in program memory. This operation is supported by XAssem320.

Instruction table

The TMS32010 instruction set was classified into a number of groups and subgroups to facilitate the crossassembler translation process. A permanent instruction table was constructed to store the mnemonic, op. code and group code of each instruction. Directives are treated in much the same way as machine instructions, and are also stored in the instruction table. The format of an entry in the table is G$$$$CCC where G is the decimal group code, $$$$ is the mnemonic string and CCC is the decimal op. code.

The group code is used to indicate the appropriate assembly process. The op. code is the numerical value which is assembled with the operand values to generate the corresponding TMS32010 instruction code. Table 1 gives examples of the TMS32010 instruction types[4] which require different assembly processes.

Symbol table

This table holds numerical values, which may be specified in binary, decimal, hexadecimal or octal form, and their representative symbols. The EQU directive is used in the source program to define an operand symbol. The symbol and its assigned value are both stored at the next free location in the symbol table specified by the table pointer.

Once a symbol is defined by the EQU directive it can be used throughout the source program as an operand to represent either immediate data, an addressing mode or a data memory address. It cannot be used to represent a program memory address as required by program control instructions such as the branch instruction. Thus, to translate the value of a symbol operand, a search is made of the symbol table to obtain its value. If the symbol is not located in the table then the operand is translated to zero and an error flag is set to indicate an 'undefined symbol error' in the output listing.

The SET directive allows symbols having an already defined numerical value in the table to be redefined with a new value.

Table 1. Examples of TMS32010 instruction words

Source statement		Bit position in instruction word
		15 14 13 12 11 10 9 8 7 6 5 4 3 2 1 0
PUSH		<- - - - - - - - - - - -OP - - - - - - - ->
XOR	D, R	<- - - - OP - - - - -> M<- - -D - ->
ADD	D, S, R	<- - OP- -> <-S- ->M<- - -D - ->
BNZ	A	<- - - - - - - - - - - -OP - - - - - - - ->
		<- OP -> <- - - - - - - -A - - - - - ->
MPYK	D	<-OP-> <- - - - - - D - - - - - ->
LACK	D	<- - - - -OP- - - - -> <- - -D - - ->

OP = op. code; A = program address; D = operand data; S = shift value;
R = register pointer (concatenated with operand data);
M = addressing mode (derived from operand data)

Label table

A label name is used in the source program as an operand to represent a program memory address. A symbolic name defined as a label in the source statement is placed into the label table with a numerical address derived from the program location pointer. The location pointer is a counter which is used to monitor the program address of each source instruction. This counter is initialized by the AORG directive at the beginning of the source program using any of the recognized numerical formats. Multiple definitions of labels are detected by XAssem320 and result in the label definition being ignored and an error being indicated in the output listing.

Forward reference table

A label name may be used as an operand before it has been defined in the program, e.g. as in a forward branch. When such a forward reference is detected, the operand is initially translated to zero and the operand name is placed into the forward reference table. The assembly process is performed with the zero operand value and the program address, the assembled hex code and the source statement are written into the temporary listing file in the same way as for any other instruction. However, in the case of a forward reference, the line in the temporary listing is also marked with a forward reference flag. This process is carried out for every forward reference operand, irrespective of the number of times the same name has been previously placed into the forward reference table.

Output process

By the time the translation process is complete, the following situation exists.

- A temporary listing has been generated which shows the translated code and machine address beside each source statement. Each line that contains an untranslated forward reference is marked with a forward reference flag.
- The forward reference table holds the name of each forward reference operand in the sequence in which they were detected during the translation process. The table pointer is redirected to the first entry in the table.
- The label table holds the label and corresponding program address of every label defined in the source program.

During the output each line of the temporary listing is copied directly to the output listing. However, if the line is marked with a forward reference flag, the next entry in the forward reference table (a forward reference operand) is removed and searched for in the label table.

If the name is located in the label table then the label value replaces the code which represents the untranslated forward reference operand. The forward reference flag is removed from the line and the line is copied to the output listing. If the name is not located in the label table then no substitution takes place and the code remains with the untranslated value of zero. The forward reference flag is left on the line to indicate an 'unresolved forward reference' error and the line is copied to the output listing.

Once every line from the temporary listing has been copied to the output listing the translation of the source program is complete. A pseudocode algorithm for the output process is given in Appendix 2.

INTERFACING

Data transfer between the Paisley College Prime system and several user terminals is performed via a Micom contention exchange acting as a multichannel, bidirectional I/O buffer. This method is commonly used in a multiuser environment to connect several possible users to a smaller number of system ports. Replacing a user terminal with an intelligent I/O device such as a single-board micro provides a simple means of communication and data transfer between the Prime and the external device.

A method of data transfer has been devised to allow object code data files created on the Prime system to be transferred to the TI evaluation module (EVM) and extended development system (XDS). The method described here has been implemented with no additional hardware and the minimum amount of software. The techniques involved may be applied directly to any system incorporating Prime Series 50 computers, or indeed any system supporting a data terminal port where the terminal driving routines are available.

Communication from the Prime system to the user terminals is made via Micom through a three-wire RS232 data link providing asynchronous bidirectional serial data transfer at a rate defined by the system operator (typically 300–2400 baud). Connection of the EVM or XDS systems between the terminal and the Prime allows serial downloading of data from the Prime system. The user maintains control of both the host Prime system and the EVM or XDS from the terminal by switching in and out of a transparency mode[5, 6]. Figure 1 shows the data paths between the Prime, EVM or XDS and the terminal for both modes of operation.

OBJECT FILE FORMATTING AND DOWNLOADING

Before transfer from the Prime, the '.HEX' object file generated by the crossassembler must be formatted to be recognizable by the EVM and the XDS. The format chosen

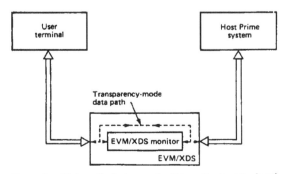

Figure 1. Data paths between the Prime, the terminal and the EVM or XDS

for this purpose was the TI 'normal ASCII' format[6]. This format allows easy manipulation of the object code within ASCII text files on the Prime system, using file handling procedures readily available to the BASIC programmer. In the TI normal ASCII format, each record within a data file is split into smaller data fields. Each field contains ASCII hex characters preceded by a tag character which specifies the type of data field about to be downloaded. The type of field is dependent on whether the object code is absolute or relocatable. Since XAssem320 generates absolute code, the object file is formatted using only the five tag characters which are associated with absolute code.

A BASIC program (Format320) checks the existence and validity of the input '.HEX' and output '.OBJ' files before generating the formatted output file.

Program requirements and development

Through use of a dummy file 'token' the formatting program may be used as a standalone program or as an extension to the crossassembler program. In the latter, XAssem320 generates the 'token' file containing the file name of the hex file to be processed. In this case no file name is required from the user and a check can be made for the existence of the given file. If the token file does not exist then the hex file has been created without XAssem320 and a file name is requested from the user. This facility allowed development of the format converter and downloader to proceed fairly independently of the crossassembler.

Having verified the validity of the input and output files, the process of formatting commences. File name extensions are used to identify the file types, with '.HEX' indicating a source object file and '.OBJ' indicating a target object file.

The hexadecimal data is converted to its decimal equivalent through use of a hex–dec routine prior to performing checksum calculations. The checksum is then converted from decimal to a hexadecimal value for transmission to the object file using a dec–hex routine. This routine is also used to convert the decimal count of the number of data words to be downloaded as a hex number following the 'K' tag character.

The formatted object file which can now be recognized by the EVM and the XDS systems may now be transferred from the Prime. Data transfer is accomplished by a BASIC program Download320 which uses a terminal output routine (TNOUA) of the Prime operating system[7]. This routine will transfer a data word specified as a parameter in the subroutine call to the terminal device, which in this application is the EVM or XDS system. Note that, since the Prime represents all data internally with the most significant bit set, then any ASCII data from the Prime requires the most significant bit to be masked off so that it can be recognized by the receiving device.

It was found necessary to introduce a short delay between each character sent to the EVM, to allow the Micom output buffer time to respond to the EVM software handshake characters XON and XOFF. Without this delay the EVM input buffer overflowed due to the extra characters being transmitted from the Prime following the XOFF character from the EVM. The problem did not occur with the XDS, since it sends the XOFF character well in advance of its input buffer becoming full.

RESULTS

The crossassembler was validated using a suite of test programs containing all legal instructions and directives, and each type of error. In addition the crossassembler was tested through practical use by members of a research group developing software for the TMS32010 microprocessor.

An example source program called ADAXDS.SRC was used to test an A/D interface connected to the TMS32010 microcomputer. Appendix 3 shows the terminal session

Douglas R Campbell has been with the Department of Electrical and Electronic Engineering at Paisley College of Technology, UK, for six years as a lecturer and senior lecturer. He received a BSc in electrical engineering in 1972 and a PhD in the field of identification techniques applied to distributed parameter systems in 1976 from the University of Strathclyde, UK, and later worked as a principal research engineer for Rediffusion Simulation Ltd, UK, on aspects of aircraft flight simulation. His current research interests include digital signal processing and computer applications.

Chris Canning is a software development engineer in British Telecom's Network Management Division. He has held this post since graduating with a degree in electrical and electronic engineering from Paisley College of Technology, UK, in 1985. He is currently a member of a project team involved in the development of network management products for private voice and data networks. His interests lie in the fields of data communications, realtime programming and micro and minicomputer systems. His previous activities have included work on database design, hardware design for laser detection systems and high volume computer peripheral testing.

Kenneth Miller is a software and hardware development engineer with GP Industrial, Plymouth, UK. He graduated with a degree in electrical and electronic engineering from Paisley College of Technology, UK, in 1985. His specialist interests lie in the field of microprocessor applications and software development. Currently he is involved in projects applying 16-bit technology for use in industrial electronics environments, particular emphasis being placed on development tools for programmable logic devices.

during the development process. Appendices 4–6 show the output listing file ADAXDS.LST, the hex file ADAXDS.HEX generated by XAssem320, and the object file ADAXDS.OBJ generated by Format320.

CONCLUSION

Software to support the development of TMS32010 assembler programs on a Prime computer system has been written using the BASIC programming language. The software has been tested and proved successful in its operation. Since it was written in a high-level language it is fairly easy to modify to the particular requirements of an organization, e.g. by adding new assembler directives, by adding new instructions to support a change within the processor family to the TMS32020, or by transferring the software to a different host computer family.

REFERENCES

1   **McGowan, C L and Kelly, J R** *Top down structured programming techniques* Petrocelli, Princetown, NJ, USA (1975)
2   **Aho, A V and Ullman, J D** *Principles of compiler design* Addison-Wesley, Wokingham, UK (1977)
3   **Heath, R and Patel, S R** 'How to write a universal cross-assembler' *IEEE Micro* (August 1981) pp 45–66
4   *TMS32010 users guide* Texas Instruments, Houston, TX, USA (1983)
5   *EVM users guide* Texas Instruments, Houston, TX, USA (1983)
6   *XDS users guide* Texas Instruments, Houston, TX, USA (1983)
7   *PRIME users guide* Prime Computers, Natick, MA, USA (1982)

APPENDIX 1: ALGORITHMS FOR TRANSLATION PROCESS

```
While (not end of source program) {
   Read next line
   If line number exists, remove
   Isolate fields, delimiter = ' ' (min of 1, max of 4)
   While (not end of Instruction Table) {
      Read next entry in table
      If 1st field matches, no label present, identify fields
      If 2nd field matches, label present, identify fields
   }
   If match found, read opcode and group code from Instruction Table
   Else set error flag: 'illegal instruction'
   Isolate operand fields, delimiter = ',' (max of 3)
   Do for each operand {
         If operand is numeric, convert to decimal value
         If operand is an addressing symbol, translate to decimal value
         If operand is a symbol {
            If group code indicates a data memory instruction {
               Search Symbol Table
               If symbol found, remove decimal value
               Else value is zero, set error flag: 'undefined symbol'
            }
            If group code indicates a program memory instruction {
               Search Label Table
               If symbol found, remove decimal value
               Else }
                  Translate value to zero                 .
                  Write symbol in Forward Reference Table
                  Set forward reference flag
               }
            }
         }
      }
   }
   If group code indicates a Directive {
      Select internal process indicated from opcode
      Perform process
   }
   If group code indicates a Machine Instruction {
      If label field present {
         Search Label Table for label name
         If label already exists in Table {
            Set error flag: 'duplicate label'
            Ignore label definition
```

```
        }
        Else write label in Table with value of location pointer
    }
    Select assembly process from group code
    Assemble Instruction Code from opcode and operand data
    }
    Convert code and program address (location pointer) to hex
    Write line to temporary listing file
    Adjust location pointer
    Clear error and forward refererence flags
}
```

APPENDIX 2:   ALGORITHM FOR OUTPUT PROCESS

```
While (not end of temporary listing) {
    Read next line
    If forward reference flag present {
        Read next name in Forward Reference Table
        Search Label Table for name
        If found {
            Remove decimal value from Label Table
            Convert to hex
            Substitute onto listing line
            Remove forward reference flag
        }
    }
    Write line to Output Listing
}
Copy contents of Symbol Table to Output Listing
Copy contents of Label Table to Output Listing
Write number of errors to Output Listing
```

APPENDIX 3:   DEVELOPMENT SESSION (USER RESPONSES ARE SHOWN IN ITALICS)

OK, *BASICV XASSEM320*
:
- TMS32010 CROSS-ASSEMBLER -

enter source file				*!ADAXDS.SRC*
warning:	ADAXDS.LST	exists		
ok to replace			Y/N	*!Y*
warning:	ADAXDS.OBJ	exists		
ok to replace			Y/N	*!N*
renamed:	ADAXDS.OBJ.BAK			
assembling:	ADAXDS.SRC			
54 lines				
0 errors				
listing file:	ADAXDS.LST	created		
ok to list			Y/N	*!N*
ok to format			Y/N	*!Y*
object file:	ADAXDS.OBJ	created		
ok to download			Y/N	*!N*
OK,				

APPENDIX 4:   ADAXDS.LST

Assembled on 30-05-86 at 10:01		4	00A		AORG	10
- - - - - - - - - - - - - - - - - - -		5		INPUT	EQU	0
		6		OUTPUT	EQU	34
1	∗∗∗ tms320 evm text editor ∗∗	7		ONE	EQU	127
2	∗∗ adc/dac test routine	8		MINUS	EQU	126
3	∗∗ - - - - - - - - - - - - - - - - -	9		CLEAR	EQU	125

10			MAX	EQU	124
11			OFFSET	EQU	123
12	00A	7E01		LACK	1
13	00B	507F		SACL	ONE
14	00C	7F89		ZAC	
15	00D	507C		SACL	MAX
16	00E	107F		SUB	ONE
17	00F	507E		SACL	MINUS
18	010	7E7F		LACK	> 7F
19	011	507D		SACL	CLEAR
20	012	7EFF		LACK	> FF
21	013	087D		ADD	CLEAR, 8
22	014	507D		SACL	CLEAR
23	015	007F		ADD	ONE
24	016	507B		SACL	OFFSET
25	017	4000		IN	0, 0
26	018	4B7D		OUT	CLEAR, 3
27	019	4100	READ	IN	0, 1
28	01A	7F80		NOP	
29	01B	4100		IN	0, 1
30	01C	F600	WAIT	BIOZ	WAIT
31	01D	001C			
32	01E	4200		IN	INPUT, 2
33	01F	2000		LAC	INPUT
34	020	FA00		BLZ	POS
35	021	0025			
36	022	7A7B		OR	OFFSET
37	023	F900		B	CONT
38	024	0026			
39	025	797D	POS	AND	CLEAR
40	026	5000	CONT	SACL	INPUT
41	027	5022		SACL	OUTPUT
42	028	2022		LAC	OUTPUT
43	029	787E		XOR	MINUS
44	02A	FD00		BGEZ	PLUS
45	02B	002F			
46	02C	7A7B		OR	OFFSET
47	02D	F900		B	DAC
48	02E	0030			
49	02F	797D	PLUS	AND	CLEAR
50	030	5022	DAC	SACL	OUTPUT
51	031	4B22		OUT	OUTPUT, 3
52	032	F900		B	READ
53	033	0019			
54				END	

Symbol Table

		=	> 0000	0
INPUT		=	> 0000	0
OUTPUT		=	> 0022	34
ONE		=	> 007F	127
MINUS		=	> 007E	126
CLEAR		=	> 007D	125
MAX		=	> 007C	124
OFFSET		=	> 007B	123

Label Table

origin	=	> 00A	10
READ	=	> 019	25
WAIT	=	> 01C	28
POS	=	> 025	37
CONT	=	> 026	38
PLUS	=	> 02F	47
DAC	=	> 030	48

----

0 Errors

APPENDIX 5:   ADAXDS.HEX

*=, 000A, 7E01, 507F, 7F89, 507C, 107F, 507E, 7E7F, 507D, 7EFF, 087D, 507D, 007F, 507B, 4000, 4B7D, 4100, 7F80, 4100, F600, 001C, 4200, 2000,
FA00, 0025, 7A7B, F900, 0026, 797D, 5000, 5022, 2022, 787E, FD00, 002F, 7A7B, F900, 0030, 797D, 5022, 4B22, F900, 0019,

APPENDIX 6:   ADAXDS.OBJ

```
K002ATADAXDS 9000AB7E01B507FB7F89B507CB107FB507EB7E7FB507D7F244F
B7EFFB087DB507DB007FB507BB4000B4B7DB4100B7F80B4100BF600B001C7F257F
B4200B2000BFA00B0025B7A7BBF900B0026B797DB5000B5022B2022B787E7F2B9F
BFD00B002FB7A7BBF900B0030B797DB5022B4B22BF900B00197F4A9F
        30-05-86      10:02      PRIME TI LOADER
```

Software controller for an arithmetic processor

8-bit microprocessors such as the 6802 are not usually powerful enough for modern instrumentation and control applications, but this is no reason to discard them. **K V Ranga Rao and O Subramanyam** show how 6802 system performance can be increased using an arithmetic processor

The paper explores the use of the Am9511A arithmetic processor (AP) by developing a software controller package bridging a 6802 microprocessor and the AP unit. The controller program emulates a stack machine for application to formula computation. The instructions of the emulated stack machine and the implementation of the controller are discussed. Execution phases of the binary instruction Z = X + Y and an output instruction are elucidated. A benchmark test of the stack machine against some proprietary microcomputers was performed.

microsystems   arithmetic processing unit   stack machine

The computational requirements of instrumentation, control and digital signal processing applications cannot be met by an 8-bit microprocessor. It is not usually economical, however, to discard such a processor and switch over to a 16-bit or 32-bit CPU for this reason alone. Any change from one processor to another, even among the same family, calls for retraining of staff and involves additional investment and procurement delays; these factors are of extreme importance when executing time-bound projects and assignments.

To resolve such a situation for a 6802 CPU, the existing 8-bit computational power can be augmented by interfacing the 6802 to a floating-point arithmetic processing unit, e.g. the Am9511A.

ARITHMETIC PROCESSOR

The Am9511A arithmetic processing (AP) unit is a monolithic MOS large-scale integration (LSI) device that provides fixed-point and floating-point arithmetic and a variety of floating-point mathematical and trigonometric operations (Table 1). All transfers, including operand, result, status and command information, take place over an 8-bit bidirectional bus. Operands are pushed onto an internal stack and a command is issued to perform operations on the data in the stack. Results are then available for retrieval from the stack, or additional commands may be entered. The block diagram and pin-out of the AP unit are shown in Figure 1.

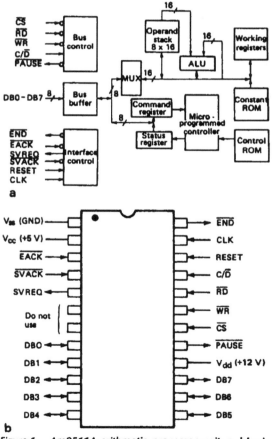

Figure 1.   Am9511A arithmetic processor unit: a, block diagram; b, pin-out diagram

Naval Science and Technological Laboratory, Vigyan Nagar, Visakhapatnam 530006, India

Transfers to and from the AP unit may be handled by the 6802 microprocessor either using conventional programmed I/O output or by a direct memory access (DMA) controller for improved performance. Upon execution of each command, the AP unit issues an end of execution signal (END) which may be used as an interrupt to the CPU for coordinating program execution. In the project under discussion, programmed I/O was employed; the same software package with fewer modifications can be adopted in DMA mode.

The relevant and important control lines (all inputs) are

- chip select (CS)
- read (RD)
- write (WR)
- command/data select (CD)

Table 1. Am9511A operations

Command mnemonic	Hex code (SR = 1)	Hex code (SR = 0)	Execution	Summary description
16-bit fixed-point operations				
SADD	EC	6C	16–18	Add TOS to NOS. Result to NOS. Pop stack.
SSUB	ED	6D	30–32	Subtract TOS from NOS. Result to NOS. Pop stack.
SMUL	EE	6E	84–94	Multiply NOS by TOS. Lower result to NOS. Pop stack.
SMUU	F6	76	80–98	Multiply NOS by TOS. Upper result to NOS. Pop stack.
SDIV	EF	6F	84–94	Divide NOS by TOS. Result to NOS. Pop stack.
32-bit fixed-point operations				
DADD	AC	2C	20–22	Add TOS to NOS. Result to NOS. Pop stack.
DSUB	AD	2D	38–40	Subtract TOS from NOS. Result to NOS. Pop stack.
DMUL	AE	2E	194–210	Multiply NOS by TOS. Lower result to NOS. Pop stack.
DMUU	B6	36	182–218	Multiply NOS by TOS. Upper result to NOS. Pop stack.
DDIV	AF	2F	196–210	Divide NOS by TOS. Result to NOS. Pop stack.
32-bit floating-point primary operations				
FADD	90	10	54–368	Add TOS to NOS. Result to NOS. Pop stack.
FSUB	91	11	70–370	Subtract TOS from NOS. Result to NOS. Pop stack.
FMUL	92	12	146–168	Multiply NOS by TOS. Result to NOS. Pop stack.
FDIV	93	13	154–184	Divide NOS by TOS. Result to NOS. Pop stack.
32-bit floating-point derived operations				
SQRT	81	01	782–870	Square root of TOS. Result to TOS.
SIN	82	02	3796–4808	Sine of TOS. Result of TOS.
COS	83	03	3840–4878	Cosine of TOS. Result to TOS.
TAN	84	04	4894–5886	Tangent of TOS. Result to TOS.
ASIN	85	05	6230–7938	Inverse sine of TOS. Result to TOS.
ACOS	86	06	6304–8284	Inverse cosine of TOS. Result to TOS.
ATAN	87	07	4992–6536	Inverse tangent of TOS. Result to TOS.
LOG	88	08	4474–7132	Common logarithm of TOS. Result to TOS.
LN	89	09	4298–6956	Natural logarithm of TOS. Result to TOS.
EXP	8A	0A	3794–4878	e raised to power in TOS. Result to TOS.
PWR	8B	0B	8290–12032	NOS raised to power in TOS. Result to NOS. Pop stack.
Data and stack manipulation operations				
NOP	80	00	4	No operation. Clear or set SVREQ.
FIXS	9F	1F	90–214	Convert TOS from floating-point format to fixed-point format.
FIXD	9E	1E	90–336	Convert TOS from floating-point format to fixed-point format.
FLTS	9D	1D	62–156	Convert TOS from fixed-point format to floating-point format.
FLTD	9C	1C	56–342	Convert TOS from fixed-point format to floating-point format.
CHSS	F4	74	22–24	Change sign of fixed-point operand on TOS.
CHSD	B4	34	26–28	Change sign of fixed-point operand on TOS.
CHSF	95	15	16–20	Change sign of floating-point operand on TOS.
PTOS	F7	77	16	Push stack. Duplicate NOS in TOS.
PTOD	B7	37	20	Push stack. Duplicate NOS in TOS.
PTOF	97	17	20	Push stack. Duplicate NOS in TOS.
POPS	F8	78	10	Pop stack. Old NOS becomes new TOS. Old TOS rotates to bottom.
POPD	B8	38	12	Pop stack. Old NOS becomes new TOS. Old TOS rotates to bottom.
POPF	98	18	12	Pop stack. Old NOS becomes new TOS. Old TOS rotates to bottom.
XCHS	F9	79	18	Exchange TOS and NOS.
XCHD	B9	39	26	Exchange TOS and NOS.
XCHF	99	19	26	Exchange TOS and NOS.
PUPI	9A	1A	16	Push floating-point constant π onto TOS. Previous TOS becomes NOS.

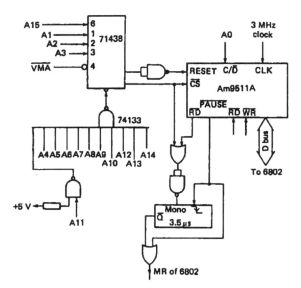

Figure 2. Interface between 6802 and Am9511A

- reset
- clock

The chip select line when in '1' state maintains the data bus tristate. The data direction is controlled by two mutually exclusive active-low signals, read and write. The command/data select line indicates the type of data: either a command or data for computation. Reading of command information indicates the status of the AP unit and writing of command information is done to execute an instruction. The CD line is normally connected to A0 of the main processor to simplify the decoding hardware. CS is obtained from a decoder. Figure 2 shows the complete interface between the AP unit and the 6802 microprocessor. A monostable was used because a deadlock problem between the 6802 and the Am9511A was noticed. This occurred because of the speed incompatibility between the two processors. A simple interconnection of the PAUSE signal from the AP unit to the 'memory ready' (MR) of the 6802 sometimes causes permanent stretching of the clock ϕ_2, leading to unreliable operation.

The interface circuit contains a monostable multivibrator which limits the stretching of the 6802 ϕ_2 to 3.5 µs. The choice of 3.5 µs was purely arbitrary; the stretching time must be sufficiently large to cater for the worst case. The minimum read time from the AP unit is $(3.5\ T_{cy} + 50)$ ns, which is approximately 0.925 µs with $T_{cy} = 250$ ns for a 4 MHz clock rate.

The strength of the AP unit lies in its ability to handle floating-point numbers in hardware. The concept of floating-point notation has both an advantage and a disadvantage associated with it. The advantage is the ability to represent the significant digits of data with values spanning a large dynamic range, limited only by the capacity of the exponent field. The shortcoming is that only the significant digits can be retained. Figure 3 indicates the data formats that can be used in the AP unit. The range of values that can be represented is from 2.7×10^{-20} to 9.2×10^{18}.

SOFTWARE CONTROLLER

An application-independent software package compatible with the above hardware was developed. The software package consists essentially of a controller program emulating a stack machine, which is the best architecture for computation of formulae. The emulated stack machine uses the 6802 memory for its data and instructions. The architecture of the machine is shown in Figure 4.

The software controller package picks up specially built variable-byte (2–6 byte) instructions from the main memory and executes the instructions in a sequence as any normal hardware processor does. The instruction range of the emulated stack machine is given in Table 1. The total design concept is evolved on the basis that all variables encountered in the formulae are mapped as a set of hexadecimal numbers running from 00 to F4. In turn these numbers are mapped as real addresses in the memory. Figure 5 details the evolution process from formula to the actual addresses illustrating the program concept.

The instructions that the emulated stack machine can handle can be classified into four categories:

- data transfer type
- command type (for AP unit)
- control type
- I/O type

Data transfer

In this type there are five instructions:

- A binary operation on two variables X and Y is performed and the result is returned to the variable Z.

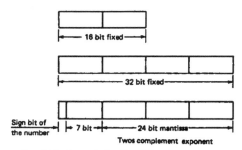

Figure 3. Data formats for the AP unit

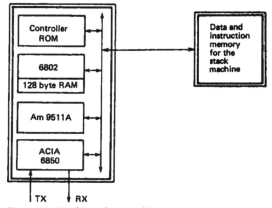

Figure 4. Stack machine architecture

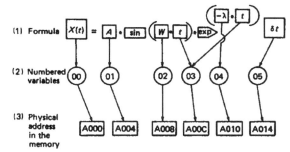

Figure 5. Evolution process for the expression X(t) = A exp (−αt) sin wt, showing how it is translated into memory locations

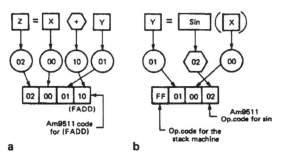

a   b

Figure 6. Machine coding formats: a, for a binary operation (see also Appendix 1); b, for a unary operation (see also Appendix 2)

Figure 6a and Appendix 1 indicate how a binary operation is machine coded.

● A unary operation on a variable X is performed and the result is returned to the variable Y. Figure 6b and Appendix 2 indicate the machine coding procedure for a unary operation.
● Move variable X to the top of the stack.
● Fetch the result from the top of the stack into variable X.
● Assign a constant value to the variable X in the floating-point format.

Command

In this type all AP unit instructions are covered and Am9511A command code is delivered to the AP unit. This is a 2 byte instruction.

Control

In this type of instruction, the program flow can be altered conditionally or unconditionally depending upon the status of the top of stack (plus, minus or zero). This is a 3 byte instruction. The first byte is the op. code and the others indicate the branch address.

I/O

The power of the software package lies in the two I/O-type instructions, as they link it to the external world.

● Variable X can be input through an RS232C link. This is a 2 byte instruction, one byte being the op. code and the other the variable number.

● Variable X can be output through an RS232C link; the format is the same as that for input. Table 2 gives the instruction repertoire of the stack machine with op. codes and formats.

Controller implementation

The machine code for the emulated stack machine is assumed to start at the memory location 8000H. This address is a purely arbitrary choice. Figure 7 shows machine code for an equation Z = X + Y. As the power is switched on, the 6802 initiates the Am9511 and sets the value 8000H in a program counter. The instruction passes through three distinct phases: fetch, decode and execute.

The flowchart in Figure 8 indicates the macroscopic view of the controller implementation. This flowchart is augmented by the functional description of the subroutines given in Table 3. The flowchart typically contains the execution phases of the binary instruction Z = X + Y as well as an output instruction. These are explained below.

Execution phases of Z = X + Y

Consider the execution of instruction ⟨02000110⟩. In the fetch phase, the byte contained in the memory location 8000H is obtained; this number is examined to see whether it lies between FF and F5. In the case of ⟨02000110⟩, the number is 02 and it is not in the range FF–F5. The decoding subroutine therefore concludes that it is a binary instruction; otherwise it would have to decode further to classify the exact function and nature of the instruction. The binary instruction has two operands lying at PC + 1 and PC + 2, the operation to be performed is at PC + 3, and the destination variable is at PC. When all information regarding the instruction in the decode phase is obtained, the program enters the execute phase.

In the execution phase the physical values of the operands are obtained from the 6802's main memory starting from A000H. This address is arbitrarily chosen. Figure 9 gives the variable array map.

Since the machine code only contains the variable number (i.e. 00 to F4H) in order to fetch the actual data, the variable number should be translated to the physical memory address. This is achieved by concatenating an 8-bit number to the given 8-bit variable number, shifting the

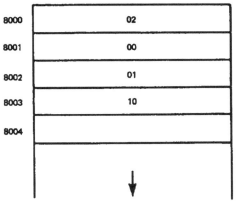

Figure 7. Machine code for the equation Z = X + Y

resulting 16-bit number left twice and adding the base value (A000H). Consider for example the number 02H. On concatenation it becomes 0002H, and on shifting left twice it becomes 0008H. A 16-bit addition is then performed by adding A000H, which yields A008H — the physical memory address of the variable 02. A simple package was written to perform the mapping.

Since arithmetic operations must be performed by the arithmetic processor, the value of the operands have to be moved onto the Am9511 stack (identical to the stack of the emulated stack machine). This is achieved by a small procedure designated 'move'. The variable X (variable number 00) is translated into the physical address, then the four consecutive bytes are moved onto the Am9511 stack. Similarly, information in the PC + 2 byte is recognized as the second operand Y (variable

number 01) and transferred onto the Am9511 stack. Now PC + 3 contains the operation to be performed between the Am9511 TOS (top of stack) and NOS (next of stack). The code contained in the memory location PC + 3 is fetched and output to the Am9511 to perform the operation. The 6802 waits until the operation is complete. The result, which is available on the Am9511 TOS, is fetched and posted at the physical memory location corresponding to the variable, Z (variable number 02) in this example, defined in the PC byte.

This completes the execution of one instruction. Subsequently the PC value is incremented by four to access the next instruction. The only instructions which do not involve the participation of the AP unit are the jump instructions, which affect only the control flow by appropriately changing the PC value.

Table 2. Instruction repertoire of stack machine (dest. = destination; opd = operand; TOS = top of stack; NOS = next of stack)

Mnemonic	Format and hex code	Description
$Z \leftarrow (X, Y) +$	⟨dest.⟩⟨opd 1⟩⟨opd 2⟩⟨AP code⟩ ⟨02⟩ ⟨00⟩ ⟨01⟩ ⟨10⟩ 02000110	Binary operation '+' between two variables X and Y numbered as 00H, 01H; result is in Z numbered as 02H
$Y \leftarrow (X)$ sin	⟨op. code⟩⟨dest.⟩⟨opd 1⟩⟨AP code⟩ ⟨FF⟩ ⟨01⟩ ⟨00⟩ ⟨02⟩ FF010002	Unary operation 'sin' on the variable X numbered as 00H; result is returned to Y numbered as 01H
$X \leftarrow 1.0$	⟨op. code⟩⟨dest.⟩⟨constant⟩ ⟨F5⟩ ⟨00⟩ ⟨01800000⟩ F50001800000	Variable X numbered as 00H is assigned a constant (1.0) as a 32-bit floating-point number
$TOS \leftarrow X$	⟨op. code⟩⟨source⟩ ⟨FD⟩ ⟨00⟩ FD00	Value of variable X is transferred to the top of the stack
$X \leftarrow TOS$	⟨op. code⟩⟨dest.⟩ ⟨FC⟩ ⟨00⟩ FC00	Contents of the top of stack are assigned to the variable X and NOS becomes TOS
$TOS \leftarrow (TOS, NOS) +$ or $TOS \leftarrow (TOS)$, sin	⟨op. code⟩⟨AP code⟩ ⟨FE⟩ ⟨10⟩ FE10 or ⟨FE⟩ ⟨02⟩ FE02	Binary or unary operation between TOS and NOS or TOS, according to the AP code; result is placed on TOS
JMP	⟨op. code⟩⟨address⟩ ⟨F6⟩ ⟨9400⟩ F69400	Unconditional jump to the address specified (e.g. 9400H)
JMP =	⟨op. code⟩⟨address⟩ ⟨FB⟩ ⟨9400⟩ FB9400	If the TOS contents are zero, a branch is executed to the address specified
JMP +	⟨op. code⟩⟨address⟩ ⟨FA⟩ ⟨9400⟩ FA9400	If the TOS contents are positive, a branch is executed to the address specified
JMP −	⟨op. code⟩⟨address⟩ ⟨F9⟩ ⟨9400⟩ F99400	If the TOS contents are negative, a branch is executed to the address specified
Out X	⟨op. code⟩⟨source⟩ ⟨F8⟩ ⟨00⟩ F800	Value of variable X is transmitted on an RS232C link as a series of ASCII characters
In X	⟨op. code⟩⟨dest.⟩ ⟨F7⟩ ⟨00⟩ F700	Variable X is assigned the value as received on the RS232C link

Table 3. Functional description of controller subroutines

Subroutine	Parameters	Description
ADRS	Register A, index register	Register A contains the variable number and the index register is returned with the physical address of the variable
MOVE	Register A	Contents of the variable defined by Register A are transferred to TOS
GET	Register A	The contents of TOS are moved to the variable defined by Register A
EXEC	Register A	Contents of register A are taken as AP code and output onto the AP unit; waits until the completion of the AP unit instruction
UNPACK	Register A, index register	Index register points to the 4 byte floating-point number; this number is multiplied by 10 000 and converted into a 32-bit integer, and then to a string of BCD numbers; starting address of the string is posted back into the index register and the number of bytes put into register A
ASKI	Register A, index register	Index register defines the starting address of a string of BCD characters and register A defines the number of bytes in the string; BCD numbers are converted into ASCII characters and output onto an ACIA until the string is exhausted
STRING	Index register	Receives a string of ASCII characters from the ACIA and places them in temporal order starting from the memory location defined by the index register, until a CR or LF character is received
PACK	Index register	Converts the string of ASCII characters whose starting address is defined by the index register and terminated by either CR or LF into a 4 byte floating-point number in a format acceptable to the AP unit; this is done using the AP unit itself; index register is returned with the address of the floating-point number

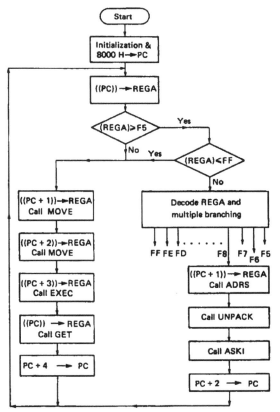

Figure 8. Macroscopic view of the controller implementation

Output instruction

The I/O instructions are amongst the most important in the set. To illustrate the computational complexity of the I/O instructions a typical output instruction, OUT X, is considered.

This instruction is coded as, for example < F832 >. The first byte (F8) indicates that it is an output instruction while the second byte is X (variable number 32H). The physical memory address for the variable address 32H is A0C8H. Let the contents of A0C8, A0C9, A0CA, A0CB be < 02A00000 >, which is the decimal equivalent of 2.5.

The floating-point number < 02A00000 > is first multiplied by < 0E9C4000 >, which is the same as multiplying by 10 000; thus the number becomes 25000.00. This floating-point number is converted into a 32-bit fixed-point number using the Am9511. In this example the result < 000061A8 > is obtained. This 32-bit integer is converted into a binary coded decimal (BCD) number using a special subroutine. Since the converted number is multiplied by 10 000, the decimal point is fixed between the fourth and fifth digits, starting from the least significant digit.

These BCD numbers are then converted into a set of ASCII characters and transmitted along with a decimal point on the RS232 link using a 6850 ACIA. A similar procedure is adopted while executing the instruction INPUT Y.

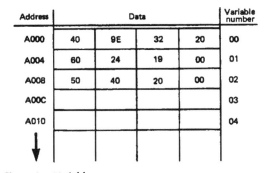

Address	Data				Variable number
A000	40	9E	32	20	00
A004	60	24	19	00	01
A008	50	40	20	00	02
A00C					03
A010					04

Figure 9. Variable array map

The space occupied by the software is around 2 kbyte, of which 1 kbyte is consumed by the I/O instructions.

Using the hardware and software, the function $f(t) = A \exp(-\alpha t) \sin wt$ was evaluated and output through a D/A converter for demonstration purposes. Figure 10 shows the waveform obtained with $A = 10$, $\alpha = 0.5$ and $w = 0.6$. Table 4 compares the times taken by different machines to evaluate the above expression.

CONCLUSIONS

Only one AP unit has been considered in this paper, but further AP units could be connected as peripherals to the same 6802 microprocessor, and computational power can be further augmented by efficient programming techniques. Further work using interrupts and DMA with two or three processors is suggested.

ACKNOWLEDGEMENTS

The authors wish to thank Commodore N K Ramanarasiah, the director of the Naval Science and Technological Laboratory, and Shir V Krishna Brahmam, the deputy director, for administrative support during this work. They are also grateful to Dr P A Janakiraman, assistant professor in the Department of Electrical Engineering, Indian Institute of Technology, Madras, for his valuable guidance and many fruitful discussions.

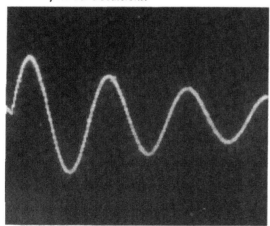

Figure 10. Waveform obtained from the function $f(t) = A \exp(-\alpha t) \sin wt$ with $A = 10$, $\alpha = 0.5$ and $w = 0.6$

Table 4. Relative performance of the stack machine, referred to as WSG1, and other machines in evaluating the expression $A \exp(-\alpha t) \sin wt$

Computer	Time taken to execute expression 25000 times (s)	Time taken to execute expression once (ms)
WSG 1 (stack machine)	165	6.6
PDP-11/23	177	7.08
HP9826	214	8.56
PDP-11/03	758	30.32
Tektronics 4051	3012.5	120.5

Kaluri Venkata Ranga Rao received a BE degree in electrical engineering from Andhra University, Waltair, India, in 1974 and an ME in automation from the Institute of Science, Bangalore, India, in 1977. From 1977 to 1985 he worked in the Indian Naval Science and Technological Laboratory as principal scientist and a divisional head, and carried out research and development work in instrumentation, simulation and signel processing. He is currently working in the Department of Electrical Engineeing at the Indian Institute of Technology, Madras, where his interests are the application of identification and pattern recognition techniques to robotics.

Oruganti Subramanyam obtained BE in electronics and communications engineering from Andhra University, Waltair, India, and an MTech in communications and radar engineering from the Indian Institute of Technology, Delhi, India. His areas of interest lie in developing of microprocessor-based hardware systems. He is presently working as a scientist at the Naval Science and Technological Laboratory, India.

BIBLIOGRAPHY

MOS microprocessors and peripherals data book Advanced Micro Devices, Sunnyvale, CA, USA (1983)

Gear, C W Computer organisation and programming (1969) McGraw-Hill, New York, USA

Peatman, J B Microcomputer based design (1977) McGraw-Hill, New York, USA

Microprocessor products data book Fairchild, Munich, FRG (1982)

'Math processor chips boost microcomputer computing power' EDN (20 August 1980)

Technical manual on the Am9511A Advanced Micro Devices, Sunnyvale, CA, USA (1984)

APPENDIX 1: PROCEDURE FOR TRANSLATING MNEMONIC IN THE CASE OF A BINARY OPERATION (FIGURE 6A)

$Z \leftarrow (X, Y) +$

(1) Identify the variables [X, Y, Z]
(2) Assign convenient numbers to the variables between F4 and 00H [00H, 01H, 02H]
(3) Obtain the AP unit code for FADD (see Table 1) [10H]
(4) From the instruction repertoire of the stack machine (Table 2), assemble the code as ⟨destination⟩ ⟨operand 1⟩ ⟨operand 2⟩ ⟨AP code⟩ [02000110]

APPENDIX 2: PROCEDURE FOR TRANSLATING THE MNEMONIC IN THE CASE OF A UNARY OPERATION (FIGURE 6B)

$Y \leftarrow (X)$ sin

(1) Identify the variables [X, Y]

(2) Assign convenient numbers to the variables between F4H and 00H [00H, 01H]
(3) Obtain the AP unit code for SIN (see Table 1) [02H]
(4) From the instruction repertoire of the stack machine (Table 2), assemble the code as ⟨opcode⟩ ⟨destination⟩ ⟨operand⟩ ⟨AP code⟩ [FF010002]

'R & D reports' surveys the recent scientific and technical literature, highlighting papers on the research, development and application of microprocessor-based systems.

Computer architectures

Godfrey, M D
'Innovation in computational architecture and design' *ICL Tech. J.* Vol 5 No 1 (May 1986) pp 18–31

The motivations for innovation in computational architecture and design are identified to be VLSI technology and application architectures. The paper explains a range of architectures — from MIMD to SISD or Von Neumann (but not MISD) — covering multiprocessors, arrays, dataflow machines, vector processors and RISCs.

Computer integrated manufacturing

Biemens, F P M
'The design of distributed transport systems as a major standard interface in computer integrated manufacturing' *Comput. in Industry* Vol 7 No 4 (August 1986) pp 319–331

Design automation

Collett, R
'ASICs: take your pick' pp 29–36

Collett, R
'Programmable logic declares war on gate arrays' pp 32–39*

Holley, M
'Smart tools ease PLD design' pp 72–75

Khokhani, K, Rogoyski, E, Chou, A and Lin, J
'Advanced algorithms enhance board layout' pp 56–60

Lai, L-W L
'Bridging the gap between VLSI design and test' pp 61–64

Marshall, J and Van Dyne, D
'Integrating CAE, CAD and CASE' pp 40–46

Meng, B
'The case for CASE' pp 77–80
Digital Des. Vol 16 No 7 (June 1986)
*Vol 16 No 8 (July 1986)

CAD, CAE, CASE, CAT — computer-aided design, engineering, software engineering and test — are all now familiar to microsystem designers as availability of design automation tools and manufacturing facilities enable them to design custom-made rather than use off-the-shelf devices.

On the hardware side, five categories of application-specific ICs (ASICs) are examined by Collett: programmable logic devices (PLDs), gate arrays, standard cells, silicon compiled chips and handcrafted full-custom ICs.

Many designers will opt for PLDs rather than gate arrays, Collett argues in a subsequent article. Quick turnaround time has been the primary advantage of PLDs, but their architectures have often been too constraining. Manufacturers are now addressing the problem by adding extra logic to the basic AND-OR structure of PLDs. Design tools for PLDs are also advancing, says Holley, reducing design times from days to hours.

A number of CAE workstations have emerged to support board design and VLSI test tasks. The emphasis of these tools is on increasing design productivity and they involve extensive computing power explain, respectively, Khokhani et al. and Lai.

While hardware design continues to leap forward, there is a crisis in software development and productivity, says Meng. Computer-aided software engineering (CASE) is not new, but it has been confined largely to microprocessor development. Now software engineers, like their hardware counterparts, increasingly have CAE tools they can use. The principal difficulty remaining is the integration of different CASE tools.

Integration of design automation tools is the theme taken by Marshall and Van Dyne. Refinements of individual tools will only produce diminishing returns unless data transfer between them is also automated, they say. Some companies are now beginning to offer integrated design tools.

Development systems

Albetengo, G
'A workstation for the development of iAPX186 based multiprocessor systems' *Int. J. Mini & Microcomput.* Vol 8 No 1 (1986) pp 26–29

A workstation based on a DEC PDP-11/03 minicomputer has been built that monitors up to seven iAPX186 microprocessors by means of a simple interface circuit and a supervisory program resident in the targets.

Hardware

Furht, B
'Evaluation and selection of 16-bit microprocessors' *Int. J. Mini & Microcomput.* Vol 8 No 1 (1986) pp 14–27

Presents the criteria, methodology and data used in selecting a 16-bit microprocessor, covering the 8086 and 80286, MC68000 and 68010, Z8001 and 8002, and the NS16016 and 16032.

Wilson, D
'Gallium arsenide — a semicustom approach' *Digital Des.* Vol 16 No 7 (June 1986) pp 89–91

High speed and low power consumption are the factors motivating the infant technology of GaAs. Three types of GaAs devices are being developed — gate arrays, static RAMs and off-the-shelf logic parts — in the main targetted for military use. Currently, however, GaAs is expensive and the lack of automatic test equipment together with nonstandard packaging limit its use. Bipolar ECL parts will be the principal competitors, says Wilson, who examines the likely impact of GaAs.

R&D reports

Multiprocessors

Sanvicente, E, Valero, M, Lang, T and Alegre, I
'Exact and approximate models for multiprocessors with single bus and distributed memory' *Int. J. Mini & Microcomput.* Vol 8 No 2 (1986) pp 45–48

Packaging

Bracey, S
'A cost-effective high lead count chip interconnection package' *J. Semicustom ICs* Vol 3 No 4 (June 1986) pp 28–35

Describes a new package, the SLICC 50 and the SLICC 25, which the author believes will become industry standards for lead counts of 50 or over, and which he says will supersede the pin grid array.

Garner, R and Taylor, T
'Surface mount packaging' *Microelectronics J.* Vol 17 No 3 (May/June 1986) pp 5–13

Hutchins, C L
'Surface mounted devices: advantages and issues' *Microelectronics J.* Vol 17 No 3 (May/June 1986) pp 42–47

Peel, M E
'SMT — ignored problems' *Microelectronics J.* Vol 17 No 3 (May/June 1986) pp 36–41

Robot software

Pagello, E, Bison, P, Mirolo, C, Perini, G and Trainito, G
'A message passing approach to robot programming' *Comput. in Industry* Vol 7 No 3 (June 1986) pp 237–247

In robotics software no standards are available, no widely accepted language exists and no long-term experience has been acquired. Classical concurrent procedural languages such as AL and AUTOPASS were developed as robot languages but, says the author, have never been fully implemented because of their complexity. This, the authors continue, suggests that attempting to constrain robotics software in a disciplined and uniform framework is premature. The authors explain in the paper how it is more convenient to build different software modules, one for each activity such as sensory feedback, modelling etc, possibly coded in different languages, and allow them to communicate through message exchange.

Sata, T, Kimura, F, Hiraoka, H and Enomoto, M
'An approach to model-based robot software for industrial applications' *Comput. in Industry* Vol 7 No 3 (June 1986) pp 211–225

Robots in industry are usually operated by the teaching/playback method to perform simple, repetitive, predefined operations. This is an inflexible approach and the authors urge the development of powerful programming systems for industrial robots. Conventional robot programming languages are low level. The authors present some basic principles that they say may be useful for constructing practical high-level robot software.

Semiconductors

Colaco, S, Davies, R, Healey, D and Choy, O
'Multilevel differential logic — the bipolar alternative' *J. Semicustom ICs* Vol 3 No 4 (June 1986) pp 21–27

The authors claim that multi-level differential current-mode logic, which uses an advanced silicon bipolar technology, offers performance levels that cannot be matched by MOS technology devices and adds low power capability to the traditional advantages of bipolar such as linear capability and high drive off the chip. Developed by Ferranti Electronics, the technology forms the basis of its recently launched DS series of uncommitted logic arrays.

Software

Kitchenham, B A, Kitchenham, A P and Fellows, J P
'The effects of inspections on software quality and productivity' *ICL Tech. J.* Vol 5 No 1 (May 1986) pp 112–122

Relph, R, Hahn, S and Viles, F
'Benchmarking C compilers' *Dr Dobb's J. Software Tools* Vol 11 No 8 (August 1986) pp 30–66

Reviews 17 C compilers for MS-DOS from 15 different companies.

Shaw, G W II
'A FORTH standards proposal: extended control structures' *Dr Dobb's J. Software Tools* Vol 11 No 7 (July 1986) pp 30–36

Sherman, B
'Attention to basics reduces risk in ADA compiler choice' *Comput. Des.* Vol 25 No 12 (15 June 1986) pp 87–90

ADA compilers are expensive and are difficult to implement. Further, says Sherman, the existence of stringent validation requirements imposed by the US Department of Defense has given buyers a false sense of security when choosing an ADA compiler. To reduce the risk of buying the wrong compiler a thorough knowledge of the performance parameters, such as the validation process and levels of code optimization, is required, Sherman argues.

Wiener, R S
'Interfacing assembly language to MODULA-2 — a case study: creating rapid screen displays for PCs' *J. Pascal, Ada & Modula-2* Vol 5 No 4 (July/August 1986) pp 21–26

Standards

Campbell-Grant, I R
'Open systems application layer standards for text and office systems' *JIERE* Vol 56 No 6/7 (June/July 1986) pp 233-236

Presents a 'status report' on the development of standards in the 'application' layer of the ISO's OSI model enabling the interconnection and interworking of text and office systems.

System design

Andra, G C, Ippolito, G and Tessitore, L
'The architecture of a microprocessor-based channel processor' *Int. J. Mini & Microcomput.* Vol 8 No 2 (1986) pp 49-52

Describes the Z80-based architecture of a GPIB controller used to control a minicomputer. The controller has been designed at Olivetti GID in Italy and a prototype is being tested.

Li, H F, Cheung, Y S and Chiu, P P K
'Microcomputer system specification using interval logic and a modified labelled-net model' *IEE Proc. E* Vol 133 No 4 (July 1986) pp 223-234

Testing

Reddy, S M and Reddy, M K
'Testable realizations for FET stuck-open faults in CMOS combinational logic circuits' *IEEE Trans. Computers* Vol C-35 No 8 (August 1986) pp 742-754

Vendl, D and Gearhardt, K
'Front-end tools ease test generation chores' *Comput. Des.* Vol 25 No 12 (15 June 1986) pp 97-100

IC designers are being forced to consider test problems at a much earlier stage in the design cycle. The key to realizing more testable designs, say Vendl and Gearhardt, is effective, easy-to-use tools that handle the front end of test pattern development. The authors, from NCR, present some of the company's workstation design tools.

VLSI

Chu, T-A
'On the models for designing VLSI asynchronous digital systems' *Integration* Vol 4 No 2 (June 1986) pp 99-113

Traditional design approaches are impractical for asynchronous circuits because it is difficult to control the relative delays of logic components, says Chu, and the problem is especially severe for VLSI circuits. Two models, that have failed in VLSI applications, finite state machines and Petri-nets, are discussed and a new model is proposed.

Green, D H and Chughtai, M A
'Use of multiplexers in direct synthesis of ASM-based designs' *IEE Proc. E* Vol 133 No 4 (July 1986) pp 194-200

The algorithmic state machine (ASM) approach to digital system design is suited to synthesis by means of modern flexible components. In addition to implementations of random logic, more powerful units such as multiplexers, programmable array logic, field programmable logic arrays and field programmable logic sequencers can be considered. The authors describe how ASM-based designs can be translated directly from their tabular descriptions into a variety of implementations.

Hurson, A R
'VLSI time and space complexities of a class of systolic multiplier units' *Comput. Syst. Sci. Eng.* Vol 1 No 3 (July 1986) pp 131-143

Single chip multipliers are now possible with gate complexities of the order of 10^5, but improved algorithms are necessary to exploit this potential, says Hurson. Previously proposed algorithms are reviewed and a new algorithm introduced.

Wang, C T
'VLSI architecture for device simulation' *Integration* Vol 4 No 2 (June 1986) pp 135-153

Discusses possible VLSI architectures for solving the nonlinear equations frequently encountered in designing a VLSI chip, such as in device and circuit simulation.

Books received

These books have been received recently by the Editorial Office. They may be reviewed in a later issue.

Kingslake, R
An introductory course in computer graphics Chartwell-Bratt, Bromley, UK (1986) £4.95, pp 144

Fundamental concepts of computer graphics presented for computer science and engineering students.

Swann, P
Quality innovation: an economic analysis of rapid improvements in microelectronic components Frances Pinter (1986) £22.50, pp 181

IEEE standard Fastbus modular high-speed data acquisition and control system (ANSI/IEEE Std 960) IEEE/Wiley, USA (1985) £24.20, pp 215

IEEE trial-use standard specifications for microprocessor operating systems interfaces (IEEE Std 855) IEEE/Wiley, USA (1985) £19.45, pp 173

These books present the American National Standard for Fastbus and the *draft* American National Standard for MOSI (microprocessor operating systems interfaces). The goal of MOSI is to facilitate writing of portable applications programs for systems.

book reviews

Software text may miss audience

Eli Fathi and Cedric Armstrong

'Microprocessor software project management' Marcel Dekker, New York, USA (1985) $69.00 pp 368

The worst thing about this book is its title, which at one stroke incorrectly limits its scope and wrongly defines its contents. The authors note that the book is based on a course and is intended to 'appeal to management as well as technical staff'.

Now it is very easy to be critical of a book that is targetted at software project management and devotes only one out of its ten chapters to principles of project management. It is equally hard to imagine that this book will be useful as a course book since it includes only two worked examples of techniques, one on producing a PERT network diagram and the other, curiously enough, on representing a program using the Nassi–Schneidermann technique. However, these comments should not be taken to imply that the book is worthless — it has very considerable merits particularly when addressed to the appropriate audience.

What the book does provide is a very useful discussion of the software development and maintenance process, which mercifully avoids the temptation to degenerate into a sterile debate about whether the software life cycle is a waterfall, a spiral or a complete myth. I feel the contents of the book should make it attractive to project managers not because of its coverage of management techniques, but because of its very clear discussion of what it is that a software project manager needs to manage. It is likely to be of particular use to managers with a hardware or other nonsoftware background who are moving into the software area. The book will also be useful to technicians, particularly those who are interested in overall software process control or software quality assurance, and are concerned with coordinating individual techniques into an overall integrated development process.

There is also no reason to restrict the potential readership of the book to microprocessor developers and managers. The book covers software in general but provides a particular insight into microprocessor issues.

It should not however be assumed that the contents of the book are flawless. There are still a number of significant omissions, usually in the project management area. There is not nearly enough consideration of the particular problems of incorporating mechanisms for project monitoring (other than time sheets) into software engineering practices, or of the major problem of producing accurate estimates of the effort and time scales necessary to complete software engineering activities. The discussion of PERT and CP/M would lead the unsuspecting reader to assume that the problems of estimating time scales and the problems of dealing with rework initiated by V&V activities have been solved.

In addition, there is a tendency for some of the chapters, particularly the ones devoted to the life cycle, to degenerate into a series of lists which results in less than stimulating reading and, even more irritatingly, there are inconsistencies between chapters with respect to the elements of the life cycle, the names of documents and the point in the life cycle when documents are produced.

Nonetheless, the book has some very good sections. The standards for documents, although they contribute to the lists and might need checking against individual national rather than North American standards, are of real practical assistance. The discussion of validation, verification and testing and test planning strategy is useful and stimulating, and it is always a relief to find a book which offers some practical advice about maintenance.

In summary, this is a worthwhile and very practical book which should be of value to a large number of managers and technicians, as long as potential readers are not put off by the title.

Barbara Kitchenham,
ICL Software Engineering,
Kidsgrove, UK

Introduction to VLSI design

Amar Mukherjee

'Introduction to NMOS and CMOS VLSI design' Prentice-Hall, Englewood Cliffs, NJ, USA (1986) £19.95 pp 370

This text gives fairly wide coverage of most of the topics relevant to VLSI design at an introductory level. It will therefore be suited to university students taking a first course in VLSI; it may also be useful to novice digital IC designers in industry. The text is divided into nine chapters covering the following areas: introduction to methodology; the MOS switch and inverter; logic design; MOS semiconductor technology; design rules; delay and power estimation; system design; memory systems; and VLSI computer-aided design (CAD) tools. It also has an appendix on the physics of semiconductor MOS devices and another on the MOSIS scalable generic CMOS design rules. Both NMOS and CMOS design are covered.

The text is relatively easy to read and gives a practical treatment of the bottom-up and top-down design aspects of VLSI. Simple algebraic models are used throughout, for the mathematical modelling of devices and for estimation of voltages, currents, speed of operation etc. This is satisfactory for first-order approximation and has an advantage in not overburdening the student who is new to the subject. There is an exercise with a variety of questions at the end of five of the chapters. The questions in these exercises are variable in content, length, quality and especially in number (from too few to almost too many). Each chapter has a good collection of relevant references, though some of these may be difficult for the average student to consult because of lack of general availability.

There are many appropriate black-and-white diagrams which accompany the text and benefit comprehension. This is a good feature. Colour line drawings of the design rules are included in the last appendix (MOSIS design rules), where the use of colour is really essential. However, it is unfortunate that colour has not been used for selected layout examples in the rest of the text, where the judicious use of colour could greatly enhance comprehension, especially for novice designers. The usual reason for restriction to black and white is that of reducing cost, which is important for a student text, but in this case the book is not as cheap as some competing texts, which do make wider use of colour illustration.

There are two major omissions: design for test (including testability) and analogue MOS design. These topics are not treated at all; they should, in my opinion, feature in any VLSI course because of their fundamental importance, but especially at the introductory level, for reasons of awareness alone. Gate array technology is not considered either. There are some minor misprints/errors which are probably inevitable in any first edition. The idiom is generally that of the VLSI university scene in the USA, with specific reference to tools, services and projects which may well only be of direct relevance in that context. Further, there are places where a knowledge of this background (or at least direct reference to a copy of the classic Mead and Conway text) is an advantage, and I wondered whether a first-time student might not have difficulty with some of the material without such assistance.

I thought that the chapter on logic design was good. Systems design was treated as a collection of example designs, mostly done over the period 1982–83 by US students for submission to MOSIS in NMOS technology. Memory systems are not well treated because of the exclusion of analogue design issues and the omission of special-purpose memory architectures (e.g. the so-called smart memories). The book could also have benefitted from a clear exposé of current research problems, as a stimulus to student project material.

The last chapter on VLSI CAD tools gives the text a distinctive mark and was a good idea. Unfortunately, the treatment is neither detailed enough

Design book useful beyond MODULA-2

Arthur Sale

'Modula-2 discipline and design' Addison-Wesley, Wokingham, UK (1986) £13.95 pp 464

Discipline and a knowledge of sound design technique are the hall marks of good engineering. In covering these topics, and in covering them well, Modula-2 discipline and design is far more than an introductory text about the MODULA-2 programming language — it is an effective introduction to software engineering. Although there is little in the book directly related to realtime or embedded systems programming, the characteristics of MODULA-2 and the emphasis on the production of correct programs make this a very good first text for both students and practising engineers wishing to acquire skill in realtime programming.

The author has taken care to place the learning tasks to be carried out in context, and he explains well by analogy what is involved in learning to program. The early chapters of the book lay out carefully the MODULA-2 features needed to deal with small programming tasks. In these early chapters, the author is careful to explain the order in which programs are developed using stepwise refinement. He also shows the difference between good programming style and 'hacking'.

The presentation of design and program refinement and the practical constraints to look out for is good. The glimpses of insight I have gained

over many years of teaching and using PASCAL are presented here clearly and coherently by the author.

Parameterless procedures and the idea of proof of program correctness are both introduced early on, to good effect, and used to present the topic of program design. The difficulty of proving a program correct is admitted, but stating a proof as the solution to a problem and then implementing it (in a number of ways) is used to give a 'handle' to the design problem.

The middle part of the book is more conventional, dealing with language features with little on how to use them. The closing chapters present substantial programs to inculcate good practice and then present the practical aspects of two MODULA-2 implementations (Apple Macintosh and Cambridge Unix 4.1/ 4.2BSD). This, and the way in which the use of editing etc. was introduced in the early chapters, gives the reader a feel for the way the language fits into the system environment.

I would have liked to see some graphical formalism used as well, structure diagrams for example, but this might well have made the book too long. Nonetheless I would use the book without hesitation for a beginning class in MODULA-2 programming. I recommend the book highly.

David Jenkins
Paisley College of
Technology, UK

to provide a standalone technical source, nor is the coverage complete enough to constitute a good overview. Instead, some topics have been selected and have then been given very variable length of treatment. Thus, the later half of the chapter is devoted to routing algorithms, whilst the earlier half attempts to cover CIF, design rule checking, circuit extraction and simulation; there is no discussion of placement algorithms, SPICE, design capture, data modelling etc, which I

would have thought were equally important areas.

In summary, this is a book which can be recommended for use in introductory VLSI design courses. It is readable, has good diagrams and fair coverage, but needs supplementing in the areas of design for test and analogue design. The price is a bit high, and the text is not suitable for advanced work.

David Renshaw
University of Edinburgh, UK

Processors explained and compared

George Loveday

'Microprocessor sourcebook' Pitman, London, UK (1986) £9.95 pp 247

Trevor Raven

'16-bit microprocessor handbook' Newnes, Twickenham, UK (1986) £9.95 pp 172

Amongst the latest additions to the ever increasing number of books concerned with microprocessors, these two books occupy different niches within the field. Whilst the *Microprocessor sourcebook* deliberately omits more advanced 'state-of-the-art' material in favour of clear explanations of fundamental terms and is, to quote the preface, aimed at 'personnel and students working in the service and test areas of the microelectronic and allied industries', the *16-bit microprocessor handbook* looks in some depth at four significant 16-bit microprocessor families and systems which use them, and is aimed more squarely at practising hardware system designers.

The *Microprocessor sourcebook* has a dictionary or encyclopaedia-type format, with entries arranged in alphabetical order. 265 topics are given clear explanation; the book is well laid out, with entry titles highlighted in bold print and explanations indented, and with a very large number of line drawings by way of illustration. I opened the book with some trepidation, having an inherent mistrust of books which claim to be 'sourcebooks' and which have a dictionary format, but in the event I was pleasantly surprised. The diagrams are excellent, and fit in well with the explanatory text, which is well written and which provides a useful description for each entry.

The book is essentially for reference, and could usefully be purchased by a student to accompany a more conventional text, or by a nonmicroprocessor specialist needing a quick reference for technical terms. The individual entries are longer than in some previously published books

of this type, and are consequently more useful.

The 'core' of the book lies under the heading 'microprocessor', and consists of descriptions of several of the more popular 8-bit microprocessors and a brief description of each of three 16-bit microprocessors. The 8-bit microprocessor descriptions cover architecture, addressing modes, control signals, instruction set, interrupt structure, and pin-out diagram for each of 6800/6802, 6502/65C02, 8080/8085, Z80 and 6809. I have mixed feelings over the wisdom of including pin-out diagrams and detailed instruction sets in a book of this type — such detail is of limited usefulness to a novice, and less useful than a full data sheet to an expert — but it does give a 'feel' for the device. The diagrams which illustrate addressing modes in this section are excellent, and the control signal and interrupt descriptions, although brief, are clear and unambiguous.

My main criticisms of the book are the omissions. I appreciate that it is impossible to include everything in a medium-length paperback, but there are some minor inconsistencies. For example five pages are devoted to a description of a parallel programmable interface, a total of 6½ pages to the description of a serial interface, but only just over a page to the description of a programmable timer. The book is largely hardware oriented, so that whilst some software topics are included (compiler, interpreter, etc.) with a brief description, others (linker, operating system) are omitted. To compensate, there are some unexpected but welcome inclusions — sensor, opto device, converter etc. — which leave the reader with the impression that microprocessors are to be used in the real world rather than being considered in isolation.

Overall, I feel the book is good value for money and, for a person learning about microprocessors for the first time, will usefully complement a more conventional text. Whilst a conventional text will usually provide detailed material concerned with programming and

interfacing a single processor within one manufacturer's microprocessor family, the *Microprocessor sourcebook* will provide alternative explanations, in less depth but perhaps with reference to other devices, for many topics.

The *16-bit Microprocessor handbook* is a different sort of book, more conventionally laid out and with a narrower subject area covered in more depth. The book is a small one, shorter than many manufacturers' individual microprocessor manuals, and it covers four 16-bit families: Intel's 8086, Zilog's Z8000, Motorola's 68000 and Texas Instruments' 99000. It also includes some information on a variety of microcomputer systems and operating systems. A glossary of terms is included at the back of the book. The descriptions of the four processor families occupy between 20 and 40 pages each and concentrate on the CPUs themselves, with little reference to support devices and interfaces.

I was disappointed with this book, and I find it difficult to judge just who the book is aimed at. Coverage of the four 16-bit families is patchy — I could find no mention of the Intel 80286 or Motorola 68010 (whilst the 32-bit Motorola 68020 does get mentioned); only the 68000 addressing modes are explained in detail (8086 addressing modes are dispensed with in a scant nine lines, Z8000 addressing modes in 13 lines); and I could find only a meagre 13 lines on the 68000 interrupt structure.

The most obvious omission, however, is of other manufacturers' processors — I would have expected some mention of the National Semiconductor 32000 family, and would have hoped for inclusion of the Inmos Transputer and possibly of the NEC V Series. Information on all these families has been available for some time now, and I find it unfortunate that they have not been included. Since many 16-bit processors are used with coprocessors and memory management units, perhaps these devices could have been emphasized more strongly although, to be fair, the book does mention the basic concepts involved.

Unix — with enthusiasm and skill

P C Poole and N Poole

'Using Unix by example' Addison-Wesley, Wokingham, UK (1985) £12.95 pp xi + 416

I like this book — an introduction to Unix for students and professional programmers, viewing Unix as a combination of kernel, tools and languages for problem solving — very much. It has a rich feel, over 400 pages of detailed information and detailed real working examples. After a brief introduction we get right in, with no useful detail omitted. The feeling is very much that of being led by a pair of patient and unflagging Unix hackers who communicate not just facts and techniques but their own enthusiasm and skill.

The coverage is comprehensive. Early on the authors deal with the file

---

Loveday, Raven *(continued)*

The section of the book concerned with computer systems gives specifications for a number of machines using the processors mentioned earlier in the book, and will give the reader a good idea of the relative performance of PCs based on different CPUs. What this section does not do, is to indicate the market dominance of IBM and, in certain niches, Apple. The operating systems section gives a reasonable review of the most used systems: CP/M-86/ Concurrent, MS-DOS and Unix.

Despite my criticisms, I feel that the *16-bit microprocessor handbook* does have some good points. The descriptions are reasonably clear and concise and in some cases are augmented by a useful discussion of the reasons behind the inclusion of a particular feature. The low price of the book will allow engineers to add it to their library and refer to it for comparison purposes. It is as a comparative study rather than as a design reference book, that I feel this book is most valuable.

Ian Whitworth,
Royal Military College of Science,
Shrivenham, UK

system, basic commands and the command interpreters. In the section on editing, which begins with the line editor **ed**, there is a very good introduction to screen editing with **vi**. **vi** is complex, and I am impressed by the way the authors introduce a good subset of its facilities in a clear and comprehensive way, enabling the reader to get to grips with it very quickly. The book also deals with file manipulations such as comparing, finding and sorting; process manipulations such as starting and stopping jobs; and with the Unix mail system for communication between users. The many examples are excellent, and some are clever enough to be interesting, but without being tricky. The final glossary, appendices and index are very useful.

There is an unusual intermediate section of 78 pages on programming, in which three different programs are developed in some detail in each of the three languages PASCAL, FORTRAN and C. This shows the use of the compilers, and deals with both compile-time and runtime errors. At first this seemed too much detail, and presumably for many people one or two (or perhaps all) of the languages would be irrelevant, but the alternative is to deal in generalities and that is not how this book works. The languages chapter ends with a section on programming the shell.

One of the main problems in writing about Unix is caused by the many versions in existence. The book covers the two main dialects, Berkeley 4.2 and AT&T system V.2. Each command description indicates whether it is available in one or both systems. The actual textual layout indicating these distinctions could be improved, but the interleaving is fine and, for example, I found the adjacent descriptions of multiple interactive shell invocations — shell layers (V.2) and foreground/background (4.2) — very clear.

The book was typeset under Unix by the authors, but has a mucky appearance which does not reflect current capabilities. As is common in such machine maintained documents,

there is overreliance on text where diagrams would help.

To follow up this thorough introduction to Unix and current Unix practice by and for real programmers, I look forward to a second volume detailing the system-call interface and programming tools. That said, the question remains as to whether this book is suitable for students or programmers to learn Unix from. The context in which Unix is presented is narrow, the perspective blinkered and the style a bit too self congratulatory. Thus for example the rationale behind Unix is introduced via the evolution of time sharing from batch. This may be the authors' history too, but not necessarily that of their readers. An experienced Macintosh user, or arcade game player, would find the shift to the Unix view difficult, and would not be helped by this book's lack of framework and philosophy.

The authors often interpret too much — 'do this, then this, then you'll feel the need to do this, and so use this' — leaving no space for the reader to build up a personal view which may be different from theirs. The view of Unix as a few simple ideas carried through in elegant combination is never presented so that, for example, processes are presented as just another feature, and there is no reference anywhere to Kernighan and Ritchie's original and beautiful paper. Current Unix systems may indeed be no different on the surface from VMS or PC-DOS, but this is because a proliferation of features has obscured Unix's basic elegance and conceptual integrity. A modern Unix text must offer some critique of the system to help the learner develop clear intuitions, and to help us all keep in mind that further progress will come from reconceptualizing the base, not from adding more commands.

For those wishing to get to grips with Unix as a way of turning out code this book is excellent; but for those who want an idea of what Unix is all about, and how it fits into what is known and what is possible, it will only be a beginning.

Bruce Anderson
University of Essex,
Colchester, UK

Control sought over VLSI junctions

Research to overcome the limitations imposed by channelling and radiation-enhanced diffusion in silicon implantation for VLSI is being undertaken at the UK Atomic Energy Authority's Harwell Research Laboratory.

Current VLSI fabrication technology relies on implanting silicon with impurity atoms such as boron and arsenic using a particle accelerator. Unfortunately the amount of control which can be obtained over the p–n junction depth is limited by two phenomena — channelling and radiation-enhanced diffusion — which affect the ion-implanted atoms; but junction depth critically affects packing density and switching speed.

Channelling occurs when the direction of the ion beam emerging from the accelerator coincides with one of the major crystal axes of the wafer, causing a substantial increase in the penetration depth of the implanted ions. This effect can be reduced by misaligning the wafers by 5° or so, but incident ions can still be scattered into various channel directions and give rise to greater depths of penetration.

Radiation-enhanced diffusion arises from tiny defects created in a chip during the implantation process. These move around inside the body of the chip and cause an undesirable migration of impurity atoms. A technique known as rapid thermal annealing (RTA) uses heat generated by quartz halogen lamps to reduce the total annealing time thus reducing, but not eliminating, chip defects.

Recent research at Harwell has shown that, by bombarding a chip with nondopant germanium or tin ions beyond the intended depth of the doped region it may be possible to overcome both channelling and radiation-enhanced diffusion and so solve the problem of junction depth control. This technique is currently being studied at Harwell under the project name Gerta (germanium bombardment and RTA).

The main objectives of the project are to investigate the practical and potential economic industrial value of the research for improving junction depth control in VLSI; to optimize process conditions for a range of likely applications; and to provide expertise to the European semiconductor industry to enable it to exploit the Gerta process in the manufacture of submicron devices.

Harwell is still seeking participants for the Gerta project, which is due to begin this month; interested organizations should contact I M Buckley-Golder at *Microelectronics Materials Centre, Building 552, AERE Harwell, Oxon OX11 0RA, UK. Tel: (0235) 24142* □

Old minis threaten AI LISP markets

Anticipated growth in the artificial intelligence (AI) marketplace may not be sufficient to sustain the fortunes of specialist LISP vendors, says market research firm IRD.

LISP vendors are relying on a growth in demand for AI applications, especially in expert systems, to keep people buying LISP hardware which is particularly suited for developing and running these applications. But specialized LISP hardware is expensive — often $50 000 or more per user — and many companies will opt to trade off somewhat inferior performance for significant cost savings by using their installed base of conventional minicomputers etc. to run AI applications, says IRD.

Also, when parallel processing machines start to appear on the market in a few years' time, the current generation of LISP hardware will be rendered almost obsolete. 'This is an ironic situation,' says Ken Bosomworth, a researcher for the IRD report *Artificial intelligence markets*. 'The market for artificial intelligence software is only going to grow stronger — to this extent the LISP hardware vendors are correct in their market analyses — but it does not follow that AI hardware will grow at the same pace.' (*International Resource Development Inc., 6 Prowitt Street, Norwalk, CT 06855, USA. Tel: (203) 866-7800*) □

More RISC systems enter the marketplace

RISC (reduced instruction set computer) microprocessors have been put into new workstations by Hewlett-Packard and US-based Silicon Graphics. Following on the heels of IBM's RISC implementation in the PC RT (*Microprocessors Microsyst.* Vol 10 No 3 (April 1986) page 188), these developments add further momentum to the growing acceptance of this type of architecture — see also the story on Acorn's RISC processor on the facing page.

Hewlett-Packard's HP 9000 model 480, a £95 000 Unix-based system aimed at the CAD, CAE and computer integrated manufacturing (CIM) markets, marks the first use of the company's 'Precision Architecture' in a technical computer. Precision Architecture is an open architecture, says the manufacturer, with I/O designs and semiconductor circuitry generally available.

The designers of the model 480 have been able to maintain compatibility with the other members of the HP 9000 family while delivering what Hewlett-Packard president John A Young calls 'price: performance and cost-of-ownership benefits on a new scale'. Support for the high-level languages C, PASCAL and FORTRAN has also been incorporated into the system.

Silicon Graphics has used a 32-bit RISC processor manufactured by Plexus Computers of the USA and developed for OEM use by another US company, MIPS Computer Systems, in a range of 3D graphics workstations. Both the CPU and an accompanying VLSI floating-point coprocessor, also used in the system, belong to the R2000 family of chips, CPU boards and memory boards. Speeds of up to 10 times that of a VAX 11/780 minicomputer have been achieved, says Silicon Graphics. □

New VME specialist launches own boards

VMEbus board-level products and 'midrange' systems, together with a portable operating system for Motorola CPUs, have been launched by UK-based VME Trade.

The board-level product range comprises a series of intelligent peripheral controllers, all having an MC68000 CPU running at 10 MHz and 512 kbyte of dual-ported RAM. The boards, which are manufactured by a number of firms including Dual Systems of the USA, include: an I/O controller for terminal handling; a universal controller for a 5¼ in floppy disc, ST506 Winchester disc and tape streamer on the same card; an ESDI controller for 5¼ in Fujitsu and NEC drives; an SMD (storage module drive) controller for Fujitsu Eagle drives, etc; a nine-track magnetic tape controller; and a 2 Mbyte memory board with onboard self cache for reads of 85 ns.

Each board has onboard ROM for instructing the controller as required, allowing the 68000 CPU to handle other tasks.

As well as being sold separately, the boards listed above form the basis of the VME-5000 series of systems configured by VME Trade. These systems are described as '32-bit lead-in systems' to allow users to use existing S100 boards and peripherals with 68000, 68010 and 68020 microprocessors.

The base system has 512 kbyte of RAM, eight RS232C ports, a 68000 CPU with two SSD encryption sockets and a 20 Mbyte hard disc. It also includes a four-slot or 15-slot S100 bus. The systems can be configured upwards to include a 68020 processor with 68881 floating-point coprocessor, 16 Mbyte of RAM, 1200 Mbyte disc and 96 I/O ports with a 20-slot S100 chassis. A full SCSI bus is available for non-SMD drives and tape subsystems.

Operating systems for the VME-5000 systems can be chosen from Pick, OS-9, CP/M-68k, Mirage, the FORTH environment and VME-d/os. The last of these is VME Trade's operating system for Motorola CPUs,

Acorn aims RISC chip at OEMs

A RISC (reduced instruction set computer) microprocessor has been developed by UK firm Acorn Computers and is being manufactured and marketed by VLSI Technology (VTI) of the USA. The ARM (Acorn RISC machine) processor features a 32-bit data bus and a 26-bit address bus, and has an instruction set of 44 basic instructions.

Acorn describes the ARM as an 'open chip for OEMs' — one of the first 'open' RISC architectures to be made commercially available. An evaluation system based on Acorn BBC or Master Series microcomputers has been released, and another using the IBM PC or compatibles will be introduced in late 1986.

ARM is designed for efficient execution of high-level languages and interrupt processing, says Acorn, making it suitable for applications that require realtime response to external interrupt sources and high processing throughput. The processor has a quoted average execution rate of 4M instructions per second using a two-phase 8 MHz clock.

Each instruction has a field containing condition code that causes an instruction to be missed out if the condition specified by the field is not true; this results in efficient code which executes quickly, says

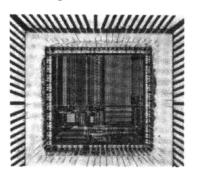

Acorn's ARM processor: an 'open' RISC architecture

Acorn. To support the movement of processing functions from hardware to software, ARM has 25 registers, each of 32 bit, which partially overlap. This overlapping is designed to allow fast interrupts to be executed without the need to store the contents of the register array.

The ARM processor is manufactured in 3 µm CMOS and is packaged in a JEDEC type B ceramic leadless chip carrier. Sampling price, which is designated VL86C010 by manufacturer VTI, is $99. As well as the processor chip, an associated set of optional ICs that can act as controllers for memory, video, sound and I/O are available.

Evaluation systems for ARM combine a hardware system (incorporating 4 Mbyte of RAM) with software packages which include five high-level languages — C, FORTRAN 77, PROLOG, LISP and BASIC — and an assembler. The BBC micro based system costs around £5200 and the IBM PC based version will be priced comparably.

While the ARM chip and its evaluation systems are only being manufactured by VTI at present, says Acorn, a second source will be announced in due course. (Acorn Computers Ltd, Fulbourn Road, Cherry Hinton, Cambridge CB1 4JN, UK. Tel: (0223) 245200. VLSI Technology Inc., 10220 South 51st Street, Phoenix, AZ 85044, USA. Tel: (602) 893-8574) □

VME Trade *(continued)*

described as 'completely portable, and compatible with Alpha Micro's Amos'. According to VME Trade, hundreds of application packages are available which can be run under VME-d/os.

VME Trade was set up in January 1986 'to meet the needs of a number of systems houses who wanted to be independent of the Alpha Micro environment', says the company's Barry Lloyd. Its aim is to become 'the major supplier of VME products to the trade'. (VME Trade Ltd, 41 North Road, London N7 9DP, UK. Tel: 01-609 9661. Dual Systems Corp., 2530 San Pablo Avenue, Berkeley, CA 94702, USA. Tel: (415) 549-3854) □

product news

6300-gate arrays meet telecommunications speed requirements

ECL (emitter coupled logic) gate arrays with 6300 equivalent gates have been launched by FRG-based Fairchild. A member of the FGE series of gate arrays designed for high-speed computer and telecommunications applications, the FGE6300 features internal propagation delays quoted by the manufacturer as 225 ps. It incorporates 560 internal cells and allows 220 I/O signals.

The FGE series is, according to Fairchild, the only ECL gate array family that can meet 565 MHz telecommunications system frequency requirements. The new 6300-gate device is stated to consume 30% less power per gate than previous FGE chips, which have equivalent gate counts from 100 to 2840.

The FGE6300 is packaged in a proprietary multilayer ceramic 301-pin grid array (5 cm square) designed to allow operation at speeds over 600 MHz without special cooling. Decoupling capacitors can be mounted on the package to reduce noise. The FGE6300 is fabricated using 'essentially the same' 1.5 μm process and exactly the same macro library that has been used in previous FGE devices, says Fairchild.

Power dissipation can be controlled using speed-power options, which allow the designer to assign the macro functional switching speed and drive current individually for each source and output of the internal cells. Thus ECL speed can be maximized where needed but overall power dissipation can be kept to a level that accommodates air cooling.

Power consumption is further reduced by on-chip internal termination to −2 V, says the manufacturer.

Circuit design, placement and routing for the gate arrays can be performed on the FairCAD design system at any of Fairchild's local design centres. Design and proto-typing of the FGE6300 are already available; production delivery begins in late 1986 for commercial devices (temperature range 0–125°C) and in first-quarter 1987 for military versions (−10°C to 125°C). (*Fairchild Semiconductor GmbH, Am Burgfrieden 1, 8090 Wasserburg Am Inn, Munich, FRG. Tel: (08071) 104–232. Fairchild Semiconductor Ltd, 230 High Street, Potters Bar, Herts, UK. Tel: (0707) 51111*) □

ASICs emulate standard chips

ASIC library elements that emulate the functionality of standard LSI and VLSI products have been launched by US-based LSI Logic. The elements, known as 'megafunctions', are proprietary gate-level functions for incorporation into LSI Logic's array-based or cell-based product lines and are available on the company's LDS design systems.

The 'megafunction' range includes ASICs which emulate products by Advanced Micro Devices, Intel and Motorola; the devices emulated include, for example, microprogram controllers, DMA controllers and UARTs. Also in the range are a number of generic logic elements: twos-complement multipliers, carry select adders, three-port adders, barrel shifters, comparators, ALUs, FIFOs and contact addressable memories.

'The availability of these mega-functions means that ASIC designers no longer need to evaluate their designs solely in terms of gates,' explained LSI Logic's John Berry. 'A design engineer can choose from a substantial list of industry standard LSI and VLSI components and place those directly within their circuit net list, similarly to board-level techniques.'

'Megafunctions' are available at all LSI Logic design centres and support the LL3000, LL5000, LL7000, LL8000 and LL9000 series channelled logic arrays. They can also be used, after modification, in LST20 standard cell, LSC20 structured cell and LCA10000 channelless compacted array chip designs. (*LSI Logic Corp., 1551 McCarthy Blvd, Milpitas, CA 95035, USA. Tel: (408) 433-8000. LSI Logic Ltd, Grenville Place, The Ring, Bracknell, Berks RG12 1BP, UK. Tel: (0344) 426544*) □

Software overhead for RAM is reduced

Hitachi's 1 kbyte 'smart dual-port RAM'

'Smart dual-port RAMs' (SDPRAMs) designed to improve the efficiency of communications in multiprocessor systems have been produced by Hitachi. The devices are intelligent RAMs configured to reduce software overheads, says the manufacturer, providing interprocessor communication paths of greater speed and functionality than in normal single-processor systems.

The first such device is the HD63310, a 1k × 8 bit RAM which may be used either as a dual-port RAM or as two FIFO (first in, first out) memories. The two ports can perform read and write operations independently and simultaneously. Two asynchronous multiplexed or nonmultiplexed microprocessor bus interfaces are included, as are semaphore registers to control RAM access. Other features include four programmable FIFO status pins which provide DMA transfer control signals, and two multipurpose interrupt outputs.

Access and cycle times for the HD63310 are 200 ns and 250 ns respectively. Power consumption is quoted as 100 mW (maximum) during operation. The device comes in a 48-pin plastic dual in-line package. (*Hitachi Ltd, New Marunouchi Building No 5, 1-chome Marunouchi, Chiyoda, Tokyo, Japan. Hitachi Electronic Components (UK) Ltd, 21 Upton Road, Watford, Herts WD1 7TB, UK. Tel: (0923) 46488*) □

Signal processor 'avoids bottlenecks'

A cascadable signal processor (CSP) capable of 10 MHz data processing speeds is the first product to emerge from the Silicon Systems Division of UK-based Inmos. Fabricated in 1.5 µm CMOS, the IMS A100 contains an array of 32 multiplier–accumulators (MACs), each of 16 × 16 bit capacity, together with registers and control logic.

The CSP represents the beginning of the third phase of the Inmos strategy, the company says. The first two phases, following the company's philosophy of avoiding direct competition with the semiconductor giants, were to develop the transputer family and a family of 'high-performance' memory products. CSPs, according to Inmos, mark the company's entry into 'specific markets which complement the transputer family's technology'. The A100 is intended to be applied to communications, control, radar, sonar, image processing and speech processing.

In designing the product, Inmos sought to escape the bottlenecks which occur at the MACs in conventional digital signal processors. The designers considered not only the speed of the individual multipliers, but also the memory bandwidth problems associated with such repeated operations.

The architecture eventually selected was a transversal filter: when implemented as a dataflow machine with each node comprising a MAC and local store this type of device can be used to evaluate most DSP algorithms, and it offers a cascadable architecture. The A100 can be cascaded to produce transversal filters of several thousand stages without degradation in throughput, says Inmos, and may thus be used as a building block for a wide range of signal processing tasks.

Using one or more A100s, says Inmos, it is possible to perform high-speed correlations, convolutions or Fourier transforms (via prime-radix and decomposition techniques) as well as many one- or two-dimensional filters. The A100 is designed to handle continuous data

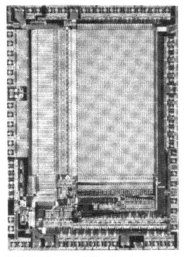

IMS A100 cascadable signal processor integrates thirty-two 16 × 16 bit MACs with registers and control logic

rates of up to 2.5M samples per second for 16-bit data and 16-bit coefficients, or 10M samples per second for 16-bit data and 4-bit coefficients. Performance increases almost in proportion to the number of devices used for most signal processing algorithms, says the manufacturer.

Input data word size is 16 bit, while coefficients are programmable to be 4, 8, 12 or 16 bit wide. Both data and coefficients use twos-complement numerical formats. Coefficients can be updated randomly and asynchronously to the system clock in less than 100 ns for normal operation, and they are buffered for continuous operation in adaptive applications. Real and complex fixed-point and block floating-point processing are supported.

A standard nonmultiplexed memory interface provides interfacing to any microprocessor or memory bus based architecture. Coefficients and status registers are accessed via this interface, which can also be used to supply data to the devices.

The A100 can be used either in dedicated standalone applications

or in more flexible microprocessor-controlled systems. According to Inmos the synchronization, control and I/O bandwidth problems associated with high-performance signal processing systems have been largely eliminated. Thus conventional processors such as the 68000 family or special-purpose devices such as the transputer can be used to control a system performing realtime signal processing at data rates of over 10 MHz while still processing system-level tasks, says Inmos.

The A100 comes in a single 84-pin package. An evaluation board comprising a T414 (32 bit) transputer and several A100s is also available. *(Inmos International plc, Whitefriars, Lewins Mead, Bristol BS1 2NP, UK. Tel: (0272) 290861)* □

32000s developed under SVID

GNX, a second generation of software development tools for the Series 32000 microprocessor family, has been introduced by National Semiconductor. The GNX package has been written to conform to AT&T's Unix system V interface definition (SVID), allowing software to be moved to the Series 32000 link from other architectures merely by recompilation.

Code is produced for execution on the 32008, 32016, 32032 and 32332 processors. The package includes C, FORTRAN 77 and PASCAL compilers, an assembler, support utilities and debuggers. The manufacturer plans to add in more compilers at a later date.

GNX is available to run on Digital Equipment VAX systems running under VMS or Unix, on National Semiconductor's own development systems, and in source form for porting to other development platforms or for OEM distribution. *(National Semiconductor Corp., 2900 Semiconductor Drive, PO Box 58090, Santa Clara, CA 95052-578090, USA. Tel: (408) 733-2600. National Semiconductor, Industriestrasse 10, D-8080 Furstenfeldbruck, FRG. Tel: (08141) 103376)* □

products in brief

Name	Description	Manufacturer/designer	Distributor/contact
Backplanes			
STE backplanes	Range of double-sided and multilayer backplanes, extender cards and a stub terminator module for STEbus systems. Double-sided boards have 5, 7 and 10 slots with 64-way type 'C' solder connectors; multilayer boards have 14 and 21 slots with a 64-way pressfit connector	Bicc-Vero Electronics Ltd, Flanders Road, Hedge End, Southampton SO3 3LG, UK. Tel: (04215) 66300	
Compilers			
BASIC compiler	Multitasking BASIC compiler written specifically for the company's Z80A STEbus CPU boards. Claimed to be around 50 times faster than interpreted BASIC. Versions are available for use in CP/M or CP/M+ operating systems, and one for EPROM-based systems (although not with full multitasking)	Arcom Control Systems Ltd, Unit 8, Clifton Road, Cambridge CB1 4WH, UK. Tel: (0223) 242224	
Development Systems			
DS24	Incircuit emulator added to Xilinx's logic cell development system to support programmable gate arrays. Can be used on up to four devices concurrently. Comprises a microcomputer-based controller and up to four emulation pods. For operation requires an IBM PC XT or AT	Xilinx Inc., 2069 East Hamilton Avenue, San Jose, CA 95125, USA	Ambar-Cascom Ltd, Rabans Close, Aylesbury, Bucks HP19 3RS, UK. Tel: (0296) 34141
EV64180	Evaluation board for the HD64180 'system-on-a-chip' microprocessor. Has 8 kbyte of monitor programs, 512 kbyte dynamic RAM, also EPROM and static RAM in the bottom 128 kbyte of memory space which can be allocated to DRAM. Fitted with an RS232C interface	Hitachi Ltd, New Marunouchi Building No 5, 1-chome Marunouchi, Chiyoda, Tokyo, Japan	Hitachi Electronic Components (UK) Ltd, 21 Upton Road, Watford, Herts WD1 7TB, UK. Tel: (0923) 46488
ICE-5100/252	Emulator for the 8051 family of microcontrollers. Runs on the IBM PC XT, AT or any compatible with DOS 3.0 or later versions. Comprises base unit with user probe, and provides realtime debug	Intel Corp., 3065 Bowers Avenue, Santa Clara, CA 95051, USA	Intel Corp. (UK) Ltd, Pipers Way, Swindon SN3 1RJ, UK. Tel: (0793) 696020
RTSYS	Links the OS-9 operating system with VMEbus hardware for development work. The minimum configuration has a 10 MHz 68010 card, 0.5 Mbyte dynamic RAM plus hard and floppy disc drives. Five VME slots are available for expansion	High Technology Electronics Ltd, 303–305 Portswood Road, Southampton SO2 1LD, UK. Tel: (0703) 581555	

Section headings in this issue's 'Products in brief' are

Backplanes	**Image processing boards**	**Microprocessors**	**PROMs**
Compilers	**Interface devices**	**Multiplier–accumulators**	**RAMs**
Development systems	**Memory boards**	**Programmable arrays**	**Single-board computers**
First-in–first-out memories	**Microcontrollers**	**Programming modules**	**Test systems**
Graphics devices			

Name	Description	Manufacturer/designer	Distributor/contact
TR6301	Training and evaluation board for the HD6303X and HD6303Y microprocessors. Can be used as a training board in colleges, or for developing and testing small programs, for which a miniassembler/disassembler is provided. The board has an integral keyboard and display and an RS232C serial port	Hitachi Ltd, New Marunouchi Building No 5, 1-chome Marunouchi, Chiyoda, Tokyo, Japan	Hitachi Electronic Components (UK) Ltd, 21 Upton Road, Watford, Herts WD1 7TB, UK. Tel: (0923) 46488

First-in–first-out (FIFO) memories

74F403, 74F413	FIFO buffer memory circuits organized as 16 word × 4 bit (403) and 64 word × 4 bit (413), introduced in Fairchild's advanced Schottky TTL (FAST) family of logic devices. Fall-through times are 265 ns and 1.1 µs respectively. Operation is over the temperature range from 0°C to 70°C. Version 403 is designed for communication between serial or parallel systems, the 413 for parallel systems	Fairchild Semiconductor GmbH, Am Burgfrieden 1, 8090 Wasserburg Am Inn, FRG. Tel: (08071) 104232	

Graphics devices

Bus interface cards	VME, Q-bus and Multibus adaptor cards for the company's GIP graphics image processor. Also available is an adaptor to link the processor with an IBM AT. GIP is a bit slice microcodeable coprocessor board designed for OEMs and systems manufacturers	benchMark Technologies Ltd, benchMark House, 2 Lower Teddington Road, Hampton Wick, Kingston-upon-Thames, Surrey KT1 4ER, UK. Tel: 01-943 4393	
DP8515/6	16-bit video shift registers for high performance raster scan video systems. Clock speed is 225 MHz. Included on-chip are four words of first-in-first-out buffer which operate in front of the register. Both parts have TTL inputs and ECL outputs: outputs of the 8515 are 10k compatible; 8516 outputs are 100k compatible	National Semiconductor Corp., 2900 Semiconductor Drive, PO Box 58090, Santa Clara, CA 95052-578090, USA. Tel: (408) 733-2600	National Semiconductor, Industriestrasse 10, D-8080 Furstenfeldbruck, FRG. Tel: (08141) 103486

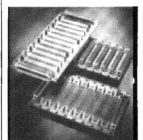   

From left: Bicc-Vero's double-sided and multilayer backplanes for STEbus; the High Technology Electronics RTSYS development system; and the EV64180 and TR6301 evaluation boards from Hitachi

Name	Description	Manufacturer/designer	Distributor/contact
GRC01/02	VMEbus graphics controller cards that use the Hitachi 63484 chip supported by the OS-9 operating system. Can draw 2 Mpixel s^{-1}, producing 16-colour displays with 1280 × 1024 × 4 pixel resolution. GRC01 has 512 kbyte dual-ported video RAM, GRC02 has 2 Mbyte. Has a 32-bit interface via a P2 port	MicroSys GmbH, Amzinger Strasse, 800 Munich, FRG. Tel: (089) 638-0132	Dage (GB) Ltd, Eurosem Division, Rabans Lane, Aylesbury, Bucks HP19 3RG, UK. Tel: (0296) 33200
Palettemate	Colour graphics card that plugs into the Acorn BBC microcomputer. Allows 16 colours to be selected from a palette of 4096 colours	Wild Vision, Mari House, 20–22 Jesmond Road, Newcastle-upon-Tyne NE2 4PQ, UK. Tel: (091) 281 7861	
TS68483	Graphics display chip that will interface to most 8- and 16-bit microprocessors, with on-chip video shift registers for dot rates below 15 Mdot s^{-1}. The built-in graphics command set reduces software overhead	Thomson Semiconducteurs, 43 Avenue de l'Europe, 78140 Velizy-Villacoublay, France. Tel: (39) 469719	Pronto Electronic Systems, City Gate House, 399–425 Eastern Avenue, Gants Hill, Ilford, Essex IG2 6LR, UK. Tel: 01-554 6222
VG-640	VME version of the 'G' series of graphics boards. Uses 32016 processors with 110 kbyte of RAM and 128 kbyte of ROM-based firmware	Matrox Electronic Systems, 1055 St. Regis, Dorval, Quebec, Canada H9P 2T4. Tel: (514) 685 2630	Perdix Microtronics, Unit 4, Airport Trading Estate, Biggin Hill, Kent TN16 3BW, UK. Tel: (0959) 71011

Name	Description	Manufacturer/designer	Distributor/contact
Image processing boards			
Series 151	VMEbus image processing modules that connect to the IBM PC AT via a proprietary interface, allowing the PC to act as a system controller. Four modules are available: AD1150 A/D interface, FB150 frame buffer, ALU150 pipelined image processor and RTC150 realtime convolver. 'Faster than realtime' performance is provided by means of a hardware implementation of area-of-interest processing: user defined subregions can be processed through the pipeline at 10 MHz per pixel without the need to conform to RS170 video standards	Imaging Technology Inc., 600 West Cummings Park, Woburn, MA 01801, USA. Tel: (617) 938-8444	Amplicon Electronics Ltd, Richmond Road, Brighton, East Sussex BN2 3RL, UK. Tel: (0273) 608331
Interface devices			
DT1403	16-bit VMEbus D/A board with four converters each with a settling time of 10 µs and output range of ± 10 V. Converters include deglitching circuits, and their outputs are designed in a force/sense configuration to maintain output accuracy and integrity	Data Translation Inc., 100 Locke Drive, Marlboro, MA 01752, USA	Data Translation Ltd, The Business Centre, Molly Millars Lane, Wokingham, Berks RG11 2QZ, UK. Tel: (0734) 793838

products in brief

Name	Description	Manufacturer/designer	Distributor/contact
Interface devices (continued)			
DT1407	Analogue I/O board for VMEbus with a 16-bit 100 kHz A/D subsystem, four DI inputs, two 12-bit 125 kHz D/A converters, an onboard programmable clock and two eight-line digital I/O ports. Data can be acquired from a user specified channel or a sequence of channels can be scanned automatically	Data Translation Inc., 100 Locke Drive, Marlboro, MA 01752, USA	Data Translation Ltd, The Business Centre, Molly Millars Lane, Wokingham, Berks RG11 2QZ, UK. Tel: (0734) 793838
HD68230	Parallel interface timer provides versatile double-buffered parallel interfaces which can operate in unidirectional or bidirectional modes, either 8 or 16 bit wide. Has a programmable 24-bit timer that can be used as a 'time-out' controller, and a 5-bit prescaler	Hitachi Ltd, New Marunouchi Building No 5, 1-chome, Marunouchi, Chiyoda, Tokyo, Japan	Hitachi Electronic Components (UK) Ltd, 21 Upton Road, Watford, Herts WD1 7TP, UK. Tel: (0923) 46488
RIC	16-bit realtime interface coprocessor based on the 80186 designed for the company's IBM Industrial Computer. Has 128 kbyte of dual ported memory with parity for error detection. A memory-resident realtime control program provides multitasking, supporting up to 253 tasks running together. A programmer's development kit is supplied	Bytech Ltd, 2 The Western Centre, Western Road, Bracknell RG12 1RW, UK. Tel: (0344) 482211	
Memory modules			
EDH891M2CL	1 Mbit buffered military CMOS RAM module with access times of 150 ns or 200 ns. Can be user configured as 128 kbit × 8 or 64 kbit × 16 at PCB interconnect levels	Electronic Designs Inc., Hopkinton Industrial Park, 35 South Street, Hopkinton, MA 01748, USA. Tel: (617) 435-9077	Electronic Designs Europe, Shelley House, The Avenue, Lightwater, Surrey GU18 5RF, UK. Tel: (0276) 72637
PMEBB-1	Bubble memory subsystem for VMEbus comprising a 1 Mbyte bubble master card plus up to eight slave storage units each providing up to 2 Mbyte. The system has a custom hybrid controller interface with a two-chip gate array to perform timing and control functions and to provide data transfer between bubble memory and the onboard Z80H. Typical access time is 11 ms	Plessey Microsystems Ltd, Water Lane, Towcester, Northants NN12 7JN, UK. Tel: (0327) 50312	Dean Microsystems Ltd, 7 Horseshoe Park, Pangbourne, Berks RG8 7JW, UK. Tel: (07357) 5155

From left: 1 Mbit memory modules from Electronic Designs; Plessey's PMEBB-1 bubble memory board; and Hitachi's HD68230 parallel interface timer

Name	Description	Manufacturer/designer	Distributor/contact
VME 48607	4 Mbyte double-height multilayer dynamic RAM modules for VMEbus systems. Can handle 8-, 16-, 24- and 32-bit data transfers as well as 24- and 32-bit addressing. Write/read access times are 80 ns single write, 60 ns block write, 240 ns single read and 230 ns block read	Bicc-Vero Electronics Ltd, Flanders Road, Hedge End, Southampton SO3 3LG, UK. Tel: (04215) 66300	

Microcontrollers

80C451/83C451	8-bit CMOS microcontrollers for the 8051 family. 56 I/O lines eliminate the need for external hardware for latching, decoding or buffering in I/O intensive applications. Port 6 is configured for various data input control and flag operations, behaving as a 'mailbox' port. Supplied in a 68-pin plastic DIP. 80C451 is a ROM-less version, 83C451 has a 4 kbit × 8 ROM	Mullard Ltd, Mullard House, Torrington Place, London WC1E 7HD, UK. Tel: 01-580 6633	

Microprocessors

Am29C116	CMOS version of the Am291160 16-bit microprocessor. Power consumption is reduced by some 75% over the original bipolar device to 1 W. Includes a barrel shifter, 32 working registers, a three-input ALU and a priority encoder. Packaging: 52-pin DIP	Advanced Micro Devices Inc., 901 Thompson Place, Sunnyvale, CA 94086, USA	Advanced Micro Devices (UK) Ltd, AMD House, Goldsworth Road, Woking, Surrey GU21 1JT, UK. Tel: (04862) 22121

Multiplier–accumulators (MACs)

WTL 2010 series	16 × 16 parallel MACs in CMOS, with speeds quoted as 45 ns. Devices are pin-for-pin compatible with TRW's TDC 1010 and the Am29570, and perform double-precision subtraction, addition and multiplication. Packaging: DIP, pin grid array or LCC	Weitek Corp., Scott Blvd, Santa Clara, CA, USA	Trident Microsystems Ltd, Trident House, 53 Ormside Way, Redhill, Surrey RH1 2LS, UK. Tel: (0737) 65900

Programmable arrays

EP 320	Erasable programmable logic device (PLD) built with Intel's sub 2 μm CHMOS II-E EPROM technology. Claimed to have the smallest die size of any PLD. Standby current is 10 μA; at 1 MHz, the device draws 10 mA. I/O time is 35 ns. Packaged in a ceramic windowed DIP	Altera Corp., 3525 Monroe Street, Santa Clara, CA 95051, USA. Tel: (408) 984-2800	Ambar-Cascom Ltd, Rabans Close, Aylesbury, Bucks HP19 3RS, UK. Tel: (0296) 34141
PAL C22V10	CMOS PAL (programmable array logic) device claimed to be industry's first fully erasable and reprogrammable PAL. Packaged in a 24-pin windowed ceramic DIP allowing ultraviolet erasure. Propagation delay is 25 ns. The array implements a new concept called the 'programmable macro cell', enabling each output to be determined individually	Cypress Semiconductor Corp., 3910 North 1st Street, San Jose, CA 95134, USA. Tel: (408) 943-2600	Advanced Technology Devices, 466-478 Cranbrook Road, Gants Hill, Ilford, Essex IG2 6LE, UK. Tel: 01-554 5700

products in brief

Name	Description	Manufacturer/designer	Distributor/contact
Programming modules			
G-Stack	Set/gang EPROM programmer for the Universe 1000 programmer range. Incorporates 32-pin ZIF sockets for up to eight devices to be programmed concurrently	Elan Digital Systems Ltd, 16–20 Kelvin Way, Crawley, West Sussex RH10 2RS, UK. Tel: (0293) 510448	
PP41	Gang programmer for up to eight 24-pin or 28-pin EPROMs or E²PROMs, featuring 512 kbit internal RAM expandable to 1 Mbit, dual communications ports and editing and data handling facilities	Stag Electronic Designs Ltd, Stag House, Tewin Court, Welwyn Garden City, Herts AL7 1AU, UK. Tel: (0707) 332148	
Sprint	A plug-in IBM PC card that connects to a universal ZIP–DIP socket adaptor for programming high-speed CMOS and NMOS programmable devices up to 1024 kbyte. Software is resident in the development machine, eliminating downloading of code from an external programmer	Cypress Semiconductor Corp., 3910 North 1st Street, San Jose, CA 95134, USA. Tel: (408) 943-2600	Advanced Technology Devices, 466–478 Cranbrook Road, Gants Hill, Ilford, Essex IG2 6LE, UK. Tel: 01-554 5700
PROMs			
CY7C261	8 kbit × 8 CMOS reprogrammable PROM. Uses an EPROM memory cell. Available with access times of 35 ns, 45 ns or 55 ns. Operating current is 100 mA; standby current is 20 mA	Cypress Semiconductor Corp., 3910 North 1st Street, San Jose, CA 95134, USA. Tel: (408) 943-2600	Advanced Technology Devices, 466–478 Cranbrook Road, Gants Hill, Ilford, Essex IG2 6LE, UK. Tel: 01-554 5700
MBM28C64/ 65-25/35	64 kbit CMOS E²PROM that uses a 5 V power supply for all operations including write, allowing data to be written remotely. Rewriting is possible in under 10 ms and can be performed 10 000 times during the life of the chip, says the manufacturer. Supplied in a 28-pin DIP	Fujitsu Ltd, 6–1 Marunouchi 2-chome, Chiyoda-ku, Tokyo 100, Japan	Fujitsu Microelectronics Ltd, Hargrave House, Belmont Road, Maidenhead, Berks SL6 6NE, UK. Tel: (0628) 76100
RAMs			
EDH816H64C	1 Mbit high-speed static RAM module. The module does not have on-substrate buffering, thus enabling fast access times of 55 ns and 70 ns. Suitable for high-density graphics and signal processing applications. Can be configured as 64 kbit × 16, 128 kbit × 8 and 256 kbit × 4	Electronic Designs Inc., Hopkinton Industrial Park, 35 South Street, Hopkinton MA 01748, USA. Tel: (617) 435-9077	Electronic Designs Europe, Shelley House, The Avenue, Lightwater, Surrey GU18 5RF, UK. Tel: (0276) 72637
MB81C86	256 kbit static RAM claimed to be the fastest such device available commercially — access times are 55 ns or 70 ns maximum — due to the 1.3 μm gate length and the use of low-resistivity polycide for gate electrodes. Power consumption in active mode is 550 mW; in standby mode it is 55 mW	Fujitsu Ltd, 6–1 Marunouchi 2-chome, Chiyoda-ku, Tokyo 100, Japan	Fujitsu Microelectronics Ltd, Hargrave House, Belmont Road, Maidenhead, Berks SL6 6NE, UK. Tel: (0628) 76100

Name	Description	Manufacturer/designer	Distributor/contact
SRM 20256C	256 kbit asynchronous CMOS static RAM organized as 32 kword × 8 bit. Access time is 100 ns maximum. Standby power requirement is 2 μA. Available in a 28-pin plastic DIP or SOP	Seiko Epson Corp., 3-3-5 Owa Suwa-Shi, Nagano-ken, 392 Japan	Hero Electronics Ltd, Dunstable Street, Ampthill, Beds MK45 2JS, UK. Tel: (0525) 405015
TC 511000	1 Mbit CMOS dynamic RAM, organized as 1 Mword × 1 bit, available in an 18-pin plastic DIP or a 20-pin plastic SOJ. Cycle time is 55 ns. Operating power is 275 mW or 5.5 mW standby	Toshiba, 1-chome Uchisaiwai-cho, Chiyoda-ku, Tokyo, Japan	Toshiba (UK) Ltd, Toshiba House, Frimley Road Camberley, Surrey GU16 5JJ, UK. Tel: (0276) 62222

Single-board computers

Name	Description	Manufacturer/designer	Distributor/contact
CT-68X	68010-based board for VMEbus products. Unix system V has been ported to the board. Has 128 kbyte or 512 kbyte dual-ported RAM, EPROM sockets, an SCSI interface and onboard selftest and diagnostic firmware	Integrated Micro Products, 1 Industrial Estate, Medomsley Road, Consett, Durham DH8 6TJ, UK. Tel: (0207) 503481	Unit-C Ltd, Dominion Way, West Broadwater, Worthing, West Sussex BN14 8NT, UK. Tel: (0903) 205233
GPC68020	68020-based 32-bit multitasking single board computer for Multibus I users. Available in two versions: with 12.5 MHz or 16.67 MHz CPU rate. Onboard memory can be up to 2 Mbyte of dual-ported RAM	Microbar Inc., 1120 San Antonio Road, Palo Alto, CA 92303, USA. Tel: (415) 964-2862	Data Design Techniques Ltd, 68/70 Tewin Road, Welwyn Garden City, Herts AL7 1BD, UK. Tel: (0707) 334774

Test systems

Name	Description	Manufacturer/designer	Distributor/contact
HP 3065AT	Combinational board tester designed to perform in-circuit component tests and functional tests on production circuit boards with VLSI, application-specific ICs and surface mount devices. Capable of high-speed data capture, clock speeds for testing 32-bit microprocessors and bus emulation testing. Interfaces to CAE sources	Hewlett-Packard Ltd, Miller House, The Ring, Bracknell, Berks RG12 1XN, UK. Tel: (0344) 424898	Literature Section, Hewlett-Packard Ltd, Eskdale Road, Winnersh Triangle, Wokingham, Berks RG11 5DZ, UK. Tel: (0734) 696622
MST16/32	Test system for 8086-, 8088- and 68000-based boards. Provides predefined tests for ROM, RAM and I/O, custom tests programmed in BASIC or pseudoassembler, and the ability to execute and monitor application programs	Scicon, Sanderson House, 49 Berners Street, London W1P 4AQ, UK. Tel: 01-580 5599	Antron Electronics Ltd, Hamilton House, 39 Kings Road, Haslemere, Surrey GU27 2QA, UK. Tel: (0428) 54541

From left: MST16/32 microprocessor system tester from Scicon; Elan G-Stack programmer for the Universe 1000; Fujitsu's MB81C86 256k static RAM and MBM28C65 E^{2}PROM

calendar

Date	Title	Contact	Place	Other details
1986				
19–26 October	Semiconductor Technology	International Information Service Ltd, Room 103, Wing On Plaza, Tsimshatsui East, Kowloon, Hong Kong	Xiangshan Hotel, Beijing, China	International conference on semiconductor and IC technology, organized by the Chinese Institute of Electronics and the University of California, USA
27–28 October	CCVLSI '86	CCVLSI '86, Dept of Electrical Engineering, McGill University, 3480 University Street, Montreal, Quebec, Canada H3H 2A7	Montreal, Canada	Canadian conference on VLSI
27–29 October	Interface International in Europe	World Trade Center, Strawinskylaan 1245, 1077 XX Amsterdam, The Netherlands	Parc des Expositions, Paris, France	Conference discussing and analysing communications technology issues such as ISDN, ISO and CCITT standards, future roles and policies of the PTTs, multinational networks, videotex, software, voice–data integration and communication satellites
27–30 October	International Conference on Computer Languages	Joseph Urban, Center for Advanced Computer Studies, University of Southwestern Louisiana, PO Box 44330, Lafayette, LA, USA. Tel: (318) 231-6304	Konover, Hotel, Miami Beach, FL, USA	Sponsored by the IEEE Computer Society
27–30 October	Satech 86	Satech 86, 2472 Eastman Avenue, Building 34, Ventura, CA 93003, USA	Boston, MA, USA	Covers intelligent manufacturing facilities and MAP
27–30 October	Systec 86	Münchener Messe und Ausstellungs GmbH, Messelgelände, Postfach 121009, D-800 München 12, FRG. Tel: (089) 5107-0	Munich Trade Fair Centre, FRG	First international trade fair for computer integration in logistics, development, design, manufacture and quality assurance
28–30 October	Gallium Arsenide IC Symposium	James A Hutchly, Research Triangle Institute, Box 12194, Research Triangle Park, NC 27709, USA	Grenelfe, FL, USA	
28–30 October	Test + Transducer '86	Norma Thewlis, Trident International Exhibitions Ltd, 21 Plymouth Road, Tavistock, Devon PL19 8AU, UK. Tel: (0822) 4671	Wembley Conference Centre, London, UK	Exhibition and conference covering materials testing, solid-state transducers, optical sensors for robots, automotive sensors, data acquisition and microprocessors, test in hazardous environments etc
28–29 October	Secure Communication Systems	Institution of Electrical Engineers, Savoy Place, London WC2R 0BL, UK. Tel: 01-240 1871	London, UK	Second international conference covering commercial and military system design, authentication and security in data networks, video, audio and speech encryption, impact of VLSI on security etc.
2–6 November	FJCC 86	Stanley Winkler, FJCC 86, 1730 Massachusetts Avenue, NW Washington, DC 20036-1903, USA	Dallas, USA	IEEE/ACM joint computer conference and exhibition, covering database management systems, artificial intelligence, software engineering, operating systems, VLSI, graphics, electronic education, languages, parallel computing and networks
4–6 November	6th International Conference on Custom and Semicustom ICs	Prodex Ltd, 9 Emson Close, Saffron Walden, Essex, CB10 1HL, UK	Heathrow Penta Hotel, London, UK	

Date	Title	Contact	Place	Other details
5–7 November	ISDN Europe 86	IGI Europe Inc., c/o AKM, PO Box 6, CH-4005 Basel, Switzerland. Tel: (061) 25-51-11	World Trade and Convention Center, Basel, Switzerland	Conference covering ISDN terminal equipment, access, protocols and standards, services, implementations, internetworking, PBXs and LANs, field trials plus broadband ISDN and future directions
10–12 November	Mini and Microcomputers and their Applications	A S Gouda, IBM, 11400 Burnet Road, Department D46, Building 802, Austin, TX 78759, USA	Austin, TX, USA	31st international symposium sponsored by the Society for Mini and Microcomputers
11–14 November	Compec '86	Reed Exhibitions, Surrey House, 1 Throwley Way, Sutton, Surrey SM1 4QQ, UK. Tel: 01-643 8040	Olympia, London, UK	Exhibition of computers, peripherals and systems for professional and business users
11–14 November	Structured Design and Programming	ICS Publishing Co., 3 Swan Court, Leatherhead, Surrey KT22 8AD, UK. Tel: (0372) 379211	London, UK	Tutorial course on systematic techniques for structured design and coding in realtime engineering and scientific applications
17 November	Electronic Interference: Practical Design and Construction Techniques	Institution of Electrical and Electronics Incorporated Engineers, Savoy Hill House, Savoy Hill, London WC2R 0BS, UK. Tel: 01-836 3357	London, UK	Symposium covering: good engineering design; circuit layout and internal wiring; power supply design and layout; system installation and environmental considerations; test and diagnostic techniques; etc.
17–18 November	Computer Networking Symposium	IEEE Computer Society Administrative Office, 1730 Massachusetts Avenue, NW Washington, DC 20036-1903, USA	Washington, DC, USA	IEEE symposium covering long-haul networks, local area networks PBX systems, satellite systems, video systems, protocols, teleconferencing, standards design, network testing, network procurement and internetworking
17–21 November	AutomAsia 86	Andry Montgomery Ltd, 11 Manchester Square, London W1M 5AB, UK. Tel: 01-486 1951	Singapore	Third South East Asian conference and show on automated manufacturing technology and robotics
18–20 November	International Open Systems Conference	Online International, 989 Avenue of the Americas, New York, NY 10018, USA. Tel: (212) 279-8890	Moscone Center, San Francisco, USA	Conference geared towards assessing the possibilities of OSI systems using MAP and TOP as case studies
20–21 November	SMT '86	French Trade Exhibitions, French Chamber of Commerce House, 54 Conduit Street, London W1R 9SD, UK. Tel: 01-439 3964	Paris, France	Convention on surface-mount technology, organized in association with Pronic '86
21–22 November	8th Annual FORTH Convention	FORTH Interest Group, PO Box 8231, San Jose, CA 95155, USA. Tel: (408) 277-0668	Doubletree Hotel, Santa Clara, USA	US FORTH convention including exhibition, vendor booths, hands-on tutorials, lectures and user group meetings
26–28 November	International Symposium on Local Communication Systems, LAN and PBX	G Cluzel, Laboratoire LSI, Université Paul Sabatier 118, route de Narbonne, 31062 Toulouse, France. Tel: (33) 61 55 67 68	Toulouse, France	International symposium sponsored by the International Federation for Information Processing (IFIP), technical committee TC6. Simultaneous French-English translation available
2–4 December	Realtime Systems Symposium	K G Shin, Dept of Electrical Engineering and Computer Science, University of Michigan, Ann Arbor, MI 48109, USA	New Orleans, LA, USA	

calendar

Date	Title	Contact	Place	Other details
9 December	Industrial Applications of Expert Systems	Sira Ltd, South Hill, Chislehurst, Kent BR7 5EH, UK. Tel: 01-467 6515	Chislehurst, Kent, UK	Tutorial course covering the capabilities and limitations of expert system technology in relation to management and industrial processes, the principles and methods of expert systems, the tools available for building industrial expert systems and for developing applications

1987

Date	Title	Contact	Place	Other details
14–16 January	Multi 87	Society for Computer Simulation, PO Box 17900, San Diego, CA 92117, USA. Tel: (619) 277-3888	San Diego, CA, USA	1987 SCS 'multiconference' covering modelling and simulation on microcomputers, emergency planning, multiprocessor and array processors (Mapcon), simulation of CIM systems and robotics, and AI simulation
28–31 January	India Comm 87	Cahners Exhibitions, Oriel House, 26 The Quadrant, Richmond-upon-Thames, Surrey TW1 3DL, UK. Tel: 01-949 3777	Pragati Maidan, New Delhi, India	Exhibition designed to encourage computer and communications trade between India and the Western world
4–6 February	International Workshop on Industrial Automation Systems	Prof. Masao Sakauchi, Institute of Industrial Science, University of Tokyo 22-1, Roppongi 7-chome, Minato-ku, Tokyo 106, Japan. Tel: (03) 402-6231	Roppongi, Tokyo, Japan	Workshop on practical and basic techniques applicable to machine vision, machine intelligence and signal processing. Includes a session on industrial applications of digital signal processors and microprocessors
4–6 February	Software and Hardware Applications of Microcomputers	Fathy F Yassa, Corporate Research & Development Center, General Electric Co., PO Box 8, KWC510, Schenectady, NY 12301, USA	University Park Holiday Inn, Fort Collins, CO, USA	Covers the applications, software, interfacing, hardware and communications etc. of microcomputers. Sponsored by the Society for Mini and Microcomputers
10–12 February	Smartex '87	Tom Archer, Smart Group, Kebbell House, Delta Gain, Carpenders Park, Watford, Herts WD1 5EF, UK. Tel: 01-427 2377	Barbican Centre, London, UK	Specialist show for the SMT industry, including the second surface mount and related technologies conference
10–12 February	Systems Design & Integration Conference	Electronic Conventions Management, 8110 Airport Blvd, Los Angeles, CA 90045, USA. Tel: (213) 772-2965	Santa Clara, CA, USA	Conference and exhibition on systems design, software engineering and integration
25–27 February	ISSCC '87	Lewis Winner, 301 Almeria Avenue, Coral Gables, FL 33134, USA. Tel: (305) 446-8193	New York Hilton, NY, USA	34th IEEE international solid-state circuits conference, covering digital VLSI design, fabrication and test, logic arrays, architecture, microprocessors and coprocessors, analogue components, memories, signal processing etc.
10–12 March	Semicon Europa '87	Cochrane Communications Ltd, CCL House, 59 Fleet Street, London EC4Y 1JU, UK. Tel: 01-353 8807	Zuspa Convention Centre, Zurich, Switzerland	13th semiconductor production equipment and materials show, this year placing an emphasis on test equipment. Organized by the Semiconductor Equipment and Materials Institute (SEMI)
22–26 March	Computer Graphics '87	National Computer Graphics Association, 2722 Merrilee Drive, Suite 200, Fairfax, VA 22031, USA. Tel: (703) 698-9600	Philadelphia Civic Center, PA, USA	Conference and exposition on the theory and practice of computer graphics. Includes sessions on artificial intelligence, architecture, user interfaces and industry standards, and a demonstration of MAP

Microprocessors and Microsystems

The journal welcomes original papers from both academic and industrial contributors on the research, design, development, evaluation and application of all microprocessor-based systems and on the development and use of microsystem software. Papers should illustrate practical experience and show the applicability of the work described. Typically, full-length papers are approximately 5000–7000 words long plus illustrations. In addition to full-length papers, the journal welcomes shorter design notes, tutorial papers and case studies of up to 3000 words.

REFEREEING

All submitted articles are refereed by two independent reviewers to ensure both accuracy and relevance, though it is the authors' sole responsibility that statements used are accurate. The author is also responsible for obtaining permission to quote material and to republish tables and illustrations.

PREPARATION OF SCRIPTS

Three copies of the manuscript, typed *double spaced* on one side of A4 paper should be sent to:

● The Editor, Microprocessors and Microsystems, PO Box 63, Westbury House, Bury Street, Guildford, Surrey GU2 5BH, United Kingdom.

Each page of the manuscript should be numbered. Wide margins should be left so that the paper can be prepared for the typesetters. Please remove tables and figures from the main body of the script and attach them at the end of the paper. Each table or figure should be reproduced on a single sheet. Please list figure captions on a separate sheet and attach this sheet at the end of the paper.

English is the sole language used by the journal, and we follow the Oxford English Dictionary. All papers should be written in English. To maintain consistency throughout each volume, every paper published is stylized by the journal's editorial staff.

Biographical notes

It is the journal's practice to include biographical notes on the authors of published papers. Biographical notes can be up to 100 words, briefly describing career details and current research interests, and should be accompanied by a black-and-white portrait photograph. To speed processing of the paper it is helpful if biographical notes can be attached to the submitted manuscript.

UNITS

SI units should be used. In circumstances where this is not possible, please provide a conversion factor at the first mention of the unit.

ILLUSTRATIONS

Line drawings

We use our own professional studio to ensure that line drawings are consistent with house style. We would prefer, however, to receive one set of unlettered drawings (black ink on tracing paper) so we can put on the lettering ourselves. Drawings, if possible, should be of a size consistent with the journal, i.e. either 169 mm or 366 mm wide. Single drawings should not extend over one page (500 mm) in height.

Computer printouts

Illustrations showing line printer listings, plotter output, etc should preferably be on unlined paper. Printouts will be reduced by us to the relevant size. Do not mark them as they will be used to make photographic copies for the typesetters. Only include sufficient lines for the reader to interpret the format and nature of the printout. Overlong printouts can cause confusion. Fuller explanation of the printout should appear in the caption and the text.

Photographs

Black-and-white glossy photographs (including Polaroid prints of VDU screens) should be supplied unmounted. They should be labelled clearly on the back with a soft pencil. Photocopies of the photographs should be provided for the referees.

REFERENCES

The journal style is to indicate the use of a reference in the text with a superscript as each one arises and give the full reference with the same number at the end of the paper. If a reference is cited more than once, the same number should be used each time. With a bibliography, the references are given in alphabetical order (dependent on the first author's surname). It would be helpful if you could follow this style. References take the following form:

(To journals)

1 **Buckroyd, A** 'Production testing of microprocessor-based equipment' *Microprocessors and Microsystems* Vol 5 No 7 (September 1981) pp 299–303

(To books)

2 **Gallacher, J** 'Testing and maintenance' in **Hanna, F K (ed.)** *Advanced techniques for microprocesor systems* Peter Peregrinus, Stevenage, UK (1980)

PROOFS

Correspondence and proofs for corrections will be sent to the first named author, unless otherwise indicated. Authors will receive a copy of the galley proofs and copies of redrawn or relettered illustrations. It is important that these proofs should be checked and returned *promptly*.

COPYRIGHT

Before publication, authors are requested to assign copyright to Butterworth & Co (Publishers) Ltd. This allows the company to sanction reprints of the whole or part of the volume and authorize photocopies. The authors, however, still retain their traditional right to reuse or to veto third-party publication.

OFFPRINTS AND REPRINTS

The first named author will receive 25 offprints of the paper free of charge as well as a complimentary copy of the journal. Further reprint copies, a minimum of 100, can be ordered at any time from the Reprints Department, Butterworth Scientific Ltd, Westbury House, PO Box 63, Bury Street, Guildford, Surrey GU2 5BH, UK.

Journal of

MOLECULAR GRAPHICS

published in association with the
Molecular Graphics Society

Editor: Dr. W.G. Richards (University of Oxford)

Computer graphics is an important and useful technique for chemists, molecular biologists, pharmaceutical researchers and others engaged in investigating molecular structure, function and interaction. The **Journal of Molecular Graphics** assists researchers in using computers to visualize, manipulate and interact with molecular models, by publishing papers from a wide range of disciplines.

Scope

- hardware and software molecular graphics systems

- new algorithms and procedures

- new representations of molecular structures

- useful parametric plots

- molecular modelling using molecular graphics

- results of projects using molecular graphics

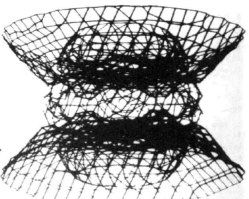

For further details and a sample copy, please contact:

Geraldine Hills, Butterworth Scientific Ltd., PO Box 63, Westbury House, Bury Street, Guildford, Surrey GU2 5BH. UK

microprocessors and microsystems

vol 10 no 9 november 1986

Butterworths

editorial advisory board

Microprocessors and Microsystems is an international journal published in February, March, April, May, June, August, September, October, November, December. *Editorial Offices:* Butterworth Scientific Ltd, PO Box 63, Westbury House, Bury Street, Guildford, Surrey GU2 5BH, UK. Tel: (0483) 31261. Telegrams and telex: 859556 SCITEC G. *Publishing Director:* John Owens. *Production:* Nick Wilson

Microprocessors and Microsystems is published by Butterworth Scientific Ltd. *Registered Office:* Butterworth Scientific Ltd, 88 Kingsway, London WC2 6AB, UK

Subscription enquiries and orders, UK and overseas: Quadrant Subscription Services Ltd, Oakfield House, Perrymount Road, Haywards Heath, West Sussex RH16 3DH, UK. Tel: (0444) 459188; *North America:* Butterworth Publishers, 80 Montvale Avenue, Stoneham, MA 02180, USA

Annual subscription (10 issues): £98.00 overseas rate (£24.00 for private individuals); $176.00 US rate ($43.00 for private individuals) UK subscription rates available on request.

Prices include packing and delivery by sea mail. Airmail prices available on request. Copies of this journal sent to subscribers in Bangladesh, India, Pakistan, Sri Lanka, Canada and the USA are air-speeded for quicker delivery.

Back issues: Prior to current volume available from Wm Dawson & Sons Ltd, Cannon House, Folkestone, Kent CT19 5EE, UK. Tel: (0303) 57421

US mailing agents: Mercury Airfreight International Ltd Inc., 10B Englehard Avenue, Avenel, NJ 07001, USA. Second class postage paid at Rahway, NJ. US Postmaster: Send address corrections to *Microprocessors and Microsystems* c/o Mercury Airfreight International Ltd Inc., address as above.

Reprints: Minimum order 100, available from the publisher.

Copyright: Readers who require copies of papers published in this journal may either purchase reprints or obtain permission to copy from the publisher at the following address: Butterworth Scientific Ltd, PO Box 63, Westbury

microprocessors and microsystems

vol 10 no 9
november 1986

Editor Steve Hitchcock

Assistant Editor Andrew Taylor

Publisher Amanda Harper

THE UNIVERSITY
OF MICHIGAN

JAN 07 1987

ENGINEERING
LIBRARY

475 **Distributed programs: an overview of implementations**
Lack of progress in software engineering has been the major constraint on multiprocessor development, but advances are now being made. **Dick Whiddett** reviews the field of distributed programming, its implementations and methodologies

485 **Vision system based on a single-chip microcomputer**
Vision sensors which use dynamic RAM are cheaper and easier to interface than their alternatives — videcon or CCD. **Andrew Russell** describes a DRAM-based 'intelligent' vision system in which all interfacing and image processing functions are provided by an 8751 single-chip microcomputer

491 **Embedded microprocessor software: case study of an automatic computer exchange**
Multitasking, realtime debugging and I/O methods are among the embedded software development techniques used by **Franco Civello** in constructing a system to control an automatic computer exchange. Here he discusses the principles and practice of such a system

500 Design note
12-bit digital audio time delay using the 6809
Commercial time delay units are not usually flexible enough to suit computer control, as may be required in laboratory situations. So **B T G Tan and L P Tay** have designed a programmable audio delay system based on the Apple II with a 6809 coprocessor

506 **R&D reports**
A survey of the recent scientific and technical literature

510 **Book reviews**
Communicating sequential processes — the Locus system — digital VLSI design

516 **Product news**
32-bit graphics processor — 68020 upgrade

518 **Products in brief**

526 **Calendar**

news file

ISDN standards spur

A standard based on a British Telecom line code for the U interface has been proposed for integrated services digital network (ISDN) systems by the ISDN standards committee of the American National Standards Institute. Although the standard still has to be ratified internationally, and this is unlikely before 1988, the ruling by the American group is expected to spur the market for ISDN chips where manufacturers have been holding back large-scale production until a definitive standard emerged.

NMOS dynamic RAMs revived

Improving market conditions in the UK have encouraged Motorola's East Kilbride division to re-enter the NMOS dynamic RAM market one year after announcing a 'phase-down' of production. But having converted much of its former NMOS wafer fabrication plant to CMOS capability, Motorola has been forced to buy in DRAM dice. An agreement was recently concluded with Japanese company Toshiba for the supply of the dice, while Motorola will assemble, test and burn in the devices. 64 kbit and 256 kbit devices will be available (models MCM4164CP and MCM6256AP respectively). The 256 kbit device offers page mode configuration, and a nibble mode version is promised early in 1987.

VHSIC design agreement

Users of the Genesil silicon development system will have access to 1.2 μm CMOS 'VHSIC' technology developed by National Semiconductor following an agreement with Silicon Compilers, who developed Genesil. The VHSIC technology that will be used has been developed under the US government's ongoing programme to provide very high-speed IC devices for military applications. With Genesil, Silicon Compilers pioneered the technique of silicon compilation, a software tool that automates IC

design by fitting the IC designer's architectural description to a custom layout. Under the agreement designs generated with systems that have the VHSIC process installed can then be fabricated by National at its 1.2 μm facilities in Santa Clara, CA, USA.

STDbus UK vendor group

A UK vendor group has been formed to 'highlight' the role played by STDbus in industrial automation and to promote wider use of the bus. Founder members of the STDbus UK Vendor Group are: Analog Devices, Apoloco, C-Matic Systems, PACS, Technitron and Wordsworth Technology. Originally developed in the USA as a manufacturer and processor-independent small industrial bus for control and communication systems, STDbus now has over 150 manufacturers worldwide with some 3 million cards installed, says the group.

First 80386 microcomputer

Mark Potts (left) and Paul Bion of UK company TFB Rair show off the Turbo 386 which was claimed at its launch to be the world's first microcomputer to be based on Intel's 32-bit 80386 microprocessor. The 'supermicro', which retails from £19 000, is intended for multiuser business and office automation systems and is being marketed to systems integrators and OEMs as a replacement for minicomputer hardware.

European heads Unix group

Dr Pamela Gray of UK Unix company Sphinx has been elected President of the US-based International Conference of Unix Users (/usr/group), becoming the first European and the first woman to head the group. Also elected to the governing board was Frank King of IBM, the first time a senior representative of that company has served on the board of the Unix group. Gray sees the main task during her year in office being to 'internationalize' the group, a non-profit organization formed in 1980 to promote Unix in the commercial market. The group is affiliated to independent Unix groups in the UK and Canada, and a drive will be made to recruit other groups to establish an international network, says Gray.

ADA compiler for 68000

A validated ADA crosscompiler supporting 68000, 68010 and MC68881 processors has been announced by UK-based Systems Designers. The compiler runs on VAX/VMS systems and is supplied with ADA tools and the target runtime software. It was validated by the UK National Computer Centre in compliance with US-established ADA standards. The company claims to have already received orders worth more than $150 000 for the compiler, which is intended to be used in the development of 'embedded' microprocessors for weapon systems, avionics and in-flight systems.

Distributed programs: an overview of implementations

Lack of progress in software engineering has been the major constraint on multiprocessor system development, but advances are now being made. **Dick Whiddett** reviews the field of distributed programming, its implementations and methodologies

The background to and progress in the development of 'distributed programs' which execute on a distributed multiple-processor architecture are reviewed. Three basic concurrent programming methodologies are introduced and illustrated. The general problems associated with the use of distributed architectures are considered. Finally, the problems and techniques associated with implementing the various programming methodologies on different architectures are discussed. The implicit constraints imposed on the high-level software by the low-level communications architecture are then examined.

microsystems   distributed processing   concurrency

The development of microprocessor-based single-board computers in the late 1970s initiated a rush of proposals for multicomputer and distributed systems. Unfortunately, these systems are still largely unrealized. The differential between the maturity of hardware and software engineering has contributed to this situation. Hardware engineering is a relatively mature topic with a number of well defined standards and interfaces. Thus, multicomputers could easily be constructed from the available technology and it was assumed that any accommodation to a distributed environment could be made in software. The simplicity of hardware problems led to an underestimation of the difficulty of producing properly engineered software solutions.

Intense research activity in recent years is now yielding a more mature understanding of the problems of a distributed environment in the areas of operating systems, database systems and computer control systems; recent reviews can be found in books by Chambers[1] and Bochman[2]. Progress has also been made in the field of programming methodologies to support a wide range of distributed applications. The aim of a 'distributed programming language' is to specify the operation of a

Department of Computing, University of Lancaster, Bailrigg, Lancaster LA1 4YR, UK

'distributed program', i.e. a single program which defines the operation of a distributed system.

In the interests of clarity, the following conventions are observed in this paper. The term 'architecture' will be used solely in connection with hardware aspects; 'methodologies' will refer to software aspects, particularly to higher-level features. 'Implementations' or 'facilities' will refer to common underlying support software provided for the use of applications programs. 'Systems' will refer to a combination of all of these aspects.

The implementation of all distributed systems is constrained by the underlying hardware and basic communications software. This paper considers only systems produced by combining a communications network with conventional processors. Alternative architectures such as dataflow machines[3] fall outside the scope of this article.

Three communications architectures have tended to dominate:

- random or hierarchical networks based on serial communications links, e.g. Darpanet[4]
- ring networks, in which each processor is connected to only two neighbours and all messages are passed around the ring from source to destination, e.g. the Cambridge Ring[5] and the IBM Token Ring[6]
- bus networks, where all processors are connected to a common communications medium and monitor all messages, e.g. Ethernet[7].

In general, communications systems are developed as layers of software protocols[8]. The bottom layers usually combine to provide one of two forms of 'transport service'.

- Connectionless or datagram systems offer a 'best effort to deliver' service for blocks of data. However, data may get lost, corrupted or arrive in the wrong order. The simplicity of implementation and the high reliability of local area networks (LANs) means that many systems are based on this service.
- Connection-oriented or virtual circuit systems allow two processes to establish a virtual link across the

0141-9331/86/09475-10 $03.00 © 1986 Butterworth & Co. (Publishers) Ltd

network. This provides an enhanced service which guarantees correct, reliable delivery of data.

The relative merit of the two systems has been a matter of debate and depends on the data transmission rates and expected error rates.

Three methodologies for concurrent programming have developed: procedure-, message- and operation-oriented methods. Andrews and Schneider[9] recently provided an extensive review of language developments. Each of the three program styles is examined here with reference to the implementation of a simple microprocessor-based instrument. The final section of the paper considers how the various methodologies may be mapped onto distributed systems and examines the constraints imposed by the various communications architectures.

MULTIPROCESSED SOFTWARE METHODOLOGIES

This paper is concerned with programming methodologies which explicitly allow the programmer to generate and control the multiple processes which are needed to program a distributed system consisting of multiple processors. There are two basic aspects of coordination between processes: communication and synchronization.

Communication is the transfer of data values from one process to another.

Synchronization involves the transmission of (possibly null) status information concerning the state of a process or of the system.

The degree of synchronization between processes varies with the program structure and the coordination methodology used. Some methodologies provide direct synchronization between pairs of processes which exchange signals or messages. With these implementations the processes are tightly constrained, and either party to the exchange will wait until the other is ready; both processes then proceed in parallel after the information exchange.

Other methodologies are more asynchronous, and information being exchanged may be stored in a buffer by underlying support software or simply discarded. The sender of the information does not know if, or when, it is received by the target process; neither does the receiver know when it was sent nor what the other process has done since.

Alternatively, the methodology may not provide any explicit synchronization mechanism, so processes must deduce the status of other processes indirectly from the values of common data variables. In practice both synchronous and asynchronous coordination of processes is often required and the programmer must implement suitable schemes using the operations available.

The use of multiple processes is illustrated by the following example which will be used throughout the paper to demonstrate the various implementation techniques. Consider an instrument which is required to sample its input data at some constant and frequent rate. The individual data values are not required for output; only their means and standard deviations for given periods are needed. These values are collected and

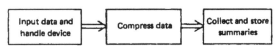

Figure 1. Data logger as three processes

periodically stored on some magnetic medium or are transmitted to a supervisory computer. The system may be simply implemented using three asynchronous processes to perform the three functions of sampling, data manipulation and data storage as shown in Figure 1. This organization is more suitable than a monolithic program since the three processes work on different timescales: whilst the sampling process must proceed at fixed regular intervals, the storage or transmission process may take an unpredictable time due to external factors such as disc head positioning delays or communication line errors. Timing constraints may necessitate the use of multiple processors even in a system as simple as this.

Both aspects of process coordination are illustrated by this example. The various processes communicate to pass on data as it is processed. The logger input process must be explicitly synchronized with some external hardware clock device so that it may sample its input at fixed intervals. Since each of the other processes may only proceed after receiving adequate input data, they are also synchronized to some degree. The degree of synchronization is dependent on the method and implementation of the communication mechanism between processes. For example, a process may either forward every item of data as it becomes available or it may accumulate and forward blocks of data to give a more loosely coupled program.

Within a system with shared memory, coordination of processes frequently involves access to shared data areas. Program segments that access shared data are the most hazardous to implement and are referred to as 'critical sections'. The safest general solution for sharing data is to adopt a policy of 'mutual exclusion' where access is restricted to one process at a time. This policy is over restrictive when a number of processes wish only to read data, but should be enforced if data is to be written or updated. Mutual exclusion need not be applied to all shared data simultaneously, but may be implemented separately over blocks of related data; in the data logger example, it would be applied separately to the two interprocess communication channels.

Early attempts to produce concurrent programs were based on semaphores[10], low-level primitives from which mutual exclusion and synchronization protocols could be constructed. Programs using semaphores suffered from two major weaknesses.

- They were very poorly structured and did not ensure that mutual exclusion in shared data areas was enforced.
- The mechanisms that were provided failed to distinguish the two modes of process coordination: communication and synchronization. The result was further confused with the program structure and data variables.

A number of programming methodologies and languages have been developed to provide structured multiprocessed systems. These have developed into two schools: the procedure- or monitor-based approach and message-based methods. Monitors provide a mechanism for the programmer to encapsulate shared data with the procedures by which it may be accessed. Mutual exclusion of access to monitor data is automatically provided by the compiler and runtime language support package. The message methodology prohibits the programmer from using shared data. Problems of access to shared data are kept within the operating system kernel. The programmer is provided with a message facility which acts as an intermediary between processes which need to synchronize or exchange data.

The two approaches have been shown to have equal expressive power[11]. The more appropriate one to adopt therefore depends on which set of basic operations may be most efficiently implemented on the hardware or the underlying software. The two methods are not mutually incompatible *a priori*, and 'operation-oriented' methodologies have been developed which combine aspects of both. These three approaches will now be considered in more detail.

Monitors

The concept of a monitor developed over a number of years[10, 12, 13] and was first implemented in the language CONCURRENT PASCAL[14] and later in MODULA[15]. Monitors are also provided as extensions to some commercially available languages such as PASCAL and PL/M. These languages define two forms of components: processes and monitors. Processes are the active program elements which operate on monitors, which are passive components containing shared data.

A monitor is a program module which encapsulates the definition of some data variables with procedures for their access. This simplifies programming since the processes accessing the monitor only need to know which procedures are provided, the particular implementation details being confined to the monitor definition. A typical monitor structure is given in Figure 2, which implements a circular buffer of items between two processes. (Illustrative examples in this paper are expressed in an arbitrary PASCAL-like notation that is intended to be self explanatory.)

```
monitor buff;
var
    buffer: array [0 .. maxbuf] of object;
    nextin, nextout: 0 .. maxbuf; count: 0 .. maxbuf + 1;
    waitmore, waitroom: queue;
entry procedure produce (ob: object);
begin
    if count = maxbuf + 1 then wait(waitroom);
    buffer[nextin] : = ob;
    nextin : = (nextin + 1) mod (maxbuf + 1);
    count  : = count + 1;
    if count = 1 then signal (waitmore);
end;
entry procedure consume (var ob:object);
begin
    if count = 0 then wait (waitmore);
    ob : = buffer [nextout];
    nextout : = (nextout + 1) mod (maxbuf + 1);
    count   : = count − 1;
    if count = maxbuf then signal (waitroom);
end;
begin {initialize}
    count : = 0; nextin : = 0; nextout : = 0
end. {buff}
```

Figure 2.   Monitor implementing a buffer

A producer process may insert items into the buffer by calling the procedure 'produce'. The items may later be extracted by another process calling 'consume'. The body of the monitor is executed when it is created and may be used to initialize the monitor variables. Implementing the data logger using a monitor-based system would require the use of two such monitors through which the data is transferred, giving the structure shown in Figure 3. Mutual exclusion of access to monitor variables is provided by the compiler and runtime support software. A process calling a monitor procedure gains exclusive use of the monitor until it exits from the monitor. If a second process attempts to enter a monitor that is currently in use by another process, the second process is delayed until the first process releases the monitor.

Monitors only provide process communication. A separate mechanism is required for process synchronization, for instance to prevent a process from attempting to extract data from the buffer before any has been inserted. Most monitor methodologies define a new type of variable (such as 'event' or 'queue') with two basic operations defined for it, such as 'wait' and 'signal'. These operations interface to the underlying process scheduling mechanisms which suspend or resume the execution of the appropriate process. Implementations of this form of mechanism vary in a number of details, such as

- whether or not signals are queued if no process is waiting, and precisely when they take effect
- the number of processes that can wait in a queue, how many of them may receive each signal, and the order in which they are resumed
- for queues located within a monitor, which processes may continue to execute within it and in what order.

The example in Figure 2 uses these operations to allow for the cases when the process speeds are too disparate and the buffer becomes full or empty.

A number of other constructs for determining when a process should delay or continue have been proposed[16, 17]. In general these require a process accessing a monitor to evaluate an expression to determine when to continue its operation, rather than waiting for an explicit signal from another process.

Message methodologies

Many operating systems have provided some primitive operations for the communication and synchronization of processes using messages. These concepts are now becoming more formalized and are incorporated in programming languages[18, 19].

All message methodologies provide at least two basic operations of the general form

send <message> { <destination> }

and

receive <message> { from <source> } { about <subject> }

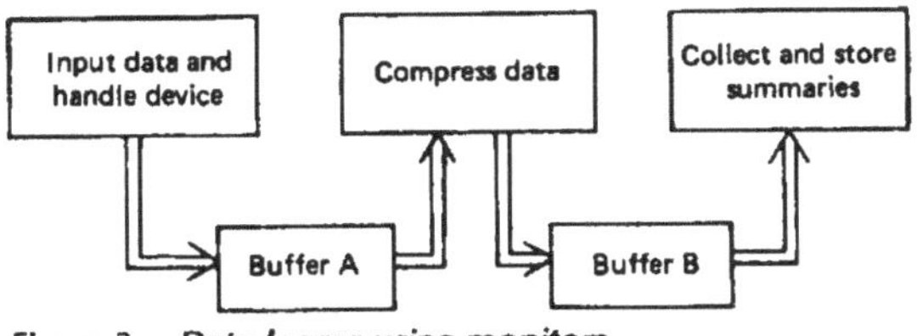

Figure 3.   Data logger using monitors

where optional fields are enclosed in braces { }. The semantics of these two operations may vary considerably depending on five factors:

- form of data within message
- patterns of communications supported
- details of naming conventions
- possible selection criteria for receipt
- synchronization constraints.

Many of these aspects are independent, leading to a wide variety of possible and actual implementations.

Form of data. Messages may be restricted to a particular size and particular variable types or they may be a variable-size collection of different types of values. The constraint is that the sender and receiver must agree on the form of the message, i.e. there must be some agreed protocol by which the receiver can determine the structure of the message from its content.

Communications patterns. Three patterns of message passing may be supported:

- one-to-one, where pairs of processes communicate and exchange messages
- N-to-one, where a process is prepared to accept a message from one of a set of processes; typically this pattern is used by a utility process which provides a service for a number of customer processes
- one-to-N, where a process may 'broadcast' a message to be received by a number of processes; broadcasts are useful in distributed systems to disseminate status or update information or to solicit information from an unknown source

Naming conventions. The above patterns of communication are closely linked to the details of naming conventions. Some methodologies require that the originator and receiver of a message mutually identify each other before communications may proceed; this is common in the one-to-one pattern. Others are more flexible and only require one party to identify the other; usually the originator will identify the receiver, whilst the receiver will accept any message directed to it.

Indirect communication between processes is sometimes provided by ports[20]. A port acts as a buffer area for messages and processes communicate with the port. This means that neither partner needs to know the identity of the process with which it is communicating, and its partner may even change without it being aware of the fact.

Selection criteria. The most primitive message facilities deliver the messages in approximately the order in which they are sent. More sophisticated ones allow messages to be given varying priorities or allow for messages to be received conditional on the contents.

Synchronization constraints. The final set of differences between message implementations relate to the degree of synchronization between the two processes involved. The tightest constraint is synchronous message passing; one process is delayed until its partner specified for the transaction is ready to proceed. When both are ready the message is transferred and both proceed. Asynchronous methodologies provide some buffering of messages so that a process may continue execution after sending a message even if the receiving process is not ready to accept it.

Message-based programming implementations

The first programming language with a formal bias based on the message concept was CSP. CSP programs employ synchronous message transfer between mutually identified pairs of processes. The message may be of any simple or structured type within the language. Message operations are similar in nature to input and output commands. A pair of commands match if the two processes name each other and the output item is of the same type as the input, in which case the two commands are executed simultaneously and the data is transferred. Either process may be delayed waiting for the matching command to become ready.

This tight coupling of processes is inappropriate for many applications, such as the logger example where processes cannot wait for others or where a process may need to interact with other processes in random order. Recent attempts to introduce nondeterminancy into programming languages have focussed on the use of 'guarded commands'[21]. Some flexibility in communications patterns is provided by incorporating input commands into a guarded command structure. In general, a guarded command consists of a series of Boolean expressions, or guards, and corresponding statements. The 'alternative' form of guarded command is executed by evaluating all the guards simultaneously and then nondeterministically selecting one of those which succeeded (i.e. was evaluated to true). The corresponding statements are then executed. In the 'iterative' form of guarded command the process is repeated until all guards fail. In the 'alternative' form only one successful guard is selected and its statement executed; the command aborts if no guards succeed.

An input or output command may be included in the guard of a command, possibly combined with other Boolean expressions. The evaluation of the guard may produce one of three results.

- The message exchange may proceed without delay, i.e. the partner process has already issued a corresponding message command and the input component of the guard evaluates to true. If the other parts of the guard also evaluate to true then the guard succeeds.
- The message exchange may never take place, for example if the partner has already terminated, and the guard evaluates to false and the command fails.
- The partner process still exists but has not yet executed a corresponding command. In this case the guard neither succeeds nor fails at this point.

The evaluation of the guards results in one of three situations.

- One or more guards succeed, in which case one guard is selected and the corresponding statements are executed.
- All guards fail, in which case the guarded command is terminated or aborted.
- The result is indeterminate since some guards may yet succeed. In this case execution is delayed and guards are repeatedly re-evaluated until a definite result is obtained.

Figure 4 illustrates the use of a message facility with guards. It uses a process to implement a message buffer

```
process buff;
var    buffer: array [0 .. maxbuf] of object;
       nextin; nextout: 0 .. maxbuf; count: 0 .. maxbuf + 1;
begin
   nextin : = 0; nextout : = 0; count : = 0;
   do count < maxbuf + 1; receive buffer[nextin] from producer = >
                     {data available and consumer ready?}
              nextin : = nextin + 1 mod (maxbuf + 1);
              count : = count + 1;
                     {pointers updated}
   or count > 0; send buffer[nextout] to consumer = >
                     {buffer available and producer ready?}
              nextout : = nextout + 1 mod (maxbuf + 1);
              count   : = count − 1;
                     {pointers updated}
   od
end. {buff}
```

Figure 4.   Buffer implemented by a process and guarded commands

between processes analogous to the monitor of Figure 2. The buffer process has an internal data structure to provide the storage area; it continually executes the iterative guarded command until both communicating processes have terminated. The buffer process exchanges data nondeterministically with both processes. Two expressions are included in the guards to prevent the overflow of underflow of the buffer. To implement the logger using a tightly synchronized message system would require a general structure similar to that of Figure 3 where each of the five software components is realized as a process.

Operation-oriented methodologies

Monitor and message facilities have tended to merge with the development of programs for distributed systems based on communications networks. These may be considered as 'operation-oriented' methodologies. They maintain the modular approach of monitors of encapsulated data structures which may only be accessed through a few extremely accessible procedures. However, their implementation is more akin to a message facility since the execution of the procedures is often performed by a separate process internal to the module. Procedure parameters and results are passed between the processes as messages.

There is a spectrum of implementation techniques used for operation-oriented methodologies. These range from 'remote procedure calls' (RPCs), which result in monitor-like implementations, to the 'rendezvous' which is similar to the CSP concept.

Distributed programs using RPCs may be implemented using a standard language and linking in special routines to access remote procedures[22]. When a remote procedure is called the parameters are assembled into a message which is sent to the remote machine. At the remote site the messages are interpreted and executed in a non-deterministic order by local server processes which implement mutual exclusion where necessary. Any results are then passed back in a separate message. The caller is usually delayed during the execution of the remote agent task giving effectively a single thread of control for the

process. The language 'distributed processes' (DP)[23] implements an RPC-like system and uses guarded commands to coordinate the execution of the remote operations.

The rendezvous mechanism which is provided in the ADA programming language[24] is more akin to CSP. Processes invoke remote operations by calling a service in a similar manner to calling a remote procedure. The name of the server process as well as the service and parameters must be provided. The calling process is delayed until it receives a reply. The operation is not performed until the remote server process is ready to accept a call for the particular service. The server then accepts the call, executes the appropriate commands using the parameters supplied and then returns the results to the caller. The two processes then continue their independent operation. Nondeterminism is introduced into ADA by using guarded commands to select which call to accept. Implementing the logger in ADA would produce a program structure very similar to a CSP program and would require the use of buffer processes like the one in Figure 5.

The significant difference between the rendezvous and synchronous message systems is that during the rendezvous the two processes are synchronized and the server process may communicate information back to the caller whilst being unaware of its identity. To simulate a rendezvous using a message system, a separate reply message must be generated by the program. Thus the server process must be provided with the identity of the calling process and the language interface must allow the use of variable destination names for messages.

Summary

This section has briefly reviewed the major techniques that have been developed for the expression of concurrency within a program.

● Monitors provide communication by accessing shared variables. This is essentially asynchronous and non-deterministic due to the random order of execution of monitor procedures. Thus an additional mechanism, such as events or queues, is necessary to provide process synchronization.

```
task body buff is
buffer : array (0 .. maxbuf) of object;
count  : integer range 0 .. bufsize: = 0;
nextin, nextout: integer range 0 .. maxbuf : = 0;
begin
  loop
    select
      when count < bufsize = >          {room in buffer}
        accept insert (ob:in object);   {accept rendezvous}
              buffer(nextin) : = ob;    {input data}
        end insert                      {end rendezvous}
        nextin : = (nextin + 1) mod bufsize;
        count : = count + 1;            {do housekeeping}
    or                                  {next select option}
      when count > 0 : = >              {data in buffer}
        accept extract (ob:out object);
              ob : = buffer(nextout);   {extract data}
        end extract;                    {end rendezvous}
        nextout : = (nextout + 1) mod bufsize;
        count   : = count − 1;          {do housekeeping}
    end select;
  end loop;
end buff
```

Figure 5.   Cyclic buffer in ADA

- Operations provide communication by the rendezvous which also provides process synchronization. Thus an additional mechanism, such as guarded commands, is necessary to provide some degree of nondeterminism and looser synchronization.
- Messages provide communication by message exchange. Synchronization is either provided directly by the message facility or it may be programmed using reply messages. Nondeterminism is again provided by guarded commands or by some other mechanism which allows a process to test the availability of messages.

MAPPING LANGUAGES ONTO A DISTRIBUTED ARCHITECTURE

A distributed architecture has inherent problems which must be overcome by all software methodologies. However, it is usually assumed that despite the additional problems there will be an overall improvement in system performance in terms of cost, performance, reliability or flexibility. This section considers the general problems for software implementations before discussing the particular implementation techniques for the various software methodologies.

Configuration and partitioning

The existence of multiple disjoint processor address spaces within a system introduces the need to partition the software components to accommodate the hardware configuration. Communication between processes residing on the same processor is usually much more efficient than interactions that involve interprocessor communications. Many design tools allow the designer to exploit this advantage by partitioning the software at an early stage in the design of the overall system. Mascot 3[25] and HCDM[26] are examples of general tools which aid the design of a system using a static modular allocation policy.

The language *MOD[27] allows the programmer to partition a computation into a collection of processes and also to define the details of communication paths between the processors. ADA has been criticized both for failing to provide a suitable partitioning construct, and for including features which inhibit partitioning. A variety of restrictions or extensions have been proposed to solve these problems[28, 29, 30].

The incorporation of configuration-specific information into a design at an early stage restricts its portability. This inhibits the use of cross development techniques where software is produced and tested on hardware that differs from the target system, and it makes upgrading the target hardware more complicated. The problems may be avoided by developing configuration independent software and then specifying the target hardware and allocation strategy at the linkage editing phase, as in the Martlet system[3]. Similarly the Conic system[32] provides linkage-time system cofiguration and also the ability to change the software configuration while the system remains online; this is a useful feature in communication or control applications where it is inconvenient or impossible to halt the target system.

Choosing the optimum site for a process can be difficult if it interacts with a number of other modules, or if

the patterns of process interaction can vary over time[33], so some systems attempt more dynamic partitioning and may relocate software modules during program execution to reflect their usage[34]. However, little is known about the relationship between local load scheduling and resource allocation policies and the global system performance.

Data representation

Because of the disjoint nature of process address spaces on a distributed system, the use of physical addresses in communications is meaningless. The components of messages or parameters to remote procedure calls must consist of data values; reference or pointer types are not permitted and optimizations such as only passing references to large data structures are not available. Any parameters passed in a communication must be explicit, and any returned information must be explicitly passed back.

The problems are compounded in heterogeneous systems in which the various processors use different internal representations of data types. Differences may occur in the machine's word lengths, representations of real numbers, character sets or the ordering of bytes in character strings. At a higher level, compilers on different machines may use incompatible representations of data structures such as records or arrays.

One solution to this problem is to translate all messages into a standard representation before transmission and then back to the local representation on receipt[35].

Where translations are required, a connection-oriented communications protocol may be an advantage so that the particulars of the translation need only be determined once, when the connection is established. This is particularly useful in large open networks such as Darpanet where the required translations are determined by a process of negotiation between the sites involved[36]. More generally, these functions are provided by level 6, the presentation layer, in the ISO open systems interconnect (OSI) model[37].

Name allocation

The system must provide a naming scheme or 'name space' to allow program components such as processes or resources to refer to each other or interact using unique names. A uniprocessor implementation allows names to be intimately associated with physical memory addresses and name resolution of static objects within a single program may be performed by the linkage editor. Interconnecting more dynamic objects, such as files, requires the support of the operating system which needs to maintain suitable tables to map names to physical addresses.

These schemes may be extended to a distributed system by giving each processor a unique name which is incorporated into the name of all objects resident at the processor. This allows a simple strategy for routing communications to their destinations to be used which may be implemented by the lower-level communication protocols.

The above solution is not suitable in a more dynamic environment in which objects may be relocated; in this case location independent names must be used. DCS (distributed computer system)[38] is an early example of a system that tackled the problem directly. This was a loop system which had 'interface units' between the loop and each processor. Each interface unit contained an associative memory with the names of the processes resident at the processor that it served. This combined fast message handling with processor independent names, and allowed processes to migrate to another processor without informing the processes with which the process communicated. The same strategy may also be applied on a bus architecture since the destinations of all messages are examined at every site. Location independent names may be supported on a general network by maintaining directory information for every object at each site[39]. However, this is expensive and difficult to recover in the event of a system failure.

The problem of generating unique names is often solved by incorporating the identity of the generating node and the time of generation into the name[40]; these may be used as location independent provided that the routing protocols treat them as such. Systems oriented to high reliability and security often employ large name spaces of 64 bit. This is much larger than the number of objects likely to need naming during the life of the system, giving two advantages.

- Names are never reused so cases of mistaken access cannot occur.
- Random allocation of names from the name space greatly reduces the chance of generating a valid name by either erroneously or maliciously corrupting a valid name.

Failure control

Distributed systems have more complex failure modes in terms of hardware and software because of the possibilities of partial system failure or because of the introduction of errors by the communications system. The failure of the central processor is usually sudden and catastrophic for a uniprocessor system, allowing no possibility of recovery or adaptation. The failure of a processor in a distributed system is not catastrophic and may not even effect some subsystems. Some systems attempt error recovery and continued operation in a degraded mode which requires much additional programming.

Recovery is usually implemented by periodically recording the status of the system (checkpointing) and then restarting from this known configuration after an error (rolling back). The technique is more difficult to apply in distributed systems due to the infeasibility of checkpointing the entire system simultaneously[41]. Restoration involves rolling back all sites until a consistent state is reached; this may provoke a 'domino effect'[42] which can be limited by synchronizing checkpointing with communication.

Various structuring techniques have been proposed to aid recovery of distributed systems[43, 44, 45]. These schemes are predicated upon the existence of 'stable storage'[46], a nonvolatile, redundant storage system which allows information to survive a system failure, and 'atomic actions' which transform the system from one consistent state to another[47]. These techniques have now been embedded into the experimental language ARGUS[48],

which is oriented towards distributed database operations. These techniques attempt to recover the functioning of a system after transient failure or in systems with redundant standby components. Recovery by reconfiguration of surviving components currently requires ad hoc solutions to be implemented for the predictable failure modes.

The logger in a distributed system would map simply onto a multiple-processor architecture. The underlying hardware configuration is liable to constrain the input and output processes to be resident at particular processors. However, the calculation process could coreside with either process, could use a third processor or could be dynamically relocatable within the system. The optimum placement depends on the detailed balance of the processing requirement against the reduction in communications overheads. These calculations must allow for the various format transformations in heterogeneous systems. The complexities of partitioning such a simple system indicate the scale of problems that may be encountered with multiple processes interacting in complex and varying patterns. The problems become further compounded if redundancy or reconfiguration is to be included, which emphasizes the need for a process independent name space.

For distributed systems the distinction between the three software methodologies becomes even more problematic since they must all be mapped onto underlying communications software based on messages. Message-based software will therefore be considered first, although a variety of implementation techniques for other structures can be distinguished.

Implementing message methodologies

In an earlier section five significant aspects of message implementations were discussed with reference to uniprocessor implementations. These were the form of the data within a message, the patterns of communications supported, details of the naming conventions, the possible selection criteria for receipt, and synchronization constraints. These aspects may be restricted by the underlying communications architecture. The restrictions on the form of messages and problems of process names were discussed in the previous section.

Both one-to-one and N-to-one patterns of communication may be supported on any underlying architecture. The connection-oriented approach would be more effective if dialogues between processes may involve several messages or if large messages need to be transmitted in sections.

The implementation of a one-to-N or broadcast mechanism requires the use of a bus or ring system using a connectionless protocol that provides 'wild card' addresses that are recognized by every site.

Given the successful delivery of a message to a process, the distributed nature of the hardware architecture does not impose any additional constraints on message acceptance in an asynchronous message facility. However, it is more difficult to implement in a synchronous message methodology. The extensive communications protocols and the resulting propagation delays between processes on any form of network mean that asynchronous message methodologies are more appropriate than synchronous ones. The close synchronization of processes required in CSP, and in related languages such as OCCAM[49], is predicated on the more direct connections found in multiprocessors or networks of transputers[50] rather than in general networks. The implementation of communication commands in the guard of a guarded command can be problematic since it requires the negotiated agreement of both parties as to when to proceed. This means that a simple message exchange at the program level leads to a multimessage dialogue at the time of execution. The problem is exacerbated if both input and output commands may appear in guards, since neither party to a communication will commit itself to wait indefinitely for the other and very complex protocols are required[51].

As noted above, the logger maps very simply onto an asynchronous message methodology, which in turn maps simply onto a small multiple-processor architecture. An asynchronous message implementation automatically provides any buffering or demon processes needed to move messages around so that the implementation of the logger is trivially simple.

Using a synchronous message methodology necessitates the introduction of buffer processes. These can be allocated their own processors, but it may be more efficient for them to reside on the same processor as their producer process and effectively implement an asynchronous message facility.

Implementing distributed monitors

Monitors may be implemented on distributed hardware in three ways.

- A single copy of the monitor migrates around the sites and is accessed locally. Verjus[52] proposed that the monitor should circulate around a virtual ring of sites; however, this may lead to unfair scheduling and starvation of individual sites. Fairer scheduling may be implemented if the monitor migrates on demand and access requests are queued by the underlying support software[34, 39].
- Several copies of a monitor exist which are resynchronized or resolved occasionally[52]. This approach depends on the possibility of partitioning the monitor variables in some way and developing stringent controls over the behaviour of the variables within each partition such that overall consistency is always maintained. Similar techniques are also employed in distributed databases, which are reviewed by Kohler[53].
- A single copy of the monitor always resides at one site and is accessed by remote procedure calls. The implementation of a monitor system in this manner is indistinguishable from the implementation of an operation-oriented system.

Each of these methods is dependent on some form of message facility to provide the transport of either monitor data, synchronization and update messages, or procedure parameters and results. Although the first two methods may be used on most network architectures they are most efficiently implemented on those supporting a broadcast mechanism.

The logger may be implemented using each of these mechanisms. Using migrating monitors it may be viable for the calculation and output processes of the logger to reside on different processors and for the data to be moved by underlying monitor access mechanisms. Whichever scheduling mechanism is used, moving monitors between sites is bound to be a time-consuming operation which may be too slow to meet the input process timing constraints. The input and calculation processes may therefore be constrained to reside at the same processor. An alternative is to have a pool of buffer monitors that circulate between the two processes which may then reside on separate processors. Unfortunately this is contrary to the monitor philosophy of encapsulating logically connected items.

The second implementation technique, of maintaining several copies of the same monitor, is more consistent with the overall philosophy of logical encapsulation. The buffer area of the monitor may be partitioned between the producer and consumer process according to whether it is in use or not. The index variables ('nextin' and 'nextout' in Figure 2) may then be constrained to reference only one partition. When the copies of the monitor are resynchronized the new input data will be passed to the copy of the monitor local to the consumer process. At the same time the constraints on the index variables may be adjusted to reflect the current buffer usage. The drawback of this approach is the complexity of the resynchronization protocol and the difficulty of finding general methods of partitioning the variables.

The final alternative, that of using remote procedure calls to access the monitor, is covered in more detail below. The buffer monitor should be located locally to the producer process since local procedure access is faster than remote procedure access.

Implementing remote operations

An advantage of operation-oriented systems is that the semantics of calling an operation may be very similar to calling a procedure; this simplifies the transition to a distributed environment for nonspecialist programmers. The significant difference between a local procedure call and a remote operation is that the execution of the operation is performed in the remote process environment. There may be a single remote process environment within which every call is evaluated (as in ADA), or an anonymous local process may be created, or allocated from a pool, and assigned to each remote request as in DP. The caller sends the request and awaits the reply; the implementation determines whether the operation is local to the processor or requires transmission over the communications network.

The implementation of remote operations may use either connection-oriented (virtual circuit) or connection-less (datagram) transport service and is generally unconstrained by the services provided. A connection-oriented approach provides a very reliable service but it is very expensive for the small amount of data involved. RPC mechanisms have built upon standard connectionless protocols, but error control mechanisms need to be integrated into the service to compensate for the poorer quality of transport service[54]. Reliable operations are usually implemented by allocating a unique name to each invocation of a remote operation or transaction; the client process periodically sends repeated requests using the same name until an acknowledgement is received. The server process keeps track of the names of the transactions it executes and ignores any duplicated requests.

Even connectionless protocols involve a substantial overhead and recently systems have recognized that RPCs are a special mode of communication significantly different from the usual 'byte-stream' communications[40, 55]. The use of integrated RPC transport services can reduce the communications delays by two orders of magnitude. However, even using high-speed links such as Ethernet, the communication delays are a significant overhead and remote operations remain two orders of magnitude slower when performed on separate machines.

SUMMARY AND DISCUSSION

The aim of this paper has been to introduce the major practical themes which have developed in programming distributed systems. Attempting to cover so large an area has necessitated some simplification and the omission of minor detail. The important topics of timing constraints, scheduling and performance evaluation have generally been omitted in this discussion.

The implementation of dynamic general-purpose distributed programs is still a poorly developed subject. Progress is being made in the distributed implementation of specific application areas which is leading to a better understanding of the general techniques. However, further work on alternative techniques needs to be carried out.

Although distributed systems have been discussed for many years now, practical systems still tend to be of limited size and fixed configuration. The full benefits of distributed systems will only be felt after the automation of scheduling, partitioning and failure control is acheived. Progress in the field of distributed systems would now benefit from a greater emphasis on the latter aspects and on their hardware support. These aspects have tended to be neglected in comparison to the lower-level communications aspects.

Current communications architectures provide fairly static configurations, and current research tends to be concentrating on improving reliability and bandwidth. The static model is quite suitable for implementing asynchronous message facilities and simple communications-level RPC mechanisms. However, it is not so suited to the current thrusts of language development. Current communications architectures are not suited to either synchronous message systems (the direction being taken by the CSP family of languages) or to the conditional communication implicit in guarded commands and ADA's rendezvous. Implementing distributed programs is a very large problem and researchers tend to work either from the top down (i.e. through language development) or from the bottom up (from communications protocols). Unfortunately the approaches seem to be targetted on different goals at present. Some agreement on common goals needs to be established to link the concurrent lines of research.

REFERENCES

1 **Chambers, F B, Duce, D A and Jones, G P** *Distributed computing* Academic Press, London, UK (1984)

2 **Bochman, G V** *Concepts for distributed systems design* Springer-Verlag, Berlin, FRG (1983)

3 **Treleaven, P C, Brownbridge, D R and Hopkins, R P** 'Data driven and demand driven computer architectures' *Comput. Surv.* Vol 14 No 1 (March 1982) pp 93-143

4 **McQuillian, J M and Walden, D C** 'The ARPA network design decisions' *Computing Networks* Vol 1 (August 1977)

5 **Wilkes, M R and Needham, R M** 'The Cambridge model distributed system' *Operat. Syst. Rev.* Vol 14 No 21 (1980)

6 *Token ring access method and physical layer specification: IEEE standard 802.5* IEEE, New York, USA (December 1984)

7 **Metcalf, R M and Boggs, D R** 'Ethernet — distributed packet switching for local computer networks' *Commun. ACM* Vol 19 No 7 (July 1976) pp 395-404

8 **Tanenbaum, A S** *Computer networks* Prentice-Hall, Englewood Cliffs, NJ, USA (1981)

9 **Andrews, G R and Schneider, F B** 'Concepts and notations for concurrent programming' *Comput. Surv.* Vol 15 No 1 (March 1983) pp 3-43

10 **Dijkstra, E W** 'Cooperating sequential processes' in **Genuys, F** (Ed.) *Programming languages* Academic Press, New York, USA (1968)

11 **Lauer, H C and Needham, R M** 'On the duality of operating system structures' reprinted in *Operat. Syst. Rev.* Vol 13 No 2 (April 1979) pp 3-19

12 **Brinch Hansen, P** *Operating systems principles* Prentice Hall, Englewood Cliffs, NJ, USA (1973)

13 **Hoare, C A R** 'Monitors: an operating system structuring concept' *Commun. ACM* Vol 17 No 10 (October 1974) pp 549-557

14 **Brinch Hansen, P** 'The programming language Concurrent Pascal' *IEEE Trans. Software Eng.* Vol SE-1 No 2 (June 1975) pp 199-206

15 **Wirth, N** 'Modula: a language for modular multi-programming' *Software Pract. Exper.* Vol 7 (1977) pp 3-35

16 **Lampson, B W and Redell, D D** 'Experience with processes and monitors in Mesa' *Commun. ACM* Vol 23 No 2 (February 1980) pp 105-117

17 **Kessels, J L W** 'An alternative to event queues for synchronization in monitors' *Commun. ACM* Vol 20 No 7 (July 1977) pp 500-503

18 **Hoare, C A R** 'Communicating sequential processes' *Commun. ACM* Vol 21 No 8 (August 1978) pp 666-677

19 **Feldman, J A** 'High level programming for distributed computing' *Commun. ACM* Vol 22 No 6 (June 1979) pp 353-368

20 **Balzer, R M** 'Ports — a method for dynamic inter-program communication and job control' *Proc. AFIPS Spring Joint Comput. Conf.* Vol 38 (1981)

21 **Dijkstra, E W** 'Guarded commands, nondeterminancy and formal derivation of programs' *Commun. ACM* Vol 18 No 8 (August 1975) pp 453-457

22 **Carpenter, B E and Cailliau, R** 'Experience with remote procedure calls in a real time system' *Software Pract. Exper.* Vol. 14 No 9 (September 1984) pp 901-907

23 **Brinch Hansen, P** 'Distributed processes: a concurrent programming concept' *Commun. ACM* Vol 21 No 11 (November 1978) pp 934-941

24 **Ichbiah, J P et al.,** 'Preliminary ADA reference manual' *Sigplan Notices* Vol 14 No 6 Part A (June 1979)

25 **Bate, G** 'Mascot 3: an informal introduction tutorial' *Software Eng. J.* Vol 1 No 3 (May 1986) pp 95–102

26 **Theuretzbacher, N** 'HCDM: a hierarchical design method for chill based systems' *Proc. IFAC Symp. Software Comput. Control* Pergamon, Oxford, UK (1986)

27 **Cook, R** '*mod — a language for distributed programming' *IEEE Trans. Software Eng.* Vol SE-6 No 6 (November 1980) pp 563–571

28 **Stammers, R A** 'ADA on distributed hardware' in **Reijns, G L and Dagless, E L** (Eds) *Concurrent languages in distributed systems* Elsevier, Amsterdam, The Netherlands (1985)

29 **Downes, V A and Goldsack, S J** 'The use of the ADA language for programming a distributed system' in **Hasse, V H** (Ed.) *Real time programming* Pergamon, Oxford, UK (1980)

30 **Jessop, W H** 'ADA packages and distributed systems' *Sigplan Notices* Vol 17 No 2 (February 1982) pp 28–36

31 **Halsall, F, Grimsdale, R L, Shoja, G C and Lambert, J E** 'Development environment for the design and test of applications software for a distributed multiprocessor computer system' *IEE Proc. E* Vol 103 No 1 (January 1983) pp 25–31

32 **Kramer, J, Magee, J, Sloman, M and Lister, A** 'Conic: an integrated approach to distributed computer control systems' *IEE Proc. E* Vol 130 No 1 (January 1983) pp 1–10

33 **Bokhari, S H** 'Dual processor scheduling with dynamic reassignment' *IEEE Trans. Software Eng.* Vol SE5 No 4 (July 1979) pp 341–349

34 **Casey, L M** 'Computer structures for distributed systems' *PhD Thesis* Edinburgh University, UK (1977)

35 **White, J E** 'Elements of a distributed programming system' *Comput. Lang.* Vol 2 (1977) pp 117–134

36 **Cohen, D** *Specifications for the network voice protocol* Information Science Institute of Southern California, Los Angeles, CA, USA (March 1976)

37 **Zimmerman, H** 'OSI reference model: the ISO model of architecture for open systems interconnection' *IEEE Trans. Commun.* Vol COM-28 (April 1980) pp 425–432

38 **Farber, D J and Larson, K C** 'The system architecture of the distributed computer system — the communication system' *Proc. Symp. Comput. Commun. Network and Teletraffic* (1972) pp 21–27

39 **Whiddett, R J** 'Dynamic distributed systems' *Software Pract. Exper.* Vol 13 (1983) pp 355–371

40 **Birrell, A D and Nelson, B J** 'Implementing remote procedure calls' *ACM Trans. Comput. Syst.* Vol 2 No 1 (February 1984) pp 39–59

41 **Lamport, L** 'Time, clocks and the ordering of events in a distributed system' *Commun. ACM* Vol 21 No 7 (July 1978) pp 558–565

42 **Russell, D L** 'State restoration in systems of communicating processes' *IEEE Trans. Software Eng.* Vol SE-6 No 2 (March 1980) pp 193–194

43 **Shrivastava, S K** 'Structuring distributed systems for recovery and crash resistance' *IEEE Trans. Software Eng.* Vol SE7 No 4 (July 1981) pp 436–447

44 **Strom, R E and Yemini, S** 'Optimistic recovery in distributed systems' *ACM Trans. Comput. Syst.* Vol 3 No 3 (August 1985) pp 204–226

45 **Jefferson, D R** 'Virtual time' *ACM Trans. Prog. Lang. Syst.* Vol 7 No 3 (July 1985) pp 404–425

46 **Needham, R M, Herbert, A J and Mitchell, J B** 'How to connect stable memory to a computer' *Operat. Syst. Rev.* Vol 17 No 1 (January 1983)

47 **Best, E and Randell, B** 'A formal model of atomicity in asynchronous systems' *Acta Informatica* Vol 16 (1981) pp 93–124

48 **Liskov, B and Scheifler, R** 'Guardians and actions: linguistic support for robust distributed programs' *ACM Trans. Prog. Lang. Syst.* Vol 5 No 3 (July 1983) pp 381–404

49 **May, D** 'Occam' *Sigplan Notices* Vol 18 No 4 (April 1983) pp 69–79

50 **May, D and Shepherd, R** 'Occam and the transputer' in **Reijns, G L and Dagless, E L** (Eds) *Concurrent languages in distributed systems* Elsevier, Amsterdam, The Netherlands (1985)

51 **Buckley, G N and Silberschatz, A** 'An effective implementation of the generalized input-output construct in CSP' *ACM Trans. Prog. Lang. Syst.* Vol 5 No 2 (April 1983) pp 223–235

52 **Verjus, J-P** 'Synchronization in distributed systems — an informal introduction' in **Parker, Y and Verjus, J-P** (Eds) *Distributed computer systems* Academic Press, New York, USA (1983)

53 **Kohler, W H** 'A survey of techniques for synchronization and recovery in decentralized computer systems' *Comput. Surv.* Vol 13 No 2 (June 1981) pp 149–184

54 **Ayache, J M** 'Software protocols in Rebus' *Proc. IFAC Symp. Software. Comput. Control, Madrid, Spain* Pergamon, Oxford, UK (1982)

55 **Spector, A** 'Performing remote operations on a local computer network' *Commun. ACM* Vol 25 No 4 (1982) pp 246–260

Dick Whiddet heads the Micro Unit in the Department of Computing, University of Lancaster, UK. After graduating in physics from the University of Bristol, UK, he worked in the field of digital electronics. The advent of microprocessors prompted his return to higher education at the Department of Computing at Lancaster, whence he graduated with an MA and a PhD for work on distributed systems. Prior to his current post he worked for the University of Birmingham, UK, and Cadbury Schweppes. His main areas of research are in the hardware–software relationship and implementation models for distributed systems.

Vision system based on a single-chip microcomputer

Vision sensors which use dynamic RAM are cheaper and easier to interface than their alternatives — videcon or CCD. **Andrew Russell** describes a DRAM-based 'intelligent' vision system in which all interfacing and image processing functions are provided by an 8751 single-chip microcomputer

The paper describes a compact and inexpensive binary vision system in which all interfacing and data processing functions are performed by an Intel 8751 single-chip microcomputer. The vision sensor is a 64 kbit dynamic RAM chip which is capable of providing a picture resolution of up to 256 × 128 pixels. Picture processing algorithms are implemented within the vision system and object statistics are transferred to the host computer over a serial interface. The resulting system is implemented using only four integrated circuits and is eminently suitable for component identification and inspection in a flexible manufacturing system environment.

microsystems   computer vision   DRAM optical sensors   8751

Computer vision systems are being used in increasing numbers for a variety of industrial inspection, part identification and control tasks. Dynamic random-access memory (DRAM) circuits have been developed as binary optical sensors for these applications[1,2]. DRAM-based vision systems are very low in cost and have direct compatibility with digital electronics. These advantages are not shared by the alternative types of system available — 'videcon' or CCD (charge coupled device) vision sensors — which are relatively expensive, were originally designed for compatibility with television displays and therefore do not provide an output which can be readily accessed by a computer. For many inspection and identification tasks the higher resolution of videcon or CCD sensors is not required, and in such applications a DRAM-based system can be a more cost effective solution.

This paper describes an 'intelligent' vision sensor in which all interfacing and image processing functions are performed by an Intel 8751 single-chip microcomputer. The 8751 contains a complete 8-bit microprocessor as well as EPROM, RAM, two timers, a full duplex I/O port

Department of Electrical and Computer Engineering, University of Wollongong, NSW 2500, Australia

and parallel I/O lines[3]. These resources within the 8751 are used to

- directly control the DRAM optical sensor, an IS32 OpticRAM manufactured by Micron Technology Inc.
- perform address 'descramble' and interpolation functions on the data in the DRAM
- either transmit the image to a host computer in compressed form or perform image processing algorithms and transmit the resulting statistics to a host computer.

The 8751-based vision system implemented contains only four integrated circuits including the OpticRAM. The large quantity of interfacing electronics required by similar DRAM vision systems is eliminated. In addition, a truly 'intelligent' sensor is created by incorporating vision processing functions within the 8751.

USING A DRAM AS A VISION SENSOR

A DRAM stores information in an array of memory cells, each consisting of a capacitor and a transistor[4]. Figure 1 shows the memory cell layout. Data is read from or written to a memory cell by the following operations.

- An 8-bit row address is established on the DRAM address lines.

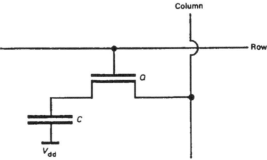

Figure 1.   DRAM single-transistor memory cell

0141-9331/86/09485-05 $03.00 © 1986 Butterworth & Co. (Publishers) Ltd

- Row address strobe ($\overline{RAS}$) is asserted, causing the row address decoder to select one of 256 row lines. The 256 transistors Q connected to the selected row line are 'switched on' and transfer charge from the associated capacitor C to a column line.
- Charge from the memory cell is regeneratively amplified and fed back onto the column lines to re-establish the original charge on the capacitors.
- An 8-bit column address is presented on the DRAM address lines.
- Column address strobe ($\overline{CAS}$) is asserted, initiating the selection of one out of 256 column sense amplifiers and directing its output to the data out (DOUT) pin of the DRAM. If a memory write operation is required data from the data in (DIN) pin would be routed to the selected sense amplifier and hence to the appropriate memory cell.

Charge on the memory cell capacitors tends to leak away. If data is to be retained the charge must be sensed before it has decayed away completely, and restored to its original level. The operation of restoring memory cell charge is called 'refresh' and occurs when a read or write cycle is performed on the same row as the cell. If light is incident on the capacitors their rate of charge decay is increased. Thus if all capacitors are charged and a suitable length of time is allowed to elapse before reading the memory cells it will be found that some of the bits have been corrupted. Those bits which are corrupted will come from capacitors subjected to a higher level of illumination than those which are not corrupted. If the physical layout of the memory cells can be determined it will be possible to locate those areas of the circuit where the light intensity is above a certain threshold and thus to produce a binary image of the incident illumination.

The 65 536 memory cells in the IS32 integrated circuits are grouped into two regions with an area containing sense amplifiers between them. For most applications a large gap in the visual field will be unacceptable; therefore only one of the two groups of cells is used.

CAMERA SYSTEM

A DRAM optical sensor may be interfaced to a microcomputer by direct connection to the processor address bus or indirectly via an I/O port[5]. Connection through an I/O port is slower and requires a more complicated control program. These drawbacks are balanced by a considerable reduction in circuit complexity. The aim of this project was to produce a simple, inexpensive vision system and therefore the DRAM was connected through an I/O port.

A schematic diagram of the camera system is shown in Figure 2. The eight OpticRAM address lines are controlled by port 1 of the 8751. Five additional I/O lines are required from port 3 to provide signals for DIN, $\overline{RAS}$, $\overline{CAS}$, W and to read data from the DOUT line. Thus all functions of the IS32 can be software controlled through ports 1 and 3 of the 8751. Instructions are received from and data transmitted to a host computer via the asynchronous serial interface. Received data line RXD and transmitted data line TXD are interfaced to RS232 voltage levels by line receiver and line driver chips. In addition, four lines from port 2 are used to read a DIL switch which sets baud rate, parity and stop bits for serial communications.

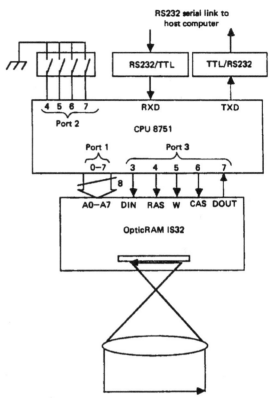

Figure 2. Computer vision system

This circuit demonstrates the capability of the Intel 8751 to implement complex control functions with a minimum of additional components.

CONTROLLING THE IS32 IN SOFTWARE

Memory refresh

This process restores the charge level on memory cell capacitors and is only stopped during image acquisition to make the memory cells sensitive to light. Timing for the refresh operation is controlled by one of the 8751's internal 16-bit counters. Counter 0 is programmed to generate an interrupt every 1.3 ms. The timer interrupt service routine performs a RAS-only refresh cycle on the 128 rows used to form the image. The service routine then restarts the timer and performs a return from interrupt. A large portion of the available processing time is used by the refresh operation and therefore efficient coding of this part of the program is essential. The program loop which performs the refresh cycle is

```
LOOP: CLR RAS
      SETB RAS
      DEC P1
      DJNZ P1, LOOP
```

Each 8751 I/O port is bit addressable using a powerful set of Boolean instructions. The CLR and SETB instructions provide a low-going pulse on the output line connected to $\overline{RAS}$. These two instructions both execute in one instruction cycle time. Other Boolean instructions are available which provide further logical and test capabilities.

Arithmetic and logical operations can be performed on the last value written to an I/O port. Both the DEC and DJNZ instructions operate directly on data stored in the I/O port to decrement the row address by 2. Memory cells in the half of the IS32 that is being used all have even row addresses. An additional function of the DJNZ instruction is to control the number of iterations of the program loop. A branch back to LOOP occurs if the result of the decrement is nonzero. The whole refresh operation takes approximately 0.7 ms representing 35% of the total computer processing time.

Acquiring an image

Recording an image involves writing 1s to the memory cells and then stopping the refresh process for a measured amount of time to allow memory cells illuminated above a certain threshold to discharge. The sequence of events is

(1) write to 1's to the memory cells
(2) inhibit interrupts
(3) perform a timing loop to measure the required exposure time
(4) re-enable interrupts.

The memory cells now contain a binary representation of the incident light image.

Reading and writing

Subroutines were written to transfer data between the 8751 and OpticRAM. These subroutines control the output of 8751 ports 1 and 3 to perform read cycles and write cycles on the DRAM. Once again Boolean bit set and clear instructions are used except in those cases where more than one output line is required to change state simultaneously. In these cases it is quicker to write a byte of data to the I/O port.

DESCRAMBLE AND INTERPOLATION OF THE IMAGE

The IS32 is a development of the µT4264 64 kbit DRAM. For this reason positioning of memory cells on the silicon chip surface was presumably governed by considerations of convenient and efficient layout. The memory cells are not positioned physically on the chip in the same order as they are addressed electrically. To overcome this problem a look-up table was used to convert physical addresses into electrical addresses. The 8751 provides a move constant (MOVC) instruction which allows indexed addressing into program memory using either the program counter or a 16-bit data pointer register (DPTR) as 'base' value. Thus, to index into a table of row addresses having a base address equal to ROW__TABLE the following instructions are used:

```
MOV    DPTR,#ROW__TABLE
MOVC   A,@A + DPTR
```

Accumulator A contains the physical DRAM row address required before the instructions are executed. The MOV instruction loads DPTR with the row table base address. MOVC causes A to be loaded with the contents of the program store location whose address is equal to the contents of DPTR added to the old contents of A. The correspondence between physical and electrical memory cell addresses is given in the IS32 data sheet[6]. Figure 3 shows how the DRAM cells are positioned on the chip. A regular array of light-sensitive elements with equal separation in both row and column directions is required. To achieve this requirement the pixels circled in Figure 3 were selected. However, half of the circles do not coincide with a memory cell. In these cases a majority 'vote' of the three adjacent memory cells is used to determine the pixel value. For example, the value of the absent pixel at point X in Figure 3 is taken to be the majority vote of pixels (R2, C1), (R2, C2) and (R4, C1). This addressing scheme was implemented in the 8751 and gives an image having 64 rows and 256 columns with approximately equal row and column spacing. It would be possible to extend the interpolation method to fill in all gaps in the memory cell array and thus provide a 128 × 512 pixel image.

Processing the image data

The vision system must be able to transmit a complete image to a host computer. This function allows an image to be displayed, helping the operator make adjustments to lens focus and camera orientation. The host computer could also apply more sophisticated processing techniques to the image or provide a means of storing the images. Two image transfer functions have been implemented. The first transmits the image as 8-bit sections compatible with the graphics display of an Acorn BBC microcomputer. An alternative, more compact method of

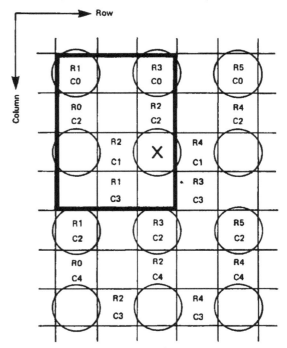

Figure 3. Physical placement of memory cells

transmitting a complete image employs run length coding. This involves counting the number of successive pixels which have the same colour (black or white) and transmitting the accumulated count when a colour change occurs. Run length coding is a very efficient way of transmitting binary pictures which have few transitions between black and white.

To provide object location and identification capabilities picture processing algorithms have been implemented within the 8751. Statistics are accumulated which allow a host computer to calculate area, perimeter, centre of area and the axis of minimum moment of inertia of an object appearing in the image. Details of the binary image processing techniques employed in this vision system appear in References 7 and 8; a brief outline is presented here.

A simple method of ensuring a well defined silhouette image of an object is to provide strong diffuse back lighting which produces a black image of the object against a white background. The vision system acquires an image of the object as described previously and then the following operations are performed.

The picture is first scanned line by line, starting at the top left-hand corner, until the first black pixel is found. The location of this pixel is recorded as (I0, J0) and the statistics I and J are initialized as

$$I = I0 - 0.5$$
$$J = J0 - 0.5$$

The program then steps round the boundary of the object in a clockwise direction. After each step statistics I, J, and P1–P3 are updated as follows.

● If the step was to the right

$$I = I + 1$$
$$P3 = P3 - J^2$$

● If the step was upwards

$$J = J - 1$$
$$P1 = P1 - I$$
$$P2 = P2 - I^2$$

● If the step was to the left

$$I = I - 1$$
$$P3 = P3 + J^2$$

● If the step was down

$$J = J + 1$$
$$P1 = P1 + I$$
$$P2 = P2 + I^2$$

A record of the number of steps taken is maintained to provide an estimate of the object perimeter. This process is repeated until the program has stepped all the way round the object boundary. The scanning and stepping operations are illustrated in Figure 4.

Accumulated statistics are then transmitted to the host computer where they can be used to calculate the parameters

$$Area = P1$$

$$I \text{ coordinate of centre of area} = \frac{P2}{2 * P1}$$

$$J \text{ coordinate of centre of area} = \frac{P3}{2 * P1}$$

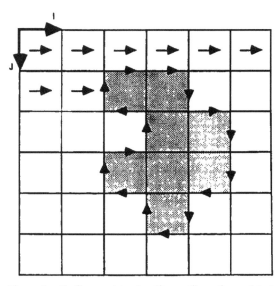

Figure 4. Finding and tracing the outline of an object silhouette

For the sake of brevity the equations for calculating P4–P7 and hence the axis of minimum moment of inertia have been omitted. These equations and other details of the picture processing techniques are given in References 7 and 8.

The 8751 contains a full duplex asynchronous serial interface. Using a system clock of 11 MHz the interface is run at a maximum of 9600 baud (faster if nonstandard baud rates can be accommodated). During the initialization process, which takes place after a system reset, four switches are read via port 2. These switches are used to set the baud rate, parity and stop bits for the serial interface.

EXPERIMENTAL RESULTS

Well defined binary images were recorded by the vision system and transferred to a BBC microcomputer for display. Figure 5 shows an example image. Using a serial transmission speed of 9600 baud, image transfer takes less then 3.5 s for a 64 × 256 image. In addition, the system can calculate and transmit the object statistics of a picture containing one object in under 3 s.

CONCLUSIONS

This paper has described a binary vision system which uses a DRAM as vision sensor. Control of the DRAM,

Figure 5. An image of some small electronic components

processing of the images and communications with a host computer are all functions performed by an Intel 8751 microcomputer. The resulting system is implemented using only four integrated circuits. For many applications the entire circuit can be mounted in the camera head thus producing a truly 'intelligent' sensor which requires only four connecting wires to provide power and a serial communication link.

ACKNOWLEDGEMENT

The work reported here was supported by the Research Grant Committee of the University of Wollongong under grant 03/103/401, 'The automation of batch assembly'.

REFERENCES

1   **Ciarcia, S** 'Build the Micro D-Cam solid-state video camera. Part 1: the optic RAM and the Micro D-Cam hardware' *Byte* Vol 8 No 9 (September 1983)
2   **Ciarcia, S** 'Build the Micro D-Cam solid-state video camera. Part 2: computer interfaces and control software' *Byte* Vol 8 No 10 (October 1983)
3   *MCS-51 family of single-chip microcomputer user's manual* Intel, Santa Clara, CA, USA (July 1981)
4   *Memory data book and designer's guide* Mostek (June 1980)
5   **Russell, R A** 'Computer vision system for applications in robotics education' *Microprocessors Microsyst.* Vol 7 No 7 (September 1983)
6   *IS32 OpticRAM data sheet* Micron Technology
7   **Cunningham, R** 'Segmenting binary images' *Robotics Age* Vol 3 No 4 (July/August 1981)
8   **Wilf, J M** 'Chain-code' *Robotics Age* Vol 3 No 2 (March/April 1981)

Andrew Russell received his BEng and PhD degrees in 1972 and 1976 respectively from the University of Liverpool, UK. He is currently a lecturer in the Department of Electrical and Computer Engineering at Wollongong University, Australia. His research interests include the application of sensory feedback in robotics, VLSI design and alternative energy sources.

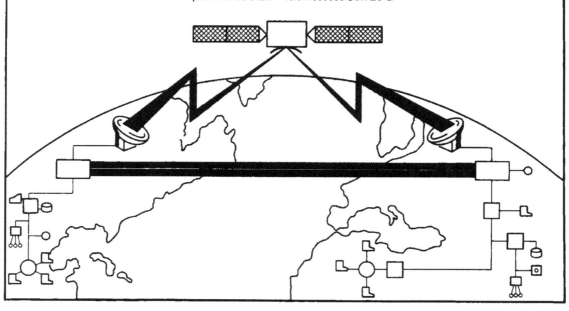

Embedded microprocessor software: case study of an automatic computer exchange

Multitasking, realtime debugging and I/O methods are among the embedded software development techniques used by **Franco Civello** in constructing a system to control an automatic computer exchange. Here he discusses the principles and practice of such a system

A computer exchange control system has been designed to fulfil the specific requirements of the Brighton Polytechnic Computer Centre. This project raised various software issues that are common to a wide range of embedded applications. Some of these issues are reviewed in the paper, in particular the creation of a multitasking environment, I/O methods, timing and synchronization, debugging and bootstrapping. Before the software aspects are examined, the application and system structure are described in some detail. The role and function of the embedded microprocessor system and its interactions with the rest of the system are discussed.

embedded systems   control   multitasking   debugging network switching

A private automatic computer exchange (PACX), manufactured by Gandalf, is used at the Computer Centre at Brighton Polytechnic to allow terminal users to select one of the computing services provided by the Centre. These include various minicomputer systems, lines to the public switched telephone network and some dedicated lines connected to external networks and sites.

The original PACX is shown in Figure 1. It comprises two units, viz.

● a switching unit (SU) which is effectively a time-division multiplexer between terminal lines and computer lines (ports). The main part of the SU is a microprogrammed unit that maintains a memory array in which the active connections between terminals and ports are represented. The clock-driven cycle of operation consists of scanning the array and, for each active connection found in the array, opening the corresponding multi-

plexer gates for a minimum time interval. The logic levels present on the lines are then latched for the rest of the cycle

● a microprocessor system that controls the SU through a serial port, causing connections and disconnections between terminals and ports and allowing the terminal user to select a service by typing a numeric service code. The microprogram in the SU acknowledges these commands by updating the contents of its memory array

When a terminal user presses the BREAK key, the SU automatically connects his/her terminal to one of a fixed set of ports, which are hardwired into the control micro (Figure 1). The control program can therefore read the service code typed at the user terminal, search its RAM database for a free port matching the user request and, if one is found, command the SU to drop the current connection for the terminal user and connect it to the port found. The serial line labelled 'statistics' in Figure 1 is used by the SU to send out a message to the controller for each new connection or disconnection. The controller can also request the SU to output the current status of any port or terminal.

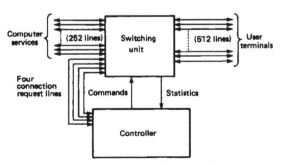

Figure 1.   Structure of the original PACX exchange

Computing and Cybernetics Department, Brighton Polytechnic, Moulsecoomb, Brighton BN2 4GJ, UK

AIMS OF THE PROJECT

Having used PACX for some years, the Computer Centre identified several areas that needed enhancement. The enhancements needed were

- an improved user interface that would replace service codes with names and perform a basic form of dialogue to allow users to see the available services and correct typing mistakes
- speed sensing of the terminal baud rate, to avoid connecting a terminal and a computer port working at different speeds
- the option for the user to queue up for connection to a full service
- restricted access to some sensitive services
- a reservation system to allow certain terminal pools used for timetabled student classes to have priority access to a service during the scheduled period
- an autodialling facility to allow authorized users to access external sites by providing the telephone number they wish to be dialled
- a facility for keeping a permanent record of terminal and port usage, to collect statistics of interest to the Centre management
- a VDU console to allow the operations staff to monitor and control the operation of the exchange; this would replace the unfriendly and restrictive control panel provided by the old system

Although the manufacturers of PACX were already marketing a new version with more extensive control functions, the Centre decided to produce a customized version of the controller to fulfil the precise requirements that had been identified. The new system became operational 18 months later; the manpower involved in its development was approximately two man years.

STRUCTURE OF THE NEW SYSTEM

Figure 2 illustrates the hardware organization of the new system. The control microcomputer of the old system has been replaced by a more complex structure consisting of

- a microprocessor system that replaces and enhances the old controller; this has a Motorola 6809 with RAM

(56k), ROM (8k), a programmable timer and several serial and parallel interfaces linking it to the rest of the system (Table 1 shows the subset of the 6809 programming model[1] relevant to this paper)
- eight speed sensing microprocessors with the sole function of relieving the controller from the task of identifying terminal baud rates; these are Motorola 6800 micros with 4 kbyte of ROM and a small amount of RAM
- a microprocessor system with a disc unit attached to it, running the Flex operating system; this provides permanent memory for the programs and the database that describes the configuration of the exchange
- an autodialling unit; this is a microprocessor-based system that uses four autodialling modems to connect requesting users to external sites.

Motorola hardware was adopted because a development system for 6800 and 6809 micros was already in use in the Centre and staff expertise in building and programming such systems was readily available.

The structure of the system was derived from its functional requirements and some pragmatic considerations. As the control of the exchange required access to a complex and integrated structure of tables, all the activities in this area were localized on a single micro (the controller). A baud rate detecting 6800-based microcomputer had already been designed, built and programmed by the Centre. This and the CPU-intensive nature of speed detection (done via software delay loops), led to the adoption of a separate speed sensing micro on each connection request line. The autodialling function was also moved to a separate system that controlled the dialling equipment, but communication with the controller was required for user authorization and connection.

Finally, a second processor for disc storage was introduced to leave the disc and file handling software out of the main controller, which needed to dedicate all its processing power to the control of the exchange. With no special realtime requirements imposed on it, the disc processor could also run the single-user disc operating system Flex which was also used on the development system, making software installation a simple matter of moving discs across to the disc processor.

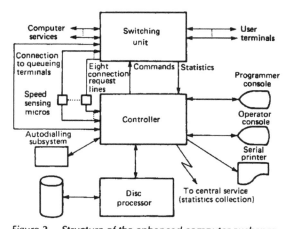

Figure 2. Structure of the enhanced computer exchange

Table 1. 6809 programming model

Registers	PC (16-bit program counter)
	A (8-bit accumulator)
	B (8-bit accumulator)
	D (16-bit accumulator, A/B)
	X, Y (16-bit index registers)
	U (16-bit user stack pointer)
	S (16-bit hardware stack pointer)
	CC (8-bit condition code register including IRQ mask bit)
Interrupts	All interrupts vectored via high-memory table
	All registers stacked on interrupt
Interrupt request pin	IRQ, maskable (sets IRQ mask bit)
Software interrupts	SWI (sets IRQ mask bit)
	SWI2, SWI3 (do not set IRQ mask bit)

CENTRAL CONTROLLER

All the software running on the controller was designed and implemented in house using assembly language. The controller maintains a database in its volatile memory to model the current status of the SU. Some of the information is of a permanent nature (the association between computer ports and service names, for example) and a permanent copy of it is kept on the disc unit for bootstrapping.

The database is central to the operation of the controller; it is used for a variety of purposes, such as finding free ports for terminal connection, keeping track of which terminals are queueing for which services and holding information on reserved services. Internally, the database is structured as a collection of tables, one for each type of object being modelled. Each table consists of an array of records, each describing a single object. A port table, for example, contains one record for each computer port attached to the PACX (Figure 3). Relationships between objects are represented by pointers between records in a network-like database structure[2]. Sets of entities included in an instance of a relationship are represented by chains of pointers from the 'owner' of the set to all the 'member' records. This technique is used, for example, to link each 'service' record to all the physical ports linked to the computer providing the service (Figure 4).

MULTITASKING ENVIRONMENT

The software running on the controller has to perform many functions, some conceptually simple, others involving complex algorithms and data structures. Close examination of the controller's functions reveals that many separate activities can be identified, each with a specific, well defined task to accomplish. One such activity is the processing of operator requests to monitor the status of the system; another is the receipt and collection of messages from the SU; yet another is the processing of user requests for connection to a service. At least 15 separate activities were identified at the design stage. This is typical of any embedded system that has to deal with a complex external system; in fact each separate activity is

Port identifier	Pointer to service record	Pointer to next port in service set	Pointer to current reservation record	Pointer to next port in reservation set

Baud rate	Time of last connection	Total number of connections	Total time connected	Port status	Terminal identifier (if connected)

Figure 3. Fields in each computer port record

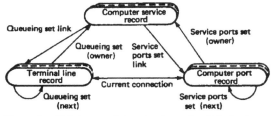

Figure 4. Database pointer structures (partial view)

often associated with each of the interfaces or ports by which the embedded micro communicates with the enclosing system.

The design of such software is best tackled using a modular approach in which each function is designed and coded as a separate program. The control flow of each program is often an endless cycle consisting of

```
loop
    await data from external device
    process data
    output reply
endloop
```

A multitasking executive creates the environment in which such concurrent programs (tasks) can share the resources of a single machine[3].

Multitasking executives are commercially available for most microprocessors[3-5], but a custom-made solution is more likely to fulfil the precise requirements of an application, as an off-the-shelf package is likely to include features that the software designer would not need to make use of and/or omit other facilities that may be important for the specific application. Another advantage of the tailor-made approach is that in-depth knowledge of the software controlling the hardware is achieved, giving better control of the system; this is especially important in the debugging and testing stages of a software project.

The first phase of the software project to enhance the exchange controller was the production of a multitasking executive (MTE) that offered the facilities deemed essential to the application. This section considers the concepts underpinning the design of a multitasking executive and gives a practical illustration by examining the structure and operation of the MTE.

Scheduling function

The main function of a multitasking executive is to share CPU time amongst tasks.

The basic mechanism for switching between tasks is to associate with each task an area of RAM where the volatile environment (context) of the task can be saved when the task gives up the CPU and whence it can be restored when the task is restarted (context switching). The decisions which determine the scheduling policy adopted fall into two categories:

● When should a task release the CPU?
● Which task should be given control next?

These two questions are now considered in relation to the features of the embedded system as a whole.

When a task is running on the CPU, there are two ways to start a context switch: either the task itself voluntarily relinquishes control or an external interrupt forces it to do so. The former usually takes place when the task has to wait for some external event or data to be able to proceed. The relinquishing action is often hidden inside the routines that tasks invoke to input or output data from or to the embedding system. If no data is available, for example, the input routine calls the scheduler to initiate a context switch. In the latter case, it is up to the interrupt servicing routine to invoke the scheduler after processing the interrupt. This approach is called 'task pre-emption' as it implies that tasks may be forced to release the CPU

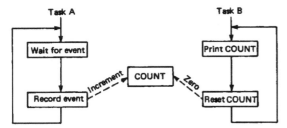

Figure 5. Two tasks accessing a shared variable

unknowingly and at unpredictable moments, due to the asynchronous nature of interrupts.

Task pre-emption requires mechanisms for mutual exclusion of tasks accessing shared resources. Figure 5 illustrates this point. Task A counts events by incrementing a variable COUNT and task B periodically prints the value of COUNT and resets it to zero. Should task B be pre-empted after printing the current value but before zeroing COUNT, task A may increment COUNT before the next activation of B. COUNT will then be zeroed, with the effect of nullifying the last increment and failing to register the last event. Similar but less desirable 'race conditions' may occur in the exchange controller, where several tasks operate concurrently on a shared database. Corruption of data or pointers may occur, leading to data inconsistencies, erroneous behaviour and possibly system failure.

Problems of this nature can be solved by protecting shared data structures with semaphores[6]. Each critical section of code must be enclosed within a 'wait' and 'signal' call to the executive, specifying the name of the semaphore as a parameter. Many semaphores may be required in a system with complex task interactions.

On a system that does not use pre-emption, use of semaphores is not required if tasks never relinquish control while updating a shared data structure. This is feasible on an embedded micro if the application is carefully designed and coded.

Another problem is the question of which task to run next. The activities in an embedded micro have different degrees of urgency, depending on the delay that the external processes or devices can tolerate. Some systems have very stringent realtime requirements in that the delay between an event occurring and the activation of the corresponding task must be within a given threshold above which erroneous or undesirable effects may result. On a system of this type, task pre-emption is mandatory to allow an interrupt routine to cause an immediate switch to the task that is to take action. A mechanism must therefore exist to associate each interrupt with the task to be dispatched when the interrupt occurs.

A further complication arises if interrupts are allowed to occur when a previous interrupt is being serviced. When such nesting of interrupts is allowed, some form of prioritization of activities must be enforced. A hardware solution is found on some 16- and 32-bit microprocessors. Interrupts are divided into classes, and each class is assigned to a priority level. A CPU register holds the current priority level (of the running task) and only interrupts of a higher level are allowed to occur. The most urgent activities can therefore be carried out at high priority levels, to avoid interference by lower-priority interrupts.

Software priorities can also be adopted on any micro by associating a numerical priority with each task and maintaining the list of 'ready to run' tasks in priority order. Priorities can be static, i.e. fixed for each task, or dynamically modifiable. The latter type makes the system more responsive to changing situations, as task priority can be altered at run time. (An interrupt routine could raise the priority of a task to cause its immediate execution).

However, many embedded systems do not have stringent realtime requirements, either because the process under observation or control is much slower in comparison to the processing speed of the CPU, or simply because there are no special safety or cost constraints on the software response time to external events. Such is the case for the SU controller, in which the main consideration of this type is the time that a terminal user has to wait to be connected to a service; this time is many orders of magnitude larger than the processing speed of any micro, and the frequency of requests is also low as users tend to remain connected to the same service for at least one minute.

On this class of system, the 'ready' list can be maintained as a round-robin queue, in which tasks are dispatched when they reach the front of the queue and put at the back when they are removed[6]. Task pre-emption can also be dispensed with, as each task has enough time at its disposal to check whether an event has occurred. The interrupt routine responsible for signalling the event can simply set a flag which the task polls at each activation.

MTE scheduling policy and mechanisms

The scheduling policy used was strongly influenced by Broughton[7]. As hinted above, priorities were not used in the MTE. Tasks are held in a circular list (task table) and are dispatched in strict sequential order. This makes the scheduling algorithm extremely simple and fast. As the functions performed by the controller tasks are not time critical, the worst-case delay between two successive dispatches of the same task does not cause any loss of incoming data or unacceptable response times to events.

Pre-empting of tasks is not allowed under the MTE. Tasks voluntarily relinquish use of the CPU whenever they need further data from external devices or periodically in loops which are not time critical. MTE simply dispatches the next task in the list.

Interrupt handling and task scheduling are therefore separate, noninteracting functions. Interrupt handlers are only concerned with performing I/O operations and returning control to the interrupted task after servicing the interrupt. This method was chosen for two reasons: because it makes the design of the scheduling function much simpler and because semaphores are not required as tasks are never pre-empted while executing a critical section of code. It is up to the task programmer to ensure that tasks do not release the CPU while in a critical section (updating a shared data structure, for example).

Careful programming should guarantee that all tasks receive a fair share of CPU time, but a mechanism exists to avoid tasks holding the CPU for too long. Periodical clock interrupts trigger a 'task watchdog' routine, which checks that the running task has not held the CPU for more than a task dependent number of clock cycles; if the task has exceeded this limit, a message is sent to the system console and the offending task is 'locked', i.e. prevented from using the CPU until 'unlocked' via the console when the cause of the problem has been found and removed.

Task control and states

Tasks can at any moment in time be in one of a set of scheduling states. Figure 6 shows the task states and state transitions under the MTE. A description of each state is given below.

Inactive. This is the initial state of each task, before the first dispatch (activation) by the executive scheduler.

Active. The task is ready to use the CPU or waiting for some event (see state transitions below).

Running. The task is currently using the CPU.

Suspended. The task has suspended itself or another task has requested its suspension. Suspended tasks are not scheduled until another task resumes them.

Locked. The task is suspended and must be restarted from its entry point.

Unlocked. A locked task has been unlocked by another task. Unlocked tasks resume execution from their original entry points; this is called task reactivation. The reason for having this state in addition to the 'inactive' state is that some fields in the task control block (see below) of an inactive task must be converted from relative to absolute addresses, whereas the same fields appear already in absolute form in the task control block of a task that has been locked. The executive therefore treats the transitions from inactive to running (activation) and from unlocked to running (reactivation) in different ways.

State transitions

Transitions between states are originated by a task call to the executive. The only exceptions are the 'activation' and 'reactivation' transitions which are initiated by the executive itself. Tasks call the executive by issuing a software interrupt (SWI2) instruction, followed by a single byte specifying the function requested. Any parameters that may be required by the call are passed via CPU registers. A parameter required by all the task control functions is the numerical identifier of the task to which the function applies; this may be the same task as is issuing the call.

SWI2 is used in preference to SWI as the latter automatically disables interrupts, which is unnecessary because interrupts are allowed to occur and be serviced even when the executive is using the CPU. This is a direct consequence of having separated the scheduling function from the interrupt servicing routines. SWI2 saves the entire machine state on the hardware stack and transfers control to the executive routine called 'task call processor', which examines the function code* of the call and uses a jump table to pass control to the relevant subroutine. The subroutine will service the call and pass control to the task scheduler. This implies that the calling task has to wait a complete cycle through the task table before its next dispatch.

Executive services

The task programmer uses macro calls to invoke the executive services available to tasks.

Pause. The calling task wishes to release the CPU and be made 'active'. As mentioned before, tasks must pause frequently to be fair to the other tasks in the system.

Suspend. A task may suspend itself or another task. The executive checks that the task's current state is 'active' and modifies it to 'suspended'.

Resume. The executive checks that the specified task is indeed suspended before changing its state to 'active'.

Lock. The specified task's state is changed to 'locked'. Locked tasks are ignored by the scheduler.

Input. The calling task is asking to be redispatched only when its input buffer contains a complete transaction. The address of a subroutine that checks the state of the input buffer is inserted in the task control block. The scheduler will call this subroutine to determine if the task is runnable. The checking subroutine could have been called by the task itself, but this method was chosen because it avoids the overhead of frequent context switching when a task is waiting for an external event. This scheme follows Broughton's description[7]. The same mechanism is used to check whether a task is waiting for a flag (Sync) or for a time of day (Delay and Appoint).

Sync. This is a low-level mechanism used for task synchronization. The calling task is dispatched when the specified memory byte becomes non-negative.

Delay. The task pauses and specifies the time interval to its next activation.

Appoint. The task pauses and specifies the time of day of its next activation.

Task representation

Each task makes itself known to the executive by a block of memory that describes the hardware and software context of the task itself. This memory area is called the task control block (TCB) and must be included in each task by the programmer using the macro TCB, whose parameters contain values to be inserted in the TCB. The

---

*The function code is pointed to by the PC of the calling task, which has been left on the system stack by the SWI2 instruction. The PC is incremented and stored back on the stack to ensure that the task will be dispatched at the correct address.

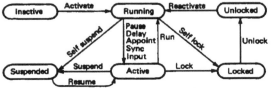

Figure 6. Task states and transitions in the MTE

information fields contained in the TCB are explained below.

Task number. This is the position of the task in the 'task table' (TT), maintained by the executive to locate the task control blocks. Each entry in TT contains the address of the corresponding TCB.

Task entry point. This field contains the address of the first instruction in the task code. The executive transfers control to this address when the task is activated. Tasks are made position independent by having an offset inserted in this field by the TCB macro rather than an absolute address. The executive calculates the absolute address at run time, before the task is activated, by adding the offset to the TCB address. The absolute address then replaces the offset. The same treatment is reserved for the next two fields in the TCB.

Task private stack pointer initial value. Each stack has its private stack and the top location of the memory block reserved for it is stored in this field. The scheduler loads the hardware stack pointer from this field before activating the task.

Task stack pointer save location. When processing a task call, the MTE stores the hardware stack pointer (S) in this location in the TCB of the calling task. As the entire task context is pushed onto the stack by the SWI2 instruction, a task is dispatched by loading S with the contents of this location and executing an RTI (return from interrupt) instruction, which pops the entire machine state off the stack.

Work area pointer. This field contains the address of a data area that tasks can address by offsets from the user stack pointer (U), allowing re-entrant tasks, i.e. tasks that use the same code but work with different dynamic data. The executive loads U with the TCB address before activating a task. It is left to the task programmer to load this field into U and use this facility.

Task name. This is a string of characters that provides a meaningful identifier for the task.

Task allowed run time. Tasks can only use the CPU for this length of time every time they are dispatched.

Elapsed CPU time since last dispatch. This field is reset to zero when the task is dispatched and checked by the task watchdog routine at each clock interrupt. The task is locked and the console operator notified if this count exceeds the allowed run time; otherwise it is simply incremented by one.

I/O port number. Tasks examine this field to find out which interface to use for their I/O operations. I/O redirection can be achieved by modifying this field.

Task delay interval. Tasks performing periodic functions find in this field the amount of time they need to 'delay' themselves before their next dispatch.

Time to next activation. This is a countdown value that is set by the 'delay' and 'appoint' routine to the desired delay interval and decremented each second. When it becomes zero, the task is made 'active'.

Task ready checking subroutine address. This address is dynamically inserted by the 'input, 'delay', 'appoint' and 'sync' routines. On finding a nonzero value in this field, the scheduler calls the addressed subroutine to find out if the event the task is waiting for has occurred. If it has, the field is zeroed and the task dispatched.

Scheduler operation

The scheduler keeps track of which task is currently using the CPU by an index into the task table. On receiving control from the task call processor, this index is incremented to point to the next entry. When a nonzero entry is found, the value in the entry points to the TCB of the next task to be run. The table is scanned in a wrap-around fashion.

Having found a task, the scheduler looks at the state of the task: if it is 'suspended' or 'locked', the task is ignored and the table scan continues; if the task is 'inactive' or 'unlocked', the scheduler dispatches it by loading S and PC from the corresponding fields in the TCB. If the task is waiting for an event or for a time interval to elapse the relevant 'time-up check' subroutine is called and the task is ignored if the return code is negative. A runnable task is dispatched by loading S from the save location in the TCB and restoring the task content from the stack (RTI).

INITIALIZATION

The executive is ROM resident. When the 'reset' interrupt occurs, an initialization routine receives control and sets about performing the required preliminary operations, such as running a diagnostic memory test, checking that some essential I/O interfaces respond correctly, initializing RAM tables, resetting the date and time of day by prompting the console operator and starting the realtime clock. The scheduler is then entered to start cycling through the task table.

Tasks are classified as 'resident' and 'nonresident'. Resident tasks have their code in ROM and a ROM descriptor that provides all the information necessary to set up their TCBs in RAM: this is done by the initialization routine for all the resident tasks. RAM TCB addresses are inserted in the task table and become known to the scheduler. Three resident tasks have been included.

Initializer. This task is responsible for loading the nonresident tasks from the disc unit attached to the disc controller. It does this by emulating a console on the DC; the host operating system is booted in and a start-up file is executed that runs a load program, which in turn downloads the nonresident tasks and data via a serial link, using a simple handshaking protocol.

Disc communication handler. This task handles communication with the DC and the associated handshaking protocol.

Realtime interactive debugger. This task provides a resident debugging environment that displays and dynamically updates memory contents on the screen of a VDU.

The initializer therefore provides the bootstrapping mechanism by which the nonresident tasks are loaded from disc into RAM. As each task is copied, its TCB address is inserted into the relevant slot in the task table. By this method, tasks can be dynamically added to a running system. In fact the system can easily be adapted to work with any type of disc processor as long as some simple communication programs and a suitable start-up file are set up.

I/O FACILITIES

A serial or parallel interface can either be polled, to determine its readiness to input or output a byte of data, or it can be configured so that it interrupts the CPU whenever it is ready to transmit more data or whenever some data has been received.

Polling ties up the CPU while the interface status is being checked; this may represent an intolerable overhead, as checking typically occurs many times before the interface is found ready. On a system with many interfaces, interrupt-driven I/O is therefore required. The communication between tasks and interrupt routines takes place via data buffers. To make task programming simpler, the filling and emptying of buffers and the required synchronization should be hidden inside re-entrant I/O routines, which can be called by the running tasks.

An important factor that the software designer needs to consider is the total amount of CPU time spent in servicing interrupts. As an example, assume that the embedded system contains 20 serial interfaces each working at 1200 bit s^{-1} (120 character s^{-1}). In the worst case when all interfaces work in both input and output at full speed, the rate of interrupt generation is

$$20 \times 2 \times 120 = 4800 \text{ s}^{-1}$$

Assuming that the average CPU time required to service an interrupt is 50 µs, the fraction of total CPU time spent will be

$$50 \times 10^{-6} \times 4800 = 0.24$$

i.e. 24%. Thus the worst-case calculation leaves 76% of CPU time available for the application tasks. The acceptability of such a figure depends on the nature of the application.

Another important consideration at the design stage is the size of the input buffers used. If the external device responsible for filling a buffer is under software control, then it can be told to stop sending data when the buffer becomes full until some room has been made by processing the data. For a VDU terminal, for example, a simple Xon/Xoff protocol will suffice, provided that Xoff is transmitted some time before the buffer is full, as the delay for the signal to reach the device may have caused overflow in the meantime.

For devices that transmit data at a constant (or maximum) rate that cannot be controlled by the embedded micro, the input buffer must never be allowed to fill up. Assuming that task A is responsible for emptying the buffer and it does so completely on each activation, the worst-case delay between successive activations of A must not cause the buffer to overflow. This provides a criterion for sizing the buffer. Let W be the worst-case

delay between successive activations of A, S be the buffer size, and R be the incoming rate for information units. Then

$$S > WR$$

If $W = 2$ s and $R = 1200$ byte s^{-1}, S must be at least 240 byte long. In practice, W can only be determined with any degree of accuracy by task A reading the system clock on each activation.

I/O mechanisms on the controller

Each I/O interface on the memory bus is described by a block in RAM memory called the I/O control block (IOCB). Each IOCB contains all the operational information and buffer space required by the I/O routines to transfer data via the interface. A central table is kept containing the addresses of all the IOCBs in the system. This table is similar in conception to the task table and provides an easy way to refer to each interface by its position in the table.

Tasks perform I/O by calling re-entrant subroutines that 'pause' when the input buffer is empty or the output buffer is full.

A wide range of operational modes is available for each interface and the I/O routines modify their behaviour according to the operational parameters defined in the IOCB. The main definable parameters are described below.

Echo. Each incoming byte of information may or may not be echoed back to the interface as it is received. Typically interfaces connected to human operators work with this option set.

Xon/Xoff. This synchronization protocol is required by certain terminals and external devices. The protocol can work in input mode, output mode or both. In input mode, Xon and Xoff are sent out to control the incoming flow of information; in output mode, they are honoured when received as a request to start or stop the outgoing flow of data.

Buffering. Input can be byte or line oriented. The former is accumulated in a circular queue while the latter is stored in a linear buffer until a line terminator is received; further input is ignored until the line has been fully delivered to a task. Other differences involve the amount of processing done on characters received: line-oriented protocol implies correct handling of 'back space' and 'line delete'.

Crosslink. Two interfaces can be internally linked by using this option. The effect is that any data input on one are output on the other and *vice versa*. Among other things, this option was widely used at the debugging stage to visualize on the console the traffic on the other interfaces, without disrupting the ongoing computation.

Interrupt handling

The IRQ interrupt pin is used for all interrupts; this implies that all interrupt servicing routines run uninterrupted. Interrupts are vectored by an external priority encoder which provides the vector value for the highest-priority active interrupt. The value is read in via a parallel port by the first-level interrupt handler and used as an offset into a jump table to point to the second-level routine to be called.

As mentioned above, interrupt handlers always return to the interrupted task and run on that task's stack. This implies that enough space must be provided on each task stack to account for the deepest possible level of stack nesting required by the interrupt handlers. As interrupts are never nested, this constraint is not severe.

Some concurrency problems arise in the concurrent use of the I/O buffers by the interrupt handlers and the I/O routines called by the application tasks. These are solved by having the I/O routines to disable the IRQ interrupt while updating critical pointers.

DEBUGGING ENVIRONMENT

Conventional debugging monitors are command-driven programs that read and execute commands typed at the console keyboard. The main debugging facilities that such programs usually provide are display and updating of CPU registers and central memory contents, program execution and breakpointing. Program execution typically takes place in trace or in realtime mode. In the former, the monitor regains control after a user-specified number of instructions and asks for user direction on what to do next; the latter mode simply passes control to the user program and the monitor loses control until a breakpoint is reached. Tracing is extremely useful when a single-threaded application has to be debugged and when the realtime speed of execution of the code does not impinge on the correctness of the result. Breakpointing is mandatory in any realtime application, as the program can run at its real speed.

To be useful in a multitasking environment, the breakpointing facility must allow the breakpointed task and all other tasks to continue undisturbed after the breakpoint has been hit. This requirement is not normally met by conventional monitors, which typically regain control of the CPU when a breakpoint has been hit and ask for user direction on the next step to take, implying that the realtime behaviour of the system is disrupted.

A debugging monitor in a multitasking environment should be under the control of the executive rather than in control of the CPU. This can be achieved by constructing the monitor program as an application task, scheduled by the executive as are all the other tasks on the system.

In the SU controller, the debugging task is present in ROM and activated when the system is bootstrapped.

Screen-based realtime debugging

Visual interaction with computer software has been exploited in various application areas, and it can indeed prove extremely useful in debugging an embedded multitasking application.

It is commonplace for conventional microprocessor monitors to include a facility to display the contents of a specified memory area on a VDU screen. Most byte-oriented machines display a number of rows, each row containing the address of its first byte and 16 byte of information, typically displayed in hexadecimal and ASCII code.

The usefulness of a memory contents display to the programmer relies on the ability to relate the information

visualized on the screen to a well known point in the computation. This is straightforward on a single-threaded monitor, as the computation is temporarily suspended by the monitor and its state can be visualized by displaying the contents of the CPU registers. A similar display of memory contents in a multitasking envionment would be of little significance, as the computational process responsible for dynamically altering the contents of the memory area on display runs asynchronously to the debugging task. In other words, the programmer would be at a loss in trying to pinpoint the state of the computation when the display took place.

This problem was tackled in two ways: first, by tying the memory display mechanism to the breakpointing facility so that the display would be easily related to the computational state at the breakpoint; secondly, by allowing the display to be dynamically refreshed by the debugging task after each scheduling cycle. Both techniques proved useful in different ways. The dynamic display in particular provided an interesting and useful tool to examine the dynamic behaviour of the system. By observing the screen, for example, the programmer can see which portions of a given memory block were being continuously updated and which were static. Their relative frequencies of modification can also be visualized. The Xon/Xoff protocol used by the I/O routines allows the screen image to be frozen and the contents of otherwise rapidly changing memory locations to be read; repeated freezing and unfreezing gives a set of readings of memory location values. An overflowing task or buffer can easily be detected using this method.

When a task is thought to be responsible for some erroneous behaviour, e.g. updating a memory location to the wrong value, confirmation can be obtained by suspending the task, modifying the location, resuming the task and observing the dynamic display of the location contents.

On the SU controller, the console for interactive debugging is separate from the operator console. The console was removed to a safe corner in the machine room when the system became operational.

The debugging task supports the following commands: display memory (in static or dynamic mode); modify memory; insert, remove and activate breakpoint; lock, unlock, suspend and resume a task; display the names of the running tasks; and display time of day.

CONCLUSIONS

Based on the experience gained during the design of the embedded microprocessor software for controlling a communication exchange, several methods and techniques have been presented that apply to a whole range of embedded applications.

The effort spent in producing the realtime executive and debugging software in house had its rewards during the testing phase of the project, where any deviation from the specified behaviour could be attributed to known software components. The reliability of the resulting software system has been confirmed to date by successful and uninterrupted operation of the system.

REFERENCES

1   **Thewlis, P J** *Microtechnology: the M6809* Blackwell, Oxford, UK (1985)

2   **Kroenke, D** *Database processing: fundamentals, modelling, applications,* SRA (1977)
3   **Foulger, R J** *Programming embedded microprocessors* NCC, Manchester, UK (1982)
4   **Mezzalama, M and Torasso, P** 'A microprocessor executive for real-time process control' *Euromicro J.* Vol 4 (1978) pp 109–114
5   *RMX/80 system user's guide* Intel, Santa Clara, USA
6   **Deitel, H M** 'An introduction to operating systems Addison-Wesley, Wokingham, UK (1984)
7   **Broughton, D C** 'Simple multitasking on microcomputers' *Small Systems Software* Vol 4 No 1 pp 12–16

BIBLIOGRAPHY

Hansen, P B *Operating systems principles* Prentice-Hall, Englewood Cliffs, NJ, USA (1973)
Van der Linden, F and Wilson, I 'Realtime executives for microprocessors' *Microprocessors Microsyst.* (July/August 1980) pp 211–218

Franco Civello is a senior lecturer in the Computing Department at Brighton Polytechnic, UK. He received a degree in electronic engineering from Padova University, Italy, in 1976 and a postgraduate diploma in computer systems engineering from Rome University, Italy, in 1978. His industrial experience involved programming and software engineering in both commercial and industrial computing. His current research interests are in the areas of software specification and design methodologies and artificial intelligence, and he is currently working as a part-time postgraduate student at Sussex University, UK, towards a PhD in the application of AI techniques to software engineering problems.

12-bit digital audio time delay using the 6809

Commercial time delay units are not usually flexible enough to suit computer control, as may be required in laboratory situations. So **B T G Tan and L P Tay** have designed a programmable audio delay system based on the Apple II with a 6809 coprocessor

The paper describes a programmable digital audio time delay system which uses the 6809 microprocessor to store and retrieve 12-bit samples in RAM. A/D and D/A conversions were accomplished by a 12-bit analogue I/O board for the Apple II microcomputer. A 6809 machine code time delay program, which was run on a 6809 coprocessor board for the Apple II, was able to attain an audio frequency response of over 14 kHz.

microsystems   audio time delay   Apple II   6809

The digital audio time delay generator is a primary tool in the design of present-day sound reinforcement systems. Most professional time delay units are dedicated units using hard-wired logic circuitry; these units are usually designed for use in sound reinforcement system installations in auditoria and concert halls, and their time delay values are not designed for rapid alteration under computer control. The present project arose out of a need for a high-quality digital time delay unit which would be easily programmable, for use in research on the psychoacoustic effects of time delays on the perception of sound sources.

The 8-bit microprocessor is a suitably flexible and inexpensive controller for a programmable time delay unit[1]. However, the signal-to-noise ratio requirements in most applications for digital time delay units demand a data word length longer than 8 bit; 8 bit would give a signal-to-noise ratio of only 48 dB or so, which is inadequate for high-quality sound reinforcement. Thus a 12-bit or 16-bit data word length is required, implying that a 16-bit microprocessor system might be necessary to perform the delay processing with sufficient speed.

However, a system based on an 8-bit data bus was judged to be preferable from the point of view of system cost and complexity. An 8-bit microprocessor would have to perform a pair of 8-bit write operations to store one 12-bit or 16-bit sample in memory and it would take a pair of 8-bit read operations to retrieve the same sample. Most current 8-bit microprocessors would not be able to cope with 16-bit data transfers at an acceptable rate for high-quality audio sampling; the solution adopted was to use a hybrid 8/16-bit microprocessor, the Motorola 6809. There are more powerful processors available which have 8-bit data buses, such as the 8088 and the 68008, but the 6809 proved to be adequate for the present purpose.

Department of Physics, National University of Singapore, Singapore 0511

Rather than building a selfcontained standalone digital delay system, it was decided to use a personal computer with an open bus architecture as the basis of the system. The Apple II was chosen, though the IBM PC could also have been used, as both computers have open buses which can be easily interfaced through their slots. The Apple II is based on the 8-bit 6502 microprocessor and has an I/O bus with eight slots[2]. In the Apple II's 64k memory map, 2k (from $C000 to $C7FF) is reserved for I/O through the eight slots.

The digital delay system included two boards to plug into the I/O slots; one board was a specially designed and constructed 12-bit analogue I/O board and the other was a commercially available 6809-based coprocessor board.

ANALOGUE I/O BOARD

The analogue I/O board was designed to perform two related functions:
- to receive an audio analogue input, convert it to a 12-bit digital sample and store it in the Apple II's memory
- to retrieve a 12-bit digital sample from the Apple II's memory and convert it to an analogue audio signal

The circuit diagram of the Analog I/O board is shown in Figure 1. The 12-bit A/D and D/A conversions were performed by an Analog Devices AD574 A/D converter and an AD565 D/A converter respectively.

There are two methods by which the AD574 can be interfaced to an 8-bit bus[3]. One method is to connect it directly to the Apple II bus with the eight least significant bits and the four remaining bits both connected to the 8-bit data bus. The AD574 is then operated in its 8-bit mode, with 12-bit data being output in two stages. A/D conversion is initiated by executing a write instruction to the AD574 address.

The other method, which was the one actually adopted, is to use the AD574 in standalone mode and direct its 12-bit output into a 6821 peripheral interface adaptor (PIA) with two 8-bit ports. The AD574 can then be operated in 12-bit mode; AD574 interfacing and programming is also simplified. One advantage of using a PIA is that the CA2 line of port A can be configured as an output for handshaking and used to initiate A/D conversion via the AD574's read/convert (R/C) pin. This eliminates one instruction in the time delay routine and increases the data sampling rate. A second PIA was used to direct the outgoing 12-bit samples from the Apple II memory to the AD565 D/A converter.

0141-9331/86/09500-06 $03.00 © 1986 Butterworth & Co. (Publishers) Ltd

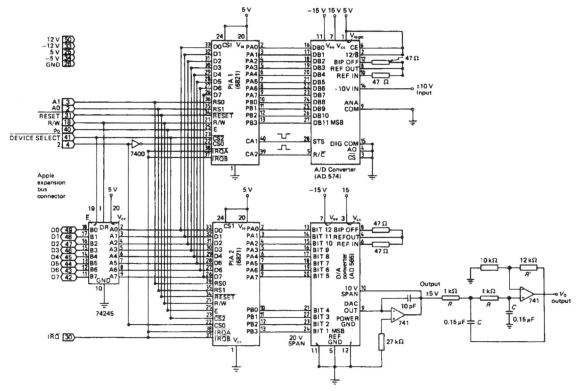

Figure 1. Circuit diagram of analogue I/O board

The addresses occupied by the two PIAs in the Apple II's memory map are $C0x0-$C0x3 or $C0x8-$C0xB (PIA 1) and $C0x4-$C0x7 or $C0xC-$C0xF (PIA 2), where the hex digit x is $n + 8$, n being the slot into which the analogue board is inserted. Normally, the four consecutive addresses occupied by a 6821 PIA are assigned to the PIA registers in the following order[4]

    PDRA/DDRA
    CRA
    PDRB/DDRB
    CRB

The register select lines of the two PIAs, RS0 and RS1, were connected to the address bus lines A1 and A0 respectively; this is the reverse of the normal practice, and was done so that the four PIA addresses would be in the order

    PDRA/DDRA
    PDRB/DDRB
    CRA
    CRB

This places the addresses for the two peripheral data registers PDRA and PDRB directly adjacent to each other and so enables them to be addressed simultaneously by the 16-bit load and store instructions of the 6809.

The AD574 A/D converter is interfaced to PIA 1. The eight least significant bits of the AD574 output are connected to port A and the remaining four bits to the four lower significant bit lines of port B of PIA 1. The AD574 A/D conversion process is initiated by its R/C̄ pin. This pin is connected to the CA2 input of port A of PIA 1. The CA2 pin is configured as an output so that it can initiate an A/D conversion at the AD574 when a high-to-low transition occurs at CA2. The PIA port is configured for handshaking, so that a high-to-low transition occurs every time a data read operation is performed there. The AD574 status pin (STS) indicates that the conversion is complete by going from high to low[3]. This pin is connected to CA1 so that PIA 1 can initiate an interrupt request for the 6809 to read the 12-bit data. The read operation then initiates another conversion through the CA2 pin. The AD574 is configured to accept a bipolar analogue input with a maximum amplitude of 10 V.

The AD565 is also configured to give a 10 V maximum output during bipolar operation[3]. Its eight least significant digital input lines are connected to port A, and the remaining four lines are connected to the four lower significant bit lines of PIA 2 port B. The output is passed through a 741 operational amplifier acting as a current-to-voltage converter, and then through another 741 acting as a second-order Butterworth low-pass filter to smooth the analogue output signal.

6809 COPROCESSOR BOARD

The 6809 coprocessor board used is manufactured by Stellation Two and is known as 'the Mill'. It uses the 6809E microprocessor, which runs off the 1.023 MHz clock of the Apple II. The 6809E runs concurrently with the Apple II's 6502, the 6502 having access to the bus during the 6809's dead cycles[5] (i.e. whenever the 6809 valid memory address is not valid). The operation of the 6809 is controlled by an onboard 8-bit control register. Each bit of the control register controls a particular board function. Each of these bits is turned off or on by writing $80 or $00 to an address from $C080 + n0 to $C087 + n0, where n is the number of the slot into which the 6809 board is inserted. By writing to the appropriate address, the 6502 or 6809 can be enabled or disabled.

When the Apple II is switched on, the 6502 is enabled and the 6809 disabled. A short program was written in BASIC to set up the starting address of the 6809 program in the Apple II memory and to activate the 6809. When the BASIC program is run, it executes the 6809 program which runs concurrently with the 6502.

DIGITAL DELAY SOFTWARE

The basic principle of the machine code program used to accomplish digital delay using the analogue I/O board is very simple. All that is needed is to load the digital samples into a contiguous block of memory. For example, the address range from $6000 to $61FF will give 512 contiguous addresses. The samples from the AD574 are stored first in $6000 and $6001 (with 2 byte for each sample) then in $6002 and $6003, and so on until $61FE and $61FF are reached. The next sample goes back to the beginning of the block at $6000 and $6001 and the whole cycle is repeated. The outgoing digital samples are retrieved from the memory block and fed to the AD565 in a similar manner.

The length of the time delay depends on two factors: the length of the memory block and the point relative to the incoming samples at which the outgoing samples are retrieved. For a given block length, the longest possible delay is obtained when the outgoing samples are retrieved from addresses immediately ahead of the incoming samples. This is accomplished in the delay programs by initially setting the pointer for the incoming samples at $6000 and that for the outgoing samples at $6002.

It is of course possible to accomplish the time delay with an 8-bit microprocessor machine code program. Figure 2 shows a program which was written for the Apple II's own 6502. The program assumes that the analogue I/O board is in slot 3. PIA 1 occupies the addresses $C0B0–$C0B3 and PIA 2 occupies $C0B4–$C0B7. The PIA initialization routine sets CA2 of PIA 1 as an output so that it can initiate the A/D conversion through the R/$\overline{C}$ input of the AD574. Port A of PIA 1 is configured for input handshaking. The AD574 requires a maximum of 35 µs for the

```
SOURCE FILE: DELAY05
----- NEXT OBJECT FILE NAME IS DELAY05.OBJ0
4000:            1           ORG   $4000      6502 TIME DELAY PROGRAM
4000:A9 00       2           LDA   #$00       PIA INITIALIZATION
4002:8D B2 CO    3           STA   $C0B2
4005:8D B3 CO    4           STA   $C0B3
4008:8D B0 CO    5           STA   $C0B0      DEFINE PIA INPUT PORTS
400B:8D B1 CO    6           STA   $C0B1
400E:8D B6 CO    7           STA   $C0B6
4011:8D B7 CO    8           STA   $C0B7
4014:A9 FF       9           LDA   #$FF
4016:8D B4 CO   10           STA   $C0B4      DEFINE PIA OUTPUT PORTS
4019:8D B5 CO   11           STA   $C0B5
401C:A9 24      12           LDA   #$24       MASK PIA INTERRUPT
401E:8D B2 CO   13           STA   $C0B2
4021:A9 04      14           LDA   #$04
4023:8D B3 CO   15           STA   $C0B3
4026:8D B6 CO   16           STA   $C0B6
4029:8D B7 CO   17           STA   $C0B7
402C:A2 00      18           LDX   #$00       X REG POINTS TO INPUT ADDRESS
402E:A0 02      19           LDY   #$02       Y REG POINTS TO OUTPUT ADDRESS
4030:AD B0 CO   20 LOOP      LDA   $C0B0      START OF DELAY LOOP; INPUT LOW BYTE
4033:9D 00 60   21           STA   $6000,X
4036:AD B1 CO   22           LDA   $C0B1      INPUT HIGH BYTE
4039:9D 01 60   23           STA   $6001,X
403C:B9 00 60   24           LDA   $6000,Y
403F:8D B4 CO   25           STA   $C0B4      OUTPUT LOW BYTE
4042:B9 01 60   26           LDA   $6001,Y
4045:8D B5 CO   27           STA   $C0B5      OUTPUT HIGH BYTE
4048:E8         28           INX
4049:E8         29           INX
404A:C8         30           INY
404B:C8         31           INY
404C:4C 30 40   32           JMP   LOOP       REPEAT LOOP

*** SUCCESSFUL ASSEMBLY: NO ERRORS
```

Figure 2. Time delay program for 6502

conversion. The delay loop takes 45 clock cycles — 43.99 µs at a clock rate of 1.023 MHz — so there is no necessity to pad the loops with extra cycles or to interrupt the 6502 to initiate the input of a new sample from the AD574. Hence the PIA interrupt output to the 6502 is masked.

With a loop delay of 43.99 µs the sampling rate is 22.73 kbaud, and hence the highest audio frequency which the time delay can handle is 11.37 kHz. The time delay depends on the length of the memory block. In the present system the block length is maximized using the 8-bit index registers (i.e. 256 byte or 128 12-bit samples), and hence the maximum time delay is 5.63 ms.

The lack of 16-bit index registers makes programs for longer time delays very cumbersome. The indirect addressing modes of the 6502 have to be used, leading to rather long sampling routines and hence long loop times, giving slower sampling rates. The 6800 microprocessor would have provided a 16-bit index register, but two index registers are needed for the indexing of the input and output addresses in the memory block.

Using the 6809, which is capable of 16-bit operations but has an 8-bit data bus, instead of the 6502 resulted in a significant improvement to the time delay program. The 6809 has two 8-bit accumulators which can be combined as one 16-bit accumulator, known as the D accumulator. Thus several 16-bit operations, including 16-bit load and store operations, can be performed. With an 8-bit data path a 16-bit load or store operation needs to transfer the

16-bit data in two 8-bit steps, but this is transparent to the user. The 6809 also has two 16-bit index registers (the X and Y registers), which considerably simplify the indexing of the input and output memory addresses for the delay samples.

Figure 3 shows a time delay program written in 6809 machine code. PIA initialization is similar to that in the 6502 program. The X and Y index registers are initially loaded with $6000 and $6002 respectively. The delay loop routine is now shorter and occupies only 35 clock cycles. When the end of the block is reached, a special end-of-block routine performs the sample processing and returns the index register addresses to the beginning of the block. This end-of-block housekeeping routine also takes 35 clock cycles, so that the transition from the end of the block to the beginning is smooth and does not result in a sampling 'hiccup'. The loop delay is 34.21 µs, giving a sampling rate of 29.23 kbaud and a maximum audio frequency of 14.61 kHz. As the nominal conversion time for the AD574 is 25 µs, this means that it is working quite close to its specified maximum performance.

Unlike the 6502 program, the memory block can be longer than 256 byte, giving longer delay times. In the 6809 program given in Figure 3, the block length is 512 byte or 256 12-bit samples, giving a time delay of 8.76 ms. Figure 4 shows a pulse modulated 4 kHz sine wave and its delayed output. The measured delay is about 8.7 ms. The time delay can of course be extended to much longer lengths, being limited only by the amount

```
2000                    ORG     $2000      6809 TIME DELAY PROGRAM
2000 4F        START    CLRA               PIA INITIALIZATION
2001 5F                 CLRB
2002 FDC0B2             STD     $C0B2
2005 FDC0B0             STD     $C0B0       DEFINE PIA INPUT PORTS
2008 FDC0B6             STD     $C0B6
200B 86FF              LDA     #$FF
200D C6FF              LDB     #$FF
200F FDC0B4             STD     $C0B4       DEFINE PIA OUTPUT PORTS
2012 8624              LDA     #$24        MASK PIA INTERRUPT
2014 C604              LDB     #$04
2016 FDC0B2             STD     $C0B2
2019 8604              LDA     #$04
201B C604              LDB     #$04
201D FDC0B6             STD     $C0B6
2020 8E6000            LDX     #$6000      STARTING ADDRESS OF MEMORY BLOCK
2023 108E6002          LDY     #$6002      Y REG POINTS TO OUTPUT ADDRESS
2027 FCC0B0    LOOP     LDD     $C0B0       START OF DELAY LOOP; INPUT TWO BYTES
202A ED81              STD,X++
202C ECA1              LDD,Y++
202E FDC0B4             STD     $C0B4       OUTPUT TWO BYTES
2031 8C61FF            CMPX    #$61FF      END OF MEMORY BLOCK?
2034 25F1              BLO     LOOP        NO, RETURN TO LOOP
2036 FCC0B0            LDD     $C0B0       YES, DO END OF BLOCK HOUSEKEEPING
2039 ED84              STD,X
203B 8E6000            LDX     #$6000
203E 108E6000          LDY     #$6000
2042 ECA1              LDD,Y++
2044 FDC0B4             STD     $C0B4
2047 20DE              BRA     LOOP        RETURN TO LOOP
     2000              END     START
       2 SYMBOLS IN TABLE:

LOOP  $2027  START $2000

SYMBOL TABLE END: 40F9

       0 STATEMENT ERROR(S). LAST PC:2048
```

Figure 3. Time delay program for 6809

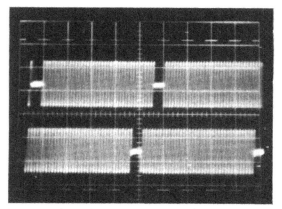

Figure 4. Time delayed pulse modulated 4 kHz sine wave: upper band is original wave (2 V cm^{-1}); lower band is delayed wave (5 V cm^{-1}); time base is 2.08 ms cm^{-1}

of free memory in the Apple II. For example, a 12 kbyte memory block would give a time delay of very nearly 420 ms which, together with the audio frequency range of over 14 kHz, makes the system perfectly adequate for a wide range of audio processing applications.

The delay program could be slightly modified so that the CMPX register instruction which tests for the end of the block could be changed from the immediate addressing mode to refer to a location which contains the block size. In this way, the block size and hence the delay time could be altered under program control, possibly by the 6502, which has concurrent access to the Apple II memory. (This could be extremely useful in situations where the delay time has to change rapidly in accordance with experimental conditions.)

In most cases 12-bit audio samples will give sufficiently good resolution. The signal-to-noise ratio from 12-bit digitization is about 72 dB, which is perfectly adequate for most applications. If 16-bit resolution is required, the same circuit design can be used with only a change in the A/D and D/A converters. The sampling rate would remain the same as for the 12-bit case, since the 6809 is already in effect taking 16-bit samples.

In its standalone mode the AD574 facilitates the input of audio samples using the 6809 interrupt. This may be necessary in a situation where the sampling rate is faster than the A/D converter's conversion time. By using the 6809's SYNC instruction[6], the 6809 can be made to wait for an end-of-conversion signal from the STS pin of the AD574. Figure 5 shows such a program, which stores 100 16-bit samples from the AD574 in the Apple II memory. During PIA initialization the PIA interrupt is enabled. The sampling routine takes 25 clock cycles, which may be faster than the conversion rate in certain circumstances. (The specified conversion rate for the AD574 is 15–35 μs.)

To initiate the 6809 interrupt properly, the 6809 coprocessor board had to be modified slightly. The 6809 IRQ line is fed by the output of one of the bits of the onboard control register described earlier. To enable the SYNC instruction to respond to an incoming interrupt request, the IRQ line from the Apple II bus was directly connected to the 6809's IRQ pin. This enables the 6809 to respond to the AD574 end-of-conversion signal through the STS and CA1 lines and thus to transfer the 16-bit samples to the Apple II memory. Strictly speaking, for the program to work properly, the loop routine delay should always be less then the A/D conversion time.

CONCLUSIONS

A programmable 12-bit audio time delay system using the 6809 for the audio processing has been successfully

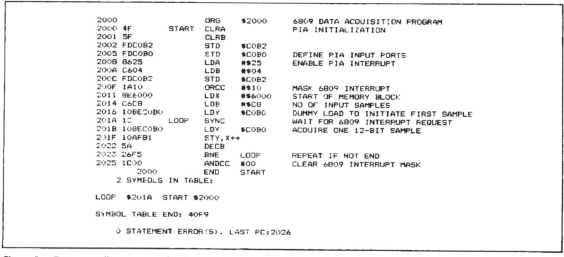

```
2000                ORG    $2000      6809 DATA ACQUISITION PROGRAM
2000 4F       START CLRA              PIA INITIALIZATION
2001 5F             CLRB
2002 FDC0B2         STD    $C0B2
2005 FDC0B0         STD    $C0B0       DEFINE PIA INPUT PORTS
2008 8625           LDA    #$25        ENABLE PIA INTERRUPT
200A C604           LDB    #$04
200C FDC0B2         STD    $C0B2
200F 1A10           ORCC   #$10        MASK 6809 INTERRUPT
2011 8E6000         LDX    #$6000      START OF MEMORY BLOCK
2014 C6C8           LDB    #$C8        NO OF INPUT SAMPLES
2016 10BEC0B0       LDY    $C0B0       DUMMY LOAD TO INITIATE FIRST SAMPLE
201A 13       LOOP  SYNC               WAIT FOR 6809 INTERRUPT REQUEST
201B 10BEC0B0       LDY    $C0B0       ACQUIRE ONE 12-BIT SAMPLE
201F 10AFB1         STY,X++
2022 5A             DECB
2023 26F5           BNE    LOOP        REPEAT IF NOT END
2025 1C00           ANDCC  #00         CLEAR 6809 INTERRUPT MASK
     2000           END    START
     2 SYMBOLS IN TABLE:

LOOP  $201A  START $2000

SYMBOL TABLE END: 40F9

     0 STATEMENT ERROR(S). LAST PC:2026
```

Figure 5. Data sampling program for 6809

demonstrated. The 6809 was able to handle the audio throughput at a rate sufficient for high-quality audio applications. The system could be used for 16-bit processing with only a change in the A/D and D/A converters from 12 bit to 16 bit. The system could be further improved by using a more powerful microprocessor such as the 68008. Further work using a 68008 coprocessor is currently under way.

REFERENCES

1 **Stajic, D** 'Microprocessor-based simulator of a variable time delay' *Microprocessors Microsyst.* Vol 6 No 2 (March 1982) pp 73–75

2 *Apple II reference manual* Apple Computers, Cupertino, CA, USA

3 *Analog Devices data acquisition databook 1984, Vol 1: integrated circuits* Analog Devices, Norwood, MA, USA (1984)

4 **Leventhal, L A** *Introduction to microprocessors: software, hardware, programming* Prentice-Hall, Englewood Cliffs, NJ, USA (1978)

5 *The Mill — principles of operation* (manual for 6809 coprocessor board) Stellation Two, USA (1981)

6 **Leventhal, L** *6809 assembly language programming* Osborne/McGraw-Hill, New York, USA (1981)

Bernard Tan graduated in 1965 with an honours degree in physics from the University of Singapore, and in 1968 with a DPhil from Oxford University, UK. He is a chartered engineer and a member of the IEE and the IERE. Since 1968 he has taught at the National University of Singapore where he is now an associate professor in physics. His research interests include microwave properties of semiconductors, computer-assisted acoustical analysis and synthesis, and microprocessor applications.

L P Tay obtained an honours degree in physics from the National University of Singapore in 1984. He is now teaching physics at River Valley High School, Singapore. He is also involved in part-time research in solid-state physics, working towards an MSc degree, at the National University of Singapore.

R & D reports

Applications

Adams, A E and Watson, A
'Implementation of GPIB standard interface to a weather satellite receiver' *J. Microcomput. Appl.* Vol 9 No 3 (July 1986) pp 209–214

An 8085-based development board and Intel GPIB interfacing chips are used to implement a communication channel for work on image analysis and pattern recognition of nonrigid objects.

Cox, G, Curphey, D, Fronek, D and Wilson, J
'Remote video sensing of highway pavements at road speeds: using the Motorola 68020 microprocessor' *Microcomput. Civil Eng.* Vol 1 No 1 (July 1986) pp 1–13

Lazzari, G and Avancini, G P
'A versatile and powerful system for control and data acquisition in the laboratory environment' *J. Microcomput. Appl.* Vol 9 No 3 (July 1986) pp 241–246

Describes a low-cost control and data acquisition system which matches FORTH and NEC's 7811 microprocessor.

Martin, S L
'Difficult speech-recognition technology shows signs of maturity' *Comput. Des.* (1 August 1986) pp 23–29

Meigh, R E and Prudence, M
'A development of a virology laboratory register using the Sinclair QL and Psion Archive' *J. Microcomput. Appl.* Vol 9 No 3 (July 1986) pp 247–249

Verma, H K, Mukherjee, S and Saha, P K
'Microprocessor-based controllers for single and multiple batch digesters for pulping' *J. Microcomput. Appl.* Vol 9 No 3 (July 1986) pp 179–195

ASICs

Agrawal, O and Shankar, K
'PAL device buries registers, brings state machines to life' *Electronic Des.* Vol 34 No 17 (24 July 1986) pp 101–106

To build state machines with programmable logic devices (PLDs), designers need PLDs with buried or internal state registers, the authors argue. This frees I/O pins, saves board space and speeds operation. The article describes a new chip from AMD with six registers that hold buried state bits, the AmPAL-23S8 20-pin PAL device.

Doerr, A H and Sabo, D G
'Silicon compilation and design for test' *Solid-State Technol.* Vol 29 No 8 (August 1986) pp 117–123

An overview by two staff members of Silicon Compilers Inc. in the USA.

Shepherd, A A
'Application specific integrated circuits: a review' *J. Semicustom ICs* Vol 3 No 4 (June 1986) pp 5–12

Stockton, J
'Megacells simplify end to end design tasks' *Solid-State Technol.* Vol 29 No 8 (August 1986) pp 127–132

Discusses the simplification of test program development as a part of the normal design process and the use of 'megacells' as building blocks in new designs.

Computer communication

Shapiro, S F
'Jumping on the MAP bandwagon: how soon and how far' *Comput. Des.* (15 August 1986) pp 16–21

Overview of the evolution of MAP to date, predicting the extent by which users can expect to benefit from it and how soon. Includes a view into the future from the chairman of the General Motors MAP Task Force.

Sloman, M, Kramer, J, Magee, J and Twidle, K
'Flexible communication structure for distributed embedded systems' *IEE Proc. E* Vol 133 No 4 (July 1986) pp 201–211

Large realtime systems generally have a long lifetime, the authors say, and so must remain flexible. In some applications, such as process control, it may not be economic or safe to shut a system down. Conic is an architecture that provides a flexible environment for building distributed embedded systems from message passing modules. It provides a high-level programming language with interprocess communication primitives suited to both local and remote communication. The paper shows how the configuration flexibility of the Conic architecture has been exploited in the design of the Conic communication system.

Education

Bromley, A G and Nicholson, T
'Pedagogic computers' *IEE Proc. E* Vol 133 No 4 (July 1986) pp 212–222

Using modern LSI components rather than MSI allows a modular approach to be taken to the design of the control part of a digital system, reducing from 20–30 hours to 2–3 hours the time a student may have to spend to build a small computer. Equipment used for this purpose and the design and implementation of several simple computer processors are described.

Fault tolerance

Yanney, R M and Hayes, J P
'Distributed recovery in fault-tolerant multiprocessor networks' *IEEE Trans. Comput.* Vol C-35 No 10 (October 1986) pp 871–879

IC design and test

Bridges, G E, Pries, W, McLeod, R D, Yunik, M, Gulak, P G and Card, H C
'Dual systolic architectures for VLSI digital signal processing systems' *IEEE Trans. Comput.* Vol C-35 No 10 (October 1986) pp 916–923

Kates, G
'GaAs pushes bit slice to new performance levels' *Comput. Des.* (15 August 1986) pp 26–27

Kinoshita, K and Saluja, K K
'Built-in testing of memory using an on-chip compact testing scheme' *IEEE Trans. Comput.* Vol C-35 No 10 (October 1986) pp 862–870

The authors review RAM faults and propose a universal fault model. A built-in test scheme is then proposed using the new fault model, taking into account chip complexity and compaction factors. The approach is extended to microcoded ROM.

Petrich, D
'Achieving accurate timing measurements on TTL/CMOS devices' *IEEE Des. Test Comput.* Vol 2 No 4 (August 1986) pp 33–42

Describes the derivation (by computer simulation) and use of correlations tables to overcome discrepancies between the measurements returned by different test systems.

Sridhar, T
'A new parallel test approach for large memories' *IEEE Des. Test Comput.* Vol 2 No 4 (August 1986) pp 15–22

A method using parallel signature analysers, which can access more data cells in parallel than can I/O pins, is analysed with respect to test time, test quality and silicon area penalty.

Unger, S H and Tan, C-J
'Clocking schemes for high-speed digital systems' *IEEE Trans. Comput.* Vol C-35 No 10 (October 1986) pp 880–895

BUILT-IN SELF-TEST: PASS OR FAIL?
IEEE Des. Test Comput. Vol 2 No 2 (April 1986)

McCluskey, E J
'Built-in self-test techniques' pp 21–28
'Built-in self-test structures' pp 29–36

Treuer, R, Fujiwara, H and Agarwal, V K
'Implementing a built-in self-test PLA design' pp 37–48

Illman, R J
'Self-tested data flow logic: a new approach' pp 50–58

Williams, T W
'Test length in a self-testing environment' pp 59–63

Daniels, R G and Bruce, W C
'Built-in self-test trends in Motorola microprocessors' pp 64–71

This special issue aims to give a 'snapshot' of the state of the art in built-in self test (BIST). McCluskey starts by reviewing the BIST design and implementation techniques applicable to most logic structures, and in his second article describes some of the options for combining BIST with functional circuitry.

Treuer *et al.* describe their NMOS implementation of a new BIST design for programmable logic arrays, which they claim achieves high fault coverage with low overhead. Illman's approach exploits the regularity of

data flow structures to implement a hybrid test technique using both random and pseudo-exhaustive test styles.

Williams of IBM shows how to estimate more accurately the pseudorandom length needed to eliminate defects in a selftest environment, while Motorola's Daniels and Bruce give an inside account of their company's BIST strategy over the last ten years.

DIGITAL DESIGN VERIFICATION
IEE Proc. E Vol 133 No 5 (September 1986)

Hanna, F K and Daeche, N
'Specification and verification of digital systems using higher-order predicate logic' pp 242–254

Gordon, M J C and Herbert, J
'Formal hardware verification methodology and its application to a network interface chip' pp 255–270

Amblard, P, Caspi, P and Halbwachs, N
'Use of time functions to describe and explain circuit behaviour' pp 271–275

Dill, D L and Clarke, E M
'Automatic verification of asynchronous circuits using temporal logic' pp 276–282

Fujita, M, Kono, S, Tanaka, H and Moto-Oka, T
'Aid to hierarchical and structured logic design using temporal logic and Prolog' pp 283–294

Sheeran, M
'Design and verification of regular synchronous circuits' pp 295–304

This special issue brings together some of the approaches that have evolved for digital design verification. Hanna and Daeche use higher-order predicate logic to specify both the structure and behaviour of a system, and to reason about their interrelationship. Gordon and Herbert use a digital logical calculus known as LSM to verify the functional correctness of a design by machine-checked formal proof. This

R&D reports

technique is implemented on an interactive system, and an example verification of a Cambridge Fast Ring chip is presented. Amblard *et al.* illustrate the use of a mechanical model for describing the time behaviour of hardware, and introduce some tools for describing the functions involved.

Temporal logic specifications are used to verify asynchronous sequential circuits by Dill and Clarke, who derive a state graph for a circuit described in terms of Boolean gates and Muller elements. Correct circuit behaviour, expressed in CTL temporal logic, is checked against the state graph by a 'model checker' program.

Fujita *et al.* present a study of a 'linear time temporal logic' (LTTL) language with PROLOG, while Sheeran presents the μFP VLSI design language and shows how it can be used in the development of regular array circuits.

Knowledge-based systems

Wigan, M R
'Engineering tools for building knowledge-based systems on microsystems' *Microcomput. Civil Eng.* Vol 1 No 1 (July 1986) pp 52–68

Reviews the range and characteristics of knowledge-based systems tools available on microcomputers, including PROLOG and LISP systems and expert system shells for both text- and rule-based approaches.

Memory

Day, J R
'A fault-driven, comprehensive redundancy algorithm' *IEEE Des. Test Comput.* Vol 2 No 3 (June 1986) pp 35–44

When a RAM chip sustains a defect that is 'theoretically repairable', commonly used failure analysis

algorithms of the 'most-repair' type may still be unable to find a repair solution. This paper describes a fault-driven algorithm which the author claims will find at least one solution for any theoretically repairable device.

Local area networks

Chianese, A and De Santo, M
'Methodology for LAN design' *Comput. Comm.* Vol 9 No 4 (August 1986) pp 177–185

A methodology based on the structured analysis and data technique (SADT) is developed for choosing a LAN that satisfies a user's requirements.

Fiol, M A, Valero, M, Andres Yebra, J L, Alegre, I and Lang, T
'Optimization of double-loop structures for local networks' *Int. J Mini & Microcomput.* Vol 8 No 2 (1986) pp 40–44

Gopalakrishnan, M and Patnaik, L M
'Integrating voice and data on SALAN; an experimental local area network' *Comput. Comm.* Vol 9 No 4 (August 1986) pp 186–194

The School of Automation local area network, SALAN, is an experimental LAN used at the Indian Institute of Science. It consists of microprocessor-based communication nodes linked to a shared coaxial cable. The paper discusses the design and implementation of a file transfer facility and a packet voice communication system.

Parallel computing

DOMESTICATING PARALLELISM *IEEE Comput.* Vol 19 No 8 (August 1986)

Mundie, D A and Fisher, D A
'Parallel processing in Ada' pp 20–25

Ahuja, S, Carriero, N and Gelernter, D
'Linda and friends' pp 26–34

Halstead, R H Jr
'Parallel symbolic computing' pp 35–43

Shapiro, E
'Concurrent Prolog: a progress report' pp 44–58

Hudak, P
'Para-functional programming' pp 60–70

Silbey, A, Milutinovic, V and Mendoza-Grado, V
'A survey of advanced microprocessors and HLL computer architectures' pp 72–85

Mundie and Fisher's paper seeks to 'place the design of ADA's parallel processing in its proper historical and technical context', with discussions of the ADA tasking model and other characteristics and limitations of ADA tasking. Ahuja *et al.* describe LINDA, an ALGOL-based language consisting of a few simple primitives designed to support and simplify the constructions of explicitly parallel programs. The authors first discuss the needs of the parallel programmer, and then the construction, current implementations and programming examples of LINDA. Higher-level parallel languages that can be implemented on top of the LINDA kernel are also covered.

Halstead explores the problems and opportunities of parallel symbolic computing and describes MULTILISP, a language used at MIT for parallel symbolic programming experiments. Shapiro reviews the history, implementation and applications of Concurrent PROLOG, while Hudak describes a programming methodology that treats a multiprocessor as a single autonomous computer onto which a program is mapped, rather than as a group of independent processors.

Finally, Silbey *et al.* classify and

exemplify high-level language computer architectures as: reduced architectures (IBM 801, Stanford MIPS, Inmos Transputer, RIMMS, VM architecture), language-directed architectures (iAPX 432, MC68020, HP Focus, NS 32032, Z80 000, DEC VLSI Vax), language corresponding architectures type A (Scheme 79/81 at MIT, IBM APL machine) and type B (Fairchild's Symbol, Stanford's DELtran), and direct-execution architectures (Pasdec — PASCAL for interactive direct execution computer — at the University of Tsukuba in Japan).

Performance

Cooper, T C, Bell, W D, Lin, F C and Rasmussen, N J
'A benchmark comparison of 32-bit microprocessors' *IEEE Micro* Vol 6 No 4 (August 1986) pp 53–58

Compares the MC68020, NS32032, AT&T 32100 and Intel 80386 using the *EDN* 16-bit benchmarks and a VMEbus test environment. Results are tabulated and discussed.

Mokhoff, N
'Supermicro look-alikes differ below the surface in processing power' *Comput. Des.* (1 September 1986) pp 57–75

Comparison of 32-bit 'supermicros' from different manufacturers, incorporating a brief market analysis and a 'system integrator's perspective'.

System security

Williams, T
'Access control plus data encryption adds up to system security' *Comput. Des.* (1 August 1986) pp 44–46

Short article reviewing the hardware methods, including encryption, that can help prevent unauthorized access to data.

Telecommunications

Allan, R
'New standards, silicon chips nudge ISDNs closer to reality' *Electronic Des.* Vol 34 No 17 (24 July 1986) pp 88–96

Telecommunications networks are evolving gradually towards integration of voice and data on a single network with the implementation of integrated services digital network (ISDN). According to Allan in this special report most experts feel that this will be the year in which ISDNs begin to penetrate — the number of international standards is growing, interface chip designs are emerging and a number of field trials are underway, he says. The report looks at ISDN standards and examines the hardware plans of the major chip manufacturers.

Books received

These books have been received recently by the Editorial Office. They may be reviewed in later issues.

Anceau, F
The architecture of microprocessors Addison-Wesley, Wokingham, UK (1986) £21.95 pp 263

Coles, R
Practical Electronics microprocessor handbook Newnes Technical Books, Twickenham, UK (1986) £13.50 pp 152

Seventeen microprocessors, including 8-bit and 16-bit general-purpose processors and 16-bit single-chip devices, are described with reference to data sheets and application examples. Based around articles that appeared in *Practical Electronics* magazine, the book can be used as a reference source or as a student primer.

Dexter, A L
Microcomputer bus structures and bus interface design Marcel Dekker, New York, NY, USA (1986) $71.50 ($59.75 in USA) pp 339

Radnai, R and Kingham, E G
Jones' instrument technology, Vol 5: automatic instruments and measuring systems Butterworth, Borough Green, Kent, UK (1986) pp 174

Looks at the general trends in electronic measuring automation. Microprocessor-based control and instrumentation systems are covered, particularly those using the IEC Interface Recommendation (IEEE 488).

Scanlon, L J
80286 assembly language on MS-DOS computers Brady Communications, New York, NY, USA (1986) £19.10 pp 331

Takagi, H
Analysis of polling systems MIT Press, Cambridge, MA, USA (1986) £22.50 pp 205

Polling systems are used in computer–terminal communication systems but are now also finding applications in local area networks. A polling system contains a number of data queues that are served in cyclic order. The book analyses the performance of polling systems with reference to a taxonomy of models.

Tasaka, S
Performance analysis of multiple access protocols MIT Press, Cambridge, MA, USA (1986) £24.95 pp 283

Communication among geographically distributed computer systems is provided by broadcast media such as satellite, radio and cable channels. Multiple access protocols are algorithms that have been proposed for these packet broadcast networks to achieve efficient sharing of a single common channel. The book evaluates the performance of various protocols proposed.

How MODULA-2 facilities support good software engineering

Gustav Pomberger

Software engineering and Modula-2
Prentice-Hall, Englewood Cliffs, NJ,
USA (1986) £12.95 pp 277

Straight away I must admit to a bias in favour of the theme of this book. The theme is that the increasing size and complexity of software systems requires the application of good software engineering principles. Good software engineering requires the support of software tools, the foremost of which is the implementation language. MODULA-2 is a well designed high-level language which supports all known software engineering concepts and lends itself equally well to systems and application programming. The volume of the language is modest and it is therefore suitable for implementation on microcomputers.

Most of the programming languages in practical use today are conceptually outdated by present software engineering standards — hence the need for the new languages such as ADA and MODULA-2.

As the author states, this book is intended for the software professional, and the reader should have a knowledge of algorithms, data structures, programming languages and the fundamentals of mathematics and logic.

The book has three main sections: the first gives an overview of MODULA-2 and is supported in two appendices by a verbatim copy of Wirth's *Report on the programming language Modula-2*; tne second deals in a fairly detailed way with the software life cycle; and the third covers the relationship between these two sections, i.e. how the facilities in MODULA-2 support good software engineering.

Pomberger rightly makes the point that the choice of the 'right' programming language for the implementation of software products influences to a much greater extent than is often assumed in practice, the quality of these software products. He deals not only with the logical criteria for the choice — program control structures, data structures, separate compilation, type checking, etc., but also with pragmatic criteria such as what the customer wants, availability of compilers, previous experience and the availability of facilities and tools.

The section on MODULA-2 is an adequate overview of the language. In 40 pages, it cannot be more. The only real omission is the handling of hardware interrupts when discussing the low-level facilities. Procedure types are covered, but I think that, in the interests of clarity, the example could have been usefully expanded to a complete short program. Also the discussion on local modules should state clearly that the reason for the existence of local modules is to deal with identifier visibility problems within either the program or library modules.

A minor error which occurs on page 80, and is mildly irritating, is that an example procedure called BuildWord is referred to in the text as ConstructWord. Similar minor errors occur in one or two other places in the book, e.g. on page 164 where the module FileProcessing is referred to as DataProcessing.

The section on the software life cycle is given due importance and occupies half the text of the book. Within this section, the subsection on design is again given due importance, occupying half of the section (i.e. a quarter of the book).

The subsection on design deals in some depth with the method of stepwise refinement, structuring of flow control, guidelines for module construction, modularization and the choice of data and program control structures, data capsules, abstract data structures and types, and verification. A most important principle for mastering complexity is the principle of abstraction. Abstraction is embodied in the method of stepwise refinement. After discussion of problem oriented and data oriented techniques, the author expresses the opinion that the technique of task oriented stepwise refinement is the most general and reasonable design concept; this reveals a practitioner of the art. Designing software is a creative process, but meaningful guidelines can be given.

Modularization is one of the most important phases of the design process. How should the program be divided? What should be the interfaces? The book lists which criteria should be considered in module construction to obtain a satisfactory decomposition of the system. Data capsules are dealt with at some length, and examples are given of solutions to a problem without and with the use of data capsules.

The pragmatism of the author comes through in his attitude to verification. The conclusion to this topic states: 'Formalism should supplement, definitely not replace, common sense and programming experience and intuition.'

In the third major section the realization of software engineering concepts in MODULA-2 is discussed. It is shown how the concept of the definition module supports the method of stepwise refinement. Further it is shown how the language definition satisfies the requirements of structured programming. Also discussed are separate compilation and team development of software, and the implementation of data capsules and abstract data types.

The book is very readable, well produced and has a useful index and bibliography. (If the reviewer may be permitted to point out one last minor error, it is that Somerville is out of alphabetical order in the reference list.)

I am pleased to add this useful book to my bookshelf and recommend it to all engaged in the design and implementation of software.

Joe Gallacher,
Microprocessor Systems
Engineering Ltd,
Aberfeldy, UK

Locus text is incomplete but useful

Gerald J Popek and Bruce J Walker

The Locus distributed system architecture MIT Press, Cambridge, MA, USA (1986) £24.95 pp 163

The Locus operating system is one of the most important developments of recent years in distributed computing and this book provides a useful collection of information about the system in a single source. Some familiarity with Unix, upon which Locus is based, is essential and the book will be most useful to experienced system designers or for use as part of an undergraduate course on the development of distributed systems. The introductory material provides an excellent summary of the reasons for developing transparent distributed systems, which is highly recommended to anyone interested in this area.

The remainder of the book is concerned with the Locus system itself, concentrating mainly on the implementation of the file system which is at its heart, but also giving brief coverage of some other aspects such as remote tasking and heterogeneity. Much of the information has already been made available in previously published papers but has here been brought up to date in the light of the developer's experiences.

Unfortunately there is so much that could be said about the system that the authors have had to be quite selective about which areas are covered in detail. This tends to make reading the sections rather hard as the information content swings from very detailed analysis of protocols to tantalizingly brief discussions of potential problem areas. Obviously the book is not a maintenance manual for someone supporting Locus but at times the contents do seem to be veering in this direction — it is part user guide, part academic paper.

There are two major omissions from the book which do tend to diminish its usefulness to the interested reader. First, no performance data are provided and thus it is hard to evaluate Locus and the claims made for it with respect to conventional and other distributed systems. Such performance data do exist and have been published in conference proceedings; they would have been a much more useful inclusion here than the tables of system calls and network messages that are appended to the text.

The second omission is of considerably more significance as it covers a topic that most people associate with the Locus system, namely that of reliability and recoverability. This book contains almost no information about the special mechanisms added to Locus to support transactions and recovery from network partitions. In fact even the sections describing the file replication mechanism do not discuss adequately the problems involved in recovering from such failures. There are a number of very difficult unsolved problems in this area and some discussion of these would have been most welcome, particularly with the benefit of the experience of the Locus teams. Perhaps a future volume is planned to cover this important area.

Another minor omission is any real comparison between the Locus approach and that taken by other systems. However, the book is provided with a good, if short, bibliography of the field which goes some way to making up for this.

The actual volume itself is well produced and is stated by the publisher to be photographed directly from the author's word processor output. This was done, it is claimed, to reduce the cost of publishing, but at £24.95 the book seems rather overpriced for a work of some 150 pages.

Lindsay Marshall
University of
Newcastle-upon-Tyne, UK

Geometrical techniques to give wireframe images

Leendert Ammeraal

Programming principles in computer graphics John Wiley, New York, USA (April 1986) £11.50 pp 168

This book is basically a collection of geometrical techniques, together with the appropriate mathematics, applicable to the production of wireframe images on vector displays. The topics covered include transformations for modelling and viewing, hidden line elimination, clipping and data structures for the representation and production of wireframe images. The title implies, to me at least, a much wider coverage of computer graphics than this. There is no discussion of graphics standards, no discussion of graphics devices, nothing on the structure of graphics programs, nothing on interactive computer graphics, and nothing on the increasingly important human factors aspects.

Full algorithms are supplied throughout to support the text and encourage the reader to implement; this is essential and the author's efforts in this direction deserve praise. The choice of C is at the expense, in my opinion, of some clarity, using PASCAL or another similar language may have made the book more suitable for both teaching and individual study.

The author's target readership is not clear; the coverage is too narrow for the book to form the basis of a computer science degree component or a similar general introduction to graphics, but the book could be used to support such courses where the content overlaps. Similar material is covered in many other texts but the book is well written and produced and will probably appeal mainly to people who require a sound introduction to some of the geometrical techniques, and associated algorithms, required for computer graphics and computer-aided design.

Helmut Bez
University of Technology,
Loughborough, UK

book reviews

CSP — language based on concurrency and communication

C A R Hoare

Communicating sequential processes
Prentice-Hall, Englewood Cliffs, NJ,
USA (April 1985) £27.95 pp 256

Communicating sequential processes is an exposition of the author's programming language (CSP) based on concurrency and communication.

'The main objective of (the author's) research into communicating processes has been to find the simplest possible mathematical theory with the following desirable properties.

(1) It should describe a wide range of interesting computer applications, from vending machines, through process control and discrete event simulation, to shared-resource operating systems.
(2) It should be capable of efficient implementation on a variety of conventional and novel computer architectures, from time-sharing computers through multiprocessors to networks of communicating microprocessors.
(3) It should provide clear assistance to the programmer in his tasks of specification, design, implementation, verification and validation of complex computer systems.'

(p 223).

In chapter 7 Professor Hoare justifies his solution by comparison with the main languages which address the same problems, OCCAM and Milner's CCS in particular. From a programming viewpoint CSP generally handles concurrency and communication in a more satisfactory manner than either OCCAM or CCS; but if one wishes to write mainly sequential programs the comparison is less favourable, ADA and PASCAL PLUS being preferable.

However, the ease with which the dining philosopher's problem is solved and an operating system is designed (chapter 6) shows that many of the author's objectives have been achieved. The CSP language is destined to be more significant than either OCCAM or CCS.

The current book continues the high quality of earlier books in Prentice-Hall's *Computer Science* series. It is aimed at the professional, postgraduate or good undergraduate computer scientist without any prerequisite theoretical knowledge. Explanations of the definitions of virtually all the constructs are comprehensive and well illustrated. At no point is Professor Hoare too theoretical. There are many examples and these are continually developed or recast.

One of my two major criticisms of the book is that there are no exercises to complement the language description in the clearly pedagogical style of the book. These would be essential for anyone wishing to learn the many different symbols well enough to benefit fully from the whole book.

The other major flaw in this gem is that the main text contains no formal definitions of any of the symbols of CSP. What the author does do is to give a number of 'laws' which the symbols satisfy. Some of these, when combined, yield the definition of the given symbol with the other laws as deducible theorems, but there is no indication of which law might produce the definition. Moreover, on one or two occasions laws are stated without all the necessary restrictions, sacrificing accuracy for readability.

Following up something you've just seen?

Please mention
Microprocessors and Microsystems

The formal definitions are deliberately relegated to sections entitled 'Mathematical theory'. The author and many others will consider this an advantage. I would much rather have seen them integrated with the informal descriptions because their juxtaposition might lead to a deeper understanding. This is most necessary for the nondeterministic aspects in chapter 3 where the difference between, for example, the internal and external choice operators $\sqcap$ and $\square$ is very hard to describe without a precise definition at hand.

Typographical and other obvious errors are very few in numbers: in the first three chapters an inaccuracy in law L5 on page 57 and the omission of a few brackets on page 131 are hardly worth mentioning.

Every so often the author includes a section entitled 'Implementation' in which a LISP definition of each construct is given. This further clarifies the CSP language, can be omitted easily when reading individual chapters and presumably, when coalesced, will provide an implementation of much of CSP.

The first couple of chapters are essentially just standard formal language theory re-expressed. It would have been nice for more knowledgeable readers to have been given pointers to an appropriate starting point, even though the author is aiming at a general readership. Parallelism comes into the chapters on the deterministic theory. The hard work comes with the nondeterministic choice symbols treated in chapter 3, where the sequence of actions which a process may perform are found to be insufficient to fully specify a process.

Chapter 4 introduces communication on channels between processes. Here piping, similar to that in Unix, is defined. This enables a particularly beautiful solution to be given to the problem of reformatting a sequence of lines of up to 80 characters into tightly packed lines of 125 characters each. In a

(continued opposite)

SDK-85 provides ideas for microprocessor 'practicals'

Borivoje Furht and Himanshu Parikh

Microprocessor interfacing and communication using the Intel SDK-85 Prentice-Hall Reston, Englewood Cliffs, NJ, USA (April 1986) £31.00 pp 499

Intended primarily as a textbook for university students at all levels in electrical engineering and computer science, and assuming a basic knowledge of microprocessors, assembly language, flow charts and circuit diagrams, this book describes a number of fully tested microprocessor experiments. Sufficient detail is given so that a person competent in the practical aspects of microprocessors could reproduce similar experiments if desired.

The book is based on the Intel SDK-85 single-board microcomputer, which includes on 8085 8-bit microprocessor, 256 byte of static RAM, a 2 kbyte ROM-based monitor and simple I/O and timer facilities. A hex keypad and a one-line display are also provided. The SDK-85 includes a prototyping area, but this is not suitable for solderless breadboarding. The book recommends the use of the EXB-85 microcomputer experiment breadboard in conjunction with the SDK-85.

The first two chapters give an introduction to the SDK-85 and its use; the rest of the text covers 12 different projects (one per chapter) gradually increasing in complexity and ranging from the design of a slot machine to a microprocessor-controlled robot arm. Around a third of the book is dedicated to appendices, consisting mainly of data sheets. These are normally available free from the manufacturers so I hope that they have not substantially increased the price of the book (although I suspect that they probably have). There is a fairly good index at the end of the book, although it does not include main entries under 'microprocessor' or 'interfacing'!

In general each project introduces the student to an aspect of microprocessor-based design (e.g. interrupts, data communication etc.). The projects and concepts they introduce are simply and well explained. Full assembler program listings, with a reasonable number of comments, are included. Flowcharts are used to explain overall program structure; most of these fit onto one page and are thus quite easy to follow, but one is split onto four pages and is an admirable example of why flowcharts should only be used in the simplest of cases. Circuit and other diagrams are also included as required.

For each project, from one to four experiments are described. Additional questions and problems are included at the end of each chapter. Some projects require external hardware (such as a robot arm or extra peripheral chips on the breadboard) whilst others are self contained. Programs for the projects can be developed on a mainframe computer such as a Vax, or even on a microcomputer with the necessary crossassembler, and downloaded into the SDK-85. The ideal alternative would be to use a microprocessor development system, although this may not be available because of the added expense.

For the book to be used by university students, it must also appear in paperback form (if it has not already done so). A version of the book without the program listings could be more suitable for students since then they could attempt to write the programs from scratch themselves if desired. In its present form the book would only really be directly suitable for student use if the SDK-85, or at least an 8080- or 8085-based microcomputer, were used for the experiments.

Otherwise its main use will be by university staff organizing microprocessor-based 'practicals'. In this context it would make a very good 'ideas' book whatever its price. I would recommend it for this purpose even if, as is likely, the SDK-85 itself is not to be used in the practicals. The projects could equally well be undertaken on a 16-bit system if required.

The book claims to be a suitable textbook for a newly proposed course on interfacing and communication in the IEEE Curriculum of Computer Engineering and Science. This may be an important incentive for the use of the book in the USA. It also claims to be useful for engineers and programmers in industry and hobbyists who use microprocessors. It could be used by a keen hobbyist wanting to learn without tutoring, but it is unlikely to get more than a browse from the majority of industrial readers.

Jonathan Bowen
Oxford University
Computing Laboratory, UK

Hoare
(*continued*)

conventional programming language it is usually necessary to favour input or output by having the outermost loop iterating over the characters of its lines or to have a possibly infinite buffer in which to store all of the text after unformatting it.

Successful termination, interrupts, checkpoints and the most important aspects of conventional sequential programming (assignment etc.) are described in chapter 5. They are used in chapter 6 to construct an operating system; this is the main example given in the book to adequately justify CSP.

The examples given are so varied — including airline booking systems and networks — and hardware is currently developing so quickly that it is hard to envisage a computer scientist not needing to know about concurrency and communication. This book is a good introduction to a language that can be used to think clearly in, and solve problems in, these areas.

C D Walter
UMIST, Manchester, UK

book reviews

FORTH gains not a textbook but a reference source

M G Kelly and N Spies

FORTH: a text and reference Prentice-Hall, Englewood Cliffs, NJ, USA (February 1986), £19.10 pp 487

The author's stated intention was to produce both a textbook for learners and a reference work for more experienced programmers. This book more nearly achieves the reference objective, and for this reason deserves to be put among the top three books currently available on the FORTH language. To my mind, however, the differing needs of these two classes of user has resulted in the book's failure as a text and a reduction in its stature as a reference.

There would seem to be two techniques commonly used by textbooks, which equate quite well to the alternatives of top-down and bottom-up programming. The top-down school of teaching, to which this book belongs, cheerfully uses structures it has yet to explain or define and hopes the student will take those areas not detailed on trust. The bottom-up school of teaching insists on organizing its material so that only one concept is introduced to the student at a time, building always upon established material. Whilst preferring my programming top down, I complain if my training is not done bottom up. One of my major objections to the 'text' aspect of this book is that its teaching is top down to such a degree that the DO... LOOP structure is not formally explained until page 151.

The first 90 pages consist of an admirably useful discussion on stack usage, fixed, floating and unsigned numbers. However, this does not make a good introduction to a language whose major advantages are its powers of abstraction. Other problems in using this as a teaching text are that its need, as a reference book, to compare and contrast published FORTH standards with a commercial implementation (MMS FORTH is used within the book) must inevitably generate some confusion for the learner.

On the positive side, the exercises

are many. Worked answers are given, and I particularly liked the way that in some chapters the answers are routines which are put together in the last question to solve a significant problem. This teaches the technique of successive prototyping admirably, extending goals as knowledge of a problem and its solution are learnt.

The book succeeds much more as a reference work than as a textbook. In this light its early chapters become a detailed description of the advantages of the different numerical representations available on computers. (This book is the only one I know of to give a comprehensive description of FORTH assembler.)

There are a number of typographical errors and some of the examples will not work in the way defined due to minor errors. However, it is to be hoped that the publishers will rectify this. FORTH is commonly criticized for not providing features such as floating point, string handling and array manipulation within the common FORTH standard. Most FORTH programmers rapidly develop a toolbox of words to perform the functions they need within these areas, and the authors successfully

show how this can be done and in the process provide such a toolbox. Their major programming example is a simple yet relatively powerful screen editor written in 130 lines of FORTH.

This generally well produced work could, however, benefit in many cases from replacing prose with diagrams. The dominance of prose is perhaps a feature of the current generation of books produced by technologists using word processors; the next generation produced using Macintosh machines will probably suffer from the reverse failing. What the book lacks in diagrams, it makes up for in appendices, which include a full glossary of the FORTH words used and of FORTH and general computer terms, and a list of commercially available FORTH systems and books.

In short, this is not the textbook I would recommend to a raw beginner, but programmers who have learnt FORTH and wish to know more about the language, and how to get the best out of it, will find this a valuable work.

C L Stephens
Computer Solutions Ltd
Byfleet, UK

Uneven treatment for control systems engineering

Stephen P Banks

Control systems engineering Prentice-Hall, Englewood Cliffs, NJ, USA (February 1986) £29.95 pp 614

A number of books are already available on the subject of control engineering theory, both classical and modern, but the wider field of control systems engineering, which is by far the most likely context within which the subject of control will be met in industry, has not often been addressed. This book therefore fulfils a clear need and is welcome for that. The scope of the subject is, however, potentially wide and decisions have to be taken on what to put in and what to leave out. The author would seem to have had

difficulties with the latter: the book is longer than most at over 600 pages.

As well as the usual foundation of theoretical principles, most people would expect such a book perhaps to include information on system identification and modelling together with some more practically oriented information related to design and implementation. The author has set about this task by dividing the book into three sections entitled 'Modelling and simulation', 'Control theory' and 'Microprocessor implementation'. So far, so good, but it is in content and balance that the achievement of the objectives is less clear.

Few would dispute that it is still generally necessary for engineers in
(continued opposite)

514   *microprocessors and microsystems*

VLSI proceedings bas many significant contributions

E Hörbst (Ed.)

VLSI 85: VLSI design of digital systems
Elsevier, Amsterdam The Netherlands
(1986) £53.50 pp 443

The IFIP international conference VLSI85, held in Tokyo during August 1985, was the most recent of a series of conferences considering the more fundamental and theoretical aspects of VLSI design methodologies and chip architectures. This text is the published proceedings of that conference, and readers selecting the perhaps ambiguous title should therefore not expect to find a standard text on the design of digital systems incorporating VLSI.

The book contains 40 papers in 11 sections covering a range of diverse topics including, for example, silicon compilation, simulation for VLSI, the impact of 'ULSI', signal processing architectures and algorithms and tools for cell and chip layout. A number of invited papers are included. Contributions are from an international list of authors, although naturally weighted towards Japan. Not surprisingly many of the Japanese contributions are concerned with advanced memory system architecture. It is interesting to note, however, that several contributions from Japan reflect modern algorithm and processor architecture developments.

A number of the invited papers are disappointing in their technical content, range and length, reducing in one case to no more than one page (including references) introducing the important concept of hierarchy within VLSI design. An invited paper on VLSI testability does no more than repeat standard work. Such papers do not contribute to the fundamental research into VLSI architectures, algorithms and design methodologies that this conference should reflect.

The text does however contain many significant contributions. Section 2 of the book on silicon compilation reviews the present state of the art in this increasingly important field. Section 5 provides examples of developing computer and digital signal processing chip architectures. A demonstration of the use of shift-register-based residue arithmetic circuits highlights the fact that advances in system performance are achieved not only by technology developments, but also by considering the fundamental form of many processing algorithms. In many papers the authors show that redundancy will increase chip yield significantly, but only with the optimum architecture.

Functional-level system design is described in section 7a. This section highlights work in functional specification and design, now known to be the limiting factor in VLSI. Experimental hardware description languages are discussed. Further sections consider the details of chip layout, discussing the layout of self-checking circuits, routing, compaction and symbolic layout. Papers discussing the generation of rules for layout and the use of 'expert systems' are welcome inclusions.

This book is aimed primarily at the active research worker, both industrial and academic, in the field of VLSI. The book covers a wide range of topics, from abstract system design concepts to the final chip layout implementation. It does contain many significant contributions, but not all the contributions reflect the current state of the art. To achieve maximum benefit the book should be read in conjunction with the proceedings of the annual design automation, acoustics and signal processing and solid-state circuit conferences. This is a text for the reference library.

John Fox
Plessey Research (Caswell) Ltd,
Towcester, UK

Banks

(continued)

control systems to have a good working knowledge of analogue techniques, but the chapter which comes closest to dealing with this subject is, in effect, a manual on analogue computers and their use for simulation. However useful a survivor of the breed may be to demonstrate principles in a teaching environment, a book of this sort would be better off with a more generalized description of the use of operational amplifiers and analogue techniques as they might be met with today.

The treatment of digital simulation starts from ground level with a description of what digital computers are all about, and then goes on to deal with the mathematical foundations very thoroughly, including finite-element and stochastic techniques. There is not much to guide the reader on how to actually use a computer, particularly the ubiquitous PC, to carry out modelling and display the results. This contrasts a little strangely with the depth of detail in the final section, where assembly language programming and interfacing of a Z80 are described; for very few readers can this be worth the 100 or more pages it is allocated, and I personally would have preferred to see some of the space used for groundwork on the subject of software engineering.

Classical frequency-response methods, on the other hand, rate about 35 pages and are followed by nonlinear theory, optimal control, stochastic systems and adaptive, selftuning and variable-structure systems.

Subjects which do not appear are reliability and fault tolerance, which in systems relating to such fields as aerospace, power generation and traffic control, for example, often turn out to be the most important aspects of the whole task.

In summary, this is a good work of reference, dealing with a wide range of the mathematical concepts underlying control systems engineering. If the total content of the book coincides with your requirement in terms of subject matter, then you will find it good value for money.

P A L Ham
NEI Parsons Ltd
Newcastle-upon-Tyne, UK

product news

Graphics processor can be used standalone or with host

A 32-bit processor with 'special capabilities for supporting high-performance computer graphics applications' has been launched by Texas Instruments (TI). The TMS34010 graphics system processor (GSP) is aimed at such applications as PC displays, workstations, laser printers, electronic publishing, fax, image capture, mass storage and robot vision.

The TMS34010 can be used as an applications processor with a host or as a standalone processor, says TI. Performance of up to 6M instructions per second (MIPS) and a draw rate of up to 48M pixels per second are specified, and develop-

ment tools based on IBM PC, TI Professional or DEC Vax computers are being offered.

A 1 Gbit DRAM bit addressable memory is used to speed addressing, while an on-chip CRT controller eliminates the need for a separate memory system controller. The 34010 instruction set supports migration of graphics algorithms through the c language, graphics standards (AKS, CGI etc.) and user interfaces. Built-in hardware support for window clipping allows rapid window management, says TI, with management of variable-size pixel arrays optimized through pixel processing and the microcoded

instruction set.

The GSP chip has 31 general-purpose registers, direct DRAM/VRAM control and integrated control of pixel displays up to 64k × 64k pixels. It is compatible with industry standard DRAMs and VRAMs and standard interface devices, says the manufacturer.

The 34010 is manufactured in CMOS, with a power dissipation of 0.5 W at 6 MIPS, and packaged in a 68-lead plastic chip carrier. (*Texas Instruments Inc., PO Box 1444, Houston, TX 77001, USA. Texas Instruments Ltd, Manton Lane, Bedford MK41 7PA, UK. Tel: (0234) 63211*) ☐

Special 'hand-sized' keys allowing handicapped people who cannot use a normal keyboard to use computers are being produced by Cleveland Information Technology Centre in the UK. Developed by the Centre's electronics supervisor Peter Backhouse in response to requests from local hospitals, the 'macro keys' are designed to be wired to the user board of an Acorn BBC microcomputer. A number of software packages for the handicapped have been written on the BBC; these aim to improve coordination by having the patient perform simple tasks such as recognizing colours or letters. Currently available software uses up to four of the special keys at once, although the BBC itself is capable of handling up to eight keys. The keys measure 143 × 95 × 55 m and weigh about 110 g. They are being made in small quantities for sale at £4.75 each, interface boxes and analogue port adaptors costing an extra £4.55 and £2.72 respectively. (Cleveland Information Technology Centre, 34 Albert Road, Middlesbrough, Cleveland TS1 1QD, UK. Tel: (0642) 221280)

Gate array designs can move to standard cell

Standard cells in 3 µm CMOS have been added to SGS Semiconductor's range of semicustom products. Compatibility with the company's existing gate array series will allow customers to produce designs in gate array form and then move them to standard cells for full production. Designs are produced on standard CAD workstations.

The standard cells are currently available with a total range of 170 logic functions, and this is due to be expanded shortly to include more complex functions such as RAM, ROM and PLA library cells. A 1.5 µm CMOS process will also be introduced soon, says SGS. Longer-term developments in the standard cell range are expected to include microprocessor cores and peripherals plus a new SGS-developed CAD system for logic design and layout.

A range of packaging options is available for the devices, including dual and quad in-line plastic and ceramic packs and pin grid arrays with from 14 to 180 pins. (*SGS-ATES Componenti Elettronici SpA, Stradale Primosole 50, 95121 Catania, Sicily, Italy. Tel: (3995) 599 111. SGS, Planar House, Walton Street, Aylesbury, Bucks, UK. Tel: (0296) 5977*) ☐

Industrial system has front and rear busos

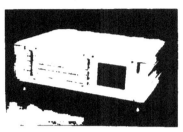

Kemitron's STE/RIO system holds five horizontally mounted double Eurocards

An industrial computer system based on STEbus has been launched by Kemitron of the UK. The system uses double Eurocards with an STE interface on one connector and a rear I/O bus on the other; this dual-bus configuration is reflected in the sytem name, STE/RIO.

Five horizontally mounted double Eurocards can be accommodated in STE/RIO; this approach is designed to facilitate routing of I/O signals to the rear of the case. The front of the 19 in × 3U rack holds the five-slot backplane and a disc drive module giving 3.5 in and 5.25 in hard and floppy disc options. The rear face holds up to 16 panels each containing 20 two-part screw terminals for signal connection to I/O boards.

The system's processor card holds a 6 MHz HD64180 8-bit CPU, 768 kbit of RAM or ROM with DMA, four serial channels, maths processor, counter–timer, watchdog, realtime clock, floppy disc controller, hard disc interface and STEbus. Other boards available include a 32-channel digital I/O–counter–timer card with feedback sensing and optoisolation and a 64/32-channel single-ended or differential analogue I/O card with sample-and-hold amplifier.

STE/RIO runs the CP/M 3.0 operating system and comes in either laboratory-style or sealed IP65 cases. (*Kemitron Ltd, Hawarden Industrial Park, Manor Lane, Deeside, Clywd CH5 3PP, UK. Tel: (0244) 536123*) □

68020 and 68881 are upgraded

A 25 MHz version of the MC68020 32-bit microprocessor, together with a 20 MHz version of the related MC68881 floating-point coprocessor, have been announced by Motorola. This chip combination is claimed to be capable of performances 'well in excess of 1M Whetstone', a level which systems designers such as Sun Microsystems have reported using just the 16.67 MHz devices.

The 25 MHz CPU operates at 12.5M instructions per second (MIPS) in burst mode, says the manufacturer, with a sustained throughput of 5 MIPS. 68020 features include an on-chip instruction cache and three-stage instruction pipeline. The 68881 gives over 40 floating-point functions and 80-bit precision, and operates concurrently to the CPU.

Both devices are manufactured in 1.5 µm CMOS and are currently available in sample qualities. Full production is due by the end of this year. (*Motorola Inc., 3501 Ed Bluestein Blvd, Austin, TX 78721, USA. Motorola Ltd, 88 Tanners Drive, Blakelands, Milton Keynes MK14 5BP, UK. Tel: (0908) 614614*)

□

PMX entends capability to 25 MHz

Daisy Systems has enhanced its Physical Modelling Extension (PMX) development system to provide simulation of systems running advanced components at up to 25 MHz. The enhancement comes in the form of PMX Fastboard, which plugs directly into any existing PMX chassis to provide what Daisy claims to be the fastest physical modelling capability available.

Fastboard supports variable vector playback rates from 200 kHz to 25 MHz in increments of 20 ns. It features 64k vector depth for each of 94 logic signal channels; this is sufficient to handle devices of the complexity of, for example, Intel's 80386, which requires 88 logical signals.

Designers who need to simulate systems incorporating a number of complex components can do this by installing several Fastboards on one PMX chassis, says Daisy. (*Daisy Systems Corp., 139 Kifer Court, Sunnyvale, CA 94086, USA. Tel: (408) 773-9111. Daisy Systems, Berk House, Basing View, Basingstoke, Hants RG21 2HZ, UK. Tel: (0256) 53625*) □

32-bit rugged systems use VME and VSB

32-bit computer modules using VMEbus and the VME Subsystem Bus (VSB) have been introduced by Plessey Microsystems. VSB has been incorporated as a 32-bit local bus to maximize system performance from the system's 68020 CPU.

The systems are designed for use in military and rugged industrial environments. Boards initially available for the system are a 68020 processor board, dual-ported static RAM, EPROM and a VME-to-MIL-STD-1553B interface. Static RAM and EPROM boards are dual ported to the VME and VSB buses to minimize contention for the system bus in multiprocessor systems and to allow rapid access to 32 bit wide local memory.

The boards are available in two versions, military and 'rugged', the latter being assembled with industrial-grade components. If desired they can be accommodated in an ATR box to provide a complete system. (*Plessey Microsystems Ltd, Water Lane, Towcester, Northants NN12 7JN, UK. Tel: (0327) 50312*) □

products in brief

Name	Description	Manufacturer/designer	Distributor/contact
Development systems			
Microrack 20/20 NS 6U and WS 9U	VMEbus development systems comprising a KM6 card frame, a 20-slot backplane with 'off-board' termination, a 400 W power supply, cooling facilities and a metal enclosure, designed to accommodate up to 20 standard VMEbus boards. WS 9U has an additional card frame for housing mass storage devices	Bicc-Vero Electronics, Flanders Road, Hedge End, Southampton SO3 3LG, UK. Tel: (04215) 66300	
Digital signal processors			
MB87064	CMOS DSP similar to Fujitsu's MB8764, but designed as a lower-cost component for higher-volume applications. Features a pipelined multiplier supporting concurrent operations with compound instructions and multiple data paths, 128×16 bit blocks of built-in RAM and a 16-bit parallel interface. Instruction cycle time is 100 ns; power consumption is 300 mW and packaging is in a 42-pin ceramic DIP	Fujitsu Ltd, 6-1 Marunouchi 2-chome, Chiyoda-ku, Tokyo 100, Japan	Fujitsu Microelectronics Ltd, Hargrave House, Belmont Road, Maidenhead, Berks SL6 6NE, UK. Tel: (0628) 76100
Graphics modules			
SYS68K/AGC-1	1280×1024 pixel graphics display controller module for VMEbus. Comprises two double-Eurocard boards, one with a colour raster tube controller (ACRTC-63484) and VMEbus interfacing and the other providing 2 Mbyte of video DRAM and shift registers	Force Computer GmbH, Screischutzstrasse 92, 8000 Munich 81, FRG. Tel: (4989) 951-041	Force Computers UK Ltd, 1 Holly Court, 3 Tring Road, Wendover, Bucks HP22 6PE, UK. Tel: (0296) 625456
Interface devices			
DAD-48	A/D and D/A interface board for STDbus. Has eight 16-bit A/D inputs and four 12-bit analogue output channels	Computer Dynamics Inc., 105 South Main Street, Greer, SC 29651, USA. Tel: (803) 877-7471	Amplicon Electronics Ltd, Richmond Road, Brighton, East Sussex BN2 3RL, UK. Tel: (0273) 608331
HD68562	Single-chip serial communications controller with two independent multiprotocol full-duplex synchronous or asynchronous serial receiver/transmitters. Supports all current serial communications protocols, says the manufacturer. Software overhead is reduced by an on-chip CRC generator–checker	Hitachi Ltd, New Marunouchi Building No 5, 1-chome Marunouchi, Chiyoda, Tokyo, Japan	Hitachi Electronic Components (UK) Ltd, 21 Upton Road, Watford, Herts WD1 7TB, UK. Tel: (0923) 46488

Section headings in this issue's 'Products in brief' section are

Development systems	**Networking products**	**PROMs**
Digital signal processors	**Peripheral controllers**	**RAMs**
Graphics modules	**Processor boards**	**Single-chip microcomputers**
Interface devices	**Programmable arrays**	**Software products**
Memory modules	**Programming modules**	

Name	Description	Manufacturer/designer	Distributor/contact
I8SER	68000-based VMEbus I/O module with 32 kbyte of dual-ported RAM, designed to simplify applications using a high-level control protocol and firmware (including synchronous communications link drivers). Includes four Z8530 serial I/O controllers and works in RS232C or RS422 modes with baud rates programmable up to 1 Mbaud. Four DMA channels are provided	High Technology Electronics Ltd, 303–305 Portswood Road, Southampton SO2 1LD, UK. Tel: (0703) 581555	
IPL Multi I/O	VME interface card designed for small systems. Includes a Centronics port, eight relay outputs, an LCD interface, eight optoisolated inputs, four differential line inputs, two TTL-compatible inputs and a 16-key keypad interface	Integrated Photomatrix Ltd, The Grove Trading Estate, Dorchester, Dorset DT1 1SY, UK. Tel: (0305) 63673	
PM2201	GPIB (general-purpose interface bus) interface board designed to allow Philips PM3100, IBM PC and PC AT and compatible computers to be used as instrumentation system controllers. Up to 15 instruments may be interconnected under control of a PC. GPIB functions are called up using a high-level language added to the PC's BASIC or GWBASIC interpreter	Philips Electrologica BV, PO Box 245, Oude Apeldoomseweg 41, Apeldoorn, The Netherlands	Philips Test and Measurement Dept, Pye Unicam Ltd, York Street, Cambridge CB1 2PX, UK. Tel: (0223) 358866
SYS68K/ISIO-1	68010, VMEbus-based serial I/O board with eight I/O channels, 128 kbyte dual ported RAM and an onboard RS232-compatible driver–receiver. CPU runs at 10 MHz without the use of wait states. An onboard bus interrupt module supports fully asynchronous operation	Force Computers GmbH, Daimlerstrasse 9, D-8012 Ottobrun/München, FRG. Tel: (089) 60091	
UVC3101-8, UVC3101-10	High-speed A/D and D/A converters, respectively, designed as an R-2R network with switched current sources. The A/D converter is 8-bit, the D/A converter is 10-bit. Maximum clock speed for the devices is 38.5 MHz. Suitable for signal processing applications or decoding television signals	ITT Semiconductors (UK), 145–147 Ewell Road, Surbiton, Surrey KT6 6AW, UK. Tel: 01-390 6578	ITT Multicomponents, The Mill House, Barry Avenue, Windsor, Berks SL4 1QS, UK. Tel: (0753) 840201

From left: Bicc-Vero's Microrack 20/20 NS 6U VME development system; the Fujitsu MB87064 digital signal processor; and HTE's I8SER intelligent VMEbus I/O module

products in brief

Name	Description	Manufacturer/designer	Distributor/contact
Interface devices (*continued*)			
XR88C681, XR68C681	CMOS dual universal asynchronous receiver/transmitters (UARTs) for use with 8080/85/86, Z80, 68XX and 65XX families (88C681) and with 68000-based systems (68C681). Available in 28- and 40-pin DIPs. Industrial and military versions can be supplied	Exar Corp., 750 Palomar Avenue, Sunnyvale CA 94086, USA. Tel: (408) 732-7970	Micro Call Ltd, Thame Park Road, Thame, Oxon OX9 3XD, UK. Tel: (084 421) 5405
Memory modules			
SYS68K/ SRAM-3A and -3B	512 kbyte and 1 Mbyte static memory boards with VMEbus and VMXbus interfacing and onboard battery backing. Two memory areas each of half the total capacity can be assigned to react to VME only, VMX only or VME and VMX transfers. Typical access times are: VMEbus write 82 ns, read 225 ns; VMXbus write 75 ns, read 250 ns	Force Computers GmbH, Daimlerstrasse 9, D-8012 Ottobrunn, Munich, FRG. Tel: (089) 60091-0	Force Computers UK Ltd, 1 Holly Court, 3 Tring Road, Wendover, Bucks HP22 6PE, UK. Tel: (0296) 625456
VME 48055/6	1 Mbyte dynamic RAM on a single-height multilayer VMEbus board. Uses ZIL packaged 256 × 1 bit DRAMs; handles 8- and 16-bit transfers and 24-bit addressing. Typical write/read access times are 190 ns or 280 ns	Bicc-Vero Electronics Ltd, Flanders Road, Hedge End, Southampton SO3 3LG, UK. Tel: (04215) 66300	
Networking products			
CT-net	Ethernet controller board for 68000-based computers. Can be piggybacked onto the CT-VIDC or CT-VICP providing a combined disc and Ethernet or I/O and Ethernet controller. Throughput rate is increased by onboard FIFO using DMA into user configurable transmit and receive buffers. Comes with Uniplus+ V.2	Integrated Micro Products Ltd, 1 Industrial Estate, Medomsley Road, Consett, Co. Durham DH8 6TJ, UK. Tel: (0207) 503481	
Gesnet-1A	Z80-based local area network controller board. Links up to 50 G-64 bus based microcomputer systems for industrial and process control applications. Arbitration scheme is collision-sense multiple access/collision avoidance (CSMA/CA) on cable lengths up to 300 m, switching to an Ethernet-like CSMA/CD collision detection mode up to 900 m. Onboard firmware implements the first four layers of the Open System Interconnection specification	Gespac Inc., 100 West Hoover Avenue #11, Mesa, AZ 85202, USA. Tel: (602) 962-5559	
HYC9068	LAN driver chip for use in coaxial 'Arcnet' baseband LANs. Compatible with the COM9026 LAN controller and its companion timing device, the chip allows a hub or active repeater to have up to eight ports without reflections. Packaged in a 20-pin SIP	Standard Microsystems Corp., 35 Marcus Blvd, Hauppage, NY 11788, USA	Manhattan Skyline Ltd, Manhattan House, Bridge Road, Maidenhead, Berks SL6 8DB, UK. Tel: (0628) 75851

Name	Description	Manufacturer/designer	Distributor/contact
Peripheral controllers			
MBL82284	Bipolar clock generator–driver for Fujitsu's MBL80286 16-bit microprocessor running at 6 MHz or 8 MHz. Frequency source can be a crystal or an external TTL signal. Ready and Reset signals are synchronized with clock timing. Packaging: 18-pin DIP	Fujitsu Ltd, 6-1 Marunouchi 2-chome, Chiyoda-ku, Tokyo 100, Japan	Fujitsu Microelectronics Ltd, Hargrave House, Belmont Road, Maidenhead, Berks SL6 6NE, UK. Tel: (0628) 76100
MBL82288	NMOS bus controller for the MBL80286 running at 6 MHz or 8 MHz, providing bus commands and control signals for memory and I/O functions. Optionally can provide compatible timing mode for Multibus after decoding the output of the bus status signals from the microprocessor. Packaging: 20-pin DIP	Fujitsu Ltd, 6-1 Marunouchi 2-chome, Chiyoda-ku, Tokyo 100, Japan	Fujitsu Microelectronics Ltd, Hargrave House, Belmont Road, Maidenhead, Berks SL6 6NE, UK. Tel: (0628) 76100
PDC-001	6809-based programmable drive controller designed for use in servo drives and stepper motor positioning systems. Configured as an STEbus peripheral, the board has 32 kbyte EPROM space, eight logic output channels, four optoisolated logic inputs (one of which can interrupt the processor), two 8-bit D/A converter outputs and an optoisolated incremental encoder (74LS2000)	Scazon Systems, 23 Agard Street, Derby DE1 1DZ, UK	Dean Microsystems Ltd, 7 Horseshoe Park, Pangbourne, Berks RG8 7JW, UK. Tel: (07357) 5155
UIPC 02	68010-based VMEbus peripheral and communications controller in which the board can be customized using modules that plug into the J2 connector; rows A and C are used for I/O functions while row B supports full 32-bit VME implementation. User configurable options include SCSI interface, Winchester/FFD/QIC 02 controller, eight RS232C serial ports, prototyping and debug modules	Lynx Computer International, 12 Deer Park Road, London SW19 3RJ, UK. Tel: 01-543 6611	Universal Engineering and Computing Systems Ltd, 5/11 Tower Street, Newtown, Birmingham B19 3UY, UK. Tel: 021-359 1749

 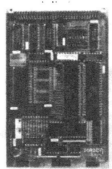 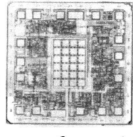  

From left: the Bicc-Vero VME 48055 RAM board; Scazon's PDC-001 STE drive controller; Fujitsu's MBL82284/8 clock generator-driver and bus controller, showing the chip structure of the clock generator; and the Integrated Micro Products CT-Net Ethernet controller board

products in brief

Name	Description	Manufacturer/designer	Distributor/contact
Processor boards			
Celeste/008	68008-based single-board computer for STEbus. Provides two software tristable RE423/485 serial ports with RTS/CTS handshaking, baud rates programmable from 50 to 38.4 kbaud or speeds to 1 Mbit s^{-1}, and FIFO buffers on each channel. Includes two 8-bit parallel ports, four control lines, 16-bit and 24-bit programmable timers, and space for 192 kbyte of memory. Features prioritized vectored interrupts	Control Universal Ltd, 137 Ditton Walk, Cambridge CB5 8QF, UK. Tel: (0223) 244448	Dean Microsystems Ltd, 7 Horseshoe Park, Pangbourne, Berks RG8 7JW, UK. Tel: (07357) 5155
GesMPU-11	Single-Eurocard implementation on the G64 bus of the CPU used in DEC's PDP-11/70 minicomputer. Clock rate is 15 MHz and address space of 512 kbyte for memory and 2 kbyte for synchronous or asynchronous I/O. Kernel, supervisory and user execution modes are provided. Implementation uses a two-chip CPU and pipelined hardware	Gespac Inc., 100 West Hoover Avenue, Suite 11, Mesa, AZ 85202, USA. Tel: (602) 962-5559	Pronto Electronic Systems Ltd, City Gate House, 399–425 Eastern Avenue, Gants Hill, Ilford, Essex IG2 6LR, UK. Tel: 01-554 6222
Programmable arrays			
TC21SC, TC22SC, TC23SC	Standard cells in 1.5 µm (23SC) and 2 µm CMOS, with gate complexities from 10k to 50k. Maximum toggle frequencies of 100 MHz (21SC, 22SC) and 150 MHz (23SC) and inner gate speeds of 1.5 ns (21SC, 22SC) and 1 ns (23SC) are available. 21SC has a macrocell library and TC17G compatible design rules; 22SC library includes a 16-bit RAM, 64-bit ROM, PLA, ALU, MPU and 74 series compatible macros; 23SC library has RAM, ROM, CPU, microcomputer peripherals and 2900 series macros	Toshiba, 1-chome, Uchisaiwai-cho, Chiyoda-ku, Tokyo, Japan	Toshiba UK Ltd, Toshiba House, Frimley Road, Camberley, Surrey GU16 5JJ, UK. Tel: (0276) 62222
Programming modules			
ZM2500	Modular firmware enhancement allowing the PPZ Universal Programmer to cope with 1 Mbit EPROMs — both 40-pin devices and 28-pin paged-mode devices	Stag Electronic Designs Ltd, Stag House, Tewin Court, Welwyn Garden City, Herts AL7 1AU, UK. Tel: (0707) 332148	

From left: Control Universal's Celeste/008 single-board computer; the Gespac GesMPU-11 PDP-11/70 implementation for G64; and Stag's PPZ programmer, now with ZM2500 enhancement

Name	Description	Manufacturer/designer	Distributor/contact
PROMs			
HD63701Y	16 kbyte CMOS one-time PROM with 'antipirating' mechanism and 'zero turnaround time' facility. Serial link emulator H3 MIX is available for prototype development	Hitachi Ltd, New Marunouchi Building No 5, 1-chome Marunouchi, Chiyoda, Tokyo, Japan	Hitachi Electronic Components (UK) Ltd, 21 Upton Road, Watford, Herts WD1 7TB, UK. Tel: (0923) 46488
HM58C65	8 k × 8 bit CMOS E^2PROM with a single-rail supply and on-chip latches and timer. Erasing times are 10 ms (byte and page modes) and 20 ms (chip mode); write times are 10 ms (byte and page modes); access times are 200 ns or 250 ns; operating current is 10 mA (typical) and standby current is 1 mA. Packaging: 28-pin DIP or SOP	Hitachi Ltd, New Marunouchi Building No 5, 1-chome Marunouchi, Chiyoda, Tokyo, Japan	Hitachi Electronic Components (UK) Ltd, 21 Upton Road, Watford, Herts WD1 7TB, UK. Tel: (0923) 46488
LH5764/J	64 kbit CMOS one-time PROM, pin compatible with Intel's I2764. Power consumption is 150 mW (active) and 0.55 mW (standby); access time is down to 200 ns; programming voltage is 12.5 V; organization is 8192 bit × 8; packaging is in a 28-pin DIP	Sharp Corp., 2613-1 Ichinomoto-cho Tnri, Nara 632, Japan. Tel: (07436) 5-1321	Altek Microcomponents Ltd, 22 Market Place, Wokingham, Berks RG11 1AP, UK. Tel: (0734) 791579
RAMs			
F100422 (F100K version), F10422 (F10K version)	1024-bit (256 × 4 bit) ECL static RAMs with maximum address access times quoted as 7 ns, designed for high-speed scratchpad, control and buffer storage applications. Devices include on-chip address decoding, separate data input and noninverting data output lines, and four active-low bit-select lines. Bit-select access time is 5 ns (max.) and typical power dissipation is 0.79 mW bit^{-1} for the F100422 or 0.92 mW bit^{-1} for the F10422	Fairchild Semiconductor GmbH, Am Burgfrieden 1, 8090 Wasserburg Am Inn, Munich, FRG. Tel: (08071) 103-349	Fairchild Semiconductor Ltd, 230 High Street, Potters Bar, Herts, UK. Tel: (0707) 51111
HM-65642	8 k × 8 bit static RAM in CMOS using edge-activated circuit design. Address access time down to 100 ns or 150 ns; active current requirement of 10 mA; standby current of 100 μA or 50 μA. Packaging: 28-pin ceramic DIP, currently with military temperature tolerance to MIL 883 burn-in	Harris MHS Semiconductor Ltd, Eskdale Road, Winnersh Triangle, Wokingham, Berks RG11 5TR, UK. Tel: (0734) 698787	RR Electronics Ltd, St Martins Way, Cambridge Road, Bedford, UK. Tel: (0234) 47211
M5M4C264P	256 kbit CMOS dual-port dynamic RAM for video applications. At one port the device appears like a conventional 64 k × 4 bit DRAM, says the manufacturer, while the other is connected to an internal 1024-bit data register through a 256 × 4 bit serial I/O control buffer, allowing transfer rates of up to 25 MHz. Access time: 120 ns maximum. Current requirement: 100 mA (active) and 5 mA (standby). Packaging: 24-pin plastic DIP	Mitsubishi Electric Corp., 2-3 Marunouchi 2-chome, Chiyoda-ku, Tokyo 100, Japan	Mitsubishi Electric (UK) Ltd, Hertford Place, Denham Way, Maple Cross, Rickmansworth, Herts WD3 2BJ, UK. Tel: (0923) 770000

Name	Description	Manufacturer/designer	Distributor/contact
RAMs (*continued*)			
HM53462	Dual-port dynamic RAM in 2 μm CMOS for video applications, featuring a logic operator and serial write capability. Write mask mode eliminates the need for read and modification phases in a normal rewrite operation. Organization is 64 kbit × 4 (RAM) and 256 bit × 4 (SAM); access times are 100, 120 or 150 ns (RAM) and 25, 30 or 40 ns (SAM); current requirement is 125 mA; packaging is in a 24-pin DIP	Hitachi Ltd, New Marunouchi Building No 5, 1-chome Marunouchi, Chiyoda, Tokyo, Japan	Hitachi Electronic Components (UK) Ltd, 21 Upton Road, Watford, Herts WD1 7TB, UK. Tel: (0923) 46488
P4C188	16 kbit ×4 CMOS static RAM with access times of 20 ns. Power consumption is 550 mW active, 193 mW standby	Performance Semiconductors Corp., 610 East Weddell Drive, Sunnyvale, CA 94089, USA. Tel: (408) 734-9000	Kudos Electronics Ltd, Handpost Corner, Finchampstead Road, Wokingham, Berks RG11 3LP, UK. Tel: (0734) 794515
Single-chip microcomputers			
80C31	CMOS 8-bit microcomputer designed to reduce system power consumption by bringing the clock frequency down to any value (from 12 MHz to DC) without loss of data. Features include idle and power-down modes, a single 5 V power supply and bus hold circuitry to eliminate pull-up resistors	Harris MHS Semiconductor Ltd, Eskdale Road, Winnersh Triangle, Wokingham, Berks RG11 5TR, UK. Tel: (0734) 698787	RR Electronics Ltd, St Martins Way, Cambridge Road, Bedford, UK. Tel: (0234) 47211
Software products			
BRU	Unix utility, written in c, for creating back-up files and verifying that files are readable and correct. Replaces the existing utilities **tar**, **cpio**, **volcopy** and **dd** but gives greater data integrity, says the manufacturer	Root Technical Systems, Saunderson House, Hayne Street, London ED1A 9HH, UK. Tel: 01-606 7799	
RAMdisk	STEbus system utility that reorganizes a chunk of RAM from system memory into a disc-like structure, so that conventional RAM can be used like a floppy disc (but with access some 200–400 times faster). Runs under CP/M on Arcom's Z80-based STEbus systems	Arcom Control Systems Ltd, Unit 8, Clifton Road, Cambridge CB1 4WH, UK. Tel: (0223) 242224	
X8080 and X8086, versions 1.6	Crossassemblers for the 8080/8085 and the 8086 family, respectively, running under PC-DOS/MS-DOS on IBM PC compatibles, under Unix and Idris on PDP-11s and 68000-based machines, and under VMS and Unix on Vax systems. Features include a symbol table of over 32 k entries which can be swapped to disc, with user control over the number of entries resident in memory	Real Time Systems Ltd, PO Box 70, Viking House, Nelson Street, Douglas, Isle of Man, UK	

calendar

Date	Title	Contact	Place	Other details
1986				
26–28 November	International Symposium on Local Communication Systems, LAN and PBX	G Cluzel, Laboratoire LSI, Université Paul Sabatier 118, route de Narbonne, 31062 Toulouse, France. Tel: (33) 61 55 67 68	Toulouse, France	International symposium sponsored by the International Federation for Information Processing (IFIP), technical committee TC6. Simultaneous French–English translation available
2–4 December	Realtime Systems Symposium	K G Shin, Dept of Electrical Engineering and Computer Science, University of Michigan, Ann Arbor, MI 48109, USA	New Orleans, LA, USA	
9 December	Industrial Applications of Expert Systems	Sira Ltd, South Hill, Chislehurst, Kent BR7 5EH, UK. Tel: 01-467 6515	Chislehurst, Kent, UK	Tutorial course covering the capabilities and limitations of expert system technology in relation to management and industrial processes, the principles and methods of expert systems, the tools available for building industrial expert systems and for developing applications
1987				
14–16 January	Multi 87	Society for Computer Simulation, PO Box 17900, San Diego, CA 92117, USA. Tel: (619) 277-3888	San Diego, CA, USA	1987 SCS 'multiconference' covering modelling and simulation on microcomputers, emergency planning, multiprocessor and array processors (Mapcon), simulation of CIM systems and robotics, and AI and simulation
20–21 January	Buscon and Syscon/87-West	Multidynamics Inc., 17100 Norwalk Blvd, Suite 116, Cerritos, CA 90701-2750, USA. Tel: (213) 402-1618	Hilton Hotel, Los Angeles Airport, CA, USA	Bus board user show and conference, and subsystems conference and exposition for OEM peripherals
21–23 January	The OSI Reference Model and Network Architecture	Frost & Sullivan Ltd, Sullivan House, 4 Grosvenor Gardens, London SW1W 0DH, UK. Tel: 01-730 3438	Cumberland Hotel, London, UK	Seminar on the role and significance of OSI in the design, implementation and operation of distributed data processing systems
28–31 January	India Comm 87	Cahners Exhibitions, Oriel House, 26 The Quadrant, Richmond-upon-Thames, Surrey TW1 3DL, UK. Tel: 01-949 3777	Pragati Maidan, New Delhi, India	Exhibition designed to encourage computer and communications trade between India and the Western world
4–6 February	International Workshop on Industrial Automation Systems	Prof. Masao Sakauchi, Institute of Industrial Science, University of Tokyo 22-1, Roppongi 7-chome, Minato-ku, Tokyo 106, Japan. Tel: (03) 402-6231	Roppongi, Tokyo, Japan	Workshop on practical and basic techniques applicable to machine vision, machine intelligence and signal processing. Includes a session on industrial applications of digital signal processors and microprocessors
4–6 February	Software and Hardware Applications of Microcomputers	Fathy F Yassa, Corporate Research & Development Center, General Electric Co., PO Box 8, KWC510, Schenectady, NY 12301, USA	University Park Holiday Inn, Fort Collins, CO, USA	Covers the applications, software, interfacing, hardware and communications etc. of microcomputers. Sponsored by the Society for Mini and Microcomputers
10–12 February	MDS '87	Microsystem Design, 31–33 High Holborn, London WC1V 6BD, UK	Wembley Conference Centre, London, UK	Microsystem design show

Date	Title	Contact	Place	Other details
10-12 February	Smartex '87	Tom Archer, Smart Group, Kebbell House, Delta Gain, Carpenders Park, Watford, Herts WD1 5EF, UK. Tel: 01-427 2377	Barbican Centre, London, UK	Specialist show for the SMT industry, including the second surface mount and related technologies conference
10-12 February	Systems Design & Integration Conference	Electronic Conventions Management, 8110 Airport Blvd, Los Angeles, CA 90045, USA. Tel: (213) 772-2965	Santa Clara, CA, USA	Conference and exhibition on systems design, software engineering and integration
25-27 February	ISSCC '87	Lewis Winner, 301 Almeria Avenue, Coral Gables, FL 33134, USA. Tel: (305) 446-8193	New York Hilton, NY, USA	34th IEEE international solid-state circuits conference, covering digital VLSI design, fabrication and test, logic arrays, architecture, microprocessors and coprocessors, analogue components, memories, signal processing etc.
3-5 March	Dexpo Europe 87	Montbuild Ltd, 11 Manchester Square, London W1M 5AB, UK. Tel: 01-486 1951	Olympia 2, London, UK	Fifth European exhibition and conference on Digital Equipment (DEC) compatible hardware, software, systems etc.
4-6 March	International Open Systems Conference	Online International Ltd, Pinner Green House, Ash Hill Drive, Pinner, Middx HA5 2AE, UK. Tel: 01-868 4466	Barbican Centre, London, UK	Conference on the construction and use of open systems, current directions and issues, and strategic and management aspects of open systems. Includes a MAP seminar
10-12 March	Semicon Europa '87	Cochrane Communications Ltd, CCL House, 59 Fleet Street, London EC4Y 1JU, UK. Tel: 01-353 8807	Zuspa Convention Centre, Zurich, Switzerland	13th semiconductor production equipment and materials show, this year placing an emphasis on test equipment. Organized by the Semiconductor Equipment and Materials Institute (SEMI)
22-26 March	Computer Graphics '87	National Computer Graphics Association, 2722 Merrilee Drive, Suite 200, Fairfax, VA 22031, USA. Tel: (703) 698-9600	Philadelphia Civic Center, PA, USA	Conference and exposition on theory and practice of computer graphics. Includes sessions in artificial intelligence, architecture, user interfaces and industry standards, and a demonstration of MAP
30 March -2 April	ICSE '87	William Riddle, Software Design & Analysis Inc., 1760 Bear Mountain Drive, Boulder, CO 80303, USA. Tel: (303) 499-4782	Monterey, CA, USA	Ninth IEEE international conference on software engineering, with software tools fair
6-9 April	ICASSP 87	Prof. Yu-H Hu, Dept of Electrical Engineering, University of Texas at Arlington, TX 76019, USA. Tel: (817) 273-3483	Registry Hotel, Dallas, TX, USA	IEEE international conference on acoustics, speech and signal processing, including coverage of VLSI for signal processing (custom VLSI for DSP, microprocessor-based implementations, systolic arrays etc.)
8-10 April	Microelectronics Conference — VLSI 1987	VLSI 87 Conference Manager, The Institution of Engineers, 11 National Circuit, Barton, ACT 2600, Australia. Tel: (062) 73-3633	Melbourne, Australia	Will cover design methods, tools, layout, automation and testing; chip architecture; process simulation and modelling; VLSI technology, processing and manufacture; future trends in VLSI; and applications of complex ICs
28-30 April	British Electronics Week	Evan Steadman Communications Group, The Hub, Emson Close, Saffron Walden, Essex CB10 1HL, UK. Tel: (0799) 26699	Olympia, London, UK	Incorporates the All-Electronics/ECIF Show, Automatic Test Equipment, Circuit Technology, Electronic Product Design, Fibre Optics, and Power Sources & Supplies

calendar

Date	Title	Contact	Place	Other details
4–7 May	ICS 87	Prof. Lana P Kartashev, 3000 34th Street South, Suite B-309, St Petersburg, FL 33711, USA	San Francisco, CA, USA	Second international conference on supercomputing, covering hardware technologies and design, supercomputer languages, operating systems and software tools, computations, artificial intelligence and operations research
11–15 May	CompEuro 87	Prof. W E Proebster, c/o IBM, PB 80 08 80, D-7000 Stuttgart 80, FRG	Congress Centre, Hamburg, FRG	First conference and exhibition on 'computer technology, systems, applications and their interaction' organized by the IEEE, Gessellschaft für Informatik, Verband Deutscher Elektrotechniker and others. This year's main topics are: the impact of VLSI on computers; the influence of computers on VLSI; microelectronics and VLSI; status and trends in computer systems; and designing systems with VLSI today (special course)
11–15 May	ISATA 87	ISATA Secretariat, 42 Lloyd Park Avenue, Croydon CR0 5SB, UK. Tel: 01-686 7026	Florence, Italy	16th international symposium on automotive technology and automation, concentrating on automotive microelectronics, vehicle management systems and computer-aided testing
13–15 May	Avignon '87	Agence de l'Informatique, Tour Fiat Cedex 16, 92084 Paris La Défense, France, Tel: (331) 47-96-43-14	Palace of the Popes, Avignon, France	Sixth international workshop on expert systems and their applications
18–21 May	Eighth Symposium on Computer Arithmetic	Luigi Dadda, Dept of Electronics, Piazza Leonardo da Vinci 32, Politecnico di Milano, I-20133 Milano, Italy. Tel: (39) 2 2399-3510	Como, Italy	Topics include mathematical foundations of computer arithmetic; arithmetic algorithms, their analysis and implementation in VLSI; arithmetic in signal and image processing and in fifth-generation computing; arithmetic processors; error control and analysis; and high-level support for numerical computations
18–22 May	Computers at the University	Symposium Secretary, University Computing Centre, 41000 Zagreb, Engelsova bb, Yugoslavia. Tel: (041) 510-099	Hotel Croatia, Dubrovnik/Cavtat, Yugoslavia	Ninth international symposium covering computing in research and education, including: informatics, software engineering, information systems and databases, modelling and simulation, CADCAM, AI, expert systems etc.
1–5 June	GRETSI '87	Secretariat du Colloque GRETSI, 7 Chemin des Presses, BP 85, 0681 Cagnes-sur-Mer Cedex, France. Tel: (93) 20-01-40	Nice, France	Eleventh symposium on signal and image processing, with simultaneous translation from French into English
2–4 June	UK Telecommunications Networks — Present and Future	INCUT 87 Conference Services, Institution of Electrical Engineers, Savoy Place, London WC2R 0BL, UK. Tel: 01-240 7735	London, UK	Covers network evolution, the regulatory framework, the standardization process, value-added services and future evolution of the UK telecommunication network
3–5 June	Sixth European Microelectronics Conference	The Secretariat, Concorde Services Ltd, 10 Wendell Road, London W12 9RT, UK. Tel: 01-743 3106	Bournemouth, UK	Conference and exhibition on hybrids and surface mount technology, organized by the International Society for Hybrid Microelectronics
23–25 June	Software Engineering Tools	Online International Ltd, Pinner Green House, Ash Hill Drive, Pinner, Middx HA5 2AE, UK. Tel: 01-868 4466	Wembley Conference Centre, London, UK	Conference and exhibition

Microprocessors and Microsystems

The journal welcomes original papers from both academic and industrial contributors on the research, design, development, evaluation and application of all microprocessor-based systems and on the development and use of microsystem software. Papers should illustrate practical experience and show the applicability of the work described. Typically, full-length papers are approximately 5000–7000 words long plus illustrations. In addition to full-length papers, the journal welcomes shorter design notes, tutorial papers and case studies of up to 3000 words.

REFEREEING

All submitted articles are refereed by two independent reviewers to ensure both accuracy and relevance, though it is the authors' sole responsibility that statements used are accurate. The author is also responsible for obtaining permission to quote material and to republish tables and illustrations.

PREPARATION OF SCRIPTS

Three copies of the manuscript, typed *double spaced* on one side of A4 paper should be sent to:

● The Editor, Microprocessors and Microsystems, PO Box 63, Westbury House, Bury Street, Guildford, Surrey GU2 5BH, United Kingdom.

Each page of the manuscript should be numbered. Wide margins should be left so that the paper can be prepared for the typesetters. Please remove tables and figures from the main body of the script and attach them at the end of the paper. Each table or figure should be reproduced on a single sheet. Please list figure captions on a separate sheet and attach this sheet at the end of the paper.

English is the sole language used by the journal, and we follow the Oxford English Dictionary. All papers should be written in English. To maintain consistency throughout each volume, every paper published is stylized by the journal's editorial staff.

Biographical notes

It is the journal's practice to include biographical notes on the authors of published papers. Biographical notes can be up to 100 words, briefly describing career details and current research interests, and should be accompanied by a black-and-white portrait photograph. To speed processing of the paper it is helpful if biographical notes can be attached to the submitted manuscript.

UNITS

SI units should be used. In circumstances where this is not possible, please provide a conversion factor at the first mention of the unit.

ILLUSTRATIONS

Line drawings

We use our own professional studio to ensure that line drawings are consistent with house style. We would prefer, however, to receive one set of unlettered drawings (black ink on tracing paper) so we can put on the lettering ourselves. Drawings, if possible, should be of a size consistent with the journal, i.e. either 169 mm or 366 mm wide. Single drawings should not extend over one page (500 mm) in height.

Computer printouts

Illustrations showing line printer listings, plotter output, etc should preferably be on unlined paper. Printouts will be reduced by us to the relevant size. Do not mark them as they will be used to make photographic copies for the typesetters. Only include sufficient lines for the reader to interpret the format and nature of the printout. Overlong printouts can cause confusion. Fuller explanation of the printout should appear in the caption and the text.

Photographs

Black-and-white glossy photographs (including Polaroid prints of VDU screens) should be supplied unmounted. They should be labelled clearly on the back with a soft pencil. Photocopies of the photographs should be provided for the referees.

REFERENCES

The journal style is to indicate the use of a reference in the text with a superscript as each one arises and give the full reference with the same number at the end of the paper. If a reference is cited more than once, the same number should be used each time. With a bibliography, the references are given in alphabetical order (dependent on the first author's surname). It would be helpful if you could follow this style. References take the following form:

(To journals)

1 **Buckroyd, A** 'Production testing of microprocessor-based equipment' *Microprocessors and Microsystems* Vol 5 No 7 (September 1981) pp 299–303

(To books)

2 **Gallacher, J** 'Testing and maintenance' in **Hanna, F K (ed.)** *Advanced techniques for microprocesor systems* Peter Peregrinus, Stevenage, UK (1980)

PROOFS

Correspondence and proofs for corrections will be sent to the first named author, unless otherwise indicated. Authors will receive a copy of the galley proofs and copies of redrawn or relettered illustrations. It is important that these proofs should be checked and returned *promptly*.

COPYRIGHT

Before publication, authors are requested to assign copyright to Butterworth & Co (Publishers) Ltd. This allows the company to sanction reprints of the whole or part of the volume and authorize photocopies. The authors, however, still retain their traditional right to reuse or to veto third-party publication.

OFFPRINTS AND REPRINTS

The first named author will receive 25 offprints of the paper free of charge as well as a complimentary copy of the journal. Further reprint copies, a minimum of 100, can be ordered at any time from the Reprints Department, Butterworth Scientific Ltd, Westbury House, PO Box 63, Bury Street, Guildford, Surrey GU2 5BH, UK.

microprocessors and microsystems

vol 10 no 10 december 1986

Butterworths

editorial advisory board

Microprocessors and Microsystems is an international journal published in February, March, April, May, June, August, September, October, November, December. *Editorial Offices:* Butterworth Scientific Ltd, PO Box 63, Westbury House, Bury Street, Guildford, Surrey GU2 5BH, UK. Tel: (0483) 31261. Telegrams and telex: 859556 SCITEC G. *Publishing Director:* John Owens. *Production:* Nick Wilson

Microprocessors and Microsystems is published by Butterworth Scientific Ltd. *Registered Office:* Butterworth Scientific Ltd, 88 Kingsway, London WC2 6AB, UK

Subscription enquiries and orders, UK and overseas: Quadrant Subscription Services Ltd, Oakfield House, Perrymount Road, Haywards Heath, West Sussex RH16 3DH, UK. Tel: (0444) 459188; *North America:* Butterworth Publishers, 80 Montvale Avenue, Stoneham, MA 02180, USA

Annual subscription (10 issues): £98.00 overseas rate (£24.00 for private individuals); $176.00 US rate ($43.00 for private individuals)
UK subscription rates available on request.

Prices include packing and delivery by sea mail. Airmail prices available on request. Copies of this journal sent to subscribers in Bangladesh, India, Pakistan, Sri Lanka, Canada and the USA are air-speeded for quicker delivery.

Back issues: Prior to current volume available from Wm Dawson & Sons Ltd, Cannon House, Folkestone, Kent CT19 5EE, UK. Tel: (0303) 57421

US mailing agents: Mercury Airfreight International Ltd Inc., 10B Englehard Avenue, Avenel, NJ 07001, USA. Second class postage paid at Rahway, NJ. US Postmaster: Send address corrections to *Microprocessors and Microsystems* c/o Mercury Airfreight International Ltd Inc., address as above.

Reprints: Minimum order 100, available from the publisher.

Copyright: Readers who require copies of papers published in this journal may either purchase reprints or obtain permission to copy from the publisher at the following address: Butterworth Scientific Ltd, PO Box 63, Westbury House, Bury Street, Guildford, Surrey GU2 5BH, UK. For readers in the USA, permission to copy is given on the condition that the copier pay the stated per copy fee through the Copyright Clearance Center Inc., 26 Congress Street, Salem, MA 01979, USA, Tel: (617) 744-3350, for copying beyond that permitted by Sections 107 and 108 of the US Copyright Law. Fees appear in the code at the foot of the first page of major papers.

ISSN 0141 9331
MCRPD 10 (10) 529-584 (1986)

© Butterworth & Co (Publishers) Ltd 1986

Butterworths
Leading the Campaign
against
Copyright Erosion

Typeset by Tech-Set, Gateshead, Tyne & Wear, and printed Greenland M UK.

microprocessors and microsystems

vol 10 no 10
december 1986

Editor Steve Hitchcock

Assistant Editor Andrew Taylor

Publisher Amanda Harper

Microcode copyright ruling

A US court has ruled that a microprocessor's microcode is covered by the laws of copyright. The ruling is the outcome of the first part of a two-stage case brought by Intel against NEC; Intel is alleging that NEC engineers copied the microcode to the 8086/88 to use in the V20 and V30 processors. Having won the first stage by establishing the principle of copyright for microcode, Intel's lawyers now have to prove that the Japanese company did in fact infringe Intel copyright, but Intel management claims to be 'confident' that the rest of the case will be decided in its favour.

Europe's IC 'opportunity'

Integrated circuit design technology provides the 'last window of opportunity' for Europe to establish an indigenous semiconductor manufacturing industry, according to Murray Duffin of Italian-based electronics company SGS. Duffin's warning was given during a keynote presentation at the recent Euromicro '86 conference in Venice, Italy. In 1986 it is possible to manufacture up to 10 million gates on a chip, but the limitation to progress is design, Duffin said. People no longer want standard commodity products but application-specific devices. Duffin urged greater political cooperation between European governments to build on the success of current collaborative projects such as Esprit and Eureka and to allow a framework to encourage growth of a European semiconductor industry.

● Euromicro '86 report: page 557

Parallel processing group

The British Computer Society has formed a new specialist group to promote the development of parallel architectures, languages and applications in the UK. The group intends to host evening and one-day meetings to publish newsletters and an annual directory of members. A central repository for technical material relating to parallel processing will also be set up. Further

details of the group are available from Dr Nigel Tucker, Paradis Consultants, East Berriow, Berriow Bridge, North Hill, Nr Launceston, Cornwall PL15 7NL, UK.

'Steady' growth for networks

Manufacturing Automation Protocol (MAP) will be the major factor behind the impetus for growth of local area network (LAN) markets towards 1990 says market research firm Frost & Sullivan. But its report warns that LANs 'will not achieve the explosive growth that many are forecasting'. Instead, 'steady' growth averaging 35% per year in dollar terms is predicted, from a base of $100M this year to a value of $431M in 1989.

Two years ago only 3% of LANs by number were MAP-compatible systems, but this will become 40% by 1989 says the report. In contrast, proprietary LANs, those that will interconnect a single vendor's products, will shrink from two-thirds of present LAN installations to slightly over half by 1989. The prominence of MAP will also encourage greater use of broadband as the interconnection medium by the 1990s. Currently twisted pair and baseband connections are more widely used but this will be reversed, the report says.

24% annual ASIC increase

Europe will have a $3000M market for custom and semicustom ICs by 1991, resulting from a 24% annual growth rate from $818M in 1985, forecasts another report from Frost & Sullivan. Most of the credit for the increase is ascribed to the cost-cutting effect of computer-aided engineering (CAE) in the semiconductor industry. Largest ASIC supplier to the European market is Ferranti, says F&S, with the market currently dominated by full custom circuits (41%) and gate arrays (33%), well ahead in volume of standard cells, fused programmable logic or silicon compilers. Automotive, military and aerospace users will form the fastest growing market sectors over the next five years, says the F&S report. (Frost & Sullivan Ltd, Sullivan House, 4 Grosvenor Gardens, London SW1W 0DH, UK. Tel: 01-730 3438)

Software engineering centre

The 'Software Tools Demonstration Centre' is the name of a new establishment set up by the UK Department of Trade and Industry at the National Computing Centre (NCC) in Manchester, UK. The centre's aim is to raise the standards and level of use of software engineering, and the NCC hopes to achieve this by promoting selected products to potential users in an environment that is not dominated by the commercial interests of the software supplier. In particular the centre is expected to act as a 'shop window' for software which develops from the UK's Alvey and Europe's Esprit projects.

Dense-Pak enters Europe

US hybrid memory specialist Dense-Pak Microsystems has set up a European sales and marketing office in the UK. Dense-Pak, whose major activity is purchasing unpackaged memory chips from semiconductor vendors, packaging them as surface-mount devices and selling them in various combinations as standard or application-specific hybrid chips, also intends to include a design centre in the UK office for the development and manufacture of custom memory devices. (Dense-Pak Microsystems, Woodstock House, The Street, Bramber, Sussex BN4 3WE, UK. Tel: (0903) 814382)

More languages on RISC

Component kits, CPU boards and computer systems based on R2000, the 32-bit RISC microprocessor made by MIPS Computer Systems, are to have COBOL and PL/I added to their repertoire. Language Processors is to supply the front-end technology for its versions of the two languages; this will be combined with an optimizer and back-end technology developed by MIPS. The deal signed between the two companies provides options for additional languages and future MIPS products, and is estimated to be worth some $2M over three years.

Design for testability — a review of advanced methods

As IC designs become more complex, so do the problems of testing the resulting silicon. **G Russell and I L Sayers** discuss recent developments in DFT that are overcoming these problems

In an attempt to curtail the almost exponential growth in testing cost as circuit complexity increases, attention has focussed over the past decade on design for testability (DFT). Although DFT techniques reduce the testing cost there is a penalty to be paid in terms of the overheads incurred through their use. The paper first presents several recently evolved hybrid techniques that combine several DFT techniques with the objective of maximizing the advantages of each method whilst minimizing their overheads. It has been predicted that, as a result of the decrease in device size through the improvements in fabrication technology, the incidence of intermittent faults will increase. Current test strategies are not generally suitable for detecting this type of fault, and the paper discusses the application of concurrent circuit testing techniques, employing information redundancy, to the problem. The vast number of DFT techniques available, each with its own advantages and disadvantages, means that the designer faces a formidable task in selecting the best technique for a particular circuit. Several expert systems developed to analyse the circuit and suggest the most appropriate technique are presented. This approach has been developed further by integrating the expert system into a silicon compiler environment which ensures that the circuit is testable by virtue of its construction.

**microprocessors   design for testability   built-in test
concurrent circuit testing   expert systems   silicon compilers**

Over the past decade improvements in fabrication techniques have permitted more complex systems to be integrated onto a single silicon chip. Although this capability has accrued many advantages, it has created a problem which has unfortunately become a major issue in the design of such systems, namely that of testing the system immediately after fabrication and also in the field. The problem arises from the overall complexity of the system to be tested and is aggravated by restricted access to the internal nodes of the system. Recent investigations[1, 2]

into complex system testing have identified the major factors to which the rise in testing costs may be attributed, with increasing circuit complexity, as

- the increase in the cost of test pattern generation and fault simulation
- the increase in the volume of test data to be stored and processed
- the increase in test application time

Several approaches have been adopted in an attempt to curtail the increase in testing costs, viz.

- development of sophisticated test generation algorithms[3]
- design for testability (DFT)[4]
- built-in test methods[5]

The development of more sophisticated test generation schemes has been carried out both at gate level and at higher levels of abstraction in an attempt to improve the efficiency of test pattern generation. Several systems have evolved, e.g. Podem-X[6] which is capable of generating tests for unpartitioned modules comprising approximately 50 000 gates. The D algorithm[7], from which most present-day test generation algorithms have evolved, has also been modified so that it can be used at higher levels of abstraction[8] (where systems are described either in terms of functional blocks, e.g. counters and decoders, or in terms of behavioural descriptions written in procedural or nonprocedural languages).

A major limitation to the efficiency of computer-aided design (CAD) tools is the use of general-purpose computers as the host machines; these do not use any of the parallelism or concurrency of CAD algorithms which would improve their efficiency. Consequently, special-purpose machines have been developed for a range of CAD tools including test pattern generation[9] and fault simulation[10], where the algorithm is mapped onto the hardware, resulting in a vast improvement in performance. More recently, investigations have been made into the use of expert systems for test generation. These systems[11] suggest techniques to test a particular function inside a circuit; thereafter decisions are made and suggestions given concerning the means of applying the desired tests.

Department of Electrical and Electronic Engineering, The Merz Laboratories, University of Newcastle upon Tyne NE1 7RU, UK

The knowledge base in an expert system for test generation comprises

- the commonly used test generation methods categorized in terms of the types of modules to which they can be applied (i.e. random or sequential logic, RAMs and ROMs, arrays with or without testability devices)
- the type of circuit description upon which a given test generation technique can be applied (i.e. gate, functional, state table or instruction set description of a system)
- the types of faults covered (i.e. stuck at 1 or 0, stuck open, short circuit)
- the types of pattern generated (i.e. functional, global, local or sensitivity patterns for RAMs)

The knowledge base will also contain a library of test patterns for commonly used functions and a knowledge of the different DFT schemes. The development of more sophisticated test generation schemes, however, can only offer an interim solution to the test generation problem since this approach is directed at the symptoms of generating tests for faults in VLSI circuits, i.e. complexity, and not at the root cause of the problem which is the controllability and observability of signal nodes internal to the circuit.

The adoption of DFT techniques attacks the root cause of the problem, namely the diminishing controllability and observability of signals on internal nodes as circuit complexity increases. DFT techniques permit either direct access to internal nodes by including test points which may be multiplexed, or indirect access through the use of scan path registers[12], or they may permit the circuit to be reconfigured for the purposes of test pattern generation and testing. Although DFT techniques reduce the problems of test generation to some extent, they also incur certain penalties, e.g. placing constraints on the circuit design, increasing the chip area and pin count, affecting circuit performance, inhibiting the circuit to be tested at speed. In some instances, support software is required to ensure adherence to a particular set of DFT rules. In addition, the techniques require the generation of vast amounts of test data and testing time can be protracted.

More recently, several built-in test schemes have evolved with the objectives of removing the task of test pattern generation and of reducing the amount of test data to be processed during the testing phase. These techniques incorporate hardware on the chip, usually some type of linear feedback shift register, to generate the test vectors and also some means of compressing the test responses from all the test vectors into a single signature[13] or syndrome[14] which can readily be checked to determine if the circuit is fault free.

HYBRID TECHNIQUES

The major disadvantages of the scan path techniques are long test application times and the need to generate and store vast volumes of test data; built-in test techniques, however, overcome these disadvantages although they tend to incur a higher area penalty. Recently several hybrid techniques have evolved which attempt to capitalize on the advantages of each method without incurring their disadvantages to any great extent.

The generic name associated with these hybrid methods is S^3 (self test using signature analysis and scan path); the basic configurations used in this technique are summarized by Yacoub[15]. The physical implementations of the technique are first classified as being external or internal. An S^3 implementation classified as external requires little or no change to the design style provided that it already incorporates a scan path and that the pseudorandom binary sequence (PRBS) generator and signature analyser (SA) are connected to the circuit through the primary inputs and outputs or scan in and out ports.

Within the category of internal implementations, the selftest circuitry is implemented on chip and can either be centralized, distributed or mixed. The centralized configuration has only one PRBS generator and one signature analysis register, requiring each test to be shifted completely through the scan registers before the next test can be applied. The distributed technique, however, has the capability to configure several generators and analysis registers; the trade-off made is testing time against additional hardware requirements. The mixed approach, as the name infers, was developed with the aim of reducing hardware overheads whilst maintaining reasonably short testing times. As a practical example of this built-in test approach two implementations, LOCST[16] and SASP[17], are described below; a general description of basic implementations of the S^3 philosophy is given by Komonytsky[18].

LOCST (LSSD on-chip self test)

The LOCST system was developed by IBM to reduce the number of different sets of test data (input vectors and output responses) required for different test environments, i.e. chip manufacture test, card test, operational system test and field return test. For testing chips immediately after manufacture, however, LOCST is only used in production to identify faulty chips rapidly before the more rigorous and lengthy LSSD tests are implemented.

The basic block diagram of the LOCST system is shown in Figure 1; it is implemented, essentially, from the testability enhancement components currently incorporated in IBM circuits, namely LSSD hardware, 'boundary scan' latches and the 'on-chip monitor' (OCM) which is the standard maintenance interface. When used in selftest mode the first 20 shift register latches (SRLs) in the circuit scan path are configured into a 20-bit LFSR to generate the input sequences; the feedback polynomial chosen is one which can produce a 'maximal length' sequence for a 20-bit register whilst keeping the area overhead to an absolute minimum.

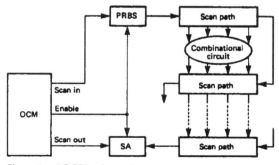

Figure 1. LOCST schematic

Differing test sequences can be produced by the LFSR by altering the initial or 'seed' value in the register. The reconfiguration of the initial sections of the scan path to an LFSR is controlled by the OCM. The signature analysis register in the system is configured from the last 16 SRLs in the scan path of the circuit, again under the control of the OCM. The selftest procedure using LOCST consists of loading all SRLs in the circuit scan path with pseudorandom data, activating the system clocks for a single cycle; this essentially applies random pattern stimuli to the combinational circuitry, partitioned by sections of SRLs, and captures the responses of the circuit to these stimuli in the SRLs attached to the output of each partition. Thereafter another test vector from the PRBS generator is loaded into the scan path; the process of loading the SRLs with a new test vector again scans the test results from the previous vector into the signature analysis register. This procedure is repeated for a given number of cycles, whereupon the final signature is scanned out for comparison.

During the LOCST test procedures the 'boundary scan' latches on the input are inhibited, thus preventing any external signals from entering the system when in selftest mode. The final fault-free signature is derived through the use of 'gold' units. The fault coverage of this technique depends upon the amount of interior and exterior logic on the chip. Interior logic is defined as combinational blocks whose inputs are fed by latches and whose outputs terminate on latches; the latches make up parts of the serial scan path through the system and hence the blocks are able to be tested using the LOCST method. Combinational blocks whose inputs and outputs are connected directly to the primary inputs and outputs of the chip are defined as exterior logic and cannot be tested by the LOCST method.

The LOCST technique was applied to several chips, one of which was used in a signal processing application. The fault coverage on interior logic was 79.7% and was obtained with less then 5000 patterns. The major limitation in this technique is the use of long serial scan paths, but the process can be made more efficient if several smaller scan paths are configured in parallel, as discussed in the SASP method, feeding a multi-input signature register.

SASP (signature analysis and scan path)

The SASP technique was the result of an investigation which attempted to quantify the effects of some of the penalties incurred by certain DFT techniques, e.g. scan path and BILBO (built-in logic block observer), with respect to testing time and area overhead. The result of the investigation indicated that a trade-off existed between the increase in additional area for the test hardware and subsequent testing time; subsequently a hybrid technique was developed which exhibited an improved performance characteristic in terms of the area/time trade-off over both the scan path and BILBO techniques.

A block diagram of the hardware configuration for the SASP technique is shown in Figure 2. The circuit is partitioned into blocks by scan path registers whose outputs are connected to a multi-input signature analysis register (SAREG) and to the multiplexer SEL1. SEL1 can select any one of the scan path outputs and connect it to an external pin, via the multiplexer SELOUT, simultaneously disabling the output from SAREG. The inputs to

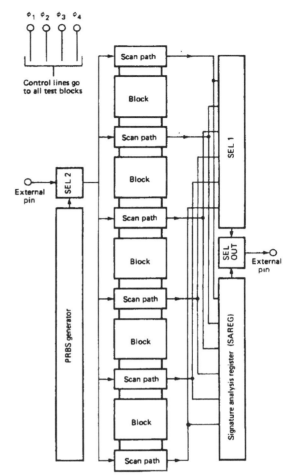

Figure 2.   SASP schematic

the scan path registers are connected to the output of the PRBS generator or to an external pin via the multiplexer SEL2.

The procedure for self testing a circuit using SASP is to first connect all the inputs to the scan paths via SEL2, to the PRBS generator, and to scan in a test vector. The test vector is then applied to the combinational blocks and the outputs are captured in the appropriate scan registers, the previous contents being overwritten. The outputs of the scan registers are subsequently clocked into the multi-input signature analysis register; a new random test vector is simultaneously entered into the scan registers. This procedure is repeated for N patterns, after which the final signature is clocked out of the system for comparison. The advantages of this technique are that combinational blocks are tested in parallel; hence long scan paths are avoided, and the built-in test facilities offered by BILBO are realized without incurring the penalty of increased chip area through the use of multifunctional registers.

One disadvantage of built-in test methods is that they have little or no fault location capability. However, the parallel test method adopted in SASP, together with the introduction of another multiplexer on the inputs to the scan registers, would permit faults to be located down to block level.

To quantitively compare the trade-offs involved between scan path, BILBO and SASP implementations of a design, a hierarchical multiplier, whose size could be changed from 8 bit to 64 bit, was selected as a test vehicle. In this instance, for a worst-case comparison, it was assumed that the test hardware was not used in the normal operation of the circuit. A comparison of the percentage area occupied by the test hardware as circuit size increases is shown in Figure 3. It is seen that, for small circuit sizes, the SASP technique incurs the highest area penalty since a PRBS generator and signature analysis register are required in addition to the register blocks required by the scan path and BILBO techniques. However, as circuit complexity increases the percentage overhead of these two blocks becomes less significant and the overall area of the test circuitry approaches that occupied by the scan path technique.

Another important aspect to be considered when implementing a DFT technique is the effect it has on the circuit testing time. The results obtained for the three techniques are shown in Figure 4 where it is assumed that, nominally, 1000 test vectors are applied to the circuits. The BILBO technique produced the shortest test time, since little time is wasted in scanning in and out the test vectors and their responses. Comparing the SASP and scan path techniques it is seen that for small circuit sizes the testing times are similar. As circuit complexity increases, however, the testing time required by SASP becomes much less than that required by the scan path method, since several blocks are tested in parallel and long serial scan paths are avoided; furthermore, the results of the test data are compressed, reducing the amount of test data to be analysed.

From the results of the above comparisons, it is seen that a trade-off exists between the area occupied by the test hardware and the testing time. To compare the three techniques a 'figure of merit' was calculated for each from the product of the area occupied by the test hardware and the testing time. The figures of merit are plotted against circuit size in Figure 5. The larger the figure of merit, the greater the penalties incurred by the test method. It is seen that the SASP technique has an improved perfor-

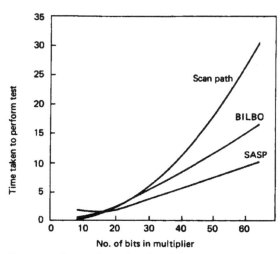

Figure 4.   Comparison of testing times

mance characteristic, in terms of the area/testing-time trade-off, over both the scan path and BILBO techniques, particularly as circuit complexity increases.

CONCURRENT CIRCUIT TESTING

Although the use of improved test generation schemes and design for testability techniques is reducing test generation costs to some extent, the basic test strategy into which they are integrated is directed at the detection of faulty devices either before or immediately after packaging. However, it has been predicted that the present trend of scaling down device sizes will lead to an increase in intermittent faults during normal device operation, resulting in a reduction of the overall reliability of systems containing these devices.

To overcome this limitation in current test strategies, and also to improve the reliability of complex VLSI

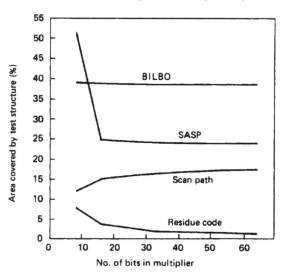

Figure 3.   Comparison of area overheads

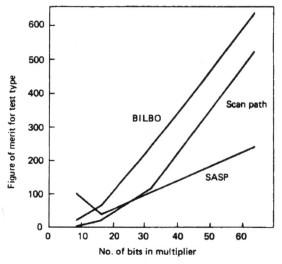

Figure 5.   Comparison of 'figures of merit'

systems, designers have been resorting to either hardware or information redundancy techniques. The area penalty incurred by hardware redundancy is considered excessive, however, so information redundancy is favoured. Although many error detection codes exist for use in information redundancy schemes, few are suitable for incorporation into VLSI designs, since they are applicable to only a limited range of digital functions or require the use of decoders to extract the check bits from the code word for verification purposes. It has been demonstrated that a class of separable codes called residue codes[19] can be incorporated cost effectively into VLSI designs[20, 21] permitting not only the detection of transient errors but also testing of the interconnectivity between function blocks. Furthermore, normal testing costs are reduced since the output test data is reduced to a simple fault/ fault-free signal and testing may be done using either random, functional or deterministic test patterns.

The choice of base size is important to the efficient implementation of residue codes for concurrent circuit testing. The main factors to be considered when deciding upon the base size are as follows.

- The area of the residue generation hardware increases with base size.
- The number of bits required to represent the residue increases with base size.
- The error detection capability for single-bit errors is independent of base size.
- Residue prediction of certain logical functions cannot be done elegantly if large base sizes are used.

In the light of the above factors, the implementation of concurrent circuit testing (CCT) for a range of VLSI functions, discussed below, was done using a base of three (Mod 3). This method has the advantage of requiring only two check bits in the code word. The Mod 3 checkers required in the implementation can easily be constructed from half and full adders and residue prediction for OR and EXOR functions can easily be implemented.

The hardware required to implement CCT using residue codes comprises

- a Mod 3 residue generator which produces the appropriate residue for a given code word; the generator consists of a tree of 2-bit adders with end-around carry; the residue generator can only be implemented in this way provided a 'low-cost' code is used, i.e. $b = 2^p - 1$ where p is the number of check bits ($p \geqslant 2$)
- a Mod 3 comparator which compares the actual and predicted residues for a given operation; the comparator produces a two-rail code as output; since the comparator essentially decides if a function block is faulty it must be designed to be totally self checking
- a two-rail encoder which compresses the comparator outputs from the various function blocks in the circuit; this reduces the number of test pins required on the package

Figure 6 illustrates the general technique for applying CCT to an arbitrary circuit using Mod 3 residue codes.

An important factor to designers in the implementation of techniques to enhance testability in VLSI circuits is the cost incurred by the technique in terms of overheads. To quantify the additional area required to implement CCT using Mod 3 residue codes, an $N \times N$ bit parallel

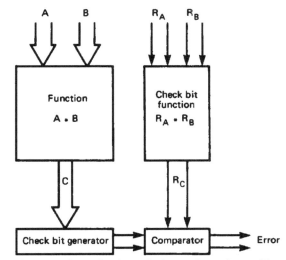

Figure 6. General schematic for testing using residue codes

multiplier and a datapath circuit were designed incorporating this feature. The parallel multiplier was designed in such a way that layouts for an 8-bit to 64-bit multiplier could be generated easily, permitting the area overhead incurred by the checking circuitry to be determined as operand size increased. A graph of the results is shown in Figure 3, where a comparison can also be made with area overheads incurred by other techniques. The percentage area overhead for CCT drops as the size of the circuit increases; this is due to the size of the residue prediction hardware remaining constant, although the residue generation hardware will increase with operand size. In general, the overall area overhead incurred by implementing CCT using Mod 3 residue codes is much less than that incurred by BILBO, SASP or the scan path method.

The datapath circuit (see Figure 1 of Reference 22) was designed as a single programmable cell to be used in the control of digital signal processing chips, where it would be embedded within the overall design. Hence the ability of the CPU to check its own operation is paramount, since few of the I/O pins would be accessible for test purposes. The datapath comprises eight 8-bit-wide registers (which are used for the program counter, the stack pointer and for general use) and an arithmetic logic unit (ALU) which can perform 22 arithmetic and three logical operations. The datapath controller performs two basic functions: first it controls the operation of the ALU and second it controls the overall operation of the datapath through the use of a microcode programmable logic array (PLA) or ROM.

The area overhead incurred by integrating CCT into the datapath circuit was 48%; this compares favourably with a 32-bit CMOS microprocessor design incorporating scan path, where the estimated area overhead was between 25% and 40%, increasing to 70% when the additional control logic etc. was included. In the datapath circuit it is estimated that, due to the large number of registers, a scan path or BILBO implementation would incur only a 20% overhead. However, these techniques can only be used for off-line testing and do not monitor the circuit continuously during normal operation; furthermore the BILBO implementation would require long simulation time to determine the fault-free signatures.

The effect of this CCT method on performance is minimal. In the case of the multiplier, since residue prediction is performed concurrently with the normal circuit operation, the only delay incurred is in the generation of the residue; this will increase with operand size. In the datapath circuit some additional delay occurs from the residue predictor in the ALU, since this has to wait in some instances for the generation of the carry or zero flags in order to predict the final residue.

Thus, as a means of enhancing circuit testability, concurrent circuit testing using Mod 3 residue codes offers the following advantages.

- A unified error detection scheme can be applied throughout a design, since it can be used on arithmetic, logical and storage functions.
- Concurrent circuit testing is performed permitting both permanent and intermittent faults to be detected.
- The area overhead incurred is much less than in hardware redundancy schemes and some standard DFT methods.
- The techniques can be applied hierarchically.
- The checking hardware is independent of the functional hardware.

Furthermore, implementation of the method in a circuit can be made transparent to the user, making it a prime candidate for incorporation into an automatic design for testability scheme which ensures circuit testability by virtue of circuit construction.

EXPERT SYSTEMS IN DFT

It is generally accepted that some sort of DFT technique must be incorporated into a design if testing costs are to be reduced. However, with the large number of methods available, each with its own advantages and disadvantages, the designer now has the added complication of identifying the technique most suitable for a particular design. In an attempt to alleviate this problem several expert systems have evolved to guide the designer's choice. If a solution cannot be found, due to the requirements of the designer being too restrictive, advice can be given upon which constraints could be relaxed to provide an acceptable solution. To provide an insight into the capabilities of these newly acquired CAD tools for DFT, two recently developed systems, TDES[23] and PLA-ESS[24], are outlined below.

TDES (testability design expert system)

The aim of the TDES system is to assist in the implementation of testable circuits. The input to the system comprises a behavioural description of the circuit to be processed in terms of PLAs, RAMs, ROMs, registers, buses etc. together with a statement of the constraints imposed upon the circuit (area overhead, number of pins etc.). The knowledge base in TDES comprises information on a range of DFT methods, rules concerning their implementation and some means of evaluating the trade-offs associated with each technique. Thereafter TDES will attempt to incorporate a testability technique into the circuit, complying wherever possible with the constraints imposed upon the circuit by the designer.

Within TDES the circuit to be processed is represented by a graph model. The nodes in the graph represent structures in the circuit; a node is defined as 'basic' if it comprises a register, combinational logic block or RAM function; otherwise it is defined as 'complex' and will have its own substructure graph model. Each node in the graph model has a label associated with it describing the attributes of the node, e.g. the type of structure, number of inputs and outputs, design style or any architectural features which could be used in testing the structure. The requirement to define the design style used to implement a function, particularly a combinational logic block, is important since this will affect the choice of DFT method which can be applied to that block. The arcs in the graph model represent the interconnections between nodes. The arcs also have labels assigned to them defining their attributes, i.e. source, destination, width etc.

The most important component in an expert system is the knowledge base. Within TDES this contains information on the structure of the DFT technique, i.e. the method of generating the test patterns and processing the responses, the method of gaining access to internal nodes, the way in which the structures are used to test the circuit (behavioural description of the test strategy), information on whether or not the test system is standalone or requires additional off-chip hardware or software for test pattern generation and finally a method of evaluating the cost of implementing a given DFT method.

Within the knowledge base the structural requirements for a testability design method (TDM) are described by means of a 'template' which contains information on the type of subcircuit (kernel) to which the technique can be applied. The template also contains information pertaining to the implementation of the technique in terms of the hardware required to generate test inputs and evaluate output responses, together with the means of connecting the test hardware to the kernel to be tested. The template of a TDM is also described as a graph model; in this instance, however, the arcs of the graph model define data transfer mechanisms between nodes which may be either simple wires or configurations of registers, multiplexers etc.

Associated with each template is a 'test plan' which defines the sequence of operations necessary to test a kernel using a particular DFT method. The test plan describes the transfer of data along the arc of a graph and the processing of the data at a node in the graph. Finally, within the data block or 'frame' associated with each DFT technique there is a statement of the trade-offs associated with the method, which can be used to assess the 'goodness' of a technique in comparison to other methods. Some of the trade-offs considered are between area overheads, fault coverage, testing time and test pattern generation costs; these attributes of a DFT technique may be constants or variables which may depend upon, for example, circuit size (in number of bits or inputs and outputs).

For the purpose of testing, the system is divided into kernels (subcircuits), which may or may not be functional blocks, but have the salient characteristic that they can be tested using some standard DFT method. TDES identifies these kernels by applying certain rules to the graph model of the circuit. Having identified the kernels in the circuit, TDES decides upon which kernels are the most difficult to test; this decision is based, again, upon a set of rules within TDES. The kernels defined as the most difficult to test are processed first, since fewer techniques are likely to be available to test these kernels, and hence fewer decisions have to be made and a decision can be reached more rapidly as to whether or not the circuit can be made testable under the constraints imposed upon the circuit. To quantify, in relative terms, the degree of difficulty encountered in testing a kernel, a cumulative weighting factor is used which is influenced by the size of the kernel, the degree of difficulty in accessing the inputs and outputs of the kernel etc.

In deciding how to apply a particular DFT technique to a kernel, a subgraph of the kernel is generated. Associated with each node in the subgraph there is an 'identity node' which defines the method of transferring data through the node together with the necessary activation signals and delays across the node. Similarly, each arc between the nodes has an 'identity transfer path' describing the activation plan to transfer data along the path and the delay that the transfer is expected to cause. The process of embedding a testability technique into a circuit consists of matching the subgraph of the kernel to the template associated with a DFT technique. If a match cannot be made additional structures may be added. The embedding of the test structures is done interactively; at each stage the 'goodness' of a technique is matched against the constraints imposed by the designer. Several possible solutions may exist for a given kernel, all of which are presented to the designer who may then select one or reject all solutions. The final output from the system defines the techniques to be used on each kernel, what overheads, if any, are incurred and also the test plan for the circuit.

PLA-ESS (PLA-expert system synthesizer)

In general, traditional test methods are not suitable for PLAs due to their high fan-in-fan-out characteristics. Consequently a number of DFT techniques have been designed to ease the testing of PLAs, each technique again having its own special requirements and overheads. Thus the designer is faced with the problem of choosing a method from a range of possible solutions which is most suitable to his/her requirements; furthermore the designer may be unaware of certain solutions to a particular testing problem which are more suitable than those he/she is currently considering. Consequently, in choosing the best DFT method for a PLA, the designer must examine a multidimensional solution space in which global trade-offs have to be made. It is to assist in this task that the PLA-ESS system was developed.

The input to PLA-ESS comprises a description of the PLA together with a requirements vector, which defines the restrictions to be imposed upon the DFT technique in terms of area overhead, fault coverage, off-chip test requirements etc. A weighting factor can be applied to each attribute in the requirements vector to indicate its relative importance. After PLA-ESS has accepted the PLA description and requirements vector, an evaluation matrix is generated which defines the attributes of each DFT method in the knowledge base of PLA-ESS with respect to the PLA being examined.

A search is then made of the evaluation matrix to determine if any entry matches the requirements vector. If there is a unique solution it is identified. If several solutions

exist, the best one is selected upon evaluation of a 'scoring' function. The 'scoring' function is a factor which reflects the trade-offs of each technique and its overall effect on the performance of the circuit, allowing the designer to make a quantitative judgement of the best technique. If a solution does not exist, the 'reasoner' is invoked to determine why a solution could not be found and how this situation may be resolved; this is usually achieved by modifying the requirements vector so that it is less constraining. The designer can seek advice from the system about which attribute of the requirements vector should be relaxed to obtain a solution. If several changes have been made the designer can request a 'trace design history'. The designer is not obliged to accept the suggestions made by the system, but can make his/her own decision and monitor the outcome. If a solution or suggestion is rejected the system will prompt for a reason and then invoke the 'reasoner' to find a more acceptable solution if one exists. Once a technique has been found which satisfies the requirements vector, the PLA is modified so that the method can be implemented and an appropriate test set generated.

TESTABILITY BY CONSTRUCTION

The traditional methods of designing IC layouts are gradually giving way to silicon compilation techniques which guarantee 'correctness by construction'. The introduction of these techniques into the design process has not only reduced design times by removing the need to perform topological analyses to detect errors in the layout, but has also highlighted the test generation phase as the ultimate time consuming task in the design process. In an attempt to rectify this situation, automatic design for testability (ADFT) schemes have been developed which not only guarantee 'correctness by construction' but also 'testability by construction'. An ADFT system resembles in many aspects an expert system directed at the DFT problem, since it contains a knowledge of DFT techniques and the logical design rules for their implementation; it has the ability to analyse designs at various levels of abstraction to locate testability problems and offer solutions. The approaches differ, however, in that the ADFT technique is embedded in a silicon compiler environment where the testability enhancement structures to be incorporated are synthesized with the functional hardware early in the design cycle.

An ADFT system[25, 26] is currently being designed at GTE Laboratories to be integrated into an existing silicon compiler environment[27]. The ADFT system comprises

- a set of rules to enforce design for testability and an associated 'rules checker'
- a testability evaluator which identifies 'hard-to-test' components
- testability structures
- a testability expert system

The functions performed by the testability evaluator are twofold: first it determines the testability of a design based on cost criteria, design constraints etc.; it then passes information on testability bottlenecks to the testability expert system which will subsequently suggest intelligent design modifications to alleviate the difficulty. The testability evaluator analyses the circuit on three levels: at structural node level where controllability and observability values are calculated for all nodes in the circuit; at path level where a path tracing algorithm is used to detect critical testing paths between the inputs and outputs of components, to determine the best place to incorporate structures for improving path testability; and at block level using an information flow approach to detect bottlenecks, with the objective of identifying sites to insert testability enhancement blocks.

The function of the testability expert system (Texpert) is to decide where and what testability enhancement structures have to be integrated into the circuit. In making decisions Texpert extracts information from several sources. These are

- the testability evaluator, which estimates the difficulty of testing a function
- the testability rule checker, which decides how well a block conforms to the design rules for testability
- the test requirements imposed by ATPG software
- the designer's requirements and constraints
- the DFT structure library, which contains parameterized testable macrocells, testability enhancement cells and an indication of the overheads incurred using these structures

Texpert uses this information to order its activities and to define the boundaries within which it can operate. When Texpert is presented with a function which has been defined as 'hard to test' it scans the DFT library to determine whether a testable version of this function exists. If a testable version exists the overheads which will result from using the testable function are examined. If the overheads are high the designer is asked if it is possible to relax the constraints. If the constraints cannot be relaxed an alternative DFT technique is examined, which may involve reconfiguring some of the functional hardware to perform a test function.

The basic philosophy underlying the concept 'testability by construction' comprises introducing testability enhancement structures at an early stage in the design. These structures are subsequently synthesized and implemented with the functional logic in the system; this has the advantage of reducing the overheads incurred by the testability enhancement structures. Also, functions which are designated 'hard to test' are identified by the ADFT system early in the design process and replaced, if possible, by a testable version of the function extracted from a DFT library. Furthermore, all of the testability enhancement structures are connected, during testing, onto a central bus system called OCTEbus (on-chip test enhancement bus). This guarantees overall controllability and observability of all function blocks in the circuit regardless of hierarchy. The connection of the test structures to OCTEbus is done automatically by Texpert, which may also share test structures between modules if the need arises to reduce area overheads. In test mode, individual testing of the components connected to OCTEbus is coordinated by an FSM controller, which may either be on or off chip. The controller selects the block to be tested, applies the necessary control and test values via OCTEbus, to the block and its associated test structures, observes the response and reports upon the results.

Thus the final output from a silicon compiler which has incorporated ADFT is a circuit that is not only correct but also testable by virtue of its construction.

CONCLUSIONS

This paper has reviewed recent developments in DFT techniques. Hybrid techniques, the objectives of which are to integrate the advantages offered by several DFT methods without incurring their overheads to any great extent, have been discussed. It has been predicted that, as advances in semiconductor technology permit smaller devices to be fabricated, the incidence of intermittent faults in integrated circuits will increase. The most reliable method of detecting intermittent faults is to continuously monitor the operation of a circuit during its lifetime. A cost effective method of performing concurrent circuit testing using Mod 3 residue codes has been discussed and its applicability to VLSI circuits demonstrated.

Over the past decade a large number of DFT techniques have evolved, each with its own advantages and disadvantages. The designer now has a formidable task in attempting to identify the technique most suited to particular requirements. To assist in this task a new class of CAD tool for DFT has been discussed; this incorporates an expert system to allow examination of a multidimensional solution space and hence an informed decision to be made on the technique best suited to a particular circuit.

Although the concept of using expert systems to assist in designing for testability is not fully developed, it has already been taken a step further by being integrated into a silicon compiler environment. The circuits generated by the system will not only be topologically correct but also testable by virtue of their construction. It is considered that, in the same way as silicon compilers have removed from the designers the 'need to know' about layout rules, such systems including automatic design for testability enhancements will remove the 'need to know' about DFT techniques, leaving the designer to concentrate on the creative aspects of the design.

REFERENCES

1 **Eichelberger, E B and Lindbloom, E** 'Trends in VLSI testing' *VLSI '83* Elsevier, Amsterdam, The Netherlands (1983) pp 339–348

2 **Goel, P** 'Test generation cost, analysis and projections' *Proc. 17th Design Automation Conf.* (June 1980) pp 77–84

3 **Snethen, T J** 'Simulator oriented fault test generator' *Proc. 14th Design Automation Conf.* (June 1977) pp 88–93

4 **Williams, T W and Parker, K P** 'Design for testability — a survey' *Proc. IEEE* Vol 71 No 1 (January 1983) pp 95–122

5 **Koenemann, B, Mucha, J and Zwiehoff, G** 'Built in logic block observation technique' *Digest Papers, 1979 Test Conf.* (1979) pp 37–41

6 **Goel, P and Rosales, B C** 'PODEM-X: an automatic test generation system for VLSI design structures' *Proc. 18th Design Automation Conf.* (June 1981) pp 260–268

7 **Roth, J P** 'Diagnosis of automatic failures: a calculus and a method' *IBM J. Res. Devel.* Vol 10 (1966) pp 278–291

8 **Levendel, Y H and Premachandran, R M** 'A test generation algorithm for computer hardware description languages' *IEEE Trans. Comput.* Vol C-31 No 7 (July 1982) pp 577–588

9 **Ambrovici, M and Menon, P R** 'A machine for design verification problems' *Digest Tech. Papers, Int. Conf. Computer Aided Design* (September 1983) pp 27–29

10 **Blank, T** 'A survey of hardware accelerators used in computer aided design' *Des. Test Comput.* (August 1984) pp 21–39

11 **Bellow, C, Robach, C and Saucier, G** 'An intelligent assistant for test program generation: the SUPERCAT system' *Digest Tech. Papers, Int. Conf. Computer Aided Design* (September 1983) pp 32–33

12 **Eichelberger, E B and Williams, T W** 'A logic design structure for LSI testability' *Proc. 14th Design Automation Conf.* (June 1977) pp 462–468

13 *A designers guide to signature analysis, Application note 222* Hewlett-Packard Wokingham, UK (1977)

14 **Savir, J** 'Syndrome testable design for combinational circuits' *IEEE Trans. Comput.* Vol C-29 No 6 (June 1980) pp 442–451

15 **Yacoub, E M** 'S³: VLSI self testing using signature analysis and scan path' *Proc. Int. Conf. Computer Aided Design* (September 1983) pp 73–76

16 **LeBlanc, J J** 'LOCST: a built in self test technique' *Des. Test Comput.* (November 1984) pp 45–52

17 **Sayers, I L, Russell, G and Kinniment, D J** 'New directions in the design for testability of VLSI circuits' *Proc. ISCAS '85* (1985) pp 1547–1550

18 **Komonytsky, D** 'LSI self-test using level sensitive scan design and signature analysis' *Digest Papers, 1982 Int. Test Conf.* (November 1982) pp 414–424

19 **Garner, H L** 'The residue number system' *IRE Trans. Electron. Comput.* Vol EC-8 (1959) pp 140–147

20 **Sayers, I L and Kinniment, D J** 'Low cost residue codes and their application to self checking VLSI systems' *IEE Proc. E* Vol 132 No 4 (July 1985) pp 197–202

21 **Montiero, P and Rao, T R N** 'A residue checker for arithmetic and logical operations' *Proc. 2nd Fault Tolerant Comput. Symp.* (1977) pp 8–13

22 **Sayers, I L, Kinniment, D J and Chester, E G** 'The design of a reliable and self testing datapath using residue coding techniques' *IEE Proc. E* Vol 133 No 3 (May 1986) pp 169–179

23 **Abadir, M S and Breuer, M A** 'A knowledge based system for designing testable VLSI chips' *Des. Test Comput.* (August 1985) pp 56–68

24 **Breuer, M A and Zhu, X** 'A knowledge-based system for selecting a test methodology for a PLA' *Proc. 22nd Design Automation Conf.* (June 1985) pp 259–265

25 **Fung, H S, Hirschhorn, S and Kulkarni, R** 'Design for testability in a silicon compilation environment' *Proc. 22nd Design Automation Conf.* (June 1985) pp 190–196

26 **Fung, H S** 'A testable-by-construction strategy for the SLIC silicon compiler' *Proc. Int. Conf. Comput. Des.: VLSI in Computers* (October 1955) pp 554–557

27 **Blackman, T, Fox, J and Rosebrugh, C** 'The SLIC silicon compiler: language and features' *Proc. 22nd Design Automation Conf.* (June 1985) pp 232–237

Gordon Russell received his BSc and PhD degrees from the University of Strathclyde, UK. Between 1975 and 1979 he was engaged in CAD research at Edinburgh University, UK. At present he is a lecturer in electrical and electronic engineering at the University of Newcastle-upon-Tyne, UK, and is also manager of the Micro-electronic Design and Test Centre. His research interests include simulation, test pattern generation, design for testability and the application of expert systems to VLSI design.

I L Sayers received his BSc and PhD degrees from Newcastle University, UK, in 1983 and 1986 respectively. Since 1985 he has been working as a lecturer in the Department of Electrical and Electronic Engineering at Newcastle. His main research interest is in concurrent error detection techniques for VLSI and WSI circuits. He is also interested in microprocessor design and applications.

Software development tool for target systems and EPROM programmers within a Unix environment

Unix can provide an ideal environment for software development, but certain vital commands are missing. **Paolo Corsini and Cosimo Antonio Prete** describe a solution

A computer running under a Unix operating system is an excellent host on which to develop software for target systems which have the same type of microprocessor as the host computer. Unfortunately, facilities for preparing executable modules able to be sent to an EPROM programmer or to be loaded onto a RAM portion of target memory space are lacking in standard Unix. These facilities can be improved in any version of Unix without the need for expensive software using the set of commands presented in this paper.

software development   Unix   EPROM

The Unix operating system[1-3] is well known and does not require presentation. More and more people are now working with the system, and many users now have access to a computer based on a standard microprocessor equipped with some version of Unix.

In such a situation the user is often tempted to use such a computer as a host system on which to develop software for target systems based on the same microprocessor[4, 5]. The user finds a powerful programming environment[6] in Unix: powerful text editors, flexible command languages[7], several programming languages (c[8], PASCAL etc.) and support for symbolic debugging facilities. In particular, the c high-level language is conducive to structured programming and the 'make'[9] command aids the user in compiling and linking programs.

The only step in software development that is not well supported is the final stage, in which the object files produced by the compiler should first be transformed into executable modules with load addresses conforming to the structure of the target system main memory (often rigidly implemented partly by means of EPROM and partly

by RAM chips) and then be prepared to be sent directly to the system and/or to an EPROM programmer.

This paper presents a set of commands that can be supported by the most common versions of Unix, and that constitute a powerful and flexible tool for supporting the final stage of software development. (How other workers have attempted to solve a similar problem can be seen in Reference 10 and also the Load and Prom commands in section 1 of Reference 11.) Such commands accept files produced by the compilers (i.e. with the standard structure of Unix 'a.out' files) and produce binary files that are the exact images of the target memories to be loaded or of the EPROM chips to be programmed. Such commands can be inserted into a Unix 'makefile'[9], allowing preparation of the final binary files to be automated.

The following section explains the commands informally but in some detail, with special reference to the 'directions for use'.

COMMAND STRUCTURE AND USE

As a working example, suppose that a user has compiled some source files and produced two relocatable object files of the 'a.out' type, named 'alpha' and 'beta', each with a 'code section' and a 'data section'. The command

```
DO myfile LINKING alpha:code, beta FROM 0x4000
            WITH alpha:data        FROM 0x8000
```

combines the two input alpha and beta files, performs relocation with respect to the entered addresses (0x4000 and 0x8000 in the above example), solves external references and produces three output files, named 'myfile0.ex', 'myfile1.ex' and 'myfile.map'. The 'myfile0.ex' file contains the code section of the file 'alpha' and the code and data sections of the file 'beta' in an absolute form

Istituto di Elettronica e Telecommunicazioni, Facolta' di Ingegneria, Universita' di Pisa, Pisa, Italy

0141-9331/86/10540–03 $03.00 © 1986 Butterworth & Co. (Publishers) Ltd

with load address 0x4000; the file 'myfile1.ex' contains an absolute form of the data section of the file 'alpha', with load address 0x8000; the file 'myfile.map' contains a table with global symbols and a summary of the characteristics (length, load addresses etc.) of the other companion absolute files. No constraint is imposed on the number of input files to be linked nor on the number or composition of the distinct modules to which specific load addresses are to be assigned.

The flexibility in assigning load addresses to the linking process allows easy solution of problems that are normally encountered in developing software for microprocessor-based target systems due to the fact that the memory space is not flexibly implemented as both EPROM and RAM chips.

Now suppose that, after the DO command has been issued one or more times, a number of files with the suffix '.ex' (named 'myfile0.ex', 'myfile1.ex' and 'yourfile0.ex') have been obtained. Moreover, suppose that the physical memory space of the target system relevant to the user's aims is 48 kbyte in size and that the files 'myfile0.ex' and 'yourfile0.ex' must be stored consecutively in such a space starting from address 0x2000, while the file 'myfile1.ex' is stored starting from address 0xA000. The command

```
CONSTRUCT image OF 48 KBYTES LOADING myfile0.ex, yourfile0.ex FROM 0x2000
                AND myfile1.ex              FROM 0xA000
```

produces a file named 'image.men' that simulates the memory space of the target system as if it were initially filled with logical 1s and afterwards loaded according to the rules given above.

It should be noted that the addresses from which the files are loaded onto the image of the target memory space do not necessarily coincide with the load addresses stated in the previous DO commands. This feature is very useful when a dynamic address translation mechanism is provided in the target system: in such cases, the addresses entered in DO commands may be 'logical addresses' while the addresses entered in CONSTRUCT commands may be 'physical addresses'.

The file 'image.mem' can be sent via a serial line from the host system to the target system if the target memory space is implemented with RAM chips. To do this, the user should write a simple routine to run on the host matching the protocol requirements supported by the monitor of his/her target system. To simplify the user's job, the internal structure of the files with the suffix '.mem' is very simple: it comprises a sequence of bytes, the first of which is the binary contents for the first 8-bit memory location, and so on.

A SEND command has been provided that sends files with suffix '.mem' via serial ports according to the Tektronics format. If the 'image.mem' file is sent via host serial port number 2, the command can be entered as

```
SEND image.mem VIA tty2
```

Now suppose that the microprocessor of the target system is a 16-bit device, and that the physical memory space of which the file 'image.mem' is an image is implemented by means of 8k × 8 bit 2764 EPROM chips. The physical memory space (Figure 1) is then a 3 × 2 matrix of chips, EPROM[0, 0], EPROM[0, 1], ..., EPROM[2, 1]. The command

```
PARTITION image.mem IN 3 FOR 2
```

outputs six files, named 'image[0, 0].mem', 'image[0, 1].mem', ..., 'image[2, 1].mem' that are the images of

EPROM[0, 0]	EPROM[0, 1]
EPROM[1, 0]	EPROM[1, 1]
EPROM[2, 0]	EPROM[2, 1]

Figure 1. Physical memory space implementation in EPROM

the chips EPROM[0, 0], EPROM[0, 1], ..., EPROM[2, 1] respectively. The parameter following the keyword FOR can take on values of 1, 2 or 4 to cover the needs of target systems based on 8-, 16- and 32-bit microprocessors. There is no constraint on the value assigned to the parameter that precedes the keyword FOR.

Each file produced by the command PARTITION can be sent to an EPROM programmer using either the SEND command or a routine written by the user according to his/her personal needs.

INTEGRATING THE COMMANDS INTO THE UNIX ENVIRONMENT

The Unix shell interpreter offers the user a powerful set of capabilities (redirection of standard input and output, connection of commands with pipelines, expansion of metacharacters, program flow control structures etc.) which make it easier to develop programs. To maintain these capabilities, each one of the commands presented here must appear to the shell as a standard Unix command. This can be accomplished simply by adding the name of the directory containing the command binary files to the 'PATH' (or 'path' for c-shell) variable.

As a practical example, let us show how a Unix make-file handles the CONSTRUCT, PARTITION and DO commands to mechanize and speed up development of the six files 'image[0, 0].mem', 'image[0, 1].mem', ..., 'image[2, 1].mem' and to be stored into 8k × 8 bit EPROM. Such files are obtained by starting from a source file 'gamma.c' written in C, and two source files 'alpha.s' and 'beta.s' written in assembly language. The text of the make file is

```
image[0, 0].mem image[0, 1].mem\
image[1, 0].mem image[1, 1].mem\
image[2, 0].mem image[2, 1].mem:image.mem
    PARTITION image.mem IN 3 FOR 2

image.mem:myfile0.ex myfile1.ex yourfile0.ex
    CONSTRUCT image OF 48 KBYTES\
        LOADING myfile0.ex yourfile0.ex FROM 0x0\
        AND myfile1.ex              FROM 0x2000

myfile0.ex myfile1.ex: alpha beta
    DO myfile LINKING alpha:code, beta FROM 0x0\
        AND alpha:data              FROM 0x1000

yourfile0.ex: gamma.o
    DO yourfile LINKING gamma.o:code FROM 0x2000\
        AND gamma.o:date FROM 0x3000

alpha: alpha.s
    as -o alpha alpha.s

beta: beta.s
    as -o beta beta.s

gamma.o: gamma.c
    cc -c gamma.c
```

The first three lines of the text state that the files 'image[0, 0].mem', 'image[0, 1].mem', . . . , 'image[2, 1].mem' are obtained by processing the file 'image.mem'; the fourth line of the text states that this processing is performed by the PARTITION command. Similarly, the subsequent four lines state that the file 'image.mem' is obtained by applying the CONSTRUCT command to the files 'myfile0.ex', 'myfile1.ex' and 'yourfile0.ex', and so on. The last six lines of the text state that the object relocatable files 'alpha', 'beta' and 'gamma.o' are obtained by processing the source files 'alpha.s', 'beta.s' and 'gamma.c' by means of the standard Unix assembler and compiler.

PORTABILITY OF THE PROPOSED COMMANDS

Let us examine the portability of the software implementing the DO, COLLECT and PARTITION commands. (The SEND command should be written by the user to meet the protocol requirements of its own target devices.)

The COLLECT and PARTITION commands elaborate on files produced primarily by the DO command and are implemented by C language programs in which only standard C functions are used (open, close, create, read, write and lseek). No portability problem arises for such commands. The DO command is also written in C and uses standard functions, but it operates on files of type 'a.out' that are produced by the Unix compilers and assemblers. Different Unix versions have some minor differences in the format of such files. The DO command described here works on 'a.out' files having the format of AT&T Unix system V release 2.0 for 3B5 and 3B2 computers (as stated in section 4 of Reference 12). The implemented DO command has been run successfully on the NCR Tower computer, with its Motorola 68010 microprocessor and Unix system V release 3.0 operating system, as well as on AT&T computers. If the user's Unix version produces 'a.out' files which have some differences from the above version, a simple file conversion should be performed by the user before applying the DO command.

CONCLUSIONS

A set of commands has been presented that allows a host computer running Unix great flexibility in preparing executable modules to be sent directly to a target system or to an EPROM programmer. The commands has been explained in an informal way. The syntax, possible short forms, default rules and C programs implementing the commands can be found in a detailed user manual[13] available from the authors.

REFERENCES

1 **Ritchie, D M and Thompson, K** 'The Unix time-sharing system' *Commun. ACM* Vol 17 No 7 (July 1974) pp 365–375
2 **Thompson, K and Ritchie, D M** *The Unix programmer's manual* Bell Laboratories, Murray Hill, NY, USA (1978)
3 **Bourne, S R** *The Unix System* Addison-Wesley, Wokingham, UK (1983)
4 **Hudson, C** 'Techniques for developing and testing microprocessor systems' *Software Microsyst.* Vol 4 No 4 (August 1985) pp 85–94
5 **Gomaa, H, Lui, J and Woo, P** 'The software engineering of a microcomputer application system' *Software Pract. Experience* Vol 12 (1982) pp 309–321
6 **Kernighan, B W and Mashey, J R** 'The Unix programming environment' *Computer* Vol 14 No 4 (April 1981) pp 12–24
7 **Bourne, S R** 'Unix time-sharing system: the Unix shell' *Bell Syst. Tech.* Vol 57 No 6 (July/August 1978) pp 1971–1990
8 **Kernighan, B W and Ritchie, D M** *The C programming language* Prentice-Hall, Englewood Cliffs, NJ, USA (1978)
9 **Feldman, S I** 'Make — a program for maintaining computer programs' *Software Pract. Experience* Vol 9 No 4 (April 1979) pp 255–265
10 *System V/68 — common link editor reference manual* Motorola, Austin, TX, USA (July 1984)
11 *System 8000 Zeus reference manual* Zilog, Campbell, CA, USA (September 1982)
12 *Unix system V release 2.0 — programmer reference manual, AT&T 3B5 computer* AT&T, Basking Ridge, NJ, USA (September 1984)
13 **Corsini, P and Prete, C A** 'Developing software for target systems under Unix environment' *Internal report* Istituto di Elettronica e Telecommunicazioni, Facolta di Ingegneria, Pisa, Italy (1986)

Paolo Corsini is professor of digital computers within the Engineering Faculty of the University of Pisa, Italy. His research interests include multimicroprocessor systems and computer architecture. He received the Dott.Ing. degree in electronic engineering, cum laude, from the University of Pisa in 1969.

Cosimo Antonio Prete has been involved in post-graduate research in computer architecture at Selenia SpA, Rome, Italy. At present, he is with the Istituto di Elettronica e Telecommunicazioni of the University of Pisa, Italy. His interests include multimicroprocessor organization and software development methodologies. He received the Dott.Ing. degree in electronic engineering, cum laude, from the University of Pisa in 1982.

Microprocessor-based digital controller for DC motor speed control

M K Refai discusses the procedure for implementing microprocessor-based PID process control algorithms, presenting the system hardware and PID algorithm for the illustrated case of DC motor control

The effectiveness of microprocessor-based systems for realizing digital random logic controllers is illustrated by the design of a controller based on an MC68B00, using E^2PROM rather than RAM or ROM to enhance flexibility and avoid memory corruption or power interrupt. Moreover, the time response of the system (about 1 ms) can cover a wide spectrum of control applications. The paper is illustrated by a DC motor speed control system.

microprocessors   digital process control   DC motors

Control is important for most industrial processes to avoid disturbances which degrade the overall process performance, and a great deal of work is being done in this field. Control mechanisms can be expensive, but the low cost and rapidly increasing power of digital circuit technology is providing the stimulus for digital controllers to be implemented in typical process examples such as low-cost automation controllers, process controllers and automatic test equipment.

Handling of discrete-time control and signal processing involves some concepts which were not previously well known. Sampling and aliasing are troublesome. Further, digital control systems have some physical restrictions which are not found in analogue or continuous data control systems.

In a survey in 1977 of electronic analogue controllers[1], 34 of the 37 controllers listed were of the proportional-integral-derivative (PID) type, either exclusively or with options (PI or P actions). Today, similar systems can be implemented with low-cost microprocessors. This paper describes the design of a PID controller based on an MC68B00 to control the speed of a DC motor. Details of the hardware and software implementation are given. For program storage the system uses E^2PROM.

MICROPROCESSOR-BASED DIGITAL CONTROL SYSTEMS

Digital processing has a relatively slow time response compared with analogue processing, which can limit its use in realtime applications. To remedy this, efficient interfaces must be used to deal with analogue input signals, such as the example illustrated by the flow diagram of Figure 1. The interface adjusts and synchronizes the signal level and provides the sample and hold circuit, as well as performing A/D and D/A conversion.

There is inherently an upper limit on the response of a digital system determined by the processor used. Microprocessor system capabilities depend on both the hardware and software limitations related to the architecture of the microprocessor. A simple scheme for using a microprocessor in a digital controller is shown in Figure 2, in which the process under control consists of any physical process (here a DC motor) and the control algorithm is executed under the control of the microprocessor.

Controller algorithm

A PID controller is a good general-purpose device. Most process loops where the plant transfer function has not been completely characterized or defined can be controlled by a PID algorithm or one of the variations[2]. The PID coefficients (K_P, K_I and K_D control gains) can be made independent of each other, but they are subject to the length of the sampling period[3].

The PID controller can be represented in both the continuous and discrete-time forms. A continuous PID controller is governed by an equation containing integral and/or derivative terms which describe the dynamic, time-varying behaviour of the input or error signal as follows

$$e_o(t) = K_p e_i(t) + K_I \int e_i(t)\, dt + K_d \frac{de_i(t)}{dt} \qquad (1)$$

Abo El Nomoros Giza, Giza, Egypt

0141-9331/86/10543-10 $03.00 © 1986 Butterworth & Co. (Publishers) Ltd

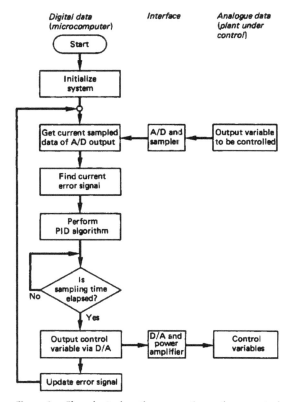

Digital data (microcomputer)   *Interface*   *Analogue data (plant under control)*

Figure 1. Flowchart for the operation of a control interface

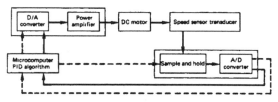

Figure 2. Schematic of a microprocessor-based process control system

where $e_o(t)$ is the control variable, $e_i(t)$ is the variable to be controlled, i.e. the error signal, that can be represented by

$$e_i(t) = \omega_d - \omega(t) \qquad (2)$$

ω_d is the desired speed and $\omega(t)$ is the load speed.

In a discrete-time system a dual-mode A/D, D/A converter must be employed to convert the error signal into digital form (sampled data) and the control variable to analogue signals to drive the DC motor, as in Figure 2. The input to the microprocessor is then the digitized error signal $e_i(nT)$ that is represented by

$$e_i(nT) = \omega_d - \omega(nT) \qquad (3)$$

where $n = 1, 2, \ldots$ and T is the sampling period.

The microprocessor can be used to implement the PID controller by describing the digital controller either by its transfer function in the Z domain, $D(Z)$, or by its

continuous equation. In this paper the latter approach is considered, hence Equation (1) is digitized by a numerical approximation method and then programmed in machine language. The integral in Equation (1) may be written as

$$X(t) = \int_{t_o}^{t} (\omega_d - \omega(t))\, dt + X(t_o) \qquad (4)$$

where $X(t_o)$ is the initial value of $X(t)$.

The trapezoidal integration rule is used to approximate the definite integral. Let $t = nT$ and $t_o = (n-1)T$, then

$$\int_{(n-1)T}^{nT} (\omega_d - \omega(t))\, dt \simeq \omega_d T - \frac{T}{2}(\omega(nT) + \omega(n-1)T) \qquad (5)$$

Thus the value of $X(t)$ can be computed using the desired input ω_d and the data for $\omega(nT)$ and $\omega(n-1)T$ at $t = nT$. For convenience it is assumed that the computation time delay (the time required to execute the PID algorithm) is equal to one sampling period T. This means that the integral computational result will be at $t = (n-1)T$, and Equation (5) is digitized by the following state equation

$$X(n+1)T = \omega_d T - \frac{T}{2}(\omega(nT) + \omega(n-1)T) + X(nT) \qquad (6)$$

where $X(nT)$ is the initial state of $X(nT)$.

The derivative part of Equation (1) is approximated by using the backward difference equation

$$\frac{de_i(t)}{dt} \simeq (e_i(nT) - e_i(n-1)T)/T \qquad (7)$$

The PID control algorithm in discrete-time form thus becomes

$$e(n+1)T = K_p e_i(nT) + K_I X(n+1)T$$
$$+ K_D(e_i(nT) - e_i(n-1)T)/T \qquad (8)$$

This algorithm can be implemented provided that the time required to perform the computation and output the result is small compared with T. If this time is not small, the value of $e_i(nT)$ must be predicted at time $(n-1)T$ and the computations performed[4] for $e(n+1)T$ during the time interval $(n-1)T$ to nT. Prediction methods require detailed knowledge of the plant under control and increase software demands on the microcontroller, however, and are rarely worthwhile.

SYSTEM DESIGN

As a control system must operate in real time, the most important design parameter is its time response. In digital systems the sampling time is the dominant parameter, and this depends mainly on the time taken to process the error signal for one data item and update the error signal for the next process.

Sample time calculation

There is no solid rule for calculating the sampling period, but in general it depends on the parameters of both the plant, which determines the time constant, and the controller, determining the algorithm computation time.

To some extent the calculation of the sampling period may be considered a standard problem. There are rules for calculating this period as shown below. (Keep in mind that setting a maximum sampling frequency is necessary to avoid errors in data representation).

With respect to the computation time of the controller algorithm, a sampling frequency about 10 times the maximum error signal frequency has been recommended to avoid sampling error[5], since this ensures that the signal will not change appreciably in any sampling period. For the case of a DC motor, the various engineering constraints upon the speed response of the motor (plant) show that the achievable closed-loop bandwidth of the continuous system f_o does not reduce but enlarges the stable operating region slightly when the sampling period T of the sampler in the loop is chosen to be smaller than the plant time constant T_m. The G16M4 DC motor, for example, is characterized by a small mechanical time constant $T_m = 0.02$ s. Then, for preliminary guidance, a sample rate[6] of three or four times greater than f_o, i.e. $T = 1/3f_o$, may be chosen such that a 10 ms sampling time, considered adequate for most types of DC motor, is obtained.

System software

It is clear that the time taken to process and update the error signal is important. A flowchart for the PID control algorithm of Equation (8) is shown in Figure 3, and the program written in MC6800 machine language is given in Appendix 1. From this it is found that to execute a complete PID algorithm requires 2343 machine cycles. Using the MC68B00 this takes ~ 1 ms, with the program in zero page. By choosing the program structure carefully its size is only 255 byte, as shown in Appendix 1. So the computation time can be reduced to accommodate a sample frequency of less than 1 kHz, which is reasonable for a wide spectrum of control applications and even allows the processor to control more than one process at a time.

System hardware

As shown in Figure 2 the interface is the heart of the system and depends on the sampling period. With the controller algorithm computation time of the order of 1 ms, the plant required a sampling period of 10 ms. The timing limits must be built around this sampling period.

As the MC6800 microprocessor has no special I/O instructions[7], memory-mapped I/O is used to handle I/O data. The processor uses no special instructions or port addresses, and only the memory decoder causes the microprocessor to function as though it were reading or writing to memory. The 'port' thus becomes effectively a memory address, i.e. there cannot be any real memory using that address. In memory-mapped I/O, a block of memory addresses is set aside to function as I/O channels. When the microprocessor executes an instruction that reads one of these locations, the input device is activated to place its data on the data bus, which is then read into the microprocessor. Similarly for writing to a memory location for output data. Any addresses can be used as I/O channels.

For a 10 ms sampling time an A/D converter with a conversion time of 1 ms for full-scale readings is adequate. For this speed of sampling a low-cost dual A/D, D/A converter would be suitable, such as the Ferranti ZN425, a monolithic 8-bit D/A and A/D converter with an R-2R ladder network, which is used here. The converter contains an internal circuit which generates a voltage reference $V_{ref} = 2.55$ V and a binary counter used for A/D conversion.

The ZN425 has an 8-bit port connected to the microprocessor data bus via 8-bit I/O latches (74373), as shown in Figure 4. These 8-bit ports control the bipolar switches for the R-2R ladder network. A 'count' control signal at pin 2 of the converter determines whether the 8-bit data port is to be used for input or output. The analogue output voltage appears at pin 14 and is connected to two op. amps. as shown in Figure 4. One of these has a potentiometer for full-scale adjustment of the output signal that controls the motor speed, while the other op. amp. is used as the voltage comparator employed in A/D conversion.

For D/A conversion the 'count' control signal must be low, when the counter outputs are isolated by the open collector transistor switches. The R-2R ladder is then controlled by the data output from the latches. In this way the converter accepts data from the 8-bit latches and converts the binary data to its analogue voltage.

For A/D conversion some control inputs of the converter must be operated with the clock signal from the internal counter. The internal counter is driven by the controlled clock input signal at pin 4 and is cleared by the convert command negative edge applied at pin 3, as shown in Figure 4. The 'count' control signal at pin 2 must be high. In this way the internal counter controls the data on the I/O port and the switches of the R-2R ladder, and the data is read into the latches.

On the negative edge of the convert command pulse the counter is set to zero and the status output to logic '1'. On the positive edge the counter starts to count up from zero. The analogue output ramps until it equals the analogue voltage applied to the other input of the comparator. At this point any further clock pulses are inhibited and the status goes low to indicate that the output data is valid.

System memory

There is a major drawback to the implementation of the process controller using RAM memory. Under adverse environmental conditions, particularly electrical interference, the RAM may be corrupted. A ROM-based process controller, however, is free from this drawback and also improves system reliability. The price for this improved reliability is that the contents of the database cannot be altered as readily as for RAM-based systems and this reduces the flexibility of the controller. The most efficient and flexible form of memory is E^2PROM, which has occasional in-system programmability and nonvolatile long-term data retention, with RAM back-up.

As discussed above, the system described uses memory-mapped I/O, so the whole address space can be treated as memory. The memory will contain all the system storage requirements, as shown in Figure 5. To save program execution time the system program is selected to be on page zero. The memory mapped I/O

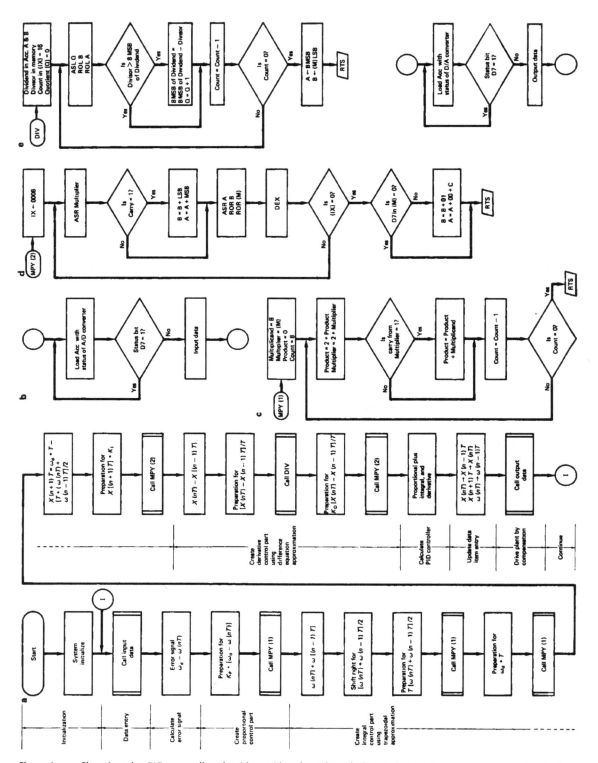

Figure 3. a, *Flowchart for PID controller algorithm with subroutines; b, input data routine; c, 8 × 8 bit multiplication subroutine; d, 16 × 8 bit multiplication subroutine; e, 8 × 16 bit division subroutine; f, output data routine*

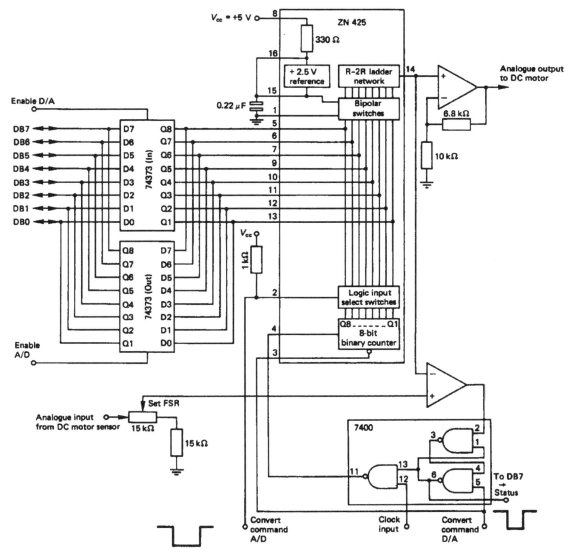

Figure 4. System interface circuit

area is selected so that the realization of decoding hardware is simple and memory space is left for extension of the system. The system program is placed in E^2PROM because it requires updating. RAM type memory is used for data manipulation. Thus, the memory map consists of

- 1 kbyte static RAM for storing stack variables, main program variables and any future software system development
- 256 byte (1k n-channel 128 × 8 bit) E^2PROM (ER 5901) for the control algorithm program, located in zero page. Also 0.5 kbyte EPROM (S6834), which contains the system vectors that the processor uses on power-up, on reset and on receiving a nonmaskable interrupt signal which causes it to preserve its present status in memory and to go into a 'halt' state

- the A/D and D/A converter memory address spaces (8E00 and 8E0F) which are used as I/O channels for control variables.

System cost

It is difficult to make a general cost analysis of a digital system as costs are both technology and manufacturer dependent. Generally, the cost of a digital system can be divided into software and hardware costs. Hardware implementation costs are the electronic components and the installation of the system. Software costs are based on estimates of the number and type of routines and the number of instructions expected per routine, as well as routine complexity and the productivity and competence of the system operator. Development of a useable and

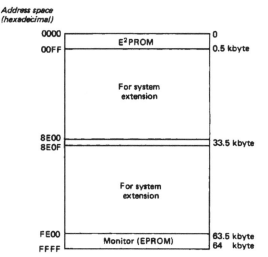

Address space
(hexadecimal)

```
0000                                          0
         E²PROM
00FF                                          0.5 kbyte

         For system
         extension

8E00                                          33.5 kbyte
8E0F

         For system
         extension

FE00                                          63.5 kbyte
         Monitor (EPROM)
FFFF                                          64   kbyte
```

Figure 5. System memory layout

reliable software cost model is hampered by the lack of good data, especially during operation and maintenance phases.

CONCLUSIONS

The advantages of microprocessors now makes the use of LSI possible even for simple control applications, with high performance and flexibility. In this paper the design of a microprocessor-based PID realtime controller has been presented. The design procedure involves the determination of an appropriate sampling rate, controller constants (P, I and D gains) and the plant constant (in this case for a DC motor) that match the desired target by changing the corresponding values in the control algorithm. It has been shown that 8-bit processing power is adequate for most industrial control systems, as the final word size which expresses the plant may be reduced to 8 bit, the size of the D/A converter. The microprocessor system illustrated above was seen to be low cost but at the same time offers high performance, versatility,

increased system throughput and extension capability without the need for extra hardware.

REFERENCES

1   **Merritt, R** 'Electronic controller survey' *Instrum. Technol.* Vol 24 No 5 (June 1977) pp 43–62
2   **Bibbero, R J** *Microprocessors in instrumentation and control* John Wiley, NY, USA (1977)
3   **De Boit, R R and Powell, R E** 'A natural 3-mode controller algorithm for DDC' *ISA J.* (Sept. 1966) pp 43–53
4   **Aylor, J H, Ramey, R L and Cook, G** 'Design and application of a microprocessor PID predictor controller' *IEEE Trans. Indust.* Vol IE-27 No 3 (August 1980) pp 133–137
5   **Krikelis, N J and Fassois, S D** 'Microprocessor implementation of PID controllers and lead–lag compensators' *IEEE Trans. Indust.* Vol IE-31 No 1 (Feb. 1984) pp 79–85
6   **Stojic, M R** 'Design of a microprocessor-based digital system for DC motor speed control' *IEEE Trans. Indust.* Vol IE-31 No 3 (August 1984) pp 243–248
7   *Motorola M6800 microprocessor application manual* (1975)

Mohamed Khalil Refai graduated in communication engineering from Einshams University, Egypt. After four years as a research engineer with the Arab Institute of Aircraft Technology in Cairo, he joined the University of Kent at Canterbury, UK, where he obtained an MSc degree in digital systems. He continued his work on multimicroprocessor systems at the University of Leeds, UK, and was awarded a PhD in November 1982. Refai then returned to Egypt to resume his former post before joining the Department of Computer and Control Systems at Al Azhar University in May 1985. His current interests are in CAD/CAM tools for digital and system design.

APPENDIX 1: MC6800 MACHINE CODE PROGRAM FROM PID CONTROL ALGORITHM

Memory location	Machine code (hex)	Label	Mnemonics (operator and operand)	Comments	Machine code storage (No. of bytes)	Execution time (No. of cycles)
0000 ↓ 0010				Free working area for algorithm internal variables and constants Routine for memory block transfer		
0011	CE 8E 04		LDX#$8E04	Start address of the block to be transferred	3	3
0014	DF 0B		STX$0B		2	5
0016	CE 00 00		LDX#$0000	Start address of transferred data in zero page	3	3

Memory location	Machine code (hex)	Label	Mnemonics (operator and operand)	Comments	Machine code storage (No. of bytes)	Execution time (No. of cycles)
0019	DF 0D		STX$0D		2	5
001B	C6 05		LDAB#$05		2	2
1D	DE 0B	L1	LDX$0B	Beginning of transfer loop	2	4
1F	A6 00		LDAAo,x		2	5
	08		INX		1	4
22 23	DF 0B		STX$0B		2	5
25	DE 0D		LDX$0D		2	4
0026	A7 00		STAAo,x		2	6
	08		INX		1	4
	DF 0D		STX$0D		2	5
002B	5A		DECB		1	2
002C	26		BNE L1	End of the transfer loop according	2	4
002D	EE			to Acc. (B)		
		*		Start input new item of Data		
002E	B6 8E 00	L2	LDAA$8E00	Load Acc. A with the status of the A/D converter	3	4
0031	2B FD		BMI L2	If D7 = 1 then wait for input data, otherwise	2	4
	B6 8E 02		LDAA$8E02	Load the data from the A/D converter	3	4
0036 0037	97 05		STAA$05	Store the input data $\omega(nT)$ in the working area	2	4
		*		Calculate error signal		
0038	16		TAB	Transfer $\omega(nT)$ from A to B	1	2
0039 003A	96 04		LDAA$04	Load Acc. A with ω_d	2	2
003B	10		SBA	Subtract $[\omega_d - \omega(nT)] \rightarrow A$	1	2
		*		Create the proportional control part		
003C	D6 00		LDAB$00	Load Acc. B with K_p	2	3
3E 3F	8D 8C		BSR MPY$_1$	Go to subroutine MPY$_1$ 8 × 8 bit multiplication	2	8
	5D		TSTB	Test if D7 is in Acc. B, otherwise	1	2
	2A		BPL L3	Branch to location L3 if D7 = 0	2	4
0042	04					
	8B 01		ADDA#$01	If D7 = 1 add 1 to MSB		
	97	L3	STAA$0D	Store in working area of	2	4
0046	0D			$K_p[\omega_d - \omega(nT)]$		
		*		Create integral control part		
0047 0048	96 05		LDAA$05	Load Acc. A with $\omega(nT)$	2	3
0049 004A	9B 06		ADDA$06	Add $\omega(nT) + \omega(nT) \rightarrow A$	2	3
004B	44		LSR A	To get $[\omega(nT) + \omega(n-1)] T1/2$	1	2
	D6 03		LDAB$03	Load Acc. B with T	2	3
004E 004F	8D 7C		BSR MPY$_1$	Go to subroutine MPY$_1$	2	8
0050	97 0B		STAA$0B		2	4

Memory location	Machine code (hex)	Label	Mnemonics (operator and operand)	Comments	Machine code storage (No. of bytes)	Execution time (No. of cycles)
0052	D7 0C		STAB$0C		2	4
54 0055	96 04		LDAA$04	Load Acc. A with ω_d	2	3
	06 03		LDAB$03	Load Acc. B with T	2	3
0058 0059	8D 72		BSR MPY$_1$	Go to subroutine MPY$_1$ 8 × 8 bit multiplication $\omega_d * T$	2	8
005A 005B	D0 0C		SUBB$0C	LSB of $[\omega_d * T - T * [(nT) + \omega(n-1) T]/2]$	2	3
005C 005D	92 0B		SBCA$0B	MSB of $\{\omega_d * T - T * [\omega(nT) + \omega(n-1) T]/2\}$	2	3
005E 005F	DB 0A		ADDB$0A	LSB of $\{\omega_d * T - T * [\omega(nT) + \omega(n-1) T]/2 + X(nT)\}$	2	3
0060 0061	99 09		ADCA$09	MSB of $\{\omega_d * T - T * [\omega(nT) + \omega(n-1) T]/2 + X(nT)\}$	2	3
0062	97 0B		STAA$0B	Store the result $X(n + 1) T$ in working area LSB	2	4
	D7 0C		STAB$0C	Store MSB of $X(n + 1) T$ in 0C	2	4
	97 0F		STAA$0F	Also store here the same $X(n + 1) T$ (LSB)	2	4
0068 0069	D7 10		STAB$10	Store here MSB of $X(n + 1) T$	2	4
006A 006B	96 01		LDAA$01		2	3
006C 006D 006E	B7 8E 0F		STAA$8E0F		3	5
006F	4F		CLR A		1	2
0070	5F		CRL B		1	2
0071 0072	8D 3B		BSR MPY$_2$	Go to subroutine MPY$_2$ 16 × 8 bit to get $K_I * [X(n + 1) T]$	2	8
	DB 0D		ADDB$0D	LSB of $K_I * [X(n + 1) T] + K_p * [\omega_d - \omega(nT)]$	2	3
	89 00		ADCA$#00	Add carry the MSB	2	2
	97 0D		STAA$0D	Store Acc. A (MSB) in working area 0D	2	4
0079 007A	D7 0E		STAB$0E	Also store Acc. B (LSB) in 000E	2	4
		*		Create derivative control part		
007B	96 09		LDAA$09	Load Acc. A with MSB of $X(nT)$	2	3
007D 007E	D6 0A		LDAB$0A	Load Acc. B with LSB of $X(nT)$	2	3
	D0 08		SUBB$08		2	3
	92 07		SBCA$07		2	3
0083	8D		BSR DIV	Go to subroutine Div. 16 + 8 bit $\{X(nT) - X(n-1) T\}/T$	2	8
	97 0F		STAA$0F		2	4
	D7 10		STAB$10		2	4
0088						
0089 008A	96 02		LDAA$02	Load Acc. A with K_D	2	3
008B 008C 008D	B7 8E 0F		STAA$8E0F		3	5
008E	4F		CLR A		1	2

Memory location	Machine code (hex)	Label	Mnemonics (operator and operand)	Comments	Machine code storage (No. of bytes)	Execution time (No. of cycles)
008F	5F		CLR B		1	2
0090	8D		BSR MPY$_2$	Go to subroutine MPY$_2$ 16 × 8 bit	2	8
0091	1C			to form $K_D* [X(nT) - X(n-1) T]/T$		
0093	0E			$+ K_p [\omega_d - \omega(nT)] + K_I * (X(n+1) T)$		
0094	99		ADCA$0D		2	3
0095	0D					
		*		Output control variable via D/A converter		
0096	5D		TST B	Test D7	1	2
	2A		BPL L4	If D7 = 0 then go to output	2	4
	04			Data to D/A converter		
	CB		ADDB$#01		2	2
	01					
	B7	L4	STAA$8E03	Store the output data in	3	5
	8E			D/A converter		
	03					
		*		Update for next sampling		
	DE		LDX$09		2	4
	09					
00A0	DF		STX$07		2	5
00A1	07					
00A2	DE		LDX$09		2	4
00A3	09					
00A4	DF		STX$07		2	5
00A5	07					
00A6	96		LDAA$05		2	3
00A7	05					
00A8	97		STAA$06		2	4
00A9	06					
00AA	20		BRA L2		2	4
00AB	83					
		*		Subroutine for 16 × 8 bit multiplication		
00AC	FE	MPY$_2$	LDX$0008		3	5
00AD	00					
00AE	08					
00AF	78	L6	ASR$8E0F		3	6
00B0	8E					
00B1	0F					
00B2	24		BCC L7		2	4
00B3	06					
	DB		ADDB$14		2	3
	14					
	99		ADCA$13		2	3
	13					
	47	L7	ASR A		1	2
	56		ROR B		1	2
	76		ROR$8E0E		3	6
	8E					
	0E					
	09		DEX		1	4
	26		BNE L6		2	4
	F0					
00C0	7D		TST$8E0E		3	6
00C1	8E					
00C2	0E					
00C3	2A		BPL L5		2	4
00C4	06					
00C5	CB		ADDB#$01		2	2
00C6	01					
00C7	89		ADCA#$00		2	2
00C8	00					

Memory location	Machine code (hex)	Label	Mnemonics (operator and operand)	Comments	Machine code storage (No. of bytes)	Execution time (No. of cycles)
00C9	39	L5	RTS		1	5
		*		Subroutine for 8 × 8 bit multiplication		
00CA	97	MPY1	STAA$13		2	4
00CB	13					
00CC	F7		STAB$8E0F		3	5
00CD	8E					
00CE	0F					
00CF	4F		CLR A		1	2
00D0	5F		CLR B		1	2
00D1	CE		LDX#$0008		3	3
00D2	00					
00D3	08					
	58	L8	ASL B		1	2
	49		ROL A		1	2
	78		ASL$8E0F		3	6
	8E					
	0F					
	24		BCC L9		2	4
	06					
	DB		ADDB$13		2	3
	13					
	89		ADCA#$00		2	2
	00					
	09	L9	DEX		1	4
00E0	26		BNE L8		2	4
00E1	F3					
00E2	39		RTS		1	5
		*		Subroutine for 8 + 16 bit division		
	86	DIV	LDAA$#00		2	2
	00					
	97		STAA$0F		2	4
	0F					
00E8	CE		LDX#$0010		3	3
00E9	00					
00EA	10					
00EB	78	L11	ASL$000F		3	6
	00					
	0F					
	59		ROL B		1	2
	49		ROL A		1	2
00F0	91		CMPA$03		2	3
00F1	03					
00F2	25		BCS L10		2	4
00F3	07					
00F4	90		SUBA$03		2	3
00F5	03					
00F6	7C		INC$000F		3	6
00F7	00					
00F8	0F					
00F9	09	L10	DEX		1	4
00FA	26		BNE L11		2	4
00FB	F0					
00FC	17		TBA		1	2
00FC	D6		LDAB$0F		2	3
00FE	0F					
00FF	39		RTS		1	5

Talking teletext receiver for the blind

It is desirable to have an alternative to Braille for communicating textual information to blind people. **O R Omotayo** describes the principles of a system that uses speech synthesis to present teletext transmissions

By converting teletext pages into speech, the blind population could be afforded an opportunity of accessing broadcast teletext information normally displayed on the screen of a domestic television receiver. The possibility is examined in this paper. A suitable teletext receiver and decoder are described, and system hardware and software for a talking teletext receiver are discussed. Some human factors affecting the design are also discussed.

microsystems   speech synthesis   teletext

Systems for transmitting textual information in digitally coded forms during the blanking period for display on the domestic television set was proposed in 1972 by the broadcasting authorities in the UK. This idea led to teletext transmission services. Many other countries[1] are now operating teletext services.

To receive teletext broadcasts the television receiver must be fitted with a teletext decoder. Such televisions are now widely available commercially. A continuously changing cycle of pages is normally transmitted and a keypad is used to enter the required page number. The number of pages in the cyclic transmission is about 800 divided into eight magazines.

Conversion of teletext pages into speech has been explored for the purpose of extending the service to blind people.

WHY SPEECH OUTPUT?

There is no doubt that Braille has been the most popular medium for the output of textual information for the blind. However, only a small proportion of the blind population — about 10% in the UK — can read Braille. The main reason many blind people have been put off learning how to read Braille appears to be the special skill required to read it. Acquiring this skill demands intensive training to which many blind people are not ready to subject themselves.

Department of Electrical Engineering, University of Ibadan, Nigeria

Even after acquiring this skill a blind person can become unable to use it. Since Braille characters are symbolic representations of the textual characters, efficient reading of Braille depends heavily on how sensitive the reader is to touching shapes. This sense of touch may become weak due to old age or an additional handicap. Thus, even a highly proficient Braille reader can lose such a laboriously acquired skill and this in itself can negate the urge to learn Braille.

This is not to say that Braille does not have a useful role to play. Indeed, computer-generated Braille (dynamic Braille) is likely to become more useful especially in the educational field. Conversion of electronic information services to Braille[2] would indeed be very useful to Braille readers. An alternative output medium must, however, be considered which would require little or no special skill to use. Speech output is a natural choice.

Having selected speech for its ease of use, it must be realized that satisfactory conversion of teletext into speech is more complex than conversion into Braille. This is because, first, a speech synthesizer is required to operate with unlimited vocabulary and the intelligibility of such synthesizers is, at present, not ideal[3]; in contrast, a dynamic Braille display can be of extremely high quality. Secondly, speech is less suited to the reproduction of two-dimensional data pages than a single-line Braille display. Nevertheless, the potential low cost of the speech synthesis process and the large number of potential blind users make the study of conversion of teletext into speech worthwhile.

Methods of synthesizing speech can be grouped broadly into two sections: copy synthesis and synthesis by rule. In copy synthesis, human speech is recorded, digitized and compressed for storage. A message is then synthesized by re-expanding and joining the stored data. Synthesizers based on this method are only capable of a limited vocabulary in most cases.

On the other hand, synthesis by rule does not use any form of stored human utterances to provide the raw material of any message, but instead generates an entire message by rule from a specification of the phonetic sequences, as well as the prosodic features (pitch and timing). Since any phoneme (the smallest unit of spoken

0141-9331/86/10553-04 $03.00 © 1986 Butterworth & Co. (Publishers) Ltd

sound) can be generated artificially in this way, synthesizers based on this method have the capability to handle unlimited vocabulary[4], although their speech intelligibility is less than that of the copy synthesis method. For this reason such a synthesizer was selected for the system described in this paper.

TELETEXT RECEIVER

A teletext receiver is illustrated schematically in Figure 1. It is the conventional remote-controlled colour television with added teletext decoder. The remote control keypad has dual-mode operation — television and teletext modes — and each mode can be selected with one key.

The major components of the teletext decoder[5] are illustrated in Figure 2. The video signal is fed into the decoder via the video input processor (VIP). The main function of the VIP is to receive the data and make it available to the teletext data acquisition and control (TAC) unit in sequence. In addition, the VIP protects the data stored in memory from being corrupted by signal noise and also provides a synchronization signal for the time base of the television.

On receiving data from the VIP, the TAC writes it into the volatile memory (RAM) by generating the memory address code as well as the Write signal with which the data is clocked into the specific memory location. Additionally, all the remote control command signals initiated on the keypad are received and processed by the TAC.

The timing signals for teletext display are generated by the teletext timing chain (TTC). To produce these signals, the TTC first subdivides a clock signal received from the VIP down to a lower-frequency signal whose frequency is the same as the television frame rate. It is from this that teletext display signals are generated.

A teletext page consists of 24 rows of 40 characters per row. Thus the data is made up of 960 characters which are stored in RAM. These characters are transmitted in 7-bit ASCII-coded format which has to be converted into a dot matrix pattern for display on the television screen. The ASCII-to-dot-matrix conversion table is kept in the nonvolatile ROM. The ROM allows many functions to be performed, such as selection of graphics, alphanumerics, flashing words, double-height characters etc.

TALKING TELETEXT RECEIVER

The main function of the proposed talking teletext receiver is to retrieve a selected teletext page, store it in memory and read the page out verbally under user control. Below the system hardware and software are described.

Hardware

The talking teletext system is illustrated schematically in Figure 3. The microcomputer stores a copy of the selected page, when input in its working memory. The page is then processed into codes for driving the voice output unit (VOU) which utters the speech.

The utterance control keypad enables the user to control the VOU. To assist the blind user to read a teletext page independently, many human factors were considered[6] in evolving the keys available on the utterance control keypad. These buttons enable the user to read a page sentence by sentence or line by line. Each sentence or line can be read phrase by phrase or word by word and any word can be spelled out. There is also a facility for repeating system utterances and another for restarting any mode of speaking. The system also announces the arrival of a selected page as well as the end of a page being read.

The voice output unit (VOU) could be built around any speech synthesizer capable of handling unlimited vocabulary. Many such synthesizers are available commercially, ranging from complete plug-in units to single-chip devices[7]. Single-chip synthesizers, however, appear to be favoured because of their small size which enhances system portability. Such a device, the Votrax SC01, was selected for the system being described in this paper, and the VOU consists simply of the SC01 chip, with a few

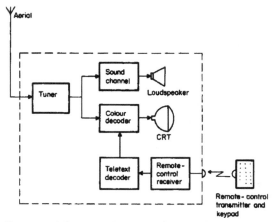

Figure 1. Schematic of teletext TV set

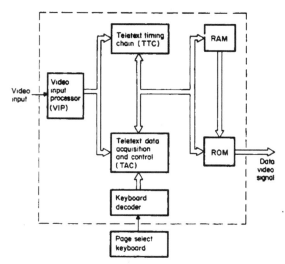

Figure 2. Schematic of teletext decoder

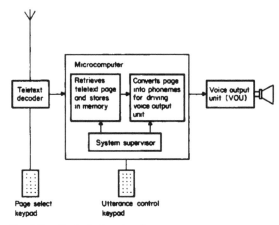

Figure 3. Basic system hardware

other components for interfacing it to the microcomputer, and an audio amplifier for speech output.

The prototype hardware of the talking teletext receiver, which acted as a development system, consisted of a microcomputer with disc drives, a teletext decoder and the VOU. The manufactured version of the system should consist of a single-board computer with adequate memory, a single-card teletext decoder and the VOU circuit board all enclosed in a portable case with headphone socket. Although the SC01 was used in this project, a better version is now available called SC02[8].

Software

The system software is outlined in Figure 4. On start-up, the system welcomes the user verbally and waits for the arrival of the first page. When any page is received, the page title is read out automatically to indicate that the page has been received. The user can then read through the page as explained above.

The speech control processes are performed by moving pointers in the page store at high speed so that, when a key is pressed for a sentence, line, phrase, word, spelling of a word etc., the speech output is almost instantaneous. For example, at the start of translating a sentence or line, a pointer P(current) is set at the beginning of the statement. At the end of translation, another pointer P(next) is set at the beginning of the next statement.

Thus, when the user depresses the word key to request that the statement be read in word mode, the system calls on a subroutine which sets a pointer P(word) to the location of P(current). The subroutine then translates the first word into speech to be uttered by the VOU. P(word) is then moved to the beginning of the next word to be spoken. In this way, a sentence or line is read word by word. If at any point the user requests the spelling of a word just spoken, another subroutine is called which starts spelling from the current position of P(word) to the end of an end-of-word marker.

To read a sentence or line in phrase mode, another subroutine is called to operate in a pattern similar to the word routine by moving a pointer P(phrase) within the page store. Spelling is only active within word mode because it is unnecessary to spell phrases, lines or

sentences. When reading a line or sentence in word or phrase mode, the pointer P(next) is used to indicate the end of the last word or phrase.

Any process for translating text into speech which is to be fast applies linguistic letter-to-sound rules[10] to convert the text into the phonemes required by the speech synthesizer generating the speech. It must also be pointed out that a teletext page is not processed directly as transmitted. The page is reformatted into a form that can be output serially, all graphics characters being removed completely.

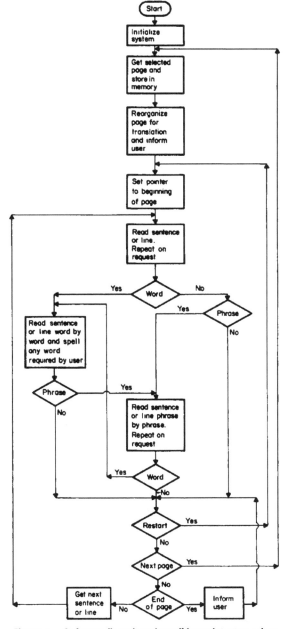

Figure 4. Software flowchart for talking teletext receiver

The software of an alternative system was also considered. This version offers more options to users than that shown in Figure 4. This multioption teletext system would allow the user to store teletext pages on disc. The system can later read these pages from the disc or it can just read the teletext pages directly as received from the decoder, as is the case with the first version. The multioption system would require a disc drive to be added to the hardware of Figure 3.

The multioption system suggested should operate as follows: on start-up, after performing all initialization procedures, the system should offer the user the choice of either on-line or off-line operation. The user who only wants to read teletext pages already stored on disc would select off-line mode. The disc containing the pages is inserted into the drive, whence the system then reads the pages.

When the on-line mode is selected, the system retrieves teletext pages directly for storage in memory and the user can either read the page immediately or store it on disc. When in this mode the user can switch from reading to storing mode and vice versa. Thus the user can listen to a page in part or fully before storing it.

HUMAN FACTORS

To satisfy a broad spectrum of potential users it is important to involve a group of them to assist in the system development. For example, the involvement of the users over a length of time led to the final version of the utterance control keys used in the system described. These keys are similar to those provided on the talking Prestel terminal described in an earlier paper[10]. Attempts were made to replace the two keypads with a single keypad to reduce the hardware components, but the users did not like this because the dual purpose of this single keypad (page selection and utterance control) was confusing. Hence, the arrangement of two keys shown in Figure 3 was finally used.

In implementing the multioption teletext system emphasis should also be placed on ease of use. Hence the system should not allow dynamic switching between on-line and off-line modes, i.e. once a mode has been selected, the system should not permit selection of the other mode. A special key should be provided on the unit for reinitializing the system before reselecting another mode. This would lessen the users' problem considerably.

CONCLUSION

This paper has reported an attempt to extend the teletext service for blind people by converting the textual electronic information into artificial speech. Many other people have also contributed to the effort of trying to extend teletext to the blind community. For example, Meli and Fallside had worked on generating good-quality speech from teletext pages[11]. The final goal is to evolve a system which would be able to convert teletext pages into good-quality speech in real time for the benefit of blind people. A lot of work remains to be done, however, to improve the quality of artificial speech to make it acceptable to users. Some barriers to be crossed to attain this goal are outlined by Rowden[12].

REFERENCES

1 **Mothersole, P L** 'Teletext and viewdata new information systems using the domestic television receiver' *Proc. IEE* Vol 126 No 12 (Dec. 1979)
2 **Cope, N and King, R W** 'Conversion of teletext and viewdata into Braille' *IEE Man-Machine Systems Conf. Publ. No 212* (1982)
3 **Omotayo, O R** 'An evaluation test for speech synthesizers' *Radio and Electronic Engineer* Vol 54 No 11/12 (1984)
4 **Damper, R I** 'Rapid message composition for large vocabulary speech output aids: a review of the possibilities' *IEE Conf. Speech Input/Output, London, UK* (March 1986) pp 225-229
5 **Beakhurst, D J and Gander, M C** 'Teletext and viewdata — a comprehensive component solution' *Proc. IEE* Vol 126 No 12 (1979)
6 **Omotayo, O R** 'Human factors aspects of designing computer voice output systems as communication aids for the disabled' *Microprocessors Microsyst.* Vol 8 No 4 (May 1984) pp 183-188
7 **Buiting, H and Boves, L** 'Speech as an additional output facility for blind operators' *IEE Conf. Speech Input/Output, London, UK* (March 1986) pp 189-193
8 *Votrax SC02 data manual* Vodex, Troy, USA
9 **Omotayo, O R** 'A talking Prestel terminal' *Microprocessors Microsyst.* Vol 8 No 8 (Oct. 1984) pp 403-412
10 **Omotayo, O R** 'Converting text into speech in real time with microcomputers' *Microprocessors Microsyst.* Vol 8 No 9 (Nov. 1984) pp 481-487
11 **Meli, R and Fallside, F** 'Speech synthesis from teletext' *IEE Colloquium Digest* No 1983/35 (April 1983)
12 **Rowden, C G** 'Barriers to the acceptance of synthesised speech as a communication aid' *IEE Conf. Speech Input/Output, London, UK* (March 1986) pp 220-224

Oluwole R Omotayo is a lecturer in the Electrical Engineering Department of the University of Ibadan, Nigeria. From 1974 to 1979 he was a lecturer at the Polytechnic, Ibadan, and in 1980 he became acting head of the Department of Electrical and Electronic Engineering of Ogun State Polytechnic in Abeokuta, Nigeria. His BSc in physics with electronics was obtained from Ahmadu Bello University, Zaria, Nigeria. Omotayo also has an MSc and a PhD in electronic engineering from the University of Southampton, UK. He is a chartered engineer (CEng) and a member of the Institution of Electronic and Radio Engineers. His research interests include microprocessor and microcomputer applications, computer-synthesized voice output and man–machine systems.

Euromicro '86

Held in Venice, Italy, during September, this year's meeting emphasized VLSI and IC design and identified a 'window of opportunity' for Europe's microelectronics designers

Integrated circuit design technology provides the last 'window of opportunity' for an indigenous European semiconductor industry to establish itself, according to Murray Duffin, of the Italian electronics company SGS. Duffin was speaking in a keynote presentation to this year's Euromicro Conference at Ca' Foscari University in Venice, and he couldn't have given this message to a more appropriate audience. Over 270 electronics and computer systems designers and engineers were attending the meeting to hear over 70 papers loosely based around the theme 'microarchitectures, developments and applications', which had encouraged a preponderance of papers on VLSI and IC design.

VLSI opportunities

When the opportunities in microelectronics arrived, the US semiconductor industry was able to grow because risk capital was readily available to finance innovation; at the same time in Japan there was an inbuilt capability to mass manufacture commodity electronic products, said Duffin. The politically and econo- mically diverse countries that comprise Europe had neither of these advantages. Today's European information technology projects such as Esprit and Eureka, however, give rise to greater optimism that Europe can develop a coherent framework on which to build a successful semiconductor industry, Duffin continued. But the time to act is now, he warned.

In 1986 is it possible to manufacture up to 10 million gates on a chip. People no longer want standard commodity products but application-specific devices. Accor- ding to Duffin the emphasis is thus firmly on architecture but the limitation to progress is design, and

present CAD tools are inadequate. This is Europe's 'window of opportunity,' argued Duffin, and if grasped it could possibly be the signal for the second industrial revolution.

Failure and test

Compared with this the rest of the Euromicro programme was subdued. Keynote speaker Professor E J McCluskey of Stanford University, CA, USA, remained true to the VLSI theme, discussing digital system failure and the causes for failure. Unusually he spoke about post- production 'explicit' testing rather than the currently more fashionable production phase, 'implicit' self-test methods. Failure models are available to evaluate causes of system failure but, McCluskey concluded, these are restricted because not all possible failure modes are accurately represented by the single-stuck fault assumption built into the models. Future research should be directed towards investigating the occurrence of non single-stuck faults, he said.

Completing the triumvirate of keynote speakers, Ulrich Trottenburg of the Gesellschaft für Mathematik und Datenverarbeitung (GMD) in the FRG described the Suprenum parallel multiprocessor system. This is a 'supercomputer for numerical applications' said Trottenburg, who leads a dozen or so German institutions from academia and industry in this collaborative project. First begun in May 1985 the project aims to combine developments in supercomputing, parallel computing and multilevel computing and will be MIMD (multiple-instruction multiple-data) based.

Aside from the keynote papers the conference took the familiar format of three parallel sessions of full papers with, at many times, a fourth session for short notes. It is therefore impossible to report the whole conference adequately and to reflect the diversity of presentation, comment and discussion. Some conference highlights are reported in 'R&D reports' on the following pages. A wider appreciation of the scope of the meeting is conveyed in

(continues overleaf)

conference report

some of the session titles: simulation, high-level systems, specialized architectures, fault tolerance, software engineering environments, hardware description languages, development tools, silicon compilation, AI applications and industrial organization, among others.

Robot pingpong

With the annual Micromouse competition being moved to its permanent home in London, UK, the meeting was robbed of one of its evening attractions. Instead, the ping-pong robots took centre stage. A large expected entry of robots was reduced by two by the time the competition was staged. When the Belgian robot crashed before hitting a ball the field was left to the restyled 'Robat Charlie' from Portsmouth Polytechnic in the UK, last year's winner (*Microprocessors Microsyst.* Vol 10 No 6 (July/August 1986) pp 332–335) to strike the ball three times in a practice session to retain the trophy.

The Euromicro conference may have passed its heyday. Attendance was slightly down on last year's meeting and was almost half that of some earlier meetings. The venue is clearly an important factor for attendance. This year in Venice unsurprisingly drew most delegates from Italy and the FRG and also significant numbers from Switzerland, The Netherlands, Belgium and the Scandinavian countries. Countries such as the UK, France, Spain and the Eastern bloc countries, however, were represented by merely a handful of delegates, and it was therefore impossible for the conference to truly reflect the range of research in these countries.

Nevertheless, as Derek Wilson illustrates below, the Euromicro Conference continues to be innovative. Inevitably in a programme of this scale new ideas will always emerge to provide 'windows of opportunity' in many individual areas of microsystem development.

Steve Hitchcock

Euromicro: past and future

Derek Wilson, vice-chairman of the Euromicro Council, discusses the highlights of recent Euromicro conferences

In recent years the aim of the Euromicro conference has been to provide a multidisciplinary conference within the general boundaries of information technology. The conference focusses on current strategic European issues and developments and has to reflect the diversity of activities prominent within the various national boundaries. The Euromicro view of Europe is not simply the EEC definition, but the classical one bounded by the Urals, the Bosphorus and a rather loose interpretation of the Mediterranean countries which have close European associations. Keynote papers are invited to reflect global activities, with speakers often coming from the USA and Japan, as well as Europe.

The first conference was held in Nice, France, in 1975. It has since been held annually, and has been staged in ten European cities — Venice, Amsterdam, Munich, Gothenburg, London, Paris, Antwerp, Madrid, Copenhagen and Brussels. This year's conference was thus the first to return to an earlier venue.

Retrospective highlights

Conference highlights are often seen in retrospect. In 1981 in Paris the conference had a distinct emphasis on concurrency, data flow and multiprocessors. A keynote paper on ADA was presented by J D Ichbiah, principal architect of the language.

The 1982 conference was the first scheduled to be held outside Europe, in Haifa, Israel, but due to the war in Lebanon the location was switched at the last minute to Antwerp in Belgium. The original programme was maintained despite the late change and took the theme of 'architecture, integration and use'.

O Zvi of Honeywell in the USA described new opportunities to use microcomputers for industrial image processing. At that time Zvi's target was to add two sets of 4096 pixels in 1 ms with a conventional 16-bit host microprocessor. Methods for dynamic software modification were considered by J De Man of Bell Manufacturing in Antwerp.

This original work, the basis of which was presented as the interpretation of modules of instances of abstract data types, has subsequently been incorporated in an Esprit project now underway.

The conference in Madrid in 1983 focussed on architecture and real-time applications, reflecting the then 'new' design freedom of VLSI to generate architectures and systems for a wide range of functions.

Esprit emerges

1984 in Copenhagen, Denmark, saw Esprit discussed for the first time in a keynote paper when H Hünke of the Esprit Task Force discussed the ambitions for the Esprit programme. An address on the increasing penetration of a conceptual and algebraic basis to software, as opposed to the 'inspirational' traditions of the software industry, was provided by Peter Naur of the University of Copenhagen at the same meeting.

'Microcomputers, usage and design' became the theme of last year's conference in Brussels, Belgium. (*Microprocessors Microsyst.* Vol 9 No 10 (1985) pp 507–510). It emerged that the newer microcomputers using the 32-bit 'supermicros' were characterized by an increasing degree of complexity that blurs the distinction between microcomputers, minis and mainframes. This was illustrated by P

Treleaven, then of Reading University, UK, whose presentation of fifth-generation microcomputing encapsulated the modern design problem as the need to 'orchestrate a single parallel computation so that it can be distributed across an ensemble of processors'. Treleaven linked the development of fifth-generation computers with the design of very high-level languages (VHLL) and VLSI hardware.

This year the conference returned to Venice, the conference location of 1976, and a different technological world. Having been introduced to the conference in 1984, the impact of Esprit became evident as many speakers reported Esprit-funded work.

The future

Trends that may be reflected in future conferences are clear. With the freedom to create electronic processing functions, the emphasis will return to the intellectual development of the subject rather than on the latest 'wizardry' associated with the number of transistors on a piece of silicon or other circuit material. This means parallel processing in its widest context will clearly be one of the major issues of the next decade.

Another major issue will be the industrialization of the personal computer, and related to this the development of Open Systems Interconnection (OSI) and implementations of OSI such as MAP and TOP. The 1987 meeting, to be held in Portsmouth, UK, is intended particularly to cover the PC issue, taking the theme 'Microcomputers: usage, methods and structures'.

Future Euromicro conferences will continue to reflect these and other initiatives with a format that provides the opportunity for leading-edge initiatives in Europe to be presented.

Derek Wilson

MICROPROCESSORS AND MICROSYSTEMS

10TH ANNIVERSARY SPECIAL ISSUE: PAST, PRESENT AND FUTURE

Volume 11 Number 1, January/February 1987

Future
- Parallel processing: a tutorial review
- Industrial networks: the role of MAP

Present
- Expert systems: design tools for VLSI test

- *PLUS* a 10-year article index

Past
- 10 year reviews: devices, systems software, telecommunications, industrial networks
- A decade of microprocessors

Reprints

Reprints of all articles in this journal are available in quantities of 100 or more.

Reprints are essential —

for the company that wants to distribute impartial comment on its activities to potential customers and clients.
for the company that wants to up-date its technical staff on new techniques and new technologies.

For full details of prices and availability of reprints, please write to:

The Reprint Department, PO Box 63, Westbury House, Bury Street, Guildford, Surrey, GU2 5BH.

R&D reports

In this issue 'R&D reports' highlights papers from the Euromicro '86 conference held in Venice, Italy, during September.

Euromicro '86 preprint proceedings is published by Elsevier, Amsterdam, The Netherlands (1986) DFl 50 pp 715

AI applications

Knodler, B and Rosenstiel, W
'A PROLOG preprocessor for Warren's abstract instruction set' pp 71–79

A PROLOG instruction set designed some years ago by Warren[1] left details of the encoding and implementation open so that the set may be realized in many different ways. The authors of this paper predict that this 'abstract' instruction set could become a standard instruction set for PROLOG and it is currently being used in several research projects. In this work the aim is to use a modified version of the instruction set to speed up execution of PROLOG programs on common microprocessors such as the 68000. It is not intended to be the fastest implementation, say the authors, but it is intended to improve the cost-performance relationship of present systems.

Buses

Van Gennip, J P C
'Interfacing VME bus to a fault-tolerant architecture in the industrial environment' pp 289–295

Control

Debaere, E H and Van Campenhout, J M
'A shared-memory MODULA-2 multi-processor for real-time control applications' pp 213–220

[1]Warren, D H D 'An abstract PROLOG instruction set' Tech. Note 309, AI Center, SRI International (October 1983)

Concurrent realtime software is typically implemented at machine level, which is complex, costly and non-portable. This multiprocessor realization of MODULA-2 is proposed to provide a high-level language environment for realtime control applications.

Halang, W A
'A precisely timed fully parallel process input/output facility for control applications' pp 657–664

Realtime computers are unable to manipulate external parallel processes simultaneously and their response times are generally unpredictable, Halang argues. These problems can be solved, he says, by endowing process control computers with I/O facilities working in parallel and making use of exact time specifications. The paper describes the additional hardware components needed to adapt systems in this way, and discusses the supporting elements needed as high-level languages and realtime operating systems.

Tempelmeier, T
'Microprocessors in factory automation — a case study of an automated guided vehicle system and its integration into a hierarchical control structure' pp 647–656

Development systems

Bemmerl, T
'Realtime high level debugging in host/target environments' pp 387–400

Microprocessor development systems do not adequately support realtime debugging of high-level languages based on a realtime multitasking kernel, says Bemmerl. Such software is often used to control embedded time-critical applications. The paper presents a prototype high-level debugging system for programs written in C or PASCAL.

Christensen, K S
'A PASCAL-like portable, interactive development system for small microcontrollers' pp 55–58

Lazzerini, B and Prete, C A
'DISDEB: an interactive high-level debugging system for a multi-microprocessor system' pp 401–408

At present distributed multimicroprocessor systems are usually debugged by running each process of the distributed program through a standard interactive debugger. This essentially sequential debugging process could be improved, however, say the authors. The architecture of a distributed debugger, DISDEB (distributed interactive symbolic debugger), is presented. DISDEB is designed specifically to debug software for the multimicroprocessor node of the Selenia Mara network, a realtime process control system developed at Selenia SpA in Italy in 1979.

Distributed systems

Gruszecki, M and Van Esbroeck, P
'Capacity and performance prediction in large distributed microprocessor systems under increasing processor speed' pp 667–674

Klar, R and Luttenberger, N
'VLSI-based monitoring of the inter-process communication in multi-microcomputer systems with shared memory' pp 195–204

Chained reference address comparator (CRAC) is a VLSI chip designed to monitor procedure- and message-oriented communication in distributed multimicrocomputer systems. This is achieved by monitoring the accesses of processors to the data structures allocated in shared memory. CRAC is designed for attachment to 8086-based microcomputers.

IC design

Ansorge, M, Piguet, C and Dijkstra, E
'Design methodology for low-power full custom RISC microprocessors' pp 427–434

Presents a design methodology for low-power VLSI circuits used in implanted medical electronics and in wrist-watch applications.

Gai, S, Lioy, A and Neri, F
'VLSI implementation of linear feedback shift registers for microprocessor applications' pp 435–440

Programmable and flexible linear feedback shift registers (LFSRs) can solve problems in fields such as data encryption, digital testing and simulation, where such functions are more easily implemented in hardware rather than software. The authors report the realization of an NMOS IC with four modules, each one a programmable LFSR that can be independently reset and programmed.

Hulin, M
'An expert system for mapping computer architectures into semi-custom integrated circuits' pp 107–122

IC synthesis

Collis, G V and Edwards, M D
'Automatic hardware synthesis from a behavioural description language: OCCAM' pp 243–250

A design automation system is being developed to study the feasibility of synthesizing a structural description of a circuit from a high-level behavioural definition. Attempts have been made to translate behavioural descriptions using high-level languages such as OCCAM and ADA. It is intended that there is minimal interaction between the system and the designer and the

authors' aim is to produce ASICs with reduced design costs in preference to highly optimized circuit structures.

Marwedel, P
'An algorithm for the synthesis of processor structures from behavioural specifications' pp 251–262

Describes a method for generating the internal structure of digital processors automatically from a PASCAL-like program specification.

Memory

Clemen, R, Eisenbraun, E, Fischer, W, Haug, W, Helwig, K, Loehlein, W, Lindner, H and Tong, M
'Fast and dense embedded arrays for microprocessors in CMOS technology' pp 441–444

Describes four array macros designed for a microprocessor that executes and controls cache-based memory operations within a processing unit.

Networks

Bender, H, Hartlmuller, P and Rzehak, H
'A local area network with dynamic switch-over between a CSMA/CD and a token-passing access protocol' pp 153–159

CSMA/CD (Ethernet) is a statistical LAN protocol that causes little overhead with low loads, but has a high overhead with high loads. In contrast, the token-passing protocol is deterministic and has a high overhead under low load conditions. The authors have attempted to combine the advantages of the two access methods and propose a VLSI-based implementation.

Dang, M, Diaz-Nava, M and Michel, G
'Design of a VLSI communicating circuit for an industrial local network

in control process and automated production' pp 173–181

Jylila, H, Lehtinen, T and Nikkila, S
'Virtual token access method and its implementations' pp 161–171

The IEEE 804.2 token-passing bus was standardized in 1985 to provide the first deterministic access delay protocol for time-critical, industrial automation applications. The complexity of the IEEE 802.4 medium access method, however, makes its implementation virtually impossible using standard microprocessor components. Expensive custom designed VLSI controllers are available instead. In response, the authors have developed a variant of the standard token bus protocol — virtual token passing (VTP) — realizable with microprocessor chip sets. Two implementations have been built on the Z80A, and two more are planned for the iAPX80186 and MC68000. The paper describes the quantitative access delay and throughput performance of these implementations.

Marsan, M A, Camarda, P and Neri, F
'Multichannel protocols for real time microcomputer networks' pp 469–477

Proposes two new access protocols which are modifications of CSMA schemes for local area networks containing several parallel broadcast channels.

Operating systems

Pulli, P
'Embedded microcontroller operating system with state-machine support' pp 59–62

Most microcontroller applications are still programmed with 'old-fashioned' techniques without true concurrent processing support, says Pulli, but the use of state machines as tools for understanding and specifying realtime software is increasing. The paper reports on a realtime operating system that supports the implementation of software state machines in an embedded microcontroller environment with, the author claims, minimal distortion.

Parallel processing

Das Gupta, S and Hwa Chang, C
'A pre-design tool for a class of parallel processing systems' pp 417–424

How good can a multiprocessor be in terms of speed and 'best' processing element designed for local processing? How can the performance of a multiprocessor that employs different types of processing element be evaluated? In the authors' view, a simulator is necessary. An MC68000-based partitionable SIMD/MIMD(PASM)

system has been simulated at Purdue University, IN, USA, but the authors of this paper argue that a more generalized simulator is necessary. The paper reports the design of a CAD tool for a generalized simulation environment.

Software

Leccisco, R, Mainetti, S and Morasca, S
'Software metrics: a critical evaluation and an application to PASCAL' pp 605–615

Software metrics are techniques for quantitative and qualitative measurements on programs and their development process. Existing software metrics were inspired by low-level language principles but have been validated against higher-level languages such as FORTRAN.

However, little is known on the application to modern languages such as PASCAL, say the authors, who have thus devised metrics for PASCAL programs.

Vadja, F
'Concurrent systems, programming primitives and languages: a comparative study' pp 185–194

The terms parallel, concurrent and distributed processing are not new but are in a 'fuzzy' state, Vadja says. Procedure-oriented languages such as PASCAL and MODULA enable concurrent accesses but their primitives do not match the implementation features of the architecture of processor networks. The message- and operation-oriented languages ADA and OCCAM show different views of process interaction and are compared in this paper.

Hardware and software of the 'teachable' 68000 processor

Walter A Triebel and Avtar Singh

The 68000 microprocessor: architecture, software and interfacing techniques Prentice-Hall, Englewood Cliffs, NJ, USA (February 1986) £37.40 pp xii + 366

Salespeople always seem to start trying to sell equipment by explaining how fast it is and how much it will improve throughput. This is a perfectly reasonable approach to a business interested only in efficiency. When buying microprocessor systems for teaching purposes, however, I am not interested in naked efficiency but in teachability. I look at equipment from the point of view of its place in the curriculum and select it on the basis of the number of points it illustrates. This is important because most 8-bit microprocessors are very limited in terms of internal architecture and are suitable for teaching only the most introductory courses.

The 68000 has one of the highest 'teachability quotients' of any microprocessor and is as suitable for final-year courses as it is for first-year courses. At the software level it has a powerful instruction set which includes operations that can be used to demonstrate the design of realtime operating systems. Equally, its hardware allows the demonstration of prioritized vectored interrupts, asynchronous bus protocols and bus arbitration.

To date, the majority of books written about the 68000 have concentrated on its software and have largely neglected its hardware, perhaps because it is easy to take an existing assembly language book on machine X and adapt it to machine Y. Triebel and Singh have produced a balanced approach to the 68000, devoting the first half of their book to programming and the second half to the hardware of the 68000 and to the interface between the chip and external components and peripherals. Thus the book is suitable for second-level courses in computer technology.

The first dozen pages of *The 68000 microprocessor* provide a general overview of the microprocessor revolution and have some very nice pictures of big computers, little computers and personal computers. It is a pleasure to discover authors who write for those who have been in prison for the last ten years and have never seen a picture of the innocuous metal boxes that make up a mainframe computer. More seriously, space should not be wasted on pictures of an IBM computer or a TI calculator in a book costing over £37 and aimed at second-year students.

After a short introduction to the 68000 itself, the authors provide three chapters on its software — addressing modes, instruction set and writing 68000 assembly language programs. These are all 'bread-and-butter' chapters; each chapter sets out to achieve an objective and does it without any extras. The authors explain things well but provide no extended examples of 68000 programs to show students how the 68000 is really used. That said, the coverage here is far better than in many of the books written on 68000 assembly language for the QL, which have even less examples and are not as well written. At least Triebel and Singh describe the LINK and UNLK instructions in reasonable detail; some authors skip over these inconveniently complex but very powerful instructions.

Like Bacon, whose book *The Motorola 68000* is devoted entirely to programming the 68000 in assembly language, Triebel and Singh use the Motorola educational microcomputer to illustrate assembly language programming on a real system. This single-board computer has become the prototype for many other low-cost educational computers based on the 68000, and therefore anything written for Motorola's computer should be easy to adapt to similar systems. However, although Triebel and Singh devote more space to this topic than Bacon, they simply elaborate on some of the documentation that comes with this computer. Bacon provides less detail but more applications. What is the good of knowing the rules if you don't know how to apply them?

The remaining chapters deal with the hardware of the 68000 microprocessor. It is impossible to write about the hardware of a microprocessor without including a discussion of the way in which it communicates with memory chips and with the outside world. The section on memory and the I/O interface provided by Triebel and Singh is relatively unexciting and closely follows Motorola's own literature on the 68000. Incidentally, the write cycle timing diagram is incorrect as it includes an extra two clock states, S8 and S9. I would guess that this is because the authors are using a very early version of the 68000 data sheet and the current device executes a shorter write cycle. No timing information is provided in the section dealing with the processor-memory interface. This is a serious omission because 90% of the art of microcomputer design lies in getting the timing right.

The popular 6821 parallel interface, 6850 serial interface and 68230 parallel interface–timer chips are all described in varying degrees of detail. Here, Bacon scores heavily over Triebel and Singh who provide no adequate programming examples for these devices.

I found the final chapter more interesting and well worth reading. The authors take the educational computer and describe its hardware in detail. At last the reader is presented with an example of a real system broken down and explained step by step.

The 68000 microprocessor is an adequate book but I found it a little 'soulless' because the authors appeared content to merely elaborate on Motorola's own literature and to add very little of their own; only in the last chapter did they depart from this pattern. There are plenty of worked examples dotted throughout the text, although many

(continues overleaf)

Digital logic testing cannot be ignored

Alexander Miczo

Digital logic testing and simulation
Harper and Row, Plymouth, UK
(1986) £24.95 pp 414

Less than a decade ago, testing of digital circuits was a task that the designer could usually ignore. Almost any design could be tested thoroughly when it entered production and use at an acceptable cost. One consequence of this was that, whilst there were numerous courses and supporting texts on logic design, very little educational or reference material was produced on test technology.

Since then, two main changes have occurred. First, the complexity of the circuits designed has increased dramatically and consequently test costs have risen rapidly. It has been suggested, for example, that test costs are related to the square of the number of logic gates in a circuit. Secondly, due largely to the inroads made into world markets by Japanese products, there is a significantly greater emphasis on quality. It is now appreciated that companies must achieve high product quality if they are to remain competitive, and this requires that products are tested thoroughly at key stages in the manufacturing process.

Thanks to these and other driving

forces, testing is no longer a task which designers can afford to ignore. Indeed, testing can now be a major contributor to the cost of getting a product to market and is one of the industry's major headaches. However, despite the considerable and readily apparent problems being experienced in industry, very little published material has been available to provide circuit designers and test engineers with the basic information they need to cope with today's complex test problems. Alexander Miczo's book therefore enters a field where material is urgently needed.

The book provides a good coverage of techniques for developing, evaluating and using tests for logic circuits. It opens with a discussion of the role of testing in the product life cycle and continues with a detailed account of test generation techniques for combinational and stored-state networks. The key commercial algorithms (e.g. the D algorithm, critical path and PODEM) are presented, along with less widely used (primarily academic) techniques such as Poage's method and the Boolean difference. A disappointment is that no distinction between the practical and the academic is clearly made.

As suggested by the title, the important topic of logic simulation is discussed at length. Correctly, this material provides the reader with the grounding in simulation technology on which he/she will depend in developing test programs and evaluating their effectiveness. Here, as elsewhere, the book addresses recently developed techniques, examples being the parallel-value-list fault simulation technique and simulation techniques for MOS circuitry. Elsewhere hardware accelerators, functional fault simulation and the use of expert systems for test development and fault diagnosis are covered.

Design-for-test techniques, from the use of *ad hoc* improvements through to scan design and built-in self test, are covered towards the end of the book. I found the treatment to be brief here in comparison to other

topics, particularly when the importance of the topic to the development of economically viable products is considered. The problem of designing printed circuit boards such that adequate test access is ensured is omitted completely, even though it is becoming increasingly difficult with the increasing use of surface-mount technology.

Generally the book is readable, although there are places where the treatment is mathematical. A more significant problem for the reader is the limited number of figures provided to support and clarify the text. Frequently, I felt a need to construct diagrams in order to obtain a clear understanding of the material covered in the text (a feeling that appears to have been anticipated by the author since he comments at one point that the reader may find it useful to create diagrams to keep track of the procedure being described).

Another minor criticism would be of the organization of the material between the chapters. Whilst the flow is logical when read from beginning to end, the reader may have difficulty locating topics when using the book for reference. For example, the discussion of failure mechanisms and fault models and that of simulation are both split between three chapters. Also the chapter entitled 'The automatic test pattern generator' contains little material on test pattern generation, a topic which is covered well in earlier chapters. Once the reader is familiar with the layout of the book, this problem should be quickly overcome.

To summarize, Miczo's book will provide its readers with a good basic understanding of the ways in which test development is performed, and of the problems which can arise in the process. Design-for-test methods are introduced which will assist the practising engineer to overcome these difficulties. I feel that both students and practising engineers will benefit by reading this book.

Colin Maunder
British Telecom Research
Laboratories, Martlesham Heath,
Ipswich, UK

Triebel and Singh
(*continued*)

of them are fairly trivial. A book costing £37 should offer much more.

The core of this book is about 300 pages long. If the authors had expanded it by, say, another 200 pages to include nontrivial hardware and software applications, they might have achieved something really worthwhile. Having said that, I have to admit that there are, as yet, few competing books which cover both the software and hardware of the 68000.

Alan Clements
Teesside Polytechnic,
Middlesbrough, UK

Two 'commendable' approaches to VLSI for signal processing

Peter Denyer and David Renshaw

VLSI signal processing: a bit-serial approach Addison-Wesley, Woking-ham, UK (1985) £19.95 pp 312

Earl E Swartzlander Jr

VLSI signal processing systems Kluwer Dordrecht, The Netherlands (1986) £36.95 pp 188

Recent advances in VLSI fabrication technology have dramatically reduced the cost of implementing realtime signal processing operations, but the associated complex algorithms impose severe compu-tational demands exceeding billions of arithmetic operations per second. Fortunately these demands can be met by new system architectures which exploit existing concurrency in many signal processing algorithms, and such architectures are often implemented using VLSI technology. However, the attendant design complexity is a dominant and limiting development cost factor, and it is therefore essential that design methodologies and manufacturing capability also advance to ensure that design capability keeps pace with algorithm development.

Denyer and Renshaw's book describes a design methodology for VLSI signal processing using bit-serial architectures, but it is not a foundation text in signal processing or in VLSI design. The basic purpose of the book is to describe methods and tools suitable for overcoming the limitations and high costs traditionally associated with VLSI's long development times and multiple design iterations.

The text is divided into two parts. Part 1 is concerned with methods and tools, and begins by introducing bit-serial architectures and systems, emphasizing their potential and advantages for VLSI implementation. The remainder of Part 1 describes a methodology for the design of bit-serial systems, and supports this through a discussion of the FIRST (fast implementation of realtime signal

transforms) silicon compiler (copies of which are obtainable from the authors at the University of Edinburgh, UK). Part 2 presents a range of practical case studies, including Fourier transform machines, transversal filters, an adaptive lattice filter, an integrated digital filter subsystem, a bit-serial multiprocessor for signal processing and a VLSI architecture for sound synthesis.

To preserve the integrity of the text the authors have dealt exclusively with NMOS technology, since this maintains a link with established teaching practice and widely available foundry services. Nevertheless, this restricted treatment does not limit the scope of the book since the architectural concepts and CAD tools, with the exception of the cell library, are technology independent. Indeed their adoption and redevelopment in other VLSI technologies are realistic.

Each chapter is well written and the text and illustrations are clearly presented. *VLSI signal processing* is certainly a useful book and I am pleased to recommend it to final-year students and practising engineers who require a clear and concise theoretical and practical treatment of VLSI signal processing in the context of a bit-serial approach to system architecture. In particular, the book will be useful to the reader having a good foundation knowledge of digital signal processing concepts and some experience of CAD techniques.

For the reader requiring a less demanding, more basic introduction to VLSI signal processing, the book by Swartzlander is to be recommended. The purpose of this book is to provide architectural guidance to designers of signal processing systems and modules and of the VLSI circuits needed to implement them. To illustrate the successful application of the architectural concepts to real signal processing systems, the book examines the algorithms, structures and tech-nologies appropriate to the development of special-purpose systems. This treatment manifests itself by the inclusion of numerous

examples and case studies. These assist the reader in appreciating the practical issues that arise in the development of real systems, and also establishes a good intuitive feeling for current state-of-the-art VLSI technology.

The first three chapters address VLSI from an internal and external architectural perspective, and the level of treatment is such that a first-year degree student could easily understand the concepts described. The next four chapters examine signal processing applications and the implementation of example systems with VLSI. Again the demand for an adequate technical background for the reader is not too stringent — the description of processing algorithms and signal processing case studies is readily assimilated and understood. Finally, chapter 8 provides an introduction to signal processing networks, and methods for the development of these are examined. Several different network types are described and criteria for comparing the performance, cost and quality of the example networks are presented.

The book is well written with clearly presented text and illustrations. It is easy to read and it is a very good introduction to the concepts of VLSI signal processing systems. The book is oriented towards logic and system design, and no attempt has been made to cover either VLSI processing or specific signal processing algorithm development.

The book should be useful to engineers and managers working in VLSI and digital signal processing, and will be good reading for graduate classes in signal processing. For the person with little knowledge of VLSI signal processing, but with a reasonable knowledge of digital systems, I strongly recommend studying Swartzlander's book first to acquire a good foundation knowledge of the topics involved, and then progressing to the book by Denyer and Renshaw.

The difference in the prices for the

(continues overleaf)

book reviews

Fundamentals of network performance analysis will endure

Joseph L Hammond and Peter J P O'Reilly

Performance analysis of local computer networks Addison-Wesley, Wokingham, UK (1986) £21.95 pp 411

Several books have been written that describe the operation of computer networks, but it is refreshing to find one that is aimed at the quantitative aspects of such systems. It is not an easy problem to tackle. Although telecommunications engineers have been familiar with teletraffic design of switched networks since the beginning of the century, the more complex problems of computer systems have, until recently, been given relatively little attention.

In addition to the performance engineering aspects, the book contains much other information. Over 100 pages are devoted to an introduction to telecommunications transmission and switching techniques. The treatment is fairly advanced but curiously selective. For example, although a whole chapter is devoted to digital PBXs, the only mention of pulse code modulation that I could find was in one of the

---

Denyer and Renshaw/Swartzlander (continued)

two books is remarkable: £36.95 for Swartzlander and £19.95 for Denyer and Renshaw. Nevertheless, both books are very useful in their own right. Swartzlander's book is very readable and provides a good introduction to VLSI signal processing systems, whereas Denyer and Renshaw's book provides a more in-depth treatment of VLSI signal processing via a bit-serial approach. If I had to justify my recommendations in terms of value for money then the book by Denyer and Renshaw would be the better of the two, but I am pleased to have a copy of both books; each is commendable in its own way.

Trevor Terrell
Lancashire Polytechnic,
Preston, UK

problems given at the end of the chapter.

The introduction to queueing theory is particularly valuable for the student. It summarizes, from an engineering viewpoint, the main results for M/G/1, M/M/1 and M/D/1 queues and also deals with priority queues. The information is sufficient to enable useful design and analysis to be carried out on a range of systems and it also serves as an introduction to more advanced mathematical works on the subject. The use of the queueing theory to derive the classical (Erlang) blocking and loss formulae is interesting and gives increased coherence to the subject.

There is a detailed account of the basic types of ring and random-access LANs and descriptions of some typical proprietary and experimental systems. Possibly the information is too detailed since there are other books (and numerous technical articles) on the subject. On the other hand, there are some surprising omissions such as the X25 protocol. True, X25 is intended for wide area systems but local networks can be connected via the increasing number of national and international packet networks. Such interconnection can have a marked effect on LAN performance. It is strange that the authors should ignore X25 protocols and at the same time include, for example, a detailed description of cyclic redundancy checks for error detection.

On the main theme of performance engineering, the authors have made a determined attack on an extremely difficult subject. A fundamental problem is to describe the traffic profile for a local network. The published data is summarized in the book but there is a real need for more research on the subject. Each application has its own traffic characteristic and only when this is known is it possible to assess the performance of the network. However, the analytical techniques described provide a good basis for the performance comparison of most types of LAN. The main criticism is

that the results are quoted in terms of averages (delay etc.). This enables some comparisons to be made but for some networks, particularly those involving realtime operations, the delay exceeded by, say, 1% of the packets is a more useful design parameter. The derivation of such statistics is of course much more involved but techniques do exist for simple cases such as M/D/1 queues and should at least be mentioned.

For more complex systems, simulation is a most valuable technique for performance engineering and yet is brought into the book almost as an afterthought. Possibly the authors have concentrated too much on the college textbook aspects (it is difficult to set examination questions involving simulation) but it is misleading to emphasize the slotted Aloha protocol simply because it is amenable to analysis within the mathematical framework covered in the book.

Overall, the book has been put together with great care and it would form an excellent basis for a final-year or postgraduate course. Those concerned with the application of computer networks will find it very useful in that it will assist them in estimating the performance of commercially available systems in their particular application. This is invaluable since the manufacturers of LANs naturally quote the performance so that it shows their system in the most favourable light. For LAN designers the book forms an excellent introduction to the subject. They will need to supplement their reading with more recent work on high-speed systems and the analysis of traffic instability on some types of slotted rings, but this is a minor criticism. For a book so well structured and in a rapidly developing field, some aspects will inevitably be out of date. The fundamentals are likely to endure for some considerable time.

Charles Hughes
University of Essex,
Colchester, UK

Second-generation 32-bit CPU and FPU are due in mid 1987

Motorola has released details of two second-generation 32-bit microprocessor products, the MC68030 CPU and the MC68882 floating-point coprocessor. A combination of these two chips will be capable of 'double the performance currently available to designers using the 68020 and 68881', claims the manufacturer.

68030 features Harvard architecture

The 68030 is scheduled for first silicon in March 1987 and is due for sampling in July. It was developed from a 68020 core by increasing internal parallelism and including dual on-chip caches with a burst fillable mode, dual internal data and address buses, an improved bus interface and a paged memory management unit (MMU). Target applications include engineering workstations, fault tolerant computers, parallel processors and intelligent industrial controllers.

According to Motorola, the new chip offers several features that have not been implemented in a microprocessor before, viz. both on-chip instruction and data caches, Harvard-style architecture, a dynamically configurable bus interface and transparent memory windows.

The dual 256 kbyte instruction and data caches are included to boost the data flow to the CPU, eliminating the usual bottleneck and increasing throughput. Operating from caches reduces access time and also reduces the overall bus requirement, as the CPU needs to spend less time accessing data from the bus. Bus access time is further reduced, says Motorola, by the burst fillable cache mode, which allows high-speed data fills of data and instruction caches.

The Harvard architecture, previously found in certain mainframe computers, allows parallel access of data and instructions. Two independent 32-bit address buses and two 32-bit data buses allow the CPU, caches, paged MMU and bus controller to operate in parallel; the parallel paths give the 68030 an internal bus bandwidth of some 80 Mbyte s^{-1}, says the manufacturer.

The 68030 bus interface is dynamically configurable as synchronous (with maximum two clock access), maximizing access time to a cache subsystem for high-performance systems, or asynchronous (as on the 68020), for slower memories, peripherals etc. Synchronous and asynchronous accesses are supported on a cycle-by-cycle basis as determined by the memory subsystem requested.

The paged MMU provides the set of functions available on the 68851 MMU, including multiple page sizes, multilevel translation trees, on-chip 22-entry address translation cache (ATC) and automatic access history maintenance. The MMU will automatically search the main memory for address translations when they are not found in the ATC.

Occasionally a system may require references to memory locations that cannot afford the time required to search tables for a correct translation. To eliminate this problem, a 'transparent memory windows' feature has been incorporated in the 68030; an application can define this to map directly through logical to physical address space, bypassing the MMU. Thus no overhead is incurred for time critical portions of the application. Window sizes from 16 Mbyte to 4 Gbyte — the largest address space supported by the 68030 — are available.

Designed in 1.2 μm CMOS, the 68030 will be available first in a 16.67 MHz version with a 20 MHz part to follow. Packaging will initially be as a 128-pin grid array.

68882 incorporates conversion control unit

The 68882 floating-point coprocessor is software, pin and functionally compatible with the 68881, says Motorola, adhering strictly to the IEEE 754 standard for binary floating-point arithmetic. The company claims, however, that performance has been increased from two to four times.

Features of the new device include: eight general-purpose floating-point data registers, each supporting a full 80-bit-precision real data format; a 67-bit arithmetic unit; a 67-bit barrel shifter; 46 instructions, including 35 arithmetic operations; and 22 constants available on on-chip ROM, including π, e and powers of 10. The 68882 can operate with any host processor on an 8-, 16- or 32-bit data bus, says the manufacturer.

A conversion control unit (CCU) has been added to the 68882; this improves performance of the FMOVE instruction and most of the arithmetic operations by speeding up the most common binary data format conversions (between the internal 80-bit format and single, double and extended precision formats used externally).

The CCU also directs the communication dialogue concurrently with the activity of the execution control unit (ECU), allowing the 68882 to pipeline the execution of floating-point instructions with the 68020 or 68030, increasing internal parallelism and hence performance. Performance is further enhanced, says Motorola, due to dual porting of the floating-point data register array, supporting concurrent loading, storing and computation by the CCU and ECU.

Alongside the four basic maths functions — add, subtract, multiply and divide — the 68882 offers a selection of transcendental and nontranscendental functions including root values, trigonometric functions, exponentials, hyperbolics and logarithmics.

The 68882 is due to see first silicon this month, with sampling scheduled for April 1987 and production for August. It will be manufactured in 1.5 μm CMOS, and will appear first in a 68-pin grid array. The first version will operate at 16.67 MHz, with a 20 MHz version to follow. (*Motorola Inc., 3501 Ed Bluestein Blvd, Austin, TX 78721, USA. Motorola Ltd, 88 Tanners Drive, Blakelands, Milton Keynes MK14 5BP, UK. Tel: (0908) 614614*) ☐

SRAM combines bipolar and CMOS

A mixed bipolar and CMOS technique known as BiCMOS, designed to combine high speed with low power requirement, is being used by Saratoga Semiconductor of the USA in the manufacture of static RAM chips. The BiCMOS process combines both technologies in the same monolithic die, thus avoiding the speed–power trade-off inherent in conventional static RAMs.

Initial products in Saratoga's BiCMOS range are the SSM 10 470-15 and 10 474-15 RAMs with 4k × 1 bit capacity and 195 mA current consumption from a 5.2 V supply, and the SSM 100 470-15 and 100 474-15 versions with 1k × 4 bit capacity and 195 mA current consumption from a 4.5 V supply. Access times are quoted as either 15 ns (address) and 8 ns (chip select) or 10 ns (address) and 6 ns (chip select); operating temperature range is 0–85°C. These devices are direct replacements for standard ECL products made by the same manufacturer.

According to Saratoga, the main advantage of BiCMOS will be the capability to implement larger RAM arrays: products with 64 kbit capacity are planned to appear soon, with larger arrays to follow.

The BiCMOS technology provides a drive capability of 24 mA, similar to that of bipolar circuits. (*Saratoga Semiconductor Corp., 10500 Ridgeview Court, Cupertino, CA 95014, USA. Tel: (408) 973-0945. UK distributor: Thame Components Ltd, Thame Park Road, Thame, Oxon OX9 3XD, UK. Tel: (084 421) 4561*) □

Audio–ROM CD

Compact disc (CD) ROM drives with combined audio and data storage, daisychain connection and IBM PC or small computer system interface (SCSI) interface facilities have been announced by Hitachi's New Media Products division.

The CDR-2500S includes its own power supply and an IBM 8-bit bus or SCSI as standard, and can optionally be provided with an audio card providing two output channels (either stereo or bilingual) and allowing a mixture of data, music and speech. Up to four drives can be daisychained, providing about 2.2 Gbyte of storage with access times of 0.5 s and 176 kbyte s^{-1} transfer rate.

Priced at £945 (one-off end user price) in the UK, the CDR-2500S is aimed at library and large database management applications. The drive has headphone/amplifier jack sockets and a volume control on the front panel. (*Hitachi New Media Products, Hitachi House, Station Road, Hayes, Middx UB3 4DR, UK. Tel: 01-848 8787*) □

PCs gain floating-point facilities

32-bit floating-point array processor boards and software for the IBM PC, XT and AT are being produced by US-based Data Translation. The Mach product range consists of the DT7010 floating-point array processor, a vector subroutine library, a microcode assembler and a simulator.

The DT7010 is based on the Am29325 floating-point processor, which incorporates a 32-bit floating-point ALU and multiplier with a full 32-bit data path. This allows the board to perform 32-bit addition, subtraction and multiplication operations in a single clock cycle at a rate of 6.5 MFLOPS (million floating-point operations per second) using the IEEE 754 arithmetic standard, says Data Translation.

The board features an address generator that speeds up repetitive operations by storing frequently used microcode instructions in a special register. Onboard microcode memory is 2k × 56 bit and data memory is 8k × 32 bit, the latter being mapped directly into the memory space of the host computer.

The Mach vector subroutine library consists of 115 subroutines, callable from user written programs in C or FORTRAN, that drive a range of image processing, digital signal processing, vector and matrix operations; examples include one- and two-dimensional fast Fourier transforms and subroutines for complex and real arrays. No microcode programming knowledge is required to use the library, says Data Translation.

Mach is intended particularly for image processing and data acquisition from sensors such as thermocouples and video cameras,

via the manufacturer's DT2821 data acquisition board. User programs incorporating subroutine calls from the Atlab library software package, which controls 2821 hardware functions including A/D channel selection, sampling speed and digitization, are written; an Atlab subroutine also stores data as it is acquired into the 7010's data memory. Calls by the user program to the vector subroutines in the Mach library instruct the 7010 to perform any of 115 different processing operations. Results of 7010 floating-point computations can be read by a 2821 D/A converter to control a real-world event.

A Mach microcode assembler and a Mach simulator are available to run on IBM PCs under PC-DOS or on Vax systems under VMS. (*Data Translation Inc., 100 Locke Drive, Marlboro, MA 01752, USA. Data Translation Ltd, The Business Centre, Molly Millars Lane, Wokingham, Berks RG11 2QZ, UK. Tel: (0734) 793838*) □

Protective chip carriers designed to prevent bending of chip 'legs' before installation, and to avoid damage by electrostatic discharges, have been introduced by FRG-based chemical company BASF. The carriers are made from Ultramid 85, a plastic based on mineral reinforced nylon 6 which have been developed specifically for the application by BASF in cooperation with Siemens. Ultramid has good mechanical properties, such as high dimensional stability, isotropic shrinkage characteristics and heat resistance, says the manufacturer; in addition its electrical properties have been modified so that any electrical discharges are carried off the chip via the carrier in less than 100 ms. The chips themselves are insulated from each other, says BASF, with a current leakage rate of less than 10^{-7} A. (BASF United Kingdom Ltd, BASF House, 151 Wembley Park Drive, Wembley, Middx HA9 8JG, UK. Tel: 01-908 3188)

Following up something you've just seen?

Please mention *Microprocessors and Microsystems*

EPROM has fast write and erase

EPROMs designed to combine the advantages of ultraviolet (UV) erasable and electrically erasable devices have been introduced by Seeq Technology of the USA. A pin-for-pin replacement for the 27128 UV erasable PROM, Seeq's DQ48128 Flash has writes perfomed by hot electron injection, as used in UV EPROMs, while erasure is by electron tunnelling as in E^{2}PROMs.

DQ48128 Flash is a 128 kbit EPROM organized as 16k × 8 bit. Programming is performed using a conventional single voltage (21 V) with a byte write time of 2 ms, and access time is 200 ns. Chip erase time, according to Seeq, is just 20 s compared with a typical 10–15 min on conventional UV EPROMs. Seeq is aiming the device at users who need

Enclosures for packaging STEbus systems have been launched by Dean Microsystems of the UK. Available so far in the STEP (STE packaging) range are STEP-42, a five-slot 3U × 42E enclosure, STEP-63, a 3U × 63E version, and STEP-1-Sub, a 10-slot 3U × 84E enclosure. The units are supplied preassembled with IEC mains inputs with fuse, switch and filter, power supply unit, backplane, all internal wiring and a back plate prepared for up to eight 25-way 'D' type connectors. Versions with two 3.5 in floppy disc drives are available. The STEP-1-Sub enclosure features 'stepped' front extrusions to allow STE boards to be set back with room for front-access I/O cabling to be routed to the rear. (Dean Microsystems Ltd, 7 Horseshoe Park, Pangbourne, Berks RG8 7JW, UK. Tel: (07357) 5155)

to be able to reprogram sections of memory *in situ*.

The 48128's particular combination of properties is made possible using a double polysilicon floating gate structure constructed via a proprietary thin-film oxide process, says the manufacturer. The programming algorithm required by the devices will be available on EPROM programmers from certain manufacturers, and its flowchart is available from Seeq or its distributors on request.

The 48128 comes in a 28-pin JEDEC standard dual in-line package and operates from a 5 V power supply. (Seeq Technology Inc., 1849 Fortune House, San Jose, CA 95131, UK. Tel: (408) 942-2313, UK distributor: Pronto Electronic Systems Ltd, City Gate House, 399–425 Eastern Avenue, Gants Hill, Ilford, Essex IG2 6LR, UK. Tel: 01-554 6222) □

Standard cells give subnanosecond gate delays

Standard cells with a gate delay quoted as 575 ps (two-input NAND gate) have been produced by US company VTC. The VL5000 cell library includes ALUs, CPUs and memories and is intended for the design of chips with equivalent gate counts from 5k to over 20k.

VL5000's subnanosecond speed is achieved via a 1 μm CMOS process using double-layer metallization, says VTC. Cell performance is optimized for driving the large fan-outs and long interconnects that are found in complex VLSI designs.

The VL5000 library comprises multipliers, RAM cells and a family of 2900 series processor macros, as well as a range of SSI and MSI functions. (VTC Inc., 2401 East 68th Street, Bloomington, MN 55420, USA. Tel: (612) 851-5200. UK distributor: Mogul Electronics, 65B Croydon Road, Caterham, Surrey CR3 6XG, UK. Tel: (0883) 47991) □

Name	Description	Manufacturer/designer	Distributor/contact
Development systems			
FDSP support kit, MON64SX monitor and MB8764 assembler	Range of development tools for Fujitsu's MB8764 digital signal processor. The assembler converts support text into MB8764 image executable code, while the support kit and monitor program provide dynamic debugging. In-circuit emulation, input data emulation, output data storage and an onboard EPROM programmer are provided. Runs on IBM PCs and compatibles under PC-DOS, MS-DOS and CPM-86; software is also available to run on Vax systems under VMS	Fujitsu Ltd, 6-1 Marunouchi 2-chome, Chiyoda-ku, Tokyo 100, Japan	Fujitsu Microelectronics Ltd, Hargrave House, Belmont Road, Maidenhead, Berks SL6 6NE, UK. Tel: (0628) 76100
HDS-300 emulator modules for M68000 series	Emulator modules for the 68000, 68008, 68010 and 68020 to be used on Motorola's HDS-300 development station. Complete system includes IBM PC, VME/10 or VMEsystem 1131 host options, hardware development station and the appropriate module, and provides realtime emulation, cache support, system performance analysis and c source-level debugging	Motorola Inc., 3501 Ed Bluestein Blvd, Austin, TX 78721, USA	Motorola Semiconductor Products Sector, 88 Tanners Drive, Blakelands, Milton Keynes MK14 5BP, UK. Tel: (0908) 614614
Graphics devices			
DP8512	Video clock using a low-frequency crystal oscillator and an on-chip digital phase locked loop to generate all clock signals. Clock signals are provided for graphics processors running at up to 20 MHz, ECL-differential-output pixel clocks up to 225 MHz and various gated TTL and ECL clocks required to transfer data from the frame buffer memory to the video shift registers or other display circuitry	National Semiconductor Corp., 2900 Semiconductor Drive, PO Box 58090, Santa Clara, CA 95052-578090, USA. Tel: (408) 733-2600	National Semiconductor, Industriestrasse 10, D-8080 Fürstenfeldbruck, FRG. Tel: (08141) 103376
GESVIG-4	Graphics controller for the G64 bus on a single-height Eurocard. Can display up to 640 × 480 pixels on a noninterlaced screen, allowing up to 256 colours from a choice of 262k. Drawing speed is up to 2.5M pixels per second. Vector and circle drawing, pattern fill, zooming and windows are supported, and a VDI-compatible software driver interface (GESGPS-3) running under OS-9 is available	Gespac Inc., 100 West Hoover Avenue, Suite 11, Mesa, AZ 85202, USA. Tel: (602) 962-5559	Gespac SA, 3 Ch. des Aulx, CH-1228 Plan-des-Ouates, Geneva, Switzerland. Tel: (4122) 71-34-00

Section headings in this issue's 'Products in brief' section are

Development systems	**Microprocessors**	**PROMs**
Graphics devices	**Networking products**	**RAMs**
I/O boards	**Peripheral controllers**	**ROMs**
Memory boards	**Processor boards**	**Software products**
Microcomputers (single chip)	**Programmable arrays**	**Test equipment**

products in brief

Name	Description	Manufacturer/designer	Distributor/contact
I/O boards			
SYS68K/ISIO-2	VMEbus serial I/O board with a 10 MHz 68010 CPU and four 68562 dual universal serial communication controllers used to interface up to eight serial I/O channels, each of which is selectable between RS232 and RS422. Uses a 128 kbyte dual-ported RAM to store commands and data and also includes 128 kbyte of EPROM. A bus interrupt module supports fully asynchronous operation on four software programmable interrupt request channels	Force Computers GmbH, Daimlerstrasse 9, D-8012 Ottobrunn, Muenchen, FRG. Tel: (089) 60091-0	Force Computers UK Ltd, 1 Holly Court, 3 Tring Road, Wendover, Bucks HP22 6PE, UK. Tel: (0296) 625456
Memory boards			
DigiRAM	3 Mbyte add-on memory board for the IBM PC AT and its faster compatibles	DigiBoard Inc., 6751 Oxford Street, St Louis, MN 55426, USA. Tel: (612) 922-8055	Data Design Techniques Ltd, Unit 16B, Norman Way, Severn Bridge Industrial Estate, Portskewett, Newport, Gwent NP6 4YU, UK. Tel: (0291) 423781
SRAM 256k	256 kbyte static RAM board for the S100 bus, made up of 8k × 8 bit devices, access time 150 ns. Features battery backing to retain data for one month, responds to 24-bit addressing and supports the S100 'Phantom' signal, allowing it to appear to a bus master in an address location normally occupied by another module	High Technology Electronics Ltd, 303–305 Portswood Road, Southampton SO2 1LD, UK. Tel: (0703) 581555	
SYS68K/SRAM-4A/B	512 kbyte and 1 Mbyte static RAM boards for VMEbus with 32-bit address and data support. Access times quoted as 88 ns (write) and 225 ns (read). Jumper selectable access address and address modifier codes are provided and memory can be split into two independently address selectable blocks	Force Computers GmbH, Daimlerstrasse 9, D-8012 Ottobrunn, Muenchen, FRG. Tel: (089) 60091-0	Force Computers UK Ltd, 1 Holly Court, 3 Tring Road, Wendover, Bucks HP22 6PE, UK. Tel: (0296) 625456
SYS68K/DRAM-5A/B	2 Mbyte or 4 Mbyte dynamic RAM boards for VMEbus, incorporating detection and correction of all single bit errors and detection of double-bit errors. Average read access time is 180 ns with maximum cache hits. Supports 16-, 24- and 32-bit addressing	Force Computers GmbH, Daimlerstrasse 9, D-8012 Ottobrunn, Muenchen, FRG. Tel: (089) 60091-0	Force Computers UK Ltd, 1 Holly Court, 3 Tring Road, Wendover, Bucks HP22 6PE, UK. Tel: (0296) 625456
UMB01	Universal memory expansion module for VMEbus, providing a maximum of 512 kbyte of memory in two 256 kbyte blocks. 16 sockets are available for 24-pin or 28-pin ROMs, EPROMs, E^{2}PROMs, CMOS SRAMs etc. Also allows for addition of a local bus interface implemented on the second DIN connector, and for battery back-up in secure applications	MicroSys GmbH, Amzinger Strasse, 800 Munich, FRG. Tel: (089) 637-0132	Dage (GB) Ltd, Rabans Lane, Aylesbury, Bucks HP19 3RG, UK. Tel: (0296) 33200

Name	Description	Manufacturer/designer	Distributor/contact
PME BB-1	1 Mbyte VMEbus bubble memory card configurable with up to eight 2 Mbyte slave boards. Implements SCSI-type commands and supports VME transfers at up to 2.6 Mbyte s^{-1} on read cycles and 3.6 Mbyte s^{-1} on write operations. Bubble access takes 11 ms (average), 8-bit and 16-bit transfers are supported, and the memory base address is user selectable within a 4 Gbyte address space	Plessey Microsystems, Water Lane, Towcester, Northants NN12 7JN, UK. Tel: (0327) 50312	
VFH-2	1 Mbyte bubble memory board for VMEbus, expandable by cartridge bubble cassette or further boards up to 32 Mbyte. Uses an 80188 controller for bubble device formatting and provides hard and soft error detection and correction. Typical access time is around 10 ms	Bubbl-Tec, PC/M Inc., 6800 Sierra Court, Dublin, CA 94568, USA. Tel: (415) 829-8700	Amplicon Electronics Ltd, Richmond Road, Brighton, East Sussex BN2 3RL, UK. Tel: (0273) 608331

Microcomputers (single chip)

Name	Description	Manufacturer/designer	Distributor/contact
TMP 80C50A	8048/9 series 8-bit microcomputer with 4 kbyte of ROM in a 40-pin DIP or 44-pin flat pack. Includes 256 kbyte of RAM, 27 I/O lines and an 8-bit timer and event counter. Operating power consumption is 10 mA from a 5 V supply at 6 MHz, with standby power of 10 μA (max.). Instruction cycle time is 1.36 μs between 0°C and 70°C	Toshiba, 1-chome Uchisaiwai-cho, Chiyoda-ku, Tokyo, Japan	Toshiba UK Ltd, Toshiba House, Frimley Road, Camberley, Surrey GU16 5JJ, UK. Tel: (0276) 62222

Microprocessors

Name	Description	Manufacturer/designer	Distributor/contact
DSP56001	56-bit general-purpose digital signal processor, identical to Motorola's recently announced DSP56000 but with 512 words of program RAM instead of the 56000's 2k words of program ROM. Simulator and assembler software is now available; chip sampling begins early 1987	Motorola Inc., 3501 Ed Bluestein Blvd, Austin, TX 78721, USA	Motorola Semiconductor Products Sector, 88 Tanners Drive, Blakelands, Milton Keynes MK14 5BP, UK. Tel: (0908) 614614

From left: MicroSys UMB01 VME memory expansion module; Force's SYS68K/DRAM-5 dynamic RAM board for VMEbus; HTE's 256k static RAM board for S100; and the Force SYS68K/ISIO-2 68010-based VME serial I/O board

Name	Description	Manufacturer/designer	Distributor/contact
EF68000	16 MHz version of the 68000 in 2 µm CMOS with a minimum clock cycle time of 60 ns and a minimum memory cycle of 240 ns. Power and instruction set are increased, says the manufacturer, with internal register multiplication of 16 bit performed in 4.2 µs. Packaged in a 64-pin DIP or 68-pin grid array	Thomson Semiconducteurs, 43 Avenue de l'Europe, 78140 Velizy-Villacoublay, France. Tel: (39) 469719	Hi-Tek Electronics Ltd, Beadle Trading Estate, Ditton Walk, Cambridge CB5 8QD, UK. Tel: (0223) 213333

Networking products

Name	Description	Manufacturer/designer	Distributor/contact
Ekko-net	Low-cost 'black box' networking system for IBM PCs that runs on a 220–240 V mains supply rather than using cables. Can be used for electronic mail and exchanging any PC files over the network, says the manufacturer. Connects to PCs via the RS232 port and runs under PC-DOS or MS-DOS. Maximum data transfer rate is 9600 baud	Cyclop Systems Ltd, 19/21 Chapel Street, Marlow, Bucks SL7 3HN, UK. Tel: (06284) 75234	

Peripheral controllers

Name	Description	Manufacturer/designer	Distributor/contact
82604	Enhanced CMOS version of Intel's WD2010 Winchester disc controller, featuring on-chip error detection and correction circuitry	Intel Corp., 3065 Bowers Avenue, Santa Clara, CA 95051, USA	Intel Corp. (UK) Ltd, Pipers Way, Swindon SN3 1RJ, UK. Tel: (0793) 696650
82702	Single-chip controller for floppy disc drives compatible with IBM PC format standards. Features the only integrated analogue data separator that needs no external components, says the manufacturer, and is software compatible with Intel's 8272A and NEC's 765 controllers. Programmable data rates of 250, 300 and 500 kbyte s^{-1} and 1 Mbit s^{-1} are provided	Intel Corp., 3065 Bowers Avenue, Santa Clara, CA 95051, USA	Intel Corp. (UK) Ltd, Pipers Way, Swindon SN3 1RJ, UK. Tel: (0793) 696650

Processor boards

Name	Description	Manufacturer/designer	Distributor/contact
GMSV06	VMEbus single-board computer featuring a 68010 CPU running at 12.5 MHz with no wait states, 68881 floating-point coprocessor, up to 2 Mbyte of dual-ported parity memory, a realtime clock with battery back-up, four-channel DMA, two serial lines and a Centronics interface. Optional 68020 daughterboard is available	General Microsystems Inc., 474 Brooks Street, Montclair, CA 91763, USA. Tel: (714) 621-7532	Universal Engineering and Computing Systems Ltd, 5/11 Tower Street, Newtown, Birmingham B19 3UY, UK. Tel: (021) 359-1749
MVME133, 133-1	68020 processor boards for VMEbus, running at 12.5 MHz (133) and 16.67 MHz (133-1). Boards include a floating-point coprocessor, 1 Mbyte DRAM array, serial debug, two multiprotocol serial RS232C ports, three 8-bit timers, a realtime clock and an A24/D32 VME interface with system controller capabilities	Motorola Inc., 3501 Ed Bluestein Blvd, Austin, TX 78721, USA	Motorola Semiconductor Products Sector, 88 Tanners Drive, Blakelands, Milton Keynes MK14 5BP, UK. Tel: (0908) 614614

Name	Description	Manufacturer/designer	Distributor/contact
PME 68-12	VMEbus single-board computer with 68000 or 68010 CPU (8 MHz or 10 MHz), memory capacity of 0.5–4 Mbyte, floppy disc controller, serial and parallel I/O, realtime clock and counter-timers. PROM-based monitor is standard and VersaDOS and P-DOS can be added	Plessey Microsystems, Water Lane, Towcester, Northants NN12 7JN, UK. Tel: (0327) 50312	
PME 68-14	Single-board computer with both GPIB (IEEE 488) and VMEbus interfaces. Features a 68000 or 68010 CPU, up to 2 Mbyte of dual-ported DRAM, two- or four-channel DMA controller, two serial ports, realtime clock, four 32-pin sites for SRAM, EPROM and E^2PROM, three counter-timers and an optional 68881 floating-point coprocessor. Onboard interrupt generator and mailbox interrupt facility allow fast multiprocessor communications	Plessey Microsystems, Water Lane, Towcester, Northants NN12 7JN, UK. Tel: (0327) 50312	

Programmable arrays

Name	Description	Manufacturer/designer	Distributor/contact
SCX6200 series	Gate arrays in 2 μm n-well CMOS giving effective channel lengths of 1.4 μm. Gate delay times average around 0.85 ns, and the manufacturer points to a high immunity to latch-up. Devices hold from 600 to 6000 gates and incorporate dedicated on-chip test circuitry	National Semiconductor Corp., 2900 Semiconductor Drive, PO Box 58090, Santa Clara, CA 95052-578090, USA. Tel: (408) 733-2600	National Semiconductor, Industriestrasse 10, D-8080 Fürstenfeldbruck, FRG. Tel: (08141) 103486
TC15G, TC17G, TC19G	Gate arrays in 3 μm, 2 μm and 1.5 μm CMOS with toggle frequencies of 50, 100 and 120 MHz and inner gate speeds of 2.5, 1.5 and 1 ns respectively. Arrays are compatible with TTL and CMOS I/O and are supported by the LDS (LSI Development System)	Toshiba, 1-chome, Uchisaiwai-cho, Chiyoda-ku, Tokyo, Japan	Toshiba UK Ltd, Toshiba House, Frimley Road, Camberley, Surrey GU16 5JJ, UK. Tel: (0276) 62222

PROMs

Name	Description	Manufacturer/designer	Distributor/contact
93Z667	64 kbit (8k × 8 bit) bipolar PROM in a 300 mm DIP, with address access times of 40 ns (commercial version) and 45 ns (military version). Has three-state outputs that provide active pull-ups when enabled and high output impedance when disabled	Fairchild Semiconductor GmbH, Am Burgfrieden 1, 8090 Wasserburg Am Inn, Munich, FRG. Tel: (08071) 103-349	Fairchild Semiconductor Ltd, 230 High Street, Potters Bar, Herts, UK. Tel: (0707) 51111

VME processor boards, from left: Motorola's MVME133 using the 68020; General Microsystems GMSV06 with 68010; and Plessey's PME 68-14 single-board computer which also includes a GPIB interface

products in brief

Name	Description	Manufacturer/designer	Distributor/contact
PROMs (continued)			
PCB8582	256 × 8 bit CMOS E^{2}PROM in an 8-pin DIP. Up to eight devices may be connected to the bus as each chip has three address input selects. Includes on-chip address increment, one point erase/write timer and power-on reset. 10k erase/write cycles are possible per byte	Mullard Ltd, Mullard House, Torrington Place, London WC1E 7HD, UK. Tel: 01-580 6633	
TC571000D, TC571001D	1 Mbit CMOS EPROMs in 32-pin ceramic DIPs, either JEDEC compatible (1000D) or compatible with 1 Mbit mask ROMs (1001D). Power dissipation is 30 mA (active) and 100 µA (standby), and access times of 150 ns or 200 ns are available. Operating temperature range is from −40°C to +85°C	Toshiba, 1-chome Uchisaiwai-cho, Chiyoda-ku, Tokyo, Japan	Toshiba UK Ltd, Toshiba House, Frimley Road, Camberley, Surrey GU16 5JJ, UK. Tel: (0276) 62222
RAMs			
DPS41288	CMOS static RAM modules in 32-pin or 48-pin DIPs, comprising up to four or up to twelve 32k × 8 bit LCC RAMs and a single high-speed CMOS decoder. Operation is from a 5 V supply and data can be retained at 2 V. OE input permits disabling of all outputs when they are OR tied. Typical access time is 45 ns at MIL-STD 883C burn-in	Dense-Pac Microsystems, Woodstock House, The Street, Bramber, Sussex BN4 3WE, UK. Tel: (0903) 813008	
M5M5256P	256 kbit (32k × 8 bit) CMOS static RAM in a 28-pin JEDEC package. Three-state outputs allow use in bus-based systems, the OE line preventing bus contention. Power consumption is typically 35 mA when active and a maximum of 2 mA on standby. Access times of 150, 120 or 100 ns are available	Mitsubishi Electric Corp., 2-3 Marunouchi 2-chome, Chiyoda-ku, Tokyo 100, Japan	Mitsubishi Electric (UK) Ltd, Hertford Place, Denham Way, Maple Cross, Rickmansworth, Herts WD3 2BJ, UK. Tel: (0923) 770000
ROMs			
TC532000P	256k × 8 bit silicon gate CMOS ROM in a 32-pin DIP. Access time is 200 ns (max.) and current consumption is 30 mA (max.) when operating and 20 µA in standby mode. Features low bit cost, making it suitable for program memory in microcomputers etc., says the manufacturer	Toshiba, 1-chome Uchisaiwai-cho, Chiyoda-ku, Tokyo, Japan	Toshiba UK Ltd, Toshiba House, Frimley Road, Camberley, Surrey GU16 5JJ, UK. Tel: (0276) 62222
Software products			
CtoP	Tool for converting software written in C into PASCAL: in most cases 70–90% of original source code is converted without the need for human intervention, says the manufacturer, with an accompanying manual providing a guide for conversion of the remaining code. Preprocessor includes many of the features of the emerging ANSI C standard	Knowledge Software Ltd, 32 Cove Road, Farnborough, Hants GU14 0EN, UK. Tel: (0252) 520667	

Name	Description	Manufacturer/designer	Distributor/contact
Lesim	Semicustom simulation package that allows an IBM PC XT or AT (with Futurenet added) to be used as a workstation for the design and simulation of Mullard's CMOS gate array and standard cell products. After schematic capture, the user can carry out both functional and timing simulation of a circuit	Mullard Ltd, Mullard House, Torrington Place, London WC1E 7HD, UK. Tel: 01-580 6633	
SD-PROLOG	Version of standard PROLOG running on IBM PCs, based on an incremental compiler that is also part of the run-time system. Provides a menu-driven environment with multiple-colour windows and features modular programming, DEC-10 'box model' debugging, context sensitive online help, pull-down menus and external interfaces including C. Supports strings and floating-point arithmetic	Systems Designers PLC, Pembroke House, Pembroke Broadway, Camberley, Surrey GU15 3EX, UK. Tel: (0276) 686200	

Test equipment

Name	Description	Manufacturer/designer	Distributor/contact
Aries test sockets	EPROM test sockets to accommodate devices of up to 32 pins, with capacities up to 1 Mbit	Aries Electronics Inc., PO Box 130, Frenchtown, NJ 08825, USA. Tel: (201) 996-6841	Aries Electronics (Europe) Ltd, Alfred House, 127 Oatlands Drive, Weybridge, Surrey KT13 9LB, UK. Tel: (0932) 57377
TeleDiagnosis	Diagnostic tool allowing Gould's K450 logic analyser to debug digital systems remotely over conventional telephone lines. Uses RS232 communications via a Hayes-compatible modem. Includes error checking algorithm	Gould Electronics, 1870 Lundy Avenue, San Jose, CA 95131, USA. Tel: (408) 263-7155	Gould Electronics Ltd, Roebuck Road, Hainault, Ilford, Essex IG6 3UE, UK. Tel: 01-500 1000
Z3200 Disk Emulator Module	Disc emulator for the Zehntel 3200 performance tester, extending its range to include testing of bus structured boards containing a disc controller. Emulates correctly operating 3¼ in and 5¼ in floppy and 5¼ in Winchester disc drives and allows insertion of specific fault conditions to test for error handling characteristics and fault tolerance of the controller circuit of the unit under test	Zehntel Performance Systems Ltd, Hanover Way, Windsor, Berks SL4 5NJ, UK. Tel: (0753) 840241	Zehntel Inc., 2625 Shadelands Drive, Walnut Creek, CA 94598, USA. Tel: (415) 932-6900

Test equipment, from left: Gould's Telediagnosis digital systems debugger; Zehntel's Z3200 performance tester, now with disc emulator module, shown here testing an IBM PC AT board; and Aries 32-pin EPROM test sockets

calendar

Date	Title	Contact	Place	Other details
1987				
14–16 January	Multi 87	Society for Computer Simulation, PO Box 17900, San Diego, CA 92117, USA. Tel: (619) 277-3888	San Diego, CA, USA	1987 SCS 'multiconference' covering modelling and simulation on microcomputers, emergency planning, multiprocessor and array processors (Mapcon), simulation of CIM systems and robotics, and AI and simulation
20–21 January	Buscon and Syscon/87-West	Multidynamics Inc., 17100 Norwalk Blvd, Suite 116, Cerritos, CA 90701-2750, USA. Tel: (213) 402-1618	Hilton Hotel, Los Angeles Airport, CA, USA	Bus board user show and conference, and subsystems conference and exposition for OEM peripherals
21–23 January	The OSI Reference Model and Network Architecture	Frost & Sullivan Ltd, Sullivan House, 4 Grosvenor Gardens, London SW1W 0DH, UK. Tel: 01-730 3438	Cumberland Hotel, London, UK	Seminar on the role and significance of OSI in the design, implementation and operation of distributed data processing systems
28–31 January	India Comm 87	Cahners Exhibitions, Oriel House, 26 The Quadrant, Richmond-upon-Thames, Surrey TW1 3DL, UK. Tel: 01-949 3777	Pragati Maidan, New Delhi, India	Exhibition designed to encourage computer and communications trade between India and the Western world
4–6 February	International Workshop on Industrial Automation Systems	Prof. Masao Sakauchi, Institute of Industrial Science, University of Tokyo 22-1, Roppongi 7-chome, Minato-ku, Tokyo 106, Japan. Tel: (03) 402-6231	Roppongi, Tokyo, Japan	Workshop on practical and basic techniques applicable to machine vision, machine intelligence and signal processing. Includes a session on industrial applications of digital signal processors and microprocessors
4–6 February	Software and Hardware Applications of Microcomputers	Fathy F Yassa, Corporate Research & Development Center, General Electric Co., PO Box 8, KWC510, Schenectady, NY 12301, USA	University Park Holiday Inn, Fort Collins, CO, USA	Covers the applications, software, interfacing, hardware and communications etc. of microcomputers. Sponsored by the Society for Mini and Microcomputers
10–12 February	MDS '87	Microsystem Design, 31–33 High Holborn, London WC1V 6BD, UK	Wembley Conference Centre, London, UK	Microsystem design show
10–12 February	Smartex '87	Tom Archer, Smart Group, Kebbell House, Delta Gain, Carpenders Park, Watford, Herts WD1 5EF, UK. Tel: 01-427 2377	Barbican Centre, London, UK	Specialist show for the SMT industry, including the second surface mount and related technologies conference
10–12 February	Systems Design & Integration Conference	Electronic Conventions Management, 8110 Airport Blvd, Los Angeles, CA 90045, USA. Tel: (213) 772-2965	Santa Clara, CA, USA	Conference and exhibition on systems design, software engineering and integration
25–27 February	ISSCC '87	Lewis Winner, 301 Almeria Avenue, Coral Gables, FL 33134, USA. Tel: (305) 446-8193	New York Hilton, NY, USA	34th IEEE international solid-state circuits conference, covering digital VLSI design, fabrication and test, logic arrays, architecture, microprocessors and coprocessors, analogue components, memories, signal processing etc.
3–5 March	Dexpo Europe 87	Montbuild Ltd, 11 Manchester Square, London W1M 5AB, UK. Tel: 01-486 1951	Olympia 2, London, UK	Fifth Euorpean exhibition and conference on Digital Equipment (DEC) compatible hardware, software, systems etc.

Date	Title	Contact	Place	Other details
4–6 March	International Open Systems Conference	Online International Ltd, Pinner Green House, Ash Hill Drive, Pinner, Middx HA5 2AE, UK. Tel: 01-868 4466	Barbican Centre, London, UK	Conference on the construction and use of open systems, current directions and issues, and strategic and management aspects of open systems. Includes a MAP seminar
10–12 March	Semicon Europa '87	Cochrane Communications Ltd, CCL House, 59 Fleet Street, London EC4Y 1JU, UK. Tel: 01-353 8807	Zuspa Convention Centre, Zurich, Switzerland	13th semiconductor production equipment and materials show, this year placing an emphasis on test equipment. Organized by the Semiconductor Equipment and Materials Institute (SEMI)
22–26 March	Computer Graphics '87	National Computer Graphics Association, 2722 Merrilee Drive, Suite 200, Fairfax, VA 22031, USA. Tel: (703) 698-9600	Philadelphia Civic Center, PA, USA	Conference and exposition on theory and practice of computer graphics. Includes sessions in artificial intelligence, architecture, user interfaces and industry standards, and a demonstration of MAP
30 March –2 April	ICSE '87	IEEE, 1730 Massachusetts Avenue, NW Washington, DC 20036-1903, USA. Tel: (202) 371-0101		
30 March –2 April	ICSE '87	William Riddle, Software Design & Analysis Inc., 1760 Bear Mountain Drive, Boulder, CO 80303, USA. Tel: (303) 499-4782	Monterey, CA, USA	Ninth IEEE international conference on software engineering, with software tools fair
6–9 April	ICASSP 87	Prof. Yu-H Hu, Dept of Electrical Engineering, University of Texas at Arlington, TX 76019, USA. Tel: (817) 273-3483	Registry Hotel, Dallas, TX, USA	IEEE international conference on acoustics, speech and signal processing, including coverage of VLSI for signal processing (custom VLSI for DSP, microprocessor-based implementations, systolic arrays etc.)
8–10 April	Microelectronics Conference — VLSI 1987	VLSI 87 Conference Manager, The Institution of Engineers, 11 National Circuit, Barton, ACT 2600, Australia. Tel: (062) 73-3633	Melbourne, Australia	Will cover design methods, tools, layout, automation and testing; chip architecture; process simulation and modelling; VLSI technology, processing and manufacture; future trends in VLSI; and applications of complex ICs
28–30 April	British Electronics Week	Evan Steadman Communications Group, The Hub, Emson Close, Saffron Walden, Essex CB10 1HL, UK. Tel: (0799) 26699	Olympia, London, UK	Incorporates the All-Electronics/ECIF Show, Automatic Test Equipment, Circuit Technology, Electronic Product Design, Fibre Optics, and Power Sources & Supplies
4–7 May	ICS 87	Prof. Lana P Kartashev, 3000 34th Street South, Suite B-309, St Petersburg, FL 33711, USA	San Francisco, CA, USA	Second international conference on supercomputing, covering hardware technologies and design, supercomputer languages, operating systems and software tools, computations, artificial intelligence and operations research
11–15 May	CompEuro 87	Prof. W E Proebster, c/o IBM, PB 80 08 80, D-7000 Stuttgart 80, FRG	Congress Centre, Hamburg, FRG	First conference and exhibition on 'computer technology, systems, applications and their interaction' organized by the IEEE, Gesselschaft für Informatik, Verband Deutscher Elektrotechniker and others. This year's main topics are: the impact of VLSI on computers; the influence of computers on VLSI; microelectronics and VLSI; status and trends in computer systems; and designing systems with VLSI today (special course)

calendar

Date	Title	Contact	Place	Other details
11–15 May	ISATA 87	ISATA Secretariat, 42 Lloyd Park Avenue, Croydon CR0 5SB, UK. Tel: 01-686 7026	Florence, Italy	16th international symposium on automotive technology and automation, concentrating on automotive microelectronics, vehicle management systems and computer-aided testing
13–15 May	Avignon '87	Agence de l'Informatique, Tour Fiat Cedex 16, 92084 Paris La Défense, France, Tel: (331) 47-96-43-14	Palace of the Popes, Avignon, France	Sixth international workshop on expert systems and their applications
18–21 May	Eighth Symposium on Computer Arithmetic	Luigi Dadda, Dept of Electronics, Piazza Leonardo da Vinci 32, Politecnico di Milano, I-20133 Milano, Italy. Tel: (39) 2 2399-3510	Como, Italy	Topics include mathematical foundations of computer arithmetic; arithmetic algorithms, their analysis and implementation in VLSI; arithmetic in signal and image processing and in fifth-generation computing; arithmetic processors; error control and analysis; and high-level support for numerical computations
18–22 May	Computers at the University	Symposium Secretary, University Computing Centre, 41000 Zagreb, Engelsova bb, Yugoslavia. Tel: (041) 510-099	Hotel Croatia, Dubrovnik/Cavtat, Yugoslavia	Ninth international symposium covering computing in research and education, including: informatics, software engineering, information systems and databases, modelling and simulation, CADCAM, AI, expert systems etc.
1–5 June	GRETSI '87	Secretariat du Colloque GRETSI, 7 Chemin des Presses, BP 85, 0681 Cagnes-sur-Mer Cedex, France. Tel: (93) 20-01-40	Nice, France	Eleventh symposium on signal and image processing, with simultaneous translation from French into English
2–4 June	UK Telecommunications Networks — Present and Future	INCUT 87 Conference Services, Institution of Electrical Engineers, Savoy Place, London WC2R 0BL, UK. Tel: 01-240 7735	London, UK	Covers network evolution, the regulatory framework, the standardization process, value-added services and future evolution of the UK telecommunication network
3–5 June	Sixth European Microelectronics Conference	The Secretariat, Concorde Services Ltd, 10 Wendell Road, London W12 9RT, UK. Tel: 01-743 3106	Bournemouth, UK	Conference and exhibition on hybrids and surface mount technology, organized by the International Society for Hybrid Microelectronics
23–25 June	Software Engineering Tools	Online International Ltd, Pinner Green House, Ash Hill Drive, Pinner, Middx HA5 2AE, UK. Tel: 01-868 4466	Wembley Conference Centre, London, UK	Conference and exhibition
24–28 August	Eurographics '87	Eurographics '87, c/o Organisatie Bureau Amsterdam bv, Europaplein 12, 1078 GZ Amsterdam, The Netherlands	Internationaal Congrescentrum RAI, Amsterdam, The Netherlands	Conference and exhibition on graphics techniques, hardware, applications and sociocultural aspects. Coverage will include object-oriented graphics, expert systems, VLSI for graphics system design, engineering workstations, and integration of graphics and text
14–17 September	Euromicro 87	Chiquita Snippe-Marlisa, p/a TH Twente, Gebouw TW/RC, Room A227, PO Box 217, 7500 AE Enschede, The Netherlands. Tel: (31) 53-338799	Portsmouth, UK	13th symposium on microprocessing and microprogramming, this year's theme being 'Microcomputers: usage, methods and structures'. Topics include: networking; interfaces and buses; data acquisition and evaluation; CIM; embedded systems; advanced microprocessor applications; operating systems and software user interfaces; fourth-generation languages; software and hardware development; silicon compilation; distributed systems and fault tolerance; concurrent processing; multiprocessor architecture and design; GaAs RISC; AI architectures and expert systems

microprocessors and microsystems

Index to Volume 10 Numbers 1–10, pages 1–584 (1986)

Author index

Title index

Microprocessors and Microsystems

The journal welcomes original papers from both academic and industrial contributors on the research, design, development, evaluation and application of all microprocessor-based systems and on the development and use of microsystem software. Papers should illustrate practical experience and show the applicability of the work described. Typically, full-length papers are approximately 5000–7000 words long plus illustrations. In addition to full-length papers, the journal welcomes shorter design notes, tutorial papers and case studies of up to 3000 words.

REFEREEING

All submitted articles are refereed by two independent reviewers to ensure both accuracy and relevance, though it is the authors' sole responsibility that statements used are accurate. The author is also responsible for obtaining permission to quote material and to republish tables and illustrations.

PREPARATION OF SCRIPTS

Three copies of the manuscript, typed *double spaced* on one side of A4 paper should be sent to:

● The Editor, Microprocessors and Microsystems, PO Box 63, Westbury House, Bury Street, Guildford, Surrey GU2 5BH, United Kingdom.

Each page of the manuscript should be numbered. Wide margins should be left so that the paper can be prepared for the typesetters. Please remove tables and figures from the main body of the script and attach them at the end of the paper. Each table or figure should be reproduced on a single sheet. Please list figure captions on a separate sheet and attach this sheet at the end of the paper.

English is the sole language used by the journal, and we follow the Oxford English Dictionary. All papers should be written in English. To maintain consistency throughout each volume, every paper published is stylized by the journal's editorial staff.

Biographical notes

It is the journal's practice to include biographical notes on the authors of published papers. Biographical notes can be up to 100 words, briefly describing career details and current research interests, and should be accompanied by a black-and-white portrait photograph. To speed processing of the paper it is helpful if biographical notes can be attached to the submitted manuscript.

UNITS

SI units should be used. In circumstances where this is not possible, please provide a conversion factor at the first mention of the unit.

ILLUSTRATIONS

Line drawings

We use our own professional studio to ensure that line drawings are consistent with house style. We would prefer, however, to receive one set of unlettered drawings (black ink on tracing paper) so we can put on the lettering ourselves. Drawings, if possible, should be of a size consistent with the journal, i.e. either 169 mm or 366 mm wide. Single drawings should not extend over one page (500 mm) in height.

Computer printouts

Illustrations showing line printer listings, plotter output, etc should preferably be on unlined paper. Printouts will be reduced by us to the relevant size. Do not mark them as they will be used to make photographic copies for the typesetters. Only include sufficient lines for the reader to interpret the format and nature of the printout. Overlong printouts can cause confusion. Fuller explanation of the printout should appear in the caption and the text.

Photographs

Black-and-white glossy photographs (including Polaroid prints of VDU screens) should be supplied unmounted. They should be labelled clearly on the back with a soft pencil. Photocopies of the photographs should be provided for the referees.

REFERENCES

The journal style is to indicate the use of a reference in the text with a superscript as each one arises and give the full reference with the same number at the end of the paper. If a reference is cited more than once, the same number should be used each time. With a bibliography, the references are given in alphabetical order (dependent on the first author's surname). It would be helpful if you could follow this style. References take the following form:

(To journals)

1 **Buckroyd, A** 'Production testing of microprocessor-based equipment' *Microprocessors and Microsystems* Vol 5 No 7 (September 1981) pp 299–303

(To books)

2 **Gallacher, J** 'Testing and maintenance' in **Hanna, F K (ed.)** *Advanced techniques for microprocesor systems* Peter Peregrinus, Stevenage, UK (1980)

PROOFS

Correspondence and proofs for corrections will be sent to the first named author, unless otherwise indicated. Authors will receive a copy of the galley proofs and copies of redrawn or relettered illustrations. It is important that these proofs should be checked and returned *promptly.*

COPYRIGHT

Before publication, authors are requested to assign copyright to Butterworth & Co (Publishers) Ltd. This allows the company to sanction reprints of the whole or part of the volume and authorize photocopies. The authors, however, still retain their traditional right to reuse or to veto third-party publication.

OFFPRINTS AND REPRINTS

The first named author will receive 25 offprints of the paper free of charge as well as a complimentary copy of the journal. Further reprint copies, a minimum of 100, can be ordered at any time from the Reprints Department, Butterworth Scientific Ltd, Westbury House, PO Box 63, Bury Street, Guildford, Surrey GU2 5BH, UK.